HARRAP'S
SPANISH
and ENGLISH
BUSINESS
DICTIONARY

HARRAP'S
SPANISH
and ENGLISH
BUSINESS
DICTIONARY

McGraw·Hill

New York Chicago San Francisco Lisbon London Madrid Mexico City
Milan New Delhi San Juan Seoul Singapore Sydney Toronto

1 2 3 4 5 6 7 8 9 0   KGP/KGP   0 9 8 7 6 5

ISBN 0-07-146337-2

McGraw-Hill books are available at special quantity discounts to use as premiums and sales promotions, or for use in corporate training programs. For more information, please write to the Director of Special Sales, Professional Publishing, McGraw-Hill, Two Penn Plaza, New York, NY 10121-2298. Or contact your local bookstore.

This book is printed on acid-free paper.

Colaboradores
Contributors

Coordinación y edición/Project Manager and Editor
Teresa Álvarez

Equipo de redacción /Editorial Team
Óscar Ramírez Molina   Liam Rodger

con/with
Pilar Bernal Macías   Joaquín Blasco   Jose A. Gálvez
Enrique González Sardinero   Elena Ron Díaz

Español de América/Latin American Spanish
Luis Ignacio de la Peña

Dirección editorial/Publishing Manager
Patrick White

Consultores especialistas/Specialist Consultants
Ross Smith
(Consultor-Jefe de equipo/Chief consultant and team leader,
PricewaterhouseCoopers Spain)
Keith Elliott   Graham Forrest   Jenny Gómez
(PricewaterhouseCoopers Spain)
Rosario Mazuela
(Términos de marketing/Marketing terms)

Corrección/Proofreading
Irene Lakhani   Alison Sadler

Preimpresión/Prepress
David Reid   Kirsteen Wright

Quisiéramos agradecer la contribución de los editores y consultores de la obra
Harrap's French Business Dictionary, cuyo material en lengua inglesa ha sido de
gran valor en la elaboración de este diccionario.
We would like to thank the contributors to the *Harrap's French Business
Dictionary* for their role in the compilation of the English language material, which
has been invaluable in the making of this dictionary.

v

Marcas registradas

Las palabras consideradas marcas registradas vienen señaladas en este diccionario con una ®. Sin embargo, la presencia o la ausencia de tal distintivo no implica juicio alguno acerca de la situación legal de la marca registrada.

Trademarks

Words considered to be trademarks have been designated in this dictionary by the symbol ®. However, no judgement is implied concerning the legal status of any trademark by virtue of the presence or absence of such a symbol.

Índice
Contents

Prefacio

Este nuevo diccionario se ha elaborado a partir de las bases de datos de Harrap y con la ayuda de expertos del mundo empresarial y financiero, particularmente PricewaterhouseCoopers España, con el objetivo de proporcionar de una forma accesible la información más completa y actualizada. Se recogen en esta obra términos de todos los ámbitos relacionados con el mundo de los negocios, desde las finanzas y la Bolsa al marketing o el comercio internacional, además del vocabulario de acuñación más reciente, como **B2B**, **viral marketing**, **burbuja bursátil** o **auditor informático**, sin olvidar el vocabulario coloquial utilizado de forma cotidiana en el trabajo (**bean counter**, **paper clip**, **chiringuito financiero** o **emilio**).

Hemos intentado ayudar al lector aportando información suplementaria en forma de **contexto** y **ayuda práctica**.

El **contexto** está representado con numerosos ejemplos de uso traducidos que figuran dentro de cada entrada, así como con varios cientos de citas extraídas de la prensa especializada española, británica y del continente americano. Estas citas aparecen al final de la entrada correspondiente y muestran un término determinado en contexto, tal y como se usa en el mundo de los negocios

Como **ayuda práctica** se ha elaborado un completo suplemento que incluye:

- Una extensa guía de comunicación comercial en inglés, que comprende modelos anotados de cartas, e-mails, fax y currículums vitae, además de expresiones útiles, convenciones de correspondencia comercial, información sobre solicitudes de trabajo y conversaciones telefónicas.

- Una sección sobre el vocabulario y las expresiones apropiadas para las reuniones de negocios en inglés.

- Un artículo con consejos e información para facilitar la tarea tanto del profesional que trabaja con un intérprete como del intérprete mismo.

- Una tabla de estados del mundo con sus respectivas monedas y lenguas oficiales.

- La lista de las divisiones administrativas de los principales países anglófonos.

Esperamos que esta nueva obra suponga una ayuda valiosa para los estudiantes de inglés comercial, así como para todo profesional que necesite comunicarse en inglés en sus relaciones empresariales con sus homólogos extranjeros.

Preface

This brand-new **Harrap's Business Dictionary** has been developed from Harrap's language databases and with the assistance of experts in business Spanish and English, particularly PricewaterhouseCoopers Spain. It aims to provide useful, up-to-date information in an accessible form. All areas of business are well represented, with terms from fields as diverse as finance, the Stock Exchange, marketing and international commerce. New and current terms such as **B2B**, **viral marketing**, **burbuja bursátil** and **auditor informático** feature in the book, as well as colloquial business terms and the language of everyday office life (**bean counter**, **paper clip**, **chiringuito financiero** and **emilio**).

We have sought to help the reader by providing extra information in the form of **context** and **practical help**.

Context is provided by giving many translated examples within entries, together with several hundred quotations from the Spanish, Latin American, British and American business press. These quotations are presented in boxes after the relevant entry and show the use of the word or expression in the real business world.

Practical help is provided in the form of a two-colour supplement which comprises:

- an extensive guide to Spanish business communication, including fully annotated sample letters, e-mails, faxes and CVs, together with useful phrases, letter-writing conventions, information on job applications and telephone conversations.

- Advice on working with an interpreter that will help make both your and the interpreter's job easier.

- Tables giving information on nations of the world and their respective currencies and official languages.

It is our hope that this new title will prove an invaluable resource for all students of business Spanish and businesspeople who liaise with their counterparts in the Spanish-speaking world.

Estructura de las entradas
Structure of Entries

Los compuestos de más de una palabra aparecen en cursiva negrita bajo el primer elemento y en orden alfabético

Compounds shown in bold italic, placed under the first element and listed in alphabetical order

petty cash n caja f para gastos menores, *Méx, RP* caja chica; **they'll pay you back out of petty cash** te pagarán con el dinero de caja ◻ *petty cash book* libro m de gastos menores; *petty cash box* caja f para gastos menores, *Méx, RP* caja chica; *petty cash management* gestión f de gastos menores; *petty cash voucher* comprobante m de caja

Cada serie de compuestos viene precedida del símbolo ◻

Series of compounds introduced by ◻

phase n fase f, etapa f; **the project is going through a critical phase** el proyecto está atravesando una etapa crucial

Los verbos frasales o con partícula vienen precedidos del símbolo ►

Phrasal verbs introduced by ►

► **phase in** vt sep *(new methods, installations, equipment)* introducir gradualmente *or* escalonadamente; **the increases will be phased in over five years** los aumentos se irán introduciendo gradualmente a lo largo de cinco años; **the reforms will have to be phased in** habrá que introducir las reformas de forma gradual

Numerosos ejemplos proporcionan el contexto necesario

Context provided by many translated examples

► **phase out** vt sep eliminar gradualmente *or* escalonadamente; **these jobs will be phased out over the next five years** estos puestos de trabajo irán desapareciendo a lo largo de los próximos cinco años

La información suplementaria a la traducción aparece en cursiva entre paréntesis

Additional information shown in italic in brackets

piggybacking n **(a)** *(in export)* transporte m multimodal *(de remolques de camión por ferrocarril)* **(b)** BANKING financiación f concatenada

Se muestra la terminación del femenino sistemáticamente

Feminine inflections shown consistently

planner n **(a)** ECON planificador(ora) m,f **(b)** **(town) planner** urbanista mf **(c)** *(in diary, on wall)* planning m

ploughback, US **plowback** n reinversión f de beneficios

Se recogen las variantes ortográficas estadounidenses

American spelling variant shown

Marcas que delimitan el campo semántico de un término determinado

Field labels indicate senses belonging to a particular subject area

point n **(a)** MKTG *point of delivery* punto m de entrega; *point of purchase* punto m de compra; *point of sale* punto m de venta **(b)** ST EXCH entero m; **the Dow Jones index is up/down two points** el índice Dow Jones ha subido/bajado dos enteros **(c)** *(for discussion, on agenda)* punto m; **let's move on to the next point** vamos a pasar al punto siguiente

Los indicadores semánticos aparecen en cursiva entre paréntesis

Sense indicators shown in italics in brackets

pool 1 n **(a)** *(of insurance companies)* mancomunidad f; *(of company cars)* parque m móvil; *(of computers)* parque informático **(b)** *(consortium)* consorcio m

2 vt *(ideas, resources)* poner en común; *(efforts)* aunar; *(capital, profits)* juntar; *(orders)* agrupar, consolidar

La forma completa de cada abreviatura aparece de forma sistemática; se muestra la traducción de todas las abreviaturas

Full form of the abbreviations given consistently; all abbreviations have translations

POS n MKTG *(abbr* **point of sale***)* punto m de venta

ADI *nf Arg* FIN *(abrev de* **Agencia de Desarrollo de Inversiones)** = Argentinian investment development agency

agencia [...]
(b) *(organismo)* agency □ **agencia de ayuda humanitaria** aid relief agency; **agencia de cooperación** development agency; **Agencia Espacial Europea** European Space Agency; **Agencia de Protección de Datos** Data Protection Agency; *Esp* **la Agencia Tributaria** *Br* ≈ the Inland Revenue, *US* ≈ the IRS

ahorrista *nmf Andes, RP* saver

alcista 1 *adj* **(a)** *(tendencia)* upward **(b)** BOLSA *(inversor)* bullish; **mercado alcista** bull market; **valores alcistas** stocks whose price is rising **2** *nmf* BOLSA *(inversor)* bull, bullish investor

> **"**
>
> Muchas de estas empresas pusieron los programas en marcha entre 1998 y 2000, cuando el mercado bursátil mantenía una tendencia **alcista** que parecía imparable.
>
> **"**

amañar *vt* Fam *(cuentas)* to fiddle

aplazamiento *nm* **(a)** *(de reunión, juicio) (antes de empezar)* postponement; *(ya empezado)* adjournment; **el presidente ordenó el aplazamiento de la reunión** the chairman adjourned the meeting **(b)** *(de pago)* deferment, deferral

áridos *nmpl* dry foodstuffs, *D* dry goods

ascender 1 *vi* **(a)** *(aumentar) (precios)* to rise, to go up **(b)** *(en empleo)* to be promoted **(a** to); **ascendió a jefe de producción** he was promoted to production manager **(c) ascender a** *(totalizar)* to come to, to total; **la facturación ascendió a 5.000 millones** turnover came to o totalled five billion; **¿a cuánto asciende el total?** what does the total come to? **2** *vt (empleado)* to promote; **fue ascendida al puesto de subdirectora** she was promoted to the position of deputy director

audiómetro **audímetro**

xi

Abreviaturas y símbolos
Abbreviations and Symbols

abbreviation	*abbr/abrev*	abreviatura
accounting	ACCT	contabilidad
adjective	*adj*	adjetivo
adverb	*adv*	adverbio
Latin American Spanish	*Am*	español de América
Argentinian Spanish	*Arg*	español de Argentina
Bolivian Spanish	*Bol*	español de Bolivia
British English	*Br*	inglés británico
Central American Spanish	*CAm*	español centroamericano
Caribbean Spanish (Cuba, Puerto Rico, Dominican Republic, Venezuela)	*Carib*	español caribeño (Cuba, Puerto Rico, República Dominicana, Venezuela)
Colombian Spanish	*Col*	español de Colombia
computing	COMPTR	informática
accounting	CONT	contabilidad
Costa Rican Spanish	*CRica*	español de Costa Rica
Cono Sur Spanish (Argentina, Chile, Uruguay, Paraguay)	*CSur*	español del Cono Sur (Argentina, Chile, Uruguay Paraguay)
law	DER	derecho
economics	ECON	economía
Ecuadorian Spanish	*Ecuad*	español de Ecuador
Peninsular Spanish	*Esp*	español de España
especially	*esp*	especialmente
specialist term	*Espec*	término especializado
European Union	EU	Unión Europea
feminine	*f*	femenino
informal	*Fam*	familiar
finance	FIN	finanzas
industry	IND	industria
computing	INFORM	informática
insurance	INS	seguros
invariable	*inv*	invariable
masculine	*m*	masculino
Mexican Spanish	*Méx*	español de México
masculine or feminine noun	*mf*	nombre masculino o femenino
masculine or feminine noun	*m,f*	nombre masculino o femenino
marketing	MKTG	marketing
noun	*n*	nombre
feminine noun	*nf*	nombre femenino
plural feminine noun	*nfpl*	nombre femenino plural
masculine noun	*nm*	nombre masculino
masculine or feminine noun	*nmf*	nombre masculino o femenino
masculine or feminine noun	*nm,f*	nombre masculino o femenino
plural masculine noun	*nmpl*	nombre masculino plural
plural noun	*npl*	nombre plural

proper noun	*n pr*	nombre propio
numeral	*núm*	número
parliament	PARL	parlamento
pejorative	*Pej/Pey*	peyorativo
plural	*pl*	plural
politics	POL	política
past participle	*pp*	participio pasado
prefix	*pref*	prefijo
preposition	*prep*	preposición
Puerto Rican Spanish	*PRico*	español de Puerto Rico
Dominican Spanish	*RDom*	español de la República Dominicana
Spanish from Argentina, Uruguay, Paraguay	*RP*	español de los países ribereños del Río de la Plata (Argentina, Uruguay y Paraguay)
South American Spanish (this excludes Mexico, Central America and the islands of the Caribbean)	*SAm*	español de América meridional
insurance	SEGUR	seguros
specialist term	*Spec*	término especializado
Stock Exchange	ST EXCH	Bolsa
telecommunications	TEL	telecomunicaciones
television	TV	televisión
printing	TYP/TIP	imprenta
European Union	UE	Unión Europea
Uruguayan Spanish	*Urug*	español de Uruguay
American English	*US*	inglés norteamericano
Venezuelan Spanish	*Ven*	español de Venezuela
intransitive verb	*vi*	verbo intransitivo
pronominal verb	*vpr*	verbo pronominal
transitive verb	*vt*	verbo transitivo
inseparable phrasal verb	*vt insep*	verbo transitivo inseparable
separable phrasal verb	*vt sep*	verbo transitivo separable
gloss [introduces an explanation]	=	glosa [precede a una explicación]
cultural equivalent [introduces a translation which has a roughly equivalent status in the target language]	≃	equivalente cultural [precede a una traducción con connotaciones equivalentes en la lengua de destino]

English–Spanish
Inglés–Español

Aa

A *adj* BANKING, ST EXCH **A rating** calificación A

A3 1 *n (paper format)* A3 *m*; **a sheet of A3** una hoja A3
2 *adj* **A3 paper** hojas A3

A4 1 *n (paper format)* A4 *m*, Din-A4 *m*; **a sheet of A4** una hoja Din-A4
2 *adj* **A4 paper** hojas Din-A4

AA [1] *n (abbr* **Advertising Association***)* = asociación británica que representa al sector del marketing y la publicidad, *Esp* ≃ AEA *f*

AA [2] *adj* BANKING, ST EXCH AA ❏ ***AA rating*** calificación *f* AA *or* doble A

AAA *adj* BANKING, ST EXCH *(en inglés se lee "triple a")* AAA ❏ ***AAA rating*** calificación *f* AAA

abandon *vt* **(a)** *(idea, project)* abandonar; **they have had to abandon expansion plans owing to a fall in profits** han tenido que abandonar sus planes de crecimiento debido a una disminución en los beneficios **(b)** INS *(ship, cargo)* abandonar **(to** a**)**; **it was decided to abandon the ship to the insurers** se decidió abandonar el buque a los aseguradores **(c)** COMPTR *(file, routine)* cancelar

abandonment *n* **(a)** *(of idea, project)* abandono *m* **(b)** INS *(of ship, cargo)* abandono *m*; **the shipping company issued a notice of abandonment to their insurers** la naviera envió un aviso de abandono a sus aseguradores

ABC *n* ACCT *(abbr* **activity-based costing***)* cálculo *m* de costos *or Esp* costes basado en las actividades

ABC1 *adj* MKTG = de alto poder adquisitivo *(según la clasificación socioeconómica británica que va de A a E)*

> "*Stuff*" had a cover price of £3.50 and was targeted at **ABC1** men aged 25-44 with an average income of around £25,000.

abeyance *n (suspense)* **the matter is still in abeyance** el asunto todavía está en el aire; **the final decision on the project is still in abeyance** todavía no han tomado la decisión final sobre el proyecto

abort COMPTR **1** *n (of program)* cancelación *f*
2 *vt (program)* cancelar, abortar

above 1 *n* **the above** *(person)* el/la citado(a) anteriormente *or* más arriba; *(people)* los/las citados(as) anteriormente *or* más arriba; *(fact, item)* lo anterior
2 *adj* de arriba, anterior; **please contact me at the above address** por favor, póngase en contacto conmigo en la dirección arriba indicada *or* indicada anteriormente
3 *adv* arriba; **mentioned above** mencionado(a) anteriormente *or* más arriba; **as above** como se indica más arriba

above-mentioned 1 *n (person)* **the above-mentioned** el/la mencionado(a) anteriormente *or* más arriba
2 *adj* mencionado(a) anteriormente; **this applies to the above-mentioned employees** esto es válido para los empleados mencionados anteriormente

above-the-line *adj* **(a)** MKTG ***above-the-line advertising*** publicidad *f* above-the-line *or* general; ***above-the-line costs*** costos *mpl or Esp* costes *mpl* above-the-line *or* de publicidad general; ***above-the-line expenditure*** gastos *mpl* de publicidad above-the-line *or* general **(b)** ACCT ***above-the-line accounts*** = cuentas incluidas en la determinación de los resultados del ejercicio; ***above-the-line costs, above-the-line expenditure*** gastos *mpl* corrientes

> British Airways is slashing its **above-the-line** advertising budget – worth an estimated £30m. And it is letting below-the-line agencies go as part of a major cost-cutting exercise.

abroad *adv* en el extranjero, fuera del país; **to be abroad on business** estar en viaje de negocios en el extranjero

absentee *n (from work)* trabajador(ora) *m,f* ausente

absenteeism *n* ausentismo *m*, *Esp* absentismo *m*

absolute *adj* **(a)** MKTG ***absolute frequency*** frecuencia *f* absoluta; **(b)** ECON ***absolute advantage*** ventaja *f* absoluta; ***absolute efficiency*** eficiencia *f* absoluta; **(c)** *(in vote)* ***absolute majority*** mayoría *f* absoluta

absorb *vt* **(a)** *(company)* absorber; **the business has been absorbed by a competitor** el negocio ha sido absorbido por un competidor (**b**) FIN *(debts)* absorber

absorption *n* (**a**) *(of company)* absorción *f* (**b**) ACCT ***absorption costing*** sistema *m* de costo *or* Esp coste integral

abstract 1 *n* *(of article)* resumen *m* ❑ FIN ***abstract of accounts*** estado *m* de cuenta abreviado **2** *vt* *(article)* compendiar, resumir

abuse *n* abuso *m* ❑ ***abuse of authority*** abuso *m* de autoridad; ***abuse of power*** abuso *m* de poder

.ac COMPTR = campo del sitio web de una institución académica o universidad

A/C, a/c *n* *(abbr* **account***)* cta.

ACAS *n* *(abbr* **Advisory, Conciliation and Arbitration Service***)* = organismo británico de arbitraje en los conflictos de trabajo

accelerated depreciation *n* ACCT amortización *f* acelerada

acceleration *n* (**a**) FIN ***acceleration clause*** cláusula *f* de vencimiento anticipado (**b**) *(for employee)* ***acceleration premium*** prima *f* de productividad

accelerator *n* COMPTR acelerador *m* ❑ ***accelerator card*** tarjeta *f* aceleradora

accent *n* acento *m*, tilde *f*

accented character *n* COMPTR letra *f* acentuada, caracter *m* acentuado

accept *vt* (**a**) *(sum, offer)* aceptar; BANKING **to accept a bill** aceptar una letra; **do you accept credit cards?** ¿aceptan tarjetas de crédito?, ¿se puede pagar con tarjeta de crédito? (**b**) *(items delivered)* aceptar; **they refused to accept (delivery of) the goods** se negaron a aceptar (la entrega de) la mercancía

Acceptable Use Policy *n* COMPTR política *f* de uso aceptable

acceptance *n* (**a**) *(of terms and conditions)* aceptación *f*; BANKING *(of bill)* aceptación *f*; **to present a bill for acceptance** presentar una letra para su aceptación ❑ ***acceptance bill*** letra *f* aceptada; ***acceptance fee*** comisión *f* de negociación (**b**) BANKING *(document)* letra *f* aceptada (**c**) *(of items delivered)* aceptación *f* (**d**) *(in quality control)* ***acceptance sampling*** muestreo *m* de aceptación; ***acceptance test*** prueba *f* or ensayo *m* de aceptación

accepted *adj* BANKING *(written on accepted bill)* aceptado(a) ❑ ***accepted bill*** letra *f* aceptada

acceptor *n* BANKING *(of bill)* aceptante *mf*

access 1 *n* (**a**) *(right to contact, use)* acceso *m*; **to have access to sth** tener acceso a algo; **I don't have access to that information** no tengo acceso a esa información
(**b**) COMPTR acceso *m*; **access denied** *(message)* acceso denegado ❑ ***access authorization***

autorización *f* de acceso; ***access code*** código *m* de acceso; ***access control*** control *m* de acceso; ***access level*** nivel *m* de acceso; ***access number*** *(to Internet Service Provider)* número *m* de acceso; ***access privileges*** privilegios *mpl* de acceso; ***access provider*** proveedor *m* de acceso (a Internet); ***access restrictions*** restricciones *fpl* de acceso; ***access time*** tiempo *m* de acceso
2 *vt* COMPTR *(data)* acceder a; **can you access last year's figures?** ¿puedes acceder a las cifras del año pasado?

accident *n* accidente *m* ❑ INS ***accident claim*** reclamación *f* or SAm reclamo *m* por siniestro; ***accident insurance*** seguro *m* de accidentes; ***accident policy*** póliza *f* de accidentes

accommodation *n* (**a**) BANKING *(loan)* crédito *m* provisional ❑ ***accommodation bill*** efecto *m* de favor (**b**) *(lodging)* alojamiento *m* ❑ ***accommodation allowance*** gastos *mpl* or Esp dieta *f* or Am viático *m* de alojamiento; ***accommodation capacity*** *(of hotel)* capacidad *f* de alojamiento (**c**) *(agreement)* acuerdo *m*; **to come to an accommodation** *(with one's creditors, debtors)* llegar a un acuerdo

accord *n* US *(agreement)* acuerdo *m*

accordance *n* **in accordance with** de acuerdo con, en conformidad con; **we must work in accordance with current regulations** debemos trabajar de acuerdo con la normativa vigente

according to *prep* (**a**) *(on the evidence of)* según, de acuerdo con; **according to the latest report, profits have risen** según el último informe, los beneficios han aumentado (**b**) *(in accordance with)* según, de acuerdo con; **according to instructions** según las instrucciones

account *n* (**a**) FIN *(statement)* cuenta *f*; **payment on account** *(advance payment)* pago *m* a cuenta; **I paid £100 on account** pagué 100 libras a cuenta ❑ ***account payable*** cuenta *f* por *or* a pagar; ***accounts payable ledger*** registro *m* de cuentas por *or* a pagar; ***account receivable*** cuenta *f* por *or* a cobrar; ***accounts receivable ledger*** registro *m* de cuentas por *or* a cobrar; ***account rendered*** cuenta *f* rendida
(**b**) *(with shop, company, ISP)* cuenta *f*; (**with** con); **to have an account with a store** tener (una) cuenta con unos grandes almacenes; **to buy sth on account** comprar algo a crédito; **to settle an account** saldar una cuenta; **to set up an account with sb** abrir una cuenta con alguien; **put it on** *or* **charge it to my account** cárguelo a *or* póngalo en mi cuenta; **cash or account?** ¿en efectivo o a la cuenta? ❑ ***account balance*** *(status)* saldo *m* de cuenta; ***account card*** tarjeta *f* de compra; ***account credit*** crédito *m* en cuenta
(**c**) ACCT **accounts** *(bookkeeping)* contabilidad *f*; *(books)* cuentas *fpl*; **the company's accounts are in order** las cuentas de la empresa están en

orden; **to keep the accounts** llevar la contabilidad; **to enter sth in the accounts** consignar algo en los libros de contabilidad ❑ **account book** libro *m* de contabilidad; **accounts clerk** *Esp* contable *mf*, *Am* contador(ora) *m,f*; **accounts department** departamento *m* de contabilidad; COMPTR **accounts package** paquete *m* de contabilidad; COMPTR **accounts software** software *m* de contabilidad

(**d**) BANKING cuenta *f*; **to open an account** abrir una cuenta; **to close an account** cerrar una cuenta; **to pay money into one's account** *Esp* ingresar *or Am* depositar dinero en la cuenta; **my salary is paid directly into my account** me ingresan *or Am* depositan el sueldo directamente en la cuenta; **to overdraw an account** dejar una cuenta en descubierto ❑ **account charges** comisión *f* de administración; **account fee** comisión *f* de mantenimiento; **account handling fee** comisión *f* de mantenimiento; **account holder** titular *mf* de una cuenta; **account manager** = gestor de cuentas; **account number** número *m* de cuenta; **account statement** estado *m* de cuenta

(**e**) MKTG *(customer)* cuenta *f*, cliente *m*; **we lost the Guinness account** perdimos la cuenta de Guinness ❑ **account director** director(ora) *m,f* de cuentas; **account executive** ejecutivo(a) *m,f* de cuentas; **account handler** ejecutivo(a) *m,f* de cuentas; **account manager** director(ora) *m,f* de cuentas

(**f**) ST EXCH **the account** = periodo de negociación en la Bolsa de Londres en el que no se liquidan las transacciones que se llevan a cabo ❑ **account day** = día de liquidación en la Bolsa de Londres; *US* **account executive** director(ora) *m,f* de cuentas

(**g**) FIN *(of expenses)* informe *m*; *(of transactions)* registro *m*

(**h**) **to set up in business on one's own account** establecerse por cuenta propia

▸ **account for** *vt insep* (**a**) *(explain)* **to account for sth** explicar algo; **the strong pound accounts for the drop in exports** la fortaleza de la libra explica la caída en las exportaciones (**b**) *(make up)* suponer; **wine accounts for 5% of all exports** el vino supone el 5% de todas las exportaciones

accountable *adj (person)* responsable (**to sb** ante alguien); (**for sth** de algo); *(for sum of money)* responsable (**for** de); **he's directly accountable to the managing director** rinde cuentas directamente al director gerente

accountancy *n esp Br* contabilidad *f* ❑ **accountancy firm** asesoría *f* contable, contaduría *f*

accountant *n Esp* contable *mf*, *Am* contador(ora) *m,f*

accounting *n* contabilidad *f* ❑ **accounting clerk** *Esp* contable *mf*, *Am* contador(ora) *m,f*; **accounting control** control *m* de contabilidad; **accounting day** *(period)* día *m* contable; **accounting entry** asiento *m or* anotación *f* contable; **accounting entry sheet** *or* **form** hoja *f* de contabilidad; **accounting firm** asesoría *f* contable, contaduría *f*; **accounting irregularity** irregularidad *f* contable; **accounting loophole** = vacío legal en las normas de contabilidad; **accounting method** método *m* contable; **accounting operation** operación *f* contable; COMPTR **accounting package** paquete *m* de contabilidad; **accounting period** periodo *m* contable; **accounting plan** plan *m* contable; **accounting policy** política *f* contable; **accounting procedure** procedimiento *m* contable; **accounting rate of return** tasa *f* de rendimiento contable; **accounting ratio** ratio *m or f or* relación *f* contable; **accounting records** registros *mpl* contables; **accounting rules** normas *fpl* contables; COMPTR **accounting software** software *m* de contabilidad; **accounting system** sistema *m* contable; **accounting year** ejercicio *m* contable

accredit *vt (representative)* acreditar

accreditation *n (of representative)* acreditación *f*

accredited *adj (representative)* acreditado(a)

accrual *n* (**a**) FIN *(of interest, debt)* acumulación *f* ❑ **accrual rate** tasa *f* de acumulación (**b**) ACCT **accruals** *(expenses, income)* gastos *mpl* devengados, ingresos *mpl* diferidos ❑ **accrual accounting** contabilidad *f* según el principio del devengo; **accruals concept** principio *m* del devengo; **accruals and deferred income** ajustes *mpl* por periodificación

accrue FIN **1** *vt (interest)* devengar
2 *vi (interest)* acumularse; **interest accrues (as) from the 5th of the month** el interés comienza a acumularse a partir del 5 de cada mes

accrued *adj* FIN **accrued benefits** *(under pension scheme)* prestaciones *fpl* acumuladas, derechos *mpl* consolidados; ACCT **accrued charges** gastos *mpl* devengados; FIN **accrued dividends** dividendos *mpl* acumulados; ACCT **accrued expenses** gastos *mpl* devengados; ACCT **accrued income** ingresos *mpl* devengados *or* acumulados; **accrued interest** interés *m* devengado *or* acumulado, cupón *m* corrido

❝

In a separate action, Rare Medium and Motient announced today that Motient repaid approximately $26.2 million, including **accrued interest**, of the $50 million aggregate principal amount of exchangeable notes issued by Motient to Rare Medium by delivering to Rare Medium five million shares of XM Satellite Radio common stock held by Motient.

❞

accumulate *vt (stock)* acumular ❑ *accumulated depreciation* amortización *f* acumulada

accumulation *n (of capital, interest)* acumulación *f*

accumulative *adj* FIN acumulativo(a)

ACH *n* US BANKING *(abbr* **Automated Clearing House)** cámara *f* de compensación automática

achieve *vt (aim, goal)* lograr, cumplir; **the company achieved all its objectives for the year** la empresa cumplió todos los objetivos del año; **the new marketing strategy achieved very little** la nueva estrategia de marketing logró muy pocos resultados

achievement *n* logro *m*; **the company is proud of its achievements this year** la empresa está orgullosa de lo que ha logrado este año

acid test ratio *n* ACCT coeficiente *m* de liquidez inmediata

acknowledge *vt* **to acknowledge (receipt of) a letter** acusar recibo de una carta; **we acknowledge receipt of your letter of 19 April** acusamos recibo de su carta del 19 de abril

acknowledg(e)ment *n* **(a)** *(of order)* acknowledgement (of receipt) acuse *m* de recibo ❑ *acknowledgement slip* acuse *m* de recibo **(b)** FIN *acknowledgement of debt* reconocimiento *m* de deuda

ACORN *n* MKTG *(abbr* **A Classification of Residential Neighbourhoods)** = clasificación de los distintos distritos residenciales del Reino Unido según los ingresos familiares, a efectos comerciales y de publicidad

acquire *vt (goods, right, property, company, shares)* adquirir; **to acquire an interest in a company** adquirir una participación en una empresa

acquired *adj (right)* adquirido(a) ❑ *acquired surplus* superávit *m* adquirido, prima *f* por fusión

acquisition *n* adquisición *f*; **making an acquisition in the software industry will greatly improve the company's future** realizar una adquisición en el sector del software mejorará considerablemente las perspectivas de la empresa ❑ ACCT *acquisition accounting* contabilidad *f* de fusiones y adquisiciones; *acquisition cost (of company, customer)* coste *m* de adquisición

acquisitive *adj* **(a)** *(company)* adquisitivo(a), = volcado(a) en adquirir otras empresas **(b)** *(society)* consumista

acquit *vt* FIN *(debt)* pagar, satisfacer

acquittance *n* FIN *(of debt)* liquidación *f*, pago *m*

across-the-board 1 *adj* generalizado(a); **an across-the-board increase** un aumento generalizado

2 *adv (increase)* de forma generalizada; **it applies across-the-board** se aplica con carácter general; **we have had to cut salaries across-the-board** hemos tenido que aplicar un recorte de sueldos generalizado

act 1 *n* **(a)** LAW **Act** *(Br* **of Parliament** *or US* **of Congress)** ley *f* **(b)** INS *act of God* caso *m* fortuito *or* de fuerza mayor

2 *vi* **to act as secretary/chairperson** desempeñar *or* ejercer funciones de secretario(a)/presidente(a); **to act on behalf of** *or* **for sb** representar a alguien

▸ **act on** *vt insep* **they received numerous letters of complaint, but did not act on them** recibieron numerosas cartas de reclamación *or* SAm reclamo, pero no hicieron nada al respecto; **to act on sb's instructions** seguir las instrucciones de alguien

acting *adj (temporary)* en funciones ❑ *acting manager* director(ora) *m,f* en funciones

action 1 *n* **(a)** *(activity)* **to take action** actuar, tomar medidas ❑ *action plan* plan *m* de acción *or* Esp actuación; *action programme* programa *m* de acción *or* Esp actuación **(b)** LAW demanda *f*; **to bring an action against sb** demandar a alguien; **action for breach of contract** demanda por incumplimiento de contrato; **action for libel** demanda por libelo; **action for damages** demanda por daños y perjuicios

2 *vt (idea, suggestion, plan)* llevar a la práctica, poner en práctica

activate *vt (account)* activar, dar de alta; *(customer)* dar de alta a

active *adj* **(a)** BANKING *(account)* activo(a) ❑ *active money* dinero *m* en circulación; *active partner (in company)* socio(a) *m,f* gerente **(b)** *(market)* activo(a); ST EXCH *(shares)* negociado(a); **there is an active demand for oils** hay una gran demanda de acciones petroleras **(c)** COMPTR *active desktop* escritorio *m* activo; *active file* archivo *m* or fichero *m* activo; *active matrix screen* pantalla *f* de matriz activa; *active program* programa *m* activo; *active window* ventana *f* activa

activity *n (in business, market, of company)* actividad *f*, movimiento *m*; *(of bank account)* movimientos *mpl*; **there has been a lot of activity on the Stock Market** ha habido mucha actividad *or* mucho movimiento en la Bolsa ❑ ACCT *activity accounting* contabilidad *f* por actividades; *activity chart* gráfico *m* de actividades; *activity ratio* tasa *f or* coeficiente *m* de actividad

activity-based costing *n* ACCT cálculo *m* de costos *or* Esp costes basado en las actividades

actual 1 *npl* **(a)** **actuals** *(real figures)* cifras *fpl* reales; **to compare budgeted amounts with actuals** comparar las cifras estimadas con las reales (**b**) ST EXCH **actuals** activos *mpl* físicos

2 *adj (real)* real, verdadero(a) □ **actual cost** costo *m or Esp* coste *m* efectivo *or* real; **actual employment** empleo *m* real; **actual figures** cifras *fpl* reales; LAW **actual possession** posesión *f* efectiva; ST EXCH **actual price** precio *m* real *or* de mercado; ST EXCH **actual quotation** cotización *f* inmediata; **actual tare** tara *f* real; INS **actual total loss** pérdida *f* efectiva total; **actual value** valor *m* real

> But what we're seeing right now is that we have gotten ahead of the curve, and we are operationally prepared from a systems and billing perspective. … We initially estimated an annual impact of approximately $7 million, and our **actuals** are tracking with this target.

actuarial *adj* actuarial □ **actuarial tables** tablas *fpl* actuariales

actuary *n* actuario(a) *m,f* de seguros

ad *n Fam (advert)* anuncio *m*; **to put an ad in the paper** poner un anuncio en el periódico □ **ad agency** agencia *f* de publicidad

adapter *n* COMPTR adaptador *m* □ **adapter card** tarjeta *f* adaptadora

add *vt (put additionally)* añadir (**to** a); *(figures)* sumar; **to add the interest to the capital** sumar los intereses al capital □ **added value** valor *m* añadido *or Am* agregado

▶ **add to** *vt insep (increase)* aumentar; **this adds to our expenses** esto aumenta nuestros gastos; **next year we hope to add to our range of products** el año que viene esperamos ampliar nuestra gama de productos

▶ **add up 1** *vt sep (figures)* sumar

2 *vi (give correct total)* cuadrar; **the figures don't add up** las cifras no cuadran; **the accounts won't add up** las cuentas no cuadrarán

▶ **add up to** *vt insep (amount to)* ascender a; **the assets add up to two million** los activos ascienden a dos millones

add-back *n* ACCT método *m* inverso

adding machine *n* máquina *f* de sumar, sumadora *f*

addition *n* (**a**) *(action)* incorporación *f*, adición *f*; *(thing added)* incorporación, añadido *m* (**to** a); **additions to the staff** incorporaciones a la plantilla *or SAm* al plantel; **he's the latest addition to the marketing team** es el nuevo miembro del equipo de marketing (**b**) **in addition (to)** además (de); **in addition to management, the meeting will also be attended by worker representatives** además de la dirección, también asistirán a la reunión representantes de los trabajadores

additional *adj (investment, expenses)* adicional; **this will require additional investment** esto supondrá una inversión adicional □ **additional charge** recargo *m*; **at no additional charge** sin recargo; **additional clause** cláusula *f* adicional; **additional discount** descuento *m* adicional; **additional expenditure** gasto *m* adicional; **additional income** otros ingresos *mpl*; **additional payment** pago *m* adicional; **additional session** *(of court, tribunal)* sesión *f* adicional; **additional sources of income** otras fuentes *fpl* de ingresos; **additional tax** *(supplementary)* impuesto *m* adicional; *(because of underpayment)* cuota *f* adicional; **additional tax assessment** liquidación *f* complementaria; **additional voluntary contribution** = aportación complementaria al plan de pensiones

add-on *n* COMPTR extra *m*, suplemento *m*

address 1 *n* (**a**) *(of person, company)* dirección *f*, domicilio *m*; *(on letter, package)* dirección, señas *fpl* □ **address book** *(printed, in e-mail program)* agenda *f*, libreta *f* de direcciones; **address label** etiqueta *f* de dirección (**b**) COMPTR dirección *f* □ **address bus** bus *m* de direccionamiento *or* direcciones; **address file** archivo *m or* fichero *m* de direcciones

2 *vt* (**a**) *(letter, envelope, parcel)* escribir *or* poner la dirección en; **make sure you address the letter correctly** asegúrate de que escribes la dirección de la carta correctamente; **who's the letter addressed to?** ¿a quién va dirigida la carta?; **the letter was addressed to the personnel manager** la carta iba dirigida al jefe de personal

(**b**) *(direct)* dirigir (**to** a); **please address all enquiries to the personnel department** para cualquier consulta, por favor diríjanse al departamento de personal

(**c**) *(speak to)* dirigirse a; **he will be addressing the meeting later** se dirigirá a los presentes más tarde

(**d**) COMPTR *(message)* dirigir, direccionar

addressable *adj* MKTG potencial □ **addressable audience** clientes *mpl* potenciales; **addressable market** mercado *m* potencial

addressee *n* destinatario(a) *m,f*

adjourn 1 *vt* **they adjourned the meeting** *(for a short time)* hicieron un receso; *(for a longer time)* aplazaron la reunión

2 *vi* **the meeting adjourned** se levantó la sesión; **the meeting adjourned for lunch** se hizo un receso para comer; **to adjourn to another room** pasar a otra habitación

adjournment *n (for a short time)* receso *m*; *(for a longer time)* aplazamiento *m*

adjudicate 1 *vt* ADMIN *(claim)* juzgar, fallar sobre; **to adjudicate sb bankrupt** declarar a alguien en quiebra

2 *vi (in dispute)* arbitrar

adjudication n (decision) sentencia f, fallo m; ADMIN (of claim) conocimiento m ❑ **adjudication of** or **in bankruptcy** declaración f de quiebra; Formerly **adjudication order** auto m de declaración judicial de quiebra

adjudicative adj LAW judicial

adjudicator n (of dispute) árbitro m

adjust vt (**a**) (prices, figures, salaries) ajustar, revisar; (accounts) regularizar; **the figures have been seasonally adjusted** las cifras han sufrido una revisión estacional; **pensions have been adjusted upwards/downwards** las pensiones han sido revisadas al alza/a la baja; **income adjusted for inflation** ingresos revisados teniendo en cuenta la inflación

(**b**) (modify) modificar; **the terms of the contract have been adjusted** se han modificado las condiciones del contrato; **production has been adjusted to meet demand** se ha modificado la producción para adaptarla a la demanda (**c**) INS **to adjust a claim** liquidar or abonar una reclamación or SAm un reclamo

adjustable adj (rate) variable ❑ US **adjustable-rate mortgage** hipoteca f (con Esp tipo or Am tasa) de interés variable

adjuster, US **adjustor** n INS perito(a) m,f tasador(ora) de seguros

adjusting entry n ACCT regularización f

adjustment n (**a**) (of prices, figures, salaries) ajuste m, revisión f; **no adjustment was made for seasonal variation** no se ha efectuado ninguna revisión por fluctuaciones estacionales (**b**) (modification) modificación f ❑ ACCT **adjustment account** asiento m de regularización

adjustor US = **adjuster**

adman n Fam publicista m, publicitario m

admin n Fam (**a**) (work) papeleo m; **there's a lot of admin in this job** en este trabajo hay mucho papeleo (**b**) (department) administración f; **admin will take care of it** se encargarán de ello en administración ❑ **admin building** edificio m de administración; **admin department** departamento m de administración

administer vt administrar ❑ US **administered price** tarifa f regulada

administrate vt (business, institution, finances, fund) administrar

administration n (**a**) (management) (of region, business, property) administración f; **to go into administration** (receivership) ser intervenido(a) ❑ ACCT **administration costs, administration expenses** costos mpl or Esp costes mpl de administración; **administration fee** comisión f de gestión (**b**) (work, department) administración f ❑ **administration building** edificio m de administración; **administration department** departamento m de administración (**c**) US (government) **the Administration** la Administración

administrative adj administrativo(a); **for administrative convenience** para facilitar el trabajo de administración ❑ **administrative building** edificio m de administración; ACCT **administrative costs** costos mpl or Esp costes mpl administrativos or de administración; **administrative department** departamento m administrativo; **administrative details** datos mpl administrativos; **administrative expenses** gastos mpl administrativos; **administrative formalities** formalidades fpl administrativas; **administrative headquarters** sede f administrativa; **administrative jargon** jerga f administrativa; **administrative law** derecho m administrativo; **administrative machinery** maquinaria f administrativa; **administrative staff** personal m administrativo; **administrative unit** unidad f administradora

administrator n (**a**) (of company) administrador(ora) m,f (**b**) (of liquidation of a company's assets) liquidador(ora) m,f, síndico(a) m,f

admission n (entry) admisión f; **the admission of Poland into the EU** la admisión de Polonia en la UE

admit vt (allow to enter, allow to join) admitir

adopt vt (**a**) (measures, approach, design) adoptar; **the company must adopt new working practices in order to increase productivity** la empresa debe adoptar un nuevo método de trabajo para aumentar su productividad (**b**) (minutes) aprobar (**c**) MKTG (product) adoptar

adoption n MKTG (of product) adopción f

ADP n COMPTR (abbr **automatic data processing**) proceso m or procesamiento m automático de datos

ADR n FIN (abbr **American Depositary Receipt**) = certificado de propiedad de un determinado número de acciones extranjeras emitido por un banco de los Estados Unidos y negociable en los mercados de valores estadounidenses

ADSL n COMPTR, TEL (abbr **Asynchronous Digital Subscriber Line**) ADSL m

adspend n Fam MKTG gastos mpl de publicidad

> **❝**
>
> Like most of its competitors, Legal & General's expansion into direct marketing has seen it increase its **adspend**.
>
> **❞**

ad valorem adj (duty, tax) ad valorem

advance 1 n (**a**) **in advance** (book, apply, inform) con antelación; (pay) por adelantado, por anticipado; **payable in advance** pagadero(a) por anticipado; **fixed in advance** fijado(a) por adelantado; **thanking you in advance** (in letter) agradeciéndole de antemano su atención

❑ **advance booking** reserva *f* (anticipada); **advance booking charter** vuelo *m* fletado con reserva anticipada; **advance notice** aviso *m* previo; **advance payment** *(payment in full)* pago *m* por adelantado; *(part payment)* fianza *f*, depósito *m*, *Esp* entrada *f*; **advance publicity** publicidad *f* previa; **advance warning** advertencia *f* previa

(**b**) FIN *(of funds)* anticipo *m*, adelanto *m*; **he asked for an advance of £200 on his salary** pidió un anticipo de 200 libras a cuenta de su sueldo; **advances on securities** *or* **against collateral** adelantos con garantía, créditos pignoraticios ❑ **advance dividend** dividendo *m* a cuenta

2 *vt* (**a**) FIN *(money)* anticipar, adelantar (**to** a); **they advanced him £500 as a gesture of good will** le adelantaron 500 libras como gesto de buena voluntad (**b**) *(prices)* aumentar

3 *vi* (**a**) *(be promoted)* ascender (**b**) *(shares)* aumentar, subir; **the stocks advanced to their highest point in May** las acciones aumentaron a su punto más alto en mayo

advantage *n* ventaja *f*; **knowledge of French is an advantage** se valorarán conocimientos de francés; **to take advantage of** *(offer, situation, opportunity)* aprovechar

adventure *n* FIN aventura *f*

adverse *adj* FIN *(balance)* negativo(a), desfavorable; **the stock markets showed an adverse reaction to the Chancellor's budget** las bolsas reaccionaron de forma negativa ante el presupuesto del ministro de economía

advert *n (for product, service, job)* anuncio *m*

advertise **1** *vt (product, service, job)* anunciar; **as advertised on TV** anunciado(a) en televisión

2 *vi (in order to sell product, service)* hacer publicidad; *(for job)* poner un anuncio; **we are currently advertising for marketing executives** hemos anunciado las vacantes de los cargos directivos de marketing

advertisement *n (for product, service, job)* anuncio *m*

advertiser *n* anunciante *mf*

advertising *n* publicidad *f* ❑ **advertising account** cuenta *f* de publicidad; **advertising agency** agencia *f* de publicidad; **advertising agent** comercial *mf* de publicidad, agente *mf* publicitario(a); **advertising approach** enfoque *m* publicitario; **Advertising Association** = asociación de agencias de publicidad británicas; **advertising awareness** notoriedad *f* de la publicidad; COMPTR **advertising banner** *(on web page)* banner *m* publicitario; **advertising budget** presupuesto *m* de publicidad; **advertising campaign** campaña *f* publicitaria; **advertising concept** concepto *m* publicitario; **advertising consultant** consultor(ora) *m,f* de publicidad; **advertising copy** copy *m or* texto *m* publicitario;

advertising costs costos *mpl or Esp* densidad *mpl* publicitarios; **advertising density** densidad *f* publicitaria; **advertising department** departamento *m* de publicidad; **advertising director** director(ora) *m,f* de publicidad; **advertising effectiveness** efectividad *f* publicitaria; **advertising executive** ejecutivo(a) *m,f* de publicidad; **advertising expenses** gastos *mpl* de publicidad; **advertising gimmick** gimmick *m or* gag *m* publicitario; **advertising insert** inserción *f* publicitaria; **advertising jargon** lenguaje *m* publicitario, jerga *f* publicitaria; **advertising leaflet** volante *m* publicitario; **advertising manager** director(ora) *m,f* de publicidad; **advertising material** material *m* publicitario; **advertising medium** medio *m* publicitario; **advertising potential** potencial *m* publicitario; **advertising psychology** psicología *f* publicitaria; **advertising rates** tarifas *fpl* publicitarias; **advertising revenue** ingresos *mpl* por publicidad; **advertising sales agency** central *f or* agencia *f* de medios **advertising schedule** programación *f* publicitaria; **advertising slogan** eslogan *m* publicitario; **advertising slot** spot *m or* espacio *m* publicitario; **advertising space** espacio *m* publicitario; **advertising standards** código *m* de conducta publicitaria; **Advertising Standards Authority** = organismo británico que vela por la calidad y el contenido de la publicidad; **advertising strategy** estrategia *f* publicitaria; **advertising target** objetivo *m* publicitario

advertorial *n* publirreportaje *m*

❝ ————————————

"The indirect endorsement they offer," says Emap Elan head of research Aida Muirhead, "appears to be a strong factor in generating purchasing interest. And the more an **advertorial** style resembles the writing style and look of the publication carrying it, the better. This prevents interrupting the flow of the reader."

———————————— ❞

advice *n* (**a**) *(opinion)* consejo *m*; **to take legal advice** consultar a un abogado (**b**) *(notice)* notificación *f*; **until further advice** hasta nuevo aviso ❑ **advice note** aviso *m* de envío *or* expedición

advise *vt* (**a**) *(give advice to)* aconsejar; **to advise sb to do sth** aconsejar a alguien hacer *or* que haga algo (**b**) *(recommend)* recomendar; **the company lawyer has advised caution** el abogado de la empresa recomienda precaución (**c**) *(inform)* informar; **we are pleased to advise you that...** tenemos el placer de informarle de que *or* comunicarle que...; **we should advise you that you have exceeded your credit limit** por la presente le informamos de que ha rebasado el límite de su crédito

adviser, advisor n asesor(ora) m,f

advising bank n banco m avisador

advisory adj asesor(ora); **in an advisory capacity** en calidad de asesor ❑ **advisory board** junta f consultiva; **advisory body** organismo m consultivo; BANKING **advisory committee** comité m asesor; **advisory service** servicio m de asesoramiento or asesoría

advocate 1 n (supporter) defensor(ora) m,f; **a strong advocate of free enterprise** un firme defensor de la libre empresa
2 vt abogar por; **he advocates reducing** or **a reduction in spending** aboga por or defiende una reducción del gasto

AER n FIN (abbr **annual equivalent rate**) TAE m or f

affair n **(a)** (business, matter) asunto m; **the affair in hand** el asunto que nos ocupa **(b) affairs** (business, matters) asuntos mpl; **her financial affairs** sus asuntos financieros

affidavit n LAW declaración f jurada

affiliate 1 n **(a)** (person) afiliado(a) m,f **(b)** US (company) filial f
2 vt afiliar; **to affiliate oneself to** or **with** afiliarse a
3 vi **to affiliate to** or **with a society** afiliarse a una sociedad

affiliated adj (member, organization) afiliado(a) ❑ **affiliated company** (empresa f) filial f; **affiliated operation** (empresa f) filial f

affiliation n afiliación f; **we gain many benefits through our affiliation to the national organization** obtenemos muchos beneficios de nuesta afiliación a la organización nacional

affinity n MKTG **affinity (credit) card** tarjeta f affinity; **affinity marketing** marketing m de afinidad; **affinity partner** partner m, = empresa u organización de otro ramo, pero con la que se mantiene una cierta relación y cuyos servicios se recomiendan a los propios clientes

> ❝
> Countless other charitable deals exist. Among the most common are **affinity credit card** deals, where a charity gets a certain amount, usually 25p for every £100 spent. …Wendy Green from the Charities Aid Foundation said cause-related marketing, as it is known in the industry, is moving away from just being **affinity marketing** of credit cards and taking on several other guises.
> ❞

affirmative adj **(a)** (proactive) **to take affirmative action (to do sth)** tomar medidas positivas (para hacer algo); **we should take affirmative action to make our intentions clear in this marketplace** deberíamos tomar medidas positivas para dejar claras nuestras intenciones en

este mercado **(b)** (promoting the disadvantaged) **to take affirmative action** aplicar una discriminación positiva

affluence n prosperidad f, riqueza f

affluent adj acomodado(a), opulento(a) ❑ **the affluent society** la sociedad de la opulencia

afford vt **(a)** (have enough money for) **to be able to afford sth** poder permitirse algo; **the company cannot afford any more new software** la empresa no tiene dinero para comprar software nuevo; **we can afford to pay all our creditors by the end of the year** podemos pagar a todos nuestros acreedores antes de final de año **(b)** (allow oneself) **we cannot afford to lose these employees** no nos podemos permitir perder a estos empleados; **we can afford to wait another few days** podemos esperar unos días más

affordability adj asequibilidad f

affordable adj asequible

affreightment n fletamento m

AFL-CIO n (abbr **American Federation of Labor and Congress of Industrial Organizations**) = federación estadounidense de sindicatos

afloat adv **to keep a business/the economy afloat** mantener un negocio/la economía a flote; **many small businesses are struggling to stay afloat** a muchos pequeños negocios les está costando mantenerse a flote

> ❝
> The chain, which operates the majority of its stores under the Dollar Zone name … spent the past year converting its variety stores to the dollar format. But the move wasn't enough to **keep the company afloat** despite the recent surge in popularity of dollar stores in the slumping economy.
> ❞

aforementioned adj susodicho(a), mencionado(a) (anteriormente); **with reference to the aforementioned items,…** en cuanto a los artículos mencionados anteriormente,…, en cuanto a los susodichos artículos

aforesaid adj susodicho(a), mencionado(a) (anteriormente)

after-hours adj ST EXCH **after-hours dealing** contratación f fuera de hora; **after-hours market** mercado m fuera de hora

aftermarket n **(a)** ST EXCH mercado m secundario **(b)** MKTG mercado m de repuestos

after-sales adj posventa ❑ **after-sales department** departamento m (de servicio) postventa; **after-sales marketing** marketing m del servicio postventa; **after-sales service** servicio m postventa

after-tax adj después de impuestos ❑ **after-tax profit** beneficio m después de impuestos; **after-tax salary** sueldo m neto

against prep (**a**) (in opposition to) contra, en contra de; **the workers are against the idea of striking** los trabajadores están en contra de hacer huelga; **to be insured against fire/theft** estar asegurado(a) contra incendios/robo, tener seguro de incendios/robo; INS **against all risks** a todo riesgo (**b**) (in relation to) **the pound rose/fell against the dollar** la libra subió/bajó frente al dólar; **to get an advance against one's salary** recibir un anticipo a cuenta del sueldo

age n edad f ❑ **age bracket** segmento m or franja f de edad; **the 15-20 age bracket** el segmento or la franja de edad comprendida entre los 15 y los 20 años; **age group** grupo m de edad; **this product is targeted at the 18-24 age group** este producto está dirigido al grupo de edad comprendido entre los 18 y los 24 años; **age limit** límite m de edad

aged debtors report n ACCT informe m de antigüedad (de las cuentas por cobrar)

agency n MKTG agencia f ❑ **agency account** cuenta f institucional, = contrato publicitario con una institución del Estado; **agency agreement** contrato m de agencia; **agency contract** = contrato con una institución del Estado; **agency fee** comisión f de agencia; US **agency shop** = empresa en la que un sindicato representa a todos los trabajadores, pero éstos deben pagar una cuota tanto si están afiliados como si no

agenda n (of meeting) orden m del día; **to draw up an agenda** redactar un orden del día; **to put a question on the agenda** incluir un asunto en el orden del día; **the first item on the agenda** el primer punto del orden del día

agent n (representative) agente mf, representante mf; (for firm) concesionario m; MKTG (for brand) representante mf; **the agent for Mercury Ltd** el/la representante de Mercury Ltd; **he is our agent in the Far East** es nuestro agente en el Lejano Oriente

aggregate 1 n total m
2 adj (amount, figure) global, total; **for an aggregate period of three years** por un periodo total de tres años ❑ **aggregate demand** demanda f agregada; **aggregate economic activity** actividad f económica global or total; **aggregate income** ingresos mpl totales; **aggregate net increment** incremento m neto acumulado; **aggregate output** rendimiento m global or total; **aggregate production** producción f global or total

aggrieved adj LAW perjudicado(a) ❑ **aggrieved party** parte f agraviada or perjudicada

agio n FIN (**a**) (price) agio m ❑ **agio account** cuenta f de agio (**b**) (business) especulación f, agiotaje m

agiotage n especulación f, agiotaje m

AGM n (abbr **annual general meeting**) asamblea f or junta f general anual

agree 1 vt (**a**) (reach agreement on) (price, conditions) acordar; **to be agreed** (date, price) por decidir; **unless otherwise agreed** a no ser que se acuerde lo contrario; **as agreed** según lo acordado (**b**) (approve) **to agree the accounts** or **the books** aprobar las cuentas or los libros; **the figures have been agreed** se han aprobado las cifras
2 vi (**a**) (books, figures) cuadrar (**b**) MKTG **to agree and counter** = negociar aceptando primero el punto de vista de la otra parte para luego contraatacar

▸ **agree on** vt insep (price, date) ponerse de acuerdo en

agreed adj (price) acordado(a) ❑ **agreed statement** declaración f conjunta

agreement n (**a**) (arrangement, contract) acuerdo m (**on** or **about** sobre); **to break an agreement** romper un acuerdo; **to have an agreement with sb** tener un acuerdo or un pacto con alguien; **to enter into** or **conclude an agreement with sb** alcanzar un acuerdo con alguien; **an agreement has been concluded between the two parties** las dos partes han alcanzado un acuerdo; **to come to an agreement** llegar a un acuerdo; **to sign an agreement** firmar un acuerdo; **to sign a legal agreement (to do sth)** firmar un contrato (para hacer algo); **to abide by the agreement** respetar las condiciones del acuerdo; **our agreement was that...** habíamos acordado que...
(**b**) (understanding) **as per agreement** según lo acordado; **by mutual agreement** por mutuo acuerdo

agribusiness n industria f agropecuaria, agroindustria f

agricultural adj agrícola ❑ **agricultural cooperative** cooperativa f agrícola; EU **agricultural levies** exacciones fpl reguladoras agrícolas

agriculture n agricultura f

agritourism *n* agroturismo *m*

agro-industrial *adj* agroindustrial

agro-industry *n* agroindustria *f*

agrotourism *n* agroturismo *m*

aid *n* ayuda *f*; **in aid of** *(fundraising event)* en *or* a beneficio de

AIDA *n* MKTG *(abbr* **attention-interest-desire-action)** AIDA *m*

aided recall *n* MKTG recuerdo *m* asistido *or* ayudado (de marca)

AIM *n* ST EXCH *(abbr* **Alternative Investment Market)** AIM *m*, Mercado *m* de Inversión Alternativa

> **"**
> Several billion pounds have been raised on the Alternative Investment Market (**AIM**) over the last four years, following the billion-plus invested on its predecessor, the Unlisted Securities Market, over a much longer period. Another half billion has flowed into venture capital trusts (VCTs) which offer 20% income tax relief and other incentives to invest in very small companies.
> **"**

AIO *n* MKTG *(abbr* **activities, interests and opinions)** AIO *m* □ ***AIO research*** investigación *f* AIO; ***AIO study*** estudio *m* AIO

air *n* **by air** en *or* por avión □ ***air cargo*** carga *f* aérea; ***air letter*** aerograma *m*; ***air link*** conexión *f* aérea; ***air miles*** millas *fpl* aéreas; **to collect air miles** juntar millas aéreas; ***air traffic*** tráfico *m* aéreo; ***air transport*** transporte *m* aéreo; ***air waybill*** conocimiento *m* de embarque aéreo

aircraft *n* avión *m*

airfreight 1 *n* transporte *m* aéreo; *(price)* flete *m* aéreo *(cargo)* carga *f* aérea □ ***airfreight company*** empresa *f* de transporte aéreo; ***airfreight consolidator*** consolidador *m* de carga aérea; ***airfreight container*** contenedor *m* para carga aérea; ***airfreight services*** servicios *mpl* de transporte aéreo
2 *vt (goods)* enviar por avión

airfreighting *n* transporte *m* aéreo

airline *n* línea *f* aérea

airmail 1 *n (service)* correo *m* aéreo; **by airmail** por correo aéreo □ ***airmail letter*** carta *f* por correo aéreo
2 *adv* **to send sth airmail** enviar algo por correo aéreo
3 *vt (letter, parcel)* enviar por correo aéreo

airport *n* aeropuerto *m* □ ***airport advertising*** publicidad *f* en aeropuertos; ***airport hotel*** hotel *m* de aeropuerto; ***airport lounge*** sala *f* (de espera) de aeropuerto; ***airport shop*** tienda *f* de aeropuerto; ***airport tax*** tasas *fpl* de aeropuerto;

airport taxi = taxi con una licencia especial para recoger pasajeros en el aeropuerto; ***airport terminal*** terminal *f* de aeropuerto

aisle *n (in shop)* pasillo *m* □ ***aisle end display*** cabecera *f* de góndola

alert box *n* COMPTR mensaje *m* de alerta

align *vt* (**a**) COMPTR *(characters, graphics)* alinear (**b**) FIN *(currency)* alinear (**on** a); **to align two different strategies** armonizar dos estrategias distintas

alignment *n* (**a**) COMPTR *(of characters, graphics)* alineación *f* (**b**) FIN *(of currencies)* alineación *f*

alimony *n US* FIN, LAW pensión *f* (matrimonial) alimenticia

allied *adj* ECON, FIN *(product, industry)* afín

all-in 1 *adj (price)* con todo incluido □ ***all-in insurance*** seguro *m* a todo riesgo; INS ***all-in policy*** póliza *f* a todo riesgo
2 *adv* todo incluido; **the computing system costs £3,000 all-in** el equipo informático cuesta 3.000 libras, todo incluido

all-inclusive *adj (price, tariff)* con todo incluido

allocate *vt* (**a**) *(resources, money, capital)* destinar, asignar (**to** a); *(duties, time)* asignar (**to** a); **10% of profits were allocated to R&D/advertising** se destinó un 10% de los beneficios a I+D/publicidad (**b**) ST EXCH *(shares)* adjudicar

allocation *n* (**a**) *(of resources, money, duties, time)* asignación *f* (**b**) ST EXCH *(of shares)* adjudicación *f*

all-or-none order *n* ST EXCH orden *f* todo o nada

allot *vt* (**a**) *(sum of money, job, task)* asignar (**to** a); **the funds have been allotted to the R&D department** los fondos se han asignado a I+D (**b**) ST EXCH *(shares)* adjudicar

allotment *n* (**a**) *(of sum of money, job, task)* asignación *f* (**b**) ST EXCH *(of shares)* adjudicación *f* □ ***allotment letter*** carta *f* de adjudicación; ***allotment right*** derecho *m* de suscripción

all-out *adj (strike)* general; *(effort)* supremo(a); **to make an all-out effort to do sth** realizar un esfuerzo supremo para hacer algo

allow *vt* (**a**) *(give)* **to allow sb a discount** conceder un descuento a alguien; **the bank allows 5% interest on deposits** el banco abona un 5% de interés por los depósitos (**b**) *(accept) (claim)* aceptar (**c**) *(take into account)* tener en cuenta, contar con; **we should allow £5,000 for unforeseen expenses** deberíamos dejar un margen de 5.000 libras para gastos imprevistos; **allow a week for delivery** el envío puede tardar una semana en llegar

▶ **allow for** *vt insep* tener en cuenta, contar con; **after allowing for** *(discount, expenses)* teniendo en cuenta; **we need to allow for some**

wastage debemos contar con una cierta cantidad de desperdicio de material; **we have to allow an extra 10% for carriage** tenemos que contar con un 10% extra para transporte; **has that been allowed for in your figures?** ¿has tenido eso en cuenta en tus cálculos?

allowable *adj (permissible)* aceptable, permisible; *(claim)* cubierto(a); *(expense)* deducible; **expenses allowable against tax** gastos deducibles

allowance *n* (**a**) ADMIN *(grant)* subsidio *m*; *(for accommodation, travel, food)* dieta *f*, asignación *f* para gastos (**b**) FIN *(discount)* descuento *m*; *(for tax)* ingresos *mpl* no sujetos a imposición; *(for bad quality)* descuento *m*

All-Share Index *n* = índice bursátil más amplio del mercado de valores británico

all-time *adj* **unemployment is at an all-time low** el desempleo se halla en un mínimo histórico; **sales have reached an all-time high** las ventas han alcanzado un máximo histórico

alphabetical order *n* orden *m* alfabético

alphanumeric *adj* COMPTR alfanúmerico(a) □ *alphanumeric keypad* teclado *m* alfanumérico; *alphanumeric numbering* numeración *f* alfanumérica

alphasort COMPTR **1** *n* orden *m* alfabético; **to do an alphasort on sth** ordenar algo alfabéticamente
  2 *vt* ordenar alfabéticamente

alpha stocks *npl* ST EXCH = valores más negociados en la Bolsa de Londres

alt *n* COMPTR **to get an e acute, press alt 130** para obtener una e acentuada, pulse alt 130; □ *alt key* tecla *f* alt

Alternative Investment Market *n* Mercado *m* de Inversión Alternativa

AMA *n* (*abbr* **American Marketing Association**) = asociación estadounidense de profesionales de marketing y ventas

amalgamate 1 *vt (companies)* fusionar □ *amalgamated union* = sindicato formado por la fusión de dos o más sindicatos
  2 *vi (companies)* unirse, fusionarse

amalgamation *n (of companies)* fusión *f*

amend *vt (resolution, motion, text)* enmendar, modificar; **the report has been amended to include the latest sales figures** se ha modificado el informe para incluir las últimas cifras de ventas

amendment *n (to resolution, motion, text)* enmienda *f*

American Express® *n* American Express®; **to pay by American Express**® pagar con American Express®; □ *American Express® card* tarjeta *f* American Express®

American-style option *n* ST EXCH opción *f* americana

Amex *n* (**a**) (*abbr* **American Stock Exchange**) Amex *m* (**b**) (*abbr* **American Express**®) Amex® □ *Amex card* tarjeta *f* Amex®

amicable settlement *n* acuerdo *m* amistoso

amortizable *adj* FIN *(debt)* amortizable

amortization *n* FIN *(of debt)* amortización *f* □ *amortization charges* cuota *f* de amortización

amortize *vt* FIN *(debt)* amortizar

amortizement *n* FIN *(of debt)* amortización *f*

amount *n (sum of money)* importe *m*, cantidad *f*; *(total)* total *m*; **amount due** importe debido; **she billed us for the amount of £50** nos envió una factura por (un importe de) 50 libras; **you're in credit to the amount of $100** dispone de un saldo a su favor de 100 dólares; **please find enclosed a cheque to the amount of $100** adjuntamos un cheque por un importe de 100 dólares □ ACCT **amount brought forward** suma *f* anterior

▶ **amount to** *vt insep* ascender a; **profits last year amounted to several million dollars** el año pasado los beneficios ascendieron a varios millones de dólares; **the company has debts amounting to over £200,000** la empresa tiene deudas que ascienden a más de 200.000 libras

ampersand *n* (signo *m*) et *m*, *Am* ampersand *m*

analog *adj* COMPTR analógico(a)

analyse, *US* **analyze** *vt (examine in detail)* analizar; *(account)* desglosar

analysis *n (detailed examination)* análisis *m inv*; *(of account)* desglose *m*

analyst *n* analista *mf*

anchor store *n* MKTG tienda *f* ancla, = tienda principal de un centro comercial

> ❝
>
> Located next to the historic Farmer's Market at the corner of 3rd St. and Fairfax in the heart of Los Angeles, The Grove is Southern California's most highly anticipated retail venue. The Grove features over 50 high-end retailers, including **anchor store** Nordstrom, as well as a spectacular 14-screen stadium-seating movie megaplex.
>
> ❞

ancillary 1 *n (of company)* (empresa *f*) subsidiaria *f*
  2 *adj* (**a**) *(supplementary)* secundario(a); **local services are ancillary to the national programme** los servicios locales están subordinados al programa nacional (**b**) *(subsidiary) (cost, advantage)* adicional □ LAW *ancillary rights* derechos *mpl* secundarios

angel *n Fam* FIN *(investor)* inversor(ora) *m,f* providencial, = inversor que respalda con su propio capital a nuevas empresas o a empresas en apuros

annex *n (to contract, document)* anexo *m*

annual *adj (holiday, payment, report)* anual ◘ *annual accounts* cuentas *fpl* anuales; *annual budget* presupuesto *m* anual; *annual congress* congreso *m* anual; *annual contribution (to pension scheme)* aportación *f* anual; ACCT *annual depreciation* amortización *f* por anualidades; *annual earnings (of company, person)* ingresos *mpl* anuales; *annual general meeting* asamblea *f or* junta *f* general anual; *annual guaranteed salary* sueldo *m or* salario *m* base (anual); *annual income* ingresos *mpl* anuales; FIN *annual instalment* anualidad *f*; *annual leave* vacaciones *fpl* al año; *annual percentage rate (of interest)* tasa *f* anual equivalente, TAE *m or f*; INS *annual premium* prima *f* anual; *annual profit* beneficio *m* anual; *annual report* memoria *f* anual; *annual returns* rendimientos *mpl* anuales; *annual revenue* recaudación *f* anual; *annual salary* sueldo *m or* salario *m* anual; **he has an annual salary of £50,000** tiene un sueldo anual de 50.000 libras; *annual sales figures* cifras *fpl* de ventas anuales; ACCT *annual statement of results* cuenta *f* de resultados anual; *annual turnover* volumen *m* de negocio anual; *annual variations* fluctuaciones *fpl* anuales; ACCT *annual writedown* amortización *f* anual

annualize *vt* anualizar; **the annualized figures** las cifras anualizadas ◘ *annualized percentage rate* tasa *f* anual equivalente, TAE *m or f*

annually *adv* anualmente

annuitant *n* INS beneficiario(a) *m,f* de una anualidad

annuity *n (regular income)* anualidad *f*; *(for life)* renta *f* vitalicia; *(investment)* póliza *f* de anualidad vitalicia **to pay sb an annuity** pagar a alguien una anualidad ◘ *annuity payment* anualidad *f*

annul *vt (contract)* anular

annulment *n (of contract)* anulación *f*

anonymous *adj* MKTG *anonymous buyer* consumidor(ora) *m,f*; COMPTR *anonymous FTP* FTP *m* anónimo; MKTG *anonymous research* estudio *m* de consumidores

ANSI *n (abbr American National Standards Institute)* = instituto estadounidense de normalización, *Esp* ≃ AENOR *m*

answer 1 *n* respuesta *f*; **in answer to your letter** en respuesta a su carta; **there's no answer** *(on telephone)* no contesta nadie

2 *vt (letter)* responder a, contestar; **to answer the telephone** contestar al teléfono

answering *adj* *answering machine* contestador *m* (automático); *answering service*

servicio *m* de atención de llamadas *or Am* llamados

answerphone *n Br* contestador *m* (automático)

anticipate *vt* **(a)** *(expect)* esperar, prever; **we anticipate a good response to our advertisement** esperamos una buena respuesta a nuestro anuncio ◘ *anticipated profit* beneficios *mpl* previstos; *anticipated sales* ventas *fpl* previstas

(b) *(be prepared for)* anticiparse a, adelantarse a; **we anticipated our competitors by launching our product first** nos adelantamos a la competencia siendo los primeros en lanzar el producto; **he anticipated the fall in price and sold early** adivinó que el precio iba a caer y vendió pronto

(c) FIN *(bill, salary)* pagar por adelantado

anticipation *n* **in anticipation of** en previsión de; **they raised their prices in anticipation of increased inflation** subieron los precios en previsión de una inflación más alta

anti-dumping *adj (laws, legislation)* antidumping

anti-glare filter, anti-glare screen *n* COMPTR filtro *m* de pantalla

anti-inflationary *adj (measures, policy)* antiinflacionista, antiinflacionario(a)

anti-raid *adj* FIN *(measures, precautions)* anti-OPA *inv*

anti-takeover *adj (measures, precautions)* antiabsorción

anti-theft tag *n* alarma *f* antirrobo, nogo *m*

antitrust *adj US* ECON antimonopolio ◘ *antitrust law* ley *f* antimonopolio

antivirus *adj* COMPTR antivirus *inv* ◘ *antivirus check* comprobación *f* antivirus; *antivirus program* (programa *m*) antivirus *m inv*

AOB *(abbr* **any other business)** ruegos *mpl* y preguntas

AOCB *(abbr* **any other competent business)** ruegos *mpl* y preguntas

APEX *adj (abbr* **advanced purchase excursion)** *APEX fare* precio *m or* tarifa *f* APEX; *APEX ticket Esp* billete *m or Am* boleto *m or esp Am* pasaje *m* (con tarifa) APEX

apologize *vi* disculparse; **to apologize to sb for sth** pedir disculpas a alguien por algo; **we apologize for any inconvenience** rogamos disculpen las molestias

apology *n* disculpa *f*; **please accept my apologies for the delay** le ruego que acepte mis disculpas por el retraso; **the director sends his apologies** el director se excusa por no poder asistir

apostrophe *n* apóstrofo *m*

appeal LAW **1** *n* recurso *m* (de apelación); **to enter** *or* **to lodge an appeal** presentar un recurso (de apelación)
2 *vi* recurrir, apelar; **to appeal against** *(decision, ruling)* interponer un recurso (de apelación) contra
3 *vt* US *(decision, ruling)* interponer un recurso (de apelación) contra

appellant LAW **1** *n* apelante *mf*, recurrente *mf*
2 *adj* **the appellant party** la parte apelante *or* recurrente

append *vt (list, document)* adjuntar (**to** a); *(signature)* estampar (**to** en); *(notes, comments)* adjuntar (**to** a); COMPTR *(to database)* añadir (**to** a); **to append a document to a file** adjuntar un documento a un archivo; **please refer to the lists appended to this document** por favor, sírvase consultar las listas adjuntas a este documento

appendix *n (to document, report, book)* apéndice *m*

applicant *n (for job, loan, patent, shares)* solicitante *mf* (**for** de); *(for trademark)* agente *mf* de la propiedad industrial

application *n* (**a**) *(for job, loan, funding, patent)* solicitud *f* (**for** de); **to submit an application** *(for job, help, loan, funding, patent)* presentar una solicitud; **to make an application for sth** solicitar algo; **closing date for applications** fecha límite de admisión de solicitudes; **full details on application** se enviará la información completa previa solicitud ❑ **application form** *(for job)* impreso *m or* formulario *m or Méx* forma *f* de solicitud
(**b**) ST EXCH **application for shares** solicitud *or* petición *f* de acciones; **to make an application for shares** presentar una solicitud *or* petición de acciones; **10% of the full share price will be payable on application** en el momento de la solicitud se deberá abonar el 10% del precio de las acciones ❑ **application form** *(for shares)* impreso *m or* formulario *m or Méx* forma *f* de solicitud
(**c**) COMPTR aplicación *f*, programa *m* ❑ **application software** software *m* de aplicación

apply *vi* (**a**) **to apply to sb for sth** solicitar algo a alguien; **apply to the personnel office** envíe la solicitud al departamento de personal; **to apply for a job** solicitar un empleo; **she has decided to apply for the job** ha decidido solicitar el empleo; **to apply for a grant** solicitar una beca; **apply within** *(sign)* razón aquí; **interested parties should apply in writing to the following address** los interesados deberán enviar una solicitud por escrito a la siguiente dirección; **I applied for the job in person** solicité el empleo en persona
(**b**) ST EXCH **to apply for shares** solicitar acciones

appoint *vt* (**a**) *(person, committee)* nombrar, designar; **to appoint sb to a post** nombrar a alguien para un cargo; **Mr Johnston has been appointed general manager** el señor Johnston ha sido nombrado director general; **he's our newly appointed sales manager** lo acaban de nombrar nuestro jefe de ventas (**b**) *(date, time, place)* fijar

appointed *adj* (**a**) *(date, time, place)* convenido(a), fijado(a) (**b**) ***appointed agent*** representante *mf* oficial

appointee *n* persona *f* nombrada *or* designada

appointment *n* (**a**) *(meeting)* cita *f*; **to make** *or* **fix an appointment with sb** fijar *or* concertar una cita con alguien; **to break an appointment** faltar *or* no acudir a una cita; **to cancel an appointment** cancelar una cita; **please telephone if you cannot make** *or* **keep your appointment** por favor, avise por teléfono si no puede acudir a la cita; **to meet** *or* **see sb by appointment** reunirse con alguien *or* ver a alguien con cita previa; **by appointment only** con cita previa; **have you got an appointment?** ¿tiene cita? ❑ **appointments book** libro *m* de citas; **appointments diary** agenda *f* (de citas)
(**b**) *(to job)* nombramiento *m*; **the new appointment has settled in well** el nuevo empleado se ha adaptado bien
(**c**) *(job held)* cargo *m*; **to hold an appointment** ostentar un cargo; **he's been offered an appointment on the board** le han ofrecido un puesto en la junta directiva
(**d**) **appointments** *(in newspaper)* ofertas *fpl* de empleo

apportion *vt (taxes, expenses)* distribuir, repartir, periodificar

apportionment *n (of taxes, expenses)* distribución *f*, reparto *m*, periodificación *f*

appraisal *n (of standards, personnel)* evaluación *f*; *(of object for insurance purposes, before auction)* tasación *f*

appraise *vt (standards, personnel)* evaluar; *(object for insurance purposes, before auction)* tasar

appraisee *n* evaluado(a) *m,f*

appreciate *vi (goods, investment, shares)* revalorizarse, apreciarse; *(value, price)* aumentar; **the euro has appreciated against other currencies** el euro se ha revalorizado *or* apreciado frente a otras divisas

appreciation *n (of goods, investment, shares)* revalorización *f*, apreciación *f*; *(of value, price)* aumento *m*

apprentice 1 *n* aprendiz(iza) *m,f*
2 *vt* **to apprentice sb to sb** colocar a alguien de aprendiz(iza) de alguien

apprenticeship *n* aprendizaje *m*; **to serve**

one's apprenticeship (with sb) hacer el aprendizaje (con alguien); **she did an apprenticeship as a carpenter** hizo un aprendizaje como carpintera, estuvo de aprendiza de carpintero

appro *n Br Fam (abbr* **approval**) **on appro** a prueba; **to buy sth on appro** comprar algo a prueba; **to send sth on appro** enviar algo a prueba

appropriate *vt (funds)* destinar, asignar (**to/ for** a/para); **£4,000 has been appropriated to upgrading the computing system** se han destinado 4.000 libras para actualizar el sistema informático

appropriation *n* (**a**) *(of funds)* asignación *f*; **government appropriations** partidas *fpl* presupuestarias estatales; **appropriation to the reserve** asignación al fondo de reserva ❑ *appropriation account* cuenta *f* de afectación (**b**) *US (budgetary)* crédito *m* presupuestario; **allotment of appropriations** distribución *f* de las partidas presupuestarias ❑ *Appropriations Committee (of Senate, House)* comité *m* de gastos, comisión *f* de presupuestos

approval *n* (**a**) *(sanction)* aprobación *f*; **the deal is subject to the approval of the board** el acuerdo depende de la aprobación del consejo; **to submit sth for approval (by sb)** someter algo para su aprobación (por parte de alguien); **for your approval** *(on document)* para su aprobación *or* visto bueno

(**b**) *(of document, minutes)* aprobación *f*

(**c**) *(trial basis)* **on approval** a prueba; **to buy sth on approval** comprar algo a prueba; **to send sth on approval** enviar algo a prueba; *US* **approvals** *(goods)* = artículos enviados a prueba a un cliente

approve *vt* aprobar; **read and approved** *(on document)* visto y conforme; **the plan must be approved by the committee** el plan debe ser aprobado por el comité

approved *adj* ADMIN **(officially) approved** homologado(a) ❑ *approved dealer* concesionario *m* autorizado

approx *adv (abbr* **approximately**) aprox.

approximate *adj* aproximado(a) ❑ *approximate price* precio *m* aproximado

approximately *adv* aproximadamente

approximation *n* aproximación *f*

APR *n* FIN *(abbr* **annual** *or* **annualized percentage rate**) TAE *m or f*

APT *n (abbr* **arbitrage pricing theory**) = teoría de fijación de precios por arbitraje

aptitude test *n* prueba *f* de aptitud

arbitrage *n* FIN, ST EXCH arbitraje *m* ❑ *arbitrage pricing theory* = teoría de fijación de precios por arbitraje

arbitrageur, arbitrager *n* FIN, ST EXCH arbitrajista *mf*

arbitrate **1** *vt* arbitrar en, actuar como árbitro en **2** *vi* arbitrar, actuar como árbitro

arbitration *n* arbitraje *m*; **to go to arbitration** someterse a arbitraje; **they referred the dispute to arbitration** decidieron someter la disputa a arbitraje; **procedure by arbitration** procedimiento *m* arbitral; **settlement by arbitration** resolución *f* mediante arbitraje ❑ *arbitration board* junta *f* arbitral; *arbitration clause* cláusula *f* de arbitraje; *arbitration court* tribunal *m* de arbitraje; *arbitration ruling* laudo *m* arbitral; *arbitration tribunal* tribunal *m* de arbitraje

arbitrator *n* árbitro *mf*, amigable componedor(ora) *m,f*; **the dispute has been referred to the arbitrator** se le ha remitido la disputa al árbitro

archive COMPTR **1** *n* archivo *m* ❑ *archive copy* copia *f* de archivo; *archive file* fichero *m* de archivo; *archive site* sitio *m* de archivos **2** *vt* archivar

archiving *n* COMPTR archivo *m*

archivist *n* archivero(a) *m,f*, archivista *mf*

area *n (region)* zona *f*, área *f*; **the London area** la zona *or* región londinense ❑ *US* TEL *area code* prefijo *m*; *area manager* jefe(a) *m,f* de zona *area of operations (sector)* sector *m* (de operaciones); MKTG *area sample* muestra *f* de área; MKTG *area sampling* muestreo *m* por áreas

Ariel *n* ST EXCH = sistema informático que permite realizar operaciones bursátiles entre suscriptores sin que intervenga la Bolsa de Londres

ARM *n US* FIN *(abbr* **adjustable-rate mortgage**) hipoteca *f* (con *Esp* tipo *or Am* tasa) de interés variable

arm's-length price *n* FIN valor *m* de mercado

ARR *n* ACCT *(abbr* **accounting rate of return**) tasa *f* de rendimiento contable

arrange **1** *vt (meeting, trip)* organizar; *(time, date)* fijar; **the meeting is arranged for noon tomorrow** la reunión está fijada para mañana a mediodía; **let's arrange a time to meet** vamos a quedar a una hora para reunirnos; **to arrange to do sth** *(with someone else)* acordar hacer algo, quedar en hacer algo; **I have arranged to have a taxi come and pick you up at 7.30** he reservado un taxi para que lo recoja a las 7.30 **2** *vi* **to arrange for sth to be done** disponer que se haga algo; **we have arranged for them to be picked up from the airport** hemos hecho las gestiones necesarias para que los recojan en el aeropuerto

arranged interview *n* entrevista *f* concertada

arrangement *n (understanding, agreement)*

acuerdo *m*; FIN *(with creditors)* acuerdo, concordato *m*; **to come to an arrangement with sb** llegar a un acuerdo con alguien; **he came to an arrangement with the bank** llegó a un acuerdo con el banco; **price by arrangement** precio a convenir; **special designs by arrangement** diseños especiales por encargo; **by prior arrangement** mediante previo acuerdo; *(appointment)* con cita previa

array *n* COMPTR matriz *f*

arrearage *n US* demora *f* en el pago

arrears *npl* atrasos *mpl*; **we're three months in arrears on the loan payments** llevamos tres meses de retraso en el pago del préstamo; **to get into arrears** retrasarse en los pagos; **we're paid a month in arrears** nos pagan a mes vencido; **interest on arrears** interés *m* de demora; **salary increase with arrears effective as from 1 March** aumento de sueldo con efecto retroactivo desde el 1 de marzo; **tax in arrears** impuestos *mpl* vencidos; **arrears of interest** intereses atrasados; **arrears of work** trabajo *m* atrasado; **she's in arrears with her correspondence** tiene correspondencia atrasada por atender

arrest *vt (stop)* detener; *(slow down)* desacelerar; **in an effort to arrest inflation** en un esfuerzo por detener/desacelerar la inflación

arrival *n (of goods, person, aeroplane)* llegada *f*; **to await arrival** *(on letter)* esperar llegada □ **arrivals list** lista *f* de llegadas; **arrival station** estación *f* de llegada; **arrival time** hora *f* de llegada

arrive *vi* **to arrive at a solution/decision** llegar a una solución/decisión; **to arrive at a price** convenir un precio

arrow key *n* COMPTR tecla *f* de dirección *or* de movimiento del cursor

article 1 *n* (**a**) LAW *(in agreement, treaty)* artículo *m*; *(in contract)* sección *f* □ **articles of apprenticeship** contrato *m* de aprendizaje; **Articles of Association** estatutos *mpl* sociales, escritura *f* de constitución; **articles and conditions** *(of sale, contract)* condiciones *fpl* (**b**) *(item)* artículo *m* 2 *vt Br (apprentice)* **to be articled to** *(trade)* trabajar de aprendiz(iza) en; *(profession)* trabajar en prácticas en; **to be articled to a firm of solicitors** hacer una pasantía en un bufete de abogados □ **articled clerk** abogado(a) *m,f* en prácticas, pasante *m,f*

"
Shareholders of Royal Ahold, the international food provider, approved all proposed amendments to the company's **Articles of Association** during an Extraordinary General Meeting of Stockholders held today. The par value of Ahold shares will now be expressed in Euro.
"

artificial person *n* LAW persona *f* jurídica

artwork *n (for advertisement)* ilustraciones *fpl*

ASA *n* (**a**) *Br (abbr* **Advertising Standards Authority**) = organismo que controla y vela por la publicidad (**b**) *US (abbr* **American Standards Association**) = instituto de normalización, en la actualidad conocido como ANSI

asap *adv (abbr* **as soon as possible**) cuanto antes, lo antes posible; **we need to reply asap** debemos responder lo antes posible

ascending *adj* COMPTR **ascending order** orden *m* ascendente; **ascending sort** ordenación *f* ascendente

ASCII *n* COMPTR *(abbr* **American Standard Code for Information Interchange**) ASCII *m* □ **ASCII code** código *m* ASCII; **ASCII file** archivo *m* or fichero *m* ASCII; **ASCII format** formato *m* ASCII; **ASCII number** número *m* ASCII

ASE *n (abbr* **American Stock Exchange**) ASE *m*, = mercado de valores estadounidense

ASEAN *n (abbr* **Association of South East Asian Nations**) ASEAN *f*

A-share *n* ST EXCH acción *f* de clase A

"
Turnover on the local currency **A-share** markets in Shanghai and Shenzhen, which are restricted to Chinese investors, has more than trebled, to a daily $6 billion – 8 billion, and prices have soared... The hard-currency **B-share** markets, supposedly reserved for foreigners but in fact havens for hot Chinese money, have almost doubled from their all-time lows earlier this year.
"

asking price, *US* **asked price** *n* precio *m* de venta; ST EXCH precio *m* de salida

aspirational *adj* MKTG *(product)* deseado(a), codiciado(a); *(consumer)* = que aspira a un alto nivel de vida y por tanto está interesado en adquirir productos de alta calidad y de prestigio; *(advertising)* = que se centra más en el prestigio que ofrece un producto que en sus cualidades □ **aspirational group** grupo *m* al que se aspira pertenecer

"
The Fosters Trading Company name is to be dropped and the clothing chain rebranded as a unisex store. ... The new stores, called d2, will stock male and female clothing and accessories and will be designed to appeal to the **aspirational** consumer.
"

assembly *n* (**a**) *(meeting)* asamblea *f* (**b**) *(construction) (of machine, furniture)* montaje *m*, ensamblaje *m*; *(end product)* unidad *f*; **a door assembly** una unidad de puerta □ **assembly**

line cadena *f* de montaje; **to work on an assembly line** trabajar en una cadena de montaje; *assembly line work* trabajo *m* en una cadena de montaje; *assembly plant* planta *f* de montaje; *assembly shop* taller *m* de montaje; *assembly workshop* taller *m* de montaje (**c**) COMPTR ❏ *assembly language* lenguaje *m* ensamblador *or* Am assembler

assess *vt* (**a**) *(damage)* evaluar, valorar; *(value)* tasar, valorar; **to assess a property for taxation** determinar el valor catastral de un inmueble; **they assessed the damages at £500** valoraron los daños en 500 libras (**b**) *(for tax purposes)* calcular, evaluar; **to assess sb's income** calcular la renta de alguien ❏ *assessed income* renta *f* imponible *or* sujeta a tributación

assessable *adj* FIN imponible, sujeto(a) a tributación *Br* **assessable income** renta *f* imponible *or* sujeta a tributación; *Br* **assessable profits** beneficios *mpl* imponibles

assessment *n* (**a**) *(of damage)* evaluación *f*, valoración *f*; *(of value)* tasación *f*, valoración (**b**) *(of tax, income)* liquidación *f* (**c**) **assessment centre** *(for job candidates)* centro *m* de selección de personal

assessor *n* tasador(ora) *m,f* ❏ *US* **assessor of taxes** inspector(ora) *m,f* fiscal

asset *n* (**a**) FIN **assets** *(of company)* activos *mpl*; *(personal)* bienes *mpl*; **assets and liabilities** el activo y el pasivo, las partidas del balance; **total assets** activo total; **to have an excess of assets over liabilities** tener un activo superior al pasivo, tener superávit ❏ *asset allocation* asignación *f* de activos; *asset management* *(of a company's property)* gestión *f* de activos; *(of money for investment)* gestión *f* de activos financieros; *asset stripper* = persona que compra empresas en quiebra para vender sus activos; *asset stripping* liquidación *f* (especulativa) de activos; *asset swap* permuta *f* de activos; *asset turnover* rotación *f* de activos; *asset utilization ratio* ratio *m or f* de explotación de activos; *asset valuation* valoración *f* de activos; ACCT *asset value* valor *m* de los activos
(**b**) *(advantage)* ventaja *f*; **she's a real asset to the company** es una valiosa aportación a la empresa

assign *vt* (**a**) *(task, funds, shares)* asignar, adjudicar (**to** a); LAW *(goods, debt, property)* ceder (**to** a); **she was assigned to investigate the complaint** le asignaron *or* encargaron que investigara la reclamación *or* SAm el reclamo; **she assigned the copyright to the school** cedió los derechos de autor a la escuela; **the property was assigned to his daughter** la propiedad fue trasferida a su hija
(**b**) *(employee)* destinar, asignar; **Robert has been assigned to the marketing department** han destinado a Robert al departamento de marketing

assignable *adj* LAW *(debts, rights)* transferible

assigned risk *n US* INS riesgo *m* señalado

assignee *n* LAW sucesor(ora) *m,f*, cesionario(a) *m,f*

assignment *n* *(of task, funds, shares)* asignación *f*, adjudicación *f*; LAW *(of goods, property)* cesión *f*, traspaso *m*; ACCT **assignment of accounts receivable, assignment of debts** cesión de cuentas por cobrar, cesión de créditos; **assignment of contract** subrogación *f* de contrato

assignor *n* LAW cesionario(a) *m,f*

assistant **1** *n* ayudante *m,f*
2 *adj* **assistant general manager** director(ora) *m,f* general adjunto(a); **assistant manager** subdirector(ora) *m,f*, director(ora) *m,f* adjunto(a)

associate **1** *n* *(in business)* socio(a) *m,f*
2 *adj* asociado(a) ❏ *associate company* empresa *f* asociada; *associate director* director(ora) *m,f* adjunto(a); *associate member* miembro *mf* asociado(a)

associated *adj* asociado(a) ❏ *associated company* empresa *f* asociada

association *n* asociación *f*; **to form an association** crear una asociación

assortment *n* *(of goods)* variedad *f*

assume *vt* *(responsibility, running of company, power, control)* asumir; **he will assume responsibility for the new department** asumirá la responsabilidad del nuevo departamento; INS **to assume all risks** asumir todos los riesgos; LAW **to assume ownership** tomar posesión

assurance *n Br* seguro *m* de vida ❏ *assurance company* compañía *f* de seguros de vida; *assurance policy* (póliza *f* de) seguro *m* de vida

assured *n* asegurado(a) *m,f (con un seguro de vida)*

assurer, assuror *n* asegurador(ora) *m,f (de seguros de vida)*

asterisk *n* asterisco *m*

at *prep* *(in e-mail address)* arroba *f*; **"gwilson at transex, dot, co, dot, uk"** "gwilson arroba transex, punto, co, punto, uk" ❏ *at sign* arroba *f*

ATM *n* (**a**) BANKING *(abbr automated teller machine)* cajero *m* automático (**b**) COMPTR *(abbr asynchronous transfer mode)* ATM *m*, modo *m* de transferencia asíncrono

attach *vt* (**a**) ADMIN *(appendix, document)* adjuntar; **the attached letter** la carta adjunta; **please find attached...** se adjunta... (**b**) *(second)* destinar *or* trasladar temporalmente; **an official attached to another department** un funcionario destinado temporalmente a otro departamento (**c**) COMPTR *(file)* adjuntar (**to** a); **to attach a file to an e-mail** adjuntar un archivo a un correo (**d**) LAW *(person)* retener por orden judicial; *(property, salary)* embargar

attachment n (**a**) ADMIN (appendix, document) anexo m (**b**) (secondment) **he's on attachment to the Manchester branch** está destinado temporalmente a la sucursal de Manchester (**c**) COMPTR (of e-mail) archivo m or fichero m adjunto, anexo m (**d**) LAW (of person) retención f por orden judicial; (of property) embargo m; **attachment of property** embargo de propiedades

attack 1 n (on market) ataque m (**on** contra); **they have just launched an attack on the telecommunications market** han emprendido un ataque contra el mercado de las telecomunicaciones
  2 vt (market) atacar

attend vt (meeting, conference) asistir a; **the conference was well attended this year** este año asistió mucha gente al congreso

▶ **attend to** vt insep (deal with) ocuparse de, atender; (client, customer) atender a; (order) procesar; **I shall attend to it** me ocuparé de ello; **are you being attended to?** ¿lo atienden?

attendance n asistencia f; **there was a good attendance at the meeting** asistió mucha gente a la reunión, la reunión tuvo gran asistencia ❑ **attendance sheet** (at meeting) hoja f de asistencia

attendee n (at meeting) asistente mf

attention n **for the attention of Mr Harvey** (in letter) a la atención del Sr. Harvey; **it has been brought to our attention that you have exceeded your overdraft limit** hemos sido informados de que ha sobrepasado el límite de su descubierto; **may I have your attention for a moment?** ¿serían tan amables de prestarme un momento de atención?

attestation n (of document) certificación f, compulsación f ❑ **attestation of employment** certificado m de empleo

attested copy n copia f compulsada

at-the-money option n ST EXCH opción f a la par, opción en dinero

attitude n MKTG (of consumer to product) actitud f ❑ **attitude research** investigación f sobre actitudes; **attitude scale** escala f de medición de actitudes; **attitude survey** estudio m de actitudes

attn (abbr **for the attention of**) A/A

attorney n (**a**) (representative) apoderado(a) m,f (**b**) US (lawyer) abogado(a) m,f

attract vt atraer; **the proposal has attracted a lot of attention** la propuesta ha suscitado or despertado mucha atención; **the campaign should attract many new investors** la campaña debería atraer muchos inversores nuevos

attractive adj (price, offer, proposition) atractivo(a), interesante

attributable profit n ACCT beneficio m imputable

attribute n MKTG (of product) característica f, atributo m ❑ **attribute list** lista f de características

auction 1 n (**sale by**) **auction** subasta f, remate m; **to sell goods** Br **by** or US **at auction** subastar or rematar bienes; **to put sth up for auction** sacar algo a subasta or remate; **the property was bought at auction** compraron la propiedad en una subasta or un remate ❑ **auction price** precio m de subasta or remate; **auction room** sala f de subastas or remates; **auction sale** venta f en pública subasta or en público remate
  2 vt subastar

▶ **auction off** vt sep subastar, liquidar mediante subasta, rematar

audience n MKTG (for product, advertisement) audiencia f ❑ **audience exposure** audiencia f expuesta; **audience measurement** medición f de la audiencia; **audience research** investigación f de la audiencia; **audience size** volumen m de audiencia; **audience study** estudio m de audiencia

audioconference n TEL audioconferencia f

audiometer n TV audímetro m

audio-typing n transcripción f (con dictáfono)

audio-typist n transcriptor(ora) m,f (con dictáfono)

audit 1 n FIN auditoría f ❑ Br **Audit Bureau of Circulation,** US **Audit Bureau of Circulations** ≃ Oficina f de Justificación de la Difusión; **audit committee** comité m de auditoría; **audit company** empresa f auditora, auditoría f; **audit manager** auditor(ora) m,f jefe(a); ADMIN **Audit Office** Tribunal m de cuentas; **audit trail** pista f de auditoría
  2 vt FIN (accounts) auditar

auditing n FIN auditoría f

auditor n auditor(ora) m,f, censor(ora) m,f de cuentas; **firm of auditors** empresa f auditora ❑ **auditor's opinion** opinión f de auditoría; **auditor's report** informe m de auditoría

auditorship n FIN auditoría f

augmented product n MKTG producto m aumentado

AUP n COMPTR (abbr **Acceptable Use Policy**) política f de uso aceptable

AUR n (abbr **asset utilization ratio**) ratio m or f de explotación de activos

austerity n ECON, FIN austeridad f ❑ **austerity measures** medidas fpl de austeridad; **austerity policy** política f de austeridad; **austerity programme** plan m de austeridad

autarky n ECON *(system, country)* autarquía f

authenticate vt (**a**) *(document, signature)* autentificar, autenticar (**b**) COMPTR autentificar, autenticar

authentication n (**a**) *(of document, signature)* autentificación f, autenticación f (**b**) COMPTR autentificación f, autenticación f

authority n (**a**) *(power)* autoridad f; **the authorities** las autoridades; **I'd like to speak to someone in authority** quisiera hablar con el responsable; **she has authority over the whole department** tiene todo el departamento a su cargo (**b**) *(permission)* autorización f; **to give sb (the) authority to do sth** autorizar a alguien a hacer algo

authorization n autorización f; **you can't do anything without authorization from the management** no se puede hacer nada sin la autorización de la dirección

authorize vt autorizar; **to authorize sb to do sth** autorizar a alguien a hacer algo

authorized adj autorizado(a) ❑ **authorized agent** representante mf autorizado(a); ST EXCH **authorized capital** capital m social autorizado; **authorized charges** tarifas fpl autorizadas; **authorized dealer** distribuidor m autorizado; **authorized distributor** distribuidor m autorizado; **authorized overdraft facility** línea f de descubierto autorizada; **authorized price** precio m autorizado; **authorized representative** *(of company)* representante mf autorizado(a); ST EXCH **authorized share capital** capital m social autorizado; **authorized signatory** signatario(a) m,f autorizado(a); **authorized signatory list** lista f de signatarios autorizados; **authorized stockist** distribuidor m autorizado; Br ST EXCH **authorized unit trust** fondo m de inversión mobiliaria autorizado

autocorrect vt COMPTR corregir automáticamente

autodial n TEL marcado m or Andes, RP discado m automático

automate vt automatizar

automated adj automatizado(a) ❑ BANKING **automated clearing house** cámara f de compensación automática; **automated reservation** reserva f automática; **automated teller machine** cajero m automático; **automated ticket** = billete de máquina expendedora automática; **automated withdrawal** cargo m automático

automatic adj automático(a) ❑ **automatic accounting** contabilidad f automatizada; COMPTR **automatic backup** copia f de seguridad automática; TEL **automatic call transfer** desvío m automático de llamadas or Am llamados; COMPTR **automatic data processing** proceso m or procesamiento m automático de datos; TEL

automatic dial marcado m or Andes, RP discado m automático; TEL **automatic dialling** marcado m or Andes, RP discado m automático; COMPTR **automatic feed** avance m automático; COMPTR **automatic input** alimentación f automática de datos; **automatic packaging** empaquetado m automático; **automatic transfer** transferencia f automática

automation n automatización f

autonomous adj autónomo(a)

autonomy n autonomía f; **the department has autonomy in this area** el departamento goza de autonomía en este ámbito

autoredial n TEL remarcado m or Andes, RP rediscado m automático

autosave COMPTR **1** n autoguardado m
2 vt guardar automáticamente

availability n disponibilidad f; **this offer is subject to availability** esta oferta es válida hasta fin de existencias

available adj disponible; *(person)* libre, disponible; **we regret that this offer is no longer available** desafortunadamente esta oferta ya no está disponible; **these items are available from stock** estos artículos están disponibles en nuestra tienda; **available on CD-ROM** disponible en CD-ROM; **available for the Mac/PC** disponible para Mac/PC; **available to download from our website** puede ser descargado desde nuestro sitio web; FIN **sum available for dividend** cantidad f disponible para el pago de dividendos ❑ **available assets** activo m disponible; **available balance** saldo m disponible; **available capital** capital m disponible; **available cash flow** capital m disponible; **available funds** saldo m disponible; MKTG **available market** mercado m potencial; COMPTR **available memory** memoria f disponible

aval n BANKING aval m bancario

avalize vt BANKING avalar

AVC n *(abbr additional voluntary contribution)* = aportación complementaria al plan de pensiones

AVCs are additional voluntary contributions – extra payments made from your salary or other net relevant earnings to top up your company pension. You can pay **AVCs** into a scheme run by your company, known as an in-house **AVC** scheme, or into a free-standing (FSAVC) policy run by another company, or you can pay **AVCs** to buy extra years of service in a final-salary company pension scheme.

AVCO n *(abbr average cost)* costo m or Esp coste m medio

average 1 n (**a**) promedio m, media f; **rough average** promedio aproximado, media aproximada; **sales average** promedio de ventas (**b**) INS avería f ❑ **average adjuster** liquidador m de averías; **average adjustment** liquidación f de averías; **average bond** garantía f de avería gruesa (**c**) ST EXCH índice m

2 adj medio(a), Am promedio ❑ **average cost per unit** costo m or Esp coste m unitario medio or Am promedio; **average due date** vencimiento m medio or Am promedio; **average price** precio m medio or Am promedio; **average revenue** ingresos mpl medios or Am promedio; MKTG **average sample** muestra f representativa; **average tare** peso m medio or Am promedio; US **average tax rate** Esp tipo m medio or Am tasa f media del impuesto sobre la renta; **average unit cost** costo m or Esp coste m unitario medio or Am promedio; **average yield** rendimiento m medio or Am promedio

3 vt (calculate the average of) calcular la media de; **household spending averages $200 per week** el consumo familiar arroja una media de 200 dólares a la semana; **the factory averages 1,000 units a day** la fábrica produce una media de 1.000 unidades al día

▶ **average out at** vt insep **profits average out at 10%** los beneficios arrojan una media de un 10%; **production averages out at 120 units per day** la producción alcanza una media de 120 unidades al día

avoidable costs npl ACCT costos mpl or Esp costes mpl evitables

avoidance clause n cláusula f resolutoria or de nulidad

await vt **awaiting your instructions** (in letter, memo) quedamos a la espera de sus instrucciones; **awaiting delivery** (of parcel, mail) pendiente de entrega

award 1 n (damages) indemnización f; (decision) fallo m; (of contract) adjudicación m

2 vt (contract) adjudicar; (pay rise, damages) conceder

awareness n MKTG (of product) conocimiento m, notoriedad f ❑ **awareness rating** grado m de notoriedad, = calificación que establece el grado de conocimiento que los consumidores tienen de un producto; **awareness study** estudio m de la notoriedad

away adv (absent) **the boss is away on business this week** el jefe está en viaje de trabajo esta semana

AWB n (abbr **air waybill**) conocimiento m aéreo

axe, US **ax 1** n Fam **to get the axe** (person) ser puesto(a) de patitas en la calle; (project) ser descartado(a) or abandonado(a); Fam **to give sb the axe** poner a alguien de patitas en la calle; Fam **to give sth the axe** abandonar algo

2 vt (person) poner de patitas en la calle a; (project) abandonar; (job, position) suprimir; **the service has been axed for economic reasons** han suprimido el servicio por motivos económicos

AZERTY keyboard n COMPTR teclado m AZERTY

Bb

B2A adj (abbr **business-to-administration**) B2A

B2B adj (abbr **business-to-business**) B2B, entre empresas

> **"**
> Up until March, it had seemed that anyone who had half a business plan and dot.com on the end of their firm's name could raise millions in venture capital in a moment. But even in the early months of the year the mood was shifting. The hottest acronym was no longer B2C – business to consumer – but **B2B**, dot.coms helping businesses function better with each other.
> **"**

B2C adj (abbr **business-to-consumer**) B2C, entre empresa y consumidor

BAA n (abbr **British Airports Authority**) = organismo aeroportuario británico, Esp ≃ Aena f

baby n US FIN **baby bond** = bono de valor nominal inferior a 1.000 dólares; **baby boomer** = persona nacida durante el periodo de explosión demográfica que siguió a la Segunda Guerra Mundial

> **"**
> They are targeting well-off **baby boomers** who are developing noses for wine and who rate choice and service at least as highly as price and convenience.
> **"**

back 1 n (of cheque) dorso m

2 adj (**a**) (overdue) **back interest** intereses mpl atrasados; **back office** (part of shop) trastienda f; (department) gestión f interna, back office m; **back office staff** personal m de back office; **back order** pedido m atrasado; **back pay** atrasos mpl, salario m atrasado; **back tax** impuestos mpl atrasados (**b**) **to put sth on the back burner** dejar algo para más tarde, Esp aparcar algo

3 vt (support) respaldar, apoyar; (financially) financiar, dar respaldo financiero a; FIN (bill, loan) avalar; **to back a winner** apostar por el caballo ganador

▶ **back up** COMPTR **1** vt sep (data, file) hacer una copia de seguridad de

2 vi hacer una copia de seguridad

backdate vt (cheque, document) poner fecha anterior a; **the pay increase is backdated to 1**

May el aumento salarial tendrá efecto retroactivo a partir del 1 de mayo

back-end load n US ST EXCH recargo m por amortización anticipada

backer n (**a**) FIN (of bill) avalista mf (**b**) (financial supporter) fuente f de financiación; **we need a backer** necesitamos que alguien nos financie

background n (**a**) (of person) (educational) formación f; (professional) experiencia f; **we need someone with a background in computers** necesitamos a alguien que tenga experiencia en informática (**b**) COMPTR segundo plano m □ **background data** datos mpl en segundo plano; **background job** tarea f en segundo plano; **background (mode) printing** impresión f subordinada; **background task** tarea f en segundo plano

backhander n Br Fam (bribe) soborno m, Andes, RP coima f, CAm, Méx mordida f

backing n (**a**) (of currency) = respaldo en metales preciosos de la emisión en papel moneda de un país (**b**) (support) apoyo m, respaldo m; (financial support) respaldo m financiero; **to give financial backing to sth** proporcionar apoyo financiero a algo

backlight n COMPTR (of screen) retroiluminación f

backlit adj COMPTR (screen) retroiluminado(a)

backlog n acumulación f; **to have a backlog of work** tener trabajo atrasado or acumulado; **we have a backlog of orders** tenemos pedidos atrasados or pendientes

backslash n COMPTR barra f invertida

backspace n COMPTR retroceso m □ **backspace key** tecla f de retroceso

back-to-back adj FIN **back-to-back credit** crédito m con garantía de otro crédito; **back-to-back loan** crédito m con garantía de otro crédito

backup n (**a**) (support) apoyo m, respaldo m (**b**) COMPTR copia f de seguridad; **to do a backup** hacer una copia de seguridad □ **backup copy** copia f de seguridad; **backup file** copia f de seguridad; **backup system** (for saving files) sistema m de copias de seguridad; (auxiliary system) sistema m auxiliar

backward adj ECON **backward integration** integración f regresiva; **backward pricing** (customer-led) = fijación de precios según las exigencias del consumidor; COMPTR **backward search** búsqueda f hacia atrás

backwardation n mercado m invertido □ **backwardation rate** = tipo de interés pagado por aplazamiento de entrega

backward-compatible adj COMPTR compatible con versiones anteriores

BACS n Br (abbr **Bankers' Automated Clearing System**) Sistema m Interbancario de Compensación; **to pay by BACS** pagar mediante el Sistema Interbancario de Compensación

> 66
>
> The banks, which have hardly rushed in the past to tackle this issue, now plan to introduce an automated direct debit transfer system through the bank clearing system, **BACS**, – but not until the end of next year.
>
> 99

bad 1 n he is **£5,000 to the bad** (overdrawn) tiene un descubierto de 5.000 libras; (after a deal) ha salido perdiendo 5.000 libras

2 adj COMPTR **bad command** (in error messages) comando m erróneo; **bad debt** deuda f incobrable; **bad debt insurance** seguro m de crédito y caución; **bad debtor** moroso(a) m,f; **bad debt provision** provisión f para deudas incobrables; **bad debts reserve** reserva f para deudas incobrables; COMPTR **bad file name** nombre m de archivo incorrecto; **bad management** mala gestión f; **bad name** mala reputación f, mala fama f; **that company has a bad name in the business** esa empresa tiene mala fama en el sector; COMPTR **bad sector** sector m dañado

> 66
>
> A deterioration in loans to mainland-related companies has forced the Bank of China's local operations to drastically increase **bad debt provisions** in the six months to June 30, causing a 46.74 per cent plunge in pretax profit to $3 billion.
>
> 99

bail n LAW fianza f; **to go** or **stand** or US **post bail for sb** pagar la fianza de alguien

▶ **bail out** vt sep (**a**) (person, company) sacar de apuros a (**b**) LAW **to bail sb out** pagar la fianza de alguien

bait-and-switch n US MKTG = estrategia de venta en la que se atrae al cliente mediante un artículo barato para luego intentar venderle otro similar, pero más caro

balance 1 n (**a**) FIN (of account) saldo m; **balance in hand** saldo disponible; **balance carried forward** saldo a cuenta nueva **balance brought forward** saldo anterior; **balance due** saldo pendiente; **to pay the balance** saldar la cantidad pendiente; **off the balance sheet reserves** fondos mpl para operaciones fuera de balance □

balance book libro m de inventarios y balances; **balance sheet** balance m de situación; **balance sheet auditing** auditoría f del balance de situación; **balance sheet consolidation** consolidación f del balance de situación; **balance sheet item** partida f del balance de situación; **balance sheet value** valor m en libros

(**b**) (remainder) resto m; **the balance of your order will be supplied within ten days** le enviaremos el resto de su pedido en un plazo máximo de diez días

(**c**) ECON **balance of payments** balanza f de pagos; **balance of payments deficit** déficit m de la balanza de pagos; **balance of trade** balanza f comercial

2 vt FIN (account) cuadrar; (budget) equilibrar; (settle, pay) saldar; **to balance the books** hacer que cuadren las cuentas □ **balanced budget** equilibrio m presupuestario

3 vi FIN (accounts) cuadrar; **I can't get the accounts to balance** no consigo que las cuentas cuadren

▶ **balance out** vi (figures) cuadrar; **debits and credits should balance out** el debe y el haber deberían cuadrar

balancing n FIN (of accounts) cuadre m

balloon 1 vi (increase dramatically) dispararse; **exports have ballooned in the last twelve months** las exportaciones se han disparado en los últimos doce meses

2 n US **balloon mortgage** hipoteca f globo; US **balloon payment** = pago final de un préstamo, que es considerablemente mayor que los anteriores

ballot 1 n (**a**) (vote) votación f; **to hold a ballot** celebrar una votación; **to take a ballot** hacer una votación (**b**) ST EXCH (when shares are oversubscribed) sorteo m

2 vt consultar por votación; **union members will be balloted on Tuesday** el martes se consultará mediante votación a los afiliados del sindicato

ballpark figure n cifra f aproximada; **a ballpark figure of £3,000** una cifra aproximada de 3.000 libras

ballpoint pen n bolígrafo m, Carib pluma f, Col, Ecuad esferográfico m, CSur birome m, Méx pluma f (atómica)

ban n (embargo) embargo m, prohibición f

bancassurance n BANKING bancaseguros f inv, bancassurance f

> 66
>
> The term imported from the continent is **bancassurance**. In essence, it is meant to describe the business model that uses a bank's high street branches to sell insurance products.
>
> 99

bancassurer *n* BANKING entidad *f or* compañía *f* de bancaseguros, bancasegurador *m*

band *n (of ages, tax, salaries)* franja *f*, banda *f*

banded pack *n* = paquete de productos que se vende a un precio inferior al que costarían éstos por separado

bandwidth *n* COMPTR ancho *m* de banda

bang *vt* ST EXCH **to bang the market** = provocar una caída repentina en el precio de los valores mediante la venta masiva de títulos

bangtail *n US* MKTG = solapa trepada de un sobre, que es a la vez un cupón de pedido, o que contiene información publicitaria

bank 1 *n* banco *m*; **the World Bank** el Banco Mundial; **the Bank of England/Mexico** el Banco de Inglaterra/México ◻ **bank acceptance** aceptación *f* bancaria; **bank account** cuenta *f* bancaria; **to open/close a bank account** abrir/cerrar una cuenta bancaria; **bank advance** crédito *m* bancario; **bank advice (notification slip)** notificación *f* al cliente; **bank annuity** = título del Estado que paga un interés perpetuo y no tiene fecha de vencimiento; **bank balance** saldo *m* bancario, haberes *mpl* bancarios; **bank base rate** *Esp* tipo *m* de interés básico, *Am* tasa *f* de interés básica; **bank bill** aceptación *f* bancaria; **bank book** libreta *f* del banco; **bank borrowing** préstamos *mpl* bancarios; **bank branch** sucursal *f* bancaria; **bank branch code** clave *f or* código *m* (de) sucursal (bancaria); **bank buying rate** *(for foreign exchange) Esp* tipo *m or Am* tasa *f* de cambio; **bank card** tarjeta *f* bancaria; **bank charges** comisión *f* bancaria, gastos *mpl* bancarios; **bank clerk** empleado(a) *m,f* de banca *or* banco, *SAm* empleado(a) *m,f* bancario; **bank credit** crédito *m* bancario; **bank debts** adeudos *mpl* bancarios, deudas *fpl* bancarias; **bank deposit** depósito *m* bancario; **bank details** datos *mpl* bancarios; **bank discount** descuento *m* bancario; **bank discount rate** tipo *m* de descuento bancario; **bank draft** cheque *m* bancario, giro *m* bancario; *US* **bank examiner** inspector(ora) *m,f* bancario(a); **bank guarantee** garantía *f* bancaria; **bank holiday** día *m* festivo; **bank interest** interés *m* bancario; **bank lending** crédito *m* bancario; **bank loan** préstamo *m or* crédito *m* bancario; **to take out a bank loan** suscribir un préstamo con el banco; **bank manager** director(ora) *m,f* de banco; **bank money** dinero *m* bancario; **bank notification** notificación *f* bancaria; **bank overdraft** descubierto *m* bancario; *US* **bank paper (banknotes)** papel *m* moneda; *(securities, drafts etc)* valores *mpl* bancarios; **bank rate** tipo *m or Am* tasa *f* de interés bancario; ACCT **bank reconciliation** conciliación *f* de estados bancarios; **bank reserves** activo *m* de caja, reservas *fpl* bancarias; **bank selling rate** valor *m* de venta; **bank shares** valores *mpl* bancarios, acciones *fpl* bancarias; **bank sort code** clave *f or* código *m* (de) sucursal (bancaria); **bank statement** extracto *m or* balance *m* de cuenta; **bank teller** cajero(a) *m,f* de banco; **bank transaction** transacción *f* bancaria; **bank transfer** transferencia *f* bancaria **bank transfer advice** notificación *f* al cliente; **bank treasurer** tesorero(a) *m,f* del banco

2 *vt (cheque, money) Esp* ingresar, *Am* depositar

3 *vi* **to bank with** tener una cuenta en; **where do you bank?, who do you bank with?** *(individual)* ¿cuál es tu banco?, ¿en qué banco tienes cuenta?; *(company)* ¿con qué banco trabajas?

bankable *adj (profitable)* rentable, productivo(a)

banker *n* banquero(a) *m,f* ◻ **banker's acceptance** aceptación *f* bancaria; *Br* **Bankers' Automated Clearing System** Sistema *m* Interbancario de Compensación; **banker's card** tarjeta *f* bancaria; **banker's cheque, banker's draft** cheque *m* bancario, giro *m* bancario; **banker's order** domiciliación *f* bancaria, *Am* débito *m* bancario

banking *n (activity)* operaciones *fpl* bancarias; *(profession)* banca *f*, sector *m* bancario; **he does his banking with us** es cliente nuestro; **she's in banking** trabaja en la banca ◻ *US* **banking account** cuenta *f* bancaria; **banking business** actividad *f* bancaria; **banking consortium** consorcio *m* bancario; **banking charter** licencia *f* bancaria; **banking controls** controles *mpl* bancarios; **banking hours** horario *m* bancario *or* de los bancos; **banking house** entidad *f* bancaria; **banking law** legislación *f* bancaria; **banking legislation** legislación *f* bancaria; **banking machinery** mecanismos *mpl* bancarios; **banking mechanism** mecanismo *m* bancario; **banking pool** = grupo de bancos que financian un proyecto conjuntamente; **banking product** producto *m* bancario; **banking services** servicios *mpl* bancarios; **banking system** banca *f*, sistema *m* bancario

banknote *n* billete *m* (de banco)

bankroll *US* **1** *n (funds)* fondos *mpl*, capital *m*

2 *vt (deal, project)* financiar

bankrupt 1 *n* quebrado(a) *m,f* ◻ **bankrupt's certificate** declaración *f* de quiebra

2 *adj* en quiebra, en bancarrota; **to go bankrupt** quebrar, ir a la quiebra; **to be bankrupt** estar en quiebra; **to adjudicate** *or* **declare sb bankrupt** declarar a alguien en quiebra

3 *vt (company, person)* conducir a la quiebra, llevar a la ruina; **the deal bankrupted the business** la operación llevó *or* condujo a la empresa a la quiebra

bankruptcy *n* quiebra *f*, bancarrota *f*; **to present** *or* **file a petition for bankruptcy** presentar una petición *or* solicitud de declaración de quiebra ◻ *Br* **bankruptcy court** tribunal *m* de quiebras; ***bankruptcy proceedings*** proceso *m or* procedimiento *m* de quiebra

banner *n* COMPTR *(for advertising on Internet)* banner *m*, pancarta *f* (publicitaria) ❑ ***banner ad, banner advertisement*** banner *m* publicitario; ***banner campaign*** campaña *f* de banners publicitarios

> “
>
> At group level Unilever has an agreement with service provider America Online to advertise its products to subscribers. Separate from this, its most expensive new-media venture in the UK was a five-week **banner campaign** earlier this year for a new Lynx deodorant fragrance called Apollo.
>
> ”

bar *n* (**a**) ***bar chart*** gráfico *m* de barras; ***bar code*** código *m* de barras (**b**) COMPTR *(menu bar)* barra *f*

bargain 1 *n* (**a**) *(agreement)* pacto *m*, trato *m*; **a bad bargain** un mal negocio; **to strike** *or* **make a bargain with sb** cerrar un trato con alguien, hacer un pacto *or* trato con alguien; **to drive a hard bargain** saber regatear (**b**) *(good buy)* ganga *f*, *Esp* chollo *m* ❑ ***bargain counter*** mostrador *m* de saldos *or* oportunidades; ***bargain offer*** oferta *f* de ocasión; ***bargain price*** precio *m* de saldo

2 *vi* (**a**) *(negotiate)* negociar (**with** con); **the unions are bargaining with management for an 8% pay rise** los sindicatos están negociando con la patronal un aumento de sueldo del 8% (**b**) *(haggle)* regatear; **to bargain with sb** regatear con alguien; **to bargain over sth** regatear algo

bargaining *n (negotiation)* negociación *f*; *(haggling)* regateo *m* ❑ ***bargaining chip*** baza *f* de negociación; **to use sb/sth as a bargaining chip** utilizar a alguien/algo como baza de negociación; ***bargaining position*** posición *f* en la negociación; **we are in a strong bargaining position** nos encontramos en una sólida posición para negociar; ***bargaining power*** poder *m* de negociación; **they have considerable bargaining power** tienen un poder de negociación considerable; ***bargaining table*** mesa *f* de negociaciones

> “
>
> As you might expect, larger companies have a distinct negotiating advantage, often using their leverage to qualify for high-volume discounts or get better deals. However, that doesn't mean that small- to medium-sized manufacturers can't beef up their **bargaining power**. For example, by joining or forming a purchasing cooperative, you can mass your company's orders with several other companies' orders, enabling all to receive a better price.
>
> ”

barrel *n (of oil)* barril *m*

barrier *n* barrera *f*; **barrier to entry** barrera de entrada

barrister *n Br* LAW **barrister (at law)** abogado(a) *m,f (que ejerce en tribunales superiores)*

barter 1 *n* trueque *m*; **a system of barter** un sistema de trueque ❑ ***barter economy*** economía *f* de trueque; ***barter society*** sociedad *f* de trueque; ***barter system*** sistema *m* de trueque

2 *vt* trocar, intercambiar

3 *vi* hacer trueques, practicar el trueque

base 1 *n* (**a**) ST EXCH ***base date*** fecha *f* base; BANKING ***base lending rate*** *Esp* tipo *m* de interés básico, *Am* tasa *f* de interés básica; *US* ***base pay*** sueldo *m* base; ***base rate*** *Esp* tipo *m or Am* tasa *f* de interés básico; *US* ***base salary*** sueldo *m* base; ***base year*** año *f* base (**b**) *(headquarters)* **the company's base** la sede central de la empresa (**c**) *(basis)* **the company's customer base** la clientela de la empresa; **the country lacks an industrial base** el país carece de tejido industrial

2 *vt (locate)* **to be based in** *(company)* estar radicado(a) en; *(operation)* desarrollarse en; **where are you based?** ¿dónde tienes tu trabajo?; **the job is based in Tokyo** el trabajo es en Tokio

baseline *n* (**a**) ***baseline costs*** costos *mpl or Esp* costes *mpl* de base; ***baseline sales*** = ventas del producto principal (**b**) COMPTR *(in DTP)* línea *f* de base

BASIC *n* COMPTR *(abbr* **Beginners' All-Purpose Symbolic Instruction Code)** BASIC *m*

basic *adj* ***basic commodity*** artículo *m* de primera necesidad; ***basic consumer goods*** artículos *mpl* de consumo básicos; INS ***basic cover*** seguro *m* básico; ***basic industry*** sector *m* básico; ***basic offer*** oferta *f* básica; ***basic pay*** salario *m or* sueldo *m* base *or* básico; ***basic personal allowance*** mínimo *m* personal básico; ***basic population*** población *f* básica *or* estable; ***basic rate*** *(of income tax) Esp* tipo *m* básico, *Am* tasa *f* básica; ***basic salary*** sueldo *m* base *or* básico; ***basic statistics*** estadísticas *fpl* básicas; ***basic wage*** sueldo *m* base *or* básico

basic-rate *adj Br* ***basic-rate tax*** *Esp* tipo *m* medio *or Am* tasa *f* media (del impuesto sobre la renta); ***basic-rate taxpayer:*** **most people are basic-rate taxpayers** la mayoría de la gente paga *Esp* el tipo medio *or Am* la tasa media del impuesto sobre la renta

basis *n* (**a**) *(foundation)* base *f*; **basis for depreciation** base de la amortización; **on the basis of these figures** teniendo en cuenta estas cifras ❑ *Br* ***basis of assessment*** *(of income tax)* base impositiva; *US* FIN ***basis point*** punto *m* básico (**b**) *(system)* **employed on a part-time basis** empleado(a) a tiempo parcial; **paid on a weekly basis** pagado(a) semanalmente

basket *n* ECON, FIN ❑ *basket clause* = cláusula de contenido general en un contrato; *basket of currencies* cesta *f* de monedas *or* divisas, *Am* canasta *f* de monedas

batch *n* (*of goods*) lote *m*, partida *f* ❑ COMPTR *batch file* archivo *m* or fichero *m* por lotes; *batch number* número *m* de lote; *batch processing* proceso *m* por lotes *batch production* producción *f* por lotes

baud *n* COMPTR baudio *m*; *at 58,600 baud* a 58.600 baudios ❑ *baud rate* velocidad *f* de transmisión

bay *n* COMPTR hueco *m*, bahía *f*

BBB *n* (*abbr* **Better Business Bureau**) = oficina de ética comercial en Estados Unidos

BBS *n* COMPTR (*abbr* **bulletin board system**) BBS *f*

Bcc COMPTR (*abbr* **blind carbon copy**) Cco

BCE *n* (*abbr* **Board of Customs and Excise**) = dirección de aduanas e impuestos sobre el consumo en el Reino Unido

BD *n* (*abbr* **bank draft**) cheque *m* bancario, giro *m* bancario

BE *n* (*abbr* **Bank of England**) Banco *m* de Inglaterra

b/e *n* (*abbr* **bill of exchange**) letra *f* de cambio

bean counter *n* US Fam contable *mf* chupatintas

bear 1 *n* (**a**) ST EXCH especulador(ora) *m,f* bajista *or* a la baja; *to go a bear* especular a la baja ❑ *bear closing* cierre *m* a la baja, *Am* cierre en baja; *bear market* mercado *m* bajista *or* a la baja; *bear operations* operaciones *f* especulativas a la baja; *bear position* posición *f* bajista; *bear sale* venta *f* a la baja; *bear speculation* especulación *f* a la baja; *bear trading* negociación *f* a la baja; *bear transaction* transacción *f* a la baja (**b**) *Fam bear hug* (*offer for company*) abrazo *m* del oso
2 *vt* (**a**) ST EXCH *to bear the market* jugar a la baja (**b**) *to bear interest* devengar intereses; *his investment bore 8% interest* su inversión devengó un 8% de interés (**c**) (*pay*) *to bear the costs (of sth)* hacerse cargo de los costos *or Esp* costes (de algo)
3 *vi* ST EXCH jugar a la baja

bearer *n* (*of news, letter, cheque*) portador(ora) *m,f*; (*of passport*) titular *mf*; *cheque made payable to the bearer* cheque al portador ❑ FIN *bearer bill* efecto *m* al portador; FIN *bearer bond* bono *m* or título *m* al portador BANKING *bearer cheque* cheque *m* al portador; FIN *bearer paper* título *m* al portador; FIN, ST EXCH *bearer securities* títulos *mpl* al portador; FIN, ST EXCH *bearer share* acción *f* al portador

bearish *adj* ST EXCH (*market*) bajista; *to be bearish* (*of person*) jugar a la baja ❑ *bearish tendency* tendencia *f* bajista *or* a la baja

bed *n* (**a**) *Fam to get into bed with sb* (*form partnership with*) asociarse con alguien (**b**) ST EXCH *bed and breakfasting* = vender acciones y volverlas a comprar al día siguiente con el fin de mostrar pérdidas a efectos fiscales

before-tax *adj* antes de impuestos, bruto(a) ❑ *before-tax income* renta *f* bruta

behalf *n* *on behalf of sb* (*write*) en nombre de alguien; (*phone*) de parte de alguien; *to make a payment on behalf of sb* realizar un pago a favor de alguien

behaviour, US **behavior** *n* MKTG (*of buyer, consumer*) comportamiento *m*, conducta *f* ❑ *behaviour segmentation* segmentación *f* por comportamiento

behavioural study, US **behavioral study** *n* MKTG estudio *m* de comportamiento

Belgian franc *n* Formerly franco *m* belga

belly *n* Fam *to go belly up* (*of company*) irse a pique

below-the-line 1 *n* MKTG below-the-line *m*
2 *adj* (**a**) MKTG below-the-line ❑ *below-the-line advertising* publicidad *f* below-the-line; *below-the-line costs* gastos *mpl* de publicidad below-the-line; *below-the-line promotion* promoción *f* below-the-line (**b**) ACCT (*expenses*) por debajo de la línea ❑ *below-the-line accounts* cuentas *fpl* por debajo de la línea, cuentas no incluidas en la determinación del resultado de ejercicio

> ❝
> Ayres will handle new product development and manage advertising and relationship marketing campaigns. There is likely to be an increased emphasis on **below-the-line** activity because of the high proportion of custom that comes from repeat visitors.
> ❞

benchmark 1 *n* punto *m* de referencia ❑ *benchmark market* mercado *m* de referencia
2 *vt* comparar (**against** con)

benchtest 1 *n* prueba *f* en el banco, prueba de control de calidad
2 *vt* someter a una prueba en el banco a

beneficiary *n* beneficiario(a) *m,f*; *beneficiary under a trust* beneficiario(a) de un fideicomiso

benefit 1 *n* (**a**) Br ADMIN (*state payment*) prestación *f*, subsidio *m*; *to be on benefit* cobrar un subsidio; *to pay out benefits* pagar prestaciones ❑ *Benefits Agency* = oficina de prestaciones sociales (**b**) (*to employee*) **benefits** prestaciones *f* extrasalariales ❑ *benefits package* paquete *m* de prestaciones extrasalariales (**c**) (*advantage*) ventaja *f* ❑ MKTG *benefit segmentation* segmentación *f* por beneficios
2 *vt* (*person, country, trade*) beneficiar, favorecer; *a steady exchange rate benefits trade* un tipo

de cambio estable beneficia *or* favorece al comercio; **the change will benefit all employees** el cambio beneficiará a todos los empleados

3 *vi* **to benefit from sth** beneficiarse de algo, sacar provecho de algo; **to benefit from a rise in prices** beneficiarse de una subida de los precios

benevolent *adj* **benevolent fund** = fondo benéfico para los jubilados de una determinada profesión; **benevolent society** cofradía *f* benéfica

bequeath *vt* LAW legar (**to** a)

bequest *n* LAW legado *m*

best-before date *n* Br fecha *f* de caducidad

best-in-class MKTG **1** *n* **it's a best-in-class** es el mejor de su clase
2 *adj* de primera línea

best-of-breed *n* MKTG producto *m* de calidad superior

best-perceived *adj* MKTG con mejor imagen, mejor percibido(a); **the best-perceived product** el producto con mejor imagen

> ❝
> But most important for Adidas is that it has toppled Reebok as the UK's **best-perceived** sports goods brand, knocking Nike into third place. This is a crucial victory for Adidas, which is engaged in a mammoth battle with Nike.
> ❞

best price *n* mejor precio *m*

best-selling *adj* de más ventas, que más vende; **it's one of our best-selling products** es uno de nuestros productos que más se vende; **a best-selling album** un álbum superventas

better *vt* *(improve)* mejorar; *(surpass)* superar; **we must try to better last year's figures** debemos intentar mejorar las cifras del año pasado; **the company has bettered the competition for the second year running** es el segundo año en el que la empresa supera a la competencia □ **Better Business Bureau** = oficina de ética comercial en Estados Unidos

betterment *n* LAW *(of property)* = aumento en el valor de una propiedad motivado por las mejoras realizadas en la zona

b/f ACCT *(abbr* **brought forward***)* a cuenta nueva

biannual *adj* bianual

bid 1 *n* (**a**) *(offer)* oferta *f*; *(at auction)* puja *f*, oferta *f*; **to make a bid of £250,000 for a property** ofrecer 250.000 libras por un inmueble; **to make the first** *or* **opening bid** hacer la oferta inicial, abrir la puja
(**b**) *(tender)* oferta *f* (de licitación); **the firm put in** *or* **made a bid for the contract** la empresa hizo una oferta *or* licitó por el contrato

(**c**) ST EXCH *US* **the bid and asked** la oferta y la demanda □ **bid bond** fianza *f* de licitación; **bid price** precio *m* de oferta, precio comprador
(**d**) *(attempt)* intento *m*, tentativa *f*; **in a bid to reopen negotiations** en un intento de reanudar las negociaciones

2 *vt* *(at auction)* pujar; **we had to bid another £1,000** tuvimos que aumentar la puja *or* oferta otras 1.000 libras

3 *vi* (**a**) *(at auction)* **to bid for sth** pujar por algo; **to bid a high price** pujar por lo alto; **to bid over sb** *or* **more than sb** hacer una puja más alta que la de alguien, pujar más que alguien (**b**) *(tender)* licitar, hacer una oferta de licitación; **to bid for** *or* **on a contract** licitar por un contrato; **several firms bid for** *or* **on the project** varias empresas han licitado por el proyecto

bidder *n* (**a**) *(at auction)* postor(ora) *m,f*; **the highest bidder** el mejor postor; **there were no bidders** no hubo ofertas, nadie pujó (**b**) *(for tender)* licitador(ora) *m,f*

bidding *n* (**a**) *(at auction)* puja *f*; **the bidding was very brisk** la puja ascendió muy rápidamente, la puja estuvo animada; **to start the bidding for sth at £5,000** comenzar *or* abrir la puja por algo con 5.000 libras; **to open the bidding** abrir la puja; **to raise the bidding** aumentar la puja; **the bidding is closed** la puja está cerrada; **the bidding went against me** perdí la puja (**b**) *(tendering)* licitación *f* □ *US* ST EXCH **bidding price** precio *m* de oferta, precio comprador

biennial *adj* bienal

BIFU *n* (*abbr* **Banking, Insurance and Finance Union**) = sindicato británico de empleados del sector financiero

big *adj* Fam **to earn big money** ganar mucha *Esp* pasta *or* Am plata *or* Méx lana □ Br Fam ST EXCH **Big Bang** = apelativo popular que designa la reforma de la Bolsa de Londres llevada a cabo en 1986; *US* **the big board** la Bolsa de Nueva York; **big business** *(major companies)* las grandes empresas; **DVDs are big business at the moment** los DVDs son un buen negocio en estos momentos; Br **the Big Four** = los cuatro bancos más grandes, o las cuatro firmas de auditoría principales; Fam **big idea** idea *f* innovadora; **new product development is all about coming up with a big idea** para poder desarrollar un nuevo producto hace falta una idea rompedora *or* innovadora

> ❝
> Call centres are **big business**, accounting for roughly one job in 50 in Britain. By 2008, that figure is expected to reach one in 30 as companies try to improve their contact with customers without taking on the expense of local offices or branches.
> ❞

big-budget *adj* de gran presupuesto

bilateral *adj* bilateral □ **bilateral agreement** acuerdo *m* bilateral

bill 1 *n* (**a**) *(notice of payment due)* factura *f*; *(for gas, electricity)* factura, recibo *m*; *(in hotel)* cuenta *f*; *Br (in restaurant)* cuenta *f*; **can we have the bill, please?** *(in restaurant)* la cuenta, por favor; **to make out a bill** hacer una factura; **to pay a bill** pagar una factura; **to foot the bill** pagar la cuenta
  (**b**) *US (banknote)* billete *m*; **a five-dollar bill** un billete de cinco dólares
  (**c**) FIN *(promissory note)* letra *f* de cambio □ **bill book** libro *m* registro de facturas emitidas; **bill broker** corredor(ora) *m,f* de letras de cambio; **bill for collection** efecto *m* al cobro, letra *f* al cobro; **bill discounter** = agente mercantil dedicado al descuento de letras o efectos; CUSTOMS **bill of entry** declaración *f* de aduanas; **bill of exchange** letra *f* de cambio; **bills of exchange statement** = declaración de datos de las letras de cambio que se poseen **bill in foreign currency** efecto *m* en moneda extranjera; **bills in hand** efectos *mpl* en cartera; **bill of lading** conocimiento *m* de embarque; **bills payable** efectos *mpl* a pagar; **bill payable at sight** letra *or* efecto a la vista; ACCT **bills payable ledger** registro *m* de efectos a pagar; **bills receivable** efectos *mpl* a cobrar ACCT **bills receivable ledger** registro *m* de efectos a cobrar; **bill of sale** escritura *f or* contrato *m* de compraventa CUSTOMS **bill of sight** permiso *m* de inspección; CUSTOMS **bill of sufferance** permiso *m* de descarga restringido; **bill without protest** letra *f* sin gastos
  (**d**) LAW proyecto *m* de ley
  2 *vt* enviar la factura a, facturar; **they billed me twice for the spare parts** me facturaron dos veces por las piezas de recambio; **he bills his company for his travelling expenses** factura los gastos de desplazamiento a su empresa

billboard *n* valla *f* publicitaria □ **billboard advertising** publicidad *f* en vallas; **billboard site** = emplazamiento para vallas publicitarias

biller *n US* = administrativo encargado de la facturación

billhead *n US* formulario *m* de factura

billing *n* facturación *f* □ **billing date** fecha *f* de facturación; **billing office** departamento *m* de facturación

billion *n* mil millones *mpl*; **10 billion dollars** 10.000 millones de dólares

BIM *n (abbr* **British Institute of Management)** = Instituto Británico de Dirección Empresarial

bi-media *adj* de radio y televisión

bimonthly 1 *adj (twice a month)* bimensual; *(every two months)* bimestral
  2 *adv (twice a month)* dos veces al mes, bimensualmente; *(every two months)* bimestralmente

binary *adj* binario(a) □ **binary code** código *m* binario

binder *n (for papers)* carpeta *f*

binding *adj* vinculante; **the contract is legally binding** el contrato tiene fuerza legal; **the agreement is binding on all parties** el acuerdo es vinculante para todas las partes; **it is binding on the buyer to make immediate payment** obliga al comprador a hacer efectivo el pago de manera inmediata

bit *n* COMPTR bit *m*; **bits per second** bits por segundo

bitmap COMPTR **1** *n* mapa *m* de bits
  2 *adj* en/de mapa de bits □ **bitmap font** fuente *f* de mapa de bits

bitmapped *adj* COMPTR en/de mapa de bits

biweekly 1 *adj (twice a week)* bisemanal; *(every two weeks)* quincenal
  2 *adv (twice a week)* dos veces por semana; *(every two weeks)* quincenalmente

B/L, b/l *n (abbr* **bill of lading)** conocimiento *m* de embarque

black 1 *n* **to be in the black** *(person, company, account)* tener saldo positivo
  2 *adj* **black book** = plan o estrategia para defender a una empresa de una opa; **black economy** economía *f* sumergida; ST EXCH **black knight** sociedad *f* hostil, caballero *f* negro; **black market** mercado *m* negro; **to buy sth on the black market** comprar algo en el mercago negro; **black marketeer** estraperlista *mf*; **Black Monday** lunes *m* negro **black money** *(earned on black market)* = dinero procedente del mercado negro; *(undeclared)* dinero *m* negro, dinero B

blackleg *n Br Fam (strikebreaker) Esp* esquirol(ola) *m,f, Am* rompehuelgas *mf inv*

blacklist 1 *n* lista *f* negra
  2 *vt* poner en la lista negra

blank 1 *n* (*in document*) espacio *m* en blanco; **fill in the blanks** rellene *or Am* llene los espacios en blanco

2 *adj* (**a**) **blank cheque** cheque *m* en blanco; FIN **blank credit** crédito *m* en blanco; FIN **blank endorsement** endoso *m* en blanco; **blank form** impreso *m or* formulario *m or Méx* forma *f* en blanco; FIN **blank transfer** certificado *m* de depósito de valores en blanco (**b**) COMPTR (*screen*) en blanco; (*disk*) virgen □ **blank unformatted disk** disquete *m* virgen sin formatear

blanket *adj* general, total; **a blanket rule for all employees** una regla de aplicación general a todos los empleados; **our insurance policy guarantees blanket coverage** nuestra póliza de seguros garantiza una cobertura total □ **blanket agreement** convenio *m* colectivo; MKTG **blanket family name** marca *f* paraguas; **blanket mortgage** hipoteca *f* abierta; **blanket order** pedido *m* general; INS **blanket policy** póliza *f* integral

blind *adj* US **blind pool** = empresa de reciente creación que vende acciones en una oferta pública sin especificar cómo se gastará el dinero de los inversores; MKTG **blind test** test *m* ciego; MKTG **blind testing** tests *mpl* ciegos; **blind trust** = fideicomiso cuyos fiduciarios no mantienen ningún tipo de relación con el beneficiario

blink rate *n* COMPTR (*of cursor*) velocidad *f* de parpadeo

blip *n* (*temporary problem*) pequeño problema *m*; **the company suffered a blip in February when it lost that contract** la empresa tuvo un pequeño contratiempo en febrero cuando no consiguió ese contrato; **the economy experienced a blip last year but is now back on track** la economía sufrió un bache pasajero el año pasado, pero ya se ha recuperado

blister pack *n* blíster *m*

blitz *n* MKTG = campaña publicitaria muy intensa; **we are already preparing for the pre-Christmas advertising blitz** ya nos estamos preparando para la supercampaña publicitaria de antes de Navidad

> "Yes we want sales in Edinburgh but we're not going to launch a billboard **blitz**. It will be gradually, year by year."

block 1 *n* (**a**) (*group*) grupo *m*; (*of shares*) paquete *m* □ **block booking** reserva *f* de grupo; ST EXCH **block issue** emisión *f* en serie; **block purchase** compra *f* en bloque; **block structure** estructura *f* de bloque; ST EXCH **block trading** negociación *f* de bloques (de acciones); **block vote** voto *m* por delegación (**b**) (*freeze*) **to put a block on sth** (*cheque, account, prices, imports*) bloquear algo (**c**) COMPTR bloque *m*; **to perform a block copy**

on sth seleccionar y copiar algo

2 *vt* (**a**) FIN (*account, prices, imports*) bloquear; (*cheque*) anular □ **blocked currency** divisa *f* bloqueada (**b**) COMPTR seleccionar; **to block text** seleccionar un bloque de texto

blocking *adj* **blocking majority** mayoría *f* de bloqueo; **blocking minority** minoría *f* de bloqueo

blue chip *n* ST EXCH acción *f* de gran liquidez

blue-chip *adj* FIN **blue-chip company** empresa *f* puntera; **blue-chip investment** inversión *f* en una empresa puntera; ST EXCH **blue-chip stocks** *or* **shares** acciones *fpl* de gran liquidez

blue-collar *adj* **blue-collar union** sindicato *m* obrero; **blue-collar worker** trabajador(ora) *m,f* manual

blue-sky *adj* US ST EXCH **blue-sky law** = ley que regula la información que se debe hacer pública al emitir bonos, acciones, etc.; **blue-sky security** = título prácticamente sin valor

Bluetooth® *n* COMPTR Bluetooth® *m*

blurb *n* (*for advertising, on book jacket*) texto *m* publicitario

board *n* (**a**) (*of company*) consejo *m* de administración, junta *f* directiva; **to be on the board** formar parte del consejo de administración *or* de la junta directiva; **the bank is represented on the board** el banco tiene representación en la junta directiva □ **Board of Customs and Excise** = dirección de aduanas e impuestos sobre el consumo en el Reino Unido; **board of directors** consejo *m* de administración, junta *f* directiva; **board of enquiry** comisión *f* investigadora; **board meeting** reunión *f* del consejo, reunión *f* de la junta; **board member** miembro *mf* del consejo, miembro de la junta; **board of referees** junta *f* arbitral; *Br Formerly* **Board of Trade** = ministerio responsable de la supervisión del comercio y de la promoción de las exportaciones; **board of trustees** junta *f* de síndicos (**b**) COMPTR placa *f*; **on board** instalado(a)

boarding *n* embarque *m* □ **boarding card, boarding pass** tarjeta *f* de embarque, *Col* pasabordo *m*; **boarding time** hora *f* de embarque

boardroom *n* sala *f* de juntas; **he has been promoted to the boardroom** le han dado un puesto en el consejo de administración; **the decision was taken at boardroom level** tomaron la decisión en el consejo de administración

body *n* (**a**) (*of letter, document, e-mail*) cuerpo *m*, texto *m* (**b**) (*organization*) organismo *m*, entidad *f* □ LAW **body corporate** persona *f* jurídica

bogus company *n* sociedad *f* fantasma

boiler room *n* US Fam = agencia que vende instrumentos financieros por teléfono y que utiliza métodos poco éticos o ilegales

bold TYP **1** n (letra f) negrita f; **in bold** en negrita
2 adj en negrita; **bold face** or **type** (letra) negrita

▸ **bolster up** vt sep FIN (currency, economy) reforzar, fortalecer

bona fide adj (genuine) auténtico(a), genuino(a); (offer, agreement) serio(a), de buena fe

bonanza adj próspero(a), de bonanza; **2001 was a bonanza year for us** 2001 fue un año próspero para nosotros

bond 1 n (**a**) FIN bono m, obligación f; **long-term/medium-term/short-term bond** bono or obligación a largo/medio/corto plazo □ **bond equivalent yield** rendimiento m explícito equivalente; **bond fund manager** director(ora) m,f de un fondo de inversión de renta fija; **bond investment** inversión f en valores de renta fija; **bond issue** emisión f de bonos; **to make a bond issue** colocar una emisión de bonos; **bond market** mercado m de valores de renta fija; **bond yield** tasa f de rendimiento de un bono
(**b**) CUSTOMS **to be in bond** encontrarse en depósito aduanero; **to put goods in bond** dejar mercancías en un depósito aduanero; **to take goods out of bond** retirar mercancías de un depósito aduanero □ **bond note** certificado m de depósito
(**c**) LAW fianza f; **to enter into a bond (with sb)** acordar una fianza (con alguien)
2 vt CUSTOMS (goods) poner en depósito aduanero

bonded adj CUSTOMS (goods) en depósito aduanero □ **bonded warehouse** depósito m aduanero

bondholder n FIN obligacionista mf, tenedor(ora) m,f de bonos

bond-trading adj BANKING **bond-trading department** departamento m de negociación de bonos

bonus n (**a**) (on salary) plus m, prima f; **to work on a bonus system** trabajar según un sistema de primas; **to get a Christmas bonus** recibir una prima de Navidad □ MKTG **bonus pack** paquete m con promoción; **bonus scheme** sistema m de primas (**b**) ST EXCH (on shares) dividendo m extraordinario □ **bonus issue** emisión f gratuita de acciones; **bonus share** acción f gratuita, acción liberada (**c**) INS (to policy holder) bonificación f

book 1 n (for keeping accounting records) libro m; **the books** (of company) los libros, la contabilidad; **to keep the books** llevar la contabilidad □ ACCT **book debts** deudas fpl contables; **book entry** anotación f contable, asiento m contable; **book entry transfer** = traspaso de acciones o valores mediante anotación en cuenta; **book value** valor m contable
2 vt (**a**) (engage) contratar; **we are heavily booked** tenemos una agenda muy apretada (**b**)

(seat, room, table, ticket) reservar; **to book sb into a hotel** hacer una reserva para alguien en un hotel; **fully booked** completo(a)

▸ **book up** vt sep **the restaurant/hotel is booked up** el restaurante/hotel está completo

booking n reserva f □ **booking agency** agencia f de reservas de entradas; **booking fee** suplemento m or recargo m por reserva; **booking number** número m de reserva; **booking office** taquilla f, Am boletería f

bookkeeper n tenedor(ora) m,f de libros, Esp contable mf, Am contador(ora) m,f

bookkeeping n contabilidad f

booklet n folleto m

bookmark COMPTR **1** n marcador m, favorito m
2 vt añadir a la lista de marcadores or favoritos

bookwork n (accounts) trabajo m de contabilidad; (secretarial duties) trabajo m administrativo

Boolean adj COMPTR booleano(a) □ **Boolean operator** operador m booleano; **Boolean search** búsqueda f booleana

boom 1 n auge m, boom m; **boom and bust** auge y crisis □ **boom town** (growing) ciudad f en auge; (prosperous) ciudad próspera
2 vt US (develop) desarrollar; (publicize) promover
3 vi (town, country, industry) crecer rápidamente; **business is booming** los negocios van viento en popa; **car sales are booming** las ventas de coches se han disparado

boomerang effect n efecto m bumerán or bumerang

booming adj (economy, business) en auge

boomlet n US Fam breve periodo m de auge

boost 1 n **to give sth a boost** (sales, productivity, economy) dar un impulso a algo; **to give sb's morale a boost** levantar la moral de alguien; **the announcement gave the pound a boost on the foreign exchanges** el anuncio dio un impulso a la libra en los mercados de divisas; **a boost in sales** un incremento en las ventas
2 vt (sales, productivity, economy) impulsar, estimular; (income) aumentar; **we must do something to boost staff morale** tenemos que hacer algo para levantar la moral de los empleados

▸ **boot up** COMPTR **1** vt sep (computer) arrancar
2 vi (computer) arrancar

boot disk n COMPTR disco m de arranque

booth n (at exhibition, trade fair) stand m, puesto m

border n (of country, region) frontera f

borrow 1 vt (from bank) pedir prestado(a); **to borrow money from sb** pedir dinero prestado a alguien; **I had to borrow some money from the bank to buy it** tuve que pedir un préstamo al banco para comprarlo; **you can borrow up to three times your salary** puedes pedir un crédito de hasta el triple de tu sueldo

2 vi *(from bank)* pedir un préstamo; **(from** a); **to borrow on** *or* **at interest** pedir un préstamo con interés

▸ **borrow against** vt insep FIN **the company borrowed against its assets** la empresa pidió un préstamo utilizando sus activos como garantía

borrowed adj prestado(a) ❑ **borrowed capital** capital m prestado

borrower n FIN prestatario(a) m,f

borrowing n endeudamiento m; **financed by borrowing** financiado(a) mediante créditos ❑ **borrowing capacity** capacidad f de endeudamiento; **borrowing limit** límite m de endeudamiento; **borrowing power** capacidad f de endeudamiento; **borrowing rate** Esp tipo m or Am tasa f de interés de los créditos; **borrowing requirements** necesidades fpl de crédito

> A trawl up and down the high street paying a visit to the myriad lenders you will find there can be as good a place as any. This way you will find out how much you are able to borrow, what rates are on offer and which lenders are able to cater to your particular needs. Your own bank might offer its existing customers improved interest rates or increased **borrowing power**.

boss n jefe(a) m,f; **to be one's own boss** trabajar por cuenta propia

Boston matrix n MKTG matriz f de Boston

bottleneck n *(in production)* cuello m de botella, atasco m

bottom 1 n **the bottom has fallen out of the market** el mercado se ha desplomado

2 adj **bottom line** *(profits)* resultado m neto; **the bottom line** *(the essential thing)* lo primordial, lo esencial; **black bottom line** resultado neto positivo; **red bottom line** resultado neto negativo; **bottom price** precio m más bajo

▸ **bottom out** vi *(recession, slump, price)* tocar fondo; **the dollar has bottomed out** el dólar ha tocado fondo; **sales bottomed out at £40,000** las ventas se desplomaron hasta las 40.000 libras

bottom-of-the-range adj MKTG de gama baja, de baja calidad

bought ledger n ACCT libro m mayor de compras

bounce Fam **1** vt **(a)** *(cheque)* rechazar, devolver, Méx, RP rebotar **(b) to bounce an idea off sb** preguntar a alguien su opinión sobre una idea **(c)** COMPTR **bounce(d) message** mensaje m rebotado

2 vi **(a)** *(cheque)* ser rechazado(a) or devuelto(a) or Méx, RP rebotado(a); **I hope this cheque won't bounce** espero que no me rechacen or devuelvan or Méx, RP reboten el cheque **(b)** COMPTR *(e-mail)* rebotar

▸ **bounce back** vi *(stock market)* recuperarse; **the pound has bounced back against the dollar** la libra se ha recuperado frente al dólar

bound adj *(obliged)* obligado(a); **bound by contract** obligado(a) por contrato

Bourse n Bolsa f *(de países no anglosajones, especialmente de los europeos)*

boutique n boutique f

box 1 n **(a)** *(container)* caja f ❑ **box file** caja f clasificadora **(b)** *(postal address)* apartado m de correos, Am casilla f postal, Andes, RP casilla de correos, Col apartado aéreo; **Box number 301** *(in advertisements)* apartado de correos 301 **(c)** *(on form)* casilla f

2 vt *(goods)* meter en cajas; **the goods are boxed before being dispatched** los productos se meten en cajas antes de despacharlos

boxed adj *(goods)* en estuche, en caja

boycott 1 n boicot m

2 vt boicotear

BP n US *(abbr* **basis point**) punto m básico

bpi COMPTR *(abbr* **bits per inch**) bpp

BPR n *(abbr* **business process reengineering**) rediseño m de los procesos de negocio, reingeniería f del proceso empresarial

bps COMPTR *(abbr* **bits per second**) bps

bracket n **(a)** ADMIN *(of income, tax, salaries)* banda f, tramo m; **the high/low income bracket** el tramo de renta alto/bajo; **what tax bracket are you in?** ¿en qué tramo impositivo estás? **(b)** *(punctuation mark) (round)* paréntesis m inv; *(square)* corchete m; *(curly)* llave f; **angle brackets** paréntesis angulares

Brady bond n bono m brady

brain-drain n fuga f de cerebros

> AN IT **brain-drain** could hit Tony Blair's plans for Britain to be a leading site for e-commerce, according to e-business consultant Steve Allan. Allan, who has moved to The Netherlands because of the new IR35 tax regulations, said that European businesses are taking advantage of the exodus of British contractors to catch up and overtake the UK.

brainstorming n brainstorming m, tormentas fpl de ideas, lluvias fpl de ideas, ❑ **brainstorming session** brainstorming m, tormenta f de ideas, lluvia f de ideas,

branch n **(a)** *(of shop, bank, company)* sucursal f;

this shop has branches all over the country la tienda tiene sucursales por todo el país ❏ **branch manager** director(ora) *m,f* de sucursal; **branch office** sucursal *f* (**b**) COMPTR ramificación *f*, bifurcación *f*

▶ **branch out** *vi* ampliar horizontes, diversificarse; **they're branching out into CD-ROMs** han ampliado su oferta a CD-ROMs; **we all agree on the need to branch out into sports equipment** todos estamos de acuerdo en que tenemos que diversificarnos hacia el equipamiento deportivo

brand MKTG **1** *n (of product)* marca *f* ❏ **brand acceptability, brand acceptance** aceptación *f* de marca; **brand advertising** publicidad *f* de marca; **brand awareness** notoriedad *f* de la marca; **brand bonding** = creación de una relación especial entre una marca y sus consumidores; **brand building** construcción *f* de marca; **brand competition** competencia *f* entre marcas; **brand concept** concepto *m* de la marca; **brand extension** ampliación *f* or extensión *f* de marca; **brand familiarity** conocimiento *m* de marca; **brand identifier** identificador *m* de marca; **brand identity** identidad *f* de marca; **brand image** imagen *f* de marca; **brand imitation** imitación *f* de marca; **brand leader** marca *f* líder; **brand lifecycle** ciclo *m* de vida de la marca; **brand loyalty** fidelidad *f* a la marca; **brand management** gestión *f* de la marca; **brand manager** director(ora) *m,f* de marca; **brand mapping** = valoración del posicionamiento de una marca; **brand mark** símbolo *m* de marca; **brand name** (nombre *m* de) marca *f*; **brand name product** producto *m* de marca; **brand name recall** recuerdo *m* de marca; **brand perception** percepción *f* de marca; **brand piracy** usurpación *f* de marca; **brand policy** política *f* de marca; **brand portfolio** cartera *f* de marcas; **brand positioning** posicionamiento *f* de marca; **brand preference** preferencia *f* de marca; **brand recognition** reconocimiento *m* de marca; **brand sensitivity** sensibilidad *f* de marca; **brand strategy** estrategia *f* de marca; **brand strengths** fortalezas *fpl* de la marca; **brand switcher** = consumidor que cambia de marca; **sales promotions are particularly effective in attracting brand switchers** las promociones de ventas son especialmente útiles para atraer a los consumidores que cambian a menudo de marca **brand switching** cambio *m* de marca

2 *vt (product)* dar nombre comercial a; **the product is branded differently in our three main markets** el producto lleva marcas diferentes en nuestros tres mercados principales

branded *adj* MKTG **branded goods** artículos *mpl* de marca; **branded product** producto *m* de marca

branding *n* MKTG creación *f* de marcas; **decisions about branding affect our investment**

in promotion and packaging las decisiones sobre la marca que demos a los productos afectan a nuestras inversiones en publicidad y packaging ❏ **branding campaign** campaña *f* de imagen de marca

brand-led *adj* MKTG condicionado(a) por la marca

❝ ──────────────────

Merloni is hoping to adopt a more **brand-led** approach to its advertising in the white goods market, which is growing by about six per cent year on year.

────────────────── ❞

brand-loyal *adj* MKTG fiel *or* leal a una marca

brand-sensitive *adj* MKTG sensible a la marca

breach 1 *n* **breach of contract** incumplimiento *m* de contrato; **to be in breach of contract** haber incumplido un contrato; **breach of discipline** incumplimiento *m* de las normas; **breach of guarantee** = incumplimiento de una de las cláusulas de una póliza de seguros por parte del asegurado; **breach of trust** abuso *m* de confianza; **breach of warranty** = incumplimiento de una de las cláusulas de una póliza de seguros por parte del asegurado

2 *vt* LAW *(agreement)* incumplir

breadwinner *n* **she's the breadwinner in the family** es la que gana el pan de la familia

break 1 *n* (**a**) *(in negotiations)* ruptura *f* (**b**) *(interval, rest)* descanso *m*; **all employees are entitled to two fifteen-minute breaks** todos los empleados tienen derecho a dos descansos de quince minutos (**c**) COMPTR **break key** tecla *f* de interrupción

2 *vt (agreement, contract)* incumplir

▶ **break down 1** *vt sep* FIN *(account, figures, expenses, statistics)* desglosar; *(bill, estimate)* detallar; **to break down bulk** dividir la mercancía en lotes pequeños

2 *vi* (**a**) *(negotiations, relations)* romperse; **talks between unions and management have broken down** las negociaciones entre los sindicatos y la patronal se han roto (**b**) *(machine)* estropearse, averiarse

▶ **break even** *vi (person, company)* cubrir gastos

▶ **break into** *vt insep (market)* penetrar en, introducirse en; **many companies are trying to break into the Japanese market** muchas empresas están intentando penetrar *or* introducirse en el mercado japonés

▶ **break up 1** *vt sep (conglomerate, trust, company, empire)* desmembrar; *(coalition)* romper

2 *vi (meeting)* terminar; *(partnership)* disolverse; *(talks, negotiations)* romperse

breakage *n (damage)* desperfectos *mpl*, daños *mpl*; **to pay for breakages** pagar por los artículos rotos, correr con los desperfectos *or* daños

break-bulk *adj US (cargo, goods)* fraccionado(a), en pequeños lotes

breakdown *n (of charges, figures, expenses, statistics)* desglose *m*; **I need a breakdown of the bill** necesito una factura detallada

break-even 1 *n* umbral *m* de rentabilidad; ACCT punto *m* de equilibrio; **to reach break-even** alcanzar el umbral de rentabilidad
   2 *adj* FIN **break-even analysis** análisis *m* del punto de equilibrio; **break-even deal** = transacción en la que sólo se cubren gastos; **break-even point** umbral *m* de rentabilidad; ACCT punto *m* de equilibrio; **break-even price** precio *m* para cubrir gastos; **break-even transaction** = transacción en la que sólo se cubren gastos

> **"**
> Certainly, digital TV is costing the two partners a lot of money: more than £800 million has been invested so far and at least £300m more will be needed. But the two companies claim that initiatives such as merging digital's management with the rest of ITV, and introducing new channels such as ITV Sport, will give the impetus needed to get to **break-even point** and beyond.
> **"**

breakthrough *n (of market)* penetración *f*

break-up *n (of company, empire)* desintegración *f*, desmembración *f* ❑ **break-up bid** = oferta que se hace sobre una empresa para vender sus componentes por separado; **break-up price** = precio que alcanza una empresa cuando sus componentes se venden por separado; **break-up value** valor *m* de fragmentación

Brent crude *n* (crudo *m*) brent *m*

bribe 1 *n* soborno *m*
   2 *vt* sobornar

bribery *n* soborno *m*; **to be open to bribery** aceptar sobornos, dejarse sobornar

bricks-and-mortar *adj* = que ofrece sus servicios en un local, no a través del teléfono o Internet

bridge loan *n* crédito *m* puente

bridging *adj* **bridging finance** financiación *f* provisional *or* puente; **bridging loan** crédito *m* provisional *or* puente

brief 1 *n* (**a**) LAW informe *m* de instrucción (**b**) *(instructions)* instrucciones *fpl*; **my brief is to develop sales** mi cometido es aumentar las ventas; **the client's brief stated that the advertising should target the 18-34 age group** las instrucciones del cliente estipulaban que la publicidad debía dirigirse a la franja de edad entre los 18 y los 34
   2 *vt* (**a**) LAW *(lawyer)* entregar la instrucción de

una causa a (**b**) *(inform)* informar, poner al corriente a (**on** sobre, de); *(instruct)* dar instrucciones a; **have you been briefed?** *(brought up to date)* ¿le han puesto al corriente?; *(given instructions)* ¿le han dado instrucciones?

briefcase *n* maletín *m*, portafolios *m inv*

briefing *n* (**a**) *(meeting)* sesión *f* informativa (**b**) *(information)* información *f*; *(written)* informe *m* ❑ **briefing room** sala *f* de reuniones

▸ **bring down** *vt sep (prices, rate of inflation)* bajar, reducir

▸ **bring forward** *vt sep* (**a**) ACCT *(item)* pasar a cuenta nueva; **brought forward** a cuenta nueva (**b**) *(date, meeting)* adelantar; **the conference has been brought forward to the 28th** el congreso se ha adelantado al 28

▸ **bring in** *vt sep (of investment, sale)* generar; **to bring in interest** generar intereses; **this investment has brought in 6%** esta inversión ha producido un 6%; **tourism brings in millions of dollars each year** el turismo genera millones de dólares cada año

▸ **bring out** *vt sep (shares)* emitir; *(product, book)* sacar

brisk *adj (market, trading)* animado(a), activo(a); **business is brisk** el negocio va muy bien

brochure *n* folleto *m*

broker 1 *n* FIN *(for insurance, goods)* agente *mf*, corredor(ora) *m,f*; ST EXCH agente de bolsa, corredor(ora) *m,f* de bolsa ❑ **broker's commission** corretaje *m*, comisión *f*; **broker's contract** contrato *m* de correduría; **broker dealer** agente *mf or* corredor(ora) *m,f* de bolsa *(que puede actuar como sociedad de valores o como agente)*
   2 *vt* **to broker an agreement** servir de mediador para la consecución de un acuerdo

brokerage *n* FIN (**a**) *(profession of broker)* correduría *f* ❑ **brokerage house** agencia *f* de valores (**b**) *(fee)* corretaje *m*, correduría *f*

broking *n* FIN *(profession)* correduría *f*

brown goods *npl* (aparatos *mpl* de) línea *f* marrón

browse COMPTR **1** *n* **browse mode** modo *m* de consulta
   2 *vt* **to browse the Web** navegar por la Web
   3 *vi* navegar

browser *n* COMPTR navegador *m*, buscador *m*

browsing *n* COMPTR navegación *f*; **fast/secure browsing** navegación rápida/segura

BS *n* *(abbr* **British Standard***)* = indica que la cifra que le sigue remite al número de la norma establecida por la asociación británica de normalización

b/s *n* *(abbr* **bill of sale***)* escritura *f or* contrato *m* de compraventa

B-share *n* ST EXCH acción *f* de clase B

BSI n (abbr **British Standards Institution**) = asociación británica de normalización, Esp ≃ AENOR f

bt/fwd adj ACCT (abbr **brought forward**) a cuenta nueva

bubble n **bubble economy** economía f de la especulación; **bubble pack, bubble wrap** embalaje m de burbujas

bubble-jet printer n impresora f de inyección

buck n Fam (dollar) dólar m; **to make a fast** or **quick buck** hacer dinero fácil; **bucks** (money) Esp pasta f, Am plata f, Méx lana f, RP guita f

bucket shop n Fam (a) FIN = agencia de cambio y bolsa fraudulenta (b) (travel agency) agencia f de viajes baratos

budget 1 n presupuesto m; **to balance the budget** equilibrar or ajustar el presupuesto; **we are within budget** estamos dentro del presupuesto; **the project was finished within budget** se concluyó el proyecto sin sobrepasar el presupuesto; **we are already well over budget** ya hemos sobrepasado considerablemente el presupuesto □ **budget account** (with a shop) cuenta f de cliente; (with a bank) cuenta f para domiciliaciones; **budget allocation** partida f presupuestaria; **budget appropriation** crédito m presupuestario; **budget constraints** limitaciones fpl or restricciones fpl presupuestarias; **budget cuts** recortes mpl presupuestarios; **budget deficit** déficit m presupuestario; **budget estimates** estimaciones fpl or previsiones fpl presupuestarias; **budget forecast** estimación f or previsión f presupuestaria; **budget planning** planificación f presupuestaria; **budget restrictions** limitaciones fpl or restricciones fpl presupuestarias; **budget surplus** superávit m presupuestario
2 adj ECON, FIN presupuestario(a)
3 vt presupuestar; **our main competitor is budgeting a loss this year** nuestro principal competidor ha anunciado pérdidas para este año; **how much has been budgeted for advertising?** ¿cuánto se ha presupuestado para publicidad?
4 vi preparar un presupuesto; **to budget for** (include in budget) presupuestar; **we hadn't budgeted for these expenses** (hadn't foreseen) no contábamos con estos gastos

budgetary adj presupuestario(a) □ **budgetary control** control m presupuestario; **budgetary limit** límite m presupuestario; **budgetary mechanism** mecanismo m presupuestario; **budgetary policy** política f presupuestaria; **budgetary resources** recursos fpl presupuestarios; **budgetary standards** normas fpl presupuestarias; **budgetary strength** potencial m presupuestario; **budgetary variance** desviación f presupuestaria; **budgetary year** ejercicio m presupuestario

budgeting n elaboración f del presupuesto

buffer n (a) (protection) **a buffer against inflation** una protección contra la inflación □ **buffer state** estado m tapón; **buffer stock** (of raw materials) stock m de regulación (b) COMPTR buffer m, búfer m □ **buffer memory** memoria f buffer

bug n COMPTR error m

bug-ridden adj COMPTR plagado(a) de errores

build vt MKTG **to build a brand** construir una marca

> ❝
> It follows the much vaunted launch that month of The Independent's first **brand building** campaign for nearly two years, using cinema and posters. The agency change is the latest in a series of measures by the paper's new management to build a stronger **brand** and halt the circulation slide.
> ❞

▶ **build into** vt sep **to build sth into a product** incorporar algo en un producto; **the alarm will be built into the system** el sistema llevará incorporada una alarma

▶ **build up** vt sep (a) (develop) (business) ampliar; (reputation) forjar; (production) aumentar (b) (advertise) promocionar (c) (stock) acumular

building n (a) (structure) edificio m □ **buildings insurance** seguro m de hogar or de la casa (b) (action) construcción f □ **building contract** contrato m de obras; **building contractor** contratista mf de obras; **building industry** industria f de la construcción; US Formerly **building and loan association** ≃ caja f de ahorros; Br **building plot** solar m; **building sector** sector m de la construcción; **building site** obra f; Br **building society** ≃ caja f de ahorros; **building society passbook** libreta f de la caja de ahorros; **the building trade** la construcción

build-up n (a) (advertising) campaña f de promoción; **they gave the product a big build-up** el producto vino precedido de una gran campaña de promoción; **after all the build-up** después de toda la expectación creada (b) (of stock) acumulación f

built-in adj (incorporated) incorporado(a) □ **built-in obsolescence** obsolescencia f incorporada or programada

bulk 1 n (a) (large quantity) **in bulk** al por mayor; **to buy in bulk** comprar al por mayor; **to ship sth in bulk** hacer un envío de algo al por mayor □ **bulk buying** compra f al por mayor; **bulk carrier** carguero m (de mercancía) a granel, granelero m; **bulk discount** descuento m por compra al por mayor; **bulk goods** mercancías fpl a granel; MKTG **bulk mailing** buzoneo m; **bulk order**

pedido *m* al por mayor; **bulk rate** *(for postage)* = tarifa reducida para envíos masivos (**b**) COMPTR *(of information)* volumen *m*
2 *vt (packages)* agrupar

bulk-buy *vt* comprar al por mayor

bulking *n (of packages)* grupaje *m*

bull 1 *n* ST EXCH alcista *mf* ❑ **bull market** mercado *m* alcista; **bull operations** operaciones *fpl* especulativas al alza; **bull position** posición *f* alcista; **bull speculation** especulación *f* al alza; **bull trading** negociación *f* al alza; **bull transaction** transacción *f* al alza
2 *vt* **to bull the market** jugar al alza
3 *vi (person)* jugar al alza; *(stocks)* cotizar al alza

❝
INVESCO is expecting a **bull market** in Asia on the back of corporate restructuring. Sam Lau, director of investment at INVESCO Asia says: 'Economic recovery is on its way. It is in its early stages and is still fragile, but key indicators show an improvement in demand'. Lau adds that corporate restructuring will provide better returns to shareholders and share prices will rise to reflect that.
❞

bulldog bond *n* FIN = bono emitido en el Reino Unido en libras esterlinas por una empresa extranjera

bullet *n* (**a**) TYP topo *m* (**b**) *US* FIN *(loan)* = préstamo cuyo interés se paga a plazos y cuyo principal se reembolsa en un solo pago a su vencimiento; *(repayment)* = reemboloso del principal de un préstamo en un solo pago a su vencimiento ❑ **bullet bond** bono *m* reembolsable de una sola vez

bulletin board *n* COMPTR tablón *m* de anuncios

bullion *n* oro *m*/plata *f* en lingotes; **gold/silver bullion** oro/plata en lingotes *or* barras ❑ **bullion reserve** reserva *f* metálica, reserva de oro y plata

bullish *adj* ST EXCH *(market, trend)* al alza, alcista; **to be bullish** *(person)* jugar al alza ❑ **bullish tendency** tendencia *f* alcista

❝
Steady demand for coconut oil has also boosted prices as the more **bullish** market outlook for soybean and palm oil spilled over to other vegetable oils. Coconut oil exports in February trebled its volume from 49,246 tons to 142,200 tons, according to the United Coconut Associations of the Philippines.
❞

bullishness *n* ST EXCH tendencia *f* alcista

bullying *n* intimidación *f*

bumf *n* *Fam (documentation)* información *f*; *(useless papers)* papelerío *m*, papelotes *mpl*; *(junk mail)* propaganda *f*

bumper *adj (profits, year)* excepcional

bundle *vt* MKTG **to bundle sth with sth** incluir algo en algo; **to come bundled with sth** venir acompañado(a) de algo

❝
Tretton won't confirm how many PlayStation2 units would be available in the United States this holiday season, but sources suggest that the number will be around 2 million. As for the final price, much will depend on exactly what is included in the box. While Sony has made little secret of its plans to have Internet connectivity and some form of hard drive for storage, the real question is whether this will be **bundled with** the final product or sold separately as accessories.
❞

bundling *n* MKTG *(of products)* venta *f* conjunta, empaquetado *m* conjunto

buoyancy *n* ST EXCH *(of market, prices, currency)* fortaleza *f*

buoyant *adj* ST EXCH *(market, currency)* fuerte, boyante; *(prices)* alto(a)

burden *vt* cargar; **burdened with tax/debts** cargado(a) de impuestos/deudas

bureau *n* oficina *f* ❑ **bureau de change** oficina *f* de cambio (de moneda)

bureaucracy *n* burocracia *f*

bureaucratic *adj* burocrático(a)

burn 1 *n* **burn rate** *(of company)* = ritmo al que una empresa nueva gasta su capital inicial en gastos fijos antes de producir ganancias
2 *vt (CD-ROM)* tostar, grabar

bus¹ *n (vehicle)* autobús *m*, bus *m*, *Andes* buseta *f*, *Bol, Arg* colectivo *m*, *CAm, Méx* camión *m*, *CAm, Carib* guagua *f*, *Urug* ómnibus *m*, *Ven* microbusete *m*

bus² *n* COMPTR bus *m* ❑ **bus board** placa *f* del bus; **bus controller** controlador *m or* controladora *f* del bus

business *n* (**a**) *(trade)* negocios *mpl*; *(commerce)* comercio *m*; **to be in the oil business** trabajar en la industria petrolera; **what's his line of business?, what business is he in?** ¿a qué se dedica?; **to set up in business** poner *or* abrir un negocio; **to be in/go into business for oneself** tener/poner *or* abrir un negocio por cuenta propia; **she's in business** se dedica a los negocios; **the company has been in business for twenty years** la empresa lleva veinte años funcionando; **they've been in business together for twenty years** tienen un negocio juntos desde hace veinte años; **to go out of business** ir a la quiebra; **supermarkets have put many small shops out of business** los supermercados han llevado a la quiebra a muchas tiendas pequeñas; **business is slow** las ventas están muy paradas; **to be away on business** estar en viaje de negocios; **to go to London on business** ir a Londres en viaje de negocios; **to lose business** perder clientes; **to do business with sb** hacer negocios con alguien; **to do good business** vender mucho; **it's good/bad for business** es bueno/malo para el negocio; **we have lost business to foreign competitors** nos han quitado clientes los competidores extranjeros; **how's business?** ¿cómo va el negocio?; **business is business** el negocio es el negocio ❑ **business account** cuenta f comercial; **business accounting** contabilidad f de empresas; **business activity** actividad f comercial; **business acumen** perspicacia f or vista f para los negocios; **business address** (of company) domicilio m comercial; (of person) dirección f de trabajo; **business administration** administración f de empresas; **business agent** agente mf comercial; **business angel** inversor(ora) m,f providencial, = inversor que respalda con su propio capital a nuevas empresas o a empresas en apuros; COMPTR **business application** aplicación f comercial or de negocios; **business appointment** cita f de negocios; **business area** zona f comercial; **business associate** socio(a) m,f; **business bank** banco m de negocios; **business banking** banca f de negocios; **business buyer** encargado(a) m,f de compras; **business call** visita f de negocios; **business card** tarjeta f de visita; **business centre** (in hotel) centro m de negocios; (city) centro m comercial; **business circles** círculos mpl empresariales; **business class** clase f preferente; **business college** facultad f de ciencias empresariales; **business community** comunidad f empresarial, RP comunidad empresaria; **business computer** Esp ordenador m or Am computadora f de empresa; **business computing** informática f de gestión; **business concern** entidad f comercial; **business consultancy** asesoría f or consultoría f empresarial; **business correspondence** correspondencia f de trabajo; **business correspondent** corresponsal mf de negocios; **business cycle** ciclo m económico; **business data processing** informática f de gestión; **business economist** administrador(ora) m,f de empresas; **business enterprise** entidad f comercial; **business ethics** ética f empresarial; **business expenses** gastos mpl de trabajo; **business failure** quiebra f; COMPTR **business graphics** gráficos mpl para presentaciones; **business hotel** hotel m de empresas or negocios; **business hours** (of company) horario m de trabajo; (of shop) horario m comercial; **business intelligence system** = sistema informático que ayuda a los directores de una empresa gestionando, organizando y analizando su información; **business lawyer** abogado(a) m,f de empresa; **business letter** carta f de negocios; **business lounge** (in airport) sala f

VIP; **business lunch** comida f de negocios; **business management** gestión f or administración f de empresas; **business manager** administrador(ora) m,f de empresa; **business market** mercado m de empresa; **business meeting** reunión f de negocios; **business mission** objetivos mpl de la empresa; **business name** razón f social; **business news** información f económica; **business operation** operación f comercial; **business park** parque m empresarial; **business partner** socio(a) m,f; **business plan** plan m de empresa; **business policy** política f económica; **business portfolio** cartera f de empresas; **business premises** local m comercial; **business process reengineering** rediseño m de los procesos de negocio, reingeniería f del proceso industrial; **business proposition** propuesta f de negocio; **business relations** relaciones fpl comerciales; **business school** escuela f de comercio; **business sector** sector m empresarial, RP sector empresario; **business services** servicios mpl de empresa; COMPTR **business software** software m empresarial or de negocios; **business strategy** estrategia f empresarial; **business studies** (ciencias fpl) empresariales fpl; **business transaction** operación f comercial; **business trend** tendencia f empresarial; **business trip** viaje m de negocios **business world** mundo m empresarial or de la empresa, RP mundo empresario

(b) (company, firm) empresa f, negocio m; **to run a business** dirigir una empresa; **to have one's own business** tener su propia empresa or propio negocio; **a profitable business** una empresa or un negocio rentable; **the small business sector** el sector de la pequeña empresa; **business for sale** (sign) se traspasa

(c) (on agenda) asuntos mpl; **any other business** ruegos mpl y preguntas

❝ Nat West is setting up a database of **business angels**… experienced business people able and willing to invest in small enterprises. There are also patron angels (people looking for longterm projects to invest in but wanting no personal involvement) and occupational angels (mainly retired or redundant people with up to £50,000 to invest, and looking for day-to-day involvement.) ❞

businessman n (executive, manager) hombre m de negocios; (owner of business) empresario m; **to be a good businessman** tener cabeza para los negocios

businesspeople npl gente f de negocios, ejecutivos(as) mpl,fpl

businessperson n (executive, manager) (man) hombre m de negocios; (woman) mujer f de negocios; (owner of business) empresario(a) m,f

business-to-business *adj* entre empresas

businesswoman *n (executive, manager)* mujer *f* de negocios; *(owner of business)* empresaria *f*; **to be a good businesswoman** tener cabeza para los negocios

bust *adj Fam* **to go bust** irse a pique; **the company went bust after a year** la empresa se fue a pique al cabo de un año

busy *adj* (a) *(person)* ocupado(a); **the manager is busy with a customer** el director está atendiendo a un cliente (b) *(period)* ajetreado(a); **the summer is our busiest period** el verano es cuando tenemos más movimiento *or* ajetreo (c) *US (telephone line)* ocupado(a); **I keep getting the busy signal** (el teléfono) da ocupado, *Esp* (el teléfono) está comunicando

button *n* COMPTR *(on mouse, screen)* botón *m*

buy 1 *n* (a) *(purchase)* **a good/bad buy** una buena/mala compra; **to make a good/bad buy** hacer una buena/mala compra (b) ST EXCH *buy order* orden *f* de compra; **to give a buy order** dar una orden de compra
  2 *vt* comprar; **to buy sth from sb** comprar algo a alguien; **to buy sth on credit** comprar algo a crédito; **to buy earnings** comprar por los beneficios potenciales; **to buy stock** comprar acciones
  3 *vi* FIN **to buy spot** comprar al contado; **to buy wholesale** comprar al por mayor; **to buy in bulk** comprar al por mayor

▸ **buy in** *vt sep* (a) *(stock up on)* aprovisionarse de, abastecerse de; *(obtain from a supplier)* comprar a un proveedor (b) ST EXCH *(shares)* adquirir

▸ **buy into** *vt insep* (a) *(company, sector)* adquirir una parte *or* acciones de; **we hope to buy into telecommunications next year** esperamos comprar acciones de telecomunicaciones el año que viene (b) *(believe)* creer en

▸ **buy out** *vt sep (partner)* comprar la parte de; **he was bought out for $50,000** le compraron su parte por 50.000 dólares; **she bought out all the other shareholders** compró la participación de todos los demás accionistas

▸ **buy up** *vt sep* (a) *(goods, supplies)* acaparar, comprar la totalidad de (b) FIN *(company, shares, stock)* acaparar; **the company bought up £50,000 worth of shares** la empresa se ha hecho con acciones por valor de 50.000 libras

buyback *n* (a) ST EXCH recompra *f* de las acciones propias (b) *(of car, currency)* recompra *f* ❑ *buyback agreement* contrato *m* de recompra

> Management got the job done, hacking the UK payroll from 17,000 in 1990 to 2,200 today, shutting plants and shovelling cash out of the door. In just nine years, the dividends, special dividends and share buybacks have returned to investors the entire £3.6 billion paid to the government for the assets. And the shareholders still own a company trading at three times the £1.75 price paid at flotation.

buyer *n* (a) *(consumer)* comprador(ora) *m,f*; **first-time buyers can have difficulty getting a mortgage** a los que compran su primera vivienda les puede resultar difícil obtener una hipoteca; **buyer beware** por cuenta y riesgo del comprador; **it's a case of buyer beware if you buy something from a street vendor** las compras a vendedores ambulantes corren por cuenta y riesgo del comprador ❑ MKTG *buyer behaviour* comportamiento *m* del comprador; *buyer credit* crédito *m* de comprador; *buyer credit guarantee* garantía *f* del crédito de comprador; FIN *buyer's market* mercado *m* favorable al comprador; *buyer's option (call option)* opción *f* de compra; MKTG *buyer readiness* predisposición *f* del consumidor
  (b) *(for company, shop)* comprador(ora) *m,f*; **head buyer** jefe(a) *m,f* de compras

buy-in *n* ST EXCH = compra de acciones al mejor precio por parte de un corredor, porque el vendedor original no ha cumplido su compromiso

buying *n* compra *f*; **buying and selling** compraventa *f*; **buying back** recompra *f*; ST EXCH **buying in** = compra de acciones al mejor precio por parte de un corredor, porque el vendedor original no ha cumplido su compromiso ❑ MKTG *buying behaviour* comportamiento *m* de compra; MKTG *buying behaviour model* modelo *m* de comportamiento de compra; MKTG *buying decision* decisión *f* de compra; *buying department* departamento *m* de compras; MKTG *buying incentive* incentivo *f* de compra; MKTG *buying inducement* inducción *f* a la compra; MKTG *buying motive* motivo *m* de compra; ST EXCH *buying order* orden *m* de compra; *buying power* poder *m* adquisitivo; ST EXCH *buying quotation, buying rate (of shares)* tipo *m* comprador *or* de compra; MKTG *buying situation* contexto *m* de compra

> But with economic clouds gathering in America, the strong **buying power** of Europe's consumers is expected to bolster growth. Indeed, even in the German manufacturing sector, growth in foreign orders is nowhere near as bad as in 1992-93, the last recession. Orders for consumer goods are holding up well.

buy-out *n (of company)* adquisición *f* (de todas las acciones); **he was planning a buy-out of his partner in the business** planeaba adquirir todas las acciones de su socio

buy-sell agreement *n* = contrato en el que

se estipulan las condiciones de sucesión en un negocio tras la muerte, jubilación o invalidez de su propietario actual

by-bidder *n* = persona que puja en una subasta para aumentar el precio

by-bidding *n* = puja en una subasta para aumentar el precio

bye-laws, by-laws *npl (of company)* estatutos *mpl*

by-line *n (on press article)* pie *m* de autor

by-product *n (of industrial process)* subproducto *m*

byte *n* COMPTR **(eight-bit) byte** byte *m*

Cc

CA n (**a**) Br (abbr **chartered accountant**) censor(ora) m,f jurado(a) de cuentas, Am contador(ora) m,f público(a) (**b**) (abbr **Consumers' Association**) asociación f de consumidores

C/A, **c/a** n (**a**) BANKING (abbr Br **current** or **cheque** or US **checking account**) c/c (**b**) BANKING (abbr **capital account**) cuenta f de capital (**c**) (abbr **credit account**) cuenta f de crédito

cable modem n COMPTR módem m (de) cable, cable módem m

CAC 40 n ST EXCH **the CAC 40 (index)** el (índice) CAC 40

cache COMPTR **1** n **cache (memory)** memoria f caché
　2 vt (data) meter en la caché

cached adj COMPTR en la caché

CAD n (**a**) COMPTR (abbr **computer-assisted design**) CAD m (**b**) (abbr **cash against documents**) pago m contra documentos

CAD/CAM n COMPTR (abbr **computer-assisted design/computer-assisted manufacture**) CAD/CAM m

CAE n COMPTR (abbr **computer-assisted engineering**) ingeniería f asistida por Esp ordenador or Am computadora

cafeteria benefit n US = prestación complementaria para empleados

CAFTA n (abbr **Central American Free Trade Agreement**) TLC CA-EU m, CAFTA m

CAL n COMPTR (abbr **computer-aided learning, computer-assisted learning**) enseñanza f asistida por Esp ordenador or Am computadora

calculate 1 vt calcular
　2 vi **let me calculate... it should take about three weeks** deja que lo calcule... debería llevar tres semanas

calculated risk n riesgo m calculado

calculation n cálculo m; **to make a calculation** hacer or efectuar un cálculo; **to be out in one's calculations** equivocarse en el cálculo or en los cálculos

calculator n calculadora f

calendar n calendario m □ **calendar month** mes m natural; **calendar year** año m natural, Am año m calendario

call 1 n (**a**) FIN (claim) requerimiento m de pago;

call (up) requerimiento de capital; **call for capital** requerimiento de capital; **payable at call** pagadero(a) en cualquier momento □ **call letter** carta f de solicitud del pago del dividendo pasivo; **call loan** préstamo m a la vista; **call money** dinero m a la vista
　(**b**) ST EXCH (option) opción f de compra; **call on a hundred shares** opción de compra sobre cien acciones; **call of more** opción de compra doble □ **call feature** cláusula f de amortización anticipada; **call option** opción f de compra **call price** precio m de rescate; **call warrant** garantía f de opción de compra
　(**c**) (telephone) **call** llamada f (telefónica), Am llamado m (telefónico); **to receive a call** recibir una llamada or Am un llamado; **to make a call** hacer una llamada or Am un llamado; **to give sb a call** llamar a alguien; **you have a call from Canada** tienes una llamada or Am un llamado de Canadá, te llaman de Canadá; **there was a call for you** te han llamado; **he's on a call** está hablando por teléfono; **will you accept the call?** (when charges are reversed) ¿acepta la llamada or Am el llamado?; **to put a call through (to sb)** pasar una llamada or Am un llamado (a alguien); **to return sb's call** devolverle la llamada or Am el llamado a alguien □ **call centre** centro m de atención telefónica, call center m; **call connection** establecimiento m de la llamada or Am del llamado; **call forwarding** desvío m de llamada or Am llamado; **call holding** atención f simultánea de llamadas or Am llamados; **call waiting service** servicio m de llamada or Am llamado en espera
　(**d**) (of representative) visita f; **to pay** or **make a call on sb** hacer una visita a alguien
　2 vt (**a**) FIN **to call a loan** exigir el pago or la amortización de un préstamo (**b**) (on telephone) llamar (**c**) (order) **to call a strike** convocar una huelga; **to call a meeting** convocar una reunión
　3 vi (on telephone) llamar; **who's calling, please?, may I ask who's calling?** ¿de parte de quién?; **could you call again later?** ¿puede llamar más tarde?

▶ **call back 1** vt sep volver a llamar; **I'll call you back later** luego te llamo
　2 vi llamar; **could you call back later, please?** ¿podría llamar más tarde?

▶ **call for** vt insep (demand) exigir; **workers are calling for a wage increase** los trabajadores exigen un aumento salarial

▶ **call in** vt sep (**a**) (person) (into building, office) hacer pasar; **call Miss Smith in, please** haga pasar a la Srta. Smith; **an accountant was called in to look at the books** trajeron a un Esp contable or Am contador para que revisara la contabilidad (**b**) FIN **to call in one's money** pedir la devolución del dinero; **to call in a loan** pedir la devolución or el pago de un préstamo; **to call in a guarantee** ejecutar una garantía (**c**) (currency) retirar de (la) circulación

▶ **call off** vt sep (meeting, deal) suspender; (strike) desconvocar

▶ **call on** vt insep (**a**) (request) **to call on sb to do sth** pedir a alguien que haga algo; **they are calling on the government to take action** piden al gobierno que actúe (**b**) (visit) visitar; **the sales reps call on their clients monthly** los comerciales van a ver or visitan a sus clientes todos los meses

▶ **call up** vt sep (**a**) (on telephone) llamar (**b**) COMPTR (help screen, file) visualizar

callable adj FIN (debt, bond) exigible; (loan) amortizable

called-up capital n FIN capital m desembolsado

calling in n (**a**) FIN (of debt, loan) exigencia f del pago (**b**) (of currency) retirada f de (la) circulación

CAM n COMPTR (abbr **computer-assisted manufacture**) CAM f, fabricación f asistida por Esp ordenador or Am computadora

campaign MKTG **1** n campaña f
2 vi **to campaign for/against** hacer campaña a favor de/en contra de ▫ **campaign plan** planificación f de la campaña

cancel 1 vt (**a**) (meeting, flight) suspender; (reservation, agreement, order) cancelar, anular; (debt) condonar, cancelar; (cheque) anular, invalidar; LAW (contract) rescindir (**b**) ACCT anular, neutralizar; **to cancel each other** (of two entries) anularse, neutralizarse (**c**) COMPTR cancelar ▫ **cancel button** botón m de cancelar
2 vi COMPTR cancelar; **press "esc" to cancel** pulse "esc" para cancelar

cancellation n (of meeting, flight) suspensión f; (of reservation, agreement, order) cancelación f, anulación f; (of debt) condonación f, cancelación; (of cheque) anulación; LAW (of contract) rescisión f ▫ **cancellation charge** tarifa f de cancelación; **cancellation clause** (in contract) cláusula f de rescisión; **cancellation fee** tarifa f de cancelación de reserva; **cancellation form** formulario m de anulación or cancelación; **cancellation insurance** seguro m de cancelación

C&F, C and F (abbr **cost and freight**) C&F

C&I, C and I n (abbr **cost and insurance**) C&I

candidate n (for job) candidato(a) m,f

cannibalization n MKTG canibalización f

cannibalize vt MKTG canibalizar

canteen n comedor m, cantina f

canvass 1 vt (**a**) (for survey) (person) encuestar; (area) hacer encuestas en (**b**) (in sales drive) (person) tratar de captar; (area) hacer una campaña de captación en
2 vi (**a**) (survey) hacer encuestas (**b**) (seek customers) hacer una campaña de captación; **to canvass for customers** tratar de captar clientes

canvasser n (**a**) (surveying opinion) encuestador(ora) mf (**b**) (seeking customers) captador(ora) m,f

canvassing n (**a**) (surveying opinion) encuestas fpl, realización f de encuestas (**b**) (seeking customers) captación f

CAP n EU (abbr **Common Agricultural Policy**) PAC f

cap 1 n (limit) tope m, límite m
2 vt (spending) poner un tope a, limitar; **these measures have been effective in capping overall expenditure** las medidas han conseguido limitar los gastos globales

capability n capacidad f

capacity n (**a**) (of factory, industry) capacidad f productiva; (output) rendimiento m (máximo); **the factory has not yet reached capacity** la fábrica aún no ha alcanzado su capacidad productiva; **to work at full capacity** trabajar a pleno rendimiento or plena capacidad ▫ **capacity output** rendimiento m máximo (**b**) (of container) capacidad f (**c**) (position) **in the capacity of** en calidad de; **he's acting in an advisory capacity** actúa or interviene en calidad de asesor; **to act in one's official capacity** actuar or intervenir oficialmente or de manera oficial

capex n (abbr **capital expenditure**) inversión f en activos fijos

capital n (**a**) FIN capital m; (assets) patrimonio m, capital; **to live on one's capital** vivir del capital que se posee ▫ **capital account** cuenta f de capital; **capital accumulation** acumulación f de capital; **capital adequacy ratio** coeficiente m de garantía or solvencia; **capital allowances** desgravaciones fpl sobre bienes de capital; **capital asset pricing model** modelo m de determinación del precio de los activos de capital; **capital assets** activo m inmovilizado; **capital bond** = bono del estado británico; **capital budget** presupuesto m de capital; **capital budgeting** análisis m inv de inversiones; **capital charge** carga f de capital; **capital clause** (in memorandum of association) = cláusula que establece la cantidad de capital autorizado; **capital contribution** aportación f de capital; **capital cost** costo m or Esp coste m del capital or de la inversión; ACCT **capital employed** capital *m* utilizado; **capital equipment** bienes *mpl* de equipo *or* de producción; **capital expenditure** inversión *f* en activos fijos; **capital flight** evasión *f* or fuga *f* de capitales; **capital gains** plusvalías *fpl* (de capital), ganancias *fpl* de capital; **capital gains distribution** distribución *f* de las ganancias de capital *or* plusvalías; **capital gains tax** impuesto *m* sobre la plusvalía *or* las ganancias de capital; **capital goods** bienes *mpl* de capital; **capital goods market** mercado *m* de bienes de capital; **capital grant** subvención *f* de capital; **capital growth** crecimiento *m* del capital; **capital income** rendimientos *mpl or* renta *f* del capital; **capital inflow** entrada *f* or afluencia *f* de capital; **capital injection** inyección *f* or aportación *f* de capital; **capital investment** *(individual)* inversión *f* (de capital); *(in general)* inversiones *fpl* (de capital); ACCT **capital items** partidas *fpl* de capital; **capital levy** impuesto *m* sobre el capital; **capital loss** pérdida *f* de capital, minusvalía *f*; **capital market** mercado *m* de capitales; **capital movements** movimiento *m* de capitales; **capital outlay** gastos *mpl or* desembolso *m* de capital; **capital profits** beneficios *mpl* del capital; **capital project evaluation** evaluación *f* de proyectos de capital; **capital reserves** reservas *fpl* de capital; ACCT **capital and reserves** capital *m* y reservas, fondos *mpl* propios; **capital share** participación *f* en el capital; **capital shortfall** insuficiencia *f* de capital; *US* **capital stock** capital *m* social *or* en acciones; **capital structure** estructura *f* del capital; **capital tax** impuesto *m* sobre el capital; **capital transaction** transacción *f* de capital; **capital transfer tax** impuesto *m* sobre transmisiones patrimoniales; **capital turnover** rotación *f* del capital (**b**) *(letter)* mayúscula *f* □ **capital letter** letra *f* mayúscula

> The fact only 2 per cent of people pay **capital gains tax** shows how little this avenue of investment is considered, and how simple it can be to avoid the tax – especially as the Budget raised the limit up to which capital gains tax is not applied to £7,900 per person per year.

capital-intensive *adj* con grandes necesidades de capital; **to be capital-intensive** requerir mucho capital

capitalism *n* capitalismo *m*

capitalist *n & adj* capitalista *m,f*

capitalization *n* (**a**) FIN capitalización *f* □ **capitalization issue** emisión *f* gratuita de acciones; **capitalization ratio** coeficiente *m* de capitalización; **capitalization of reserves** incorporación *f* de reservas (**b**) ACCT *(of expenses)* activación *f*

capitalize *vt* (**a**) FIN *(convert into capital)* capitalizar, convertir en capital; *(provide with capital)* financiar, capitalizar □ **capitalized value** valor *m* capitalizado (**b**) FIN *(estimate value of)* **they capitalized her investments at £50,000** valoraron sus inversiones en un capital de 50.000 libras; **the company is capitalized at £100,000** el valor en capital de la empresa es de 100.000 libras (**c**) ACCT *(expenses)* activar

capital-labour ratio *n* relación *f or* razón *f* capital-trabajo

capital-output ratio *n* relación *f or* razón *f* capital-producto

capitation *n* FIN capitación *f* □ **capitation tax** impuesto *m* de capitación, impuesto por cabeza

CAPM *n* (*abbr* **capital asset pricing model**) = modelo de determinación del precio de los activos de capital

capped-rate *adj (mortgage)* con tope máximo de interés

caps *npl* COMPTR (*abbr* **capital letters**) mayúsculas *fpl* □ **caps lock** mayúsculas *fpl* fijas; **caps lock key** tecla *f* de mayúsculas fijas

caption *n (under graph, photo)* pie *m*

captive *adj* MKTG cautivo(a) □ **captive audience** público *m* cautivo, audiencia *f* cautiva; **captive fund** fondo *m* cautivo; **captive market** mercado *m* cautivo **captive product** producto *m* cautivo

captive-product pricing *n* MKTG fijación *f* de precios de productos cautivos

capture *vt (market)* acaparar, hacerse con; **in one year they have captured a large part of the mail-order market** en un año han acaparado *or* se han hecho con gran parte del mercado de venta por correo

car *n* coche *m*, *Am* carro *m*, *CSur* auto *m* □ **car industry** industria *f* automovilística; **car factory** fábrica *f or* planta *f* de automóviles; *Br* **car hire** alquiler *m* de coches *or Am* carros *or CSur* autos, *Méx* renta *f* de carros; **car manufacturer** fabricante *m* de automóviles; **car rental** alquiler *m* de coches *or Am* carros *or CSur* autos, *Méx* renta *f* de carros

carbon copy *n* copia *f* en papel carbón

card *n* (**a**) *(with printed information)* tarjeta *f*; *(for card index)* ficha *f* □ **card file** fichero *m* de tarjetas; **card index** fichero *m* de tarjetas; BANKING **card payment** pago *m* con tarjeta; (**b**) COMPTR *(circuit board)* tarjeta *f* □ **card slot** ranura *f* para tarjeta

card-index 1 *vt* archivar en un fichero de tarjetas
2 *adj* **card-index file** fichero *m* de tarjetas

cardphone *n* TEL teléfono *m* de tarjetas

career *n* carrera *f* (profesional); **she wanted a**

career in banking/engineering quería una carrera en el sector de la banca/ingeniería; **it was a good/bad career move** fue bueno/malo para mi/tu/*etc* trayectoria profesional □ *careers adviser* asesor(ora) *m,f* de orientación profesional; *career break* interrupción *f* de la carrera profesional; **to take a career break** interrumpir la carrera profesional; *career counselling* orientación *f* profesional; *careers counsellor* asesor(ora) *m,f* de orientación profesional; *career development* desarrollo *m* profesional; *Br Career Development Loan* = préstamo bancario para financiar cursos de formación profesional en el Reino Unido, que se comienza a amortizar a la finalización de los mismos; *careers guidance* orientación *f* profesional; *careers office* oficina *f* de orientación profesional; *career plan* plan *m* de futuro profesional; *careers service* servicio *m* de orientación profesional; *career structure* estructura *f* de la carrera profesional

care of *prep (in addresses)* **write to me care of Mr McLean** escríbeme a la dirección del Sr. McLean

cargo *n* cargamento *m*; **to take on** *or* **embark cargo** embarcar carga; **cargo outward** cargamento de ida; **cargo homeward** cargamento de vuelta □ *cargo boat* barco *m* de carga, carguero *m*; *cargo plane* avión *m* de carga; *cargo ship* buque *m* de carga, carguero *m*

carnet *n* CUSTOMS *(pass)* carnet *m*, cuaderno *m*

carriage *n (transportation)* transporte *m*, porte *m*; *(cost of transportation)* portes *mpl*; **to pay the carriage** pagar los portes; **carriage forward** porte debido; **carriage free** porte pagado, franco(a) de porte; **carriage and insurance paid** porte y seguro pagados; **carriage paid** porte pagado □ *carriage charge(s)* portes *mpl*; *carriage costs* gastos *mpl* de transporte

carrier *n* (a) *(company)* transportista *m,f*; **sent by carrier** enviado(a) por transportista (b) COMPTR,TEL *(for signal)* portadora *f*

carry *vt* (a) *(keep in stock)* tener (en almacén); **do you carry computer accessories?** ¿venden accesorios informáticos? (b) *(interest)* producir; **the investment carries 10% interest over three years** la inversión produce el 10% de interés en tres años (c) *(proposal, motion)* aprobar; **the motion was carried unanimously** la moción se aprobó por unanimidad (d) *(transport)* llevar, transportar

▸ **carry forward** *vt sep* ACCT *(item)* pasar a cuenta nueva; **carried forward** suma y sigue

▸ **carry on** *vt sep (trade, business)* dirigir, gestionar

▸ **carry out** *vt sep (market research)* llevar a cabo, realizar; *(instructions)* seguir, cumplir; *(order)* cumplir

▸ **carry over** *vt sep* (a) ACCT *(balance)* trasladar al siguiente ejercicio; **to carry over a loss to the following year** trasladar una pérdida *or* un rendimiento negativo al siguiente ejercicio, repercutir una pérdida *or* un rendimiento negativo en el ejercicio siguiente
(b) ST EXCH **to carry shares over** retrasar el pago de las acciones hasta el día siguiente; **carried over** *(stock)* con el pago retrasado hasta el día siguiente
(c) *(defer)* aplazar; **that will have to be carried over to the next meeting** eso tendremos que dejarlo para la siguiente reunión; **you may carry over your holiday entitlement to the following year** puedes trasladar las vacaciones que te corresponden al año siguiente

carrying *n* (a) *(transport)* transporte *m*, porte *m* □ *carrying capacity (of vehicle)* capacidad *f* de carga (b) US ACCT *carrying cost, carrying value* valor *m* neto contable *or* en libros (c) US *carrying charge (on credit purchase)* recargo *m*, comisión *f*

carry-over *n* ACCT pérdida *f* trasladada al ejercicio siguiente

cartage *n (transport)* transporte *m*, porte *m*; *(cost)* portes *mpl*

cartel *n* cartel *m*, cártel *m*; **to form a cartel** formar un cartel *or* cártel; **an oil/steel cartel** un cartel *or* cártel petrolero/siderúrgico □ *cartel laws* legislación *f* sobre carteles

cartellization *n* cartelización *f*

cart note *n* (a) *(for transporting goods)* hoja *f* de embarque, guía *f* de carga (b) *(for taking goods from customs)* conduce *m*

cartridge *n* COMPTR cartucho *m*; **ink/toner cartridge** cartucho de tinta/tóner

cascade taxation *n* impuestos *mpl* *or* tributación *f* en cascada

CASE *n* COMPTR *(abbr* **computer-assisted software engineering***)* ingeniería *f* de software asistida por *Esp* ordenador *or Am* computadora

case *n* (a) *(container)* **(packing) case** cajón *m* (b) LAW causa *f*, caso *m* (c) *case study* estudio *m* de casos, estudio monográfico (d) COMPTR **to be case insensitive** no distinguir entre mayúsculas y minúsculas; **to be case sensitive** distinguir entre mayúsculas y minúsculas

cash 1 *n (coins, banknotes)* (dinero *m* en) efectivo *m*; *(money in general)* dinero, *Am* plata *f*; **to pay (in) cash** pagar en efectivo; **to buy/sell sth for cash** comprar/vender algo al contado; ACCT **cash at bank** efectivo en bancos; **cash against documents** pago *m* contra documentos; ACCT *Br* **cash on delivery** entrega *f* contrarreembolso; **cash in hand** efectivo disponible; ACCT **cash in till** efectivo en caja; **cash with order** pago con el pedido □ *cash account* cuenta *f* de caja; *cash advance* adelanto *m* *or* anticipo *m* en metálico;

cash balance *(status)* estado *m* de cuenta; *(amount remaining)* saldo *m* de caja; ACCT **cash basis accounting** contabilidad *f* de caja; **cash benefits** prestaciones *fpl* en efectivo; **cash bonus** bonificación *f or* prima *f* en efectivo; **cash book** registro *m or* libro *m* de caja; **cash box** caja *f* (para el dinero); **cash budget** presupuesto *m* de caja; **cash and carry** *(shop)* almacén *m* (de venta) al por mayor *or Am* al mayoreo, cash and carry *m*; **cash compensation** compensación *f* en efectivo; ACCT **cash contribution** aportación *f* en efectivo; MKTG **cash cow** vaca *f* lechera, mina *f*; **cash crop** cultivo *m* comercial; ST EXCH **cash deal** operación *f* al contado; **cash deficit** déficit *m* de caja; FIN **cash deposit** depósito *m or Esp* ingreso *m* en efectivo; **cash desk** (mostrador *m* de) caja *f*; **cash discount** descuento *m or* rebaja *f* por pronto pago; **cash dispenser** cajero *m* automático; **cash dividend** dividendo *m* en efectivo; FIN **cash equivalents** equivalentes *mpl* en efectivo; ACCT **cash expenditure** gastos *mpl* de caja *or* en efectivo; **cash flow** flujo *m* de caja, cash-flow *m*; **cash flow forecast** previsión *f* de flujo de caja *or* cash-flow; **cash flow management** gestión *f* del flujo de caja *or* cash-flow; **cash flow problems** problemas *mpl* de liquidez; **cash flow rate** coeficiente *m* de flujo de caja; **cash flow situation** situación *f* del flujo de caja *or* cash-flow; ACCT **cash flow statement** estado *m* de flujo de caja; FIN **cash incentive** incentivo *m* en efectivo; ACCT **cash inflow** flujo *m* de entrada de caja; ACCT **cash item** partida *f* de caja; **cash machine** cajero *m* automático; **cash management** gestión *f* de caja; **cash offer** oferta *f* en efectivo; **they made us a cash offer for the house** nos hicieron una oferta en efectivo *or* en dinero por la casa; ACCT **cash order** orden *f* de pago en metálico; ACCT **cash outflow** flujo *m* de salida de caja; **cash outgoings** salidas *fpl* de caja; ACCT **cash overs** excedentes *mpl* líquidos; **cash payment** pago *m* en efectivo; **cash price** precio *m* al contado; **cash purchase** compra *f* al contado; ACCT **cash ratio** coeficiente *m* de caja; ACCT **cash receipt** recibo *m* por pago en efectivo; ACCT **cash receipts** entradas *fpl* de caja, cobros *mpl* por caja; ACCT **cash receipts and payments** entradas *fpl* y salidas de caja; ACCT **cash received** *(balance sheet item)* efectivo *m*, cobros *mpl* por caja; **cash register** caja *f* registradora; ACCT **cash report (form)** informe *m* de caja; **cash requirements** requerimientos *mpl* de caja; **cash reserves** reservas *fpl* de caja *or* efectivo; **cash returns** rendimientos *mpl* en efectivo; **cash sale** venta *f* al contado; **cash settlement** liquidación *f* en efectivo; **cash shortage** insuficiencia *f* de liquidez, faltante *m* de caja; ACCT **cash statement** estado *m* de caja, cuenta *f* de tesorería; ACCT **cash surplus** superávit *m* de tesorería, excedente *m* de efectivo; **cash terms** condiciones *fpl* de pago al contado; **cash transaction** operación *f* al contado; **cash value** valor *m* en efectivo;

ACCT **cash voucher** comprobante *m* de caja; **cash withdrawal** reintegro *m* (en efectivo)
  2 *vt (cheque, bill)* cobrar, hacer efectivo(a)

▸ **cash in** *vt sep (bond, savings certificate)* hacer efectivo(a), canjear (en dinero)

▸ **cash up** *vi Br* hacer la caja *or* el arqueo

cashable *adj* FIN que se puede cobrar en efectivo

cash-and-carry arbitrage *n* ST EXCH arbitraje *m* directo

cashback *n* **(a)** *(in mortgage lending)* reintegro *m* en efectivo **(b)** *(in supermarket)* = servicio que ofrece la posibilidad de sacar dinero de una cuenta en el momento de pagar con tarjeta de débito una compra; **would you like any cashback?** ¿quiere sacar dinero de la cuenta?

cash-based accounting *n* contabilidad *f* de caja

cashier *n* cajero(a) *m,f* □ *US* **cashier's check** caja *f*

cashless society *n* sociedad *f* que no maneja dinero en efectivo

cashpoint *n* cajero *m* automático

cask *n* tonel *m*, barril *m*

CASM *n* COMPTR *(abbr* **computer-assisted sales and marketing***)* ventas *fpl* y marketing asistidos por *Esp* ordenador *or Am* computadora

cassette drive *n* COMPTR unidad *f* de cinta

casting vote *n* voto *m* de calidad; **the chairman has the casting vote** el presidente tiene voto de calidad; **to give the casting vote** hacer uso del voto de calidad

casual *adj (employment)* eventual; **to employ sb on a casual basis** dar empleo a alguien de manera eventual □ **casual labour** trabajo *m* eventual; **casual worker** trabajador(ora) *m,f* eventual

casualization of labour *n* ECON precarización *f* del mercado laboral

CAT *Br (abbr* **Charges, Access and Terms***)* **CAT standard** = normas sobre ciertos productos hipotecarios y crediticios establecidas por el gobierno británico para la protección del consumidor que se comprometen a cumplir las entidades que ofrecen dichos productos

catalogue, *US* **catalog 1** *n* catálogo *m*; **to buy sth by catalogue** comprar algo por catálogo □ **catalogue number** *(in library)* signatura *f*; **catalogue price** precio *m* de catálogo
  2 *vt* catalogar

catch *vt Br Fam* ST EXCH **to catch a cold** sufrir un bache

category *n* categoría *f* □ MKTG **category leader** líder *m* de la categoría

▸ **cater for** *vt insep* **(a)** *(requirements)* tener en cuenta; **we cater for the needs of small**

companies atendemos las necesidades de la pequeña empresa; **does the building cater for disabled staff?** ¿tiene el edificio accesibilidad para personal discapacitado? (**b**) *(provide meals for)* dar servicio de comidas *or* catering a

caveat *n* LAW advertencia *f*; **to enter a caveat** realizar una advertencia al juez; **caveat emptor** por cuenta y riesgo del comprador; **caveat subscriptor** por cuenta y riesgo del suscriptor

CBD *n* (*abbr* **cash before delivery**) pago *m* antes de la entrega

CBI *n* (*abbr* **Confederation of British Industry**) = organización empresarial británica, ≃ *Esp* CEOE *f*

CBT *n* (*abbr* **Chicago Board of Trade**) = Bolsa de futuros de Chicago

cc (*abbr* **carbon copy**) cc; **cc Anthea Baker** con copia para Anthea Baker; *Fam* **to cc sb sth, to cc sth to sb** enviar una copia de algo a alguien

CCA *n* ACCT (*abbr* **current cost accounting**) contabilidad *f* de costos *or Esp* costes corrientes

CCI *n* (*abbr* **Chamber of Commerce and Industry**) cámara *f* de comercio e industria

cd/fwd ACCT (*abbr* **carried forward**) suma y sigue

CD *n* (*abbr* **compact disc**) CD *m*

CD-I, CDI *n* COMPTR (*abbr* **compact disc interactive**) CD-I *m*

CDL *n abbr* **Career Development Loan**) = en el Reino Unido, préstamo bancario para financiar cursos de formación profesional que se comienza a amortizar a la finalización de los mismos

CD-R *n* (**a**) (*abbr* **compact disc recorder**) CD-R *m*, grabadora *f* de CD-ROM (**b**) (*abbr* **compact disc recordable**) CD-R *m*, disco *m* compacto regrabable

CD-ROM *n* COMPTR (*abbr* **compact disc-read only memory**) CD-ROM *m*; **available on CD-ROM** disponible en CD-ROM □ **CD-ROM burner** estampadora *f or* grabadora *f* de CD-ROM; **CD-ROM drive** unidad *f* de CD-ROM, lector *m* de CD-ROM, *Andes, RP* lectora *f* de CD-ROM; **CD-ROM newspaper** periódico *m* en CD-ROM; **CD-ROM reader** lector *m* de CD-ROM, *Andes, RP* lectora *f* de CD-ROM; **CD-ROM writer** estampadora *f or* grabadora *f* de CD-ROM

CD-RW *n* (*abbr* **compact disc rewritable**) CD-RW *m*

CD-text *n* (*abbr* **compact disc text**) CD-texto *m*; CD-text *m*

cease *vt Br* **to cease trading** *(as company)* cerrar el negocio, suspender la actividad comercial; *(on Stock Exchange)* suspender la cotización

ceiling *n* ECON techo *m*, tope *m*; **to reach a ceiling** *(prices, interest rates)* tocar techo; **to have a**

ceiling of tener un techo *or* tope de; **to fix a ceiling to sth** poner un techo *or* tope a algo; **the government has set a 3% ceiling on wage rises** el gobierno ha marcado un techo *or* tope del 3% para los incrementos salariales □ **ceiling price** precio *m* máximo autorizado

> **❝**
> A rise in global oil prices would not have a direct impact on the Malaysian economy, but higher prices for a sustained period could boost to the country's coffers. According to economists, as a net oil exporter, Malaysia will benefit from a rise in oil prices, but the Government's **ceiling price** on retail oil prices will ensure the country's inflation remains in check amid spiralling global oil prices.
> **❞**

cell *n* COMPTR *(on spreadsheet)* celda *f*

cellphone *n US* teléfono *m* móvil, *Am* teléfono celular

cellular phone *n* teléfono *m* móvil, *Am* teléfono celular

census *n* censo *m*; **to conduct** *or* **take a census** realizar *or* elaborar un censo □ **Census Bureau** = organización encargada de la elaboración de censos en los Estados Unidos

center *US* = **centre**

central *adj* **central account** cuenta *f* central *or* centralizada; FIN **central bank** banco *m* central; **central buying** compras *fpl* centralizadas; **Central European Bank** Banco *m* Central Europeo; **Central Office of Information** = organismo público que publica documentos de información sobre el Reino Unido; COMPTR **central processing unit** unidad *f* central de proceso *or Am* procesamiento; **central purchasing** compras *fpl* centralizadas; **central purchasing department** departamento *m* central de compras; **central purchasing group** departamento *m* central de compras; **central purchasing office** oficina *f* central de compras; **central reservations unit** central *f* de reservas; BANKING, ST EXCH **Central Securities Depository** Depósito *m or* Depositario *m* Central de Valores; **central works council** comité *m* intercentros

centralized *adj* centralizado(a) □ **centralized management** dirección *f or* administración *f* centralizada; **centralized purchasing** compras *fpl* centralizadas

centre, *US* **center 1** *n (place, building)* centro *m*
2 *vt* COMPTR centrar

CEO *n esp US* (*abbr* **chief executive officer**) consejero(a) *m,f* delegado(a), director(ora) *m,f* gerente; **President and CEO** Presidente(a) *m,f* y Consejero(a) Delegado(a)

certificate *n* certificado *m* □ **certificate of**

airworthiness certificado *m* de aeronavegabilidad; **certificate of approval** certificado *m* de aprobación; **certificate of compliance** certificado *m* de conformidad; **certificate of conformity** certificado *m* de conformidad; INS **certificate of damage** certificado *m* de averías *or* daños; **certificate of deposit** certificado *m* de depósito; FIN **certificate of dishonour** certificado *m* de impago; **certificate of guarantee** certificado *m* de garantía; **certificate of incorporation** certificado *m* de constitución; **certificate of insurance** certificado *m* de seguro; **certificate of origin** certificado *m* de origen; **certificate of proficiency** certificado *m* de aptitud; **certificate of quality** certificado *m* de calidad; **certificate of receipt** certificado *m* de recibo; **certificate of registration** *(of ship)* patente *f* de navegación; US **certificate of residence** certificado *m* de residencia; **certificate of transfer** certificado *m* de transferencia; **certificate of value** certificado *m* de valor

certificated *adj* **certificated bankrupt** oficialmente en quiebra *or* bancarrota

certification *n* (**a**) *(act)* certificación *f* ❑ **certification mark** sello *m* de calidad, marca *f* de certificación (**b**) *(document)* certificado *m*

certified *adj* (**a**) US **certified financial planner** asesor(ora) *m,f* financiero(a) independiente; **certified public accountant** *Esp* censor(ora) *m,f* jurado(a) de cuentas, *Am* contador(ora) *m,f* público(a)
(**b**) **certified accounts** cuentas *fpl* certificadas; **certified cheque** cheque *m* certificado
(**c**) LAW **certified copy** copia *f* certificada; **certified true copy** *(document)* copia *f* auténtica compulsada; *(appearing on document)* es fiel copia del original
(**d**) US **certified letter** carta *f* certificada; US **certified mail** correo *m* certificado; **to send sth by certified mail** enviar algo por correo certificado

certify *vt* (**a**) *(confirm)* certificar; **certified by a notary** certificado(a) por notario; **this is to certify that...** *(on document)* por la presente certifico que...; **to certify the books** certificar las cuentas (**b**) *(cheque, invoice)* conformar

CET *n* EU *(abbr* **common external tariff**) AEC *m*

CF *(abbr* **carriage forward**) porte *m* debido

c/f ACCT *(abbr* **carried forward**) suma y sigue

CFO *n* US *(abbr* **Chief Financial Officer**) director(ora) *m,f* financiero(a)

CFP *n* US *(abbr* **certified financial planner**) asesor(ora) *m,f* financiero(a) independiente

CFR *(abbr* **cost and freight**) CFR

CFSP *n* EU *(abbr* **Common Foreign and Security Policy**) PESC *f*

CFTC *n* FIN, ST EXCH *(abbr* **Commodity Futures Trading Commission**) = comisión creada en 1973 con el fin de controlar las transacciones comerciales en los mercados de futuros estadounidenses

CGI *n* COMPTR (**a**) *(abbr* **common gateway interface**) CGI *m*, interfaz *f* común de pasarela (**b**) *(abbr* **computer-generated images**) imágenes *fpl* generadas por *Esp* ordenador *or* *Am* computadora

CGT *n* *(abbr* **capital gains tax**) impuesto *m* sobre la plusvalía *or* las ganancias de capital

CH *n* *(abbr* **clearing house**) cámara *f* de compensación

chaebol *n* ECON chaebol *m*

> **"**
>
> The Fair Trade Commission (FTC), the nation's antitrust watchdog, has begun to use its scalpel to root out unfair business practices by the nation's five largest business groups in the initial stages of an operation which will later be applied to 24 other groups or **chaebol**. The punitive action by the government agency is expected to serve as a key means to press **chaebol** groups to expedite their restructuring work in compliance with the government call.
>
> **"**

chain *n* (**a**) *(of stores, restaurants)* cadena *f* ❑ **chain bank** US BANKING grupo *m* bancario; **chain store** tienda *f* (de una cadena) (**b**) **chain of distribution** cadena *f* de distribución

chair 1 *n (chairperson) (of formal meeting)* presidente(a) *m,f*; *(of informal discussion, workshop)* moderador(ora) *m,f*; **to be in the chair** ocupar la presidencia; **to address the chair** dirigirse a la presidencia, dirigirse al presidente/a la presidenta; **to support the chair** apoyar a la presidencia; **to take the chair** ocupar la presidencia, presidir
2 *vt (formal meeting)* presidir; *(informal discussion, workshop)* moderar

chairman *n (of formal meeting)* presidente *m*; *(of informal discussion, workshop)* moderador *m*; *(of company)* presidente *m*; **to act as chairman** ocupar la presidencia; **chairman and managing director** presidente y consejero delegado, presidente y máximo responsable ejecutivo; **Mr Chairman** Señor Presidente; **Chairman of the Board** presidente del consejo de administración ❑ **chairman's report** informe *m* del presidente (del consejo de administración)

chairmanship *n* presidencia *f*; **under the chairmanship of Mr Greene** bajo *or* durante la presidencia del Señor Greene

chairperson *n (of formal meeting)* presidente(a) *m,f*; *(of informal discussion, workshop)* moderador(ora) *m,f*; *(of company)* presidente(a) *m,f*

chairwoman n (of formal meeting) presidenta f; (of informal discussion, workshop) moderadora f; (of company) presidenta f; **Madam Chairwoman** Señora Presidenta

challenge n (threat, opportunity) reto m

challenger n MKTG competidor m

chamber n **Chamber of Commerce** Cámara f de Comercio; **Chamber of Commerce and Industry** Cámara f de Comercio e Industria; **Chamber of Trade** Cámara f de Comercio

Chancellor of the Exchequer n Br ministro(a) m,f de Economía y Hacienda

change 1 n (a) (transformations) **change management** gestión f del cambio (b) (coins) **(small) change** (dinero m) suelto m; **can you give me change for £20?** ¿me podría cambiar 20 libras? □ **change machine** máquina f de cambio (c) (money returned) cambio m; **keep the change** quédese con el cambio
2 vt (money) cambiar; **to change dollars into euros** cambiar dólares en euros

channel n (a) (means) cauce m, canal m; **to go through the official channels** seguir los trámites oficiales; **to open up new channels for trade** abrir nuevas vías para el comercio □ **channel of distribution** canal m de distribución; MKTG **channel management** gestión f de los canales de distribución (b) COMPTR (of communication, data flow, for IRC) canal m

CHAPS n Br BANKING (abbr **clearing house automated payment system**) CHAPS m, = sistema electrónico de transferencias interbancarias en libras esterlinas

Chapter 11 n FIN (part of bankruptcy laws) = sección de la ley de quiebras estadounidense que regula el proceso de declaración oficial de bancarrota; **to file for Chapter 11** = solicitar la aplicación de la sección 11 de la ley de quiebras

> **❝**
>
> AMF Bowling Worldwide, Inc. today announced that it has emerged from **Chapter 11** after completing its exit financing arrangements with Deutsche Bank Alex Brown and its affiliate Bankers Trust Company. AMF Bowling Worldwide, Inc. and its U.S. subsidiaries filed voluntary petitions for reorganization under **Chapter 11** on July 2, 2001.
>
> **❞**

character n COMPTR carácter m; **characters per inch** caracteres por pulgada; **characters per second** caracteres por segundo □ **character code** código m de carácter; **character generator** generador m de caracteres; **character insert** inserción f de carácter; **character recognition** reconocimiento m de caracteres; **character set** juego m de caracteres; **character smoothing** suavizado m de caracteres; **character space** espacio m; **character spacing** espaciado m de caracteres; **character string** cadena f de caracteres

charge 1 n (cost) precio m, tarifa f; (to an account) adeudo m, cargo m; **to make a charge for sth** cobrar por algo; **there is no extra charge for installation** la instalación es gratuita; **what's the charge?** ¿cuánto cuesta?, ¿cuánto cobran?; **at a small charge** por una módica cantidad or suma; US **will that be cash or charge?** ¿pagará en efectivo o con tarjeta?; ACCT **charge to provisions** cargo contra provisiones □ US **charge account** cuenta f de crédito; **charge card** tarjeta f de compra
2 vt (a) (defer payment of) **charge it to my account** cárguelo en mi cuenta; **charge it to the company's account** póngalo en la cuenta de la empresa; **I charged all my expenses to the company** cargué todos los gastos a la cuenta de la empresa
(b) (person, sum, commission) cobrar; **they charged us $50 for delivery** nos cobraron 50 dólares por el envío; **how much will you charge for the lot?** ¿cuánto cobra por todo?; **you will be charged for postage** los gastos de envío correrán a su cargo
3 vi (demand payment) cobrar; **we don't charge for postage and packing** no cobramos gastos de envío

▶ **charge off** vt US cancelar; **we were obliged to charge off the whole operation** tuvimos que dar por perdida toda la operación

▶ **charge up** vt sep **to charge sth up to sb's account** cargar algo en la cuenta de alguien; **could you charge it up?** ¿podría cargarlo en mi cuenta?

chargeable adj (a) (to an account) imputable; **to be chargeable to sb** (payable by) correr a cargo de alguien; **who is it chargeable to?** ¿a nombre de quién hago la factura?; **could you make that chargeable to Crown Ltd?** ¿podría hacer la factura a nombre de Crown Ltd? □ **chargeable expenses** gastos mpl imputables or repercutibles; **chargeable weight** peso m imponible
(b) FIN gravable □ **chargeable asset** activo m imponible; **chargeable gain** plusvalía f imputable, beneficios mpl imputables

chargehand n encargado(a) m,f, supervisor(ora) m,f

charitable trust n fundación f benéfica

charity n (organization) entidad f benéfica; **all proceeds will go to charity** toda la recaudación se dedicará a obras de beneficencia □ **charity card** = tarjeta de crédito vinculada a una entidad benéfica; **charity organization** organización f benéfica

chart 1 n (diagram) gráfica f ▫ ACCT **chart of accounts** plan m contable; **chart analysis** análisis m inv gráfico or de gráficas; **chart analyst** analista mf de gráficos
2 vt (**a**) (on diagram) representar gráficamente; **this graph charts sales over the last ten years** esta gráfica representa or refleja las ventas de los últimos diez años (**b**) (follow) (progress, rise) describir; **the director charted a way out of financial collapse** el director describió or expuso una salida del colapso financiero

charter 1 n (**a**) (of company) escritura f de constitución, carta f fundacional (**b**) (of aeroplane, boat) fletamiento m ▫ **charter company** compañía f de vuelos chárter; **charter flight** vuelo m chárter; **charter plane** avión m chárter
2 vt (**a**) (company) constituir, otorgar carta fundacional a (**b**) (aeroplane, boat) fletar

chartered adj (**a**) Br **chartered accountant** Esp censor(ora) m,f jurado(a) de cuentas, Am contador(ora) m,f público(a); US **chartered bank** banco m autorizado; **chartered company** = empresa británica creada por cédula real; **chartered surveyor** tasador(ora) m,f de la propiedad (**b**) (aeroplane, boat) fletado(a)

chartist n ST EXCH chartista mf

▶ chase up vt sep (debt) reclamar; **I'll chase them up about it** les llamaré para recordárselo

chat COMPTR **1** n chat m ▫ **chat room** sala f de conversación or chat
2 vi chatear

chattel mortgage n hipoteca f sobre bienes muebles

cheap 1 adj barato(a) ▫ **cheap money** dinero m barato; **cheap rate** tarifa f reducida or económica
2 adv **to buy sth cheap** comprar algo barato; **it works out cheaper to buy 10 kilos** sale más barato or económico comprar 10 kilos

cheaply adv barato; **they can manufacture more cheaply than we can** pueden fabricar con un costo or Esp coste más bajo que el nuestro

check 1 n (**a**) (restraint) freno m; **to put a check on production** poner freno a la producción (**b**) (verification) control m ▫ MKTG **check question** pregunta f de control; MKTG **check sample** muestra f testigo or de control (**c**) US (in restaurant) cuenta f (**d**) US (cheque) cheque m (**e**) COMPTR **check box** casilla f de verificación

2 vt (**a**) (price increases, inflation, production) frenar (**b**) (verify, examine) (accounts, figures) comprobar, revisar; (document) revisar; **to check the books** comprobar or revisar la contabilidad; **all the sales are checked** todas las ventas son comprobadas or revisadas (**c**) US (baggage) dejar en consigna

▶ check in 1 vt sep (baggage) (at airport) facturar, Am despachar; (at left-luggage) dejar en consigna
2 vi (at hotel) registrarse; (at airport) facturar, Am despachar

▶ check off vt sep (goods) hacer el inventario de; **to check sth off a list** marcar algo en una lista (como comprobado)

▶ check out vi (leave hotel) **I'd like to check out now, please** quisiera pagar la cuenta, por favor; **you should check out by 11 a.m.** la habitación tiene que quedar libre a las 11 de la mañana

▶ check over vt sep (goods) revisar

checkbook US = **chequebook**

check-in n (at airport) facturación f, Am despacho m; **latest check-in time is 30 minutes prior to departure** se podrá facturar hasta 30 minutos antes de la salida ▫ **check-in desk** mostrador m de facturación

checking account n US cuenta f corriente

checkless society US = **chequeless society**

check-out n (**a**) (in supermarket) (mostrador m de) caja f (**b**) (in hotel) **check-out time is at 12 noon** la habitación tiene que quedar libre a las 12 del mediodía

cheque, US **check** n cheque m; **a cheque for ten pounds** un cheque de diez libras; **cheque to order** cheque a la orden; **cheque to bearer** cheque al portador; **to cash a cheque** hacer efectivo or cobrar un cheque; **to endorse a cheque** endosar un cheque; **to make out a cheque (to sb)** extender un cheque (a alguien); **who should I make the cheque out to?** ¿a nombre de quién extiendo el cheque?; **will you take a cheque?** ¿le puedo extender un cheque or pagar con un cheque?; **to pay by cheque** pagar con cheque; **to pay a cheque into the bank** Esp ingresar or Am depositar un cheque en el banco; **to stop a cheque** suspender el pago de un cheque ▫ **cheque account** cuenta f corriente; Br **cheque counterfoil** talón m or matriz f or resguardo m de cheque Br **cheque (guarantee) card** = tarjeta que avala los cheques; **cheque form** formulario m de cheque; **cheque number** número m de cheque; **cheque stub** talón m or matriz f or resguardo m de cheque

chequebook, US **checkbook** n talonario m (de cheques), chequera f ▫ **chequebook account** cuenta f corriente

chequeless society, *US* **checkless society** *n* = sociedad en la que el cheque ha sido desplazado por otros sistemas electrónicos de pago

cherry pick *vt* seleccionar sólo lo mejor de

chief *adj* **chief accountant** jefe(a) *m,f* de contabilidad; **Chief Financial Officer** director(ora) *m,f* financiero(a); *Br* **chief executive**, *esp US* **chief executive officer** consejero(a) *m,f* delegado(a), director(ora) *m,f* gerente

child *n Br* ADMIN **child benefit** prestaciones *fpl* familiares por hijos; **child labour** trabajo *m* infantil

Chinese walls *npl* murallas *fpl* chinas

chip *n* COMPTR chip *m*

CHIPS *n US* BANKING (*abbr* **Clearing House Interbank Payment System**) CHIPS *m*, = sistema electrónico de transferencias interbancarias en dólares

choice 1 *n* MKTG (*selection, range*) selección *f*, surtido *m*; **the product of choice** el producto predilecto □ **choice set** gama *f* (de productos)
2 *adj (food, product)* selecto(a)

chooser *n* COMPTR selector *m*

Christmas bonus *n* prima *f* de Navidad

chronic *adj (shortage, unemployment)* crónico(a)

churn 1 *n* MKTG (número *m* de) clientes *npl* perdidos
2 *vt Fam* ST EXCH *(portfolio)* = realizar operaciones de compraventa de acciones con el único objetivo de generar comisiones para el agente

> The improvements mean that fewer customers are leaving the cable companies than before. Telewest's **churn** has fallen 10% since Singer took over two years ago. NTL's performance has been similar, but both companies say they can still improve. "Do I still get absolutely legitimate grumps and groans from customers? Yes. We're better but we're not there yet," Singer says.

churning *n Fam* ST EXCH = realización de operaciones de compraventa con el único objetivo de generar comisiones para el agente

CI *n* (*abbr* **certificate of insurance**) certificado *m* de seguro

CIF *n* (*abbr* **cost, insurance and freight**) CIF

CIM *n* (**a**) MKTG (*abbr* **Chartered Institute of Marketing**) = organización profesional británica de los directivos de marketing (**b**) (*abbr* **Convention Internationale concernant le transport des Marchandises par chemin de fer**) □ **CIM waybill** carta *f* de porte CIM (**c**) (*abbr* **computer-integrated manufacture**) fabricación *f* integrada por *Esp* ordenador *or Am* computadora

cinema advertising *n* publicidad *f* en el cine

CIO *n* (*abbr* **Congress of Industrial Organizations**) = uno de los dos sindicatos que integran el AFL-CIO, la mayor organización sindical estadounidense

CIP (*abbr* **carriage and insurance paid to**) CIP

circular 1 *n* (**a**) *(letter)* circular *f* (**b**) *(advertisement)* circular *f*
2 *adj* **circular letter** circular *f*; **circular letter of credit** carta *f* de crédito dirigida a todas las sucursales (del banco)

circulate 1 *vt* (**a**) *(banknotes)* poner en circulación (**b**) *(document, prospectus) (from person to person)* hacer circular, pasar; *(by mass mailing)* enviar; **please circulate the minutes of this morning's meeting** por favor hagan circular las actas de la reunión de esta mañana
2 *vi (money)* circular; **to circulate freely** circular libremente

circulating *adj* circulante □ ACCT **circulating assets** activo *m* circulante; FIN **circulating capital** capital *m* circulante

circulation *n* (**a**) *(of capital)* circulación *f* (**b**) **to be in circulation** *(of money)* estar en circulación; **notes in circulation** papel moneda en circulación (**c**) *(of newspaper)* difusión *f*; **a newspaper with a large circulation** un periódico de gran difusión □ **circulation figures** cifras *fpl* de difusión

citizen *n* ciudadano(a) *m,f* □ ADMIN **Citizens' Advice Bureau** = oficina británica de asesoría para los ciudadanos; ADMIN **Citizens' Charter** = iniciativa gubernamental británica introducida en 1991 para garantizar una calidad mínima en los servicios públicos

City *n* **the City** la City (de Londres); **he's in the City** trabaja en la City □ **the City Companies** = conjunto de entidades de la City londinense, de cometido benéfico y social, cuyo origen se remonta a los gremios medievales

civil *adj* LAW **civil action** proceso *m* civil; **Civil Aviation Authority** = organismo regulador de la aviación civil en Gran Bretaña; **civil engineer** ingeniero(a) *m,f* civil *or* de caminos, canales y puertos; **civil engineering** ingeniería *f* civil *or* de caminos, canales y puertos; **civil law** derecho *m* civil; **Civil and Public Services Association** = sindicato de funcionarios británicos; **civil servant** funcionario(a) *m,f*; **civil service** *(system)* administración *f* pública; *(personnel)* funcionarios *mpl*, funcionariado *m*; **Civil Service Union** = sindicato de funcionarios británicos; ADMIN **civil status** estado *m* civil

claim 1 *n* (**a**) *(demand) (for damages, compensation)* reclamación *f*, *SAm* reclamo *m*; *(as a right)* reivindicación *f*; **to put in a claim for damages** presentar *or* interponer una demanda por daños y perjuicios; **to make a legal claim for sth** reclamar algo ante los tribunales; **they're putting**

in a claim for better working conditions reivindican mejores condiciones de trabajo ❑ **claims book** libro *m* de reclamaciones *or SAm* reclamos; **claims register** libro *m* de reclamaciones *or SAm* reclamos sindicales

(**b**) INS reclamación *f*; **to make** *or* **put in a claim (for sth)** dar parte al seguro (de algo) ❑ **claims adjuster** tasador(a) *m,f* de daños; **claim form** *(for insurance) (after theft, fire, holiday cancellation)* formulario *m* de reclamación *or SAm* reclamo; *(after car accident)* parte *m* de accidente

(**c**) MKTG *(assertion)* afirmación *f*; **they have been making all sorts of claims about their new product** según ellos su nuevo producto es capaz de todo tipo de proezas

2 *vt* (**a**) *(demand) (damages, compensation)* reclamar; *(as a right)* reivindicar; **to claim damages (from sb)** reclamar daños y perjuicios (a alguien); **workers are claiming the right to strike** los obreros reivindican el derecho a la huelga (**b**) MKTG afirmar, asegurar; **they claim that their product is the best on the market** según ellos su producto es el mejor en el mercado

▸ **claim back** *vt sep (tax)* pedir la devolución de

claimant *n* ADMIN, INS *(for social security)* solicitante *mf*; *(for insurance)* reclamante *mf*; LAW *(for damages)* demandante *mf*, reclamante

clampdown *n* medidas *fpl* contundentes (**on** contra); **there has been a clampdown on credit** se ha puesto freno a los créditos

classified *adj* (**a**) *(secret)* reservado(a), confidencial ❑ **classified information** información *f* confidencial (**b**) **classified advertisements** *(in newspaper)* clasificados *mpl*, anuncios *mpl* por palabras

clause *n (of law, agreement, insurance policy)* cláusula *f*

claused bill *n* conocimiento *m* de embarque sucio

▸ **claw back** *vt sep* FIN *(expenditure)* recobrar, recuperar

clawback *n* FIN *(of expenditure, tax relief, stock relief)* recuperación *f*; *(sum)* reembolso *m*, devolución *f*

clean *adj* FIN **clean bill (of exchange)** letra *f* limpia; **clean bill of lading** conocimiento *m* de embarque limpio

clear 1 *adj* (**a**) *(net)* neto(a); **clear of taxes** libre de impuestos ❑ **clear loss** pérdida *f* neta; **clear profit** beneficio *m* neto (**b**) **clear day** día *f* completo; **three clear days** tres días completos; **ten clear days' notice** un aviso con días de antelación (**c**) *(accounts)* claro(a)

2 *vt* (**a**) *(debt, account)* liquidar; *(mortgage)* amortizar; (**b**) *(authorize) (ship)* permitir el paso de; *(goods through customs)* despachar; **to clear customs** *(person, goods)* pasar la aduana (**c**)

(make profit of) **she cleared 10% on the deal** ganó un 10% con la transacción; **I clear £1,000 monthly** gano 1.000 libras limpias al mes (**d**) BANKING *(cheque)* compensar, dar por bueno; FIN *(bill)* compensar (**e**) COMPTR **to clear the screen** borrar la pantalla

4 *vi (cheque)* ser compensado(a); **it takes three working days for cheques to clear** los cheques tardan tres días en ser compensados

▸ **clear off** *vt sep (debt, stock)* liquidar

clearance *n* (**a**) CUSTOMS *(of goods)* despacho *m*; **to effect customs clearance** efectuar el despacho de aduanas ❑ **clearance certificate** certificado *m* de despacho aduanero *or* de aduanas; **clearance inward(s)** despacho *m* de entrada; **clearance outward(s)** despacho *m* de salida; **clearance papers** certificado *m* de despacho aduanero *or* de aduanas (**b**) BANKING *(of cheque)* compensación *f* (**c**) **clearance sale** liquidación *f* *(de existencias)*

cleared value *n* valor *m* compensado

clearer *n* BANKING banco *m* compensador *or* de compensación

clearing *n (of cheque)* compensación *f*; *(of account)* liquidación *f*; *(of debt)* liquidación *f*; **under the clearing procedure** siendo compensado(a) ❑ **clearing account** cuenta *f* transitoria *or* de compensación; **clearing agreement** acuerdo *m* de compensación; **clearing bank** banco *m* compensador *or* de compensación; **clearing house** FIN cámara *f* de compensación; *(for information, materials)* centro *m* coordinador; **to pass a cheque through the clearing house** pasar un cheque por la cámara de compensación; **clearing member** miembro *m* liquidador; **clearing system** sistema *m* de compensación; **clearing transaction** operación *f* de compensación

clerical *adj* administrativo(a) ❑ **clerical error** error *m* administrativo; **clerical job** trabajo *m* administrativo; **clerical staff** personal *m* administrativo; **clerical work** trabajo *m* de oficina **clerical worker** administrativo(a) *m,f*

clerk 1 *n* (**a**) *(in office)* oficinista *mf*; *(in bank)* empleado(a) *m,f* (**b**) US *(in store)* dependiente(a) *m,f* (**c**) US *(receptionist)* recepcionista *mf* (**d**) **clerk of works** maestro(a) *m,f* de obras

2 *vi* US trabajar de dependiente(a)

CLI *n (abbr* **cost-of-living index)** costo *m or Esp* coste *m* de la vida

click COMPTR **1** *n* clic *m*

2 *vt* hacer click en

3 *vi* hacer click (**on** en); **to click and drag** hacer clic y arrastrar

clickable image *n* COMPTR imagen *f* interactiva

clicks-and-mortar *adj* COMPTR *(company, operation)* = que combina el comercio electrónico con el tradicional

> E-tailers once ridiculed traditional traders for the sluggishness with which they set up internet sites. However, these **"clicks-and-mortar"** operations now look best placed to make e-commerce more reliable. They already boast stocked warehouses and supply infrastructure to keep their real world shops in business.

client n (**a**) (of company, lawyer) cliente mf ❑ BANKING **client account** cuenta f de un cliente; **client base** base f de clientes; **client confidence** confianza f de los clientes; **client file** expediente m del cliente; **client list** relación f de clientes (**b**) COMPTR (part of network) cliente m

clientele n clientela f

client-server database n COMPTR base f de datos cliente/servidor

climb 1 n subida f; **a climb in production costs is expected in the next quarter** se espera que los costos or Esp costes de producción suban durante el próximo trimestre
  2 vi subir

clinch vt (deal) cerrar

clip art n COMPTR clip art m, imágenes fpl prediseñadas

clipboard n (writing board) carpeta f con sujetapapeles; COMPTR portapapeles m inv

clock n COMPTR reloj m ❑ **clock speed** velocidad f de reloj

▸ **clock in, clock on** vi fichar (a la entrada), RP marcar tarjeta (a la entrada)

▸ **clock off, clock out** vi fichar (a la salida), RP marcar tarjeta (a la salida)

▸ **clock on** vi = **clock in**

▸ **clock out** vi = **clock off**

clocking-in, clocking-on n **clocking-in before 8 a.m. is not allowed** no está permitido fichar or RP marcar tarjeta antes de las 8 de la mañana ❑ **clocking-in card** tarjeta f de control (horario), Am tarjeta de reloj

clocking-off, clocking-out n **clocking-off time is 5.30** la hora de fichar or RP marcar tarjeta (para salir) es a las 5.30

clocking-on = **clocking-in**

clocking-out = **clocking-off**

clone n COMPTR clónico m, Am clon m

close 1 n ST EXCH (of stock market) cierre m; (closing price) cotización f al cierre; **at close of business** al cierre de la sesión ❑ COMPTR **close box** cuadro m de cierre
  2 vt (**a**) ACCT **to close the books** saldar los libros; **to close the yearly accounts** cerrar las cuentas anuales (**b**) (meeting) terminar; (account, deal) cerrar (**c**) ST EXCH **to close a position**

cerrar una posición
  3 vi ST EXCH **the shares closed at 420p** las acciones cerraron a 420 peniques; **the share index closed two points down/up** la bolsa cerró con una caída/subida de dos enteros

▸ **close down 1** vt sep cerrar; **the factory was closed down after a drop in orders** cerraron la fábrica debido a una caída en los pedidos
  2 vi (factory, business) cerrar

▸ **close off** vt sep (account) cerrar

▸ **close out** vt sep US (goods) liquidar

▸ **close with** vt insep (finalize agreement with) cerrar el trato con

closed adj (**a**) (shut) (shop, factory) cerrado(a) (**b**) US (exclusive) **closed corporation** = sociedad anónima con un número reducido de accionistas, sus acciones no cotizan y su transmisión está restringida; **closed shop** = centro de trabajo que emplea exclusivamente a trabajadores de un sindicato en particular

closed-end adj **closed-end investment fund** fondo m de inversión cerrado; **closed-end mortgage** hipoteca f cerrada

closed-ended adj MKTG (question) cerrado(a), (de) tipo test

closedown n cierre m (definitivo)

closeout n US liquidación f

closing 1 n (**a**) (of shop) cierre m (**b**) (of meeting) finalización f; (of account, deal) cierre m (**c**) ST EXCH (of position) cierre m
  2 adj (**a**) (concluding) (ceremony) de clausura; (remarks) final ❑ **closing speech** discurso m de clausura
  (**b**) (final) BANKING **closing account balance** saldo m final de la cuenta; **closing bid** oferta f final; **closing date** fecha f límite; ACCT **closing entry** asiento m de cierre; **closing stock** existencias fpl al cierre
  (**c**) ST EXCH **closing price** precio m de cierre, cotización f al cierre; **closing quotations** cotizaciones fpl al cierre; **closing range** variación f al cierre; **closing session** sesión f de cierre; **closing trade** operaciones fpl or negociación f al cierre; **closing transaction** transacción f de cierre

closing-down n (of factory, business, shop) cierre m (definitivo) ❑ **closing-down costs** costos mpl or Esp costes mpl de cierre; **closing-down price** precio m de liquidación; **closing-down sale** liquidación f por cierre del negocio

closing-off n ACCT (of accounts) cierre m

closing-out n US cierre m (definitivo) ❑ **closing-out sale** liquidación f por cierre del negocio

closure n (of factory, business, shop) cierre m (definitivo)

club class n (in air travel) clase f preferente or preferencial or club

cluster n (**a**) COMPTR (of disk sectors) cluster m; (of terminals) agrupamiento m (**b**) MKTG **cluster analysis** (in statistics) análisis m inv cluster; **cluster marketing** marketing m de grupos; **cluster sample** muestra f por grupos; **cluster sampling** muestreo m por grupos

CMO n US FIN (abbr **collateralized mortgage obligation**) obligación f con garantía hipotecaria

CMR n (abbr **Convention Relative au Contrat de Transport International de Marchandises par Route**) **CMR waybill** carta f de porte CMR

Co, co (abbr **company**) cía.

.co COMPTR = en las direcciones de Internet, abreviatura que utilizan las empresas británicas

c/o (abbr **care of**) **John Watson, c/o Fred Smith, 44 Bank St** (on envelope) Fred Smith, Att. John Watson, 44 Bank St

coastal adj costero(a) □ **coastal trade** cabotaje m, comercio m de cabotaje; **coastal traffic** tráfico m de cabotaje

coated paper n papel m couché or cuché

COBOL n COMPTR (abbr **Common Business-Oriented Language**) COBOL m

co-branding n MKTG marcas fpl compartidas

co-chair vt copresidir

co-creditor n FIN coacreedor(ora) m,f

COD, cod adv (abbr Br **cash** or US **collect on delivery**) contra reembolso; **all goods are sent COD** enviamos todos los productos contra reembolso

code 1 n (**a**) (Br **dialling** or US **dialing**) **code** prefijo m, Am característica f (**b**) (rules) código m; **code of conduct** código de conducta; **code of ethics** (in profession) código ético or deontológico; **code of practice** código de conducta
2 vt COMPTR codificar

coded adj COMPTR codificado(a)

codetermination n IND codecisión f

coding n COMPTR (providing codes) codificación f; (system of codes) códigos mpl

co-director n codirector(ora) m,f

coffers npl FIN (funds) arcas fpl

co-founder n (of company) cofundador(ora) m,f

COGS n ACCT (abbr **cost of goods sold**) costo for Esp coste m de las mercancías vendidas

COI n (abbr **Central Office of Information**) = organismo gubernamental británico encargado de llevar a cabo campañas informativas

coin 1 n (**a**) (item of metal currency) moneda f; **a 50p coin** una moneda de 50 peniques (**b**) (metal currency) moneda f; **£50 in coin** 50 libras en moneda(s)
2 vt **to coin money** acuñar moneda

coinage n (**a**) (monetary system) sistema m monetario (**b**) (coins) monedas fpl

co-insurance n coaseguro m, coseguro m

co-insure vt coasegurar

co-insurer n coasegurador(ora) m,f

COLA n US FIN (abbr **cost-of-living adjustment**) ajuste m del costo or Esp coste de vida

cold adj (**a**) MKTG **cold call** (on phone) llamada for Am llamado m en frío or sin previo aviso; (in person) visita f en frío or sin previo aviso; **cold calling** contacto m en frío or sin previo aviso; **cold call sales** ventas fpl en frío
(**b**) COMPTR **cold start** arranque m en frío
(**c**) **cold storage** (of food) conservación f en cámara frigorífica; **to put sth into cold storage** poner algo en cámara frigorífica; **cold storage dock** muelle m para el almacenamiento refrigerado; **cold store** (room) cámara f frigorífica

collaborate vi colaborar (**on** en)

collaboration n colaboración f

collapse 1 n (of market, prices, currency) desplome m, hundimiento m
2 vi (of market, prices, currency) desplomarse, hundirse

collate vt (compare) cotejar; (assemble) recopilar

collateral FIN **1** n garantía f (prendaria), pignoración f; **what can you provide as collateral?** ¿qué puede ofrecer como garantía?; **to lodge sth as collateral** utilizar algo como garantía; **the bank prefers not to lend without collateral** el banco prefiere no realizar préstamos sin garantía
2 adj **collateral loan** préstamo m pignoraticio or con garantía prendaria; **collateral security** garantía f prendaria or pignoraticia

> **"**
> Rapid restructuring is likely to lift asset prices, which buoys economic activity. Rational market participants are aware which assets need to be reallocated - for example, the property held as **collateral** that must be sold when companies are restructured.
> **"**

collateralize vt US FIN garantizar □ **collateralized mortgage obligation** obligación f con garantía hipotecaria

colleague n (in same company) compañero(a) m,f de trabajo; (in same industry) colega mf de profesión

collect 1 adj US **collect call** llamada for Am llamado m a cobro revertido; **to make a collect call** hacer una llamada or Am un llamado a cobro revertido
2 vt (salary) percibir; (debt) cobrar; (taxes) recaudar; US **collect on delivery** entrega f contra reembolso

3 *adv US* **to call sb collect** llamar a alguien a cobro revertido; **to send a parcel collect** enviar un paquete contra reembolso

collecting *adj* **collecting agency** agencia *f* especializada en el cobro de deudas; **collecting bank** banco *m* cobrador; **collecting banker** empleado(a) *m,f* de un banco cobrador; **collecting department** departamento *m* de cobros *or* cobranzas

collection *n* (**a**) *(of debts)* cobro *m*; *(of taxes)* recaudación *f* (**b**) FIN *(of bill)* cobro *m*; **to hand a bill in for collection** presentar una letra de cambio para cobrarla; **a bill for collection** una letra al cobro □ **collection bank** banco *m* de cobro; **collection charges** gastos *mpl* de cobro; **collection fees** gastos *mpl* de cobro; **collection period** periodo *m* de cobro; **collection rate** tipo *m* aplicable en el momento del cobro

collective 1 *n* (farm) cooperativa *f*
2 *adj* colectivo(a) □ **collective agreement** convenio *m* colectivo; **collective bargaining** negociación *f* colectiva; **collective bargaining agreement** convenio *m* colectivo; **collective liability** responsabilidad *f* colectiva; **collective ownership** propiedad *f* colectiva; **collective responsibility** responsabilidad *f* colectiva; **collective risk** riesgo *m* colectivo

> **"**
> Northwest Airlines, the country's fourth largest airline, and its pilots' union have reached a tentative agreement to extend their current five-year **collective bargaining** agreement by 12 months. The agreement provides for a 4.5% salary increase this September and another 5.5% increase in September 2003.
> **"**

collectivism *n* ECON colectivismo *m*

collectivist *n* ECON colectivista *mf*

collectivity *n* ECON colectividad *f*

collector *n* (**a**) *(of cheque)* cobrador(ora) *m,f* (**b**) *(of taxes)* recaudador(ora) *m,f*

colon *n* *(punctuation mark)* dos puntos *mpl*

colour, *US* **color** *n* COMPTR **colour graphics** gráficos *mpl* en color; **colour printer** impresora *f* en color; **colour printing** impresión *f* en color

column *n* ACCT columna *f*

.com COMPTR .com

combination *n* *(of lock)* combinación *f* □ **combination lock** cierre *m* de combinación

combine *n* FIN grupo *m* empresarial

combined *adj* **combined transport bill of lading** conocimiento *m* de embarque (de transporte) combinado; **combined transport company** empresa *f* de transporte combinado; **combined transport document** conocimiento *m* de em-

barque (de transporte) combinado

Comecon *n* Formerly (*abbr* **Council for Mutual Economic Aid**) COMECON *m*, CAME *m*

▸ **come out** *vi* COMPTR *(exit)* salir; **to come out of a document** salir de un documento

comma *n* *(punctuation mark)* coma *f*

command *n* (**a**) COMPTR comando *m* □ **command file** archivo *m or* fichero *m* de comandos; **command key** tecla *f* de comando **command line** línea *f* de comando (**b**) ECON **command economy** economía *f* dirigida

comment(s) card *n* MKTG hoja *f* de sugerencias

commerce *n* comercio *m*

commercial 1 *n* *(advertisement)* anuncio *m* (publicitario)
2 *adj* comercial; **a commercial venture** una empresa comercial □ **commercial agency** agencia *f* comercial; **commercial agent** agente *mf* comercial; **commercial aircraft** avión *m* comercial; **commercial attaché** agregado(a) *m,f* comercial; **commercial bank** banco *m* comercial; **commercial bill** letra *f* (de cambio) comercial; **commercial break** pausa *f* publicitaria; **commercial broker** corredor(ora) *m,f* de comercio; **commercial centre** centro *m* de comercio; **commercial channel** canal *m* comercial; **commercial charter** alquiler *m* comercial; **commercial contract** contrato *m* mercantil; **commercial designer** diseñador(ora) *m,f* de anuncios; **commercial directory** directorio *m or* guía *f* comercial *or* de empresas; **commercial dispute** disputa *f* comercial; **commercial district** centro *m* de negocios; **commercial documents** documentos *mpl* comerciales; **commercial efficiency** eficacia *f* comercial; **commercial jurisdiction** jurisdicción *f* mercantil; **commercial law** derecho *m* mercantil; **commercial lease** arrendamiento *m* comercial; **commercial loan** préstamo *m* comercial *or* mercantil; **commercial monopoly** monopolio *m* comercial; **commercial paper** papel *m* comercial, efecto *m* de comercio; **commercial port** puerto *m* comercial; **commercial premises** locales *mpl* comerciales; **commercial process** proceso *m* comercial; **commercial route** ruta *f* comercial; **commercial traveller** viajante *mf* de comercio; **commercial tribunal** tribunal *m* de comercio; **commercial value** valor *m* comercial; **commercial vehicle** vehículo *m* comercial

commercialism *n* (**a**) *(practice of business)* comercio *m* (**b**) *(profit-seeking)* comercialismo *m*

commercialization *n* comercialización *f*

commercialize *vt* comercializar

commercialized *adj* *(product)* comercializado(a); **it has become too commercialized** se ha vuelto demasiado comercial

commercially *adv* comercialmente; **commercially available** a la venta, disponible en las tiendas

commission 1 *n* (**a**) *(payment)* comisión *f*; **to get 3% commission** llevarse un 3% de comisión; **to work on a commission basis** trabajar a comisión; **this post offers a basic salary plus generous commission** el puesto ofrece un salario básico más una generosa comisión □ **commission agency** casa *f* de comisiones; **commission agent** comisionista *mf*; **commission merchant** comisionista *mf*; ACCT **commission note** aviso *m or* factura *f* de comisión; **commission sale** venta *f* a comisión

(**b**) *(committee)* comisión *f*, comité *m* □ **commission of inquiry** comisión *f* de investigación

(**c**) *(order)* encargo *m*; **work done on commission** trabajo hecho por encargo; **to carry out a commission** llevar a cabo un encargo

2 *vt (order)* encargar; **to commission sb to do sth** encargar a alguien hacer algo *or* que haga algo

Commissioner of the Inland Revenue *n* *Br* inspector(ora) *m,f* de Hacienda

commitment *n* FIN compromiso *m* □ **commitment fee** comisión *f* de *or* por compromiso; **commitment of funds** asignación *f* de fondos

committed costs *npl* ACCT costos *mpl or Esp* costes *mpl* comprometidos

committee *n* comité *m*, comisión *f*; **to be** *or* **sit on a committee** ser miembro de un comité □ **committee meeting** reunión *f* del comité

commoditization *n* = conversión en producto de consumo corriente

commodity *n* (**a**) ECON *(product)* producto *m or* bien *m* básico; *(foodstuff)* alimento *m* básico; **rice is the staple commodity of China** el arroz es el alimento básico en China

(**b**) ST EXCH producto *m* básico, commodity *f*; **to trade commodities** comerciar con productos básicos; **coffee is considered to be the main agricultural commodity** se considera que el café es el principal producto básico agrícola □ **commodity broker, commodity dealer** corredor(ora) *m,f* de productos básicos; **commodity exchange** bolsa *f* de productos básicos; **commodity futures** contrato *m* de futuros sobre productos básicos; **commodity market** mercado *m* de productos básicos; **commodity money** dinero *m* mercancía; **commodity prices** precios *mpl* de los productos básicos

> " He says the main reason why the recovery will continue is to do with **commodity prices** and capital flows, which he says have yet to recover. We are at the bottom of the **commodity price** market – these countries produce raw materials and so it is a very

important part of their economy, he says. And people have stopped pulling their money dramatically out of emerging markets. "

common *adj* (**a**) EU *Common Agricultural Policy* Política *f* Agrícola Común; **common budget** presupuesto *m* comunitario; **common customs tariff** arancel *m* aduanero común; **common external tariff** arancel *m* externo común; **Common Fisheries Policy** Política *f* Pesquera Común; **Common Foreign and Security Policy** Política *f* Exterior y de Seguridad Común; *Formerly* **the Common Market** el Mercado Común

(**b**) *(shared)* US **common carrier** *(transport company)* empresa *f* de transporte público; *(telecommunications company)* empresa *f* de telecomunicaciones; FIN **common currency** moneda *f* común; ACCT **common fixed costs** costos *mpl or Esp* costes *mpl* fijos comunes; **common ground** puntos *mpl* en común; **the two groups need to build on common ground before continuing their discussions** los dos grupos necesitan encontrar puntos en común antes de continuar con las discusiones; **common ownership** propiedad *f* colectiva

(**c**) US ST EXCH **common equities, common stock** acciones *fpl* ordinarias

comms *n* COMPTR **comms package** software *m* de comunicaciones; **comms port** puerto *m* de comunicaciones

communal *adj* **communal property, communal tenure** propiedad *f* comunal

communicate *vi (be in touch)* comunicarse; *(get in touch)* ponerse en contacto

communication *n* (**a**) *(contact)* comunicación *f*; **to enter into communication with sb** entrar en comunicación con alguien □ **communications channel** canal *f* de comunicación; **communications director** director(ora) *m,f* de comunicación *or* de relaciones públicas; **communications expert** experto(a) *m,f* en comunicaciones; **communications link** enlace *m* de comunicación *or* comunicaciones; **communications management** gestión *f* de comunicación *or* relaciones públicas; **communications manager** director(ora) *m,f* de comunicación *or* relaciones públicas; **communication network** red *f* de comunicaciones; **communications officer** responsable *mf* de comunicaciones; COMPTR **communications package** paquete *m* de comunicaciones; **communications sector** sector *m* de las comunicaciones; **communication skills** dotes *fpl or* aptitud *f* para la comunicación; **you need to have good communication skills** hay que ser buen comunicador; COMPTR **communications software** software *m* de comunicaciones **communication strategy** estrategia *f* de comunicación *or* relaciones públicas;

communications study estudio *m* de comunicaciones

(**b**) *(message)* comunicado *m*

communicator *n* comunicador(ora) *m,f*; **she's a good communicator** es buena comunicadora

Community EU **1** *n* the (European) Community la Comunidad (Europea)

2 *adj* comunitario(a) ❏ ***Community carnet*** carnet *m* comunitario; ***Community directive*** directiva *f* comunitaria ***Community law*** derecho *m* comunitario

community *n* comunidad *f*; **the business community** el sector empresarial, los empresarios; **the international community** la comunidad internacional ❏ *US* FIN ***community chest*** = fondo comunitario para actividades benéficas a nivel local; ***community transit*** transporte *m* comunitario

commutation *n US* = desplazamiento diario al lugar de trabajo

commute *vi* to commute (to work) desplazarse diariamente al lugar de trabajo

commuter *n* = persona que se desplaza diariamente al trabajo ❏ ***commuter belt*** barrios *mpl* de la periferia; ***commuter train*** = tren de cercanías que las personas utilizan para desplazarse diariamente al lugar de trabajo

commuting *n* = desplazamiento diario al lugar de trabajo

compact COMPTR **1** *adj* compacto(a) ❏ ***compact disc*** disco *m* compacto, compact disc *m*; ***compact disc interactive*** disco *m* compacto interactivo; ***compact disc recorder*** grabadora *f* de discos compactos; ***compact disc rewritable*** disco *m* compacto regrabable

2 *vt (file)* compactar, comprimir

Companies House, Companies Registration Office *n Br* registro *m* mercantil

company *n* empresa *f*, compañía *f*; **to form** *or* **incorporate a company** constituir (en sociedad) una empresa; **to liquidate a company** liquidar una empresa; **in company time** en horas de trabajo ❏ ***company accounts*** cuentas *fpl* de la empresa; ***Companies Act*** Ley *f* de Sociedades Mercantiles; *US* ***company apartment*** apartamento *m or Esp* piso *m* de empresa; ***company car*** coche *m or Am* carro *m or RP* auto *m* de empresa; ***company census*** censo *m* de empresas; ***company credit card*** tarjeta *f* de crédito de empresa; ***company director*** consejero(a) *m,f* de la empresa; ***company doctor*** *(doctor)* médico(a) *m,f* de la empresa; *(businessperson)* especialista *mf* en la salvación de empresas con problemas; *Br* ***company flat*** apartamento *m or Esp* piso *m* de empresa; ***company funds*** fondos *mpl* de la empresa; ***company law*** derecho *m* de sociedades; ***company lawyer*** abogado(a) *m,f* de la empresa; ***company manager*** gerente *mf* de la empresa; ***company name*** denominación *f or* razón *f* social; ***company planning*** planificación *f* de la empresa; ***company policy*** política *f* de empresa; ***company profile*** perfil *m* de la empresa; ***company recovery plan*** plan *f* de recuperación empresarial; ***company reserves*** reservas *fpl* sociales; ***company rules*** normas *fpl* de la empresa; ***company savings scheme*** plan *m* de ahorro de la empresa; ***company secretary*** jefe(a) *m,f* de administración; *US* ***company town*** = ciudad que depende de una sola empresa para su supervivencia económica

comparable worth *n* valor *m* equivalente

comparative *adj* MKTG ***comparative advantage*** ventaja *f* comparativa; ***comparative advertising*** publicidad *f* comparativa; ***comparative test*** prueba *f* comparativa; ***comparative testing*** pruebas *fpl* comparativas

compare 1 *vt* comparar (**with** *or* **to** con); **we must compare last year's figures with this year's** debemos comparar las cifras del año pasado con las de éste

2 *vi* **how does last month's output compare with this month's?** ¿cómo fue la producción del mes pasado en comparación con la de éste?; **we compare well with our competitors** comparativamente somos mejores que nuestros competidores

comparison *n* MKTG ***comparison advertising*** publicidad *f* comparativa; ***comparison shopping*** compras *fpl* comparativas

compassionate leave *n* = permiso por enfermedad grave o muerte de un familiar

compatibility *n* COMPTR compatibilidad *f*

compatible *adj* COMPTR compatible (**with** con); **IBM-compatible** compatible IBM ❏ ***compatible computer*** *Esp* ordenador *m or Am* computadora *f* compatible

compensable *adj* compensable ❏ ***compensable loss*** daños *mpl* indemnizables

compensate *vt (for loss, injury, damage)* indemnizar (**for** por)

compensating *adj* FIN ***compensating payment*** pago *m* compensatorio

compensation *n* (**a**) *(for loss, injury, damage)* indemnización *f* ❏ ***compensation deal*** acuerdo *m* de indemnización; ST EXCH ***compensation fund*** fondo *m* de compensación (**b**) *(remuneration)* retribución *f*, remuneración *f* ❏ ***compensation package*** *(total pay and benefits)* paquete *m* de beneficios; *Br (for redundancy)* indemnización *f* por despido

compensatory *adj* compensatorio(a) ❏ EU ***compensatory amounts*** montantes *mpl* compensatorios; EU ***compensatory levy*** tasa *f* compensadora; *US* ***compensatory time*** crédito *m* horario

compete vi (one company) ser competitivo(a); (two companies) competir (**with** con); **they compete with foreign companies for contracts** compiten por contratos con empresas extranjeras; **we have to compete on an international level** tenemos que ser competitivos a nivel internacional

competence, competency n (**a**) (ability) capacidad f; **this lies within his competence** está capacitado para hacer esto (**b**) (of company) competencia f (**c**) **competencies** (skills) cualidades fpl; **her competencies were re-assessed at her annual appraisal** sus cualidades fueron analizadas de nuevo en su evaluación anual

competent adj (capable) competente (**in** en); (qualified) capacitado(a); **is she competent to handle the accounts?** ¿está capacitada para encargarse de la contabilidad?

competing adj (companies) que compiten; (products) que están en competencia

competition n (between companies, candidates) competencia f; **the competition** (rivals) la competencia; **the company has to stay ahead of the competition** la empresa tiene que mantenerse por delante de la competencia □ **competition authorities** autoridades fpl de defensa de la competencia; **Competition Commission** = comisión antimonopolios británica

competitive adj ECON (product, company, price) competitivo(a); **to offer competitive terms** ofrecer condiciones competitivas; **industry must become more competitive** la industria tiene que ser más competitiva □ **competitive advantage** ventaja f competitiva **competitive advertising** publicidad f competitiva; **competitive analysis** análisis m inv competitivo; **competitive awareness** conocimiento m de la competencia; **competitive bidding** licitación f pública; **competitive edge** ventaja f competitiva **competitive marketplace** mercado m competitivo; **competitive position** posición f competitiva; **competitive positioning** posicionamiento m competitivo; **competitive pricing** fijación f de precios competitivos; **competitive scope** ámbito m competitivo; **competitive strategy** estrategia f competitiva

> 〝
> The new, new thing is really serious. The impact of publicity on the Internet is fast and global – instantaneously everywhere. I first noticed it in action three years ago when a client called to complain that its competitor was getting tons of publicity and the client wasn't. I was stunned, because we had just done a **competitive analysis** showing our client had dramatically more publicity.
> 〞

competitively adv **to be competitively priced** tener un precio competitivo

competitiveness n (of product, company, price) competitividad f

competitor n competidor(ora) m,f; **we must keep up with our main competitors** tenemos que mantenernos a la misma altura que nuestros competidores, tenemos que mantenernos a la altura de la competencia □ **competitor analysis** análisis m inv de la competencia

complain vi (make formal protest) quejarse; **several customers have complained about the quality of service** varios clientes se han quejado de la calidad del servicio, ha habido varias quejas de clientes sobre la calidad del servicio

complaint n queja f, reclamación f, SAm reclamo m; **to lodge** or **make a complaint (against sb/about sth)** presentar una queja (contra alguien/sobre algo) □ **complaints department** departamento f de reclamaciones or SAm reclamos; **complaints office** oficina f de reclamaciones or SAm reclamos

complete 1 adj completo(a); **the new software offers a complete service for the business user** el nuevo software ofrece un completo paquete de soluciones para el usuario empresarial
2 vt (order) completar; (contract, work) concluir, finalizar

completion n (of work, contract, sale) finalización f; **the project is nearing completion** el proyecto está a punto de concluir; **payment on completion of contract** pago a la finalización del contrato □ **completion date** fecha f de finalización; **completion guarantee** garantía f de finalización

complex n (of buildings) complejo m

compliance n (conformity) cumplimiento m; **she acted in compliance with the terms of the contract** actuó en conformidad con los términos del contrato □ **compliance certificate**, **compliance test** prueba f de conformidad

compliant adj en conformidad (**with** con)

compliments slip n nota f de cortesía

comply vi **to comply with** (specifications) cumplir, ajustarse a; (contract, order) cumplir; **they must comply with existing regulations** deben cumplir el reglamento existente

component n componente m

composite index n ST EXCH índice m compuesto

composition n LAW (agreement)(with creditors, on bankruptcy) acuerdo m

compound 1 adj ACCT **compound entry** asiento m compuesto; FIN **compound interest** interés m compuesto; **compound (net) annual return** rendimiento m (neto) anual
2 vt LAW (settle) **to compound a debt** liquidar una deuda pagando sólo una parte

comprehensive adj (insurance) a todo riesgo

compress vt COMPTR (data, file) comprimir

compression n COMPTR compresión f ▫ **compression rate** índice m de compresión

comp time n US Fam crédito m horario

comptroller n US (financial director) director(ora) m,f financiero(a); (of accounts) interventor(ora) m,f, Am contralor(ora) m,f ▫ **Comptroller General** Interventor(ora) m,f General, Am Contralor(ora) m,f General

compulsorily adv obligatoriamente **he was compulsorily retired at age 70** le obligaron a jubilarse a los 70 años

compulsory adj obligatorio(a) ▫ **compulsory liquidation** liquidación f forzosa; Br ADMIN **compulsory purchase** expropiación f forzosa; **compulsory purchase order** orden m de expropiación forzosa; **compulsory redundancy** despido m forzoso **compulsory retirement** jubilación f forzosa; LAW **compulsory sale** venta f forzosa; **compulsory standards** normas fpl de obligado cumplimiento

computer n Esp ordenador m, Am computadora f; **to be computer literate** tener conocimientos de informática; **to put sth on computer** introducir or meter algo en Esp el ordenador or Am la computadora ▫ **computer analyst** analista mf informático; **computer animation** animación f por Esp ordenador or Am computadora; **computer department** departamento m informático; **computer engineer** ingeniero(a) m,f informático(a); **computer equipment** equipo m informático; **computer expert** experto(a) m,f en informática; **computer graphics** (display) gráficos mpl informáticos; (technique) infografía f; **computer hardware** hardware m; **computer literacy** conocimientos mpl de informática; **computer manager** gerente mf de informática; **computer network** red f informática; **computer operator** operador(ora) m,f de Esp ordenadores or Am computadoras; **computer population** parque m de Esp ordenadores or Am computadoras; **computer printout** copia f impresa; **computer program** programa m informático; **computer programmer** programador(ora) m,f (informático(a)); **computer programming** programación f (informática or de Esp ordenadores or Am computadoras); **computer science** informática f; **computer scientist** informático(a) m,f; **computer system** sistema m informático; **computer virus** virus m inv informático

computer-aided, computer-assisted adj asistido(a) por Esp ordenador or Am computadora ▫ **computer-aided audit techniques** técnicas fpl de auditoría asistida por Esp ordenador or Am computadora; **computer-aided design** diseño m asistido por Esp ordenador or Am computadora; **computer-aided engineering** ingeniería f asistida por Esp ordenador or Am computadora; **computer-aided interview** entrevista f asistida por Esp ordenador or Am computadora; **computer-aided learning** enseñanza f asistida por Esp ordenador or Am computadora; **computer-aided manufacture** fabricación f asistida por Esp ordenador or Am computadora; **computer-aided presentation** presentación f asistida por Esp ordenador or Am computadora; **computer-aided trading** comercio m asistido por Esp ordenador or Am computadora; **computer-aided translation** traducción f asistida por Esp ordenador or Am computadora

computer-based training n formación f asistida por Esp ordenador or Am computadora

computer-enhanced adj mejorado(a) por Esp ordenador or Am computadora

computer-generated adj generado(a) por Esp ordenador or Am computadora ▫ **computer-generated images** imágenes fpl generadas por Esp ordenador or Am computadora

computer-integrated manufacture n fabricación f asistida por Esp ordenador or Am computadora

computerization n informatización f, Am computarización f, Am computadorización f

computerize vt informatizar, Am computarizar, Am computadorizar

computerized adj informatizado(a), Am computarizado(a), Am computadorizado(a) ▫ ACCT **computerized accounts** contabilidad f informatizada or Am computarizada; **computerized banking** banca f informatizada or Am computarizada; **computerized data** datos mpl informatizados or Am computarizados; **computerized information system** sistema m informático de información, Am sistema m de información computarizado; ST EXCH **computerized trading system** sistema m informático de contratación, Am sistema m de negociación computarizado

computer-literate adj **to be computer-literate** tener conocimientos de informática

computing n informática f, Am computación f

conceal vt FIN (assets) ocultar

concealed unemployment n desempleo m or Esp paro m encubierto

concealment n LAW (of facts) ocultación f ▫ FIN **concealment of assets** ocultación f de activos

concept n concepto m ▫ MKTG **concept development** desarrollo m de concepto; **concept test** prueba f del concepto; **concept testing** pruebas fpl del concepto

concern n (business) empresa f; (interest) interés m; **a manufacturing concern** una empresa manufacturera; **the whole concern is for sale**

toda la empresa está a la venta; **we have a concern in the restaurant** tenemos una participación en el restaurante

2 *vt (affect)* concernir; **to whom it may concern** *(on letter)* a quien pueda interesar, a quien corresponda; **the persons concerned** los interesados; **the department concerned** el departamento responsable *or* competente

concert party *n* ST EXCH grupo *m* concertado de inversores, = grupo de inversores que conviene comprar por separado acciones de una empresa para después ponerlas en común y hacerse con el control de la misma

concession *n* (**a**) *Br (discount)* descuento *m*; **we offer a 10% concession to retailers** ofrecemos un 10% de descuento a los minoristas □ *concession close (sales technique)* oferta *f* para cerrar la compra (**b**) *(within larger store)* concesión *f* (**c**) *(right)* concesión *f*, derechos *mpl* de explotación; **a mining concession** una concesión minera

concessionaire *n* concesionario(a) *m,f*

concessionary *adj* con descuento

concessioner *n* concesionario(a) *m,f*

conciliation *n* IND conciliación *f* □ *conciliation board* junta *f* de conciliación; *conciliation magistrate* juez *mf* de conciliación; *conciliation service* órgano *m* de conciliación

conciliator *n* IND conciliador(ora) *m,f*

conclude *vt* (**a**) *(meeting, session)* concluir (**b**) *(deal)* cerrar; *(treaty)* firmar

conclusion *n* (**a**) *(of meeting, session)* conclusión *f* (**b**) *(of deal, treaty)* firma *f*

condition *n* (**a**) *(stipulation)* condición *f*; **on condition that...** a condición de que... □ *conditions of application* requisitos *mpl* de solicitud; *conditions of employment* términos *mpl* del contrato (de trabajo); *conditions of sale* condiciones *fpl* de venta (**b**) *(state)* estado *m*, condiciones *fpl*; **in good/bad condition** *(goods, machine)* en buen/mal estado, en buenas/malas condiciones

conditional *adj (offer)* condicional; **the offer is conditional on your acceptance of our terms of employment** la oferta depende de que acepte las condiciones del contrato □ *conditional acceptance* aceptación *f* condicional

confederation *n* confederación *f* □ *Confederation of British Industry* = organización empresarial británica, ≃ *Esp* CEOE *f*

conference *n* (**a**) *(convention)* congreso *m* □ *conference centre (building)* palacio *m* de congresos; *(part of complex)* centro *m* de congresos; *conference coordinator (of particular conference)* coordinador(ora) *m,f* del congreso; *(job title)* coordinador(ora) *m,f* de congresos; *conference delegate* delegado(a) *m,f* del congreso;

conference hall salón *m* de congresos; *conference interpreter* intérprete *mf* de conferencias; **the conference organizers** la organización *or* los organizadores del congreso; *conference pack* carpeta *f* con el material del congreso (**b**) *(meeting)* reunión *f*; **to be in conference with** estar reunido(a) con □ TEL *conference call* multiconferencia *f*; *conference room* sala *f* de juntas *or* reuniones; *conference table* mesa *f* de reuniones; **we hope to get management to the conference table** esperamos que la dirección se siente en la mesa de negociaciones

confidential *adj (report, memo)* confidencial

config.sys *n* COMPTR config.sys *m*

configuration *n* COMPTR configuración *f*

configure *vt* COMPTR configurar

confirm 1 *vt* confirmar; **we confirm receipt of** *or* **that we have received your letter** acusamos recibo de su carta

2 *vi* **they said they would come, but they haven't confirmed yet** dijeron que vendrían, pero todavía no lo han confirmado; **please confirm in writing** por favor, confírmelo por escrito

confirmation *n* confirmación *f*; **to receive confirmation of sth** recibir confirmación de algo; **all bookings subject to confirmation** todas las reservas están pendientes de confirmación □ *confirmation of receipt* acuse *m* de recibo

confirmed letter of credit *n* carta *f* de crédito confirmada

confirming *adj confirming bank, confirming house* banco *m* confirmador

conflict *n* conflicto *m*; **the unions are in conflict with the management** los sindicatos están en conflicto con la dirección; **a conflict of interests** un conflicto de intereses; **her presence on the boards of two competing companies led to a conflict of interests** había un problema de incompatibilidad por su presencia en el consejo de administración de dos empresas en competencia

conform *vi* ajustarse; **to conform to the law** cumplir la ley; **all cars must conform to regulations** todos los coches deben cumplir con la normativa vigente

conformity *n* conformidad *f*; **in conformity with** de conformidad con..., conforme a...

conglomerate *n* conglomerado *m* de empresas

congress *n* congreso *m*

con man *n* Fam timador *m*, estafador *m*

connect 1 *n* COMPTR conexión *f* □ *connect time* tiempo *m* de conexión

2 *vt* (**a**) COMPTR *(component, cable)* conectar (**to** a)

(**b**) TEL pasar, *Esp* poner (**with** con); **will you connect me with reservations, please?** ¿me puede pasar *or Esp* poner con el departamento de reservas?

3 *vi* COMPTR (**a**) *(component, cable)* conectarse (**to** a) (**b**) *(to Internet)* conectarse (**to** a)

connection *n* (**a**) *(colleague, business contact)* contacto *m*; **she has some useful connections in the publishing world** tiene varios contactos útiles en el mundo editorial (**b**) TEL conexión *f*; **we had a bad connection** la conexión era mala (**c**) *(to Internet)* conexión *f*; **to establish a connection** conectarse; **to have a fast/slow connection** tener una conexión rápida/lenta (**d**) COMPTR *(of two components)* conexión *f* ▫ **connection kit** kit *m* de conexión

conquer *vt (market, market share)* conquistar

conquest *n (of market, market share)* conquista *f*

consensus *n* consenso *m*; **there was a consensus of opinion to reject the board's offer** hubo consenso a la hora de rechazar la oferta del consejo ▫ **consensus management** gestión *f* por consenso

conservatism concept *n* ACCT principio *m* de prudencia

consideration *n (payment)* retribución *f*; **for a small consideration** a cambio de una pequeña retribución; **in consideration of your services** en retribución por sus servicios

consign *vt (goods)* consignar, enviar

consignee *n* consignatario(a) *m,f*

consigner *n* consignador(ora) *m,f*

consignment *n* (**a**) *(goods)* envío *m* **a consignment of machinery** un envío de maquinaria (**b**) *(despatch)* envío *m*, consignación *f*; **to give goods to sb on consignment** dar a alguien mercancías en consignación; **goods for consignment abroad** mercancías listas para ser enviadas al extranjero ▫ **consignment invoice** factura *f* de consignación; **consignment note** carta *f* de porte, hoja *f* de ruta

consignor *n* consignador(ora) *m,f*

consistency concept *n* ACCT principio *m* de uniformidad

console *n* COMPTR consola *f*

consolidate *vt* (**a**) FIN *(companies)* fusionar; *(shares)* consolidar; *(debts, funds, loans)* consolidar; **the company has consolidated its position as the market leader** la empresa ha consolidado su posición como líder en el mercado (**b**) *(orders, consignments)* agrupar

consolidated *adj* (**a**) FIN *(funds, debt)* consolidado(a) ▫ **consolidated accounts** cuentas *fpl* consolidadas; **consolidated annuities** = obligaciones con intereses y sin fecha de vencimiento del gobierno británico; **consolidated**

balance sheet balance *m* consolidado; **consolidated debt** deuda *f* consolidada; **consolidated entry** partida *f* consolidada; **consolidated funds** = fondos consolidados del Tesoro británico; **consolidated loan** préstamo *m* consolidado; **consolidated profit and loss account** cuenta *f* de resultados consolidada; **consolidated statement of net income** cuenta *f* de resultados consolidada; **consolidated stock** = obligaciones con intereses y sin fecha de vencimiento del gobierno británico

(**b**) *(orders, consignments)* agrupado(a)

(**c**) *(in name of company)* = nacido(a) de la fusión de dos empresas

consolidation *n* (**a**) FIN *(of companies)* fusión *f*; *(of shares)* consolidación *f*; *(of debts, funds, loans)* consolidación *f* (**b**) *(of orders, consignments)* agrupamiento *m*

consolidator *n (transport company)* consolidador *m*, agrupador *m*

consols *npl* FIN = obligaciones con intereses y sin fecha de vencimiento del gobierno británico

consortium *n* FIN consorcio *m*

constant *adj (currency)* constante; **the dividend of $5 per share that was paid in 1999 was worth only $2.50 in constant dollars of 1989** el dividendo de 5 dólares por acción pagado en 1999 equivalía solo a 2,50 dólares constantes de 1989

constitute *vt (committee)* constituir; *(chairperson)* nombrar; **to constitute sb arbitrator** nombrar a alguien árbitro

constraint management *n* gestión *f* de restricciones

constructive *adj* IND **constructive dismissal** = despido forzado por presiones del empresario; FIN **constructive fraud** fraude *m* implícito; FIN **constructive interest** intereses *mpl* implícitos

consular *adj* consular ▫ **consular fees** derechos *mpl* consulares; **consular invoice** factura *f* consular

consult 1 *vt* consultar; **to consult sb about sth** consultar algo a alguien; **I have to consult my boss before taking a decision** antes de tomar cualquier decisión tengo que consultarla con mi jefe

2 *vi* consultar; **we have to consult with our supplier about this problem** tenemos que consultar el problema con nuestro proveedor

consultancy *n (company, advice)* asesoría *f*, consultoría *f* ▫ **consultancy fees** honorarios *mpl* de asesoría *or* consultoría **consultancy service** servicio *m* de asesoría *or* consultoría

consultant *n* asesor(ora) *m,f*, consultor(ora) *m,f*

consultation *n (discussion)* consulta *f*; **the matter will be decided in consultation with**

our partners el asunto será resuelto tras consultar con nuestros socios; **there was no consultation with the unions about the changes** los cambios no se consultaron con los sindicatos

consumable 1 n **consumables** bienes mpl consumibles, material m consumible; COMPTR consumibles mpl

2 adj ❏ **consumable goods** bienes mpl consumibles

consumer n consumidor(ora) m,f ❏ **consumer acceptance** aceptación f del consumidor; **consumer adviser** asesor(ora) m,f del consumidor; **Consumers' Assocation** = organización de consumidores y usuarios británica, ≃ Esp OCU f; **consumer audit** evaluación f del consumidor; **consumer behaviour** comportamiento m del consumidor; **consumer behaviour study** estudio m del comportamiento del consumidor; **consumer benefit** beneficio m para el consumidor or los consumidores; **consumer brand** marca f de consumo; **consumer confidence** confianza f del consumidor; **consumer credit** crédito m al consumo; **consumer debt** deuda f de or por consumo; **consumer demand** demanda f de consumo; **consumer durables** bienes mpl de consumo duraderos; **consumer expenditure** gasto m de or en consumo; **consumer goods** bienes mpl de consumo; **consumer group** organización f de consumidores; **consumer industry** industria f de bienes de consumo; **consumer journalism** periodismo m en defensa del consumidor; **consumer loan** crédito m or préstamo m personal; **consumer loyalty** fidelidad f del consumidor; **consumer magazine** revista f del consumidor; **consumer market** mercado m de consumo; **consumer motivation** motivación f del consumidor; **consumer organization** organización f de consumidores; **consumer panel** panel m de consumidores; **consumer preference** preferencia f del consumidor; US **consumer price index** índice m de precios al Esp consumo or Am consumidor; **consumer product** producto m de consumo; **consumer profile** perfil m del consumidor; **consumer protection** protección f del consumidor; **consumer protection agency** agencia f de protección del consumidor; **consumer purchasing power** poder m adquisitivo del consumidor; **consumer research** estudio m de mercado; **consumer resistance** resistencia f del consumidor; **consumer satisfaction** satisfacción f del consumidor; **consumer society** sociedad f de consumo; **consumer sovereignty** soberanía f del consumidor; **consumer spending** consumo m privado; **consumer survey** encuesta f a consumidores; **consumer test** prueba f or test m del consumidor; **consumer test group** grupo m de consumidores (test(e)ados); **consumer testing** pruebas fpl del consumidor; **consumer trends** tendencias fpl de consumo

> "
>
> That is a bit extreme, but making assumptions about people can be counter-productive and lead to a puzzling, if not insulting, experience. It is a case of traditional brand-value building competing with the current digital-channels marketing mantra of tailoring the retail offering to an audience of one. The Internet has given retailers more direct access to **consumer behaviour** and is capable of producing staggering amounts of "clickstream" and other data for analysis.
>
> "

consumerism n (consumer protection) protección f al consumidor; ECON (consumption) consumismo m

consumption n consumo m

contact 1 n (**a**) (communication) contacto m; **to be in contact with sb** estar en contacto con alguien; **to get in contact with sb** ponerse en contacto con alguien (**b**) (acquaintance) contacto m; **she has some useful business contacts** tiene algunos contactos útiles en el mundo empresarial ❏ **contact person** persona f de contacto

2 vt ponerse en contacto con, contactar con; **we'll contact you later on this week** nos pondremos en contacto contigo más entrada la semana

container n (**a**) (for storage, sale) (large) contenedor m; (small) recipiente m

(**b**) (for containerized transport) contenedor m ❏ **container berth** muelle m para carga y descarga de contenedores; **container depot** depósito m de contenedores; Br **container lorry** camión m de transporte de contenedores; **container port** terminal f de contenedores, puerto m de contenedores; **container ship** buque m de transporte de contenedores; **container shipping** transporte m marítimo en contenedores; **container truck** camión m de transporte de contenedores (**c**) MKTG **container premium** producto m con envase reutilizable

containerization n (of cargo, port) contenerización f, contenedorización f

containerize vt (cargo, port) contenerizar, contenedorizar ❏ **containerized freight** carga f contenerizada or contenedorizada

contango ST EXCH **1** n (practice) contango m, reporte m; (percentage) interés m aplicable a la prolongación de pago; **contangoes are low** los intereses aplicables a la prolongación de pago están bajos ❏ **contango day** día m del reporte; **contango rate** interés m aplicable a la prolongación de pago

2 vi pagar el interés de prolongación de pago

contents insurance n seguro m del contenido

contest *vt* LAW **to contest a will** impugnar un testamento □ **contested claim** reclamación *f* impugnada, *SAm* reclamo *m* impugnado

context-sensitive *adj* COMPTR contextual □ *context-sensitive help* ayuda *f* contextual

contingency *n* contingencia *f*, eventualidad *f*; **to allow for every contingency** tomar precauciones ante cualquier eventualidad □ **contingency fund** fondo *m* de emergencia *or* para contingencias; ACCT **contingency and loss provision** fondo *m* contra contingencias y pérdidas; **contingency plan** plan *m* de emergencia; **contingency reserve** reserva *f* de emergencia *or* para contingencias; ACCT **contingency theory** teoría *f* de la contingencia

contingent *adj* (**a**) *(possible)* eventual □ **contingent liabilities** ACCT pasivo *m* contingente; FIN responsabilidad *f* contingente; ST EXCH **contingent order** orden *f* condicional; **contingent profit** beneficio *m* aleatorio; ST EXCH **contingent value right** derecho *m* al valor de rescate (**b**) *(dependent)* contingente; **to be contingent on** *or* **upon sth** depender de algo; **a salary increase is contingent upon group performance** una subida de sueldo depende de los resultados del grupo (**c**) *US* **contingent worker** trabajador(ora) *m,f* eventual

continuous *adj* continuo(a) □ **continuous budget** presupuesto *m* continuo; **continuous flow production** producción *f* continua; **continuous improvement** mejora *f* continua; **continuous innovation** innovación *f* continua; COMPTR **continuous input** entrada *f* continua; COMPTR **continuous mode** modo *m* continuo; COMPTR **continuous paper** papel *m* continuo; COMPTR **continuous processing** procesado *m* continuo; **continuous production** producción *f* continua; MKTG **continuous research** investigación *f* continua; COMPTR **continuous stationery** papel *m* continuo; ST EXCH **continuous trading** contratación *f* continua

contra ACCT **1** *n* **per/as per contra** según la cuenta de contrapartida
2 *adj* **contra account** cuenta *f* de contrapatida; **contra entry** asiento *m* de contrapartida

contraband *n* contrabando *m* □ **contraband goods** mercancías *fpl* de contrabando

contract 1 *n* (**a**) *(agreement)* contrato *m*; **to draw up a contract** redactar un contrato; **to sign a contract** firmar un contrato; **to cancel a contract** rescindir un contrato; **to be bound by contract** estar obligado(a) por un contrato; **to enter into a contract with sb** entablar una relación contractual con alguien; **to break one's contract** incumplir el contrato; **to be under contract (to sb/to do sth)** estar contratado(a) (por alguien/para hacer algo) □ **contract of apprenticeship** contrato *m* de aprendizaje; **contract bond** fianza *f* de contratista; **contract of**

carriage contrato *m* de transporte; **contract of employment** contrato *m* de trabajo; **contract law** derecho *m* contractual; ST EXCH **contract note** notificación *f* de la celebración de una transacción; **contract of service** contrato *m* de trabajo
(**b**) *(won by tender)* contrata *f*; **to put work out to contract** subcontratar un trabajo; **to give or award a contract to sb** dar *or* conceder una contrata a alguien; **to tender for a contract** presentarse a una licitación de contratación, licitar por un contrato; **to secure a contract for sth** conseguir la contrata de algo; **they were given a contract to build the new road** les concedieron una contrata para construir la nueva carretera, fueron subcontratados para construir la nueva carretera □ **contract date** fecha *f* de finalización de la contrata; **contract labour** mano *f* de obra contratada; **contract price** precio *m* según el contrato; **contract staff** personal *m* contratado; **contract work** trabajo *m* de contrata
2 *vt* (**a**) *(person, company)* **to contract sb to do sth** contratar a alguien para hacer algo (**b**) *(debt)* contraer
3 *vi* **to contract for the supply of sth** firmar un contrato para suministrar algo; **to contract for work** firmar un contrato para hacer un trabajo

▶ **contract in** *vi* *(into insurance policy, pension plan)* suscribirse

▶ **contract out 1** *vt sep* *(work)* externalizar, *RP* tercerizar (**to** a); **the work was contracted out** se externalizó *or RP* tercerizó el trabajo
2 *vi Br (insurance policy, pension plan)* darse de baja (**of** de)

contracting party *n* parte *f* contratante

contractor *n* contratista *m,f*

contractual *adj* *(agreement, obligations)* contractual; **on the present contractual basis** en las condiciones de empleo actuales □ **contractual agreement** acuerdo *m* contractual; **contractual allowance** descuento *m* contractual; **contractual claims** reclamaciones *fpl or SAm* reclamos *mpl* contractuales; **contractual cover** cobertura *f* contractual; **contractual date** fecha *f* de finalización de la contrata; **contractual guarantee** garantía *f* contractual; **contractual labour** mano *f* de obra contratada; **contractual liability** responsabilidad *f* contractual; **contractual price** precio *m* según el contrato

contrarian *n* = operador que va contra las tendencias dominantes en el mercado □ **contrarian investor** = inversor que va contra las tendencias dominantes en el mercado

❝ ───────

But being a **contrarian investor** by nature, he also likes to invest in trusts that are out of favour and sell them when sentiment is more positive. Currently, he is overweight in Asia and emerging markets. He likes to hold between 35 and 40 trusts in the fund. **"**

contribute 1 *vt* contribuir con, aportar; **she contributes 10% of her salary to the pension scheme** contribuye con *or* aporta el 10% de su sueldo al plan de pensiones
  2 *vi (make contribution)* contribuir; **to contribute to a charity** realizar un donativo a una organización benéfica

contribution *n* (**a**) *(payment) (to charity)* donación *f*; *(to non-state pension scheme)* aportación *f*; *(to National Insurance)* cotización *f*; **employer's and employee's contributions** cotizaciones de los trabajadores y los empresarios; **we made a small contribution towards the costs** contribuimos al costo total con una pequeña cantidad (**b**) ACCT *(in management accounting)* contribución *f*; *(made to share capital)* aportación *f* ❏ *contribution margin* margen *m* de contribución; *contribution ratio* tasa *f* de contribución

contributory 1 *n* ST EXCH deudor(ora) *m,f*, = persona obligada a contribuir al haber social de una sociedad en liquidación
  2 *adj* **contributory insurance** seguro *m* contributivo; **contributory pension plan** *or* **scheme** plan *m* de pensiones contributivo

control 1 *n* (**a**) *(of company, organization)* control *m*; **to have control of a business** controlar un negocio; **public spending is under the control of our department** el gasto público está bajo control de nuestro departamento; **the control process showed that objectives were being met** el proceso de control mostró que se estaban cumpliendo los objetivos
  (**b**) *(of exchange rates, prices)* control *m*; **to impose controls on sth** imponer controles sobre algo; **there are to be new government controls on financial practices** va a haber nuevos controles gubernamentales sobre las actividades financieras; **inflation must be kept under control** hay que controlar *or* contener la inflación ❏ *control account* cuenta *f* de control; *control commission* comisión *f* de control; MKTG *control group* grupo *m* de control; MKTG *control market* mercado *m* de control; MKTG *control question* pregunta *f* de control
  (**c**) COMPTR (tecla *f* de) control *m* ❏ *control bus* bus *m* de control; *control key* tecla *f* de control; *control panel* panel *m* de control
  2 *vt* (**a**) *(company, organization)* controlar (**b**) *(exchange rates, prices)* controlar, regular; *(inflation)* controlar, contener; **to control the rise in the cost of living** controlar *or* contener la subida del costo *or* *Esp* coste de la vida

controllable costs *npl* costos *mpl* *or* *Esp* costes *mpl* controlables

controlled *adj* ECON **controlled economy** economía *f* dirigida; **controlled price** precio *m*

controlado; **to sell sth at the controlled price** vender algo al precio controlado

controller *n* FIN interventor(ora) *m,f*, *Am* contralor(ora) *m,f*

controlling *adj* **controlling factor** factor *m* determinante; **controlling interest, controlling share** *(in company)* control *m* accionarial, participación *f* mayoritaria; **controlling shareholding** cartera *f* de control

convene 1 *vt* *(conference, meeting)* convocar; **to convene a meeting of shareholders** convocar una reunión de accionistas
  2 *vi* *(board, people)* reunirse; **the meeting convened at 11 a.m.** la reunión comenzó a las 11 de la mañana

convener, convenor *n* *Br* *(of trade union)* jefe(a) *m,f* de la sección sindical; *(of meeting)* convocante *mf*

convenience *n* **at your earliest convenience** *(in letter)* en cuanto le sea posible; **please reply at your earliest convenience** por favor responda en cuanto le sea posible ❏ MKTG *convenience brand* marca *f* cotidiana *or* de artículos de uso diario; MKTG *convenience goods* artículos *mpl* cotidianos *or* de uso diario; MKTG *convenience sampling* muestreo *m* de conveniencia

convenor = **convener**

convention *n* (**a**) *(agreement)* convenio *m*, convención *f*; **to sign a convention (on sth)** firmar un convenio *or* una convención (sobre algo) (**b**) *(conference)* congreso *m*

convergence *n* ECON convergencia *f* ❏ EU *convergence criteria* criterios *mpl* de convergencia

conversational *adj* COMPTR *(mode)* conversacional

conversion *n* (**a**) FIN *(of securities)* conversión *f* ❏ *conversion cost* costo *m* *or* *Esp* coste *m* de conversión; *conversion issue* emisión *f* convertible; *conversion loan* empréstito *m* de conversión; *conversion premium* prima *f* de conversión; *conversion price* precio *m* de conversión; *conversion rate* tasa *f* de conversión
  (**b**) COMPTR *conversion program* programa *m* de conversión *conversion software* software *m* de conversión
  (**c**) *Br* *(of building society into bank)* conversión *f*

convert 1 *n* *US* FIN bono *m* convertible
  2 *vt* (**a**) *(currency, bonds, securities)* convertir; **to convert pounds into euros** *(as calculation)* convertir libras en euros; *(by exchanging them)* cambiar libras en euros (**b**) COMPTR *(file)* convertir (**to/into** en)

convertibility *n* convertibilidad *f*

convertible *adj* FIN *(loan, security)* convertible ❏ *convertible bond* bono *m* convertible; *convertible currency* moneda *f* *or* divisa *f* convertible

convertible loan stock obligaciones *fpl* convertibles

convey *vt (goods)* transportar

conveyance *n* LAW *(transfer)* traspaso *m*, transmisión *f; (deed)* escritura *f* de traspaso

conveyancing *n* LAW *(procedure)* contratación *f* inmobiliaria; *(drawing up documents)* tramitación *f* de una operación de compraventa inmobiliaria

cook *vt Fam* **to cook the books** falsificar las cuentas

cookie *n* COMPTR cookie *m or f*

cooling-off period *n* periodo *m* de reflexión

> **"**
> The directives require suppliers of mail-order goods (as distinct from services) to provide written information about the company and terms of sale, as well as delivering goods promised within a 30-day period. Perhaps more importantly, however, they also give consumers a seven-day **cooling-off period** after the goods are delivered, during which time they can change their mind and receive a full refund.
> **"**

co-op *n (abbr* **co-operative**) cooperativa *f*

co-operative 1 *n* cooperativa *f*
2 *adj* cooperativo(a) ❏ *co-operative advertising* publicidad *f* cooperativa; *co-operative bank* banco *m* cooperativo; *co-operative credit society* cooperativa *f* de crédito; *co-operative group* grupo *m* cooperativo; *co-operative society* cooperativa *f*

coordinate *vt (work)* coordinar

coordination *n (of work)* coordinación *f*

co-owner *n* copropietario(a) *m,f*

co-ownership *n* copropiedad *f*

copartner *n* socio(a) *m,f*

copartnership *n* sociedad *f* comanditaria

co-processor *n* COMPTR coprocesador *m*

coproprietor *n* copropietario(a) *m,f*

copy 1 *n* (**a**) *(of document, letter)* copia *f;* **to make a copy of sth** hacer una copia de algo ❏ *copy typist* mecanógrafo(a) *m,f*
(**b**) *(of book, newspaper)* ejemplar *m*
(**c**) *(in advertising)* textos *mpl* publicitarios; **the story made good copy** la noticia dio mucho de sí ❏ *copy deadline* fecha *f* límite de edición; *copy editor* corrector(ora) *m,f* de estilo
(**d**) MKTG *copy test* prueba *f or* test *m* de copy, prueba de texto; *copy testing* pruebas *fpl* de copy *or* texto
(**e**) COMPTR **copy and paste** copiar y pegar ❏ *copy block* copia *f* de bloque; *copy command*

comando *m* de copiar; *copy disk* disco *m* de copia; *copy protection* protección *f* contra copia
2 *vt* (**a**) *(document, letter)* copiar; *(photocopy)* fotocopiar (**b**) COMPTR copiar; **to copy sth to disk** copiar algo en un disco; **to copy and paste sth** copiar y pegar algo
3 *vi* COMPTR **to copy and paste** copiar y pegar

copy-protected *adj* COMPTR protegido(a) contra copia

copyright 1 *n* copyright *m*, derechos *mpl* de autor, propiedad *f* intelectual; **copyright reserved** reservados todos los derechos; **to be out of copyright** ya no estar sujeto a derechos de autor; **it's still subject to copyright** todavía está protegido por los derechos de autor; **she has the sole copyright to her invention** tiene la propiedad intelectual exclusiva de la invención ❏ *copyright deposit* depósito *m* legal; *copyright infringement* violación *f* de los derechos de autor; *copyright notice* nota *f* sobre los derechos de autor
2 *adj* protegido(a) por las leyes de la propiedad intelectual
3 *vt* registrar como propiedad intelectual

copywriter *n* redactor(ora) *m,f* creativo(a) *or* de publicidad

copywriting *n* redacción *f* publicitaria

cordless *adj* inalámbrico(a) ❏ COMPTR *cordless keyboard* teclado *m* inalámbrico; COMPTR *cordless mouse* Esp ratón *m or Am* mouse *m* inalámbrico; *cordless telephone* teléfono *m* inalámbrico

core *n core assets* activos *mpl* principales; MKTG *core brand* marca *f* principal; *core business* negocio *m* principal; *core competence* habilidad *f* principal; *core holding* inversión *f* central *or* principal; *core market* mercado *m* principal; MKTG *core message* mensaje *m* principal *or* central; *core skills* habilidades *fpl* principales; *core time (in flexitime)* tiempo *m* mínimo

corner 1 *n* monopolio *m*; **to have a corner in sth** ejercer un monopolio sobre algo, acaparar algo
2 *vt (market)* monopolizar, acaparar; **in two years they've cornered the market in software packages** en dos años han monopolizado *or* acaparado el mercado de paquetes de software

cornering *n (of market)* monopolización *f*

Corp, corp *n (abbr* **corporation**) ≃ S.A.

corpocracy *n* (**a**) *(society)* = sociedad dominada por las grandes corporaciones (**b**) *(company)* = empresa que no asume riesgos, altamente burocratizada y con baja productividad

corporate *adj* corporativo(a) ❏ *corporate advertising* publicidad *f* corporativa; *corporate assets* activos *mpl* sociales; *corporate banking* banca *f* corporativa; **corporate body** persona *f* jurídica; **corporate bond** bono *m* empresarial; **corporate budget** presupuesto *m* corporativo; **corporate buy-out** adquisición *f* corporativa; **corporate card** tarjeta *f* de empresa; **corporate culture** cultura *f* empresarial *or* corporativa; **their corporate culture emphasizes the need for continuous improvement in customer service** su cultura empresarial pone énfasis en la necesidad de una mejora continua del servicio al cliente; **corporate entertainment** eventos *mpl* para empresas; **corporate environment** entorno *m* empresarial; **corporate film** película *f* corporativa; **corporate finance** gestión *f* financiera de las sociedades; **corporate finance manager** director(ora) *m,f* financiero(a) corporativo(a); **corporate governance** buen gobierno *m* empresarial, gobernanza *f* corporativa; **corporate governance committee** comité *m* de buen gobierno empresarial; **corporate hospitality** actos *mpl* sociales de la empresa; **corporate identity** identidad *f* corporativa; **corporate image** imagen *f* corporativa *or* de empresa; **the company cares about its corporate image** la empresa cuida mucho su imagen corporativa; **corporate income** ingresos *mpl* de la sociedad; **corporate income tax** impuesto *m* de sociedades; **corporate institution** persona *f* jurídica; **corporate law** derecho *m* de sociedades; **corporate lawyer** abogado(a) *m,f* de empresa; *US* **corporate licensing** licencias *fpl* para empresas; **corporate literature** folletos *mpl* corporativos; **corporate member** *(of association)* miembro *m* corporativo; **corporate misery index** índice *m* de miseria empresarial; **corporate model** modelo *m* corporativo; **corporate name** razón *f* social; **corporate planning** planificación *f* empresarial; **corporate raider** tiburón *m*; **corporate recovery** recuperación *f* empresarial; **corporate responsibility** responsabilidad *f* corporativa; **the idea of corporate responsibility is now taken seriously by an increasing number of companies** cada vez más empresas se toman en serio la idea de la responsabilidad corporativa; **corporate restructuring** reestructuración *f* empresarial; **two subsidiary companies will be sold off as part of the corporate restructuring plan** van a vender dos filiales como parte del plan de reestructuración empresarial; **corporate sector** sector *m* empresarial *or* RP empresario; **corporate social responsibility** responsabilidad *f* social corporativa; **corporate sponsorship** patrocinio *m* corporativo; **corporate strategy** estrategia *f* empresarial *or* corporativa; **corporate structure** estructura *f* social; **corporate tax** impuesto *m* de sociedades; **corporate video** *Esp* vídeo *m* *or* *Am* video *m* corporativo; *US* **corporate welfare** subsidios *mpl* a las empresas

> ❝
> As if investors didn't have enough to worry about, a brokerage house has invented a new measure to show that the corporate profit recovery could take longer than the market and some analysts think. A key economic measure in the last decades of the 20th century was the "misery index," which combined inflation and unemployment to show how badly consumers were hurting. But the key gauge for the first decade of the new century could be something called the "**corporate misery index**." ❞

corporation *n* *(company)* sociedad *f*, corporación *f* ▫ *US* **corporation income tax,** *Br* **corporation tax** impuesto *m* de sociedades

corporatism *n* corporatismo *m*

corporatist *adj* corporatista

correct 1 *adj* *(amount, figure)* exacto(a); *(information)* correcto(a); **these sales figures are not correct** estas cifras de ventas no son correctas
2 *vt* *(mistake, spelling)* corregir

correcting entry *n* ACCT asiento *m* de corrección

correction *n* **(a)** *(of error, in document)* corrección *f* ▫ **correction fluid** líquido *m* corrector **(b)** ST EXCH *(adjustment)* corrección *f*

correspond *vi* **(a)** *(be equivalent)* corresponder **(with** *or* **to** con *or* a); **the two sets of figures don't correspond** los dos grupos de cifras no se corresponden **(b)** *(write letters)* mantener correspondencia **(with** con)

correspondence *n* **(a)** *(letterwriting)* correspondencia *f*; **to be in correspondence with sb** mantener correspondencia con alguien **(b)** *(letters)* correspondencia *f*; **to read one's correspondence** leer la correspondencia ▫ **correspondence tray** bandeja *f* de la correspondencia

correspondent *n* corresponsal *mf* ▫ **correspondent bank** banco *m* corresponsal

corresponding entry *n* ACCT asiento *m* correspondiente

corrupt COMPTR **1** *adj* *(disk, file)* dañado(a), corrompido(a)
2 *vt* *(disk, file)* dañar, corromper

COS *n* *(abbr* **cash on shipment)** pago *m* contra embarque

co-sign *vt* LAW firmar conjuntamente

co-signatory *n* LAW firmante *mf* conjunto(a) **(to** *or* **of** de)

cost 1 *n* **(a)** *(price)* costo *m*, *Esp* coste *m*; **cost and freight** costo *or* *Esp* coste y flete; **cost, insurance and freight** costo *or* *Esp* coste, seguro y flete; **cost per thousand** costo *or* *Esp* coste por mil ▫ **cost accountant** *Esp* contable *mf* de costes, *Am* contador(ora) *m,f* de costos; **cost accounting** contabilidad *f* de costos *or Esp* costes; **cost allocation** asignación *f* de costos *or Esp* costes; **cost analysis** análisis *f inv* de costos *or Esp* costes; **cost assessment** evaluación *f* de costo *or Esp* coste; ACCT **cost base** base *f* del costo *or Esp* coste; ACCT **cost centre** centro *m* de costo *or Esp* coste; ACCT **cost curve** curva *f* de costos *or Esp* costes; **cost equation** ecuación *f* de costos *or Esp* costes; **cost factor** factor *m* del costo *or Esp* coste; ACCT **cost of goods purchased** costo *m or Esp* coste *m* de la mercancía comprada; ACCT **cost of goods sold** costo *m or Esp* coste *m* de la mercancía vendida; **cost of living** costo *m or Esp* coste *m* de la vida; **cost management** gestión *f* de costos *or Esp* costes; **cost overrun** sobrecosto *m*, *Esp* sobrecoste *m*; **the project had a cost overrun of £20m** el costo *or Esp* coste del proyecto superó en 20 millones de libras la cifra presupuestada inicialmente; **cost price** precio *m* de costo *or Esp* coste; **cost pricing** fijación *f* del precio en función del costo *or Esp* coste; ACCT **cost of sales** costo *m or Esp* coste *m* de ventas; **cost standard** estándar *m* de costos *or Esp* costes; **cost structure** estructura *f* de costos *or Esp* costes; **cost unit** unidad *f* de costo *or Esp* coste, unidad de costeo; **cost variance** variación *f* de costo *or Esp* coste

(**b**) LAW **costs** costas *fpl* (judiciales); **to pay costs** pagar las costas (judiciales)

2 *vt* (**a**) *(be priced at)* costar; **how much does it cost?** ¿cuánto cuesta?; **it costs $25** cuesta 25 dólares (**b**) *(estimate cost of) (article, job)* calcular el costo de; **how much was it costed at?** *(job)* ¿en cuánto se estimó el costo *or Esp* coste?

3 *vi Fam (be expensive)* salir caro(a); **we can do it but it will cost** podemos hacerlo, pero va a salir caro

cost-benefit *adj* **cost-benefit analysis** análisis *m inv* de costo-beneficio *or Esp* coste-beneficio; **cost-benefit ratio** relación *f* costo-beneficio *or Esp* coste-beneficio

cost-competitive *adj (product)* con costos *or Esp* costes competitivos; **we're not cost-competitive** nuestros costos *or Esp* costes no son competitivos

cost-conscious *adj* consciente de los costos *or Esp* costes

cost-cutter *n (method of reducing costs)* método *m* de reducción de costos *or Esp* costes; **the new chief is a tough cost-cutter** el nuevo jefe es partidario a ultranza de la reducción de costos

cost-cutting *adj* de reducción de costos *or Esp* costes

cost-effective *adj* rentable

cost-effectiveness *n* rentabilidad *f* □ **cost-effectiveness analysis** análisis *m inv* de rentabilidad

costing *n (process, estimate)* cálculo *m* de costos *or Esp* costes

cost-of-living *adj* **cost-of-living adjustment** *(in salary)* ajuste *m* del costo *or Esp* coste de vida; **cost-of-living allowance** compensación *f* por el costo *or Esp* coste de vida; **cost-of-living increase** *(in salary)* aumento *m* por el costo *or Esp* coste de vida; **cost-of-living index** índice *m* del costo *or Esp* coste de la vida

> ❝
>
> The taxpayer asked the IRS if it was possible to modify his payment plan by adding an annual 4% **cost-of-living adjustment** (COLA) and by including a one-time "catch-up" amount. The IRS denied the request. It held the taxpayer could not modify the annual payment without triggering the 10% penalty for premature distributions.
>
> ❞

cost-plus FIN **1** *n* costo *m or Esp* coste *m* incrementado
2 *adj* **on a cost-plus basis** basado(a) en el costo *or Esp* coste incrementado □ **cost-plus pricing** fijación *f* de precios mediante el método de costo *or Esp* coste incrementado

cost-push inflation *n* ECON inflación *f* de costos *or Esp* costes

cost-reduce *vt* reducir el costo *or Esp* coste de

cost-volume-profit analysis *n* ACCT análisis *m inv* costo-volumen-beneficio *or Esp* coste-volumen-beneficio

co-trustee *n* LAW cofiduciario(a) *m,f*

cottage industry *n* industria *f* artesanal

council *n* (**a**) *(local government) (of town)* ayuntamiento *m*, municipio *m*; *(of region, county)* autoridades *fpl* regionales, *Esp* ≃ diputación *f* provincial (**b**) *(assembly)* consejo *m* □ **Council of Europe** Consejo *m* de Europa; **Council for Mutual Economic Aid** Consejo *m* de Asistencia *or* Ayuda Mutua Económica

counsel *n* LAW abogado(a) *m,f*; **counsel for the defence** abogado(a) *m,f* defensor(ora); **counsel for the prosecution** fiscal *mf*

counter *n (in shop, supermarket)* mostrador *m*; *(in bank)* ventanilla *f*; FIN **to buy shares over the counter** comprar acciones sin cotización oficial; **to buy/sell sth under the counter** comprar/vender algo bajo mano □ BANKING **counter services** servicios *mpl* de ventanilla; **counter staff** *(in bank, post office)* personal *m* de ventanilla; **counter transaction** transacción *f* en la ventanilla

counter-appraisal *n US* segunda evaluación *f*

counterbid *n* contraoferta *f*

counterclaim LAW **1** n contrademanda f; **to make a counterclaim (against sb)** presentar or interponer una contrademanda (contra alguien)
2 vi presentar or interponer una contrademanda

counterclaimant n LAW contrademandante mf

counterfeit 1 n falsificación f
2 adj falso(a)
3 vt falsificar

counterfoil n Br (of cheque) matriz f, talón m, resguardo m

counter-guarantee n ST EXCH contragarantía f

countermand vt (order) revocar

counteroffer n contraoferta f

counterpart n (person) homólogo(a) m,f; (document) duplicado m

counterparty risk n BANKING riesgo m de contraparte

counterproductive adj contraproducente; **closing the factory would be counterproductive to the region's economy** el cierre de la fábrica sería contraproducente para la economía de la región

countersign vt refrendar

countertrade 1 n comercio m compensatorio or de compensación
2 vt (goods) ofrecer a cambio

countertrading n comercio m compensatorio or de compensación

countervailing adj FIN compensatorio(a)

country n país m □ **country of origin** país m de origen; **country risk** riesgo m país

coupon n (a) FIN (on bearer bond) cupón m □ **coupon bond** bono m al portador; **coupon yield** rendimiento m del cupón (b) (exchangeable voucher) cupón m, vale m; **(money-off) coupon** vale-descuento m □ **coupon offer** oferta f en cupones

courier n mensajero(a) m,f; **to send sth by courier** enviar algo por mensajería; **to arrive by courier** llegar por mensajería

course n (of study) curso m; **to do** or **take a course in sth** hacer un curso de algo

court n tribunal m; **to go to court** ir a juicio or a los tribunales; **to take sb to court** llevar a alguien a juicio or a los tribunales; **to settle a dispute out of court** resolver un conflicto extrajudicialmente □ Br **Court of Appeal** Tribunal m de Apelación; US **Court of Appeals** Tribunal m de Apelación; **court case** caso m judicial, proceso m; **court of first instance** tribunal m de primera instancia; EU **Court of Justice of the European Communities** Tribunal m de Justicia de las Comunidades Europeas; **court order** orden f judicial; **court ruling** fallo m or decisión f judicial

courthouse n US juzgado m

courtroom n (room) sala f de juicios; (people) tribunal m

covenant LAW **1** n (a) (promise of money) = acuerdo por el que una persona se compromete a realizar donaciones a una entidad benéfica, la cual, además, recibe los impuestos con que haya sido gravada la cantidad donada (b) (agreement) pacto m, convenio m
2 vt donar (por el sistema de "covenant")
3 vi **to covenant for a sum** comprometerse contractualmente a pagar una cantidad; **to covenant with sb for sth** comprometerse contractualmente con alguien a algo

cover 1 n (a) (in insurance) cobertura f; **to have cover against sth** estar asegurado(a) or tener seguro contra algo □ **cover note** nota f de cobertura, póliza f provisional
(b) FIN (collateral) garantía f; **to operate with/ without cover** operar con/sin garantía; □ **cover ratio** tasa f de cobertura
(c) **to send sth under separate cover** enviar algo por separado □ US **cover letter** (in general) carta f explicatoria; (enclosed with CV) carta de presentación; **cover page** (of fax) página f de portada; **cover sheet** (of fax) página f de portada
2 vt (a) (insure) cubrir, asegurar (**for** or **against** contra); **to be fully covered** tener cobertura total; **the insurance covers serious illness** el seguro cubre enfermedades graves (b) **to be covered** (creditor) tener garantía; **to cover a loan** garantizar un crédito; ST EXCH **to cover a position** cubrir una posición (c) (be enough for) cubrir; **to cover one's expenses** cubrir gastos; **to cover a deficit** cubrir un déficit; ACCT **to cover a loss** cubrir una pérdida

coverage n INS cobertura f

covered adj (position) cubierto(a) □ ST EXCH **covered (short) position** posición f cubierta

covering adj (a) **covering letter** carta f de presentación (b) ST EXCH **covering purchases** compras fpl de cobertura

co-worker n US compañero(a) m,f de trabajo

c/p (abbr **carriage paid**) porte m pagado

CPA n US (abbr **Certified Public Accountant**) Esp censor(ora) m,f jurado(a) de cuentas, Am contador(ora) *m,f* público(a)

cpa *n* (*abbr* **critical path analysis**) análisis *m inv* del camino crítico

CPI *n* (*abbr* **Consumer Price Index**) IPC *m*, *Méx* INPC *m*

cpi COMPTR (*abbr* **characters per inch**) cpp

cps COMPTR (*abbr* **characters per second**) cps

CPSA *n Br* (*abbr* **Civil and Public Services Association**) = sindicato de funcionarios británicos

CPT (*abbr* **carriage paid to**) CPT

CPU *n* COMPTR (*abbr* **central processing unit**) CPU *f* ❑ **CPU board** placa *f* de la CPU

crack *vt* (*market*) penetrar en

▸ **crack open** *vt sep* (*market*) penetrar en

crash 1 *n* (**a**) (*financial*) quiebra *f* (financiera), crack *m* (**b**) (*of computer*) bloqueo *m*
2 *adj* **crash course** curso *m* intensivo; **crash programme** programa *m* intensivo
3 *vi* (**a**) (*business*) quebrar; (*prices, shares*) hundirse; (*economy*) venirse abajo; **shares crashed from 75p to 11p** las acciones cayeron de 75 a 11 peniques (**b**) (*computer network, system*) bloquearse; (*computer*) colgarse

crate *n* (*for storage, transport*) caja *f*

crawler *n* COMPTR rastreador *m*

crawling peg *n* FIN paridad *f* móvil, ajuste *m* de la paridad

cream *vt US* **to cream the market** explotar al máximo el mercado

▸ **cream off** *vt sep* (*money, profits*) quedarse con

create *vt* crear; **foreign investment has created many new jobs in the area** la inversión extranjera ha creado muchos empleos en la zona; **new markets are constantly being created** se crean nuevos mercados constantemente

creation *n* (*of jobs, new markets*) creación *f*

creative 1 *n* (*department*) departamento *m* creativo; (*work*) trabajo *m* creativo; (*person*) creativo(a) *m,f*; **we prefer creative to be handled out of house** preferimos subcontratar el trabajo creativo
2 *adj* creativo(a) ❑ FIN **creative accounting** contabilidad *f* creativa, maquillaje *m* de cuentas; **creative copy strategy** estrategia *f* creativa publicitaria; **creative department** departamento *m* creativo; **creative director** director(ora) *m,f* creativo; **creative marketing** marketing *m* creativo; **creative team** equipo *m* creativo

creativity *n* creatividad *f*

credit *n* (**a**) (*for future payment*) crédito *m*; **to give sb credit** conceder un crédito a alguien; **to buy/sell sth on credit** comprar/vender algo a crédito; **her credit is good** tiene un buen historial crediticio *or* de crédito ❑ **credit account** cuenta *f* de crédito; **credit advice** aviso *m* de crédito *or* abono; **credit agency** agencia *f* de calificación crediticia; **credit agreement** convenio *m or* acuerdo *m* de crédito; **credit application form** formulario *m* de solicitud de crédito; **credit bank** banco *m* de crédito; **credit broker** intermediario(a) *m,f* de crédito; *US* **credit bureau** agencia *f* de calificación crediticia; **credit call** llamada *for Am* llamado *m* con tarjeta de crédito; **credit card** tarjeta *f* de crédito; **credit card fraud** fraude *m* con tarjetas de crédito; **credit card number** número *m* de tarjeta de crédito; **credit card transaction** transacción *f* con tarjeta de crédito; **credit ceiling** límite *m* de crédito; **credit control** control *m* crediticio *or* de crédito; **credit controller** supervisor(ora) *m,f* de crédito; **credit crunch** restricciones *fpl* al crédito; **credit enquiry** consulta *f* de historial crediticio; **credit facilities** facilidades *fpl* de pago; **to give sb credit facilities** ofrecer facilidades de crédito alguien; **credit file** historial *m* crediticio *or* de crédito; **credit freeze** *Esp* congelación *f or Am* congelamiento *m* de créditos; **credit guarantee fund** fondo *m* de garantía de crédito; **credit history** historial *m* crediticio *or* de crédito; **to obtain information on sb's credit history** obtener información sobre el historial crediticio de alguien; **credit institution** entidad *f or* institución *f* de crédito; **credit insurance** seguro *m* de crédito; **credit limit** límite *m or* tope *m* de crédito; **credit line** línea *f* de crédito, descubierto *m* permitido; **credit management** gestión *f* de(l) crédito; **credit manager** gerente *mf* de crédito; **credit margin** margen *m* de crédito; **credit options** opciones *fpl* de crédito; **credit organization** entidad *f or* institución *f* de crédito; **credit period** periodo *m* del crédito; **credit purchase** compra *f* a crédito; **credit rating** calificación *f* crediticia *or* de solvencia; **credit rating agency** agencia *f* de calificación crediticia; **credit restrictions** restricciones *fpl* al crédito; **credit risk** riesgo *m* crediticio; **credit sale** venta *f* a crédito; **credit scoring** calificación *f* crediticia *or* de solvencia; **credit squeeze** restricciones *fpl* al crédito; **credit terms** condiciones *fpl* de crédito; **credit transaction** transacción *f* de crédito; **credit union** cooperativa *f* de crédito
(**b**) **to be in credit** (*person, account*) tener saldo positivo; ACCT **debit and credit** debe *m* y haber ❑ ACCT, BANKING **credit balance** saldo *m* acreedor; **credit column** columna *f* del haber; **credit entry** ACCT abono *m*, asiento *m* al haber; BANKING (asiento *m* de) abono; ACCT **credit item** partida *f* del haber; **credit memo** nota *f* de abono; **credit note** nota *f* de abono; **credit side** (*of account*) haber *m*; **credit transfer** transferencia *f*; **credit voucher** comprobante *m* de crédito
2 *vt* **to credit an account with £200, to credit £200 to an account** depositar *or Esp* ingresar 200 libras en una cuenta

> "
> The Money Store, which has 140 employees at branches in Glasgow, Birmingham, Bristol, Manchester, Newcastle and Warrington, is focused on customers such as the self-employed and divorced who can suffer difficulties in getting a **credit rating** from high street lenders.
> "

creditor *n* acreedor(ora) *m,f* ❑ ECON *creditor country* país *m* acreedor; *creditors' meeting* asamblea *for* junta *f* de acreedores; ECON *creditor nation* nación *f* acreedora; *creditors' turnover* periodo *m* medio de pago

creditworthiness *n* solvencia *f*

creditworthy *adj* solvente

creeping *adj (inflation)* reptante

crisis *n* crisis *f inv*; **to take crisis measures** tomar medidas de emergencia ❑ *crisis management* gestión *f* de crisis

critical *adj critical illness insurance* = seguro de enfermedad con cobertura de enfermedad grave; *critical path* camino *m* crítico; *critical path analysis* análisis *m inv* del camino crítico; *critical path method* método *m* del camino crítico; *critical path model* modelo *m* del camino crítico

CRN *n Br (abbr customs registered number)* = número de identificación de aduanas

CRO *n (abbr Companies Registration Office)* = registro mercantil británico

cross *vt (cheque)* cruzar ❑ *crossed cheque* cheque *m* cruzado, *Esp* talón *m* cruzado

cross-border *adj* transfronterizo(a) ❑ *cross-border business* negocios *mpl* transfronterizos; *cross-border trade* comercio *m* transfronterizo

cross-currency *adj cross-currency interest rate swap* permuta *f* financiera *or* swap *m* de divisas con diferentes tipos de interés; *cross-currency swap* permuta *f* financiera de divisas, swap *m* de divisas

cross-hedge *n* ST EXCH cobertura *f* cruzada

cross-holding *n* FIN participación *f* recíproca, cruce *m* de participaciones

> "
> This did not satisfy Mr Pébereau, who had made compromises which included BNP retaining its 37% stake in SocGen but reducing its voting rights to less than 20%. He also offered SocGen a **cross-holding** in BNP which would make it his bank's biggest shareholder.
> "

cross-impact analysis *n* MKTG análisis *m inv* de impacto cruzado

cross-media ownership *n* propiedad *f* cruzada de los medios de comunicación

cross-pricing *n* precios *mpl* cruzados

cross-selling *n* ventas *fpl* cruzadas

crown *n Crown Agent* = funcionario de la agencia británica de ayuda del desarrollo; *Br Crown Court* Tribunal *m* Superior de lo Penal

crude 1 *n (oil)* crudo *m*
  2 *adj crude oil* petróleo *m* crudo

crunch *vt* COMPTR *(numbers, data)* devorar

CSC *n* ADMIN *(abbr Civil Service Commission)* = organismo británico responsable de la contratación de funcionarios por oposiciones

CSD *n* BANKING, ST EXCH *(abbr Central Securities Depository)* DCV *m*

C-share *n* ST EXCH acción *f* de clase C

CSR *n (abbr corporate social responsibility)* RSC *f*, responsabilidad *f* social corporativa

CUG *n* TEL *(abbr closed user group)* grupo *m* cerrado de usuarios

culture *n (within company)* cultura *f*

cumulative *adj (error)* acumulado(a), acumulativo(a) ❑ MKTG *cumulative audience* audiencia *f* acumulada; *cumulative balance* saldo *m* acumulado; *cumulative costs* costos *mpl or Esp* costes *mpl* acumulados; *cumulative debit* débito *m* acumulado; *cumulative dividend* dividendo *m* acumulativo; FIN *cumulative interest* interés *m* acumulable; ST EXCH *cumulative preference share* acción *f* preferente acumulativa; *cumulative profit* beneficio *m* acumulado; *cumulative revenue* ingresos *mpl* acumulados; ST EXCH *cumulative share* acción *f* acumulativa

curb *vt (expenditure, inflation)* frenar, contener; *(imports)* frenar

curly quotes *npl* comillas *fpl* tipográficas

currency *n* moneda *f*; *(foreign)* divisas *fpl* ❑ *currency of account* moneda *f* de cuenta; *currency assets* activos *mpl* en divisas; *currency bloc* bloque *m* de monedas; *currency conversion* conversión *f* de moneda; *currency dealer* cambista *mf*, agente *mf* de cambios; *currency exchange market* mercado *m* de cambio de moneda; *currency expansion* expansión *f* monetaria; *currency exposure* riesgo *m* cambiario; *currency fluctuation* fluctuación *f* de divisas; *currency interest-rate swap* permuta *f* financiera de divisas con el mismo tipo de interés; *currency loan* préstamo *m* en moneda extranjera; *currency manipulation* manipulación *f* de divisas; *currency market* mercado *m* de divisas; *currency note* pagaré *m* del Tesoro; *currency pool* reserva *f* de divisas; *currency risk* riesgo *m* cambiario; *currency snake* serpiente *f* monetaria; *currency speculation* especulación *f* en divisas; *currency speculator* especulador(ora) *m,f* en divisas; **currency standard** patrón *m* monetario; **currency swap** permuta *f* or swap *m* de divisas; **currency transfer** transferencia *f* de moneda extranjera

current *adj* **current account** cuenta *f* corriente; **current affairs** (temas *mpl* de) actualidad *f*; **current affairs magazine** revista *f* de actualidad *or* de información general; COMPTR **current application** aplicación *f* activa; **current assets** activo *m* circulante; **current cost** costo *m* corriente *or* de reposición, *Esp* coste *m* corriente *or* de reposición; **current cost accounting** contabilidad *f* de costos *or Esp* costes corrientes; **current earnings** ingresos *mpl* corrientes; **current expenditure** gasto *m* corriente; **current** *Br* **financial** *or US* **fiscal year** año *m* fiscal en curso; **current income** (*actual earnings*) ingresos *mpl* reales; **current liabilities** pasivo *m* corriente *or* circulante; ACCT **current net value** valor *m* neto actual; **current rate of exchange** tipo *m* de cambio actual; ACCT **current ratio** coeficiente *m* de solvencia; ACCT **current value** valor *m* actual; ACCT **current value accounting** contabilidad *f* a valores actuales; **current year** año *m or* ejercicio *m* en curso; FIN **current yield** rendimiento *m* corriente

curriculum vitae *n* currículum *m* vitae

cursor *n* COMPTR cursor *m*; **move the cursor to the right/left** mueva el cursor a la derecha/izquierda ▫ **cursor control** control *m* del cursor; **cursor movement key** tecla *f* de movimiento *or* desplazamiento del cursor

curve *n* curva *f*; **the graph shows an upward/downward curve** la gráfica muestra una curva ascendente/descendente; *US Fam* **to throw sb a curve (ball)** poner a alguien en un aprieto; **he threw me a curve (ball) when he accepted a higher offer** me puso en un aprieto cuando aceptó una oferta mayor

custodian *n US* ST EXCH depositario(a) *m,f*

custody account *n US* cuenta *f* de custodia

custom *n* (a) (*of business*) **to lose sb's custom** perder a alguien como cliente; **to take one's custom elsewhere** comprar en otra parte; **we value your custom** gracias por seguir confiando en nostros (b) **custom house** aduana *f*

customer *n* cliente *mf* ▫ **customer account** cuenta *f* de cliente; **customer acquisition** captación *f* de clientes; **customer appeal** atractivo *m* para el cliente; **customer base** clientela *f* fija, clientes *mpl* fijos; **customer care** atención *f* al cliente; **customer code** código *m* de cliente; **customer confidence** confianza *f* del cliente; **customer database** base *f* de datos de clientes; **customer list** lista *f* de clientes; **customer loyalty** fidelidad *f* del cliente; **customer loyalty discount** descuento *m* por fidelidad; **customer profile** perfil *m* del cliente; **customer record** ficha *f* del cliente; **customer reference number**

número *m* de referencia del cliente; **customer relations** relaciones *fpl* con los clientes; **customer relations manager** director(ora) *m,f* de atención al cliente; **customer satisfaction** satisfacción *f* del cliente; **customer satisfaction questionnaire** cuestionario *m* de satisfacción del cliente; **customer service** atención *f* al cliente; **customer service department** departamento *m* de atención al cliente; **customer support** atención *f* or asistencia *f* al cliente

customer-centred,   customer-driven, customer-focused *adj* (*company*) centrado(a) en el cliente

> **❝**
>
> More importantly, perhaps, Mr Dunstone has created a clean, **customer-driven** business, with a highly-motivated work force. The formula is already rolling through Europe and further afield, with visible success.
>
> **❞**

customizable *adj* COMPTR personalizable

customization *n* (*of product, service*) personalización *f*

customize *vt* (*service, product*) personalizar, adaptar al gusto del cliente; COMPTR personalizar ▫ **customized marketing** marketing *m* personalizado

customs *npl* aduana *f*; **to go through customs** pasar la aduana; **to take sth through customs** pasar algo por la aduana ▫ **customs agency** agencia *f* de aduanas; **customs agent** agente *mf* de aduanas; **customs allowance** cantidad *f* libre de impuestos; **customs barriers** barreras *fpl* arancelarias; **customs broker** agente *mf* de aduanas; **customs charges** gastos *mpl* de aduana; **customs classification** clasificación *f* arancelaria; **customs clearance** despacho *m* aduanero; **customs clearance area** zona *f* de despacho aduanero; **customs clearance authorization** autorización *f* aduanera; **customs control** control *m* aduanero; **customs declaration** declaración *f* en la aduana *or* de aduanas; **customs duties** derechos *mpl* arancelarios; **customs examination** inspección *f* aduanera; **Customs and Excise** = dirección de aduanas e impuestos sobre el consumo en el Reino Unido; **customs formalities** trámites *mpl* aduaneros; **customs house** aduana *f*; **customs inspection** inspección *f* aduanera (*de mercancías*); **customs inspector** inspector(ora) *m,f* or agente *mf* de aduanas; **customs invoice** factura *f* de artículos importados; **customs legislation** legislación *f* aduanera; **customs manifest** manifiesto *m or* guía *f* de aduanas; **customs note** declaración *f* de aduanas; **customs office** aduana *f*; **customs officer** inspector(ora) *m,f* or agente *mf* de aduanas; **customs papers** documentos *mpl* aduaneros; **customs permit** permiso *m* de aduanas; **customs preferential duty** preferencias *fpl* aduaneras; **customs procedure** formalidades *fpl* aduaneras; **customs receipt** recibo *m* de aduanas; *Br* **customs registered number** = número de identificación de aduanas; **customs regulations** reglamento *m* de aduana; **customs seal** precinto *m* aduanero; **customs service** servicio *m* de aduanas; **customs system** sistema *m* aduanero; **customs tariff** arancel *m* aduanero; **customs transit** tránsito *m* aduanero; **customs union** unión *f* aduanera; **customs value** valor *m* en aduana; **customs visa** permiso *m* aduanero; **customs zone** zona *f* aduanera

cut 1 *n* (**a**) *(in wages, prices, taxes, production, staff)* reducción *f*; **he took a cut in pay** aceptó un recorte salarial (**b**) COMPTR **cut and paste** cortar y pegar ❏ **cut sheet feed** alimentación *f* hoja a hoja; **cut sheet feeder** alimentador *m* hoja a hoja
2 *vt* (**a**) *(wages, prices, taxes, production, staff)* reducir (**b**) COMPTR cortar; **to cut and paste sth** cortar y pegar algo
3 *vi* COMPTR **to cut and paste** cortar y pegar
▸ **cut back 1** *vt sep (prices, production)* reducir, recortar; **arms spending has been cut right back** se ha reducido *or* recortado sustancialmente el gasto en armamento
2 *vi (financially)* reducir *or* recortar gastos
▸ **cut back on** *vt insep* reducir, recortar
▸ **cut down** *vt sep (spending)* reducir, recortar
▸ **cut down on** *vt insep* reducir, recortar
▸ **cut in** *vt sep Fam* **to cut sb in (on a deal)** dejar que alguien participe (en un negocio); **we could cut him in for £5,000** podríamos darle una participación de 5.000 libras
▸ **cut off** *vt sep* (**a**) *(stop)* cortar; **we are cutting off all overseas investment** estamos cortando todas las inversiones en el extranjero (**b**) *(on telephone)* cortar; **I was cut off** *(during conversation)* fui interrumpido; *(disconnected from phone)* se cortó (la comunicación)
▸ **cut out** *vt sep (oust)* **to cut sb out of a deal** excluir a alguien de un trato

cutback *n (in production, budget)* reducción *f*, recorte *m*

cut-price, *US* **cut-rate** *adj (goods)* rebajado(a)

cut-throat *adj (competition)* salvaje, sin escrúpulos

cutting edge *n* **to be at the cutting edge of technology** estar a la vanguardia de la tecnología

CV *n Br (abbr* **curriculum vitae***)* CV *m*, currículum *m*

CVP *n (abbr* **cost-volume profit***)* CVB *m*

CVR *n* FIN *(abbr* **contingent value right***)* derecho *m* al valor de rescate

cwo *(abbr* **cash with order***)* pago *m* con el pedido

CWU *n (abbr* **Communication Workers Union***)* = sindicato británico de trabajadores de telecomunicaciones

cyber- *pref* COMPTR ciber-

cyberbanking *n* COMPTR banca *f* electrónica

cybernaut *n* COMPTR cibernauta *mf*

cyberspace *n* COMPTR ciberespacio *m*; **in cyberspace** en el ciberespacio

cybersquatting *n* COMPTR ocupación *f* ilegal de dominios, *Esp* ciberokupación *f*

> **❝**
>
> Mohamed Al Fayed has been given something to cheer about after winning a landmark **cybersquatting** case. A US district court judge has ruled that Mr Al Fayed's famous London department store, Harrods, can now take possession of 60 Harrods-related internet addresses that were registered in "bad faith".
>
> **❞**

cycle *n (in economy, trade)* ciclo *m*

cyclical 1 *n* **cyclicals** valores *mpl* cíclicos, acciones *fpl* cíclicas
2 *adj* ST EXCH **cyclical stocks** valores *mpl* cíclicos, acciones *fpl* cíclicas; **cyclical unemployment** desempleo *m or Esp* paro *m* cíclico; **cyclical variations** variaciones *fpl* cíclicas

Dd

D/A *npl* (*abbr* **documents against acceptance**) documentos *mpl* contra aceptación

DAB *n* (*abbr* **digital audio broadcasting**) radiodifusión *f* digital

dabble *vi* **to dabble on the Stock Exchange** jugar a la Bolsa

DAF (*abbr* **delivered at frontier**) DAF

daily *adj* diario(a) ❏ **daily allowance** dietas *fpl*, *Am* viáticos *mpl*; ACCT **daily balance interest calculation** cálculo *m* de intereses sobre saldos diarios; ST EXCH **Daily Official List** = boletín de la Bolsa de Londres; **daily takings** ingresos *mpl* diarios; ST EXCH **daily trading report** informe *m* diario del mercado

> **"**
> Ordinary Shares will be acquired under the tender offer at a common price that will be set within a specified tender price range. The bottom of the tender price range, which is the lowest price at which tenders will be accepted, will be the average middle market quotation of Ordinary Shares as derived from the **Daily Official List**.
> **"**

daisy-wheel *n* margarita *f* ❏ **daisy-wheel printer** impresora *f* de margarita

damage 1 *n* (**a**) (*to goods, ship, cargo*) daños *mpl*; **the insurance will pay for the damage** el seguro se hará cargo de *or* pagará los daños ❏ INS **damage certificate** certificado *m* de averías *or* daños; **damage claim** reclamación *f or SAm* reclamo *m* por daños; **damage report** informe *m* de daños; **damage survey** valoración *f* de daños (**b**) LAW **damages** daños *mpl* y perjuicios; **to award damages to sb for sth** conceder a alguien una indemnización por daños y perjuicios por algo; **to be awarded damages** recibir una indemnización por daños y perjuicios; **to sue sb for damages** presentar una demanda por daños y perjuicios contra alguien; **to be liable for damages** ser responsable de los daños; **to claim £1,000 damages** reclamar una indemnización de 1.000 libras por daños y perjuicios (**c**) **damage limitation** limitación *f* de daños; **the sale of the subsidiary is an exercise in damage limitation** la venta de la filial es una acción para minimizar los daños

2 *vt* (*goods*) dañar

damaged *adj* (*goods*) dañado(a); **damaged in transit** dañado(a) durante el transporte

▶ **damp down** *vt sep* (*market*) enfriar; (*consumption*) moderar

danger money *n* prima *f or* plus *m* de peligrosidad

dash *n* (*symbol*) signo *m* menos; TYP **em-dash** raya *f*; TYP **en-dash** signo *m* menos

DAT *n* COMPTR (*abbr* **digital audio tape**) DAT *f*, cinta *f* digital de audio ❏ **DAT cartridge** cartucho *m* DAT; **DAT drive** unidad *f* DAT

data *n* datos *mpl*, información *f*; COMPTR datos *mpl*; **an item of data** un dato; **to collect data on sb/sth** reunir información sobre alguien/algo ❏ **data acquisition** recogida *f* de datos; **data analysis** análisis *m inv* de datos; **data bank** banco *m* de datos; **data bus** bus *m* de datos; **data capture** captura *f or Esp* recogida *f* de datos; **data carrier** portadora *f* de datos; **data collection** recogida *f* de datos; **data communications** transmisión *f* (electrónica) de datos; **data compression** compresión *f* de datos; **data decryption** desencriptado *m or* desencriptación *m* de datos; **data encryption** encriptación *f* de datos; **data entry** proceso *m or* entrada *f* de datos; COMPTR **data entry form** formulario *m* de datos; **data exchange** intercambio *m* de datos; **data export** exportación *f* de datos; **data import** importación *f* de datos; **data input** entrada *f* de datos; **data link** enlace *m* para transmisión de datos; **data loss** pérdida *f* de datos; **data management** gestión *f* de datos; **data manipulation** manipulación *f* de datos; **data memory** memoria *f* de datos; **data mining** minería *f or* extracción *f* de datos; **data network** red *f* de datos; **data organization** organización *f* de datos; **data path** ruta *f* de acceso a los datos; **data privacy** confidencialidad *f* de los datos; **data processing** proceso *m or* procesamiento *m* de datos; **data processing centre** centro *m* de proceso *or* procesamiento de datos; **data processing manager** gerente *mf* de procesamiento de datos; **data processing system** sistema *m* de procesamiento de datos; **data processor** (*machine*) procesador *m* de datos; (*person*) procesador(ora) *m,f* de datos; **data protection** protección *f* de datos; *Br* **Data Protection Act** = ley de protección de datos; **data recovery** recuperación *f* de datos; **data retrieval** recuperación *f* de datos; **data security** seguridad *f* de los datos; **data set** conjunto *m* de datos; **data sharing** compartimiento *m* de datos; **data source** fuente f de datos; **data storage** almacenamiento m de datos; **data throughput speed** velocidad f de transmisión de datos; **data transfer** transferencia f de datos

database n COMPTR base f de datos; **to enter sth into a database** introducir algo en una base de datos ❑ **database management** gestión f de bases de datos; **database management system** sistema m de gestión de bases de datos

datacomms n COMPTR transmisión f de datos ❑ **datacomms network** red f de transmisión de datos; **datacomms software** software m de transmisión de datos

date 1 n (**a**) (day) fecha f; **date as postmark** fecha del matasellos ❑ **date of birth** fecha f de nacimiento; **date of delivery** fecha f de entrega; **date of invoice** fecha f de la factura; **date of issue** fecha f de emisión; **date of receipt** fecha f de recepción; **date of signature** fecha f de la firma; **date stamp** sello m con la fecha
(**b**) **up to date** (method, approach) moderno(a); (news, information) reciente, actualizado(a); (well-informed) al día (**on** en); **I'm up to date with my work** estoy al día con mi trabajo; **to bring/keep sb up to date (on sth)** poner a alguien al día or al corriente (de algo); **to bring/keep sth up to date** poner/mantener algo al día
(**c**) **to date** hasta la fecha; **interest to date** interés m hasta la fecha
(**d**) **out of date** (passport, cheque) caducado(a)
(**e**) FIN (of bill) fecha f de vencimiento; **three months after date, at three months' date** tres meses a partir de la fecha ❑ **date of maturity** fecha f de vencimiento
2 vt (letter, cheque) fechar; **the cheque is dated 24 March** el cheque tiene fecha del 24 de marzo

datebook n US agenda f

daughter company n empresa f filial or subsidiaria

dawn n ST EXCH **dawn raid** = compra masiva de acciones al comienzo de la sesión; **dawn raider** = operador que realiza una compra masiva de acciones al comienzo de la sesión

Dax n ST EXCH **the Dax (index)** el (índice) Dax

day n día m; (working hours) jornada f; **to have/take a day off** tener/tomarse un día libre; **to work an eight-hour day** trabajar una jornada de ocho horas; **to be paid by the day** cobrar

por día trabajado; **we can give you four days' grace** le podemos dar cuatro días de periodo de gracia ❑ **day of action** día m de huelga; **day of grace** día f de gracia; **days of grace** periodo m de gracia; **day labour** trabajo m a jornal; **day labourer** jornalero(a) m,f; **day off** día m libre; ST EXCH **day order** orden f de compra de un día; **day release** = sistema que permite a un trabajador realizar cursos de formación continua un día a la semana; **to be on day release** asistir a un curso de formación continua; **day shift** (in factory) turno m de día; **to be on day shift, to work the day shift** trabajar de día, trabajar en el turno de día; ST EXCH **day trade** operación f en el mismo día; ST EXCH **day trader** especulador(ora) m,f a corto plazo; **day work** trabajo m diurno

day-after recall n MKTG impacto m del día siguiente ❑ **day-after recall test** test m del impacto del día siguiente

daybook n ACCT libro m diario

dayside n US personal m de día

day-to-day adj diario(a), cotidiano(a); **he is responsible for the day-to-day running of the business** es responsable de la gestión diaria del negocio; **we can barely afford the day-to-day expenses** casi no podemos permitirnos los gastos diarios or ordinarios

DBA n (abbr **Doctor of Business Administration**) (person) doctor(ora) m,f en Administración de Empresas; (qualification) doctorado m en Administración de Empresas

dbase n COMPTR (abbr **database**) base f de datos

DBMS n (abbr **database management system**) sistema m de gestión de bases de datos

DCF n ACCT (abbr **discounted cash flow**) flujo m de caja descontado

D/D n (abbr **direct debit**) domiciliación f bancaria or de pago, Am débito m bancario, Bol, RP débito directo

DDP (abbr **delivered duty paid**) DDP

DDU (abbr **delivered duty unpaid**) DDU

dead adj FIN **dead account** cuenta f inactiva; Fam ST EXCH **dead cat bounce** recuperación f temporal; **dead freight** flete m falso; **dead letter** (undelivered letter) = carta que no se puede repartir ni devolver; (law) letra f muerta; INS **dead loss** siniestro m total; **dead market** mercado m muerto; **dead money** capital m improductivo or ocioso; **dead period** periodo m muerto; **dead season** temporada f baja; **dead weight** peso m muerto

unsustainable. They have been **dead cat bounces** – some of the recent examples have been dropped from quite a height. **"**

deadline n (day) fecha f límite; (time) plazo m; **to meet/miss a deadline** cumplir/no cumplir un plazo; **to work to a deadline** trabajar con un plazo; **deadline for payment** fecha límite de pago

deadlock 1 n punto m muerto; **to reach a dead-lock** llegar a un punto muerto; **talks with the union were in deadlock** las conversaciones con el sindicato habían llegado a un punto muerto; **they have succeeded in breaking the deadlock** han conseguido salir del punto muerto
2 vt **to be deadlocked** (talks, negotiations) estar en un punto muerto

deadweight n peso m muerto ◻ **deadweight cargo** cargamento m pesado

deal 1 n (agreement) acuerdo m; (in business) trato m; (on Stock Exchange) operación f; **to do** or **make a deal (with sb)** hacer un trato (con alguien); **to negotiate a deal** negociar un acuerdo; **to call off a deal** suspender un acuerdo; **it's a deal!** ¡trato hecho!
2 vi (do business) comerciar; **our firm has been dealing for over 50 years** nuestra empresa lleva 50 años en el negocio; **to deal in leather** dedicarse al negocio de la piel; **to deal on the Stock Exchange** operar en el mercado de valores; FIN, ST EXCH **to deal in options** dedicarse a la compraventa de opciones
▸ **deal with** vt insep (a) (do business with) hacer negocios con (b) (get supplies from) trabajar con (c) (handle) (problem, query, order, complaint) ocuparse de

dealer n (trader) comerciante mf; (in cars) concesionario m; (on Stock Exchange) operador(ora) m,f, agente mf de bolsa; (in foreign exchange) cambista mf, agente de cambio

dealership n (a) (showroom) concesionario m (b) (franchise) concesión f

dealing n (a) ST EXCH contratación f ◻ **dealing room** sala f de cambios (b) (trading) negocio m; **dealings** tratos mpl; **to have dealings with sb** estar en tratos con alguien

dealmaker n (person) intermediario(a) m,f comercial

dealmaking n intermediación f comercial

dear adj (a) (expensive) caro(a) **dear money** dinero caro (b) (in letter) **Dear Sir** Muy Sr. mío; **Dear Sirs** Muy Sres. míos; **Dear Madam** Muy Sra. mía; **Dear Sir or Madam** Muy Sres. míos; **Dear Mr Martin** Estimado Sr. Martin; **Dear Ms Carrington** Estimada Sra. Carrington

death n muerte f; **death in service (benefit)** indemnización f por fallecimiento del trabajador

◻ INS **death benefit** indemnización f por fallecimiento; Br **death duties** impuesto m de sucesiones; US **death tax** impuesto m de sucesiones

debenture n FIN obligación f ◻ **debenture bond** obligación f hipotecaria; **debenture holder** obligacionista mf; **debenture issue** emisión f de obligaciones; **debenture loan** empréstito m de obligaciones; **debenture register** registro m de obligacionistas; **debenture stock** obligaciones fpl

debit 1 n cargo m, adeudo m; ACCT **debit and credit** debe m y haber; **your account is in debit** el saldo de su cuenta es negativo ◻ **debit account** cuenta f deudora; **debit advice** nota f de adeudo or de cargo; **debit balance** saldo m deudor; **debit card** tarjeta f de débito; ACCT **debit column** columna f del debe; **debit entry** asiento m de adeudo or de cargo; **debit interest** interés m deudor; ACCT **debit item** asiento m de adeudo or de cargo; **debit note** nota f de adeudo or de cargo; **debit side** (columna f del) debe m
2 vt (account, person) adeudar, debitar; **to debit sb's account with $200, to debit $200 to sb's account** adeudar or debitar 200 dólares de la cuenta de alguien; **has this cheque been debited to my account?** ¿ha sido adeudado or debitado ya este cheque de mi cuenta?

debriefing n interrogatorio m

debt n deuda f; **to be in debt** estar endeudado(a); **to be £12,000 in debt** tener una deuda de 12.000 libras; **to be in debt to sb** estar endeudado(a) con alguien; **to pay off a debt** saldar una deuda; **to be out of debt** no tener deudas; **to get** or **run into debt** endeudarse; **to reschedule** or **restructure a debt** reestructurar una deuda; **debt owed by us** deuda pasiva; **debt owed to us** deuda activa **to be up to the neck** or **one's ears in debt** estar endeudado(a) hasta las cejas ◻ **debt burden** peso m or carga f de la deuda; **debt capacity** capacidad f de endeudamiento; **debt collection** cobro m de deudas; **debt collection agency** agencia f de cobro de deudas; **debt collector** cobrador(ora) m,f de deudas or de morosos; **debt due** deuda f vencida; **debt equity swap** capitalización f de la deuda, conversión f de la deuda en capital; **debt financing** financiación f de la deuda; **debt of honour** deuda f de honor; **debt instrument** instrumento m de deuda; **debt limit** límite m de endeudamiento; **debt rating** calificación f de la deuda; **debt ratio** tasa f or ratio m or f de endeudamiento; **debt reduction programme** programa m de reducción de la deuda; **debt rescheduling, debt restructuring** reestructuración f de la deuda; **debt relief** alivio m (de la carga) de la deuda; Br **debt service** servicio m de la deuda; US **debt servicing** servicio m de la deuda; **debt swap** intercambio m or swap m de deuda

debt-equity ratio *n* coeficiente *m* de endeudamiento

debtor *n* deudor(ora) *m,f* ❑ ACCT **debtor account** cuenta *f* deudora; ECON **debtor country** país *m* deudor *or* endeudado; ECON **debtor nation** nación *f* deudora *or* endeudada; **debtor in possession** deudor(ora) *m,f* en posesión; **debtor side** *(of account)* debe *m*; **debtors' turnover** periodo *m* medio de cobro

> **"**
> Now, of course, the United States is in no position to repeat its midcentury largesse. America has become a **debtor nation** and provides stimulus to the global economy by going deeper into debt as it buys goods from others. And the United States, like other debtors, is beginning to express its enmity toward those from whom it borrows to buy.
> **"**

debug *vt* COMPTR *(program)* depurar, eliminar errores en

debugger *n* COMPTR *(program)* depurador *m*

debugging *n* COMPTR *(of program)* depuración *f*, eliminación *f* de errores

decasualization *n* **the decasualization of labour** la eliminación de la precariedad en el empleo

decasualize *vt (workers)* dar contratos permanentes a; *(labour)* eliminar la precariedad en

decentralization *n* descentralización *f*

decentralize *vt* descentralizar

decision *n* decisión *f*; **to make a decision** tomar una decisión ❑ **decision model** modelo *m* de decisiones; **decision table** tabla *f* de decisión; **decision theory** teoría *f* de las decisiones; **decision tree** árbol *m* de decisión

decision-maker *n (politician)* responsable *m* político; *(manager)* responsable *m* de tomar decisiones; **to be a good/bad decision-maker** ser bueno(a)/malo(a) a la hora de tomar decisiones

decision-making *n* toma *f* de decisiones; **this job calls for a lot of decision-making** en este trabajo hay que tomar muchas decisiones ❑ **decision-making model** modelo *m* de toma de decisiones; **decision-making power** poder *m* para *or* de tomar decisiones, facultad *f* de decisión; **the decision-making process** el proceso de toma de decisiones; **decision-making tool** herramienta *f* para la toma de decisiones; **decision-making unit** unidad *f* con capacidad de decisión

> **"**
> But women's international economic and political power is still minimal and much too limited to make the fundamental economic

changes, especially in accounting and reward systems, to recognize women's real economic contributions and thus give women the **decision-making** power they have earned and deserve.
> **"**

decision-tree model *n* modelo *m* del árbol de decisiones

declaration *n* declaración *f* ❑ **declaration of bankruptcy** declaración *f* de quiebra; **declaration of dividend** declaración *f* de dividendos; **declaration of income** declaración *f* de la renta; **declaration of intent** declaración *f* de intenciones; **declaration inwards** declaración *f* de entrada; ST EXCH **declaration of options** declaración *f* de opciones; **declaration outwards** declaración *f* de salida; **declaration of solvency** declaración *f* de solvencia; **declaration of value** *(for customs)* declaración *f* del valor

declare *vt* (**a**) CUSTOMS *(goods)* declarar ❑ **declared value** valor *m* declarado (**b**) *(announce)* **to declare sb bankrupt** declarar a alguien en quiebra; FIN **to declare a dividend of 10%** fijar un dividendo del 10%; ST EXCH **to declare an option** ejecutar una opción

decline 1 *n (decrease)* descenso *m*; *(deterioration)* declive *m*; **to be on the decline** *(industry)* estar en declive ❑ MKTG **decline stage** *(of product)* fase *f* de decadencia
  2 *vi* (**a**) *(decrease)* disminuir; *(industry)* estar en declive; *(demand, production, profits, sales)* descender (**b**) *(refuse)* rehusar

declining *adj (sales, profits)* decreciente; *(industry)* en declive, en decadencia ❑ ACCT **declining balance depreciation** depreciación *f* por saldos decrecientes; ACCT **declining balance method** método *m* de amortización de saldos decrecientes

decode *vt* COMPTR descodificar, descifrar; **the file is automatically decoded when it is received** el archivo se descodifica automáticamente al recibirse

decoder *n* COMPTR descodificador *m*

decoding *n* COMPTR descodificación *f*

decompress *vt* COMPTR *(file)* descomprimir

decontrol 1 *n (of prices)* liberalización *f*
  2 *vt (trade, prices, wages)* liberalizar

> **"**
> She favours the Tobin tax, taxing foreign exchange speculation, but only if it can be made to be practical and thinks that countries have to be careful how to **decontrol** their banks and foreign exchange markets. Governments may have to step in to stop capital stampeding out of a country in panic with capital controls.
> **"**

decrease 1 *n* disminución *f*; **sales are on the**

decrease las ventas están disminuyendo *or* decreciendo
   2 *vi* disminuir

decreasing *adj* decreciente □ ACCT **decreasing rate** ritmo *m* decreciente

decrypt *vt* COMPTR desencriptar

decryption *n* COMPTR desencriptado *m*, desencriptación *m*

DECT *n* TEL (*abbr* **digital enhanced cordless telecommunications**) DECT *m*

dedicated *adj* (*assigned for particular purpose*) dedicado(a) □ TEL **dedicated line** línea *f* dedicada; **dedicated word processor** procesador *m* de textos

deduct *vt* (*take off*) descontar, deducir; (*tax*) deducir; **to deduct £10 from the price** descontar 10 libras del precio; **to be deducted at source** (*tax*) deducirse en origen; **after deducting expenses** después de descontar los gastos

deductible 1 *n* US INS franquicia *f*
   2 *adj* deducible; **deductible for tax purposes** desgravable

deduction *n* (*removal*) deducción *f* (**from** de); (*from salary*) retención *f*; **after deduction of taxes** descontados los impuestos; **deduction (of income tax) at source** retención en origen del impuesto de la renta; **after deductions, I'm left with a salary of £20,000** descontadas las retenciones, me queda un sueldo de 20.000 libras

deed *n* LAW escritura *f*, título *m* de propiedad; **to draw up a deed** redactar una escritura □ **deed of arrangement** concordato *m*; **deed of assignment** escritura *f* de cesión; **deed of covenant** = escritura que formaliza el pago de una donación periódica a una entidad, generalmente benéfica, o a un individuo; **deed of partnership** escritura *f* de constitución de una sociedad colectiva; **deed of sale** escritura *f* de compraventa; **deed of title** escritura *f* or título *m* de propiedad; **deed of transfer** escritura *f* de traspaso

> ❝
> And at work, are there any expenses you could set against tax such as training fees to professional bodies or travelling costs? Are your donations to charities benefiting from tax relief via the Gift Aid scheme or **deeds of covenant**?
> ❞

deep discount *n* descuento *m* elevado

deep-discount bond *n* bono *m* de descuento elevado

de facto *adj* & *adv* de hecho; **de facto possession** posesión de hecho; **de facto and de jure** de facto y de jure, de hecho y de derecho

defalcation *n* desfalco *m*

default 1 *n* (**a**) LAW (*failure to appear in court*) incomparecencia *f* (**b**) FIN **to be in default of payment** estar en mora □ **default interest** interés *m* moratorio *or* de mora (**c**) COMPTR **default drive** unidad *f* (de disco) predeterminada *or* por defecto *or* por omisión; **default font** fuente *f* predeterminada *or* por defecto *or* por omisión; **default settings** valores *mpl* predeterminados *or* por defecto *or* por omisión, configuración *f* predeterminada *or* por defecto *or* por omisión
   2 *vi* (**a**) LAW (*fail to appear in court*) no comparecer (**b**) FIN incumplir un pago; **to default on a payment** incumplir un pago (**c**) COMPTR **to default to sth** seleccionar algo por defecto *or* por omisión

> ❝
> Jenkins told Newsbytes that ZipLink had a total of 99 employees before warning earlier this month that its cash reserves would allow it to operate only until Nov. 17 unless more funds were found. The company said today that, in addition to failing in its bid to raise new cash, it also faced a **default** on payments by its second-largest customer, the free-ISP marketing company Spinway Inc.
> ❞

defaulter *n* moroso(a) *m,f*

defaulting *adj* FIN moroso(a), incumplidor(ora) □ **defaulting party** parte *f* morosa *or* incumplidora

defeasance *n* LAW anulación *f*

defect *n* defecto *m*

defective *adj* defectuoso(a)

defend *vt* defender; **the company must defend its share of the market** la empresa tiene que defender su cuota de mercado; **they are defending themselves against the takeover bid** se están defendiendo contra la OPA

defensive *adj* ST EXCH **defensive stocks** valores *mpl* defensivos; **defensive tactics** táctica *f* defensiva

defer *vt* (*decision, meeting, judgement*) aplazar; (*payment*) diferir, aplazar

deferment, deferral *n* (*of decision, meeting, payment, judgement*) aplazamiento *m*

deferred *adj* diferido(a) □ **deferred annuity** anualidad *f* diferida; **deferred assets** activo *m* diferido; **deferred charges** gastos *mpl* diferidos *or* amortizables; **deferred credit** crédito *m* diferido; **deferred debit** débito *m* diferido; **deferred income** ingresos *mpl* diferidos; **deferred liabilities** pasivo *m* diferido, pasivo exigible a largo plazo; **deferred ordinary share** acción *f* diferida; **deferred pay** (*of employee*) salario *m* diferido; **deferred payment** pago *m* diferido *or* aplazado; **deferred rebate** reembolso *m* diferido; **deferred results** resultados *mpl* diferidos; **deferred share** acción *f* diferida; **deferred taxation** impuestos *mpl* diferidos

deficit *n* FIN déficit *m*; **to be in deficit** tener déficit; **the balance of payments shows a deficit of £800 million** la balanza de pagos arroja un déficit de 800 millones de libras □ **deficit spending** gasto *m* financiado mediante déficit

defined *adj* **defined contribution** aportación *f* definida; **defined benefits** prestación *f* definida

definite *adj (order, price)* definitivo(a)

deflate FIN, ECON *vt (prices)* deflactar; **to deflate the economy** producir una deflación en la economía

deflation *n* FIN, ECON deflación *f*

deflationary *adj* FIN, ECON *(measures, policy)* deflacionario(a), deflacionista □ **deflationary gap** brecha *f* deflacionaria

deflator *n* FIN, ECON deflactor *m*

defragmentation *n* COMPTR desfragmentación *f*

defraud *vt (the State)* defraudar; *(company, person)* estafar; **he defrauded the government of £15,000 in unemployment benefit** defraudó al gobierno 15.000 libras a través del subsidio de desempleo

defray *vt* **to defray sb's expenses** sufragar *or* costear los gastos de alguien; **to defray the cost of sth** sufragar el costo *or* Esp coste de algo; **all charges to be defrayed by the purchaser** todos los gastos corren a cargo del comprador

defunct *adj (company, industry)* desaparecido(a)

defund *vt* dejar de financiar

degearing *n* desapalancamiento *m* financiero

degressive *adj* degresivo(a) □ **degressive tax** impuesto *m* degresivo, = modalidad de impuesto sobre la renta de tarifa única aplicable a ingresos que superan un mínimo exento

dehire *vt* US *(dismiss)* dejar de emplear a

deindex *vt* FIN desindexar

deindexation *n* FIN desindexación *f*

deindustrialization *n* desindustrialización *f*

deindustrialize *vt* desindustrializar

deinstall *vt* COMPTR desinstalar

deinstallation *n* COMPTR desinstalación *f*

deinstaller *n* COMPTR desinstalador *m*

de jure *adj & adv* LAW de jure, de derecho

delay 1 *n* retraso *m*, demora *f*; **we apologize for the delay in dealing with your letter** pedimos disculpas por el retraso *or* la demora en atender su carta; **there will be a 20-minute delay before the meeting** la reunión comenzará con un retraso de 20 minutos; **all flights are subject to delay** todos los vuelos pueden llevar retraso *or esp Am* demora
2 *vt (project, decision)* retrasar; **to be delayed** *(flight, train)* llevar retraso *or esp Am* demora

delayering *n* desjerarquización *f*, recorte *f* de cuadros (inter)medios; **middle management has been cut back through delayering** se ha producido un recorte de cuadros medios

del credere *n* riesgo *m* de impago □ **del credere agent** agente *mf* de garantía; **del credere clause** cláusula *f* de garantía; **del credere commission** comisión *f* de garantía

delegate 1 *n* delegado(a) *m,f*
2 *vt* delegar; **to delegate sb to do sth** delegar en alguien para hacer algo; **he must learn to delegate more work to his team** tiene que aprender a delegar más trabajo en su equipo

delegation *n* (a) *(of person, powers)* delegación *f* (b) *(group of delegates)* delegación *f*; **to send a delegation** enviar una delegación

delete 1 *n* COMPTR suprimir *m* □ **delete command** comando *m* suprimir; **delete key** tecla *f* de suprimir
2 *vt* (a) COMPTR borrar, suprimir (b) *(cross out)* tachar; **delete where applicable, delete as appropriate** *(on form)* táchese lo que no corresponda (c) *(from stock, catalogue)* retirar
3 *vi* COMPTR borrar, suprimir

deleveraging *n* desapalancamiento *m* financiero

delinquency *n* FIN morosidad *f*, impago *m*

delinquent FIN **1** *n* moroso(a) *m,f*
2 *adj (person, loan, debt)* moroso(a)

delist *vt* (a) ST EXCH suspender la cotización de (b) MKTG *(product)* descatalogar

delisting *n* (a) ST EXCH suspensión *f* de la cotización (b) MKTG *(of product)* descatalogación *f*

deliver 1 *vt* (a) *(hand over) (letter, parcel, goods)* entregar (**to** a); *(leaflets, junk mail)* repartir; **you can have the furniture delivered for a £25 charge** por 25 libras le entregamos los muebles; **delivered free** con entrega gratuita; **delivered free on board** franco a bordo; **delivered to domicile** entregado(a) a domicilio; **delivered at frontier** entrega *f* en frontera (b) *(provide) (service)* prestar; FIN **to deliver a profit** producir beneficios; FIN **to deliver shares** entregar acciones
2 *vi (supplier)* repartir; **we deliver the next day** entregamos el pedido en 24 horas

delivered weight *n* peso *m* entregado

deliverer *n* *(of order)* empresa *f* de entregas *or* reparto; *(of leaflets, junk mail)* repartidor(ora) *m,f*

delivery *n* *(of letter, parcel, goods)* entrega *f*; *(of leaflets, junk mail)* reparto *m*; *(consignment)* envío *m*; **to accept** *or* **take delivery of sth** recibir algo; **awaiting delivery** pendiente de entrega; **for immediate delivery** para entrega inmediata; **to pay on delivery** pagar en el momento de la entrega; **free delivery** entrega gratuita; **next day delivery** entrega al día siguiente ▫ *delivery address* dirección *f* de entrega; *delivery charges* gastos *mpl* de envío *or* transporte; *delivery date* fecha *f* de entrega; ST EXCH *delivery month* mes *m* de entrega; *delivery note* nota *f* de entrega, *Esp* albarán *m*; *delivery order* orden *f* de entrega; *delivery point* punto *m* de entrega; *delivery schedule* calendario *m* de entrega; *delivery service* servicio *m* de entrega; *delivery time* tiempo *m* de entrega; *delivery van* furgoneta *f* de reparto

del key *n* COMPTR tecla *f* de suprimir

de-man *vt* reducir la plantilla de, recortar personal en

demand *n* (**a**) *(request)* exigencia *f*; *(for pay rise)* reivindicación *f or* demanda *f* salarial; **payable on demand** exigible a la vista, pagadero(a) a su presentación; **there have been demands for the manager's resignation** han exigido *or* pedido la dimisión del director ▫ FIN *demand bill* letra *f* a la vista; *US demand deposit* depósito *m* a la vista, depósito disponible; *US demand deposit account* cuenta *f* corriente; FIN *demand draft* giro *m* a la vista; FIN *demand note* pagaré *m* a la vista
(**b**) ECON demanda *f* (**for** de); **supply and demand** la oferta y la demanda; **to be in great demand** estar muy solicitado(a), tener mucha demanda; **there isn't much demand for that model** ese modelo no tiene mucha demanda ▫ *demand analysis* análisis *m inv* de la demanda; *demand assessment* evaluación *f* de la demanda; *demand curve* curva *f* de demanda; *demand equation* ecuación *f* de (la) demanda; *demand factor* factor *m* de demanda; *demand forecasting* previsión *f* de la demanda; *demand function* función *f* de la demanda; *demand management* gestión *f* de la demanda

demand-led *adj* ECON arrastrado(a) por la demanda

demand-pull inflation *n* ECON inflación *f* de demanda

demand-side economics *n* política *f* (económica) de actuación sobre la demanda

de-manning *n* reducción *f* de plantilla, recorte *m* de personal

demarcation *n* delimitación *f* de atribuciones; **a clear demarcation of responsibilities is essential in any organization** es fundamental que cualquier organización tenga una clara delimitación de atribuciones ▫ *demarcation dispute* = enfrentamiento entre los grupos sindicales y la patronal sobre la delimitación de las tareas que sus miembros deben realizar en el trabajo

demarket *vt* reducir la demanda de

demarketing *n* reducción *f* de la demanda

dematerialization *n* FIN desmaterialización *f*

dematerialize *vt* FIN desmaterializar

demerge *vt* separar, disolver

demerger *n* separación *f*, disolución *f*; **several new companies were formed after the demerger of the holding group** varias empresas surgieron de la separación *or* disolución del holding

❝
One market minnow is braving the tight IPO climate. In a little-noticed announcement last week, Hay & Robertson, the firm that owns the Admiral and Mountain brands, and markets trendy Kangol gear, is to embark on a three-way **demerger** designed to restore shareholder value.
❞

demo *n* (*abbr* **demonstration**) demo *f*; **we have received a demo of the new software** hemos recibido una demo *or* una versión de demostración del nuevo software ▫ COMPTR *demo disk* disco *m* de demostración

demographic **1** *n* *(segment)* grupo *m* demográfico
2 *adj* demográfico(a) ▫ *demographic analysis* análisis *m inv* demográfico; *demographic data* datos *mpl* demográficos; *demographic profile* perfil *m* demográfico; *demographic segment* segmento *m* demográfico; *demographic segmentation* segmentación *f* demográfica

demographics *npl* *(demographic data)* datos *mpl* demográficos, estadísticas *fpl* demográficas

❝
The French, Germans and Italians largely rely on their generous state pension schemes. The British have sensibly moved much faster into private or company schemes; but the **demographics** still mean a pensions crunch everywhere in the developed world.
❞

demography *n* demografía *f*

demonetarization = demonetization

demonetarize = demonetize

demonetization *n* FIN *(of currency)* desmonetización *f*

demonetize *vt* FIN *(currency)* desmonetizar

demonstrate *vt* *(system, equipment)* hacer una demostración de; **he demonstrated how the new system worked** nos hizo una demostración de cómo funciona el nuevo sistema

demonstration *n* *(of system, equipment, product)* demostración *f*; **they gave us a demonstration**

of the new model nos hicieron una demostración del nuevo modelo ❑ **demonstration model** modelo *m* de muestra

demote *vt* degradar, relegar; **he was demoted from area manager to sales representative** fue degradado *or* relegado de gerente de área a comercial

demotion *n* degradación *f*

demotivate *vt* desmotivar

demotivating *adj* desmotivador(ora); **the spate of redundancies has been very demotivating for the workforce** la oleada de despidos ha desmotivado mucho a los trabajadores

demurrage *n* sobrestadía *f*

demutualization *n Br* desmutualización *f*

demutualize *vi* desmutualizarse

> **"**
>
> However, if the lender is allowed to increase sales arbitrarily, it effectively has a blank cheque to draw on the borrower's money. … People who borrow from a building society which **demutualizes** are particularly vulnerable to this. Building societies, theoretically at least, act solely in their members' interests and have no interest in overcharging.
>
> **"**

denationalization *n* desnacionalización *f*

denationalize *vt* desnacionalizar

denominate *vt* FIN expresar, denominar; **denominated in dollars** expresado(a) *or* denominado(a) en dólares

denomination *n* FIN valor *m* (nominal); **coins of all denominations** monedas de todos los valores (nominales); **small/large denominations** valores (nominales) pequeños/grandes

department *n* (**a**) *(in company)* departamento *m*; *(in shop)* sección *f*; **the sales/personnel department** el departamento de ventas/personal; **the toy department** la sección de juguetería ❑ **department manager** *(in company)* director(ora) *m,f* de departamento; *(in shop)* encargado(a) *m,f* de sección; **department store** grandes almacenes *mpl*
(**b**) *(of government)* ministerio *m*, *Méx* secretaría *f* ❑ *US* **Department of Energy** Ministerio *m* de Energía; *US* **Department of the Interior** Ministerio *m* del Interior; *US* **Department of Justice** Ministerio *m* de Justicia; *US* **Department of Labor** Ministerio *m* de Trabajo; *US* **Department of State** Departamento *m* de Estado; *US* **Department of Trade** Ministerio *m* de Comercio; *Br* **Department of Trade and Industry** Ministerio *m* de Industria y Comercio; *Br* **Department of Work and Pensions** Ministerio *m* de Trabajo y Pensiones

departmental *adj* *(in company)* de departamento; *(in shop)* de sección; *(of government)* ministerial, *Méx* de secretaría ❑ **departmental manager** *(in company)* director(ora) *m,f* de departamento; *(in shop)* encargado(a) *m,f* de sección; **departmental meeting** reunión *f* de departamento

departure *n* *(of plane, train)* salida *f*; *(from place)* partida *f*; *(from tradition)* alejamiento *m*; *(from plan)* cambio *m*; **our departure was delayed for three hours** nuestra salida se retrasó tres horas; **the introduction of bonuses was a departure from standard company policy** la introducción de pluses supuso un cambio en la política de la compañía; ❑ **departure list** lista *f* de salidas; **departure lounge** *(in airport)* sala *f* de embarque; **departure time** hora *f* de salida

dependant *n* ADMIN, LAW **his/her dependants** las personas a su cargo; **do you have any dependants?** ¿tiene personas a su cargo?

deplete *vt* *(stocks)* reducir considerablemente; **unexpectedly high demand is depleting stocks** una demanda inesperadamente alta está haciendo que se agoten las existencias

depletion *n* *(of stocks)* agotamiento *m*

deposit *n* (**a**) BANKING depósito *m*, *Esp* ingreso *m*; **to make a deposit** hacer *or* realizar un depósito *or Esp* ingreso; **on deposit** en una cuenta de ahorros, en depósito ❑ *Br* **deposit account** cuenta *f* or depósito *m* a plazo fijo; **deposit bank** banco *m* de depósitos; **deposit book** libreta *f* de depósitos; **deposit receipt** resguardo *m* or comprobante *m* de depósito *or Esp* ingreso; **deposit slip** resguardo *m* or comprobante *m* de depósito *or Esp* ingreso
(**b**) *(down payment)* pago *m* inicial, *Esp* entrada *f*, *Am* cuota *f* inicial; *(against damage)* señal *f*, fianza *f*; **to pay** *or* **put down a deposit on sth** pagar la entrega inicial *or Esp* entrada (de algo); **he left £10 as a deposit** dejó 10 libras de fianza ❑ **deposit receipt** resguardo *m* or comprobante *m* de fianza
2 *vt* (**a**) *(money)* *(in bank account)* depositar, *Esp* ingresar (**b**) *(document)* *(with a bank, solicitor)* depositar (**with** con); FIN **to deposit sth as security** depositar algo como garantía; **you must deposit 10% of the value of the house** tienes que hacer una entrega inicial del 10% del valor de la casa, *Esp* tienes que dar una entrada equivalente al 10% del valor de la casa

depositary *n* depositario(a) *m,f*

deposition *vt* MKTG *(product)* quitar el posicionamiento de, desposicionar

depositor *n* BANKING depositante *mf*

depository *n* (**a**) *(warehouse)* depósito *m*, almacén *m* (**b**) *(for shares, bonds)* depositario(a) *m,f*

depot *n* depósito *m*, almacén *m*

depreciable *adj* (**a**) *US* FIN amortizable □ **depreciable base** base *f* de amortización (**b**) *(subject to depreciation)* depreciable

depreciate 1 *vt* (**a**) ACCT *(asset)* amortizar (**b**) *(currency)* devaluar
2 *vi (goods, property)* depreciarse; **the pound has depreciated against the euro** la libra se ha depreciado *or* devaluado con respecto al euro

depreciated *adj* (**a**) ACCT *(cost)* amortizado(a); (**b**) *(currency)* depreciado(a)

depreciation *n* (**a**) ACCT amortización *f* □ **depreciation accounting** contabilización *f* de la amortización; **depreciation charges** cuotas *fpl* de amortización; **depreciation period** período *m* de amortización; **depreciation provision** fondo *m* de amortización; **depreciation rate** tasa *f* de amortización; **depreciation schedule** plan *m* de amortización (**b**) *(of goods, property, currency)* depreciación *f*; *(of equipment)* pérdida *f* de valor; *(amount)* depreciación, minusvalía *f*

depressed *adj (market, trade, industry)* deprimido(a); *(prices, profits, wages)* reducido(a), disminuido(a); **this is one of the most depressed sectors of the economy** este es uno de los sectores más deprimidos de la economía; **the economy has been in a depressed state for nearly two years** la economía está pasando por una fase de recesión que dura ya casi dos años

> ❝
> What makes the difference in the UK is that people are more likely to get on their bikes from **depressed** areas to booming ones such as Cambridge than they are to seek work in Cologne. And if there are serious regional imbalances, the UK government has the power to spend proportionately more money on the needy regions – as it does in Northern Ireland.
> ❞

depression *n* depresión *f*; **the country's economy is in a state of depression** la economía del país está pasando por una fase de depresión

dept *n* (*abbr* **department**) dpto.

depth *n* MKTG *(of product)* impacto *m* □ **depth interview** entrevista *f* en profundidad, entrevista a fondo

> ❝
> The **depth interview** is a personal, face-to-face, qualitative interview lasting from 50 to 90 minutes. Usually, depth interviews are tape-recorded and transcribed. The **depth interview** is the most powerful and comprehensive of the various qualitative techniques.
> ❞

deputize 1 *vt* **to deputize sb (to do sth)** nombrar a alguien como sustituto (para hacer algo)
2 *vi* **to deputize for sb** suplir a alguien; **if you can't make the meeting, I'll deputize** si no pudieras acudir a la reunión, yo te supliré *or* yo iré en tu lugar

deputy *n (assistant)* asistente *mf*, lugarteniente *mf*; *(temporary replacement)* sustituto(a) *m,f*, suplente *mf*; **to act as deputy for sb** sustituir a alguien □ **deputy chairman** vicepresidente(a) *m,f*; **deputy director** director(ora) *m,f* adjunto(a); **deputy manager** director(ora) *m,f* adjunto(a); **deputy managing director** director(ora) *m,f* general adjunto(a)

DEQ (*abbr* **delivered ex quay**) DEQ

deregulate *vt* liberalizar, desregular

deregulation *n* liberalización *f*, desregulación *f*

derivative *n* ST EXCH derivado *m*, producto *m* financiero derivado; **to deal in derivatives** dedicarse a la compraventa de derivados □ **derivative market** mercado *m* de derivados

DES (*abbr* **delivered ex ship**) DES

descending *adj* COMPTR **descending order** orden *m* descendente; **descending sort** ordenación *f* descendente

description *n (of goods)* descripción *f*

deselect *vt* COMPTR deseleccionar

design 1 *n (composition)* diseño *m*; *(style)* modelo *m*; **our latest design** nuestro último modelo □ **design agency** agencia *f* de diseño; **design department** departamento *m* de diseño; **design engineer** ingeniero(a) *m,f* de diseño; **design engineering** ingeniería *f* de diseño; **design fault** defecto *m* de diseño; **design team** equipo *m* de diseño
2 *vt (plan)* diseñar; **they have designed a product to appeal to younger customers** han diseñado un producto con atractivo para los consumidores jóvenes; **this financial package is designed to meet the needs of small businesses** el paquete financiero está pensado para dar respuesta a las necesidades de la pequeña empresa

designate *vt* designar

designer *n* diseñador(ora) *m,f*

desire *n* MKTG *(of consumer for product)* deseo *m*

desk *n (in office)* mesa *f*, escritorio *m* □ **desk calculator** calculadora *f* de escritorio; **desk diary** agenda *f*; **desk job** trabajo *m* de oficina; MKTG **desk research** trabajo *m* de documentación; **desk tray** bandeja *f* de escritorio

deskill *vt* desprofesionalizar

> Software has already made it easy for managers to do their own admin, and artificial intelligence promises to take over tasks much further up the value chain, eventually replacing large numbers of managerial and professional jobs while **deskilling** many others.

deskilling *n* desprofesionalización *f*, = pérdida de la aportación humana en un trabajo como resultado de la introducción de una nueva tecnología

desktop *n* COMPTR *(screen area)* escritorio *m*; **you will find the icon on your desktop** el icono aparece en el escritorio □ **desktop calculator** calculadora *f* de escritorio; COMPTR **desktop computer** *Esp* ordenador *m or Am* computadora *f* de sobremesa; **desktop publishing** autoedición *f*; **desktop publishing operator** autoeditor(ora) *m,f*; **desktop publishing package** programa *m* de autoedición

despatch = **dispatch**

despatcher = **dispatcher**

despatching = **dispatching**

destination *n* (lugar *m* de) destino *m* □ COMPTR **destination disk** disco *m* de destino; COMPTR **destination drive** unidad *f* (de disco) de destino MKTG **destination purchase** compra *f* prevista

destock 1 *vt* reducir el inventario de
2 *vi* reducir el inventario

destocking *n* reducción *f* de inventario

detail 1 *n* detalle *m*; **details** *(information)* detalles *mpl*; *(name, address, phone number etc)* datos *mpl* (personales); **for further details please contact...** para obtener información más detallada, diríjase a...; **please send me details of your range of products** les ruego me envíen información detallada sobre su gama de productos; **let me take down your details** permítame que anote sus datos
2 *vt (enumerate, specify)* detallar

determine *vt (date, price)* fijar; *(conditions)* determinar

Deutschmark *n Formerly* marco *m* alemán

devaluation *n* ECON devaluación *f*

devalue *vt* ECON devaluar; **the franc has been devalued by 3%** han devaluado el franco un 3%

develop 1 *vt* (**a**) *(idea, method, product)* desarrollar; *(business, market)* ampliar, expandir; *(skills)* perfeccionar (**b**) ECON *(country, region)* desarrollar
2 *vi* (**a**) *(evolve)* desarrollarse; **we have developed into one of the leading companies in the field** nos hemos convertido en una de las principales compañías del sector (**b**) ECON *(country, region)* desarrollarse

developer *n (of land)* promotor(ora) *m,f* (inmobiliario(a))

developing country *n* país *m* en (vías de) desarrollo

development *n* (**a**) *(of idea, method, product)* desarrollo *m*; *(of business, market)* ampliación *f*, expansión *f*; *(of skills)* perfeccionamento *m*
(**b**) ECON *(of country, region)* desarrollo *m* □ **development agency** agencia *f* de cooperación; **development aid** ayuda *f* al desarrollo; *Br* **development area** = zona deprimida en la que el gobierno fomenta la creación de nuevas industrias; **development assistance** ayuda *f* al desarrollo; **development capital** capital *m* de desarrollo; **development company** *(for property)* promotor(ora) *m,f* inmobiliario; **development costs** costos *mpl or Esp* costes *mpl* de desarrollo; **development grant** subvención *f* al desarrollo; **development loan** crédito *m* al desarrollo; **development plan** plan *m* de desarrollo; **development potential** potencial *m* de desarrollo; **development programme** programa *m* para el desarrollo; **development site** solar *m* edificable; **development stage** *(of product)* fase *f* de desarrollo

device *n* COMPTR *(peripheral)* dispositivo *m*, periférico *m*

devolution *n* (**a**) *(of duty, responsibility)* delegación *f* (**b**) LAW *(of property, estate)* cesión *f*, traspaso *m* (**c**) *(in politics)* transferencia *f* de poder político, traspaso *m* de competencias

devolve *vi* (**a**) *(duty)* corresponder; *(power)* recaer (**on** *or* **upon** en); **the responsibility devolves on him** es su responsabilidad (**b**) LAW *(property, estate)* pasar (**on** *or* **upon** a); **the property devolves on** *or* **upon the son** el patrimonio pasa al hijo *or* recae en el hijo

DG *n* (**a**) ADMIN *(abbr* **Director General***)* director(ora) *m,f* general (**b**) EU *(abbr* **Directorate General***)* DG *f*, Dirección *f* General

diagnostic audit *n* auditoría *f* de diagnósticos

diagram *n* diagrama *m*; *(graph)* gráfico *m*

diagrammatic *adj* gráfico(a), esquemático(a)

dial 1 *n US* **dial code** prefijo *m* (telefónico); *US* **dial tone** tono *m*
2 *vt (number)* marcar, *Andes, RP* discar; *(operator, country)* llamar; **the number you have dialled has not been recognized** el número marcado no existe; **for more information, dial 825195** para más información llame al 825195
3 *vi* marcar, *Andes, RP* discar; **to dial direct** llamar directamente

dialling, *US* **dialing** *n Br* **dialling code** prefijo *m* (telefónico); *Br* **dialling tone** tono *m*

dialogue, *US* **dialog** *n* diálogo *m* □ COMPTR **dialogue box** cuadro *m* de diálogo; **dialogue mode**

modo *m* (de) diálogo *dialogue window* ventana *f* de diálogo

dial-up *n* COMPTR *dial-up access* acceso *m* telefónico *or* por línea conmutada; *dial-up account* cuenta *f* con acceso telefónico *or* por línea conmutada; *dial-up connection* conexión *f* por línea telefónica *or* conmutada; *dial-up line* línea *f* conmutada; *dial-up modem* módem *m* para línea telefónica *or* conmutada; *dial-up service* servicio *m* por línea telefónica *or* conmutada

diarize *vt* incluir en la agenda

diary *n* agenda *f*

Dictaphone® *n* dictáfono *m*

dictate 1 *vt* (**a**) *(letter)* dictar; **to dictate sth to sb** dictar algo a alguien (**b**) *(determine)* imponer; **market conditions are dictated by the economic situation** la situación económica impone las condiciones del mercado
2 *vi* (**a**) *(dictate text)* dictar (**b**) *(give orders)* **to dictate to sb** dar órdenes a alguien

dictating machine *n* dictáfono *m*

dictation *n* dictado *m*

differential 1 *n* diferencial *m*; **wage** *or* **pay differentials** diferenciales salariales
2 *adj* diferencial □ *differential duties* aranceles *mpl* diferenciales; *differential pricing* desdoblamiento *m* de precios; *differential rate* tarifa *f* diferencial; *differential tariff* arancel *m* diferencial

differentiated marketing *n* marketing *m* diferenciado

differentiation *n* diferenciación *f* □ *differentiation strategy* estrategia *f* de diferenciación

digicash *n* dinero *m* electrónico

digit *n* dígito *m*

digital *adj* COMPTR digital □ *digital analog(ue) converter* convertidor *m* analógico digital; *digital audio tape* cinta *f* digital (de audio); *digital data* datos *mpl* digitales; *digital display* monitor *m* digital; *digital exchange* centralita *f* digital; *digital optical disk* disco *m* óptico digital; *digital readout* pantalla *f* digital; *digital signal* señal *f* digital; *digital signature* firma *f* electrónica; *digital versatile disk* disco *m* versátil digital; *digital video disk* disco *m* de *Esp* vídeo *or* *Am* video digital

> ❝
> E-commerce transactions are encrypted, but it is hard to verify that buyers and merchants are who they say they are. That is why Visa is urging a swifter adoption of the Secure Electronic Transaction (SET) protocol and a rapid move towards **digital signatures**.
> ❞

digitally *adv* digitalmente

digitization *n* COMPTR digitalización *f*

digitize *vt* COMPTR *(data)* digitalizar □ *digitized image* imagen *f* digitalizada

digitizer *n* COMPTR digitalizador *m*

dilution *n* FIN, ST EXCH dilución *f* □ *dilution of equity* dilución *f* (del valor de las acciones); *dilution of shareholding* dilución *f* (del valor de las acciones)

dilutive *adj* FIN dilutivo(a) □ *dilutive effect* efecto *m* dilutivo

diminish 1 *vt* *(price, quality, value)* disminuir
2 *vi* disminuir; **their profits have diminished** han disminuido sus beneficios

diminishing *adj* *(price, quality, value)* cada vez menor □ ACCT *diminishing balance (method)* (método *m* del) saldo *m* decreciente; *diminishing marginal productivity* productividad *f* marginal decreciente; *diminishing returns* rendimientos *mpl* decrecientes

dinosaur *n* *(outdated product)* anacronismo *m* decimonónico

dip 1 *n* *(in prices, value, figures)* descenso *m*; **the winter months saw a sharp dip in profits** los meses de invierno presenciaron una fuerte caída de los beneficios
2 *vi* *(prices, value, figures)* descender; **shares dipped on the London Stock Market yesterday** las acciones experimentaron ayer un descenso en la Bolsa londinense

diplex *adj* TEL díplex *inv*

dir (**a**) ADMIN *(abbr* **director***)* dir., dir.a (**b**) COMPTR *(abbr* **directory***)* directorio *m*

direct 1 *adj* COMPTR *direct addressing* direccionamiento *m* directo; *direct advertising* publicidad *f* directa; *direct banking* banca *f* directa; *direct competition* competencia *f* directa; *direct costs* costos *mpl or Esp* costes *mpl* directos; *direct cost accounting* contabilidad *f* de costos *or Esp* costes directos; *direct costing* cálculo *m* de costos *or Esp* costes directos; BANKING *direct debit* domiciliación *f* bancaria *or* de pago, *Am* débito *m* bancario; **they prefer their customers to pay by direct debit** prefieren que sus clientes domicilien los pagos; *direct debit advice* aviso *m* de domiciliación bancaria *or Am* débito bancario; *direct debit mandate* orden *f* de domiciliación bancaria *or Am* débito bancario; *US* BANKING *direct deposit* *Esp* ingreso *m* en cuenta, *Am* depósito *m* directo; **to pay by direct deposit** pagar por *Esp* ingreso en cuenta *or Am* depósito directo; TEL *direct dialling* marcación *f* directa, *Andes, RP* discado *m* directo; *direct expenses* gastos *mpl* directos; *direct fixed costs* gastos *mpl* fijos directos; *direct flight* vuelo *m* directo *or* sin escalas; *direct investment* inversión *f* directa; *direct labour* mano *f* de obra directa; *direct labour cost* costos *mpl or Esp* costes *mpl* de mano de obra directa; TEL *direct*

line línea *f* directa; **direct mail** correo *m* directo, correo comercial; **direct mail advertising** publicidad *f* directa por correo; **direct mail campaign** campaña *f* publicitaria por correo; **direct marketing** marketing *m* directo; **direct marketing agency** agencia *f* de marketing directo; **direct product profitability** rentabilidad *f* directa del producto; **direct purchase** compra *f* directa; **direct purchasing** compras *fpl* directas; **direct response advertising** publicidad *f* de respuesta directa; **direct sale** venta *f* directa; **direct selling** venta *f* directa; **direct tax** impuesto *m* directo; **direct taxation** impuestos *mpl* directos, imposición *f* directa
   2 *vt (company, work)* dirigir; **to direct sb to do sth** mandar *or* indicar a alguien que haga algo

direct-dial *adj* **direct-dial number** número *m* directo; **direct-dial telephone** teléfono *m* directo

direction *n* **(a)** *(of company)* dirección *f*; **he will take over the direction of the group as of next week** se hará cargo de la dirección del grupo a partir de la próxima semana **(b)** **directions** *(instructions)* instrucciones *fpl* □ **directions for use** instrucciones *fpl* de uso

directive *n* directiva *f*

director *n* *(of company)* director(ora) *m,f*; *(board member)* consejero(a) *m,f* □ **directors' remuneration** remuneración *f* de los consejeros; **directors' report** informe *m* del consejo de administración

directorate *n* **(a)** *(post)* dirección *f* **(b)** *(board)* consejo *m* de administración **(c)** EU **Directorate General** Dirección *f* General

director-general *n* director(ora) *m,f* general

directorship *n* dirección *f*, puesto *m* de director(ora); **during his directorship** durante su dirección; **he has been offered a directorship** le han ofrecido un puesto de director

directory *n* *(of telephone numbers)* guía *f* (telefónica), listín *m* (de teléfonos), *Am* directorio *m* telefónico *or* de teléfonos; *(of addresses)* *Esp* callejero *m*, *Am* guía *f* de la ciudad; COMPTR *(of files)* directorio *m* □ *Br* **directory enquiries,** US **directory assistance** (servicio *m* de) información *f* telefónica; COMPTR **directory structure** estructura *f* de directorio

dirigisme *n* ECON, POL dirigismo *m*

dirty *adj* **(a)** *(bill of landing)* sucio(a) **(b)** **dirty money** dinero *m* sucio

disability *n* discapacidad *f*, invalidez *f* □ **disability allowance** subsidio *m* por discapacidad *or* invalidez; **disability benefit** seguro *m* de discapacidad *or* de invalidez; INS **disability clause** cláusula *f* de invalidez; **disability pension** pensión *f* de *or* por invalidez

disbursal *n* US *(action, payment)* desembolso *m*

disburse *vt* desembolsar

disbursement *n* *(action, payment)* desembolso *m*

discharge 1 *n* **(a)** FIN *(of bankrupt)* rehabilitación *f* **discharge in bankruptcy** rehabilitación *f* del quebrado **(b)** *(dismissal)* despido *m* **(c)** FIN *(of debt, account, obligation)* liquidación *f*; **in full discharge** como pago completo **(d)** *(of cargo)* descarga *f*, desembarque *m*; *(of passengers)* desembarque
   2 *vt* **(a)** FIN *(bankrupt)* rehabilitar **(b)** *(dismiss)* despedir **(c)** FIN *(debt, account, obligation)* saldar, liquidar; *(fine)* pagar **(d)** *(cargo)* descargar, desembarcar; *(passengers)* desembarcar

discharged bankrupt *n* quebrado(a) *m,f* rehabilitado(a)

disciplinary *adj* disciplinario(a) □ **disciplinary action** expediente *m* disciplinario; **to take disciplinary action against sb** abrirle a alguien un expediente disciplinario; **disciplinary board** comité *m* disciplinario; **disciplinary hearing** audiencia *f* or vista *f* disciplinaria; **disciplinary measures** medidas *fpl* disciplinarias; **disciplinary procedure** procedimiento *m* disciplinario

disclaimer *n* **(a)** *(denial of responsibility)* negación *f* de responsabilidad; **to issue a disclaimer** hacer público un comunicado negando toda responsabilidad **(b)** LAW renuncia *f*

disclosure *n* divulgación *f* (de información financiera) □ **disclosure of accounts** divulgación *f* de cuentas; **disclosure requirements** obligaciones *fpl* de presentación de información financiera; **disclosure threshold** *(for donation)* = límite a partir del cual hay que revelar el importe de una donación

disconnect *vt* *(machine)* desconectar

discontinue *vt* *(production)* suspender; *(product)* dejar de fabricar, discontinuar □ **discontinued item** artículo *m* que ya no se fabrica; **discontinued line** modelo *m* que ya no se fabrica

discount 1 *n* **(a)** *(reduction in price)* descuento *m*, rebaja *f*; **to give sb a discount** hacer un descuento a alguien; **to buy/sell sth at a discount** *(goods)* comprar/vender algo con descuento; ST

EXCH *(shares)* comprar/vender algo al descuento *or* a un precio reducido; **to allow a discount of 10% (on sth)** permitir un descuento del 10% (en algo); **discounts and allowances** descuentos y bonificaciones; ❏ *discount card* tarjeta *f* de descuento; *US discount house (store)* tienda *f* de saldos; *discount price* precio *m* con descuento; *discount pricing* fijación *f* de precios con descuento; **a large volume of sales is needed to make discount pricing successful** hace falta un gran volumen de ventas para que la venta con descuento tenga éxito; *discount rate* tarifa *f* de descuento; *discount store* tienda *f* de saldos; *discount voucher* cupón *m or* vale *m* de descuento

(**b**) FIN *(of security)* descuento *m* ❏ *discount bank* banco *m* de descuento; *discount bond* bono *m* con descuento; *Br discount house* sociedad *f* mediadora del mercado de dinero, casa *f* de descuento; *discount loan* crédito *m* de descuento; *discount market* mercado *m* de descuento; *discount mechanism* mecanismo *m* de descuento; *discount operation* operación *f* de descuento; *discount rate Esp* tipo *m or Am* tasa *f* de descuento

2 *vt* (**a**) *(price, goods)* rebajar (**b**) FIN *(sum of money, bill, banknote)* descontar

discountable *adj* FIN descontable

discounted *adj* FIN *discounted bill* letra *f* descontada; ACCT *discounted cash flow* flujo *m* de caja descontado; *discounted rate Esp* tipo *m or Am* tasa *f* de descuento; *discounted value* valor *m* descontado

discounter *n (broker)* broker *m,f* dedicado(a) al descuento de letras; *(shop)* tienda *f* que vende con descuento

discounting *n (price reduction)* descuentos *mpl*; FIN descuento *m* de facturas ❏ *discounting bank* banco *m* de descuento; *discounting banker* empleado(a) *m,f* de un banco de descuento

discrepancy *n* discrepancia *f* (**between** entre); **there's a discrepancy in the accounts** existe una discrepancia en las cuentas

discretion *n (judgement)* criterio *m*; **at the manager's discretion** a discreción del director

discretionary *adj* BANKING discrecional ❏ *discretionary account* cuenta *f* discrecional; *discretionary costs* costos *mpl or Esp* costes *mpl* discrecionales; *discretionary fund* fondo *m* discrecional; *US discretionary income* ingresos *mpl* discrecionales; ST EXCH *discretionary order* orden *f* discrecional; *discretionary portfolio* cartera *f* discrecional; *discretionary powers* poderes *mpl* discrecionales

discriminate *vi* **to discriminate in favour of sb/sth** discriminar a favor de alguien/algo; **to discriminate against sth/sb** discriminar algo/a alguien; **she was being discriminated**

against la estaban discriminando

discriminating *adj* ADMIN *(duty, tariff)* diferencial

discrimination *n (bias)* discriminación *f*

discuss *vt (talk about)* hablar de; *(debate)* discutir, debatir; **I want to discuss it with my lawyer** quiero consultarlo con mi abogado; **we can discuss the matter of pay rises at the next meeting** podemos discutir el asunto de las subidas de sueldo en la próxima reunión

discussion *n (talk)* conversación *f*; *(debate)* discusión *f*, debate *m*; **the matter is under discussion** el asunto se está debatiendo; **to come up for discussion** *(in meeting)* discutirse ❏ COMPTR *discussion group* grupo *m* de discusión

diseconomy *n* deseconomía *f*

disemploy *vt US* dejar de emplear a

dishonour, *US* **dishonor** *vt* FIN *(bill, cheque)* no pagar, devolver ❏ *dishonoured cheque* cheque devuelto *or* rechazado *or Méx, RP* rebotado

disincentive *n* ECON traba *f*; **heavy taxation is a disincentive to expansion** los altos impuestos desincentivan la expansión; **to act as a disincentive to sth** desincentivar algo

disincorporate **1** *vt (company)* disolver, liquidar

2 *vi (of company)* disolverse

disinflation *n* ECON desinflación *f*

disinflationary *adj* ECON desinflacionista, desinflacionario(a)

disintermediation *n* desintermediación *f*

disinvestment *n* desinversión *f*

disk *n* COMPTR disco *m*; **to put sth on disk** poner algo en un disquete *or* disco; ❏ *disk access time* tiempo *m* de acceso al disco; *disk box* caja *f* en forma de disco; *disk capacity* capacidad *f* del disco; *disk controller* controlador *m* del disco; *disk controller card* tarjeta *f* controladora del disco; *disk copy* copia *f* en un disco; *disk drive* unidad *f* de disco, disquetera *f*; *disk error* error *m* de disco; *disk file* archivo *m or* fichero *m* en el disco; *disk fragmentation* fragmentación *f* del disco; *disk mailer* sobre *m* para el envío de discos; *disk memory* memoria *f* de disco; *disk operating system* sistema *m* operativo de disco; *disk space* espacio *m* en disco

diskette *n* COMPTR disquete *m*; **on diskette** en disquete ❏ *diskette box* caja *f* de disquetes

dismiss *vt* (**a**) *(from job) (employee)* despedir; *(official)* destituir, cesar (**b**) LAW *(case)* sobreseer; *(appeal)* desestimar

dismissal *n* (**a**) *(from job) (of employee)* despido *m*; *(of official)* destitución *f*, cese *m*; **dismissal without notice** despido en el acto ❏ *dismissal procedure* procedimiento *m* de despido (**b**) LAW *(of case)* sobreseimiento *m*; *(of appeal)* desestimación *f*

dispatch, despatch 1 n (of letter, parcel, goods) envío m, expedición f □ **dispatch department** departamento m de envíos or de expedición; **dispatch note** nota f de envío
2 vt (letter, parcel, goods) enviar, despachar; (messenger) enviar

dispatcher, despatcher n (sender) remitente mf

dispatching, despatching n (of letter, parcel, goods) expedición f

dispenser n (machine) máquina f expendedora; **cash dispenser** cajero automático

display 1 n (**a**) (of goods) muestra f, exposición f □ **display advertisement** anuncio m publicitario; **display advertising** publicidad f visual; **display area** zona f de exposición; **display material** material m de exposición; **display pack** expositor m; **display space** espacio f de exposición; **display stand** expositor m; **display unit** expositor m; **display window** escaparate m, Am vidriera f, Chile, Col, Méx vitrina f
(**b**) COMPTR (screen) pantalla f □ **display area** área f de visualización; **display card** tarjeta f de monitor; **display speed** velocidad f de visualización; **display unit** monitor m
2 vt (**a**) (goods) exponer (**b**) COMPTR visualizar

displayed price n precio m marcado or expuesto

disposable 1 n disposables productos mpl desechables
2 adj (**a**) (available) disponible □ **disposable funds** fondos mpl disponibles; **disposable income** renta f disponible; **disposable personal income** renta f disponible per cápita; LAW **disposable portion** porción f disponible (**b**) (packaging, product) desechable (**c**) **disposable goods** productos mpl desechables

disposal n (**a**) (of goods, property, securities) venta f; **for disposal** a la venta (**b**) (availability) disposición f; **to have sth at one's disposal** tener algo a su disposición

dispute 1 n (**a**) (disagreement) disputa f; (between management and workers) conflicto m (laboral); **to be in dispute with sb over sth** estar en conflicto con alguien por algo; **their right to remain in the country is in dispute** su derecho a permanecer en el país es motivo de conflicto (**b**) LAW litigio m
2 vt (debate) debatir, discutir; (call into question) cuestionar

disruptive strike n huelga que causa trastornos públicos

dissolution n (of company, partnership) disolución f

dissolve vt (company, partnership) disolver

distrain vi **to distrain on sb's goods** embargar los bienes de alguien

distraint n LAW embargo m

distress n US **distress merchandise** mercancías fpl vendidas en apuros or a cualquier precio; US **distress sale** venta f en apuros or a cualquier precio

distressed area n zona f deprimida

distributable adj (profits, reserves, dividend) distribuible

distribute vt (goods) distribuir; (work, profits, reserves, dividend) distribuir, repartir; **Hammond Ltd is the only company allowed to distribute our products** Hammond Ltd es la única empresa autorizada a distribuir nuestros productos

distribution n distribución f; (of dividend) distribución, reparto m; **wholesale and retail distribution** distribución mayorista y minorista □ **distribution agency** oficina f de distribución; **distribution agent** agente mf de distribución; **distribution centre** centro m de distribución; **distribution chain** cadena f de distribución; **distribution channel** canal m de distribución or comercialización; **distribution contract** contrato m de distribución; **distribution costs** gastos mpl de distribución; **distribution cycle** ciclo m de distribución; **distribution depot** depósito m or almacén m de distribución; **distribution list** (of memo) lista f de distribución; **distribution market** mercado m de distribución; **distribution method** método m de distribución; **distribution network** red f de distribución; **distribution outlet** punto m de distribución; **distribution planning** planificación f de la distribución; **distribution policy** política f de distribución; **distribution process** proceso m de distribución; **distribution ratio** ratio m or f de distribución; **distribution rights** derechos mpl de distribución; **distribution system** sistema f de distribución

distributor n distribuidor(ora) m,f; (of particular make of car) concesionario m □ **distributor's brand** marca f del distribuidor; **distributor discount** descuento m al distribuidor; **distributor's margin** margen m del distribuidor; **distributor panel** panel m de distribuidores

distributorship n **to have the distributorship for sth** ser el distribuidor de algo

district n (of country) (administrative area) distrito m; (more generally) zona f, región f; (of town, city) barrio m □ US **district attorney** fiscal mf del distrito; Br ADMIN **district council** junta f municipal; US LAW **district court** tribunal m federal; **district manager** director(ora) m,f regional; **district tax collector** recaudador(ora) m,f regional de impuestos

disturbed adj ST EXCH (market) turbulento(a)

div n (abbr **dividend**) dividendo m

diversification n diversificación f (**into** hacia); **the company's recent diversification**

into cosmetics la reciente diversificación de la empresa hacia el área de los cosméticos ❑ *diversification strategy* estrategia *f* de diversificación

diversify **1** *vt (production)* diversificar; **we must aim to diversify our product portfolio** nuestro objetivo debe ser la diversificación de nuestra cartera de productos
2 *vi (company)* diversificarse; **the company diversified in the 1960s and started producing food products as well as tobacco** la empresa se diversificó en los años 60 y comenzó a elaborar productos alimenticios además de tabaco; **to diversify into a new market** entrar en un nuevo mercado; **to diversify into a new product** diversificarse hacia un producto nuevo

> **"**
> First, contrary to popular belief, high yield does not necessarily equate with high risk - as a well-**diversified** portfolio of high yield bonds has shown to deliver higher income with reduced volatility over longer periods of time.
> **"**

divest *vt (company)* desinvertir

divestment *n (of company, assets)* desinversión *f*

dividend *n* FIN dividendo *m*; **the company has declared a dividend of 10%** la empresa ha fijado un dividendo del 10%; **dividend on shares** dividendo en acciones; **dividend per share** dividendo por acción; **cum dividend,** US **dividend on** con dividendo; **ex dividend,** US **dividend off** sin dividendo ❑ *dividend announcement* anuncio *m* del dividendo; *dividend cover* cobertura *f* del dividendo; *dividend mandate* orden *f* de pago de dividendos; *dividend policy* política *f* de dividendos; *dividend share* acción *f* de dividendo; *dividend tax* impuesto *m* sobre dividendos; *dividend warrant* cheque *m* para pago de dividendos; *dividend yield* rendimiento *m or* rentabilidad *f* del dividendo

dividend-price ratio *n* US ST EXCH relación *f* dividendo-precio

division *n (of company)* división *f*; *(of property, inheritance)* reparto *m* ❑ *division of labour* división *f* del trabajo

divisional *adj (in a company)* de (la) división ❑ *divisional director* director(ora) *m,f* de división; *divisional management* dirección *f* de división; *divisional manager* gerente *mf* de división

divisionalization *n* separación *f* en divisiones

DJIA *n* ST EXCH *(abbr* **Dow Jones Industrial Average***)* índice *m* Dow Jones de (Valores) Industriales

DNS *n* COMPTR *(abbr* **Domain Name System***)* DNS

m, = sistema de nombres de dominio

dock **1** *n* muelle *m* ❑ *dock dues* derechos *mpl* portuarios; *dock strike* huelga *f* de estibadores; *dock warehouse* almacén *m* portuario; *Br dock worker* estibador *m*
2 *vt* **(a)** *(ship)* atracar **(b)** *(wages)* recortar; **you'll be docked £25** te descontarán 25 libras
3 *vi (ship)* atracar

docker *n Br* estibador *m*

docket *Br* **1** *n (on package) (indicating contents)* etiqueta *f*; *(on delivery)* nota *f* de entrega, *Esp* albarán *m*; *(at customs)* certificado *m* de aduana
2 *vt (package)* etiquetar

docking station *n* COMPTR *(for notebook)* estación *f* base

doctor's certificate *n* justificante *m* (del) médico

document *n* documento *m*; **documents against acceptance** documentos contra aceptación; **documents against payment** documentos contra pago ❑ *document case* portafolios *m inv*; *document collator* clasificador *m*; *document cover* funda *f* de plástico para documentos; COMPTR *document file* documento *m*; *document handling* gestión *f* de documentos; *document of payment* documento *m* de pago; *document reader* lector *m* de documentos; *document wallet* carpeta *f*

documentary *adj* documentario(a) ❑ *documentary bill* letra *f* documentaria; *documentary charges* gastos *mpl* documentarios; *documentary credit* crédito *m* documentario; *documentary credit application* solicitud *f* de crédito documentario; *documentary credit department* departamento *m* de crédito documentario; *documentary evidence* justificación *f* documental; *documentary letter of credit* carta *f* de crédito documentaria; *documentary remittance* remesa *f* documentaria; *documentary support* justificación *f* documental

documentation *n* documentación *f*

dog *n* MKTG *(product)* producto *m* perro, = producto con baja cuota de mercado

> **"**
> For the marketing executive guessing the future is more than a routine parlour game to be indulged in at the beginning of each new year. Getting it right or getting it wrong is the difference between being regarded as a star or a **dog**.
> **"**

DOL *n* US *(abbr* **Department of Labor***)* Ministerio *m* de Trabajo

dole *n Br Fam* subsidio *m* de desempleo, *Esp* paro *m*; **to be on the dole** cobrar el subsidio de desempleo *or Esp* el paro; **to go on the dole** apuntarse para cobrar el desempleo, *Esp* apuntarse al paro □ **dole money** subsidio *m* de desempleo, *Esp* paro *m*

dollar *n* dólar *m* □ ECON **dollar area** área *f* del dólar; **dollar balances** saldos *mpl* en dólares; **dollar bill** billete *m* de un dólar; **dollar crisis** crisis *f* del dólar; **dollar diplomacy** diplomacia *f* del dólar; **dollar exchange rate** *Esp* tipo *m* or *Am* tasa *f* de cambio del dólar; **dollar premium** prima *f* del dólar; **dollar rate** tipo *m* de cambio del dólar; **dollar sign** signo *m* del dólar

dollar-cost averaging *n (calculation of average dollar cost)* promedio *m* del costo or *Esp* coste en dólares; ST EXCH promedio *m* del valor en dólares

dollarization *n* dolarización *f*

> The thought of dumping their own yo-yoing currencies for the strong and stable U.S. dollar has made many beleaguered central bankers swoon. And we're not just talking crisis economies such as Ecuador, which in 2000 jilted its inflation-prone sucre in favor of the dollar: Last April, Canada's second-largest bank proclaimed that **dollarization** is the "only viable option" to boost the country's ailing economy.

dollarize *vt* dolarizar

domain *n* COMPTR dominio *m* □ **domain name** nombre *m* de dominio; **Domain Name System** Sistema *m* de Nombres de Dominio

domestic *adj (affairs, policy)* interior; *(currency, economy)* nacional □ **domestic airline** línea *f* aérea de vuelos nacionales; *US* **domestic mail** correo *m* interior; **domestic market** mercado *m* nacional or interno; **domestic product** *(household product)* producto *m* para el hogar; **domestic products** productos *mpl* nacionales; **domestic route** *(in air travel)* ruta *f* nacional; **domestic sales** ventas *fpl* nacionales; **domestic trade** comercio *m* interior

domicile 1 *n* ADMIN, FIN, LAW domicilio *m*
2 *vt* **(a)** ADMIN, LAW *(person)* **domiciled in Ireland** domiciliado(a) en Irlanda **(b)** FIN **bills domiciled in France** letras domiciliadas en Francia □ **domiciled bill** letra *f* domiciliada

domiciliation *n* FIN domiciliación *f* □ **domiciliation advice** aviso *m* de domiciliación; **domiciliation file** fichero *m* de domiciliación; **domiciliation papers** documentos *mpl* de domiciliación

dominant brand *n* MKTG marca *f* dominante

donation *n* donativo *m*, donación *f*

done deal *n* acuerdo *m* cerrrado; **the merger is not a done deal yet** todavía no ha sido cerrado el acuerdo de la fusión

donee *n* LAW donatario(a) *m,f*

donor *n* LAW donante *mf*

door drop *n* MKTG buzoneo *m*

door knocking *n* ventas *fpl* a domicilio

door-to-door *adj* **door-to-door delivery** entrega *f* a domicilio; **door-to-door salesman** vendedor *m* a domicilio; **door-to-door selling** venta *f* a domicilio

dormant *adj* BANKING *(account)* inactivo(a)

DOS *n* COMPTR *(abbr* **disk operating system)** DOS *m* □ **DOS command** comando *m* DOS; **DOS prompt** indicador *m* or señal *f* de DOS

dosh *n Br Fam (money) Esp* pasta *f*, *Am* plata *f*, *Méx* lana *f*, *RP* guita *f*

dossier *n* dossier *m*, expediente *m*

dot *n (in e-mail address)* punto *m*

dotcom *n (company)* empresa *f* punto com or puntocom

> Having launched his website Teenfront.com from his bedroom aged 14 he had been offered a substantial chunk of cash in return for signing it over to London-based dotcom Rools.com. And if you are wondering why anyone would trust a schoolboy to run his own office and hand him a seven-figure cheque remember this was July 2000 – the height of the **dotcom** bubble.

dot-matrix printer *n* impresora *f* matricial or de agujas

double *adj* **(a)** ST EXCH **double option** doble opción *f* **(b)** INS **double insurance** doble seguro *m*; FIN **double taxation** doble imposición *f* or tributación *f*; **double taxation agreement** or **treaty** convenio *m* or acuerdo *m* de doble imposición **(c)** **double time** *(pay)* paga *f* doble; **I get double time on Sundays** los domingos cobro el doble **(d)** **inflation is now in double figures** la inflación se ha situado en los dos dígitos

double-A rating *n* ST EXCH calificación *f* AA or doble A

double-click COMPTR **1** *n* doble clic *m*
2 *vt* hacer doble clic en
3 *vi* hacer doble clic (**on** en)

double-digit *adj (inflation, growth)* de dos dígitos

double-entry *adj* ACCT **double-entry bookkeeping** contabilidad *f* por partida doble; **double-entry method** método *m* de partida doble

doubtful *adj* FIN **doubtful debt** deuda *f* de cobro dudoso **doubtful loan** crédito *m* dudoso

Dow Jones *n* ST EXCH **Dow Jones (Industrial) Average** or **Index** índice *m* Dow Jones (de Valores Industriales)

down 1 *adv (reduced, lower)* **the price of gold is**

down ha bajado el precio del oro; **the pound is down two cents against the dollar** la libra ha bajado dos centavos frente al dólar; **sales are 5% down on last year** las ventas han bajado 5% con respecto al año pasado

2 adj (**a**) (not working) **to be down** (of computer) no funcionar; **the network is down/has gone down** se ha caído la red; **the lines are down** no hay línea ❑ **down arrow** flecha f abajo; **down arrow key** tecla f de flecha abajo (**b**) **down payment** pago m inicial, Esp entrada f, Am cuota f inicial; **to make a down payment on sth** pagar la Esp entrada or Am cuota inicial de algo, efectuar el pago inicial de algo; **he made a down payment of £500** hizo un pago inicial de 500 libras, Esp dio una entrada de 500 libras

downgrade vt (job, person) rebajar de categoría

download COMPTR **1** n descarga f ❑ **download kit** kit m de descarga; **download protocol** protocolo m de descarga

2 vt bajar(se), descargar(se)

3 vi descargarse; **films take a long time to download** las películas tardan or Am demoran mucho en descargarse

downloadable adj COMPTR descargable

downloading n COMPTR descarga f

downmarket 1 adj popular, barato(a)

2 adv **to move downmarket** dirigirse a un público más popular

downside n (trend) a la baja; **prices have tended to be on the downside** los precios han tenido una tendencia a la baja ❑ ST EXCH **downside potential** potencial m bajista ST EXCH **downside risk** riesgo m bajista, riesgo a la baja

downsize vt (company) hacer ajuste or reajuste de plantilla en, reducir plantilla en, redimensionar

downsizing n ajuste m or reajuste m de plantilla, redimensionamiento m; **we see downsizing as our only option if the company is to remain competitive** contemplamos el ajuste or reajuste de plantilla como la única solución para seguir siendo competitivos

> ❝
> Men who were anxious about changes in the structure of their organisation were also approximately twice as likely to have time off sick. But those working in a company in which **downsizing** was likely were conversely far less likely to take time off – presumably fearing that more sickly workers would be far more likely to be made redundant.
> ❞

downstream adv (in production process) en una fase posterior

downswing n (fase f de) contracción f, bajón

m; **the recent downswing in interest rates** la reciente contracción or el reciente bajón en Esp los tipos or Am las tasas de interés

downtick n (**a**) (small decrease) ligero descenso m (**b**) ST EXCH = venta de un título a un precio inferior al de su cotización inmediatamente anterior

downtime n (**a**) (of machine, factory, worker) paro m técnico (**b**) (time spent on task) tiempo m; **how much downtime have you spent on this project?** ¿cuánto tiempo te ha llevado este proyecto?

downtrend n tendencia f a la baja

downturn n (in market, economy) desaceleración f; (in demand, sales) bajón m; **Asian economies have experienced a significant downturn in recent years** las economías asiáticas han experimentado una desaceleración significativa en los últimos años; **there has been a downturn in profits** se ha producido un bajón en los beneficios

downward adj **the economy is on a downward path** la economía está experimentando una tendencia a la baja ❑ FIN **downward movement** movimiento m a la baja; **downward market trend** tendencia f a la baja del mercado; **downward trend** tendencia f a la baja

downward-compatible adj COMPTR compatible con versiones anteriores

Dow theory n ST EXCH teoría f de Dow

DP n COMPTR (abbr **data processing**) proceso m or procesamiento m de datos

dpi COMPTR (abbr **dots per inch**) ppp

drachma n Formerly dracma m or f

draft n (**a**) (of letter, proposal, speech) borrador m; (of law) anteproyecto m ❑ **draft agreement** borrador m or proyecto m de acuerdo; **draft budget** proyecto m de presupuesto; **draft contract** borrador m de contrato; **draft letter** borrador m de la carta; COMPTR **draft mode** modo m borrador; COMPTR **draft printout** copia f impresa en borrador; COMPTR **draft quality** calidad f borrador; COMPTR **draft quality printing** impresión f en calidad borrador; COMPTR **draft version** borrador m

(**b**) FIN letra f de cambio, giro m; **to make a draft on sb** girar una letra a cargo de alguien

2 vt (letter, proposal, speech) hacer un borrador de; (law, contract) hacer un proyecto de; **to draft a bill** redactar un anteproyecto de ley

draftsman US = **draughtsman**

draftswoman US = **draughtswoman**

drag COMPTR **1** n **drag and drop** arrastrar y soltar

2 vt (icon) arrastrar; **to drag and drop sth** arrastrar y soltar algo

3 vi **to drag and drop** arrastrar y soltar

dragon bond n ST EXCH bono m dragón, = bono en dólares estadounidenses emitido en Asia

drain n (depletion) merma f, mengua f (**on** de); **it is a drain on the company's resources** absorbe muchos de los recursos de la empresa

DRAM n COMPTR (abbr **dynamic random access memory**) DRAM f

draughtsman, US **draftsman** n delineante m

draughtswoman, US **draftswoman** n delineante f

draw 1 n COMPTR **draw program** programa m de dibujo
2 vt (**a**) (salary) percibir; **to draw money from the bank** retirar or sacar dinero del banco (**b**) FIN (cheque) extender; (bill) girar; **to draw a cheque on the company's account** extender un cheque con cargo a la cuenta de la empresa (**c**) (interest) devengar
3 vi FIN **to draw at sight** girar a la vista

▸ **draw down** vt sep (funds) disponer de

▸ **draw out** vt sep (money) retirar, sacar

▸ **draw up** vt sep (document, bill) redactar, preparar; (budget, programme, procedure) elaborar, preparar; (plan, itinerary) elaborar, preparar; (bill of exchange) extender

drawback n CUSTOMS reintegro m or devolución f de derechos de aduana

drawdown n FIN disposición f de crédito

drawee n FIN (of bill) librado(a) m,f

drawer n FIN (of cheque, bill) librador(ora) m,f; **to refer a cheque to drawer** devolver un cheque al librador

drawing n (**a**) (of sum) Esp retirada f, Am retiro m (**b**) FIN (of cheque, bill) libramiento m □ **drawing account** cuenta f corriente or de depósitos a la vista; **drawing rights** derechos mpl de giro

dress-down Friday n = viernes en el que los empleados tienen permiso para acudir al trabajo con ropa informal

drift n (of prices, salaries) tendencia f al alza

drip advertising n MKTG publicidad f repetida

drip-feed vt (company) financiar poco a poco

drive n (**a**) (campaign) campaña f; **the company is having a sales drive** la empresa está metida en una campaña de ventas (**b**) COMPTR (for disk) unidad f de disco; **a:/c: drive** unidad a:/c:

▸ **drive down** vt sep ECON (prices, inflation) hacer bajar; **to drive prices down** hacer que los precios bajen

▸ **drive up** vt sep ECON (prices, inflation) hacer subir; **to drive prices up** hacer que los precios suban

driver n COMPTR controlador m

drop 1 n (**a**) (in prices, inflation) caída f, descenso m (**in** de); **sales show a drop of 10%** las ventas muestran una caída del 10% (**b**) (delivery) entrega f; **I have four drops to make** tengo que hacer cuatro entregas □ **drop shipment** envío m directo
2 vt COMPTR (icon) soltar
3 vi (prices, inflation) caer, bajar; **sales have dropped by 10%** las ventas han caído or bajado un 10%; ST EXCH **shares dropped a point** las acciones cayeron un entero; **the pound dropped three points against the dollar** la libra bajó tres enteros frente al dólar

drop-dead adj **drop-dead fee** = comisión por la no utilización de un préstamo bancario previamente pactado para financiar una adquisición; **drop-dead rate** = tipo del "drop-dead fee"

drop-down menu n COMPTR menú m desplegable

drug n **a drug on the market** (product) un producto sin salida

dry adj **dry cargo** carga f seca; **dry goods** Br (grain, pulses, tea, coffee) áridos mpl; US (drapery) artículos mpl de confección

DSL n COMPTR (abbr **Digital Subscriber Line**) línea f digital por suscripción

DTI n (abbr **Department of Trade and Industry**) = ministerio británico de industria y comercio

DTP n COMPTR (abbr **desktop publishing**) autoedición f □ **DTP operator** autoeditor(ora) m,f; **DTP software** software m de autoedición

dual adj EU **dual circulation** (of currencies) doble circulación f; EU **dual circulation period** periodo m de doble circulación; **dual currency** doble divisa f; **dual exchange market** mercado m de cambio doble; ST EXCH **dual listing** doble cotización f; **dual ownership** copropiedad f; **dual pricing** (within a company) sistema m de doble precio; *(showing prices in two currencies)* doble indicación *f* de precios

dual-band *adj* TEL de banda dual

dual-branded *adj* MKTG con dos firmas, con dos marcas

dual-currency *adj (system)* con dos monedas

dud *adj (banknote, coin)* falso(a); *(cheque)* sin fondos

due 1 *n* **dues** *(membership fees)* cuota *f*
2 *adj (owed)* pagadero(a); *(debt)* vencido(a); *(bill)* vencido(a); **when is the next instalment due?** ¿cuándo vence el siguiente plazo?; **I'm due three days' holiday** tengo derecho a tres días de vacaciones; **I'm due a rise** *(I will receive one)* me van a subir el sueldo; *(I deserve one)* me deberían subir el sueldo ▫ **due date** (fecha *f* de) vencimiento *m*; **due diligence** diligencia *f* debida

due-date *vt* **due-dated October 1, 2005** con vencimiento el 1 de octubre de 2005

dull *adj* FIN *(market)* flojo(a); **business is dull** el negocio está parado ▫ **dull season** temporada *f* baja

duly *adv (properly)* como corresponde, debidamente; **a duly authorized representative** un representante debidamente autorizado; **he said he'd be punctual and he duly arrived on the stroke of eight** dijo que llegaría puntual y llegó, como correspondía, a las ocho en punto; **I duly received your letter of 8 March** recibí su carta del 8 de marzo como estaba previsto

dummy 1 *n (product)* producto *m* simulado; *(book)* maqueta *f*
2 *adj* falso(a) ▫ **dummy company** empresa *f* fantasma; **dummy pack** envase *m* de muestra

dump 1 *n* **dump bin** cesta *f or Am* canasta *f* de productos
2 *vt (goods)* inundar el mercado con, hacer dumping con
3 *vi* hacer dumping

dumper *n (company)* empresa *f* que hace dumping

dumping *n (of goods)* dumping *m*

dun *vt* apremiar; **to dun sb for money** *or*

payment apremiar a alguien para que pague

dunning notice *n* carta *f* de cobranza

duopoly *n* duopolio *m*

duopsony *n* duopsonio *m*

duplex *adj* TEL dúplex

duplicate 1 *n (of document, receipt)* duplicado *m*, copia *f*; **in duplicate** por duplicado
2 *adj (key, document)* duplicado(a); *(receipt, certificate)* por duplicado; **a duplicate receipt** un recibo por duplicado ▫ **duplicate copy** duplicado *m*, copia *f*
3 *vt (document, receipt)* duplicar, hacer un duplicado de; *(on photocopier)* fotocopiar

durable 1 *n* **durables** bienes *mpl* duraderos
2 *adj* duradero(a) ▫ **durable goods** bienes *mpl* duraderos

duration *n (of lease)* duración *f*

Dutch auction *n* subasta *f* a la baja

dutiable *adj (taxable)* imponible; CUSTOMS sujeto(a) a derechos arancelarios

duty *n* CUSTOMS derecho *m*, impuesto *m*; **to pay duty on sth** pagar derechos *or* impuestos por algo; **liable to duty** sujeto(a) a derechos arancelarios; **duty paid** derechos pagados

duty-free CUSTOMS **1** *n* **(a)** *(goods)* artículos *mpl* libres de impuestos **(b)** *(shop)* tienda *f* libre de impuestos
2 *adj (goods)* exento(a) *or* libre de impuestos ▫ **duty-free allowance** cantidad *f* libre de impuestos; **duty-free entry** franquicia *f* aduanera; **duty-free import** importación *f* libre de impuestos; **duty-free shop** tienda *f* libre de impuestos **duty-free zone** zona *f* franca

duty-paid *adj* CUSTOMS *(goods)* con los derechos pagados

DVD *n* COMPTR *(abbr* **Digital Versatile Disk, Digital Video Disk***)* DVD *m* ▫ **DVD drive** unidad *f* de DVD

dynamic *adj (company, economy)* dinámico(a) ▫ COMPTR **dynamic data exchange** intercambio *m* dinámico de datos; **dynamic HTML** HTML *m* dinámico; **dynamic RAM** RAM *f* dinámica

Ee

EAGGF *n* EU (*abbr* **European Agriculture Guidance and Guarantee Fund**) FEOGA *m*, Fondo *m* Europeo de Orientación y de Garantía Agrícola

E & OE *Br* ACCT (*abbr* **errors and omissions excepted**) s.e.u.o.

early *adj* (**a**) **at your earliest convenience** (*in correspondence*) en cuanto le sea posible, a la mayor brevedad; **what is your earliest possible delivery date?** ¿cuál es su fecha de entrega más inmediata? ❑ *early closing:* (*of shops*) **it's early closing today** hoy cierran temprano; FIN *early redemption* amortización *f* anticipada; *early retirement* jubilación *f* anticipada; **to take early retirement** acogerse a la jubilación anticipada, jubilarse antes de tiempo
(**b**) MKTG *early adopters* adoptadores *mpl* iniciales, primeros adoptadores *mpl*; *early majority* mayoría *f* inicial, primera mayoría

earmark *vt* (*funds*) destinar, asignar (**for** a); **this money has been earmarked for research** esta partida ha sido destinada *or* asignada a investigación

earn *vt* (**a**) (*money*) ganar; **how much do you earn?** ¿cuánto gana?; **to earn a** *or* **one's living** ganarse la vida (**b**) (*interest*) producir, devengar; **their money is earning a high rate of interest** obtienen un interés muy alto por su dinero

earned *adj* FIN *earned income* rentas *fpl* del trabajo; *earned income allowance* deducción *f* de los rendimientos del trabajo; *US* ADMIN *earned income credit* = prestación disponible para los trabajadores con las rentas más bajas; *earned interest* interés *m* devengado; ACCT *earned surplus* beneficios *mpl* retenidos

earner *n* (*person*) (**wage**) **earner** asalariado(a) *m,f*; **one of the biggest earners in the company** una persona con uno de los sueldos más altos de la empresa; **this product is the biggest profit earner in our range** este producto es el que más beneficios da de nuestra gama

earning *adj* *earning capacity, earning potential* (*of person*) capacidad *f* de ganar dinero; (*of company*) capacidad de generar ingresos, poder *m* lucrativo

earnings *npl* (*of person*) ingresos *mpl*, renta *f*; (*of company*) beneficios *mpl*, ganancias *fpl*; **earnings before interest and tax** beneficios antes de intereses e impuestos ❑ *earnings forecast* previsión *f* de beneficios; *earnings growth* crecimiento *m* de beneficios; *earnings per share* dividendo *m* por acción, beneficio *m* por acción; *earnings retained* beneficios *mpl* no distribuidos

earnings-related *adj* (*benefit, allowance*) calculado(a) según los ingresos, en función de los ingresos ❑ *earnings-related pension* pensión *f* contributiva

earnout *n* = cantidad extra que se paga al vendedor de una empresa si durante un determinado periodo después de la venta ésta produce unos beneficios superiores a una cifra especificada

EAS *n* (*abbr* **Enterprise Allowance Scheme**) = programa británico que ofrece ayuda financiera a las personas que comienzan un negocio

easy *adj* (**a**) **by easy payments, on easy terms** con facilidades de pago (**b**) ST EXCH (*market*) poco activo(a), con tendencia a la baja (**c**) *Fam easy money* dinero *m* fácil

EBIT *npl* (*abbr* **earnings before interest and tax**) EBIT *m*, beneficios *mpl* antes de intereses e impuestos

EBITDA *npl* (*abbr* **earnings before interest, taxes, depreciation and amortization**) EBITDA *m*, beneficios *mpl* antes de intereses, impuestos, depreciación y amortización

e-book *n* COMPTR libro *m* electrónico

EBRD *n* (*abbr* **European Bank for Reconstruction and Development**) BERD *m*

e-broker *n* ST EXCH corredor(ora) *m,f* de Bolsa electrónico(a)

e-broking *n* ST EXCH corretaje *m* de Bolsa electrónico

e-business *n* COMPTR comercio *m* electrónico

EC *n Formerly* (*abbr* **European Community**) CE *f*

ECA *n* (*abbr* **Economic Complementation Agreement**) ACE *m*

e-cash *n* COMPTR dinero *m* electrónico

ECB *n* (*abbr* **European Central Bank**) BCE *m*

ECGD *n* (*abbr* **Export Credit Guarantee Department**) = departamento británico de garantía de créditos a la exportación

echelon *n* nivel *m*; **the higher echelons of industry** las altas esferas del mundo de la industria

ECM *n US* (*abbr* **European Common Market**) MCE *m*

ECN *n* ST EXCH (*abbr* **electronic communications network**) = red de comunicaciones electrónica

ECOFIN *n* FIN (*abbr* **Economic and Financial Council of Ministers**) Ecofin *m*

e-commerce *n* COMPTR comercio *m* electrónico; **e-commerce is continuing to grow** el comercio electrónico sigue creciendo

econometric *adj* econométrico(a) ❑ *econometric model* modelo *m* econométrico

econometrician *n* económetra *mf*

econometrics *n* econometría *f*

economic *adj* (**a**) *(relating to the economy)* económico(a) ❑ *economic activity tables* tablas *fpl* de actividad económica *or* sector económico; *economic adviser* asesor(ora) *m,f* económico(a); *economic agent* agente *m* económico; *economic aid* ayuda *f* económica; *economic*

analysis análisis *m* económico; *economic appraisal* evaluación *f* económica; *economic authorities* autoridades *fpl* económicas; *economic boom* auge *m* económico; *economic climate* situación *f* económica, clima *m* económico; *economic cost* costo *m or Esp* coste *m* económico; *economic council* consejo *m* económico; *economic crisis* crisis *f* económica; *economic cycle* ciclo *m* económico; *economic development* desarrollo *m* económico; *economic downturn* desaceleración *f or* ralentización *f* económica; *economic efficiency* eficiencia *f* económica; *economic embargo* embargo *m* económico; *economic factor* factor *m* económico; *economic forces* fuerzas *fpl* económicas; *economic forecast* previsión *f* económica; *economic growth* crecimiento *m* económico; *economic growth rate* tasa *f* de crecimiento económico; *economic indicator* indicador *m* económico; *economic integration* integración *f* económica; *economic interest group* grupo *m* de interés económico; *economic life* (*of machinery, product*) vida *f* útil; *economic lot size* tamaño *m* económico del lote; *economic machinery* maquinaria *f* económica; *economic measure* medida *f* económica; EU *Economic and Monetary Union* Unión *f* Económica y Monetaria; *economic order quantity* volumen *m* óptimo de pedido; *economic performance* resultados *mpl* económicos; *economic plan* plan *m* económico; *economic planning* planificación *f* económica; *economic player* actor *m* económico; *economic policy* política *f* económica; *economic principles* principios *mpl* económicos; *economic profit* beneficio *m* económico; *economic prospects* perspectivas *fpl* económicas; *economic rate of return* tasa *f* de rendimiento económico; *economic recession* recesión *f* económica; *economic recovery* recuperación *f* económica; *economic research* investigación *f* económica; *economic revival* recuperación *f* económica; *economic sanctions* sanciones *fpl* económicas; *economic sector* sector *m* económico; *economic situation* situación *f* económica; *economic slump* depresión *f* económica; *economic stranglehold* bloqueo *m* económico; *economic strategy* estrategia *f* económica; *economic trend* tendencia *f* económica; *economic union* unión *f* económica; ACCT *economic value added* valor *m* económico añadido; *economic warfare* guerra *f* económica

(**b**) *Br (profitable)* rentable; **to make sth economic** hacer que algo sea rentable ❑ *economic batch* lote *m* económico; *economic batch quantity* volumen *m* óptimo de pedido por lotes

economical *adj* (*method, approach, machine*) económico(a); *(person)* ahorrativo(a)

economically *adv* (**a**) *(relating to the economy)*

económicamente (**b**) *(with economy)* económicamente; **economically viable** *(campaign, product, project)* económicamente viable

economics 1 *n (science)* economía *f*, ciencias *fpl* económicas
2 *npl (profitability)* rentabilidad *f*; *(financial aspects)* aspectos *mpl* económicos; **we must consider the economics of the project before making any decisions** debemos estudiar la rentabilidad del proyecto antes de tomar ninguna decisión

economism *n* economicismo *m*

economist *n* economista *mf*

economize *vi* economizar (**on** en); **the recession has led to a need to economize throughout the company** la recesión ha hecho que sea necesario economizar en todos los ámbitos de la empresa

economy *n* economía *f*; **to make economies** economizar, recortar gastos; **it's (a) false economy** lo barato sale caro; **economies of scale** economías de escala □ **economy brand** marca *f* económica; **economy class** clase *f* económica *or* turista; **economy drive** *(cost-cutting campaign)* campaña *f* de ahorro; **I'm on an economy drive at the moment** me toca ahorrar por el momento; **economy measure** medida *f* de ahorro; **as an economy measure** como medida de ahorro; **economy pack** envase *m or* pack *m* familiar

ecotax *n* ecotasa *f*, impuesto *m* ecológico

ecotourism *n* ecoturismo *m*, turismo *m* verde

ECP *n* EU *(abbr* **eurocommercial paper***)* efecto *m* comercial en eurodivisas

ECSC *n (abbr* **European Coal and Steel Community***)* CECA *f*

ECSDA *n* FIN *(abbr* **European Central Securities Depositories Association***)* ECSDA *f*, Asociación *f* Europea de Depositarios Centrales de Valores

ECU, ecu *n* Formerly EU *(abbr* **European Currency Unit***)* ecu *m*

ed (**a**) *(abbr* **editor***)* ed. (**b**) *(abbr* **edited***)* editado(a) (**c**) *(abbr* **edition***)* ed.

EDGAR *n* FIN *(abbr* **electronic data gathering, analysis and retrieval***)* EDGAR *m*, = base de datos de la comisión del mercado de valores estadounidense

EDI *n* (**a**) FIN *(abbr* **European Data Interchange***)* IDA *m* (**b**) COMPTR *(abbr* **Electronic Data Interchange***)* EDI *m*, Intercambio *m* Electrónico de Datos

edit *vt* COMPTR *(text)* editar

editing *n* COMPTR edición *f* □ **editing window** ventana *f* de edición

edition *n (of book, newspaper)* edición *f*

editor *n* (**a**) COMPTR *(software)* editor *m* (**b**) *(of newspaper, journal) (manager)* director(ora) *m,f*; *(journalist)* redactor(ora) *m,f*; *(of article, book)* editor(ora) *m,f*

editorial 1 *n* (**a**) *(article)* editorial *m* (**b**) *(department)* redacción *f*
2 *adj (decision, job, skills)* editorial □ **editorial column** editorial *m*; **editorial content** contenido *m* editorial; **editorial freedom** libertad *f* de redacción; **editorial opinion** *(in press)* opinión *f* editorial; **editorial policy** *(in press)* política *f* editorial

editorialize *vi* editorializar; **as *The Times* editorialized,...** como afirmó el *Times* en su editorial,...

editorship *n (of newspaper)* dirección *f*; **during her editorship** durante su etapa como directora

EDR *n* FIN *(abbr* **European Depository Receipt***)* recibo *m* de depósito europeo

.edu COMPTR = en las direcciones de Internet, abreviatura que designa las páginas de universidades y entidades educativas

EEA *n* EU *(abbr* **European Economic Area***)* EEE *m*

EEB *n* EU *(abbr* **European Environmental Bureau***)* OEMA *f*

EEC *n* Formerly *(abbr* **European Economic Community***)* CEE *f*

EEOC *n (abbr* **Equal Employment Opportunity Commission***)* = comisión estadounidense para la igualdad de oportunidades en el empleo

case, when Mitsubishi Motor Manufacturing of America agreed to pay $34 million to settle a class action lawsuit filed by the **EEOC** in April 1996.
                                                                          "

EEZ *n (abbr* **Exclusive Economic Zone**) ZEE *f*

effect 1 *n* (**a**) **to put sth into effect** *(regulation, law)* aplicar algo; **to come into** *or* **take effect** entrar en vigor; **to remain in effect** continuar en vigor; *Br* **a new regulation is being introduced with effect from 1 January** una nueva normativa entrará en vigor a partir del 1 de enero (**b**) *(meaning)* **we have made provisions to this effect** hemos tomado medidas en este sentido **2** *vt (payment, sale, purchase)* efectuar

effective *adj* (**a**) ECON *(yield, return, production)* efectivo(a); *(value)* real ❑ **effective annual rate** *Esp* tipo *m* efectivo anual, *Am* tasa *f* efectiva anual; **effective capacity** capacidad *f* real; **effective income** *(after tax)* ingresos *mpl* netos; **effective life** *(of product, structure)* vida *f* útil; **effective tax rate** *Esp* tipo *m* impositivo real, *Am* tasa *f* impositiva real
(**b**) *(regulation, law)* **to become effective** entrar en vigor; **the new regulation is effective as from...** la nueva normativa entrará en vigor a partir de... ❑ **effective date** fecha *f* de entrada en vigor
(**c**) *(achieving results)* eficaz ❑ **effective management** gestión *f* eficiente

efficiency *n (of person, company, method)* eficiencia *f*; *(of machine)* rendimiento *m* ❑ **efficiency bonus** prima *f* de productividad

efficient *adj (person, company)* eficiente; *(method)* eficaz; **we must make more efficient use of the marketing team** debemos utilizar el equipo de marketing de una forma más eficaz

EFT *n* COMPTR *(abbr* **electronic funds transfer**) TEF *f*, transferencia *f* electrónica de fondos

EFTA *n (abbr* **European Free Trade Association**) EFTA *f*, AELC *f*

EFTPOS *n* COMPTR *(abbr* **electronic funds transfer at point of sale**) transferencia *f* electrónica de fondos en el punto de venta

EFTS *n* COMPTR *(abbr* **electronic funds transfer system**) sistema *m* electrónico de transferencia de fondos

EGA *n* COMPTR *(abbr* **enhanced graphics adaptor**) EGA *m*

EGM *n (abbr* **extraordinary general meeting**) junta *f* or asamblea *f* general extraordinaria

e-government *n* gobierno *m* electrónico

"
Departments have raised several concerns about meeting the **e-government** deadline and the report makes several recommendations. Just over half of the 524 services
"

that government departments routinely provide are currently delivered online. But the report pointed out that few are transactional services that allow the public to interact with government.
                                                                          "

EIA *n (abbr* **environmental impact assessment**) EIA *f*

EIB *n (abbr* **European Investment Bank**) BEI *m*

eighty/twenty rule, **80/20 rule** *n* FIN regla *f* 80/20

elastic *adj* ECON *(market, supply, demand)* elástico(a)

elasticity *n* ECON *(of market, supply, demand)* elasticidad *f*

electronic *adj* electrónico(a) ❑ **electronic banking** banca *f* electrónica; **electronic cash** dinero *m* electrónico; COMPTR **electronic catalogue** catálogo *m* electrónico; **electronic commerce** comercio *m* electrónico; **electronic data interchange** intercambio *m* electrónico de datos; **electronic data processing** tratamiento *m* or procesamiento *m* electrónico de datos; **electronic directory** directorio *m* electrónico; **electronic funds transfer** transferencia *f* electrónica de fondos; **electronic funds transfer at point of sale** transferencia *f* (electrónica de fondos) en el punto de venta; **electronic funds transfer system** sistema *m* electrónico de transferencia de fondos; COMPTR **electronic journal** revista especializada *m* electrónica; COMPTR **electronic mail** correo *m* electrónico; COMPTR **electronic mailbox** buzón *m* electrónico, *Am* casilla *f* de correo electrónico; **electronic mall** centro *m* comercial electrónico; **electronic money** dinero *m* electrónico; **electronic newspaper** periódico *m* electrónico; COMPTR **electronic office** oficina *f* informatizada or electrónica; **electronic payment** pago *m* electrónico; **electronic payment terminal** terminal *m* de pago electrónico; **electronic point of sale** punto *m* de venta electrónico; COMPTR **electronic purse** monedero *m* electrónico; COMPTR **electronic shopping** compras *fpl* en línea; ST EXCH **electronic trading** negociación *f* electrónica; **electronic transfer** transferencia *f* electrónica

"
Shop globally. Buy locally. That's the message from a number of Nashville merchants who are finding e-Commerce success in a locally-targeted **electronic mall**. GetItNashville.com is an electronic shopping mall that features Nashville businesses and targets local shoppers.
"

eligibility *n (for job, grant, benefit)* elegibilidad *f* (**for** para); **to determine sb's eligibility for promotion** decidir si alguien reúne los requisitos necesarios para un ascenso

eligible *adj* (**a**) **to be eligible** *(for job)* cumplir los requisitos necesarios; **to be eligible for a pension/a tax rebate** tener derecho a una pensión/una desgravación fiscal (**b**) *Br* FIN **eligible bill** efecto *m* redescontable; **eligible list** *(of banks)* = lista de bancos autorizados por el Banco de Inglaterra a descontar efectos redescontables; *(of securities)* lista *f* de valores admisibles; **eligible paper** papel *m* redescontable

EMA *n* (*abbr* **European Monetary Agreement**) AME *m*

e-mail, email COMPTR **1** *n* correo *m* electrónico, e-mail *m*; **to contact sb by e-mail** contactar con alguien por correo electrónico; **to send sth by e-mail** enviar algo por correo electrónico *or* e-mail ◻ **e-mail account** cuenta *f* de correo (electrónico); **e-mail address** dirección *f* de correo (electrónico); **e-mail client** cliente *m* de correo electrónico; **e-mail software** software *m* de correo electrónico
2 *vt* (*person*) enviar un correo electrónico *or* e-mail a; (*document*) enviar por correo electrónico *or* e-mail; **e-mail us at...** contacte con nosotros por correo electrónico en la siguiente dirección...

e-marketer *n* especialista *mf* en marketing electrónico

> "
> To succeed in the Net Future, an **e-marketer** must harness customer expectations by maximizing the present and future value of customer interactions online and offline, in the virtual mall of the Internet and in the brick-and-mortar walls of a conventional store.
> "

e-marketing *n* marketing *m* electrónico

embargo 1 *n* embargo *m*; **to lay** *or* **put an embargo on sth** imponer un embargo a *or* sobre algo; **to be under an embargo** *(of ship, goods)* estar sometido(a) a embargo; **to lift** *or* **raise an embargo** levantar un embargo
2 *vt* someter a embargo

embark *vt* embarcar

embarkation *n* embarque *m*

embezzle 1 *vt* (*public money*) malversar; (*private money*) desfalcar
2 *vi* (*public money*) malversar fondos; (*private money*) realizar un desfalco; **to embezzle from a company** desfalcar a una compañía

embezzlement *n* embezzlement (of funds) (*of public money*) malversación *f* (de fondos); (*of private money*) desfalco *m*

embezzler *n* (*of public money*) malversador(ora) *m,f*; (*of private money*) desfalcador(ora) *m,f*

emergency *n* **emergency fund** reservas *fpl* para imprevistos; **emergency measures** medidas *fpl* de emergencia; **emergency powers** poderes *mpl* extraordinarios; **emergency tax** impuesto *m* extraordinario

emerging market *n* mercado *m* emergente

EMF *n* (*abbr* **European Metalworkers' Federation**) FEM *f*

EMI *n* (*abbr* **European Monetary Institute**) IME *m*

eminent domain *n* US expropiación *f* forzosa

emission *n* (*of bank notes, currency*) emisión *f*

emit *vt* (*bank notes, currency*) emitir

emolument *n* **emoluments** emolumentos *mpl*

e-money *n* COMPTR dinero *m* electrónico

emoticon *n* COMPTR emoticono *m*, emoticón *m*

emotional *adj* MKTG (*reaction, response*) impulsivo(a) ◻ **emotional purchase** compra *f* por impulso

> "
> The importance of image in fashion retailing cannot be underestimated: "It is 90% an **emotional purchase**," says Kindleysides. His view is supported by academic research: "Store design in this market ... is crucial in the first place for attracting customers to the store and then for creating the right atmosphere for purchase."
> "

employ 1 *n* **to be in sb's employ** trabajar al servicio *or* a las órdenes de alguien
2 *vt* (**a**) (*give work to*) emplear; (*new staff*) contratar, emplear; **they employ twenty staff** tienen una plantilla *or* SAm un plantel de veinte personas; **to employ sb as a receptionist** emplear a alguien como recepcionista, tener a alguien trabajando como recepcionista; **he has been employed with the firm for fifteen years** lleva quince años trabajando para la empresa (**b**) (*make use of*) (*tool, method, force*) emplear, utilizar; **we must employ all our resources to tackle this problem** debemos emplear *or* utilizar todos los recursos a nuestra disposición para abordar este problema

employability *n* empleabilidad *f*

employable *adj* (*person*) empleable; **a good education makes you more employable** una buena formación te prepara mejor para encontrar trabajo *or* empleo

employed 1 *npl* **the employed** los trabajadores *or* los asalariados
2 *adj* (*person*) empleado(a), con empleo

employee *n* empleado(a) *m,f*; **management and employees** (*in negotiations*) la dirección y los trabajadores *or* empleados ◻ **employee association** asociación *f* de trabajadores; **employee benefits** prestaciones *fpl* para los empleados; **employee buy-out** = adquisición de una empresa por los trabajadores *or* emplea-dos; ***employee's contribution*** *(to non-state pension scheme)* aportación *f or RP* aporte *m* del trabajador; *(to National Insurance)* cotización *f* del trabajador; ***employee incentive scheme*** plan *m* de incentivos a los trabajadores; ***employee profit-sharing scheme*** plan *m* de participación de los trabajadores en los beneficios de la empresa; **to provide an employee profit-sharing scheme** ofrecer un plan de participación de los trabajadores en los beneficios de la empresa; ***employee representative*** representante *mf* de los trabajadores; *US **Employee Retirement Income Security Act*** = ley que regula los planes de pensiones privados en los Estados Unidos; ***employee shareholding*** participación *f* de los trabajadores en el capital social de la empresa; *Br **employee share ownership plan***, *US **employee stock ownership plan*** plan *m* de oferta de acciones a los empleados

employer *n (person)* empresario(a) *m,f; (company)* empresa *f;* **employers** *(as a body)* la patronal, los empresarios ❑ ***employers' association*** organización *f* empresarial *or* patronal; ***employer's contributions*** *(to employee benefits)* cotizaciones *fpl* por parte de la empresa; ***employers' federation*** federación *f* empresarial; ***employer's liability*** *(for accidents at work)* responsabilidad *f* de la empresa; ***employers' liability insurance*** seguro *m* de responsabilidad empresarial; ***employers' organization*** organización *f* empresarial *or* patronal

employment *n (occupation)* empleo *m; (recruitment)* contratación *f;* **to be without employment** no tener empleo, estar desempleado(a) *or Am* desocupado(a); **to give sb employment** dar trabajo *or* empleo a alguien; **to look for** *or* **seek employment** buscar trabajo *or* empleo ❑ *Br **Employment Act*** = ley sobre la igualdad de oportunidades en el empleo; ***employment agency*** agencia *f* de colocación; ***employment bureau*** agencia *f* de colocación; ***employment costs*** gastos *mpl* de personal; *EU **employment guidelines*** directrices *fpl* para el empleo; ***employment law*** derecho *m* laboral; ***employment legislation*** legislación *f* laboral; ***employment policy*** política *f* de empleo; ***employment protection*** protección *f* del empleo; ***employment regulations*** normativas *fpl* sobre empleo; ***employment and training contract*** contrato *m* en prácticas; ***employment tribunal*** tribunal *m* de lo social

> ❝
> Many economists say the Berlusconi government's proposals are quite mild because they will end up removing the application of Article 18 in the case of very few workers, and will not even affect those currently employed. However, the unions see Article 18

as the cornerstone of **employment protection** law and believe even a modest change could open the way to a more rigorous set of reforms.
> ❞

empower *vt* (**a**) *(authorize)* **to empower sb to do sth** facultar *or* autorizar a alguien a hacer algo (**b**) *(give power to)* **to empower sb** otorgar poder *or* fuerza a alguien; **the new measures will empower women in the labour market** las nuevas medidas potenciarán el papel de la mujer en el mercado laboral

empowerment *n* **these changes gave greater empowerment to employees** estos cambios dieron mayor autonomía a los empleados

> ❝
> The flexibility to work where and how you want to is another key benefit of **empowerment**. Again, employers can expect to see an increasingly motivated workforce as a result. Media buyer Kate Parry became Just Media's first teleworker as she became disillusioned with working in London. The company set her up with a laptop computer, a fax and a printer. I am able to speak with my clients and my colleagues efficiently from my home office; communication is the key to our success, so it is very important that I can do this in a suitable environment, she says.
> ❞

empty return *n* devolución *f* de envases vacíos

EMS *n (abbr* **European Monetary System**) SME *m*

EMU *n (abbr* **Economic and Monetary Union**) UEM *f*

emulate *vt* COMPTR emular

emulation *n* COMPTR emulación *f*

enable *vt* COMPTR *(device, option)* activar

enabled *adj* COMPTR *(device, option)* activado(a)

enc (**a**) *(abbr* **enclosure**) material *m* adjunto (**b**) *(abbr* **enclosed**) adjunto(a)

encash *vt Br (cheque)* hacer efectivo(a), cobrar

encashable *adj Br (cheque)* cobrable

encashment *n Br (of cheque)* cobro *m*

enclose *vt (in letter)* adjuntar; **to enclose sth in a letter** adjuntar algo en una carta; **please find enclosed my CV, enclosed please find my CV** adjunto encontrará mi CV; **I enclose a cheque for £20** adjunto un cheque por 20 libras; **the enclosed cheque** el cheque adjunto

enclosure *n (in letter)* material *m* adjunto

encode *vt* COMPTR codificar

encoder *n* COMPTR codificador *m*

encoding *n* COMPTR codificación *f*

encrypt *n* COMPTR encriptar

encryption *n* COMPTR encriptación *f*

end 1 *n* fin *m*, final *m*; **to bring sth to an end** *(speech, meeting)* terminar *or* acabar algo; **at the end of the month/year** a finales *or* fin de mes/año ❑ COMPTR **end key** tecla *f* fin; **end product** producto *m* final
2 *vt (speech, meeting)* terminar, acabar
3 *vi* terminar, acabar

end-consumer *n* consumidor(ora) *m,f* final

endgame *n* MKTG objetivo *m*

endnote *n* COMPTR nota *f* de fin de documento

end-of-month *adj* de final de mes ❑ **end-of-month balance** saldo *m* de final de mes; **end-of-month payments** pagos *mpl* de final de mes; **end-of-month settlement** liquidación *f* a mes vencido; **end-of-month statement** extracto *m* de cuenta de final de mes

end-of-season sale *n* rebajas *fpl* de fin de temporada

end-of-year *adj (at end of calendar year)* de fin de año; *(at end of financial year)* de fin de ejercicio ❑ ACCT **end-of-year balance sheet** balance *m* general de fin de ejercicio; **end-of-year bonus** prima *f* de fin de año

endorse, indorse *vt* **(a)** FIN *(document, cheque, bill of exchange)* endosar **(b)** *(approve) (action)* apoyar, respaldar; *(candidature)* avalar, respaldar **(c)** *(product)* promocionar; **sportswear endorsed by top athletes** ropa deportiva promocionada por atletas del más alto nivel

endorsee *n* FIN endosatario(a) *m,f*

endorsement *n* **(a)** FIN *(of document, cheque, bill of exchange)* endoso *m*; *(in insurance policy)* adición *f*; **endorsement in blanco** endoso en blanco ❑ FIN **endorsement fee** comisión *f* por endoso **(b)** *(approval) (of action)* apoyo *m*, respaldo *m*; *(of candidature)* aval *m*, respaldo *m* **(c)** *(of product)* promoción *f*; **that film star has made a fortune from her endorsement of cosmetics** esa estrella de cine ha hecho una fortuna promocionando cosméticos

endorser *n* FIN *(of document, cheque)* endosante *mf*

endow *vt* FIN *(person, company)* = donar capital o propiedades que proporcionen una renta regular

endowment *n* FIN *(action)* donación *f*; *(fund)* fondo *m* de seguro mixto ❑ **endowment fund** fondo *m* de seguro mixto; **endowment insurance** seguro *m* de vida mixto *or* de ahorro; **endowment mortgage** hipoteca-inversión *f*, = crédito hipotecario por intereses ligado a un seguro de vida; **endowment policy** póliza *f* de tipo mixto

❝
The **endowment mortgage** crisis has escalated in the past year with three in five borrowers now told their investment policy will not pay off their home loan. Figures to be published this week by the Association of British Insurers will show that life assurers have issued "red" or "amber" warning letters to 60 per cent of endowment mortgage holders telling them to save more. If borrowers do not take action they are likely to face shortfalls of thousands of pounds when their mortgage comes to an end and the **endowment** is not enough to pay off the loan.
❞

end-user *n* usuario(a) *m,f* final ❑ **end-user certificate** certificado *m* del destinatario final; **end-user specialist** especialista *mf* en usuarios finales

energy energía *f* ❑ **energy audit** auditoría *f* energética; **energy consumption** consumo *m* de energía; **energy consumption bill** factura *f* energética

enforce *vt (policy, decision)* hacer cumplir, aplicar; *(contract)* hacer cumplir, ejecutar

enforceable *adj* LAW ejecutable, exigible por ley ❑ **enforceable deed** escritura *f* ejecutable; **enforceable judgement** sentencia *f* ejecutoria

engage *vt (staff)* contratar; **to engage the services of sb** contratar *or* emplear los servicios de alguien

engaged *adj* **(a)** *(busy)* ocupado(a); **I'm otherwise engaged** tengo otros compromisos; **to be engaged in discussions (with sb)** estar en discusiones (con alguien) **(b)** *Br* **to be engaged** *(phone)* estar ocupado(a) *or Esp* comunicando; **the line** *or* **number is engaged** este número está ocupado; **I got the engaged tone** *or* **signal** estaba ocupado *or Esp* comunicando

engagement *n* **(a)** *(appointment, meeting)* compromiso *m*; **he had a previous** *or* **prior engagement** tenía un compromiso previo **(b)** *(of staff, services)* contratación *f*; **engagement (letter)** contrato *m*

engineer *n* ingeniero(a) *m,f*

engineering *n* ingeniería *f*; **an engineering company** una empresa de ingeniería ❑ **engineering department** departamento *m* de ingeniería

engross *vt* LAW *(make clear copy of)* redactar en forma legal

enhance *vt* **(a)** FIN *(pension, value)* aumentar **(b)** COMPTR *(image, quality)* mejorar

enhanced *adj* **(a)** FIN *(pension, value)* más alto(a) **(b)** COMPTR *(image, quality)* mejorado(a) ❑ **enhanced graphics adaptor** adaptador *m* de gráficos mejorado; **enhanced keyboard** tecla-do *m* expandido

enhancement *n* (**a**) FIN *(of pension, value)* aumento *m* (**b**) COMPTR *(of image, quality)* mejora *f*

enquire = **inquire**

enquiry = **inquiry**

enter 1 *n (key)* tecla *f* intro *or* enter ❑ **enter key** tecla *f* intro *or* enter
2 *vt* (**a**) *(market, country)* entrar en; **all goods entering the market are subject to duty** todas las mercancías que entren en el mercado estarán sujetas al pago de aranceles (**b**) ACCT *(item)* anotar; **to enter an item/figures in the ledger** anotar una entrada/cifras en el libro mayor (**c**) COMPTR *(data)* introducir

▶ **enter into** *vt insep (business)* empezar, iniciar; *(negotiations)* dar comienzo a, iniciar; *(contract)* firmar; **to enter into partnership with sb** asociarse con alguien; **to enter into an agreement with sb** firmar un acuerdo con alguien

▶ **enter up** *vt sep* ACCT **to enter up an item/figures in the ledger** anotar una entrada/cifras en el libro mayor

enterprise *n (undertaking)* empresa *f*, iniciativa *f*; *(company)* empresa ❑ Br **Enterprise Allowance Scheme** = programa que ofrece ayuda financiera a las personas que comienzan un negocio; **enterprise culture** cultura *f* empresarial; **enterprise economy** economía *f* de (libre) empresa; **enterprise society** sociedad *f* de libre empresa; **enterprise zone** ≃ zona *f* de urgente reindustrialización

> ❝
> We also need to further develop an **enterprise culture**. We're in lockstep with Wal-Mart by being very action-oriented. This applies in our speed to market, streamlined decisionmaking, and empowerment of people down to lower levels.
> ❞

enterprising *adj (person)* emprendedor(ora), innovador(ora); *(idea, project)* innovador(ora)

entertainment *n* **entertainment allowance** gastos *mpl* de representación; **entertainment expenses** gastos *mpl* de representación; **entertainment tax** impuesto *m* de espectáculos

entitle *vt* **to be entitled to sth** *(allowance, benefit)* tener derecho a algo; **his disability entitles him to a pension** su minusvalía le da derecho a percibir una pensión

entitlement *n* derecho *m*; **entitlement to a full pension** derecho al cien por cien de la jubilación

entrant *n (to market)* empresa *f* entrante; **stocks in two new entrants to the market performed well** las acciones de dos empresas nuevas en el mercado demostraron un buen comportamiento

entrepôt *n (port)* puerto *m* franco ❑ **entrepôt port** puerto *m* franco

entrepreneur *n* empresario(a) *m,f*

entrepreneurial *adj (activities, decision, attitude)* empresarial; *(skills, flair)* para los negocios

entrepreneurship *n (businesspeople)* empresariado *m*; *(business skills)* espíritu *m* de empresa

entry *n* (**a**) ACCT *(action)* asiento *m*, registro *m*; *(item)* asiento; **to make an entry** realizar un asiento (**b**) COMPTR *(of data)* introducción *f* (**c**) CUSTOMS *(of goods into country)* entrada *f* ❑ **entry barrier** barrera *f* de entrada; **entry permit** permiso *m* de entrada; **entry visa** visado *m or Am* visa *f* de entrada (**d**) *(of company or product on market)* introducción *f* (**e**) **entry level** *(of job)* nivel *m* de incorporación

envelope *n* sobre *m*; **in a sealed envelope** en un sobre cerrado

environment *n* COMPTR, ECON entorno *m*; **a pleasant working environment** un entorno de trabajo agradable

environmental *adj* **environmental audit** auditoría *f* medioambiental; **environmental damage** daños *mpl* medioambientales *or* ecológicos; **environmental economics** economía *f* medioambiental; **environmental impact assessment** evaluación *f* del impacto ambiental; **environmental policy** política *f* medioambiental; **environmental protection** protección *f* del medio ambiente

environmentally-friendly *adj* ecológico(a), que no daña el medio ambiente

EOC *n* ADMIN *(abbr* **Equal Opportunities Commission**) = organismo público británico que vela por la existencia de igualdad de oportunidades entre sexos, razas, etc

EONIA *n (abbr* **Euro Overnight Index Average**) EONIA *m*

EPOS *n (abbr* **electronic point of sale**) punto *m* de venta electrónico

EPS *n* (**a**) *(abbr* **earnings per share**) dividendo *m* por acción, beneficio *m* por acción (**b**) COMPTR *(abbr* **encapsulated PostScript**) EPS *m*

equal *adj* igual ❑ ADMIN **Equal Employment Opportunities Commission** = organismo público estadounidense que vela por la existencia de igualdad de oportunidades entre sexos, razas, etc; **equal opportunities** igualdad *f* de oportunidades; ADMIN **Equal Opportunities Commission** = organismo público británico que vela por la existencia de igualdad de oportunidades entre sexos, razas, etc; **an equal opportunity** *or* **opportunities employer** una entidad *or* organización no discriminatoria; **equal partners** = socios de una mercantil con iguales derechos y obligaciones; **equal pay** igualdad *f* salarial *or* de retribuciones; **Equal Pay Act** = ley británica que garantiza la igualdad salarial; **equal rights** igualdad *f* de derechos; **equal sign, equals sign** (signo *m* (de)) igual *m*

equality *n* igualdad *f* ❏ **equality of opportunity** igualdad *f* de oportunidades

equalization *n* FIN *(of dividends)* compensación *f*; *(of taxes, wealth)* nivelación *f*, igualación *f* ❏ **equalization fund** fondo *m* de estabilización; **equalization payment** pago *m* compensatorio

equalize *vt* FIN *(dividends)* compensar; *(taxes, wealth)* nivelar, igualar

equip *vt (factory)* equipar (**with** con); *(person)* dotar (**with** de); **we must equip our staff with the skills needed to use new technology** debemos dotar a nuestros empleados de las técnicas necesarias para el uso de las nuevas tecnologías

equipment *n* equipo *m* ❏ **equipment financing** financiación *f* de equipo; **equipment leasing** arrendamiento *m* de bienes de equipo; **equipment subsidy** subvención *f* de bienes de equipo

equity *n* FIN, ST EXCH *(of shareholders, company)* fondos *mpl* propios, patrimonio *m* neto; **equities** acciones *fpl* (ordinarias) ❏ **equity capital** fondos *mpl* propios, capital *m* aportado por los accionistas; **equity dilution** dilución *f* de capital; **equity financing** financiación *f* mediante la emisión de acciones; **equity investment** inversión *f* en capital social; **equity issue** ampliación *f* de capital; **equity leader** *(person)* director(ora) *m,f* de operaciones de renta variable; **equity loan** crédito *m* personal con garantía patrimonial; **equity** *or* **equities market** mercado *m* de renta variable; **equity risk premium** prima *m* por riesgo de los títulos de renta variable; **equity share** acción *f* ordinaria, título *m* de renta variable; **equity share capital** capital *m* en acciones ordinarias; **equity swap** permuta *fpl* de acciones; **equities trader** operador(ora) *m,f* de títulos de renta variable; **equity trading** negociación *f* de títulos de renta variable; **equity unit trust** fondo *m* de inversión de renta variable; **equity warrant** warrant *m*, derecho *m* especial de suscripción; **equity withdrawal** *(from mortgage)* = endeudamiento mediante créditos personales con garantía inmobiliaria no invertidos en la adquisición de la vivienda

equity-based unit trust *n* fondo *m* de inversión colectiva en títulos de renta variable

equity-linked *adj* FIN, ST EXCH *(policy)* ligado(a) al mercado de renta variable

equivalence of exchange *n* FIN paridad *f* cambiaria *or* monetaria

equivalent *adj* equivalente; **to be equivalent to sth** equivaler a algo

erase *vt* COMPTR, FIN borrar

ERDF *n* FIN *(abbr* **European Regional Development Fund**) FEDER *m*

ergonomic *adj* ergonómico(a)

ergonomics *n* ergonomía *f*

ERM *n* Formerly FIN *(abbr* **Exchange Rate Mechanism**) mecanismo *m* de tipos de cambio

ERP *n (abbr* **Enterprise Resource Planning**) ERP *m*

error *n* error *m*; ACCT **errors and omissions excepted** salvo error u omisión ❏ COMPTR **error code** código *m* de error; COMPTR **error detection** detección *f* de errores; COMPTR **error message** mensaje *m* de error

escalate *vi (prices)* aumentar vertiginosamente

escalation clause, escalator clause *n (in contract)* cláusula *f* de escala móvil

escape *n* (**a**) COMPTR escape *m* ❏ **escape key** tecla *f* de escape (**b**) **escape clause** cláusula *f* de escape *or* de salvaguardia

escrow *n* LAW plica *f*; **to be held in escrow** estar depositado(a) como garantía; **to put sth in escrow** depositar algo como garantía ❏ *esp US* **escrow account** cuenta *f* de depósito en garantía, cuenta de plica; **escrow agent** depositario(a) *m,f* de plica

escudo *n* Formerly escudo *m*

ESF *n* EU *(abbr* **European Social Fund**) FSE *m*

ESOP *n (abbr* **employee** *Br* **share** *or US* **stock ownership plan**) = plan de oferta de acciones a los empleados

est *adj (abbr* **established**) fundado(a); **A. Jones (est 1885)** A. Jones, fundada en 1885

establish *vt (system)* crear, establecer; *(business)* constituir, fundar; *(agency)* crear, constituir; **he quickly established himself in business** afianzó su negocio rápidamente

established *adj (system)* contrastado(a); *(business)* reconocido(a); **once the company becomes established** cuando la empresa esté bien establecida; **established 1890** fundado(a) en 1890

establishment *n* (**a**) *(company)* establecimiento *m*; **a business establishment** un establecimiento comercial (**b**) *(creation) (of system)* creación *f*, establecimiento *m*; *(of business)* constitución *f*, fundación *f*; *(of agency)* creación, constitución (**c**) **the Establishment** *(dominant group)* la clase dirigente; **the financial establishment** la clase económica dirigente

estate *n* (**a**) LAW *(possessions)* patrimonio *m* (**b**) *(of deceased person)* patrimonio *m* ❏ *Br* **estate duty,** *US* **estate tax** impuesto *m* sobre sucesiones (**c**) *(of bankrupt)* masa *f* de la quiebra (**d**) *(land)* finca *f* ❏ *Br* **estate agency, estate agent's** (agencia *f*) inmobiliaria *f*; *Br* **estate agent** agente *mf* de la propiedad (inmobiliaria)

estimate 1 *n* (**a**) *(calculation)* estimación *f*, cálculo *m* aproximado; **these figures are only a rough estimate** estas cifras son sólo un cálculo aproximado; **give me an estimate of how much you think it will cost** dime aproximadamente cuánto crees que costará; **at the lowest estimate it will take three months to complete** como mínimo se tardará tres meses en terminarlo
(**b**) *(of cost)* presupuesto *m*; **to put in an estimate (for sth/for doing sth)** presentar un presupuesto (para algo/para hacer algo); **to ask for an estimate (for sth/doing sth)** pedir un presupuesto (para algo/para hacer algo); **get several estimates before deciding which company to use** pide varios presupuestos antes de decidir con qué empresa lo vas a hacer
2 *vt* estimar (**at** en), calcular (**at** en); **the cost was estimated at £2,000** calcularon *or* estimaron que el costo *or* Esp coste sería de dos mil libras

estimation *n* *(calculation)* cálculo *m*, estimación *f*

estimator *n* tasador(ora) *m,f*

ETA *n* (*abbr* **estimated time of arrival**) hora *f* estimada de llegada

e-tail *vt* vender (al detalle) por Internet

e-tailer *n* tienda *f* electrónica

❝
Argos was last night recognised as the country's leading **e-tailer**, winning the most awards at this year's Visa E-tail Awards, as voted for by Visa customers. The 'Bricks to Clicks' award acknowledged Argos' e-tailing expertise, through its successful integration of its High Street, catalogue and Internet operations, and confirmed its position at the forefront of multi-channel retailing in the UK.
❞

e-tailing *n* venta *f* electrónica, venta (al detalle) por Internet

ETD *n* (*abbr* **estimated time of departure**) hora *f* estimada de salida

Ethernet® *n* COMPTR Ethernet® *f*

ethical *adj* ético(a) ❑ FIN **ethical investment** inversiones *fpl* éticas; FIN **ethical investment fund** fondo *m* de inversión ético

ETUC *n* (*abbr* **European Trade Union Confederation**) CES *f*

EU *n* (*abbr* **European Union**) UE *f*

EURIBOR *n* FIN (*abbr* **Euro Interbank Offered Rate**) Euribor *m*

euro, Euro *n* euro *m*; **the euro area** *or* **zone** la zona (del) euro ❑ ST EXCH **Euro Interbank Offered Rate** tipo *m* medio interbancario en euros; ST EXCH **Euro Overnight Index Average** =

media ponderada en euros de las operaciones interbancarias de crédito a un día; ST EXCH **Euro Stoxx** EuroStoxx *m*

Eurobank *n* eurobanco *m*

Eurobarometer *n* EU eurobarómetro *m*

Eurobond *n* eurobono *m*

Eurocard® *n* Eurocard® *f*

Eurocertificate *n* eurocertificado *m*

Eurocheque *n* eurocheque *m*

Euro-commercial paper *n* efectos *mpl* comerciales en eurodivisas

Eurocrat *n* eurócrata *mf*

Eurocredit *n* eurocrédito *m*

Eurocurrency *n* eurodivisa *f* ❑ **eurocurrency market** mercado *m* de eurodivisas

❝
The fund aims to give shareholders access to income at wholesale **euro-currency** market interest rates in the euro currency. The fund invests in a spread of short-term money market instruments with a weighted average maturity of 60 days.
❞

Eurodollar *n* eurodólar *m*

Euroland *n* Eurolandia *f*

Euroloan *n* europréstamo *m*

Euromarket *n* euromercado *m*

Euro-MP *n* eurodiputado(a) *m,f*

European *adj* europeo(a) ❑ **European Bank for Reconstruction and Development** Banco *m* Europeo de Reconstrucción y Desarrollo; **European Central Bank** Banco *m* Central Europeo; **European Central Securities Depositories Association** Asociación *f* Europea de Depositarios Centrales de Valores; ADMIN **European Coal and Steel Community** Comunidad *f* Europea del Carbón y el Acero; **European Commission** Comisión *f* Europea; **European commissioner** comisario(a) *m,f* europeo(a); **European Community** Comunidad *f* Europea; EU **European company** sociedad *f* europea; **European Convention on Human Rights** Convención *f* Europea de Derechos Humanos; **European Court of Human Rights** Tribunal *m* Europeo de Derechos Humanos; **European Court of Justice** Tribunal *m* de Justicia Europeo; *Formerly* **European currency snake** serpiente *f* monetaria europea; *Formerly* **European Currency Unit** unidad *f* de cuenta europea; **European Depository Receipt** recibo *m* de depósito europeo; **European Development Fund** Fondo *m* Europeo de Desarrollo; **European Economic Area** Espacio *m* Económico Europeo; *Formerly* **European Economic Community** Comunidad *f* Económica Europea; **European Environmental Bureau** Oficina *f*

Europea del Medio Ambiente; *Formerly **European Exchange Rate Mechanism*** Mecanismo *m* del Tipo de Cambio del SME; ***European Free Trade Association*** Asociación *f* Europea de Libre Comercio; ***European Investment Bank*** Banco *m* Europeo de Inversiones; ***European Metalworkers' Federation*** Federación *f* Europea (de Trabajadores) del Metal; ***European Monetary Agreement*** Acuerdo *m* Monetario Europeo; *Formerly **European Monetary Cooperation Fund*** Fondo *m* Europeo de Cooperación Monetaria; ***European Monetary Institute*** Instituto *m* Monetario Europeo; *Formerly **European Monetary System*** Sistema *m* Monetario Europeo; ***European Monetary Union*** Unión *f* Monetaria Europea; ***European Parliament*** Parlamento *m* Europeo; ***European Regional Development Fund*** Fondo *m* Europeo de Desarrollo Regional; ***European Social Fund*** Fondo *m* Social Europeo; ***European standards*** normas *fpl* europeas; ***European Standards Commission*** Comisión *f* Europea de Normalización; ***European Trade Union Confederation*** Confederación *f* Europea de Sindicatos; ***European Union*** Unión *f* Europea; ***European unit of account*** unidad *f* de cuenta europea

European(-style) option *n* ST EXCH opción *f* europea

Eurosterling *n* eurolibra *f*

Euroyen *n* euroyen *m*

EVA *n* (*abbr* **economic value added**) valor *m* económico añadido

evade *vt* **to evade tax** evadir impuestos

evaluate *vt* (*damages, value, cost*) evaluar

evaluation *n* (*of damages, value, cost*) evaluación *f*

event *n* (*corporate activity*) actividad *f* ❑ **event advertising** = publicidad realizada en acontecimientos deportivos, conciertos, etc; **event(s) management** organización *f* de eventos; **event(s) manager** organizador(ora) *m,f* de eventos; **event promotion** promoción *f* de eventos *or* actividades

evergreen *adj* FIN **evergreen facility** descubierto *m* bancario permanente; **evergreen fund** fondo *m* de crédito permanente

evoked set *n* MKTG = conjunto de marcas que un consumidor considera al plantearse hacer una compra

ex 1 *prep* (**a**) (*out of*) **ex quay** en muelle; **ex ship** sobre buque; **ex warehouse** en almacén; **ex wharf** en muelle; **ex works** en fábrica
(**b**) FIN, ST EXCH (*without*) **ex all, ex allotment** sin beneficios; **ex bonus** sin derecho de suscripción; **ex cap, ex capitalization** sin derecho de suscripción; **ex coupon** ex cupón; **this stock goes ex coupon on 1 August** esta acción cotiza

ex cupón el 1 de agosto; **ex dividend** sin dividendo; **ex interest** sin interés; **ex new, ex rights** ex derecho; **ex scrip** sin derecho de suscripción
2 (*abbr* **excluding**) no incluido(a); **ex VAT** sin IVA, IVA no incluido

exceed *vt* (*amount, number*) superar, exceder; (*budget*) sobrepasar; **demand exceeds supply** la demanda supera *or* excede la oferta; **her salary exceeds mine by £4,000 a year** gana 4.000 libras más que yo al año

exceptional *adj* ACCT **exceptional item** (*cost*) gasto *m* extraordinario; (*income*) ingreso *m* extraordinario; **exceptional tax** impuesto *m* extraordinario

excess *n* (**a**) (*in weight, expenditure*) exceso *m*; **there has been an excess of expenditure over revenue** los gastos han superado a los ingresos ❑ **excess capacity** exceso *m* de capacidad; **excess charges** recargo *m*; **excess demand** exceso *m* de demanda; **excess fare** suplemento *m*; **excess liquidities** exceso *m* de liquidez; **excess profits** (*considered to be too high*) beneficios *mpl* excesivos; (*unexpected*) beneficios *mpl* extraordinarios; **excess profits tax** impuesto *m* sobre beneficios extraordinarios; BANKING **excess reserves** exceso *m* de reservas; ST EXCH **excess shares** acciones *fpl* excedentes; **excess supply** exceso *m* de oferta; **excess weight** exceso *m* de peso
(**b**) *Br* INS franquicia *f* ❑ **excess clause** cláusula *f* de excedentes; **excess policy** póliza *f* con franquicia

exchange 1 *n* (**a**) FIN (*of currency*) cambio *m*; *US* **exchanges** (*bills*) letras *fpl* de cambio ❑ **exchange adjustments** ajuste *m* del tipo de cambio; **exchange broker** corredor(ora) *m,f* de comercio; **exchange controls** controles *mpl* de cambio; **exchange cross rate** tipo *m* de cambio cruzado; **exchange dealer** agente *mf* de cambios, cambista *mf*; **exchange equalization account** cuenta *f* de igualación de cambios; **exchange gain** diferencias *fpl* positivas de cambio; **exchange index** índice *m* bursátil; **exchange law** legislación *f* monetaria; **exchange loss** diferencias *fpl* negativas de cambio; **exchange market** mercado *m* de cambios *or* divisas; **exchange offer** oferta *f* de cambio; **exchange policy** política *f* de cambio, política *f* cambiaria; **exchange premium** ganancia *f* cambiaria; **exchange rate** tipo *m or* tasa *f* de cambio; **at the current exchange rate** al tipo de cambio actual; ST EXCH **exchange rate arbitrage** arbitraje *m* de cambio; *Formerly* EU **Exchange Rate Mechanism** mecanismo *m* de tipos de cambio; **exchange rate parity** paridad *f* en el tipo de cambio; **exchange rate stability** estabilidad *f* en el tipo de cambio; **exchange rate swap** swap *m or* permuta *f* de divisas; **exchange reserves** reservas *fpl* de divisas; **exchange restrictions**

restricciones *fpl* cambiarias *or* de cambio; **exchange risk** riesgo *m* cambiario; **exchange transaction** operación *f* en divisas, transacción *f* cambiaria; **exchange value** contravalor *m*
(**b**) *(of goods, shares, commodities)* intercambio *m* ❏ *Br* **exchange of contracts** = intercambio entre el vendedor y el comprador de una propiedad de los contratos vinculantes de una compraventa, ≃ firma *f* del contrato de arras
2 *vt* (**a**) *(shares, commodities)* intercambiar; *(defective goods)* cambiar (**b**) *Br* **to exchange contracts** *(when buying property)* = intercambiar los contratos vinculantes de la compraventa de una propiedad, ≃ firmar el contrato de arras

exchequer *n Br* ADMIN **the Exchequer** *(money)* el erario público; *(government department)* ≃ Hacienda ❏ **exchequer bill** bono *m* del Tesoro

excisable *adj* ADMIN imponible

excise *n* ADMIN *(tax)* impuestos *mpl* especiales ❏ **excise bond** fianza *f* específica; **excise documents** documentos *mpl* de los impuestos especiales; **excise duty** impuestos *mpl* especiales; **excise tax** impuestos *mpl* especiales

excl *(abbr* **excluding)** no incluido(a); **excl VAT** sin IVA, IVA no incluido

exclamation mark, US **exclamation point** *n* signo *m* de exclamación *or* admiración

excluding *prep* no incluido(a); **excluding VAT** sin IVA, IVA no incluido

exclusive 1 *adj* exclusivo(a) ❏ **exclusive agreement** contrato *m* de exclusividad; **exclusive distribution** distribución *f* exclusiva; **exclusive distribution agreement** contrato *m* de distribución exclusiva; **exclusive economic zone** zona *f* económica exclusiva; **exclusive licence** licencia *f* exclusiva; **exclusive rights** derechos *mpl* exclusivos; **exclusive selling rights** derechos *mpl* exclusivos de venta; **exclusive shipment** = envío de mercancías sujeto a condiciones especiales de transporte; **exclusive territory** *(for franchisee)* territorio *f* exclusivo
2 *adv* **exclusive of tax** impuestos no incluidos; **exclusive of delivery** excluyendo *or* sin incluir los gastos de envío; **£350, exclusive of delivery** 350 libras, más gastos de envío

exclusivity *n* uso *m* exclusivo, exclusividad *f* ❏ **exclusivity agreement** contrato *m* de exclusividad; **exclusivity clause** cláusula *f* de exclusividad

❝
Also, there are five divisions of Kroger representing 514 stores which have contractual conflicts due to an **exclusivity clause** they have in their contracts with News American Marketing In-Store (NAMIS). This **exclusivity clause** is what our counterclaims center on in our legal conflict with NAMIS. If

Kroger's contractual conflict remains unresolved, we will lose the 514 stores by mid-September. We are optimistic that we will renew our relationship with these stores when the NAMIS contract expires.
❞

ex-directory *adj Br* **ex-directory number** = número que no figura en la guía telefónica

exec *n Fam* *(abbr* **executive)** ejecutivo(a) *m,f*

executable file *n* COMPTR archivo *m or* fichero *m* ejecutable

execute *vt* (**a**) FIN *(transfer)* realizar (**b**) COMPTR ejecutar ❏ **execute cycle** ciclo *m* de ejecución

execution *n* COMPTR ejecución *f* ❏ **execution speed** velocidad *f* de ejecución

executive 1 *n* (**a**) *(person)* ejecutivo(a) *m,f* (**b**) *(board, committee)* ejecutivo *m*
2 *adj* *(ability)* ejecutivo(a); *(job)* directivo(a); *(car, plane)* para ejecutivos ❏ **executive board** comité *m* ejecutivo, directorio *m* ejecutivo; **executive director** director(ora) *m,f* ejecutivo(a); **executive functions** funciones *fpl* directivas; **executive member** miembro *m* del comité ejecutivo; **executive officer** directivo(a) *m,f* de empresa; **executive pension plan** = plan de pensiones especial para directivos; **executive power** poder *m* ejecutivo; **executive secretary** secretario(a) *m,f* ejecutivo(a); **executive share option scheme** = plan de compra de acciones de la empresa para directivos

executor *n* LAW *(of will)* albacea *mf* (testamentario(a))

exempt 1 *adj* exento(a) (**from** de); **exempt from taxes** exento(a) de impuestos
2 *vt* *(from obligation, taxes)* eximir (**from** de); **to be exempted from tax** *(goods)* estar exento(a) de impuestos

exemption *n* *(from obligation)* exención *f* (**from** de); *(from tax)* exención *f* tributaria *or* fiscal ❏ **exemption clause** cláusula *f* de exención

exercisable *adj* ST EXCH *(option)* ejercible

exercise 1 *n* (**a**) *(of one's rights)* ejercicio *m* (**b**) ST EXCH *(of option)* ejercicio *m* ❏ **exercise date** fecha *f* de ejercicio; **exercise notice** notificación *f* de ejercicio; **exercise price** precio *m* de ejercicio
2 *vt* (**a**) *(rights)* ejercer (**b**) ST EXCH **to exercise an option** ejercer una opción

ex gratia *adj (payment)* voluntario(a)

ex-growth *adj (company, share)* estancado(a), sin perspectivas de crecimiento; **to go ex-growth** estancarse

❝
Vodafone's performance indicators vindicate neither bulls nor bears. We shall need several more quarters to judge whether the

company has or has not gone **ex-growth**. During the long meanwhile the shares will remain volatile.

"

exhibit 1 n (at trade show) (stand) stand m, puesto m; (item) objeto m or producto m expuesto **2** vt (object, goods) exhibir

exhibition n (a) (show) exposición f □ **exhibition hall** sala f de exposiciones; **exhibition stand** stand m de una exposición (**b**) (of goods) muestra f

exhibitor n (at exhibition) expositor(ora) m,f

Ex-Im bank n US banco m de exportación e importación

existing adj MKTG **existing customer** cliente(a) m,f actual; **existing market** mercado m actual

exit 1 n (**a**) **exit barrier** barrera f de salida; **exit charge(s)** comisión f por amortización or cancelación anticipada; **exit interview** entrevista f de despedida or salida; **exit permit** permiso m de salida; **exit visa** visado m or Am visa f de salida (**b**) COMPTR salida f
2 vt COMPTR (program, session) salir de
3 vi COMPTR salir

ex officio ADMIN **1** adj (member) en virtud del cargo
2 adv (act) en virtud del cargo

expand 1 vt (company, business, market) ampliar, expandir; (production, output, staff) ampliar; COMPTR (memory) ampliar, expandir; **to expand a company into a multinational** convertir una empresa en una multinacional
2 vi (company, business, market) ampliarse, expandirse; (production, output, staff) ampliarse; **the mobile phone sector is continuing to expand** el sector de los teléfonos móviles or Am celulares se sigue expandiendo; **we want to expand into publishing** queremos introducirnos en el sector editorial; **Texaco expanded into oil production in the later part of last century** Texaco se introdujo en el sector productor de petróleo a finales del siglo pasado

expandable adj COMPTR (memory) ampliable, expandible; **98MB expandable to 392MB** 98MB ampliables or expandibles a 392MB

expanded adj COMPTR □ **expanded keyboard** teclado m expandido; **expanded memory** memoria f expandida

expanding adj (company, market) en expansión

"

Waste is the great new growth industry, and as British landfill sites are phased out, in accordance with EU regulations, there will be a need for more and more recycling: "It's an **expanding** market, it's not seasonal, and I could sell exclusively within the UK."

"

expansion n (**a**) (of company, business, market) expansión f; (of economy) crecimiento m (**b**) COMPTR (of memory) ampliación f, expansión f □ **expansion board** placa f de expansión; **expansion card** tarjeta f de expansión or ampliación (de memoria); **expansion port** puerto m de expansión; **expansion slot** ranura f de expansión

expansionist adj expansionista

expectation n expectativa f; **the company's performance did not confirm the financial community's expectations** los resultados de la empresa no cumplieron las expectativas de la comunidad financiera; **we have certain expectations of our employees** esperamos ciertas cosas de nuestros empleados

expected adj esperado(a), previsto(a) □ **expected monetary value** valor m monetario previsto; **expected value** valor m previsto

expend vt (money) gastar (**on** en)

expenditure n (**a**) (spending) gasto m; **this will involve us in fairly heavy expenditure** esto nos obligará a realizar un desembolso considerable (**b**) (amount spent) gasto m (**on** en)

expense n (**a**) (cost) gasto m; **at great expense** con un gran gasto; **it's not worth the expense** no vale lo que cuesta □ **expense account** cuenta f de gastos; **to put sth on the expense account** apuntar algo en la cuenta de gastos; **the company gives him an expense account for basic entertaining** la empresa le proporciona una cuenta básica para gastos de representación; **expense budget** presupuesto m para gastos de representación
(**b**) **expenses** gastos; **to meet** or **cover sb's expenses** correr con or costear los gastos de alguien; **to put sth on expenses** apuntar algo en la cuenta de gastos (de la empresa); **it's on expenses** corre a cargo de la empresa; **to cut down on expenses** reducir or recortar gastos; **to incur expenses** contraer gastos; **all expenses paid** con todos los gastos pagados □ **expenses claim form** formulario m de gastos

expensive adj caro(a)

experience n experiencia f; **do you have any experience of dealing with the public?** ¿tiene experiencia en la atención al público?; **she has considerable management experience** tiene mucha experiencia como directiva; **no experience necessary** (in job advert) no es necesaria or no se necesita experiencia □ MKTG **experience curve** curva f de experiencia; MKTG **experience effect** efecto m de experiencia

expert n experto(a) m,f; **he is an expert in this field** es experto en este campo □ **expert panel** equipo m de expertos; **expert's report** dictamen m pericial; COMPTR **expert system** sistema m experto

expertise *n* destreza *f*, pericia *f*

expiration *n* vencimiento *m* ❏ *US* **expiration date** *(of product)* fecha *f* de caducidad

expire *vi* expirar, vencer

expiry *n* vencimiento *m* ❏ **expiry date** fecha *f* de caducidad

explanatory note *n* nota *f* aclaratoria

explore *vt (market)* estudiar, explorar

export 1 *n* (**a**) *(product)* artículo *m* de exportación; **exports** *(of country)* exportaciones *fpl*
(**b**) *(activity)* exportación *f*; **for export only** sólo para exportación ❏ **export agent** agente *mf* exportador(ora); **export aid** ayuda *f* a la exportación; **export ban** prohibición *f* de exportación; **to impose an export ban on sth** imponer una prohibición de exportación a algo; **export company** empresa *f* exportadora; **export concessionaire** = titular de una concesión de exportación; **export credit** crédito *m* a la exportación; **export credit guarantee** garantía *f* de créditos para la exportación; *Br* **Export Credit Guarantee Department** departamento *m* de garantía de créditos a la exportación; **export credit rate** *Esp* tipo *m* or *Am* tasa *f* de los créditos a la exportación; **export declaration** declaración *f* de exportación; **export department** departamento *m* de exportación; **export director** director(ora) *m,f* de exportaciones; **export division** división *f* de exportación; **export drive** = campaña publicitaria para fomentar la exportación; **export duty** derechos *mpl* de exportación; **export earnings** ingresos *mpl* por exportación; **export gold-point** punto *m* oro; **export goods** mercancías *fpl* para exportación; **export incentive** incentivo *m* a la exportación; **export label** *(brand)* = marca con la que se vende un producto en otros países; **export levy** exacción *f* a la exportación; **export licence** permiso *m* or licencia *f* de exportación; **export list** arancel *m* de salida; **export management** gestión *f* de exportaciones; **export manager** director(ora) *m,f* de exportaciones; **export market** mercado *m* de exportación; **export office** departamento *m* de exportación; **export order** pedido *m* de exportación; **export permit** permiso *m* de exportación; **export potential** potencial *f* de exportación; **export price** precio *m* de exportación; **export prohibition** prohibición *f* de exportación; **export quota** cuota *f* de exportación; **export refund** restitución *f* a la exportación; **export reject** = producto cuya calidad no se considera suficiente para la exportación y se vende en el mercado interior; **export restrictions** restricciones *fpl* a la exportación; **export revenue** ingresos *mpl* por exportaciones; **export sales** ventas *fpl* de exportación; **export subsidy** subvención *f* a la exportación; **export tax** impuesto *m* sobre la exportación; **export**

trade comercio *m* de exportación
2 *vt* (**a**) *(goods)* exportar (**b**) COMPTR exportar (**to** a)
3 *vi* exportar; **the firm exports all over the world** la empresa exporta a todo el mundo

exportable *adj* exportable

exportation *n (of goods)* exportación *f*

exporter *n* exportador(ora) *m,f*; **Britain is now one of the world's biggest exporters of aircraft** el Reino Unido es hoy en día uno de los mayores exportadores de aviones del mundo

Export-Import bank *n US* banco *m* de exportación e importación

exporting *adj* exportador(ora), de exportación ❏ **exporting country** país *m* exportador

exposé *n (article)* artículo *m* de denuncia; *(TV programme)* programa *m* de denuncia

exposure *n* (**a**) *(publicity)* publicidad *f*; **to get** *or* **receive a lot of exposure** *(company, product)* recibir mucha publicidad; **exposure to the media is important for a new product** es importante que el nuevo producto reciba la atención de los medios de comunicación (**b**) FIN riesgo *m*

express *adj (letter, delivery)* urgente, exprés

ext *(abbr* **extension**) ext.

extend *vt* (**a**) *(grant)* **to extend credit to sb** conceder un crédito a alguien; **the banks won't extend any more credit to the company** los bancos no concederán más crédito(s) a la empresa (**b**) *(deadline, contract)* prolongar, prorrogar; *(expiry of bill)* aplazar, prorrogar el plazo de

extended *adj* (**a**) **extended credit** crédito *m* ampliado, crédito prorrogado; **extended guarantee** garantía *f* ampliada; **extended leave** baja *f*; **extended warranty** garantía *f* ampliada (**b**) COMPTR **extended keyboard** teclado *m* extendido; **extended memory** memoria *f* extendida

extension *n* (**a**) *(of credit, contract)* prórroga *f*; *(of deadline)* prórroga *f*, ampliación *f*; **we need an extension to complete the project** necesitamos una prórroga para terminar el proyecto (**b**) *(for telephone)* extensión *f*, *RP* interno *m*; **can I have extension 946?** ¿me puede comunicar *or Esp* poner con la extensión 946?, *RP* ¿me puede dar con el interno 946? ❏ **extension number** número *m* de extensión *or RP* interno (**c**) COMPTR *(of file)* extensión *f*

external *adj* (**a**) *(trade)* exterior; *(debt)* externo(a), exterior ❏ **external account** *(of nation)* cuenta *f* corriente de la balanza de pagos; *(of individual)* cuenta *f* de no residente; **external audit** auditoría *f* externa; **external auditing** auditoría *f* externa; **external auditor** auditor(ora) *m,f* externo(a); **external deficit** déficit *m* exterior, déficit de la balanza de pagos; FIN **external financing** financiación *f* ajena; **external growth**

crecimiento *m* mediante adquisiciones
(**b**) COMPTR **external cache** caché *f* externa; **external device** periférico *m* externo; **external drive** disco *m* externo; **external modem** módem *m* externo

extn (*abbr* **extension**) Ext., *RP* Int.

extra 1 *n* (*additional charge*) suplemento *m*, recargo *m*
2 *adj* adicional; **to charge extra** cobrar un recargo ◻ **extra charge** suplemento *m*, recargo *m*; **extra cost** coste *m* adicional

extract *vt* COMPTR (*zipped file*) extraer

extraordinary *adj* (**a**) FIN **extraordinary general meeting** junta *f or* asamblea *f* general extraordinaria; **to call an extraordinary general meeting of the shareholders** convocar una junta *or* asamblea extraordinaria de accionistas (**b**) ACCT **extraordinary expenses** gastos *mpl* extraordinarios; **extraordinary income** ingresos *mpl* extraordinarios; **extraordinary item** partida *f* extraordinaria; **extraordinary profit or loss** ganancia *f* o pérdida *f* extraordinaria

"

In the first quarter of 2002, Italian energy group Edison reported net consolidated profit of 420m euros which included **extraordinary income** of 425m euros derived from the sale of a 22.2 per cent stake in Italian insurance company Fondiaria.

"

extrapolate 1 *vt* extrapolar; **we can extrapolate sales figures of the last ten years to predict future trends** podemos extrapolar las cifras de ventas de los diez últimos años para predecir las tendencias futuras
2 *vi* extrapolar; **to extrapolate from sth** hacer una extrapolación a partir de algo

extrapolation *n* extrapolación *f*

extrinsic value *n* ST EXCH valor *m* tiempo *or* temporal

EXW (*abbr* **exworks**) EXW

e-zine *n* revista *f* electrónica

Ff

faa *adj* (*abbr* **free of all average**) libre de toda avería

face *n* (**a**) *face value*, *US* *face amount* (*of banknote, traveller's cheque, stamp, share*) valor *m* nominal (**b**) *US* *face time* (*meeting*) tiempo *m* de contacto personal

> **"**
> America Online executives covered both bases as Chairman-CEO Steve Case and President-COO Bob Pittman hit the Allen dealmaker fest and George Vradenburg, senior vice president-global and strategic policy, accompanied Clinton on his tour of Los Angeles' Watts district. Any **face time** between Vradenburg and the President likely included discussion of AOL's desire to gain access to the cable industry's high-speed broadband pipe.
> **"**

facilitate *vt* (*meeting, focus group*) facilitar

facilitator *n* (*of meeting, focus group*) facilitador(ora) *m,f*

facility *n* (**a**) (*service*) servicio *m*; **facilities for payment** formas *fpl* de pago; **we offer easy credit facilities** ofrecemos facilidades de crédito (**b**) **facilities** (*equipment, resources*) instalaciones y servicios; **we don't have the facilities to hold a conference here** no contamos con los medios adecuados para organizar un congreso

facsimile *n* facsímil *m*

factor *n* (**a**) (*in multiplication*) factor *m*; **the sales increased by a factor of ten** las ventas aumentaron en un factor diez (**b**) ECON *factors of production* factores *mpl* de producción (**c**) (*factoring company*) factor *m*, empresa *f* de factoring *or* factoraje

factorage *n* (*charge*) = comisión que recibe una empresa de factoring

factoring *n* factoring *m*, compra *f* de deudas ◻ *factoring agent* empresa *f* de factoring *or* factoraje; *factoring charges* = comisión que recibe una empresa de factoring; *factoring company* empresa *f* de factoring, factor *m*;

> **"**
> "A **factoring company** essentially buys your invoices and charges a commission in exchange for rapid settlement," he says. "It is

chiefly used by companies with a turnover up to £1m, the kind of organisation that most often depends on a streamlined cashflow. With overseas **factoring**, commission rates are likely to be higher because chasing a debt abroad can be expensive and time consuming."
> **"**

factory *n* fábrica *f*, *Am* planta *f* ◻ *factory inspection* inspección *f* de fábrica; *factory inspector* inspector(ora) *m,f* de trabajo; *factory outlet* tienda *f* de fábrica, factory outlet *m*; *factory overheads* gastos *mpl* generales de fabricación; *factory price* precio *m* de fábrica; *Br factory shop* tienda *f* de fábrica; *factory unit* unidad *f* de fabricación; *factory work* trabajo *m* de *or* en una fábrica; *factory worker* trabajador(ora) *m,f* de producción, obrero(a) *m,f* industrial

fail *vi* (*project, scheme, negotiations*) fracasar; (*company*) quebrar; (*crops*) perderse

failure *n* (*of project, scheme, negotiations*) fracaso *m*; (*of company*) quiebra *f*; (*of crops*) pérdida *f* ◻ *US failure investment* inversión *f* fallida; *failure rate* tasa *f* de quiebras

fair 1 *n* (*exhibition*) feria *f* (comercial)
2 *adj* *fair average quality* calidad *f* corriente; *fair copy* copia *f* en limpio; *fair deal* trato *m* justo; *fair market value* valor *m* justo de mercado; *fair pay* retribución *f* justa; *fair trade* comercio *m* justo; *fair wage* retribución *f* justa; *fair wear and tear* desgaste *m* natural

fair-trade *adj* de comercio justo ◻ *fair-trade agreement* acuerdo *m* de comercio justo

faith *n* **in good faith** de buena fe; **to buy sth in good faith** comprar algo de buena fe

faithfully *adv* **yours faithfully** (*in letter*) (le saluda) atentamente

fake 1 *n* (*product, document*) falsificación *f*
2 *adj* falso(a)
3 *vt* (*document, signature*) falsificar

fall 1 *n* (*of prices, shares, interest rate, value, currency*) caída *f* (**in** de)
2 *vi* (*prices, shares, interest rate, value, currency*) caer, bajar

▶ **fall back** *vi* (*shares*) caer, bajar; **shares fell back one point** las acciones cayeron un punto

▶ **fall off** *vi* (*profits, sales*) disminuir

fallen angel *n* ST EXCH ángel *m* caído

falling *adj (shares, market, interest rate, value)* a la baja, en descenso; **the problems caused by the falling pound** los problemas provocados por la caída de la libra; **owing to falling demand/prices** debido a la caída de la demanda/los precios

falling-off *n (in demand)* descenso *m*; *(in production)* disminución *f*

fallout *n (consequences)* secuelas *fpl*

false *adj* falso(a) ❑ **false bill** factura *f* falsa; **false claim** reclamación *f* fraudulenta, *SAm* reclamo *m* fraudulento; ACCT **false entry** asiento *m* falso

falsification *n* falsificación *f*

falsify *vt (document, balance sheet)* falsificar

family *n Br Formerly* ADMIN **family allowance** ayuda *f* familiar; ADMIN **family benefits** prestaciones *fpl* familiares; MKTG **family brand** marca *f* de familia; **family business** negocio *m* familiar; *Br* ADMIN **family credit** = prestación suplementaria a familias con bajos ingresos que tienen al menos un hijo; ADMIN **family income** renta *f* familiar, ingresos *mpl* familiares; **family leave** permiso *m* por asuntos familiares; MKTG **family lifecycle** ciclo *m* de vida familiar; **family model** modelo *m* familiar

family-sized *adj (packet, box)* de tamaño familiar

Fannie Mae *n Fam* = denominación coloquial de la "Federal National Mortgage Association", organismo estadounidense que negocia con hipotecas en el mercado secundario y garantiza el pago de las mismas

> **❝**
> These government mandated mortgage market "wholesalers", **Fannie Mae** and Freddie Mac – or savings and loan institutions similar to building societies – have been expanding their trillion dollar balance sheets at annualised rates of greater than 20%.
> **❞**

FAO 1 *n (abbr* **Food and Agriculture Organization)** FAO *f*
  2 *prep (abbr* **for the attention of)** a la atención de

FAQ 1 *n* COMPTR *(abbr* **frequently asked questions)** preguntas *fpl* más frecuentes ❑ **FAQ file** documento *m* con las preguntas más frecuentes
  2 *adj (abbr* **free alongside** *or* **at quay)** franco muelle

faq *n (abbr* **fair average quality)** calidad *f* corriente

FAS *(abbr* **free alongside ship)** FAS

fast mover *n* MKTG producto *m* de rápida rotación

fast-moving *adj* MKTG de rápida rotación ❑ **fast-moving consumer goods** bienes *mpl* de consumo de rápida rotación

fast-track 1 *adj* (**a**) *(executive, employee)* destinado al ascenso por la vía rápida (**b**) *(application, procedure)* por la vía rápida
  2 *vt (application, procedure)* hacer por la vía rápida; **he's been fast-tracked for promotion** lo han ascendido por la vía rápida

fast-tracking *n* (**a**) *(of executive, graduate, employee)* promoción *f* or ascenso *m* por la vía rápida (**b**) *(of application, procedure)* procesado *m* por la vía rápida

fat cat *n (in industry)* = alto ejecutivo con un salario desproporcionado

> **❝**
> Shell, the self-styled socially responsible oil group, yesterday rekindled the row over boardroom pay by disclosing that its new executive chairman, Phil Watts, won an 82% pay rise to £1.59m last year. The increase in Mr Watts' salary package, including a £455,000 performance bonus, dwarfed the 58% rise given to BP's chief executive Lord Browne which itself retriggered the **fat cat** furore.
> **❞**

fault tree *n* árbol *m* de fallos *or Am* fallas

faulty *adj* defectuoso(a)

favorable *US* = **favourable**

favorites *npl* COMPTR *(websites)* favoritos *mpl*

favourable, *US* **favorable** *adj (terms)* favorable, ventajoso(a); **on favourable terms** en términos ventajosos

fax 1 *n (machine)* fax *m*, telefax *m*; *(document, message)* fax; **to send sb a fax** enviar un fax a alguien; **to send sth by fax** enviar algo por fax ❑ **fax card** tarjeta *f* de fax; COMPTR **fax modem** módem *m* fax; **fax number** número *m* de fax
  2 *vt (message, document)* mandar por fax; **to fax sb** mandar un fax a alguien

FCA *(abbr* **free carrier)** FCA

FCFS *(abbr* **first come, first served)** por riguroso orden de llegada

FCL-FCL *(abbr* **full container load-full container load)** FCL-FCL

FCL-LCL *(abbr* **full container load-less than container load)** FCL-LCL

FDI *n (abbr* **foreign direct investment)** inversión *f* directa extranjera

feasibility *n (of plan)* viabilidad *f* ❑ **feasibility report** informe *m* de viabilidad; **feasibility stage** *(of product development)* fase *f* de viabilidad; **feasibility study** estudio *m* de viabilidad; **feasibility test** prueba *f* de viabilidad

featherbed *vt* ECON *(industry, business)* proteger por medio de subsidios

> Despite US recession, Euro-zone slump, the collapse in American tourists and foot and mouth fears, consumers just keep on spending – so much so that towns in Northern Ireland are reporting a surge in shoppers offloading their punts. Some of this is down to the side effects of the monumental currency switch. At least IR£500 million (£392m) in so-called 'mattress money' is **featherbedding** the economy by boosting consumer spending.

featherbedding *n* (**a**) ECON *(of industry, business)* = protección gubernamental por medio de subsidios (**b**) *(in industrial relations)* = práctica que consiste en contratar mano de obra que no es necesaria o limitar el rendimiento de los obreros a fin de crear puestos de trabajo o proteger los ya existentes

feature 1 *n (of product)* característica *f*
2 *vt (product)* contar con; **all our products feature a money-back guarantee** todos nuestros productos cuentan con una garantía de devolución

Fed *US Fam* (**a**) *(abbr* **Federal Reserve Board**) junta *f* de gobierno de la Reserva Federal (**b**) *(abbr* **Federal Reserve (System)**) Reserva *f* Federal (**c**) *(abbr* **Federal Reserve Bank**) banco *m* de la Reserva Federal (**d**) *(abbr* **Federal**) *Fed funds* fondos *mpl* federales

> Hong Kong Monetary Authority interest rates are following the US **Fed Funds** rate in a downward direction, already at 2.0%, and with strong hints by the **Fed**'s Governor Laurence Meyer last week of more monetary easing to come.

federal *adj Federal Aviation Administration* ≃ Dirección *f* General de Aviación Civil; LAW *federal court* tribunal *m* federal; *Federal Debt* deuda *f* federal; *Federal Deposit Insurance Corporation* = organismo federal estadounidense asegurador de depósitos bancarios; *Federal funds* fondos *mpl* federales; *Federal Housing Administration* Departamento *m* Federal de la Vivienda; *Federal Insurance Contributions Act* = ley estadounidense sobre las cotizaciones a la seguridad social; *Federal Mediation and Conciliation Service* = organismo estadounidense de arbitraje en los conflictos de trabajo; *Federal Reserve Bank* banco *m* de la Reserva Federal; *Federal Reserve Board* junta *f* de gobierno de la Reserva Federal; *Federal Reserve (System)* Reserva *f* Federal; *Federal Trade Commission* Comisión *f* Federal de Comercio

> The **Federal Reserve Board** sets monetary policy, develops banking regulations and examines banks for compliance with laws and regulations. The White House's announcement today that Mr. Olson would serve on the Federal board is well received by the Minnesota bankers because Mr. Olson thoroughly understands the issues facing Minnesota banks.

federation *n* federación *f*

fee *n (for services)* tarifa *f*; *(of lawyer)* minuta *f*, honorarios *mpl*; *(of doctor)* honorarios *mpl*; *(for agency)* comisión *f*; **to draw one's fees** cobrar los honorarios; **to do sth for a small fee** hacer algo por un módico precio; **to charge a fee** cobrar una cantidad; **a monthly fee** una cuota mensual; LAW **property held in fee simple** bienes de pleno dominio

feed *vt* COMPTR *(paper)* introducir; **to feed data into a computer** introducir datos en *Esp* un ordenador *or Am* una computadora

feedback *n* reacción *f*; **positive/negative feedback** reacción positiva/negativa; **we welcome feedback from our customers** apreciamos la opinión de nuestros clientes; **this will provide us with much-needed feedback on public opinion** esto nos proporcionará la información que tanto necesitamos sobre la opinión pública

feeder *n* COMPTR *(for printer, scanner, photocopier)* alimentador *m*

FEPC *n (abbr* **Fair Employment Practices Commission**) = organismo oficial que fomenta la igualdad de oportunidades en el empleo

fetch *vt (price)* venderse por, alcanzar; **it fetched a high price** se vendió por una suma considerable; **it fetched £100,000** alcanzó las 100.000 libras

FHA *n (abbr* **Federal Housing Administration**) = departamento federal de la vivienda en EE.UU.

FHLMC *n (abbr* **Federal Home Loan Mortgage Corporation**) = organismo estadounidense que negocia con hipotecas en el mercado secundario y garantiza el pago de las mismas

fiat (money) *n US* moneda *f* fiduciaria

> And, at the base of the financial system, with the abandonment of gold convertibility in the 1930s, legal tender became backed – if that is the proper term – by the **fiat** of the state. The value of **fiat money** can be

inferred only from the values of the present and future goods and services it can command. And that, in turn, has largely rested on the quantity of **fiat money** created relative to demand. ⟥

fibre-optic, US **fiber-optic** adj de fibra óptica ◻ **fibre-optic cable** cable m de fibra óptica

fibre optics n fibra f óptica

FICA n (abbr **Federal Insurance Contributions Act**) = ley estadounidense sobre las contribuciones a la seguridad social

fictitious adj **fictitious assets** activo m ficticio; **fictitious bill** factura f falsa; **fictitious cost** gasto m ficticio; **fictitious person** persona f jurídica

fiddle Fam **1** n amaño m, chanchullo m; **to be on the fiddle** tener un chanchullo (montado)
2 vt (accounts, expenses) amañar

fidelity guarantee n INS póliza f de fidelidad

fiduciary FIN **1** n (trustee) fiduciario(a) m,f
2 adj fiduciario(a) ◻ **fiduciary account** cuenta f fiduciaria; **fiduciary issue** emisión f fiduciaria

field n (**a**) (sphere of activity, knowledge) campo m; **what field are you in?, what's your field?** ¿a qué tipo de actividad te dedicas?; **she's an expert in her field** es una experta en su campo ◻ **field of activity** tipo m de actividad
(**b**) (practice as opposed to theory) **in the field** sobre el terreno; **to work in the field** hacer trabajo de campo, trabajar in situ ◻ **field engineer** ingeniero(a) m,f de campo; **field experiment** prueba f de campo; **field marketing** = práctica que consiste en enviar representantes de ventas a tiendas y almacenes para construir marca y mejorar ventas; **field research** estudios mpl de campo; **field study** (scientific) estudio m de campo; **field test** prueba f sobre el terreno; **field trials** (for machine) pruebas fpl sobre el terreno; **field work** trabajo m de campo
(**c**) COMPTR (in database) campo m ◻ **field name** nombre m de campo

field-test vt probar or testear sobre el terreno

FIFO (abbr **first in, first out**) (**a**) ACCT PEPS, primeras entradas, primeras salidas (**b**) (in industrial relations)= principio según el cual los trabajadores con más antigüedad de una empresa son los primeros en ser despedidos

fifty-fifty **1** adj **a fifty-fifty venture** una operación al cincuenta por ciento
2 adv **to share the costs fifty-fifty** compartir los gastos al cincuenta por ciento

figure n cifra f; **figures** (statistics) cifras; **the figures for next year look good** las cifras para el año que viene son prometedoras; **to work out the figures** hacer cuentas; **to find a mistake in the figures** encontrar un error en las cuentas; **his salary is in six figures** gana más de 100.000

file 1 n (**a**) (folder) carpeta f; (ring binder) carpeta de anillas or Méx argollas
(**b**) (documents) expediente m, ficha f; **to have** or **keep sth on file** tener algo archivado; **it's on file** lo tenemos archivado; **we will keep your CV on file** guardaremos su currículum ◻ US **file cabinet** archivador m, Méx archivero m; US **file clerk** archivero(a) m,f, archivista mf; **file copy** copia f de archivo
(**c**) COMPTR archivo m, fichero m ◻ **file compression** compresión f de archivos or ficheros; **file conversion** conversión f de archivos or ficheros; **file extension** extensión f del archivo or fichero; **file format** formato m de archivo or fichero; **file lock** bloqueo m de archivo or fichero; **file management** gestión f de archivos or ficheros; **file management system** sistema m de gestión de archivos or ficheros; **file manager** administrador m de archivos or ficheros; **file menu** menú m de archivo or fichero; **file merge** fusión f de archivos or ficheros; **file name** nombre m de archivo or fichero; **file name extension** extensión f (del nombre) del archivo or fichero; **file protection** protección f de archivos or ficheros; **file server** servidor m de archivos or ficheros; **file sharing** (menu item) compartir archivos or ficheros; **file structure** estructura f del archivo or fichero; **file transfer** transferencia f de archivos or ficheros; **file transfer protocol** protocolo m de transferencia de archivos or ficheros; **file viewer** visualizador m de archivos or ficheros
2 vt (**a**) (documents) archivar; **file these documents under "sales"** archiva estos documentos en "ventas"; **what name is it filed under?** bajo qué nombre está archivado?
(**b**) (complaint, claim, request) presentar; FIN **to file one's petition in bankruptcy** presentar una declaración de quiebra, declararse en quiebra; **to file an application for a patent** presentar una solicitud de patente; **to file a claim for damages** presentar una demanda por daños y perjuicios; US **to file one's tax return** presentar la declaración de renta
3 vi (**a**) (classify documents) archivar; **I spent the whole morning filing** pasé toda la mañana archivando documentos (**b**) FIN **to file for bankruptcy** presentar una declaración de quiebra, declararse en quiebra

filing n (**a**) (of documents) archivo m, archivado m; **there is a lot of filing to be done** tengo muchas cosas que archivar ◻ **filing cabinet** archivador m, Méx archivero m; Br **filing clerk** archivero(a) m,f, archivista mf; **filing system** sistema m de archivo; **filing tray** bandeja f de la documentación para archivar (**b**) (of complaint, claim, request) presentación f; (for bankruptcy) petición f de declaración de quiebra

fill vt (post, vacancy) cubrir; **the post has already been filled** la vacante ya ha sido cubierta

▶ **fill in** vt sep (form, cheque stub, application) rellenar, cumplimentar, Am llenar; (date, details) escribir

▶ **fill out** vt sep (form, application) rellenar, cumplimentar, Am llenar

filter n COMPTR filtro m

Fimbra n Formerly (abbr **Financial Intermediaries, Managers and Brokers Regulatory Association**) = asociación profesional británica de intermediarios, gestores y agentes financieros

final adj (last) último(a); (definitive) definitivo(a) □ **final acceptance** aceptación f definitiva; **final accounts** cuentas fpl anuales definitivas; **final assessment** liquidación f definitiva; **final copy** versión f definitiva; FIN **final date** (for payment) fecha f de vencimiento; **final demand** último aviso m de pago; ST EXCH **final dividend** dividendo m definitivo; **final instalment** último plazo m; **final offer** última oferta f; **final payment** último pago m; **final product** producto m final; FIN **final settlement** liquidación f final; **final statement** balance m final

finalization n (of details, plan, agreement) ultimación f; (of date, deal) concreción f

finalize vt (details, plan, agreement) ultimar; (date, deal) concretar

finance 1 n (a) (money, field) finanzas fpl; **we don't have the necessary finance** no contamos con los recursos económicos necesarios □ **Finance Act** Ley f Presupuestaria; **Finance Bill** Proyecto m de Ley Presupuestaria; **finance charges** cargos mpl de or por financiación; **finance company** compañía f financiera; **finance costs** costos mpl or Esp costes mpl de financiación; **finance department** departamento m financiero; **finance director** director(ora) m,f financiero(a); Br **finance house** compañía f financiera; **Finance Minister** Ministro(a) m,f de Economía

(b) **finances** (funds) finanzas fpl; **the company's finances are a bit low at the moment** en estos momentos la empresa se encuentra en una mala situación financiera

2 vt financiar; **the company has agreed to finance staff training** la empresa se ha comprometido a financiar la formación de la plantilla

financial adj financiero(a) □ **financial accountant** contable mf financiero(a), Am contador(ora) m,f financiero(a); **financial accounting** contabilidad f financiera; **financial administration** gestión f financiera; **financial adviser** asesor(ora) m,f financiero(a); **financial aid** ayuda f financiera; **financial analyst** analista mf financiero(a); **financial appraisal** evaluación f financiera; **financial arrangement** régimen m de financiación; **financial assistance** ayuda f financiera; **financial authorities** autoridades fpl financieras; **financial backer** capitalista mf,

inversor(ora) m,f; **financial backing** respaldo m financiero; **financial centre** centro m financiero; **financial chart** gráfico m financiero; **financial circles** círculos mpl financieros; **financial community** comunidad f financiera; **financial compensation** indemnización f, compensación f económica; **financial consultant** consultor(ora) m,f financiero(a); **financial control** control m financiero; **financial controller** interventor(ora) m,f (financiero(a)); ACCT **financial costs** costos mpl or Esp costes mpl financieros; **financial crisis** crisis f financiera; **financial deal** acuerdo m financiero; **financial difficulties** problemas mpl financieros; **to be in financial difficulties** tener problemas financieros; **financial director** director(ora) m,f financiero(a); **financial engineering** ingeniería f financiera; **financial expenses** gastos mpl financieros; ST EXCH **financial future** futuro m financiero; ST EXCH **financial futures market** mercado m de futuros financieros; **financial gearing** apalancamiento m financiero; **financial group** grupo m financiero; **financial healthcheck** valoración f de la situación financiera; **financial imbalance** déficit m financiero; **financial institution** entidad f financiera; **financial instrument** instrumento m financiero; **financial intermediary** intermediario(a) m,f financiero(a); **financial journal** publicación f financiera; **financial law** derecho m financiero; **financial management** gestión f financiera; **financial manager** director(ora) m,f financiero(a); **financial market** mercado m financiero; **financial means** medios mpl financieros; **financial ombudsman** defensor(ora) m,f del cliente; **financial news** información f financiera; **financial partner** socio(a) m,f capitalista; **financial period** ejercicio m económico; **financial plan** plan m financiero; **financial planning** planificación f financiera; **financial pool** pool m financiero; **financial position** situación f financiera; **financial press** prensa f financiera; **financial pressure** apuros mpl económicos; **financial product** producto m financiero; ACCT **financial ratio** ratio m financiero; ACCT **financial report** informe m financiero; ACCT **financial reporting** información f financiera; Br **Financial Reporting Council** = comisión que comprueba la exactitud de la información financiera publicada por las empresas; **financial resources** recursos mpl financieros; **financial review** valoración f de la situación financiera; **financial services** servicios mpl financieros; **Financial Services Authority** = organismo oficial encargado de la regulación de los servicios financieros en el Reino Unido; **financial situation** situación f financiera; **financial statement** balance m (general); **financial strategy** estrategia f financiera; **financial support** respaldo m financiero; **financial syndicate** consorcio m financiero; **Financial Times All-Share Index** índice m general de la Bolsa de Londres; **Financial**

Times (Industrial) Ordinary Share Index índice *m* de valores industriales de la Bolsa de Londres; **Financial Times-Stock Exchange 100 Share Index** índice *m* de valores de las 100 sociedades de mayor capitalización de la Bolsa de Londres; **financial transaction** transacción *f* financiera; *Br* **financial year** *(for budget)* ejercicio *m* (económico); *(for tax)* año *m* fiscal

financially *adv* económicamente, financieramente; **financially sound** económicamente sólido(a); **is the company financially sound?** ¿tiene la empresa solidez económica *or* patrimonial?

financier *n* financiero(a) *m,f*

financing *n* financiación *f*, financiamiento *m* ◻ **financing capacity** capacidad *f* de financiación

find COMPTR **1** *n* **find command** comando *m* de búsqueda
  2 *vt* **to find and replace** buscar y reemplazar

finder's fee *n* comisión *f* de intermediación financiera

findings *npl (of research, tribunal, report)* conclusiones *fpl*; **as a result of the findings, the R&D department proceeded with their plans for a new model** en vista de las conclusiones, el departamento de I+D siguió adelante con sus planes para el nuevo modelo

fine (trade) bill *n* letra *f* (de cambio) de máxima garantía

finish *n* ST EXCH **price at the finish** cambio *m* de cierre; **trading at the finish** contratación *f* al cierre de la sesión; **shares were up at the finish** la sesión cerró en positivo

finished product *n* producto *m* acabado

fire *vt (dismiss)* despedir; **to get fired** ser despedido(a)

firewall *n* COMPTR cortafuegos *m inv*, *Am* firewall *m*

firm 1 *n* empresa *f*; *(of lawyers)* bufete *m*, despacho *m*; *(of consultants)* despacho *m*
  2 *adj (offer, sale, deal)* en firme; *(market)* firme, estable; **oil shares remain firm at $20** las acciones petroleras se mantienen estables en los 20 dólares; **to place a firm order for sth** hacer un pedido en firme de algo ◻ **firm currency** moneda *f* convertible; **firm order** pedido *m* en firme; **firm sale** venta *f* en firme

firmware *n* COMPTR firmware *m*

first 1 *n* **(a)** BANKING, FIN **first of exchange** primera *f* de cambio
  (b) first in, first out ACCT primeras entradas, primeras salidas; *(in industrial relations)* = principio según el cual los trabajadores con más antigüedad de una empresa son los primeros en ser despedidos; **first in, last out** ACCT primeras entradas, últimas salidas; *(in industrial relations)* = principio según el cual los trabajadores con

menos antigüedad en una empresa son los primeros en ser despedidos; **on a first come, first served basis** por riguroso orden de llegada
  2 *adj* primero(a) ◻ **first class** *(on train)* primera *f* (clase *f*), (clase) preferente *f*; *Br (for mail)* servicio *m* postal de primera clase; **first quarter** *(of year)* primer trimestre *m*; **first refusal** derecho *m* de tanteo; **if he ever decides to sell it, we have first refusal** si alguna vez decide venderlo, nos lo va a ofrecer a nosostros primero; **the First World** el primer mundo *m*

first-class 1 *adj* **(a)** *(compartment, ticket, seat)* de primera (clase) **(b)** *(letter)* con tarifa postal de primera clase ◻ **first-class mail** *or Br* **post** servicio *m* postal de primera clase; **first-class stamp** sello *m* de primera clase **(c)** FIN **first-class paper** efectos *mpl* comerciales de primera clase
  2 *adv* **(a)** *(travel)* en primera (clase) **(b)** *Br* **to send sth first-class** enviar algo con un sello de primera clase

first-loss insurance *n* INS = tipo de póliza de seguros en la que sólo se asegura una parte de los bienes, dado que la pérdida total sería prácticamente imposible

first-notice day *n* ST EXCH primer día *m* de aviso

first-time *adj* **first-time buyer** *(of property)* comprador(ora) *m,f* de primera vivienda; **first-time user** = persona que utiliza un producto por primera vez

> “
> A focus on the **first-time buyer** market in Ireland is being replicated in Britain, where the average cost of the starter home built by McInerney last year was £88,000.
> ”

fiscal *adj* fiscal ◻ **fiscal agent** agente *m* fiscal *or* financiero; ECON **fiscal drag** rémora *f* fiscal, progresividad *f* en frío; **fiscal measure** medida *f* fiscal; *US* ACCT **fiscal period** periodo *m* fiscal; **fiscal policy** política *f* fiscal; **fiscal pressure** presión *f* fiscal; *US* **fiscal year** año *m* fiscal

fiscality *n* fiscalidad *f*

Five-Year Plan *n* ECON plan *m* quinquenal

fix *vt (price, interest rate)* fijar; **to fix the budget** fijar el presupuesto

▶ **fix up** *vt sep (meeting)* organizar

fixed *adj (price, rate)* fijo(a) ◻ **fixed annuity** anualidad *f* fija; ACCT **fixed assets** activo *m* fijo; **fixed capital** capital *m* fijo *or* inmovilizado; **fixed charge** gravamen *m* sobre los activos fijos; **fixed costs** costos *mpl or Esp* costes *mpl* fijos; **fixed deposit** depósito *m* a plazo fijo; COMPTR **fixed disk** disco *m* fijo; **fixed exchange rate** *Esp* tipo *m* de cambio fijo, *Am* tasa *f* de cambio fija; **fixed income** renta *f* fija, ingresos *mpl* fijos; **fixed interest rate** *Esp* tipo *m or Am* tasa *f* de interés fijo; *fixed investment* inversión *f* en capital fijo, inmovilizaciones *fpl* financieras; *fixed maturity* vencimiento *m* a plazo fijo; *fixed parity* paridad *f* fija; *fixed property* activo *m* fijo *or* inmovilizado; *fixed rate Esp* tipo *m or Am* tasa *f* de interés fijo; *fixed salary* sueldo *m* fijo; *fixed savings* ahorros *mpl* a plazo fijo; *fixed wage* salario *m* fijo; FIN *fixed yield* rendimiento *m* fijo

fixed-income *adj US* a interés fijo ▫ *fixed-income investment* inversión *f* en renta fija; *fixed-income securities* títulos *mpl or* valores *mpl* de renta fija

fixed-interest *adj Br (investments, securities)* a interés fijo ▫ *fixed-interest market* mercado *m* de renta fija

fixed-rate *adj (loan, mortgage)* a interés fijo ▫ *fixed-rate bond* bonos *mpl or* obligaciones *fpl* con *Esp* tipo *or Am* tasa de interés fijo; *fixed-rate borrowing* créditos *mpl* a *Esp* tipo *or Am* tasa de interés fijo; *fixed-rate financing* financiación *f* con *Esp* tipo *or Am* tasa de interés fijo; *fixed-rate investment* inversión *f* con *Esp* tipo *or Am* tasa de interés fijo; *fixed-rate rebate* devolución *f* lineal; *fixed-rate securities* títulos *mpl or* valores *mpl* de renta fija

fixed-term *adj* a plazo fijo ▫ FIN *fixed-term bill* letra *f* a plazo fijo; *fixed-term contract* contrato *m* temporal *or Am* temporario; *fixed-term credit* crédito *m* a plazo fijo; *fixed-term deposit* depósito *m* a plazo fijo

fixed-yield *adj* FIN de rentabilidad fija

fixture *n* = bien mueble adherido a un bien inmueble ▫ *fixtures and fittings* instalaciones *fpl* y accesorios *or* enseres

flag *n flag airline* línea *f* aérea de bandera; *flag of convenience* pabellón *m or* bandera *f* de conveniencia

flagging *adj (economy)* debilitado(a)

flagship *n (product)* producto *m* estrella *or* insignia *or* bandera; **this latest model is the flagship of their new range** este nuevo modelo es el producto estrella de su nueva gama; **the London store is the flagship of the chain** la tienda de Londres es el buque insignia de la cadena ▫ *flagship branch (of store)* tienda *f* estrella *or* insignia *or* bandera; *(of bank)* sucursal *f* principal; *flagship brand* marca *f* estrella *or* insignia *or* bandera; *flagship product* producto *m* estrella *or* insignia *or* bandera; *flagship store* tienda *f* estrella *or* insignia *or* bandera;

> **"**
> The design of Virgin Vie's **flagship store** in Oxford Street – which is based on the principles of Japanese landscape gardening – draws customers into the store via a window water feature.
> **"**

flame COMPTR **1** *n* llamarada *f*, mensaje *m* ofensivo ▫ *flame war* guerra *f* de llamaradas *or* mensajes ofensivos
2 *vt* lanzar llamaradas *or* mensajes ofensivos a
3 *vi* lanzar llamaradas *or* mensajes ofensivos

flamer *n* COMPTR = autor de un mensaje ofensivo

flaming *n* COMPTR envío *m* de mensajes ofensivos

flank attack *n* MKTG *(on market)* ataque *m* lateral *or* por los flancos

flash pack *n (discounted)* paquete *m* con descuento

flat *adj (market)* poco activo(a); *(fare, charge)* fijo(a) ▫ *flat bed (of vehicle)* plataforma *f*; *flat fee* tarifa *f* fija; COMPTR *flat file* archivo *m or* fichero *m* sin formato; COMPTR *flat monitor* monitor *m* de pantalla plana; *flat price* precio *m* único; *flat rate* FIN tarifa *f* única; COMPTR tarifa *f* plana; *flat screen* pantalla *f* plana

flatbed scanner *n* COMPTR escáner *m* plano *or* de sobremesa

flat-rate *adj* fijo(a) ▫ *flat-rate connection (to Internet)* conexión *f* con tarifa plana

flat-screen *adj* COMPTR de pantalla plana ▫ *flat-screen monitor* monitor *m* de pantalla plana

flaw *n (in product, plan)* defecto *m*, *Esp* fallo *m*, *Am* falla *f*

fledgling *adj (company, industry)* naciente

fleet rating *n* INS tarificación *f* de flota

Fleet Street *n* = calle de Londres en la que en un tiempo estuvieron las oficinas de los periódicos más importantes de Gran Bretaña; **the Fleet Street papers** = los principales periódicos de Gran Bretaña

> **"**
> But Morgan said: "The Sun can bluster away about it being a war, and glory in their Lara Logan bazooka exposés selling better than our famine in Malawi investigations, but we're not interested in what they say or what they do. They, like the rest of **Fleet Street**, do not have a clue what we are up to and that's the way I like it."
> **"**

flexcash *n*, **flexdollars** *npl US* = dinero que paga el empresario al empleado para que éste contrate prestaciones tales como seguros de vida y de salud

flexdollars *npl* = **flexcash**

flexibility *n (of budget, prices, approach, employees)* flexibilidad *f*

flexible *adj (prices, approach, employees)* flexible ▫ *flexible budget* presupuesto *m* flexible; *flexible manufacturing system* sistema *m* de fabricación flexible; *flexible mortgage* hipoteca *f* flexible; *flexible working hours* horario *m* de trabajo flexible

flexitime, **flextime** n horario m flexible

flier n (**a**) US Fam (speculative venture) operación f arriesgada; **to take a flier** (financial risk) realizar una operación arriesgada (**b**) (leaflet) hoja f de propaganda

flight n (**a**) (of plane) vuelo m ◳ **flight coupon** cupón m de vuelo; **flight number** número m de vuelo; **flight personnel** personal m de vuelo; **flight time** duración f de(l) vuelo (**b**) **flight capital** capital m evadido; **flight of capital** fuga f de capitales

flip chart n flip chart m, pizarra f caballete or de conferencia

float 1 n (**a**) (petty cash) efectivo m en caja; Br (in cash register) reserva f de cambio (**b**) US BANKING (uncleared cheques) valor m total de cheques en gestión de cobro (**c**) ST EXCH salida f a Bolsa (**d**) (of currency) flotación f; **clean float** flotación f limpia; **dirty float** flotación f sucia

   2 vt (**a**) FIN, ST EXCH (company) sacar a Bolsa; (loan, bonds, share issue) emitir; **they decided to float the company** (on Stock Exchange) decidieron la salida a Bolsa de la empresa (**b**) (currency) hacer flotar (**c**) (idea, proposal) lanzar

floatation = **flotation**

floater n US (insurance policy) seguro m de carga transportada

floating 1 n (**a**) FIN, ST EXCH (of company) salida f a Bolsa; (of loan, bonds, share issue) emisión f (**b**) (of currency) flotación f (**c**) (of idea, proposal) lanzamiento m

   2 adj (**a**) FIN (currency, exchange rate) flotante ◳ ACCT **floating assets** activo m flotante; FIN **floating capital** capital m circulante; BANKING **floating charge** garantía f flotante; FIN **floating debt** deuda f flotante; INS **floating policy** póliza f flotante; **floating rate** Esp tipo m or Am tasa f de interés flotante (**b**) COMPTR **floating accent** acento m flotante; COMPTR **floating point** coma f flotante

floating-rate adj con interés flotante ◳ **floating-rate bond** bono m con Esp tipo or Am tasa de interés flotante; BANKING **floating-rate certificate of deposit** certificado m de depósito con Esp tipo or Am tasa de interés flotante; **floating-rate interest** Esp tipo m or Am tasa f de interés flotante; **floating-rate investment** inversión f con Esp tipo or Am tasa de interés flotante; **floating-rate note** obligación f con Esp

tipo or Am tasa de interés flotante; **floating-rate securities** valores mpl con Esp tipo or Am tasa de interés flotante

flood vt (market) inundar; **the market is flooded with computer games** el mercado está inundado de juegos de ordenador or Am computadora

floor n (**a**) (in shop) **floor ad** = anuncio en el interior de una tienda; **floor display** = exposición de productos y materiales de promoción en el interior de una tienda; **floor manager** (in store) gerente mf de planta; (of TV show) regidor(ora) m,f; US **floor sample** = muestra que se utiliza en una exposición en el interior de una tienda y luego se suele vender rebajada; **floor space** superficie f comercial, superficie de venta; **floor stand** expositor m
   (**b**) (of Stock Exchange) parqué m ◳ **floor price** precio m mínimo; **floor trader** corredor(ora) m,f de parqué; **floor trading** contratación f en el parqué

floorwalker n US (in department store) supervisor(ora) m,f

floppy COMPTR **1** n disquete m
   2 adj **floppy disk** disquete m; **floppy (disk) drive** disquetera f, unidad f de disquetes

florin n Formerly florín m

flotation, **floatation** n (**a**) FIN, ST EXCH (of company) salida f a Bolsa; (of loan, bonds, share issue) emisión f (**b**) (of currency) flotación f

flourish vi (business, economy, trade) prosperar

flourishing adj (business, economy, trade) próspero(a), floreciente

flow 1 n (of capital) circulación f; (of information) flujo m; **flow of money** flujo de dinero ◳ **flow chart**, **flow diagram** diagrama m de flujo, organigrama m; COMPTR **flow path** ruta f de flujo; ACCT **flow sheet** diagrama m de flujo
   2 vi (capital, money) circular

flow-through method n US (of accounting) = método que reduce las tarifas de servicio de forma proporcional al ahorro en impuestos

fluctuate vi (market, currency, value, price) fluctuar

fluctuating adj (market, currency, value, precio) fluctuante

fluctuation n (of market, currency, value, precio) fluctuación f ❑ **fluctuation band** banda f de fluctuación; **fluctuation margin** margen m de fluctuación

flurry n there has been a late flurry of activity on the Stock Market últimamente ha habido una actividad frenética en la Bolsa

fly-by-night adj (company) no fiable, Am no confiable

flyer n (leaflet) hoja f de propaganda, flyer m, Am volante m

flying picket n IND piquete m móvil

FMCG npl MKTG (abbr **fast-moving consumer goods**) productos mpl de rápida rotación

FMCS n (abbr **Federal Mediation and Conciliation Service**) = organismo estadounidense de arbitraje en los conflictos de trabajo

FNMA n (abbr **Federal National Mortgage Association**) = organismo estadounidense que negocia con hipotecas en el mercado secundario y garantiza el pago de las mismas

FO n ADMIN (abbr **Foreign Office**) = ministerio de asuntos exteriores británico

FOB, fob (abbr **free on board**) FOB ❑ **FOB port of embarkation** FOB puerto de embarque

focus 1 n (of activity, business) centro m, aspecto m central ❑ **focus group** MKTG grupo m de discusión, focus group m; **focus group interview** dinámica f de grupo de discusión

  2 vi to focus on centrarse en; **we are currently focusing on the European market** en estos momentos nos estamos centrando en el mercado europeo

> **"**
> Focus group research commissioned for the task force suggests both young and old people regard too many parks as unwelcoming because they are either rundown, poorly maintained or potentially dangerous.
> **"**

fold vi Fam (business) irse al garete

folder n (a) (file, document wallet) carpeta f; (ring binder) carpeta f de anillas or Méx argollas (b) COMPTR (directory) carpeta f

folding money n Fam billetes mpl

folio n ACCT (sheet) folio m; (book) libro m en folio, infolio m

▶ **follow up 1** vt sep (letter, order, enquiry) hacer el seguimiento de; (customer) hacer el seguimiento de; (advantage, success) acrecentar; (opportunity) aprovechar; **follow up your initial phone call with a letter** confirma tu llamada inicial por escrito

  2 vi (in selling) hacer un seguimiento; **they never followed up on my letter** no tomaron

ningún tipo de medidas en respuesta a mi carta

follower n MKTG seguidor m, = producto o empresa con una cuota de mercado pequeña

following 1 adj siguiente; **the following methods of payment are acceptable** se aceptan los siguientes sistemas de pago

  2 prep en respuesta a; **following your letter** en respuesta a su carta; **following our meeting last week, I have decided to offer you the job** a raíz de la reunión que mantuvimos la semana pasada he decidido ofrecerle el puesto de trabajo

follow-me product n MKTG producto m gancho

follow-up n (of orders, enquiry, customer) seguimiento m; MKTG (of advertisement) anuncio m de seguimiento, follow up m ❑ **follow-up letter** carta f de seguimiento; **follow-up visit** visita f de seguimiento; **follow-up work** trabajo m de seguimiento

font n COMPTR tipo m (de letra), fuente f

food n food and drink comida f y bebida; **exotic/imported food(s)** alimentos mpl exóticos/de importación ❑ **the food industry** la industria alimentaria; **food manufacturer** (company) empresa f elaboradora de alimentos, fabricante m de alimentos; **food packaging** (containers) envases mpl alimentarios; (activity) envasado m de alimentos; **food processing** procesado m de alimentos **food products** productos mpl alimenticios; US **food stamp** = cupón que se entrega a personas con bajos ingresos para la adquisición de alimentos

food-processing adj (industry, sector) elaborador(ora) de alimentos, de procesado de alimentos

foodstuffs npl alimentos mpl, productos mpl alimenticios

footer n COMPTR (on document) pie m de página

footfall n MKTG (people entering shop) número m de clientes que visitan un punto de venta

> **"**
> Heathrow Airport, with a **footfall** of 1.2 million business travellers a month, allows corporate advertisers to make use of a medium which reaches business people with lower wastage than standard roadside outdoor sites.
> **"**

footnote n nota f a pie de página

footprint n (of building) superficie f, área f; **this is a graph of our company's manufacturing footprint in Europe** esto es un gráfico de la superficie que nuestra empresa dedica a producción en Europa ❑ **footprint migration** (of company) = evolución de la presencia geográfica de una empresa

FOOTSIE, Footsie *n* (*abbr* **Financial Times-Stock Exchange 100 Index**) Footsie *m*

> "
>
> Computer services group Logica is poised to be booted out of the **Footsie** after a profit warning left the shares down 51 pence at 243 pence for a two-day loss of 93 pence, wiping £415 million off its value. The shares peaked at 2724 pence in 2000. The firm, which supplies systems that make text-messaging possible, is also axing 700 jobs.
>
> "

FOR (*abbr* **free on rail**) franco sobre vagón

force *n* (**a**) (*power*) **Europe is becoming a powerful economic force** Europa se está convirtiendo en una poderosa potencia económica; **he is the driving force behind the merger** es el motor de la fusión; **the company is a force to be reckoned with** es una de las empresas a tener en cuenta
(**b**) (*personnel*) **our sales force** nuestro personal de ventas
(**c**) **to be in force** (*law, regulation*) estar en vigor; **to come into force** entrar en vigor
(**d**) INS **force majeure** fuerza *f* mayor; **force majeure clause** cláusula *f* de fuerza mayor

▶ **force down** *vt sep* (*prices, inflation*) hacer bajar

▶ **force up** *vt sep* (*prices, inflation*) hacer subir

forced *adj* **forced currency** circulación *f* forzada, curso *f* forzoso; **forced loan** empréstito *m* forzoso; **forced sale** venta *f* forzosa; **forced saving** ahorro *m* forzoso

forecast 1 *n* previsión *f* □ ACCT **forecast balance sheet** balance *m* previsional; **forecast operating budget** presupuesto *m* de explotación previsto; **forecast plan** plan *m* previsional; **forecast sales level** nivel *m* de ventas previsto
2 *vt* prever, pronosticar; **he forecasts sales of £2m** prevé unas ventas de 2 millones de libras

forecaster *n* ECON analista *mf* económico(a)

foreclose LAW **1** *vt* **to foreclose a mortgage** ejecutar una hipoteca
2 *vi* **to foreclose on sb** embargar a alguien; **to foreclose on a mortgage** ejecutar una hipoteca

foreclosure *n* LAW ejecución *f*

foreign *adj* (*from another country*) extranjero(a); (*trade, policy*) exterior □ **foreign account** cuenta *f* extranjera *or* en el extranjero; **foreign affairs** política *f* exterior; **foreign agent** representante *mf* en el extranjero; **foreign bill** letra *f* or efecto *m* sobre el extranjero; *Br* **Foreign and Commonwealth Office** Ministerio *m* de Asuntos Exteriores *or Am* Relaciones Exteriores; *Br* **Foreign and Commonwealth Secretary** ministro(a) *m,f* de Asuntos Exteriores *or*

Am Relaciones Exteriores; **foreign currency** divisa *f*, moneda *f* extranjera; **foreign currency account** cuenta *f* en divisas; **foreign currency assets** activos *mpl* en divisas; **foreign currency earnings** ingresos *mpl* en divisas; **foreign currency holding** existencias *fpl* en divisas; **foreign currency loan** empréstito *m* en divisas; **foreign currency option** opción *f* sobre divisas; **foreign currency reserves** reservas *fpl* de divisas; **foreign debt** deuda *f* exterior *or* externa; **foreign direct investment** inversión *f* directa extranjera; **foreign exchange** (*currency*) divisas *fpl*; (*system*) mercado *m* de divisas *or* de cambios; **foreign exchange broker** agente *mf* de cambio, cambista *mf*; **foreign exchange control** control *m* de cambios; **foreign exchange dealer** agente *mf* de cambio, cambista *mf*; **foreign exchange gain** ganancias *fpl* por operaciones en divisas; **foreign exchange inflow** entrada *f* de divisas; **foreign exchange loss** pérdidas *fpl* por operaciones en divisas; **foreign exchange market** mercado *m* de divisas *or* de cambios; **foreign exchange option** opción *f* sobre divisas; **foreign exchange outflow** salida *f* de divisas; **foreign exchange rate** tipo *m* de cambio de divisas; **foreign exchange reserves** reservas *fpl* en divisas; **foreign exchange risk** riesgo *m* de tipo de cambio; **foreign exchange trading** operaciones *fpl* en divisas; **foreign exchange transfer** transferencia *f* de divisas; **foreign goods** mercancías *fpl* extranjeras; **foreign investment** inversión *f* extranjera; **foreign investor** inversor(ora) *m,f* extranjero(a); **foreign labour** mano *f* de obra extranjera; **foreign market** mercado *m* exterior; *Br* **Foreign Office** Ministerio *m* de Asuntos Exteriores *or Am* Relaciones Exteriores; **foreign policy** política *f* exterior; **foreign produce** alimentos *mpl* frescos extranjeros; **foreign rights** derechos *mpl* de venta en el extranjero; **foreign trade** comercio *m* exterior

> "
>
> These legal reforms are "essential to get credit flowing again and to restore the confidence of domestic and **foreign investors**, without which it will be very difficult to revive investment and growth", she said. Order must also be restored to the **foreign exchange market**, where reports say the central bank plans continued interventions to help support the weak peso.
>
> "

foreman *n* encargado *m*

forementioned *adj* LAW, ADMIN susodicho(a)

forensic accounting *n* peritaje *m* contable judicial

forex *n* (*abbr* **foreign exchange**) mercado *m* de divisas □ **forex trading** operaciones *fpl* en divisas

> On the world's adrenaline-charged foreign exchange markets, $1.5 trillion changes hands every day. To set that figure in context, the global trade in merchandise and commercial services last year was $6.5 trillion – or 4.3 days of **forex trading**.

forfaiting n BANKING = compra con descuento de los instrumentos de pago de un importador a un exportador

forfeit 1 n (**a**) LAW (for non-performance of contract) sanción f, penalización f ▫ **forfeit clause** cláusula f de penalización (**b**) LAW **to declare goods forfeit** decomisar la mercancía
2 vt LAW (lose) perder el derecho a; (confiscate) decomisar; **to forfeit a deposit** renunciar al depósito; **to forfeit a patent** perder una patente

forfeiture n (**a**) ST EXCH (of shares) pérdida f legal de acciones (**b**) (of sum, rights) pérdida f (**c**) LAW (loss) pérdida f

forge vt falsificar

forged adj (banknote, letter) falso(a), falsificado(a); (signature) falsificado(a)

forgery n (**a**) (activity) falsificación f (**b**) (thing forged) falsificación f; **the signature was a forgery** la firma estaba falsificada

form 1 n (**a**) (for applications, orders) formulario m, impreso m, Méx forma f; **to fill in** or **fill out a form** rellenar or Am llenar un formulario or un impreso or Méx una forma ▫ **form letter** carta f general (**b**) COMPTR (on Internet) formulario m ▫ **form document** formulario m; **form feed** avance m de página
2 vt (company, committee) fundar, formar

formal adj (official) formal ▫ **formal agreement** acuerdo m formal; **formal consent** aprobación f oficial; **formal demand** requerimiento m oficial; **formal notice** notificación f oficial

format 1 n (**a**) COMPTR formato m (**b**) (of advertisement, publication) formato m, presentación f
2 vt COMPTR (disk, page, text) formatear

formation n (of company) fundación f, formación f

formatting n COMPTR (of disk) formateo m; (of page, text) formato m

for-profit organization n US entidad f or organización f con ánimo de lucro

forthcoming adj **the funds were not forthcoming** no nos concedieron los fondos

Fortune 500 npl lista f Fortune 500

> Mr. Stenglein has represented various **Fortune 500** companies, including General Electric, PG&E Corporation, Hughes Electronics, Occidental Chemical Corporation, U.S. Trust Company and General Electric Capital Corporation.

forum n (**a**) COMPTR fórum m, foro m (**b**) LAW **forum shopping** = búsqueda de una jurisdicción legal favorable

forward 1 adj (**a**) FIN a plazo, a término ▫ **forward account** cuenta f a plazo; **forward buying** compra f a plazo or a término; **forward contract** contrato m a plazo or a término; **forward dealing** negociación f a plazo or a término; **forward delivery** entrega f a plazo or a término; **forward exchange market** mercado m de divisas a plazo or a término; **forward exchange transaction** operación f de divisas a plazo or a término; **forward market** mercado m a plazo or de futuros; **forward price** precio m a plazo or a término; ST EXCH **forward purchase** compra f a plazo or a término; **forward rate** cotización f a plazo or a término, tipo m de cambio a plazo or a término; **forward rate agreement** acuerdo m sobre Esp tipos de interés futuros or Am tasas de interés futuras; ST EXCH **forward sale** venta f a plazo or a término; **forward trading** negociación f a plazo or a término
(**b**) (in direction) ECON **forward integration** integración f progresiva; COMPTR **forward search** búsqueda f hacia adelante; **forward slash** barra f inclinada
2 adv ACCT **to carry the balance forward** pasar el saldo a cuenta nueva; **(carried) forward** suma y sigue
3 vt (**a**) (goods) enviar, expedir; **to forward sth to sb** enviar algo a alguien; **to forward the goods to Paris** enviar la mercancía a París (**b**) (letter) reexpedir, remitir; (e-mail) remitir; **please forward** (on letter) = expresión que se escribe en una carta para indicar que ésta debe ser enviada a una nueva dirección

forwardation n FIN forwardation f, reporte m

forwarder n (company) empresa f transportista or de transporte; **forwarder and consolidator** empresa de transporte y agrupación de carga

forwarding n envío m, expedición f ▫ **forwarding address** (for goods) dirección f de entrega; (for letter) = nueva dirección a la que remitir el correo; **forwarding agent** transitario(a) m,f; **forwarding charges** gastos mpl de entrega; **forwarding department** departamento m de expedición; **forwarding house** empresa f transportista or de transportes; **forwarding instructions** instrucciones fpl de envío; **forwarding office** oficina f de expedición; **forwarding station** estación f de salida

FOT adj (abbr **free on truck**) franco sobre camión

foul adj (bill of lading) con reservas

found vt (company) fundar, crear

foundation n (**a**) (of company) fundación f, creación f (**b**) (institution, endowment) fundación f

founder n (of company) fundador(ora) m,f ❑ **founder member** socio(a) m,f fundador(ora); **founder's share** acción f del fundador/de la fundadora

founding n (of business) fundación f ❑ **founding member** socio(a) m,f fundador(ora); **founding partner** socio(a) m,f fundador(ora)

fourth adj cuarto(a) ❑ **fourth quarter** (of year) cuarto trimestre m; **the Fourth World** cuarto mundo m

FQDN n COMPTR (abbr **Fully Qualified Domain Name**) nombre m de dominio totalmente cualificado

Fr (abbr **franc**) Fr

FRA n FIN (abbr **Future Rate Agreement, Forward Rate Agreement**) FRA m

fraction n FIN (of share) fracción f

fractional adj FIN **fractional currency** moneda f fraccionaria; **fractional interest** propiedad f parcial; **fractional money** moneda f fraccionaria

fragile adj (goods) frágil

fragmentation n COMPTR (of hard disk) fragmentación f

framework n (structure) marco m; **within the framework of the EU** dentro del marco de la UE

franc n franco m ❑ **franc area** Formerly zona f (monetaria) del franco

franchisable adj franquiciable

franchise 1 n (for shop, fast-food outlet) franquicia f; (for radio, TV station) licencia f; **several high-street shops are run as franchises** varias tiendas del centro funcionan como franquicias ❑ **franchise agreement** contrato m de franquicia; **franchise outlet** franquicia f
2 vt franquiciar

franchisee n (of shop, fast-food outlet) franquiciado(a) m,f, concesionario(a) m,f; (of radio, TV station); concesionario(a) m,f

franchiser, franchisor n franquiciador(ora) m,f

franchising n franquicias fpl, franchising m ❑ **franchising operation** franquicia f

franchisor = **franchiser**

franco 1 adj franco, libre ❑ **franco price** precio m franco hasta el almacén de destino
2 adv gratuitamente

frank vt (letter) franquear

franking machine n Br (máquina f) franqueadora f

fraud n LAW, FIN fraude m; **to obtain sth by fraud** conseguir algo por medios fraudulentos

fraudulent adj fraudulento(a) ❑ **fraudulent balance sheet** balance m fraudulento; **fraudulent bankruptcy** quiebra f fraudulenta; **fraudulent trading** comercio m fraudulento; **fraudulent transaction** transacción f fraudulenta

fraudulently adv de forma fraudulenta, fraudulentamente

FRB n (abbr **Federal Reserve Board**) junta f de gobierno de la Reserva Federal

FRCD n BANKING (abbr **floating-rate certificate of deposit**) certificado m de depósito con Esp tipo or Am tasa de interés flotante

Freddie Mac n Fam = denominación coloquial de la "Federal Home Loan Mortgage Corporation", organismo estadounidense que negocia con hipotecas en el mercado secundario y garantiza el pago de las mismas

free 1 adj (**a**) (without charge) gratuito(a), gratis; **free overside** franco puerto de desembarque; **free in and out** franco de carga y descarga; **free alongside ship, free at quay, free on wharf** franco al costado del buque; **free at frontier** franco frontera; **free of all average** libre de toda avería; CUSTOMS **free of duty** libre de derechos; **free of tax** libre de impuestos; **free on board** franco a bordo; **free carrier** franco transportista; **free on rail** franco sobre vagón; **free on truck** franco sobre camión ❑ **free credit** crédito m gratuito; **free delivery** entrega f gratuita; ST EXCH **free float** = acciones de una empresa que cotizan libremente en el mercado; **free gift** obsequio m (promocional); **free home delivery** entrega f a domicilio gratuita; CUSTOMS **free import** importación f libre de derechos; ST EXCH **free issue** emisión f gratuita; CUSTOMS **free list** lista f de mercancías exentas de aranceles; **free sample** muestra f gratuita; **free trial** prueba f gratuita; **free trial period** periodo m de prueba gratuito
(**b**) (unrestricted) libre ❑ **free agent** = persona libre de obligaciones legales o contractuales; **free collective bargaining** negociación f colectiva libre; **free competition** libre competencia f; **free enterprise** libre empresa f; **free market** libre mercado m; **free market economics** liberalismo m económico; **free market economy** economía f de libre mercado; **free marketeer** partidario(a) m,f de la economía de libre mercado, librecambista mf; **free movement** (of capital, workers) libertad f de circulación, libre circulación f; **free port** puerto m franco or libre; **free trade** libre comercio m, libre cambio m; **free trade agreement** acuerdo m de libre comercio or cambio; **free trade area** área f de libre comercio or cambio; **free trade association** asociación f de libre comercio or cambio; **free trade policy** política f de libre comercio or

cambio; *free trader* partidario(a) *m,f* de la economía de libre mercado, librecambista *mf*; *free trade zone* área *f* de libre comercio *or* cambio; *free zone* zona *f* franca

2 *adv* gratis, gratuitamente; **they will deliver free of charge** harán la entrega de forma gratuita

3 *vt (prices, trade)* liberalizar; *(funds)* liberar

> **"**
>
> Mr Ralph himself described the sale of Sidex as "the privatisation of the decade" and "hugely important in terms of creating the fully functioning **free market economy** which the European Union has set as a fundamental criterion for Romanian accession to the EU." He recommended the letter be sent since "it would send a strong signal of British government support in the hope that this would stimulate increased British investment in and trade with Romania".
>
> **"**

freebie *n Fam* regalito *m*

freedom *n* libertad *f* □ *freedom of communication* libertad *f* de comunicación; *freedom of information* libertad *f* de información; *Freedom of Information Act* ley *f* del derecho a la información; *freedom of the press* libertad *f* de prensa; *freedom of trade* libertad *f* de comercio

free-flowing *adj (capital)* de libre circulación

Freefone® *n Br* TEL **a Freefone® number** un (número de) teléfono gratuito; **call Freefone 400** llame al número gratuito 400

freehold *n* propiedad *f* absoluta

freeholder *n* propietario(a) *m,f* absoluto(a)

freelance 1 *n* colaborador(ora) *m,f* externo(a), free-lance *mf*

2 *adj* free-lance

3 *adv* **to work freelance** trabajar como colaborador(ora) externo(a) *or* free-lance

4 *vi* trabajar como colaborador(ora) externo(a) *or* free-lance

freenet *n* COMPTR red *f* ciudadana, *Am* freenet *f*

Freepost® *n Br* ≃ franqueo *m* pagado

freeware *n* COMPTR freeware *m*, software *m* gratuito (de dominio público)

freeze 1 *n (of prices, wages, assets, credit, currency) Esp* congelación *f*, *Am* congelamiento *m*

2 *vt (prices, wages, assets, credit, currency)* congelar

3 *vi* COMPTR *(screen, computer)* colgarse

freezing *n (of prices, wages, assets, credit, currency) Esp* congelación *f*, *Am* congelamiento *m*

freight 1 *n* (**a**) *(transport)* transporte *m or* flete *m* de mercancías; **to send sth by freight** enviar algo por flete □ *freight price* precio *m* del flete (**b**) *(goods)* flete *m*, carga *f* □ *US freight car*

vagón *m* de mercancías; *freight depot* estación *f* de mercancías *or* de carga; *freight forwarder* empresa *f* transitaria; *freight insurance* seguro *m* de flete; *freight manifest* manifiesto *m* de flete; *freight note* factura *f* de flete; *freight plane* avión *m* de carga; *freight rate* tarifa *f* de flete; *freight release* justificante *m* de pago de fletes; *freight service* servicio *m* de transporte de mercancías; *freight shipping* buques *mpl* de carga; *freight ton* tonelada *f* de flete; *freight traffic* tráfico *m* de mercancías; *US freight train* tren *m* de mercancías, tren de carga; *freight vehicle* vehículo *m* de carga

(**c**) *(cost)* flete *m*, porte *m*; **freight by weight** flete a peso; **freight (charges) paid** flete pagado, portes *mpl* pagados; **freight forward** flete debido, flete en destino

2 *vt (goods)* fletar, enviar

freightage *n* flete *m*

freighter *n* (**a**) *(company)* empresa *f* de transportes (**b**) *(ship)* carguero *m*; *(aeroplane)* avión *m* de carga

freightliner *n* = servicio rápido de mercancías en el Reino Unido

French franc *n Formerly* franco *m* francés

frequency *n* MKTG frecuencia *f* □ *frequency rate* ratio *m* de frecuencia

frequent *adj* *frequent flyer* viajero(a) *m,f* frecuente; *frequent flyer club* club *m* de viajeros frecuentes; *frequent flyer programme* programa *m* de viajeros frecuentes; *frequent user card* tarjeta *f* de usuario frecuente

frictional unemployment *n* desempleo *m or Esp* paro *m* friccional

friction feed *n* COMPTR avance *m or* alimentación *f* de papel por fricción

friendly *adj Br* FIN *friendly society* mutua *f*, mutualidad *f*; *friendly takeover bid* oferta *f* pública de adquisición amistosa, OPA *f* amistosa

fringe *n US* **fringes** *(fringe benefits)* ventajas *fpl* adicionales *or* extras □ *Br fringe benefits* ventajas *fpl* adicionales *or* extras; *fringe market* mercado *f* secundario

FRN *n* BANKING *(abbr* **floating-rate note**) obligación *f* con *Esp* tipo *or Am* tasa de interés flotante

front 1 *n* (**a**) *front desk (reception)* recepción *f*; *front man (of organization)* cabeza *f* visible; *US Fam front money* capital *m* inicial *(para crear una empresa)*; *front office* oficina *f* de atención al cliente (**b**) *Fam* **to pay up front** pagar por adelantado; **they want £5,000 up front** quieren 5.000 libras por adelantado

2 *vt* (**a**) *(lead) (organization)* dirigir (**b**) *US Fam (advance)* adelantar; **the cashier can front you the money** el cajero le puede adelantar el dinero

frontage *n (of shop)* fachada *f*

front-end *adj* (**a**) *(initial)* **front-end fee** comisión *f* inicial *or* de apertura; **front-end loading** sistema *m* de cuota de entrada (**b**) COMPTR **front-end computer** *Esp* ordenador *m or Am* computadora *f* frontal; **front-end processor** procesador *m* frontal

> 66
> The charges for buying into a trust are usually at the standard rate. Dunedin, however, has no **front-end fee** for its share plan other than stamp duty.
> 99

frontier *n* frontera *f* ❑ **frontier zone** zona *f* fronteriza

front-runner *n* favorito(a) *m,f*

front-running *n* ST EXCH = compra de valores para uso propio por parte de un corredor de Bolsa antes de realizar la compra encargada por un cliente del mismos tipo de valores

frozen *adj* (**a**) FIN *(account, credit, wages, prices, assets)* congelado(a) (**b**) COMPTR colgado(a)

FRS *n US* (*abbr* **Federal Reserve System**) Reserva *f* Federal

frustration of contract *n* LAW frustración *f* del (fin del) contrato

FSA *n* (*abbr* **Financial Services Authority**) = organismo oficial británico encargado de la regulación de los servicios financieros

FT *n* (*abbr* **Financial Times**) Financial Times *m*

FTC *n* (*abbr* **Federal Trade Commission**) Comisión *f* Federal de Comercio

FT index *n* (**a**) (*abbr* **Financial Times (Industrial) Ordinary Share Index**) Índice *m* de valores industriales de la Bolsa de Londres (**b**) (*abbr* **Financial Times-Stock Exchange 100 Index**) índice *m* FTSE de la Bolsa de Londres

FTP *n* COMPTR (*abbr* **File Transfer Protocol**) FTP *m* ❑ **FTP server** servidor *m* FTP; **FTP site** sitio *m* FTP

FT-SE index *n* (*abbr* **Financial Times-Stock Exchange 100 Index**) Índice *m* FTSE de la Bolsa de Londres

fulfil, *US* **fulfill** *vt* *(contract, order)* ejecutar; *(obligation)* cumplir con

fulfilment, *US* **fulfillment** *n* *(of contract, order)* ejecución *f*; *(of obligation)* cumplimiento *m*

full 1 *n* (**a**) *(complete, whole)* **to pay in full** pagar el total; **we paid the bill in full** pagamos la factura en su totalidad; **they refunded my money in full** me devolvieron todo el dinero (**b**) *(detailed)* **he gave us a full report** nos hizo un informe completo; **I asked for full information** pedí toda la información

  2 *adj* **full assessment system** sistema *m* de evaluación integral; ACCT **full consolidation** consolidación *f* por integración global; **full**

container load carga *f* por contenedor completo; **full cost accounting (method)** contabilidad *f* de costos *or Esp* costes totales; **full costing** costeo *m* total *or* por absorción; INS **full cover** cobertura *f* total; **full demand** = el nivel máximo existente de demanda de los productos y servicios de una empresa; FIN **full discharge** pago *m* total; **full employment** pleno empleo *m*; **full fare** precio *m or* tarifa *f* normal; ST EXCH **full listing** = admisión a cotización en Bolsa; **full load** carga *f* completa; **full pay** retribución *f* completa; **full payment** pago *m or* liquidación *f* total; LAW **full power of attorney** poder *m* notarial sin restricciones; **full price** precio *m* completo; **full rate** tarifa *f* completa; *esp Br* **full stop** *(punctuation)* punto *m*; **full time** *(employment)* jornada *f* completa; **full warranty** garantía *f* total; **full weight** peso *m* total

> 66
> Tenon Group, the AIM-listed accountancy consolidator, has said it will move up to a **full listing** on the London Stock Exchange – but not until September 2003 at the earliest, writes Philip Smith. The original intention had been for the company to make the switch this year, but chief executive Ian Buckley admitted that would no longer be possible and could be as late as March 2004.
> 99

full-cost pricing *n* MKTG = fijación de precios basándose en los costes totales

full-employment economy *n* economía *f* de pleno empleo

full-line strategy *n* MKTG = estrategia unificada para la gama completa de una línea de productos

full-time 1 *adj* *(job, employee)* a tiempo completo; **to be in full-time employment** tener un trabajo a tiempo completo ❑ **full-time contract** contrato *m* a tiempo completo

  2 *adv* a tiempo completo

fully *adv* INS **fully comprehensive** a todo riesgo; FIN, ST EXCH **fully diluted earnings per share** beneficio *m* por acción después de disolución; **fully paid capital** capital *m* totalmente desembolsado; **fully paid-up security** valor *m* plenamente desembolsado; **fully paid-up share** acción *f* plenamente desembolsada; **fully secured creditor** acreedor *m* con plena garantía

full-year *adj* *(profits, results)* anual

function *n* (**a**) *(role)* *(of machine, person)* función *f*; **in his function as a magistrate** en su calidad de magistrado; **to resign one's functions (as...)** renunciar a sus funciones (de...) ❑ COMPTR **function key** tecla *f* de función (**b**) *(celebration)* celebración *f*; *(official occasion)* acto *m* (**c**) *(department)* **our personnel/accounting function**

nuestra sección de personal/de cuentas

functional *adj (practical)* funcional; *(operational)* operativo(a); **to be functional** estar en funcionamiento, funcionar ❑ *functional analysis chart* cuadro *m* de análisis por funciones; *functional budget* presupuesto *m* de departamento; *functional layout* organización *f* por departamentos; *functional organization* organización *f* por departamentos; *functional strategy* estrategia *f* departamental

fund FIN **1** *n* **(a)** *(reserve of money)* fondo *m*; **funds flow statement** estado *m* de origen y aplicación de fondos; **fund of funds** fondo de fondos ❑ *fund management* gestión *f* de fondos; *fund manager* gestor(ora) *m,f* de fondos **(b) funds** *(cash resources)* fondos *mpl*; **to be short of or low on funds** no tener suficientes fondos; **insufficient funds** *(to honour cheque)* saldo *m* insuficiente; *Br* **the Funds** títulos *mpl* del Estado; **to make a call for funds** solicitar fondos
2 *vt (project, company)* financiar; *(public debt)* consolidar; **to fund money** aportar dinero público; **funded from cashflow** financiado(a) con efectivo

fundable *adj* FIN *(debt)* consolidable

fundamental market analyst *n* = analista que estudia los factores básicos del mercado

funded *adj* FIN *(assets)* financiado(a) ❑ *funded capital* capital *m* en fondos; *funded debt* deuda *f* consolidada; *funded pension scheme* fondo *m* de pensiones

fundholder *n (investor)* inversor(ora) *m,f*; *(in funds to be distributed)* entidad *f* pública de financiación; *(in public funds)* inversor(ora) en deuda pública

funding *n (for project) (act of resourcing)* financiación *f*, financiamiento *m*; *(resources)* fondos *mpl*; *(of debt)* consolidación *f*; *(of income)* generación *f* de rentas; **BP will put up half of the funding** BP financiará la mitad ❑ *funding loan* empréstito *m* de consolidación; *funding operation* = conversión de las deudas a corto plazo en deudas a largo plazo; *funding plan* plan *m* de financiación

fundraiser *n (person)* recaudador(ora) *m,f or* captador(ora) *m,f* de fondos; *(event)* acto *m* para recaudar *or* captar fondos

fundraising *n* recaudación *f* de fondos, captación *f* de fondos

fungible ST EXCH **1** *n* **fungibles** títulos *mpl* fungibles
2 *adj* fungible ❑ *fungible securities* títulos *mpl* fungibles

furnish *vt (supply) (provisions)* proporcionar, suministrar; *(information, reason)* proporcionar; **to furnish sb with sth** proporcionar algo a alguien

further **1** *adj* **for further information, phone this number** para más información, llame a este número; **please send me further information concerning the project** por favor, envíenme más información sobre el proyecto; **I would like further details of the programme** desearía recibir más información sobre el programa; **until further notice** hasta nuevo aviso
2 *adv* **further to** *(in letter)* en respuesta a; **further to your letter of 15 June** en respuesta a su carta del 15 de junio; **further to our telephone conversation** en relación a nuestra conversación telefónica
3 *vt (cause, career)* favorecer

future **1** *n* **(a)** *(of person)* futuro *m*, porvenir *m*; **a job with a (good) future** un trabajo con (mucho) futuro; **there is a future ahead for bilingual people in publishing** las personas bilingües tienen futuro en el mundo editorial
(b) ST EXCH **futures** *(financial instruments, contracts, securities)* futuros *mpl*; *(transactions)* transacciones *fpl* de futuros ❑ *futures contract* contrato *m* de futuros; *futures exchange* mercado *m* de futuros; *futures market* mercado *m* de futuros; *futures option* opción *f* de futuros; *futures and options* futuros *mpl* y opciones; *futures and options fund* fondo *m* de futuros y opciones; *futures order* orden *f* de futuros; *Future Rate Agreement* contrato *m* a plazo sobre *Esp* tipos de interés *or Am* tasas de interés; *futures trading* negociación *f* de futuros; *futures transaction* transacción *f* de futuros
2 *adj* FIN **future delivery** entrega *f* a plazo *or* a término; **goods for future delivery** mercancías para entrega a plazo *or* a término; *future value* valor *m* futuro

> **❝**
> The first step consists of a feasibility study for the creation of a regulated **futures market** for categories of fine wines. This innovative project, announced at a conference/debate organized by Paris Europlace at Bordeaux, is based on a finished product – namely homogeneous categories of sought-after fine wines – that is ready to be consumed. The first contract is expected to be a **future** on the top growths of the Bordeaux region, based on a 12-bottle case en primeur for delivery in 32 months' time.
> **❞**

FX *n (abbr* **foreign exchange***) (currency)* divisas *fpl*; *(system)* mercado *m* de divisas *or* de cambios *mpl* ❑ *FX broker, FX dealer* agente *mf* de cambio, cambista *mf*; *FX market* mercado *m* de divisas *or* de cambios; *FX option* opción *f* sobre divisas; *FX transfer* transferencia *f* de divisas

FY *n (abbr* **fiscal year***)* año *m* fiscal

Gg

G7 n G7 m ❏ **G7 meeting** reunión f del G7; **G7 summit** cumbre f del G7

G8 n G8 m ❏ **G8 meeting** reunión f del G8; **G8 summit** cumbre f del G8

GA n INS (abbr **general average**) avería f gruesa

GAAP npl ACCT (abbr **generally-accepted accounting principles**) PCGA mpl

gag n **gag law** ley f de silencio; **gag order** orden f de silencio; **to issue a gag order** emitir una orden de silencio

gagging order n orden f de silencio; **to issue a gagging order** emitir una orden de silencio

> 66
>
> Patty Hearst, the newspaper heiress kidnapped by urban guerrillas in California in 1974 and later jailed for participating with them in a bank robbery, could find herself back in court this week for contempt. Despite a **gagging order**, she has given an interview about the pending trial in August of a group member, Kathy Soliah (now Sarah Jane Olsen), captured last year after a quarter of a century on the run.
>
> 99

gain 1 n (a) (profit) beneficio m, ganancia f (b) (increase) aumento m (**in** de); FIN **gain in value** aumento de valor, plusvalía f; **there has been a net gain in profits this year** este año se ha registrado un aumento neto en los beneficios; **there has been a gain of 100 points on the Dow Jones** el Dow Jones ha registrado un aumento de 100 puntos; **to gain a share of the market** ganar cuota de mercado
2 vt ganar; **the share index has gained two points** el índice de cotizaciones ha subido dos puntos

gain-sharing adj US con participación en los beneficios

galloping inflation n ECON inflación f galopante

gamble vi **to gamble on the Stock Exchange** jugar a la Bolsa

gameplan n MKTG plan m or estrategia f de juego

game theory n MKTG teoría f de juegos

GAO n US (abbr **General Accounting Office**) Oficina f General de Contabilidad

gap n **a gap in the market** un hueco or Am una brecha en el mercado; **there's a technology gap between our two countries** existe una gran distancia or Am una brecha tecnológica entre nuestros dos países ❏ MKTG **gap analysis** análisis m inv de las necesidades del mercado; **gap financing** crédito m puente; MKTG **gap level** nivel m de las necesidades del mercado; MKTG **gap study** estudio m de las necesidades del mercado

> 66
>
> Six insurance companies yesterday formed a European pool to cover damage caused by acts of terror, plugging a **gap in the market** left since the September 11 attacks. Allianz, Zurich, Swiss Re, Hannover Re, XL Capital and Scor said they had established a company called Special Risk Insurance and Reinsurance Luxembourg.
>
> 99

gapping n =práctica por la cual un banco reduce los tipos de interés de las cuentas de ahorro antes de hacerlo en los préstamos hipotecarios

garnish vt US LAW embargar

garnishee n LAW embargado(a) m,f ❏ **garnishee order** orden f de embargo

garnishment n LAW embargo m ❏ **garnishment order** orden f de embargo

gatekeeper n MKTG (in purchasing department) mediador(ora) m,f, filtro m

> 66
>
> … the supplier's marketing department must try to identify and reach technical specialists, engineers, technical buyers etc. This will depend on how accessible these people are, and on how effective are the **gatekeepers** whose role includes filtering out what they, or the influencer, deem to be undesirable or unnecessary information.
>
> 99

gateway n COMPTR pasarela f, puerta f de enlace

GATT n (abbr **General Agreement on Tariffs and Trade**) GATT m

GAW n US (abbr **guaranteed annual wage**) sueldo m base

gazump vt Br Fam = vender un inmueble ya apalabrado con un comprador a otro que paga más; **we've been gazumped** han vendido la casa que teníamos ya apalabrada a otros que pagan más

gazumping *n* = venta de un inmueble ya apalabrado con un comprador a otro que paga más

> **"**
>
> Estate agents go around telling people ... that the property from which they are hoping to move is incredibly saleable in the present market conditions. ... What if their present home is snapped up in 20 minutes flat, but they can't find what they want? So they don't put their existing property on the market until they have found what they want – which, with thousands of people doing just the same, could be some time. ... This encourages **gazumping**, which is, after all, only the market's way of raising prices to the point where demand meets supply. Hence the silly prices.
>
> **"**

GB *n* COMPTR (*abbr* **gigabyte**) GB *m*

GDP *n* ECON (*abbr* **gross domestic product**) PIB *m*

gear *vt (link)* indexar; **salaries are geared to the cost of living** los sueldos están indexados al costo de vida, los sueldos están referenciados al IPC

▶ **gear up** *vt sep* (**a**) *(prepare)* preparar; **the company is geared up for expansion** la empresa está preparada para la expansión (**b**) *(increase)* aumentar; **we must gear up production to meet the demand** debemos aumentar la producción para satisfacer la demanda

gearing *n Br* FIN *(leverage)* apalancamiento *m* ❏ **gearing adjustment** ajuste *m* por apalancamiento; **gearing ratio** coeficiente *m* de apalancamiento

GEMM *n Br* ST EXCH (*abbr* **gilt-edged market maker**) creador *m* de mercado para obligaciones del Estado, sociedad *f* de contrapartida de obligaciones del Estado

general *adj* ❏ *US* ACCT **General Accounting Office** Oficina *f* General de Contabilidad; BANKING **general account manager** gestor(ora) *m,f* de particulares; ACCT **general accounts** cuentas *fpl* generales; **general and administrative expenses** gastos *mpl* generales y de administración; **general agent** apoderado(a) *m,f*; **General Agreement on Tariffs and Trade** Acuerdo *m* General sobre Aranceles y Comercio; **general audit** auditoría *f* general; INS **general average** avería *f* gruesa; **general broker** agente *mf* general de Bolsa; **general business** *(on agenda)* ruegos *mpl* y preguntas; ACCT **general cash book** libro *m* de caja; **general expenses** gastos *mpl* generales; **general headquarters** sede *f* central; ACCT **general ledger** libro *m* mayor; LAW

general lien derecho *m* de retención; **general management** dirección *f* general; **general management committee** junta *f* de directores generales; **general manager** director(ora) *m,f* general; **general meeting** asamblea *f* general; *Br* **General, Municipal and Boilermakers' Union** = uno de los mayores sindicatos británicos, que representa a trabajadores de sectores muy diversos; FIN **general obligation bond** bono *m* de responsabilidad general; *Br* **general overheads,** *US* **general overhead** gastos *mpl* generales; **general partnership** sociedad *f* colectiva; **general price level** nivel *m* general de precios; **general strike** huelga *f* general; **general tax code** Ley *f* General Tributaria; **general trend** tendencia *f* general; **general union** sindicato *m* general; **general wage level** nivel *m* general de salarios

generate *vt* (**a**) COMPTR generar (**b**) *(income)* generar; **we must try to generate new sources of income** debemos intentar generar nuevas fuentes de ingresos

generic MKTG **1** *n* genérico *m*
2 *adj* genérico(a) ❏ **generic advertising** publicidad *f* genérica; **generic brand** marca *f* genérica; **generic market** mercado *m* genérico; **generic name** nombre *m* genérico; **generic product** producto *m* genérico

gentleman's agreement *n* pacto *m* de *or* entre caballeros

genuine *adj (article)* auténtico(a), genuino(a); *(diamond, gold, leather)* auténtico(a)

geodemographic *adj* MKTG geodemográfico(a) ❏ **geodemographic data** datos *mpl* geodemográficos; **geodemographic profile** perfil *m* geodemográfico; **geodemographic segment** segmento *m* geodemográfico; **geodemographic segmentation** segmentación *f* geodemográfica

geodemography *n* MKTG perfil *m* geodemográfico

geographic *adj* MKTG geográfico(a) ❏ **geographic pricing** fijación *f* de precios según zonas geográficas; **geographic segment** segmento *m* geográfico; **geographic segmentation** segmentación *f* geográfica

geomarketing *n* geomarketing *m*

get *vt* (**a**) *(obtain)* conseguir (**from** *or* **off** de); *(buy)* comprar (**from** *or* **off** a); **I got this computer cheap** esta impresora me salió barata, compré esta impresora bien de precio
(**b**) *(earn)* ganar; **to get £35,000 a year** ganar 35.000 libras anuales
(**c**) *(letter, phone call, reply)* recibir; **I got a letter from my mother** recibí una carta de mi madre; **I got his answer yesterday** recibí su respuesta ayer
(**d**) *(contact by telephone)* hablar con; **I couldn't**

get her at the office no contestaba en la oficina; **get me Washington 330 330** *(to operator)* póngame con el 330 330 de Washington

▶ **get through** *vi* **to get through to sb** *(on telephone)* (lograr) comunicarse con alguien

giant *n (company)* gigante *m*; **computer giant Microsoft is in the news this week** el gigante de los ordenadores Microsoft es noticia esta semana

giant-sized *adj (pack, box)* de tamaño gigante

GIF *n* COMPTR *(abbr* **Graphics Interchange Format***)* GIF *m*

gift *n* **(a)** LAW *(donation)* donación *f*; **I gave the money as a gift** doné el dinero □ *Br* **gift aid** = sistema según el cual una persona hace una donación a una organización caritativa y ésta recibe además la cantidad que el donante tendría derecho a deducirse de su declaración de la renta; **gift and inheritance tax** impuesto *m* de donaciones y sucesiones; **gift inter vivos** donación *f* inter vivos

(b) *(present)* regalo *m*, obsequio *m* □ *US* **gift certificate** vale *m* de regalo; **gift token, gift voucher** vale *m* de regalo

gigabyte *n* COMPTR gigabyte *m*

gilts *npl Br* ST EXCH valores *mpl* del Estado □ **gilts market** mercado *m* de valores del Estado

gilt-edged *adj* ST EXCH **gilt-edged bonds** *(high-grade bonds)* títulos *mpl or* valores *mpl* de máxima garantía; *Br (government bonds)* títulos de deuda pública, valores del Estado; **gilt-edged investment** *(in government bonds)* inversión *f* en valores del Estado; *Br* **gilt-edged market** mercado *m* de valores del Estado; *Br* **gilt-edged market maker** creador *m* de mercado para obligaciones del Estado, sociedad *f* de contrapartida de obligaciones del Estado; **gilt-edged stock, gilt-edged securities** *(high-grade bonds)* títulos *mpl or* valores *mpl* de máxima garantía; *Br (government bonds)* títulos *mpl* de deuda pública, valores *mpl* del Estado

"
Five years ago, the prospect of a 10 per cent profit in the course of a year would not have set investors' pulses racing. However, in the context of the dire performance of the UK stock market in the past two years, and the poor prospective returns from **gilt-edged stock** and cash deposits, a 10 per cent return from the FTSE 100 in 2002 takes on a new appeal, and would go some way to restoring two years of capital destruction since the index peaked at 6930 in December 1999.
"

Ginnie Mae *n Fam* =denominación coloquial del organismo oficial estadounidense que negocia con hipotecas en el mercado secundario y garantiza el pago de las mismas

giro *n Br* **(a)** *(system)* giro *m* bancario, transferencia *f* bancaria; **to pay by bank giro** pagar con giro bancario □ **giro account** cuenta *f* de giros postales; **giro cheque** cheque *m* postal; **giro transfer** transferencia *f* bancaria **(b)** *Fam (unemployment benefit)* cheque *m* del desempleo *or Esp* paro

Girobank *n Br* = banco especializado en giros bancarios, ≃ Caja Postal

give *vt (pay)* dar, pagar; **to give a good price for sth** pagar un buen precio por algo; **I'll give you $500 for it** te doy 500 dólares por él; **what will you give me for it?** ¿cuánto me das por él?

give-and-take policy *n* toma y daca *m*

giveaway *n Fam (free gift)* obsequio *m* □ **giveaway material** material *m* de regalo; **giveaway paper** periódico *m* gratuito

giveback *n US* = recorte salarial concedido por un sindicato por la mala situación económica

given *adj* determinado(a); **at a given price** a un precio determinado

give-up *n US* ST EXCH = comisión compartida por dos o más agentes de Bolsa por una operación entre dos empresas

glamour stock *n* ST EXCH acción *f* favorita

glare *n* COMPTR **glare filter** filtro *m* de pantalla; **glare screen** filtro *m* de pantalla

glass ceiling *n* techo *m* de cristal

"
In the seven years Morag Stuart has been a qualified lawyer, she has seen a marked shift in attitudes towards women in the legal profession which indicate the so-called **glass ceiling** is finally cracking. While in the past some female solicitors would have been held back because of their gender, now Ms Stuart, 29, believes that attitude is simply not tolerated.
"

global *adj* **(a)** *(worldwide)* mundial, global □ MKTG **global audience** audiencia *f* mundial *or* global; BANKING **global banking** banca *f* mundial; FIN **global bond** bono *m* global; **global consumption** consumo *m* mundial *or* global; FIN **global custody** custodia *f* global; **global economy** economía *f* mundial *or* global; FIN **global equities market** mercado *m* global de acciones; **global finance** finanzas *fpl* mundiales; **global market** mercado *m* mundial *or* global; **global marketing** marketing *m* mundial *or* global; **global marketplace** mercado *m* mundial *or* global; **global player** empresa *f* transnacional; **the global village** la aldea global; **global warming** calentamiento *m* global

(b) *(comprehensive)* global □ COMPTR **global change** cambio *m* global; COMPTR **global search**

and replace buscar *m* y reemplazar todos; *global strategy* estrategia *f* global

> British American Tobacco, the world second largest tobacco company, is close to striking a deal with the Ministry of Sound, the nightclub-to-publishing business, that will give BAT a **global strategy** for marketing its cigarettes to young people.

globalization *n* globalización, *f*, mundialización *f* ❑ MKTG *globalization strategy* estrategia *f* globalizadora

globalize *vt* globalizar

globalized economy *n* economía *f* globalizada

> Judith Robertson knows a thing or two or three about transitions: she's one of a new breed of people in the investment management business who appear able to glide effortlessly from posting to posting in the **globalized economy**, making the transition from Toronto to Vancouver to San Francisco to London to San Francisco and back to Toronto.

glut 1 *n (on market)* saturación *f*; *(of commodity)* exceso *m*; **there's a glut of oil on the market** el mercado está saturado de petróleo; FIN **glut of money** superabundancia *f* de capital
2 *vt (market, economy)* saturar; **the market is glutted with luxury goods** el mercado está saturado de productos de lujo

GMB *n Br (abbr* **General, Municipal and Boilermakers' Union)** = uno de los mayores sindicatos británicos, que representa a trabajadores de sectores muy diversos

GMC *n (abbr* **general management committee)** junta *f* de directores generales

GNMA *n (abbr* **Government National Mortgage Association)** = organismo oficial estadounidense que negocia con hipotecas en el mercado secundario y garantiza el pago de las mismas

gnome *n Fam* **the gnomes of Zurich** los banqueros suizos

> Who could have suspected that Gordon Brown would realise the aspiration of all his Labour predecessors: to finance a centre-left programme largely out of economic growth? Who could have thought that he would do so after three years without the slightest hint of a financial or economic crisis, without any bother from the **gnomes of Zurich** or bankers' ramps, or other mysterious forces of international capitalism that were always thought certain to undermine a Labour government?

GNP *n* ECON *(abbr* **gross national product)** PNB *m*

go *vi* **to go live** *(of company)* salir al mercado

▸ **go down** *vi (prices, value)* bajar, disminuir; **to go down in value** disminuir de *or* perder valor

▸ **go up** *vi (prices, value)* aumentar, subir; **the cost of living is going up** el costo *or Esp* coste de la vida está subiendo; **to go up in value** aumentar de valor

go-between *n* mediador(ora) *m,f*

gofer *n Fam* recadero(a) *m,f*, chico(a) *m,f* de los recados *or RP* mandados

go-go stock *n* ST EXCH = acción muy especulativa y arriesgada que ofrece la posibilidad de un alto rendimiento

going *adj* **(a)** *(profitable)* **a going concern** una empresa rentable; **for sale as a going concern** se traspasa **(b)** *(current) (price)* vigente; **she's getting the going rate for the job** le pagan la tarifa vigente por el trabajo

going-concern *adj* ACCT *going-concern concept* principio *m* de empresa en marcha; *going-concern status* condición *f* de empresa en marcha

going-rate pricing *n* MKTG imitación *f* de los precios de la competencia

gold *n* oro *m* ❑ FIN *gold bond* bono *m* respaldado con oro; *gold bullion* lingotes *mpl* de oro, oro *m* en lingotes; *gold bullion standard* patrón *m* lingote oro; *gold card* tarjeta *f* oro; *gold coin (currency)* oro *m* acuñado; *gold currency* oro *m* en moneda de curso legal; *gold exchange standard* patrón *m* de cambio oro; *gold export point* punto *m* de exportación del oro; *gold fixing* fijación *f* del precio del oro; *gold franc* franco *m* de oro; *gold import point* punto *m* de importación del oro; *gold ingot* lingote *m* de oro; *gold loan* empréstito *m* con garantía de oro; *gold market* mercado *m* del oro; *gold mine* mina *f* de oro; *(source of profit)* mina (de oro); *gold money* dinero *m* en oro; *gold point* punto *m* oro; *gold pool* fondo *m* de oro; *gold reserves* reservas *fpl* de oro; *gold share* acción *f* aurífera; *gold standard* patrón *m* oro

gold-collar worker *n* = empleado altamente cualificado y muy necesario para una empresa

golden *adj golden handcuffs* prima *f* de permanencia; *golden handshake (retirement bonus)* gratificación *f* voluntaria por jubilación; *golden hello* = cuantiosa gratificación ofrecida como incentivo para ingresar en una empresa; *golden parachute* contrato *m* blindado; *golden share* acción *f* de oro, participación *f* de control; *golden umbrella* contrato *m* blindado

gondola *n (for displaying goods)* góndola *f* ❑ **gondola end** cabecera *f* de góndola

good *adj (cheque)* válido(a); *(investment, securities)* seguro(a); *(contract, deal)* beneficioso(a); **their credit is good for £5,000** tienen hasta 5.000 libras de crédito

goods *npl* (**a**) LAW *(possessions)* bienes *mpl* ❑ *Br* **goods and chattels** enseres *mpl* (**b**) *(articles)* mercancía(s) *f(pl)*, artículos *mpl*, productos *mpl*; **send us the goods by rail** envíenos los productos *or* la mercancía por ferrocarril ❑ **goods depot** almacén *m or* depósito *m* de mercancías; **goods rate** tarifa *f* de mercancías; **goods service** servicio *m* de mercancías; **goods station** estación *f* de mercancías; **goods traffic** tráfico *m* de mercancías; **goods train** tren *m* de mercancías; **goods in transit** mercancías *fpl* en tránsito; **goods vehicle** = vehículo de carretera para el transporte de mercancías

good-till-cancelled order *n* ST EXCH orden *f* abierta

goodwill *n* fondo *m* de comercio ❑ **goodwill accounting** contabilización *f* del fondo de comercio

❝
Accounting convention assumes that **goodwill**, the premium a company pays for an acquisition, is a wasting asset. Why not create an impairment test that would consider market conditions and profitability projections to determine the value of **goodwill**? A 15-person team of accounting firms and investment bankers recently floated such a proposal, which is currently under consideration by the Financial Accounting Standards Board (FASB).
❞

gopher *n* (**a**) COMPTR gopher *m* (**b**) *Fam (person)* recadero(a) *m,f*, chico(a) *m,f* de los recados *or RP* mandados

go-slow *Br* **1** *n* huelga *f* de celo, *CSur* trabajo *m* a reglamento
2 *adj* **go-slow strike** huelga *f* de celo, *CSur* trabajo *m* a reglamento

.gov COMPTR = campo del sitio web de los organismos oficiales

govern *vt (country, city, bank)* gobernar; *(company, organization)* dirigir

governance *n* buen gobierno *m*, gobernanza *f*

governing *adj* gobernante ❑ **governing body** consejo *m* de gobierno

government *n (of country)* gobierno *m* ❑ **government action** iniciativas *fpl or* medidas *fpl* gubernamentales; **government aid** ayuda *f* estatal *or* del Estado; **government auditor** auditor(ora) *m,f* del Estado; **government bond** obligación *f or* bono *m* del Estado; **government borrowings** deuda *f* pública; *Br Formerly* **government broker** = agente de Bolsa a las órdenes del Banco de Inglaterra que compra y vende títulos del Estado; **government expenditure** gasto *m* público; **government grant** subvención *f* del Estado; **government loan** préstamo *m* del Estado; *US* **Government Printing Office** = imprenta (oficial) del Estado; **government property** propiedad *f* del Estado; **government resources** recursos *mpl* del Estado; **government revenue** ingresos *mpl* del Estado; **government securities** títulos *mpl* del Estado; **government spending** gasto *m* público; **government stock** títulos *mpl* del Estado

GPO *n US (abbr* **Government Printing Office**) = imprenta (oficial) del Estado

GPRS *n* TEL *(abbr* **General Packet Radio Service**) GPRS *m*

GPS *n (abbr* **Global Positioning System**) GPS *m*

grace *n* **days of grace** = periodo de gracia que se concede para el pago de una letra de cambio o la prima de un seguro tras su vencimiento ❑ **grace period** periodo *m* de gracia

grade **1** *n* (**a**) *(in profession)* grado *m*, rango *m*; *(on salary scale)* tramo *m*, banda *f*; **the top grades of the civil service** los escalafones superiores de la administración pública (**b**) *(of product)* clase *f*, calidad *f* ❑ **grade label** sello *m* de calidad
2 *vt (products)* clasificar

graded *adj (advertising rates)* escalonado(a); *(tax)* progresivo(a)

graduate *Br* **1** *n* licenciado(a) *m,f* ❑ **graduate entry** = nivel salarial de los licenciados al empezar un trabajo; **graduate recruitment scheme** programa *f* de captación de licenciados; **graduate training scheme** programa *m* de formación para licenciados *(que se incorporan a un trabajo)*
2 *vi* licenciarse, obtener la licenciatura; **she graduated in economics** se licenció *or* obtuvo la licenciatura en ciencias económicas

graduated *adj (payments, tax)* progresivo(a) ❑ **graduated payment mortgage** hipoteca *f* con pagos progresivos

grain *n* cereal *m*, grano *m* ❑ **grain market** mercado *m* de cereales

grammar checker *n* COMPTR corrector *m* gramatical *or* de gramática

granny bond *n Br Fam* FIN = bono de ahorro de interés fijo disponible para personas mayores de 60 años

grant **1** *n* (**a**) *(financial aid)* subvención *f* (**b**) *(transfer) (of property, land)* cesión *f*, concesión *f*
2 *vt (subsidy, loan, overdraft)* conceder

grant-aided *adj* subvencionado(a)

grant-in-aid *n* subvención *f*, subsidio *m* (*del estado a un organismo regional*)

graph *n* gráfico *m*, gráfica *f*; **to plot a graph** trazar un gráfico *or* una gráfica ▫ **graph paper** papel *m* milimetrado

graphic *adj* **graphic artist** artista *mf* gráfico(a); **graphic designer** diseñador(ora) *m,f* gráfico(a), grafista *mf*; COMPTR **graphic interface** interfaz *m* *or f* gráfico(a)

graphical user interface *n* COMPTR interfaz *m* *or f* gráfico(a) de usuario

graphics *npl* COMPTR gráficos *mpl* ▫ **graphics accelerator** acelerador *m* gráfico; **graphics accelerator card** tarjeta *f* aceleradora gráfica; **graphics application** aplicación *f* gráfica; **graphics card** tarjeta *f* gráfica; **graphics display** representación *f* gráfica; **graphics mode** modo *m* gráfico; **graphics package** software *m* de gráficos; **graphics palette** paleta *f* gráfica; **graphics software** software *m* de gráficos; **graphics spreadsheet** hoja *f* de cálculo con gráficos; **graphics tablet** tableta *f* gráfica; **graphics window** ventana *f* de gráficos

grass-roots *adj* de base, básico(a); **there is no grass-roots support for the party leadership's policy** la política de la dirección del partido no cuenta con el apoyo de las bases; **the grass-roots feeling is that…** la gente de la calle piensa que…; **at grass-roots level** entre las bases ▫ MKTG **grass-roots forecasting** previsión *f* a un nivel básico

gratis 1 *adj* gratuito(a), gratis
2 *adv* gratis

gratuity *n* (**a**) *(tip)* propina *f* (**b**) *Br (payment to employee)* gratificación *f*

graveyard shift *n* turno *m* de noche; **I work the graveyard shift** trabajo en el turno de noche

gray *US* = **grey**

green *adj* **green audit** auditoría *f* ambiental; **green card** *US (work permit)* permiso *m* de trabajo, carta *f* verde; *(car insurance)* carta *f* verde; Formerly EU **green currency** moneda *f* verde; **green marketing** marketing *m* ecológico; Formerly EU **the green pound** libra *f* verde, = valor de la libra en el mercado agrícola europeo; **green product** producto *m* ecológico; **green rate, green tariff** = tarifa que se paga por los suministros del gas y de la electricidad que son ecológicos; FIN **green taxation** tributación *f* ecológica; **green tourism** turismo *m* verde

greenback *n US Fam* billete *m* (de dólar) *(dólar estadounidense)*, *RP* verde *m*

greenfield site *n* terreno *m* edificable *(fuera del casco urbano)*

> "
> Anyone under the illusion that the British countryside is in safe hands had better think again, and fast. The developers are on the offensive, claiming they need to build on more **greenfield sites**. The government has bowed to the pressure and is proposing an ill-thought-out reform of planning controls, which would guarantee that the south-east would be concreted over. Behind these so-called reforms is the architect of another fiasco, Lord Falconer of the Dome.
> "

greenmail *n* FIN órdago *m*, = acción de chantajear a una empresa obligándola a recomprar un importante lote de acciones bajo amenaza de OPA

grey, *US* **gray 1** *n* COMPTR **shades of grey** tonos *mpl* de gris
2 *adj* **grey import** importación *f* paralela; ST EXCH **grey knight** = en el proceso de una OPA, agente cuyas intenciones son desconocidas para todos; **grey market** mercado *m* gris; **grey zone** zona *f* gris

greyscale, *US* **grayscale** *n* COMPTR escala *f* de grises

grievance *n* *(complaint)* queja *f*; **the workers put forward a list of grievances** los trabajadores informaron de sus quejas ▫ **grievance procedure** procedimiento *m* de resolución de conflictos

gross 1 *n* gruesa *f*, doce docenas *fpl*
2 *adj* (**a**) *(overall, total)* bruto(a) ▫ **gross actuarial return** rendimiento *m* actuarial bruto; **gross amount** importe *m* bruto; **gross annual interest return** interés *m* anual bruto; **gross assets** activo *m* bruto; INS **gross average** avería *f* gruesa; **gross dividend** dividendo *m* bruto; **gross domestic product** producto *m* Esp interior *or* Am interno bruto; **gross earnings** ingresos *mpl* íntegros; **gross income** *(in accounts)* total *m* ingresos; *(of individual)* renta *f* íntegra; **gross loss** pérdida *f* bruta; **gross margin** beneficio *m* *or* margen *m* bruto; **gross national income** renta *f* nacional bruta; **gross national product** producto *m* nacional bruto; **gross operating profit** beneficio *m* bruto de explotación; **gross proceeds** ingresos *mpl* brutos; **gross profit** beneficio *m* bruto; **gross profit margin** margen *m* bruto; **gross receipts** ingresos *mpl* brutos; **gross redemption yield** rendimiento *m* bruto al vencimiento; **gross registered tonnage** tonelaje *m* de registro bruto; **gross return** beneficio *m* bruto; **gross salary** salario *m* bruto; **gross value** valor *m* bruto; **gross wage** sueldo *m* bruto; **gross weight** peso *m* bruto; **gross yield** rendimiento *m* bruto

(**b**) LAW **gross negligence** negligencia *f* grave, imprudencia *f* temeraria

3 vt (of company) tener unos beneficios brutos de; **the sale grossed £30,000** la venta generó un beneficio bruto de 30.000 libras; **she grosses £40,000 a year** gana 40.000 libras brutas al año; **our firm grossed $800,000 last year** nuestra empresa tuvo unos beneficios brutos de 800.000 libras el año pasado

grossed-up adj FIN **grossed-up dividend** dividendo m expresado en bruto; FIN **grossed-up price** precio m bruto

ground n terreno m ❑ **ground handling agent** (at airport) empresa f de servicios de tierra; **ground rent** = alquiler que se paga al dueño del solar donde está edificada una vivienda

group n (of people, companies) grupo m; **the Shell Group** el Grupo Shell ❑ **group advertising** publicidad f colectiva; **group booking** reserva f de grupo; **group contract** contrato m colectivo; **group discount** descuento m de grupo; **Group of Eight** Grupo m de los Ocho; **group insurance** seguro m colectivo; **group interview** (for job) entrevista f en grupo; **group leader** jefe(a) m,f de grupo; **group manager** director(ora) m,f de grupo; **group meeting** reunión f de grupo; **Group of Seven** Grupo m de los Siete; **group subscription** suscripción f colectiva; FIN **group turnover** facturación f del grupo

groupage n agrupamiento m, consolidación f ❑ **groupage bill** conocimiento m de embarque para envíos consolidados; **groupage rate** tarifa f reducida aplicable a envíos consolidados

grouped consignment n envío m agrupado or consolidado

grow 1 vt **to grow the business** hacer crecer el negocio; **to grow a company** hacer crecer una empresa
2 vi (increase) crecer; **our market share has grown by 5% in the last year** nuestra cuota de mercado ha crecido en un 5% en el último año

> **❝**
> He thinks he can **grow the business** into a significant piece of change, much of it coming perhaps from the Microsoft arena where, as much as Lachman is a self-admitted Unix bigot, he knows he has to enter.
> **❞**

growing-equity mortgage n US FIN = hipoteca con tipo fijo y mensualidades crecientes

growth n (of business, market, industry) crecimiento m; **the experts predict a 2% growth in imports** los expertos prevén un crecimiento del 2% en las importaciones; **to go for growth** decidirse por el crecimiento; **the recent growth in the number of small businesses** el reciente aumento en el número de pequeños

negocios ❑ **growth area** área f de crecimiento; **growth company** empresa f en expansión; **growth curve** curva f de crecimiento; **growth developer** motor m de crecimiento; **growth driver** motor m de crecimiento; **growth factor** factor m de crecimiento; **growth fund** fondo m de crecimiento; **growth index** índice m de crecimiento; **growth industry** industria f en expansión; **growth market** mercado m en expansión; **growth phase** fase f de crecimiento; **growth potential** potencial m de crecimiento; **growth rate** tasa f de crecimiento; **growth sector** sector m en expansión; ST EXCH **growth shares, growth stock** valores mpl de crecimiento; **growth strategy** estrategia f de crecimiento; **growth trend** tendencia f creciente

growth-share matrix n MKTG matriz f crecimiento-cuota

GST n (abbr **goods and services tax**) = impuesto del estado en Canadá y Australia

guarantee 1 n (a) (document, promise) garantía f; **this printer has a five-year guarantee** esta impresora tiene cinco años de garantía; **under guarantee** en garantía ❑ **guarantee certificate** certificado m de garantía; **guarantee commission** comisión f por venta de garantía; **guarantee label** etiqueta f de garantía
(b) (security) garantía f, aval m; **to give sth as a guarantee** ofrecer algo como aval ❑ **guarantee company** (limited company) sociedad f limitada; **guarantee fund** fondo m de reserva or garantía
(c) (person) avalista mf, garante mf; **to act as guarantee (for sb)** ser el/la de garante (de alguien)
2 vt (a) (product, appliance) garantizar; **the printer is guaranteed for two years** la impresora tiene una garantía de dos años (b) (loan, debt) garantizar, avalar; (cheque) garantizar

guaranteed adj (debt) garantizado(a), avalado(a); (cheque) garantizado(a); **guaranteed by** (on financial document) garantizado(a) por ❑ FIN **guaranteed bill** letra f avalada; FIN **guaranteed bond** bono m garantizado; **guaranteed delivery period** plazo m de entrega garantizado; **guaranteed income** rendimiento m garantizado (de una póliza de prima única); **guaranteed income bond** obligación f de renta garantizada; **guaranteed loan** préstamo m garantizado or avalado; **guaranteed minimum pension** = pensión contributiva mínima garantizada; **guaranteed minimum wage** salario m mínimo interprofesional

guarantor n avalista mf, garante mf; **to stand as guarantor for sb** avalar a alguien

guaranty n US (a) (security) aval m (b) (written guarantee) garantía f

guerilla attack n MKTG ataque m de guerrilla(s)

guest *n (of hotel)* cliente *mf* ❑ *guest worker* = extranjero con permiso de trabajo

GUI *n* COMPTR (*abbr* **graphical user interface**) interfaz *m or f* gráfico(a) de usuario

guided interview *n* MKTG cuestionario *m* de respuestas cerradas, test *m*

guilder *n Formerly* florín *m*

guillotine *n (for cutting paper)* guillotina *f*

gyrations *npl (in market)* altibajos *mpl*

Hh

habitual buying behaviour *n* MKTG comportamiento *m* de compra habitual

hack *vi* COMPTR **they hacked their way into the system** accedieron al sistema burlando los códigos de seguridad

hacker *n* COMPTR *(illegal user)* pirata *mf* informático(a), hacker *mf*; *(expert user)* usuario(a) *m,f* experto(a), hacker *mf*

haggle *vi* regatear; **to haggle over sth** regatear por algo; **to haggle over the price of sth** regatear el precio de algo

haircut *n Fam* ST EXCH recorte *m*

> ❝
> The stock plunged after the company said that December-quarter earnings will be tiny because of slower-than-expected sales of new products such as the PowerMac Cube. That surely was reason for some decline in the stock − but in my opinion not for a $12 billion **haircut**, which is what the stock got.
> ❞

half-commission man *n* intermediario(a) *m,f* a media comisión, = persona que presenta clientes a un agente de Bolsa y se lleva la mitad de la comisión por la venta de acciones a dichos clientes

half-day *n* media jornada *f*; **tomorrow is my half-day** mañana solo trabajo media jornada; **to work half-days** trabajar a media jornada

half-yearly 1 *adj* semestral, bianual
2 *adv* semestralmente, cada seis meses

halo effect *n* MKTG efecto *m* halo

▶ **hammer out** *vt sep (agreement)* alcanzar, llegar a; *(contract)* formalizar

hammered *adj* ST EXCH *(stockbroker)* insolvente

hammering *n* ST EXCH *(of stockbroker)* declaración *f* de insolvencia

hand *n* **to change hands** *(business)* cambiar de dueño ❑ **hand baggage, hand luggage** equipaje *m* de mano; **a piece of hand baggage or luggage** un bulto como equipaje de mano

▶ **hand in** *vt sep (give)* entregar; **he handed in his resignation** presentó su dimisión

handbook *n* manual *m*

hand-held COMPTR **1** *n Esp* ordenador *m* or *Am* computadora *f* de bolsillo

2 *adj* **hand-held computer** *Esp* ordenador *m* or *Am* computadora *f* de bolsillo; **hand-held scanner** escáner *m* de mano

handle *vt* **(a)** *(deal with)* encargarse de; **we're too small to handle an order of that size** somos una empresa demasiado pequeña para hacernos cargo de un pedido de esa envergadura; **we can handle orders for overseas** podemos gestionar pedidos internacionales; **she's good at handling difficult customers** sabe cómo tratar a los clientes difíciles
(b) *(trade in)* tratar en; **we don't handle chemical products** no tratamos en productos químicos
(c) **handle with care** *(on parcel)* frágil

handler *n (of goods)* tratante *mf*, comerciante *mf*

handling *n* **(a)** *(of goods)* manejo *m*, manipulación *f* ❑ **handling capacity** *(of airport, port)* capacidad *f* de tráfico; **handling charges** gastos *mpl* de gestión *or* tramitación **(b)** *(of order, contract)* gestión *f*, tramitación *f*

hand-made *adj* hecho(a) a mano

handout *n (brochure)* folleto *m*; *(sample)* muestra *f* gratuita

handset *n* **(a)** *(of telephone)* auricular *m* **(b)** *(mobile phone)* terminal *m*

hands-free *adj* TEL de manos libres ❑ **hands-free device** dispositivo *m* de manos libres

handshake *n* COMPTR diálogo *m* de establecimiento de comunicación

hands-off *adj (approach, manager)* poco intervencionista

hands-on *adj (approach, style)* práctico(a); **the director has a hands-on style of management** al director le gusta implicarse en todos los aspectos de la empresa ❑ **hands-on training** formación *f* práctica

> ❝
> His departure is a setback for the Business, which was relaunched after Christmas as a joint venture with the Press Association. Sources said Northedge, who had expected to be given a fuller role at the revamped title, felt Neil's **hands-on** approach to editorial would not accommodate him.
> ❞

handwork n trabajo m manual

Hang Seng index n ST EXCH Índice m Hang Seng

harbour, US **harbor** n puerto m □ **harbour dues** derechos mpl portuarios or de puerto; **harbour facilities** instalaciones fpl portuarias; **harbour station** estación f marítima

hard adj (a) MKTG **hard sell** venta f agresiva; **to give sth the hard sell** hacer una promoción agresiva de algo; **try not to give your clients the hard sell** intenta evitar presionar a los clientes a que compren; **hard sell techniques** técnicas fpl de venta agresivas
(b) FIN **hard loan** préstamo m a condiciones de mercado
(c) **hard commodities** metales mpl y minerales; **hard currency** divisa f fuerte
(d) COMPTR **hard copy** copia f impresa; **hard disk** disco m duro; **hard drive** unidad f de disco duro; **hard return** retorno m manual

hard-core adj MKTG **hard-core loyal** cliente m más fiel; **hard-core loyalty** fidelidad f total

harden vi (prices, market) consolidarse, estabilizarse

hardening n (of prices, market) consolidación f, estabilización f

hardness n (of prices, market) estabilidad f

hardware n COMPTR hardware m

hash n (signo m) número m; (on telephone, IRC channel) almohadilla f, Am numeral m

hatchet man n Fam = directivo que realiza un duro reajuste de plantilla

❝
Logan is the man on the barricades. When he first arrived at Time Inc. in 1992, some of the older staffers saw it as the ultimate expression of the changes ushered in by the Warner merger. Fears swirled that he would be a financial **hatchet man**. And he imposed unprecedented financial discipline. **❞**

haul 1 n (transport) transporte m
2 vt (transport) transportar

haulage n (a) (transportation) transporte m (de mercancías) □ **haulage company** empresa f de transportes, transportista m; **haulage contractor** transportista mf; **haulage firm** empresa f de transportes, transportista m (b) (costs) (gastos mpl de) transporte m

haulier, US **hauler** n (company) empresa f de transportes, transportista m; (person) transportista mf

HD COMPTR (a) (abbr **hard disk**) disco m duro (b) (abbr **high density**) alta densidad f

head n (a) (person) jefe(a) m,f; **head of department** (in company, shop) jefe(a) de departamento □ **head buyer** jefe(a) m,f de compras; **head cashier** cajero(a) m,f principal or jefe; **head foreman** capataz mf general; **head office** sede f, central f (b) **heads of agreement** (draft) borrador m de un acuerdo

headed (note)paper n papel m con membrete

header n (on document) encabezamiento m

headhunt vt captar, cazar; **to be headhunted by sb** ser captado(a) por alguien

❝
It has also suffered from the loss of key senior staff who were **headhunted** by crosstown rival, Scottish Life, to launch a separate protection specialist which is expected to be operational later this year. **❞**

headhunter n cazatalentos mf inv

headhunting n captación f or caza f de altos ejecutivos

heading n (a) (of letter, invoice) membrete m (b) (in body of text) encabezamiento m, título m; **see under the next heading** ver el siguiente apartado (c) (on balance sheet) partida f; **see under the heading 'sales'** ver la partida 'ventas'

head-on attack n MKTG ataque m frontal

headquarter US **1** vt **to be headquartered in Chicago** tener la sede or central en Chicago
2 vi (company) **to headquarter in Houston** tener la sede or central en Houston

headquarters npl sede f, central f; **the company has its headquarters in Zurich** la empresa tiene la sede or central en Zurich

health n (in the workplace) higiene f □ **health cover** cobertura f sanitaria; **health inspector** inspector(ora) m,f de Sanidad; **health insurance** seguro m de enfermedad; **health insurance contributions** cotizaciones fpl al seguro de enfermedad; US **health plan** seguro m de enfermedad; **health and safety** seguridad f e higiene; Br **health and safety committee** comité m de seguridad e higiene; Br **Health and Safety Executive** ≃ Inspección f de Trabajo, = organismo oficial encargado de supervisar la seguridad en los centros de trabajo; Br **Health and Safety Inspector** ≃ Inspector(ora) m,f de Trabajo; Br **Health and Safety Officer** ≃ delegado(a) m,f de seguridad e higiene; Br **health and safety regulations** normas fpl de seguridad e higiene; Br **Health and Safety at Work Act** = ley de seguridad e higiene en el trabajo; **health sector** sector m de Sanidad; Br **the Health Service** el sistema nacional de salud británico

heart share n MKTG = fidelidad de los clientes basada en vínculos emocionales con una marca

heavy adj (taxation) alto(a), elevado(a); (loss, expenditure, payments) importante; **heavy losses**

grandes *or* importantes pérdidas; **they expect heavy trading on the Stock Exchange** se espera un alto nivel de contratación en la Bolsa; **closures have resulted in heavy job losses** los cierres se han traducido en importantes pérdidas de puestos de trabajo ❑ *heavy equipment* equipo *m* pesado; *Br heavy goods vehicle* vehículo *m* pesado *or* de gran tonelaje; *heavy industry* industria *f* pesada; *heavy investment* inversión *f* importante; ST EXCH *heavy market* mercado *m* deprimido *or* a la baja

hedge ST EXCH **1** *n* **hedge fund** fondo *m* de inversión de alto riesgo, hedge fund *m*; *hedge ratio* coeficiente *m* de cobertura; *hedge transaction* operación *f* de cobertura
2 *vt (shares, transactions)* realizar una operación de cobertura de
3 *vi* **to hedge against currency fluctuations** cubrir el riesgo de las fluctuaciones cambiarias

❝
ADB [Asian Development Bank] officials argued that developing countries could borrow extremely cheaply by denominating their loans in yen – at interest rates of 0.7 per cent – and **hedging** against the currency risk. But Mr Chino said the bank would review its lending policies following the latest round of international consultations on the subject.
❞

hedger *n* ST EXCH operador(ora) *m,f* de cobertura

hedging *n* ST EXCH cobertura *f* de riesgos ❑ *hedging instrument* instrumento *m* de cobertura de riesgos

help *n* COMPTR *help button* botón *m* de ayuda; *help desk (for queries)* servicio *m* de asistencia; *help file* archivo *m or* fichero *m* de ayuda; *help key* tecla *f* de ayuda; *help line* servicio *m* de asistencia; *help menu* menú *m* de ayuda; *help message* mensaje *m* de ayuda; *help screen* pantalla *f or* ventana *f* de ayuda; *help window* ventana *f* de ayuda

Helsinki agreement *n* acuerdos *mpl* de Helsinki

hereafter *adv (in legal document)* en adelante, en lo sucesivo

hereby *adv (in legal document)* por la presente; **we hereby declare that...** por la presente declaramos que...

heterogeneous *adj (market, goods)* heterogéneo(a)

hexadecimal *adj* COMPTR hexadecimal

HGV *n Br (abbr* **heavy goods vehicle***)* vehículo *m* pesado *or* de gran tonelaje ❑ *HGV licence* permiso *m* para conducir vehículos pesados *or* de gran tonelaje, *Esp* ≃ permiso *m* de conducir del tipo C

HICP *nm* ECON *(abbr* **Harmonized Index of Consumer Prices***)* IAPC *m*

hidden *adj* FIN *hidden cost* coste *m* oculto; *hidden defect* vicio *m* oculto; *hidden extras* gastos *mpl* extras; *hidden price increase* aumento *m* encubierto de precio; *hidden reserves* reservas *fpl* ocultas; *hidden tax* impuesto *m* encubierto

high 1 *n (peak)* máximo *m*; **the Stock Market reached a new high** la Bolsa ha alcanzado un nuevo máximo; **prices are at an all-time high** los precios han alcanzado un máximo histórico; ST EXCH **the highs and lows** las cotizaciones máximas y mínimas
2 *adj* **(a)** *(cost, price, interest rate)* alto(a), elevado(a); **to fetch a high price** alcanzar un precio elevado; **to pay a high price** pagar un alto precio; **areas of high unemployment** zonas con un alto nivel de desempleo ❑ *Br higher rate (of income tax) Esp* tipo *m* máximo, *Am* tasa *f* máxima; *the high season* la temporada alta
(b) *(important)* alto(a); **to hold a high position** tener un puesto importante; **to have a high profile** ser muy prominente *or* destacado(a) ❑ *high finance* altas finanzas *fpl*
(c) *Br* **the high street** *(street)* la calle principal; *(shops)* el comercio; **the high street has been badly hit by the recession** el comercio se ha visto gravemente afectado por la recesión
3 *adv* **to run high** *(prices)* estar alto(a); **salaries can go as high as £100,000** los sueldos pueden alcanzar las 100.000 libras

high-density *adj* COMPTR *(disk, graphics, printing)* de alta densidad

high-end *adj (goods)* de gama alta

higher-rate *adj Br* **higher-rate taxpayers** contribuyentes *mpl* del tramo impositivo máximo ❑ *higher-rate tax Esp* tipo *m* impositivo máximo, *Am* tasa *f* impositiva máxima

high-flier *n* **(a)** *(ambitious person)* persona *f* con ambición **(b)** ST EXCH acción *f* de altos vuelos

high-grade *adj (goods)* de primera calidad; *(minerals, coal)* de alto grado (de pureza)

high-growth company *n* empresa *f* de crecimiento rápido

high-income *adj* de altos ingresos ❑ *high-income group* grupo *m* de alto poder adquisitivo

high-involvement *adj* MKTG = que obliga al consumidor a dedicarle tiempo y esfuerzo antes de decidirse a comprarlo

high-level *adj (talks, meeting)* de alto nivel ❑ *high-level decision* decisión *f* de alto nivel; *high-level staff* altos ejecutivos *mpl*, altos cargos *mpl*

highlight *vt (with highlighter pen)* resaltar, marcar *(con rotulador fluorescente)*; COMPTR *(text)* seleccionar

highlighter n (pen) rotulador m fluorescente, Col, RP resaltador m, Méx marcador m

highly adv (**a**) (at an important level) **a highly-placed official** un alto cargo (**b**) (very well) muy bien; **to be highly paid** estar muy bien pagado(a)

highly-geared adj con un alto coeficiente de apalancamiento or endeudamiento

> ❝
> EZT invests mostly in zero dividend preference shares – historically the safest form of share in a split, offering a set return over a set period. But the trust is **highly geared**, which has magnified falls in zero share prices. The trust now has net liabilities of £5.5m.
> ❞

highly-skilled adj (employee, worker) altamente or muy cualificado

high-margin adj **high-margin product** producto m con un alto margen de beneficio

high-powered adj (person, job) de gran importancia

high-profile adj de renombre

high-quality adj (product) de alta calidad

high-resolution adj COMPTR de alta resolución

high-speed adj COMPTR de alta velocidad

high-street adj Br **the high-street banks** = los bancos principales que trabajan con el público en general; **high-street shops** las tiendas principales del centro (de la ciudad)

high-tech, hi-tech adj (product, industry, approach, solution) de alta tecnología

high-yield adj (bond, security) de alta rentabilidad

hire 1 n (**a**) Br (of car, equipment) alquiler m, Méx renta f ❑ **hire car** coche m or Am carro m or CSur auto m de alquiler, Méx carro m rentado; **hire charges** tarifas fpl de alquiler or Méx renta; **hire company** empresa f de alquiler or Méx renta (**b**) esp Br **hire purchase** compra f a plazos; **to buy sth on hire purchase** comprar algo a plazos; **hire purchase agreement** contrato m de compra a plazos
2 vt (**a**) (worker, lawyer) contratar (**b**) Br (car, equipment) alquilar, Méx rentar; **to hire sb's services** contratar los servicios de alguien
3 vi (engage workers) contratar personal; **the personnel manager has the power to hire and fire** el jefe de personal tiene poder para contratar y despedir a la gente

▸ **hire out** vt sep Br (car, equipment) alquilar, Méx rentar; **to hire out one's services** ofrecer sus servicios

hired adj Br (car, equipment) alquilado(a), Méx rentado(a)

historical cost n ACCT costo m or Esp coste m histórico ❑ **historical cost accounting** (sistema m de) contabilidad f a costos or Esp costes históricos

hit COMPTR **1** n (visit to web site) acceso m, visita f; (in search) resultado m; **this website counted 20,000 hits last week** esta página web registró 20.000 accesos durante la semana pasada
2 vt (key) pulsar

hi-tech = **high-tech**

▸ **hive off** vt sep **part of the industry was hived off to private ownership** se privatizó parte del sector; **the subsidiary companies will be hived off** las empresas filiales se privatizarán por separado

HMSO n Br (abbr **His/Her Majesty's Stationery Office**) = imprenta (oficial) del Estado

HNC n Br (abbr **Higher National Certificate**) = título de escuela técnica de grado medio

HND n Br (abbr **Higher National Diploma**) = título de escuela técnica de grado superior

hoarding n Br (billboard) valla f publicitaria ❑ **hoarding site** (espacio m para) vallas fpl publicitarias

hold 1 n **to put sb on hold** (on telephone) poner a alguien en espera; **to be on hold** estar en espera
2 vt (**a**) (possess) **to hold shares** tener acciones; **to hold 5% of the shares in a company** tener el 5% de las acciones de una empresa; **to hold office** (chairperson, deputy) ocupar el cargo; **to hold a seat on the board** tener un puesto en la junta directiva; **she holds the post of treasurer** ostenta el puesto de tesorera
(**b**) (conversation) mantener; (negotiations) celebrar; **the meeting will be held at 2 o'clock** la reunión se celebrará a las 2; **interviews will be held in early May** las entrevistas se celebrarán a principios de mayo
(**c**) COMPTR (store) almacenar; **the commands are held in memory** los comandos se almacenan en memoria; **how much data will this disk hold?** ¿cuánta información cabe en este disco?
(**d**) (on telephone) **hold the line, please** espere un momento, no cuelgue; **hold all my calls for the next hour** no me pases llamadas durante la próxima hora
3 vi (**a**) (on telephone) esperar; **the line's** Br **engaged** or US **busy just now – I'll hold** la línea está ocupada en estos momentos – espero
(**b**) (remain) mantenerse; **prices held at the same level as last year** los precios se mantuvieron al mismo nivel que el año pasado; **the pound held firm against the dollar** la libra se mantuvo sólida frente al dólar

▸ **hold over** vt sep (payment, meeting) aplazar, diferir; **payment was held over for six months** aplazaron seis meses el pago; **we'll hold these**

items over until the next meeting aplazaremos estos temas hasta la próxima reunión

▸ **hold up 1** vt sep (delay) retrasar; **the goods were held up at customs** las mercancías estuvieron retenidas en la aduana
2 vi (stay at the same level) mantenerse; **the shares held up well** las acciones se mantuvieron bien; **the market is holding up well** el mercado se está manteniendo bien

holder n (of job, shares, insurance policy, account) titular mf; (of degree) poseedor(ora) m,f

holding n FIN (shares in company) participación f; **he has holdings in several companies** tiene participaciones en varias empresas □ **holding company** sociedad f de cartera, holding m; **holding costs** costes mpl de conservación

> The treasury announced that Paolo Scaroni, the Italy-born chief executive of UK glass maker Pilkington, is to take over from Franco Tato as chief executive of state-run electricity giant Enel. Piero Gnudi, chairman of Italian state **holding company** Iri, is to become Enel's chairman.

hole-in-the-wall machine n Br Fam BANKING cajero m (automático)

holiday n (**a**) Br (vacation) vacaciones fpl; **a month's holiday** un mes de vacaciones; **to be on/go on holiday** estar/irse de vacaciones; **to get paid holidays** tener vacaciones retribuidas □ **holiday entitlement** vacaciones fpl (**b**) (day off) Esp (día m de) fiesta f, Am feriado m (**c**) (public) día m festivo

home n (**a**) (house) casa f; (family abode) hogar m; **to work at** or **from home** trabajar en or desde casa □ **home address** domicilio m; **home banking** banca f a domicilio, banca en casa; **home computer** Esp ordenador m doméstico, Am computadora f doméstica; **home computing: the growth of home computing** el aumento de Esp los ordenadores or Am las computadoras en el hogar; **home delivery** entrega f or reparto m a domicilio; US **home equity loan** segunda hipoteca f (sobre la misma vivienda); **home improvement loan** crédito m para mejoras del hogar; **home loan** crédito m hipotecario, hipoteca f; **home owner** propietario(a) m,f de vivienda; **home ownership: home ownership is increasing** están aumentando las viviendas en propiedad; MKTG **home party selling** venta f en reuniones de amigas; **home shopping** telecompra f
(**b**) (country) ECON **home consumption** consumo m interior; **home freight** flete m de retorno or vuelta; **home market** mercado m interior or nacional; Br **Home Office** Ministerio m del Interior; **home produce** productos mpl agrícolas nacionales; **home sales** ventas fpl en el mercado interior; Br **the Home Secretary** el/la ministro(a) del Interior; **home trade** comercio m interior
(**c**) COMPTR inicio m □ **home key** tecla f de inicio; **home page** (initial page) portada f, página f inicial or de inicio; (personal page) página personal
(**d**) US **home office** (of company) oficina f central

homeowner n propietario(a) m,f de vivienda

homeward adj □ **homeward cargo** carga f de retorno; **homeward freight** carga f de retorno; **homeward journey** viaje m de vuelta a casa

homeworker n persona f que trabaja en el (propio) domicilio

homeworking n trabajo m en el (propio) domicilio

homogeneous adj homogéneo(a)

honorarium n honorarios mpl

honorary adj (member) honorífico(a), honorario(a); **honorary president** or **chairman** presidente m de honor

honour, US **honor** vt (cheque, bill of exchange) pagar, liquidar; (agreement, contract) cumplir

horizontal adj **horizontal communication** comunicación f horizontal; FIN **horizontal equity** equidad f horizontal; **horizontal integration** integración f horizontal; FIN **horizontal spread** diferencia f horizontal

horse-trading n Fam negociaciones fpl entre bastidores, tira m y afloja, Esp chalaneo m; **a lot of horse-trading was required to clinch the deal** fue necesario mucho tira y afloja para conseguir firmar el contrato

> AT&T's rejection of Comcast came as no surprise to analysts, but many had expected the **horse-trading** for AT&T Broadband to continue with higher offers for the unit, either from Comcast or other cable companies. [AT&T] is playing a game of poker at this point, said InfoTech Broadband Analyst Erv Paw. "They're trying to get the price up."

hospitality n (industry) hostelería f (y restauración); **he's in charge of hospitality at the conference** se encarga de los actos sociales del congreso □ **hospitality business** sector m or negocio m de la hostelería (y restauración); **hospitality industry** sector m de la hostelería (y restauración); **hospitality management** gestión f de servicios de restauración; **hospitality room, hospitality suite** sala f de recepción

host COMPTR **1** n **host computer** host m, sistema m central; **host system** sistema m host
2 vt (website) hospedar, alojar

hostile takeover bid n OPA f hostil

> Mr Levy has had a mixed history in the US to date - and that's a considerable understatement. The roots of his satisfaction with the current coup will lie in the acrimonious mid-1990s fall-out with his former business partner, the once venerable FCB (now part of the Interpublic Group), which resulted in a failed **hostile takeover bid**.

hosting n COMPTR (of website) hospedaje m, alojamiento m

hot adj (a) TEL **hot line** línea f directa, teléfono m rojo; **hot line support** asistencia f por línea directa (b) FIN **hot money** dinero m especulativo (c) COMPTR **hot key** tecla f personalizada; **hot link** enlace m directo (d) **hot desking** sistema m de mesa compartida, = sistema de trabajo en el que los trabajadores carecen de un escritorio propio y ocupan el que se encuentre libre

hotel n hotel m ❏ **hotel accommodation** alojamiento m hotelero; **the town needs more hotel accommodation** la ciudad necesita más alojamiento hotelero; **hotel administration** dirección f de hoteles; **hotel bill** factura f de hotel; **the hotel business** la hostelería, Am la hotelería; **hotel chain** cadena f de hoteles; **hotel complex** complejo m hotelero; **hotel desk** mostrador m de recepción (del hotel); **hotel group** grupo m de hoteles; **hotel industry** sector m hotelero, hostelería f; **hotel management** (training) dirección f de hoteles; (people) dirección f del hotel; **hotel manager** director(ora) m,f de hotel; **hotel reception** recepción f; **hotel receptionist** recepcionista mf de hotel; **hotel staff** plantilla f de hotel; **the hotel trade** el negocio hotelero; **hotel warrant** licencia f de hotel

hour n hora f; **to pay sb by the hour** pagar a alguien por horas; **to be paid £5 an hour** cobrar 5 libras por hora; **an eight-hour day** una jornada de ocho horas

hourly adj (rate, pay, output) por hora; **the hourly wage has been increased** se ha aumentado la tarifa por hora

house n (a) (company) casa f, empresa f ❏ **house bill** conocimiento m de embarque de la empresa; US MKTG **house brand** marca f de la casa; **house magazine** boletín m interno (de una empresa) (b) ST EXCH **the House** la Bolsa de Londres

household n ECON unidad f familiar, hogar m ❏ **household budget** presupuesto m familiar; **household consumption** consumo m familiar; **household expenses** gastos mpl del hogar; **household goods** enseres mpl domésticos; **household name** marca f famosa or muy conocida

householder n cabeza mf de familia

house-to-house adj (selling) (de) puerta a puerta ❏ **house-to-house canvassing** venta f (de) puerta a puerta

housing n vivienda f; **the budget allocation for housing has been cut** se ha recortado la partida presupuestaria para la vivienda ❏ **housing allowance** subsidio m por vivienda; Br ADMIN **housing association** cooperativa f de viviendas; Br ADMIN **housing benefit** = subsidio para el pago del alquiler; **housing list** lista f de espera (para viviendas públicas de alquiler); **housing market** mercado m inmobiliario; **housing shortage** escasez f de viviendas

HP n (abbr **hire purchase**) compra f a plazos

HQ n (abbr **headquarters**) sede f, central f

HR npl (abbr **human resources**) RR.HH. mpl ❏ **HR manager** director(ora) m,f de RR.HH.

HRM n (abbr **human resource management**) gestión f de HH.RR.

HSE n (abbr **Health and Safety Executive**) = organismo oficial británico encargado de supervisar la seguridad en los centros de trabajo, ≃ Inspección f de Trabajo

HTML n COMPTR (abbr **Hyper Text Markup Language**) HTML m ❏ **HTML editor** editor m de HTML

HTTP n COMPTR (abbr **Hyper Text Transfer Protocol**) HTTP m ❏ **HTTP server** servidor m de HTTP

huckster n US Fam Pej (advertising copywriter) publicitario(a) m,f, publicista mf

human adj **human capital** capital m humano; **human engineering** ergonomía f, ingeniería f humana; **human factor** factor m humano; **human resource management** gestión f de recursos humanos; **human resources** recursos mpl humanos; **human resources manager** director(ora) m,f de recursos humanos

hurdle rate n tasa f crítica de rentabilidad

> In general, three pieces of information form the foundation for analyzing investments: the initial cost, the resulting cash flows, and the discount rate (that is, the required rate of return for a given investment, often referred to as the **hurdle rate** in capital budgeting).

hype Fam **1** n (publicity) bombo m, revuelo m publicitario
2 vt (publicize) dar mucho bombo a

▶ **hype up** vt sep Fam (publicize) dar mucho bombo a

hyperinflation n hiperinflación f

hyperlink n COMPTR hiperenlace m

hypermarket *n* hipermercado *m*

hypermedia *n* COMPTR hipermedia *f*

hypersegmentation *n* MKTG hipersegmentación *f*

hypertext *n* COMPTR hipertexto *m* ❑ ***hypertext link*** enlace *m* hipertextual

hyphen *n* guión *m*

hyphenate *vt* escribir con guión

hyphenation *n* partición *f* silábica *or* de palabras

hypothecation *n* pignoración *f*

Ii

IAP *n* COMPTR (*abbr* **Internet Access Provider**) proveedor *m* de acceso a Internet

IASC *n* (*abbr* **International Accounting Standards Committee**) IASC *m*

IBAS *n* (*abbr* **Independent Banking Advisory Service**) = servicio independiente británico de asesoría bancaria

IBOR *n* (*abbr* **interbank offered rate**) tipo *m* interbancario

IBRD *n* (*abbr* **International Bank for Reconstruction and Development**) BIRD *m*

ICC *n* (**a**) (*abbr* **International Chamber of Commerce**) ICC *f*, CCI *f* (**b**) *US* (*abbr* **Interstate Commerce Commission**) = organismo oficial que controla el comercio entre diferentes estados

ICD *n* (*abbr* **inland clearance depot**) depósito *m* aduanero interior, puerto *m* seco

ICFTU *n* (*abbr* **International Confederation of Free Trade Unions**) CIOSL *f*

icon *n* COMPTR icono *m* ◻ ***icon bar*** barra *f* de iconos; ***icon editor*** editor *m* de iconos

ICT *n* (*abbr* **Information and Communication Technologies**) TIC *fpl*

ICVC *n* FIN (*abbr* **investment company with variable capital**) ≃ SICAV *f*

IDB *n* FIN (*abbr* **inter-dealer broker**) mediador(ora) *m,f* de la deuda

IDD *n* TEL (*abbr* **international direct dialling**) marcación *f* directa internacional, *Andes, RP* discado *m* directo internacional

IDE *n* COMPTR (*abbr* **integrated drive electronics**) IDE *m*

identification *n* identificación *f* ◻ ***identification code*** (*of product*) código *m* de identificación; ***identification label*** (*of product*) etiqueta *f* de identificación

identifier *n* COMPTR identificador *m*

identify *vt* (*gap in market, opportunity*) identificar

identity *n* identidad *f* ◻ ***identity card*** carné *m* or documento *m* de identidad; ***identity papers*** documentos *mpl* de identificación

idle 1 *adj* (*employee*) ocioso(a), desocupado(a); (*factory, machine*) inactivo(a); ST EXCH (*markets*) inactivo(a); **to lie idle** (*money*) permanecer improductivo(a); **to let one's money lie idle** dejar

que el dinero permanezca improductivo ◻ ***idle time*** tiempo *m* muerto

2 *vt US* (*make unemployed*) dejar sin empleo or *Esp* en el paro or *Am* desocupado(a)

IFA *n Br* (*abbr* **independent financial adviser**) asesor(ora) *m,f* financiero(a) independiente

> **"**
>
> In the past, when a manager moved on, many investors would wait to see how the new one fared, while others would not even realise there had been a change. Since the start of the bear market, however, independent financial advisers (**IFA**s) have encouraged investors to view 'star' managers as the only chance of making money. If they move, you should follow – treating them as guardians of your money.
>
> **"**

IFC *n* FIN (*abbr* **International Finance Corporation**) CFI *f*

ILEC *n* TEL (*abbr* **incumbent local exchange carrier**) = compañía telefónica local en Estados Unidos que ofrecía sus servicios antes de la liberalización del mercado de 1996

illegal *adj* (*against the law*) ilegal, ilícito(a); COMPTR (*character, file name, instruction*) ilegal

illegally *adv* ilegalmente, de forma ilegal

illicit *adj* (*trading, profits*) ilícito(a)

illiquid *adj* irrealizable, ilíquido(a) ◻ ***illiquid assets*** activo *m* no realizable or ilíquido

illiquidity *n* iliquidez *f* ◻ ***illiquidity premium*** prima *f* por iliquidez

illustration *n* COMPTR ***illustration software*** software *m* de diseño gráfico

illustrator *n* ilustrador(ora) *m,f*

ILO *n* (*abbr* **International Labour Organization**) OIT *f*

ILWU *n* (*abbr* **International Longshoremen's and Warehousemen's Union**) = sindicato norteamericano de estibadores

image *n* imagen *f*; **their brief is to update the product's image** su trabajo consiste en actualizar la imagen del producto; **the company is suffering from an image problem** la empresa tiene un problema de imagen ◻ ***image bank*** banco *m* de imágenes; MKTG ***image building*** creación *f* de imagen; COMPTR ***image digitizer***

digitalizador *m* de imágenes; COMPTR *image file* archivo *m or* fichero *m* de imagen; COMPTR *image format* formato *m* de imagen; MKTG *image pricing* = fijación del precio de basándose en la imagen percibida del producto; COMPTR *image processing* tratamiento *m* de imagen; COMPTR *image processor* procesador *m* de imágenes; COMPTR *image refresh rate* velocidad *f* de refresco de imágenes; MKTG *image rights* derechos *mpl* de imagen

imager *n* COMPTR reproductor *m* de imágenes

IMF *n* ECON (*abbr* **International Monetary Fund**) FMI *m*

imitative product *n* MKTG producto *m* de imitación

immediate *adj* inmediato(a) □ *immediate debit* débito *m* inmediato; *immediate delivery* entrega *f* inmediata

immobilization *n* FIN *(of capital)* inmovilización *f*

immobilize *vt* FIN *(capital)* inmovilizar

immovable LAW **1** *n* **immovables** propiedad *f* inmobiliaria
   2 *adj* *immovable property* propiedad *f* inmobiliaria

immunity *n* inmunidad *f* (**from** contra); **immunity from prosecution** inmunidad procesal; **immunity from taxation** inmunidad tributaria

impact *n* impacto *m*; **high wages had a considerable impact on production costs** los altos salarios tuvieron un impacto considerable sobre los costos *or Esp* costes de producción □ ST EXCH *impact day* = día en el que se anuncian las condiciones de una nueva emisión de acciones; MKTG *impact study* estudio *m* de impacto

impairment *n* US ACCT deterioro *m* patrimonial

imperfect *adj* imperfecto(a); **it's slightly imperfect** *(of item for sale)* tiene algunas pequeñas imperfecciones □ *imperfect competition* competencia *f* imperfecta

impersonal accounts *npl* ACCT cuentas *fpl* no personales

implement *vt (plan, strategy, policy)* poner en práctica, llevar a cabo, implementar; *(law)* aplicar

implementation *n (of plan, strategy, policy)* puesta *f* en práctica, implementación *f*; *(of law)* aplicación *f*; MKTG *(of product)* implementación *f*

implicit *adj (cost, interest)* implícito(a)

import 1 *n* (**a**) *(product)* artículo *m* de importación; **imports** *(of country)* importaciones *fpl*
   (**b**) *(activity)* importación *f*; **import and export** importación y exportación □ *import agent* importador *m*, importadora *f*; *import ban* prohibición *f* sobre la importación; **to impose an import ban on sth** imponer una prohibición sobre la importación de algo; *import control*

control *m* de importaciones; *import credit* crédito *m* a la importación; *import declaration* declaración *f* de importación; *import duty* derechos *mpl* de importación *or* de aduana; *import firm* empresa *f* importadora; *import goldpoint* punto *m* oro; *import goods* mercancías *fpl* de importación; *import licence* licencia *f* de importación; *import list (of products that may be imported)* lista *f* de importación; *(of prices)* arancel *m* de entrada; *import permit* permiso *m* de importación; *import potential* potencial *m* importador; *import price* precio *m* de importación; *import prohibition* prohibición *f* sobre la importación; *import quotas* contingente *m* de importación; *import restrictions* restricciones *fpl* sobre la importación; *import surcharge* recargo *m* a la importación; *import surplus* exceso *m* de importaciones; *import tax* arancel *m* aduanero; *import trade* comercio *m* de importación; *import wholesaler* mayorista *mf* importador(ora)
   2 *vt* (**a**) *(goods)* importar (**from** de) (**b**) COMPTR importar (**from** de)

importation *n* (**a**) *(of goods)* importación *f*; **for temporary importation** para importación temporal (**b**) *US (imported article)* artículo *m* de importación

importer *n (person)* importador(ora) *m,f*; *(company)* importador *m*, importadora *f*; *(country)* país *m* importador, importador; **an oil importer** un país importador de petróleo; **this country is a big importer of luxury goods** este país es un gran importador de artículos de lujo; **we are a net importer of technology** somos un país netamente importador de tecnología □ *importer's margin* margen *m* del importador

import-export *n* importación-exportación *f*, comercio *m* exterior □ *import-export company* empresa *f* de importación-exportación

importing 1 *n* importación *f*
   2 *adj* importador(ora) □ *importing country* país *m* importador; *importing house* importador *m*, importadora *f*

impose *vt* **to impose a tax on sth** gravar algo con un impuesto; **to impose a ban on sth** prohibir algo; **the EU is in favour of imposing a ban on tobacco advertising** la UE está a favor de prohibir la publicidad del tabaco

imposition *n (of tax, ban)* imposición *f*

impost *n* impuesto *m*

impound *vt* LAW *(goods, documents)* embargar, confiscar

imprest *n* *imprest account* cuenta *f* de anticipos; *imprest fund* fondo *m* fijo de caja; *imprest system* sistema *m* de fondo fijo (de caja)

improve *vi* mejorar; *(prices, markets)* estar en alza; **business is improving** la actividad comercial está mejorando; **the pound improved**

against the dollar la libra se fortaleció con respecto al dólar

▶ **improve on, improve upon** vt insep **to improve on sb's offer** mejorar la oferta de alguien

impulse n **impulse buy** compra f impulsiva or por impulso; **impulse buyer** comprador(ora) m,f impulsivo(a) or por impulso; **impulse buying** compra f impulsiva or por impulso; **impulse purchase** compra f impulsiva or por impulso; **impulse purchaser** comprador(ora) m,f impulsivo(a) or por impulso; **impulse purchasing** compra f impulsiva or por impulso

inactive adj (money) improductivo(a); (bank account) inactivo(a), sin movimientos; (Stock Market) inactivo(a)

in-box n COMPTR (for e-mail) buzón m or bandeja f de entrada

Inc adj US (abbr **Incorporated**) ≃ S.A.

incapacity n incapacidad f; **his incapacity for work** su incapacidad para trabajar ◻ Br **incapacity benefit** prestación f por incapacidad

incent vt US incentivar

incentive n incentivo m; **the company offers various incentives** la empresa ofrece diversos incentivos ◻ **incentive bonus** prima f de productividad; **incentive marketing** marketing m de incentivos; **incentive pay** incentivos mpl; **incentive scheme** plan m de incentivos; **incentive travel** viaje m de incentivos

incentivize vt incentivar

> **"**
>
> Such thinking was based on the seminal management book In Search of Excellence by former McKinsey employees Tom Peters and Bob Waterman. Enron employees read it avidly. They were also big fans of another book, The War for Talent, by McKinsey consultants Ed Michaels, Helen Handfield-Jones and Beth Axelrod, which used Enron as a textbook example of how to **incentivize** staff.
>
> **"**

incidental 1 n **incidentals** gastos mpl imprevistos

2 adj **incidental costs, incidental expenses** gastos mpl imprevistos; **incidental income** otros ingresos mpl

in-clearing book n BANKING = libro en el que se registran todos los efectos liquidados enviados por la cámara de compensación

include vt incluir; (in letter) adjuntar; **the price includes VAT** el precio incluye el IVA; **up to and including 31 December** hasta el 31 de diciembre incluido

inclusive adj (price, sum) con todo incluido;

from 4 to 12 February inclusive del 4 al 12 de febrero, ambos inclusive; **inclusive of all taxes** todos los impuestos incluidos; **inclusive of VAT** IVA incluido

income n (**a**) (of person) (from work) ingresos mpl; (from shares, investment) rendimientos mpl, réditos mpl; (from property) renta f; **to be on a low/high income** tener un bajo/alto nivel de ingresos; **their combined income totals $200,000** la suma de sus ingresos asciende a 200.000 dólares; **the income from her investments** los rendimientos de sus inversiones ◻ **income bracket, income group** tramo m de renta; **most people in this area belong to the lower/higher income group** la mayoría de la gente en esta zona tiene una renta baja/alta; **income property** propiedades fpl generadoras de rentas; Br ADMIN **income support** = ayuda gubernamental a personas con muy bajos ingresos o desempleadas pero sin derecho al subsidio de desempleo; **income tax** impuesto m sobre la renta; **income tax is deducted at source** se realiza una retención de IRPF sobre el sueldo; **income tax allowance** deducción f de la base imponible, mínimo m exento; **income tax inspector** inspector(ora) m,f de tributos (especializado en IRPF); **income tax return** declaración f de la renta or del impuesto sobre la renta

(**b**) (of company) ingresos mpl; ACCT **income from operations** beneficios mpl de explotación ◻ ACCT **income account** cuenta f de resultados; **income bond** bono m de ingreso; **income and expenditure account** cuenta f de ingresos y gastos; **income fund** fondo m de renta; **incomes policy** política f de rentas; ACCT **income smoothing** maquillaje m de la cifra de negocios, = manipulación contable de los ingresos para presentar un aumento constante de los mismos de un ejercicio a otro; US ACCT **income statement** cuenta f de resultados; **income stock** título m de renta alta; **income stream** fuente f regular de ingresos; **income velocity of capital** velocidad f de circulación de la renta; **income velocity of circulation** velocidad-renta f de la circulación del dinero

incoming 1 n FIN **incomings** ingresos mpl; **comings and outgoings** ingresos y gastos

2 adj (telephone call, fax) entrante; (mail, e-mail) recibido(a); **there's an incoming fax addressed to you** está entrando un fax dirigido a ti ◻ **incoming inventory** existencias fpl que llegan al almacén

in-company adj en la empresa, en el lugar de trabajo ◻ Br **in-company training** formación f en la empresa or en el lugar de trabajo; Br **in-company training scheme** plan m de formación en la empresa or en el lugar de trabajo

incompatible adj COMPTR incompatible (**with** con)

inconvenience *n* molestia *f*; **we apologize for any inconvenience** disculpen las molestias

inconvertible *adj* FIN inconvertible

incorporate 1 *vt (company, bank)* constituir (en sociedad)
 2 *vi (form a corporation)* constituirse (en sociedad); *(merge)* fusionarse

incorporated *adj US* **Bradley, Wells & Jones Incorporated** Bradley, Wells & Jones S.A. □ *incorporated company* sociedad *f* anónima; *incorporated sector* sector *m* de las empresas privadas

incorporation *n (of company)* constitución *f* en sociedad

incoterm *n (abbr* **international commercial term)** incoterm *m*

increase 1 *n (in rate, sales, salary, prices)* aumento *m* (**in** de); **an increase in productivity/the cost of living** un aumento de (la) productividad/del costo *or Esp* coste de (la) vida; **to be on the increase** ir en aumento
 2 *vt (rate, sales, salary, price)* aumentar; **we must increase output to 500 units a week** debemos aumentar la producción a 500 unidades por semana
 3 *vi (rate, sales, salary, price)* aumentar; **to increase by 10%** aumentar en un 10%; **to increase in value** aumentar de valor; **to increase in price** subir *or* aumentar de precio; **the growth rate is likely to increase** es probable que aumente la tasa de crecimiento

increased *adj* mayor; **increased demand will lead to increased productivity** una mayor demanda tendrá como consecuencia una mayor productividad

increment *n* incremento *m*; **a salary with yearly increments of £2,000** un sueldo con incremento anual de 2.000 libras

incremental *adj* progresivo(a) □ *incremental cash flow* flujo *m* de caja incremental; *incremental cost* coste *m* marginal *or* incremental; *incremental increase* incremento *m* progresivo

incubator *m* **(business)** incubator vivero *m* de empresas

incur *vt (risk)* correr; *(loss)* experimentar, sufrir; *(debts)* contraer; *(expenses)* incurrir en; **the expenses incurred amount to several thousand pounds** se incurrió en gastos por valor de varios miles de libras

incurred *adj* ACCT □ *incurred expenditure, incurred expenses* gastos *mpl* soportados

indebted *adj* endeudado(a); **to be heavily indebted to sb** tener importantes deudas con alguien

indebtedness *n* endeudamiento *m*

indemnification *n* (**a**) *(act of compensation)* indemnización *f* (**b**) *(sum reimbursed)* indemnización *f*

indemnify *vt* (**a**) *(compensate)* **to indemnify sb for sth** indemnizar a alguien por algo; **you will be indemnified for any losses incurred** se le indemnizará por toda pérdida que pueda sufrir (**b**) *(insure)* **to indemnify sb against sth** asegurar a alguien contra algo; **to be indemnified against sth** estar asegurado(a) contra algo

> **“**
> Correctional Properties Trust will receive a total of $18,000,000, including the sale proceeds and lease termination fee. In addition, WCC has agreed to **indemnify** the Company against related liabilities and to pay all of Correctional Properties Trust's expenses associated with the sale of the Facility to the State, whether or not a closing occurs.
> **”**

indemnity *n* (**a**) *(compensation)* indemnización *f* □ FIN *indemnity bond* caución *f* de indemnidad (**b**) *(insurance)* indemnización *f*

indent 1 *n* (**a**) *Br (order)* pedido *m*, orden *f* de compra (**b**) *(in text)* sangría *f*, sangrado *m* (**c**) *(contract)* contrato *m*; *Formerly (of apprentice)* contrato *m* de aprendizaje
 2 *vt* (**a**) *(goods)* encargar, pedir (**b**) *(line of text)* sangrar; **indent the first line** sangrar la primera línea
 3 *vi* (**a**) *(order goods)* hacer un pedido; **to indent on sb for sth** hacer un pedido de algo a alguien (**b**) *(at start of paragraph)* hacer una sangría *or* un sangrado

independent *adj* independiente □ *independent administration* administración *f* independiente; *Br independent financial adviser* asesor(ora) *m,f* financiero(a) independiente; *independent income* rentas *fpl*, ingresos *mpl* independientes; *independent port* puerto *m* privado; *independent retailer* minorista *mf* independiente

index 1 *n* (**a**) *(in book, database)* índice *m* (**b**) *(on index cards)* índice *m* □ *index box* fichero *m*; *index card* ficha *f* (**c**) ECON, FIN, ST EXCH índice *m* □ *index arbitrage* arbitraje *m* de índices; *index fund* fondo *m* de índice; *index of growth* índice *m* de crecimiento; *index option* opción *f* sobre índice bursátil
 2 *vt* (**a**) COMPTR *(database)* indizar (**b**) FIN *(salary, pension, payment)* indexar, indizar (**to** a) □ *indexed bond* bono *m* indexado *or* indizado; *indexed loan* empréstito *m* indexado *or* indizado; *indexed portfolio* cartera *f* indexada *or* indizada

> **“**
> Trading in the final hour in both Dublin and London was frantic as **index funds** bid the shares up to a close of euro 5.00 (£3.94)

with bids for stock at euro 4.98. … Whether the magical euro 5.00 will trigger more selling by private investors remains to be seen but the shares are well-supported. **"**

indexation n FIN indexación f, indización f □ *indexation clause* cláusula f de indexación, claúsula de revisión salarial ligada al IPC

index-link vt FIN indexar, indizar

index-linked adj FIN indexado(a), indizado(a); **this pension is index-linked to the cost of living** esta pensión está indexada al costo or Esp coste de la vida, esta pensión está referenciada al IPC □ *index-linked bond* bono m indexado a la inflación; *index-linked fund* fondo m indexado

index-linking n FIN indexación f, indización f

indicator n (sign) indicador m

"

The market often anticipates interest changes likely to come as a result of changes in economic **indicators** such as the inflation rate or the exchange rate. Thus, often gilt prices start to change direction before interest rate movements take place, as investors successfully anticipate the government's intentions.

"

indict vt LAW acusar (formalmente) (**for** de)

indictment n LAW (act) acusación f formal; (document) acta f or escrito m de acusación formal; **indictment for fraud** acusación formal de fraude

indigenous company n empresa f nacional

indirect adj indirecto(a) □ *indirect costs* costos mpl or Esp costes mpl indirectos; *indirect investment* inversión f indirecta; *indirect labour* mano f de obra indirecta; MKTG *indirect promotional costs* costos mpl or Esp costes mpl indirectos de las campañas; *indirect selling* ventas fpl indirectas; *indirect tax* impuesto m indirecto; *indirect taxation* impuestos mpl indirectos

individual adj individual □ *individual company accounts* cuentas fpl individuales de empresa; *individual entity* persona f física; *individual owner* propietario(a) m,f individual; *individual ownership* propiedad f individual; *individual savings account* cuenta f de ahorro personal (con ventajas fiscales)

indorse = **endorse**

inducement n (incentive) incentivo m; **he was offered considerable financial inducements to leave his company** le ofrecieron jugosos incentivos para que abandonara la empresa

induction course n curso m or cursillo m introductorio

industrial 1 adj (**a**) industrial □ *industrial accident* accidente m laboral; *industrial accident insurance* seguro m contra accidentes laborales; *industrial action* movilizaciones fpl, medidas fpl de presión de los trabajadores; **to take industrial action** movilizarse, ejercer medidas de presión; *industrial centre* núcleo m industrial; *industrial change* reconversión f industrial; *industrial complex* complejo m industrial; *industrial concern* explotación f industrial; *industrial design* diseño m industrial; *industrial disease* enfermedad f laboral; *industrial dispute* conflicto m laboral; *industrial engineering* ingeniería f industrial; *industrial espionage* espionaje m industrial; Br *industrial estate* polígono m industrial; *industrial goods* bienes mpl de producción; *industrial group* grupo m industrial; *industrial injury* lesión f laboral; Formerly *industrial injuries benefit* prestación f por lesiones laborales; *industrial insurance* seguro m contra accidentes laborales; *the industrial machine* la maquinaria industrial; *industrial market* mercado m industrial; *industrial marketer* especialista mf en marketing industrial; *industrial marketing* marketing m industrial; US *industrial park* polígono m industrial; *industrial plant* equipamiento m industrial; *industrial pool* grupo m industrial; *industrial potential* potencial m industrial; *industrial product* producto m industrial; *industrial psychology* psicología f industrial; *industrial relations* relaciones fpl laborales; *industrial town* ciudad f industrial; *industrial trade* comercio m industrial; *industrial training* formación f industrial (en la empresa); *industrial tribunal* tribunal m laboral, Esp tribunal de lo social; *industrial union* sindicato m sectorial; *industrial unrest* conflictividad f laboral; *industrial vehicle* vehículo m industrial; *industrial warrant* derecho m de suscripción de acciones industriales; *industrial waste* residuos mpl industriales
(**b**) ECON *industrial unit* planta f industrial
(**c**) FIN *industrial bank* banco m industrial; *industrial monopoly* monopolio m industrial; ST EXCH *industrial shares* acciones fpl industriales
2 n ST EXCH **industrials** acciones fpl industriales

industrialism n industrialismo m

industrialist n industrial mf

industrialization n industrialización f

industrialize 1 vt industrializar
2 vi industrializarse

industrialized adj industrializado(a) □ *industrialized countries* países mpl industrializados

industry n (in general) industria f; (particular sector) sector m, industria; **the aircraft industry** el sector aeronáutico, la industria aeronáutica; **the tourist industry** el sector turístico □

industry expert experto(a) *m,f* sectorial; **industry forecast** previsión *f* sectorial; **industry sector** sector *m* industrial; **industry union** sindicato *m* sectorial

industry-wide *adj (campaign)* intersectorial; *(redundancies)* generalizado(a) ❏ **industry-wide agreement** acuerdo *m* interprofesional

inefficiency *n* ineficiencia *f*

inefficient *adj* ineficiente

inelastic *adj (demand)* inelástico(a)

❝
The telcos have one basic advantage over their suffering dot-com cousins: while many Internet firms were built on demand that has yet to materialize (people will love buying groceries over the Internet – right?), the telecom sector is blessed with what economists call **inelastic** demand. In other words, people will always want to make phone calls and transmit data, regardless of how low the market sinks.
❞

inertia selling *n* MKTG venta *f* por inercia

inexpensive *adj* económico(a), barato(a)

infect *vt* COMPTR infectar

inferior *adj* (a) *(goods, quality)* inferior (b) *(in rank)* inferior; **she holds an inferior position in the company** tiene un puesto inferior en la empresa

inflate 1 *vt* (a) *(expense account, figures)* inflar (b) ECON *(prices)* inflar; **to inflate the currency** provocar una inflación monetaria
2 *vi (prices)* inflarse; **the government decided to inflate** el gobierno decidió adoptar medidas inflacionarias *or* inflacionistas

inflated *adj* ECON *(prices, salary)* desorbitado(a) ❏ **inflated currency** moneda *f* inflacionaria *or* inflacionista

inflation *n* ECON inflación *f*; **inflation is down/up on last year** la inflación ha disminuido/aumentado con respecto al año pasado; **inflation now stands at 5%** la inflación se sitúa actualmente en el 5% ❏ **inflation differential** diferencial *m* de inflación; **inflation tax** impuesto *m* a la inflación

inflationary *adj* ECON inflacionario(a), inflacionista ❏ **inflationary gap** déficit *m* inflacionario *or* inflacionista; **inflationary policy** política *f* inflacionaria *or* inflacionista; **inflationary pressure** presión *f* inflacionaria *or* inflacionista; **inflationary spiral** espiral *f* inflacionaria *or* inflacionista; **inflationary surge** repunte *m* inflacionario *or* inflacionista

❝
Inflation is picking up as the value of the peso plummets, with fuel and supermarket prices rising weekly. Unions are planning a

series of mass protests to call for pay rises, threatening an **inflationary spiral** that could spell the end of Mr Duhalde's period in office.
❞

inflationism *n* ECON inflacionismo *m*

inflationist 1 *n* ECON inflacionista *mf*
2 *adj* inflacionista

inflation-proof *adj* protegido(a) contra la inflación

in-flight magazine *n* revista *f* de a bordo

inflow *n* afluencia *f*, entrada *f*; **the inflow of capital** la entrada *or* afluencia de capital; **the inflow of cheap imports** la afluencia de artículos de importación baratos

influence peddling *n* tráfico *m* de influencias

❝
During Bill Clinton's presidency, Republicans were loud in accusing the White House of being too cozy with campaign contributors and lobbyists and relentlessly looking to shape policy to appeal to this or that group of minority voters. **Influence peddling** seemed rife, as did special treatment and access for corporate bigwigs who shelled out for the Democrats.
❞

influencer *n* MKTG influenciador *m*

influx *n* afluencia *f* (masiva)

info *n* Fam información *f*; **a piece of info** una información, un dato

infoaddict *n* Fam COMPTR infoadicto(a) *m,f*

infobahn *n* COMPTR infopista *f*, autopista *f* de la información

infohighway *n* COMPTR infopista *f*, autopista *f* de la información

infomercial *n* publirreportaje *m*

inform *vt (in letter)* **I am pleased to inform you that...** me complace informarle de que...; **I regret to inform you that...** siento comunicarle *or* informarle de que...; **we are informed that...** nos informan de que...

informal economy *n* ECON economía *f* informal

❝
The European Commission estimates 7-16 percent of the European economy is **informal**, giving a range of approximately EUR500 billion–1.1 trillion ($448.8 billion to $987 billion) that is effectively a cash economy. The smallest **informal economies** are estimated to be in Scandinavia, Ireland, Austria and the Netherlands, each at around a very honest, and modest, 5 percent of GDP. But that balloons to over 20 percent in Italy and Greece.
❞

information n (a) *(news, facts)* información f; **a piece of information** una información, un dato; **I am sending you this brochure for your information** le envío este folleto para tu información ▫ *information bureau* oficina f de información; *information card* tarjeta f informativa; *information centre* centro m de información; ADMIN *information copy* ejemplar m informativo; *information desk* mostrador m de información; *information market* mercado m de la información; *information office* oficina f de información; *information officer* documentalista mf; *information overload* sobrecarga f de información; *information pack* documentación f; ST EXCH *information prospectus* prospecto m de emisión; *information service* servicio m de información; *information sheet* hoja f informativa; *information theory* teoría f de la información

(b) COMPTR información f ▫ *information gathering* recolección f de información; *information highway* autopista f de la información; *information processing* proceso m de datos; *information retrieval* recuperación f de la información; *information science* informática f; *information society* sociedad f de la información; *information storage* almacenamiento m de información; *information superhighway* autopista f de la información; *information system* sistema m informático; *information technology* tecnologías fpl de la información, informática f

(c) US TEL información f, Am informaciones fpl

> 66
>
> We need, too, to build a genuine **information society**, in which internet access is available to all. Europe must move quickly to ensure widespread availability of broadband internet links. Further liberalisation of the telecommunications market should help us deliver this goal. The internet is one of the tools that can help bind the enlarged union together.
>
> 99

informative advertising n MKTG publicidad f informativa

infrared adj COMPTR infrarrojo(a) ▫ *infrared keyboard* teclado m infrarrojo; *infrared mouse* Esp ratón m or Am mouse m de infrarrojos

infrastructure n ADMIN infraestructura f

infringe vt *(agreement, rights)* violar, vulnerar; **to infringe copyright** violar los derechos de autor; **to infringe a patent** violar una patente

infringement n *(of agreement, rights)* violación f, vulneración f; **infringement of copyright** violación de los derechos de autor; **infringement of a patent** violación de una patente

ingot n lingote m

inherent vice n INS vicio m propio

inherit 1 vt heredar (**from** de); **she inherited one million dollars** heredó un millón de dólares 2 vi heredar

inheritable adj heredable

inheritance n herencia f; **to come into an inheritance** heredar, recibir una herencia ▫ *inheritance tax* impuesto m sobre sucesiones

inhibitor n MKTG inhibidor m

in-home adj MKTG *in-home placement testing* = prueba consistente en que una persona utilice durante un periodo determinado el producto que se quiere probar en lugar del que suele usar, normalmente a cambio de un incentivo; *in-home shopping* compra f desde el hogar

in-house 1 adj *(policy, rules)* interno(a); *(staff)* de plantilla, SAm de plantel ▫ *in-house journal* boletín m interno (de una empresa); *in-house magazine* revista f de empresa; *in-house team* plantilla f; *in-house training* formación f en el lugar de trabajo

2 adv en la empresa; **we prefer to train our staff in-house** preferimos formar a nuestros empleados en la empresa

initial 1 adj inicial ▫ *initial capital* capital m inicial; *initial cost* costo m or Esp coste m inicial; *initial expenditure* desembolso m inicial; *initial investment* inversión f inicial; ST EXCH *initial margin* depósito m de garantía; US ST EXCH *initial public offering* oferta f pública inicial; *initial stock* oferta f inicial; *initial value* valor m inicial

2 vt *(letter, document, changes)* poner las iniciales en

initialization n COMPTR inicialización f

initialize vt (a) COMPTR inicializar (b) *(letter, document, changes)* poner las iniciales en, visar; **the contract needs to be initialized** hay que firmar el contrato con las iniciales

initiate vt *(talks, debate)* iniciar; *(policy, measures)* emprender, poner en marcha; LAW **to initiate proceedings against sb** emprender una acción legal contra alguien

initiator n MKTG iniciador(ora) m,f

inject vt *(money)* inyectar (**into** en); **they've injected billions of dollars into the economy** le han inyectado a la economía miles de millones de dólares

injection n *(of money)* inyección f (**into** en); **an injection of capital** una inyección de capital

injunction n LAW requerimiento m judicial; **to take out an injunction against sb** obtener un requerimiento judicial contra alguien

injured party n LAW **the injured party** la parte perjudicada

ink n tinta f ▫ *ink cartridge* (for pen, printer) cartucho m de tinta; *ink pad* tampón m

inkjet printer *n* COMPTR impresora *f* de chorro de tinta

inland *adj* interior, nacional ❏ FIN ***inland bill*** letra *f* (de cambio) interior; ***inland clearance depot*** depósito *m* aduanero interior, puerto *m* seco; ***inland freight*** flete *m* interior; ***inland haulage*** transporte *m* interior *or* nacional de mercancías; ***inland mail*** correo *m* interior *or* nacional; *Br* **the Inland Revenue** ≃ Hacienda, *Esp* ≃ la Agencia Tributaria, *Méx* ≃ el Servicio de Administración Tributaria

inner reserve *n* provisiones *fpl* internas

innovating company *n* empresa *f* innovadora

innovation *n* innovación *f*; **innovations in management techniques** innovaciones en técnicas de gestión

innovative *adj* innovador(ora) ❏ ***innovative product*** producto *m* innovador

innovator *n* innovador(ora) *m,f*

input 1 *n* (**a**) *(of production)* materias *fpl* primas ❏ ACCT ***input VAT*** IVA *m* soportado
(**b**) COMPTR *(action, data)* input *m*, entrada *f* ❏ ***input box*** ventana *f* de texto; ***input device*** dispositivo *m* de entrada; ***input form*** formulario *m or Méx* forma *f* de datos; ***input grid*** rejilla *f or Am* grilla *f* de datos
(**c**) *(during meeting, discussion)* aportación *f*, aporte *m*; **we'd like some input from marketing before committing ourselves** nos gustaría saber qué piensan en marketing antes de decidirnos
2 *vt* COMPTR **to input data** introducir datos

input/output *n* COMPTR entrada *f* y salida ❏ ***input/output device*** dispositivo *m* de entrada y salida

inquire, enquire 1 *vt* preguntar
2 *vi* preguntar; **to inquire about…** informarse sobre…

inquiry, enquiry *n* *(request for information)* consulta *f*; **to make inquiries (about sth)** consultar *or* informarse (sobre algo); **with reference to your inquiry of 5 May,…** *(in letter)* en referencia a su consulta del 5 de mayo,… ❏ ***inquiry office*** oficina *f* de información

inscribed securities *npl* ST EXCH títulos *mpl* nominativos

insert 1 *n* (**a**) COMPTR inserción *f* ❏ ***insert command*** comando *m* de inserción; ***insert key*** tecla *f* de inserción; ***insert mode*** modo *m* de inserción (**b**) *(leaflet)* encarte *m*
2 *vt* *(clause, advertisement, page number)* insertar

insertion *n* COMPTR inserción *f* ❏ ***insertion marker*** marcador *m* de inserción; ***insertion point*** punto *m* de inserción

insider *n* FIN, ST EXCH **the insiders** las personas con información privilegiada ❏ ***insider dealing,***

insider trading transacciones *fpl* con información privilegiada

> Investors should benefit from stronger protection against **insider dealing** and stock market manipulation through the first ever set of Europe-wide rules, under plans agreed yesterday by the European Union. The new legislation, approved yesterday by European finance ministers, is a further step towards the EU's goal of creating a single market for securities by the end of next year.

insolvency *n* insolvencia *f*; **to declare insolvency** declararse insolvente ❏ ***insolvency provision*** provisión *f* (salarial) para insolvencias

insolvent *adj* insolvente; **to be declared insolvent** *(person, firm)* ser declarado(a) insolvente

insourcing *n* subcontratación *f* *(de un servicio realizado en la propia empresa)*

inspect *vt* *(documents, goods, premises, accounts, staff)* inspeccionar, examinar

inspection *n* *(of documents, goods, premises, accounts, staff)* inspección *f*, examen *m*; **to buy goods on inspection** = comprar mercancías con la posibilidad de devolverlas si no se está totalmente satisfecho ❏ CUSTOMS ***inspection order*** orden *f* de inspección

inspector *n* inspector(ora) *m,f* ❏ *US* ***inspector general*** inspector(ora) *m,f* general; *Br* ***Inspector of Taxes*** inspector(ora) *m,f* de tributos

instability *n* inestabilidad *f*

install, *US* **instal** *vt* (**a**) *(machinery, equipment)* instalar; **to install sb in a post** colocar a alguien en un puesto (**b**) COMPTR *(software)* instalar

installation *n* COMPTR instalación *f* ❏ ***installation disk*** disco *m* de instalación

installer *n* COMPTR *(program)* instalador *m*

instalment, *US* **installment** *n* *(part payment)* plazo *m*, *CSur* cuota *f*; **to pay in** *or* **by instalments** pagar a plazos *or CSur* en cuotas ❏ ***instalment loan*** crédito *m* a plazos *or CSur* en cuotas; *US* ***installment plan*** compra *f* a plazos *or CSur* en cuotas; **to buy sth on the installment plan** comprar algo a plazos *or CSur* en cuotas

instant *adj* *(access to savings)* inmediato(a)

instant-access *adj* *(bank account)* a la vista

> The internet-only savings accounts, as usual, offer the best rates to savers prepared to eschew trips to high street branches. Egg offers its internet-only savers 5 per cent, including an introductory offer, which puts it

well out in the lead among **instant-access** accounts and is comfortably above official interest rates.
"

instantaneous audience *n* MKTG audiencia *f* simultánea

institute *vt* LAW **to institute proceedings against sb** emprender una acción legal contra alguien

institution *n (organization)* institución *f*; **the institutions of the state** las instituciones del Estado

institutional *adj* MKTG **institutional advertising** publicidad *f* institucional; FIN **institutional buying** compras *fpl* institucionales *(de acciones)*; **institutional investment** inversiones *fpl* institucionales; **institutional investor** inversor *m* institucional; **institutional savings** ahorro *m* institucional

in-store *adj* MKTG **in-store advertising** publicidad *f* en el punto de venta; **in-store advertising space** espacio *m* publicitario en el punto de venta; **in-store demonstration** demostración *f* en el punto de venta; **in-store promotion** promoción *f* en el punto de venta

instruction *n* COMPTR **instructions** *(in program)* instrucciones *fpl* ❑ **instruction manual** manual *m* de instrucciones

instrument *n* FIN instrumento *m*; LAW documento *m* legal; **an instrument of payment** un instrumento de pago ❑ **instrument of commerce** instrumento *m* de comercio; **instrument of incorporation** acta *f* de constitución; **instrument to order** título *m* a la orden

insufficient *adj* insuficiente ❑ **insufficient capital** capital *m* insuficiente; BANKING **insufficient funds** saldo *m* insuficiente; **insufficient resources** recursos *mpl* insuficientes

insurable *adj* asegurable ❑ **insurable interest** interés *m* asegurable; **insurable value** valor *m* asegurable

insurance *n* seguro *m*; **to take out insurance (against sth)** hacerse un seguro (contra algo), asegurarse (contra algo); **how much do you pay in insurance?** ¿cuánto pagas de seguro?; **you can extend the insurance when you renew the policy** puede ampliar el seguro cuando renueve la póliza; **she got £2,000 in insurance** cobró 2.000 libras por el seguro ❑ **insurance adviser** asesor(ora) *m,f* de seguros; **insurance agent** agente *mf* de seguros; **insurance banker** = banco que ofrece servicios de seguros; **insurance broker** corredor(ora) *m,f* de seguros; **insurance certificate** certificado *m* de seguro; **insurance charges** gastos *mpl* de seguro; **insurance claim** reclamación *f* or SAm reclamo *m* al seguro; **to make an insurance claim** hacer una reclamación or SAm reclamo al seguro;

insurance company aseguradora *f*, compañía *f* de seguros; **insurance cover** cobertura *f* del seguro; **insurance form** impreso *m* del seguro; **insurance group** grupo *m* asegurador; **insurance inspector** inspector(ora) *m,f* de seguros; **insurance money** dinero *m* del seguro; **insurance policy** póliza *f* de seguros; **to take out an insurance policy** contratar una póliza de seguros; **insurance pool** consorcio *m* asegurador; **insurance portfolio** cartera *f* de productos de seguros; **insurance premium** prima *f* (del seguro); **insurance proposal** solicitud *f* de seguro; **insurance rate** cuota *f* del seguro; **insurance value** valor *m* asegurable

insure 1 *vt* asegurar (**against** contra); **to insure one's life** hacerse un seguro de vida; **we're insured against flooding** tenemos un seguro contra inundación
2 *vi* **to insure against sth** contratar un seguro contra algo

insured 1 *n* **the insured** el/la asegurado(a)
2 *adj* asegurado(a) (**against** contra) ❑ **insured value** valor *m* asegurado

insurer *n* asegurador(ora) *m,f*

intangible 1 *n* **intangibles** bienes *mpl* inmateriales
2 *adj* ACCT **intangible assets** bienes *mpl* intangibles; **intangible fixed assets** inmovilizado *m* inmaterial; **intangible property** bienes *mpl* inmateriales

integrate *vt* integrar

integrated *adj* integrado(a) ❑ COMPTR **integrated circuit board** placa *f* de circuito integrado; **integrated management system** sistema *m* integrado de gestión; COMPTR **integrated package** paquete *m* integrado; **integrated port facilities** servicios *mpl* portuarios integrados; COMPTR **integrated services digital network** red *f* digital de servicios integrados; COMPTR **integrated software** software *m* integrado; **integrated transport network** red *f* integrada de transporte

integration *n* integración *f*

"
"If Bertelsmann want to pursue their pan-European strategy do they have to go in and bid against the US players for ITV?" said Nicola Stewart, analyst at West LB Panmure …But she said US companies would take a close look at ITV. "There is a lot of logic in having vertical **integration** between content and distribution assets, especially if there is a common language involved, which has put off the European groups", she said.
"

integrative growth *n* crecimiento *m* por integración

intellectual property *n* propiedad *f* intelectual

intelligent terminal *n* COMPTR terminal *m* inteligente

intensive distribution *n* distribución *f* intensiva ❏ **intensive distribution strategy** estrategia *f* de distribución intensiva

intention to buy *n* MKTG intención *f* de compra

intention-to-buy-scale *n* MKTG grado *m* de intención de compra

interactive *adj* COMPTR interactivo(a) ❏ **interactive CD** CD *m* interactivo; **interactive digital media** medios *mpl* digitales interactivos; **interactive highway** autopista *f* interactiva; **interactive marketing** marketing *m* interactivo

interactivity *n* COMPTR interactividad *f*

interbank *adj* interbancario(a) ❏ **interbank deposit** depósito *m* interbancario; **interbank deposit rate** *Esp* tipo *m or Am* tasa *f* de interés para depósitos interbancarios; **interbank interest rate** *Esp* tipo *m* de interés interbancario, *Am* tasa *f* de interés interbancaria; **interbank loan** crédito *m* interbancario; **interbank market** mercado *m* interbancario; **interbank money** dinero *m* interbancario; **interbank offered rate** *Esp* tipo *m or Am* tasa *f* de oferta interbancaria; **interbank reference rate** *Esp* tipo *m or Am* tasa *f* interbancaria de referencia; **interbank transfer** transferencia *f* interbancaria; **interbank wholesale market** mercado *m* interbancario

interbranch *adj* entre oficinas, entre sucursales

intercept interview *n* MKTG encuesta *f* por interceptación

intercompany *adj* entre empresas ❏ **intercompany transactions** transacciones *fpl* entre empresas

inter-dealer broker *n* ST EXCH = entidad mediadora de la Bolsa de Londres autorizada para tratar exclusivamente con operadores bursátiles, no con el público

interdepartmental *adj* interdepartamental

interest *n* (**a**) FIN *(on loan, investment)* interés *m* (**on** sobre); **interest accrued** interés acumulado; **interest on arrears** interés de mora; **interest on capital** renta *f* de capital **interest due** intereses vencidos; **interest due and payable** intereses vencidos y pagaderos; **interest paid** intereses pagados; **interest payable** intereses pagaderos; **interest received** intereses percibidos; **to bear** *or* **yield interest** producir interés; **to bear** *or* **yield 5% interest** producir un interés del 5%; **to pay interest** pagar intereses ❏ **interest charges** cargos *mpl* en concepto de intereses; **interest day** día *m* de pago de intereses; **interest and dividend income** ingresos *mpl*

por intereses y dividendos; **interest payment date** día *m* de pago de intereses; **interest rate** *Esp* tipo *m or Am* tasa *f* de interés; **the interest rate is 4%** *Esp* el tipo *or Am* la tasa de interés es del 4%; **interest rate differential** diferencial *m* de *Esp* tipos *or Am* tasas de interés; ST EXCH **interest rate swap** swap *m* de *Esp* tipos *or Am* tasas de interés; **interest table** tabla *f* de *Esp* tipos *or Am* tasas de interés

(**b**) *(stake)* interés *m*, participación *f*; **our firm's interests in Europe** las participaciones que nuestra empresa tiene en Europa; **to have a financial interest in sth** tener intereses financieros *or* una participación financiera en algo; **to have an interest in the profits** tener una participación en los beneficios; **his interest in the company is £10,000** su participación en la empresa es de 10.000 libras

(**c**) *(activity)* actividad *f*; **since the late 1980s the firm has had major interests in plastics and engineering** desde finales de los ochenta la empresa tiene importantes intereses en los sectores de plásticos e ingeniería

interest-bearing *adj (account)* que produce *or* devenga intereses ❏ **interest-bearing capital** capital *m* que produce intereses; **interest-bearing loan** préstamo *m* remunerado; **interest-bearing securities** valores *mpl* que producen intereses

interested party *n* LAW **the interested party** la parte interesada

interest-free *adj* sin intereses ❏ **interest-free credit** crédito *m* sin intereses; **interest-free loan** préstamo *m* sin intereses

interface *n* COMPTR interface *m*, interfaz *f*

interim *adj* provisional, *Am* provisorio(a) ❏ **interim accounts** cuentas *fpl* provisionales; **interim budget** presupuesto *m* provisional; FIN **interim dividend** dividendo *m* a cuenta; *US* ACCT **interim income statement** cuenta *f* provisional de resultados; **interim payment** pago *m* a cuenta; *Br* ACCT **interim profit and loss account** cuenta *f* provisional de resultados; **interim report** informe *m* de coyuntura; ACCT **interim statement** estado *m* provisional

> "
> Shares in Dixons, the UK retailer, jumped 2.88 per cent to £12.50 after the company declared a special **interim dividend** of 7.5p per ordinary share to be paid on December 13. Sir Stanley Kalms, Dixons' chairman, said total retail sales for the 18 weeks to September 4 were up 20 per cent over the same period last year and 9 per cent higher on a like-for-like basis.
> "

intermediary *n* intermediario(a) *m,f*, mediador(ora) *m,f*

intermediate *adj* FIN **intermediate broker** corredor(ora) *m,f* intermediario(a); **intermediate credit** créditos *mpl* a medio plazo; **intermediate goods** bienes *mpl* intermedios

internal *adj* (**a**) *(within company)* interno(a); *(within country)* interior, interno(a) ▫ **internal audit** auditoría *f* interna; **internal auditing** auditorías *fpl* internas; **internal auditor** auditor(ora) *m,f* interno(a); **internal check** control *m* interno; **internal company document** documento *m* interno de empresa; **internal debt** deuda *f* interior *or* interna; **internal growth** crecimiento *m* interno; **internal mail** correo *m* interno; **internal marketing** marketing *m* interno; **internal memo** nota *f* interna; **internal promotion** promoción *f* interna; **internal rate of return** tasa *f* interna de rentabilidad; **internal regulations** normas *fpl* internas; **internal revenue** ingresos *mpl* internos; *US* **the Internal Revenue Service** ≃ Hacienda, *Esp* ≃ la Agencia Tributaria, *Méx* ≃ el Servicio de Administración Tributaria; **internal telephone** teléfono *m* interno

(**b**) COMPTR interno(a); **internal drive** unidad *f* de disco interna; **internal modem** módem *m* interno; **internal unit** unidad *f* interna

internally *adv (within company)* internamente

international *adj* internacional ▫ **International Accounting Standards Committee** Comisión *f* Internacional de Normas Contables; **International Bank for Reconstruction and Development** Banco *m* Internacional para la Reconstrucción y el Desarrollo; TEL **international call** llamada *f or Am* llamado *m* internacional; **International Chamber of Commerce** Cámara *f* de Comercio Internacional; **international commodity agreements** acuerdos *mpl* internacionales de *or* sobre productos básicos; **international community** comunidad *f* internacional; **International Confederation of Free Trade Unions** Confederación *f* Internacional de Sindicatos Libres; **international currency** moneda *f* internacional; TEL **international** *Br* **dialling** *or US* **dialing code** indicativo *m* internacional; **international division** departamento *m* de comercio exterior; **International Finance Corporation** Corporación *f* Financiera Internacional; **International Labour Office** Oficina *f* Internacional del Trabajo; **International Labour Organization** Organización *f* Internacional del Trabajo; **international law** derecho *m* internacional; **International Monetary Fund** Fondo *m* Monetario Internacional; **international monetary reserves** reservas *fpl* monetarias internacionales; **international money markets** mercados *mpl* monetarios internacionales; **international money order** giro *m* postal internacional; **international operations** *(of company)* operaciones *fpl* internacionales; **international reply coupon** cupón *m* de respuesta internacional; **international rights** derechos *mpl* internacionales; **International Standards Organization** Organización *f* Internacional de Normalización; **international trade** comercio *m* internacional; **International Trade Organization** Organización *f* Mundial del Comercio; **international trademark register** Registro *m* Internacional de Marcas; **international trading corporation** sociedad *f* de comercio internacional

> **“**
>
> The International Federation of Airline Pilots' Associations (IFALPA) has formally requested an investigation by the **International Labour Organisation** (ILO) into the practices of Cathay Pacific Airways management in the ongoing dispute with its pilots. The group charges that Cathay Pacific management has violated international standards of workers protection agreed to by many nations including China.
>
> **”**

Internet *n* COMPTR **the Internet** Internet *f*; **to surf the Internet** navegar por Internet ▫ **Internet access** acceso *m* a Internet; **Internet access provider** proveedor *m* de acceso a Internet; **Internet account** cuenta *f* de Internet; **Internet address** dirección *f* de Internet; **Internet banking** banca *f* por Internet, banca *f* electrónica; **Internet café** cibercafé *m*; **Internet connection** conexión *f* a Internet; **Internet number** número *m* de Internet; **Internet phone** teléfono *m* por Internet; **Internet presence provider** proveedor *m* de presencia en Internet; **Internet protocol** protocolo *m* de Internet; **Internet Relay Chat** charla *f* interactiva por Internet; **Internet service provider** proveedor *m* de servicios de Internet; **Internet Society** Sociedad *f* Internet; **Internet surfer** internauta *mf*; **Internet surfing** navegación *f* por Internet; **Internet telephone** teléfono *m* por Internet; **Internet telephony** telefonía *f* por Internet; **Internet user** internauta *mf*

interoffice *adj* entre oficinas

interpersonal *adj* interpersonal ▫ **interpersonal skills** relaciones *fpl* interpersonales

interpret 1 *vt* interpretar
   2 *vi* interpretar

interpreter *n* intérprete *mf*

intervention *n* EU **intervention price** precio *m* mínimo garantizado; **intervention rate** cambio *m* de intervención

interventionism *n* ECON intervencionismo *m*

interventionist 1 *n* intervencionista *mf*
   2 *adj* intervencionista

interview 1 *n* *(for job, in market research)* entrevista *f*; **to give sb an interview** hacer una entrevista a alguien; **to invite** *or* **call sb for**

interview invitar a alguien a or llamar a alguien para una entrevista; **interviews will be held at our London offices** las entrevistas se celebrarán en nuestras oficinas de Londres
2 vt (for job) entrevistar; (in market research) encuestar; **shortlisted candidates will be interviewed in March** los candidatos preseleccionados serán entrevistados en marzo

interviewee n (for job) entrevistado(a) m,f; (in market research) encuestado(a) m,f; **the first four interviewees are coming this afternoon** los cuatro primeros candidatos vienen esta tarde

interviewer n (for job) entrevistador(ora) m,f; (in market research) encuestador(ora) m,f; **there will be a panel of three interviewers** habrá tres personas para hacer las entrevistas

intestate adj **to die intestate** morir intestado(a)

in-the-money option n opción f con dinero

intra-Community adj EU intracomunitario(a)

intra-company adj interno(a)

intra-day adj intradía

Intranet n COMPTR intranet f

intrapreneur n emprendedor(ora) m,f interno(a)

> 〟
> "Steve brings extensive knowledge of business development in health sciences from working as an **intrapreneur** at Monsanto, building several businesses from scratch. His strategic vision will be vital in making Kiva Genetics the leader in the genetics market", said Hugh Rienhoff.
> 〟

in-tray n bandeja f para correo entrante

intrinsic value n ST EXCH valor m intrínseco

introduce vt (product, reform, new methods) introducir; (laws, legislation) presentar, introducir; ST EXCH **to introduce shares** realizar una emisión restringida de acciones (de empresas determinadas y a clientes seleccionados)

introduction n (**a**) ST EXCH emisión f restringida de acciones (de empresas determinadas y a clientes seleccionados) (**b**) MKTG **introduction stage** (of product) fase f de introducción

introductory adj MKTG **introductory offer** oferta f de introducción; **introductory price** precio m de lanzamiento

intruder n COMPTR intruso(a) m,f

invalid adj (contract, document) nulo(a); (objection) no válido(a); COMPTR (file name) inválido(a)

invalidate vt (contract, document) anular, invalidar

invalidity n (**a**) Br ADMIN **invalidity benefit** prestación f por invalidez; **invalidity pension** pensión f de invalidez (**b**) (of contract, document) invalidez f

inventory 1 n (**a**) (list) inventario m; **to draw up** or **take an inventory (of sth)** hacer un inventario (de algo) □ **inventory book** libro m de inventarios; **inventory of fixtures** inventario m de enseres; **inventory of goods** inventario m de mercancías; **inventory method** método m de inventario; **inventory value** valor m de inventario
(**b**) (stock) existencias fpl □ **inventory account** cuenta f de existencias; **inventory control** control m de existencias; **inventory level** nivel m de existencias; **inventory management** gestión f de existencias; **inventory shortage** falta f de existencias; **inventory turnover** rotación f de existencias; **inventory valuation** valoración f de existencias
2 vt inventariar, hacer un inventario de

inverted commas n comillas fpl

invest FIN**1** vt invertir (**in** en); **to invest money in a business** invertir dinero en un negocio; **they invested five million dollars in new machinery** invirtieron cinco millones de dólares en maquinaria nueva □ **invested capital** capital m aportado
2 vi invertir (**in** en); **to invest in shares/in the oil industry** invertir en acciones/en la industria petrolífera; **to invest in property** invertir en inmuebles; **we're going to invest in three new machines** vamos a invertir en tres máquinas nuevas; **the company has invested heavily in its Asian subsidiary companies** la empresa ha realizado importantes inversiones en sus filiales asiáticas; **she's been investing on the Stock Market** ha estado invirtiendo en Bolsa

investment n FIN inversión f; **are these shares a good investment?** ¿son una buena inversión estas acciones?; **property is no longer such a safe investment** las propiedades inmobiliarias ya no son una inversión tan segura; **I would prefer a better return on investment** preferiría una inversión con un mayor rendimiento; **the company has investments all over the world** la empresa tiene inversiones por todo el mundo □ **investment account** cuenta f de inversión; **investment advice** asesoría f de inversiones; **investment adviser** asesor(ora) m,f de inversiones; **investment analyst** analista mf de inversiones; **investment appraisal** análisis m de inversiones; **investment bank** banco m de inversión; **investment banker** directivo(a) m,f de banco de inversión; **investment banking** banca f de inversión; **investment boom** auge m de inversiones; **investment capital** capital m de inversiones; **investment certificate** certificado m de inversión; **investment company** sociedad f de inversión; **investment consultancy** asesoría f de inversión; **investment curve** curva f de inversión; **investment fund** fondo *m* de inversión; **investment grant** ayuda *f* a la inversión; **investment house** sociedad *f* de inversión; **investment income** rendimientos *mpl (de una inversión)*; **investment institution** sociedad *f* de inversión; **investment instrument** instrumento *m* de inversión; **investment management** gestión *f* de inversiones; **Investment Management Regulatory Organization** = organismo británico que controla las actividades de los bancos de negocios y de los gestores de fondos de pensiones; **investment market** mercado *m* de inversiones; **investment objectives** objetivos *mpl* de inversión; **investment officer** director(ora) *m,f* de inversiones; **investment performance** comportamiento *m* de la inversión; **investment plan** plan *m* de inversiones; **investment policy** política *f* de inversiones; **investment portfolio** cartera *f* de inversiones; **investment product** producto *m* de inversión; **investment programme** programa *m* de inversiones; **investment return** rendimiento *m* de la inversión; **investment securities, investment stock** valores *mpl* de inversión; **investment subsidy** ayuda *f* a la inversión; **investment trust** sociedad *f* de inversión

investment-grade *adj* FIN adecuado(a) para la inversión

investor *n* FIN inversor(ora) *m,f*

invisible ECON **1** *n* **invisibles** invisibles *mpl*
2 *adj* **invisible assets** activos *mpl* invisibles *or* intangibles; **invisible balance** balanza *f* de operaciones invisibles; **invisible earnings** ganancias *fpl* invisibles; **invisible exports** exportaciones *fpl* invisibles; **invisible imports** importaciones *fpl* invisibles; **invisible trade** comercio *m* de invisibles

> ❝
> Shell, BAE Systems and HSBC are among the leading British-based firms active in the Middle East either directly or through subsidiaries. They help draw in some £3bn in physical trade a year with a further £3bn estimated to come from **invisibles** such as insurance and shipping.
> ❞

invitation *n* **invitation to tender** concurso *m* público

invite *vt* **(a)** *(ask)* **to invite sb for interview** citar a alguien para una entrevista; **we invite applications from all qualified candidates** invitamos a todos los candidatos que cumplan los requisitos a enviar sus solicitudes **(b)** FIN **to invite bids** *or* **tenders** sacar a concurso, llamar a licitación

invoice 1 *n* factura *f*; **to make out an invoice** extender *or* hacer una factura; **to settle an invoice** saldar una factura; **as per invoice** según factura; **payment should be made within 30 days of invoice** el pago se deberá efectuar en un plazo no superior a 30 días a partir de la fecha de facturación; **payable against invoice** pagadero previa presentación de factura ❑ **invoice clerk** encargado(a) *m,f* de facturación; **invoice date** fecha *f* de facturación; **invoice department** departamento *m* de facturación; **invoice discounting** descuento *m* de facturas; **invoice price** precio *m* facturado; **invoice value** valor *m* en factura
2 *vt (goods)* facturar; *(person, company)* mandar la factura a; **to invoice sb for sth** enviarle una factura a alguien por algo

invoicing *n (of goods)* facturación *f* ❑ **invoicing address** domicilio *m* de facturación; **invoicing instructions** instrucciones *fpl* de facturación; **invoicing machine** máquina *f* facturadora; COMPTR **invoicing software** programas *mpl or* software *m* de facturación

inward *adj* **inward bill of lading** conocimiento *m* de entrada; **inward charges** *(of ship)* costes *mpl* de entrada (al puerto); **inward customs clearance** despacho *m* de aduanas *(para mercancías que entran en el país)*; **inward investment** inversión *f* del exterior; **inward manifest** manifiesto *m* de entrada; ACCT **inward payment** pago *m* recibido

I/O *n* COMPTR *(abbr* **input/output**) E/S *f*

IOSCO *n (abbr* **International Organisation of Securities Commissions**) OICV *f*

IOU *n (abbr* **I owe you**) pagaré *m*

IP *n* COMPTR *(abbr* **Internet Protocol**) **IP address** dirección *f* IP; **IP number** número *m* IP

IPO *n* ST EXCH *(abbr* **initial public offering**) oferta *f* pública inicial

> ❝
> Over in the US, Wit Capital appeared to be on to a good thing. It offered Internet subscribers first bite of the cherry on **IPOs**, as Americans call flotations. This would allow them to get the share of a float usually reserved for institutional investors and, as Wit had access to all those lovely technology **IPOs**, which appear to go to an astonishing premium, this would be lucrative for all concerned.
> ❞

IPP *n* COMPTR *(abbr* **Internet Presence Provider**) PPI *m*, proveedor *m* de presencia en Internet

IRA *n* US *(abbr* **individual retirement account**) cuenta *f* de retiro *or* jubilación individual

IRC *n* COMPTR *(abbr* **Internet Relay Chat**) IRC *m* ❑ **IRC channel** canal *m* IRC

Irish pound *n Formerly* libra *f* irlandesa

iron *n (mineral)* hierro *m*; **the iron and steel industry** la industria siderúrgica ❑ **iron ore**

mineral *m* de hierro; **Iron and Steels Confederation** = sindicato de trabajadores de la siderurgia del Reino Unido

IRR *n abbr* (**internal rate of return**) TIR *f*

irrecoverable *adj (debt)* irrecuperable

irredeemable FIN **1** *n* **irredeemables** instrumentos *mpl* de deuda perpetua
 2 *adj (funds)* no reembolsable; *(share)* no amortizable; *(bill)* inconvertible □ **irredeemable bond** obligación *f* perpetua

irregularity *n (in accounts)* irregularidad *f*; **there were some irregularities in the paperwork** había algunas irregularidades en los papeles

irregulars *npl US* artículos *mpl* defectuosos

irrevocable *adj* BANKING *(credit, letter of credit)* irrevocable

IRS *n US (abbr* **Internal Revenue Service**) **the IRS** ≃ Hacienda, *Esp* ≃ la Agencia Tributaria, *Méx* ≃ el Servicio de Administración Tributaria

ISA *n Br (abbr* **individual savings account**) = plan de ahorro personal exento de impuestos con un tope de ahorro anual prefijado

> **❝**
> Halifax is among those who are hopeful rather than confident of an extension of 10 per cent dividend tax credits on equity **ISAs** beyond April 2004. It wants to see the £7,000 annual **ISA** allowance extended to cash savers, who are currently subject to a £3,000 annual limit.
> **❞**

ISBN *n (abbr* **International Standard Book Number**) ISBN *m*

ISDN 1 *n* COMPTR *(abbr* **integrated services digital network**) RDSI *f* □ **ISDN card** tarjeta *f* RDSI; **ISDN line** línea *f* RDSI; **ISDN modem** módem *m* RDSI
 2 *vt Fam* enviar por RDSI

> **❝**
> DSL is losing out to **ISDN** as broadband connection method of choice among UK business, said a survey by Rhetorik. It found that less than 2% of IT decision-makers at 361 UK firms had installed DSL as their primary method. More than 40% of public and private sector companies had adopted **ISDN**. Half of firms with 500-1,000 employees used **ISDN**, as did 45% of smaller firms

with up to 250 employees. Reliability, availability and speed of access were cited as reasons for adoption.
> **❞**

island *n* MKTG *(for displaying goods)* isla *f*

ISO *n (abbr* **International Standards Organization**) ISO *f*

ISOC *n* COMPTR *(abbr* **Internet Society**) Sociedad *f* Internet

ISP *n* COMPTR *(abbr* **Internet Service Provider**) PSI *m*, proveedor *m* de servicios Internet

issuable *adj* FIN, ST EXCH apto(a) para su emisión

issuance *n* FIN, ST EXCH emisión *f*

issue 1 *n* (**a**) FIN, ST EXCH *(of banknotes, money orders, shares)* emisión *f* □ **issue premium** prima *f* de emisión; **issue price** precio *m* de emisión; **issue value** valor *m* de emisión (**b**) **issue card** *(from warehouse)* registro *m* de salida
 2 *vt* FIN, ST EXCH *(bill, letter of credit, shares, money orders, banknotes)* emitir; *(new edition, prospectus)* publicar; **to issue a draft on sb's account** emitir un cheque bancario contra la cuenta de alguien

issued *adj* FIN, ST EXCH **issued capital** capital *m* emitido; **issued securities** títulos *mpl* emitidos; **issued share capital** capital *m* emitido en acciones

issuer *n* FIN, ST EXCH emisor *m*

issuing *adj* FIN, ST EXCH emisor(ora) □ **issuing bank** banco *m* emisor; **issuing company** sociedad *f* emisora; **issuing house** entidad *f* emisora de acciones en Bolsa; **issuing monopoly** monopolio *m* emisor

IT *n* COMPTR *(abbr* **information technology**) tecnologías *fpl* de la información, IT *fpl*, informática *f*; **our IT expert** nuestro informático

item *n* (**a**) *(article)* artículo *m*; **please send us the following items** sírvanse enviarnos los siguientes artículos (**b**) ACCT partida *f*; **item of expenditure** gasto *m* (**c**) *(on list, agenda, in contract)* punto *m*; **there are two important items on the agenda** hay dos puntos importantes en el orden del día

itemize *vt* detallar □ **itemized account** cuenta *f* detallada; **itemized bill** factura *f* detallada; **itemized billing, itemized invoicing** facturas *fpl* detalladas

ITO *n (abbr* **International Trade Organization**) OIC *f*

Jj

J/A, j/a *n* BANKING (*abbr* **joint account**) cuenta *f* conjunta *or* mancomunada

jargon *m* jerga *f*

Java *n* COMPTR Java® *m* ❑ *Java script* lenguaje *m* Java

Jaycees *npl* US **the Jaycees** = cámara de comercio para jóvenes empresarios

J-curve *n* ECON curva *f* en forma de J

jet lag *n* desfase *m* horario, jet-lag *m*

jet-lagged *adj* afectado(a) por el desfase horario, con jet-lag

jingle *n* MKTG melodía *f* (*de un anuncio*), jingle *m*

JIT *adj* (*abbr* **just in time**) justo a tiempo, JIT ❑ *JIT distribution* distribución *f* justo a tiempo *or* JIT; *JIT production* producción *f* justo a tiempo *or* JIT; *JIT purchasing* compras *fpl* justo a tiempo *or* JIT

job *n* (**a**) (*employment, post*) (puesto *m* de) trabajo *m*, empleo *m*; **to look for a job** buscar trabajo *or* empleo; **I've lost my job** he perdido mi trabajo; **to be out of a job** estar sin trabajo *or* empleo ❑ US *job action* movilizaciones *fpl*, medidas *fpl* de presión *or* acción de los trabajadores; *job advertisement* anuncio *m* de trabajo; ADMIN *job analysis* análisis *m* de puestos de trabajo; *job application* solicitud *f* or demanda *f* de empleo; *job application form* impreso *m* or formulario *m* or *Méx* forma *f* de solicitud *or* demanda de empleo; *job assignment* asignación *f* de tareas; *job classification* clasificación *f* de empleos; *job creation* creación *f* de empleo; *job creation scheme* programa *m* or plan *m* de creación de empleo; *job description* responsabilidades *fpl* del puesto; *job enrichment* enriquecimiento *m* del trabajo; *job evaluation* evaluación *f* del trabajo; *job hunter* demandante *mf* de empleo; *job hunting* búsqueda *f* de empleo; **to go/be job hunting** salir a buscar/estar buscando trabajo; *job interview* entrevista *f* de trabajo; *job losses* despidos *mpl*; *job market* mercado *m* de trabajo; *job offer* oferta *f* de empleo; *job opportunities* ofertas *fpl* de empleo; *job prospects* perspectivas *fpl* de trabajo; *job protection* protección *f* del empleo; *job rotation* rotación *f* de empleos; *job satisfaction* satisfacción *f* laboral, satisfacción *f* en el trabajo; **although the pay is quite low, there is a high level of job satisfaction** aunque la retribución es bastante baja, el nivel de satisfacción en el trabajo es alto; *job*

security seguridad *f* del empleo; **talks of a merger caused speculation about job security** las conversaciones sobre una fusión dieron pie a especulaciones sobre la seguridad de los puestos de trabajo; *job seeker* demandante *mf* de empleo; *job sharing* empleo *m* compartido; *job specification* responsabilidades *fpl* del puesto; *job title* cargo *m*, nombre *m* del puesto; *job vacancy* vacante *f* laboral

(**b**) (*piece of work, task*) tarea *f*, trabajo *m*; **to do a job** hacer una tarea *or* un trabajo

(**c**) *job lot* lote *m* (*de artículos dispares*) **to buy sth as a job lot** comprar algo como un lote; **they sold off the surplus as a job lot** liquidaron todos los excedentes en un solo lote

> **"**
>
> Professionals in this program also participate in ongoing **job enrichment** and professional development activities designed to increase competence and confidence and to provide a forum for group information sharing and problem solving.
>
> **"**

▶ **job out** *vt sep* subcontratar; **they jobbed out the work to three different firms** subcontrataron el trabajo a tres empresas distintas

jobber *n* (**a**) (*piece worker*) trabajador(ora) *m,f* a destajo (**b**) *Br Formerly* ST EXCH corredor(ora) *m,f* *or* agente *mf* de Bolsa (**c**) (*wholesaler*) vendedor(ora) *m,f* al por mayor

jobbing **1** *adj* a destajo
2 *n Br Formerly* corretaje *m*

Jobcentre *n Br* oficina *f* de empleo

jobholder *n* empleado(a) *m,f*

job-hop *vi* US ir de un trabajo en otro

jobless **1** *npl* **the jobless** los desempleados, *Esp* los parados, *Am* los desocupados
2 *adj* desempleado(a), *Esp* parado(a), *Am* desocupado(a)

Jobseekers allowance *n Br* subsidio *m* or prestación *f* por desempleo

job-share **1** *n* empleo *m* compartido; **I'm in a job-share with another colleague** comparto el empleo con otro compañero
2 *vi* compartir el empleo

join *vt* (*company*) entrar a trabajar en, incorporarse a; (*union*) afiliarse a; EU **to join the single currency** integrarse en la moneda única

joining fee *n* COMPTR tarifa *f* de alta

joint *adj* conjunto(a) ❑ BANKING **joint account** cuenta *f* conjunta *or* mancomunada; **joint agreement** *(between any two parties)* acuerdo *m* mutuo; *(between unions and management)* convenio *m* colectivo; **joint beneficiary** beneficiario(a) *m,f* pro indiviso; **joint commission** comisión *f* mixta; **joint committee** comisión *f* mixta; **joint creditor** coacreedor(ora) *m,f*; **joint debtor** codeudor(ora) *m,f*; **joint decision** decisión *f* conjunta; **joint enterprise** agrupación *f* temporal de empresas; LAW **joint estate** copropiedad *f*; FIN **joint filing** *(of tax returns)* declaración *f* conjunta; LAW **joint heir** coheredero(a) *m,f*; LAW **joint liability** responsabilidad *f* conjunta; **joint management** gestión *f* conjunta; **joint negotiations** negociaciones *fpl* con representación paritaria; **joint obligation** obligación *f* conjunta; **joint occupancy** utilización *f* conjunta; **joint ordering** pedidos *mpl* conjuntos; **joint owner** copropietario(a) *m,f*; **to be joint owners of sth** ser copropietarios de algo; **joint ownership** copropiedad *f*; **joint partnership** sociedad *f* colectiva; INS **joint policy** póliza *f* conjunta; **joint production** producción *f* conjunta; LAW **joint property** propiedad *f* colectiva; **joint purchase** compra *f* conjunta; **joint report** informe *m* conjunto; **joint representation** representación *f* paritaria; LAW **joint and several creditor** acreedor(ora) *m,f* solidario(a); LAW **joint and several debtor** deudor(ora) *m,f* solidario(a); LAW **joint and several guarantor** avalista *mf or* garante *mf* solidario(a); LAW **joint and several liability** responsabilidad *f* solidaria; LAW **joint responsibility** responsabilidad *f* conjunta; **joint shares** acciones *fpl* de propiedad conjunta; **joint signature** firma *f* colectiva; **joint statement** declaración *f* conjunta; **joint stock** capital *m* social; **joint surety** coavalista *mf*, cogarante *mf*; **joint tenancy** coarriendo *m*; **joint tenant** coarrendatario(a) *m,f*; **joint venture** empresa *f* conjunta, joint venture *f*; **joint venture agreement** acuerdo *m* de (constitución de) empresa conjunta *or* joint venture; **joint venture company** (sociedad *f* resultante de una) empresa *f* conjunta, joint venture *f*

jointly *adv* conjuntamente; **we manage the firm jointly** dirigimos la empresa conjuntamente; LAW **jointly liable** conjuntamente responsables; **jointly and severally liable** responsables solidariamente

joint-stock *adj Br* FIN **joint-stock bank** banco *m* por acciones; **joint-stock company** sociedad *f* anónima

journal *n* (**a**) ACCT *(for transactions)* libro *m* diario ❑ **journal entry** asiento *m* en el libro diario (**b**) *(magazine)* revista *f*

journalism *n* periodismo *m*

journalist *n* periodista *mf*

journalistic *adj* periodístico(a)

JPEG *n* COMPTR *(abbr* **Joint Photographic Experts Group)** JPEG *m*

judge LAW **1** *n* juez *mf*, juez(a) *m,f*
  2 *vt* juzgar; **the case will be judged tomorrow** la causa se oirá mañana

judg(e)ment *n* (**a**) LAW fallo *m*; **to pass judgement on sb/sth** pronunciar *or* emitir el veredicto sobre alguien/algo; **to sit in judgement** *(of court)* deliberar (**b**) MKTG **judgement sample** muestra *f* predeterminada; **judg(e)ment sampling** muestreo *m* intencional *or* discrecional

judg(e)mental *adj* **judgemental forecasting** = previsiones basadas en la experiencia; **judgemental method** = método de previsión basado en la experiencia

judicature *n* *(judge's authority)* competencia *f*; *(court's jurisdiction)* jurisdicción *f*; *(judges collectively)* judicatura *f*

judicial *adj* judicial; **to bring** *or* **take judicial proceedings against sb** iniciar un pleito contra alguien ❑ **judicial enquiry** investigación *f* judicial; **judicial power** poder *m* de los jueces; **judicial review** = revisión por un tribunal superior de un fallo judicial o de una ley

judiciary **1** *n* *(judicial authority)* poder *m* judicial; *(judges collectively)* judicatura *f*
  2 *adj* judicial

jumbo *adj Fam* FIN **jumbo bond** bono *m* jumbo *(volumen mínimo de emisión de 500 millones)*; *Fam* **jumbo certificate of deposit** certificado *m* de depósito jumbo *(de 100.000 dólares o más)*; *US Fam* **jumbo loan** préstamo *m* jumbo *(de un mínimo de 1.000 millones de dólares)*; *Fam* ST EXCH **jumbo trade** = contratación o venta de acciones de gran volumen

> “
>
> Further, there is now more variety for investors. The previous record for weekly issuance last June was owed entirely to a sole **jumbo bond** offering from Deutsche Telekom AG. By contrast, the recent $15 billion week is the product of a number of issuers, including DaimlerChrysler AG's $7.1 billion deal, as well as deals from Heller Financial Inc., General Motors Corp., and self-issues from Citigroup and Goldman Sachs.
>
> ”

jump **1** *n* *(rise)* salto *m* (**in** en); **there has been a sudden jump in house prices** se ha producido una repentina escalada en los precios de la vivienda
  2 *vi* *(rise)* dispararse, aumentar rápidamente

jumpy *adj* ST EXCH *(market)* nervioso(a)

junior **1** *n* *(in rank)* subalterno(a) *m,f*
  2 *adj (in rank)* de rango inferior; **to be junior to sb** tener un rango inferior a alguien ❑ *US* **Junior**

Chamber of Commerce = cámara de comercio para jóvenes empresarios; **junior executive** directivo(a) *m,f* de rango inferior; *Br* **junior partner** socio(a) *m,f* secundario(a)

junk *n* FIN, ST EXCH **junk bond** bono *m* basura; **junk e-mail** correo *m* basura; **junk mail** propaganda *f* (postal)

> **"**
>
> The U.S. **junk bond** market is absorbing a huge amount of new bond supply from corporate "fallen angels", yet analysts aren't fretting that the huge influx is likely to drag down the sector. ... Analysts say over the next year they expect tens of billions of dollars of additional bonds to fall into what J.P. Morgan Chase & Co. says is a US$802-billion **junk bond** market.
>
> **"**

jurisdiction *n* competencia *f*; **this matter does not come within our jurisdiction** esta cuestión está fuera de nuestra competencia

juror *n* (miembro *m* del) jurado *m*

jury *n* jurado *m*; **to serve on a jury** formar parte de un jurado

justice *n* justicia *f*; **a court of justice** un tribunal de justicia; **to bring sb to justice** llevar a alguien a juicio □ *US* **the Justice Department, the Department of Justice** el Ministerio de Justicia

justification *n* COMPTR justificación *f*; **left justification** justificación *f* a la izquierda; **right justification** justificación *f* a la derecha

justified *adj* COMPTR justificado(a); **left/right justified** justificado(a) a la izquierda/derecha

justify *vt* COMPTR justificar

just-in-time *adj* □ **just-in-time distribution** distribución *f* justo a tiempo; **just-in-time production** producción *f* justo a tiempo; **just-in-time purchasing** compras *fpl* justo a tiempo

> **"**
>
> Production cannot be "**just-in-time**" when parts are imported from thousands of miles away in Japan. At Georgetown, Toyota keeps three days' worth of stocks of imported parts, compared with 1.5 days' worth of American parts — or four hours' worth at its Japanese plants.
>
> **"**

JV *n* (*abbr* **joint venture**) empresa *f* conjunta, joint venture *f*

Kk

K *n* (**a**) (*abbr* **thousand, thousand pounds**) **he earns 30K** gana treinta mil (**b**) COMPTR (*abbr* **kilobyte**) K *m*; **how many K are left?** ¿cuántos K quedan?

kaffir *n Fam* ST EXCH = acción de las empresas surafricanas extractoras de oro en la Bolsa de Londres

Kai zen *n* kai zen *m*

kangaroo *n Fam* ST EXCH = acción australiana, especialmente de empresas mineras, tabaqueras o de propiedades rurales, en la Bolsa de Londres

KB *n* COMPTR (*abbr* **kilobyte**) KB *m*

Kb *n* (*abbr* **kilobit**) Kb *m*

Kbps COMPTR (*abbr* **kilobits per second**) kbps

keen *adj* (*competition*) feroz; (*prices*) competitivo(a)

keep *vt* (**a**) **to keep the books** llevar las cuentas; **to keep a note of sth** anotar algo (**b**) (*have in stock*) tener; **we don't keep computer accessories** no tenemos accesorios para el ordenador

▶ **keep down** *vt sep* (*prevent from increasing*) mantener bajo(a); **our aim is to keep prices down** nuestro objetivo es mantener los precios lo más bajos que podamos; **we must keep our expenses down** tenemos que mantener nuestros gastos al mínimo

▶ **keep up** *vt sep* (*prices*) mantener

keiretsu *n* keiretsu *mpl*

> "
> The first building blocks are Kvault Software, an email archiving specialist, and 45one.com, which threatens to be the "destination site for decision-critical news, analysis and comment" on the technology and media industries. … Mr Chamberlain says we're looking at "**keiretsu** synergy" here, a new version of Japan's corporate network system - a system which the Japanese, as it happens, are currently trying to disentangle.
> "

kerb *n Fam* ST EXCH **to buy/sell on the kerb** = comprar/vender acciones tras el cierre de la Bolsa de Londres; **business done on the kerb** = operaciones efectuadas tras el cierre de la Bolsa de Londres ❑ **kerb broker** agente *mf* que

opera en un mercado informal; **kerb market** mercado *m* (financiero) informal

> "
> Syed Wasimuddin, spokesman for the State Bank of Pakistan, told Dow Jones Newswires that the main difference from last year was the increased purchases from the interbank market compared with the money changers' **kerb market**. The central bank bought $1.526 billion from the interbank market during July-March period, compared with $839 million in the corresponding period a year earlier. It purchased $1.068 billion from the money changers' **kerb market** in the period, compared with $1.561 billion a year earlier, the spokesman said.
> "

kerbstone market *n Fam* ST EXCH mercado *m* informal

key 1 *n* COMPTR (*button*) tecla *f*; (*of sort, identification*) criterio *m* ❑ **key combination** combinación *f* de teclas

2 *adj* (**a**) (*important*) clave; **a key factor** un factor clave ❑ MKTG **key account** cuenta *f* clave, cliente *m* principal; **key accounts manager** director(ora) *m,f* de cuentas clave; MKTG **key brand** marca *f* clave; **key industry** industria *f* or sector *m* clave; **key person** persona *f* clave; **key position** puesto *m* clave; **key post** puesto *m* clave; **key sector** sector *m* clave; **key staff** personal *m* clave (**b**) *Br* **key money** (*deposit*) fianza *f*, depósito *m* (*que a menudo no se devuelve*)

3 *vt* COMPTR (*data, text*) teclear, *Am* tipear

▶ **key in, key up** *vt sep* COMPTR (*data, text*) teclear, *Am* tipear

key-account *adj* MKTG **key-account management** gestión *f* de cuentas clave or clientes principales; **key-account manager** director(ora) *m,f* de cuentas clave or clientes principales; **key-account sales** ventas *fpl* a cuentas clave or clientes principales

keyboard 1 *n* (*of typewriter, computer*) teclado *m* ❑ **keyboard layout** disposición *f* del teclado; **keyboard map** mapa *m* de caracteres; **keyboard operator** operador(ora) *m,f* de teclado; **keyboard shortcut** atajo *m* de teclado; **keyboard skills** = habilidad para escribir con ordenador

2 *vt (data, text)* teclear, *Am* tipear

3 *vi* teclear, *Am* tipear

keyboarder *n* COMPTR teclista *mf*, operador(a) *m,f*

key-escrow *n* COMPTR depósito *m* de la clave

"

Under **key-escrow**, your private key would be held in trust by a third party, and if you came under suspicion it would be made available to the authorities. ... Where can we find a suitably trustworthy third party, anyway? In some countries where **key-escrow** has been mooted, the banking institutions have been seen as the logical TTP. People trust them with their money, so why not with a crypto key?

"

keying *n* COMPTR tecleado *m, Am* tipeo *m (de datos en el ordenador)* ❑ **keying error** error *m* tipográfico *or Am* de tipeo; **keying speed** velocidad *f* de tecleado *or Am* tipeo

Keynesian *adj* ECON keynesiano(a)

keypad *n* COMPTR teclado *m* numérico

keystroke *n* COMPTR pulsación *f*; **keystrokes per minute/hour** caracteres *mpl* por minuto/hora

keyword *n* COMPTR palabra *f* clave ❑ **keyword advertising** publicidad *f* mediante palabras clave

kick *vt Fam* **to kick sb upstairs** ascender a alguien para que no moleste

kickback *n Fam* **he got a kickback for doing it** le *Esp* untaron *or Andes, RP* coimearon *or CAm, Méx* dieron una mordida para que lo hiciera

killing *n Fam* **to make a killing** forrarse

kilobit *n* COMPTR kilobit *m*

kilobyte *n* COMPTR kilobyte *m*

kindly *adv (in letter)* **kindly remit the balance by cheque** sírvase remitir la diferencia mediante un cheque; **kindly reply by return of post** sírvase contestar a vuelta de correo

kite *Fam* FIN **1** *n* **to fly** *or* **to send up a kite** lanzar un globo sonda (para tantear el terreno)

2 *vt US* **to kite a cheque** emitir un cheque sin fondos suficientes

kiting *n US Fam* FIN *(cheque fraud)* emisión *f* fraudulenta de cheques

"

The bank holding company will ... more easily identify potential fraud and reduce losses from check **kiting**, a sophisticated scam involving repeated deposits of bad checks through multiple accounts. Check **kiting** scams can cost financial institutions millions of dollars if not detected early in the process.

"

▸ **knock down** *vt sep (price)* rebajar; **I knocked her down to £300** conseguí que me lo dejara en 300 libras

knockdown price *n Br* **for sale at knockdown prices** rebajado(a) a precio de saldo; **I got it for a knockdown price** lo compré a precio de saldo

knocking copy *n* MKTG publicidad *f* comparativa *(que ataca o desacredita a la competencia)*

knock-on effect *n* repercusiones *fpl*; **businesses are feeling the knock-on effect of a strong pound** las empresas están sintiendo las repercusiones de una libra fuerte

know-how *n* conocimientos *mpl* (técnicos), pericia *f*

knowledge *n* conocimiento *m* ❑ **knowledge management** gestión *f* del conocimiento

krona *n* corona *f* (sueca)

krone *n (in Norway)* corona *f* (noruega); *(in Denmark)* corona *f* (danesa)

Krugerrand *n* krugerrand *m*, = moneda de oro sudafricana

Ll

label 1 n etiqueta f; (of record company) sello m discográfico, casa f discográfica □ **label of origin** etiqueta f de origen
  2 vt etiquetar

labelling, US **labeling** n etiquetado m, etiquetaje m

labor, laborer etc US = **labour, labourer** etc

labour, US **labor** n (a) (work) trabajo m
  (b) (manpower) mano f de obra; (workers) trabajadores mpl; **capital and labour** el capital y los trabajadores □ US **labor code** reglamentación f del trabajo; US **labor contract** contrato m de trabajo; **labour costs** costos mpl or Esp costes mpl de mano de obra; US **Labor Day** el Día del Trabajo; **labour dispute** conflicto m laboral; Br Formerly **labour exchange** bolsa f de trabajo; **labour force** (of country) población f activa; (of company) efectivos mpl; **labour law** derecho m laboral or del trabajo; **labour laws** leyes fpl laborales; **labour legislation** legislación f laboral; **labour market** mercado m laboral or de trabajo; **labour regulations** reglamentación f laboral; **labour relations** relaciones fpl laborales; **labour shortage** escasez f de mano de obra; US **labor union** sindicato m

labourer, US **laborer** n obrero(a) m,f

labour-intensive, US **labor-intensive** adj **to be labour-intensive** absorber mucha mano de obra

labour-saving, US **labor-saving** adj **to be labour-saving** ahorrar trabajo □ **labour-saving device** aparato m que permite ahorrar trabajo

lack 1 n (of capital, workers) falta f, carencia f (**of** de)
  2 vt carecer de; **we lack the necessary resources** carecemos de los recursos necesarios

laddered portfolio n US = cartera de valores con fechas de vencimiento escalonadas

❝
A **laddered portfolio** of individual bonds has an additional advantage: if you need to sell some of them to raise cash at a time when the bond market is slumping, you can select the more profitable ones for sale and hold the others to maturity. When redeeming bond fund shares, you may be forced to swallow a capital loss if the market is against you.
❞

laden adj cargado(a) □ **laden weight** peso m cargado

lading n (a) (of ship) carga f (b) (of goods) carga f

lag n intervalo m, lapso m; **there was a lag between completion of the text and publication** hubo un lapso de tiempo entre la terminación del texto y su publicación

laggard n MKTG consumidor m conservador

laisser-faire, laissez-faire n ECON liberalismo m, no intervencionismo m □ **laisser-faire policy** política f de mínima intervención estatal

lame duck n Fam (company) empresa f con serias dificultades

❝
Cordiant looks like a **lame duck** to me, the executive said. "It's got some great individual assets but in its current form it's a wounded animal that I don't think anyone will go for."
❞

LAN n COMPTR (abbr **local area network**) LAN f, red f de área local

land 1 n (a) LAW tierras fpl, terrenos mpl □ **land agent** (manager) administrador(ora) m,f de fincas; (seller) agente mf inmobiliario(a), corredor(ora) m,f de fincas; **land bank** banco m or caja f rural; ACCT **land charges** tributos mpl territoriales; **land ownership** propiedad f de la tierra; **land register** registro m de la propiedad inmobiliaria; **land registration** inscripción f de la propiedad inmobiliaria; **land registration certificate** certificado m de registro de la propiedad inmobiliaria; **land registry** registro m de la propiedad inmobiliaria; **land registry (office)** registro m de la propiedad; **land tax** contribución f territorial or rústica
  (b) TEL **land line** línea f terrestre
  2 vt (goods) descargar; (passengers) desembarcar

landed adj (a) (of land) **landed estate** finca f; **landed property** bienes mpl raíces, terrenos mpl rústicos or rurales; **landed proprietor** terrateniente mf (b) **landed cost** (of goods) precio m en muelle

landing n (**a**) *(of goods)* descarga f ❑ *landing certificate* certificado m de descarga; *landing charges* gastos mpl de descarga; *landing order* permiso m de descarga (**b**) *(of plane)* aterrizaje m; *(of passengers)* desembarco m ❑ *landing card* tarjeta f de inmigración; *landing permit* permiso m de aterrizaje; *landing and port charges* derechos mpl portuarios

land-office business n US empresa f floreciente

landowner n terrateniente mf

landscape n COMPTR formato m apaisado; **to print sth in landscape** imprimir algo en apaisado ❑ *landscape mode* modo m apaisado

lapse 1 n LAW (**a**) *(of right, patent)* extinción f (**b**) **a lapse of time** un lapso de tiempo; **after a lapse of three months** tras un lapso de tres meses
2 vi (**a**) LAW *(right, patent)* extinguirse (**b**) *(subscription)* caducar, vencer; *(fund, insurance policy)* vencer; **he let his insurance lapse** dejó que su seguro venciera

lapsed adj *(subscription)* caducado(a), vencido(a); *(fund, insurance policy)* vencido(a) ❑ ST EXCH *lapsed option* opción f vencida

laptop n COMPTR Esp ordenador m or Am computadora f portátil

large-cap adj US *(share, company)* de alta or gran capitalización ❑ *large-cap index* índice m de empresas con un nivel alto de capitalización

laser n COMPTR láser m ❑ *laser disc* láser disc m, disco m láser; *laser printer* impresora f láser

last adj (**a**) ST EXCH *last trading day* día m último de negociación (**b**) **last in, first out** el último en entrar es el primero en salir

late adj (**a**) *(behind schedule)* atrasado(a); **if payment is late** si el pago se retrasa ❑ *late delivery* entrega f atrasada; *late delivery penalty* penalización f por retraso en la entrega; *late payment* pago m atrasado; *late payment interests* intereses mpl de demora; *late payment penalty* penalización f por retraso en el pago
(**b**) *(in time)* tarde ❑ MKTG *late adopter* = consumidor que tarda en adquirir nuevos productos; *late cancellation* cancelación f de última hora; *late entrant:* **they are a late entrant into the market** han entrado tarde en el mercado; MKTG *late majority* mayoría f tardía
(**c**) ST EXCH *late trading* negociación f a última hora

latent defect n vicio m oculto

launch 1 n *(of product, website)* lanzamiento m; *(of project)* puesta f en marcha; **the launch of a new job creation scheme** la puesta en marcha de un nuevo plan para la creación de empleos
2 vt (**a**) *(product, website)* lanzar; *(project)* poner en marcha; **to launch a £3m cash bid** lanzar una oferta de 3 millones de libras en metálico (**b**) *(company)* *(set up)* crear; **they've launched the company onto the stock market** han sacado a Bolsa la empresa

launching n *(of product, website)* lanzamiento m; *(of project)* puesta f en marcha

launder vt *(money)* blanquear

> ❝
> The drug traffickers create links with front companies and people in the United States and Spain from where they draw money from their bank accounts and send international money transfers to the Panamanian company. With this great blow, the DAS and the DEA dismembered the largest asset-laundering organization in the world, which managed to **launder** more than 200 million dollars in a single year in Colombia alone.
> ❞

laundering n *(of money)* blanqueo m

LAUTRO n INS *(abbr Life Assurance and Unit Trust Regulatory Organization)* = organismo británico regulador de la actividad de las compañías de seguros de vida y de los fondos de inversión

law n (**a**) *(rule)* ley f ❑ *law of diminishing returns* ley f de rendimientos decrecientes; *law merchant* derecho m mercantil; ECON *the law of supply and demand* la ley de la oferta y la demanda (**b**) *(system of justice)* derecho m; Br **to go to law** acudir a los tribunales ❑ *law court* tribunal m de justicia; *law department* departamento m jurídico; *law firm* bufete m de abogados; Br *the Law Society* = el colegio de abogados de Inglaterra y Gales

> ❝
> Norman Price, one of the industrialists seconded to the DTI's future and innovation unit, which carried out the survey, said there was a danger that companies invested in their established businesses at the expense of new activities. Increased capital investment in mature business might bring productivity improvements, but such investment was subject to the **law of diminishing returns**.
> ❞

lawful adj *(legal)* legal; *(rightful)* legítimo(a) ❑ *lawful currency* moneda f de curso legal; *lawful owner* propietario(a) m,f legítimo(a); *lawful trade* comercio m legítimo

lawsuit n pleito m; **to bring a lawsuit against sb** entablar un pleito contra alguien

lawyer n abogado(a) m,f

▸ **lay in** vt sep *(goods, stock)* abastecerse de, aprovisionarse de

▶ **lay off** *vt sep* (**a**) *(make redundant)* despedir *(por reducción de plantilla)* (**b**) INS **to lay off a risk** reasegurar un riesgo

lay-away plan *n US* plan *m* de compra a plazos

lay-off *n* despido *m (por reducción de plantilla)* ❑ *US* **lay-off pay** indemnización *f* por despido

layout *n* (**a**) *(of building)* distribución *f* (**b**) *(of plan)* esquema *m* (**c**) *(of text)* composición *f; (of advertisement)* diseño *m*

❝
Analysts argue that M&S has failed to make its store **layouts** help shoppers bring clothing together to make outfits.
❞

LBO *n* FIN (*abbr* **leveraged buy-out**) compra *f* apalancada

L/C *n* (*abbr* **letter of credit**) carta *f* de crédito

LCD *n* COMPTR (*abbr* **liquid crystal display**) LCD *m* ❑ **LCD screen** pantalla *f* de cristal líquido, pantalla LCD

LCL *n* (*abbr* **less-than-container load**) LCL, = contenedor de grupaje

LDC *n* ECON (*abbr* **less-developed country**) país *m* menos desarrollado

lead *n* (**a**) **leads and lags** adelantos *mpl* y atrasos ❑ *lead time (for production)* tiempo *m or* periodo *m* de producción; *(for delivery)* tiempo de entrega (**b**) MKTG *lead user* = primer usuario de un producto, que a menudo participa en su diseño

leader *n* (**a**) *(head) (of group, association)* líder *mf*, dirigente *mf* (**b**) MKTG *(product, company)* líder *m*; *US (loss leader)* artículo *m* de reclamo, = producto que se vende por debajo del precio de coste para atraer a la clientela (**c**) ST EXCH valor *m* puntero (**d**) *esp Br (in newspaper)* editorial *m*

leadership *n (qualities)* liderazgo *m*

leading *adj* principal, destacado(a); **a leading shareholder** uno de los principales accionistas; **one of Europe's leading electronics firms** una de las principales empresas europeas de electrónica ❑ *leading indicators* indicadores *mpl* avanzados *or* de tendencia; *US* *leading price indicator* indicador *m* de tendencia de valores; FIN *leading share* valor *m* puntero

leaflet *n (small brochure)* volante *m; (piece of paper)* octavilla *f* ❑ *leaflet drop* buzoneo *m*

lean production *n* producción *f* ajustada

learning curve *n* curva *f* de aprendizaje

❝
As a result, the company became an early adopter of Microsoft's recently-launched .NET platform and in just three months fortified its comprehensive content repository with a technical backbone designed to maximize content delivery and services. Following a short **learning curve**, HealthGate optimized its architecture with the .NET technology and transformed more than 20,000 files into validated, well-formed XML.
❞

lease 1 *n* (contrato *m* de) arrendamiento *m or* alquiler *m*; **the lease runs out in May** el contrato (de alquiler) vence en mayo; **to sign a lease** firmar un contrato de alquiler ❑ *lease agreement (for property, equipment)* contrato *m* de arrendamiento *or* alquiler; ACCT *lease charges* canon *m* de arrendamiento *or* alquiler; *lease contract (for property, equipment)* contrato *m* de arrendamiento *or* alquiler; *lease financing* financiación *f* mediante arriendo; ACCT *lease revenue* ingresos *mpl* por arrendamientos
2 *vt* (**a**) *(of owner) (house, land, equipment)* arrendar, alquilar, *Méx* rentar (**to** a) (**b**) *(of leaseholder) (house, land, equipment)* arrendar, alquilar, *Méx* rentar; **we lease it from them** se lo arrendamos *or* alquilamos *or Méx* rentamos a ellos

▶ **lease back** *vt sep* hacer una operación de cesión-arrendamiento *or* retroarriendo con

▶ **lease out** *vt sep* arrendar, alquilar, *Méx* rentar

lease-back *n* **(sale and) lease-back** cesión-arrendamiento *m*, retroarriendo *m*

leased line *n* COMPTR línea *f* arrendada *or* alquilada

leasehold 1 *n* arriendo *m*
2 *adj* arrendado(a)

leaseholder *n* arrendatario(a) *m,f*

leasing *n (of property, equipment, land, system)* arrendamiento *m* (financiero), leasing *m* ❑ *leasing company* sociedad *f* de arrendamiento financiero *or* leasing

leave *n (holiday)* vacaciones *fpl; (other absence)* permiso *m*, *Am* licencia *f*; **to go on leave** irse de vacaciones/permiso *or Am* licencia; **to take two weeks' leave** tomarse dos semanas de vacaciones/permiso *or Am* licencia ❑ *leave of absence* licencia *f*, permiso *m*

LED *n* COMPTR (*abbr* **light-emitting diode**) LED *m*, diodo *m* emisor de luz

ledger *n* ACCT libro *m* mayor

left arrow *n* COMPTR flecha *f* izquierda ❑ *left arrow key* tecla *f* de flecha izquierda

left-click 1 *vt* hacer click con el botón izquierdo en
2 *vi* hacer click con el botón izquierdo (**on** en)

leftover stock *n* excedente *m* de existencias

legacy 1 *n* (**a**) LAW herencia *f*, legado *m*; **to leave sb a legacy** dejar una herencia a alguien; **to come into a legacy** heredar (**b**) COMPTR *legacy retirement* retirada *f* de sistemas de legado
2 *adj* COMPTR *(systems, software)* de legado

legal 1 *adj (lawful)* legal; *(judicial)* legal, jurídico(a); **to have a legal claim to sth** tener derecho legal a algo; **this is the legal procedure** este es el procedimiento legal ❑ *legal action* acción *f* judicial; **to take legal action against sb** presentar una demanda contra alguien; *legal advice* asesoría *f* jurídica *or* legal; **to take legal advice** asesorarse jurídicamente; *legal adviser* asesor(ora) *m,f* jurídico(a); *legal aid* asistencia *f* jurídica de oficio; *legal costs* costas *fpl* (judiciales); *legal currency* moneda *f* de curso legal; *legal department (in company)* departamento *m* jurídico; *legal director* director(ora) *m,f* del departamento jurídico; *legal dispute* disputa *f* legal; *legal document* documento *m* legal; *legal entity* persona *f* jurídica; *legal executive* = persona que trabaja asesorando a clientes y preparando casos en un bufete de abogados, pero que tiene formación jurídica; *legal expenses* costas *fpl* (judiciales); *legal flaw* laguna *f* legal; *legal guarantee* garantía *f* legal; *US legal holiday* día *m* festivo; *legal owner* propietario(a) *m,f* legal; *US legal pad* bloc *m* de notas *(de 216mm x 356mm)*; *legal proceedings* procedimiento *m or* actuación *f* judicial; **to take legal proceedings against sb** entablar un pleito contra alguien; *legal rate* tasa *f* legal; *legal redress* reparación *f* legal; *legal reserve* encaje *m* legal; *legal secretary* secretario(a) *m,f* con conocimientos jurídicos; *legal status* personalidad *f* jurídica; *legal system* sistema *m* legal; *legal tender* moneda *f* de curso legal; **to be legal tender** ser moneda de curso legal; *legal value* valor *m* legal
   2 *n US (paper size)* = tamaño de papel de 216mm x 356mm

legality *n* legalidad *f*

legalization *n* legalización *f*

legalize *vt* legalizar

legally *adv* legalmente; **to act legally** actuar dentro de la ley; **to be legally binding** ser (legalmente) vinculante; **to be legally responsible for sth** tener la responsabilidad legal de algo

legal-tender value *n* FIN valor *m* de curso legal

legislate *vi* legislar; **to legislate in favour of/against sth** legislar a favor de/en contra de algo

legislation *n* legislación *f*; **the legislation on immigration** la legislación sobre inmigración

legislative *adj* legislativo(a) ❑ *legislative power* poder *m* legislativo

leisure industry *n* industria *f* del ocio

lend 1 *vt* prestar; **to lend sth to sb, to lend sb sth** prestar algo a alguien; **to lend money at interest** prestar dinero con interés; **to lend money against security** prestar dinero contra un aval
   2 *vi* prestar dinero; **to lend at 12%** prestar dinero al 12%

lender *n (person)* prestamista *mf*; *(institution)* entidad *f* de crédito; **lender of last resort** prestamista de última instancia

lending *n* préstamos *mpl*, créditos *mpl*; **bank lending has increased** los créditos bancarios han aumentado ❑ *lending bank* banco *m* de crédito; *lending country* país *m* acreedor; *lending limit* límite *m* de crédito; *lending policy (of bank, country)* política *f* crediticia; *lending rate Esp* tipo *m or Am* tasa *f* de interés de préstamos *or* créditos

less *prep* **the purchase price less 10%** el precio de venta menos un 10%; **interest less tax amounts to £50** los intereses menos los impuestos ascienden a 50 libras

lessee *n* arrendatario(a) *m,f*

lessor *n* arrendador(ora) *m,f*

let *esp Br* **1** *n (property)* propiedad *f* en alquiler *or Méx* renta; **a short/long let** un alquiler *or Méx* una renta por un periodo corto/largo
   2 *vt* alquilar, *Méx* rentar; **to let** *(sign)* se alquila, *Méx* se renta

let-out clause *n* cláusula *f* de salvaguardia

LETS *n (abbr Local Exchange Trading System)* sistema *m* de intercambio *or* trueque local

letter *n* **(a)** *(communication)* carta *f*; **to notify sb by letter** avisar a alguien por carta; **your letter of 4 October** su carta del 4 de octubre ❑ *letter of acknowledgement* carta *f* de acuse de recibo; ST EXCH *letter of allotment* acta *f* de adjudicación; *letter of apology* carta *f* de disculpa; *letter of application (for job)* carta *f* de solicitud; ST EXCH *(for shares)* carta *f* de solicitud; *letter of appointment* carta *f* de nombramiento; *letter of complaint* carta *f* de reclamación *or SAm* reclamo; *letter of confirmation* carta *f* de confirmación; *letter of consent* consentimiento *m* escrito; *letters of credence (of ambassador)* cartas *fpl* credenciales; *letter of dismissal* carta *f* de despido; *letter of guarantee* carta *f* de garantía; INS *letter of indemnity* carta *f* de indemnidad; *letter of notification* carta *f* de notificación; *letter opener* abrecartas *m inv*; COMPTR *letter quality* calidad *f* de carta; **near letter quality** calidad (de impresión) casi de carta *or* próxima a la de carta; **letter rate** franqueo *m (para cartas)*; **letter of recommendation** carta *f* de recomendación; **letter of reference** carta *f* de recomendación; **letter scales** pesacartas *m inv*; **letter tray** bandeja *f* para cartas

(**b**) **letters patent** (certificado *m* de) patente *f*

(**c**) BANKING **letter of advice** carta *f* de aviso; **letter of credit** carta *f* de crédito; **letter of exchange** letra *f* de cambio; **letter of guaranty** carta *f* de garantía; **letter of intent** carta *f* de intenciones

(**d**) *(paper size)* = tamaño de papel de 216mm x 279mm, utilizado sobre todo en Estados Unidos

letterhead *n (heading)* membrete *m*; *(paper)* hoja *f* de papel con membrete

letting *adj Br* alquiler *m* ❑ **letting agency** inmobiliaria *f (que sólo alquila viviendas)*; **letting agent** agente *mf* inmobiliario(a) *(que sólo alquila viviendas)*

level 1 *n (of salaries, prices)* nivel *m*; **to maintain prices at a high level** mantener los precios altos

2 *vt* igualar

▸ **level off, level out** *vi (prices, demand, sales)* estabilizarse

leverage 1 *n FIN (gearing)* apalancamiento *m*; *(as percentage)* relación *f* deudas-capital propio ❑ **leverage ratio** coeficiente *m* de apalancamiento

2 *vt (take advantage of)* aprovechar

leveraged *adj* **the company is highly leveraged** la empresa está muy apalancada ❑ **leveraged buy-out** compra *f* apalancada; **leveraged management buy-out** compra *f* apalancada por la gerencia

> Despite IPC's debt, which stems mostly from its **leveraged buy-out** from Reed two years ago, it is believed the publisher feels Prima and Best are such strong brands that it could not pass up the opportunity to acquire them. Adding the two titles to its portfolio will substantially increase advertising revenue across the group, IPC believes.

levy 1 *n* (**a**) *(action)* exacción *f* (**b**) *(tax)* impuesto *m*, tasa *f* (**on** sobre); **to impose a levy on imports** aplicar un impuesto sobre las importaciones

2 *vt (tax)* aplicar (**on** a); **to levy a duty on goods** gravar las mercancías con un impuesto

liability *n* (**a**) LAW *(responsibility)* responsabilidad *f* (**for** de); **to admit liability for sth** responsabilizarse de algo (**b**) *(eligibility)* sujeción *f*; **liability for tax** sujeción *f* a impuestos (**c**) ACCT, FIN pasivo *m*, deuda *f*; **liabilities** *(debts)* pasivo *m*, deudas *fpl*; **to meet one's liabilities** hacer frente a

los compromisos contraídos

liable *adj* (**a**) LAW *(responsible)* responsable (**for** de); **to be held liable for sth** ser considerado(a) responsable de algo; **to be liable for sb's debts** responder de las deudas de alguien; **employers are liable for their staff's mistakes** los empresarios son responsables de los errores de sus empleados (**b**) *(eligible)* sujeto(a) (**to/for** a); **to be liable for tax** *(person, goods)* estar sujeto(a) a tributación

liaise *vi* **to liaise with sb** *(be in contact with)* estar en contacto con alguien; *(work together with)* colaborar con alguien

liaison *n (contact)* contacto *m*; *(co-operation)* coordinación *f*

libel LAW **1** *n* libelo *m*, difamación *f (escrita)*; **to sue sb for libel** demandar a alguien por libelo *or* difamación ❑ **libel case** demanda *f* por libelo *or* difamación; **libel laws** legislación *f* sobre libelo *or* sobre la difamación; **libel suit** demanda *f* por libelo *or* defamación

2 *vt* difamar

libellous *adj* LAW difamatorio(a)

liberate *vt* FIN liberar

LIBOR *n Br* FIN *(abbr* **London Inter-Bank Offer Rate)** Líbor *f*

licence, US **license**[1] *n (to manufacture, sell)* licencia *f*, autorización *f*; **to manufacture/sell sth under licence** fabricar/vender algo con licencia *or* con autorización ❑ **licence agreement** acuerdo *m* de licencia; **licence holder** titular *mf* de licencia

license[2] *vt* conceder una licencia a, autorizar; **to be licensed to manufacture/sell sth** tener licencia *or* autorización para fabricar/vender algo

licensed *adj* con licencia, autorizado(a) ❑ **licensed brand name** marca *f* comercial con licencia; **licensed product** producto *m* con licencia

licensee *n* licenciatario(a) *m,f*

licensing *n* contrato *m or* acuerdo *m* de licencia ❑ **licensing agreement** contrato *m or* acuerdo *m* de licencia; **licensing requirements** condiciones *fpl* de licencia

lien *n* LAW *(on property)* derecho *m* de retención, gravamen *m*, prenda *f*; **to have a lien on a cargo** tener derecho de retención sobre un cargamento; **vendor's lien** gravamen del vendedor; **lien on shares** prenda sobre acciones

lieu *n* **we get days off in lieu of overtime** nos dan días de fiesta a cambio de las horas extra **I'm working on Saturday, so I'm going to take Monday off in lieu** trabajo el sábado, así que voy a tomarme el lunes de vacaciones; **two weeks' salary in lieu of notice** dos semanas de sueldo a modo de notificación de despido

life n (**a**) **life annuity** anualidad f vitalicia, renta f vitalicia; **life pension** pensión f vitalicia; **life tenancy** arrendamiento m vitalicio, alquiler m vitalicio; **life tenant** arrendatario(a) m,f vitalicio(a)
 (**b**) INS **life assurance** seguro m de vida; **life assurance policy** póliza f de seguro de vida; **Life Assurance and Unit Trust Regulatory Organization** = organismo británico que regula la actividad de las compañías de seguros de vida y de los fondos de inversión; **life expectancy tables** tablas fpl de esperanza or expectativa de vida; **life insurance** seguro m de vida; **life insurance policy** póliza f de seguro de vida
 (**c**) FIN (of loan) vida f del préstamo □ **life expectancy** (of machine) vida f útil

lifecycle n MKTG (of product) ciclo m de vida □ **lifecycle curve** curva f del ciclo de vida

lifestyle n MKTG **lifestyle analysis** análisis m de estilos de vida; **lifestyle data** información f sobre los estilos de vida; **lifestyle group** grupo m según el estilo de vida; **lifestyle segmentation** segmentación f por estilos de vida

lifetime n FIN, ST EXCH (of option) vigencia f

LIFFE n (abbr **London International Financial Futures Exchange**) LIFFE m, = mercado internacional de futuros financieros de Londres

> London robusta coffee futures fell to a seven-week low in late trading on Thursday. Traders said investment funds had been liquidating positions and there had also been some selling from producer countries. The **LIFFE** July contract broke through $495 a tonne, closing $27 down at $488/tonne. This was the lowest for a second-month contract in London since 19 March.

LIFO (abbr **last in, first out**) el último en entrar es el primero en salir

light 1 n COMPTR **light pen** lápiz m óptico
 2 adj (**a**) (market) poco activo(a); (trading) escaso(a) □ **light industry** industria f ligera (**b**) MKTG **light user** usuario(a) m,f ocasional

lightning strike n IND huelga f relámpago

limit 1 n (**a**) (restriction) límite m; **the limit on Japanese imports** el límite a las importaciones japonesas; **to put** or **set a limit on sth** poner or establecer or imponer un límite a algo □ FIN **limit down** límite m a la baja; FIN **limit up** límite m al alza (**b**) ST EXCH **limit order** orden f limitada
 2 vt limitar; **we're trying to limit costs** estamos tratando de limitar costos or Esp costes

limitation n limitación f; LAW **limitation of liability** limitación de responsabilidad

limited adj (**a**) (market, expenditure) limitado(a) □ **limited edition** edición f limitada; LAW

limited liability responsabilidad f limitada; **limited warranty** garantía f limitada (**b**) **limited (liability) company** sociedad f (de responsabilidad) limitada; **limited partner** socio(a) m,f comanditario(a); **limited partnership** sociedad f comanditaria

limiting clause n cláusula f restrictiva

line n (**a**) (telephone connection) línea f; **hold the line, please** espere un momento, no cuelgue; **the line's very bad** se oye muy mal; **the line's** Br **engaged** or US **busy** Esp está comunicando, Am la línea está ocupada; **I have Laura Milligan on the line** tengo a Laura Milligan al teléfono; **she's on the other line** está hablando por la otra línea □ **line rental** alquiler m or Méx renta f de la línea
 (**b**) (of goods) línea f; **a new line of office furniture** una nueva línea de mobiliario de oficina □ MKTG **line addition** = nuevo producto que se añade a una línea ya existente; **line differentiation** diferenciación f por líneas; **line extension** = nuevo producto que se añade a una serie ya existente para aprovechar la popularidad de ésta; **line filling** = práctica comercial que consiste en llenar con nuevos productos todos los huecos posibles en una determinada línea de productos para no dejar oportunidades a la competencia; **line stretching** = práctica comercial que consiste en ampliar una línea de productos ya existente hacia una gama más alta, más baja o en ambos sentidos
 (**c**) (in hierarchy) **line management** dirección f de línea; **line manager** gerente mf or jefe(a) m,f de línea; **your line manager** tu superior inmediato; **line organization** organización f lineal
 (**d**) COMPTR **line break** salto m de línea; **line command** comando m de línea; **line end** fin m de línea; **line end hyphen** guión m de fin de línea; **line feed** avance m de línea; **line printer** impresora f de líneas; **line printout** impresión f por líneas; **line space** espacio m entre líneas; **three line spaces** triple espacio; **line spacing** interlineado m; **line width** ancho m de línea
 (**e**) (production line) cadena f de producción; **the new model will be coming off the line in May** el nuevo modelo saldrá de la cadena en mayo
 (**f**) **line of credit** línea f de crédito, descubierto m permitido

linear adj lineal □ **linear metre** metro m lineal

> This form of calculation is very useful to the retailer. It helps him to work out present and expected sales, and to find out how much profit he has made. For example: a unit displaying tins of soup has a total **linear** measurement of 5 metres. From it the retailer sells tins of soup to the value of £200 per month so each **linear metre** of space sells £40.

link n COMPTR enlace m, vínculo m (**to** a) ❑ **link editor** editor m de enlaces or vínculos

linker n COMPTR editor m de enlaces or vínculos

liquid adj (**a**) FIN líquido(a) ❑ **liquid assets** activo m disponible; **liquid capital** capital m disponible; **liquid debt** deuda f líquida; **liquid resources** recursos mpl líquidos or disponibles; **liquid securities** valores mpl líquidos (**b**) **liquid crystal display** pantalla f de cristal líquido; **liquid crystal screen** pantalla f de cristal líquido (de tamaño grande, como la pantalla de un monitor, etc.); **liquid paper** (correction fluid) líquido m corrector

liquidable adj FIN liquidable

liquidate FIN **1** vt (company, capital, debt) liquidar; ST EXCH **to liquidate a position** realizar una inversión
    2 vi (company) entrar en liquidación

liquidation n FIN (of company, debt, capital) liquidación f; **to go into liquidation** (company) entrar en liquidación

liquidator n (of company) liquidador(ora) m,f

liquidity n FIN liquidez f ❑ BANKING **liquidity ratio** coeficiente m or ratio m or f de liquidez

---
> Deposits also grew by over 5bn tugriks from 24.9bn tugriks and loans increased to 13.8bn tugriks from 10bn tugriks. Mr Peter Morrow added that cash and short term investments of 14.8bn tugriks provide a strong **liquidity ratio** of 42 per cent, well above Mongol Bank's required 18 per cent.
---

lira n Formerly lira f

LISA n Br (abbr **long-term individual savings account**) = plan de pensiones que invierte en acciones

list 1 n (**a**) (of bills, assets, liabilities, names) lista f; FIN, ST EXCH **list of applicants** (for loan, shares) lista de solicitantes (**b**) ST EXCH **list of quotations** lista f de cambios (**c**) BANKING **list of investments** cartera f de inversiones; **list of bills for collection** lista f de efectos por cobrar (**d**) **list price** (in catalogue) precio m de catálogo
    2 vt (**a**) (enter in list) hacer una lista de; (make inventory of) inventariar; ST EXCH **to be listed on the Stock Exchange** cotizar en Bolsa (**b**) (price) **what are the new laptops listed at?** ¿cuál es el precio de catálogo de los nuevos portátiles? (**c**) COMPTR listar

listed adj ST EXCH **listed company** empresa f cotizada; **listed securities, listed stock** valores mpl admitidos a cotización en Bolsa

listing n (**a**) ST EXCH derecho m de cotización en Bolsa; **to have a listing** cotizar en Bolsa ❑ **listing agreement** contrato m de admisión a cotización; **listing particulars** prospecto m para la admisión a la cotización (**b**) COMPTR copia f impresa ❑ **listing paper** papel m continuo

literature n (information) documentación f

litigant n LAW litigante mf, pleiteante mf

litigate LAW **1** vt (case) llevar a juicio
    2 vi litigar, pleitear

litigation n LAW litigio m, pleito m

livelihood n medio m de vida; **to lose one's livelihood** perder el medio de vida

lively adj FIN (market, trading) animado(a)

living n (livelihood) **what does he do for a living?** ¿a qué se dedica?; **to make a living** ganarse la vida ❑ **living allowance** dietas fpl, Am viáticos mpl; **living conditions** condiciones fpl de vida; **living expenses** gastos mpl (cotidianos); **living standards** nivel m de vida **living wage** salario m decente or digno; **£400 a month is not a living wage** 400 libras al mes no es un salario digno

Lloyd's name n Br INS inversor(ora) m,f institucional de Lloyd's of London

---
> The number of **Lloyd's Names** has fallen from its 35,000 peak to just 12,500 — although only 2,490 of them participated in the last underwriting year. Their numbers dropped off dramatically after 1996 when a rescue package was introduced for Lloyd's at a time when many Names faced personal ruin following £8bn of asbestos-related claims.

LMBO n (abbr **leveraged management buyout**) compra f apalancada por la gerencia

load 1 n (**a**) (of ship, lorry) carga f ❑ **load bed** (of lorry) plataforma f de carga; **load factor** factor m de ocupación; **load limit** límite m de carga (**b**) ST EXCH = gastos de gestión de un fondo de inversión
    2 vt (**a**) (ship, lorry, goods) cargar; **the ship is loading grain** están cargando el barco de cereales (**b**) INS (premium) aumentar (**c**) COMPTR cargar
    3 vi (**a**) (ship, lorry) cargar; **the ship is loading** están cargando el barco (**b**) COMPTR (software, program) cargarse

▶ **load up** vt sep (**a**) (ship, lorry) cargar (**with** con) (**b**) COMPTR cargar

load-carrying capacity n capacidad f de carga

loaded adj (**a**) (ship, lorry, goods) cargado(a) ❑ **loaded return** regreso m con carga (**b**) INS **loaded premium** sobreprima f

loading n (of ship, lorry, goods) carga f ❑ **loading bay** zona f de carga y descarga; **loading dock** zona f de carga; **loading permit** permiso m de carga; *loading platform* muelle *m* de carga; *loading point* punto *m* de carga; *loading time* tiempo *m* de carga

loan 1 *n (money) (from bank)* crédito *m; (from individual)* préstamo *m*; **to take out a loan** obtener un crédito; **to apply for a loan** solicitar un crédito; ACCT **loans and advances to customers** créditos y anticipos a clientes **loan at call** crédito reembolsable a demanda; **loan at interest** préstamo remunerado *or* con interés; **loan at notice** crédito a plazo; **loan on collateral** préstamo con garantía; **loan on mortgage** préstamo hipotecario; **loans outstanding** préstamos pendientes de reembolso; **loan repayable on demand** crédito reembolsable a demanda; **loan against securities** préstamo con garantía de valores; **loan without security** préstamo sin garantía; **loan on trust** préstamo fiduciario; **loan to value** *(ratio)* = ratio entre el principal de un préstamo y el valor del activo que lo respalda ❑ BANKING *loan account* cuenta *f* de crédito; *loan agreement* póliza *f* de crédito; *loan application* solicitud *f* de crédito; *loan application form* impreso *m or* formulario *m or Méx* forma *f* de solicitud de crédito; *loan back* = crédito con cargo al saldo acumulado del fondo de pensiones; ACCT *loan capital* recursos *mpl* ajenos (a largo plazo); *loan certificate* título *m* de préstamo; *loan charges* gastos *mpl* del crédito; *loan company* institución *f* crediticia; *loan department* departamento *m* de créditos; *loan guarantee scheme* = programa gubernamental británico de respaldo de créditos a las pequeñas empresas; *loan insurance* seguro *m* de préstamo; *loan market* mercado *m* de seguros; *loan maturity* vencimiento *m* del préstamo; FIN *loan note* pagaré *m* del préstamo; *loan office* institución *f* crediticia; *loan origination fee* comisión *f* de apertura del préstamo; *loan repayment insurance* seguro *m* de amortización; *loan risk cover* seguro *m* contra riesgo crediticio; *Fam loan shark* usurero(a) *m,f; loan stock* obligaciones *fpl; loan transaction* contratación *f* de un préstamo
2 *vt* prestar

loan-back, loanback *n* = crédito con cargo al saldo acumulado del fondo de pensiones ❑ *loanback pension* = pensión que permite la obtención de un crédito con cargo al saldo acumulado

lobby 1 *n* grupo *m* de presión, lobby *m*
2 *vt* presionar; **a group of financiers went to lobby the minister** un grupo de financieros fue a presionar al ministro
3 *vi* presionar; **ecologists are lobbying for the closure of the plant** los ecologistas están ejerciendo presión para que se cierre la fábrica

lobbying *n* presiones *fpl* políticas

local *adj* local ❑ *local agent* distribuidor(ora)

m,f local; COMPTR *local area network* red *f* de área local; *local authority* administración *f* local; COMPTR *local bus* bus *m* local; TEL *local call* llamada *f or Am* llamado *m* local *or* urbana; *local council* ayuntamiento *m*, municipio *m; local currency* moneda *f* nacional; *Local Exchange Trading Scheme* sistema *m* de intercambio *or* trueque local; *local tax* impuesto *m* municipal; *local time* hora *f* local; **at 6 a.m. local time** a las 6 de la mañana hora local

> **"**
>
> Communities in several countries have also organized indirect exchange systems, most notably using the **Local Exchange Trading System** (LETS), which began in Canada in 1983. LETS is similar to a credit union, but members begin their account balances at zero and exchange with other members. Those who purchase goods incur a debit, while those who sell obtain a credit; debits and credits are denominated in the national currency.
>
> **"**

localization *n* COMPTR localización *f*

localize *vt* COMPTR localizar

locate *vi (company, factory)* establecerse, instalarse

location *n (of company, factory)* lugar *m*, ubicación *f*; **the company has moved to a new location** la empresa se ha trasladado a otro lugar ❑ MKTG *location pricing* fijación *f* de precios según la localización geográfica

lock *vt* COMPTR bloquear
▶ **lock into** *vt sep* **to be locked into** *(company, pension scheme, contract)* estar atado(a) a
▶ **lock out** *vt sep* **the workers were locked out** hubo un cierre patronal
▶ **lock up** *vt sep (capital)* inmovilizar

lockout *n (of workers)* cierre *m* patronal

loco *adv* entregable en

lodge *vt* **(a)** *(claim)* presentar; **she lodged a complaint with the authorities** presentó una queja ante las autoridades **(b)** *(money)* depositar; **to lodge securities with a bank** depositar valores en un banco

log 1 *n (record)* registro *m*; COMPTR registro *m* de actividad; **keep a log of all phone calls** anota todas las llamadas telefónicas ❑ COMPTR *log file* registro *m* de actividad
2 *vt (information)* registrar
▶ **log in** = **log on**
▶ **log off, log out** COMPTR **1** *vt sep* salir de
2 *vi* salir
▶ **log on, log in** COMPTR **1** *vt sep* entrar en, abrir una sesión en
2 *vi (user)* entrar, abrir una sesión; *(to remote*

user) establecer comunicación; **to log onto a system** entrar en un sistema

▶ **log out** = **log off**

logical *adj* COMPTR lógico(a)

logic circuit *n* COMPTR circuito *m* lógico

logistics *n* logística *f* ❑ *logistics management* gestión *f* logística

logo *n* logo *m*, logotipo *m*

Lombard rate *n* BANKING *Esp* tipo *m* or *Am* tasa *f* Lombard

London *n* Londres ❑ *London Inter-Bank Offer Rate* *Esp* tipo *m* ofertado *or* *Am* tasa *f* ofertada por el mercado interbancario de Londres; *London International Financial Futures Exchange* Mercado *m* Internacional de Futuros Financieros de Londres; *London School of Economics* Escuela *f* de Economía y Ciencia Política de Londres; *London Stock Exchange* Bolsa *f* de Londres

long 1 *n* ST EXCH **longs** = títulos con vencimiento a largo plazo
   2 *adj* **long credit** crédito *m* a largo plazo; *US Fam* **long green** crédito *m* a largo plazo; **long lease** arrendamiento *m* a largo plazo; ST EXCH **long position** posición *f* larga; **to take a long position** tomar una posición larga
   3 *adv* ST EXCH **to go long** tomar una posición larga

long-dated *adj* FIN a largo plazo ❑ *long-dated bill* letra *f* a largo plazo; *long-dated securities* títulos *mpl* a largo plazo

long-distance 1 *adj* **a long-distance (telephone) call** una llamada a *or Am* un llamado de larga distancia
   2 *adv* **to telephone long-distance** hacer una llamada a *or Am* un llamado de larga distancia

longitudinal *adj* MKTG *(research, study)* longitudinal

long-lived assets *npl* ACCT activos *mpl* de larga vida

long-range *adj (forecast)* a largo plazo

longshoreman *n* US estibador *m*

longstanding *adj (customer, agreement)* de muchos años ❑ *longstanding accounts* clientes *mpl* de muchos años

long-term *adj* a largo plazo ❑ FIN *long-term bond* bono *m* a largo plazo; *long-term bond rate* rentabilidad *f* del bono a largo plazo; ACCT *long-term borrowings* créditos *mpl* a largo plazo; ACCT *long-term capital* capital *m* a largo plazo; *long-term credit* crédito *m* a largo plazo; *long-term debt* deuda *f* a largo plazo; *long-term financing* financiación *f* a largo plazo; *long-term interest rate* *Esp* tipo *m* or *Am* tasa *f* de interés a largo plazo; *long-term investments* inversiones *fpl* a largo plazo; *long-term*

liabilities deudas *fpl* a largo plazo; *long-term loan* préstamo *m* a largo plazo; *long-term maturity* vencimiento *m* a largo plazo; *long-term objective* objetivo *m* a largo plazo; *long-term planning* planificación *f* a largo plazo; **the long-term unemployed** los parados de larga duración; *long-term unemployment* desempleo *m* de larga duración

look-up table *n* COMPTR tabla *f* de referencia

loophole *n (in law, contract)* laguna *f* legal

loose *adj* **(a)** *(goods)* suelto(a), a granel **(b)** *loose insert* encarte *m*

lorry *n Br* camión *m* ❑ *lorry driver* camionero(a) *m,f*

lose 1 *vt (custom, market share, job, money)* perder; **his shop is losing money** su tienda está perdiendo dinero; **they are losing their markets to the Koreans** los coreanos les están quitando el mercado
   2 *vi* **the dollar is losing in value** el dólar está perdiendo valor

▶ **lose out** *vi* salir perdiendo (**to** en beneficio de); **to lose out on a deal** salir perdiendo en una operación; **will the Americans lose out to the Japanese in computers?** ¿perderán los americanos la partida de los ordenadores ante los japoneses?

loser *n* ST EXCH *(shares)* perdedor *m*

loss *n* **(a)** *(of custom, market share, job)* pérdida *f*; **he's seeking compensation for loss of earnings** ha presentado una reclamación de indemnización por pérdida de ingresos; **the closure will cause the loss of hundreds of jobs** el cierre provocará la pérdida de cientos de puestos de trabajo
   (b) *(financial)* **losses** pérdidas *fpl*; **to make a loss** tener pérdidas; **to run at a loss** *(business)* arrojar pérdidas; **to sell sth at a loss** vender algo con pérdidas; **the company announced losses** *or* **a loss of £4m** la empresa anunció pérdidas por valor de 4 millones de libras; **we made a loss of 10% on the deal** perdimos un 10 por ciento en la transacción; ACCT *loss attributable* pérdida atribuible; ACCT *loss carry back* traslado *m* de pérdidas a un ejercicio anterior; ACCT *loss carry forward* traslado de pérdidas a un ejercicio posterior; ACCT *loss transferred* pérdidas trasladadas ❑ MKTG *loss leader* reclamo *m* de ventas; MKTG *loss leader price* precio *m* de reclamo; MKTG *loss leader pricing* utilización *f* or fijación *f* de precios de reclamo; MKTG *loss pricing* utilización *f* or fijación *f* de precios de reclamo
   (c) INS siniestro *m*; **to estimate the loss** realizar una valoración del siniestro; **the following losses are not covered by the policy** la póliza no cubre los siguientes siniestros ❑ *loss adjuster* *(in insurance)* perito(a) *m,f* tasador(ora) de siniestros; *loss assessment* evaluación *f* del siniestro; *loss ratio* índice *m* de siniestralidad;

loss risk riesgo *m* de siniestro (**d**) *(of product being manufactured or transported)* pérdida *f* □ ***loss in transit*** pérdida *f* en ruta

loss-making *adj Br (company)* deficitario(a), con pérdidas; *(venture, scheme)* deficitario(a)

lost-time accident *n* accidente *m* con pérdida de tiempo

lot *n* (**a**) FIN, ST EXCH *(of bonds, shares)* lote *m*; **in lots** en lotes; **to buy/sell sth in one lot** comprar/vender algo en un lote □ ***lot number*** número *m* de lote; ***lot size*** tamaño *m* del lote (**b**) *(at auction)* lote *m*; **lot 49 is a set of five paintings** el lote 49 consta de cinco cuadros (**c**) *US (piece of land)* terreno *m*

lottery *n* (**a**) FIN ***lottery bonds*** obligaciones *fpl* a prima; ***lottery loan*** empréstito *m* de obligaciones con prima de reembolso; ***lottery loan bond*** obligación *f* a prima (**b**) *Br* ***lottery funding*** *(from National Lottery)* financiación *f* procedente de la lotería

low 1 *n* mínimo *m*; **the share index has reached a new low** el índice bursátil ha sufrido un nuevo mínimo; **inflation is at an all-time low** la inflación ha alcanzado un mínimo histórico; ST EXCH **the highs and lows** cotizaciones *fpl* máximas y mínimas

2 *adj (cost, price, interest rate, salary)* bajo(a); **prices are at their lowest** los precios están más bajos que nunca

3 *adv* **to buy low** comprar barato; ST EXCH comprar a la baja

low-ball *vt US Fam (customer)* = dar un precio o un presupuesto muy bajo sin intención de atenerse a él; *(estimate)* = rebajar de forma deliberadamente engañosa

low-cost *adj (purchase, purchasing)* a bajo costo *or Esp* coste; *(country)* de bajo costo *or Esp* coste

low-end *adj* MKTG de gama baja

lower[1] *vt (prices)* rebajar; *(interest rate)* reducir

lower[2] *adj* ***lower case*** minúsculas *fpl*, *Spec* caja *f* baja; ***lower limit*** mínimo *m*

lower-case *adj* en minúsculas, *Spec* en caja baja

lower-income group *n* tramo *m* de ingresos medios bajos

low-grade *adj* de baja calidad

low-income group *n* tramo *m* de ingresos bajos

low-interest *adj (credit, loan)* a bajo interés

low-involvement *adj* MKTG *(purchasing)* = que requiere una mínima participación por parte del cliente

low-load *adj* □ ***low-load fund*** fondo *m* de inversión con unos gastos de gestión bajos

loyal *adj (customer)* fiel

loyal-customer discount *n* MKTG descuento *m* por fidelización

loyalty *n* MKTG ***loyalty card*** tarjeta *f or* carné *m* de fidelización; ***loyalty discount*** descuento *m* por fidelización *or* fidelidad; ***loyalty magazine*** revista *f* para clientes; ***loyalty programme*** programa *m* de fidelización; ***loyalty scheme*** plan *m* de fidelización

> **"**
> In a bid to capitalise on the growth of relationship marketing, AT&T is preparing to launch a managed **loyalty programme** linking the functions of a **loyalty card**, call centre, customer database analysis and campaign management.
> **"**

LSE *n* (**a**) *(abbr* **London School of Economics***)* Escuela *f* de Economía y Ciencia Política de Londres (**b**) *(abbr* **London Stock Exchange***)* Bolsa *f* de Londres

Ltd *Br (abbr* **limited***)* S.L.; **Dragon Software Ltd** Dragon Software S.L.

lucrative *adj* lucrativo(a)

luggage *n* equipaje *m*; **a piece of luggage** un bulto (de equipaje) □ ***luggage allowance*** equipaje *m* permitido; ***luggage label*** etiqueta *f* identificativa del equipaje

lump sum *n* cantidad *f* única; **to be paid in a lump sum** recibir un pago único

luncheon voucher *n Br* vale *m* de comida

luxury *adj* de lujo □ ***luxury brand*** marca *f* de lujo; ***luxury goods*** productos *mpl or* artículos *mpl* de lujo; ***luxury goods industry*** sector *m* de artículos de lujo; ***luxury tax*** impuesto *m* especial sobre artículos de lujo

Mm

MABE *n* (*abbr* **Master of Agricultural Business and Economics**) máster *m* en agronomía

machine 1 *n* (**a**) *(device)* máquina *f* ❏ *machine hour* hora *f* máquina; *machine operator* operario(a) *m,f* de máquina; *machine production* producción *f* de máquina; *machine shop* taller *m* de máquinas; *machine tool* máquina *f* herramienta; *machine work* trabajo *m* de máquina (**b**) *(computer)* máquina *f* ❏ *machine code* código *m* máquina; *machine language* lenguaje *m* máquina; *machine translation* traducción *f* automática
  2 *vt (manufacture)* producir a máquina

machine-down time *n* tiempo *m* de máquina parada, = tiempo muerto de la máquina

machine-produced *adj* hecho(a) a máquina

machine-readable *adj* COMPTR legible por *Esp* ordenador *or Am* computadora

machinery *n* (**a**) *(machines)* maquinaria *f*; *(mechanism)* mecanismo *m* (**b**) *(of organization, government)* maquinaria *f*

machining *n* fresado *m*, labrado *m*

machinist *n* (**a**) *(operator)* operario(a) *m,f* (**b**) *(repairer)* mecánico(a) *m,f*

macro *n* COMPTR macro *f* ❏ *macro language* lenguaje *m* macro

macroeconomics *n* macroeconomía *f*

macroenvironment *n* MKTG macroentorno *m*, macroambiente *m*

macromarketing *n* macromarketing *m*

MACRS *n* US ACCT (*abbr* **modified accelerated cost recovery system**) = método de amortización acelerada basado en el sistema de doble saldo decreciente

MAD *n* ACCT (*abbr* **mean absolute deviation**) desviación *f* absoluta media

mad dog *n* Fam *(company)* empresa *f* de rápido crecimiento *(siempre que obtenga una cuantiosa financiación)*; **there are several rising mad dogs in the IT sector** en el sector de la informática hay varias empresas que pueden crecer muy rápido si obtienen financiación

made *adj* **made in Spain** *(on product)* fabricado(a) en España

magnate *n* magnate *mf*; **a press/an oil magnate** un magnate de la prensa/del petróleo

magnetic *adj* COMPTR *magnetic card* tarjeta *f* magnética; *magnetic card reader* lector *m* de tarjetas magnéticas; *magnetic disk* disco *m* magnético; *magnetic media* soporte *m* magnético; *magnetic strip* banda *f* magnética; *magnetic tape* cinta *f* magnética

MAI *n* (*abbr* **multilateral agreement on investment**) AMI *m*, acuerdo *m* multilateral de inversiones

maiden name *n* apellido *m* de soltera

mail 1 *n* (**a**) *(letters, parcels)* correo *m*; **has the mail arrived?** ¿ha llegado el correo? ❏ US *mail clerk* empleado(a) *m,f* de la oficina de clasificación del correo; *mail room* oficina *f* de clasificación del correo
  (**b**) *(postal service)* correo *m*; **to put sth in the mail** echar algo al correo; **to send sth by mail** enviar algo por correo ❏ *mail order* venta *f* por correo; **to buy sth by mail order** comprar algo por correo; *mail specialist (mail-order company)* empresa *f* de venta por correo; MKTG *mail survey* encuesta *f* por correo; *mail transfer* giro *m* postal
  (**c**) COMPTR *(e-mail)* correo *m* (electrónico) ❏ *mail address* dirección *f* de correo (electrónico); *mail bomb* bomba *f* de correo (electrónico); *mail file* archivo *m* or fichero *m* de correo (electrónico); *mail forwarding* reenvío *m* de correo (electrónico); *mail gateway* pasarela *f* de correo (electrónico); *mail path* ruta *f* de correo (electrónico); *mail reader* lector *m* de correo (electrónico); *mail server* servidor *m* de correo (electrónico)
  2 *vt* (**a**) *esp US (letter, parcel)* enviar *or* mandar (por correo) (**b**) *(by e-mail) (file)* enviar *or* mandar (por correo electrónico); *(person)* enviar *or* mandar un correo (electrónico) a

mailbox *n* COMPTR buzón *m*

mailer *n* MKTG *(mailshot)* mailing *m*

mailing *n* MKTG *(mailshot)* mailing *m*; **to do** *or* **send a mailing** hacer *or* lanzar un mailing ❏ *mailing card* tarjeta *f* para mailing; *mailing list* MKTG lista *f* de direcciones *or* destinatarios *(para envío de publicidad)*; COMPTR lista *f* de correo *or* de distribución; **are you on our mailing list?** ¿tenemos su nombre en nuestra lista de direcciones?; *mailing shot* mailing *m*; **to do** *or* **send a mailing shot** hacer *or* lanzar un mailing

mailmerge *n* COMPTR combinación *f* de correspondencia

mail-order adj de venta por correo ❑ **mail-order catalogue** catálogo m de venta por correo; **mail-order company** empresa f de venta por correo; **mail-order goods** artículos mpl de venta por correo; **mail-order organization** empresa f de venta por correo; **mail-order purchasing** compra f por correo; **mail-order retailing, mail-order selling** venta f por correo

mailshot Br MKTG **1** n mailing m; **to do** or **send a mailshot** hacer or lanzar un mailing
2 vt hacer or lanzar un mailing a

> A common tactic used by unauthorised firms is to use a publicly available share register to **mailshot** a large bulk of UK investors in one go, inviting them to send off for research on a firm whose shares they already own. The small print on the form will then give the company the investor's consent to be contacted directly.

main adj principal ❑ **main branch** (of bank) oficina f principal; (of shop) tienda f principal; **main claim** (in negotiations) reivindicación f principal; ACCT **main cost centre** centro m principal de costos or Esp costes; ST EXCH **main market** mercado m principal (de la Bolsa de Londres); **main office** (in a town, region) oficina f central; (headquarters) sede f central or social; ECON **main product** producto m principal

mainframe n COMPTR **mainframe (computer)** Esp ordenador m or Am computadora f central

maintain vt (exchange rate, output, contact) mantener; **we must maintain our position as market leader** debemos mantener nuestra posición como líderes del mercado

maintenance n (a) (of building, equipment) mantenimiento m ❑ **maintenance contract** contrato m de mantenimiento; **maintenance costs** costos mpl or Esp costes mpl de mantenimiento; **maintenance department** departamento m de mantenimiento; **maintenance engineer** técnico(a) m,f de mantenimiento; **maintenance equipment** equipo m de mantenimiento; **maintenance programme** programa m de mantenimiento; **maintenance staff** personal m de mantenimiento
(b) (financial support) manutención f; LAW pensión f alimenticia ❑ **maintenance allowance** (for divorced partner) pensión f alimenticia; Br (for student) beca f de manutención

major 1 n US (big company) gran empresa f; **the oil majors** las grandes petroleras
2 adj principal ❑ **major shareholder** accionista mf principal

majority n mayoría f ❑ **majority decision** decisión f por mayoría; **majority holding** participación f mayoritaria; **majority interest** participación f mayoritaria; **majority investor** accionista mf mayoritario(a); Br **majority shareholder,** US **majority stockholder** socio(a) m,f or accionista mf mayoritario(a); **majority vote** votación f por mayoría

majority-owned subsidiary n filial f de participación mayoritaria

make 1 n (of product) marca f; **what make of printer is it?** ¿qué marca es la impresora?
2 vt (a) (construct) hacer, fabricar (b) (earn) ganar; **she makes £50,000 a year** gana 50.000 libras al año; **to make a loss** tener or sufrir pérdidas; **to make a profit** obtener or sacar beneficios

▶ **make out** vt sep (list) elaborar, hacer; (bill) expedir; **to make out a cheque (to sb)** extender un cheque (a alguien)

▶ **make over** vt sep ceder, traspasar (**to** a)

▶ **make up** vt sep (a) (loss) recuperar; (deficit) equilibrar (b) (parcel, order) preparar; (list) elaborar, hacer; (bill) expedir

▶ **make up for** vt insep compensar; **European sales made up for our losses in the UK** las ventas en Europa compensaron nuestras pérdidas en el Reino Unido

maker n (manufacturer) fabricante mf ❑ **maker's price** precio m de fábrica; **maker's trademark** marca f registrada del fabricante

making-up n ST EXCH **making-up day** día m de la liquidación (en la Bolsa de Londres); **making-up price** valor m de liquidación

maladjustment n ECON desajuste m

maladministration n mala gestión f

mall n **(shopping) mall** centro m comercial

malpractice n negligencia f profesional, malas prácticas fpl profesionales ❑ **malpractice insurance** seguro m contra la negligencia profesional

man vt (switchboard) atender; (machine) manejar; **to man a nightshift** cubrir el turno de noche; **to man the phone** atender el teléfono; **the office is manned by a skeleton staff** la oficina funciona con un mínimo de personal; **the company is manned mainly by university graduates** la mayoría de los trabajadores de la empresa son licenciados universitarios

manage vt (a) (company, factory, project) dirigir; (shop) llevar, regentar; (property, estate) administrar (b) (economy, resources, budget) gestionar, administrar; (money) administrar; **to manage sb's affairs** gestionar los asuntos de alguien

managed adj ACCT **managed costs** costos mpl or Esp costes mpl controlados; FIN **managed currency** moneda f controlada; **managed fund** fondo m administrado; **managed investment fund** fondo m de inversión administrado; **managed mutual fund** fondo m administrado de inversión colectiva; **managed trade** comercio *m* controlado

management *n* (**a**) *(action) (of company, project, factory)* dirección *f*, gestión *f*, gerencia *f*; *(of property, estate)* administración *f*; *(of economy, money, resources)* gestión, administración; **all their problems are due to bad management** todos sus problemas se deben a una mala gestión; **he knew next to nothing about the management of a bookshop** no sabía apenas nada sobre cómo llevar una librería ❑ **management accountant** *Esp* contable *mf* de gestión, *Am* contador(ora) *m,f* de gestión; **management accounting** contabilidad *f* de gestión; **management accounts** cuentas *fpl* de gestión; **management audit** control *m* de gestión; **management auditor** inspector(ora) *m,f* administrativo(a); **management chart** organigrama *m* directivo; **management committee** comité *m* de gestión; **management company** sociedad *f* gestora; **management consultancy** *(activity)* consultoría *f* en administración de empresas; *(company)* consultora *f* en administración de empresas; **management consultancy report** informe *m* de la consultora en administración de empresas; **management consultant** consultor(ora) *m,f* en administración de empresas; **management control** control *m* de gestión; **management error** error *m* de gestión; **management by exception** dirección *f* por excepción; *US* **management expenses** comisión *f* de gestión; **management expert** experto(a) *m,f* en gestión; **management fee** comisión *f* de gestión; COMPTR **management information system** sistema *m* de gestión de la información; **management by objectives** dirección *f* por objetivos; **management operating system** sistema *m* operativo de gestión; **management report** informe *m* de gestión; **management science** ciencias *fpl* de gestión; **management skills** dotes *fpl* de gestión; **management studies** estudios *mpl* de gestión empresarial *or* de administración de empresas; **management style** estilo *m* de gestión; **management system** sistema *m* de gestión; **management techniques** técnicas *fpl* de gestión; **management theory** teoría *f* de gestión empresarial; **management tool** instrumento *m* de gestión; **management training** formación *f* de cargos de gestión

(**b**) *(managers, employers)* **the management** la dirección, la gerencia; **negotiations between management and unions have broken down** las negociaciones entre la dirección y los sindicatos se han roto ❑ **management buy-in** = adquisición de una empresa por directivos externos; **management buy-out** = adquisición de una empresa por sus propios directivos; **as a result of a management buy-out, the business was rescued** la empresa sobrevivió gracias a su adquisición por la gerencia; **management team** equipo *m* de dirección

manager *n* (**a**) *(person in charge) (of company, bank branch)* director(ora) *m,f*, gerente *mf*; *(of shop, bar, restaurant)* encargado(a) *m,f* (**b**) *(member of management structure)* gerente *mf* (**c**) *(administrator) (of property, estate, funds, money)* administrador(ora) *m,f*; *(of assets)* gestor(ora) *m,f*, administrador(ora) (**d**) COMPTR *(of disk)* administrador *m*

manageress *n (of company, bank, hotel)* directora *f*; *(of shop, bar, restaurant)* encargada *f*

managerial *adj* directivo(a), de gestión ❑ **managerial functions** funciones *fpl* directivas *or* de gestión; **managerial grid** rejilla *f* gerencial; **managerial position** puesto *m* directivo *or* de gestión; **managerial skills** capacidad *f* directiva *or* de gestión; **managerial staff** personal *m* directivo *or* de gestión; **managerial structure** estructura *f* directiva *or* de gestión

managing director *n* director(ora) *m,f*, gerente

M&A *n* (*abbr* **mergers and acquisitions**) fusiones *fpl* y adquisiciones

“

Despite a red-hot market for venture-backed initial public offerings, mergers and acquisitions abounded in the first half of 1999, refuting the notion that the rise in **M&A** deals in the past several years was in response to a poor IPO market. ... And, as the bull market continues to drive valuations of entrepreneurial companies to record heights, **M&A**s have emerged as a more attractive exit option for venture capitalists.

”

mandate *n (authority)* autoridad *f*; *(instruction)* mandato *m* ❑ BANKING **mandate form** orden *f* de pago, autorización *f*

mandatory *adj* obligatorio(a) ❑ BANKING **mandatory liquid assets** reserva *f* obligatoria *(no utilizada en transacciones, que el Banco de Inglaterra obliga a tener a los bancos de compensación)*; **mandatory powers** poderes *mpl* ejecutivos; ST EXCH **mandatory quote period** horario *m* oficial de negociación

man-day *n* día-hombre *m*, día *m* de mano de obra

man-hour *n* hora-hombre *f*, hora *f* de mano de obra

manifest *n (of ship, aeroplane)* manifiesto *m*

manipulate *vt* **to manipulate the accounts** manipular las cuentas; ST EXCH **to manipulate the market** manipular el mercado

“

They said there had been speculation that someone may be **manipulating** the market, noting that three-month prices had climbed to $6,200 per tonne last week while tin trading volatility jumped to as high as 25 percent. **"**

manpower *n* mano *f* de obra; **we don't have the necessary manpower** no disponemos de la mano de obra necesaria ▫ *manpower forecasting* previsión *f* de mano de obra; *manpower management* gestión *f* de la mano de obra; *manpower planning* planificación *f* de la mano de obra

manual 1 *n (handbook)* manual *m*
2 *adj* manual ▫ COMPTR *manual input* entrada *m* manual; *manual labour* trabajo *m* manual; *manual operation* operación *f* manual; *manual trade* oficio *m* manual; *manual work* trabajo *m* manual; *manual worker* obrero(era) *m,f*, trabajador(ora) *m,f* manual

manually *adv* a mano, manualmente

manufactory *n US* fabricante *mf*

manufacture 1 *n* fabricación *f*, manufactura *f*
2 *vt (cars, clothes)* fabricar ▫ *manufactured goods* productos *mpl or* bienes *mpl* manufacturados; *manufactured products* productos *mpl* manufacturados

manufacturer *n* fabricante *mf* ▫ *manufacturer's agent* representante *mf* del fabricante; *manufacturer brand* marca *f* del fabricante; *manufacturer's liability* responsabilidad *f* del fabricante; *manufacturer's price* precio *m* de fábrica; *manufacturer's recommended price* precio *m* recomendado por el fabricante

manufacturing *n* fabricación *f*; **the decline of manufacturing** el declive de la producción industrial *or* de la industria manufacturera ▫ ACCT *manufacturing account* cuenta *f* de producción; *manufacturing base* base *f* productiva; *manufacturing capacity* capacidad *f* de fabricación; *manufacturing company* empresa *f* manufacturera; *manufacturing costs* costos *mpl or Esp* costes *mpl* de fabricación; *manufacturing defect* defecto *m* de fábrica *or* fabricación; *manufacturing fault Esp* fallo *m or Am* falla *f* de fabricación; *manufacturing industry* industria *f* manufacturera *or* de transformación; *manufacturing licence* licencia *f* de fabricación; *manufacturing method* método *m* de fabricación; *manufacturing monopoly* monopolio *m* de fabricación; *manufacturing overheads* costos *mpl or Esp* costes *mpl* de fabricación; *manufacturing plant* planta *f* de fabricación; *manufacturing process* proceso *m* de fabricación; *manufacturing rights* derechos *mpl* de fabricación; *manufacturing stage* fase *f* de fabricación; *manufacturing town* ciudad *f* industrial *or* manufacturera

man-year *n* ECON año-hombre *m*, año *m* de mano de obra

MAP *n (abbr* **maximum average price)** precio *m*

medio máximo *(impuesto por el gobierno sobre los suministros básicos como la electricidad y el gas)*

mapping *n* representación *f*

margin *n* (**a**) FIN margen *m*; **to have a low/high margin** tener un margen bajo/alto; **the margins are very tight** se trabaja con márgenes muy ajustados ▫ *margin of error* margen *m* de error; *margin of fluctuation (of a currency)* margen *m* de fluctuación; *margin of interest* margen *m* de rendimiento
(**b**) ST EXCH depósito *m* de garantía ▫ *margin call* petición *f* de aportación de garantía; *margin dealing* = compraventa de valores utilizando créditos para pagar una parte de su importe; *margin default* impago *m* de garantías; *margin requirement* depósito *m* de garantía mínimo

"
Competition in most low- and middle-price lines currently comes from places little expected – China and Germany – where private labeling is being used to crack American markets. In fact, competitors in Black & Decker's consumer lines are suffering from 1%/year price deflation. Low **margins** also are presenting difficulties in building and protecting brands.
"

marginal *adj (business, profit)* marginal ▫ *marginal cost* costo *m or Esp* coste *m* marginal; *marginal costing, marginal cost pricing* fijación *f* de precios de acuerdo con el costo *or Esp* coste marginal; *marginal disinvestment* desinversión *f* marginal; *marginal profit* beneficio *m* marginal; *marginal productivity* productividad *f* marginal; *Br marginal relief (on corporation tax)* desgravación *f* marginal; *marginal return on capital* rendimiento *m* marginal sobre el capital; *marginal revenue* ingresos *mpl* marginales; *marginal utility* utilidad *f* marginal; *marginal value* valor *m* marginal

marginalism *n* ECON marginalismo *m*

marine *adj* marino(a) ▫ *marine bill of lading* conocimiento *m* de embarque marítimo; *marine insurance* seguro *m* marítimo; *marine insurance policy* póliza *f* de seguro marítimo

marital *adj* ADMIN, LAW marital, conyugal ▫ *marital home* hogar *m* conyugal; *marital rights* derechos *mpl* conyugales; *marital status* estado *m* civil

maritime *adj* marítimo(a) ▫ *maritime freight* flete *m* marítimo; *maritime freight consolidator* consolidador(ora) *m,f* de carga marítima; *maritime insurance* seguro *m* marítimo; *maritime law* derecho *m* marítimo; *maritime shipment* envío *m* de mercancías por mar; *maritime trade* comercio *m* marítimo

mark¹ *n* Formerly *(currency)* marco *m* (alemán)

mark² **1** *n (level)* barrera *f*; **sales topped the 5**

million mark las ventas superaron la barrera de los 5 millones
  2 *vt (goods)* marcar

▸ **mark down** *vt sep (price, goods)* rebajar; **everything has been marked down to half price** todo está rebajado a la mitad de precio; ST EXCH **prices have been marked down** los precios están a la baja

▸ **mark up** *vt sep (price)* subir; *(goods)* subir el precio de; ST EXCH **prices have been marked up** los precios están al alza

markdown *n (action)* rebaja *f*, reducción *f* (de precio); *(article)* artículo *m* rebajado

marked price *n* precio *m* marcado

marker barrel *n* barril *m* de referencia

market 1 *n* (a) ECON, MKTG mercado *m*; **it isn't on the market yet** aún no está a la venta; **to come onto the market** salir al mercado; **to put sth on the market** sacar algo al mercado; **to take sth off the market** retirar algo del mercado *or* de la venta; **to be in the market for sth** querer comprar algo; **to find a market for sth** encontrar un mercado para algo; **to corner the market in sth** monopolizar *or* acaparar el mercado de algo; **to find a ready market** dar con un mercado idóneo *or* bien dispuesto; **there's always a (ready) market for software** siempre hay mercado para el software; **to price oneself out of the market** perder mercado o ventas por precios elevados; **the bottom has fallen out of the market** el mercado se ha desplomado □ *market analysis* análisis *m* de mercados; *market analyst* analista *mf* de mercados; *market appeal* atractivo *m* comercial; *market appraisal* evaluación *f* de mercado; *US market basket* cesta *for Am* canasta *f* de la compra; *market challenger* empresa *f* retadora, empresa aspirante a ser líder del mercado; *market choice (availability of different products)* oferta *f* de mercado; *(product)* producto *m* favorito; *market competition* competencia *f* de mercado; *market conditions* condiciones *fpl* del mercado; *market crisis* crisis *f* de mercado; *market demand* demanda *f* del mercado; *market depression* depresión *f* del mercado; *market development* desarrollo *m* del mercado; *market division (by agreement)* reparto *m* del mercado; *market dynamics* dinámica *f* del mercado; *market economy* economía *f* de mercado; *market entry* entrada *f* en el mercado; *market expansion* ampliación *f* del mercado; *market exposure* presencia *f or* exposición *f* en el mercado; *market fluctuation* fluctuación *f* del mercado; *market follower* empresa *f* seguidora en el mercado; *market forces* fuerzas *fpl* del mercado; *market forecast* previsión *f* de mercado; *market growth* crecimiento *m* del mercado; *market indicator* indicador *m* de mercado; *market intelligence* información *f* de mercado;

market leader líder *mf* del mercado; *market manager* director(ora) *m,f* de mercado; *market mechanism* mecanismo *m* de mercado; *market minimum (in sales forecast)* mínimo *m* de mercado; *(wage)* = sueldo mínimo que dicta el mercado; *market orientation* orientación *f* al *or* hacia el mercado; *Formerly* LAW *market overt* mercado *m* abierto; *market participant* participante *mf* en el mercado; *market penetration* penetración *f* en el mercado; *market penetration pricing* precios *mpl* de penetración en el mercado; *market penetration strategy* estrategia *f* de penetración en el mercado; *market pioneer* pionero(a) *m,f* del mercado; *market positioning* posicionamiento *m* en el mercado; *market potential* potencial *m* de mercado; *market price* precio *m* de mercado; *market profile* perfil *m* del mercado; *market prospects* perspectivas *fpl* de mercado; *market rate* precio *m* de mercado; *market rate of discount Esp* tipo *m or Am* tasa *f* de descuento del mercado; *market research* estudios *mpl* de mercado, investigación *f* de mercado; *market research has shown that the idea is viable* los estudios de mercado han demostrado que la idea es factible; *market research company* empresa *f* de estudios *or* investigación de mercado; *market researcher* investigador(ora) *m,f* de mercado; *Market Research Society* = asociación profesional británica de investigadores de mercado; *market segment* segmento *m* de mercado; *market segmentation* segmentación *f* del mercado; *market share* cuota *f* de *or* participación *f* en el mercado; *market size (of product)* volumen *m* de mercado; *(of market)* tamaño *m* del mercado; *market structure* estructura *f* del mercado; *market study* estudio *m* de mercado; *market study report* informe *m* del estudio de mercado; *market survey* estudio *m* de mercado; *market test* test *m or* prospección *f* de mercado; *market thrust* intento *m* de penetración en el mercado; *market trends* tendencias *fpl* del mercado; *market value* valor *m* de mercado

(b) ST EXCH mercado *m* (de valores), bolsa *f*; **the market has risen ten points** la bolsa *or* el mercado ha subido diez puntos; **to play the market** jugar a la bolsa □ *market capitalization* capitalización *f* bursátil; *market commentator* comentarista *mf* de mercados; *market correction* corrección *f* de mercado; *market crisis* crisis *f* bursátil; *market fund* fondo *m* de inversión en bolsa; *market indicator* indicador *m* bursátil; *market maker* creador(ora) *m,f* de mercado; *market order* orden *f* al mercado; *market price* precio *m* de mercado; *market price list* índice *m* de precios del mercado; *market quotation* cotización *f* en el mercado; *market rating* calificación *f* bursátil, rating *m*; *market report* información *f* bursátil; *market risk* riesgo *m* de mercado; *market size* volumen *m* del mercado;

market trend tendencia *f* del mercado; **market value** valor *m* de mercado

2 *vt* comercializar

> The primary commodity price index, developed by the economists Enzo R. Grilli and Maw Cheng Yang, takes the international cost of a **market basket** of 24 of the most commonly consumed "renewable and non-renewable resources" – foodstuffs, non-food agricultural goods, and metals – and adjusts for inflation.

marketability *n* MKTG comerciabilidad *f*; **these changes will improve the shares' marketability** estos cambios harán que las acciones sean más comercializables

marketable *adj* **(a)** MKTG *(goods)* comercializable **(b)** ST EXCH negociable ❑ **marketable securities** valores *mpl* negociables

market-driven *adj* determinado(a) por el mercado ❑ **market-driven economy** economía *f* de mercado

> The nub of it is that the chair must be able to hold the line between the demands of the **market-driven** telecoms industry and the cultural objectives of broadcasting. ... The great challenge for the chair will be to keep those two objectives in tension, while having the gravitas to lead a review of media ownership rules every three years.

marketer *n* **(a)** *(seller)* operador(ora) *m,f* de mercado; **a leading beauty products marketer** una empresa puntera en venta de productos de belleza **(b)** MKTG *(marketing specialist)* encargado(a) *m,f* de marketing

marketing *n* *(study, theory)* marketing *m*, mercadotecnia *f*; *(of product)* comercialización *f* ❑ **marketing agreement** acuerdo *m* de comercialización; **marketing analyst** analista *mf* de marketing; **marketing approach** enfoque *m* de marketing; **marketing audit** auditoría *f* de marketing; **marketing auditor** auditor(ora) *m,f* de marketing; **marketing budget** presupuesto *m* de marketing; **marketing campaign** campaña *f* de marketing; **marketing channel** canal *m* de comercialización; **marketing communications channel** canal *m* de comunicación de marketing; **marketing company** empresa *f* de marketing; **marketing concept** concepto *m or* enfoque *m* de marketing; **marketing consultancy** *(service, activity)* consultoría *f* de marketing; *(company)* consultora *f* de marketing; **marketing consultant** consultor(ora) *m,f* de marketing; **marketing costs** gastos *mpl* de comercialización; **marketing department** departamento *m*

de marketing; **marketing efficiency** eficacia *f* del marketing; **marketing efficiency study** estudio *m* de eficacia del marketing; **marketing environment** entorno *m* de marketing; **marketing executive** ejecutivo(a) *m,f* de marketing; **marketing expert** experto(a) *m,f* en marketing; **marketing fit** = producto o servicio que se adapta bien a la estrategia de marketing de una empresa; **marketing implementation** implementación *f* de marketing, puesta *f* en práctica de la estrategia de marketing; COMPTR **marketing information system** sistema *m* de información para marketing; **marketing intelligence** información *f* comercial; **marketing intelligence system** sistema *m* de información comercial; **marketing management** dirección *f* de marketing; **marketing manager** director(ora) *m,f* de marketing; **marketing mix** marketing mix *m*, = síntesis de los elementos básicos de mercado; **marketing myopia** miopía *f* en (el) marketing; **marketing network** red *f* de comercialización; **marketing orientation** orientación *f* al *or* hacia el mercado; **marketing plan** plan *m* de marketing; **marketing planner** planificador(ora) *m,f* de marketing; **marketing planning** planificación *f* de marketing; **marketing policy** política *f* de marketing; **marketing questionnaire** cuestionario *m* de marketing; **marketing research** investigación *f* de marketing; **marketing spectrum** espectro *m* de marketing; **marketing spend** gastos *mpl* de marketing; **marketing strategy** estrategia *f* de marketing; **marketing study** estudio *m* de marketing; **marketing subsidiary** delegación *f* de marketing, filial *f* de comercialización; **marketing target** target *m or* objetivo *m* de marketing; **marketing team** equipo *m* de marketing; **marketing techniques** técnicas *fpl* de marketing; **marketing tool** herramienta *f* de marketing

marketization *n* mercadización *f*

market-led *adj* *(behaviour, decision)* provocado(a) por el comportamiento del mercado; *(business, company)* orientado(a) hacia el mercado

marketplace *n* ECON mercado *m*; **the international/European marketplace** el mercado internacional/europeo; **the products in the marketplace** los productos del mercado

marking *n* ST EXCH **marking to market** valoración *f* a precios de mercado

markka *n* *Formerly* marco *m* finlandés

mark-up *n* margen *m* comercial; **we operate a 2.5 times mark-up** aplicamos un margen (comercial) del 250% ❑ **mark-up pricing** fijación *f* de precios mediante porcentajes; **mark-up ratio** porcentaje *m* del margen comercial

mart *n* **(a)** *(market)* mercado *m*; *US (shop)* tienda *f*, negocio *m* **(b)** *(auction room)* sala *f* de subastas *or* remates

marzipan layer *n* *Fam* = grupo de directivos

de una empresa que se encuentran justo por debajo de la junta directiva

> **"**
>
> The main grievances inside the firm seem to be coming from what insiders call the **marzipan layer**. This is the group of senior staff who have not been made new partners in the transition to a quoted company. The resentment that comes from people in all sections of the firm, from traders to fund managers, focuses on the 40 new partners, many of whom seem to have leapfrogged their colleagues.
>
> **"**

mass n **mass circulation** circulación f masiva; **mass consumption** consumo m en masa; **mass dismissal** despido m masivo; MKTG **mass display** presentación f masiva; **mass distribution** distribución f en masa; **mass distribution sector** sector m de distribución en masa; **mass mailing** mailing m masivo; **mass market** mercado m de masas; **mass marketing** comercialización f a gran escala; **mass media** medios mpl de comunicación de masas; **mass production** fabricación f en serie, producción f en cadena; **it goes into mass production next week** se empezará a fabricar en serie la semana que viene; **mass redundancies** despidos mpl masivos; COMPTR **mass storage** almacenamiento m masivo; **mass unemployment** desempleo m generalizado or masivo, Am desocupación f generalizada or masiva

massage vt (figures, numbers) maquillar

mass-market adj de alto consumo

mass-produce vt fabricar en serie

master 1 n (expert) maestro(a) m,f; **master of works** maestro m de obras
2 adj (**a**) (expert) **master builder** maestro m albañil (**b**) (main) **master budget** presupuesto m general; **master copy** original m; COMPTR **master disk** disco m maestro; **master document** documento m original; COMPTR **master file** archivo m or fichero m maestro **master plan** plan m maestro; **master production schedule** plan m maestro de producción

masterbrand n MKTG marca f estrella

> **"**
>
> As well as Kellogg and Nestlé, Cadbury has made a concerted effort to increase the prominence of its name on all confectionery and spin-off products and spent £870,000 on the **masterbrand** "Tastes Like Heaven" campaign in the year to May.
>
> **"**

MasterCard® n MasterCard®; **to pay by MasterCard®** pagar con MasterCard® □ **MasterCard® card** tarjeta f MasterCard®

masthead n (of newspaper) cabecera f

match vt **to match funding** aportar la misma cantidad de fondos

matched adj ST EXCH **matched bargain** transacción f casada; US **matched orders** órdenes fpl casadas

matching n (**a**) ACCT correlación f; □ **matching principle** principio m de correlación de ingresos y gastos (**b**) US ST EXCH = sincronización de los ingresos procedentes de una cartera de valores con las obligaciones futuras conocidas

material n (**a**) **materials** (equipment) materiales mpl; **materials and labour** materiales y mano de obra □ **materials cost** costo m or Esp coste m de materiales; **material defect** defecto m sustancial; **materials management** dirección f de materiales; **material requirements planning** planificación f de los requerimientos de materiales (**b**) MKTG (for marketing, promotion) material m

maternity n **maternity benefit** subsidio m de maternidad; **maternity leave** baja f or permiso m or Am licencia f por maternidad

maths co-processor n COMPTR coprocesador m matemático

matrix n matriz f □ **matrix management** gestión f matricial; **matrix organization** organización f matricial; COMPTR **matrix printer** impresora f matricial or de agujas

mattress money n FIN dinero m debajo del colchón

> **"**
>
> **Mattress money** is fast becoming the el Nino of European economics. The previously dormant stashes of cash, have been jarred into life by their imminent loss of status as legal currency. They can now be invoked to explain any number of bewildering economic phenomena, from rising house prices in France to a building boom in Spain, or even the overall weakness of the euro exchange rate.
>
> **"**

maturation n US FIN (of bill, investment, insurance policy) vencimiento m

mature 1 adj (**a**) **mature economy** economía f madura (**b**) MKTG (market) maduro(a) (**c**) FIN (bill) vencido(a), pagadero(a); (insurance policy, bond) vencido(a); **a mature investment** una inversión que ha alcanzado su madurez
2 vi FIN (bill, insurance policy, bond) vencer; (investment) alcanzar su madurez, vencer

maturity n (**a**) FIN (of bill, insurance policy) vencimiento m; (of investment) vencimiento, madurez f □ **maturity date** fecha f de vencimiento; **maturity value** valor m al vencimiento (**b**) MKTG (of market) madurez f

maxi-ISA n Br = plan de ahorros personal exento de impuestos con un tope de ahorro anual prefijado (más alto que el de una "mini-ISA")

maximization n maximización f; **our aim for this year is the maximization of profits** nuestro objetivo para este año es la maximización de los beneficios

maximize vt (**a**) (profit) maximizar, elevar al máximo (**b**) COMPTR (window) agrandar

maximum 1 n máximo m; **to raise production to a maximum** aumentar la producción al máximo; **the space has been used to the maximum** el espacio se ha aprovechado al máximo
2 adj máximo(a) ◻ **maximum efficiency** eficiencia f máxima; **maximum fluctuation** oscilación f máxima, fluctuación f máxima; INS **maximum foreseeable loss** siniestro m máximo previsible; **maximum load** carga f máxima; **maximum output** producción f máxima; **maximum price** precio m máximo

MB n COMPTR (abbr **megabyte**) MB m

Mb n COMPTR (abbr **megabit**) Mb m

MBA n (abbr **Master of Business Administration**) MBA m, máster m en administración de empresas

MBI n (abbr **management buy-in**) = adquisición de una empresa por directivos externos

MBO n (**a**) (abbr **management buy-out**) = adquisición de una empresa por sus propios directivos (**b**) (abbr **management by objectives**) dirección f por objetivos

MBps COMPTR (abbr **megabytes per second**) MBps

Mbps COMPTR (abbr **megabits per second**) Mbps

MBS n FIN (abbr **mortgage-backed security**) título m con garantía hipotecaria

m-commerce n comercio m móvil

> The company has predicted that **m-commerce** will become more widespread within the next few years, leading to USD25bn generated through mobile payments in 2006 – about 15% of total e-commerce consumer spending. Mobile commerce will comprise of automated payments at vending machines, parking meters, ticket machines, shop counters or taxis as well as mobile Internet payments and transactions between individuals.

MD n (abbr **managing director**) director(ora) m,f gerente

MDAX n ST EXCH índice m MDAX

mdse n US (abbr **merchandise**) mercancías fpl, género m

meal ticket n US vale m de comida

mean 1 n (average) media f
2 adj (average) medio(a) ◻ **mean absolute deviation** desviación f absoluta media; **mean price** precio m mediano

means 1 n (method) medio m ◻ **means of communication** medio m de comunicación; **means of payment** sistema m de pago, medio m de pago; **means of production** medios mpl de producción; **means of transport** medio m de transporte
2 npl (income, wealth) medios mpl ◻ ADMIN **means test** (for benefits) estimación f de ingresos **the grant is subject to a means test** la beca está sujeta a una estimación de ingresos

means-test vt ADMIN **to means-test sb** comprobar los recursos económicos de alguien; **all applicants are means-tested** se comprueban los recursos económicos de todos los solicitantes

> Even though vast chunks of state spending – from university grants to income support – are **means-tested**, the term still carries a real stigma, especially for pensioners. The universal principle – embodied in the welfare state through the state pension, child benefit and NHS – has a binding effect. Poor people feel they are getting something as of right and rich people get something back for their taxes, discouraging them from opting out altogether.

measure n (action, step) medida f; **to take measures to do sth** tomar medidas para hacer algo

measurement n (**a**) (of performance, productivity) medición f (**b**) (of freight) cubicación f ◻ **measurement tonnage** arqueo m

mechanical adj mecánico(a) ◻ **mechanical fault** Esp fallo m mecánico, Am falla f mecánica

mechanically adv (by machine) mecánicamente ◻ **mechanically recovered meat** carne f separada mecánicamente

mechanism n (**a**) (of machine) mecanismo m (**b**) (process, procedure) mecanismo m, procedimiento m

mechanization n mecanización f

mechanize vt mecanizar

media n medios mpl (de comunicación); **he works in the media** trabaja para los medios de comunicación; **the news media** los medios informativos ◻ **media advertising** publicidad f en medios de comunicación; **media analysis** estudio m de medios; **media analyst** analista mf de medios; **media buyer** comprador(ora) m,f de espacios publicitarios (en medios de comunicación); **media buying** compra f de espacios publicitarios (en medios de comunicación); **media**

consultant asesor(ora) *m,f* de medios de comunicación; **media coverage** cobertura *f* mediática; **media department** departamento *m* de medios; **media event** acontecimiento *m* mediático; **media exposure** atención *f* mediática; **media group** grupo *m* de medios de comunicación; **media hype** despliegue *m* mediático; **media mix** equilibrio *m* publicitario en medios; **media plan** plan *m* de medios; **media planner** planificador(ora) *m,f* de medios; **media planning** planificación *f* de medios; **media research** análisis *m* de medios de comunicación; **media schedule** plan *m* de medios; **media studies** ciencias *fpl* de la información *or* comunicación; **media vehicle** soporte *m* mediático

> ❝
> This study gives us insight that helps not only to determine the appropriate **media mix** for reaching teens, but more importantly the role of each medium, and how the dots connect within that mix. This new information will guide us into the future as consumer media habits continue to morph toward more diverse and fragmented mediums.
> ❞

media-conscious *adj* a media-conscious politician un político consciente de la importancia de los medios (de comunicación)

media-friendly *adj* to be media-friendly tratar bien a los medios de comunicación

> ❝
> Over that period, Merrill's merger business had shot to the top of the league tables in 1997 and 1998. Mr. Levy, with his sturdy frame and ready smile, was something of an anomaly within Merrill: a **media-friendly**, larger-than-life banker who stood strikingly apart from his gray, dull-suited peers.
> ❞

mediagenic *adj* mediático(a), interesante como tema informativo

mediate *vi* mediar (**in/between** en/entre)

mediation *n* mediación *f*; **to go to mediation** recurrir a una mediación

mediator *n* mediador(ora) *m,f*

medical *adj* **medical certificate** (confirming state of health) certificado *m* médico; (excusing holder from work) justificante *m* médico; **medical insurance** seguro *m* médico *or* de enfermedad; **medical officer** médico *mf* de empresa

medium 1 *n* (means of communication) medio *m*; **the choice of media open to us is limited by the budget** la oferta de medios a los que tenemos acceso está limitada por el presupuesto ❑ ECON **medium of exchange** medio *m* de cambio

2 *adj* medio(a); **in the medium term** a medio *or* Am mediano plazo

medium-dated *adj* (gilts, securities) a medio plazo, Am a mediano plazo

medium-sized *adj* mediano(a)

medium-term *adj* (forecast, loan) a medio plazo, Am a mediano plazo ❑ **medium-term credit** crédito *m* a medio *or* Am mediano plazo; EU **medium-term financial assistance** ayuda *f* financiera a medio *or* Am mediano plazo; **medium-term liabilities** pasivo *m* a medio *or* Am mediano plazo; **medium-term maturity** vencimiento *m* a medio *or* Am mediano plazo; FIN **medium-term note** pagaré *m* a medio *or* Am mediano plazo

meet 1 *vt* (a) (by arrangement) reunirse con; **to arrange to meet sb** quedar con alguien; (formal meeting) quedar en reunirse con alguien; **I arranged to meet him at 3 o'clock** he quedado con él a las 3 en punto

(b) (become acquainted with) conocer; **it was a pleasure to meet you** ha sido un placer conocerle; **I hope to meet you soon** espero tener pronto el placer de conocerle; **meet Mr Jones** le presento al señor Jones

(c) (satisfy) (need) satisfacer; (order) servir, cumplir; **to meet sb's requirements** satisfacer los requisitos de alguien; **to meet demand** satisfacer la demanda; **to meet sb's expenses** cubrir los gastos de alguien; **the cost will be met by the company** la empresa correrá con los gastos

2 *vi* (assemble) reunirse; **the delegates will meet in the conference room** los delegados se reunirán en la sala de conferencias; **the committee meets once a month** el comité se reúne una vez al mes

▶ **meet with** *vt insep* esp US (by arrangement) reunirse con; **I'm meeting with him tomorrow to discuss the budget** voy a reunirme con él mañana para discutir el presupuesto

meeting *n* reunión *f*; (of shareholders) asamblea *f*, junta *f*; (of workforce) asamblea; **to hold a meeting** celebrar una reunión; **the meeting will be held tomorrow at 3 o'clock** la reunión se celebrará mañana a las 3 en punto; **the meeting voted in favour of the measure** los reunidos votaron a favor de la medida; **to call a meeting of shareholders/the workforce** convocar una junta de accionistas/una asamblea de trabajadores; **to open the meeting** comenzar la reunión; **to close the meeting** terminar la reunión; **to address the meeting** dirigirse a los presentes; **to put a resolution to the meeting** someter una resolución a la reunión/junta/asamblea ❑ **meeting place** lugar *m* or punto *m* de encuentro

meg *n* COMPTR Fam mega *m*

megabit *n* COMPTR megabit *m*

megabyte n COMPTR megabyte m

megamerger n megafusión f

member n (of group, classification) miembro m, integrante mf; (of club, association, shareholder) socio(a) m,f; (of trade union) afiliado(a) m,f ▫ US **member bank** banco m comercial miembro de la Reserva Federal; EU **member country** país m miembro; ST EXCH **member firm** agencia f de bolsa afiliada; EU **member state** estado m miembro

membership n (a) (state of being a member) (of group, club, association) pertenencia f, Am membresía m; (of trade union) afiliación f, Am membresía; **his country's membership of UNESCO is in question** se cuestiona la pertenencia de su país a la UNESCO; **they have applied for membership to the EU** han solicitado su adhesión a la UE; **membership of the union will entitle you to vote in meetings** la pertenencia al sindicato te concederá el derecho a voto en las reuniones; **to apply for membership** solicitar el ingreso ▫ **membership card** carné m de socio/afiliado; **membership fee** cuota f de socio/afiliado

(**b**) (members) (of group, classification) miembros mpl, integrantes mfpl, Am membresía m; (of club, association) socios mpl, Am membresía m; (of trade union) afiliación f, afiliados mpl, Am membresía m; **the opinion of the majority of the union's membership** la opinión de la mayoría de los afiliados del sindicato

memo n memorándum m; (within office) nota f, **I've received a memo from head office** he recibido una nota de la central ▫ ACCT **memo account** cuenta f de orden; COMPTR **memo field** campo m memo; **memo pad** bloc m de notas

memorandum n (a) (business communication) memorándum m; (in office) nota f (**b**) (of contract, sale) escritura f (**c**) LAW **memorandum of agreement** contrato m preliminar; **memorandum and articles of association** estatutos mpl sociales; **memorandum of association** escritura f de constitución; BANKING **memorandum of satisfaction** documento m de cancelación

memory n COMPTR memoria f ▫ **memory bank** banco m de memoria; **memory buffer** buffer m de memoria; **memory capacity** capacidad f de memoria; **memory card** tarjeta f de memoria; **memory chip** chip m de memoria; **memory dump** volcado m de memoria; **memory expansion** ampliación f de memoria; **memory expansion card** or **board** tarjeta f de ampliación de memoria; **memory management** gestión f de memoria; **memory manager** gestor m de memoria; **memory space** memoria f; **memory upgrade** ampliación f de memoria; **memory variable** variable f de memoria

mentor n mentor(ora) m,f

mentoring n mentoring m, tutorización f

> White people seem to be picked up much earlier and promoted more quickly if they show talent, whereas ethnic minorities often hit a plateau in middle management, says Mitchell. So now there are **mentoring schemes**, in addition to training programmes, to help black and Asian staff move on and up within the corporation.

menu n COMPTR menú m ▫ **menu bar** barra f de menús; **menu item** ítem m de menú **menu option** opción f del menú

MEP n (abbr **Member of the European Parliament**) eurodiputado(a) m,f; **David Green MEP** el eurodiputado David Green

mercantile adj (class, expansion, interests) mercantil; **a mercantile nation** una nación de comerciantes ▫ **mercantile agency** empresa f de información comercial; **mercantile agent** agente mf comercial; **mercantile agreement** acuerdo m comercial; **mercantile bank** banco m de comercio; **mercantile broker** agente mf de cambio, cambista mf; **mercantile company** compañía f mercantil; **mercantile law** derecho m mercantil; **mercantile operation** operación f comercial, transacción f comercial; **mercantile paper** letra f de cambio comercial; **mercantile system** mercantilismo m

mercantilism n mercantilismo m

mercantilist adj mercantilista

merchandise 1 n mercancías fpl, géneros mpl
2 vt comercializar

merchandiser n (object) expositor m; (person) especialista mf en merchandising

merchandising n (activity) merchandising m, promoción f; (items) artículos mpl de merchandising or promoción ▫ **merchandising allowance** bonificación f por promoción (de las empresas a los comerciantes); **merchandising techniques** técnicas fpl de merchandising

merchant n (trader) negociante mf; (shopkeeper) comerciante mf ▫ Br **merchant bank** banco m mercantil or de negocios; Br **merchant banker** banquero(a) m,f (en un banco mercantil); **merchant ship** buque m or barco m mercante **merchant wholesaler** mayorista mf

merchantable quality n calidad f comercializable; **all goods must be of merchantable quality** todas los artículos deben tener una calidad comercializable

merchanting n Br compraventa f

merge 1 vt (**a**) (banks, companies) fusionar (**b**) COMPTR (files) unir, fusionar
2 vi (banks, companies) fusionarse; **they have merged with their former competitor** se han fusionado con su antiguo competidor

merger *n* fusión *f*; **the two companies are holding merger talks** las dos empresas están negociando una fusión ❑ *merger accounting* contabilidad *f* de fusiones; *mergers and acquisitions* fusiones *fpl* y adquisiciones; *merger premium* prima *f* de fusión

merit *n (advantage)* mérito *m*; **promotion is on** or **by merit alone** el ascenso se otorga exclusivamente en función de los méritos ❑ *merit bonus* prima *f* por méritos *(que se entrega a los directivos por aumentar las ventas, aumentar la productividad, reducir gastos, etc)*; *merit increase* aumento *m* de sueldo por méritos; *merit rating* valoración *f* de méritos; *merit system* sistema *m* de contratación y ascenso por méritos

> Second, consider the Equal Pay Act, which generally requires that men and women be paid alike for substantially equal work, unless you can justify pay distinctions on the basis of a bona fide **merit system**, seniority system or a factor other than gender. "If the male is paid more than the female, even though you base that on prior salary history, it's going to raise a red flag," Duffie says.

message *n* mensaje *m*; **to leave a message (for sb)** dejar un recado *or* mensaje (a *or* para alguien); **would you like to leave a message?,** **can I take a message?** ¿quiere dejar algún recado?; **can you give her a message?** ¿le puede dar un recado? ❑ COMPTR *message box* ventana *f or* cuadro *m* de diálogo *message handling* tratamiento *m* de mensajes

messenger *n* mensajero(a) *m,f*; **by special messenger** por mensajero ❑ *messenger boy* chico *m* de los recados

Messrs *npl (abbr* **Messieurs)** Sres., señores *mpl*

method *n* método *m* ❑ *methods analysis* estudio *m* de métodos; *methods engineer* analista *mf* de métodos de trabajo; *methods engineering* análisis *m* de métodos de trabajo; *methods office* departamento *m* de análisis de métodos de trabajo; *method of operation* método *m* de funcionamiento; *method of payment* sistema *m* de pago; *method study* estudio *m* de métodos

methodical *adj* metódico(a)

methodology *n* metodología *f*

me-too *adj* MKTG *me-too product* producto *m* de imitación; *me-too strategy* estrategia *f* de imitación

metric *adj* métrico(a); **to go metric** cambiar al sistema métrico ❑ *metric hundredweight* = unidad equivalente a 50 kg; *metric system* sistema *m* métrico; *metric ton* tonelada *f* métrica

mezzanine *n* *mezzanine debt* deuda *f* de entresuelo; *mezzanine finance* financiación *f* de entresuelo

> When it comes to financing mergers, the red-hot market for junk bonds has for years squeezed out **mezzanine debt** as the method of choice. Nowadays, though, as the high-yield market has turned lukewarm to issuers of smaller-sized deals, savvy Wall Street players and financial buyers are quickly moving to capitalize on the new-found role for **mezzanine debt**.

mfd *(abbr* **manufactured)** fabricado(a)

mgmt *(abbr* **management)** dirección *f*

mgr *(abbr* **manager)** *(of bank, company, hotel)* dir.; *(of shop, bar, restaurant)* encargado(a) *m,f*

mgt *(abbr* **management)** dirección *f*

MHz COMPTR *(abbr* **megahertz)** MHz

MIBOR *n (abbr* **Madrid Interbank Offer Rate)** MIBOR *m*

micro *n* COMPTR *Esp* microordenador *m*, *Am* microcomputadora *f*

microbusiness *n* microempresa *f*

microcap fund *n* FIN fondo *m* de inversión en empresas de muy pequeña capitalización

microchip *n* COMPTR microchip *m*

microcomputer *n Esp* microordenador *m*, *Am* microcomputadora *f*

micro-computing *n* microinformática *f*

microcredit *n* FIN microcrédito *m*

microeconomics *n* microeconomía *f*

microenterprise *n* microempresa *f*

microfiche *n* microficha *f*

microfilm *n* microfilm *m* ❑ *microfilm reader* lector *m* de microfilms

microlending *n* FIN microcréditos *mpl*

microloan *n* FIN microcrédito *m*

micromanage *vt* supervisar hasta el último detalle de

> By her own admission, Shapiro was not a good administrator and manager of the staff.... That she spent almost as much time out of the office than in attests to how she attempted to run Giants. Her accusation that the board has sought to **micromanage** Giants is inaccurate. In fact, the board only became more involved in management when Ms. Shapiro failed to do so; and in addition, she refused to follow board directions on hiring and compensation.

micromarketing *n* micromarketing *m*

microprocessing *n* microprocesamiento *m*

microprocessor *n* microprocesador *m*

microsegment *n* MKTG microsegmento *m*

microsegmentation *n* MKTG microsegmentación *f*

mid *adj* **in mid June** a mediados de junio

mid-cap *adj* ST EXCH *(share, company)* de mediana capitalización ◻ *mid-cap index* índice *m* de empresas de mediana capitalización

middle *adj* **the middle classes** la clase media; *middle management* mandos *mpl* intermedios; *middle manager* mando *m* intermedio; ST EXCH *middle price* precio *m* mediano

middle-income *adj (group, bracket)* de ingresos medios

middleman *n* intermediario *m* ◻ *middleman's market* mercado *m* de intermediarios

mid-month account *n* ST EXCH cuenta *f* de mediados de mes

mid-range *adj (product, car etc)* de gama media

mileage allowance *n* ≃ *Esp* (dieta *f* de) kilometraje *m*, *Am* (viáticos *mpl* por) kilometraje

millage *n US* tasa *f* expresada en milésimas de dólar

mind share *n* MKTG cuota *f* de mente

❝

With personal-video-recording services such as those offered by TiVo Inc. and ReplayTV Inc. capturing more and more **mind share**, supporting time-shifted programming is beginning to show up on the future service lists of video-on-demand vendors. At its most basic level, the concept is simple: Record all programming and make it available on-demand, at any time, with pause, rewind and fast-forward functions.

❞

mine 1 *n* mina *f*
2 *vt (coal, gold)* extraer; *(coal seam)* explotar
3 *vi* **to mine for coal/gold** extraer carbón/oro

minicomputer *n Esp* miniordenador *m*, *Am* minicomputadora *f*

MiniDisc® *n* COMPTR MiniDisc® *m* ◻ *MiniDisc*® *player* reproductor *m* or lector *m* de MiniDisc®

mini-ISA *n Br* = plan de ahorros personal exento de impuestos con un tope de ahorro anual prefijado (más bajo que el de una "maxi-ISA")

minimal *adj* mínimo(a) ◻ *minimal value* valor *m* mínimo

minimize *vt* minimizar, reducir al mínimo; **we must try to minimize overheads** debemos intentar reducir al mínimo los gastos fijos

minimum 1 *n* mínimo *m*; **a minimum of two years' experience** un mínimo de dos años de experiencia, dos años de experiencia como mínimo; **to reduce sth to a minimum** reducir algo al mínimo; **to keep expenses to a minimum** mantener los gastos al mínimo
2 *adj* mínimo(a); **the minimum number of shares** el número mínimo de acciones ◻ *minimum charge* tarifa *f* mínima; *minimum deposit* depósito *m* mínimo; ST EXCH *minimum fluctuation* oscilación *f* mínima; *Br Formerly* *minimum lending rate Esp* tipo *m* mínimo or *Am* tasa *f* mínima de interés; *minimum living wage* salario *m* mínimo vital; *minimum output* producción *f* mínima; *minimum payment* cuota *f* mínima; *minimum price* precio *m* mínimo; *minimum rate* tarifa *f* mínima; *minimum stock level* nivel *m* mínimo de existencias; *minimum wage* salario *m* mínimo (interprofesional), sueldo *m* mínimo; *minimum weight* peso *m* mínimo

minister *n (politician) (in charge of department)* ministro(a) *m,f*; *(junior)* secretario(a) *m,f* de Estado

ministerial *adj* ministerial; **to hold ministerial office** ostentar una cartera ministerial ◻ *ministerial functions* funciones *fpl* ministeriales; *ministerial order* orden *f* ministerial; *ministerial responsibility* responsabilidad *f* ministerial

ministry *n (department)* ministerio *m*

mini tower *n* COMPTR minitorre *f*

minor *adj (profit, improvement, change)* de poca importancia, menor ◻ *minor shareholder* accionista *mf* minoritario(a)

minority *n* minoría *f* ◻ *minority holding, minority interest* participación *f* minoritaria; *minority investor* inversor(ora) *m,f* minoritario(a); *Br minority shareholder*, *US minority stockholder* accionista *mf* minoritario(a)

mint 1 *n Br* FIN **the (Royal) Mint** ≃ la Casa de la Moneda, *Esp* ≃ la Fábrica Nacional de Moneda y Timbre ◻ *mint par* = paridad entre el tipo de cambio y el valor metálico de las monedas
2 *vt (coins)* acuñar

mintage *n (process of minting)* acuñación *f*

minute 1 *n* **minutes** *(of meeting)* acta *f*, actas *fpl*; **to approve the minutes of the last meeting** aprobar el acta de la última reunión; **to take the minutes of a meeting** levantar el acta de una reunión ◻ *minute book* libro *m* de actas
2 *vt (make note of)* hacer constar en acta; *(send note to)* notificar; **the meeting will be minuted** se levantará acta de la reunión

mips *n* COMPTR *(abbr* **million instructions per second***)* mips, millón *m* de instrucciones por segundo

MIRAS *n Br Formerly (abbr* **Mortgage Interest Relief at Source***)* = desgravación fiscal de intereses por adquisición o reforma de vivienda habitual

mirror site n COMPTR sitio m espejo or réplica

MIS n (**a**) COMPTR (abbr **management informa-tion system**) MIS m, sistema m de gestión de la información (**b**) MKTG (abbr **marketing informa-tion system**) sistema m de información de marketing

misapplication n (of money) malversación f

misapply vt (money) malversar

misappropriate vt (for oneself) apropiarse in-debidamente de; (for a wrong use) malversar

misappropriation n (for oneself) apropiación f indebida; (for a wrong use) malversación f de fondos ❑ **misappropriation of funds** malver-sación f de fondos

misbrand vt MKTG **to misbrand a product** eti-quetar un producto de forma engañosa o frau-dulenta

> ❝
>
> The president of a "low-fat" baked-goods company went to jail after pleading guilty to **misbranding** products. According to the Food and Drug Administration, the com-pany had simply purchased regular day-old pastries from a Chicago bakery and re-packaged them under its "Skinny" line. While all the items were supposed to con-tain one or two grams of fat and 125 to 165 calories, at least one, a carob doughnut, had 23 1/2 grams of fat and 411 calories.
>
> ❞

misbranding n = denominación o etiquetado engañoso o fraudulento de un producto

miscalculate vt calcular mal or erróneamente

miscalculation n error m de cálculo

miscarriage n Br (of mail, goods) extravío m

miscellaneous adj diverso(a), misceláneo(a) ❑ **miscellaneous expenses** gastos mpl varios; **miscellaneous shares** acciones fpl diversas

misconduct n (**a**) (mismanagement) mala ges-tión f; **they accused her of misconduct of the company's affairs** la acusaron de gestionar mal la empresa (**b**) (**professional**) **misconduct** conducta f (profesional) poco ética

misdate vt poner la fecha equivocada a

misdirect vt (letter) mandar a una dirección equivocada

misentry n ACCT ingreso m o cargo m erróneo (en una cuenta)

misery index n US índice m de malestar eco-nómico or de miseria

> ❝
>
> One, admittedly artificial, indicator of finan-cial conditions is the "**misery index**", which is an average of the depreciation of the cur-rency, the change in the stock market index,

and the change in domestic interest rates (in basis points). This index shows that the major developing countries have seen sub-stantial declines in interest rates, exchange rate appreciation, and stock market in-creases since December 1998.
>
> ❞

misleading advertising n publicidad f engañosa

mismanage vt administrar or gestionar mal

mismanagement n mala administración f, mala gestión f

misroute vt (parcel) entregar en la dirección equivocada

mission n (**a**) (delegation) delegación f; **a Chi-nese trade mission** una delegación comercial china (**b**) (of company) misión f ❑ **mission state-ment** declaración f de (la) misión, misión f

> ❝
>
> The purpose of the NCC, which was estab-lished with government funds in 1975, is to safeguard the interests of consumers – particularly, according to its **mission state-ment**, "the inarticulate and disadvantaged". It has battled on their behalf against sharp practice, especially in the insurance, bank-ing, supermarket and utilities sectors. Now, however, consumers could be forgiven for wondering whose side it is on.
>
> ❞

missionary selling n MKTG = prospección de clientes a domicilio

mission-critical adj indispensable para el cumplimiento de la misión de la empresa

> ❝
>
> What you can say about the new economy is that it changes the way we work. Email has long been **mission-critical**, but six months from now you will have to be web-literate to even survive within BP.
>
> ❞

mistake n error m, equivocación f; **to make a mistake** equivocarse, cometer un error

misuse 1 n (of equipment, resources) uso m inde-bido; (of authority) uso indebido, abuso m; (of funds) malversación f
2 vt (equipment) usar indebidamente (authority) usar indebidamente, abusar de; (funds) malver-sar

mixed adj **there was mixed trading on Wall Street today** hubo indecisión en Wall Street hoy ❑ **mixed cargo** cargamento m mixto; **mixed costs** costos mpl or Esp costes mpl semi-variables; **mixed economy** economía f mixta; INS **mixed policy** póliza f combinada; **mixed risks** riesgos mpl combinados

mixed-media adj multimedia inv

MJPEG *n* COMPTR (*abbr* **Moving Joint Photographic Expert Group**) MJPEG *m*

MLM *n* (*abbr* **multi-level marketing**) marketing *m* de multinivel

MLR *n Br* FIN (*abbr* **minimum lending rate**) *Esp* tipo *m* activo mínimo de interés, *Am* tasa *f* activa mínima de interés

MMC *n Formerly* (*abbr* **Monopolies and Mergers Commission**) = comisión antimonopolios británica

MMF *n* ST EXCH (*abbr* **money market fund**) FIAMM *m*

MO *n* (*abbr* **money order**) transferencia *f*, giro *m*

mobbing *n* acoso *m* moral, mobbing *m*

mobile 1 *n* (*mobile phone*) móvil *m*, *Am* celular *m*
2 *adj* **mobile customs unit** aduana *f* móvil; **mobile phone** teléfono *m* móvil, *Am* teléfono celular

mobilization *n* (*of capital*) movilización *f*

mobilize *vt* (*capital*) movilizar

mock-up *n* reproducción *f*, modelo *m* (*de tamaño natural*)

mode *n* COMPTR modo *m*

model *n* (**a**) (*small version*) maqueta *f* (**b**) (*example, product*) modelo *m*; **this is our latest model** este es nuestro último modelo; **we plan to bring out a new model next season** tenemos previsto sacar un nuevo modelo la próxima temporada ❏ **model factory** fábrica *f* modelo (**c**) ECON modelo *m*

modem COMPTR **1** *n* módem *m*; **to send sth to sb by modem** enviar algo a alguien por módem ❏ **modem cable** cable *m* del módem; **modem card** tarjeta *f* del módem
2 *vt* **to modem sth (to sb)** enviar algo (a alguien) por módem

moderate *adj* (*price, rise*) moderado(a); (*income*) modesto(a)

moderate-income *adj* de ingresos modestos

moderator *n* (*at meeting*) moderador(ora) *m,f*; (*mediator*) mediador(ora) *m,f*

modernization *n* modernización *f*

modernize *vt* modernizar

modified rebuy *n* modificación *f* de compra

monadic *adj* MKTG **monadic test** test *m* monádico; **monadic testing** tests *mpl* monádicos

monetarism *n* ECON monetarismo *m*

monetarist *n & adj* ECON monetarista *mf*

monetary *adj* monetario(a) ❏ **monetary adjustment** alineación *f* monetaria; **monetary aggregate** masa *f* monetaria; **monetary agreement** acuerdo *m* monetario; **monetary alignment** ajuste *m* monetario; **monetary area** zona *f* monetaria; **monetary assets** activos *mpl* monetarios; **monetary base** base *f* monetaria; ECON **monetary bloc** bloque *m* monetario; **monetary compensatory amounts** montantes *mpl* compensatorios monetarios; **monetary control** control *m* monetario; **monetary inflation** inflación *f* monetaria; **monetary parity** paridad *f* monetaria; **monetary policy** política *f* monetaria; **monetary policy committee** comité *m* de política monetaria; **monetary reform** reforma *f* monetaria; **monetary reserves** reservas *fpl* monetarias; **monetary standard** patrón *m* monetario; **monetary surplus** excedente *m* monetario; **monetary system** sistema *m* monetario; **Monetary Union** Unión *f* Monetaria; **monetary unit** unidad *f* monetaria

monetization *n* monetización *f*

monetize *vt* monetizar

money *n* (**a**) (*cash, currency*) dinero *m*, *Am* plata *f*; (*currency*) moneda *f*; **counterfeit money** dinero falso; **to make money** (*person*) ganar *or* hacer dinero; (*business*) dar dinero; **to be worth a lot of money** (*thing*) valer mucho dinero; (*person*) tener mucho dinero; **the deal is worth a lot of money** el contrato va a dar mucho dinero; **I got my money back** (*I got reimbursed*) me devolvieron el dinero; (*I recovered my expenses*) recuperé el dinero ❏ **money of account** moneda *f* de cuenta; **money broker** cambista *mf*; BANKING **money at call** dinero *m* a la vista; **money laundering** blanqueo *m* de dinero *or* de capitales; *US* **money manager** director(ora) *m,f* de inversiones; **money market** mercado *m* monetario; *US* **money market certificate** certificado *m* del mercado monetario; **money market fund** fondo *m* de inversión en activos del mercado monetario; **money measurement** medida *f* monetaria; **money order** transferencia *f*, giro *m*; **money rate** *Esp* tipo *m* *or Am* tasa *f* de interés del dinero; BANKING **money at short notice** dinero *m* a corto plazo; **money supply** oferta *f* *or* masa *f* monetaria **money trader** cambista *mf*
(**b**) ST EXCH **to be in the money** estar con dinero; **at the money** en dinero; **out of the money** fuera de dinero

> ❝
> But these problems, together with those seen in the euro switchover, do post a warning. We now know that the far simpler changeover to the euro resulted in large bank payments going astray and a serious liquidity problem in the Euroland **money markets**, which required large injections of cash.
> ❞

money-back *adj* **money-back guarantee** garantía *f* de devolución *or* reembolso (del dinero); **money-back offer** oferta *f* de devolución *or* reembolso (del dinero)

moneychanger *n* (**a**) (*person*) cambista *mf* (**b**) *US* (*machine*) máquina *f* de cambio

moneylender *n* prestamista *mf*

moneymaker *n (business, product)* negocio *m* rentable *or* lucrativo

moneymaking *adj* lucrativo(a)

moneyman *n Fam* financiero *m*

money-off *adj* **money-off coupon** cupón *m* de descuento; **money-off deal** oferta *f* de descuento; **money-off voucher** vale *m* de descuento

money-spinner *n Br Fam* mina *f* de oro

moneyspinning *adj Br Fam* muy lucrativo(a)

monitor 1 *n* COMPTR monitor *m*
  2 *vt* MKTG hacer un seguimiento de, monitorear

monitoring *n* MKTG seguimiento *m*, monitoreo *m*

monometallic *adj* FIN monometálico(a)

monometallism *n* FIN monometalismo *m*

Monopolies and Mergers Commission *n Formerly* =comisión antimonopolios británica

monopolize *vt* monopolizar

monopoly *n* monopolio *m*; **to have a monopoly of** *or* **on sth** tener el monopolio de algo; **to form a monopoly** formar un monopolio ❑ **monopoly control** control *m* monopolístico *or* monopólico; **monopoly market** mercado *m* monopolizado

monopsony *n* ECON monopsonio *m*

month *n* mes *m*

monthly 1 *adj* mensual ❑ **monthly instalment** plazo *m* mensual; **monthly payment** mensualidad *f*; **monthly repayment** plazo *m* mensual; **monthly statement** *(from bank)* extracto *m* (bancario) mensual
  2 *adv* mensualmente

moonlight *vi Fam* **he's moonlighting for another company** tiene un trabajo en negro en otra empresa

moonlighting *n Fam* pluriempleo *m (a menudo ilegal)*

moral hazard *n* INS riesgo *m* moral

> **"**
>
> The US Congress is reluctant to fund President Clinton's promise of $210m ...for the initiative, and Japan fears that a write off of its $10bn share will create a **moral hazard**. An added condition for indebted countries to fulfil, linking debt relief to poverty reduction, has also caused delays as poor countries struggle to prepare "poverty reduction strategy papers" to the satisfaction of their creditors. The result is that most of the neediest countries are getting nothing from the process.
>
> **"**

moratorium *n* FIN moratoria *f* (**on** en); **to**

declare a moratorium (on sth) decretar *or* declarar una moratoria (en algo)

mortality tables *npl* INS tablas *fpl* de mortalidad

mortgage 1 *n* FIN hipoteca *f*, crédito *m* hipotecario; **a 25-year mortgage at 7%** una hipoteca a 25 años al 7%; **to take out a mortgage** obtener una hipoteca; **to secure a debt by mortgage** garantizar una deuda mediante una hipoteca; **to pay off a mortgage** liquidar una hipoteca; **they can't meet their mortgage repayments** no pueden hacer frente a los plazos de su hipoteca ❑ **mortgage bank** banco *m* hipotecario, banco de crédito inmobiliario; **mortgage bond** cédula *f or* obligación *f* hipotecaria, bono *m* con garantía hipotecaria; **mortgage broker** agente *mf* hipotecario(a); **mortgage charge** carga *f* hipotecaria, gravamen *m* hipotecario; **mortgage debenture** cédula *f or* obligación *f* hipotecaria, bono *m* con garantía hipotecaria; **mortgage deed** escritura *f* hipotecaria; **mortgage lender** entidad *f* de préstamo hipotecario, prestamista *m* hipotecario; **mortgage loan** préstamo *m* hipotecario; **mortgage market** mercado *m* hipotecario; **mortgage payments** plazos *mpl* de la hipoteca; **mortgage rate** *Esp* tipo *m* (de interés) hipotecario, *Am* tasa *f* (de interés) hipotecaria; **mortgage registrar** registrador(ora) *m,f (del Registro Público de la Propiedad)*; **mortgage repayments** plazos *mpl* de la hipoteca; **mortgage repossession** ejecución *f* hipotecaria; **mortgage security** garantía *f* hipotecaria
  2 *vt* hipotecar

mortgageable *adj* hipotecable

mortgage-backed security *n* FIN valores *mpl* con respaldo hipotecario

mortgagee *n* acreedor(ora) *m,f* hipotecario(a)

mortgagor *n* deudor(ora) *m,f* hipotecario(a)

most-favoured nation, *US* **most-favored nation** *n* nación *f* más favorecida; **this country has most-favoured nation status** este país goza de estatus de nación más favorecida

> **"**
>
> Ukraine's exports would benefit from the proximity of a large single market, said Ms Franey, as well as from demand sparked by economic growth in the candidates. And once they join the EU, the candidates will have to grant Ukraine the same privileges it already enjoys in relations with the EU – notably **most-favoured nation** status, and benefits under the Generalised System of Preferences.
>
> **"**

motherboard *n* COMPTR placa *f* madre, motherboard *m or f*

mother company n empresa f matriz, casa f matriz

motion n (**a**) *(in meeting, debate)* moción f; **to propose a motion** proponer una moción; **to carry a motion** aprobar una moción; **to second a motion** apoyar una moción (**b**) IND *(movement)* movimiento m ◻ ***motion analysis*** análisis m de movimientos; ***motion study*** estudio m de movimientos (**c**) LAW *(request)* petición f

motivate vt motivar

motivation n motivación f ◻ MKTG ***motivation research*** estudio m de la motivación; ***motivation study*** estudio m de la motivación

motivational adj MKTG ***motivational research*** investigación f motivacional; ***motivational study*** estudio m motivacional

motivator n motivador(ora) m,f

motive n *(intention)* motivo m, razón f

mount vt *(campaign)* organizar; *(exhibition)* montar; **to mount a bid to do sth** intentar hacer algo

▶ **mount up** vi (**a**) *(increase)* aumentar, crecer; **the bill was mounting up** la factura seguía aumentando (**b**) *(accumulate)* acumularse

mouse n COMPTR Esp ratón m, Am mouse m ◻ ***mouse button*** botón m del Esp ratón or Am mouse; ***mouse driver*** controlador m del Esp ratón or Am mouse; ***mouse mat, mouse pad*** tapete m, alfombrilla f

mousetrap n US **to build a better mousetrap** crear un producto mejor

> **"**
>
> The common philosophy among many Southeast Asian executives is that if their products are good – if they **build a better mousetrap** – consumers will know how to get to them. But these executives need to change their focus from achieving short-term sales to building long-term relationships with the key stakeholders in their businesses.
>
> **"**

movable, moveable LAW **1** n **movables** bienes mpl muebles

   2 adj ***movable assets*** activos mpl muebles; ***movable effects*** bienes mpl muebles; ***movable property*** bienes mpl muebles

move 1 n (**a**) *(change of job)* cambio m; *(change of premises)* traslado m (**b**) *(step, measure)* paso m, medida m; **the new management's first move was to increase all salaries** la primera medida que tomó la nueva dirección fue aumentar todos los sueldos; **at one time there was a move to expand** en su día se dieron los primeros pasos para la expansión

   2 vt (**a**) *(transfer)* trasladar; **she's been moved to the New York office/to accounts** la han

trasladado a la oficina de Nueva York/a contabilidad (**b**) *(sell)* dar salida a; **we must move these goods quickly** tenemos que dar salida pronto a estas mercancías

   3 vi (**a**) *(change premises, location)* trasladarse; **the company has moved to more modern premises** la empresa se ha trasladado a un local más moderno; **he's moved to a job in publishing** se ha cambiado a un trabajo en el sector editorial (**b**) *(sell)* venderse; **the new model isn't moving as quickly as planned** el nuevo modelo no se está vendiendo con la rapidez que esperábamos

▶ **move up** vi ST EXCH *(of shares)* subir; **shares moved up three points today** las acciones han subido tres puntos hoy

moveable = **movable**

movement n *(of capital, share prices, market)* movimiento m; **the upward/downward movement of interest rates** el movimiento ascendente/descendente de los tipos de interés

mover n **the movers and shakers** *(key people)* los que mueven los hilos

> **"**
>
> The **movers and shakers** of real estate development are among the late arrivals to the great Web party that has revolutionized business practices in almost every sector of our economy. In fact, many in the real estate business are still "arriving" – on their way. As an industry we have not yet tapped even half of the Internet's remarkable potential for advertising and marketing real estate.
>
> **"**

moving average n media f móvil

MP3 n *(abbr* **MPEG1 Audio Layer 3***)* MP3 m ◻ ***MP3 file*** archivo m or fichero m MP3; ***MP3 player*** reproductor m de MP3

MPA n *(abbr* **Master of Public Administration***)* Máster m en Administración Pública

MPC n *(abbr* **monetary policy committee***)* comité m de política monetaria

> **"**
>
> Most City economists believe the Bank of England monetary policy committee will leave base rates on hold at 5 per cent at their two-day meeting tomorrow…. It is believed the **MPC** will feel economic indicators show overall inflationary pressures are under control, despite concerns about last week's statement from Halifax, Britain's biggest mortgage lender, that house prices had risen 9.4 per cent in the year to August.
>
> **"**

MPEG n COMPTR *(abbr* **Moving Pictures Expert Group***)* MPEG m

mps n (abbr **master production schedule**) plan m maestro de producción

mrp n (**a**) (abbr **manufacturer's recommended price**) PVP m recomendado por el fabricante (**b**) (abbr **material requirements planning**) planificación f de los requerimientos de materiales, MRP f

MRS n (abbr **Market Research Society**) = asociación profesional británica de investigadores de mercado

MS-DOS® n (abbr **Microsoft Disk Operating System**) MS-DOS® m

MTFA n EU (abbr **medium-term financial assistance**) préstamo m a medio plazo (que solicita un banco central a otro dentro del Sistema Monetario Europeo)

MTN n FIN (abbr **medium-term note**) pagaré m a medio or Am mediano plazo

multi-access adj COMPTR multiusuario inv, de acceso múltiple

multibrand strategy n MKTG estrategia f multimarca

multicurrency n EU multidivisa f

multifunctional adj multifuncional ❑ BANKING **multifunctional card** tarjeta f multifuncional (de débito y de crédito); COMPTR **multifunctional key** tecla f multifuncional; COMPTR **multifunctional keyboard** teclado m multifuncional

multilateral adj multilateral ❑ **multilateral agreement** acuerdo m multilateral; **multilateral trade agreement** acuerdo m multilateral de comercio

multi-level marketing n marketing m de multinivel

multimedia COMPTR **1** n multimedia f or m
2 adj multimedia inv ❑ **multimedia bus** bus m multimedia; **multimedia computer** Esp ordenador m or Am computadora f multimedia **multimedia designer** diseñador(ora) m,f multimedia; **multimedia facility** instalaciones fpl multimedia; **multimedia group** grupo m multimedia; **multimedia network** red f multimedia

multimillion adj **a multimillion pound/dollar project** un proyecto multimillonario

multinational **1** n multinacional f
2 adj multinacional ❑ **multinational company** empresa for compañía f multinacional; **multinational enterprise** empresa f multinacional; **multinational marketing** marketing m multinacional

multi-part stationery n COMPTR papel m múltiple

multiple 1 n (chain store) cadena f (de tiendas)
2 adj múltiple ❑ ST EXCH **multiple application** solicitud f múltiple de acciones (por una sola persona); **multiple exchange rate** Esp tipo m or Am

tasa f de cambio múltiple; COMPTR **multiple mailboxes** buzones mpl múltiples, Am casillas fpl de correo múltiples; FIN **multiple management** gestión f múltiple de carteras; FIN **multiple option facility** crédito m con múltiples opciones de financiación; **multiple ownership** multipropiedad f; **multiple pricing** precios mpl múltiples (según el mercado); **multiple shop, multiple store** establecimiento m de una cadena

multiple-choice adj MKTG (question, questionnaire, survey) de opción múltiple

multiplex TEL **1** n múltiplex m inv
2 vt multiplexar

multiplexer n TEL múltiplex m inv

multiplexing n TEL multiplexión f

multiskilling n (of employee) polivalencia f

multi-station adj COMPTR multipuesto inv

multitasking 1 n (**a**) (of employee) (ejecución f de) tareas fpl múltiples (**b**) COMPTR multitarea f
2 adj COMPTR de multitarea

multi-user adj COMPTR multiusuario inv ❑ **multi-user software** software m multiusuario; **multi-user system** sistema m multiusuario

municipal adj municipal ❑ US FIN **municipal bond** bono m municipal; **municipal buildings** casa f consistorial

must-have 1 n artículo m imprescindible
2 adj **a must-have product** un artículo imprescindible

> **"**
>
> The Consumer Confidence Index does not establish your customers' need for a new home but it does put more pressure on how their money will be spent. Being the builder of a **must-have product** rather than a "choice" is absolutely essential as the willingness to make a major financial investment is now a more difficult commitment for today's consumer.
>
> **"**

mutual adj mutuo(a) ❑ **mutual agreement** acuerdo m mutuo; **mutual benefit society** mutua f, mutualidad f; US **mutual fund** fondo m de inversión mobiliaria; **mutual insurance** seguro m mutuo; **mutual insurance company** mutua f de seguros; **mutual status** condición f de sociedad mutua

> **"**
>
> Nationwide made much of its **mutual status** in the recent row over charges for cash machines, setting itself up as the good guy against the shareholder-owned bad guy, Barclays.
>
> **"**

mutualization n mutualización f

mutualize *vt* mutualizar

mystery *n* **mystery shopper** comprador(ora) *m,f* ficticio(a), cliente *mf* misterioso(a); **mystery shopping** compra *f* oculta, compra *f* fantasma

Nn

N/A, n/a ADMIN (*abbr* **not applicable**) *(on form)* no corresponde

NAFTA *n* (*abbr* **North American Free Trade Agreement**) NAFTA *f*, TLC *m*

naked *adj* FIN *(unsecured)* descubierto(a) ❏ FIN **naked debenture** obligación *f* sin garantía prendaria; ST EXCH **naked option** opción *f* al descubierto; ST EXCH **naked sale** venta *f* al descubierto

NAM *n* (*abbr* **National Association of Manufacturers**) = asociación nacional de fabricantes estadounidenses

Name *n* Br INS inversor(ora) *m,f* institucional de Lloyd's of London

name 1 *n* **(a)** *(of person, company, account)* nombre *m*; **the shares are in my name** las acciones están a mi nombre; **the company trades under the name of Scandia** la empresa realiza sus operaciones comerciales bajo el nombre de Scandia ❏ **name brand** marca *f* conocida; ST EXCH **name day** día *m* de intercambio de nombres, día de los boletos; MKTG **name licensing** concesión *f* de licencia de marca
  (b) *(reputation)* nombre *m*, reputación *f*; **to have a good/bad name** tener buena/mala fama; **they have a name for prompt service** tienen fama de ofrecer un servicio rápido
  2 *vt* *(appoint)* nombrar; **she's been named president** la han nombrado presidenta

NAO *n* (*abbr* **National Audit Office**) ≃ Tribunal *m* de Cuentas

narcodollars *npl* narcodólares *mpl*

narration, narrative *n* ACCT descripción *f*

narrow *adj* *(market)* estrecho(a) ❏ **narrow money** circulación *f* fiduciaria

NASD *n* ST EXCH (*abbr* **National Association of Securities Dealers**) = asociación nacional estadounidense de operadores de Bolsa

Nasdaq *n* ST EXCH (*abbr* **National Association of Securities Dealers Automated Quotation**) (índice *m*) Nasdaq *m*

nation *n* *(people)* nación *f*, pueblo *m*; *(country)* nación, país *m*

national 1 *n* *(person)* ciudadano(a) *m,f*, súbdito(a) *m,f*
  2 *adj* nacional ❏ **national accounting** contabilidad *f* nacional, cuentas *fpl* nacionales; **national airline** compañía *f* aérea nacional; **National Audit Office** ≃ Tribunal *m* de Cuentas; **national bank** banco *m* nacional; **the national debt** la deuda pública; *Br Formerly* **National Enterprise Board** ≃ Instituto *m* Nacional de Industria; BANKING **National Giro** giro *f* postal; **national government** gobierno *m* nacional; *Br* **National Health Service** Servicio *m* Nacional de Salud (británico); **national income** renta *f* nacional; *Br* **National Insurance** Seguridad *f* Social (británica); *Br* **National Insurance contributions** aportaciones *fpl* or cotizaciones *fpl* a la Seguridad Social; *Br* **National Insurance number** número *m* de afiliación a la Seguridad Social; *US* **National Labor Relations Board** Junta *f* Nacional de Relaciones Laborales, = organismo federal estadounidense encargado del arbitraje y la conciliación en los conflictos de trabajo; **national market** mercado *m* nacional; **national press** prensa *f* nacional; **national product** producto *m* nacional; **National Savings and Investments** = entidad de ahorro estatal británica; **National Savings Certificate** = bono destinado a los pequeños inversores emitido por el gobierno británico

nationalization *n* nacionalización *f*

nationalize *vt* nacionalizar

natural *adj* natural ❏ INS **natural disaster** catástrofe *f* natural; **natural economy** economía *f* natural; COMPTR **natural language** lenguaje *m* natural; **natural life** *(of company, product)* vida *f* útil; LAW **natural person** persona *f* física; **natural resources** recursos *mpl* naturales; **natural wastage** *(in job numbers)* bajas *fpl* naturales

> 20 percent of staff, although he said it was too early to say where the ax will fall, or how many people will go. "Staff are being offered voluntary redundancy, and we are hoping to achieve some of the reductions by **natural wastage**, but the numbers involved mean that some layoffs may be inevitable, he said.

NAV n (abbr **net asset value**) valor m activo neto

navigate COMPTR **1** vt navegar por; **to navigate the Net** navegar por Internet
2 vi navegar

navigation n navegación f ❏ COMPTR **navigation bar** barra f de navegación **navigation company** compañía f naviera; **navigation dues** tasas fpl portuarias

NBA n Formerly (abbr **net book agreement**) acuerdo m de precios mínimos (fijados por la editorial)

NBV n ACCT (abbr **net book value**) valor m neto contable or en libros

NDP n ACCT (abbr **net domestic product**) PIN m

near adj **near miss** (in industrial accident reporting) cuasi accidente m; ST EXCH **near money** cuasidinero m, Am cuasimoneda f; ST EXCH **near month** mes m más próximo

need n MKTG necesidad f; **needs and wants** necesidades y deseos ❏ **needs analysis** análisis m de necesidades; **needs assessment** evaluación f de necesidades; **need identification** identificación f de necesidades; **need level** nivel m de necesidades; **need market** mercado m de necesidades; **need recognition** reconocimiento m de la necesidad; **need set** conjunto m de necesidades; **needs study** estudio m de necesidades

needs-and-wants exploration n MKTG investigación f de necesidades y deseos

needs-based adj MKTG basado(a) en las necesidades ❏ **needs-based market** mercado m basado en las necesidades; **needs-based segmentation** segmentación f por necesidades

negative adj negativo(a) ❏ **negative amortization** amortización f negativa; **negative amortization loan** préstamo m de amortización inicial negativa; **negative equity** patrimonio m negativo; FIN **negative income tax** impuesto m compensatorio teórico (para las personas con los ingresos más bajos); Br FIN **negative interest rate** Esp tipo m de interés negativo, Am tasa f de interés negativa; **negative net worth** patrimonio m negativo; FIN **negative pledge clause** cláusula f de pignoración negativa; **negative prescription** prescripción f negativa; FIN **negative saving** ahorro m negativo

> "
> About 65,000 homeowners in Hong Kong are in **negative equity**, involving loans of HK$127 million (about US$16.3 million), 23% of total outstanding mortgage loans held by banks, the Hong Kong Monetary Authority said Tuesday. The number of people in **negative equity**, whose outstanding loan exceeds the current market value of their property, represents 14% of total mortgage borrowers, the territory's quasi-central bank said in a statement.
> "

neglected adj ST EXCH (shares) depreciado(a) (por los inversores)

negligence n negligencia f; **through negligence** por negligencia ❏ INS **negligence clause** cláusula f de negligencia

negotiability n negociabilidad f

negotiable adj (salary, fee, bill) negociable; **not negotiable** (on cheque) no negociable ❏ **negotiable instrument** instrumento m negociable; **negotiable paper** efecto m negociable; FIN **negotiable stock** títulos mpl negociables

negotiate 1 vt (business deal, loan, fee, bill) negociar; **price to be negotiated** precio a convenir
2 vi negociar (**with** con); **the unions will have to negotiate with the management for higher pay** los sindicatos tendrán que negociar con la patronal (para conseguir) un aumento salarial

negotiated settlement n acuerdo m de compromiso

negotiating table n mesa f de negociaciones; **it's time to sit round the negotiating table and discuss our differences** es hora de que nos sentemos a la mesa de negociaciones y discutamos nuestras diferencias

negotiation n negociación f; **under negotiation** en proceso de negociación; **to be in negotiation with sb** estar en negociaciones con alguien; **to enter into negotiations (with sb)** entablar negociaciones (con alguien); **to break off/resume negotiations** romper/reanudar las negociaciones; **the pay deal is subject to negotiation** la remuneración está pendiente de negociación

negotiator n negociador(ora) m,f

nervous adj (market) nervioso(a)

nest egg n Esp ahorrillos mpl, Am ahorritos mpl

> "
> Nervous about your **nest egg**? If it's loaded with stocks, you should be. Stocks could easily sink further, tread water, or rise slowly. To minimize the damage to your portfolio, you need some holdings that don't move in tandem with equities. The most obvious vehicle

is bonds, but you can further protect yourself against market swings by including other alternatives, such as hedge funds, real estate, and oil and gas.

"

.net COMPTR .net

Net *n Fam* COMPTR **the Net** la Red

net 1 *adj (weight, price, profit, interest)* neto(a); **the net result is...** el resultado neto es...; **net, due and payable** líquido, vencido y exigible □ *net amount* importe *m* neto; *net assets* activo *m* neto, patrimonio *m* neto; *net asset value* valor *m* patrimonial neto; *Formerly* **Net Book Agreement** acuerdo *m* de precios mínimos *(fijados por la editorial)*; ACCT *net book value* valor *m* neto contable *or* en libros; *net capital expenditure* gastos *mpl* netos de capital; ACCT *net cash flow* flujo *m* de caja neto; ST EXCH *net change* variación *f* neta; *net contributor* contribuidor(ora) *m,f* neto(a); *net cost* costo *m or Esp* coste *m* neto; ACCT *net current assets* activo *m* circulante neto; *net discounted cash flow method* método *m* de capitalización de flujos de caja; *net dividend* dividendo *m* neto; ECON *net domestic product Esp* producto *m* interior neto, *Am* producto interno neto; *net earnings (of company)* beneficios *mpl* netos; *(of worker)* renta *f* neta; *net income (in accounts)* ingresos *mpl* netos; *(of individual)* renta *f* neta, ingresos *mpl* netos; *net interest income* ingresos *mpl* financieros netos; *net interest margin* margen *m* neto de intereses; *net loss* pérdida *f* neta; *net margin* margen *m* neto; *net national income* renta *f* nacional neta; *net national product* producto *m* nacional neto; *net operating profit* beneficio *m* neto de explotación; *net present value* valor *m* actual neto; ACCT *net present value rate* tasa *f* de actualización; *net proceeds* beneficios *mpl* netos, beneficios *mpl* líquidos; *net profit* beneficio *m* neto, ganancia *f* neta; *net profit margin* margen *m* de beneficio neto, margen *m* de ganancia neta; *net profit ratio* tasa *f* neta de beneficio; ACCT *net realizable value* valor *m* neto de realización; *net receipts* ingresos *mpl* netos; *net registered tonnage* tonelaje *m* de registro neto; *net residual value* valor *m* residual neto; *net result* resultado *m* neto; *net return* rendimiento *m* neto; *net salary* sueldo *m* neto; *net tangible assets* activos *mpl* fijos materiales netos; *net tonnage* tonelaje *m* de registro neto; *net total* total *m* neto; *net value* valor *m* neto; ACCT *net variance* desviación *f* neta *(entre el coste real y el coste estándar)*; *net working capital* capital *m* circulante neto; *net worth* patrimonio *m* neto

2 *n* FIN rendimiento *m* neto □ *net payable* importe *m* neto a pagar

3 *vt (of person, company)* tener unos ingresos netos de; *(of sale)* suponer un ingreso neto de; *(profit)* suponer un beneficio neto de; **he nets**

£20,000 **a year** gana 20.000 libras netas *or* limpias al año

4 *adv* **net of tax** después de impuestos; **net of VAT** después del IVA

<hr>

Net asset value (NAV), worked out by dividing the value of the portfolio, less borrowings, by the number of shares in issue, tells you how much each share can claim of the trust's assets. Discount or premium to NAV, the gap between the share price and the asset value, helps measure a trust's popularity.

"

nethead *n Fam* COMPTR loco(a) *m,f* por Internet

netiquette *n* COMPTR netiqueta *f*

netizen *n* COMPTR ciudadano(a) *m,f* de la Red, ciuredano(a) *m,f*

netspeak *n* COMPTR jerga *f* de Internet

network 1 *n* COMPTR red *f* □ *network administrator* administrador(ora) *m,f* de red; *network card* tarjeta *f* de red; *network computer Esp* ordenador *m or Am* computadora *f* de red; *network driver* controlador *m* de red; *network management* gestión *f* de red; *network manager* gestor(ora) *m,f* de red; *network operating system* sistema *m* operativo de red; *network server* servidor *m* de red; *network software* software *m* de red; *network traffic* tráfico *m* de la red

2 *vt* COMPTR conectar en red □ *networked system* sistema *m* en red

3 *vi (make contacts)* establecer contactos

networking *n* **(a)** COMPTR conexión *f* en red; **to have networking capabilities** *(terminal)* poderse conectar a una red **(b)** *(making contacts)* establecimiento *m* de contactos profesionales

<hr>

Daimler-Chrysler has 13,000 people working in its Auburn Hills, Michigan headquarters. Kathryn Lee, staff labor programs administrator, is proud that her company supports a Women's Network Group and provides a number of opportunities for after-hours **networking**, including guest speakers and presentations.

"

new *adj* nuevo(a) □ *new borrowings* endeudamiento *m* adicional; MKTG *new buy situation* nueva situación *f* de compra *(en la que el comprador tiene contacto por primera vez con el producto y con el vendedor)*; *new capital* capital *m* adicional; *new economy* nueva economía *f*; ST EXCH *new issue* nueva emisión *f* de acciones; ST EXCH *new issue market* mercado *m* de nuevas emisiones; *the new media* los nuevos medios; FIN *new money* dinero *m* fresco; MKTG *new product* producto *m* nuevo; MKTG *new product*

development desarrollo m de nuevos productos; MKTG **new product marketing** marketing m de nuevos productos; **new shares** acciones fpl nuevas

newbie n Fam COMPTR novato(a) m,f

newly industrialized country n país m de reciente industrialización

news n (a) (information) noticias fpl (b) (programme) (on TV) informativo m, telediario m, Am noticiero m, Andes, RP noticioso m; (on radio) noticiario m, informativo, Am noticiero, Andes, RP noticioso ❏ **news agency** agencia f de noticias; **news analyst** comentarista mf (político, financiero, etc.); **news bulletin** boletín m de noticias; **news conference** rueda f de prensa; **news desk** (programme) programa m de noticias; **news editor** redactor(ora) m,f de informativos; **news service** servicios mpl informativos (c) COMPTR noticias fpl ❏ **news article** artículo m (de Usenet); **news reader** lector m de noticias; **news server** servidor m de grupos de noticias

newsgroup n COMPTR grupo m de noticias

newsletter n boletín m informativo

newsocracy n sociedad f mediatizada

newspaper n (publication) periódico m; (daily) periódico, diario m ❏ **newspaper advertisement** anuncio m de periódico; **newspaper advertising** publicidad f en prensa; **newspaper article** artículo m de periódico; **newspaper clipping, newspaper cutting** recorte m de periódico; **newspaper report** artículo m de periódico

newssheet n boletín m informativo

new-to-the-company product n MKTG producto m nuevo para la empresa

new-to-the-world product n MKTG producto m nuevo (para el mundo)

next-day delivery n entrega f al día siguiente

NF BANKING (abbr **no funds**) sin fondos

NGDO n (abbr **non-governmental development organization**) ONGD

NGO n (abbr **non-governmental organization**) ONG f

NHS n (abbr **National Health Service**) = servicio de salud pública británico

NI n Br (abbr **National Insurance**) Seguridad f Social (británica)

NIC n (a) Br (abbr **National Insurance contributions**) aportaciones fpl or cotizaciones fpl a la seguridad social (b) (abbr **newly-industrialized country**) PRI m, país m de reciente industrialización

niche n MKTG (in market) nicho m ❏ **niche market** nicho m de mercado; **niche marketing** marketing m de nichos or segmentación; **niche player** empresa f orientada hacia un nicho de mercado;

niche product producto m para un nicho de mercado

nickel-and-dime store n US = tienda de productos muy baratos

NIF n BANKING (abbr **note issuance facility**) servicio m de emisión de pagarés

night n noche f ❏ US BANKING **night depository** cajero m nocturno; **night rate** tarifa f nocturna; Br BANKING **night safe** cajero m nocturno; **night shift** turno m de noche; **to be on night shift** trabajar de noches; **night work** trabajo m de noche

Nikkei Index n ST EXCH índice m Nikkei

nil 1 n cero m; **the balance is nil** el saldo es cero **2** adj nulo(a), cero ❏ **nil balance** saldo m cero; **nil growth** crecimiento m cero; **nil premium** prima f cero; **nil profit** rendimiento m cero

nine-to-five 1 adv **to work nine-to-five** trabajar de nueve a cinco, tener horario de oficina **2** adj **a nine-to-five mentality** = una mentalidad de funcionario (que cumple el horario de trabajo al pie de la letra); **a nine-to-five job** un trabajo de oficina (de nueve a cinco)

nine-to-fiver n US **to be a nine-to-fiver** trabajar de nueve a cinco

NIOSH n (abbr **National Institute for Occupational Safety and Health**) = organismo federal estadounidense encargado de la prevención de enfermedades y accidentes laborales

NLRB n (abbr **National Labor Relations Board**) = organismo federal estadounidense encargado del arbitraje y la conciliación en los conflictos de trabajo

NNP n (abbr **net national product**) PNN m

no-claims bonus n INS bonificación f por no siniestralidad

node n COMPTR nodo m

no-fault insurance n US seguro m a todo riesgo

noise n COMPTR ruido m

no-load fund n ST EXCH fondo m de inversión sin comisiones

nominal adj (**a**) (neglible, token) (price, fee, rent) simbólico(a); **a nominal contribution of one pound a year** una contribución simbólica de una libra al año; **a nominal amount** una cantidad simbólica
(**b**) (in name only) nominal; **he was the nominal president of the company** era el presidente nominal de la empresa
(**c**) ACCT **nominal account** cuenta f general de gastos; FIN **nominal capital** capital m nominal; FIN **nominal interest rate** Esp tipo m or Am tasa f de interés nominal; **nominal ledger** libro m mayor; **nominal partner** socio(a) m,f nominal; **nominal price** precio m nominal; **nominal quote** cotización f nominal; **nominal rate** Esp tipo m or Am tasa f de interés nominal; **nominal value** valor m nominal; **nominal wages** salario m nominal; **nominal yield** rendimiento m nominal

nominate vt (**a**) (appoint) nombrar, designar; **to nominate sb to a post** nombrar or designar a alguien para un puesto; **he was nominated chairman** lo nombraron presidente (**b**) (propose) proponer; (for award) proponer como candidato(a), nominar; **to nominate sb for a post** proponer a alguien (como candidato) para un puesto

nomination n (proposal) propuesta f; (for an award) candidatura f, nominación f

nominee n (**a**) (to post) (proposed) candidato(a) m,f; (appointed) persona f nombrada (**b**) ST EXCH **nominee account** cuenta f del depositario; **nominee company** sociedad f depositaria; **nominee name** nombre m del depositario; **nominee shareholder** tenedor m de participaciones accionariales; **nominee shareholding** tenencia f de participaciones accionariales

non-acceptance n BANKING (of bill of exchange) no aceptación f, falta f de aceptación

non-accruing loan n préstamo m que no contabiliza intereses impagados or Am impagos

non-adopter n MKTG no adoptador m, = persona que nunca compra determinados productos ni adopta ciertos estilos

nonassessable adj INS (policy) no gravable

non-bank adj no bancario(a)

non-business marketing n marketing m altruista

noncallable adj FIN (bond) no rescatable

nonclearing member n ST EXCH miembro m no liquidador

non-competition clause n cláusula f de no concurrencia

non-contributory pension n pensión f no contributiva

non-convertible adj (currency) no convertible, inconvertible

non-core adj (businesses, activities, assets) secundario(a)

non-cumulative adj FIN (shares) no acumulativo(a) ▫ **non-cumulative quantity discount** descuento m no acumulativo por volumen

non-current liabilities npl ACCT pasivo m exigible a largo plazo, pasivo circulante

nondeductible adj FIN no desgravable

non-delivery n (of goods) no entrega f; **in the event of non-delivery** en el supuesto de no entrega

non-durable goods npl material m fungible

non-dutiable adj CUSTOMS franco(a) or exento(a) de aranceles or derechos de aduanas

non-equity share n ST EXCH título m de renta fija

non-execution n (of contract) incumplimiento m

non-executive director n consejero(era) m,f sin cargo ejecutivo

nonfood 1 n nonfoods artículos mpl no comestibles
2 adj (item) no comestible; (sector) de artículos no comestibles

non-forfeiture clause n INS cláusula f de no caducidad

non-fulfilment n (of contract) incumplimiento m

non-governmental adj **non-governmental development organization** organización f no gubernamental de desarrollo; **non-governmental organization** organización f no gubernamental

non-interlaced adj COMPTR no entrelazado(a)

non-liability n LAW no responsabilidad f ▫ **non-liability clause** cláusula f de no responsabilidad

nonmarketable adj FIN no trasferible

non-negotiable adj (demand, cheque, note) no negociable

non-participating adj INS (policy) sin participación en beneficios; ST EXCH (share) sin derecho a participación

non-payment n impago m, falta f de pago; **in case of non-payment** en el supuesto de impago or falta de pago

non-performing loan n BANKING crédito m moroso

non-probability adj MKTG **non-probability method** (of sampling) método m no probabilístico; **non-probability sample** muestra f no probabilística; **non-probability sampling** muestreo m no probabilístico

non-productive adj ECON no productivo(a)

non-profit-making organization, non-profit organization n Br organización f sin ánimo de lucro

non-qualifying policy n = póliza sin desgravación fiscal

non-quoted adj ST EXCH no cotizado(a)

non-random adj MKTG **non-random sample** muestra f no aleatoria; **non-random sampling** muestreo m no aleatorio

non-recourse finance n FIN financiación f sin posibilidad de recurso

non-recurring expenditure n gastos mpl extraordinarios

non-refundable n a fondo perdido, sin posibilidad de reembolso

non-resident account n BANKING cuenta f de no residente

non-returnable adj (bottle, container) no retornable; (packaging) desechable; (deposit) no reembolsable, sin posibilidad de reembolso; **sales goods are non-returnable** no se admite la devolución de los artículos rebajados

non-tariff barrier n barrera f no arancelaria

non-taxable adj ADMIN (revenue) exento(a) de impuestos

non-trading adj **non-trading company** empresa f no comercial; **non-trading day** día m festivo; **non-trading hours** (for shop) horario m no comercial; ST EXCH **during non-trading hours** fuera del horario cle contratación

non-union, non-unionized adj (worker) no sindicado(a)

nonvoting adj FIN, ST EXCH (share) sin derecho a voto

non-warranty n no garantía f, exención f de garantía □ **non-warranty clause** cláusula f de exención de garantía

no-par adj FIN sin valor nominal

no-quibble guarantee n garantía f sin condiciones

normal adj MKTG **normal distribution curve** curva f de distribución normal; ST EXCH **normal market size** = criterio de clasificación utilizado en la compraventa de valores en la Bolsa de Londres; **normal retirement age** edad f normal de jubilación

North American Free Trade Agreement n Tratado m de Libre Comercio de América del Norte

notarial adj LAW (functions, procedure, deed) notarial

notarize vt LAW autenticar, legalizar □ **notarized contract** contrato m otorgado ante notario; **notarized copy** copia f notarial or legalizada ante notario; **notarized deed** escritura f notarial

notary n LAW **notary (public)** notario(a) m,f, Andes, CRica, RP escribano(a) m,f

note 1 n (a) (information, reminder) nota f □ FIN **note of hand** pagaré m, letra f a propio cargo (b) esp Br (banknote) billete m; **a ten-pound note** un billete de diez libras □ FIN **note issue** emisión f de papel moneda; **note issue facility** servicio m de emisión de pagarés 2 vt (observe, notice) notar, advertir; **you will note that there is an error in the account** advertirá que existe un error en la cuenta

notebook n COMPTR **notebook (computer)** Esp ordenador m or Am computadora f portátil

not-for-profit organization n organización f sin ánimo de lucro

notice n (a) (notification) aviso m; **until further notice** hasta nuevo aviso □ **notice of receipt** acuse m de recibo; **notice of withdrawal** aviso m de retirada
(b) (warning) aviso m; (of resignation, redundancy) notificación f, (pre)aviso m; **to give** or **hand in one's notice** presentar la dimisión, despedirse; **fifty people have been given their notice** cincuenta personas han recibido notificaciones de despido; **what notice do you require?** ¿con cuánta antelación tengo que avisar de que dejo el trabajo?; **employees must give three months' notice** los empleados deben avisar con tres meses de antelación si desean dejar su trabajo; **to give sb notice (of sth)** (of decision, resignation, redundancy) notificar a alguien (de algo); **can be delivered at three days' notice** se puede entregar en un plazo de tres días; BANKING **deposit at seven days' notice** depósito con preaviso de siete días □ **notice of dismissal** aviso m de despido
(c) (intent to vacate premises) **notice (to quit)** notificación f de desalojo; **to be under notice to quit** haber recibido una notificación de desalojo; **to give sb a month's notice** (landlord) darle a alguien un plazo de un mes para abandonar el inmueble

> **"**
> The toughest part came when a meeting that took two months to schedule with a director of e-business for a large manufacturer didn't go the way she hoped it would. The official told Kovacs and York that he had given his **notice to quit** because he was fed up. He'd wasted 18 months setting up a Web storefront only to hear from management that it was being scrapped.
> **"**

notification *n* notificación *f*; **to give sb notification of sth** dar a alguien notificación de algo; **you will receive notification by mail** recibirá notificación por correo

notify *vt* notificar; **to notify sb (of sth)** notificar (algo) a alguien

notional *adj* teórico(a), hipotético(a) ❑ **notional income** ingresos *mpl* teóricos; **notional rent** renta *f* teórica

novation *n* LAW novación *f*

NOW account *n* US BANKING cuenta *f* a la vista con interés

NPD *n* MKTG (*abbr* **new product development**) desarrollo *m* de productos nuevos

NPV *n* ACCT (*abbr* **net present value**) VAN *m* ❑ **NPV rate** tasa *f* de actualización

NRV *n* FIN (*abbr* **net realizable value**) valor *m* neto de realización

NSF BANKING (*abbr* **not sufficient funds**) sin fondos suficientes

nuisance tax *n* US impuesto *m* indirecto *(visto como algo negativo)*

> His most recent bit of mischief is a proposal to put a measure on the November ballot that seeks to impose a nickel-a-bullet tax on every round of ammunition sold in California. Perata's justification for another **nuisance tax** is that it would raise money to offset the costs of emergency and trauma centers that treat people with gunshot wounds.

null *adj* LAW *(invalid)* nulo(a); **null and void** nulo(a) (y sin valor); **to declare a contract null and void** declarar un contrato nulo (y sin valor); **the contract was rendered null and void** el contrato quedó invalidado

nullification *n* anulación *f*, invalidación *f*

nullify *vt (claim, contract)* anular, invalidar

number 1 *n* número *m* ❑ COMPTR **number crunching** cálculos *mpl* numéricos largos y complicados; **number key** tecla *f* numérica; **numbers lock** bloqueo *m* numérico; **numbers lock key** tecla *f* de bloqueo numérico

2 *vt (consecutively)* numerar ❑ **numbered account** cuenta *f* numerada

numeric COMPTR **1** *n* **numerics** caracteres *m* numéricos

2 *adj* numérico(a) ❑ **numeric field** campo *m* numérico; **numeric keypad** teclado *m* numérico

numerical *adj* numérico(a) ❑ COMPTR **numerical analysis** análisis *m inv* numérico; **numerical data** datos *mpl* numéricos; **numerical distribution** distribución *f* numérica; **numerical keypad** teclado *m* numérico

num lock *n* COMPTR (*abbr* **numbers lock**) bloq num; **the num lock is on** los números están bloqueados ❑ **num lock key** tecla *f* de bloqueo numérico

NYMEX *n* ST EXCH (*abbr* **New York Mercantile Exchange**) NYMEX *m*, = mercado de petróleo y metales de Nueva York

NYSE *n* ST EXCH (*abbr* **New York Stock Exchange**) Bolsa *f* de Nueva York

Oo

objective n objetivo m; **to achieve** or **attain one's objective** conseguir or alcanzar el objetivo; **our objective for this year is to increase sales by 10%** nuestro objetivo para este año consiste en aumentar las ventas en un 10%

objectivity n objetividad f

object-oriented, object-orientated adj COMPTR orientado(a) a objeto

obligate vt US FIN (funds, credits) afectar

obligation n US FIN obligación f

obligee n FIN (creditor) acreedor(ora) m,f; (bondholder) obligatario(a) m,f

oblique n (slash) barra f oblicua

o.b.o. (abbr **or best offer**) negociable, o mejor oferta

observational research n MKTG investigación f por observación

obsolescence n obsolescencia f ❑ INS **obsolescence clause** = cláusula de una póliza de seguros que regula los cambios en la cobertura en caso de obsolescencia del objeto asegurado

obsolescent adj que se está quedando obsoleto(a), obsolescente

obtain 1 vt obtener, conseguir
2 vi (practice) imperar; (rule) regir; **practices obtaining in British banking** las prácticas imperantes en la banca británica; **this new system will obtain as from next week** este nuevo sistema se aplicará a partir de la semana que viene

obvious defect n defecto m evidente

occupancy n (**a**) (of building) periodo m de alquiler or Méx renta (**b**) LAW ocupación f

occupant n (of building) ocupante mf; (tenant) inquilino(a) m,f

occupation n (**a**) (profession) profesión f, ocupación f; **please state your name and occupation** por favor, indique su nombre y profesión; **what is his occupation?** ¿a qué se dedica? (**b**) (of building) ocupación f; **the premises are ready for immediate occupation** el inmueble está listo para entrar a vivir

occupational adj profesional, laboral ❑ **occupational accident** accidente m laboral; **occupational disease** enfermedad f profesional; **occupational hazard** IND riesgo m laboral; Fam gaje m del oficio; Br **occupational pension fund** fondo m de pensiones de empleo or de empresa;

Br **occupational pension scheme** plan m de pensiones de empleo or de empresa; **occupational safety** seguridad f en el puesto de trabajo

occupier n Br ocupante mf

occupy vt ocupar

OCR n COMPTR (**a**) (abbr **optical character reader**) OCR m, lector m óptico de caracteres (**b**) (abbr **optical character recognition**) OCR m, reconocimiento m óptico de caracteres ❑ **OCR font** fuente f OCR; **OCR reader** lector m OCR; **OCR software** software m de OCR

OD 1 n (abbr **overdraft**) descubierto m, saldo m negativo or deudor
2 adj (abbr **overdrawn**) en descubierto

ODA n (abbr **Overseas Development Administration**) = organismo británico de ayuda al desarrollo en el Tercer Mundo

odd-even adj MKTG **odd-even price** precio m psicológico (no acabado en un número redondo); **odd-even pricing** fijación f de precios psicológicos

odd lot n (**a**) (of goods) lote m de artículos variados (**b**) ST EXCH (of shares) lote m con menos de 100 acciones

odd-lot adj ST EXCH **odd-lot order** = orden de compraventa de lotes de acciones de número inferior a 100; **odd-lot trading** = compraventa de lotes de acciones de número inferior a 100

odd-lotter n US ST EXCH = inversor que negocia en lotes de menos de 100 acciones

odd-numbers adj **odd-numbers price** precio m no acabado en un número redondo; **odd-numbers pricing** precios mpl no acabados en un número redondo

OE n (abbr **original equipment**) equipo m original

OECD n (abbr **Organization for Economic Co-operation and Development**) OCDE f

OEIC n (abbr **open-ended investment company**) ≃ SIMCAV f

OEM n (abbr **original equipment manufacturer**) fabricante m de equipo original, OEM m

OFEX n ST EXCH (abbr **off-exchange**) = plataforma de contratación electrónica para acciones no listadas y cotizadas de Londres

off-balance sheet adj ACCT extracontable, no

incluido(a) en el balance de situación ❑ **off-bal-ance sheet item** elemento *m* no incluido en el balance de situación, partida *f* extracontable; **off-balance sheet transaction** transacción *f* no incluida en el balance de situación, transacción extracontable

off-brand *adj* de marca desconocida

> **"**
>
> In 1960 Harry Zimmerman introduced value. He opened his first Service Merchandise catalog showroom, providing consumers an alternative to both discount stores that offered **off-brand** merchandise and traditional retailers who required full retail mark-up.
>
> **"**

offer 1 *n* oferta *f*; **to make sb an offer (for sth)** hacer a alguien una oferta (por algo); **the house is under offer** han hecho una oferta por la casa; **what is on offer in the negotiations?** ¿qué ofrecen en las negociaciones?; **these goods are on offer this week** estos artículos están de oferta esta semana; **£500 or nearest offer** 500 libras negociables ❑ INS **offer of cover** oferta *f* de cobertura; **offer price** *(of shares, in takeover)* precio *m* de oferta; ST EXCH **offer by prospectus** oferta *f* de venta directa de acciones; ST EXCH **offer to purchase** oferta *f* pública de adquisición de acciones; ST EXCH **offer for sale** oferta *f* pública de venta de acciones
2 *vt* ofrecer (**for** por); **he was offered the post** le ofrecieron el puesto; **to offer goods for sale** tener productos en venta; **to offer one's services** ofrecer sus servicios

offered price *n* precio *m* de oferta

offeree *n* FIN, LAW = destinatario de la oferta

offering *n* *(of new shares)* oferta *f* ❑ US **offering circular** circular *f* de información

offeror *n* FIN, LAW ofertante *mf*, oferente *mf*

off-exchange *adj* ST EXCH *(transaction, contract, market)* fuera de bolsa

office *n* (**a**) *(place) (premises)* oficina *f*; *(room)* despacho *m*, oficina; *(of lawyer)* despacho, bufete *m*; *(of architect)* estudio *m*; **he's out of the office at the moment** en este momento no se encuentra en la oficina; **for office use only** *(on form)* uso interno exclusivamente ❑ **office account** cuenta *f* (bancaria) de la oficina *(de una empresa)*; **office address** dirección *f* de la oficina; **office automation** ofimática *f*; **office block** bloque *m* de oficinas; **office building** edificio *m* de oficinas; **office equipment** equipo *m* de oficina; **office expenses** gastos *mpl* de oficina; **office furniture** mobiliario *m* de oficina; **office hours** horas *fpl* or horario *m* de oficina; **office IT** ofimática *f*; **office job** trabajo *m* de oficina; **office junior** auxiliar *mf* de oficina; **office management** gestión *f* de oficinas; **office manager**

gerente *mf* de oficina; **office rent** alquiler *m* or Méx renta *f* de oficina; **office space** espacio *m* para oficinas; **office staff** personal *m* de oficina; **office supplies** material *m* de oficina; **office work** trabajo *m* de oficina; **office worker** oficinista *mf*
(**b**) *(position)* cargo *m*; **to be in office, to hold office** *(in a job)* ocupar el cargo; *(in power)* estar en el poder; **to be out of office** estar fuera del gobierno; **to leave office** dejar el cargo
(**c**) *(government department)* oficina *f*; **the local tax office** la oficina local de Hacienda ❑ **the Office of Fair Trading** = organismo británico que vela por los intereses de los consumidores y regula las prácticas comerciales; **the Office of Management and Budget** = organismo que ayuda al presidente estadounidense a elaborar los presupuestos del estado

officeholder *n* **the previous officeholder** la persona que ocupaba el cargo anteriormente

officer *n* *(in local government)* responsable *mf*; *(in trade union)* delegado(a) *m,f*; *(of company)* directivo(a) *m,f*; *(of association, institution)* directivo(a), dirigente *mf*

official 1 *n* *(representative)* representante *mf*; *(in public sector)* funcionario(a) *m,f*; **a bank official** un representante del banco; **a trade union official** un delegado sindical; **a government official** un funcionario del gobierno
2 *adj* oficial; **his appointment will be made official tomorrow** su nombramiento se hará oficial mañana; **she's here on official business** está aquí por motivos oficiales; **to go through (the) official channels** seguir los trámites oficiales; **to act in one's official capacity** actuar en el ejercicio de sus funciones; **she was speaking in her official capacity as General Secretary** hablaba en calidad de Secretaria General ❑ **official assignee** *(in bankruptcy)* síndico(a) *m,f*; ST EXCH **official broker** corredor(ora) *m,f* or broker *mf* oficial *(de la Bolsa de Londres)*; ST EXCH **official brokerage company** = sociedad de valores oficial de la Bolsa de Londres; **official document** documento *m* oficial; **official exchange rate** Esp tipo *m* or Am tasa *f* de cambio oficial; **official letter** carta *f* oficial; **official liquidator** comisario(a) *m,f* de quiebra; ST EXCH **official list** lista *f* oficial; ST EXCH **official market** bolsa *f* oficial; **official price** *(of commodity)* precio *m* oficial; ST EXCH **official quotation** cotización *f* oficial; BANKING **official rate** cambio *m* oficial; FIN **official rate of interest** Esp tipo *m* or Am tasa *f* de interés oficial; **official receiver** síndico(a) *m,f*; **the official receiver has been called in** han solicitado la declaración de quiebra; **official receivership** administración *f* judicial; **official report** informe *m* oficial; Br **Official Secrets Act** ≃ ley *f* de secretos oficiales or de Estado; **official strike** huelga *f* oficial

officialese *n* Fam jerga *f* administrativa

"

However, five centuries later, it is a matter of debate whether the incomprehensible **officialese** widely used by the French authorities is any easier to understand than Latin – or possibly, double Dutch. Never use one word when half a dozen will do, appears to be the rule of thumb, and make sure as many as possible are archaic and totally incomprehensible without the aid of a dictionary. But help may finally be at hand. A government body has just been set up with the task of simplifying the language of French bureaucracy.

"

officially adv oficialmente; **he has now been officially appointed** su nombramiento ya se ha hecho oficial

off-line 1 adj (**a**) COMPTR (processing) fuera de línea; (printer) desconectado(a); **to be off-line** estar desconectado(a), no estar conectado(a); **to go off-line** desconectarse □ **off-line mode** modo m desconectado; **off-line reader** lector m off-line (**b**) IND (production) individualizado(a) **2** adv fuera de línea; **to work off-line** trabajar desconectado(a)

offload vt (goods) descargar

offloading n (of goods) descarga f □ **offloading platform** muelle m de descarga

off-peak 1 adj (electricity, travel, phone call) en horario de tarifa reducida, en horas valle □ **off-peak hours** horario m de tarifa reducida, horas fpl valle **2** adv en horario de tarifa reducida, en horas valle

off-price adj US (goods) a precios reducidos; (store) de precios reducidos(porque vende restos de serie, artículos de tiendas en quiebra, etc.)

off-season 1 n temporada f baja **2** adj de temporada baja □ **off-season tariff** tarifa f de temporada baja **3** adv en temporada baja

offset 1 n ACCT compensación f □ **offset agreement** acuerdo m compensatorio **2** vt (compensate for) compensar; **to offset losses against tax** deducir las pérdidas de los impuestos; **any wage increase will be offset by inflation** cualquier aumento salarial se verá contrarrestado por la inflación; **we'll have to offset our research investment against long-term returns** tendremos que compensar la inversión en investigación con las ganancias a largo plazo

offsetting entry n ACCT asiento m de regularización

offshoot n (subsidiary) filial f

offshore 1 adj (interests, account, shares) en paraíso fiscal, offshore □ **offshore banking**

operaciones fpl bancarias en paraísos fiscales; **offshore company** empresa f inscrita en paraíso fiscal; **offshore fund** fondo m colocado en paraíso fiscal; **offshore investment** inversión f en paraíso fiscal **2** adv **to keep sth offshore** tener algo en un paraíso fiscal

off-the-peg research n MKTG investigación f basada en datos existentes

off-the-shelf adj (goods) estándar □ **off-the-shelf company** empresa f "lista para usar", = empresa inscrita en el Registro Mercantil, pero que no realiza operaciones comerciales ni tiene directivos

OFT n (abbr **Office of Fair Trading**) = organismo británico que vela por los intereses de los consumidores y regula las prácticas comerciales

"

Following the publication today of a proposed decision by the Office of Fair Trading (**OFT**) that the company has behaved anti-competitively, a British Sky Broadcasting Group plc spokesman said: BSkyB has not infringed the Competition Act and welcomes its first opportunity to put its case to the **OFT**.

"

OHP n (abbr **overhead projector**) retroproyector m, proyector m de transparencias □ **OHP slide** transparencia f

OID n FIN (abbr **original issue discount bond**) bono m emitido con descuento

oil n (**a**) (petroleum) petróleo m □ **oil company** compañía f petrolera; **oil crisis** crisis f del petróleo; **oil industry** industria f petrolera, industria f del petróleo; **oil magnate** magnate m del petróleo; **oil market** mercado m del petróleo; **oil port** puerto m petrolero; **oil prices** precios mpl del petróleo; **oil products** productos mpl derivados del petróleo; **oil reserves** reservas fpl de petróleo; **oil revenue** ingresos mpl del petróleo; **oil royalty** derechos mpl petroleros, Am regalías fpl petroleras; **oil shares** acciones fpl petroleras; **oil tycoon** magnate m del petróleo (**b**) ST EXCH **oils** acciones fpl petroleras

oil-backed bond n bono m petrolero

oilfield n yacimiento m petrolífero or petrolero, explotación f petrolífera or petrolera

oil-producing country n país m productor de petróleo

old-age pension n pensión f de jubilación

oligopolist n ECON oligopolista mf

oligopolistic adj ECON oligopolista

oligopoly n ECON oligopolio m

oligopsony n ECON oligopsonio m

OMB *n* (*abbr* **Office of Management and Budget**) = organismo que ayuda al presidente estadounidense a elaborar los presupuestos del estado

ombudsman *n* defensor(ora) *m,f* del pueblo

OMO *n* FIN (*abbr* **open market operation**) operación *f* de mercado abierto, *Am* OMA *f*

omnibus survey *n* MKTG encuesta *f* omnibús

oncosts *npl* costos *mpl or Esp* costes *mpl* fijos

one *n* ST EXCH unidad *f*; **to issue shares in ones** emitir acciones por unidades

one-day fall *n* ST EXCH caída *f* de un día

one-level (distribution) channel *n* MKTG canal *m* de distribución con un solo intermediario

one-man business *n* empresa *f* individual

one-off *Br* **1** *n* (*article*) pieza *f* única
   2 *adj* (*article*) único(a); (*order*) excepcional; **a one-off job** un trabajo aislado

one-price store *n* tienda *f or* comercio *m* de precio único

one-sided *adj* (*contract*) unilateral, desigual

one-stop *adj* **one-stop buying** compra *f* integral, = compra de servicios o artículos variados a un solo proveedor; **one-stop shop** (*service*) servicio *m* integral; **one-stop shopping** compra *f* integral, = compra de servicios o artículos variados a un solo proveedor

one-to-one marketing *n* marketing *m* one-to-one

one-way *adj* (*packaging*) desechable

on-line COMPTR **1** *adj* on-line, en línea; **to be on-line** (*person*) estar conectado(a) (a Internet); **to go on-line** (*connect to Internet*) conectarse (a Internet); **the company went on-line in November** (*got Internet presence*) la empresa comenzó a ofrecer sus servicios por Internet en noviembre; **to put the printer on-line** conectar la impresora ❑ **on-line bank** banco *m* on-line *or* en línea; **on-line banking** banca *f* on-line *or* en línea; ST EXCH **on-line broker** broker *mf* on-line *or* en línea; **on-line cash desk terminal** cajero *m* automático on-line *or* en línea; **on-line catalogue** catálogo *m* on-line *or* en línea; **on-line communication** comunicación *f* on-line *or* en línea; **on-line help** ayuda *f* on-line *or* en línea; FIN **on-line investing** inversiones *fpl* on-line *or* en línea; FIN **on-line investor** inversor(ora) *m,f or* inversionista *mf* on-line *or* en línea; **on-line marketing** marketing *m* on-line; **on-line mode** modo *m* on-line *or* en línea; **on-line registration** inscripción *f* on-line *or* en línea; **on-line retailer** minorista *mf* on-line *or* en línea; **on-line retailing** venta *f* (al menor) on-line *or* en línea; **on-line selling** venta *f* on-line *or* en línea; **on-line service** servicio *m* on-line *or* en línea; **on-line shop**

tienda *f or* comercio *m* on-line *or* en línea; **on-line shopping** compras *fpl* on-line *or* en línea; **on-line terminal** cajero *m* automático on-line *or* en línea; **on-line time** tiempo *m* de conexión; ST EXCH **on-line trading** negociación *f* on-line *or* en línea
   2 *adv* on-line, en línea; **to buy/order on-line** comprar/hacer pedidos on-line *or* en línea; **to shop on-line** comprar on-line *or* en línea; **to work on-line** trabajar on-line *or* en línea

> **“**
> UK-based Interactive Music & Video Shop is an **on-line retailer** selling 230,000 music and video products. As well as selling through its site *invs.com*, it handles **on-line retailing** for partners that include Sony.
> **”**

o.n.o *adv* (*abbr* **or nearest offer**) **£300 o.n.o.** 300 libras negociables

on-pack *adj* MKTG **on-pack offer** oferta *f* on-pack; **on-pack promotion** promoción *f* on-pack

on-screen **1** *adj* COMPTR en pantalla ❑ **on-screen help** ayuda *f* en pantalla
   2 *adv Esp* en el ordenador, *Am* en la computadora; **to work on-screen** trabajar *Esp* en el ordenador *or Am* en la computadora

on-target earnings *npl* beneficios *mpl* según los objetivos

on-the-job *adj* (*training*) en el puesto de trabajo; **he's got plenty of on-the-job experience** tiene mucha experiencia práctica

OPEC *n* (*abbr* **Organization of Petroleum-Exporting Countries**) OPEP *f*

OPEIC *n* FIN (*abbr* **open-ended investment company**) ≃ SIMCAV *f*

open **1** *adj* abierto(a) ❑ FIN **open account** cuenta *f* abierta; **open cheque** cheque *m* abierto, cheque *m* no cruzado; ST EXCH **open contract** contrato *m* abierto; INS **open cover** póliza *f* abierta; **open credit** crédito *m* abierto; **open economy** economía *f* abierta; COMPTR **open file** archivo *m or* fichero *m* abierto; TEL **open line** línea *f* abierta; ECON **open market** mercado *m* libre; ST EXCH **to buy shares on the open market** comprar acciones en el mercado abierto; **open money market** mercado *m* monetario libre; ST EXCH **open outcry** corro *m* a viva voz; INS **open policy** póliza *f* abierta; **open port** puerto *m* abierto; ST EXCH **open position** posición *f* abierta; MKTG **open question** (*in survey*) pregunta *f* abierta; IND **open shop** *Br* (*open to non-union members*) = empresa que acepta trabajadores no afiliados al sindicato; *US* (*with no union*) empresa *f* sin afiliación sindical; **open ticket** *Esp* billete *m or Am* boleto *m or esp Am* pasaje *m* abierto
   2 *vt* abrir; (*negotiations, conversation*) entablar, iniciar; (*debate*) dar comienzo a, abrir; **to open a line of credit** abrir una línea de crédito; **to**

open a loan suscribir un préstamo
3 *vi* (**a**) *(shop, business)* abrir (**b**) ST EXCH abrir; **the FTSE opened at 1083** el FTSE abrió con 1083

>
> However, Mills recognized that most businesses would still prefer the **open shop**, but argued that sophisticated conservatives, if forced to recognize unions and make concessions on wages and working conditions, would in return try to use labor leaders as a tool to repress rank-and-file discontent.
>

▶ **open up 1** *vt sep (office, shop)* abrir; **to open up a country to trade** abrir un país al comercio
2 *vi (office, shop)* abrir

open-door policy *n (for importing goods)* política *f* permisiva *or* de puertas abiertas

open-ended *adj (agreement)* indefinido(a); *(mortgage)* abierto(a), sin plazo de vencimiento ❏ **open-ended contract** contrato *m* indefinido; **open-ended credit** crédito *m* abierto; **open-ended investment company** ≃ sociedad *f* de inversión mobiliaria de capital variable; MKTG **open-ended question** pregunta *f* abierta; **open-ended trust** sociedad *f* de inversiones con cartera libre

opening *n* (**a**) *(of shop, office)* inauguración *f*, apertura *f*; *(of account)* apertura; *(of negotiations)* inicio *m*, apertura ❏ ACCT **opening balance** saldo *m* de apertura; ACCT **opening balance sheet** balance *m* de apertura; ACCT **opening entry** asiento *m* de apertura; **opening hours** *(of shop)* horario *m* comercial; *(of tourist attraction)* horario *m* de visita; *(of bank, office)* horario *m* de atención al público; ACCT **opening stock** existencias *fpl* iniciales
(**b**) *(opportunity)* oportunidad *f*; *(job)* (puesto *m*) vacante *f*; *(in market)* hueco *m*; **there are lots of good openings in the industry** hay muchas oportunidades laborales en el sector; **there's an opening with Lakeland Ltd** hay una vacante en Lakeland Ltd; **they exploited an opening in the market** aprovecharon un hueco en el mercado
(**c**) ST EXCH **opening day** día *m* de apertura; **opening price** *(of share)* precio *m* de apertura; **opening range** límites *mpl* de apertura; **opening session** sesión *f* de apertura; **opening transaction** operación *f* de apertura

open-market *adj* **open-market policy** política *f* de mercado abierto; **open-market value** valor *m* en el mercado abierto

open-plan office *n* oficina *f* diáfana

operate 1 *vt* (**a**) *(machine)* manejar, hacer funcionar (**b**) *(business)* dirigir; **she operates her business from home** dirige su negocio desde casa
2 *vi* (**a**) *(machine)* funcionar; **the factory is operating at full capacity** la fábrica está funcionando *or* trabajando a plena capacidad
(**b**) *(be active) (company)* actuar, operar; **the company operates in ten countries** la empresa desarrolla su actividad en diez países; **the company operates out of Philadelphia** la empresa tiene su sede en Filadelfia
(**c**) *(be in effect)* **the pay rise will operate from 1 January** el aumento de sueldo entrará en vigor *or* se hará efectivo a partir del 1 de enero; **the rule doesn't operate in such cases** la norma no se aplica en estos casos

operating *adj* **the factory has reached full operating capacity** la fábrica ha alcanzado su capacidad plena de funcionamiento ❏ *US* **operating account** cuenta *f* de explotación; **operating assets** activo *m* circulante; **operating budget** presupuesto *m* de explotación; *US* **operating capital** capital *m* circulante operativo; **operating cash flow** caja *f* operativa generada; **operating costs** costos *mpl or Esp* costes *mpl* de explotación; **operating costs analysis** análisis *m inv* de costos *or Esp* costes de explotación; **operating cycle** ciclo *m* operativo; **operating deficit** déficit *m* de explotación; **operating expenses** gastos *mpl* de explotación; **operating free cash flow** flujo *m* neto de caja; **operating income** ingresos *mpl* de explotación; **operating leverage** apalancamiento *m* operativo; **operating loss** pérdidas *fpl* de explotación; **operating margin** margen *m* de explotación; **operating monopoly** monopolio *m* de explotación; **operating officer** director(ora) *m,f*; **operating process** proceso *m* operativo; **operating profit** beneficio *m* de explotación; **operating ratio** coeficiente *m* de explotación; **operating rules** reglas *fpl* de funcionamiento; **operating statement** cuenta *f* de explotación **operating subsidy** subvención *f* de explotación; COMPTR **operating system** sistema *m* operativo; COMPTR **operating system command** comando *m* del sistema operativo; COMPTR **operating system software** software *m* del sistema operativo

operation *n* (**a**) *(functioning) (of machine, system, device, process, market forces)* funcionamiento *m*; **to be in operation** *(machine, company)* estar en funcionamiento; *(law, regulation)* estar en vigor *or* vigencia; **the plant is in operation round the clock** la fábrica funciona las veinticuatro horas; **to put sth into operation** *(machine)* poner algo en funcionamiento; *(plan)* poner algo en práctica; *(law, regulation)* poner algo en vigor *or* vigencia
(**b**) *(act, activity)* operación *f*; **they are to close down their operations in Mexico** van a cerrar sus operaciones comerciales en México; **the company is moving its soft drinks operation** la empresa va a trasladar su fábrica de refrescos ❏ **operations breakdown** desglose *m* de actividades; **operations management** gestión *f*

operativa; *operations manager* director(ora) *m,f* operativo(a); *operations strategy* estrategia *f* operativa
  (**c**) *(running, management) (of company, system)* gestión *f; (of process)* aplicación *f; (of machine)* manejo *m*
  (**d**) *(company)* empresa *f*
  (**e**) MKTG *(campaign)* operación *f*, campaña *f*

operational *adj* operativo(a); **the design team was operational within six months** a los seis meses ya estaba operativo el equipo de diseñadores ❑ *operational audit* auditoría *f* operativa; *operational costs* gastos *mpl* de explotación, costos *mpl or Esp* costes *mpl* de explotación; ACCT *operational cost accounting* contabilidad *f* basada en los gastos de explotación; ACCT *operational cost accounts* cuentas *fpl* de gastos de explotación; ACCT *operational cost centre* = centro de gastos de explotación; *operational efficiency* eficiencia *f* operativa; *operational marketing* marketing *m* operativo; *operational planning* planificación *f* operativa; *operational research* análisis *mpl* operativos

operative 1 *n (manual worker)* operario(a) *m,f*
  2 *adj* (**a**) *(law, rule, regulation)* vigente; **to become operative** entrar en vigor (**b**) *(system, scheme)* operativo(a); **the system will soon be operative** el sistema pronto estará operativo *or* en funcionamiento

operator *n* (**a**) TEL **(switchboard) operator** telefonista *mf*, operador(ora) *m,f* (**b**) *(of machine)* operario(a) *m,f* (**c**) *(company)* empresa *f*; **there are too many small operators in real estate** hay demasiadas empresas pequeñas en el sector inmobiliario (**d**) ST EXCH agente *mf*, corredor(ora) *m,f*; **operator for a fall/rise** agente que juega a la baja/al alza

opex *n (abbr* **operating expenses)** gastos *mpl* de explotación, OPEX *mpl*

opinion *n* MKTG *opinion former* creador(ora) *m,f* de opinión, *Am* formador(ora) *m,f* de opinión; *opinion leader* líder *m* de opinión; *opinion measurement* estudios *mpl* de opinión; *opinion measurement technique* técnica *f* de estudios de opinión; *opinion poll, opinion survey* sondeo *m* de opinión

opportunity *n* (**a**) *(chance)* oportunidad *f*, ocasión *f*; **the opportunities for advancement are excellent** las oportunidades de promoción son excelentes (**b**) MKTG oportunidad *f*; *opportunities and threats* oportunidades y amenazas MKTG *opportunities to hear* oportunidades de oír; MKTG *opportunities to see* oportunidades de ver ❑ ECON *opportunity cost* costo *m or Esp* coste *m* de oportunidad; MKTG *opportunity and issue analysis* análisis *m inv* DAFO; MKTG *opportunity and threat analysis* análisis *m inv* de oportunidades y amenazas

opposite number *n (person)* homólogo(a) *m,f*

opposition *n* **the opposition** *(competitors)* la competencia

▶ **opt in** *vi Br* unirse (**to** a), decidir participar (**to** en)

▶ **opt into** *vt insep* unirse a, decidir participar en; **to opt into an association/the EU** decidir ingresar en una asociación/en la UE

▶ **opt out** *vi* decidir no unirse, decidir no participar; **many opted out of joining the union** muchos decidieron no afiliarse al sindicato

optical COMPTR *adj* óptico(a) ❑ *optical character reader* lector *m* óptico de caracteres; *optical character recognition* reconocimiento *m* óptico de caracteres; *optical disk* disco *m* óptico; *optical drive* unidad *f* de disco óptico; *optical fibres* fibras *fpl* ópticas; *optical mouse Esp* ratón *m or Am* mouse *m* óptico; *optical reader* lector *m* óptico; *optical reading* lectura *f* óptica; *optical scanner* lector *m* óptico

optimal *adj* óptimo(a) ❑ MKTG *optimal price* precio *m* óptimo; MKTG *optimal psychological price* precio *m* psicológico óptimo; *optimal resource allocation* asignación *f* óptima de recursos

optimizer *n* COMPTR optimizador *m*

optimum 1 *n* nivel *m* óptimo
  2 *adj* óptimo(a) ❑ *optimum conditions* condiciones *fpl* óptimas; *optimum employment of resources* aprovechamiento *m* óptimo de recursos

option *n* (**a**) ST EXCH opción *f*; **to take an option (on sth)** adquirir una opción (sobre algo); **to take up an option** ejercer el derecho de opción; **to declare an option** notificar que se va a ejercer una opción; **option to buy** opción de compra; **option to double** opción de compra o venta doble; **option to sell** opción de venta; **option on shares** opción sobre acciones ❑ *option day* fecha *f* de vencimiento de una opción; *option deal* operación *f* a prima; *options desk* departamento *m* de opciones; *options market* mercado *m* de opciones; *option money* precio *m* de opción; *option price* precio *m* de opción; *option spread* spread *m*; *options trading* negociación *f* de opciones
  (**b**) COMPTR opción *f* ❑ *option box* caja *f* de opciones; *option button* botón *m* de opción *option key* tecla *f* de opción; *options menu* menú *m* de opciones

optional *adj* optativo(a) ❑ *optional extra* accesorio *m* opcional

optional-feature pricing *n* MKTG sistema *m* de precios según accesorios

optionee *n* ST EXCH tenedor(ora) *m,f* de opción

order 1 *n* (**a**) *(request for goods, goods ordered)* pedido *m*; **another company got the order** otra empresa se llevó el pedido; **to have sth on order** haber hecho un pedido de algo, haber encargado algo; **to place an order (with sb/for sth)** hacer un pedido (a alguien/de algo); **to make sth to order** hacer algo por encargo; **to deliver an order** entregar un pedido; **to fill an order** rellenar *or* cumplimentar *or* Am llenar un pedido; **as per order** según pedido ❑ *order book* (book) libro *m* de pedidos; *(total orders recorded)* cartera *f* de pedidos; *order cycle* ciclo *m* del pedido; *order cycle time* duración *f* del ciclo de pedido; *order department* departamento *m* de pedidos; *order flowchart* diagrama *m* del ciclo de pedido; *order form* hoja *f* de pedido, formulario *m* or *Méx* forma *f* de pedido; *order number* número *m* de pedido

(**b**) *(command, instruction)* orden *f*; **to give sb orders to do sth** dar órdenes a alguien de que haga algo ❑ ST EXCH *order to buy* orden *f* de compra; ST EXCH *order to sell* orden *f* de venta

(**c**) FIN *(document)* orden *f*; **cheque to order** cheque a la orden; **pay to the order of J. Martin** páguese a J. Martin; **pay J. Martin or order** páguese a J. Martin o a *(en un cheque)*; **by order and for account of J. Martin** de orden y por cuenta de J. Martin ❑ *order to pay* orden *f* de pago

(**d**) *(condition)* **in (good) working order** en buen estado de funcionamiento; **out of order** *(sign)* no funciona

(**e**) LAW orden *f*; **he was served with an order for the seizure of his property** le fue entregada una orden de embargo

(**f**) *(in meeting)* **order!** ¡silencio!; **to rule a question out of order** declarar improcedente una pregunta; **to call sb to order** llamar a alguien al orden; **he called the meeting to order** llamó al orden a los asistentes

2 *vt* (**a**) *(goods)* pedir, encargar (**from** a) (**b**) *(command)* **to order sb to do sth** mandar *or* ordenar a alguien hacer algo; LAW **he was ordered to pay costs** el juez le ordenó pagar las costas

order-driven *adj* ST EXCH *(market)* dirigido(a) por órdenes

order-to-remittance cycle *n* ciclo *m* del pedido al pago

ordinary *adj* ACCT *ordinary activities* (balance sheet item) actividades *fpl* ordinarias; FIN *ordinary creditor* acreedor(ora) *m,f* común; *ordinary rate* (of postage) tarifa *f* ordinaria; *Br* FIN, ST EXCH *ordinary share* acción *f* ordinaria; *ordinary share capital* capital *m* en acciones ordinarias

organic *adj* orgánico(a) ❑ *organic growth* crecimiento *m* orgánico

organigram *n* organigrama *m*

organization *n* (**a**) *(running)* organización *f*; *(structure)* organización, estructura *f*; **we are unhappy with the organization of the company** no estamos conformes con la estructura de la compañía ❑ *organization chart* organigrama *m*; *organization and methods* organización *f* y métodos; *organization tree* organigrama *m* de árbol

(**b**) *(association, official body)* organización *f* ❑ *Organization for Economic Cooperation and Development* Organización *f* para la Cooperación y el Desarrollo Económico; *Organization for Security and Co-operation in Europe* Organización *f* para la Seguridad y la Cooperación en Europa

(**c**) ADMIN *(personnel)* personal *m*

(**d**) IND *(of labour)* organización *f*

organizational *adj (skills, methods, expenses)* organizativo(a), de organización ❑ ECON *organizational behaviour* comportamiento *m* organizativo; *organizational buyer* comprador(ora) *m,f* de empresa; *organizational chart* organigrama *m*; *organizational marketer* encargado(a) *m,f* de marketing de una empresa

organize 1 *vt* (**a**) *(put into order)* organizar; **to organize people into groups** organizar a gente en grupos (**b**) *(workers)* sindicar, *Am* sindicalizar ❑ *organized labour* trabajadores *mpl* sindicados *or Am* sindicalizados

2 *vi (workers)* sindicarse, *Am* sindicalizarse

organizer *n (of event)* organizador(ora) *m,f*

organizing *n* organización *f* ❑ *organizing committee* comité *m* organizador

orientate *vt* orientar; **it is orientated towards the youth market** está orientado al mercado juvenil

origin *n* origen *m*; **country of origin** país *m* de origen ❑ *origin of goods label* certificado *m* de origen

original 1 *n (of document, bill of exchange)* original *m*

2 *adj* original ❑ FIN *original capital* capital *m* inicial; ACCT *original cost* costo *m* or *Esp* coste *m* histórico; ACCT *original document* documento *m* original; **original equipment manufacturer** fabricante *mf* de equipo original; **original invoice** factura *f* original; FIN **original issue discount bond** bono *m* emitido con descuento; **original packaging** embalaje *m* original; **original value** valor *m* original

OS *n* COMPTR (*abbr* **operating system**) sistema *m* operativo

O/S *adj* (*abbr* **out of stock**) agotado(a)

OSCE *n* (*abbr* **Organization for Security and Co-operation in Europe**) Organización *f* para la Seguridad y la Cooperación en Europa

OSHA *n* (*abbr* **Occupational Safety and Health Administration**) = organismo gubernamental estadounidense encargado de higiene y seguridad en el trabajo, ≃ Inspección *f* de Trabajo

OTC *adj* ST EXCH (*abbr* **over-the-counter**) extrabursátil

OTE *npl* (*abbr* **on-target earnings**) beneficios *mpl* según los objetivos

OTH *n* MKTG (*abbr* **opportunity to hear**) oportunidad *f* de oír

OTS *n* MKTG (*abbr* **opportunity to see**) oportunidad *f* de ver

out 1 *adj* ACCT **out book** libro *m* de gastos; COMPTR **out box** buzón *m* de salida
2 *adv* **to be out (on strike)** estar en huelga

outage *n* (*power cut*) apagón *m*, corte *m* de luz

outbid *vt* **to outbid sb (for sth)** (*at auction*) pujar *or* ofertar más que alguien (por algo)

outbound freight *n* flete *m* de salida

outflow *n* FIN (*of currency, capital*) salida *f*

outgoing *adj* (**a**) (*government, minister*) saliente; (*tenant*) anterior (**b**) (*train, ship, plane*) saliente (**c**) (*telephone call, mail, e-mail*) saliente ▢ **outgoing inventory** existencias *fpl* salientes; **outgoing shift** turno *m* saliente

outgoings *npl* gastos *mpl*; **the outgoings exceed the incomings** los gastos son superiores a los ingresos

outlay 1 *n* (*expenditure, investment*) desembolso *m*; (*investment*) inversión *m*; **to get back** *or* **recover one's outlay** recuperar la inversión inicial
2 *vt* (*spend*) desembolsar; (*invest*) invertir; **to outlay $10,000 capital** invertir 10.000 dólares de capital

outlet *n* (*point of sale*) punto *m* de venta; (*market*) mercado *m*; **there are not many sales outlets in Japan** no hay muchos puntos de venta en Japón; **the main outlet for our product** el principal mercado para nuestro producto ▢ **outlet village** parque *m* comercial (*que suele estar a las afueras de la ciudad y vende marcas conocidas a precios reducidos*)

outlook *n* (*prospect*) perspectivas *fpl*; **the out-** **look is gloomy** (*for economy*) las perspectivas económicas son muy malas

❝
She too is concerned about the impact of this upon the **outlook** for the economy – with ABN forecasting GDP growth to decline marginally to 2.4% in 2002, from 2.5% in 2001 – but she notes that this is the first currency crisis that Mboweni has faced in his year of office so far, which could make him particularly susceptible to a knee-jerk reaction.
❞

out-of-court settlement *n* LAW acuerdo *m* extrajudicial

out-of-house worker *n* trabajador(ora) *m,f* externo(a) *or* a domicilio

out-of-pocket expenses *npl* gastos *mpl* extras

out-of-the-money option *n* ST EXCH opción *f* fuera de dinero

out-of-town *adj* (*retail park, development*) de las afueras de la ciudad

outperform *vt* FIN obtener un mayor rendimiento que

outplacement *n* recolocación *f*

❝
Outplacement services provide a solution to organizational changes that result in the discharge or displacement of employees. E-Cruiter.com's Allen And Associates division provides professional assistance to people seeking to re-enter the job market following corporate downsizing. **Outplacement** services are a key part of the rapidly growing HCM market, which according to leading industry analysts is expected to reach $200 billion by 2003.
❞

output 1 *n* (**a**) (*of worker, factory, machine*) producción *f*; **this represents 25% of the total output** esto representa un 25% de la producción total; **our output is not keeping pace with demand** nuestra producción no satisface la demanda; **this machine has an output of 6,000 items per hour** esta máquina tiene una producción de 6.000 unidades por hora; **output per hour** producción por hora; **output per person** producción por persona ▢ **output bonus** prima *f* de producción; **output ceiling** techo *m* de producción; **output ratio** coeficiente *m* de producción; ACCT **output tax** impuesto *m* sobre ventas
(**b**) COMPTR (*of data, information*) salida *f* ▢ **output buffer** memoria *f* intermedia de salida, búfer *m* de salida; **output device** dispositivo *m* de salida; **output file** archivo *m* *or* fichero *m* de salida;

output formatting formateo *m* de salida; **output medium** soporte *m* de salida; **output port** puerto *m* de salida

2 *vt* (**a**) *(of factory, worker, machine)* producir (**b**) COMPTR *(data, information)* sacar; **to output a file to the printer** enviar un archivo *or* fichero a la impresora

outreach *n* ADMIN = programa de la administración que busca informar de las prestaciones a las que tienen derecho a personas que no las conocen □ **outreach worker** = trabajador social que presta asistencia a personas que pudiendo necesitarla no la solicitan

> ❝
> An equalities panel has been appointed to consider issues for the small ethnic minority population in the area, and an equalities officer has begun work. For lone parents, projects are being set up with family centres and there are plans to set up an **outreach** service to help lone parents towards jobs, benefits and better health care.
> ❞

outright 1 *adv* **to buy sth outright** comprar algo (con) dinero en mano

2 *adj* **outright loan** préstamo *m* a fondo perdido

outsell *vt (of goods, retailer)* superar en ventas a; **the brand of cigarettes that outsells all the others** la marca de cigarrillos que supera en ventas a todas las demás

outside *adj* (**a**) **outside worker** trabajador(ora) *m,f* externo(a) *or* a domicilio (**b**) ST EXCH **outside broker** agente *mf or* corredor(ora) *m,f* no perteneciente a la Bolsa; **outside brokerage** correduría *f* de agentes *or* corredores no pertenecientes a la Bolsa; **outside market** mercado *m* fuera de la Bolsa; **outside price** precio *m* máximo (**c**) TEL **outside line** línea *f* exterior

outsider *n* ST EXCH agente *mf or* corredor(ora) *m,f* no perteneciente a la Bolsa

outsource *vt* subcontratar, externalizar, *Am* tercerizar, *Am* terciarizar; **equipment maintenance has been outsourced to another company** el mantenimiento de los equipos está subcontratado *or* externalizado *or Am* tercerizado *or Am* terciarizado

outsourcing *n* subcontratación *f*, externalización *f*, *Am* tercerización *f*, *Am* terciarización *f*

> ❝
> Organizations are increasingly turning to **outsourcing** in an attempt to enhance their competitiveness. Chrysler, for example, outsources 100% of the manufacture of half of its minicompact and subcompact cars. Furthermore, Chrysler and Ford currently produce less than one-half of the value of all their vehicles in-house. Similarly, Boeing has begun to rely more heavily on **outsourcing** partners to manufacture its aircraft.
> ❞

outstanding *adj (business, amount, invoice, account, payment)* pendiente; *(interest)* devengado(a) □ **outstanding balance** saldo *m* pendiente; BANKING **outstanding cheque** cheque *m* en gestión de cobro; **outstanding credits** créditos *mpl* pendientes de cobrar; **outstanding debts** deudas *fpl* pendientes; **outstanding shares** acciones *fpl* en circulación

out-supplier *n* proveedor(ora) *m,f* externo(a)

out-tray *n* bandeja *f* de trabajos terminados

outturn *n* FIN resultados *mpl*

> ❝
> Helped mainly by better than expected fiscal revenues and also lower interest payments, the fiscal **outturn** for 1999 was just below the initial target of 2 per cent of GDP.
> ❞

outward *adj* **outward bill of lading** conocimiento *m* exterior; **outward cargo** cargamento *m* de ida; **outward freight** flete *m* de ida; ECON **outward investment** inversión *f* en el exterior **outward mail** correo *m* saliente; **outward manifest** manifiesto *m* de salida; **outward mission** misión *f* comercial a un país extranjero; **outward voyage** viaje *m* de ida

outwork *n* trabajo *m* en *or* desde casa

outworker *n* trabajador(ora) *m,f* externo(a) *or* a domicilio

outyear 1 *n* año *m* fiscal siguiente al año de presupuesto

2 *adj* del año fiscal siguiente al año de presupuesto

overage *n* US excedente *m*

overall *adj* global; **she has overall responsibility for sales** es la responsable global de ventas □ **overall budget** dotación *f* presupuestaria global; **overall consumption** consumo *m* global; **overall demand** demanda *f* global; **overall objective** objetivo *m* global; **overall plan** plan *m* global

overassess *vt* FIN realizar una liquidación tributaria excesiva de; **I've been overassessed** me han emitido una liquidación excesiva

overassessment *n* FIN liquidación *f* tributaria excesiva

overbid 1 *n* pago *m* excesivamente alto

2 *vi* pagar un precio excesivamente alto

overbook 1 *vt (flight, hotel)* sobrecontratar; **they've overbooked this flight** han sobrecontratado este vuelo, este vuelo tiene overbooking

2 *vi (airline, hotel)* sobrecontratar, hacer overbooking

overbooking n sobrecontratación f, overbooking m

overborrow vi (company) endeudarse excesivamente

overborrowed adj (company) excesivamente endeudado(a)

overborrowing n (of company) endeudamiento m excesivo

overbought adj ST EXCH (market) sobrecomprado(a)

" ———————————————

Mr Greenspan's dilemma is that he would probably like to raise interest rates – inflation indicators from the labour market are mixed but the productivity miracle cannot continue for ever while signals from the energy sector are less equivocal. He would also like to see the US stock markets down from their current **overbought** levels. But he must achieve both without causing a nervous market to panic.

——————————————— "

overbuy vt ST EXCH (market) sobrecomprar

overcapacity n ECON exceso m de capacidad

overcapitalization n FIN sobrecapitalización f

overcapitalize vt FIN sobrecapitalizar

overcharge 1 vt **to overcharge sb (for sth)** cobrar de más a alguien (por algo); **they overcharged me for the repair** me cobraron de más por la reparación
  2 vi **to overcharge (for sth)** cobrar de más (por algo)

overconsumption n ECON consumo m excesivo, sobreconsumo m

overdemand n demanda f excesiva, sobredemanda f

overdevelop vt ECON sobredesarrollar

overdevelopment n ECON sobredesarrollo m

overdraft n BANKING (amount borrowed) descubierto m, saldo m negativo or deudor; **to arrange an overdraft** acordar un (límite de) descubierto; **to have an overdraft** tener un descubierto; **to allow sb an overdraft** conceder a alguien un descubierto; **to pay off one's overdraft** liquidar un descubierto ❑ **overdraft facility** servicio m de descubierto; **overdraft limit** límite m de descubierto; **overdraft loan** descubierto m

overdraw BANKING **1** vt (account) girar en descubierto; **to be overdrawn** tener un descubierto; **your account is overdrawn** su cuenta tiene saldo negativo; **to be $230 overdrawn** tener un descubierto de 230 dólares ❑ **overdrawn account** cuenta f en descubierto
  2 vi girar en descubierto

overdue adj (account, payment) vencido(a); **the**

bill/rent is overdue la factura/el pago del alquiler ha vencido; **our repayments are two months overdue** debemos dos plazos atrasados ❑ FIN **overdue bill** letra f no atendida, efecto m impagado or Am impago

overemployment n ECON sobreempleo m

overestimate vt sobreestimar

overextend vt FIN sobrevalorar

overflow n COMPTR (of data) desbordamiento m

overfreight n exceso m de carga

overfunding n sobrefinanciación f

overgear vt (company) endeudar excesivamente; **to be overgeared** estar excesivamente endeudado(a)

overgearing n FIN endeudamiento m excesivo

overhead 1 n gasto m general; **our overheads are** or US **our overhead is too high** nuestros gastos generales son demasiado altos ❑ ACCT **overhead absorption rate** tasa f de absorción de los gastos generales; **overhead budget** presupuesto m para gastos generales; **overhead costs, overhead expenses** gastos mpl generales; FIN **overhead variance** desviación f en los gastos generales
  2 adj **overhead projector** retroproyector m, proyector m de transparencias

overheat vi (economy) recalentarse

overindustrialization n sobreindustrialización f

overinsurance n aseguramiento m excesivo

overinsure vt asegurar en exceso

overinvest FIN **1** vt sobreinvertir
  2 vi sobreinvertir (**in** en)

overinvestment n FIN sobreinversión f

overissue FIN **1** n emisión f excesiva
  2 vt emitir en exceso

overlap n MKTG solapamiento m

overload vt (market) sobrecargar

overmanned adj con exceso de empleados

overmanning n exceso m de empleados

overnight adj FIN **overnight loan** depósito m a un día; **overnight rate** Esp tipo m or Am tasa f del depósito a un día

over-packaging n exceso m de embalaje

overpay vt pagar en exceso a, pagar de más a

overpayment n (of taxes, employee) pago m excesivo

overperform vi ST EXCH (shares) estar sobrevalorado(a)

over-position vt MKTG sobreposicionar, = exagerar la calidad, el rendimiento o las prestaciones de

over-positioning n MKTG sobreposición f, =

exageración de la calidad, el rendimiento o las prestaciones de un producto

overprice *vt* poner un precio excesivo a

overpriced *adj* excesivamente caro(a)

overproduce *vt & vi* producir en exceso

overproduction *n* sobreproducción *f*, superproducción *f*

overrate *vt* ADMIN sobrevalorar

overriding *adj (importance)* primordial; *(factor)* preponderante ❏ LAW **overriding clause** cláusula *f* derogatoria; **overriding commission** *(paid to broker)* comisión *f* extra

overrun *n* **(cost) overrun** costos *mpl or Esp* costes *mpl* superiores a los previstos; **(production) overrun** excedente *m* (de producción)

overseas 1 *adj (visitor)* extranjero(a); *(trade, debt)* exterior; *(travel)* al extranjero ❏ **overseas agent** representante *mf* en el extranjero; **overseas business** operaciones *fpl* en el extranjero; **overseas debt** deuda *f* exterior *or* externa; **overseas development** desarrollo *m* exterior; **Overseas Development Administration** = organismo británico de ayuda a los países en vías de desarrollo; **overseas investment** inversión *f* extranjera; **overseas market** mercado *m* exterior
2 *adv* fuera del país

oversold *adj* ST EXCH *(market)* muy bajo(a) de precio *(por exceso de títulos)*

overspend 1 *n* gasto *m* superior a lo previsto
2 *vt* **to overspend one's budget** salirse del presupuesto
3 *vi* gastar de más

overspending *n* gastos *mpl* superiores a lo previsto

overstaffed *adj* con exceso de personal; **the plant is overstaffed** la fábrica tiene demasiado personal

overstaffing *n* exceso *m* de personal

overstate *vt* ACCT sobrevalorar

overstock 1 *n* US **overstocks** exceso *m* de existencias
2 *vt (market)* saturar; *(warehouse)* abarrotar (**with** de)
3 *vi* almacenar más existencias de las necesarias

overstocked *adj* **the market is overstocked with foreign goods** el mercado está saturado de productos extranjeros; **to be overstocked with sth** *(warehouse, shop)* tener exceso (de existencias) de algo

oversubscribe *vt* FIN, ST EXCH **the share issue was oversubscribed** la demanda superó la oferta de venta de acciones

oversubscription *n* FIN, ST EXCH suscripción *f* cubierta con exceso

overtax *vt* FIN *(goods)* gravar en exceso; *(person)* cobrar demasiados impuestos a

overtaxation *n* FIN impuestos *mpl* excesivos

over-the-counter *adj* ST EXCH extrabursátil
❏ **over-the-counter market** mercado *m* extrabursátil

overtime 1 *n* **(a)** *(work)* horas *fpl* extraordinarias *or* extra(s); **an hour's overtime** una hora extra; **the salary does not include overtime** el sueldo no incluye horas extraordinarias; **to do overtime** hacer horas extra(s) ❏ **overtime ban** prohibición *f* de trabajar horas extra(s); **overtime pay** horas *fpl* extra(s); **overtime rate** tarifa *f* por horas extra(s) **(b)** *(pay)* horas *fpl* extra; **after 6pm we're on overtime** a partir de las 6 de la tarde se cuenta como horas extra(s); **to be paid overtime** cobrar horas extra(s)
2 *adv* **to work overtime** hacer horas extra

> **"**
> National long distance services were hit earlier this week as Indian Telecom Service workers took action because of concern about the Indian Telecom Department's corporatization on October 1. According to local media reports, officials agreed on Thursday to cancel an **overtime ban** – that had seen workers leave their jobs each day at 5pm – and put in extra hours.
> **"**

overtrading *n (by a company)* exceso *m* de operaciones comerciales *(que suelen llevar a falta de liquidez)*; ST EXCH exceso de transacciones *(en la cuenta de un cliente)*

overvaluation *n* sobrevaloración *f*

overvalue 1 *n (of currency)* sobrevaloración *f*
2 *vt (assets, object, currency)* sobrevalorar

overweight 1 *n* exceso *m* de peso
2 *adj* **(a)** *(luggage, parcel)* **this suitcase is two kilos overweight** esta maleta tiene un exceso de peso de dos kilos **(b)** FIN **to be overweight in sth** estar excesivamente ponderado(a) en algo **(c)** *(overstaffed)* con exceso de personal

overwithhold *vt* US **to overwithhold taxes** retener demasiados impuestos

overwrite COMPTR **1** *n* **overwrite mode** modo *m* de sobreescritura
2 *vt (file)* sobreescribir

owe *vt* deber; **to owe sb sth, to owe sth to sb** deber algo a alguien; **the sum owed to her** la cantidad que le deben

owing *adj* **the money owing to me** el dinero que se me adeuda; **I have a lot of money/ £500 owing to me** me deben mucho dinero/ 500 libras

own *vt* **(a)** *(possess)* poseer; **a 50% owned company** una empresa en propiedad al 50% **(b)** *(be* *responsible for)* **to be owned by** corresponder a, ser responsabiliad de; **the staff evaluation function is owned by the human resources manager** la evaluación del personal corresponde al *or* es responsabilidad del director de recursos humanos

own-brand MKTG **1** *n* marca *f* blanca

2 *adj* ***own-brand label*** etiqueta *f* de marca blanca; ***own-brand product*** producto *m* de marca blanca

own-branding *n* MKTG utilización *f* de marcas blancas

owner *n* dueño(a) *m,f*, propietario(a) *m,f* ❑ ACCT

owner's capital account cuenta *f* de acciones de los propietarios *(de una empresa)*

owner-occupied *adj Br* ocupado(a) por el/la propietario(a)

owner-occupier *n Br* propietario(a) *m,f* de la vivienda que habita

ownership *n* propiedad *f*; **under new ownership** *(sign)* nuevos propietarios; **to be in private/public ownership** ser de propiedad privada/pública

own-label *adj* blanco(a) ❑ ***own-label brand*** marca *f* blanca

P *n* **the four Ps** las cuatro P, = producto, precio, promoción y distribución

P2P *adj* (*abbr* **peer to peer**) P2P

P45 *n Br* = impreso oficial que se entrega a la persona que deja un trabajo; **to be handed one's P45** ser despedido(a)

P60 *n Br* = certificado (anual) de rendimientos del trabajo y retenciones fiscales

PA *n* (*abbr* **personal assistant**) secretario(a) *m,f* personal

p.a. *adv* (*abbr* **per annum**) anual, al año

pace of work *n* ritmo *m* de trabajo

pack 1 *n* paquete *m*
  2 *vt* (**a**) *(goods) (for transportation)* embalar; *(for sale)* envasar; **the equipment is packed in polystyrene chips** el equipo está embalado con bolitas de poliestireno (**b**) COMPTR *(database)* compactar

package 1 *n* (**a**) *(pay deal, contract)* paquete *m*; **the package includes private health insurance** el paquete incluye seguro médico privado; **the offer is part of a larger package** la oferta forma parte de un paquete más amplio; **a package of measures to halt inflation** un paquete de medidas para detener la inflación; **we offered them a generous package worth over £100,000** les hicimos una oferta generosa por valor de más de 100.000 libras □ **package deal** acuerdo *m* global
  (**b**) COMPTR *(software)* paquete *m* (de software)
  (**c**) *(parcel)* paquete *m*; *US (packet)* paquete *m*
  2 *vt (for transportation)* embalar; *(for sale)* envasar

packaging *n (for transport, freight)* embalaje *m*; *(of product)* envasado *m* □ **packaging charges** cargos *mpl* de embalaje; **packaging costs** gastos *mpl* de embalaje; **packaging plant** planta *f* de envase *or* envasadora

packet *n* COMPTR *(of data)* paquete *m*

packing *n* embalaje *m*; **postage and packing** gastos *mpl* de envío □ **packing case** cajón *m*; **packing charges** gastos *mpl* de embalaje; **packing costs** gastos *mpl* de embalaje; **packing list** lista *f* de cosas para embalar; **packing materials** embalaje *m*; **packing slip** lista *f* de contenidos *(de un paquete)*

Pac Man defense *n US Fam* = estrategia defensiva ante una OPA hostil consistente en lanzar una oferta contra la empresa atacante

pad *n* **(writing) pad** bloc *m*

page¹ *n (of book, document, computer file)* página *f* □ **page break** salto *m* de página; **page design** diseño *m* de página; COMPTR **page down** avance *m* de página; COMPTR **page down key** tecla *f* de avance de página; **page format** formato *m* de página; COMPTR **page layout** maquetación *f*; COMPTR **page preview** previsualización *f*; COMPTR **page scanner** escáner *m* de páginas; COMPTR **page up** retroceso *m* de página; COMPTR **page up key** tecla *f* de retroceso de página

page² *vt (by loudspeaker)* avisar por megafonía; *(by electronic device)* llamar por el buscapersonas *or Esp* busca *or Méx* localizador *or RP* radiomensaje

▶ **page down** *vi* COMPTR avanzar una página

▶ **page up** *vi* COMPTR retroceder una página

pager *n* buscapersonas *m inv, Esp* busca *m, Méx* localizador *m, RP* radiomensaje *m*

paginate *vt* paginar

pagination *n* paginación *f*

paid *adj* (**a**) *(person, work)* remunerado(a); **to get paid sick/maternity leave** cobrar la baja por enfermedad/maternidad □ **paid holidays** vacaciones *fpl* remuneradas; **paid leave** baja *f* remunerada (**b**) *(goods, bill)* pagado(a); **paid (on**

bill) pagado ❑ ACCT **paid cash book** libro *m* de gastos

paid-up *adj (member)* al corriente de cuotas ❑ FIN **paid-up capital** capital *m* liberado en acciones, capital desembolsado; **paid-up policy** póliza *f* liberada *or* con prima; **paid-up shares** *Esp* acciones *fpl* desembolsadas, *Am* acciones liberadas

"
A member's liability is limited to the amount, if any, which remains unpaid upon the member's shares. Since normal practice is for a member to be issued with **paid-up shares**, the member's liability is limited to the extent that the shares which he or she has in the company are rendered valueless.
"

paired comparison *n* MKTG comparación *f* entre dos productos *(realizada por el consumidor)*

palette *n* COMPTR paleta *f*

pallet *n* palet *m*, palé *m* ❑ **pallet truck** carretilla *f* elevadora (de horquilla)

palletization *n* paletización *f*

palletize *vt* paletizar ❑ **palletized goods** mercancías *fpl* paletizadas

palletizer *n* paletizadora *f*

palmtop *n* COMPTR palm(top) *m or f*, asistente *m* personal

pamphlet *n* folleto *m*

P & L *n* (**a**) *(abbr* **profit and loss***)* pérdidas *fpl* y ganancias, PyG *fpl* ❑ **P & L account** cuenta *f* de pérdidas y ganancias; **P & L form** cuenta *f* de resultados a efectos fiscales; **P & L statement** cuenta *f* de pérdidas y ganancias (**b**) *(abbr* **profit and loss account, profit and loss statement***)* cuenta *f* de resultados; **we can see from the P & L that developing the product is not a viable option** de la cuenta de resultados se desprende que no es posible desarrollar el producto (**c**) *(abbr* **profit and loss form***)* cuenta *f* de resultados a efectos fiscales

p & p *n Br (abbr* **postage and packing***)* gastos *mpl* de envío

panel *n* MKTG *(for market research)* grupo *m* de discusión ❑ **panel discussion** debate *m*; **panel member** participante *mf* en un grupo de discusión; **panel research** investigación *f* mediante grupos de discusión

panic *n* **panic buying** compra *f* provocada por el pánico; **panic selling** venta *f* provocada por el pánico

paper *n* (**a**) *(material)* papel *m*; **papers** *(documents)* papeles *mpl*, documentación *f* ❑ **paper copy** copia *f* en papel (**b**) FIN *(securities)* valores *mpl* ❑ **paper company**

sociedad *f* instrumental *or* vehículo; **paper loss** pérdida *f* teórica *or* sobre el papel; **paper profit** beneficio *m* teórico *or* sobre el papel; **paper securities** papel *m* comercial (**c**) *(banknotes)* papel *m* moneda ❑ **paper currency** papel *m* moneda; **paper money** papel *m* moneda (**d**) COMPTR **paper advance** *(on printer)* avance *m* del papel; **paper feed** alimentación *f* de papel; **paper format** formato *m* de papel; **paper jam** atasco *m* de papel; **paper tray** bandeja *f* de papel

"
Wall Street's rapid rise has meant many Americans feel richer and they have been prepared to spend their **paper profits** from the US equity markets by borrowing against them or running down their savings. If Mr Greenspan's policy decisions spark a crisis of confidence, Wall Street could nose dive with a consequent impact on consumer spending.
"

paperless *adj* informatizado(a), electrónico(a) ❑ **paperless office** oficina *f* completamente informatizada; ST EXCH **paperless trading** negociación *f* electrónica

paperwork *n* papeleo *m*

par *n* FIN *(of bills, shares)* valor *m* nominal, paridad *f*; **at par** a la par; **to issue shares at par** emitir acciones a la par; **above par** sobre la par; **below par** bajo par ❑ **par of exchange** tipo *m or Am* tasa *f* de cambio; ST EXCH **par value** valor *m* nominal

paragraph *n* párrafo *m* ❑ COMPTR **paragraph break** salto *m* de párrafo; COMPTR **paragraph mark** marca *f* de párrafo, calderón *m*

parallel *adj* paralelo(a) ❑ COMPTR **parallel cable** cable *m* paralelo; **parallel imports** importaciones *fpl* paralelas; COMPTR **parallel interface** interfaz *f* paralela; **parallel market** mercado *m* paralelo; COMPTR **parallel output** salida *f* paralela; COMPTR **parallel port** puerto *m* paralelo; COMPTR **parallel printer** impresora *f* en paralelo; **parallel rate of exchange** tipo *m or Am* tasa *f* de cambio paralelo; MKTG **parallel selling** ventas *fpl* paralelas

parameter *n* COMPTR parámetro *m*

parcel *n* (**a**) *(package)* paquete *m*; **to make up a parcel** hacer un paquete ❑ **parcel delivery** entrega *f* de paquetes; **parcel delivery company** empresa *f* de paquetería *or CAm, SAm* encomiendas; **parcel post** servicio *m* de paquete postal *or CAm, SAm* encomienda; **to send sth by parcel post** enviar algo por paquete postal *or CAm, SAm* encomienda; **parcel rates** tarifas *fpl* de paquete (**b**) ST EXCH *(of shares)* paquete *m*

▸ **parcel up** *vt sep* embalar, empaquetar

parent company *n* empresa *f* matriz

Pareto rule n FIN ley f de Pareto

pari passu adj FIN, ST EXCH en igualdad de condiciones (**with** que)

parity n FIN paridad f; **the two currencies were at parity** había paridad entre las dos monedas; **euro-dollar parity** paridad euro-dólar ❑ **parity of exchange** paridad f de cambio; **parity grid** parrilla f de paridades; **parity ratio** coeficiente m de paridad; **parity value** valor m de paridad

parking n ST EXCH aparcamiento m, Am estacionamiento m

parlay vt US (money, project, investment) convertir, transformar (**into** en); **she parlayed the local newspapers into a press empire** construyó un emporio periodístico a partir de los periódicos locales

> ❝
> Young & Rubicam **parlayed** a well-received campaign for the National Football League and the United Way into a corporate-image account from the NFL without a review. The New York-based shop will develop ads for the league, its players and its public services efforts, an agency representative said.
> ❞

part 1 n (for machine) pieza f ❑ **parts and labour warranty** garantía f sobre piezas de recambio y mano de obra

   2 adj **in part payment** como parte del pago; **they'll take your old one in part exchange** aceptan el viejo como parte del pago ❑ **part load** carga f incompleta; **part owner** copropietario(a) m,f; **part ownership** copropiedad f; **part shipment** embarque m parcial

partial adj parcial ❑ BANKING **partial acceptance** (of bill) aceptación f parcial; **partial exemption** (from tax) exención f parcial; INS **partial loss** pérdida f parcial; **partial payment** pago m parcial

participant n (in negotiation) participante mf

participating adj **participating interest** participación f en el capital; **to hold a participating interest in a company** poseer una participación en el capital de una empresa; **participating loan** préstamo m participativo

participation n ST EXCH **participation certificate** certificado m de participación; **participation rate** tasa f de participación

particular n INS **particular average** avería f particular; FIN **particular lien** gravamen m específico

partly adv en parte ❑ FIN **partly paid-up capital** capital m parcialmente desembolsado; **partly paid-up shares** acciones fpl parcialmente liberadas; **partly secured creditor** acreedor(ora) m,f con garantía parcial

partner n socio(a) m,f; **our European partners** nuestros socios europeos

partnership n (**a**) (company) sociedad f comanditaria

   (**b**) (association) colaboración f; **to enter** or **go into partnership (with sb)** formar sociedad or asociarse (con alguien); **to dissolve a partnership** disolver una sociedad ❑ **partnership agreement** acuerdo m de colaboración; **partnership share** participación f en una sociedad; **partnership at will** = sociedad colectiva sin plazo fijo de duración y que puede ser abandonada a voluntad de sus miembros

   (**c**) (position in firm) **to offer sb a partnership in the firm** ofrecer a alguien la posición de socio en la empresa

part-time 1 adj (contract, job, staff, employee) a tiempo parcial; **to be in part-time employment** trabajar a tiempo parcial

   2 adv a tiempo parcial

party n LAW (participant) parte f; **the contracting parties** las partes contratantes

PASCAL n COMPTR PASCAL m

pass 1 n (permit) pase m ❑ **pass book** libreta f or cartilla f de banco

   2 vt (bill, resolution, invoice) aprobar; **to pass a dividend** no declarar un dividendo

passenger n (in vehicle, aircraft, ship) pasajero(a) m,f ❑ **passenger and cargo plane** avión m de pasajeros y carga; **passenger and cargo ship** buque m de pasajeros y carga; **passenger and goods train** tren m de pasajeros y mercancías; **passenger list** lista f de pasajeros; **passenger service** servicio m de pasajeros; **passenger ship** barco m de pasajeros; **passenger train** tren m de pasajeros

passing adj **passing customer** cliente(a) m,f de paso; **passing trade** clientela f de paso

passive management n gestión f indiciaria

passport n pasaporte m

pass-through adj US **pass-through securities** títulos mpl de transferencia de ingresos; **pass-through tax entity** sujeto m impositivo con responsabilidad fiscal personal

password n COMPTR contraseña f ❑ **password protection** protección f por contraseña

password-protected adj COMPTR protegido(a) por contraseña

paste vt COMPTR pegar (**into/onto** en)

patch n (**a**) COMPTR (correction) parche m (**b**) MKTG (of sales representative) zona f

patent 1 n patente f; **to take out a patent on sth** patentar algo; **patent applied for, patent pending** (on product) patente solicitada, en espera de patente ❑ **patent agent** agente mf de patentes; **patent holder** titular mf de la patente; **patent law** derecho m de patentes; **patent office** registro m de la propiedad industrial, Esp ≃ Oficina f de Patentes y Marcas;

patent rights propiedad *f* industrial ; **patent specifications** especificaciones *fpl* de patente
  2 *adj (patented)* patentado(a) ◻ **patent goods** mercancías *fpl* patentadas ; **patent medicine** específico *m*, especialidad *f* farmacéutica
  3 *vt* patentar

patented *adj* patentado(a)

patentee *n* titular *mf* de la patente

paternity leave *n* baja *f* or permiso *m* or *Am* licencia *f* por paternidad

> ❝
>
> Ian Swinson worked out a monthlong **paternity leave** before becoming the creative director of eScene Networks, a streaming media applications firm in San Francisco. "If they had said no, there's a good chance I wouldn't have joined", Swinson says. "And I would've left if they hadn't given me the time off [after I started]."
>
> ❞

path *n* COMPTR camino *m*, localización *f*

patron *n* *Formal (of shop)* cliente(a) *m,f*

patronage *n* (a) *Formal (custom)* clientela *f* (b) *(sponsorship) (of arts)* mecenazgo *m* ; *(of charity)* patrocinio *m*

patronize *vt* *Formal (shop)* frecuentar

pattern *n* *(design)* dibujo *m* ◻ **pattern book** muestrario *m*

pawn 1 *n* **to put sth in pawn** empeñar algo ; **to take sth out of pawn** desempeñar algo ◻ **pawn ticket** resguardo *m* de la casa de empeños
  2 *vt* empeñar

pawnbroker *n* prestamista *mf (de casa de empeños)*

pawnshop *n* casa *f* de empeños

pay 1 *n* *(wages)* sueldo *m*, paga *f* ; **the pay's good / bad** el sueldo es bueno/malo ◻ **pay advice slip** nómina *f* ; **pay agreement** acuerdo *m* salarial ; **pay bargaining** negociación *f* salarial ; **pay Br cheque** *or US* **check** cheque *m* del sueldo ; **pay claim** reivindicación *f* salarial ; **pay cut** recorte *m* salarial ; **pay day** día *m* de pago ; **pay deal** acuerdo *m* salarial ; **pay dispute** conflicto *m* salarial ; *US* **pay envelope** *(envelope)* sobre *m* de la paga ; *(money)* paga *f* ; **pay equity** igualdad *f* salarial ; **pay formula** fórmula *f* para calcular los aumentos salariales ; **pay freeze** *Esp* congelación *f* or *Am* congelamiento *m* salarial ; **pay increase** aumento *m* salarial *or* de sueldo ; ACCT **pay ledger** registro *m* de nóminas ; **pay packet** *(envelope)* sobre *m* de la paga ; *(money)* paga *f* ; **pay policy** política *f* salarial ; **pay rise** aumento *m* salarial *or* de sueldo ; **pay scale** escala *f* salarial ; **pay settlement** acuerdo *m* salarial ; **pay slip** nómina *f* ; **pay talks** negociaciones *fpl* salariales
  2 *vt* (a) *(person)* pagar ; **to pay sb £100** pagar a alguien 100 libras ; **to be paid by the hour/the**

week cobrar por horas/semanas ; **she's paid $5,000 a month** cobra *or* le pagan 5.000 dólares al mes
  (b) *(sum of money)* pagar ; **you pay £100 now, the rest later** pague 100 libras ahora y el resto más tarde ; **to pay money into sb's account** *Esp* ingresar *or Am* depositar dinero en la cuenta de alguien
  (c) *(bill, dividend, fine, taxes)* pagar ; *(debt)* saldar, liquidar ; **the account pays interest** la cuenta da intereses ; **interest is paid quarterly** los intereses se abonan trimestralmente ; **to pay cash** pagar en efectivo ; **to pay a cheque into the bank** *Esp* ingresar *or Am* depositar un cheque en el banco
  3 *vi* pagar ; **how would you like to pay?** ¿cómo lo va a pagar? ; **to pay by cheque** pagar con un cheque ; **to pay in cash** pagar en efectivo ; **to pay in advance** pagar por adelantado ; **to pay in full** liquidar ; FIN **to pay on demand** *or* **on presentation** pagar a la vista ; FIN **pay to bearer** páguese al portador

▸ **pay back** *vt sep (lender)* devolver el dinero a ; *(money)* devolver ; *(loan)* amortizar, liquidar

▸ **pay in** *vt sep (money, cheque)* *Esp* ingresar, *Am* depositar

▸ **pay off 1** *vt sep* (a) *(worker)* pagar el finiquito a (b) *(loan)* amortizar, liquidar ; *(debt)* saldar, liquidar ; *(mortgage)* amortizar, redimir
  2 *vi (work, efforts)* dar fruto ; **moving the company out of London really paid off** el traslado de la empresa fuera de Londres dio muy buenos resultados

▸ **pay out 1** *vt sep* gastar
  2 *vi* pagar

▸ **pay up 1** *vi* pagar
  2 *vt (capital)* desembolsar

payable 1 *adj* pagadero(a) ; **payable in 24 monthly instalments / in advance** pagadero(a) en 24 mensualidades/por adelantado ; **to make a cheque payable to sb** extender un cheque a favor *or* a nombre de alguien ; **please make your cheque payable to Ms A. Johnston** por favor, extienda el cheque a nombre de la Sra. A. Johnston ; **payable in cash** pagadero(a) en efectivo ; **payable at sight** pagadero(a) a la vista ; **payable on delivery / with order** pagadero(a) contra entrega/por adelantado ; **payable to bearer** pagadero(a) al portador ; **payable to order** pagadero(a) a la orden
  2 *n US* **payables** efectos *mpl* por pagar

pay-as-you-earn, *US* **pay-as-you-go** *n* retención *f* en nómina del impuesto sobre la renta

payback *n* FIN recuperación *f*, reembolso *m* ◻ **payback period** periodo *m* de amortización *or* reembolso

PAYE *n Br (abbr* **pay-as-you-earn**) retención *f* en

nómina del impuesto sobre la renta

> "
>
> Finally, 5 October is the date for notifying the taxman that you are liable to income or capital gains tax. There's no need to do this if you've been sent a tax return, nor if **PAYE** covers all your income. But if you have new freelance income or have started a new business, you should be putting your hand up to the Revenue by six months after the end of the tax year in which you started – hence 5 October.
>
> "

payee n (of postal order, cheque) beneficiario(a) m,f; (of bill) tomador(ora) m,f

payer n (**a**) (in general) pagador(ora) m,f; **that company is a good/bad payer** esa empresa es buena/mala pagadora (**b**) (of cheque) pagador(ora) m,f

paying 1 n pago m
2 adj (**a**) (who pays) **a paying customer** un(a) cliente(a) que paga or de pago ◻ **paying bank** banco m pagador (**b**) (profitable) **it's not a paying proposition** no es una propuesta rentable

paying-in n **paying-in book** talonario m de pagos or depósitos; **paying-in slip** talón m de pago

payload n (of vehicle) carga f útil

paymaster n oficial m pagador; **the World Bank acts as paymaster of the project** el Banco Mundial financia el proyecto ◻ **Paymaster General** Br = funcionario encargado del pago de sueldos y pensiones a los funcionarios públicos; US = funcionario encargado del pago de sueldos al personal de las Fuerzas Armadas

payment n pago m; **48 monthly payments** 48 pagos or cuotas mensuales; **to make a payment** efectuar un pago; **to present a bill for payment** presentar una letra al cobro; **to stop payment on a cheque** revocar un cheque; **on payment of £100** previo pago de 100 libras; **on payment of a deposit** previo pago de una fianza; **in payment of your invoice** como pago de su factura; **in easy payments** con facilidades de pago; **payment on account** pago a cuenta; **payment in advance** pago por adelantado; **payment in arrears** pago atrasado; **payment in cash** pago en efectivo; **payment by cheque** pago con cheque; **payment on delivery** pago contra entrega; **payment against documents** pago contra documentos; **payment in full** liquidación f; **payment by instalments** pago a plazos; **payment in kind** pago en especie ◻ **payment advice** notificación f de abono en cuenta; **payment day** día m de pago; **payment facilities** sistemas mpl or formas fpl de pago; **payment order** orden f de pago; **payment proposal** propuesta f de pago; **payment schedule** calendario m de pago

payoff n (**a**) (of loan) amortización f, liquidación f; (of debt) liquidación; (of mortgage) amortización (**b**) (bribe) soborno m (**c**) (severance payment) indemnización f, compensación f (**d**) (benefit) beneficio m

payout n (**a**) INS pago m, desembolso m (**b**) (of dividends) beneficios mpl

payroll n (**a**) (list of employees) nómina f; **to be on the payroll** estar en nómina; **how many do you have on the payroll?** ¿cuántos tienes en nómina?; **she's been on our payroll for over twenty years** lleva más de veinte años en nómina; **they were taken off the payroll** (voluntarily) dejaron la empresa; (were laid off) los despidieron; **to do the payroll** pagar las nóminas or los salarios ◻ ACCT **payroll ledger** registro m de nóminas (**b**) (money paid) nómina f, salario m ◻ **payroll tax** impuesto m sobre la nómina

> "
>
> In the 12-month period ending in January 1998, turnover at the Space Coast Credit Union was a horrifying 62 percent. Of 250 employees on the **payroll** that year, the Florida credit union lost 155.
>
> "

PB n US BANKING (abbr **pass book**) libreta f or cartilla f de banco

PC n (abbr **personal computer**) PC m

p/c n (abbr **petty cash**) caja f para gastos menores, Méx, RP caja chica

PC-compatible adj COMPTR compatible con (el) PC

PCMCIA n COMPTR (abbr **PC memory card international association**) PCMCIA f

PCN n TEL (abbr **personal communications network**) RCP f

PDA n COMPTR (abbr **personal digital assistant**) PDA m

PDF n COMPTR (abbr **portable document format**) PDF m

PDL n COMPTR (abbr **page description language**) lenguaje m de descripción de páginas

peak 1 n (**a**) (of price, inflation, demand) punto m máximo, (máximo) apogeo m; **production was at its peak** la producción alcanzó su máximo ◻ **peak hours** (of traffic) horas fpl Esp punta or Am pico; (of electricity, gas) horas de mayor consumo; (of TV watching) horas de mayor audiencia; **peak output** producción f máxima; **peak price** precio m máximo; **peak rate** tarifa f punta; **peak season** temporada f alta; **peak year** año m récord (**b**) Br MKTG (on TV) **peak time** franja f de máxima audiencia; **peak time advertising** publicidad f en la franja de máxima audiencia
2 vi (price, demand, production, inflation) tocar

techo; **profits peaked in July** los beneficios alcanzaron su máximo en julio

peg vt FIN, ST EXCH (prices) (fix) fijar; (stabilize) estabilizar; **to peg sth to the rate of inflation** vincular algo al índice de la inflación; **oil was pegged at $20 a barrel** el precio del petróleo se fijó en 20 dólares; **export earnings are pegged to the exchange rate** los ingresos por exportaciones están determinados por el tipo de cambio

penal adj □ **penal interest** interés m de demora; **penal rate** (charged as penalty) interés m de demora

penalty n (for late delivery, payment) penalización f, recargo m □ **penalty clause** cláusula f de penalización; **penalty interest** intereses mpl de demora; US **penalty rate** (for overtime) tarifa f de horas extras

pence npl peniques mpl

pending 1 adj (negotiations, documents) pendiente; LAW (case) pendiente de resolución □ **pending tray** bandeja f de asuntos pendientes
2 prep a la espera de; **pending your decision** a la espera de su decisión

penetrate vt (market) introducirse en, penetrar en

penetration n (of market) penetración f □ **penetration rate** tasa f de penetración; **penetration strategy** estrategia f de penetración

penny n Br (coin, unit of currency) penique m; US (coin) centavo m □ Br **penny shares** acciones fpl de poco valor; US **penny stock** acciones fpl de poco valor

pen-pusher n Fam Pej chupatintas m inv

pen-pushing n Fam trabajo m de chupatintas

pension n pensión f; **to be on a pension** cobrar una pensión □ **pension fund** fondo m de pensiones; **pension plan** plan m de pensiones; **pension scheme** plan m de jubilación or de pensiones

> 〝
> These interlocking shareholders have an interest in each other's prosperity, partly because they do business with one another, partly because they have invested in each other. Unlike a **pension fund** in either Britain, America or even Japan, these interlocking shareholders have strong economic reasons to care about the performance of the firms in which they own shares.
> 〟

▶ **pension off** vt sep jubilar

pensionable adj (person, job) con derecho a cobrar pensión; **of pensionable age** en edad de jubilación □ **pensionable age** edad f de jubilación

pensionary 1 n (person receiving a pension) pensionista mf
2 adj (receiving a pension) que cobra una pensión

pensioner n Br **(old-age) pensioner** pensionista mf

people-focused adj centrado(a) en la persona

> 〝
> Deloitte & Touche's selection for this prestigious list is reflective of the firm's dedication to continuous improvement, the quality of its human resources programs, and its **people-focused** culture, which provides the opportunity for all individuals to realize their full professional and personal potential.
> 〟

PEP n Formerly FIN (abbr **personal equity plan**) = plan personal de inversión en valores de renta variable fiscalmente incentivado por el gobierno británico

peppercorn rent n Br alquiler m or arrendamiento m (por un precio) simbólico

per prep por; **per annum** al año, por año; **per capita** per cápita; **the highest per capita income in Europe** la renta per cápita más alta de Europa; **per capita consumption** el consumo per cápita; US **per diem** (per day) al día, por día; (expenses) dietas fpl; LAW **per pro** por poderes; **per pro signature** firma por poderes; **per week** a la semana; **as per invoice** según factura; **as per your instructions** según sus instrucciones; **as per sample** conforme a la muestra

p/e ratio n ACCT (abbr **price/earnings ratio**) relación f precio-beneficio

perceive vt MKTG (product, brand) percibir

perceived adj MKTG **perceived performance** funcionamiento m or rendimiento m percibido; **perceived quality** calidad f percibida; **perceived risk** riesgo m percibido; **perceived service** servicio m percibido; **perceived value** valor m percibido; **perceived value pricing** precios mpl según el valor percibido

percent 1 n porcentaje m, tanto m por ciento; **a nine percent interest rate** una tasa de interés del nueve por ciento
2 adv por ciento; **prices went up ten percent** los precios subieron un diez por ciento

percentage n porcentaje m, tanto m por ciento; **a high percentage of the staff** un alto porcentaje de la plantilla; **to get a percentage on all sales** percibir un tanto por ciento de todas las ventas

percentile n percentil m

perception n (of product, brand) percepción f

perfect competition *n* ECON competencia *f* perfecta

perforated *adj* COMPTR **perforated paper** papel *m* perforado

perform *vi* (**a**) *(company)* rendir; *(shares, investment, currency)* comportarse; **the Edinburgh branch is performing very well** la sucursal de Edimburgo está rindiendo mucho; **how did the company perform in the first quarter?** ¿cuál fue el rendimiento de la empresa en el primer trimestre?; **shares in the company performed well yesterday** las acciones de la empresa se comportaron bien ayer

(**b**) *(person) (in job, situation)* desenvolverse; **how does she perform under pressure?** ¿cómo se desenvuelve bajo presión?

performance *n* (**a**) *(of contract)* ejecución *f*; *(of task)* realización *f*, ejecución □ **performance bond** fianza *f* de ejecución de un contrato

(**b**) *(of company)* rendimiento *m*; *(of economy)* marcha *f*, desarrollo *m*; *(of investment, currency, shares)* comportamiento *m*; **the country's poor economic performance** la mala marcha de la economía del país; **the company's performance on the Stock Exchange** el comportamiento de la empresa en la Bolsa □ **performance appraisal** evaluación *f* del rendimiento; FIN **performance hurdle** = listón de rendimiento que vincula el derecho a ejercer las opciones otorgadas a los ejecutivos a su actuación personal; **performance rating** valoración *f* del rendimiento; ACCT **performance ratio** coeficiente *m* de rendimiento; **performance test** prueba *f* de rendimiento

performance-related *adj* según el rendimiento □ **performance-related bonus** prima *f* de rendimiento; **performance-related pay** sueldo *m* vinculado al rendimiento

performer *n (product, shares, company)* **to be a good/bad performer** tener un buen/mal comportamiento

period *n* periodo *m*, período *m*; **for a period of three months** durante un periodo de tres meses; **within the agreed period** dentro del plazo acordado □ FIN **period bill** letra *f* a fecha fija; **period of grace** periodo *m* de gracia

periodic *adj* **periodic inventory** inventario *m* periódico; **periodic payments** pagos *mpl* periódicos, cuotas *fpl* periódicas

periodical *n* publicación *f* periódica, boletín *m*

peripheral COMPTR **1** *n* periférico *m*

2 *adj* periférico(a) □ **peripheral device, peripheral unit** *(dispositivo m)* periférico *m*

perishability *n* carácter *m* perecedero

perishable 1 *n* **perishables** productos *mpl* perecederos

2 *adj* perecedero(a) □ **perishable cargo** cargamento *m* perecedero; **perishable goods** mercancías *fpl* perecederas

perk *n Fam (of job)* ventaja *f*; **cheap air travel is one of the perks of his job** una de las ventajas de su trabajo son los vuelos baratos

permanent *adj* permanente; *(employee, job)* fijo(a) □ **permanent address** domicilio *m* fijo, residencia *f* habitual; FIN **permanent assets** activos *mpl* fijos; **permanent contract** contrato *m* fijo *or* indefinido; **permanent credit** crédito *m* permanente; **permanent establishment** *(in tax legislation)* establecimiento *m* permanente; **permanent job** trabajo *m* fijo; **permanent member** miembro *m* permanente; **permanent post** *(with private company)* puesto *m* de trabajo fijo; *(in public service)* plaza *f* en propiedad; **permanent staff** *(of private company)* personal *m* fijo; *(in public service)* personal *m* con plaza en propiedad

permatemp 1 *n* empleado(a) *m,f* con contrato basura de larga duración

2 *adj (worker, employee)* con contrato basura de larga duración

permissible *adj (allowed)* admisible, permisible; *(tolerable)* tolerable □ **permissible overload** sobrecarga *f* permitida

permission *n* permiso *m*; **to ask for permission to do sth** pedir permiso para hacer algo; **to give sb permission to do sth** dar a alguien permiso para hacer algo □ ST EXCH **permission to deal** permiso *m* para comenzar a negociar;

permission marketing marketing *m* de permiso, permission marketing *m*

permit 1 *n* permiso *m*; CUSTOMS licencia *f*
2 *vt* permitir; **to permit sb to do sth** permitir a alguien hacer algo; **smoking is not permitted** no se permite fumar

perpetual *adj* continuo(a), constante □ **perpetual inventory** inventario *m* permanente; **perpetual loan** préstamo *m* perpetuo

perpetuity *n* FIN *(annuity)* anualidad *f* perpetua; **in perpetuity** a perpetuidad

personal *adj* personal; **personal** *(on letter)* personal y privado; **personal callers welcome** *(in advertisement)* se atienden llamadas de particulares □ INS **personal accident insurance** seguro *m* individual de accidentes; **personal account** *(with bank, of stock trader, in accounts)* cuenta *f* personal; **personal allowance** *(for tax)* mínimo *m* (exento) personal; **personal assets** bienes *mpl* personales, patrimonio *m* personal; BANKING **personal assets profile** perfil *m* de patrimonio personal; **personal assistant** *(person)* secretario(a) *m,f* personal; COMPTR asistente *m* personal; COMPTR **personal computer** *Esp* ordenador *m or Am* computadora *f* personal; COMPTR **personal computing** informática *f* personal; **personal credit** crédito *m* personal; COMPTR **personal digital assistant** asistente *m* personal; **personal effects** efectos *mpl* personales; *Formerly* **personal equity plan** = plan personal de inversión en valores de renta variable fiscalmente incentivado por el gobierno británico; **personal estate** bienes *mpl* muebles; BANKING **personal identification number** número *m* secreto personal, PIN *m*; **personal injury** lesiones *fpl*, daños *mpl* corporales; *Br Formerly* **Personal Investment Authority** = organismo oficial que regula la inversión privada; **personal legacy** legado *m* personal; BANKING **personal loan** préstamo *m or* crédito *m* personal; MKTG **personal observation** observación *f* personal; **personal organizer** *(diary)* agenda *f*; COMPTR agenda *f* electrónica; **personal pension plan** plan *m* personal de jubilación; **personal property** bienes *mpl* muebles; MKTG **personal selling** venta *f* personal; BANKING **personal withdrawals** retiros *mpl or* reintegros *mpl* de efectivo *(para uso personal)*

> The income is tax-free because your units are held in a **personal equity plan**. The government made PEPs tax-free to encourage people to invest in shares. A PEP should be regarded as a long-term investment though, so do not tie your money up if you think you may need it quickly.

personality promotion *n* MKTG promoción *f* con un personaje público

personalty *n* LAW bienes *mpl* muebles; **to convert realty into personalty** transformar los bienes inmuebles en bienes muebles

personnel *n* personal *m* □ **personnel department** departamento *m* de personal; **personnel management** gestión *f* del personal; **personnel manager** director(ora) *m, f or* jefe(a) *m,f* de personal; **personnel rating** evaluación *f* del personal

person-to-person approach *n* MKTG tratamiento *m* personalizado

peseta *n Formerly* peseta *f*

peso *n* peso *m*

PEST *n* MKTG *(abbr* **political economic sociological technological)** PEST *m*

Peter principle *n* **the Peter principle** el principio de Peter

> Of course, beware of the **Peter Principle**: You may promote someone to their level of incompetence, as has often happened with coders and insurance specialists who were elevated to the top of the heap. However, such a promotion may be worth the risk if the employee has the potential to become a manager. In that case, provide on-the-job training.

petition in bankruptcy *n* solicitud *f* de declaración de quiebra; **to file a petition in bankruptcy** declararse en quiebra; **filing of a petition in bankruptcy** declaración *f* de quiebra

petrochemical 1 *adj* petroquímico(a) □ **petrochemical industry** industria *f* petroquímica
2 *n* **petrochemicals** productos *mpl* petroquímicos

petrocurrency *n* petrodivisa *f*

petrodollar *n* petrodólar *m*

petroleum *n* petróleo *m* □ **petroleum industry** industria *f* del petróleo; **petroleum products** productos *mpl* petrolíferos *or* derivados del petróleo

petty cash *n* caja *f* para gastos menores, *Méx, RP* caja chica; **they'll pay you back out of petty cash** te pagarán con el dinero de caja □ **petty cash book** libro *m* de gastos menores; **petty cash box** caja *f* para gastos menores, *Méx, RP* caja chica; **petty cash management** gestión *f* de gastos menores; **petty cash voucher** comprobante *m* de caja

pfennig *n Formerly* pfennig *m*

PFI *n* *(abbr* **private finance initiative)** = acuerdo de financiación de centros públicos entre una entidad privada y la administración británica

phase *n* fase *f*, etapa *f*; **the project is going through a critical phase** el proyecto está atravesando una etapa crucial

► **phase in** vt sep (new methods, installations, equipment) introducir gradualmente or escalonadamente; **the increases will be phased in over five years** los aumentos se irán introduciendo gradualmente a lo largo de cinco años; **the reforms will have to be phased in** habrá que introducir las reformas de forma gradual

► **phase out** vt sep eliminar gradualmente or escalonadamente; **these jobs will be phased out over the next five years** estos puestos de trabajo irán desapareciendo a lo largo de los próximos cinco años

phone 1 n teléfono m; **to be on the phone** (speaking) estar al teléfono; (have a telephone) tener teléfono; **to answer the phone** contestar or Esp coger el teléfono; **you're wanted on the phone** te llaman ▫ **phone bill** factura f del teléfono; **phone book** guía f telefónica or de teléfonos, Am directorio m de teléfonos; **phone call** llamada f telefónica, Am llamado m telefónico; **phone number** número m de teléfono
  2 vt **to phone sb** telefonear a alguien, llamar a alguien (por teléfono); **I'll phone you** te llamaré (por teléfono)
  3 vi telefonear, llamar (por teléfono); **to phone for a taxi** llamar a un taxi

phonecard n tarjeta f telefónica

photocopier n fotocopiadora f

photocopy 1 n fotocopia f; **to take** or **make a photocopy of sth** hacer una fotocopia de algo
  2 vt fotocopiar

phreaker n = persona que manipula las líneas telefónicas para obtener llamadas gratis

physical adj FIN **physical assets** activo m fijo material; **physical capital** capital m físico; **physical distribution** distribución f física; **physical distribution management** gestión f de la distribución física; FIN **physical fixed assets** activo m fijo material; **physical inventory** inventario m físico; **physical property** propiedades fpl tangibles

PIA n Formerly (abbr **Personal Investment Authority**) = organismo oficial británico que regula la inversión privada

► **pick up** vi (business, prices) mejorar; **the market is picking up after a slow start** el mercado se va animando tras los titubeos iniciales

picket 1 n (group) piquete m; (individual) integrante mf de un piquete; **there was a picket outside the factory** había un piquete fuera de la fábrica; **twenty pickets stood outside the factory** había veinte personas en un piquete fuera de la fábrica ▫ **picket duty** turno m de piquete; **to be on picket duty** estar en el turno de piquete; **picket line** piquete m; **to be** or **stand on a picket line** estar en un piquete; **to cross a picket line** atravesar or cruzar un piquete

  2 vt **to picket a factory** hacer piquetes en una fábrica

picking n ordenación f

pick-up point n (for cargo, passengers) lugar m de recogida

piece n artículo m; **to sell sth by the piece** vender algo por unidades ▫ **piece rate** (pay) tarifa f de destajo; **to be paid piece rates** cobrar tarifa de destajo

piecework n (trabajo m a) destajo m

pieceworker n trabajador(ora) m,f a destajo

pie chart n gráfico m circular or de sectores, Méx gráfica f de pastel, SAm gráfica or gráfico de torta

pigeonhole n casillero m, casilla f

piggybacking n (a) (in export) transporte m multimodal (de remolques de camión por ferrocarril) (b) BANKING financiación f concatenada

pilferage n hurto m

pilot 1 n **pilot factory** fábrica f piloto; **pilot project** proyecto m piloto; MKTG **pilot questionnaire** cuestionario m piloto; **pilot run** serie f de prueba; **pilot scheme** proyecto m piloto; **pilot series** serie f piloto; **pilot study** estudio m piloto; MKTG **pilot survey** encuesta f piloto
  2 vt (scheme, study) hacer una prueba piloto de

pilotage n derechos mpl de practicaje

PIMS n MKTG (abbr **profit impact of marketing strategy**) PIMS m

PIN n (abbr **personal identification number**) **PIN (number)** (número m de) PIN m

pin n COMPTR pin m

pink adj US **the pink dollar**, Br **the pink pound** el poder adquisitivo de los homosexuales; US Fam **pink slip: to get a pink slip** ser despedido(a)

> At the outset, analysts argued gay clients might feel reassured that they would not be discriminated against when taking out a loan. However, G & L's problems were not in attracting investors but in finding people who wanted to take out loans, for houses and other purchases, which would bring in the cashflow that banks rely on. Without that, and up against competition from other physical banks, which increasingly recognised that the **pink dollar** was worth the same as any other, it could not survive.

pink-collar adj US **pink-collar job** = trabajo de oficina desempeñado por una mujer y mal remunerado; **pink-collar workers** = trabajadoras de oficina mal remuneradas

pipe vt COMPTR (commands) canalizar

pipeline n (**a**) (for water, gas) tubería f, conducto m; **oil pipeline** oleoducto m (**b**) **in the pipeline: there are several new projects in the pipeline** hay varios proyectos en preparación; **they have a new model in the pipeline** están preparando un nuevo modelo; **important changes are in the pipeline for next year** se están preparando cambios importantes para el año próximo

piracy n (of copyright material) piratería f

pirate 1 n (of book, software) pirata mf ❑ **pirate edition** edición f pirata
2 vt (book, software) piratear

pit n ST EXCH corro m

pitch 1 n (of product, idea) presentación f
2 vt **our new model is pitched to appeal to executives** nuestro nuevo modelo está diseñado para atraer a ejecutivos; **we need to pitch the idea in a way that will convince them to take it up** tenemos que presentar la idea de tal forma que les convenza y la acepten
3 vi pujar (**for** por)

> KFC originally invited five agencies to **pitch**. Apart from Zenith, Initiative and Optimedia, New PHD and Motive were also asked to present but were knocked out after the first round.

pixel n COMPTR píxel m

pixellated adj COMPTR (image) pixelado(a)

place 1 n lugar m, sitio m ❑ **place of birth** lugar m de nacimiento; **place of business** domicilio m social; **place of delivery** lugar m de entrega; FIN **place of issue** lugar m de emisión; **place of origin** lugar m de origen; **place of payment** lugar m de pago; **place of residence** lugar m de residencia; **place of shipment** lugar m de envío; **place of work** lugar m de trabajo
2 vt (**a**) (put) **to place an order (with sb)** hacer un pedido (a alguien); **to place a contract with sb** conceder un contrato a alguien; **to place an advertisement in a newspaper** poner un anuncio en un periódico (**b**) ST EXCH (shares) colocar

placement n (**a**) (work experience) (empleo m en) prácticas fpl; **she did a placement with a local firm** hizo unas prácticas en una empresa de la zona (**b**) ST EXCH (of shares) colocación f (**c**) MKTG (of product) colocación f (en una película o un programa de televisión)

plain paper n (unheaded) papel m sin membrete; (unruled) papel liso ❑ **plain paper fax (machine)** fax m de papel normal

plaintiff n LAW demandante mf

plan 1 n (**a**) (strategy) plan m; **to draw up** or **to make a plan** hacer un plan; **plan of action** plan de acción (**b**) (of building, town) plano m

2 vt (**a**) (arrange) planear, planificar; **to plan to do sth** planear hacer algo; **an industrial estate is planned for this site** tienen previsto construir un polígono industrial en este solar; **they're planning a new venture** están planeando embarcarse en una nueva empresa (**b**) (building, town) proyectar (**c**) ECON (economy) planificar

plane n (aeroplane) avión m ❑ **plane ticket** Esp billete m or Am boleto m or esp Am pasaje m de avión

planned adj planeado(a) ❑ **planned economy** economía f planificada; **planned maintenance** mantenimiento m planificado; **planned obsolescence** obsolescencia f planificada; **planned production** producción f prevista; **planned redundancy scheme** programa m de regulación de empleo

> This enables us to say therefore that competition creates a system of prices which embodies relevant information so that the wealth created within the market order is produced at least cost. In other words, a market economy is an efficient way of producing wealth; the reason it is more efficient than a **planned economy** in which prices are not competitive is that prices do not convey this information.

planner n (**a**) ECON planificador(ora) m,f (**b**) (**town**) **planner** urbanista mf (**c**) (in diary, on wall) planning m

planning n (**a**) (organization) planificación f; **planning and allocation of resources** planificación de asignación de recursos ❑ Br **planning permission** licencia f de obras (**b**) ECON (of economy) planificación f (**c**) (town planning) urbanismo m

planning-programming-budgeting system n ACCT sistema m de planificación, programación y presupuestación

plant n (equipment) bienes mpl de equipo; (factory) planta f; **plant and machinery** instalaciones fpl y bienes de equipo ❑ **plant capacity** capacidad f de producción (de la planta); **plant hire** alquiler m de equipo; **plant layout** distribución f de la planta; **plant manager** jefe(a) m,f de planta

plastic Fam **1** n (credit cards) tarjetas fpl de crédito; **to put sth on the plastic** comprar algo con tarjeta de crédito; **do they take plastic?** ¿se puede pagar con tarjeta de crédito?
2 adj **plastic money** tarjetas fpl de crédito, dinero m plástico

platform n COMPTR plataforma f

player n actor m; **who are the key players in this market?** ¿cuáles son los protagonistas or los principales actores en este mercado?

"

But Lexus would be wise to consider the fortunes of Audi. It has taken many years for VW to turn the brand, which already had a long history, into a major **player** in the premium market.

"

PLC, plc n (a) Br (abbr **public limited company**) ≃ S.A.; **Scotia Hotels plc** ≃ Scotia Hotels S.A. (b) (abbr **product lifecycle**) CVP m, ciclo m de vida del producto

pledge FIN **1** n garantía f, aval m; **in pledge** en garantía □ **pledge holder** depositario(a) m,f (de una garantía)
2 vt (offer as security) ofrecer en garantía or como prenda; (pawn) empeñar; **to pledge one's property** dar las propiedades en garantía; **to pledge securities** dar valores en garantía; **pledged securities** valores pignorados or dados en garantía

pledgee n FIN depositario(a) m,f (de una garantía)

pledgor n FIN prendador(ora) m,f, pignorador(ora) m,f

plenary 1 n (at conference) sesión f plenaria
2 adj (meeting) plenario(a) □ **plenary session** (at conference) sesión f plenaria; **to meet in plenary session** reunirse en sesión plenaria

plotter n COMPTR (device) plóter m, plotter m

▸ **plough back**, US **plow back** vt sep FIN reinvertir (**into** en); **to plough the profits back into the company** reinvertir los beneficios en la empresa; **ploughed back profits** beneficios reinvertidos

▸ **plough in**, US **plow in** vt sep (money) invertir

ploughback, US **plowback** n reinversión f de beneficios

▸ **plow back, plow in** US = **plough back, plow in**

▸ **plowback** US = **ploughback**

plug Fam **1** n (publicity) **their products got another plug on TV** sus productos recibieron otra recomendación en televisión
2 vt (product) hacer publicidad de, promocionar

plug-in n COMPTR plugin m, conector m

plummet vi (price, rate, currency) desplomarse, Esp caer en picado, Am caer en picada; **the value of the pound has plummeted** el valor de la libra se ha desplomado

plunge vi (price, rate, currency) desplomarse, Esp caer en picado, Am caer en picada; **sales have plunged by 30%** las ventas han caído un 30%

PMG n Br (a) (abbr **Paymaster General**) = funcionario encargado del pago de sueldos y pensiones a los funcionarios públicos (b) (abbr

Postmaster General) ≃ Director(ora) m,f General de Correos

pmt n US (abbr **payment**) pago m

P/N n (abbr **promissory note**) pagaré m

PO n (a) (abbr **Post Office**) oficina f de correos □ **PO Box** apartado m de correos, apartado postal, CAm, Méx casilla f postal, Andes, RP casilla de correos (b) (abbr **postal order**) giro m postal

poach vt (employee) robar; **several of our staff have been poached by a rival company** una empresa rival nos ha robado a varios empleados

"

Highly trained staff are being **poached** from Gateway's Republic of Ireland operation by Internet start-up companies offering inflated salaries, says Gateway's local MD Mike Maloney. The problem is creating shortages in key skill areas, which Maloney has raised with IDA Ireland, the state agency responsible for attracting multinational investment.

"

pocket adj de bolsillo □ **pocket calculator** calculadora f de bolsillo; **pocket diary** agenda f de bolsillo

pocket-sized adj de bolsillo

POD adv US (abbr **pay on delivery**) contra reembolso; **to send sth POD** enviar algo contra reembolso

POE n (a) (abbr **port of embarkation**) puerto m de embarque (b) (abbr **port of entry**) puerto m de entrada

point n (a) MKTG **point of delivery** punto m de entrega; **point of purchase** punto m de compra; **point of sale** punto m de venta (b) ST EXCH entero m; **the Dow Jones index is up/down two points** el índice Dow Jones ha subido/bajado dos enteros (c) (for discussion, on agenda) punto m; **let's move on to the next point** vamos a pasar al punto siguiente

point-and-click adj COMPTR de apuntar y hacer clic

pointer n COMPTR puntero m

point-of-purchase adj MKTG en el punto de compra □ **point-of-purchase advertising** publicidad f en el punto de compra; **point-of-purchase display** expositor m en el punto de compra; **point-of-purchase information** información f en el punto de compra; **point-of-purchase material** material m disponible en el punto de compra; **point-of-purchase promotion** promoción f en el punto de compra

point-of-sale adj MKTG punto m de venta □ **point-of-sale advertising** publicidad f en el punto de venta; **point-of-sale display** expositor m en el punto de venta; **point-of-sale information** información f en el punto de venta;

point-of-sale material material *m* disponible en el punto de venta; **point-of-sale promotion** promoción *f* en el punto de venta; **point-of-sale terminal** terminal *f* de punto de venta

poison pill *n Fam (action, clause in contract)* píldora *f* venenosa

---
❝

Poison pill provisions are triggered when a hostile suitor acquires a predetermined percentage of company stock. At that point, all existing shareholders except the suitor are granted options to buy additional stock at a dramatic discount, thus diluting the acquirer's share so as to head off a change in control of the company. ... According to statistics from Thomson Financial Securities Data, 140 companies adopted **poison pill** provisions in the first half of 2001, up 45 percent from the same period last year.

❞
---

policy *n* (**a**) *(of company, organization)* política *f*; **to adopt a policy** adoptar una política; **this is in line with company policy** esto se encuadra dentro de la política de la empresa; **our policy is to hire professionals only** tenemos por norma contratar únicamente profesionales; **the company's success is essentially down to their inspired marketing policy** el éxito de la empresa se debe fundamentalmente a su acertada política de marketing ◻ **policy document** documento *m* de política general; **policy meeting** reunión *f* de política general; **policy paper** documento *m* normativo; **policy position** política *f* general; **policy statement** declaración *f* de principios; *US Fam* **policy wonk** tecnócrata *mf* (**b**) INS póliza *f* (de seguros); **to take out a policy** hacerse un seguro ◻ **policy holder** asegurado(a) *m,f*

❝

Managing a Mayoral campaign in New York City has to be one of the most stressful jobs in the world and not, under any circumstance, a recommended activity for recovering heart patients. But no one seems to have told that to Richard Schrader, a bearded agitator turned **policy wonk** who's running Mark Green's campaign to succeed Rudolph Giuliani.

❞
---

policymaker *n* responsable *mf* político(a)

political *adj* (**a**) *(relating to politics)* político(a) ◻ **political economy** economía *f* política; **political editor** *(journalist)* redactor(ora) *m,f* (de la sección) de política; *(head of department)* jefe(a) *m,f* (de la sección) de política; **political organization** organización *f* política; **political science** ciencias *fpl* políticas, politología *f*; **political scientist** politólogo(a) *m,f* (**b**) *(tactical) (decision, appointment)* político(a)

politician *n* político(a) *m,f*

politics *n* política *f*; **to go into politics** meterse en política

poll 1 *n (survey)* encuesta *f*, sondeo *m*; **to carry out** *or* **conduct a poll on** *or* **about sth** realizar una encuesta *or* un sondeo de opinión sobre algo ◻ *Formerly* **poll tax** *(in UK)* = impuesto municipal de tarifa única abolido en 1993; *(in US)* = impuesto, abolido en 1964, cuyo pago daba derecho a estar inscrito en el censo electoral
2 *vt (person)* sondear; **most of those polled were in favour of the plan** la mayor parte de los encuestados se manifestó a favor del plan

polling *n* sondeo *m*, encuesta *f* ◻ **polling company** empresa *f* de sondeos de opinión; **polling method** método *m* de sondeo

pollster *n* encuestador(ora) *m,f*

Ponzi scheme *n US* esquema *m* Ponzi, = plan piramidal de inversión en el que los dividendos de los inversores más antiguos se financian con el dinero invertido por los más recientes

---
❝

The investors who have sued Slatkin allege that he used funds collected from new investors to pay returns to older investors, a form of fraud commonly known as a **Ponzi scheme**. Last month, one investor won a court order to freeze Slatkin's brokerage accounts and other assets, including a ranch home in Santa Barbara.

❞
---

pool 1 *n* (**a**) *(of insurance companies)* mancomunidad *f*; *(of company cars)* parque *m* móvil; *(of computers)* parque informático (**b**) *(consortium)* consorcio *m*
2 *vt (ideas, resources)* poner en común; *(efforts)* aunar; *(capital, profits)* juntar; *(orders)* agrupar, consolidar

pooling of interests *n US* agrupación *f or* consolidación *f* de intereses *or* fondos

POP *n* (**a**) COMPTR *(abbr* **post office protocol)** (protocolo *m*) POP *m* (**b**) MKTG *(abbr* **point of purchase)** punto *m* de compra

population *n* población *f* ◻ **population census** censo *m* de población; **population count** recuento *m* de población; **population explosion** explosión *f* demográfica; **population growth** crecimiento *m* de la población; **population statistics** estadística *f* de población

pop-up menu *n* COMPTR menú *m* desplegable

port *n* (**a**) *(harbour)* puerto *m* ◻ **port of arrival** puerto *m* de llegada; **port authority** autoridad *f* portuaria; **port of call** escala *f*; **port charges** tasas *fpl* portuarias; **port of departure** puerto *m* de salida; **port of destination** puerto *m* de destino; **port dues** tasas *fpl* portuarias; **port of embarkation** puerto *m* de embarque; **port**

of entry puerto *m* de entrada; ***port of loading*** puerto *m* de embarque; ***port of shipment*** puerto *m* de embarque; ***port of transit*** puerto *m* de tránsito
(**b**) COMPTR puerto *m*

portability *n* FIN *(of pension, mortgage)* transferibilidad *f*

portable 1 *n (computer)* portátil *m*
2 *adj* (**a**) *(computer)* portátil (**b**) FIN *(pension, mortgage)* transferible

portage *n (transport, cost)* porte *m*

portal *n* COMPTR portal *m*

porterage *n (of goods, parcels)* porte *m*; *(cost)* portes *mpl*, gastos *mpl* de transporte □ ***porterage facilities*** servicio *m* de portes

portfolio *n* (**a**) *(for holding documents)* cartera *f* (**b**) FIN *(of shares)* cartera *f* (de valores) □ ***portfolio analysis*** análisis *m* de carteras; ***portfolio assets*** activos *mpl* en cartera; ***portfolio diversification*** diversificación *f* de cartera; ***portfolio insurance*** seguro *m* de cartera; ***portfolio liquidity*** liquidez *f* de cartera; ***portfolio management*** gestión *f* de carteras; ***portfolio manager*** gestor(ora) *m,f* de carteras; ***portfolio mix*** combinación *f* de cartera; ***portfolio securities*** valores *mpl* de cartera
(**c**) MKTG *(sample of work)* book *m*, portafolio *m*
(**d**) ***portfolio worker*** profesional *mf* autónomo(a)

> 66
> The prototype **portfolio workers** are surely not web designers but women who do night shifts cleaning so that they can rush back to make the kids' breakfast before doing a stint as a barmaid. **Portfolio workers** forfeit security, sick pay, holiday pay and pensions in the name of personal autonomy. They carry the burdens that formerly would have rested on corporate shoulders.
> 99

portrait *n* COMPTR formato *m* vertical *or* de retrato; **to print sth in portrait** imprimir algo en vertical □ ***portrait mode*** modo *m* vertical

port-to-port *adj* puerto a puerto □ ***port-to-port shipment*** envío *m* de puerto a puerto

POS *n* MKTG *(abbr* **point of sale***)* punto *m* de venta

position 1 *n* (**a**) *(circumstances)* posición *f*, situación *f*; **our cash position is not good** nuestra situación de caja es mala; **our financial position is improving** nuestra situación financiera está mejorando
(**b**) *(job)* puesto *m*; **it's a position of great responsibility** es un puesto de una gran responsabilidad; **there were four candidates for the position of manager** había cuatro candidatos para el puesto de director

(**c**) MKTG *(of company, of product on market)* posición *f*
(**d**) ST EXCH posición *f*; **to take a long/short position** tomar una posición larga/corta □ ***position limit*** límite *m* de posición; ***position taking*** toma *f* de posiciones; ***position trader*** operador(ora) *m,f* de posición
2 *vt* COMPTR *(cursor, image)* colocar; MKTG *(product)* posicionar

positioning *n* MKTG posicionamiento *m* □ ***positioning strategy*** estrategia *f* de posicionamiento; ***positioning study*** estudio *m* de posicionamiento

positive *adj* LAW ***positive prescription*** prescripción *f* positiva; *Br* ***positive vetting*** *(security check)* = investigación exhaustiva a la que es sometido un aspirante a un cargo público por motivos de seguridad nacional

possess *vt* LAW poseer

possession *n* LAW *(of property)* posesión *f*; **to take possession (of sth)** tomar posesión (de algo)

possessor *n* LAW poseedor(ora) *m,f*

possessory *adj* LAW posesorio(a) □ ***possessory action*** pleito *m* posesorio; ***possessory right*** derecho *m* de posesión

post¹ 1 *n Br (mail)* correo *m*; **by return of post** a vuelta de correo; **to send sth by post** enviar *or* mandar algo por correo; **it's in the post** ha sido enviado por correo; **can you put the cheque in the post?** ¿puedes mandar el cheque por correo? □ ***post office*** oficina *f* de correos; ***the Post Office*** *(service) Esp* Correos *m, Am* Correo *m*; ***post office account*** ≃ cuenta *f* en la Caja Postal; ***post office box*** apartado *m* de Correos, apartado postal, *CAm, Méx* casilla *f* postal, *Andes, RP* casilla de Correo; ***post office cheque*** cheque *m* postal; COMPTR ***post office protocol*** protocolo *m* POP; *Br* ***post office savings bank*** ≃ Caja *f* Postal; ***post office transfer*** giro *m* postal
2 *vt* (**a**) *(letter, parcel) (send by post)* enviar *or* mandar (por correo); *(put in box)* echar al buzón; **I'll post it to you** te lo mandaré por correo
(**b**) ACCT consignar, contabilizar; **to post an amount** consignar una cantidad; **to post an entry** hacer un asiento
(**c**) *(publicize) (results)* hacer público, anunciar; **they have posted a near 80% rise in sales** han anunciado que las ventas aumentaron en casi un 80%
(**d**) ST EXCH *(bond, security)* depositar; **to post security** depositar una garantía

post² 1 *n (job)* puesto *m*; **the post is still vacant** el puesto sigue vacante; **he got a post as a human resources manager** consiguió un puesto como jefe de recursos humanos
2 *vt (assign)* destinar; **to be posted to a different branch** ser destinado(a) a una oficina diferente

postage *n* franqueo *m*; **postage and packing** gastos *mpl* de envío; **postage included** franqueo incluido; **postage paid** franqueo pagado ❏ *US* **postage meter** (máquina *f*) franqueadora *f*; **postage receipt** recibo *m* de gastos de franqueo; **postage stamp** sello *m* (de correos), *Am* estampilla *f*

postal *adj* postal ❏ **postal area** área *f* postal; **postal charges** gastos *mpl* postales *or* de correo; *Br* **postal code** código *m* postal; **postal delivery** entrega *f* por correo; **postal district** distrito *m* postal; **postal link** conexión *f* postal; *US* **postal meter** (máquina *f*) franqueadora *f*; *Br* **postal order** giro *m* postal; **postal rates** tarifas *fpl* postales; *US* **the Postal Service** *Esp* Correos *m inv*, *Am* Correo *m*; **postal services** servicios *mpl* postales; **postal strike** huelga *f* de correos, huelga *f* postal; **postal survey** encuesta *f* postal *or* por correo; *Br* **postal vote** voto *m* por correo

postcode *n Br* código *m* postal

postdate *vt (cheque)* extender con fecha posterior

posted price *n* precio *m* marcado *or* indicado

poster *n* MKTG cartel *m*, póster *m*, *Am* afiche *m* ❏ **poster advertising** publicidad *f* con *or* en carteles; **poster campaign** campaña *f* con carteles

> ❝
> Bartle Bogle Hegarty (BBH) has developed a **poster campaign** for the internet-based company that brings modern and contemporary art into mainstream life by portraying it in everyday situations. One poster features a Damien Hirst limited edition print.
> ❞

poste restante *n Br* lista *f* de correos, *RP* poste *m* restante

post-free *Br* **1** *adj* con el franqueo pagado
  2 *adv* libre de gastos de envío

Post-it® *n* Post-it® *m*

postmark 1 *n* matasellos *m inv*; **date as postmark** con la fecha del matasellos
  2 *vt* matasellar; **the letter is postmarked Phoenix** la carta lleva un matasellos de Phoenix

postmaster *n* COMPTR administrador(ora) *m,f or* jefe(a) *m,f* de correos

post-paid 1 *adj* con el franqueo pagado
  2 *adv* libre de gastos de envío

postpone *vt* aplazar, posponer; **the meeting was postponed until a later date** la reunión fue aplazada hasta una fecha posterior

postponement *n* aplazamiento *m*

post-purchase *adj* MKTG postcompra ❏ **post-purchase behaviour** comportamiento *m* postcompra; **post-purchase evaluation** evaluación *f* postcompra

PostScript® *n* COMPTR PostScript® *m* ❏ **PostScript® font** fuente *f* PostScript®; **PostScript® printer** impresora *f* PostScript®

post-test MKTG **1** *n* test *m* a posteriori
  2 *vt* testear a posteriori

potential 1 *n* potencial *m*, posibilidades *fpl*; **the idea has potential** la idea tiene posibilidades; **the scheme has no potential** el plan no tiene ningún potencial; **there is little potential for development in the firm** hay muy pocas posibilidades de promoción en la empresa
  2 *adj* potencial ❏ **potential buyer** comprador(ora) *m,f* potencial; **potential customer** cliente(a) *m,f* potencial

pound *n (British currency)* libra *f* (esterlina) ❏ **pound coin** moneda *f* de una libra; **pound sign** símbolo *m* de la libra; **pound sterling** libra *f* esterlina

pour *vt (supply in large amounts)* **the government poured money into the industry** el gobierno invirtió mucho dinero en el sector; **I've already poured a fortune into the company** ya he invertido un dineral en la empresa

poverty *n* **poverty line** umbral *m* de la pobreza; **to live above/below the poverty line** vivir por encima/por debajo del umbral de la pobreza; **poverty trap** trampa *f* de la pobreza

> ❝
> The government gets its data from a national survey conducted every five years. The **poverty line** is put at consumption per person of about $11 a month, just about conceivable in India though it may sound impossibly low to a westerner.
> ❞

power *n* **(a)** *(authority)* poder *m* **(over** sobre**)**; **to act with full powers** actuar con plenos poderes ❏ MKTG **power brand** marca *f* con presencia; **power breakfast** desayuno *m* de trabajo; **power dressing** = estilo de vestir utilizado por mujeres ejecutivas y que transmite profesionalidad y seguridad; **power lunch** almuerzo *m* de trabajo; **power structure** estructura *f* de poder; **power struggle** lucha *f* por el poder
  (b) LAW poder *m*, potestad *f* ❏ **power of attorney** poder *m* (notarial); **to give sb power of attorney** otorgar a alguien un poder (notarial)
  (c) COMPTR **power supply** *(for city, building)* suministro *m* eléctrico; *(for machine)* fuente *f* de alimentación; **power unit** alimentador *m* de corriente; **power user** usuario(a) *m,f* experto(a)
  (d) **power station** central *f* or Andes, Col, RP usina *f* eléctrica

> ❝
> The **power lunch** is alive and well, according to a recent survey of chief financial officers (CFOs). Nearly half (49 percent) of

executives polled said their most successful business meeting outside the office was conducted over a meal. **"**

▸ **power down** COMPTR **1** *vt sep* apagar
2 *vi* apagarse

▸ **power up** COMPTR **1** *vt sep* encender, *Am* prender
2 *vi* encenderse, *Am* prenderse

powerbroker *n* persona *f* con mucha influencia política

"
George W Bush scraped to victory in the 2000 presidential election thanks largely to an array of hugely influential rightwing lobbyists and **powerbrokers**. He knows what he owes them – and since September 11 their grip has grown yet tighter.
"

power-down *n* COMPTR apagado *m*

power-on *n* COMPTR encendido *m* ❏ *power-on key* tecla *f* de encendido

power-up *n* COMPTR encendido *m*

pp (*abbr* **per procurationem**) p.p.

PPB *n* ACCT (*abbr* **planning-programming-budgeting system**) sistema *m* de planificación, programación y presupuestación, sistema de planeamiento, programación y presupuestación

PPD *adj* (*abbr* **prepaid**) pagado(a) por adelantado

ppi COMPTR (*abbr* **pixels per inch**) ppp

PPP *n* (**a**) COMPTR (*abbr* **point-to-point protocol**) PPP *m* (**b**) *Br* (*abbr* **public-private partnership**) sociedad *f* de financiación pública y privada (**c**) ECON (*abbr* **purchasing power parity**) PPA *f*

PR *n* (*abbr* **public relations**) relaciones *fpl* públicas; **who does their PR?** ¿quién les hace las relaciones públicas? ❏ *PR agency* agencia *f* de comunicación *or* relaciones públicas; *PR company* empresa *f* de comunicación *or* relaciones públicas; *PR consultancy* agencia *f* de comunicación *or* relaciones públicas; *PR consultant* asesor(ora) *m,f* de relaciones públicas

pre-acquisition profit *n* beneficios *mpl* antes de la adquisición

prebill *vt* ACCT facturar por adelantado a

prebilling *n* ACCT facturación *f* por adelantado

precision *n* precisión *f* ❏ *precision industry* industria *f* de precisión

predate *vt* (*cheque*) antedatar

predator *n* (*company*) depredador *m*

predatory *adj* ❏ MKTG *predatory price* precio *m* desleal; *predatory pricing* fijación *f* de precios desleales

"
South African carriers Nationwide and South African Airways (SAA) have appeared before the Competition Tribunal, with Nationwide claiming that the larger airline is using **predatory pricing** techniques to force competitors out of key routes. Nationwide has filed a petition for interim relief, claiming that SAA has maintained prices on the popular Johannesburg to Cape Town and Johannesburg to Durban routes despite increasing fuel prices, yet has raised prices on other routes where it has less competition.
"

predecessor *n* predecesor(ora) *m,f*

predictive analysis *n* análisis *m* predictivo

pre-empt *vt* LAW (*land, property*) = ocupar con el objetivo de conseguir el derecho de compra

pre-emption *n* LAW opción *f* de compra prioritaria ❏ ST EXCH *pre-emption right* derecho *m* de preferencia

pre-emptive *adj* LAW preferente, prioritario(a) ❏ ST EXCH *pre-emptive right* derecho *m* preferente *or* prioritario

prefer *vt* FIN (*creditor*) dar preferencia *or* prioridad a

preference *n* (**a**) (*preferential treatment*) preferencia *f* (**b**) ST EXCH preferencia *f* ❏ *Br preference cumulative dividend* dividendo *m* preferente acumulativo; *Br preference dividend* dividendo *m* preferente; *Br preference share* acción *f* preferente *or* privilegiada (**c**) MKTG *preference test* test *m* de preferencias

preferential *adj* (*favourable*) preferente ❏ LAW *preferential claim* derecho *m* de preferencia *or* prioridad; FIN *preferential creditor* acreedor(ora) *m,f* preferente; FIN *preferential debt* deuda *f* preferente; FIN *preferential dividend* dividendo *m* preferente *or* preferencial; CUSTOMS *preferential duty* arancel *m* preferente; FIN *preferential investment certificate* certificado *m* privilegiado de inversión; *preferential price* precio *m* preferente *or* preferencial; FIN *preferential rate* tarifa *f* preferente *or* preferencial; LAW *preferential right* derecho *m* de preferencia *or* prioridad; IND *preferential shop* = empresa que, en virtud de un acuerdo laboral, da preferencia a la contratación de trabajadores sindicados; CUSTOMS *preferential tariff* tarifa *f* preferente *or* preferencial; *preferential voting* = sistema electoral en el que los votantes eligen candidatos por orden de preferencia

"
The agreement maintained a **preferential price** for Cuban sugar, lower than that of the previous five-year period, but higher than world prices.
"

preferred adj (**a**) **preferred creditor** acreedor(ora) m,f preferente; FIN **preferred debt** deuda f privilegiada (**b**) US ST EXCH **preferred stock** acciones fpl privilegiadas or preferentes

prefinancing n ACCT prefinanciación f, financiación f anticipada

preformatted adj COMPTR preformateado(a)

preinstall vt COMPTR (software) preinstalar

preinstalled adj COMPTR (software) preinstalado(a)

pre-inventory balance n ACCT balance m antes de inventario

prejudice 1 n LAW (detriment) perjuicio m; **without prejudice to your guarantee** sin perjuicio or menoscabo de su garantía; **to the prejudice of sb's rights** en perjuicio de los derechos de alguien
   2 vt (**a**) (bias) predisponer (**against/in favour of** en contra de/a favor de) (**b**) (harm) perjudicar

preliminary adj preliminar ❑ **preliminary expenses** gastos mpl preliminares; LAW **preliminary investigation** instrucción f preliminar; **preliminary study** estudio m preliminar

pre-marketing n pre-marketing m

premises npl (of factory) instalaciones fpl; (of shop) local m, establecimiento m; (of office) oficina f; **business premises** locales comerciales; **to escort sb off the premises** acompañar a alguien a la calle

premium n (**a**) INS (payment) prima f; **to pay an additional premium** pagar una prima adicional ❑ **premium discount** descuento m de prima; **premium rebate** descuento m de prima
   (**b**) (additional sum) (on price) recargo m; (on salary) prima f; ST EXCH **to pay a premium** pagar por encima de la par; **to sell sth at a premium** vender algo por encima de su valor; **to issue shares at a premium** emitir acciones por encima de la par ❑ **premium bond** = bono del gobierno británico cuyo comprador participa en el sorteo mensual de premios en metálico; **premium on redemption** prima f de reembolso
   (**c**) MKTG **premium brand** marca f de lujo; **premium price** precio m de lujo; **premium product** producto m de lujo; **premium selling** venta f de lujo; **premium service** servicio m de lujo

prepack vt empaquetar

prepackage vt empaquetar

prepackaged adj empaquetado(a)

prepacked adj empaquetado(a)

prepaid adj (cost, postage) pagado(a) por adelantado; ACCT anticipado(a), pagado(a) por adelantado ❑ **prepaid card** tarjeta f (de) prepago; **prepaid envelope** sobre m franqueado or con franqueo pagado; **prepaid income** ingresos mpl anticipados; **prepaid reply (card)** tarjeta f

de respuesta con el franqueo pagado; **prepaid tax** impuesto m anticipado

prepayment n pago m (por) adelantado, pago anticipado; ACCT pago anticipado ❑ **prepayment clause** cláusula f de penalización por pago anticipado; **prepayment penalty** penalización f por pago anticipado

preprogram vt COMPTR preprogramar

preprogrammed adj COMPTR preprogramado(a)

prerequisite n requisito m previo, prerrequisito m (**of/for** para)

presell vt (customer) vender por anticipado a; (goods) vender por anticipado

> **❝**
>
> While Game Boy Advance will get a budget in line with some of Nintendo's past software title releases, Harrison said the marketing plan calls for a sampling program and an effort to **presell** the devices about eight weeks before the summer release.
>
> **❞**

present 1 adj actual; **the present year** el presente año ❑ **present capital** capital m actual; ACCT **present value** valor m actual; INS **present value tables** tablas fpl de valor actual
   2 vt (**a**) (report, information, proposal) presentar (**b**) FIN (invoice) presentar; **to present a cheque for payment** presentar un cheque al pago; **to present a bill for acceptance** presentar una letra a la aceptación

presentation n (**a**) (showing) **presentation for acceptance** presentación f a la aceptación; **presentation for payment** presentación al pago; **payable on presentation of the coupon** pagadero(a) a la presentación del cupón; **on presentation of the invoice** a la presentación de la factura, presentando la factura; **cheque payable on presentation** cheque pagadero a su presentación
   (**b**) (formal talk) presentación f, exposición f; **to give a presentation (on sth)** hacer una exposición (sobre algo) ❑ COMPTR **presentation graphics** gráficos mpl para presentaciones; COMPTR **presentation software** software m para presentaciones
   (**c**) BANKING **presentation date** fecha f de presentación
   (**d**) MKTG **presentation pack** envase m or pack m de presentación

presentment n (of bill of exchange) presentación f

preside vi presidir; **to preside at** or **over a meeting** presidir una reunión

presidency n presidencia f

president n (of country, organization) presidente(a) m,f; US (of company) presidente(a) m,f

press *n (newspapers)* **the press** la prensa; **to get** *or* **have (a) good/bad press** tener buena/mala prensa ◻ *press agency* agencia *f* de noticias, agencia *f* de prensa; *press agent* agente *mf* de prensa; *Br* **the Press Association** Asociación *f* de la Prensa; *press attaché* jefe(a) *m,f* de prensa *(de una embajada)*; *press badge* pase *m* de prensa; *press baron* magnate *mf* de la prensa; *press campaign* campaña *f* de prensa; *press card* carné *m* de periodista; *press clipping* recorte *m* de prensa; *Press Complaints Commission* = organismo británico que gestiona las quejas del público sobre la prensa; *press conference* rueda *f* or conferencia *f* de prensa; *Press Council* = organismo que vela por la ética en el periodismo británico; *Br press cutting* recorte *m* de prensa; *press handout* circular *f* de prensa; MKTG *press insert* encarte *m*; MKTG *press kit* carpeta *f* or dossier *m* de prensa; *press lord* magnate *m* de la prensa *(con título nobiliario)*; *press office* oficina *f* de prensa; *press officer* jefe(a) *m,f* de prensa; MKTG *press pack* carpeta *f* or dossier *m* de prensa; *press pass* pase *m* or acreditación *f* de prensa; *press release* comunicado *m* or nota *f* de prensa; *press tycoon* magnate *mf* de la prensa

pressure *n* presión *f*; **copper prices came under renewed pressure** los precios del cobre han experimentado nuevas presiones ◻ *pressure group* grupo *m* de presión

prestige *n* MKTG *prestige advertising* publicidad *f* en revistas selectas; *prestige goods* artículos *mpl* de prestigio *or* de alta calidad; *prestige model* modelo *m* de prestigio *or* de alta calidad; *prestige price* precio *m* de prestigio; *prestige product* producto *m* de prestigio *or* de alta calidad; *prestige promotion* promoción *f* basada en el prestigio

presumptive *adj presumptive loss* pérdida *f* presunta; *presumptive taxation* imposición *f* en régimen de evaluación global

pre-tax *adj* antes de impuestos, bruto(a) ◻ *pre-tax margin* margen *m* antes de impuestos *or* bruto; *pre-tax profits* beneficios *mpl* antes de impuestos *or* brutos

pre-test MKTG **1** *n* test *m* previo, prueba *f* previa **2** *vt* someter a un test previo *or* una prueba previa; **all adverts should be pre-tested** se debe realizar un test previo de todos los anuncios

prevailing *adj (current)* actual; **the prevailing economic climate** el clima económico actual

price 1 *n* precio *m*; *(of shares)* cotización *f*; **to go up** *or* **rise** *or* **increase in price** subir de precio; **the price has gone up** *or* **risen** *or* **increased by 10%** el precio ha subido en un 10%; **to go down** *or* **fall** *or* **decrease in price** bajar de precio; **the price has gone down** *or* **fallen** *or* **decreased by 10%** el precio ha bajado en un 10%; **to pay a high price for sth** pagar un precio alto por algo;

to sell sth at a reduced price vender algo a precio reducido; ST EXCH **today's prices** los precios de hoy; ST EXCH **what is the price of gold?** ¿a qué precio está el oro? ◻ *price agreement* acuerdo *m* de precios; *price bid* oferta *f* (de precio); *price bracket* banda *f* de precios; ST EXCH *price break* caída *f* de precio; *price cartel* cártel *m* de precios; *price ceiling* precio *m* tope; *price comparison* comparación *f* de precios; *price competitiveness* competitividad *f* de precios; *price controls* controles *mpl* de precios; *price curve* curva *f* de precios; *price cut* reducción *f* *or* recorte *m* de precios; *price cutting* reducción *f* or recorte *m* de precios; *price differential* diferencial *m* de precios; *price discount* descuento *m* (del precio); *price discrimination* discriminación *f* en el precio; *price elasticity* elasticidad *f* en los precios; *price escalation clause* cláusula *f* de revisión de los precios; *price ex warehouse* precio *m* franco en almacén or depósito; *price ex works* precio *m* franco en fábrica; *price fixing (government control)* fijación *f* de precios; *(rigging by companies)* imposición *f* de precios; ST EXCH *price fluctuation* fluctuación *f* de precios; *price freeze Esp* congelación *f* or *Am* congelamiento *m* de precios; *price hike* aumento *m* de precios; *prices and incomes policy* política *f* de precios y rentas; *price increase* aumento *m* de precios; *price index* índice *m* de precios; *price inflation* inflación *f* de precios; *price label* etiqueta *f* del precio; *price labelling* etiquetado *m* de precios; *price leader* líder *mf* en precios; *price leadership* liderazgo *m* en precios; *price level* nivel *m* de precios; *price limit* precio *m* límite; *price list* listado *m* de precios; *price maker* agente *m* económico que determina el precio; *price mark-up* margen *m* comercial; *price mechanism* mecanismo *m* de precios; BANKING, FIN *price of money* precio *m* del dinero; ECON *price pegging* congelación *f* de precios; MKTG *price plan* planificación *f* de precios; MKTG *price point* nivel *m* de precios; *price policy* política *f* de precios; MKTG *price positioning* posicionamiento *m* del precio; *price promotion* promoción *f* de precios; *price proposal* oferta *f* (de precio); *price range* escala *f* de precios; **that's outside my price range** (eso) no está a mi alcance; *price reduction* reducción *f* de precios; *price regulation* regulación *f* de precios; *price ring* cártel *m* de precios; *price scale* escala *f* de precios; MKTG *price sensitivity* sensibilidad *f* al precio; *price setting* fijación *f* del precio; ST EXCH *price spread* diferencial *m* de precios; *price stability* estabilidad *f* de precios; MKTG *price step* incremento *m* de precio *(dentro de una escala)*; *price structure* estructura *f* de precios; *price survey* encuesta *f* de precios; *price tag* etiqueta *f* del precio; *price threshold* umbral *m* de precios; *price ticket* etiqueta *f* del precio; *price undercutting* fijación *f* de precios a la baja; *price war* guerra *f* de precios

2 *vt* (**a**) *(decide cost of)* poner precio a; **the book is priced at £17** el precio del libro es de 17 libras (**b**) *(indicate cost of)* poner el precio a; **these goods haven't been priced** a estos artículos no se les ha puesto precio; **all goods must be clearly priced** todos los artículos deben mostrar claramente el precio (**c**) *(compare cost of)* comparar el precio de; *(estimate value of)* valorar; **she priced it in several shops before buying it** comparó el precio en varias tiendas antes de comprarlo (**d**) **to price competitors out of the market** dejar a los competidores fuera del mercado bajando los precios; **to price oneself out of the market** perder mercado *or* ventas por pedir precios demasiado elevados; **we've been priced out of the Japanese market** nos hemos quedado fuera del mercado japonés (por nuestros elevados precios) (**e**) ECON *(quantity)* valorar

> 44
> National Power and its partner in duopoly, PowerGen, are the only game in town. Buy from them or buy candles. They can name their price and they do. One recent Friday, for example, generators raised the **price bid** into the pool at noon by 440 per cent above the sale price at 7am.
> 99

▶ **price down** *vt sep* rebajar (el precio de); **all items have been priced down by 10%** se han rebajado todos los artículos un 10%

▶ **price up** *vt sep* subir (el precio de)

price-earnings ratio *n* ST EXCH relación *f* precio-beneficio

price-elastic *adj* de precio elástico

> 44
> Later on, products mature and become more **price-elastic**, allowing production advantage to shift to lower-income countries that may later begin exporting on their own account.
> 99

price-inelastic *adj* de precio rígido *or* inelástico

price-sensitive *adj (product)* sensible al precio; ST EXCH **price-sensitive information** información que puede afectar el valor de las acciones de la compañía

pricing *n (prices)* precios *mpl*; *(price setting)* fijación *f* de precios □ **pricing policy** política *f* de precios; **pricing research** investigación *f* de precios

primary *adj* ECON primario(a) □ MKTG **primary data** información *f* primaria; **primary dealer** especialista *mf* en valores del Tesoro; MKTG **primary demand** demanda *f* primaria; **primary**

earnings per share beneficios *mpl* básicos por acción; **primary industry** industria *f* primaria; ST EXCH **primary market** mercado *m* primario; **primary product** producto *m* básico *or* de primera necesidad; **primary production** producción *f* primaria; **primary sector** sector *m* primario; **the primary sector industries** las industrias del sector primario

prime *adj* FIN **prime bill** letra *f* de cambio sin riesgo; **prime bond** bono *m* sin riesgo; **prime cost** costo *m or Esp* coste *m* básico de producción, precio *m* de costo *or Esp* coste; FIN **prime lending rate** *Esp* tipo *m* preferencial *or* básico, *Am* tasa *f* preferencial *or* básica; **Prime Minister** primer(era) ministro(a) *m,f*; FIN **prime rate** *Esp* tipo *m or Am* tasa *f* preferencial; MKTG **prime time** *(on TV)* franja *f* (horaria) de máxima audiencia; **prime time advertising** publicidad *f* en horario de máxima audiencia

principal *n* (**a**) LAW *(employer of agent)* poderdante *mf*, principal *mf*; **principal and agent** poderdante y apoderado(a), principal y agente (**b**) FIN *(capital)* principal *m*; **principal and interest** principal e interés

print 1 *vt (book, newspaper)* imprimir; *(money)* emitir

2 *vi (document)* imprimirse; *(printer)* imprimir □ **print ad, print advertisement** anuncio *m* impreso; **print advertising** publicidad *f* impresa; COMPTR **print format** formato *m* de impresión; COMPTR **print head** cabezal *m* de impresión; COMPTR **print job** *(file)* trabajo *m* de impresión; COMPTR **print list** lista *f* de impresión; COMPTR **print menu** menú *m* de impresión; COMPTR **print option** opción *f* de impresión; COMPTR **print preview** presentación *f* preliminar; COMPTR **print quality** calidad *f* de impresión; COMPTR **print queue** cola *f* de impresión; COMPTR **print speed** velocidad *f* de impresión

▶ **print out** *vt sep* COMPTR imprimir

printed *adj* impreso(a) □ **printed form** impreso *m*; **printed matter** impresos *mpl*; **printed paper rate** tarifa *f* de impresos

printer *n* COMPTR impresora *f* □ **printer cable** cable *m* de impresora; **printer driver** controlador *m* de impresora; **printer font** fuente *f* de impresora; **printer paper** papel *m* de impresora; **printer peripheral** periférico *m* de impresora; **printer port** puerto *m* de la impresora; **printer sharing** compartición *f* de impresora; **printer speed** velocidad *f* de impresión; **printer spooling** envío *m* a la cola de impresión

printout *n* COMPTR copia *f* impresa; *(list, results of calculation)* listado *m*

prior 1 *adj* previo(a) (**to** a); **to have a prior engagement** tener un compromiso previo; **without prior notice** sin previo aviso

2 *adv* **prior to** con anterioridad a

prioritizing question n MKTG (in survey) pregunta f de prioridad de preferencias

priority n prioridad f; **to have** or **take priority (over)** tener prioridad (sobre); **this matter has top priority** este asunto tiene la máxima prioridad ◻ ST EXCH **priority share** acción f preferente or privilegiada

private adj (**a**) (not state-run) privado(a) ◻ **private bank** banco m privado; **private company** empresa f privada (que no cotiza en bolsa); **private enterprise** la empresa or iniciativa privada; **private health insurance** seguro m médico privado; **private limited company** sociedad f (de responsabilidad) limitada; **private ownership** propiedad f privada; **private pension** pensión f privada; **private sector** sector m privado (**b**) (personal) privado(a), personal; (on envelope) personal ◻ LAW **private agreement** acuerdo m privado; LAW **private contract** contrato m privado; **private income** renta f privada; **private investment** inversión f privada; **private investor** inversor(ora) m,f privado(a); TEL **private line** línea f privada; **private means** renta f privada; **private property** propiedad f privada; **private secretary** secretario(a) m,f particular (**c**) (confidential) privado(a); **private and confidential** (on letter) privado y confidencial

private-label brand n MKTG marca f blanca

privately adv **to sell sth privately** vender algo de forma privada; **privately owned** (company) privado(a), en manos privadas

privatization n privatización f

privatize vt privatizar

privileged debt n deuda f privilegiada

privity of contract n LAW relación f contractual

prize bond n = bono del gobierno cuyo comprador participa en el sorteo mensual de premios en metálico

proactive adj proactivo(a) ◻ ADMIN **proactive staffing** = política de personal adaptada a las necesidades

---
"
Why is there a need for the director or chairman to attempt secret behind-the-scenes deals? The PCC exists to adjudicate and urge good practice, not to broker compromises. Why indeed wait for a complaint in the first place? One important change the PCC could make is for it to become **proactive** and speak out on abuses before the formality of a complaint.
"
---

probability n MKTG **probability method** (of sampling) muestreo m probabilístico; **probability sample** muestra f probabilística; **probability sampling** muestreo m probabilístico

probate LAW **1** n (of will) validación f, certificado m de testamentaría; **to value sth for probate** tasar algo a efectos del impuesto de sucesiones ◻ **probate price** = valor a efectos del impuesto de sucesiones **2** vt (will) legalizar, autenticar

probation n (trial employment) periodo m de prueba; **to take sb on probation** contratar a alguien a prueba; **to be on probation** estar a prueba

probationary adj (period) de prueba

probationer n (employee) empleado(a) m,f en periodo de prueba

problem n problema m ◻ **problem analysis** análisis m inv de problemas; MKTG **problem child** (company, product) problema f persistente, pesadilla f; **problem solving** resolución f de problemas

---
"
Long a **problem child**, Granada Computer Services is now thriving and as of April 15, it restructured its customer support functions into two separate divisions with the aim of providing a more focussed and efficient service.
"
---

procedure n procedimiento m; **what's the correct procedure?** ¿cuál es el procedimiento correcto?; **you must follow the normal procedure** debes seguir el procedimiento normal ◻ LAW **procedure by arbitration** procedimiento m de arbitraje

proceed vi (**a**) (continue) proseguir, continuar; **we are now unable to proceed with our plans for expansion** ahora nos resulta imposible seguir adelante con nuestros planes de expansión (**b**) (take place, happen) llevarse a cabo, tener lugar; **is the meeting proceeding according to plan?** ¿se está llevando a cabo la reunión según lo previsto? (**c**) (act) actuar; **how should we proceed?** ¿qué debemos hacer a continuación?

proceedings npl (**a**) (meeting) acto m; (record of meeting) actas fpl (**b**) LAW proceso m, pleito m; **to start** or **institute proceedings against sb** entablar un pleito contra alguien

proceeds npl (from sale) recaudación f, ganancias fpl

process 1 n (**a**) (method) proceso m; **to develop a process for doing sth** desarrollar un proceso para hacer algo; **a new manufacturing process** un nuevo proceso de fabricación (**b**) COMPTR proceso m **2** vt (**a**) (information) procesar; (application, claim, order) tramitar, procesar; **we process thousands of applications every week** tramitamos miles de solicitudes todas las semanas (**b**) COMPTR (data) procesar (**c**) (raw materials, waste) procesar

processing n (**a**) *(of information)* procesamiento m; *(of application, order)* tramitación f, procesamiento (**b**) COMPTR *(of data)* proceso m ❑ **processing speed** velocidad f de proceso *or* procesamiento; **processing time** tiempo m de proceso *or* procesamiento (**c**) *(of raw materials, waste)* procesamiento m

processor n COMPTR procesador m ❑ **processor chip** chip m procesador; **processor speed** velocidad f del procesador

procuration n LAW procuración f

procure vt adquirir

procurement n adquisición f

produce 1 n productos mpl (del campo); **agricultural produce** productos agrícolas
2 vt (**a**) *(manufacture, make)* producir; **we aren't producing enough spare parts** no producimos suficientes piezas de recambio; **we have produced three new models this year** hemos lanzado tres nuevos modelos este año
(**b**) *(interest, profit)* producir, devengar; **my investments produce a fairly good return** mis inversiones producen unos beneficios aceptables; **this account produces a high rate of interest** esta cuenta produce una alta tasa de interés
(**c**) *(raw materials)* producir

producer n *(of raw materials, goods)* productor(ora) m,f; **this region is Europe's biggest wine producer** esta región es la mayor productora de vino de Europa ❑ **producers' association** asociación f de productores; **producers' co-operative** cooperativa f de productores; **producer goods** bienes mpl de producción

product n producto m ❑ **product advertising** publicidad f de producto; **product analysis** análisis m inv del producto; **product attribute** característica f or atributo m del producto; **product augmentation** aumento m or mejora f del producto; **product awareness** conocimiento m del producto; **product bundling** venta f conjunta *or* empaquetado m conjunto de productos; **product bundling pricing** fijación f de precios por paquetes de productos; **product category** categoría f de productos; **product champion** encargado(a) m,f de producto *(de su promoción)*; **product design** diseño m del producto; **product development** desarrollo m del producto; **product development cost** costo m *or Esp* coste m del desarrollo del producto; **product differentiation** diferenciación f del producto; **product display** exposición f del producto; **product diversification** diversificación f de productos; **product dynamics** dinámica f de productos; **product features** características fpl del producto; **product image** imagen f del producto; **product improvement** mejora f del producto; **product information sheet** ficha f técnica del producto; **product**

innovation innovación f de productos; **product launch** lanzamiento m del producto; **product launch file** ficha f de lanzamiento del producto; **product liability** responsabilidad f civil de productos; **product liability insurance** seguro m de responsabilidad civil de productos; **product lifecycle** ciclo m de vida del producto; **product lifecycle curve** curva f del ciclo de vida del producto; **product line** línea f de productos; **product management** gestión f de producto; **product manager** jefe(a) m,f de producto; **product mix** mix m de productos; **product orientation** orientación f al *or* hacia el producto; **product performance test** prueba f de rendimiento del producto; **product placement** colocación f de producto; **product planning** planificación f de productos; **product policy** política f de productos; **product portfolio** cartera f de productos; **product positioning** posicionamiento m de producto; **product price policy** política f de precios del producto; **product profile** perfil m de producto; **product promotion** promoción f del producto; **product range** gama f de productos; **product research** investigación f de producto; **product specialist** especialista mf de producto; **product strengths** fortalezas fpl del producto; **product test** test m *or* prueba f de producto; **product testing** tests mpl or pruebas fpl de producto; **product testing panel** grupo m de discusión para el test de producto

production n producción f; **to go into production** empezar a fabricarse; **it went out of production years ago** hace años que dejó de fabricarse; **to cease production** dejar de fabricar ❑ **production budget** presupuesto m de producción; **production capacity** capacidad f de producción; **production control** control m de (la) producción; **production costs** costos mpl or Esp costes mpl de producción; **production department** departamento m de producción; **production engineering** ingeniería f de producción; **production facilities** instalaciones fpl de producción; **production facility** instalación f productiva; **production factor** factor m de producción; **production flowchart** diagrama m de producción; **production incentive** incentivo m a la producción; **production lead time** tiempo m de producción; **production line** cadena f de producción; **to work on a production line** trabajar en una cadena de producción; **this model has just come off the production line** este modelo acaba de salir de la cadena de producción; **production management** gestión f de la producción; **production manager** jefe(a) m,f de producción; ACCT **production overheads** gastos mpl de producción; **production planning** planificación f de la producción; **production plant** planta f de producción; **production schedule** programa m de producción; **production scheduling**

programación f de la producción; **production target** objetivo m de producción **production tool** herramienta f de producción; **production unit** unidad f de producción; **production worker** trabajador(ora) m,f de producción

productive adj ECON productivo(a) □ **productive forces** fuerzas fpl productivas; **productive labour** trabajo m de producción; **productive life** (of machine) vida f útil

productivity n productividad f □ **productivity agreement** acuerdo m de productividad; **productivity bargaining** negociaciones fpl de productividad; **productivity bonus** plus m de productividad; **productivity campaign** campaña f de productividad; **productivity deal** pacto m de productividad; **productivity drive** campaña f de productividad; **productivity gains** aumento f de la productividad; **productivity investment** inversión f en productividad; **productivity surplus** excedente m productivo

product/market pair n MKTG binomio m producto/mercado

profession n profesión f ocupación f; **by profession** de profesión

professional 1 n profesional mf, Méx profesionista mf
   2 adj (**a**) (relating to a profession) profesional □ **professional association** asociación f profesional; **professional body** organismo m profesional; **professional confidentiality** confidencialidad f profesional; **professional fees** tarifas fpl profesionales; **professional indemnity insurance** seguro m de responsabilidad civil profesional; **professional life** vida f profesional; **professional misconduct** violación f de la ética profesional; **professional negligence** negligencia f profesional; **professional qualifications** titulación f profesional, títulos mpl profesionales; **professional training** formación f profesional
   (**b**) (in quality, attitude) profesional; **he works in a very professional manner** trabaja de una forma muy profesional; **she is very professional in her approach** tiene un enfoque muy profesional

proficiency n dominio m (**in** de); **proficiency in a foreign language is essential** es esencial dominar una lengua extranjera

proficient adj competente (**in** en); **to be proficient in German** dominar el alemán

profile n (of candidate, employee, market, product) perfil m; **to have the ideal profile for the job** tener el perfil idóneo para el puesto

profit n beneficio m; **profits** beneficios, Am utilidades fpl; **profits were down/up this year** los beneficios cayeron/subieron este año; **to make a profit (out of sth)** obtener or sacar beneficios (de algo); **to show a profit** arrojar beneficios;

to move into profit (business) pasar a tener beneficios; **to sell sth at a profit** vender algo con beneficios; **profit and loss** pérdidas y ganancias □ **profit balance** beneficios mpl distribuibles; **profit centre** centro m de beneficios; **profit equation** ecuación f de beneficios; **profit forecast** previsión f de beneficios; **profit indicator** indicador m de beneficios; **profit and loss account, profit and loss statement** cuenta f de pérdidas y ganancias; **profit margin** margen m de beneficios; **the profit motive** el lucro; **profit optimization** optimización f de beneficios; **profit squeeze** reducción f de los márgenes de beneficio; **profit target** objetivo m de beneficios; **profit tax** impuesto m sobre los beneficios; **profit warning** advertencia f sobre los beneficios

> **"**
> City professionals are naturally wary of a company which has issued three **profit warnings** in the space of two years – the most recent arriving in July. But other market players are more optimistic. They smell more corporate action and they are probably right.
> **"**

profitability n rentabilidad f □ **profitability index** índice f de rentabilidad; **profitability value** (of a project) valor m de rentabilidad

profitable adj (business, deal, investment) rentable; **this factory is no longer profitable** esta fábrica ya no es rentable; **it wouldn't be profitable for me to sell** no me sería rentable vender

profit-centre accounting n ACCT contabilidad f por centros de beneficio

profiteer 1 n especulador(ora) m,f
   2 vi especular

profitless adj improductivo(a), infructuoso(a); **a profitless deal** una operación sin beneficios

profit-making adj (**a**) (aiming to make profit) con ánimo de lucro □ **profit-making organization** organización f con ánimo de lucro (**b**) (profitable) lucrativo(a)

profit-sharing n reparto m de beneficios □ **profit-sharing scheme** plan m de participación en los beneficios

profit-taking n realización f de beneficios

> **"**
> The question really is whether the activity at SIVB is little more than routine **profit-taking** or whether if reflects a chink in the armor of the super high-tech economy. There are those who insist that any decrease in the bank's IPO/Venture Cap business will be more than offset by an increase in its traditional lending operations.
> **"**

profit-volume ratio *n* tasa *f* de contribución de los beneficios

pro-forma 1 *n* *(invoice)* factura *f* pro forma *or* proforma
2 *adj* **pro-forma invoice** factura *f* pro forma *or* proforma

program 1 *n* **(a)** COMPTR programa *m* ❏ **program disk** disco *m* de programa; **program language** lenguaje *m* de programación; **program library** biblioteca *f* *or* librería *f* de programas **(b)** *US (scheme)* programa *f*
2 *vt* programar; **to program a computer to do sth** programar *Esp* un ordenador *or* *Am* una computadora para que haga algo
3 *vi* programar

programme *n* *Br (scheme)* programa *f*

programmer *n* COMPTR programador(ora) *m,f*

programming *n* COMPTR programación *f* ❏ **programming language** lenguaje *m* de programación

progress 1 *n* progreso *m*; **to make progress** hacer progresos; **the meeting is already in progress** la reunión ya ha comenzado; **the negotiations in progress** las negociaciones en curso ❏ **progress payment** pago *m* a cuenta; **progress report** informe *m* de situación; **a progress report on the project** un informe *or Am* reporte sobre la marcha del proyecto
2 *vi* progresar; **the talks are progressing well** las conversaciones van por buen camino

progressive *adj* progresivo(a) ❏ **progressive tax** impuesto *m* progresivo; **progressive taxation** tributación *f* progresiva

prohibitive *adj (price)* prohibitivo(a)

project 1 *n* proyecto *m*; **they're working on a new building project** están trabajando en un nuevo proyecto de construcción ❏ **project analysis** análisis *m inv* de proyectos; **project management** gestión *f* de proyectos; COMPTR **project management package** paquete *m* de gestión de proyectos; **project manager** jefe(a) *m,f* de proyecto; **project milestones** hitos *mpl* del proyecto
2 *vt (forecast)* proyectar; **he's projecting a 40% drop in sales** prevé una caída de un 40% en las ventas; **we have attempted to project next year's profits/output** hemos intentado hacer una previsión de los beneficios/de la producción del año que viene; **inflation is projected to fall** se prevé que baje la inflación

❝
Not only is actual conflict greater today, but even the potential for interpersonal conflicts in the workplace is far greater than at any time in the past. One reason for this is increased time-to-market pressures. The need to rapidly make decisions, establish

an engineering direction, and meet **project milestones** adds elements of tension and stress to an already difficult endeavor.
❞

projected *adj (forecast)* previsto(a); **the projected growth of the economy** el crecimiento previsto de la economía ❏ **projected demand** demanda *f* prevista; **projected income** ingresos *mpl* previstos; **projected population** población *f* prevista; **projected turnover** volumen *m* de negocio previsto

projection *n* *(forecast)* estimación *f*, pronóstico *m*; **here are my projections for the next ten years** éstos son mis pronósticos para los próximos diez años

promissory note *n* FIN pagaré *m*

promo *n* *Fam (promotion)* promoción *f*; *(short video) Esp* vídeo *m or Am* video *m* promocional

promote *vt* **(a)** *(person)* ascender; **to be promoted** ser ascendido(a); **she's been promoted to regional manager** ha sido ascendida a gerente regional **(b)** *(foster)* fomentar, promover; **to promote economic growth** promover el crecimiento económico **(c)** *(product)* promocionar; **to promote a new product** promocionar un nuevo producto

promoter *n* promotor(ora) *m,f*

promotion *n* **(a)** *(of person)* ascenso *m*; **to get promotion** ser ascendido(a); **there are good prospects for promotion in this company** en esta empresa hay buenas perspectivas de ascenso ❏ **promotions list** lista *f* de ascensos **(b)** *(of product)* promoción *f*; **this week's promotion** la oferta de la semana ❏ **promotions agency** agencia *f* de promociones; **promotion budget** presupuesto *m* para promociones; **promotion campaign** campaña *f* de promoción; **promotion team** equipo *m* de promociones

promotional *adj* **promotional campaign** campaña *f* de promoción; **promotional costs** costos *mpl or Esp* costes *mpl* de promoción; **promotional discount** descuento *m* de promoción; **promotional label** etiqueta *f* de promoción; **promotional literature** folletos *mpl* de promoción; **promotional material** material *m* de promoción; **promotional offer** oferta *f* de promoción; **promotional policy** política *f* de promociones; **promotional price** precio *m* de promoción; **promotional sale** venta *f* promocional; **promotional sample** muestra *f* de promoción; **promotional target** grupo *m* destinatario de la promoción; **promotional T-shirt** camiseta *f* publicitaria; **promotional video** *Esp* vídeo *m or Am* video *m* publicitario

prompt 1 *n* **(a)** *(for payment)* recordatorio *m* de pago ❏ **prompt day** día *m* de pago; **prompt note** recordatorio *m* de pago **(b)** COMPTR *(short phrase)* mensaje *m*; **return to the C:\ prompt** volver a C:\

2 adj (quick) rápido(a) ❑ **prompt payment**
pronto pago m; **prompt service** servicio m
rápido

proof n **proof of credit** garantía f de crédito;
proof of delivery acuse m de recibo; **proof of
identity** prueba f de identidad; **proof of
payment** comprobante m de pago; **proof of
postage** comprobante m de envío; **proof of
purchase** justificante m de compra

propensity n ECON **propensity to consume**
propensión f al consumo; ECON **propensity to
save** propensión f al ahorro

property n (**a**) (possession) propiedad f; **all his
property was confiscated** confiscaron todas
sus propiedades; **it's company property** es
propiedad de la empresa
(**b**) (real estate) bienes mpl inmuebles; **he's
investing his money in property** está invirtiendo (su dinero) en bienes inmuebles or propiedades ❑ Br **property assets** bienes mpl
inmuebles; **property boom** boom m inmobiliario; **property bubble** burbuja f inmobiliaria;
property charge carga f territorial; **property
developer** promotor(ora) m,f inmobiliario(a);
**property ladder: to get a foot on the prop-
erty ladder** acceder al mercado de la vivienda;
Br **property loan** préstamo m inmobiliario;
property manager administrador(ora) m,f de
fincas or Arg propiedades; **property market**
mercado m inmobiliario; **property owner** pro-
pietario(a) m,f de bienes inmuebles; US ACCT
property, plant and equipment inmovilizado
m material; **property shares** acciones fpl inmobiliarias; **property speculation** especulación f
inmobiliaria; **property tax** impuesto m sobre la
propiedad inmobiliaria
(**c**) (house, building) inmueble m

proposal n (offer) propuesta f; (plan) proyecto
m; **to make a proposal** hacer una propuesta

propose vt proponer; **to propose a motion**
proponer una moción

proprietary adj **proprietary article** artículo m
de marca registrada; **proprietary brand** marca f
registrada; **proprietary name** nombre m comercial

proprietor n propietario(a) m,f

pro rata 1 adj prorrateado(a); **the salary is
£21,000 pro rata** el sueldo es de 21.000 libras
prorrateadas
2 adv de forma prorrateada

prosecute vt LAW procesar

prosecution n LAW proceso m, juicio m; **to be
liable to prosecution** estar sujeto(a) a una acción judicial; **to bring a prosecution against sb**
interponer una demanda contra alguien, iniciar
una acción judicial contra alguien

prospect 1 n (**a**) (chance, likelihood) posibilidad f;
(outlook) perspectiva f; **the prospects for the**

automobile industry las perspectivas para la
industria del automóvil; **a job with prospects**
un trabajo con buenas perspectivas (de futuro);
it's a job without any prospects of promotion
es un trabajo sin ninguna perspectiva de ascenso
(**b**) (prospective customer) posible cliente(a) m,f,
cliente(a) m,f potencial; **he's a good prospect
for the manager's job** tiene buenas posibilidades de conseguir el puesto de director ❑ MKTG
prospect pool clientes mpl potenciales
2 vi MKTG **to prospect for new customers** buscar nuevos clientes

> **❝**
>
> The Internet allows us to inexpensively mar-
> ket, distribute and administer the products
> and services of several web site/e-com-
> merce products, each with its own market
> niche and clearly defined customer/**pro-
> spect pool**.
>
> **❞**

prospective adj (buyer, client) posible, potencial

prospectus n (**a**) (about company, product) folleto m informativo, prospecto m (**b**) ST EXCH
(about share issue) folleto m or prospecto m de
emisión

protection n (provided by insurance) protección f

protectionism n ECON proteccionismo m

protectionist n & adj ECON proteccionista mf
❑ **protectionist measures** medidas fpl pro-
teccionistas

protective adj ECON (measure, duty) protec-
tor(ora)

protest n (**a**) LAW protesto m ❑ **protest for
non-acceptance** protesto m por falta de aceptación; **protest for non-payment** protesto m
por falta de pago (**b**) INS protesta f

protocol n COMPTR protocolo m

prototype n prototipo m

provide vt (**a**) (stipulate) establecer; **the contract provides that...** el contrato establece
que... (**b**) (supply) suministrar, proporcionar;
(service, support) prestar, proporcionar; **to provide sb with sth** suministrar or proporcionar
algo a alguien; **this factory will provide 500
new jobs** la fábrica creará 500 nuevos puestos
de trabajo

▶ **provide for** vt insep (**a**) (allow for) prever; **the
bill provides for subsidies to be reduced** el
proyecto de ley prevé la reducción de las subvenciones; INS **this risk is not provided for in
the policy** este riesgo no está contemplado en
la póliza (**b**) (support) mantener; **an insurance
policy that will provide for your children's future** una póliza de seguros que garantizará el
futuro de sus hijos (**c**) (prepare) **to provide for**

sth prepararse para algo (**d**) ACCT provisionar

provident *adj* **provident fund** fondo *m* de previsión; **provident society** sociedad *f* de seguros mutuos, mutua *f*

provider *n* COMPTR proveedor *m*

provision *n* (**a**) *(supplying) (of money, supplies)* suministro *m*, abastecimiento *m*; *(of services)* prestación *f*; **the provision of new jobs** la oferta de nuevos puestos de trabajo; **provision of capital** provisión *f* de fondos
(**b**) *(allowance)* **to make provision for sth** prever algo, tener en cuenta algo ❑ ACCT **provision for bad debts** provisión *f* para deudas incobrables; ACCT **provision for depreciation** provisión *f* por depreciación; ACCT **provision for liabilities** provisión *f* para riesgos
(**c**) **provisions** *(supplies)* provisiones *fpl*
(**d**) *(in treaty, contract)* estipulación *f*, disposición *f*; **under the provisions of the UN charter** según lo estipulado en la carta de las Naciones Unidas; **a 4% increase is included in the budget's provisions** las disposiciones del presupuesto contemplan un aumento de un 4%

provisional *adj* provisional, *Am* provisorio(a)

proviso *n* condición *f*; **with the proviso that the goods be delivered within one month** a condición de que la mercancía se entregue en el plazo de un mes; **they accept, with one proviso** aceptan, pero con una condición

proxy *n* (**a**) LAW *(power)* poder *m*; *(person)* apoderado(a) *m,f*; **by proxy** por poder; **to vote by proxy** votar por poderes (**b**) COMPTR proxy *m*, servidor *m* caché

prudence principle, prudence concept *n* ACCT principio *m* de prudencia

> ❝
> The 1987 SORP stated that the **prudence concept** has to be modified because "proper accounting practice within the legal framework" includes accounting that "best commercial practice" would find imprudent. The instance cited was where debt charges continue to be included in revenue accounts for financing assets whose useful life is over.
> ❞

PSBR *n Br* ECON (*abbr* **public sector borrowing requirement**) NESP *fpl*

psychographic MKTG *adj (data, profile, segment)* psicográfico(a)

psychological *adj* **psychological contract** contrato *m* psicológico; MKTG **psychological price** precio *m* psicológico; **psychological profile** perfil *m* psicológico

psychometric *adj* psicométrico(a)

public **1** *n* **the (general) public** el público en general, el gran público; **to issue shares to the public** realizar una oferta pública de acciones
2 *adj* público(a); ST EXCH **to go public** comenzar a cotizar en Bolsa ❑ **public affairs** asuntos *mpl* públicos; **public auction** subasta *f* pública, *CSur* remate *m* público; **public authorities** autoridades *fpl* públicas; **public company** sociedad *f* anónima; *Br* **public corporation** corporación *f* pública; **public debt** deuda *f* pública *or* del Estado; BANKING **public deposits** depósitos *m* públicos; **public domain** dominio *m* público; **public enterprise** empresa *f* pública; **public expenditure** gasto *m* público; **public finance** política *f* fiscal; **public funds** fondos *mpl* públicos; **public holiday** día *m* festivo *or Am* feriado; **public inquiry** investigación *f (de puertas abiertas)*; ST EXCH **public issue** oferta *f* pública de acciones; **public liability** responsabilidad *f* civil; **public liability insurance** seguro *m* de responsabilidad civil; **public limited company** sociedad *f* anónima; **public loan** empréstito *m* público; ST EXCH **public offering** oferta *f* pública de acciones; **public opinion** la opinión pública; **public ownership** propiedad *f* pública; **public property** bienes *mpl* públicos; **public relations** relaciones *fpl* públicas; **public relations consultancy** agencia *f* de comunicación *or* relaciones públicas; **public relations manager** jefe(a) *m,f* de relaciones públicas; **public relations officer** empleado(a) *m,f* de relaciones públicas; **public sale** venta *f* pública; **public sector** sector *m* público; **public sector pay is expected to rise by only three per cent over the next year** está previsto que los sueldos del sector público suban sólo un tres por ciento durante el año que viene; **public sector borrowing requirement** necesidades *fpl* de financiamiento del sector público; **public sector deficit** déficit *m* del sector público; **public sector earnings** ingresos *mpl* del sector público; **public sector employee** funcionario(a) *m,f* (público(a)); **public servant** funcionario(a) *m,f* (público(a)); **public service** *(amenity)* servicio *m* público; *Br (civil service)* administración *f* pública; **she's in public service** trabaja en la administración pública; ST EXCH **public share offer** oferta *f* pública de acciones; **public spending** gasto *m* público; **public transport** transporte *m* público; **public utility** (empresa *f* de) servicio *m* público; *Br* **public utility company** empresa *f* de servicio público; **public works** obras *fpl* públicas; **public works contractor** contratista *mf* de obras públicas

publication *n (activity)* publicación *f*, edición *f*; *(published work)* publicación

publicity *n* publicidad *f*; **it will give us free publicity for the product** nos proporcionará publicidad gratuita del producto ❑ **publicity agent** agente *mf* publicitario(a); **publicity brochure** folleto *m* publicitario; **publicity campaign** campaña *f* publicitaria *or* de publicidad; **publicity department** departamento *m* de publicidad; **publicity expenses** gastos *mpl* publicitarios *or* de publicidad; **publicity manager** gerente *mf* de publicidad

publicize *vt (product)* dar publicidad a; **the launch of their new product has been widely publicized** le han dado mucha publicidad al lanzamiento de su nuevo producto

publicly *adv* ECON **publicly owned** de titularidad pública; **the company is 51% publicly controlled** la empresa tiene un 51% de titularidad pública ◻ US **publicly traded company** sociedad *f* cotizada en Bolsa

public-private partnership *n Br* proyecto *m* de financiación pública y privada, colaboración *m* público-privada

public-service corporation *n US* empresa *f* privada de servicios públicos

publish *vt* publicar, editar; **the magazine is published quarterly** la revista se publica trimestralmente

publisher *n (person)* editor(ora) *m,f*; *(company)* editorial *f*

publishing *n* industria *f* editorial ◻ **publishing company, publishing house** editorial *f*

▸ **pull down** *vt sep* COMPTR *(menu)* desplegar

▸ **pull out** *vi (from deal, arrangement)* retirarse (**of** de); **they've pulled out of the deal** se han retirado del acuerdo

pull-down *adj* COMPTR **pull-down menu** menú *m* desplegable; **pull-down window** ventana *f* desplegable

pull strategy *n* MKTG estrategia *f* del tirón

punitive damages *npl* LAW daños *mpl* punitivos

punt *n Formerly* libra *f* irlandesa

punter *n Fam* (**a**) *(customer)* cliente *mf* (**b**) ST EXCH *(speculator)* jugador(ora) *m,f*

> There are few better times to buy a mobile phone than at Christmas. The phone networks and stores always make it a season to be jolly by offering all kinds of deals and promotions. Some entice buyers with extra talk minutes or free text messages. Others are a little less subtle and encourage **punters** to part with their cash in exchange for free games, watches or entry to big money competitions.

purchasable *adj* a la venta; **all items are purchasable directly from the manufacturer** todos los artículos se pueden adquirir directamente del fabricante

purchase 1 *n* compra *f*, adquisición *f*; **to make a purchase** realizar una compra ◻ **purchase account** cuenta *f* de compras; **purchase account-**

ing contabilidad *f* de compras; MKTG **purchase behaviour** comportamiento *m* de compra; **purchase budget** presupuesto *m* de compras *or* adquisiciones; **purchase cost** precio *m* de compra; ACCT **purchase of debts** compra *f* de deudas; MKTG **purchase decision** decisión *f* de compra; MKTG **purchase diary** diario *m* de compras; ACCT **purchase entry** anotación *f* en el registro de compra; MKTG **purchase environment** entorno *m* de la compra; MKTG **purchase frequency** frecuencia *f* de compra; ACCT **purchase invoice** factura *f* de compra; ACCT **purchase invoice ledger** registro *m* de facturas de compra; ACCT **purchase ledger** libro *m* mayor de compras; **purchase method** forma *f* de compra; **purchase note** recibo *m* de compra; **purchase order** orden *f* de compra; **purchase price** precio *m* de compra; **purchase report** resumen *m* de compras; **purchase return** devolución *f* de compra; **purchase tax** impuesto *m* sobre la compra; **purchase value** valor *m* de compra; **purchase volume** volumen *m* de compra

2 *vt* comprar, adquirir; **to purchase sth from sb** comprar algo a alguien; **to purchase sth on credit** comprar algo a crédito; ACCT **to purchase a debt** comprar una deuda

3 *vi* comprar; **now is the time to purchase** ahora es el momento de comprar

purchaser *n* comprador(ora) *m,f* ◻ MKTG **purchaser behaviour** comportamiento *m* del comprador

purchasing *n* compra *f*, adquisición *f* ◻ **purchasing agent** agente *mf* de compras; MKTG **purchasing behaviour** comportamiento *m* de compra; **purchasing behaviour model** modelo *m* de comportamiento de compra; **purchasing costs** costos *mpl or Esp* costes *mpl* de compra; **purchasing department** departamento *m* de compras; **purchasing group** grupo *m* de compra; **purchasing manager** jefe(a) *m,f* de compras; **purchasing motivator** motivo *m or* motivador *m* de compra; ECON **purchasing power** poder *m* adquisitivo, capacidad *f* adquisitiva; **purchasing power parity** paridad *f* del poder adquisitivo; **purchasing process** proceso *m* de compra; **purchasing rights** derechos *mpl* de compra; **purchasing unit** unidad *f* de compras

> Estimating comparative levels of per capita GNP between various nations is probably best done by assessing relative levels of **purchasing power** – what a currency will buy in the country in which it is issued, using comparisons between particular products.

pure *adj* ECON, MKTG **pure competition** competencia *f* perfecta; INS **pure premium** prima *f* neta *or* pura

purposive *adj* MKTG **purposive sample** muestra

f dirigida; ***purposive sampling*** muestreo *m* dirigido

pursuant to *prep Formal* de acuerdo con

push 1 *n* ***push money*** gratificación *f* a vendedores *(del fabricante)*; MKTG ***push strategy*** estrategia *f* del empujón
  2 *vt* ST EXCH **to push shares** colocar valores dudosos

put 1 *n* ST EXCH ***put bond*** bono *m* con opción de amortización anticipada; ***put and call option*** opción *f* de compra y venta; ***put option*** opción *f* de venta
  2 *vt* (**a**) *(invest)* invertir; **she had put all her savings into property** había invertido todos sus ahorros en bienes inmuebles (**b**) *(present) (suggestion, question)* hacer; **to put a proposal to the board** presentar una propuesta al consejo de administración; **to put a motion to the vote** someter una moción a votación

▶ **put back** *vt sep* (**a**) *(postpone)* aplazar, posponer; **the meeting has been put back to Thursday** la reunión ha sido aplazada hasta el jueves (**b**) *(delay)* retrasar; **the strike has put our schedule back at least a month** la huelga ha retrasado nuestro programa por lo menos un mes

▶ **put down** *vt sep* (**a**) *(write)* poner por escrito; **to put sth down in writing** poner algo por escrito (**b**) *(pay as deposit)* dejar; **we've already put £500 down on the equipment** ya hemos dejado 500 libras como señal por el equipo

▶ **put forward** *vt sep* (**a**) *(bring forward)* adelantar; **the meeting has been put forward to early next week** la reunión se ha adelantado a principios de la próxima semana (**b**) *(suggest) (proposal)* presentar; *(suggestion)* hacer; *(candidate)* proponer; **she put her name forward for the post of treasurer** se presentó candidata al puesto de tesorera

▶ **put out** *vt sep (sub-contract)* subcontratar; **we put most of our work out** subcontratamos la mayor parte de nuestro trabajo

▶ **put through** *vt sep (on phone)* **to put sb through to sb** poner *or* pasar a alguien con alguien; **put him through, please** pásemelo, por favor; **I'll put you through to Mr Peters** le pongo *or* paso con el señor Peters

▶ **put up** *vt sep* (**a**) *(money)* aportar; **who's putting the money up for the new business?** ¿quién aporta el dinero para el negocio? (**b**) *(increase)* subir, aumentar; **this will put up the price of oil** esto hará subir el precio del petróleo

P/V *n* (*abbr* **profit-volume ratio**) tasa *f* de contribución de los beneficios

pyramid 1 *n* ***pyramid scheme*** sistema *m* piramidal de distribución; ***pyramid selling*** venta *f* piramidal
  2 *vt (companies)* organizar de forma piramidal

> ❝
>
> The 1996 Trading Schemes Act outlaws **pyramid selling schemes**, but not investment pyramids. Originators of the investment versions have insured against legal clamp down by requiring that each recruit signs a declaration that her investment is an unconditional gift.
>
> ❞

Qq

Q n (*abbr* **quarter**) T m; **our profits fell in Q3** nuestros beneficios cayeron en T3

QC n (*abbr* **quality control**) CC m

qty n (*abbr* **quantity**) cantidad f

qualification n (**a**) (*diploma*) titulación f; **please list your academic qualifications** por favor, detalle sus títulos académicos (**b**) (*skill, competence*) requisito m; **the main qualification we are looking for is a creative mind** la principal característica que estamos buscando es una mente creativa

qualified *adj* (**a**) (*having diploma*) titulado(a); **our staff are highly qualified** nuestro personal está altamente cualificado *or Am* calificado; **to be qualified to do sth** tener la titulación necesaria *or* los títulos necesarios para hacer algo ❑ **qualified accountant** contable *mf or Am* contador(ora) *m,f* titulado(a)
(**b**) (*skilled, competent*) capaz, capacitado(a); **to be qualified to do sth** estar capacitado(a) para hacer algo
(**c**) (*modified*) limitado(a), parcial ❑ BANKING **qualified acceptance** aceptación f limitada; **qualified approval** aprobación f con reservas; ACCT **qualified report** dictamen m con reservas

qualify *vt* (**a**) (*make competent*) **to qualify sb to do sth** capacitar a alguien para hacer algo; **her experience qualifies her for the post** su experiencia la capacita para el puesto (**b**) (*modify*) matizar; **they qualified their acceptance of the plan** aceptaron el plan con algunas salvedades

qualifying policy n = póliza con derecho a desgravación fiscal

qualitative *adj* cualitativo(a) ❑ MKTG **qualitative forecasting** previsiones *fpl* cualitativas; **qualitative research** investigación f cualitativa; **qualitative study** estudio m cualitativo

quality n (**a**) (*standard*) calidad f; **of good/poor quality** de buena/mala calidad; **we have a reputation for quality** tenemos una reputación de ofrecer calidad ❑ **quality assurance** garantía f de calidad; **quality certificate** certificado m de calidad; **quality circle** círculo m de calidad; **quality control** control m de calidad; **quality control department** departamento m de control de calidad; **quality goods** productos *mpl* de calidad; **quality label** etiqueta f de calidad; **quality management** gestión f de calidad; MKTG

quality positioning posicionamiento m de calidad
(**b**) (*attribute*) cualidad f; **these are the qualities we are looking for in our candidates** éstas son las cualidades que buscamos en nuestros candidatos

quality-price ratio n relación f calidad-precio

quango n (*abbr* **quasi-autonomous non-governmental organization**) = entidad creada por el gobierno británico y dotada de poderes semiautónomos

Despite the promise of a people's government, the country is increasingly run by unaccountable, secretive crony networks, writes Stuart Weir. Tony Blair and his colleagues have been full of promises to abolish the **quango** state and make "bonfires of **quangos**". But there are no dead **quangos** among the slaughtered sheep and livestock in the funeral pyres and trenches that disfigure the British countryside. No, the **quango** state is alive and well.

quantify *vt* cuantificar

quantitative *adj* cuantitativo(a) ❑ MKTG **quantitative forecasting** previsiones *fpl* cuantitativas; **quantitative research** investigación f cuantitativa; **quantitative study** estudio m cuantitativo

quantity n cantidad f; **to buy sth in large quantities** comprar algo en grandes cantidades ❑ **quantity discount** descuento m por volumen, rappel m; **quantity rebate** descuento m por volumen; **quantity surveying** estimación f, medición f; **quantity surveyor** ≃ aparejador(ora) *m,f*; ECON **quantity theory (of money)** teoría f cuantitativa del dinero

quarter n (*three-month period*) trimestre m; **profits were up during the last quarter** los beneficios aumentaron en el último trimestre

quarterly 1 n (*publication*) publicación f trimestral
2 *adj* trimestral
3 *adv* trimestralmente

quartile n cuartil m

quasi-contract n LAW cuasicontrato m

quasi-money *n* FIN cuasidinero *m*, *Am* cuasi-moneda *f*

quay *n* muelle *m*

quayage *n* muellaje *m*

query 1 *n* COMPTR *(in database)* consulta *f* ❏ *US* *query mark* signo *m* de interrogación
  2 *vt (account, invoice)* cuestionar

question mark *n* (**a**) *Br (punctuation mark)* signo *m* de interrogación (**b**) MKTG *(product)* interrogante *m*

questionnaire *n* MKTG cuestionario *m* ❏ *questionnaire survey* sondeo *m* con cuestionario

queue COMPTR **1** *n* cola *f*
  2 *vt (print jobs)* poner en cola

quick *adj* rápido(a) ❏ ACCT *quick assets* activo *m* disponible; *quick ratio* relación *f* activo disponible-pasivo corriente; *quick returns* beneficio *m* rápido; *quick sale* venta *f* rápida

> **❝**
> … individual businesses have to show **quick returns** on minimal outlays or be deliberately run down and liquidated as "cash cows".
> **❞**

quid *n Br Fam (pound sterling)* libra *f*

quiet *adj (business, market)* inactivo(a), poco animado(a); *(trading)* escaso(a); **business is very quiet** hay poca actividad

quit COMPTR **1** *vt (database, program)* salir de
  2 *vi* salir

quittance *n* FIN finiquito *m*, descargo *m*

quorum *n* quórum *m inv*; **to have a quorum** tener quórum; **we don't have a quorum** no tenemos quórum

quota *n* (**a**) *(limited quantity)* cuota *f*; **fishing quotas have been disputed** se han puesto en cuestión las cuotas de pesca (**b**) *(share)* cupo *m*, cuota *f* ❏ MKTG *quota sample* muestra *f* de cuota; MKTG *quota sampling* muestreo *m* por cuotas; MKTG *quota sampling method* método *m* de muestreo por cuotas

quotable *adj* ST EXCH cotizable

quotation *n* (**a**) *Br* ST EXCH cotización *f*; **the latest quotations** las últimas cotizaciones; **to seek a share quotation** solicitar la admisión a cotización de las acciones (**b**) *(for work)* presupuesto *m*; **to get a quotation** obtener un presupuesto; **they gave me a quotation of £500** me dieron un presupuesto de 500 libras (**c**) *quotation marks* comillas *fpl*

quotation-driven *adj Br* ST EXCH *(market)* dirigido(a) por precios

quote 1 *n (for work)* presupuesto *m*; **to get a quote** obtener un presupuesto; **they gave me a quote of £500** me dieron un presupuesto de 500 libras
  2 *vt* (**a**) *Br* ST EXCH *(shares, company)* cotizar; **gold prices were quoted at $290 an ounce** el oro se cotizó a 290 dólares la onza ❏ *quoted company* empresa *f* cotizada (en Bolsa); *quoted investment* inversión *f* en títulos cotizados; *quoted price* precio *m* de cotización; *quoted share* acción *f* cotizada
  (**b**) *(price)* dar; **to quote sb a price for sth** dar a alguien un precio por algo; **they quoted me £500 for the work** me presupuestaron 500 libras por la obra
  (**c**) ADMIN **please quote this number** *(in reply)* por favor indique este número
  3 *vi* **to quote for a job** dar un presupuesto para un trabajo

quote-driven *adj Br* ST EXCH *(Stock Market)* dirigido(a) por precios

QWERTY keyboard *n* COMPTR teclado *m* QWERTY

Rr

radio *n* radio *f* ❑ *radio advertising* publicidad *f* en radio

radiopager *n* buscapersonas *m inv, Esp* busca *m, Méx* localizador *m, RP* radiomensaje *m*

raid ST EXCH **1** *n* = operación de compraventa de valores muy agresiva
2 *vt (pension fund)* utilizar ilícitamente

raider *n* ST EXCH tiburón *m*

rail *n (train system)* ferrocarril *m*, tren *m*; **to send goods by rail** enviar mercancías por ferrocarril ❑ *rail link* conexión *f* ferroviaria *or* por ferrocarril; *rail transport* transporte *m* ferroviario

rail-air link *n* conexión *f* ferroviaria con el aeropuerto

railroad *n US (train system)* (red *f* de) ferrocarril *m*

railway *n Br (train system)* (red *f* de) ferrocarril *m*

raise 1 *n US (pay increase)* aumento *m* (de sueldo)
2 *vt* (**a**) *(price, rate, salary)* aumentar, subir; **to raise interest rates** subir *Esp* los tipos *or Am* las tasas de interés (**b**) *(capital, funds)* reunir, recaudar (**c**) *(taxes)* recaudar; *(loan)* conseguir, obtener (**d**) *(cheque)* extender

▶ **rake in** *vt sep Fam (money)* amasar; **she's raking it in!** ¡se está forrando!, *Méx* ¡se está llenando de lana!

▶ **rake off** *vt sep Fam (money, commission)* llevarse

rake-off *n Fam* tajada *f*; **to get a rake-off on each sale** sacar tajada por cada venta

rally 1 *n (of prices, shares)* recuperación *f*, repunte *m*
2 *vi (prices, shares)* recuperarse, repuntar; **the pound rallied in the afternoon** la libra se recuperó por la tarde

RAM *n* COMPTR *(abbr* **random access memory)** (memoria *f*) RAM *f*

R&D, R and D *n (abbr* **research and development)** I+D *m* ❑ *R&D tax credit* desgravación *f* por I+D

random *adj (choice)* hecho(a) al azar; *(sample)* aleatorio(a) ❑ COMPTR *random access* acceso *m* aleatorio; COMPTR *random access memory* memoria *f* de acceso aleatorio; *random check* comprobación *f* aleatoria; *random error* error *m* aleatorio; *random sample* muestra *f* aleatoria; *random sampling* muestreo *m* aleatorio; MKTG *random selection* selección *f* aleatoria; ST EXCH *random walk (theory)* (teoría *f* del) paseo *m* aleatorio

range 1 *n* (**a**) *(of prices, colours, products)* gama *f*; **we stock a wide range of office materials** tenemos una amplia gama de artículos de oficina; **this product is the top/bottom of the range** este producto es el más alto/bajo de la gama ❑ MKTG *range addition* incorporación *f* a la gama; MKTG *range stretching* ampliación *f* de la gama (**b**) ST EXCH banda *f*; **opening/closing range** banda de apertura/cierre (**c**) *(of advertising campaign)* ámbito *m*
2 *vi* **prices range from £15 to £150** los precios oscilan entre las 15 y las 150 libras

rank 1 *n* (**a**) *(grade)* rango *m*; **to pull rank: she pulled rank on him** le recordó quién mandaba (allí) ❑ *rank and file members* (of trade union) afiliados *mpl* de base (**b**) FIN *(of debt, mortgage)* graduación *f*
2 *vi* (**a**) *(creditor, claimant)* **to rank after sb** tener una prelación inferior a alguien; **to rank before sb** tener una prelación superior a alguien; **to rank equally (with sb)** tener la misma prelación que alguien (**b**) FIN *(share)* **to rank after sth** tener una cotización inferior a algo; **to rank before sth** tener una cotización superior a algo; **to rank equally (with sth)** tener la misma cotización que algo

ratable *adj =* **rateable**

rate n (**a**) *(of inflation)* índice m, tasa f; *(of tax, interest) Esp* tipo m, *Am* tasa; **the rate is 20p in the pound** *Esp* el tipo *or Am* la tasa es de 20 peniques por libra □ MKTG **rate of adoption** *(of product)* tasa f *or* índice m de adopción; MKTG **rate of awareness** *(of product)* índice m de conocimiento; **rate band** banda f *or* rango m de precios; MKTG **rate of churn** tasa f de pérdida de clientes; **rate of depreciation** tasa f de depreciación; **rate of exchange** (tipo m *or Am* tasa f de) cambio m; **rate of growth** tasa f de crecimiento; ECON **rate of inflation** tasa f de inflación; MKTG **rate of penetration** tasa f *or* índice m de penetración; **rate of production** índice m de producción; MKTG **rate of renewal** índice m de renovación; **rate of return** tasa f de rentabilidad; **rate of return analysis** análisis m *inv* de la tasa de rentabilidad; **rate of return pricing** fijación f de precios según la tasa de rentabilidad; **rate of taxation** *Esp* tipo m impositivo, *Am* tasa f impositiva; **rate of turnover** índice m de rotación; **rate of uptake** tasa f *or* índice m de adopción

(**b**) *(price, charge)* tarifa f; **the going rate** la tarifa vigente *or* actual

While most in telecom are quite aware of the high **rate of churn** and the resulting consequences, what is surprising is the increasing rate of this dynamic, says Mary Ellen Smith, Faulkner director of research services. "It is only the expanding number of services and technologies that allow some organizations to remain profitable."

"

▶ **rate up** vt sep INS **to rate sb up** subir la prima de alguien

rateable, ratable adj Br **rateable value** ≃ valor m catastral

rate-cap vt Br ADMIN = limitar la contribución que puede cobrar un municipio

rate-capping n Br ADMIN = limitación de la contribución que puede cobrar un municipio

ratification n LAW ratificación f

ratify vt LAW ratificar

rating scale n MKTG escala f (de puntuación)

ratio n *(proportion)* proporción f; *(coefficient)* coeficiente m, ratio f; **in a ratio of four to one** en una proporción de cuatro a uno

rationalization n *(of industry)* racionalización f, reconversión f

rationalize vt *(industry)* racionalizar, reconvertir

rationing n *(of funds)* restricción f; **banks are warning of mortgage rationing** los bancos advierten de una posible restricción de los créditos hipotecarios

rat race n **to get out of the rat race** huir de la lucha frenética por escalar peldaños en la sociedad

New York is pretty work orientated and the hours can be long. It's less of a **rat race** than London, though, especially the transport. Since September 11, it's like a different city – particularly because my offices are downtown near where the World Trade Center was.

"

raw adj *(data, statistics)* bruto(a) □ **raw materials** materias fpl primas

RDBMS n COMPTR *(abbr* **relational database management system***)* RDBMS m

re prep *(abbr* **regarding***)* con referencia a; **re your letter of 8 March** con referencia a *or* en relación con su carta del 8 de marzo; **re: 2003 sales figures** *(in letter heading)* REF: cifras de ventas de 2003

reach 1 n MKTG *(of campaign, advertisement)* audiencia f

2 vt (**a**) *(extend as far as)* alcanzar, llegar a; **inflation has reached record levels** la inflación ha alcanzado niveles históricos (**b**) *(agreement, decision)* alcanzar, llegar a (**c**) *(contact)* contactar con *or Am* a; **you can always reach me at this number** siempre me puedes encontrar en este número

react vi *(prices)* reaccionar

reaction n *(of prices)* reacción f

read vt leer; ADMIN **read and approved** *(on document)* leído y aprobado; **to take the minutes as read** dar por leídas las actas

▶ **read out** vt sep COMPTR *(data)* visualizar

readdress vt (**a**) *(letter)* cambiar la dirección de (**b**) COMPTR redireccionar

reader n (**a**) *(of book)* lector(ora) m,f; *US (company librarian)* documentalista mf (**b**) COMPTR lector m, *Méx, RP* lectora f

readership n *(of newspaper, magazine)* lectores mpl

read-me file n COMPTR archivo m *or* fichero m léeme

read-only adj COMPTR **it is read-only** es de sólo lectura □ **read-only disk** *(hard)* disco m de sólo lectura; *(floppy)* disquete m de sólo lectura; **read-only file** archivo m *or* fichero m de sólo lectura; **read-only lock** bloqueo m de sólo lectura; **read-only memory** memoria f de sólo lectura; **read-only mode** modo m de sólo lectura

readvertise vt *(job, position)* volver a anunciar

read-write head n COMPTR cabeza f lectora-grabadora

ready adj **ready cash** dinero m en efectivo; *Fam*

ready money dinero *m* contante y sonante; *ready reckoner* baremo *m*

real *adj* (**a**) *(actual)* real ❑ *real accounts* cuentas *fpl* de patrimonio; *real assets* bienes *mpl* inmuebles; *real cost* costo *m* or *Esp* coste *m* real; *real income* renta *f* real, ingresos *mpl* reales; *real profit* beneficio *m* real; MKTG *real repositioning* reposicionamiento *m*; *real salary* salario *m* real; *real terms* términos *mpl* reales; **salaries have fallen in real terms** los sueldos han caído en términos reales; COMPTR *real time* tiempo *m* real; FIN *real value* valor *m* real

(**b**) *real estate* bienes *mpl* inmuebles; *US real estate agency* agencia *f* de la propiedad inmobiliaria; *US real estate agent* agente *mf* inmobiliario(a); *US real estate leasing* arrendamiento *m* de inmuebles

> **"**
> The proposal also included an offer to reduce the price of supplies in **real terms** over the first five years and a pledge that during the contract period prices would remain "within the general movement of prices in the economy".
> **"**

realign *vt* FIN reajustar

realignment *n* FIN reajuste *m*; **realignment of currencies** reajuste monetario

realizable *adj* FIN realizable ❑ ACCT *realizable assets* activos *mpl* realizables; *realizable securities* valores *mpl* realizables

realization *n* FIN realización *f*

realize *vt* FIN *(convert into cash)* realizar, liquidar; *(yield financially)* producir; **to realize a high price** *(of goods)* alcanzar un precio alto; *(of seller)* obtener un precio alto; **how much did they realize on the sale?** ¿cuánto obtuvieron por la venta?; **these shares cannot be realized** estas acciones no se pueden rescatar

real-time *adj* COMPTR en tiempo real ❑ *real-time clock* reloj *m* de tiempo real

realtor *n US* agente *mf* inmobiliario(a)

realty *n US* bienes *mpl* inmuebles

reapply *vi (for job)* volver a presentar solicitud, volver a presentarse; **previous applicants need not reapply** no se aceptarán solicitudes de candidatos anteriores

reappoint *vt* volver a nombrar

reappraisal *n* (**a**) FIN *(of property)* nueva tasación *f* (**b**) *(of policy)* reconsideración *f*, replanteamiento *m*

reappraise *vt* (**a**) FIN *(property)* volver a tasar (**b**) *(policy)* reconsiderar, replantear

reasonable *adj (offer, price)* razonable

reassess *vt* (**a**) *(policy, situation)* replantearse (**b**) FIN *(damages)* volver a valorar; *(taxation)* practicar

una liquidación provisional; **you have been reassessed** se le ha practicado una liquidación provisional

reassessment *n* (**a**) *(of policy, situation)* replanteamiento *m* (**b**) FIN *(of damages)* nueva valoración *f*; *(of taxation)* liquidación *f* provisional

reassign *vt (funds)* reasignar

reassignment *n (of funds)* reasignación *f*

rebate *n* (**a**) *(refund)* devolución *f*, reembolso *m*; *(of tax)* devolución *f* (**b**) *(discount on purchase)* bonificación *f*

reboot COMPTR **1** *vt* reiniciar
2 *vi* reiniciarse

rebrand *vt* MKTG *(product)* relanzar *(con otra marca)*

rebranding *n* MKTG *(of product)* relanzamiento *m (con otra marca)*

> **"**
> We may well see more consolidation in the sector, but a merger between any of the high street banks is a rank outsider. Everyone will be watching closely the **rebranding** of Midland to HSBC.
> **"**

rebuy *n* MKTG repetición *f* de compra ❑ *rebuy rate* tasa *f* de repetición de compra

recall 1 *n* (**a**) MKTG *(of brand name)* recuerdo *m*, recordatorio *m* ❑ MKTG *recall rate* índice *m* de recuerdo; *recall study* estudio *m* de recuerdo; *recall test* test *m* de recuerdo (**b**) *(of faulty goods)* retirada *f* del mercado
2 *vt (faulty goods)* retirar del mercado

> **"**
> … there is liable to be a very different result according to whether a **recall test** is carried out within 24 hours, or a week, or three months, of an ad appearing.
> **"**

recapitalization *n* FIN *(of company)* recapitalización *f*

recapitalize *vt* FIN *(company)* recapitalizar

> **"**
> China is still deflating, its banking system needs to be **recapitalized**, but [the] government's ability to raise enough taxes to do it is poor, while consumers save and do not spend to protect their own futures.
> **"**

recapture *US* FIN **1** *n* reversión *f* al Estado
2 *vt* revertir

receipt 1 *n* (**a**) *(act of receiving)* recibo *m*, recepción *f*; **to be in receipt of sth** acusar recibo de algo; **we are in receipt of your letter of 9 June** acusamos recibo de su carta del 9 de junio; **to pay on receipt** pagar contra reembolso; **to**

acknowledge receipt of sth acusar recibo de algo; **on receipt of this letter** a la recepción de esta carta
  (**b**) *(proof of payment) (for service, rent, parcel, letter)* recibo *m*; *(for purchase)* ticket *m or* tíquet *m* (de compra), justificante *m* de compra ❑ *receipt book* talonario *m* de recibos; *receipt in full* finiquito *m*; *receipt stamp* sello *m* de recibo
  (**c**) **receipts** *(takings)* ingresos *mpl*; **receipts and expenditure** ingresos y gastos
  2 *vt* (**a**) *(mark as paid)* indicar como pagado(a); **to receipt a bill** indicar "pagado" en una factura
  (**b**) *US (give a receipt for)* entregar un recibo por

receivable 1 *n* **receivables** cuentas *fpl* pendientes de cobro, cuentas por cobrar
  2 *adj (account, bill)* a *or* por cobrar

receive *vt* recibir; *(money)* percibir; *(salary)* cobrar; ST EXCH **to receive a premium** cobrar una prima; **received with thanks** *(on bill)* recibí conforme ❑ *received cash book* libro *m* de ingresos en caja

receiver *n* (**a**) *(of goods, consignment)* destinatario(a) *m,f* (**b**) FIN *(in bankruptcy)* síndico(a) *m,f*; **to be in the hands of the receiver(s)** estar en liquidación; **the receivers have been called in at Lawson Trading** Lawson Trading ha solicitado la declaración de quiebra (**c**) *US receiver general* recaudador(ora) *m,f* general

❝
Leading fresh prepared food firm Geest has announced it has acquired the facilities of Tinsley Foods, which is **in the hands of the receivers**. Geest, which recently revealed an 18% rise in turnover for the interim period, said it planned to continue to invest in capacity to match strong consumer demand for quality fresh products.
❞

receivership *n* **to go into receivership** declararse en quiebra, suspender pagos

receiving *n* (**a**) *(of goods)* **receiving depot** depósito *m* de recepción; **receiving office** oficina *f* de recepción; **receiving station** estación *f* receptora (**b**) LAW **receiving order** auto *m* de quiebra

reception *n* (**a**) *(at hotel, in office)* recepción *f* ❑ *US reception clerk* recepcionista *mf*; *reception desk* recepción *f*; *reception room* sala *f* de recepción (**b**) *(formal party)* recepción *f*

receptionist *n* recepcionista *mf*

recession *n* ECON recesión *f*; **the economy is in (a) recession** la economía está en recesión

recessionary *adj* ECON *(conditions, policy)* recesivo(a); **to have a recessionary effect** tener un efecto recesivo, propiciar una recesión

❝
The most important part of his empire in the **recessionary** Nineties is the lower-priced Emporio Armani line, sold both in London and Glasgow, which takes all its inspiration from the street.
❞

recipient *n (of letter, e-mail message)* destinatario(a) *m,f*; *(of cheque, bill)* beneficiario(a) *m,f*

reciprocal *adj* recíproco(a) ❑ *reciprocal agreement* acuerdo *m* recíproco; MKTG *reciprocal relationships model* modelo *m* de relaciones recíprocas; *reciprocal trading* comercio *m* recíproco

reckon 1 *vt (calculate)* calcular; **to reckon the cost of sth** calcular el costo *or Esp* coste de algo
  2 *vi (calculate)* calcular

reckoning *n (calculation)* cálculo *m*

recognition *n* MKTG reconocimiento *m* ❑ *recognition score* tasa *f* de reconocimiento; *recognition test* test *m or* prueba *f* de reconocimiento

recognized *adj (agent)* acreditado(a) ❑ *recognized investment exchange* bolsa *f* de valores oficialmente reconocida

recommended retail price *n* precio *m* recomendado de venta al público, *Esp* precio de venta al público recomendado

recompense LAW **1** *n (compensation)* compensación *f*, indemnización *f*
  2 *vt* **to recompense sb for sth** recompensar a alguien por algo

reconcile *vt (figures, accounts)* cuadrar, conciliar; *(bank statements)* conciliar; ACCT *(entries)* conciliar

reconciliation *n (of figures, accounts)* conciliación *f*; *(of bank statements)* conciliación *f*; ACCT *(of entries)* conciliación *f* ❑ *reconciliation account* cuenta *f* de conciliación; ACCT *reconciliation statement* estado *m* de conciliación

reconfigure *vt* COMPTR reconfigurar

reconstruction *n (of company, economy)* reconstrucción *f*

record 1 *n* (**a**) *(account)* registro *m*; **to make a record of sth** registrar algo, hacer un registro de algo; **to keep a record of sth** llevar nota de algo; *(more officially)* llevar un registro de algo; **they keep a record of all deposits** llevan un registro de todos los depósitos; **do you have any record of the transaction?** ¿tiene algún registro de la transacción?; **our records show that payment is overdue** según nuestros datos ese pago ha vencido
  (**b**) *(past history)* historial *m*; **his past record with the firm** su historial con la empresa; **the makers have an excellent record for high quality** los fabricantes tienen una excelente tradición de calidad

(**c**) COMPTR *(in database)* registro *m*
2 *adj* récord *inv*; **unemployment is at a record high/low** el desempleo *or Am* la desocupación ha alcanzado un máximo/mínimo histórico
3 *vt (take note of)* anotar; **to record the minutes of a meeting** levantar acta de una reunión

recorded *adj* ❑ *Br* **recorded delivery** correo *m* certificado; **to send sth recorded delivery** enviar algo por correo certificado; **recorded message** *(on answering machine)* mensaje *m* grabado

recoup *vt* (**a**) *(get back) (losses)* resarcirse de; **to recoup one's investment** recuperar una inversión; **to recoup one's costs** recuperar los gastos (**b**) *(pay back) (person)* reembolsar

recourse *n* FIN, LAW recurso *m*; **to have recourse to** recurrir a; **endorsement without recourse** endoso *m* completo

recover 1 *vt* (**a**) *(debt, money, deposit)* recuperar; **to recover one's expenses** recuperar los gastos (**b**) LAW *(damages)* cobrar (**c**) COMPTR *(file, data)* recuperar
2 *vi (economy, prices, shares, business)* recuperarse

recoverable *adj (debt)* recuperable; *(packaging)* reciclable

recovery *n* (**a**) *(of debt, money, deposit)* recuperación *f* (**b**) LAW *(of damages)* cobro *m* (**c**) COMPTR *(of file, data)* recuperación *f* (**d**) *(of economy, prices, shares, business)* recuperación *f*

recruit 1 *n* nuevo(a) empleado(a) *m,f*
2 *vt* contratar

recruitment *n* contratación *f* ❑ **recruitment agency** agencia *f* de contratación; **recruitment consultant** asesor(ora) *m,f* de contratación; **recruitment drive** *(of organization, party)* campaña *f* de reclutamiento *or* incorporación; **recruitment plan** plan *m* de contratación (de empleados)

rectification *n (of mistake)* rectificación *f*; ACCT *(of entry)* rectificación *f*

rectify *vt (mistake)* rectificar; ACCT *(entry)* rectificar

recurrent expenses *npl* gastos *mpl* ordinarios

recycle *vt (materials)* reciclar; FIN *(funds)* reciclar, recircular ❑ COMPTR **recycle bin** papelera *f* de reciclaje

red 1 *n* **to be in the red** *(person, company, account)* estar en números rojos, *Am* estar en rojo; **to be £5,000 in the red** *(person, company)* tener un descubierto de 5.000 libras; *(account)* presentar un descubierto de 5.000 libras
2 *adj US* FIN **to go into red ink** *(person, company, account)* entrar en números rojos ❑ **red chip** red chip *m*, acción *f* roja; **red tape** burocracia *f*, papeleo *m* (burocrático)

> Otherwise companies will find themselves locked into expensive and time consuming legal battles without any certainty over the timespan or the result. Indeed, such a process could easily be subverted by companies on the receiving end of a hostile bid to stifle the takeover battle with a blanket of legal **red tape**.

redeem *vt* FIN (**a**) *(bond)* amortizar; *(share)* rescatar; *(coupon)* canjear (**b**) *(loan, mortgage)* amortizar; *(bill, debt)* pagar

redeemable *adj (loan)* liquidable; *(mortgage)* amortizable; *(bond)* amortizable; *(share)* rescatable

redemption *n* FIN (**a**) *(of bond)* amortización *f*; *(of share)* rescate *m*; **redemption before due date** amortización antes del vencimiento ❑ **redemption date** fecha *f* de amortización; **redemption fee, redemption premium** prima *f* de rescate, prima de reembolso; **redemption price** precio *m* de rescate, precio de reembolso; **redemption value** valor *m* de amortización; **redemption yield** rendimiento *m* al vencimiento (**b**) *(of loan)* liquidación *f*; *(of mortgage)* amortización *f*

> Income shares come in two forms. Those in the Schroder Split fund, Martin Currie Extra Return and Second St David's for instance, will be repaid at 100p at the end of the trust's life – so long as it has sufficient assets after paying all the zeros. In the meantime they get all the income. The current yield is over 7 per cent and should increase. This seems attractive, except that those who buy above **redemption price** and hold to **redemption** are bound to suffer a capital loss.

redeploy *vt (resources)* redistribuir, reorganizar; *(workers)* recolocar

redeployment *n (of resources)* redistribución *f*, reorganización *f*; *(of workers)* recolocación *f*

redial TEL **1** *n* **redial (feature)** *(botón m de)* rellamada *f*; **the latest model has automatic redial** el último modelo tiene rellamada automática *or Andes, RP* rediscado automático
2 *vt (number)* volver a marcar *or Andes, RP* discar
3 *vi* volver a marcar *or Andes, RP* discar (el número)

redirect *vt (mail)* reexpedir (**to** a)

rediscount FIN **1** *n* redescuento *m*
2 *vt* redescontar

redline *vt US (area, community)* = no conceder hipotecas o seguros a

redo *vt* rehacer, volver a hacer

redraft vt (document, letter, report) redactar de nuevo, reescribir

reduce vt reducir, disminuir; (price) rebajar; (output) reducir

reduced adj reducido(a); (goods) rebajado(a); **to buy sth at a reduced price** comprar algo rebajado □ **reduced rate** tarifa f reducida; **reduced staff** personal m reducido

reduction n (a) reducción f, disminución f; (of prices, taxes) rebaja f, reducción (b) (discount) descuento m, rebaja; **to make a reduction (on sth)** hacer un descuento (en algo)

redundancy n Br (dismissal) despido m; **the company has announced three hundred redundancies** la empresa ha anunciado trescientos despidos □ **redundancy notice** notificación f de despido; **redundancy pay** indemnización f por despido; **redundancy payment** indemnización f por despido

redundant adj Br **to make sb redundant** (of employer) despedir a alguien; **to be made redundant** ser despedido(a)

re-employ vt volver a contratar, Am recontratar

re-employment n contratación f repetida, Am recontratación f

reengineer vt (product, method, process) rediseñar; (company) reestructurar

reengineering n reingeniería f

> 66
>
> Investors are growing concerned that the company's customer base is not growing quickly enough while customers themselves are not spending enough. Telewest, which recently claimed it could survive on its current facilities as long as it executed well, is known to have discussed options with both Liberty Media and Microsoft, two of its major shareholders. It remains silent on whether a financial **reengineering** is under way.
>
> 99

re-export 1 n (activity) reexportación f; (product) producto m reexportado; **re-exports** reexportaciones □ **re-export trade** reexportación f
2 vt reexportar

re-exportation n reexportación f

ref (abbr **reference**) (at head of letter) ref.; **your ref** S/Ref.; **our ref** N/Ref.

refer vt (a) BANKING **to refer a cheque to drawer** devolver un cheque al librador; **refer to drawer** (on cheque) devolver al librador (b) (send, direct) remitir; **to refer a customer to another department** remitir a un cliente a otro departamento

▸ **refer to** vt insep (consult) (person, notes, document) consultar; **I shall have to refer to the board** necesito consultar a la junta

referee n (a) (for job) **please give the names of two referees** por favor dé los nombres de dos personas que puedan proporcionar referencias suyas; **you can give my name as a referee** puedes dar mi nombre para referencias (b) LAW tercer árbitro m (c) **referee in case of need** (on bill of exchange) interventor en caso de necesidad

reference n (a) (consultation) consulta f; **with reference to your letter of 20 March** (in letter) con or en referencia a su carta del 20 de marzo; **with reference to what was said at the meeting** con or en referencia a lo que se dijo en la reunión; **reference AB** (at head of letter) referencia AB □ **reference number** número m de referencia; **please quote this reference number** (in reply) por favor, indique este número de referencia
(b) (testimonial) (from bank) referencias fpl; (from employer) informe m, referencias; **to give sb a reference** dar referencias de alguien; **to have good references** tener buenas referencias; **to take up references** comprobar referencias; **you can use my name as a reference** puedes dar mi nombre para referencias
(c) MKTG **reference customer** cliente(a) m,f de referencia; **reference group** grupo m de referencia; **reference price** precio m de referencia; **reference sale** venta f por referencias
(d) BANKING, FIN **reference rate** Esp tipo m or Am tasa f de referencia
(e) (of commission, tribunal) competencia f, atribuciones fpl; **under these terms of reference** dentro de estas competencias; **the question is outside the tribunal's reference** la cuestión queda fuera del ámbito de competencia del tribunal

refinance FIN **1** vt (loan) refinanciar
2 vi (company) refinanciarse

refinancing n FIN refinanciación f

reflate vt (economy) reflacionar

reflation n reflación f

> 66
>
> In the United States itself, the Bush administration has unceremoniously shredded the Washington consensus on the virtues of global free trade by imposing tariffs on imported steel; Alan Greenspan, the chairman of the Federal Reserve, has gone for a hyper-Keynesian policy of **reflation** at any cost; and defence spending, as well as tax cuts, threatens the federal surplus.
>
> 99

refloat vt FIN (company) volver a sacar a Bolsa; (loan) volver a emitir

refresh COMPTR **1** *n* actualización *f*, refresco *m* ❏ *refresh rate* velocidad *f* de refresco **2** *vt (screen)* actualizar, refrescar

refresher course *n* cursillo *m* de reciclaje

refrigerate *vt* refrigerar ❏ *Br refrigerated lorry* camión *m* frigorífico; *refrigerated ship* buque *m* refrigerado; *US refrigerated truck* camión *m* frigorífico

refrigeration *n* refrigeración *f*; **to keep sth under refrigeration** mantener algo refrigerado ❏ *refrigeration plant* planta *f* refrigeradora

refrigerator *n (storeroom)* cámara *f* frigorífica

refund 1 *n* (**a**) reembolso *m*; **to get** *or* **obtain a refund** recibir la devolución del importe (**b**) LAW *(of monies)* restitución *f* **2** *vt* (**a**) *(person, money)* reembolsar; **to refund sb sth, to refund sth to sb** devolver algo a alguien; **they refunded me the postage** me reembolsaron los gastos de envío (**b**) LAW *(monies)* restituir

refundable *adj* reembolsable

refunding *n* refinanciación *f*, conversión *f* ❏ *refunding clause* cláusula *f* de refinanciación, cláusula *f* de conversión; *refunding loan* préstamo *m* de refinanciación

refusal *n* (**a**) *(of suggestion, offer, request, proposal)* rechazo *f*; **to meet with a refusal** *(offer)* ser rechazado(a); *(person)* recibir una negativa ❏ MKTG *refusal rate* tasa *f* de rechazo (**b**) *(option to buy)* **to have first refusal (on sth)** tener primera opción de compra (sobre algo); **to give sb first refusal (on sth)** conceder a alguien opción de compra (sobre algo)

> As well as bidding to run the station, Innogy is understood to be interested in acquiring a stake in it if Enron's shareholding becomes available. The existing investors in the plant are expected to be offered **first refusal**, but already Western Power has stated that it is not interested in increasing its 15.4 per cent holding.

refuse *vt* (**a**) *(suggestion, offer, request, proposal)* rechazar; **I refused to take delivery of the parcel** me negué a firmar la entrega del paquete (**b**) *(permission, visa)* denegar; *(help)* negar; **he was refused entry** le negaron la entrada; **they were refused a loan** les negaron un préstamo

regard *n* **with regard to** en cuanto a, con respecto a; **with regard to your enquiry, I am happy to inform you that...** con respecto a su consulta, me complace informarle que...

regional *adj* regional ❏ *regional council* consejo *m* regional; *Br regional development* desarrollo *m* regional; *Br regional development corporation* corporación *f* para el desarrollo

regional; *regional director* director(ora) *m,f* regional; *regional headquarters* sede *f* regional

register 1 *n* (**a**) *(list)* registro *m*; *(book)* libro *m* de registro; **to enter sth in a register** consignar algo en un registro ❏ *Br* LAW *register of companies* registro *m* de empresas, registro mercantil; ST EXCH *register of shareholders* registro *m* de accionistas (**b**) COMPTR *(of memory)* registro *m* **2** *vt* (**a**) *(name, company, shares, trademark)* registrar; *(mortgage)* inscribir, registrar; **to register a complaint** presentar una queja (**b**) COMPTR *(software)* registrar

registered *adj* (**a**) *registered agent* agente *mf* oficial; FIN *registered bond* obligación *f* nominativa; *registered capital* capital *m* social autorizado; *registered charity* entidad *f* benéfica legalmente reconocida; FIN *registered debenture* obligación *f* nominativa; *registered design* diseño *m* registrado; *registered name* nombre *m* registrado; *registered office* domicilio *m* social; *registered securities* valores *mpl* or títulos *mpl* nominativos; *registered share* acción *f* nominativa; *Br registered shareholder* accionista *mf* registrado(a); *registered stock* valores *mpl or* títulos *mpl* nominativos; *US registered stockholder* accionista *mf* registrado(a); *registered tonnage* toneladas *fpl* de arqueo; *registered trademark* marca *f* registrada; COMPTR *registered user* usuario *m,f* registrado(a); *registered value* valor *m* registrado (**b**) *(letter, parcel)* certificado(a) *(con derecho a indemnización)*; **to send sth by registered post** enviar algo por correo certificado

registrar *n* (**a**) ADMIN registrador(ora) *m,f* (**b**) *Br* LAW *registrar of companies* encargado(a) *m,f* del Registro Mercantil

registration *n (of name, shares, company, trademark)* registro *m*; *(of mortgage)* inscripción *f*, registro ❏ ST EXCH *registration body* organismo *m* de registro; COMPTR *registration card* tarjeta *f* de registro; *registration certificate* certificado *m* de inscripción; *registration fees* derechos *mpl* de registro, derechos de inscripción; *registration number* COMPTR número *m* de registro; *(of vehicle)* (número de) matrícula *f*, *RP* patente *f*; FIN *registration and transfer fees* comisiones *fpl* de registro y transmisión

registry *n* registro *m* ❏ *registry fees* derechos *mpl* de registro, derechos de inscripción; *Br* ADMIN *registry office* registro *m* civil

regressive *adj* FIN regresivo(a)

regressively *adv* FIN regresivamente

regular *adj (habitual, normal)* habitual; **to be in regular employment** tener un trabajo regular; **to go through the regular channels** seguir el procedimiento habitual ❏ *regular customer* cliente(a) *m,f* habitual; *regular income* ingresos *mpl* regulares; *regular price* precio *m* normal

regulate *vt (adjust, supervise by law)* regular; **the price is regulated by supply and demand** el precio está regulado por la oferta y la demanda; **hitherto the industry has regulated itself** hasta ahora, la industria se ha regulado a sí misma

regulating body *n* organismo *m* regulador

regulation *n (adjustment, supervision by law)* regulación *f*; *(rule)* regla *f*, norma *f*; **it's contrary to** *or* **against (the) regulations** va contra las normas; **it complies with EU regulations** cumple con la normativa *or* las normas de la UE

regulator *n (regulatory body)* regulador *m*

regulatory *adj* regulador(ora) ❑ *regulatory body* organismo *m* regulador

> ❝
> The Office of Telecommunications (OFTEL) was created to act as the **regulatory body** for the telecommunications industry in order to ensure that BT did not abuse its dominant position.
> ❞

reimburse *vt* reintegrar, reembolsar; **to reimburse sb for sth** reintegrar *or* reembolsar algo a alguien

reimport 1 *n (activity)* reimportación *f*
2 *vt* reimportar

reimportation *n* reimportación *f*

reinitialize *vt* COMPTR reinicializar

reinstate *vt* (**a**) *(person)* restituir (**b**) *(law)* reinstaurar; *(idea, system)* reintroducir

reinstatement *n* (**a**) *(of person)* restitución *f* (**b**) *(of law)* reinstauración *f*; *(of idea, system)* reintroducción *f*

reinsurance *n* INS reaseguro *m*

reinsure *vt* INS reasegurar

reinsurer *n* INS reaseguradora *f*

reinvest *vt* FIN reinvertir

reinvestment *n* FIN reinversión *f*

reissue FIN **1** *n (of banknote, shares)* nueva emisión *f*
2 *vt (banknote, shares)* emitir de nuevo

reject 1 *n (object)* artículo *m* defectuoso *or* con tara
2 *vt* rechazar

related to, relating to *prep* ADMIN, LAW relacionado(a) con; **questions related to official procedure** preguntas relacionadas con el procedimiento oficial

relational database *n* COMPTR base *f* de datos relacional

relationship marketing *n* MKTG marketing *m* de relaciones

relative *adj* relativo(a) ❑ *relative market*

share cuota *f* de mercado relativa

relaunch 1 *n (of product)* relanzamiento *m*
2 *vt (product)* relanzar

release 1 *n* (**a**) *(of debtor)* liberación *f* (**b**) CUSTOMS *(of goods from bond)* despacho *m* (**c**) FIN *(of funds)* liberación *f*
2 *vt* (**a**) *(debtor)* liberar (**b**) CUSTOMS *(goods from bond)* despachar (**c**) FIN *(funds)* liberar

reliability *n* fiabilidad *f*, *Am* confiabilidad *f*

reliable *adj (person, company, machine)* fiable, *Am* confiable; *(information)* fidedigno(a), fiable, *Am* confiable

relief *n* (**a**) *(replacement)* relevo *m* (**b**) *US* ADMIN *(state benefit)* subsidios *mpl* estatales; **to be on relief** cobrar un subsidio (**c**) *(of debt)* alivio *m*

reload *vt* COMPTR volver a cargar, recargar

relocate 1 *vt (company, person)* trasladar
2 *vi (company, person)* mudarse, trasladarse (**to** a)

relocation *n* traslado *m* ❑ *relocation allowance (for employee)* suplemento *m* por traslado; *relocation expenses (for employee)* gastos *mpl* de traslado

> ❝
> At Schwab.com, all interns are offered stock options. In addition, college-age interns earn $500 to $600 a week. And graduate students can rake in as much as $5,500 a month for full-time work, plus **relocation expenses** or a housing stipend. The question is, have students become more interested in the money and perks steered their way than in the experience of the internship?
> ❞

remainder 1 *n* (**a**) *(money, debt)* resto *m* (**b**) *(unsold product)* resto *m* de serie; *(unsold book)* ejemplar *m* no vendido
2 *vt (books)* liquidar

remarket *vt* comercializar

remarketing *n* comercialización *f*

REMIC *n US* FIN (*abbr* **real estate mortgage investment conduit**) obligación *f* con garantía real

reminder *n (for bill)* recordatorio *m*; **reminder of account due** recordatorio de pago ❑ ACCT *reminder entry* partida *f* informativa

remission *n (of debt)* condonación *f*

remit 1 *n (area of authority)* cometido *m*; **that's outside their remit** eso está fuera de su ámbito de actuación
2 *vt* (**a**) *(payment)* remitir, girar (**b**) *(cancel) (debt)* cancelar, condonar; **to remit sb's fees** eximir a alguien del pago de los honorarios; **to remit sb's income tax** eximir a alguien del pago del impuesto sobre la renta
3 *vi (pay)* enviar el pago; **please remit by cheque** se ruega pagar con cheque

remittal n FIN (of debt) cancelación f, condonación f

remittance n (money) giro m, envío m de dinero; **return the form with your remittance** devuelva el impreso con el giro □ **remittance advice** aviso m de pago; **remittance date** fecha f de envío; **remittance of funds** transferencia f de fondos, envío m de fondos

remortgage vt (with different lender) subrogar; (with same lender) novar

remote adj COMPTR (user) remoto(a) □ **remote access** (to computer, answering machine) acceso m remoto; **remote banking** telebanca f; **remote server** servidor m remoto; **remote terminal** terminal m remoto

removable adj COMPTR (disk, media) extraíble, removible

remunerate vt remunerar, retribuir

remuneration n remuneración f, retribución f (for para); **to receive remuneration for sth** percibir una remuneración por algo □ **remuneration package** paquete m de beneficios

> " ──────────────
>
> ... Vodafone pointed out that it has held its focus groups and consulted to show how it has learned from past mistakes of previously over-generous and opaque remuneration packages. As shareholders wished, 80 per cent of Gent's package was performance-related; a paltry 20 per cent (£.192 million) was base pay.
>
> ────────────── "

remunerative adj remunerativo(a)

rename vt COMPTR (file) cambiar de nombre, renombrar

render vt (bill, account) presentar; **as per account rendered** de acuerdo con su factura; **for services rendered** por los servicios prestados

renegotiate vt & vi renegociar

renegotiation n renegociación f

renew vt (membership, contract, lease) renovar; **to renew one's subscription (to sth)** renovar la suscripción a (a algo)

renewal n (of membership, contract, lease) renovación f □ INS **renewal notice** aviso m de renovación; **renewal premium** prima f de renovación

rent 1 n alquiler m, Méx renta f; **for rent** (sign) se alquila, Méx se renta □ **rent control** control m de alquileres or Méx rentas
　　2 vt alquilar, Méx rentar (**to/from** a); **to rent sth from sb** alquilar or Méx rentar algo a alguien

▶ **rent out** vt sep alquilar, Méx rentar; **to rent sth out to sb** alquilar or Méx rentar algo a alguien

rental n (**a**) (hire) alquiler m, Méx renta f □ **rental agreement** contrato m de alquiler; **rental company** empresa f de alquiler; **rental market** mercado m de alquiler; **rental property** propiedad f en alquiler; **rental value** valor m de alquiler (**b**) (money) (for house, office, equipment, telephone line) alquiler m, Méx renta f □ **rental charges** costos mpl or Esp costes mpl de alquiler; **rental income** ingresos mpl por alquileres

rent-controlled adj (apartment) de alquiler protegido or Méx renta protegida

rented adj alquilado(a), de alquiler, Méx rentado(a) □ **rented accommodation** viviendas fpl de alquiler or Méx rentadas; **we live in rented accommodation** vivimos en una vivienda de alquiler or Méx rentada; **rented car** coche m or Am carro m or CSur auto m de alquiler, Méx carro m rentado; **rented property** vivienda f de alquiler or Méx rentada

rent-free 1 adj exento(a) del pago de alquiler or Méx renta
　　2 adv sin pagar alquiler or Méx renta

rent-roll n (register) registro m de alquileres or Méx rentas; (income) ingresos mpl por alquiler or Méx renta

reopen 1 vt (shop, border) reabrir; (debate, negotiations) reanudar
　　2 vi (shop) volver a abrir; (debate, negotiations) reanudarse; **the border should reopen soon** la frontera se volverá a abrir próximamente

reorder 1 n nuevo pedido m □ **reorder level** nivel m mínimo de reabastecimiento or de existencias
　　2 vt pedir de nuevo

reorganization n reorganización f

reorganize 1 vt reorganizar
　　2 vi reorganizarse

rep n Fam (abbr **representative**) (salesperson) representante mf, comercial mf

repackage vt (goods) reempaquetar, reembalar; (company, image) renovar la imagen de

repair 1 n (**a**) (mending) (of car, machine, roof, road) reparación f; **to be under repair** estar en reparación; **to carry out repairs on sth** realizar reparaciones en algo; **closed for repairs** (sign) cerrado por reparaciones (**b**) (condition) **to be in good/bad repair** estar en buen/mal estado
　　2 vt (car, machine, roof, road) reparar

repatriate vt (funds) repatriar

repatriation n (of funds) repatriación f

repay vt (person) pagar; (money) devolver; (debt) pagar, saldar; (loan) amortizar

repayable adj (loan) pagadero(a), a devolver (**over** en); (debt) amortizable; **the amount is repayable in five years** la cantidad ha de ser devuelta en un plazo de cinco años

repayment *n (of person, debt)* pago *m*; *(of money)* devolución *f*; *(of loan)* amortización *f*; **repayments can be spread over 12 months** los pagos *or* las cuotas pueden repartirse en doce meses ❑ ***repayment mortgage*** préstamo *m* hipotecario *(con amortización del capital)*; ***repayment options*** opciones *fpl* de amortización

repeal 1 *n (of law)* revocación *f*
2 *vt (law)* derogar, abrogar

repeat 1 *n* COMPTR ***repeat function*** función *f* repetir; ***repeat order:* the success of a business depends on repeat orders** el éxito de un negocio depende de la renovación de pedidos; ***repeat purchase*** repetición *f* de compra; ***repeat sale*** repetición *f* de venta
2 *vt (order)* volver a hacer, renovar; *(offer)* repetir, hacer otra vez

repetitive *adj* ***repetitive strain*** *or* ***stress injury*** lesiones *fpl* por esfuerzo *or* movimiento repetitivo

replace *vt (substitute for)* sustituir, reemplazar (**with** *or* **by** por); *(battery, tyre, broken part)* cambiar; *(lost, damaged item)* reponer, restituir; COMPTR **replace all** *(command)* reemplazar todos

replacement *n* (**a**) *(person)* sustituto(a) *m,f*; *(engine or machine part)* (pieza *f* de) recambio *m*, repuesto *m*, *Méx* refacción *f*; *(for defective product)* artículo *m* nuevo; **I took the faulty book back to the shop and they gave me a replacement** llevé el libro defectuoso a la tienda y me dieron un ejemplar nuevo; **we are looking for a replacement for our secretary** estamos buscando una sustituta para nuestra secretaria
(**b**) *(substituting)* sustitución *f*; *(of battery, tyre, broken part)* cambio *m* ❑ ***replacement cost*** costo *m or Esp* coste *m* de reposición; ***replacement sale*** venta *f* de repuestos *or Méx* refacciones; ***replacement staff*** personal *m* sustituto; INS ***replacement value*** valor *m* de reposición

reply 1 *n* respuesta *f*, contestación *f*; **in reply to your letter** en respuesta a su carta ❑ ***reply card*** tarjeta *f* de respuesta; ***reply coupon*** cupón *m* de respuesta; ***reply form*** impreso *m* de respuesta; ***reply slip*** cupón *m* de respuesta
2 *vi* responder, contestar (**to** a)

reply-paid *adj Br (envelope)* con franqueo pagado

repo *n Fam* (**a**) BANKING, ST EXCH *(abbr* **repurchase**) recompra *f* ❑ ***repo agreement*** pacto *m* de recompra; ***repo operation*** operación *f* de recompra; ***repo rate*** tasa *f* de recompra (**b**) *US (abbr* **repossession**) *(of property)* = ejecución de una hipoteca por parte de un banco

report 1 *n* (**a**) *(account, review)* informe *m*, *Andes, CAm, Méx, Ven* reporte *m* (**on** sobre); **to draw up** *or* **make a report on sth** preparar *or* hacer un informe sobre algo; **to present a report to sb on sth** presentar un informe sobre algo a alguien ❑ ***report of the board of directors*** *(in annual accounts)* informe *m* de la junta directiva
(**b**) COMPTR *(of database)* informe *m*
2 *vt* (**a**) *(news, fact)* informar de; *(debate, speech)* informar (acerca) de; *(profits, losses, discovery)* anunciar, *CAm, Méx* reportar de; *(accident, theft, crime)* dar parte de; **to report one's findings (to sb)** informar de sus conclusiones (a alguien)
(**b**) CUSTOMS **to report a vessel** informar de la arribada
3 *vi* (**a**) *(present oneself)* presentarse (**to** en); **please report to our branch in Paris** le rogamos se presente en nuestra sucursal de París; **report to my office** preséntese en mi oficina
(**b**) *(give account)* informar (**to/on** a/sobre); *(committee)* presentar sus conclusiones
(**c**) *(be accountable)* **to report to sb** estar bajo las órdenes de alguien, *Andes, CAm, Méx, Ven* reportar a alguien; **I report directly to the sales manager** estoy bajo las órdenes directas del jefe de ventas, *Andes, CAm, Méx, Ven* reporto directamente al jefe de ventas

reporting *n* presentación *f* de informes *or Andes, CAm, Méx, Ven* reportes ❑ ST EXCH ***reporting limit*** límite *m* de notificación

reposition *vt* MKTG *(product)* reposicionar

> “
> Sales, independent for each of the four brands, operate out of new design studios, showrooms and offices. The brands have been **repositioned** with relevant distribution and marketing changes. The team is now in place but the total reorganisation task has been expensive and operational efficiency has suffered during the process of change.
> ”

repositioning *n* MKTG *(of product)* reposicionamiento *m*

> “
> It has been two years since Baymont Inns & Suites became the name of the brand that had been Budgetel Inns. It was touted then as the largest rebranding and **repositioning** in the history of the lodging industry without a change in ownership.
> ”

repossess *vt (property)* recobrar, recuperar; **our house has been repossessed** el banco ha ejecutado la hipoteca de nuestra casa

repossession *n (of property)* = ejecución de una hipoteca por parte de un banco

represent *vt* representar; **I represent the agency** represento a la agencia; **he represented the union at the meeting** representó al sindicato en la reunión

representation *n* representación *f*

representative 1 *n (of group, company, organization)* representante *mf*
2 *adj* representativo(a) **(of** de) ❑ MKTG *representative sample* muestra *f* representativa

reprocess *vt* reprocesar, volver a tratar

reprocessing *n* reprocesado *m*

reprogram *vt* COMPTR reprogramar

reprogrammable *adj* COMPTR reprogramable

repurchase 1 *n* (**a**) BANKING, ST EXCH recompra *f*; **sale with option of repurchase** venta *f* con opción de recompra ❑ *repurchase agreement* pacto *m* de recompra; *repurchase market* mercado *m* de recompra; *repurchase rate* tasa *f* de recompra; *repurchase right* derecho *m* de recompra (**b**) MKTG reposición *f* ❑ *repurchase market* mercado *m* de reposición; *repurchase period* periodo *m* de reposición
2 *vt* (**a**) BANKING, ST EXCH recomprar (**b**) MKTG volver a comprar

request 1 *n* petición *f*, solicitud *f*, *Am* pedido *m* (**for** de); **to make a request (for sth)** hacer una petición *or Am* un pedido (de algo); **samples sent on request** se envían muestras a petición *or Am* pedido
2 *vt* pedir, solicitar; **to request sb to do sth** pedir *or* solicitar a alguien que haga algo; **as requested** como se solicitaba

require *vt* (**a**) *(qualifications, standard, commitment)* necesitar, requerir; **this job requires skills and experience** este trabajo requiere capacidad y experiencia; **it is required that you begin work at 8 am** deberá comenzar su trabajo a las 8 de la mañana (**b**) *(need)* necesitar; **your presence is urgently required** se requiere su presencia urgentemente

requirement *n* (**a**) *(need, demand)* requisito *m*, necesidad *f*; **energy requirements** necesidades energéticas; **to meet sb's requirements** cumplir con los requisitos de alguien; **this doesn't meet our requirements** esto no cumple nuestros requisitos (**b**) *(condition, prerequisite)* requisito *m*, condición *f*; **she doesn't fulfil the requirements for the job** no cumple con los requisitos para el puesto

requisition *n* pedido *m*, solicitud *f*; **to put in a requisition for sth** realizar una solicitud de algo ❑ *requisition number* número *m* de solicitud

resale *n* reventa *f*; **not for resale** prohibida la venta ❑ *resale price maintenance* mantenimiento *m or* fijación *f* del precio de venta al público; *resale value* valor *m* de reventa

resaleable *adj* apto(a) para la venta; **in resaleable condition** en condiciones aptas para la venta

reschedule *vt* (**a**) *(meeting, flight, plan, order)* reprogramar; **the meeting has been rescheduled**

for next week la reunión se ha reprogramado para la próxima semana (**b**) FIN *(debt)* reprogramar, renegociar

rescind *vt (agreement, contract)* rescindir; *(law)* derogar

rescission *n (of agreement, contract)* rescisión *f*; *(of law)* derogación *f*

research 1 *n* investigación *f*; **to do research into sth** investigar algo; **research and development** investigación y desarrollo; **research and engineering** investigación y diseño ❑ *research company* empresa *f* de investigación; *research department* departamento *m* de investigación; *research programme* programa *m* de investigación; *research work* trabajo *m* de investigación
2 *vt* investigar
3 *vi* investigar; **to research into sth** investigar algo

researcher *n* investigador(ora) *m,f*

resell *vt* revender, volver a vender

reservation *n (booking)* reserva *f*, *Am* reservación *f*; **to make a reservation** hacer una reserva ❑ *reservations agent* agencia *f* de reservas; *reservations book* libro *m* de reservas; *reservation desk* mostrador *m* de reservas; *reservation form* impreso *m or* formulario *m or Méx* forma *f* de reserva; *reservation sheet* hoja *f* de reserva

reserve 1 *n* (**a**) FIN *(of money)* reserva *f*; **to draw on one's reserves** recurrir a las reservas ❑ *reserve account* cuenta *f* de reserva; *US reserve bank* banco *m* de la Reserva Federal; *reserve capital* capital *m* de reserva; *reserve currency* divisa *f* de reserva; ACCT *reserve fund* fondo *m* de reserva; *reserve ratio* coeficiente *m* de liquidez; *reserve stocks* reservas *fpl* (**b**) *reserve price (at auction)* precio *m* mínimo
2 *vt (room, table, seat)* reservar

> But an increase in the supply of dollars implied a persistent US balance of payments deficit (e.g. exporters to the USA accept payments in dollars, or payments overseas by US residents are made in dollars), and this would undermine confidence in the dollar as a **reserve currency** because dollar claims were growing in relation to US gold reserves.

reset COMPTR **1** *n* reinicio *m* ❑ *reset button, reset switch* botón *m* de reinicio
2 *vt* reiniciar

residence *n (stay, home)* residencia *f* ❑ *residence permit* permiso *m* de residencia

residual income *n* ingresos *mpl* netos

residuary *adj* LAW *residuary legacy* legado *m* *(después de la liquidación)*; *residuary legatee* heredero(a) *m,f* universal *(después de la liquidación)*

resign 1 *vt (job)* renunciar de; *(senior position)* dimitir de
  2 *vi* dimitir, renunciar; **she resigned from her job/from the committee** dimitió de su trabajo/del comité

resignation *n* dimisión *f*, renuncia *f*; **to hand in** *or Formal* **tender one's resignation** presentar la dimisión ◻ **resignation letter** carta *f* de dimisión *or* renuncia

resolution *n* **(a)** *(formal motion)* resolución *f*; *(of shareholders' meeting)* resolución, acuerdo *m*; **to put a resolution to the meeting** presentar una resolución a la asamblea; **to pass/adopt/reject a resolution (to do sth)** aprobar/adoptar/rechazar una resolución (para hacer algo); **the statutes can only be changed by resolution** los estatutos sólo se pueden modificar mediante una resolución
  (b) COMPTR *(of image)* resolución *f*; **high resolution screen** pantalla *f* de alta resolución

resource *n* recurso *m*; **there's a limit to the resources we can invest** los recursos que podemos invertir tienen un límite ◻ **resource allocation** asignación *f* de recursos; **resource management** gestión *f* de recursos

respect *n* **with respect to, in respect of** *(in letter)* con respecto a

respite *n* *(delay)* prórroga *f*; **we've been given a week's respite before we need to pay** nos han dado una prórroga de una semana para pagar

respond *vi* responder, contestar; **to respond to a letter** contestar a una carta

respondent *n* encuestado(a) *m,f*

response *n* respuesta *f*; **in reponse to your letter** en respuesta a su carta ◻ COMPTR **response time** tiempo *m* de respuesta

responsibility *n* **(a)** *(control, authority)* responsabilidad *f*; **to have responsibility for sth** ser responsable de algo; **the project is their joint responsibility** tienen la responsabilidad conjunta del proyecto; **a position of great responsibility** un puesto de gran responsabilidad
  (b) *(task, duty)* responsabilidad *f*; **your responsibilities will include product development** sus responsabilidades incluirán el desarrollo de productos; **they have a responsibility to the shareholders** son responsables frente a los accionistas ◻ ACCT **responsibility accounting** contabilidad *f* por responsabilidades

responsible *adj* **(a)** *(in control, in authority)* responsable; **who's responsible for research?** ¿quién es el responsable de investigación?; **a responsible job** *or* **post** *or* **position** un puesto de responsabilidad
  (b) *(accountable)* responsable (**to** ante); **he is responsible only to the managing director**

sólo tiene que rendir cuentas al director gerente
  (c) *(serious, trustworthy)* responsable; **the chemical industry has become more environmentally responsible** la industria química ha adoptado una actitud más responsable hacia el medio ambiente; **our bank makes responsible investments** nuestro banco realiza inversiones responsables

restart COMPTR **1** *n (of system, program)* reinicio *m*; **warm/cold restart** rearranque *m* en caliente/frío
  2 *vt (system, program)* reiniciar
  3 *vi (system, program)* reiniciarse

restitution *n* *(compensation)* restitución *f*; **the company was ordered to make full restitution of the monies** se ordenó a la empresa restituir la totalidad del dinero

restock *vt (shop)* reabastecer, reaprovisionar

restocking *n (of shop)* reabastecimiento *m*, reaprovisionamiento *m*

restore COMPTR **1** *n (of file, text, data)* restauración *f*
  2 *vt (file, text, data)* restaurar

restrict *vt (expenses, production)* restringir; **to restrict credits** restringir los créditos

restricted *adj (document, information)* confidencial

restriction *n (of expenses, production)* restricción *f*, limitación *f*; **to put** *or* **place** *or* **impose restrictions on sth** imponer restricciones sobre algo

restrictive *adj* restrictivo(a) ◻ **restrictive clause** cláusula *f* de restricción; **restrictive practices** prácticas *fpl* restrictivas

restructure *vt (economy)* reconvertir; *(company)* reestructurar; *(debt)* refinanciar, reestructurar

restructuring *n (of economy)* reconversión *f*; *(of company)* reestructuración *f*; *(of debt)* refinanciamiento *m*, reestructuración; **the car industry in Europe has undergone massive restructuring in recent years** la industria automovilística europea ha experimentado una profunda reconversión en los últimos años ◻ **restructuring plan** plan *m* de reestructuración

The Corporation also announced a comprehensive **restructuring plan** designed to significantly reduce its manufacturing cost base. The plan includes the transfer of production and service operations in the Power Tools and Accessories and Hardware and Home Improvement businesses from facilities in the United States and England to low-cost locations in Mexico, China, and Central Europe as well as actions to reduce selling, general, and administrative expenses.

result 1 n resultado m; **the company's results are down on last year's** las ganancias de la compañía son inferiores a las del año pasado; **to yield** or **show results** producir or dar resultados; **our policy is beginning to show results** nuestra política está empezando a producir or dar resultados

2 vi resultar; **to result in sth** tener algo como resultado, ocasionar algo; **a price rise would inevitably result** el resultado inevitable sería un aumento de los precios

résumé n (**a**) (summary) resumen m (**b**) US (curriculum vitae) currículum (vitae) m

retail 1 n venta f al por menor, Am menudeo m; **a wholesale and retail business** una empresa mayorista y minorista ▫ **retail audit** auditoría f de ventas; **retail auditor** auditor(ora) m,f de ventas; **retail bank** banco m minorista; **retail banking** banca f minorista or para particulares; **retail chain** (of shops) cadena f de tiendas or comercios; (of department stores) cadena de grandes almacenes; **retail company** empresa f minorista, empresa de venta al detalle; **retail customer** cliente(a) m,f particular; **retail dealer** minorista mf, detallista mf; **retail goods** productos mpl de venta al por menor, productos de venta al detalle; **retail outlet** punto m de venta; **retail panel** estudio m de ventas; Br **retail park** parque m comercial; **retail price** precio m de venta (al público); Br ECON, FIN **Retail Price Index** Esp Índice m de Precios al Consumo, Am Índice de Precios al Consumidor; **retail sales** ventas fpl al por menor, Am ventas de menudeo; **retail shipment** envío m del fabricante al minorista; **the game had an initial retail shipment of two million copies** se pusieron a la venta dos millones de unidades del juego; **retail shop, retail store** tienda f; **the retail trade** los minoristas

2 vt vender (al por menor)

3 vi venderse (al por menor); **they retail at £50 each** su precio de venta al público es de 50 libras

> **“**
> Located in a mall near P&G's headquarters in suburban Cincinnati, the 4,700-square-foot **retail outlet** is being regarded by the company as a test. However, executives say P& G does not plan on entering the **retail** arena. Instead, the company will use the store to launch new products and refine offerings.
> **”**

retailer n minorista mf, detallista mf ▫ **retailer co-operative** cooperativa f de minoristas; **retailers' group** grupo m de minoristas; **retailer margin** margen m de beneficio (del minorista)

retailing n venta f al por menor, venta al detalle, Am menudeo m ▫ **retailing mix** retailing mix m

retained adj ACCT **retained earnings** beneficios mpl no distribuidos; **retained profit** beneficios mpl no distribuidos

retainer n iguala f; **to pay sb a retainer** pagar a alguien una iguala

retaining fee n anticipo m

retire 1 vt (**a**) (person) jubilar (**b**) FIN (bill, bonds, shares) amortizar

2 vi jubilarse; **he retired at 65** se jubiló a los 65

retired adj (**a**) (person) jubilado(a) (**b**) FIN (bill, bonds, shares) amortizado(a)

retiree n US jubilado(a) m,f

retirement n (**a**) (of person) jubilación f; **to take early retirement** acogerse a or tomar la jubilación anticipada ▫ **retirement age** edad f de jubilación; **retirement pension** pensión f de jubilación; **retirement savings plan** plan m de jubilación (**b**) FIN (of bill, bonds, shares) amortización f

retiring adj (employee) saliente (por jubilación), que se jubila ▫ **retiring age** edad f de jubilación

retool 1 vt reequipar; **to retool a factory for armaments production** reconvertir una fábrica para la producción de armamento

2 vi reequiparse

retrain 1 vt (employee) reciclar

2 vi (employee) reciclarse (**as** como)

> **“**
> It is unlikely that people training for work today will be prepared for a job for life. Instead they will have to **retrain** in future, perhaps to do jobs they cannot even imagine today.
> **”**

retraining n reciclaje m (profesional) ▫ **retraining course** curso m de reciclaje

retrench FIN **1** vt (expenditure, costs) reducir

2 vi reducir gastos

retrenchment n FIN (of expenditure, costs) reducción f

retrieval n COMPTR recuperación f

retrieve vt COMPTR recuperar

retroactive adj retroactivo(a)

> **“**
> The earliest the matter can be raised again is in January when the new Congress returns, and although if the benefit is reintroduced it may well be **retroactive** to 1 January, potential donors are biding their time for the moment.
> **”**

retroactively adv retroactivamente

retry vi COMPTR reintentar

return 1 n (**a**) (of goods) devolución f; **by return of post** a vuelta de correo; **we bought the**

goods on a sale or return basis compramos la mercancía de forma condicional ❏ **return address** dirección f del remitente; **return cargo** carga f de retorno; **return freight** flete m de retorno

  (**b**) FIN (yield) rendimiento m (**on** por); **how much return do you get on your investment?** ¿qué rendimiento obtienes por tu inversión?; **to bring a good return** proporcionar un buen rendimiento ❏ ACCT **return on capital** rendimiento m del capital; ACCT **return on capital employed** rendimiento m del capital empleado; **return on capital invested** rendimiento m del capital invertido; **return on equity** rentabilidad f de los recursos propios; **return on investment** rendimiento m de las inversiones; **return on net assets** rendimiento m sobre activos netos; **return on sales** rendimiento m de ventas

  (**c**) **returns** (profit) beneficios mpl ❏ ACCT **returns book, returns ledger** libro m de devoluciones

  (**d**) (for declaring tax) declaración f de la renta

  (**e**) Br (round trip) Esp billete m or esp Am pasaje m or Am boleto m de ida y vuelta ❏ **return ticket** Esp billete m or esp Am pasaje m or Am boleto m de ida y vuelta

  (**f**) COMPTR retorno m ❏ **return key** tecla f de retorno

  2 vt (**a**) (goods) devolver; **to return sb's call** devolver la llamada a alguien, Am llamar a alguien en respuesta a su llamado; **return to sender** (on letter) devuélvase al remitente (**b**) (deposit, sum paid in excess) devolver (**c**) FIN (profit) rendir, proporcionar; (interest) devengar

returnable adj (container) retornable; **sale items are not returnable** no se admite la devolución de los artículos rebajados

revaluation n ECON, FIN (of currency) revalorización f, revaluación f; (of property) revaloración, retasación f

revalue vt ECON, FIN (currency) revalorizar, revaluar; (property) revalorar, retasar

Revenue n Br Fam **the Revenue** el Fisco, Hacienda f

revenue n FIN ingresos mpl ❏ **revenue account** (part of ledger) ventas fpl e ingresos mpl; (profit and loss account) cuenta f de pérdidas y ganancias; US **revenue bond** obligación f municipal (emitida para financiar una obra pública específica, cuyos intereses se financian con los ingresos generados por dicha obra); **revenue budget** presupuesto m de beneficios; **revenue centre** centro m de beneficios; **revenue stamp** timbre m fiscal; **revenue tariff** arancel m financiero

reverse 1 adj (**a**) IND **reverse engineering** retroingeniería f; ACCT **reverse entry** partida f inversa; ST EXCH **reverse repo operation** compra f con pacto de reventa; FIN, ST EXCH **reverse takeover** adquisición f inversa (**b**) COMPTR **reverse**

sort ordenación f inversa

  2 vt (**a**) (decision) revocar, revertir; **the unions have reversed their policy** los sindicatos han dado un giro de 180 grados en su política (**b**) Br TEL **to reverse the charges** llamar a cobro revertido, Méx llamar por cobrar

reverse-charge call n Br TEL llamada f or Am llamado m a cobro revertido, Méx llamada por cobrar

reversionary adj INS **reversionary annuity** anualidad f por reversión de renta; **reversionary bonus** bonificación f por reversión de renta

review 1 n (of policy, situation, salary) revisión f; (of finances) análisis m; **the annual review of expenditure** la memoria anual de gastos; **all our prices are subject to review** todos nuestros precios están sujetos a modificaciones; **my salary comes up for review next month** el mes que viene me revisan el sueldo

  2 vt (policy, situation, salary) revisar; (finances) analizar; **they should review their security arrangements** deberían revisar su sistema de seguridad

revise vt (policy, offer) revisar; **to revise a price upwards/downwards** revisar or corregir el precio al alza/a la baja

revival n (in economy, business, industry) recuperación f, reactivación f

revive 1 vt (economy, business, industry) reactivar
  2 vi (economy, business, industry) recuperarse, reactivarse

revocable adj LAW (contract, will, decision) revocable; (law) derogable; (order) cancelable ❏ FIN **revocable letter of credit** carta f de crédito revocable

revoke vt (law) derogar; (contract, will, decision) revocar; (order) cancelar

revolver credit n US crédito m renovable automáticamente, crédito rotativo

revolving adj Br FIN **revolving credit** crédito m rotativo; **revolving fund** fondo m rotativo

> **❝**
>
> And the whole point of credit cards and other forms of **revolving credit** is that they don't come to an end. This puts a new burden on the credit user: the need to decide not to use a form of credit, or stop using it, instead of the need to decide to use it.
>
> **❞**

rewritable adj COMPTR regrabable

rider n (to document) cláusula f adicional

RIE n (abbr **recognized investment exchange**) bolsa f de valores oficialmente reconocida

rig ST EXCH **1** n (rise) subida f artificial; (fall) caída f artificial
  2 vt **to rig the market** manipular el mercado

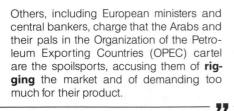

Others, including European ministers and central bankers, charge that the Arabs and their pals in the Organization of the Petroleum Exporting Countries (OPEC) cartel are the spoilsports, accusing them of **rigging** the market and of demanding too much for their product.

rigging *n* ST EXCH manipulación *f*

right 1 *n* (**a**) *(entitlement)* derecho *m*; **to have the right to sth** tener derecho a algo; **she has a right to half the profits** tiene derecho a la mitad de los beneficios □ *right of appeal* derecho *m* de apelación; *right of entry* derecho *m* de acceso; *right of first refusal* primera opción *f* de compra; *right to strike* derecho *m* de huelga (**b**) ST EXCH derecho *m* de suscripción preferente □ *rights issue* emisión *f* con derecho de suscripción preferente

2 *adj* COMPTR *right arrow* flecha *f* derecha; *right arrow key* tecla *f* de flecha derecha; *right justification* justificación *f* (a la) derecha

right-click COMPTR **1** *vt* hacer clic con el botón derecho en

2 *vi* hacer clic con el botón derecho (**on** en)

rightful *adj* legítimo(a) □ *rightful owner* propietario(a) *m,f* legítimo(a)

rightsize *vt (workforce)* hacer ajuste *or* reajuste de plantilla *or* SAm plantel en, reducir plantilla *or* SAm plantel en

We have made significant strides in **rightsizing** the business, cutting corporate overhead and realigning our product mix with the changing demands of the marketplace, said Marcus Lemonis, chairman and CEO of Recreation USA.

rightsizing *n (of workforce)* ajuste *m or* reajuste *m* de plantilla

rim country *n* US país *m* de la Cuenca del Pacífico

ring¹ *n* (**a**) *(group)* cártel *m* de empresas (**b**) *ring binder* archivador *m or* carpeta *f* de anillas (**c**) ST EXCH **the Ring** el corro

ring² *Br* **1** *vt (on telephone)* llamar (por teléfono) a, telefonear a

2 *vi (on telephone)* llamar (por teléfono), telefonear

▸ **ring back** *Br* **1** *vt sep* llamar más tarde a
2 *vi* devolver la llamada *or* Am el llamado

▸ **ring off** *vi (on telephone)* colgar

▸ **ring up 1** *vt sep* (**a**) *Br (on telephone)* llamar (por teléfono) a, telefonear a (**b**) *(on cash register)* teclear; **last year they rang up a profit of £50 million** el año pasado cosecharon unos beneficios de 50 millones de libras

2 *vi (on telephone)* llamar, telefonear

ring-fence *vt* FIN *(funds, resources)* reservar; **these funds are ring-fenced and cannot be used for any other purpose** estos fondos están reservados y no se pueden utilizar para ningún otro fin

ringing tone *n* TEL señal *f* de llamada, tono *m*

▸ **rip off** *vt sep Fam* timar, robar

rip-off *n Fam* timo *m*, robo *m*

We might find ourselves in a similar position in five years' time, when the rest of the world has real broadband access and we are stuck with services that deliver data at one tenth of the speed. This would be a **rip-off** beyond anything seen in the dial-up market, paying over the odds for a service that cannot deliver the benefits we need.

RISC *n* COMPTR *(abbr* **reduced instruction set chip** *or* **computer**) *RISC processor* procesador *m* RISC

rise 1 *n* (**a**) *(in price, interest rates)* aumento *m*, subida *f* (**in** de); **the rise in the price of petrol** el aumento en el precio de la gasolina *or* RP nafta; ST EXCH **to speculate on a rise** jugar al alza (**b**) *Br (salary increase)* aumento *m* (de sueldo)

2 *vi* aumentar, subir; **the pound has risen against the dollar** la libra ha subido respecto al dólar; **gold has risen in value by 10%** el valor del oro ha aumentado en un 10%

rising star *n* MKTG promesa *f*

risk *n* (**a**) *(possibility)* riesgo *m*, peligro *m*; **to run the risk of...** correr el riesgo de...; **it was a calculated risk** era un riesgo calculado □ *risk analysis* análisis *m* de riesgos; *US* ST EXCH *risk arbitrage* arbitraje *m* especulativo; *risk assessment* evaluación *f* de riesgos; *risk asset ratio* coeficiente *m* de riesgo; FIN *risk capital* capital *m* (de) riesgo; *risk factor* factor *m* riesgo; *risk management* gestión *f* de riesgos; *risk manager* gestor(ora) *m,f* de riesgos; *risk spreading* diversificación *f* de riesgos

(**b**) INS riesgo *m*; **to be a good/bad risk** constituir un bajo/alto riesgo; **to underwrite a risk** garantizar un riesgo □ *risk subscribed* riesgo suscrito

risk-averse *adj* prudente, = que rehuye el riesgo

risk-reward ratio *n* ST EXCH ratio *f or* relación *f* riesgo-rendimiento

rival *adj & n* rival *mf*

road *n* carretera *f*; *(in town)* calle *f*; **to be on the road** *(salesman)* estar de viaje (de ventas) □ *road haulage* transporte *m* por carretera; *road haulage company* empresa *f* de transporte por carretera; **road haulage consolidator** consolidador *m or* agrupador *m* de transporte por carretera; **road haulage depot** depósito *m* de transporte por carretera; **road link** conexión *f* por carretera; **road tax** impuesto *m* de circulación; **road traffic** tráfico *m or* tránsito *m* rodado; **road transport** transporte *m* por carretera

roadshow *n* exhibición *f* itinerante

> Maritz did not carry out the BA launch in isolation; all staff were briefed face to face on the strategy behind the new identity before it was unveiled to them at a high-tech mobile **roadshow**. Attendance was not compulsory – staff had to feel they were there through choice.

roam *vi* TEL *(mobile phone user)* usar del servicio de itinerancia *or* roaming

roaming *n* TEL *(of mobile phone)* itinerancia *f*, roaming *m*; COMPTR *(on Internet)* acceso *m* internacional

robber baron *n* Fam tiburón *m*

> Ted Turner, for example, used his billion-dollar pledge to the United Nations as public proof that he is on the side of the angels of social justice. Bill Gates has set up a $22 billion foundation, in part to rescue his reputation from the charge that he is a modern-day **robber baron**. CEOs I have talked to often explain their philanthropic involvement by saying, I am just trying to give back to the community.

robotics *n* robótica *f*

ROCE *n* (*abbr* **return on capital employed**) ROCE *m*

rock bottom *n* **to reach rock bottom** *(of company, finances)* tocar fondo; **prices have reached rock bottom** los precios han tocado fondo

rock-bottom *adj (price)* mínimo(a)

rocket *vi (prices, inflation, unemployment)* dispararse

rogue trader *n* ST EXCH agente *mf* de bolsa sin escrúpulos

> The fallout from the Allied Irish Banks scandal began to spread yesterday after it emerged that Citibank had suspended two employees for lavishly indulging the **rogue trader** who lost $691m (£487m) at AIB's subsidiary Allfirst Financial.

ROI *n* (*abbr* **return on investment**) ROI *m*,

rendimiento *m* de la inversión

▸ **roll back** *vt sep* US *(prices, inflation, unemployment)* reducir

▸ **roll out** *vt sep (launch) (product)* introducir gradualmente; *(extend) (production)* aumentar gradualmente; **the new scheme will be rolled out nationwide** el nuevo plan será introducido de forma gradual en todo el país

▸ **roll over** *vt sep* FIN refinanciar

rollback *n* US *(in prices, inflation, unemployment)* reducción *f* (**in** en)

rollercoaster market *n* mercado *m* muy volátil

rolling *adj* ACCT **rolling budget** presupuesto *m* actualizado periódicamente; ACCT **rolling plan** plan *m* renovable; **rolling stock** material *m* móvil *or* rodante

roll-on-roll-off *n (system)* acceso *m* para vehículos; *(ship)* buque *m* con acceso para vehículos

roll-out *n (of product)* introducción *f* gradual

rollover 1 *n (in taxation)* desgravación *f* por inversión; *(of loan)* renovación *f*

2 *adj* **rollover credit** crédito *m* renovable de interés variable; **rollover loan** préstamo *m* renovable de interés variable

ROM *n* COMPTR (*abbr* **read only memory**) ROM *f*

root directory *n* COMPTR directorio *m* raíz

RORO *n* (*abbr* **roll-on-roll-off**) *(system)* acceso *m* para vehículos; *(ship)* buque *m* con acceso para vehículos

ROS *n* (*abbr* **return on sales**) rendimiento *m* de ventas

rota *n* Br *(system)* sistema *m* de turnos; *(list)* lista *m* de los turnos

rotation *n (of staff, jobs)* rotación *f*

rough 1 *n (of design)* esbozo *m*, boceto *m*

2 *adj (approximate)* aproximado(a) ▫ **rough calculation** cálculo *m* aproximado; **rough copy** *or* **draft** borrador *m*; **rough drawing** esbozo *m*, boceto *m*; **rough estimate** cálculo *m* aproximado; **rough layout** distribución *f* aproximada; **rough sketch** bosquejo *m*

round 1 *n (of talks, visits)* ronda *f*

2 *adj* (**a**) **round brackets** paréntesis *mpl*; **round figure** número *m* redondo; **in round figures** en números redondos; **round sum** cifra *f* redonda; **round table** mesa *f* redonda (**b**) US **round trip** viaje *m* de ida y vuelta; **round trip ticket** Esp billete *m or* Am boleto *m or esp* Am pasaje *m* de ida y vuelta

▸ **round down** *vt sep* redondear a la baja

▸ **round up** *vt sep* redondear al alza

route 1 *n (of traveller)* ruta *f*, itinerario *m*; *(of plane, ship)* ruta

2 *vt (parcel, goods)* enviar; **we had to route the consignment through Belgium because of the flooding** tuvimos que enviar el pedido por Bélgica debido a la inundación

router *n* COMPTR router *m*, encaminador *m*

routine 1 *n* COMPTR rutina *f*
2 *adj* de rutina, rutinario(a) ◽ *routine business* trabajo *m* de rutina; *routine maintenance* mantenimiento *m* periódico

routing *n* (a) *(of parcel, goods)* envío *m* (b) COMPTR encaminamiento *m*

row *n* COMPTR *(in spreadsheet)* fila *f*

Royal Mint *n Br* FIN ≃ Casa *f* de la Moneda, *Esp* ≃ Fábrica *f* Nacional de Moneda y Timbre

royalty *n* *(for invention)* canon *m*; **royalties** *(for author, musician)* derechos *mpl* de autor

RPI *n Br* ECON *(abbr* **Retail Price Index***)* IPC *m*, *Méx* INPC *m*

RPIX *n Br* ECON *(abbr* **Retail Price Index excluding mortgage interest***)* índice *m* de inflación subyacente *(excluyendo los intereses de las hipotecas)*

RPM *n (abbr* **resale price maintenance***)* mantenimiento *m* *or* fijación *f* del precio de venta al público

RRP *n (abbr* **recommended retail price***)* PVP *m* recomendado

RSI *n (abbr* **repetitive strain injury***)* lesiones *fpl* por esfuerzo *or* movimiento repetitivo

> 66 ──────────
> A disabling ailment whose symptoms range from minor pain to loss of function in the affected body part, **RSI** affects millions of people who spend long hours at computers, switchboards and other worksites where repetitive motions are performed – typically hand-intensive exercises such as keyboarding or cutting.
> ────────── 99

RTGS *n* BANKING *(abbr* **Real-Time Gross Settlement***)* RTGS *m* ◽ *RTGS system* sistema *m* RTGS

RTM *n (abbr* **registered trade mark***)* marca *f* comercial *or* registrada

rubber cheque *n Fam* cheque *m* sin fondos

ruin 1 *n* ruina *f*
2 *vt* arruinar; **we're ruined** estamos arruinados

rule 1 *n (law, principle, regulation)* regla *f*, norma *f*; **the rules and regulations** la normativa, el reglamento
2 *vi (make decision)* decidir, dictaminar(**on** sobre); **to rule on a dispute** emitir dictamen sobre una disputa

▸ **rule off** *vt sep (account)* cerrar

ruler *n* regla *f* ◽ COMPTR *ruler line* raya *f*

ruling 1 *n (judgement)* decisión *f*, dictamen *m*
2 *adj (class)* dirigente

run 1 *n* FIN *(on currency)* venta *f* masiva(**on** de); *(on bank, stock exchange)* retirada *f* masiva de fondos; **there was a run on the dollar** se produjo una venta apresurada de dólares
2 *vt* **(a)** *(business, office, shop)* dirigir, llevar; **(b)** *(machinery)* hacer funcionar **(c)** COMPTR *(program)* ejecutar; **the computer will run most programs you're likely to use** con *Esp* este ordenador *or Am* esta computadora se puede ejecutar la mayoría del software que vaya a usar
3 *vi* **(a)** *(contract, lease)* durar; *(bill of exchange)* tener validez; **the lease has another year to run** el contrato de alquiler *or Méx* renta todavía tiene otro año de validez; **your subscription will run for two years** su suscripción tiene una validez de dos años
(b) *(machine)* funcionar (**on** con); **the new assembly line is up and running** la nueva cadena de montaje está en funcionamiento
(c) COMPTR **this software runs on DOS** este software funciona en DOS; **do not interrupt the program while it is running** no interrumpa el programa mientras se ejecuta

▸ **run down** *vt (production, stocks)* reducir, disminuir

▸ **run into** *vt insep (amount to)* ascender a; **the debts run into millions of dollars** las deudas ascienden a millones de dólares

▸ **run out** *vi (lease, contract)* vencer, cumplirse; *(money, supplies, resources)* agotarse; **to run out of sth** quedarse sin algo; **to have run out of sth** haberse quedado sin existencias de algo

▸ **run up** *vt sep (debts)* acumular; **I've run up a huge overdraft** he acumulado un descubierto enorme; **she ran up a huge bill at the jeweler's** su factura de la joyería ascendía a una fortuna

runner *n (messenger)* mensajero(a) *m,f*, recadero(a) *m,f*

running 1 *n* **(a)** *(of machine)* funcionamiento *m* ◽ *running costs* costos *mpl* *or* gastos *mpl* de mantenimiento y de consumo **(b)** *(management)* dirección *f*, gestión *f*; **she leaves the day-to-day running of the department to her assistant** delega la gestión cotidiana del departamento en su ayudante ◽ *running costs* gastos *mpl* de explotación
2 *adj* BANKING *running account* cuenta *f* corriente

runtime version *n* COMPTR versión *f* run-time

rush *n* **(a)** *rush hour Esp* hora *f* punta, *Am* hora pico **(b)** *(hurry)* prisa *f*, *Am* apuro *m*, *Col* afán *m* ◽ *rush job (done too quickly)* trabajo *m* hecho a toda prisa; **it's a rush job for Japan** *(urgent)* es un trabajo urgente para Japón; **rush order** pedido *m* urgente

▶ **rush out** *vt sep (new product)* sacar apresuradamente *or* a toda prisa

▶ **rush through** *vt sep (job, goods ordered)* despachar a toda prisa; *(application)* procesar a toda prisa

rust belt *n* = región del noreste de Estados Unidos con una alta concentración de industria pesada en declive

"

The steel dispute threatens to destroy painstaking efforts by the EU and US trade representatives to calm a series of transatlantic trade disputes. European officials believe the US administration is on the brink of sacrificing its free trade credentials to its midterm electoral prospects in America's **rust belt** states.

"

Ss

S2P *n* FIN (*abbr* **State Second Pension**) = sistema público británico de pensiones contributivas que complementa la pensión básica del Estado

sabbatical 1 *n* periodo *m* sabático
  2 *adj* sabático(a) ❑ **sabbatical year** año *m* sabático

sack *Fam* **1** *n* (*dismissal*) **to give sb the sack** echar *or* despedir a alguien; **he got the sack** lo echaron *or* despidieron
  2 *vt* (*dismiss*) echar, despedir

SAE *n* *Br* (*abbr* **stamped addressed envelope**) sobre *m* franqueado con la dirección del remitente

safe 1 *n* caja *f* fuerte
  2 *adj* (**a**) (*secure*) seguro(a) ❑ **safe custody** (*of securities, assets*) custodia *f* segura; **to place sth in safe custody** dejar algo bajo custodia (**b**) (*not dangerous*) seguro(a) ❑ **safe load** carga *f* segura

safe-deposit *n* cámara *f* acorazada ❑ **safe-deposit box** caja *f* de seguridad

safeguard 1 *n* salvaguardia *f*, garantía *f* (**against** contra) ❑ **safeguard clause** cláusula *f* de salvaguardia
  2 *vt* (*sb's interests, rights*) salvaguardar
  3 *vi* **to safeguard against sth** protegerse contra algo

safekeeping *n* **in safekeeping** bajo custodia; **to place securities in the bank for safekeeping** dejar valores bajo custodia en el banco

safety *n* seguridad *f* ❑ **safety clause** cláusula *f* de seguridad; **safety factor** factor *m* de seguridad; ST EXCH **safety margin** margen *m* de seguridad; **safety measures** medidas *fpl* de seguridad; **safety officer** delegado(a) *m,f* de seguridad; **safety precautions** medidas *fpl* de seguridad; **safety regulations** normas *fpl* de seguridad; **safety standards** criterios *mpl* de seguridad; **safety stock** existencias *fpl* de seguridad; **safety vault** cámara *f* acorazada

sag 1 *n* (*of shares, prices, demand*) caída *f*
  2 *vi* (*shares, prices, demand*) caer

sagging *adj* (*shares, prices, demand*) a la baja

salaried *adj* (*personnel, job*) asalariado(a) ❑ **salaried employee** asalariado(a) *m,f*; **salaried staff** personal *m* asalariado

salary *n* salario *m*, sueldo *m*; **to draw one's salary** percibir el salario *or* sueldo ❑ **salary advice**

(*slip*) nómina *f*; **salary curve** curva *f* salarial; **salary earner** asalariado(a) *m,f*; **salary grade** nivel *m or* grado *m* salarial; **salary increase** aumento *m* salarial *or* de sueldo; **salary level** nivel *m* salarial; **salary progression curve** curva *f* salarial; **salary range** banda *f* salarial; **salary reduction plan** = plan de jubilación en el cual el empleado deposita parte de su salario en un fondo de inversión libre de impuestos; **salary review** revisión *f* salarial; **salary scale** escala *f* salarial; **salary structure** estructura *f* salarial

sale *n* (**a**) (*act, event*) venta *f*; **sales** (*turnover*) ventas; **to work in sales** trabajar en ventas; **for sale** (*available*) en venta; (*sign*) se vende; **to put sth up for sale** poner algo a la venta; **on sale** a la venta; **sale for the account** venta a cuenta; **sale on approval** venta a prueba; **sale by auction** venta en subasta; **sale on CIF basis** venta con el CIF pagado; **sale by description** venta conforme a la descripción; **sale and lease-back** venta con arrendamiento; **sale at a loss** venta con pérdida; **sales and marketing** ventas y marketing; **sales and marketing department** departamento *m* de ventas y marketing; **sales and marketing director** director(ora) *m,f* de ventas y marketing; **sale with option of repurchase** venta con opción de recompra; **sale by order of the court** venta judicial; **sale by private agreement** venta por contrato privado; **sales and profit forecast** previsión *f* de ventas y beneficios; **sale at a reduced price** venta a precio rebajado; **sale or return** venta en depósito; **sale by sample** venta por muestrario; **sale by sealed tender** licitación *f* mediante sobre cerrado; **sale as seen** venta sin derecho a reclamación ❑ **sales account** cuenta *f* de ventas; **sales acumen** perspicacia *f* para las ventas; **sale agreement** acuerdo *m* de venta; **sales analysis** análisis *m inv* de ventas; **sales area** (*in store*) superficie *f* de ventas; (*district*) zona *f* de ventas; *Br* **sales assistant** dependiente(a) *m,f*; **sales audit** auditoría *f* de ventas; **sales budget** presupuesto *m* de ventas; **sales campaign** campaña *f* de ventas; **sales chart** gráfico *m* de ventas; *US* **sales check** comprobante *m* de venta; *US* **sales clerk** dependiente(a) *m,f*; **sales commission** comisión *f* de venta; **sales consultant** asesor(ora) *m,f* de ventas; **sales contract** contrato *m* de venta; **sales counter** mostrador *m* de ventas; **sales coverage** cobertura *f* de ventas; **sales department**

departamento *m* de ventas; *sales director* director(ora) *m,f* de ventas; *sales drive* promoción *f* de ventas; *sales effectiveness* efectividad *f* de las ventas; *sales engineer* ingeniero(a) *m,f* de ventas; *sales equation* ecuación *f* de ventas; *sales executive* ejecutivo(a) *m,f* de ventas; *sales expansion* expansión *f* de ventas; ST EXCH *sales fee* comisión *f* de venta; *sales figures* cifra *f* de ventas; *sales floor* zona *f* de ventas; *sales force* personal *m* de ventas; *sales forecast* previsión *f* de ventas; *sales growth* crecimiento *m* de ventas; *sales incentive* incentivo *m* de ventas; *sales invoice* factura *f* de venta; *sales invoice ledger* libro *m* mayor de facturas de venta; ACCT *sales ledger* libro *m* mayor de ventas; *sales letter* carta *f* de venta; *sales literature* folletos *mpl* publicitarios; *sales management* gestión *f* de ventas; *sales manager* jefe(a) *m,f* de ventas; *sales meeting* reunión *f* de ventas; *sales monopoly* monopolio *m* de ventas; *sales network* red *f* de ventas; *sales note* nota *f* de venta; *sales objective* objetivo *m* de ventas; *sales orientation* orientación *f* a *or* hacia las ventas; *sales outlet* punto *m* de venta; *sales performance* rendimiento *m* de ventas; *sales personnel* personal *m* de ventas, comerciales *mpl*; *sales philosophy* filosofía *f* de ventas; *sales pitch* estrategia *f* de ventas; *sales planning* planificación *f* de las ventas; *sales policy* política *f* de ventas; *sales potential* potencial *m* de ventas; *sale price* (selling price) precio *m* de venta; *sales programme* programa *m* de ventas; *sales projection* previsión *f* de ventas; *sales promoter* promotor(ora) *m,f* de ventas; *sales promotion* promoción *f* de ventas; *sales promotion agency* agencia *f* de promoción de ventas; *sales quota* cupo *m* de ventas; *sales ratio* índice *m* de ventas; Fam *sales rep* representante *mf* comercial *or* de ventas; *sales report* informe *m or* Am reporte *m* de ventas; *sales representative* representante *mf* comercial *or* de ventas; *sales research* investigación *f* de ventas; *sales response* respuesta *f* de ventas; *sales room* (for auction) sala *f* de subastas; *sales schedule* programa *m* de ventas; US *sales slip* recibo *m*; *sales staff* personal *f* de ventas, comerciales *mpl*; *sales subsidiary* filial *f* de ventas; *sales support* asistencia *f* de ventas; *sales support staff* personal *f* de asistencia de ventas; *sales target* objetivo *m* de ventas; US *sales tax* impuesto *m* de venta, ≃ IVA *m*; *sales team* equipo *m* de ventas; ST EXCH *sales technician* técnico(a) *m,f* de ventas; *sales technique* técnica *f* de ventas; *sales territory* territorio *m* de ventas; *sales tool* herramienta *f* de ventas; *sales volume* volumen *m* de ventas; MKTG *sales wave* ola *f* de ventas

  (**b**) *(at reduced prices)* rebajas *fpl*; Br **in the sale,** US **on sale** *(article)* rebajado(a); **the sales** las rebajas; **I got it in a sale** lo compré en las rebajas □ *sale price* (reduced price) precio *m* rebajado

saleability *n* potencial *f* de ventas

saleable *adj* vendible □ *saleable goods* productos *mpl* vendibles

saleroom *n* (for auction) sala *f* de subastas

salesman *n* (for company) comercial *m*, vendedor *m*; (in shop) dependiente *m*, vendedor

salesmanship *n* habilidad *f* para vender

> **"**
> While the investment community has been enthralled by Lord Browne's brand of cerebral **salesmanship** at BP, it is far from enamoured by the taciturn style of the 56-year-old Yorkshireman who took over at Shell last July.
> **"**

salesperson *n* (for company) comercial *mf*, vendedor(ora) *m,f*; (in shop) dependiente(a) *m,f*, vendedor(ora)

sales-response function *n* respuesta *f* de ventas

saleswoman *n* (for company) comercial *f*, vendedora *f*; (in shop) dependienta *f*, vendedora

salutation *n* (in letter) encabezamiento *m*

salvage 1 *n* (recovery) (of vessel, cargo) salvamento *m*, rescate *m*; (of waste material) recuperación *f*; (things recovered) objetos *mpl* salvados □ *salvage company* empresa *f* de salvamento; *salvage money* prima *f* de salvamento; *salvage value* valor *m* residual

  2 *vt* (vessel, cargo) salvar, rescatar; (waste material) recuperar

same-day *adj* *same-day delivery* entrega *f* en el mismo día; BANKING *same-day value* valor *m* del mismo día

sample 1 *n* MKTG muestra *f*; **up to sample** según muestra; **to send sth as a sample** enviar algo como muestra; **to buy sth from sample** comprar algo después de probar una muestra □ *sample base* base *f* de muestreo; *sample book* muestrario *m*; *sample card* carta *f* de muestras; *sample pack* paquete *m* de muestra; *sample survey* encuesta *f* por muestreo

  2 *vt* (**a**) (food) probar (**b**) MKTG (public opinion) sondear

sampler *n* MKTG (person) tomador(ora) *m,f* de muestras

sampling *n* MKTG muestreo *m* □ *sampling error* error *m* de muestreo; *sampling method* método *m* de muestreo; *sampling offer* oferta *f* de muestras; *sampling project* plan *m* de muestreo; *sampling quota* cuota *f* de muestreo

Samurai bond *n* Fam ST EXCH bono *m* Samurai

sanction 1 *n* (**a**) (penalty) sanción *f*; **to impose (economic) sanctions on a country** imponer sanciones (económicas) a un país (**b**) (approval) sanción *f*; **it hasn't yet been given official**

sanction todavía no ha sido sancionado oficialmente
2 vt (authorize) sancionar, autorizar

sandbag 1 n (in takeover bid) = estrategia para ganar tiempo ante la amenaza de una OPA hostil
2 vt obstaculizar

> ❝
>
> The CEO of Corus, controlled by Calgary-based cable giant Shaw Communications Inc., happens to be John Cassaday – the same man Mr. Fecan bounced out of the top job at CTV. Mr. Cassaday doubtless would take some pleasure in kicking Mr. Fecan out of his old CEO's office at CTV. Some say that, to avoid this humiliation, Mr. Fecan has been seeking a friendly buyer – possibly Disney – to **sandbag** any hostile takeover attempts.
>
> ❞

sandwich course n Br curso m de formación en alternancia, = curso que combina la formación teórica con la práctica laboral

SASE n US (abbr **self-addressed stamped envelope**) sobre m franqueado con la dirección del remitente

satcaster n Fam (abbr **satellite broadcaster**) emisora f vía satélite

> ❝
>
> The rulings, announced Monday by the Spanish Minister of Science and Technology Josep Pique, will force Telefonica to sell its controlling stake in free-to-air broadcaster Antena 3 if it wants to push through the merger of its **satcaster** Via Digital with rival pay TV operator Sogecable.
>
> ❞

satcasting n Fam (abbr **satellite broadcasting**) emisión f vía satélite

satellite n satélite f; **(tele)communications satellite** satélite de telecomunicaciones ❑ **satellite broadcaster** emisora f vía satélite; **satellite broadcasting** emisión f vía satélite; **satellite channel** canal m vía satélite; **satellite dish** (antena f) parabólica f; **satellite link** conexión f vía satélite; **satellite network** red f vía satélite; **satellite picture** imagen f de satélite; **satellite station** emisora f vía satélite; **satellite television** televisión f por or vía satélite

satisfaction n (a) (of demand, conditions) satisfacción f, cumplimiento m; (of contract) cumplimiento m; **the satisfaction of the union's demands** la satisfacción de las reivindicaciones sindicales (b) (of debt) satisfacción f, saldo m

satisfy vt (a) (demand, conditions) satisfacer, cumplir; (contract) cumplir (b) (debt) satisfacer, saldar

saturate vt (market) saturar

saturated adj (market) saturado(a)

saturation n (of market) saturación f ❑ **saturation advertising** publicidad f por saturación; **saturation campaign** campaña f de saturación; **saturation point** punto m de saturación; **the market has reached saturation point** el mercado ha llegado al punto de saturación

save 1 n COMPTR **to do a save of sth** guardar algo ❑ **save command** comando m (de) guardar; **save function** función f (de) guardar; **save option** opción f (de) guardar
2 vt (a) (money) ahorrar; **I save £100 a month in a special account** ahorro 100 libras al mes en una cuenta especial; **how much money have you got saved?** ¿cuánto dinero tienes ahorrado?; **buying in bulk saves 10%** comprando en grandes cantidades ahorras el 10% (b) COMPTR guardar; **to save sth to disk** guardar algo en disco; **do you want to save changes?** ¿desea guardar los cambios?; **save as** guardar como
3 vi (a) (put money aside) ahorrar; **to save on sth** ahorrar algo; **you save if you buy in bulk** comprando en grandes cantidades ahorras (b) COMPTR guardar cambios

save-as-you-earn scheme n Br FIN = plan de ahorros mediante descuentos en la nómina

saver n ahorrador(ora) m,f, Andes, RP ahorrista mf

saving n (a) (thrift, economy) ahorro m; **measures to encourage saving** medidas para fomentar el ahorro
(b) (money saved) ahorro m; **we made a saving of £500 on the usual price** lo compramos 500 libras más barato de lo que cuesta normalmente; **savings** ahorros ❑ **savings account** cuenta f de ahorros; **savings bank** ≃ caja f de ahorros; US **savings bond** = bono emitido por el gobierno estadounidense; Br **savings certificate** = bono emitido por el gobierno británico, cuyos intereses están libres de impuestos; US **savings and loan association** ≃ caja f de ahorros; **savings plan** plan m de ahorro; **savings ratio** índice m de ahorro; **savings scheme** plan m de ahorro

SAYE n FIN (abbr **save-as-you-earn**) = sistema británico de planes de ahorro mediante descuentos en la nómina

> ❝
>
> **SAYE** was introduced more than 20 years ago as a way to encourage workers to become stakeholders in their own companies and to boost private investment in the stock market. The proceeds of **SAYE** schemes are subject to capital gains tax but the investment is relatively risk free because if the company's share price falls the individual can reclaim the cash they invested rather than taking the price for the shares.
>
> ❞

SBU n (abbr **strategic business unit**) UEN f, unidad f estratégica de negocio

scalage n US deducción m por disminución

scale n (of salaries, prices) escala f

▸ **scale down** vt sep (reduce) disminuir; **production is being scaled down** están disminuyendo la producción

▸ **scale up** vt sep (increase) aumentar; **production is to be scaled up by 10%** la producción va a aumentar un 10%

scaled question n (in market research) pregunta f escalonada

scalp vt US Fam (tickets, securities) revender

scalper n US Fam (of tickets, securities) revendedor(ora) m,f

scan COMPTR **1** n escaneo m
2 vt escanear

▸ **scan in** vt sep COMPTR (graphics) escanear

scanner n COMPTR escáner m

scanning n MKTG exploración f, escáner m

scarce adj (commodities) escaso(a); **sugar is scarce at the moment** en este momento escasea el azúcar or hay una escasez de azúcar ▫ **scarce currency** moneda f escasa

scarceness, scarcity n escasez f; **there is a scarcity of labour** escasea la mano de obra, hay una escasez de mano de obra ▫ **scarcity value** valor m de escasez

schedule 1 n (**a**) (plan) programa m, calendario m; **a schedule was agreed for the work** se acordó un calendario para el trabajo; **the work was carried out according to schedule** el trabajo se llevó a cabo siguiendo el calendario; **everything went according to schedule** todo fue según las previsiones; **to be ahead of schedule** estar adelantado(a); **to be on schedule** estar al día; **to be behind schedule** estar atrasado(a); **I work to a very tight schedule** tengo que cumplir unos plazos muy estrictos (**b**) (list) (of items) lista f, inventario m; (of prices) lista or catálogo m de precios; ADMIN (of taxes) apartado m; **schedule of charges** tarifa f (**c**) LAW (clause) anexo m, apéndice m
2 vt (**a**) (plan) programar; **a meeting has been scheduled for 3 o'clock** se ha programado una reunión para las tres; **we're scheduled to arrive at 9pm** está previsto que lleguemos a las nueve de la noche (**b**) LAW (clause) anexar

scheduler n COMPTR (package) software m de planificación (de proyectos)

scheme n (**a**) (system) sistema m, plan m; **the company has a profit-sharing/a pension scheme** la empresa tiene un plan de reparto de beneficios/de pensiones (**b**) (plan) plan m; **an investment scheme** un plan de inversiones ▫ LAW **scheme of arrangement** acuerdo m preventivo

schilling n Formerly chelín m (austriaco)

scoop n (in press) primicia f; **the paper got a scoop on the story** el periódico consiguió la primicia

scorched earth policy n (against hostile takeover situation) política f de tierra quemada or Am arrasada

"
Deutsche Börse is believed to be seeking to exercise a penalty clause in the planned iX merger deal which collapsed in September. ... Financial market sources said Deutsche Börse's claim was unwise and was likely to kill off any co-operation between the two exchanges. Others accused the Deutsche Börse of pursuing a **scorched earth policy** which could put off other potential partners.
"

score n MKTG (in market research) puntuación f

scrambled adj MKTG **scrambled merchandising, scrambled retailing** venta f cruzada, = comercialización de productos en puntos de venta con los que no están asociados tradicionalmente

scrap 1 n chatarra f; **to sell sth for scrap** vender algo para chatarra ▫ **scrap dealer, scrap merchant** chatarrero(a) m,f; **scrap metal** chatarra f; **scrap value** valor m como chatarra
2 vt (**a**) (send to scrap) (car) mandar a la chatarra; (machinery) desguazar (**b**) (abandon) (idea, plans) descartar, abandonar; (system) abandonar

scrapbook n COMPTR (on Macintosh) apuntador m

scratchpad n US COMPTR bloc m de notas ▫ **scratchpad memory** memoria f del bloc de notas

screen 1 n COMPTR pantalla f; **on screen** en pantalla; **to work on screen** trabajar en pantalla; **to bring up the next screen** visualizar la siguiente pantalla ▫ **screen capture** captura f de pantalla; **screen display** monitor m; **screen dump** pantallazo m, captura f de pantalla; **screen refresh** refresco m de pantalla; **screen saver** salvapantallas m inv, protector m de pantalla; **screen shot** pantallazo m, captura f de pantalla; ST EXCH **screen trader** operador(ora) m,f que contrata electrónicamente; ST EXCH **screen trading** contratación f electrónica; ST EXCH **screen trading system** sistema f de contratación electrónica
2 vt (candidates, applications) examinar, controlar; **we screen all our security staff** examinamos los antecedentes de todo nuestro personal de seguridad

screening n (of candidates, applications) examen m, control m; **after we receive the applications, the screening process can begin** después de recibir las solicitudes, puede comenzar el proceso de examen de antecedentes

scrip *n* FIN, ST EXCH resguardo *m* provisional ❏ *scrip certificate* certificado *m* provisional; *US scrip dividend* dividendo *m* en acciones; *scrip issue* emisión *f* de acciones liberadas

scripholder *n* FIN, ST EXCH titular *mf* de resguardo provisional

scroll COMPTR **1** *n* desplazamiento *m* ❏ *scroll bar* barra *f* de desplazamiento; *scroll box* caja *f* de desplazamiento; *scroll button* botón *m* de desplazamiento; *scroll key* tecla *f* de desplazamiento; *scroll lock key* tecla *f* de bloqueo de desplazamiento; *scroll wheel* (on mouse) rueda *f* de desplazamiento
2 *vt* desplazarse por
3 *vi* desplazarse (por la pantalla)

▶ **scroll down** COMPTR **1** *vt insep* to scroll down a document desplazarse de arriba a abajo por un documento; **to scroll down a page** avanzar una página
2 *vi (person)* desplazarse hacia abajo; *(text)* avanzar hacia abajo

▶ **scroll through** *vt insep* COMPTR *(text)* recorrer, bajar

▶ **scroll up** COMPTR **1** *vt insep* to scroll up a document desplazarse de abajo a arriba por un documento; **to scroll up a page** retroceder una página
2 *vi (person)* desplazarse hacia arriba; *(text)* avanzar hacia arriba

SCSI *n* COMPTR *(abbr* small computer systems interface*)* SCSI *m* ❏ *SCSI card* tarjeta *f* SCSI

SDR *n (abbr* special drawing right*)* DEG *m*, derecho *m* especial de giro

SDRAM *n* COMPTR *(abbr* synchronous dynamic random access memory*)* (memoria *f*) SDRAM *f*

sea *n sea link* enlace *m* por mar; *sea port* puerto *m* de mar; *sea risk* riesgo *m* de mar

seal 1 *n (on deed, letter)* sello *m*; *(on goods for export)* precinto *m*
2 *vt (deed, envelope)* sellar; *(goods for export)* precintar ❏ *sealed bid, sealed tender* oferta *f* en sobre cerrado

sealed-bid pricing *n* = fijación de los precios en concursos públicos en sobre cerrado

SEAQ *n (abbr* Stock Exchange Automated Quotations System*)* SEAQ *m*, = sistema automatizado de información sobre las cotizaciones bursátiles

search COMPTR **1** *n* búsqueda *f*; **to do a search** hacer una búsqueda; **to do a search for sth** buscar algo; **search and replace** buscar y reemplazar ❏ *search engine (for Web)* motor *m* or página *f* de búsqueda
2 *vt (file, directory)* buscar; **to search and replace sth** buscar y reemplazar algo
3 *vi* buscar

season *n* **(a)** *(for trade)* temporada *f*; **it's a busy season for tour operators** es una temporada muy movida para los operadores turísticos; **Christmas is our busiest season** la Navidad es la época en la que tenemos más trabajo; **in season** en temporada; **out of season** fuera de temporada; **the low/high season** la temporada baja/alta **(b)** *season ticket (for public trasport)* abono *m*

seasonal *adj (demand, fluctuations)* estacional ❏ *seasonal adjustment* fluctuación *f* or ajuste *m* estacional; *seasonal discount* descuento *m* de temporada; *seasonal index* índice *m* estacional; *seasonal staff* trabajadores *mpl* estacionales, *Esp, Chile* temporeros *mpl*, *RP* temporarios *mpl*; *seasonal unemployment* desempleo *m* estacional; *seasonal variations* variaciones *fpl* estacionales; *seasonal worker* trabajador(ora) *m,f* estacional, *Esp, Chile* temporero(a) *m,f*, *RP* temporario(a) *m,f*

seasonally *adv* **seasonally adjusted** *(figures)* ajustado(a) para reflejar variaciones estacionales ❏ *seasonally adjusted index* índice *m* ajustado para reflejar variaciones estacionales

> **❝**
> Orders for manufactured goods in the US fell in November, pulled down by flagging demand for transportation and defence-related equipment. Factory orders dropped 3.3 per cent in November to a **seasonally adjusted** $321.7bn (£223.4bn). This followed a revised rise of 7.0 per cent in October.
> **❞**

SEC *n (abbr* Securities and Exchange Commission*)* = comisión del mercado de valores estadounidense

second¹ 1 *n* **seconds** artículos *mpl* defectuosos ❏ *second of exchange* segunda *f* de cambio
2 *adj* segundo(a) ❏ *second debenture* obligación *f* de segundo rango; *second endorser* segundo(a) endosante *mf*; *second mortgage* hipoteca *f* de segundo grado; *second quarter (of year)* segundo trimestre *m*

second² *vt (motion, speaker)* secundar

second³ *vt (employee)* trasladar temporalmente; **she's been seconded to head office** ha sido trasladada temporalmente a la sede central

secondary *adj* secundario(a) ❏ *Br secondary action* actuación *f* subordinada; ACCT *secondary cost centre* centro *m* de costos or *Esp* costes secundario; MKTG *secondary data* información *f* secundaria; ST EXCH *secondary distribution* colocación *f* en el mercado secundario; *secondary industry* industria *f* secundaria; ST EXCH *secondary market* mercado *m* secundario; ST EXCH *secondary offering* colocación *f* en el mercado secundario; *Br secondary picketing*

= piquetes de solidaridad contra empresas que trabajan con la compañía cuyos trabajadores están en huelga; **secondary product** producto *m* secundario; **secondary production** producción *f* secundaria; **secondary sector** sector *m* secundario; **secondary supplier** proveedor *m* secundario

second-class 1 *adj* de segunda clase ❑ **second-class mail** *or* Br **post** servicio *m* postal de segunda clase; **second-class stamp** sello *m or* Am estampilla *f* de segunda clase

2 *adv Br* **to send sth second-class** enviar algo con un sello *or* Am una estampilla de segunda clase

second-hand 1 *adj (goods)* usado(a), de segunda mano ❑ **second-hand dealer** comerciante *mf* de artículos usados *or* de segunda mano; **second-hand market** mercado *m* de artículos usados *or* de segunda mano; **second-hand shop** tienda *f* de artículos usados *or* de segunda mano; **second-hand trade** mercado *m* de artículos usados *or* de segunda mano

2 *adv (buy)* de segunda mano

secondment *n* traslado *m* temporal; **I'm on secondment** me han trasladado temporalmente

second-rate *adj (goods)* de segunda (categoría)

second-tier *adj* **second-tier bank** banco *m* de segundo piso; **second-tier supplier** proveedor *m* secundario

secret *adj* **secret funds** fondos *mpl* reservados; US **secret partner** socio(a) *m,f* secreto(a); **secret reserve** reserva *f* oculta

secretarial *adj (tasks)* administrativo(a); **to have a secretarial job** tener un trabajo de administrativo ❑ **secretarial course** curso *m* de secretariado; **secretarial pool** personal *m* administrativo; **secretarial school** escuela *f* de secretariado; **secretarial skills** técnicas *fpl* de secretariado; **secretarial work** trabajo *m* administrativo

secretary *n (in office)* secretario(a) *m,f*

section *n* (**a**) *(sector)* sección *f*, sector *m*; **all sections of society** todos los sectores de la sociedad (**b**) *(of document)* sección *f*; *(of law)* artículo *m*

sector *n* (**a**) *(of economy, society)* sector *m*; **the banking sector** el sector bancario, la banca; **he works in the advertising sector** trabaja en el sector publicitario; **whole sectors of society live below the poverty line** sectores enteros de la sociedad viven por debajo del umbral de la pobreza (**b**) COMPTR *(of screen, disk)* sector *m*

sectoral *adj* sectorial

sectorization *n* sectorización *f*

secure 1 *adj* (**a**) *(investment, job)* seguro(a) (**b**) COMPTR **secure electronic transaction** transac-

ción *f* electrónica segura; **secure HTTP** HTTP *m* seguro; **secure server** servidor *m* seguro; **secure sockets layer** protocolo *m* SSL

2 *vt* (**a**) *(obtain) (agreement, loan)* conseguir (**b**) *(guarantee) (debt, loan)* garantizar; **the loan is secured by mortgages on several properties** el préstamo está garantizado por las hipotecas de varias propiedades

secured *adj* FIN **secured bond** bono *m* hipotecario *or* con garantía; **secured credit card** tarjeta *f* de crédito garantizada; **secured creditor** acreedor(ora) *m,f* asegurado(a); **secured debenture** obligación *f* garantizada; **secured debt** deuda *f* garantizada; **secured loan** préstamo *m* garantizado; **secured note** pagaré *m* garantizado

securitization *n* ST EXCH titulización *f*, titularización *f*

securitize *vt* ST EXCH titulizar, titularizar

security *n* (**a**) *(for loan)* garantía *f*, aval *m*; *(person)* avalista *mf*, garante *mf*; **to pledge sth as security** entregar algo como garantía; **to stand security for sb** ser el avalista de alguien; **to lend money on security** prestar dinero con garantía; **to lend money without security** prestar dinero sin garantía; **what security do you have for the loan?** ¿con qué puede garantizar el préstamo? ❑ **security of tenure** *(of tenant)* seguridad *f* de permanencia (en la vivienda); *(in employment)* seguridad *f* en el puesto de trabajo

(**b**) ST EXCH **securities** valores *mpl*; **securities in portfolio** valores en cartera ❑ **securities department** departamento *m* de valores; **Securities and Exchange Commission** = comisión del mercado de valores estadounidense; **securities firm** sociedad *f* de valores; **securities house** sociedad *f* de valores; *Formerly* **Securities and Investment Board** = comisión del mercado de valores londinense; **securities market** mercado *m* de valores; **securities portfolio** cartera *f* de valores

(**c**) *(safety, confidentiality)* seguridad *f* ❑ **security certificate** certificado *m* de seguridad; **security code** código *m* de seguridad; **Security Council** Consejo *m* de Seguridad; **security level** nivel *m* de seguridad; **security officer** agente *mf* de seguridad; **security tag** etiqueta *f* de seguridad

seed capital, seed money *n* FIN capital *m* simiente *or* generador

seek time *n* COMPTR tiempo *m* de búsqueda

see-saw effect *n* efecto *m* de dientes de sierra

segment 1 *n* MKTG *(customer base, market)* segmento *m* ❑ ACCT **segment margin** margen *m* de segmento; **segment reporting** informes *mpl* por segmentos

2 *vt* MKTG *(customer base, market)* segmentar

segmentation *n* MKTG *(of customer base, market)* segmentación *f*

seize *vt* LAW *(goods)* incautarse de

seizure *n* LAW *(of goods)* incautación *f*

select *vt* (**a**) *(candidate)* seleccionar (**b**) *(product)* elegir, escoger (**c**) COMPTR seleccionar; **select 'I agree'** seleccione "acepto"; **to select an option** seleccionar una opción

selection *n* (**a**) *(of candidate)* selección *f* ❑ **se-lection committee** comité *m* de selección; **selection criteria** criterios *mpl* de selección (**b**) *(of product)* elección *f* (**c**) COMPTR selección *f* ❑ **selection box** cuadro *m* de selección (**d**) MKTG **selection error** error *m* de selección; **selection method** método *m* de selección

selective *adj* MKTG selectivo(a) ❑ **selective distortion** distorsión *f* selectiva; **selective distribution** distribución *f* selectiva; **selective marketing** marketing *m* selectivo; **selective perception** percepción *f* selectiva; **selective retention** retención *f* selectiva; **selective selling** venta *f* selectiva

self-assessment *n* Br *(for tax purposes)* autoli-quidación *f* tributaria ❑ **self-assessment form** formulario *m* de autoliquidación tributaria

> “
> A leading professional body yesterday called for an inquiry into the Government's tax **self-assessment** system after official fig-ures showed one in 10 taxpayers had failed to hit the deadline. The Chartered Institute of Taxation said more research was urgently needed. According to Inland Revenue fig-ures only 8.25 million tax returns, or 90.6 per cent of the total 9.11 million due, were filed ahead of the 31 January deadline.
> ”

self-employed 1 *npl* **the self-employed** los autónomos
2 *adj* autónomo(a) ❑ **self-employed person** trabajador(ora) *m,f* autónomo(a) *or* por cuenta propia

self-employment *n* autoempleo *m*, trabajo *m* por cuenta propia

self-financing 1 *n* autofinanciación *f*
2 *adj* autofinanciado(a)

self-insurance *n* autoseguro *m*

> “
> Looking for a way to manage costs and have greater control over the health benefits you provide your employees? **Self-insur-ance** may be a workable alternative. Self-in-suring means you pay health benefits with corporate assets rather than paying a pre-mium to transfer that responsibility to a third party, says James Kinder, CEO of the **Self-Insurance** Institute of America in Santa Ana, California.
> ”

self-liquidating *adj* autoliquidable ❑ **self-li-quidating premium** prima *f* autoliquidable

self-mailer *n* MKTG autoensobrado *m*, com-plet *m*

self-management *n* autogestión *f*

self-regulation *n* autorregulación *f*

self-regulatory organization *n* Br organi-zación *f* autorregulada

self-service 1 *n* *(shop)* autoservicio *f*
2 *adj* *(restaurant, petrol station)* (de) autoservicio

self-sufficiency *n* *(of nation, resources)* auto-suficiencia *f*; ECON autarquía *f*

self-sufficient *adj* autosuficiente; ECON autár-quico(a); **our country is self-sufficient in oil** nuestro país es autosuficiente en petróleo

self-tender *n* FIN autooferta *f*

self-test COMPTR **1** *n* autotest *m*
2 *vi* efectuar un autotest

sell 1 *n* ST EXCH **sell order** orden *f* de venta; **sell price** precio *m* de venta
2 *vt* vender; **to sell sth to sb, to sell sb sth** ven-der algo a alguien; **to sell sth for cash** vender algo al contado; **to sell sth at a loss** vender algo con pérdidas
3 *vi* *(product)* venderse; *(person)* vender; ST EXCH **to sell short** vender en descubierto, especular a la baja; ST EXCH **to sell at best** vender al mejor precio posible

▸ **sell forward** *vt sep* ST EXCH vender a término *or* a futuro

▸ **sell off** *vt sep* (**a**) *(goods)* *(at reduced price)* vender; *(to clear)* liquidar; **the house was sold off to pay debts** vendieron la casa para pagar deudas (**b**) *(industry)* privatizar (**c**) *(shares)* vender

▸ **sell on** *vt sep* revender

▸ **sell out 1** *vt sep* (**a**) FIN *(company, shares)* ven-der (**b**) **to be sold out** *(book, item)* estar agota-do(a); **we are sold out of champagne** se nos ha agotado el champán
2 *vi* (**a**) *(sell business)* liquidar el negocio; *(sell stock)* vender las acciones; **he sold out to some Japanese investors** les vendió el negocio a unos inversores japoneses (**b**) *(run out)* **we've sold out** se nos han agotado; **to sell out of sth** quedarse sin algo

▸ **sell up 1** *vt sep* vender, liquidar
2 *vi* *(sell business)* liquidar el negocio

sellable *adj* vendible

sell-by date *n* fecha *f* límite de venta

seller *n* (**a**) *(person)* vendedor(ora) *m,f* ❑ **seller's market** ST EXCH mercado *m* de vendedores; *(for buying property)* mercado *m* favorable a los ven-dedores; ST EXCH **seller's option** opción *f* de venta (**b**) *(article)* **to be a good/bad seller** venderse bien/mal; **it's one of our biggest sellers** es uno de los que más vendemos

selling n (of goods, shares) venta f ▢ ST EXCH **selling climax** auge m de ventas; **selling costs** gastos mpl de venta; **selling licence** licencia f de venta; **selling point** atractivo m; **selling power** poder m de ventas; **selling price** precio m de venta; ACCT **selling price variance** variación f en el precio de venta

sell-off n (a) (of goods) (at reduced price) venta f; (to clear) liquidación f (b) (of industry) privatización f (c) (of shares) liquidación f

sell-out n (event) lleno m; **the concert was a sell-out** se agotaron todas las entradas para el concierto

semantic differential n MKTG diferencial m semántico

semi-automated adj semiautomatizado(a)

semicolon n punto m y coma

semi-finished adj semiacabado(a), semielaborado(a) ▢ **semi-finished product** producto m semiacabado or semielaborado

semi-manufactured adj semimanufacturado(a) ▢ **semi-manufactured product** producto m semimanufacturado

semi-public company n empresa f mixta

semi-retired adj jubilado(a) a tiempo parcial

semi-retirement n jubilación f parcial

semi-skilled adj semicualificado(a), Am semicalificado(a) ▢ **semi-skilled labour** mano f de obra semicualificada or Am semicalificada; **semi-skilled worker** trabajador(ora) m,f semicualificado(a) or Am semicalificado(a)

semi-variable adj (costs) semivariable

send vt (person, letter, parcel, money) enviar, mandar; **to send sb sth, to send sth to sb** enviar or mandar algo a alguien; **all customers on our mailing list will be sent a catalogue** enviaremos un catálogo a todos los clientes de nuestra lista de direcciones

▸ **send away** vi **to send away for sth** pedir or encargar algo por correo

▸ **send back** vt sep (goods) devolver

▸ **send for** vt insep **to send for sth** (by mail order) pedir or encargar algo por correo

▸ **send in** vt sep enviar; **please send in a written application** (for job) por favor envíe su solicitud por escrito

▸ **send off** 1 vt sep (letter, parcel, money) mandar, enviar
  2 vi **to send off for sth** (by mail order) pedir or encargar algo por correo

▸ **send on** vt sep (mail) remitir

▸ **send out** vt sep mandar, enviar

sender n remitente mf

senior 1 n (in rank) **to be sb's senior** ser el superior de alguien
  2 adj (a) (in rank) superior; **to be senior to sb** ser el superior de alguien ▢ **senior executive** alto(a) ejecutivo(a) m,f; **senior management** alta dirección f; **senior partner** (in company) socio(a) m,f principal; **senior position** (in company) cargo m de responsabilidad; **senior vice-president** primer(era) vicepresidente(a) m,f (b) FIN **senior debt** deuda f prioritaria

seniority n (in age, length of service) antigüedad f; (in rank) rango m, categoría f ▢ **seniority bonus** plus m de or por antigüedad

sensitive adj FIN (market) sensible

separator n COMPTR separador m

sequence n COMPTR secuencia f

sequential adj COMPTR secuencial ▢ **sequential access** acceso m secuencial; **sequential processing** procesado m secuencial

sequester, sequestrate vt LAW (goods) embargar

sequestration n LAW embargo m ▢ **sequestration order** orden f de embargo

serial adj (a) COMPTR ▢ **serial cable** cable m de serie; **serial device** periférico m en serie; **serial interface** interfaz f de serie; **serial output** salida f de serie; **serial port** puerto m (en) serie; **serial printer** impresora f en serie (b) **serial number** número m de serie (c) ST EXCH **serial bond** bono m de vencimiento escalonado

Serious Fraud Office n Br = fiscalía británica de delitos monetarios

SERPS n Formerly FIN (abbr **State Earnings-Related Pension Scheme**) = sistema público británico de pensiones contributivas que complementaba la pensión básica del Estado

server n COMPTR servidor m ▢ **server administrator** administrador(ora) m,f de servidores; **server software** software m de servidor

service 1 n (a) (employment) **during his service with the company** durante sus años de trabajo en la empresa; **ten years' service** diez años de antigüedad; **bonuses depend on length of service** los pluses dependen de la antigüedad en la empresa ▢ **service agreement, service contract** contrato m de servicios; **service record** historial m, hoja f de servicios
  (b) (in shop, restaurant) servicio m; **service included** el servicio está incluido ▢ **service charge** (tarifa f por) servicio m
  (c) (facility provided) **service bureau** (company) empresa f de servicios; COMPTR servicio m de filmación; US **service charge** (for financial transaction) comisión f bancaria, gastos mpl bancarios; US **service mark** marca f de servicios; **service provider** (for Internet) proveedor m de servicios

(**d**) *(working order) (of system, equipment)* funcionamiento *m*, servicio *m*; **to bring into service** poner en funcionamiento; **to come into service** entrar en funcionamiento *or* servicio; **to be in service** estar en funcionamiento; **to be out of service** estar fuera de servicio □ ***service life*** vida *f* útil; ***service manual*** manual *m* de mantenimiento

(**e**) ECON **services** servicios *mpl*; **goods and services** bienes y servicios □ ***service company*** empresa *f* de servicios; ***service industry*** industria *f* de servicios; ***service sector*** sector *m* servicios; **analysts predict continued growth in the service sector** los analistas pronostican un crecimiento continuo en el sector servicios

2 *vt* (**a**) *(machine)* revisar (**b**) FIN *(loan, debt)* amortizar los intereses de

session *n (period of activity, meeting)* sesión *f*; **to hold a session** celebrar una reunión

SET® *n* COMPTR (*abbr* **secure electronic transaction**) *(protocolo m)* SET® *m*

set 1 *n* (**a**) COMPTR *(of characters, instructions)* juego *m* (**b**) FIN *(of bills of exchange)* juego *m* de letras de cambio

2 *adj (price)* fijo(a)

3 *vt* (**a**) *(date, limit, schedule, rule)* fijar, establecer; **to set a value on sth** poner precio *or* asignar un valor a algo; **it's up to them to set their own production targets** les corresponde a ellos fijar sus propios objetivos de producción; **the price was set at $500** fijaron un precio de 500 dólares (**b**) COMPTR *(tabs, format)* definir

▸ **set against** *vt sep (deduct, offset)* deducir, compensar; **to set losses against tax** compensar pérdidas

▸ **set aside** *vt sep (money, time, place)* reservar; **this room is set aside for meetings** la habitación está reservada para reuniones

▸ **set off against** *vt sep (deduct, offset)* deducir, compensar; **some of these expenses can be set off against tax** algunos de estos gastos son desgravables

▸ **set up 1** *vt sep* (**a**) *(company)* montar; *(system, programme, committee)* crear; *(computer)* configurar; **you'll be in charge of setting up training programmes** serás responsable de la puesta en marcha de programas de formación (**b**) *(financially, in business)* **he set his son up in a dry-cleaning business** montó una tintorería para su hijo; **she set herself up as a consultant** se estableció como asesora

2 *vi* **to set up in business** montar un negocio; **he's setting up in the fast-food business** está montando una tienda de comida rápida; **to set up on one's own** montarse su propio negocio

set-aside *n* EU retirada *f or* abandono *m* de tierras

setback *n* FIN, ST EXCH caída *f*

settings *n* COMPTR configuración *f*

settle 1 *vt* (**a**) *(day, date, place)* fijar; *(terms)* acordar (**b**) *(question, problem, dispute)* resolver; LAW **the matter was settled out of court** se llegó a un acuerdo extrajudicial; **lawyers were called in to settle the remaining differences** llamaron a abogados para resolver las diferencias pendientes (**c**) *(account, debt, bill)* liquidar, saldar; *(fine)* pagar (**d**) LAW *(money, allowance, estate)* **to settle sth on sb** otorgar algo a alguien

2 *vi* LAW **to settle out of court** llegar a un acuerdo extrajudicial

▸ **settle up** *vi (pay bill)* pagar; **I must settle up with the electrician** tengo que pagar al electricista

settlement *n* (**a**) *(of question, problem, dispute)* resolución *f* □ ***settlement by arbitration*** acuerdo *m* de arbitraje

(**b**) *(of account, debt, bill)* liquidación *f*; *(of fine)* pago *m*; **I enclose a cheque in settlement of your account** adjunto un cheque como liquidación de la cuenta □ ***settlement discount*** descuento *m* por liquidación; ***settlement in kind*** pago *m* en especie; ***settlement period*** periodo *m* de liquidación; ***settlement value*** valor *m* de liquidación

(**c**) ST EXCH liquidación *f* □ ***settlement day*** día *f* de liquidación; ***settlement note*** nota *f* de liquidación; ***settlement price*** precio *m* de liquidación; ***settlement value*** valor *m* de liquidación

(**d**) *(agreement)* acuerdo *m*; **to reach a settlement** llegar a un acuerdo

set-up *n* COMPTR ***set-up charge*** cuota *f* de conexión; ACCT ***set-up costs*** costos *mpl or Esp* costes *mpl* iniciales; ***set-up fee*** *(for account)* comisión *f* de apertura; COMPTR ***set-up program*** programa *m* de configuración

sever *vt (contract)* rescindir

several liability *n* LAW responsabilidad *f* solidaria

severally *adv* LAW **severally liable** responsable solidariamente

severance pay *n* indemnización *f* por despido

sexual *adj* ***sexual discrimination*** discriminación *f* sexual; ***sexual harassment*** acoso *m* sexual

sexy *adj Fam* MKTG *(product)* excitante

their horizons to become more exciting and relevant. Riding a wave of strong economic growth and low interest rates, appliance makers are on a tear, with the consumer remodeling frenzy showing no signs of slowing.

SF *n* (*abbr* **sinking fund**) fondo *m* de amortización

SFO *n* (*abbr* **Serious Fraud Office**) = fiscalía británica de delitos monetarios

SGML *n* COMPTR (*abbr* **Standard Generated Markup Language**) SGML *m*

SGP *n* EU (*abbr* **Stability and Growth Pact**) PEC *m*

shade *vt* US **to shade prices** hacer descuentos; **prices shaded for quantities** descuentos por cantidades

shadow printing *n* COMPTR impresión *f* con sombreado

shakeout *n* ECON reestructuración *f*

shake-up *n* Fam (*of company, organization*) reorganización *f*

> User companies must speak out to safeguard their interests ahead of an expected **shake-up** in the software industry, an analyst has warned. Research published last week by UK research firm Xephon predicts a wave of acquisitions over the next few months. This will see larger IT suppliers fighting to acquire small, innovative software companies in a bid to boost flagging revenues.

sham *adj* (*dividend*) ficticio(a)

share 1 *n* (**a**) ST EXCH acción *f*; **to allot shares** adjudicar acciones; **to issue shares** emitir acciones; **to transfer shares** traspasar acciones; **to hold** *or* **have shares (in)** tener acciones (en); **to own 51% of the shares** poseer el 51% de las acciones □ **share account** Br (*with building society*) cuenta *f* de participación; US (*with credit union*) cuenta *f* de participación; **share application form** formulario *m or Méx* forma *f* de suscripción de acciones; **share capital** capital *m* social; **share certificate** título *m* de acción; **share dealing** compraventa *f* de acciones; **share dividend** dividendo *m* en acciones; **share economy** economía *f* participada; **share fluctuation** fluctuación *f* de las acciones; **share index** índice *m* bursátil, índice de cotización; **share issue** emisión *f* de acciones; **share ledger** libro *m* registro de acciones; **share market** mercado *m* de acciones; **share option** opción *f* sobre acciones; **share portfolio** cartera *f* de acciones; **share premium** prima *f* de emisión; **share price** cotización *f*; **share price index** índice *m* bursátil, índice de cotización; **share**

register registro *m* de acciones; **share splitting** fraccionamiento *m* de acciones; **share subscription form** formulario *m or Méx* forma *f* de suscripción de acciones; **share swap** intercambio *m* de acciones

(**b**) (*portion*) participación *f*, parte *f*; **to give sb a share of the profits** dar a alguien una participación en los beneficios; **to have a share in a business** tener una participación en un negocio □ MKTG **share point** punto *m* de cuota de mercado; **share of voice** audiencia *f* potencial

2 *vt* (**a**) (*use jointly*) compartir; **to share an office with sb** compartir una oficina con alguien (**b**) (*divide*) repartir, dividir; **responsibility is shared between the manager and his assistant** el director y su ayudante se reparten la responsabilidad

3 *vi* **to share in the profits** participar de los beneficios

shared services centre *n* centro *m* de servicios compartidos

shareholder *n* Br ST EXCH accionista *mf* □ **shareholders' equity, shareholders' funds** fondos *mpl* propios, patrimonio *m* neto; **shareholders' meeting** asamblea *f or* junta *f* (general) de accionistas; **shareholders' register** registro *m* de accionistas; **shareholder value** valor *m* para el accionista

shareholding *n* Br ST EXCH participación *f* accionarial *or Am* accionaria; **he has a major shareholding in the company** tiene una participación accionarial *or Am* accionaria importante en la empresa

share-out *n* reparto *m*

share-picker *n* analista *mf* bursátil

shareware *n* COMPTR shareware *m*

shark *n* Fam (*in business*) tiburón *m*, = autor de una OPA hostil □ **shark watcher** = empresa especializada en detectar OPAS hostiles

sharp *adj* (*rise, fall*) pronunciado(a); (*change*) repentino(a)

shed *vt* **oil stocks shed 1.4% on the Nasdaq Composite yesterday** la cotización de los valores del petróleo en el Nasdaq Composite cayó ayer el 1,4%

sheet *n* (*of paper*) hoja *f* □ COMPTR **sheet feeder** alimentador *m* de hojas sueltas

sheet-fed printer *n* COMPTR impresora *f* de hojas sueltas

sheetfeed *n* COMPTR alimentación *f* de hojas sueltas

shelf *n* (*in shop*) estante *m*; (*in hypermarket*) lineal *m*; **shelves** estantería *f* □ **shelf facing** frontal *m* del lineal (de distribución); **shelf impact** impacto *m* en el lineal; **shelf life** (*of goods*) vida *f* útil; **shelf space** espacio *m* en el lineal; **shelf yield** ventas *fpl* por metro de lineal

"

In Australia, Patak's largest foreign market, it found that, although there was little Indian food around when its first shipment arrived in 1988, familiarity with Far Eastern food and many Australians' British roots helped open up supermarket **shelf space**.

"

shelve *vt (postpone) (project)* aplazar, *Esp* aparcar

shelving *n* estanterías *fpl*

shift 1 *n* (**a**) *(period worked, workers)* turno *m*; **to work shifts, to be on shifts** trabajar por turnos; **what shift are you on this week?** ¿qué turno haces esta semana?; **to be on eight-hour shifts** trabajar en turnos de ocho horas; **I'm on the night/morning shift** estoy en el turno de la noche/mañana; **she works long shifts** trabaja en turnos muy largos ❑ **shift pattern** organización *f* de los turnos; **shift work** trabajo *m* por turnos; **she does shift work** trabaja por turnos; **shift worker** trabajador(ora) *m,f* por turnos
(**b**) *(change)* cambio *m* ❑ COMPTR **shift key** tecla *f* de mayúsculas
2 *vt Fam (sell)* vender; **how can we shift this old stock?** ¿cómo vamos a conseguir dar salida a estas existencias viejas?
3 *vi Fam (sell)* venderse; **those TVs just aren't shifting at all** esos televisores no están teniendo salida

ship 1 *n* barco *m*, buque *m* ❑ **ship's certificate of registry** certificado *m* de registro del barco; **ship's papers** documentos *mpl* de a bordo; **ship's protest** protesta *f* de mar *or* del capitán
2 *vt* (**a**) *(send by ship)* enviar por barco; *(carry by ship)* transportar por barco; **we're having our luggage shipped** el equipaje nos lo mandan por barco (**b**) *(send by any means)* despachar; *(carry by any means)* transportar; **the goods will be shipped by train** *(sent)* las mercancías serán despachadas por tren; *(transported)* las mercancías serán transportadas por tren (**c**) *(make available in shops)* lanzar (**d**) *(embark) (passengers, cargo)* embarcar
3 *vi* **it ships with Windows XP** viene con Windows XP instalado

shipbroker *n* agente *m* marítimo

shipbrokerage *n* corretaje *m* marítimo

shipment *n* (**a**) *(sending of goods)* despacho *m*, envío *m* (**b**) *(cargo, goods shipped)* cargamento *m*

shipped *adj* embarcado(a) ❑ **shipped bill** conocimiento *m* de embarque incluido en el envío; **shipped weight** carga *f* embarcada

shipper *n (of goods)* consignador(ora) *m,f*

shipping *n* (**a**) *(transport) (by any means)* flete *m*, envío *m*; *(by sea)* transporte *m* marítimo ❑ **shipping address** dirección *f* de entrega; **shipping**

agency agente *m* marítimo, agencia *f* marítima; **shipping agent** consignatario(a) *m,f*; **shipping bill** solicitud *f* de devolución de derechos arancelarios; **shipping charges** gastos *mpl* de envío; **shipping clerk** expedidor(ora) *m,f*; **shipping company** compañía *f* naviera; **shipping costs** flete *m*; **shipping depot** almacén *m* de envíos; **shipping documents** documentos *mpl* de embarque; **shipping dues** derechos *mpl* de navegación; **shipping line** naviera *f*; **shipping note** nota *f* de envío; **shipping office** *(for any means of transport)* transportista *f*; *(maritime)* compañía *f* naviera
(**b**) *(ships)* navíos *mpl*, buques *mpl*

shipyard *n* astillero *m*

▶ **shoot up** *vi (prices, inflation, demand)* dispararse

shop 1 *n* (**a**) *(for goods)* tienda *f*, negocio *m*; **to keep a shop** tener una tienda; **to talk shop** hablar del trabajo; **to set up shop** *(open a shop)* abrir una tienda; *(start a business)* montar un negocio ❑ **shop assistant** dependiente(a) *m,f*; **shop front** fachada *f* de tienda; **shop window** escaparate *m*, *Am* vidriera *f*, *Chile, Col, Méx* vitrina *f*
(**b**) *(workshop)* taller *m* ❑ **the shop floor** *(place)* el área de producción; *(workers)* los trabajadores a pie de máquina, los trabajadores de producción; **shop foreman** encargado(a) *m,f*; **shop steward** delegado(a) *m,f* sindical
2 *vi* comprar, hacer compra(s); **to shop around** comparar precios (en diferentes establecimientos); **I shopped around before opening a bank account** antes de abrir una cuenta bancaria comparé las condiciones que me ofrecían varios bancos; **our company is shopping around for new premises** nuestra empresa está comparando precios antes de comprar un nuevo local

shopkeeper *n* tendero(a) *m,f*

shopping *n* compra *f*, *Am* compras *fpl*; **to do one's/the shopping** hacer la compra *or Am* las compras ❑ **shopping area** zona *f* comercial; **shopping basket** *(in shop, for Internet shopping)* cesta *f* de la compra; *US* COMPTR **shopping cart** *(in shop, for Internet shopping)* carrito *m* (de la compra); **shopping centre** centro *m* comercial; **shopping complex** complejo *m* comercial; **shopping mall** centro *m* comercial

▶ **shore up** *vt sep (currency)* apuntalar; **Brazil started selling off its foreign currency reserves in an attempt to shore up its currency** Brasil comenzó a vender sus reservas de divisas extranjeras en un intento de apuntalar su propia moneda

short 1 *n* ST EXCH **shorts** obligaciones *fpl* a corto plazo
2 *adj* (**a**) *(lacking, insufficient)* **we are short of staff/money** nos falta personal/dinero; **the**

weight is 50 grams short le faltan 50 gramos; **to be on short time** trabajar con jornada reducida; **to give sb short weight** dar a alguien peso de menos ❏ *short delivery* entrega *f* incompleta; *short payment* pago *m* insuficiente; *short ton* tonelada *f* (aproximada) *(= 907 kilos)*

(**b**) FIN *short bill* letra *f* a corto plazo; *short rate* Esp tipo *m* or Am tasa *f* a corto plazo

(**c**) ST EXCH *short account* cuenta *f* en descubierto; *short covering* cobertura *f* a corto plazo; *short hedge* cobertura *f* corta; *short interest ratio* relación *f* de las posiciones cortas; *short position* posición *f* corta; *short sale* venta *f* en or al descubierto; *short seller* vendedor(ora) *m,f* en or al descubierto; *short selling* venta *f* en or al descubierto; *short squeeze* cierre *m* masivo de posiciones cortas

3 *adv* ST EXCH **to sell short** vender al descubierto; **to buy short** comprar corto

> ❝
> A **short squeeze** occurs when institutional investors take large positions in already heavily shorted stocks and then request delivery of the shares. This transaction reduces the liquidity of the shares and forces a premature closing out of the short position. ❞

shortage *n (of labour, resources, materials, money, staff)* escasez *f*, falta *f*

shortcut *n* COMPTR atajo *m*, acceso *m* directo ❏ *shortcut key* tecla *f* de atajo or acceso directo

short-dated *adj* FIN *(bill, security)* a corto plazo

shortfall *n* déficit *m*; **there's a shortfall of $100** faltan 100 dólares

> ❝
> Companies are declining to provide pensions themselves because they can no longer afford the guarantee. Iceland, for instance, found that it had to pay £78m into a scheme valued at just over £500m to make good a **shortfall** that had appeared. Nationwide explained the problem in a different way. To maintain benefits at their promised level, it would have had to raise its contribution from 12.6 per cent of salaries to 19 per cent. ❞

shorthand *n* taquigrafía *f*; **to take notes in shorthand** tomar notas taquigráficas ❏ *shorthand typist* taquimecanógrafo(a) *m,f*

short-handed *adj* falto(a) de personal; **we're very short-handed at the moment** en este momento nos falta mucho personal

shortlist *Br* **1** *n* preselección *f*; **eight candidates are on the shortlist and have been contacted** ya nos hemos puesto en contacto con

los ocho candidatos que hay en la lista de preseleccionados

2 *vt (candidate)* preseleccionar; **to be shortlisted for sth** estar preseleccionado(a) para algo

short-staffed *adj* falto(a) de personal; **we're very short-staffed at the moment** en este momento nos falta mucho personal

short-term *adj* a corto plazo ❏ *short-term bond* bono *m* a corto plazo; *short-term borrowings* préstamos *mpl* a corto plazo; *short-term capital* capital *m* a corto plazo; *short-term contract* contrato *m* temporal; *short-term credit* crédito *m* a corto plazo; *short-term credit facilities* facilidades *fpl* de crédito a corto plazo; *short-term debt* deuda *f* a corto plazo; *short-term financing* financiación *f* a corto plazo; *short-term interest rate* Esp tipo *m* or Am tasa *f* de interés a corto plazo; *short-term investment* inversión *f* a corto plazo; *short-term liabilities* obligaciones *fpl* a corto plazo; *short-term loan* préstamo *m* a corto plazo; *short-term maturity* vencimiento *m* a corto plazo; *short-term planning* planificación *f* a corto plazo

short-termism *n* soluciones *fpl* a corto plazo

short-time *adj short-time working* trabajo *m* con jornada reducida

show 1 *n (exhibition)* exposición *f* ❏ *show house* casa *f* piloto

2 *vt (profit, loss)* registrar; **prices show a 10% increase on last year** los precios han registrado un incremento del 10% durante el último año

showcard *n (in shop)* rótulo *m*, letrero *m*

showcase 1 *n (of glass)* vitrina *f*; **a showcase for British exports** un escaparate or Am una vidriera para las exportaciones británicas

2 *vt* servir de escaparate or Am vidriera a; **the exhibition will showcase our new product range** la exposición servirá de escaparate or Am vidriera a nuestra nueva gama de productos

> ❝
> Springboard 2001: New York is one of a series of forums designed to accelerate investments in high-growth women-led businesses and facilitate new deal flow to investors. The forum will **showcase** 30 women seeking seed, early and later stage funding. Selected entrepreneurs will present their business plans to the tri-state area's venture capital, angel and corporate investors. ❞

showroom *n* sala *f* de exposición

shpt *n (abbr shipment)* cargamento *m*

shred *vt (documents)* triturar

shredder *n* trituradora *f* (de documentos)

shrink *vi (profits, savings, income, budget)* reducirse, disminuir; *(economy)* contraerse

shrinkage *n (through theft)* pérdidas *fpl* por robo; *(through damage)* pérdidas *fpl* por daños; *(while in transit)* pérdidas *fpl*

❝
According to Hollinger, results of the survey should serve as a wake-up call to the retail industry that **shrinkage** continues to be a significant source of revenue loss amounting to billions of dollars.
❞

shrink-wrap *vt* retractilar, envolver con plástico (de polietileno) adherente

shrink-wrapped *adj* retractilado(a), envuelto(a) con plástico (de polietileno) adherente

shut *vi (shop, business)* cerrar

▶ **shut down 1** *vt sep* (**a**) *(shop, business)* cerrar *(por completo)*; *(production)* suspender (**b**) COMPTR *(system, computer)* apagar
   2 *vi* (**a**) *(shop, business)* cerrar *(por completo)* (**b**) COMPTR *(system)* apagarse

shutdown *n* (**a**) *(of shop, business)* cierre *m* (**b**) COMPTR apagado *m*

shut-out *n* cierre *m* patronal

SIB *n Formerly (abbr* **Securities and Investment Board***)* = comisión del mercado de valores londinense

sick *adj* **sick building syndrome** síndrome *m* del edificio enfermo; **sick day** día *f* de baja por enfermedad; **sick leave** baja *f* por enfermedad; **to be on sick leave** estar de baja por enfermedad; **sick pay** subsidio *m* por enfermedad

❝
Further, the agency agrees with an estimate from the World Health Organization that up to 30 percent of all new and remodeled buildings worldwide have excessive air-quality problems that can lead to **sick building syndrome** or building-related illness.
❞

sickness benefit *n* subsidio *m* por enfermedad, prestación *f* por enfermedad

sideline *n* (**a**) *(business)* negocio *m* subsidiario; **they've made recycling a profitable sideline** han hecho del reciclaje una actividad subsidiaria rentable; **it's only a sideline for us** para nosotros sólo es una actividad subsidiaria (**b**) *(job)* segundo empleo *m*

sight *n* (**a**) FIN **sight bill** letra *f* a la vista; **sight deposit** depósito *m* a la vista; **sight draft** giro *m* a la vista; **sight letter of credit** carta *f* de crédito a la vista; **sight maturity** vencimiento *m* a la vista; **sight paper** efecto *m* a la vista (**b**) **to sell sth sight unseen** vender algo sin examinarlo; **to**

buy sth sight unseen comprar algo sin examinarlo

❝
The notion of store returns or exchanges is a fairly foreign one to these shoppers, and Latin Americans are even more skeptical about security and satisfaction with products bought **sight unseen**.
❞

sighting *n* FIN *(of bill)* presentación *f*

sign 1 *vt (document, cheque, bill of exchange)* firmar; **sign your name on the dotted line** firme en la línea de puntos; **to sign a deal** firmar un acuerdo; **the deal is already signed and sealed** ya se ha concluido el acuerdo
   2 *vi (write one's name)* firmar

▶ **sign for** *vt insep (delivery, parcel)* firmar el acuse de recibo de; **to sign for goods received** firmar el acuse de recibo de las mercancías recibidas; **the files have to be signed for** hay que firmar en el registro en el momento de sacar los archivos

▶ **sign on** *vi Br (register as unemployed) (initially)* registrarse para recibir el subsidio de desempleo, *Esp* apuntarse al paro; *(regularly)* ir a firmar *or* sellar; **you have to sign on every two weeks** tienes que ir a sellar cada dos semanas

▶ **sign out** *vt sep* **to sign sth out** *(file, equipment)* registrar *or* consignar el préstamo de algo

signatory *n & adj* signatario(a) *m,f*, firmante *mf*
   ❑ **signatory countries** países *mpl* firmantes

signature *n* firma *f*; **his signature was on the letter** la carta tenía su firma; **the signature of the company** la firma de la empresa; **to put one's signature to sth** firmar algo; **for signature** *(on document)* para ser firmado

silent partner *n US* socio(a) *m,f* capitalista

silver *n* plata *f* ❑ **silver money** dinero *m* de plata

SIM *n* TEL *(abbr* **subscriber identity module***)* ❑ **SIM card** *(in mobile phone)* tarjeta *f* SIM

SIMM *n* COMPTR *(abbr* **single in-line memory module***)* SIMM *m*

simple *adj* LAW **simple contract** contrato *m* simple *or* verbal; **simple debenture** obligación *f* simple; FIN **simple interest** interés *m* simple; **simple majority** mayoría *f* simple

simplex *adj* TEL símplex

simulate *vt* COMPTR simular

simulation *n* COMPTR simulación *f*

simulator *n* COMPTR simulador *m*

simultaneous *adj* MKTG **simultaneous product development** desarrollo *m* simultáneo de productos; **simultaneous translation** traducción *f* simultánea; **simultaneous translator** traductor(ora) *m,f* simultáneo(a)

sincerely adv Yours sincerely (in letter) Atentamente

single 1 n Br (ticket) Esp billete m or Am boleto m or esp Am pasaje m sencillo or de ida
  2 adj (**a**) (one only) EU **single currency** moneda f única; **the Single European Act** el Acta Única Europea; **Single (European) Market** mercado m único (europeo); INS **single premium policy** póliza f de prima única; **single tax** impuesto m único; COMPTR **single user licence** licencia f para un único usuario (**b**) (not double) **in single figures** por debajo de diez; **inflation is now in single figures** la inflación está por debajo del diez por ciento

single-A rating n ST EXCH calificación f A

single-entry adj ACCT **single-entry bookkeeping** contabilidad f por partida simple; **single-entry method** método m de partida simple

singletasking COMPTR **1** n monotarea f
  2 adj de monotarea

singly adv (packaged) individualmente, por separado; **to be sold singly** venderse individualmente or por separado

sink 1 vt (**a**) (debt, loan) amortizar (**b**) (invest) invertir; **we sank a fortune into this company** invertimos una fortuna en esta empresa
  2 vi (prices, currency, rate, profits) desplomarse; **the dollar has sunk to half its normal value** el dólar se ha desplomado hasta llegar a la mitad de su valor normal; **profits have sunk to an all-time low** los beneficios han alcanzado un mínimo histórico

sinking fund n fondo m de amortización

sister company n empresa f asociada

sit-down strike n huelga f de brazos caídos

site 1 n (**a**) (piece of land) solar m; **the development project includes sites for small businesses** la urbanización incluye locales para pequeñas empresas (**b**) (building) site obra f □ **site foreman** capataz m de obra; **site manager** director(ora) m,f de obra (**c**) (plant) fábrica f (**d**) COMPTR sitio m (**e**) MKTG (for advertising) ubicación f
  2 vt emplazar, ubicar

sit-in n sentada f

sitting tenant n inquilino(a) m,f titular or legal

situation n (**a**) (state of affairs) situación f; **the firm's financial situation isn't good** la situación financiera de la empresa no es buena; **the skills needed in an interview situation** las aptitudes necesarias en el contexto de una entrevista (**b**) (job) colocación f; **situations vacant/ wanted** (in advertisements) ofertas fpl/demandas fpl de empleo

Six Sigma® n seis Sigma® m

size n (**a**) (of place, object) tamaño m; (of clothes) talla f; (of shoes) número m (**b**) COMPTR (of file, font) tamaño m □ **size box** caja f de tamaño

skeleton n **skeleton organization** organización f con el personal mínimo; **skeleton staff** personal m mínimo

skill n (technique) capacidad f; (ability) destreza f, habilidad f; **computer technology requires us to learn new skills** la informática nos obliga a aprender nuevas técnicas

skilled adj (worker) cualificado(a), Am calificado(a); (task) especializado(a) □ **skilled labour** mano f de obra cualificada or Am calificada

skim vt MKTG (market) descremar

skimming n MKTG (of market) descremación f □ **skimming price** precio m de descremación

skip vt COMPTR (command) saltarse, omitir

slack adj (business) flojo(a), parado(a); **business is slack at the moment** el negocio anda flojo en estos momentos; **the slack season for tourists** la temporada baja del turismo

slacken vi (business) aflojar

slash 1 n (punctuation mark) barra f
  2 vt (prices, cost, taxes) recortar or reducir drásticamente; **prices have been slashed by 40%** han recortado los precios un drástico 40%

sleep vi COMPTR dormir, reposar □ **sleep mode** modo m de reposo

sleeping adj **sleeping economy** economía f dormida; Br **sleeping partner** (in company) socio m capitalista or comanditario

slide n (for presentation) diapositiva f □ **slide show** proyección f de diapositivas

sliding adj **sliding peg** paridad f móvil, ajuste m de la paridad; **sliding scale** escala f móvil

sliding-scale adj **sliding-scale depreciation** depreciación f de la escala móvil; **sliding-scale tariff** tarifa f de escala móvil; **sliding-scale taxation** tributación f progresiva

slip 1 n (printed paper) tira f de papel, hoja f de papel (pequeña y alargada)
  2 vi (prices) caer; **shares in the company slipped to 125p** las acciones de la empresa cayeron hasta los 125 peniques

slogan n MKTG eslogan m, lema m

slot n (**a**) COMPTR ranura f, Am slot m (**b**) US (job) puesto m

slow 1 adj (business, market) inactivo(a), flojo(a); **business is slow** el negocio está flojo
  2 adv **to go slow** (as protest) estar en huelga de celo

▶ **slow down 1** vt sep (growth, economy) desacelerar, ralentizar; **production is slowed down during the winter** durante el invierno se reduce la producción

2 vi *(economy)* experimentar una desaceleración, ralentizarse; **growth slowed down in the second quarter** el crecimiento se ralentizó durante el segundo trimestre

slowdown n (**a**) *(in productivity, rate)* disminución f; *(in economy)* desaceleración f, ralentización f (**b**) US *(go-slow)* huelga f de celo, RP trabajo m a reglamento

sluggish adj *(growth, economy)* lento(a); *(market, business)* inactivo(a), flojo(a); **trading is always rather sluggish on Mondays** el lunes es siempre un día de poca contratación

slump 1 n *(in prices, sales, market)* desplome m, caída f; *(economic depression)* crisis f inv; **there has been a slump in investment** ha habido una caída de las inversiones; **a slump in prices/demand** un desplome de precios/de la demanda **2** vi *(prices, currency, economy)* desplomarse

slush fund n caja f negra

> ❝
> They discussed a plan to create a **slush fund** in the administrative affairs section so they could entertain central government officials who made business trips to Okinawa. They filed for bogus business trips and used the pooled expense money whenever necessary.
> ❞

small adj (**a**) **small ads** anuncios mpl breves or por palabras; **small caps, small capitals** versalita(s) f(pl); **small letters** (letras fpl) minúsculas fpl; **the small print** la letra pequeña; **make sure you read the small print before you sign** antes de firmar asegúrese de leer la letra pequeña (**b**) **small business** pequeña empresa f; **small businessman** pequeño empresario m; **small change** cambio m, suelto m, Am sencillo m; **small firm** pequeña empresa f; **small investor** pequeño(a) inversor(ora) m,f; **small and medium-sized businesses** pequeñas y medianas empresas fpl; **small and medium-sized enterprises** pequeñas y medianas empresas fpl; **small saver** pequeño(a) ahorrador(ora) m,f, Andes, RP pequeño(a) ahorrista mf; **small shareholder** pequeño(a) accionista mf; **small shopkeeper** pequeño(a) comerciante mf; **small trader** pequeño(a) comerciante mf; **small wholesale selling** venta f al por mayor or Am al mayoreo en pequeña escala

small-cap adj US *(share, company)* de pequeña capitalización ❑ **small-cap index** índice m de empresas de pequeña capitalización

small-claims court n Br LAW = tribunal para causas de pequeña cuantía

small-scale adj *(operation, investment, project)* de poca envergadura ❑ **small-scale industry** industria f a pequeña escala or de pequeño tamaño

smart adj **smart card** tarjeta f inteligente; **smart card reader** lector m de tarjetas inteligentes; **smart money** dinero m bien invertido; **smart terminal** terminal m inteligente

SME n (abbr **small and medium-sized enterprise**) PYME f

smear campaign n *(in press)* campaña f de difamación

> ❝
> Mr Denktash not only rejected the charge out of hand but responded by launching a **smear campaign** against Mr Nadir in the state-controlled press. Volcan, a pro-government paper, regularly proclaims that Mr Nadir the international fugitive should be sent back to the UK.
> ❞

SMI n (abbr **small and medium-sized industry**) PYMI f

smiley n COMPTR emoticón m

SMS TEL **1** n (abbr **short message service**) *(service)* SMS m; *(message)* mensaje m SMS or de texto **2** vt **to SMS sb** enviar un mensaje SMS or de texto a alguien

SMTP n COMPTR (abbr **Simple Mail Transfer Protocol**) (protocolo m) SMTP m

smuggle 1 vt pasar de contrabando; **to smuggle sth through customs** pasar algo de contrabando por la aduana **2** vi dedicarse al contrabando

▸ **smuggle in** vt sep *(goods)* introducir de contrabando

▸ **smuggle out** vt sep *(goods)* sacar de contrabando

smuggler n contrabandista mf

smuggling n contrabando m

snail mail n Fam correo m caracol or tortuga, correo tradicional

> ❝
> E-mail is putting the squeeze on **snail mail** as computer users opt for the faster, cheaper and more convenient method of writing to friends, family and business associates. Feeling the pinch is the Communications Authority of Thailand (CAT), the country's postal service operator. The CAT has suffered decreasing mail volume for the past several years as more and more Thais become Internet users and discover the benefits of e-mail.
> ❞

snake n ECON serpiente f monetaria

SNG n (abbr **satellite news gathering**) SNG f, recopilación f de noticias por satélite

snowball effect *n* efecto *m* (de la) bola de nieve

soar *vi* (prices, profits, inflation) dispararse; **sales have soared since the advertising campaign** las ventas se han disparado desde la puesta en marcha de la campaña publicitaria

soaring *adj* (prices, profits, inflation, sales) desorbitado(a)

social *adj* **social assets** patrimonio *m* social; **social audit** auditoría *f* social; **social benefits** prestaciones *fpl* sociales; **social charges** (levied on employers) contribuciones *fpl* sociales; **social contract** pacto *m* social; **social cost** costo *m* or *Esp* coste *m* social; **social dumping** dumping *m* social; **social entitlements** derechos *mpl* sociales; *Br* ADMIN **social fund** = fondo social del gobierno británico para el pago de diferentes prestaciones sociales; **social integration** inserción *f* social; **social ownership** propiedad *f* colectiva; **social partners** interlocutores *mpl* or agentes *mpl* sociales; **social report** balance *m* social; **social security** seguridad *f* social; **to be on social security** estar recibiendo prestaciones sociales; **social security benefits** prestaciones *fpl* de la seguridad social; **social security contribution** cotización *f* a la seguridad social; *US* **social security number** número *m* de afiliación a la seguridad social; **social security office** oficina *f* de la seguridad social; **social security provisions** sistema *m* de seguridad social; **social security system** sistema *m* de seguridad social; **social welfare (system)** bienestar *m* social, sistema *m* de asistencia social

sociodemographic *adj* sociodemográfico(a) ❑ **sociodemographic data** datos *mpl* sociodemográficos; **sociodemographic profile** perfil *m* sociodemográfico; **sociodemographic segment** segmento *m* sociodemográfico; **sociodemographic segmentation** segmentación *f* sociodemográfica

socioeconomic *adj* socioeconómico(a) ❑ **socio-economic classification** clasificación *f* socioeconómica; **socio-economic group** grupo *m* socioeconómico

sociological *adj* sociológico(a) ❑ **sociological survey** encuesta *f* sociológica

sociology *n* sociología *f*

socio-professional *adj* socioprofesional ❑ **socio-professional group** grupo *m* socioprofesional

socket *n* (**a**) (for plug) enchufe *m*, toma *f* de corriente; (for light bulb) casquillo *m* (**b**) COMPTR zócalo *m*

SOFFEX *n* ST EXCH (abbr **Swiss Options and Financial Futures Exchange**) SOFFEX *m*, = mercado suizo de opciones y futuros

soft 1 *n* **softs** productos *mpl* agrícolas básicos

2 *adj* **soft commodities** productos *mpl* agrícolas básicos; COMPTR **soft copy** copia *f* electrónica or en formato electrónico; **soft currency** divisa *f* débil; *Br* **soft goods** (fabrics) textiles *mpl*; **soft loan** crédito *m* blando; *US* POL **soft money** = fondos destinados a los partidos políticos para ser utilizados con cualquier finalidad que no sea la de apoyar a candidatos al gobierno federal; COMPTR **soft return** retorno *m* automático; **soft sell** venta *f* no agresiva

> "
> The result has been to introduce advertising material that marketers describe as relevant to, as an extension of, or as "contextual" to the content – less intrusive and in-your-face than flashy, oversized banners or pop-up ads. The **soft sell** in other words.
> "

software *n* COMPTR software *m* ❑ **software bug** error *m* de software; **software company** empresa *f* de software; **software developer** desarrollador(ora) *m,f* de software; **software error** error *m* de software; **software failure** *Esp* fallo *m* or *Am* falla *f* de software; **software package** paquete *m* de software; **software piracy** piratería *f* informática; **software pirate** pirata *mf* informático(a); **software problem** problema *m* de software; **software producer** productor(ora) *m,f* de software

sola of exchange *n* FIN única *f* de cambio

sole *adj* (only) único(a); (exclusive) exclusivo(a) ❑ **sole agency** representación *f* exclusiva; **sole agency contract** contrato *m* de representación exclusiva; **sole agent** agente *mf* en exclusiva; **to be sole agent for Rover** tener la representación exclusiva de Rover; **sole contract** contrato *m* exclusivo; **sole dealer** agente *mf* único(a); **sole owner** único(a) propietario(a) *m,f*; **sole representative** representante *mf* exclusivo(a); **sole right** derecho *m* exclusivo; **sole supplier** suministrador(ora) *m,f* exclusivo(a); **sole trader** empresario(a) *m,f* individual

solicitor *n Br* = abogado que hace las veces de notario para contratos de compraventa y testamentos o que actúa de procurador en los juzgados ❑ **Solicitor General** (in UK) Fiscal *mf* General del Estado; (in US) Subsecretario(a) *m,f* de Justicia

solus *adj* MKTG **solus advertisement** anuncio *m* exclusivo or aislado; **solus position** espacio *m* exclusivo or aislado; **solus site** emplazamiento *m* exclusivo

solvency *n* solvencia *f* ❑ **solvency ratio** coeficiente *m* or índice *m* de solvencia

solvent *adj* solvente; **in such cases the directors must declare that the company is solvent** en casos así los consejeros deben declarar que la empresa es solvente

SOP *n* (*abbr* **standard operating procedure**) PNT *m*

sort 1 *n* (**a**) *(putting in order)* ordenación *f*; **the program will do an alphabetical sort** el programa realizará una ordenación alfabética □ *sort routine* rutina *f* de ordenación (**b**) BANKING *sort code* (*of bank*) número *m* de sucursal
2 *vt* (*put in order*) ordenar, clasificar; **to sort sth in ascending/descending order** clasificar algo por orden ascendente/descendente
3 *vi* (*put things in order*) ordenar, clasificar; (*file, data*) ordenar

sorting *n* BANKING *sorting code* número *m* de sucursal; *sorting office* oficina *f* de clasificación de correo

sound[1] *n* COMPTR *sound card* tarjeta *f* de sonido

sound[2] *adj* (*investment, business, financial position*) seguro(a), sólido(a)

soundbite *n* frase *f* lapidaria (*en medios de comunicación*)

> Yesterday's plan for the railways was launched on the trite **soundbite** that the Government wants to see a "safer, better and bigger" railway ... the aims are inherently contradictory, which demonstrates not only the huge task the Government faces in trying to improve the railways but also the wider lack of coherence on transport that has dogged New Labour ever since it was elected in 1997.

source 1 *n* (**a**) (*of revenue, income*) fuente *f*; (*of goods*) origen *m*; **income is taxed at source** el impuesto sobre la renta se deduce en origen *or* en la fuente □ ACCT *source and application of funds* origen *m* y aplicación de fondos; *sources and use of funds statement* estado *m* de origen y aplicación de fondos
(**b**) COMPTR *source code* código *m* fuente; *source disk* disco *m* original; (*floppy*) disquete *m* original; *source document* documento *m* original; *source file* archivo *m or* fichero *m* fuente; *source language* lengua *f* original *or* fuente; *source text* texto *m* original *or* fuente
2 *vt* adquirir, obtener

sourcing *n* adquisición *f*, obtención *f*; **we prefer local sourcing of materials** preferimos adquirir *or* obtener los materiales en la región

space *n* (*in text*) espacio *m* □ *space bar* (*on keyboard*) barra *f* espaciadora

spacing *n* (*in text*) (*horizontal*) espaciado *m*; (*vertical*) interlineado *m*

spam COMPTR **1** *n* correo *m* basura
2 *vt* enviar correo basura a
3 *vi* enviar correo basura

> An Australian man has been given a two-year suspended jail sentence for his part in sending mass commercial e-mail, or **spam**, and bulletin board postings to millions of Internet users. Wayne John Loughnan of Noosa Heads, Queensland, was sentenced to two years in jail on Tuesday after pleading guilty to charges of securities fraud and unlawful interference with third-party computer systems.

spammer *n* COMPTR = persona que envía correo basura

spamming *n* COMPTR envío *m* de correo basura

spare 1 *n* (*spare part*) (pieza *f* de) recambio *m or* repuesto *m*
2 *adj* (*funds, capital*) disponible □ *spare part* (pieza *f* de) recambio *m or* repuesto *m*

speak *vi* (*on telephone*) **who's speaking?** ¿de parte de quién?; **Mr Thomas? – yes, speaking** ¿el señor Thomas? – sí, soy yo *or* al aparato

spec *n* (*abbr* **specification**) especificaciones *fpl or* características *fpl* técnicas

special *adj* Br *special delivery* correo *m* urgente, Esp ≃ postal exprés *m*; *special delivery parcel* paquete *m* enviado por correo urgente; FIN *special drawing rights* derechos *mpl* especiales de giro; *special offer* oferta *f* especial; **on special offer** en oferta (especial); *special permit* permiso *m* especial; *special price* precio *m* especial; *special promotion* promoción *f* especial; *special provision* disposición *f* especial; *special rate* tarifa *f* especial; *special rate of taxation* Esp tipo *m* impositivo *or* Am tasa *f* impositiva especial; *special savings account* cuenta *f* de ahorro especial

specialist 1 *n* especialista *mf*
2 *adj* (*skills, equipment*) especializado(a) □ *specialist press* prensa *f* especializada; *specialist retailer* tienda *f* especializada

speciality, US **specialty** *n* especialidad *f*; **our speciality is electronic components** nuestra especialidad son los componentes electrónicos □ *speciality goods* artículos *mpl* especializados

specialization *n* (*process*) especialización *f*; **his specialization is computers** su especialidad es la informática

specialize *vi* especializarse (**in** en); **we specialize in electronics** somos especialistas en electrónica

specialty US = **speciality**

specie *n* FIN (*coins*) monedas *fpl*; **to pay in specie** pagar en moneda

specification *n* (**a**) (*of contract*) estipulación *f* (**b**) **specifications** (*of machine, materials*) especificaciones *fpl or* características *fpl* técnicas; (*for* *technical project)* pliego *m* de condiciones ❑ ***specifications sheet*** ficha *f* técnica (**c**) MKTG ***specification buying*** compra *f* según especificaciones técnicas

specify *vt* especificar; **unless otherwise specified** salvo que se indique lo contrario; **the rules specify a five-minute break** el reglamento estipula cinco minutos de descanso ❑ ***specified load*** carga *f* especificada

specimen *n (of goods)* muestra *f* ❑ ***specimen invoice*** modelo *m* de factura; ***specimen signature*** modelo *m* de firma

speculate *vi* FIN, ST EXCH especular; **to speculate on the Stock Market** especular en (la) Bolsa, jugar a la *or* en Bolsa; **to speculate in oils** especular en acciones petrolíferas; **to speculate for a fall** jugar a la baja; **to speculate for a rise** jugar al alza

speculation *n* FIN, ST EXCH especulación *f*; **speculation in oil** especulación en acciones petrolíferas

speculative *adj* FIN, ST EXCH especulativo(a) ❑ ***speculative buying*** compras *fpl* especulativas; ***speculative securities*** valores *mpl* especulativos; ***speculative selling*** ventas *fpl* especulativas; ***speculative shares*** acciones *fpl* especulativas

speculator *n* FIN, ST EXCH especulador(ora) *m,f*

speech recognition *n* COMPTR reconocimiento *m* del habla

speed dial *n* TEL marcado *m* rápido, marcación *f* rápida, *Andes, RP* discado *m* rápido

Speedwriting® *n* escritura *f* abreviada, = sistema de taquigrafía que usa combinaciones alfabéticas para representar grupos de sonidos

spellcheck *n* COMPTR **to do** *or* **run a spellcheck on a document** pasar el corrector ortográfico a un documento

spellchecker *n* COMPTR corrector *m* ortográfico

spend 1 *n* gasto *m*; **we must increase our marketing spend** debemos aumentar el gasto de marketing; **this year's spend has exceeded the budget by 10%** los gastos de este año se han excedido en un 10% del presupuesto
2 *vt* (**a**) *(money)* gastar; **to spend money on sth** gastar dinero en algo (**b**) *(time)* dedicar; **to spend time on sth/doing sth** dedicar tiempo a algo/a hacer algo

> 66
> Pernod Ricard, the French drinks group which recently bought part of Seagram, has announced that it will increase its marketing **spend** in Central and South America by around 20%. The move by the makers of Clan Campbell and Havana Club comes despite the region's economic instability.
> 99

spending *n* gasto *m* ❑ ***spending cuts*** recorte *m* de gastos; ***spending limit*** límite *m* de gastos; ***spending money*** dinero *m* para gastos; ECON ***spending power*** poder *m* adquisitivo

sphere *n* ámbito *m*, esfera *f*; **our sphere of activity** nuestro campo *or* ámbito de actividad; **it's not my sphere** está fuera de mi ámbito; **the question is outside the committee's sphere** el asunto está fuera de las competencias de la comisión

spike *n* US *(sharp increase)* subida *f* brusca (**in** en); **there was a spike in prices** los precios se dispararon

spin *Fam* **1** *n (on information)* **to put the right spin on a story** dar el sesgo conveniente a una noticia; **the government has been criticized for indulging in too much spin** se ha criticado al gobierno por manipular demasiado la información dada al público ❑ ***spin doctor*** = encargado de marketing político y relaciones públicas de un partido
2 *vi (spin doctor)* **to spin against someone** difundir una imagen negativa de alguien

> 66
> Meanwhile, the former royal **spin doctor**, Simon Lewis, has been reflecting on his time trying to cast Britain's leading dysfunctional family in a better light. On his first day he turned up at the Buckingham Palace gates ... and was asked by a policeman who he was. "I'm the Queen's new director of communications", said Lewis proudly. The reply: "Does that mean you're here to fix the telephones?"
> 99

spinner *n* MKTG *(for displaying goods)* expositor *m* giratorio

spin-off *n* (**a**) *(product)* (producto *m*) derivado *m*, subproducto *m* ❑ ***spin-off product*** producto *m* derivado, subproducto *m* (**b**) *(of company)* escisión *f*

> 66
> Southampton Innovations was set up as an autonomous limited company to give Ashby the freedom to hunt for winning technology within the university, patent it and then find outside chief executives to run **spin-off companies** to develop it commercially.
> 99

spiral 1 *n* espiral *f*; **an inflationary spiral** una espiral inflacionaria *or* *Esp* inflacionista
2 *vi (prices)* subir vertiginosamente

split 1 *n* FIN, ST EXCH *(of shares)* fraccionamiento *m*
2 *adj* **he works a split shift** trabaja en un turno partido ❑ FIN ***split capital investment trust*** sociedad *f* de inversión de duración limitada; ***split coupon bond*** bono *m* de cupón cero; COMPTR ***split screen*** pantalla *f* partida

3 *vt* FIN, ST EXCH **to split shares** fraccionar acciones; **the shares were split 50%, one new share for each two shares held** las acciones fueron fraccionadas al 50%, con una acción nueva por cada dos acciones antiguas

SPOC *n* (*abbr* **single point of contact**) punto *m* único de contacto *(para atención al cliente)*

spoil 1 *vt* (*goods*) deteriorar, estropear
  2 *vi* (*goods*) deteriorarse, estropearse

spoilage *n* deterioro *m*

spoiler campaign *n* MKTG contracampaña *f*

spokesman *n* portavoz *m*, *Am* vocero *m* (**for** de)

spokesperson *n* portavoz *mf*, *Am* vocero(a) *m,f* (**for** de)

spokeswoman *n* portavoz *f*, *Am* vocera *f* (**for** de)

sponsor 1 *n* patrocinador(ora) *m,f*
  2 *vt* patrocinar

sponsorship *n* patrocinio *m* ❑ *sponsorship agreement* acuerdo *m* de patrocinio; *sponsorship budget* presupuesto *m* para patrocinios; *sponsorship deal* acuerdo *m* de patrocinio

spontaneous recall *n* MKTG recuerdo *m* espontáneo

spooler *n* COMPTR (*for printing*) spooler *m* de impresión

spot *n* (**a**) FIN *spot buying* compra *f* al contado; *spot cash* dinero *m* al contado, dinero contante y sonante; **to pay spot cash** pagar al contado; *spot credit* crédito *m* a corto plazo; ST EXCH *spot deal* operación *f* al contado; ST EXCH *spot delivery* entrega *f* inmediata; ST EXCH *spot exchange rate* tipo *m* or *Am* tasa de cambio al contado; *spot goods* mercancías *fpl* al contado; ST EXCH *spot market* mercado *m* al contado *or* a término; ST EXCH *spot price* precio *m* al contado; ST EXCH *spot quotation* cotización *f* al contado; ST EXCH *spot rate* tipo *m or* tasa *f* de cambio al contado; ST EXCH *spot trading* operaciones *fpl* al contado; ST EXCH *spot transaction* operación *f* al contado (**b**) (*in advertising*) anuncio *m*, spot *m*

spread 1 *n* (**a**) (*between interest rates*) diferencial *m*, spread *m*; ST EXCH (*between buying and selling prices*) diferencial (**b**) ST EXCH (*range of investments*) abanico *m*
  2 *vt* **to spread payments over several months** distribuir los pagos a lo largo de varios meses
  3 *vi* ST EXCH especular con el diferencial de precios

spreadsheet *n* (*document, software*) hoja *f* de cálculo

square 1 *n* Fam **the Square Mile** = el barrio financiero y bursátil de Londres
  2 *adj square brackets* corchetes *mpl*
  3 *vt* (*account, bill, debt*) saldar; **to square the**

books ajustar las cuentas

> **"**
> The more solemn atmosphere reflects financial reality in the **Square Mile**. HSBC's full-year financial results tomorrow are expected to predict a difficult year ahead. The Bank Of England's Monetary Policy Committee is likely to announce on Thursday that interest rates will stay at their current low levels.
> **"**

squeeze 1 *n* **credit/profits squeeze** reducción *f* del crédito/de los beneficios
  2 *vt* **profits have been squeezed by foreign competition** los beneficios se han visto mermados por la competencia extranjera

SRO *n Br* ST EXCH (*abbr* **self-regulatory organization**) organización *f* autorregulada

SSP *n Br* ADMIN (*abbr* **statutory sick pay**) subsidio *m* por enfermedad, prestación *f* por enfermedad *(mínimo reglamentario que garantiza el Estado)*

stability *n* (*of prices, market, economy*) estabilidad *f* ❑ EU *Stability and Growth Pact* Pacto *m* de Estabilidad y Crecimiento

stabilization *n* (*of prices, market, economy*) estabilización *f* ❑ *stabilization plan* plan *m* de estabilización

stabilize 1 *vt* (*prices, market, economy*) estabilizar
  2 *vi* (*prices, market, economy*) estabilizarse

stabilizing *adj* **to have a stabilizing influence on prices** ejercer una influencia estabilizadora sobre los precios ❑ *stabilizing policy* política *f* de estabilización

stable *adj* (*prices, market, economy*) estable

staff 1 *n* personal *m*; **to be on the staff** estar en plantilla *or* SAm plantel; **staff only** (*sign*) privado ❑ *staff appraisal* evaluación *f* del personal; *staff association* asociación *f* del personal; *staff costs* gastos *mpl* de personal; *staff cutbacks* recortes *mpl* de personal; *staff increase* aumento *m* de personal; *staff management* administración *f* del personal; *staff manager* director(ora) *m,f* de personal; *staff meeting* reunión *f* del personal; *staff motivation* motivación *f* del personal; *staff organization* organización *f* del personal; *staff representative* delegado(a) *m,f* de personal; *staff shortage* falta *f* de personal; *staff training* formación *f* del personal; *staff turnover* movimiento *m* de personal
  2 *vt* (*provide with employees*) proveer de personal; **the office is staffed by volunteers** el personal de la oficina está formado por voluntarios; **the desk is staffed at all times** el mostrador está atendido en todo momento

staffer *n* Fam empleado(a) *m,f*

staffing *n* (*recruiting*) dotación *f* de personal,

contratación *f* (de personal); **the delay is due to staffing difficulties** el retraso se debe a problemas para encontrar personal ❑ *staffing levels* niveles *mpl* de personal, número *m* de empleados; *staffing policy* política *f* de contratación de personal

stag *n* ST EXCH *Br (who sells shares on quickly)* especulador(ora) *m,f* ciervo; *US (who is not a member of the exchange)* zurupeto(a) *m,f*

> **"**
>
> The **stags** were left looking forlorn as Spike Networks' A\$34 million (US\$21.86 million) share offering fell flat on Friday, its first day of trading on the Australian Stock Exchange – but directors Chris O'Hanlon and John McGuigan still had plenty of reasons to be smiling.
>
> **"**

stage *n (phase)* etapa *f*, fase *f*; **the next stage in computer technology** la siguiente etapa de la tecnología informática; **the changes were instituted in stages** los cambios fueron introducidos por etapas

stagflation *n* ECON estanflación *f*

stagger *vt (payments, holidays)* escalonar; **they plan to bring in staggered working hours** están planeando introducir un horario de trabajo escalonado; **employees' vacation times are staggered over the summer months** las vacaciones de los empleados se distribuyen escalonadamente a lo largo de los meses de verano

staggered *adj staggered delivery* entrega *f* escalonada; *staggered payments* pagos *mpl* escalonados; *staggered strike* huelga *f* escalonada

stagnant *adj (economy, prices, trade)* estancado(a)

stagnate *vi (economy, prices, trade)* estancarse

stagnation *n (of economy, prices, trade)* estancamiento *m*

stake 1 *n* (**a**) *(share) (interest)* intereses *mpl*; *(shareholding)* participación *f* (accionarial); **she has a 10% stake in the company** tiene una participación del 10% en la sociedad; **the company has a big stake in nuclear energy** la compañía está directamente interesada en la energía nuclear (**b**) *US (savings)* ahorros *mpl*
2 *vt US (aid financially)* ayudar económicamente, financiar; **he is staking the newspaper for half a million dollars** va a financiar al periódico con medio millón de dólares

stakeholder *n (in company)* parte *f* interesada; **the stakeholders in a project** las partes interesadas en un proyecto ❑ *Br stakeholder pension* = plan de pensiones regulado por el gobierno británico para complementar el estatal y que ofrece incentivos fiscales

> **"**
>
> A better deal for poorer pensioners not covered in company schemes was supposed to be delivered by the **stakeholder pension** concept. This aimed to encourage the many millions of low earners who have no savings whatsoever into at least making some provision for retirement. The motives were good but the outcome again is disappointing. Only 700,000 **stakeholder pensions** have been sold, and it is not clear whether these have been to low earners.
>
> **"**

stale *adj (cheque)* caducado(a), vencido(a)

stall *vi* **to stall (for time)** intentar ganar tiempo; **I think they're stalling on the deal until we make more concessions** creo que están retrasando el *or* dando largas al acuerdo para conseguir más concesiones de nuestra parte

stamp 1 *n* (**a**) *(for letter, parcel)* sello *m*, *Am* estampilla *f*, *CAm, Méx* timbre *m* (**b**) *(device)* tampón *m*, sello *m*; *(mark)* sello (**c**) *stamp Br duty or US tax* póliza *f*, = impuesto de transmisiones patrimoniales
2 *vt* (**a**) *(document)* estampar; *(passport)* sellar; **he stamped the firm's name on each document** le puso el sello de la empresa a cada uno de los documentos; **incoming mail is stamped with the date received** el correo recibido se sella con la fecha de llegada (**b**) *(letter, parcel)* franquear ❑ *Br stamped addressed envelope* sobre *m* franqueado y con la dirección

stand 1 *n (at exhibition)* stand *m*, puesto *m*
2 *vi* (**a**) *(be valid)* seguir en pie; **the agreement stands** el acuerdo sigue en pie; **even with this new plan, our objection still stands** incluso con el nuevo plan, nuestras objeciones siguen en pie (**b**) *(statistics)* ascender a; **inflation/unemployment stands at 5%** la inflación/el desempleo asciende a *or* se sitúa en el 5%; **their turnover now stands at three million pounds** su facturación asciende ahora a los tres millones de libras

▶ **stand down** *vi (resign)* retirarse

▶ **stand off** *vt sep Br (workers)* dejar sin trabajo a

stand-alone *adj* COMPTR independiente, autónomo(a)

standard 1 *n* (**a**) *(level)* nivel *m*; **to be up to/below standard** estar al nivel/por debajo del nivel exigido; **most of the goods are up to standard** la calidad de mayoría de los productos es satisfactoria ❑ *standards commission* comisión *f* de normalización; *standard of living* nivel *m* de vida
(**b**) *(set requirement)* norma *f*, estándar *m*; *(for currency)* patrón *m*; **to make a product comply with standards** hacer que un producto cumpla las normas; **to set standards for a product** fijar

normas para un producto; **gold/dollar standard** patrón oro/dólar

2 *adj (design, size)* estándar ❏ **standard cost** costo *m or Esp* coste *m* estándar; **standard cost accounting** sistema *m* de costo *or Esp* coste estándar; **standard costing** cálculo *m* de costos *or Esp* costes estándar; **standard deviation** desviación *f* típica *or* estándar; **standard document** documento *m* modelo; **standard ending** *(of letter)* fórmula *m* de despedida; **standard letter** carta *f* modelo; **standard opening** *(of letter)* fórmula *f* de saludo; **standard operating procedure** procedimiento *m* normalizado de trabajo; INS **standard policy** póliza *f* estándar; **standard practice** práctica *f* habitual; **standard price** precio *m* normal; **standard rate** *(of tax) Esp* tipo *m* medio *or Am* tasa *f* media del impuesto sobre la renta; **standard sample** muestra *f* estándar; **standard weight** peso *m* estándar

standardization *n* normalización *f*, estandarización *f*; *(by official body)* normalización

standardize *vt* normalizar, estandarizar; *(by official body)* normalizar

standby *n* (**a**) FIN ❏ **standby credit** crédito *m* contingente *or* standby; **standby letter of credit** carta *f* de crédito contingente *or* standby (**b**) *(for flight)* **to be on standby** estar en lista de espera *or* stand-by ❏ **standby passenger** pasajero(a) *m,f* en lista de espera *or* stand-by; **standby ticket** *Esp* billete *m or Am* boleto *m or esp Am* pasaje *m* de lista de espera *or* stand-by (**c**) COMPTR **standby mode** *(of printer)* modo *m* de reposo, modo *m* de suspensión del sistema

standing 1 *n (status)* reputación *f*; **the scandal has damaged the company's standing** la reputación de la empresa se ha visto manchada con el escándalo; **enquiries were made into his financial standing** se investigó su posición económica

2 *adj* **standing charges** *(on bill)* tarifa *f* fija; **standing committee** comisión *f* permanente; *Br* FIN **standing order** domiciliación *f* (bancaria), *Am* débito *m* bancario; **I get paid by standing order** tengo el sueldo domiciliado

standstill *n* **to be at a standstill** *(economy, production)* estar paralizado(a) ❏ **standstill agreement** acuerdo *m* de moratoria

❝
The major shareholders in Anaconda Nickel ... have come to a **standstill agreement** regarding their stakes. In the hectic hours before today's extraordinary general meeting, they agreed not to increase their stakes above 30 percent in the period up to Dec. 31 2001, or 90 days after the publication of key recommendations of a strategic review, whichever is the later.
❞

staple¹ 1 *n (for paper)* grapa *f*, *Am* grampa *f*, *Chile*

corchete *m*, *Col* gancho *m*, *RP* ganchito *m*, broche *m* ❏ **staple gun** *Esp, Méx, Carib* grapadora *f or Méx, CAm, Bol, Perú* engra(m)padora *f or Chile* corchetera *f or RP* abrochadora *f* industrial

2 *vt* grapar, *Am* engra(m)par, *Chile* corchetear, *RP* abrochar (**to** a)

staple² 1 *n (basic foodstuff)* alimento *m* básico; *(raw material)* materia *f* prima; *(main product)* producto *m* básico *or* de primera necesidad

2 *adj (foodstuffs, products)* básico(a), de primera necesidad; *(export, crop)* básico(a) ❏ **staple commodity** producto *m* básico; **their staple commodity is cotton** su producto básico es el algodón

stapler *n Esp, Méx, Carib* grapadora *f*, *Méx, CAm, Bol, Perú* engra(m)padora *f*, *Chile* corchetera *f*, *RP* abrochadora *f*

star *n* (**a**) MKTG (producto *m*) estrella *f* (**b**) ST EXCH **star analyst** mejor analista *mf* (**c**) COMPTR **star network** red *f* en estrella; **star structure** estructura *f* en estrella

start 1 *n* principio *m*, comienzo *m* ❏ COMPTR **start button** botón *m* de inicio; **start menu** menú *m* (de) inicio

2 *vt* (**a**) *(machine, device)* arrancar, poner en marcha; **to start the printer again, press this key** para reiniciar la impresora, apriete esta tecla (**b**) *(business)* montar, poner; *(project, campaign)* empezar, comenzar

3 *vi* empezar, comenzar; **she started on $500 a week** empezó con 500 dólares a la semana; **prices start at** *or* **from £20** *(in advert)* precios desde 20 libras

▸ **start up 1** *vt sep (business)* montar, poner; *(project, campaign)* empezar, comenzar; *(computer)* arrancar

2 *vi (computer)* arrancar; **to start up in business** poner *or* montar un negocio

starting *n* **starting date** fecha *f* de inicio; **starting price** *(at auction)* precio *m* de salida (a subasta); *Br* **starting rate** *(of income tax) Esp* tipo *m* impositivo mínimo, *Am* tasa *f* imposiva mínima; **starting salary** salario *m or* sueldo *m* inicial

starting-rate *adj Br* **starting-rate taxpayers** contribuyentes *mpl* que pagan *Esp* el tipo mínimo *or Am* la tasa mínima ❏ **starting-rate tax** *Esp* tipo *m* impositivo mínimo, *Am* tasa *f* impositiva mínima

start-up *n* (**a**) *(of new business)* puesta *f* en marcha; **there have been 500 start-ups this year** este año han comenzado a funcionar 500 empresas ❏ **start-up capital** capital *m* inicial; **start-up company** empresa *f* de reciente creación, nueva empresa *f*; **start-up costs** gastos *mpl* de puesta en marcha; **start-up loan** préstamo *m* para la puesta en marcha de un negocio (**b**) *(Internet company)* puntocom *f* nueva (**c**) COMPTR arranque *m* ❏ **start-up disk** disco *m* de arranque; **start-up mode** modo *m* de arranque; ***start-up screen*** pantalla *f* de arranque

state[1] *n (country, administrative region)* estado *m*
❑ *US* **state bank** banco *m* del estado, banco estatal; ***state budget*** presupuestos *mpl* del Estado;
state control control *m* estatal; **under state control** bajo control estatal; *US* **State Department** Departamento *m* de Estado; ***state monopoly*** monopolio *m* del Estado; ***state pension*** pensión *f* del Estado

state[2] *vt (conditions, reasons, demands, objections)* exponer; **please state salary expectations** por favor indique el salario que espera recibir

state-aided *adj* con ayuda estatal

state-controlled *adj (industry, company)* estatal, controlado(a) por el Estado; *(economy)* dirigido(a); **the oil company is 51% state-controlled** el Estado controla el 51% de la empresa petrolera

stated *adj (amount, limit)* indicado(a); *(date, price)* fijado(a); **it will be finished within the stated time** se terminará dentro del plazo fijado

statement *n* **(a)** *(of facts, situation, to press)* declaración *f* ❑ ***statement of intent*** declaración *f* de intenciones; ***statement of principle*** declaración *f* de principios
  (b) *(of expenses, sales figures)* balance *m*; *(from bank)* extracto *m* (bancario) ❑ ACCT ***statement of account*** *(of company)* estado *m* de cuentas; *(of client)* extracto *m* de cuenta; ***statement of affairs*** estado *m* financiero; ACCT ***statement of assets and liabilities*** balance *m* (general); ***statement of changes in financial position*** estado *m* de origen y aplicación de fondos; ***statement of expenditure, statement of expenses*** declaración *f* de gastos; *US* ACCT ***statement of financial position*** balance *m* (general); ***statement of invoices*** balance *m* de facturas; INS ***statement of loss*** declaración *f* de pérdidas; ACCT ***statement of results*** balance *m* de resultados; ***statement of sales figures*** balance *m* de cifras de ventas; ACCT ***statement of sources and applications of funds*** estado *m* de origen y aplicación de fondos

state-of-the-art *adj* puntero(a), de vanguardia; **the method incorporates state-of-the-art technology** el método incorpora tecnología punta

❝
Seats on any given flight can be sold in many different markets. The idea of investing in **state-of-the-art** technology is to better match supply with demand and ensure that each market is allocated an appropriate number of seats, especially when traffic mix and seasonal travel have to be factored in. Ultimately, we want to minimize seat wastage.
❞

state-owned *adj* público(a), estatal ❑ ***state-owned company*** empresa *f* pública *or* estatal

stationery *n (writing materials)* artículos *mpl* de papelería; *(writing paper)* papel *m* de carta ❑ *Br* ADMIN **the Stationery Office** = la imprenta del Estado

statistic *n* dato *m* (estadístico); **statistics** *(facts)* estadísticas *fpl*, datos estadísticos; *(science)* estadística *f*

statistical *adj* estadístico(a) ❑ ***statistical analysis*** análisis *m inv* estadístico; ***statistical data*** datos *mpl* estadísticos, estadísticas *fpl*; ***statistical indicator*** indicador *m* estadístico; ***statistical table*** tabla *f* estadística

statistician *n* estadístico(a) *m,f*

status *n (position)* categoría *f*, posición *f*; **what's your status in the company?** ¿cuál es tu posición en la empresa? ❑ COMPTR ***status bar*** barra *f* de estado; COMPTR ***status box*** caja *f* de estado; ***status enquiry*** *(about creditworthiness)* petición *f* de informes crediticios; COMPTR ***status line*** línea *f* de estado; ***status report*** informe *m* de la situación

statute *n* LAW ley *f*; **statutes** *(of company)* estatutos *mpl* ❑ ***statute book*** legislación *f*, código *m* de leyes; ***statute law*** derecho *m* escrito

statutory *adj (price controls, income policy, duties, regulations)* legal, obligatorio(a), reglamentario(a) ❑ *Br* ***statutory company*** entidad *f* controlada por el Estado; ***statutory holidays*** días *mpl* festivos *or Am* feriados oficiales; *Br* ***statutory maternity pay*** prestación *f* por maternidad; ***statutory report*** informe *m* financiero de presentación obligatoria; ***statutory reserve*** reserva *f* legal; ***statutory rights*** derechos *mpl* legales; *Br* ***statutory sick pay*** prestación *f* por enfermedad *(mínimo reglamentario que garantiza el Estado)*

steady 1 *adj (growth, rate, increase, decline)* constante; *(price, Stock Market)* estable; **inflation remains at a steady 5%** la inflación permanece estable al 5%
  2 *vi (growth, rate, price, Stock Market)* estabilizarse

steep *adj (rise, fall)* pronunciado(a); *(price)* excesivo(a); **a steep drop in share prices** una caída pronunciada de las acciones

steering committee *n* comisión *f* consultiva

❝
He said France could not "take refuge" behind the views of its own national scientific body – the food safety agency – to oppose a commission decision resuming British beef exports which itself had been based on the opinion of an EU scientific body, the scientific **steering committee** of veterinary experts.
❞

step costs *npl* ACCT costos *mpl or Esp* costes *mpl* escalonados

sterling *n* libra *f* esterlina; **in sterling** en libras (esterlinas); **five thousand pounds sterling** cinco mil libras (esterlinas) ❑ **sterling area** zona *f* de la libra esterlina; **sterling balances** reservas *fpl* en libras esterlinas; **sterling bloc** bloque *m* de la libra esterlina

stevedore *n* estibador *m*

sticker price *n* precio *m* de catálogo

stimulate *vt (production, demand, growth, trade)* estimular

stimulation marketing *n* marketing *m* basado en la estimulación

stimulus *n* MKTG estímulo *m* ❑ **stimulus response** respuesta *f* al estímulo

stipulate *vt* estipular; **it is stipulated that construction shall start next month** está estipulado que la construcción empezará el próximo mes; **please stipulate the quantity on your order form** por favor indique la cantidad en el formulario de pedido ❑ **stipulated quality** calidad *f* estipulada

stipulation *n* estipulación *f*; **they accepted, but with the stipulation that the time limit be extended** aceptaron, pero con la condición de que el plazo de tiempo fuera ampliado

stock 1 *n* (**a**) *esp Br (of goods)* existencias *fpl*, stock *m*; **stocks are low** quedan pocas existencias; **while stocks last** hasta agotar existencias; **to be in stock** estar en existencias; **I think the product you are looking for is in stock** creo que tenemos el producto que busca; **to be out of stock** *(product)* estar agotado(a); **we're out of stock** no nos queda, se nos ha agotado ❑ **stock book** libro *m* de inventario; **stock check** balance *m* de inventario; **stock clearance** liquidación *f* de existencias; **stock control** control *m* de existencias *or* stock; **stock controller** encargado(a) *m,f* de almacén; **stock control system** sistema *m* de control de existencias *or* stock; **stock in hand** existencias *fpl* disponibles, stock *m* disponible; **stock issued form** formulario *m or Méx* forma *f* de salida de almacén; *esp US* **stock outage** falta *f* de existencias *or* stock; **stock received form** formulario *m or Méx* forma *f* de entrada en almacén; **stock sheet** hoja *f* de almacén; **stock shortage** escasez *f* de existencias; **stock turnover** rotación *f* de existencias; **stock turnover ratio** coeficiente *m* de rotación de existencias; **stock valuation** valoración *f* de existencias; **stock wastage** pérdida *f* por deterioro de existencias

(**b**) ST EXCH *(shares)* acciones *fpl*; *(government bonds)* obligaciones *fpl* del Estado; **stocks and shares** valores *mpl* ❑ *US* **stock average** índice *m* bursátil; *US* **stock certificate** título *m* de acción; *US* **stock company** sociedad *f* anónima;

stock dividend dividendo *m* en acciones; **stock exchange** bolsa *f* (de valores); **the Stock Exchange** la Bolsa; **stock exchange committee** cámara *f* de agentes de cambio; **Stock Exchange crash** crack *m* bursátil; **Stock Exchange Daily Official List** = boletín de la Bolsa de Londres; **stock exchange dealer** agente *mf* de cambio y bolsa, corredor(ora) *m,f* de bolsa; **stock exchange order** orden *f* bursátil; **stock exchange transaction** operación *f* bursátil; **stock index** índice *m* bursátil; **stock list** *(department)* departamento *m* de cotizaciones; **stock market** mercado *m* bursátil *or* de valores; **the Stock Market** la Bolsa; **stock market boom** auge *m* bursátil; **stock market bubble** burbuja *f* bursátil; **stock market crash** crack *m* bursátil; **stock market fluctuation** fluctuación *f* de la bolsa; **stock market forecast** predicción *f* bursátil; **stock market index** índice *m* bursátil; **stock market investment** inversión *f* bursátil; **stock market manipulation** manipulación *f* de la bolsa; **stock market prices** precios *mpl* del mercado de valores; **stock market report** boletín *m* de la bolsa; **stock market value** valor *m* en el mercado de valores; **stock option** opción *f* sobre acciones; **stock option plan** plan *m* de opción de compra de acciones; **stock price level** nivel *m* de precios de las acciones; **stock purchase plan** plan *m* de opción de compra de acciones; **stock transfer** transferencia *f* de acciones

2 *vt* (**a**) *(supply)* surtir, abastecer (**with** de); **the shop is well stocked** la tienda está bien surtida *or* abastecida (**b**) *(have in stock)* vender; **we don't stock that item any more** ya no vendemos ese artículo

stockbroker *n* ST EXCH *(person)* agente *mf* de cambio y bolsa, corredor(ora) *m,f* de bolsa; *(company)* agencia *f* de cambio y bolsa ❑ **stockbroker belt** = cinturón formado por zonas residenciales exclusivas que rodean una gran ciudad; **stockbroker's clerk** agente *mf* auxiliar de bolsa

---

❝

A farmer killed in a shooting accident had acquired squatter's rights over 57 acres of prime development land in Berkshire, a high court judge ruled yesterday. The four fields, which would be worth millions with planning consent, are on the outskirts of Henwick, near Thatcham, in one of the most desirable parts of the county's **stockbroker belt**.

❞

---

stockbroking *n* ST EXCH correduría *f* de bolsa ❑ **stockbroking firm** agencia *f* de cambio y bolsa

stockholder *n US* ST EXCH accionista *mf* ❑ **stockholder's equity** fondos *mpl* propios, patrimonio *m* neto

stockholding *n* ST EXCH participación *f* accionarial *or Am* accionaria

stock-in-trade n actividad f principal

stockist n distribuidor(ora) m,f

stockjobber n (**a**) Br ST EXCH Formerly agente mf (libre) de bolsa (**b**) US Pej (broker) corredor(ora) m,f de bolsa

stockkeeper n US ganadero(a) m,f

stockkeeping n US ganadería f

stockless purchase plan n plan f de adquisición de existencias

stocklist n (**a**) (inventory) inventario m; **to make a stocklist of goods** hacer inventario de mercancías (**b**) ST EXCH lista f de acciones

stockpicker n ST EXCH analista mf de inversiones

stockpicking n ST EXCH análisis m inv de inversiones

stockpile 1 n reservas fpl
2 vt acumular, hacer acopio de

stockroom n almacén m

stocktake vi hacer inventario

stocktaking n inventario m, balance m de existencias; **to do the stocktaking** hacer inventario; **stocktaking is in February** hacemos inventario en febrero ▫ **stocktaking sale** liquidación f de existencias

stop 1 n ST EXCH **stop loss** orden f (de) stop; **stop order** orden f (de) stop; **stop payment advice** aviso m de suspensión de pago
2 vt Br (withhold) **to stop payment** suspender el pago; **to stop a cheque** bloquear el pago de un cheque; **to stop sb's wages** retener el sueldo de alguien; **the money will be stopped out of your wages** se le retendrá ese dinero de su sueldo

stop-go policy n Br ECON política f de frenado y aceleración, política de contracción y expansión

stop-loss adj ST EXCH **stop-loss order** orden f (de) stop; **stop-loss selling** venta f para limitar las pérdidas

stoppage n (**a**) (strike) paro m (**b**) Br (sum deducted) retención f; **my wages are a lot less after stoppages** si se descuentan las retenciones mi sueldo es mucho menor

storage n (**a**) (action) almacenamiento m, almacenaje m; **we are running out of storage** nos estamos quedando sin espacio en el almacén; **the goods are in storage** las mercancías están en el almacén; **to put sth into storage** almacenar algo ▫ **storage capacity** capacidad f de almacenamiento or almacenaje; **storage charges** gastos mpl de almacenamiento or almacenaje; **storage facilities** instalaciones fpl de almacenamiento or almacenaje
(**b**) COMPTR almacenamiento m ▫ **storage capacity** capacidad f de almacenamiento; **storage device** dispositivo m de almacenamiento;

storage medium medio m de almacenamiento

store 1 n (**a**) (supply) reserva f, provisión f (**b**) (warehouse) almacén m (**c**) (large shop) grandes almacenes mpl, Am grandes tiendas fpl; US (shop) tienda f ▫ MKTG **store audit** auditoría f de ventas; MKTG **store brand** marca f propia or blanca; **store card** tarjeta f de compra (a crédito); **store manager** director(ora) m,f del establecimiento
2 vt (**a**) (goods) almacenar (**b**) COMPTR almacenar

stored production n ACCT producción f almacenada

storefront n US fachada f (de tienda)

storehouse n almacén m

storekeeper n (**a**) (in warehouse) almacenista mf, almacenero(a) m,f (**b**) US (shopkeeper) tendero(a) m,f

storeroom n almacén m

straddle n ST EXCH cono m, straddle m; **to take a straddle position** comprar a un vencimiento y vender a otro

straight-line adj ACCT **straight-line depreciation** amortización f lineal; **straight-line depreciation method** método m de amortización lineal; **straight-line method** método m lineal; **straight-line rate** tarifa f constante

strapline n MKTG eslogan m de marca

> ❝
> The publication has been given a striking cover-to-cover redesign and the new **strapline** – Create the home you'll love to live in – encapsulates the mix of inspiration and practical advice that is woven together throughout the title.
> ❞

strategic adj estratégico(a) ▫ **strategic business plan** plan m estratégico de negocio; **strategic business unit** unidad f estratégica de negocio; **strategic fit** complementariedad f estratégica; **strategic group** grupo m estratégico; **strategic management** gestión f estratégica; **strategic marketing** marketing m estratégico; **strategic planning** planificación f estratégica; **strategic position** posición f estratégica; **strategic positioning** posicionamiento m estratégico; **strategic review** revisión f estratégica; **strategic segmentation** segmentación f estratégica; **strategic targeting** fijación f estratégica de objetivos; **strategic withdrawal** (of product, campaign) retirada f estratégica

strategically adv estratégicamente

strategy n estrategia f

stratified adj MKTG **stratified sample** muestra f estratificada; **stratified sampling** muestreo m estratificado

straw boss n US Fam supervisor(ora) m,f

stream *vt* COMPTR reproducir en tiempo real

streaming *n* COMPTR reproducción *f* en tiempo real

streamline *vt (production, methods, department, industry)* racionalizar; *(company)* sanear

> " ──────────────────
>
> The sweeping restructuring, including plans to scrap the second delivery, **streamline** the transport network and outsource some non-core operations is expected to cost £2.4bn. The plan is being underpinned by a package of measures announced yesterday by the government.
>
> ────────────────── "

streamlined *adj (production, methods, department, industry)* racionalizado(a); *(company)* saneado(a)

streamlining *n (of production, methods, department, industry)* racionalización *f*; *(of company)* saneamiento *m*

street *n* ST EXCH **street dealing** contratación *f* no oficial de valores; **street directory** *Esp* callejero *m*, *Am* guía *f* de calles, *Arg* plano *m* de calles; ST EXCH **street market** mercado *m* en horas no oficiales; **street price** ST EXCH cotización *f* no oficial; *(of retail goods)* precio *m* en las tiendas

strength *n (of product, company, currency, economy)* fuerza *f* ❑ MKTG **strengths, weaknesses, opportunities and threats** fortalezas, debilidades, oportunidades y amenazas

strengthen **1** *vt (financial position, currency, economy)* fortalecer
2 *vi (financial position, currency, economy)* fortalecerse

stressor *n* factor *m* de estrés

stress-related illness *n* enfermedad *f* relacionada con el estrés

strike 1 *n* **(a)** *(of workers)* huelga *f*; **to be on strike** estar en huelga; **to come out** *or* **go on strike** declararse en huelga ❑ **strike ballot** = voto para decidir si se va a la huelga; INS **strike clause** cláusula *f* de huelga; **strike fund** *Esp* caja *f* de resistencia, *Am* fondo *m* de huelga; **strike leader** líder *mf* de la huelga; **strike notice** aviso *m* de huelga; **strike pay** subsidio *m* de huelga **(b)** ST EXCH **strike price** precio *m* de ejercicio
2 *vt (agreement)* llegar a; **to strike a bargain** *or* **deal** hacer un trato
3 *vi (workers) (go on strike)* hacer huelga, declararse en huelga; *(be on strike)* estar en huelga; **they're striking for more pay** están en huelga para conseguir un aumento de sueldo

strikebound *adj* paralizado(a) por una huelga

strikebreaker *n Esp* esquirol *mf*, *Am* rompehuelgas *mf inv*

striker *n* huelguista *mf*

striking price *n* ST EXCH precio *m* de ejercicio

string *n* **(a)** COMPTR *(of characters)* cadena *f* **(b)** **to pull strings** mover los hilos; **somebody pulled strings to get him the job** alguien movió los hilos para conseguirle el trabajo; **with no strings attached** sin compromiso

strip mall *n US* calle *f* comercial

> " ──────────────────
>
> Naturally, you have to feel comfortable making transactions over the Internet. Although an online broker-banker is likely to have branches for times when you crave a tete-a-tete transaction, chances are it won't be as convenient as the bank at your local **strip mall**.
>
> ────────────────── "

stripped bond *n* ST EXCH bono *m* sin cupón

strong *adj (market, price)* pujante; *(currency, economy)* fuerte; **the pound is getting stronger** la libra está cada vez más fuerte

strongroom *n* cámara *f* acorazada

struck *adj US (industry, factory)* en huelga

structural *adj* ECON **structural adjustment programme** programa *m* de ajuste estructural; **structural change** cambio *m* estructural; EU **structural funds** fondos *mpl* estructurales; **structural unemployment** desempleo *m* estructural

structure 1 *n (method, process)* estructura *f*
2 *vt* estructurar ❑ MKTG **structured interview** entrevista *f* estructurada

stub *n (of cheque)* talón *m*, *Esp* matriz *f*

study *n (of market, feasibility)* estudio *m* ❑ **study group** grupo *m* de estudio

stuffer *n* MKTG volante *m* publicitario

► stump up *Br Fam* **1** *vt insep* **to stump up the money (for sth)** poner *or Esp* apoquinar el dinero (para algo)
2 *vi* poner dinero, *Esp* apoquinar (**for** para)

stumpage *n US* madera *f*

style *n* COMPTR **style bar** barra *f* de estilos; **style sheet** hoja *f* de estilos

subaccount *n* ACCT subcuenta *f*

sub-agency *n* subagencia *f*

sub-agent *n* subagente *mf*

subcommittee *n* subcomité *m*

subcontract 1 *n* subcontrato *m*
2 *vt (work, order)* subcontratar; **they subcontract some of the work (out) to local firms** subcontratan parte del trabajo a empresas de la zona
3 *vi* subcontratar; **they have a lot of small companies who subcontract for them** tienen muchas subcontratas con pequeñas empresas

subcontracting *n* subcontratación *f*; **we do a lot of subcontracting for larger firms** hacemos muchas subcontratas para grandes empresas ❑ *subcontracting agreement* acuerdo *m* de subcontratación

subcontractor *n* subcontratista *mf*

subdirectory *n* COMPTR subdirectorio *m*

subheading *n* subtítulo *m*

subject *adj (liable)* **to be subject to sth** *(fine, taxation, commission)* estar sujeto(a) a algo; **the price is subject to a handling charge** el precio está sujeto a una tarifa por gastos de gestión; **the terms are subject to alteration without notice** los términos se podrían modificar sin previo aviso

sublease 1 *n* subarriendo *m*
    2 *vt* realquilar, subarrendar

subledger *n* ACCT libro *m* mayor auxiliar

sublessee *n* subarrendatario(a) *m,f*

sublessor *n* subarrendador(ora) *m,f*

sublet 1 *n* subarriendo *m*
    2 *vt* realquilar, subarrendar

subletter *n* subarrendador(ora) *m,f*

subletting *n* subarrendamiento *m*

subliminal advertising *n* publicidad *f* subliminal

submarket *n* submercado *m*

submenu *n* COMPTR submenú *m*

submit *vt (tender, report)* entregar

subordinate 1 *n* subordinado(a) *m,f*
    2 *adj (job, position)* inferior; **to be subordinate to sb** estar subordinado(a) a alguien

subordinated debt *n* deuda *f* subordinada

subrogation *n* LAW subrogación *f*

subroutine *n* COMPTR subrutina *f*

subscribe 1 *vt* FIN *(shares)* suscribir ❑ *subscribed capital* capital *m* suscrito
    2 *vi* (**a**) *(to newspaper, magazine)* suscribirse (**to** a); *(to ISP)* abonarse (**to** a) (**b**) FIN **to subscribe for shares in a company** suscribir acciones de una compañía

subscriber *n* (**a**) *(to newspaper, magazine)* suscriptor(ora) *m,f*, abonado(a) *m,f*; *(to Internet service)* usuario(a) *m,f*, cliente *mf* (**b**) FIN *(to share issue)* suscriptor(ora) *m,f*, solicitante *mf* (**c**) *(of new company)* firmante *mf* de la escritura de constitución

subscription *n* (**a**) *(to newspaper, magazine)* suscripción *f*; *(to Internet service)* conexión *f*; **to take out a subscription to sth** suscribirse/conectarse a algo ❑ *subscription form* boletín *m* de suscripción; *subscription rate (to newspaper, magazine)* precio *m* de suscripción; *(to Internet service)* cuota *f* de conexión (**b**) FIN *(to share issue)* suscripción *f* ❑ *subscription list* lista *f* de suscriptores; *subscription right* derecho *m* de suscripción

subsidiarity *n* subsidiariedad *f*

subsidiary 1 *n (company)* filial *f*, subsidiaria *f*
    2 *adj (goal, position, product)* secundario(a) ❑ *subsidiary account* cuenta *f* subsidiaria; LAW *subsidiary claim* reclamación *f* subsidiaria, SAm reclamo *m* subsidiario; *subsidiary company* filial *f*, empresa *f* subsidiaria

subsidize *vt* subvencionar; **the company was subsidized to the tune of £3 million** la compañía recibió subvenciones por un valor de tres millones de libras ❑ *subsidized industry* industria *f* subvencionada

subsidy *n* subvención *f*, subsidio *m*

sub-standard *adj (goods)* deficiente

substitute *n (product)* sustituto *m* ❑ *substitute good* bien *m* sustitutivo

substitution *n* sustitución *f* ❑ FIN *substitution of debt* traspaso *m* de deuda; *substitution effect* efecto *m* de sustitución; *substitution market* mercado *m* de sustitución

subtenancy *n* subarrendamiento *m*

subtenant *n* subarrendatario(a) *m,f*

subvention *n* US subvención *f*

success *n* éxito *m* ❑ *success fee* comisión *f* por éxito *or* por resultados

successor *n* sucesor(ora) *m,f*

sue LAW **1** *vt* demandar (**for** por); **he sued the factory for damages** demandó a la fábrica por daños y perjuicios
    2 *vi* ir a juicio

suicide pill *n (in takeover)* píldora *f* suicida, = píldora venenosa que acaba con la compañía objeto de la OPA

suit *n* LAW pleito *m*, demanda *f*; **to bring** *or* **to file a suit against sb** presentar una demanda contra alguien

suite *n* COMPTR *(of software)* paquete *m* integrado

sum *n (of money)* suma *f*, importe *m* ❑ *sum advanced* anticipo *m*; *sum in excess* cantidad *f* excedente; *sum payable* importe *m* a pagar; *sum at risk (in term insurance)* capital *m* asegurado

summary *n* resumen *m* ❑ ACCT *summary balance sheet* balance *m* condensado; *summary dismissal* despido *m* inmediato; *summary report* informe *m* resumido

summit *n (meeting)* cumbre *f*; **to hold a summit** celebrar una (reunión en la) cumbre ❑ *summit conference* conferencia *f* en la cumbre

summon *vt (person, meeting)* convocar; LAW *(witness)* citar

summons LAW **1** *n* citación *f*
    2 *vt* citar

sundry 1 *n* **sundries** *(items)* artículos *mpl* varios; *(costs)* gastos *mpl* diversos
2 *adj* diversos(as) ❑ **sundry charges** gastos *mpl* diversos; **sundry expenses** gastos *mpl* diversos; **sundry income** ingresos *mpl* diversos

sunk costs *npl* costos *mpl* or *Esp* costes *mpl* hundidos

sunrise industry *n* industria *f* de tecnología punta

> **"**
>
> The war against terrorism has left corporate America in a cleft stick. On the one hand, the kneejerk reaction of business is to retrench – rapidly – after the terrorist attacks. After all, the renaissance of US industry in the 1990s has been a story not just of American dominance in **sunrise industries**, but also ruthless cost-cutting to make firms more efficient.
>
> **"**

sunset industry *n* industria *f* tradicional

superannuate *vt* (**a**) *(person)* jubilar (**b**) *(machine)* retirar, jubilar

superannuated *adj* (**a**) *(person)* jubilado(a); *(job, post)* con plan de jubilación incluido (**b**) *(machine)* anticuado(a), obsoleto(a)

superannuation *n* *(act of retiring)* jubilación *f*; *(pension)* pensión *f* (de jubilación); *(contribution)* cotización *f* ❑ **superannuation fund** fondo *m* de pensiones

supercomputer *n* COMPTR *Esp* superordenador *m*, *Am* supercomputadora *f*

superhighway *n* COMPTR (**information**) **superhighway** autopista *f* de la información

supermajority *n* mayoría *f* cualificada *or* calificada

supermarket *n* supermercado *m* ❑ **supermarket bank** = banco perteneciente a una cadena de supermercados

superstock *n* *US* ST EXCH acciones *mpl* con doble derecho a voto

superstore *n* hipermercado *m*, gran superficie *f*

supertax *n* impuesto *m* adicional *(sobre las grandes fortunas)*

supervise *vt* supervisar

supervision *n* supervisión *f*

supervisor *n* supervisor(ora) *m,f*

supervisory board *n* consejo *m* de supervisión, = consejo en el que se sientan representantes de los trabajadores y la empresa y que supervisa las acciones de la junta directiva

supplement 1 *n* (**a**) *(addition, extra charge)* suplemento *m*; **a supplement is charged for occupying a single room** hay un suplemento por el uso de una habitación individual (**b**) *(to newspaper, magazine)* suplemento *m*
2 *vt* complementar, suplementar

supplementary *adj* ACCT **supplementary entry** asiento *m* suplementario; **supplementary pension** pensión *f* suplementaria

supplier *n* proveedor(ora) *m,f* ❑ **supplier base** base *f* de proveedores; **supplier code** código *m* del proveedor; ACCT **supplier credit** crédito *m* de proveedor; **supplier file** ficha *f* del proveedor

supply 1 *n* (**a**) ECON oferta *f*; **supply and demand** la oferta y la demanda ❑ **supply curve** curva *f* de la oferta; **supply and demand mechanism** mecanismo *m* de la oferta y la demanda; **supply price** precio *m* de oferta
(**b**) *(stock)* **our supplies of stationery are running out** se nos está agotando el material de oficina; **we are expecting a new supply of microchips** estamos esperando la llegada de una nueva remesa de microchips; **this type of paper is in short supply** este tipo de papel escasea
(**c**) *(act of supplying)* suministro *m*
2 *vt* *(goods, services)* suministrar; **to supply sb with sth, to supply sth to sb** suministrar algo a alguien; **they supply all the local retailers** abastecen a todos los pequeños comerciantes de la zona

supply-side economics *n* economía *f* de la oferta

support 1 *n* (**a**) *(funding)* ayuda *f*; **they depend on the government for financial support** dependen del gobierno para obtener ayuda financiera; **what are your means of support?** ¿con qué recursos cuenta? ❑ EU **support price** precio *m* subvencionado
(**b**) *(backing)* apoyo *m*, respaldo *m* (**for** a); **to give** *or* **lend one's support to sth/sb** apoyar *or* respaldar algo/a alguien ❑ **support activities** actividades *fpl* auxiliares; **support services** servicios *mpl* de apoyo; **support staff** personal *m* auxiliar
(**c**) COMPTR asistencia *f* técnica, soporte *m* ❑ **support line** línea *f* de asistencia técnica
2 *vt* (**a**) *(financially)* *(family)* mantener; *(company, project)* financiar (**b**) *(back)* apoyar (**c**) COMPTR soportar; **this package is supported by all workstations** este paquete funciona en todas las estaciones de trabajo (**d**) FIN *(price, currency)* apoyar

supporting document *n* documento *m* justificativo, comprobante *m*

surcharge 1 *n* *(on price, imports, tax)* recargo *m*; **a 7% import surcharge** un recargo del 7% en las importaciones
2 *vt* *(price, imports, taxpayer)* aplicar un recargo a

surety *n* *(person)* fiador(ora) *m,f*, garante *mf*; *(collateral)* fianza *f*, garantía *f*; **to stand surety (for sb)** ser fiador(ora) *or* garante (de alguien)

surf *vt* COMPTR **to surf the Net** navegar por Internet

surface *n* **surface mail** correo *m* por vía terrestre *or* por superficie; **by surface mail** por vía terrestre; **surface transport** transporte *m* terrestre

surfeit *n* exceso *m* (**of** de); **there is a surfeit of imported goods** hay un exceso de importaciones

surge 1 *n* incremento *m* repentino, subida *f* repentina
   2 *vi* incrementarse *or* subir repentinamente; **stock markets surged on announcement of the decision** el anuncio de la decisión provocó un alza repentina de las bolsas

surname *n* apellido *m*

surplus 1 *n* (**a**) *(of product, stock, commodity)* excedente *m*; **EU grain surpluses** excedentes comunitarios de grano; **Japan's trade surplus** el excedente comercial de Japón □ **surplus produce** excedentes *fpl* agrícolas; **surplus stock** excedentes *mpl* (**b**) ACCT superávit *m inv*; **we have a surplus of assets over liabilities** tenemos un excedente del activo sobre el pasivo, tenemos superávit
   2 *adj (items)* excedentario(a); **they export their surplus agricultural produce** exportan sus excedentes agrícolas; **these employees are now surplus to requirements** esos empleados ahora sobran □ **surplus production** producción *f* excedentaria; **surplus stock** existencias *fpl* excedentarias

surrender 1 *n* INS *(of policy)* rescate *m* □ **surrender value** valor *m* de rescate
   2 *vt (right)* renunciar a; INS *(policy)* rescatar

surtax 1 *n* impuesto *m* adicional
   2 *vt* aplicar un impuesto adicional a

survey 1 *n* (**a**) Br *(of building) (inspection)* inspección *f*, peritaje *m*; *(report)* informe *m*, peritaje (**b**) *(study, investigation)* estudio *m*; **they carried out a survey of retail prices** realizaron un estudio sobre los precios de venta al público (**c**) *(opinion poll)* encuesta *f* □ **survey research** investigación *f* por *or* mediante encuestas
   2 *vt* (**a**) Br *(building)* tasar, peritar (**b**) *(study, investigate)* estudiar; **the report surveys the current state of the manufacturing industry** el informe estudia el estado actual de la industria manufacturera (**c**) *(poll)* encuestar; **65% of women surveyed were opposed to the measure** el 65% de las mujeres encuestadas se opuso a la medida

surveyor *n* (**a**) Br *(of building)* tasador(ora) *m,f* or perito(a) *m,f* de la propiedad (**b**) *(of land)* agrimensor(ora) *m,f*

survivor's pension *n* pensión *f* para los beneficiarios

suspect *n* MKTG cliente *m* potencial □ **suspect**

pool base *f* de clientes potenciales

suspend *vt* (**a**) *(payment)* suspender; **the government has suspended the repayment of foreign debts** el gobierno ha suspendido el pago de la deuda externa (**b**) *(employee)* suspender

suspense account *n* cuenta *f* transitoria *or* de orden

suspension *n* (**a**) *(of payment)* suspensión *f* (**b**) *(of employee)* suspensión *f* (**c**) **suspension file** archivo *m* colgante

sustainability *n* sostenibilidad *f*

sustainable *adj (agriculture, resource, environment)* sostenible □ **sustainable development** desarrollo *m* sostenible

sustained yield *n* ECON rendimiento *m* sostenido

SVGA *n* COMPTR *(abbr* **Super Video Graphics Array)** SVGA *m* □ **SVGA monitor** monitor *m* SVGA

swap 1 *n* BANKING, ST EXCH swap *m*, permuta *f* □ **swap agreement** acuerdo *m* de swap *or* permuta; **swap facilities** facilidades *fpl* de swap *or* permuta; **swap option** contrato *m* de opción sobre permuta
   2 *vt* ST EXCH intercambiar; **to swap sth for sth** intercambiar algo por algo

swaption *n* ST EXCH contrato *m* de opción sobre permuta

> "
> In addition to buying the gilts, Scottish Widows has been trying to peg its interest rate exposure by arranging deals to borrow from big companies or buy complex derivatives instruments known as **swaptions**.
> "

sweat equity *n* US = incremento del capital del patrimonio logrado mediante los esfuerzos de la dirección

> "
> While the terms of these two deals were not disclosed, it is generally believed that agencies can go for 1.5 times their revenue. In Burrell's case, that could amount to $32.7 million, according to Advertising Age. "These mergers are good because they recognize the **sweat equity** that multicultural agencies have put into the business", says the AAAA's Donahue.
> "

sweatshop *n* = fábrica donde se explota al trabajador; **illegal sweatshops** talleres *mpl* clandestinos

sweetheart deal *n* IND = acuerdo interesado entre patronal y sindicatos que puede no ser del todo favorable para los trabajadores

SWIFT *n* (*abbr* **Society for Worldwide Interbank Financial Telecommunication**) SWIFT *m* ❑ **SWIFT code** código *m* SWIFT

swingline *adj (loan, credit)* a muy corto plazo

swing shift *n US (work period, team)* turno *m* de tarde y noche

swipe 1 *n* **swipe card** tarjeta *f* con banda magnética
　2 *vt (card)* pasar

Swiss franc *n* franco *m* suizo

switch 1 *n* (**a**) ST EXCH **switch trading** arbitraje *m* (**b**) *Br* **Switch®** = sistema de tarjeta de débito aceptado en la mayoría de las tiendas del Reino Unido ❑ **Switch® card** = tarjeta de débito que usa el sistema Switch®
　2 *vt* ST EXCH **to switch a position** intercambiar contratos con diferentes fechas de vencimiento

switchboard *n* centralita *f*, *Am* conmutador *m* ❑ **switchboard operator** telefonista *mf*

switching *n* ST EXCH compraventa *f* de contratos con diferentes fechas de vencimiento

sworn statement *n* declaración *f* jurada

SWOT *n* MKTG (*abbr* **strengths, weaknesses, opportunities, threats**) DAFO *m* ❑ **SWOT analysis** análisis *m inv* DAFO

> ❝
> ... a **SWOT** (Strength, Weakness, Opportunity and Threat) analysis is a fundamental tool in corporate strategic planning. Once planners have conducted a **SWOT analysis**, they are in a position to articulate the mission, strategy, and objectives of the organization.
> ❞

symbol *n* símbolo *m*

sympathy *n* **to come out in sympathy with sb**

declararse en huelga de solidaridad con alguien ❑ **sympathy strike** huelga *f* de solidaridad *or* apoyo

syndicate 1 *n* consorcio *m*; **to form a syndicate** formar un consorcio; **the loan was underwritten by a syndicate of banks** el préstamo estaba garantizado por un consorcio bancario; **a syndicate of British and French companies** un consorcio de empresas británicas y francesas
　2 *vt* FIN **syndicated credit** crédito *m* sindicado; **syndicated loan** préstamo *m* sindicado; **syndicated shares** acciones *fpl* sindicadas

synergistic *adj* sinérgico(a)

synergy *n* sinergia *f*

syntax *n* COMPTR sintaxis *f inv* ❑ **syntax error** error *m* de sintaxis

SYSOP *n* COMPTR (*abbr* **Systems Operator**) operador(ora) *m,f* del sistema

system *n* (**a**) *(structure, method)* sistema *m*; **a new system of sorting mail** un nuevo sistema de clasificación del correo ❑ **systems and procedures** sistemas *mpl* y procedimientos
(**b**) COMPTR sistema *m* ❑ **systems analysis** análisis *m inv* de sistemas; **systems analyst** analista *mf* de sistemas; **system clock** reloj *m* del sistema; **system crash** bloqueo *m* or caída *f* del sistema; **system disk** disco *m* de sistema; **systems engineering** ingeniería *f* de sistemas; **system error** error *m* del sistema; **system failure** *Esp* fallo *m or Am* falla *f* del sistema; **system file** archivo *m or* fichero *m* del sistema; **system folder** carpeta *f* del sistema; **systems management** gestión *f* de sistemas; **system prompt** mensaje *m* del sistema; **system software** software *m* de sistema

systematic *adj* sistemático(a)

Tt

tab 1 *n (on typewriter, word processor)* tabulador *m*; **to set tabs (at)** establecer *or* fijar tabulaciones (en) ❑ **tab key** tecla *f* de tabulación, tabulador *m*; **tab points** posiciones *fpl or* puntos *mpl* de tabulación, posición *f* de las tabulaciones; **tab setting** fijación *f* de (las) tabulaciones; **tab stop** parada *f* de tabulación
2 *vt (text)* tabular

table 1 *n* (**a**) *(chart, list)* tabla *f*, cuadro *m*; **the results are set out in the following table** los resultados se exponen en el siguiente cuadro ❑ **table of account codes** tabla *f* de imputaciones; **table of contents** índice *m* de materias (**b**) *(furniture)* mesa *f*; **to get round the negotiating table** sentarse a negociar
2 *vt* **to table a motion/proposal** *Br (present)* presentar una moción/propuesta; *US (postpone)* aplazar la discusión de una moción/propuesta

tabloid *n (paper size, format)* tamaño *m or* formato *m* tabloide; *(newspaper)* diario *m* popular *or* sensacionalista *(de formato tabloide)*

tabular *adj (statistics, figures)* tabular; **in tabular form** en forma tabular

tabulate *vt* (**a**) *(present in table form)* tabular (**b**) *(classify)* clasificar

tabulator *n* tabulador *m*

tactical *adj* táctico(a)

tactics *npl* táctica *f*

tag 1 *n* (**a**) *(showing price)* etiqueta *f* (**b**) COMPTR *(code)* etiqueta *f*
2 *vt* (**a**) *(fix label to)* etiquetar; *US* **it was tagged at $39.95** la etiqueta marcaba 39,95 dólares (**b**) COMPTR etiquetar

take 1 *n* Fam *(takings)* recaudación *f*; *(share)* parte *f*
2 *vt* (**a**) *(remove)* **to take an amount out of one's income** descontar *or* deducir una cantidad de los ingresos; **to take sth off the market** retirar algo del mercado
(**b**) *(receive) (money)* **she takes home £3,000 a month** gana 3.000 libras mensuales netas
(**c**) *(accept)* aceptar; **he won't take less** no aceptará menos; **will you take a cheque?** ¿se puede pagar con cheque?, ¿aceptan cheques?; **does the machine take pound coins?** ¿la máquina acepta monedas de una libra?
(**d**) *(write down) (name and address)* tomar, anotar; *(notes)* tomar; **to take a letter** tomar nota

de una carta; **to take the minutes** levantar las actas

▶ **take back** *vt sep* (**a**) *(employee)* readmitir; **the factory took back the workers** la fábrica readmitió a los trabajadores (**b**) *(goods)* devolver; **take it back to the shop** devuélvelo (a la tienda)

▶ **take off** *vt sep* (**a**) *(deduct)* quitar, descontar; **he took 10% off the price** aplicó un 10% de descuento sobre el precio, rebajó el precio en un 10% (**b**) *(time)* **to take a day off** tomarse un día libre; **she takes Thursdays off** descansa los jueves

▶ **take on** *vt sep* (**a**) *(worker)* contratar (**b**) *(responsibility, task)* asumir; *(new contract, customer)* aceptar

▶ **take out** *vt sep (patent)* registrar; *(permit, licence)* sacarse; *(insurance policy)* contratar, suscribir; **to take out a mortgage** contratar una hipoteca; **to take out a subscription (to sth)** suscribirse (a algo)

▶ **take over 1** *vt sep (company) (buy out)* adquirir; *(become responsible for)* hacerse cargo de; **they were taken over by a Japanese firm** fueron adquiridos por una empresa japonesa; ST EXCH **to take over an issue** absorber una emisión
2 *vi (new manager)* tomar posesión; **to take over from sb** *(replace)* tomar el relevo de alguien

▶ **take up** *vt sep* (**a**) *(offer)* aceptar; **to take sb up on an offer** aceptar una oferta de alguien (**b**) FIN *(bill)* pagar; ST EXCH *(option)* ejecutar; *(shares)* suscribir (**c**) *(position)* tomar; *(post)* asumir; **she took up her duties** se incorporó a su puesto

take-home pay *n* paga *f* neta, sueldo *m* neto

takeover *n (of company)* adquisición *f* ❑ **takeover bid** oferta *f* pública de adquisición (de acciones), OPA *f*; **to be the subject of a takeover bid** ser objeto de una OPA; ST EXCH **takeover stock** valores *mpl* opables

taker *n* **there were no takers for the offer** nadie aceptó la oferta; **without more information there will be few takers** sin más información habrá pocos interesados

> The 400,000-square-foot Robinsons building had been shuttered for several years and was owned by private investors. There

were **no takers** from the retail world in subsequent years – both Target and Price Club passed on it. _"_

take-up n (of share offer) grado m de aceptación; (of benefit) número m de solicitudes; **there has been a 10% take-up of the grants** se han otorgado el 10% de las subvenciones

takings npl recaudación f; (in shop) caja f, ventas fpl; (in theatre, cinema, stadium) taquilla f, Am boletería f; **the day's takings** las ventas del día

talks npl (negotiations) conversaciones fpl

tally 1 n (record) cuenta f; **to keep a tally of sth** llevar la cuenta de algo ◻ COMPTR **tally file** archivo m or fichero m contador
2 vt (goods) hacer el recuento de
3 vi (figures, accounts) cuadrar, concordar (**with** con); **these accounts do not tally** estas cuentas no cuadran

tangible ACCT 1 n **tangibles** activos mpl tangibles, bienes mpl tangibles or materiales
2 adj tangible ◻ **tangible assets** activos mpl tangibles, bienes mpl tangibles or materiales; **tangible fixed assets** inmovilizado m fijo or material; **tangible movables** bienes mpl muebles tangibles

tankage n (storing in tanks) almacenamiento m en tanques, tancaje m; (storage fee) canon m de almacenamiento en tanque; (capacity) capacidad f de tanque

tap n FIN = valor que forma parte de una emisión continua; **long/medium/short tap** valor a corto/medio/largo plazo ◻ **tap issue** = emisión continua de determinados valores del estado; **tap stock** = valor que forma parte de una emisión continua

tape n COMPTR cinta f ◻ **tape backup** copia f de seguridad en cinta; **tape backup system** sistema m de copia de seguridad en cinta; **tape backup unit** unidad f de copias de seguridad en cinta; **tape unit** unidad f de cinta

tapering adj FIN (rate) escalonado(a) ◻ **tapering charge** facturación f decreciente

taper relief n Br = reducción progresiva del impuesto sobre la plusvalía o sobre donaciones en función de tiempo durante el que se es propietario de un bien

_"_
Everyone has this £3,000 limit and, if it's not used up in one year, the amount can be carried forward to the next. After three years, the tax payable on a gift starts reducing until it reaches nil at year seven. Small gifts of up to £250 can be made to any number of people. This is known as **taper relief**.
_"_

tare n tara f; **to allow for the tare** tener en cuenta la tara

TARGET n EU, BANKING (abbr **Trans-European Automated Real-Time Gross Settlement Transfer System**) (sistema m) TARGET m

target 1 n (objective) objetivo m, meta f; **to meet production targets** alcanzar los objetivos de producción; **to be on target** (plans) ir según lo previsto; (productivity) ir cumpliendo los objetivos
2 adj MKTG **target audience** (of product) público m objetivo or target; MKTG **target buyer** comprador(ora) m,f objetivo or target; **target company** (in takeover bid) empresa f objeto de una OPA; MKTG **target consumer** consumidor(ora) m,f objetivo or target; **target cost** costo m or Esp coste m objetivo; **target date** plazo m previsto; COMPTR **target disk** disco m de destino; MKTG **target group** grupo m objetivo or target; MKTG **Target Group Index** = informe anual sobre el uso de productos y marcas por parte de los consumidores; MKTG **target market** mercado m objetivo or target; **target marketing** marketing m selectivo; **target population** público m objetivo or target; **target price** EU (in CAP) precio m indicativo or objetivo; (at auction) precio m mínimo; **target pricing** fijación f del precio óptimo
3 vt (TV programme) destinar, dirigir (**at** a); **the benefits are targeted at one-parent families** los subsidios están destinados or dirigidos a familias monoparentales; **the campaign targets the youth market** la campaña está dirigida al mercado juvenil

targeting n MKTG determinación f del objetivo or de los objetivos

tariff n (a) (list of prices) lista f de precios; (rate) tarifa f (b) (tax) arancel m ◻ **tariff agreement** convenio m aduanero, acuerdo m arancelario; **tariff barrier** barrera f arancelaria; **tariff laws** leyes fpl arancelarias; **tariff level indices** índices mpl arancelarios

task n tarea f ◻ **task force** grupo m de trabajo; **task sheet** hoja f de tareas

taskbar n COMPTR barra f de tareas

tax 1 n (levy) impuesto m, tributo m; (taxation) impuestos mpl; **a third of my income goes in tax** la tercera parte de mis ingresos se me va en impuestos; **I paid over $5,000 in tax** pagué más de 5.000 dólares de impuestos; **there is a high tax on whisky** el whisky está gravado con un impuesto muy elevado, el impuesto sobre el whisky es muy elevado; **to put** or **levy a 10% tax on sth** gravar algo con un 10% de impuestos; **to be liable to tax** (goods) estar sujeto(a) a impuestos; (person) estar obligado(a) a pagar impuestos; **before/after tax** antes/después de impuestos; **exclusive of tax** libre de impuestos, sin impuesto ◻ **tax adjustment** ajuste m fiscal; **tax allowance** deducción f fiscal; **tax assessment** estimación f de la base imponible; **tax**

audit auditoría *f* fiscal *or* tributaria; *tax autho- rities* autoridad *f* fiscal, administración *f* fiscal, (Administración *f* de) Hacienda *f*; *tax avoid- ance* evasión *f* legal de impuestos; *tax band* banda *f* impositiva; *tax base (people)* total *m* de contribuyentes; *(money)* recaudación *f* tributa- ria; *tax benefit* ventaja *f* fiscal; *tax bite* carga *f* impositiva, presión *f* fiscal; *tax bracket* banda *f* impositiva, tramo *m* impositivo *or* de renta; *tax break* ventaja *f* fiscal; *tax burden* carga *f* fiscal; *tax ceiling (maximum amount)* máxima cantidad *f* a abonar en impuestos; *(maximum proportion)* porcentaje *m* imponible máximo; *(upper limit of tax bracket) Esp* tipo *m* impositivo máximo, *Am* tasa *f* impositiva máxima; *tax centre* centro *m* fiscal; *tax code* código *m* impositivo; *tax collec- tor* recaudador(ora) *m,f* de impuestos; *tax con- sultant* asesor(ora) *m,f* fiscal; *tax credit* crédito *m* fiscal, descuento *m* impositivo; *tax cut* re- ducción *f* de la presión fiscal; *tax deducted at source* impuesto *m* retenido en origen; *tax de- duction* deducción *f* fiscal; *tax deduction at source* retención *f* de impuestos en origen; *tax demand* notificación *f* de deuda fiscal; *US tax dollars* dólares *mpl* de los presupuestos esta- dounidenses; *tax domicile* domicilio *m* fiscal; *tax evasion* fraude *m or* evasión *f* fiscal; *tax ex- emption* exención *f* fiscal; *tax exile (person)* exiliado(a) *m,f* fiscal; *tax form* impreso *m* de de- claración de la renta; *tax fraud* fraude *m* fiscal; *EU tax harmonization* armonización *f* fiscal; *tax haven* paraíso *m* fiscal; *tax holiday* periodo *m* de exención fiscal, vacaciones *fpl* fiscales; *tax incentive* incentivo *m* fiscal; *tax inspection* inspección *f* fiscal; *tax inspector* inspector(o- ra) *m,f* fiscal *or* de Hacienda; *tax law* derecho *m* fiscal; *tax laws* legislación *f* tributaria, leyes *fpl* fiscales; *tax liability (of person)* deuda *f* fiscal, impuesto *m* a pagar; *tax loophole* laguna *f* fis- cal; *tax loss* pérdida *f* fiscal; *tax on luxury goods* impuesto *m* sobre artículos de lujo; *tax offence* delito *m* fiscal; *tax office* oficina *f* de Hacienda, agencia *f* tributaria; *tax official* fun- cionario(a) *m,f* de Hacienda; *tax privilege* ven- taja *f or* privilegio *m* fiscal; *ACCT tax provision* provisión *f* para impuestos; *tax rate Esp* tipo *m* impositivo, *Am* tasa *f* impositiva; *tax rebate* de- volución *f* fiscal; *tax reduction* reducción *f* de impuestos, reducción *f* fiscal; *tax refund* devo- lución *f* fiscal; *tax regime* régimen *m* fiscal; *tax relief* desgravación *f* fiscal; *tax resources* re- cursos *mpl* fiscales; *tax return* declaración *f* de la renta; *tax revenue* recaudación *f* tributaria *or* fiscal; *tax roll* censo *m* fiscal *or* de contri- buyentes; *tax rules* normas *fpl* fiscales, norma- tiva *f* fiscal; *tax schedule* escala *f* de gravamen, escala *f* del impuesto; *tax shelter* refugio *m or* amparo *m* fiscal; *tax shield* amparo *m* fiscal, re- fugio *m* tributario; *tax survey* estudio *m* sobre la fiscalidad de los contribuyentes; *tax system* régimen *m* fiscal; *tax threshold* mínimo *m* exen-

to, umbral *m* impositivo; *tax on value* impuesto *m* sobre el valor; *tax wrapper* = vehículo de in- versión con un tratamiento fiscal favorable; *tax on weight* impuesto *m* sobre el peso; *tax year* ejercicio *m* fiscal, año *m* fiscal

2 *vt (goods, income, services)* gravar (con un im- puesto), aplicar un impuesto sobre; *(people)* co- brar impuestos a; *(company)* imponer una carga fiscal a; **the rich should be more heavily taxed** los ricos deberían pagar más impuestos; **luxury goods are taxed at 28%** los artículos de lujo están gravados con un impuesto del 28%; **small businesses are being taxed out of existence** los elevados impuestos están haciendo que cierren los negocios pequeños

3 *vi* **tax and spend** = política gubernamental consistente en subir los impuestos para aumen- tar el gasto en servicios públicos

> **❝**
>
> **Tax cutting** can encourage people to do the right thing. **Tax relief** for charitable giv- ing, and a **tax holiday** for charities, is ac- cepted by both major parties, and does help increase the amount of charitable money.
>
> **❞**

taxable *adj* gravable, imponible ❑ **taxable base** base *f* imponible; **taxable income** ingre- sos *mpl* sujetos a gravamen, ≃ base *f* imponible; **taxable profit** beneficio *m* imponible; **taxable transaction** operación *f* gravada, operación su- jeta al impuesto

taxation *n* **(a)** *(system)* fiscalidad *f*, sistema *m* fiscal *or* tributario; *(of person, company, goods)* imposición *f*, tributación *f*; **taxation at source** retención *f* en origen **(b)** *(taxes)* **an increase in taxation** un aumento de los impuestos

tax-deductible *adj* desgravable

tax-deferred *adj US* con aplazamiento del pa- go de impuestos, con diferimiento impositivo

tax-exempt *adj (goods, income, savings)* exen- to(a) de impuestos

tax-free *adj* libre de impuestos ❑ **tax-free shopping** compras *fpl* libres de impuestos

taxman *n Br Fam* **the taxman** el fisco, Hacien- da

> **❝**
>
> David Clowes will earn £60,000 this tax year – but he will not pay the **taxman** a penny. Mr Clowes, 54, left, who runs the London Keyholding Company, has used every tax shelter he can lay his hands on to stay out of the tax collector's hands.
>
> **❞**

taxpayer *n* contribuyente *mf*

tax-sensible *adj* con bonificación fiscal

T-bill *n US (treasury bill)* letra *m* del Tesoro

TCP/IP *n* COMPTR (*abbr* **transmission control protocol/Internet protocol**) TCP/IP *m*

TD *n US* (*abbr* **Treasury Department**) Tesoro *m* (Público), ≃ (Ministerio *m* de) Hacienda *f*

team *n* equipo *m*; **a team effort** una labor de equipo ▫ **team building** creación *f* de espíritu de equipo; **team dynamics** dinámica *f* de equipo; **team leader** jefe(a) *m,f* de equipo; **team player** buen(a) trabajador(ora) *m,f* en equipo; **team spirit** espíritu *m* de equipo

teamster *n US* camionero(a) *m,f*; **the Teamsters (Union)** = el sindicato norteamericano de camioneros

teamwork *n* trabajo *m* en *or* de equipo

teaser *n* MKTG **teaser ad** publicidad *f* teaser *or* con intriga; **teaser campaign** campaña *f* teaser

techie *n Fam* COMPTR experto(a) *m,f* en informática

technical *adj* técnico(a) ▫ **technical adviser** asesor(ora) *m,f* técnico(a); ST EXCH **technical analysis** análisis *m inv* técnico; **technical assistance, technical backup** asistencia *f* técnica, servicio *m* técnico; ST EXCH **technical correction** corrección *f* técnica; **technical department** departamento *m* técnico; **technical director** director(ora) *m,f* técnico(a); **technical equipment** material *m* técnico, instrumental *m* técnico; **technical handbook** *or* **instructions** manual *m* técnico, instrucciones *fpl* técnicas; **technical manager** director(ora) *m,f* técnico(a), gerente *mf* técnico(a); **technical skill** habilidad *f* técnica; **technical standard** estándar *m* técnico; COMPTR **technical support** servicio *m* de asistencia técnica

technician *n* técnico(a) *m,f*

technique *n* técnica *f*

technology *n* tecnología *f* ▫ **technology park** parque *m* tecnológico

teething troubles *npl* problemas *mpl* de partida; **we're having teething troubles with the new system** estamos teniendo algunos problemas iniciales con el nuevo sistema

66
Who'd have thought you could make supermarket shopping work online? Top marks to Tesco for having the vision to go ahead and do it. Despite early **teething troubles**, since its revamp this service has become simple and efficient.
99

telebanking *n* banca *f* telefónica, telebanca *f*

telecommunications *npl* telecomunicaciones *fpl* ▫ **telecommunications network** red *f* de telecomunicaciones; **telecommunications satellite** satélite *m* de telecomunicaciones

telecommute *vi* teletrabajar

telecommuter *n* teletrabajador(ora) *m,f*

telecommuting *n* teletrabajo *m*

66
For employees, **telecommuting** can be a huge boon, allowing them to live anywhere they choose and forgo the frustrations usually associated with a good job in a crowded city. For the company, the promise of a **telecommuting** program is equally grand. The company can be sure its current work force will be happier and more productive, and it can look forward to hiring the best people for the job, regardless of their locations.
99

telecoms *npl* (*abbr* **telecommunications**) telecomunicaciones *fpl*

teleconference *n* teleconferencia *f*

teleconferencing *n* teleconferencias *fpl*

telecottage *n Br* = casa en el campo usada por el teletrabajador

telegenic *adj* telegénico(a)

telegram *n* telegrama *m*; **to send sb a telegram** enviar un telegrama a alguien

telegraph 1 *n* telégrafo *m* ▫ **telegraph service** servicio *m* telegráfico
2 *vt* (*news*) telegrafiar; (*money*) girar; (*person*) telegrafiar a, mandar un telegrama a

telegraphic *adj* telegráfico(a) ▫ **telegraphic address** dirección *f* telegráfica; FIN **telegraphic transfer** transferencia *f* telegráfica

telemarketing *n* telemarketing *m*

telematics *n* telemática *f*

teleorder 1 *n* telepedido *m*
2 *vt* realizar un pedido por *Esp* ordenador *or Am* computadora

telephone 1 *n* teléfono *m*; **to be on the telephone** (*talking*) estar al teléfono; (*have a telephone*) tener teléfono; **to have a good telephone manner** ser amable por teléfono; **to order sth by telephone** pedir *or* encargar algo por teléfono, hacer el pedido de algo por teléfono; **the boss is on the telephone for you** tienes al jefe al teléfono, te llama el jefe; **you're wanted on the telephone** te llaman por teléfono ▫ **telephone banking** telebanca *f*, banca *f* telefónica; **telephone bill** factura *f* del teléfono; **telephone book** guía *f* telefónica, listín *m* de teléfonos, *Am* directorio *m* de teléfonos; **telephone call** llamada *f* telefónica, *Am* llamado *m* telefónico; **telephone canvassing** captación *f* telefónica de clientes; **telephone code** prefijo *m* telefónico, *RP* característica *f* telefónica; **telephone code area** área *f* telefónica; **telephone communications** comunicaciones *fpl* telefónicas; **telephone dealing** negociación *f* telefónica (OTC); **telephone directory** guía *f*

telefónica, listín *m* de teléfonos, *Am* directorio *m* de teléfonos; **telephone exchange** central *f* telefónica; **telephone follow-up** seguimiento *m* telefónico; MKTG **telephone interview** encuesta *f* telefónica; **telephone line** línea *f* telefónica *or* de teléfono; **telephone link** enlace *m* telefónico; **telephone marketing** telemarketing *m*, marketing *m* telefónico; **telephone message** mensaje *m* telefónico; **telephone network** red *f* telefónica; **telephone number** número *m* de teléfono; **telephone order** pedido *m* por teléfono; **telephone prospecting** captación *f* telefónica de clientes; **telephone sales** *(activity)* venta *f* telefónica, televenta *f*; *(number of sales)* ventas *fpl* por teléfono; **telephone selling** venta *f* telefónica, televenta *f*; **telephone subscriber** abonado(a) *m,f* al teléfono; **telephone survey** encuesta *f* telefónica; **telephone system** sistema *m* telefónico
  2 *vt* **to telephone sb** telefonear a alguien, llamar a alguien (por teléfono); **to telephone the United States** telefonear a Estados Unidos, llamar (por teléfono) a Estados Unidos
  3 *vi* telefonear, llamar (por teléfono)

telephonist *n Br* telefonista *mf*

telephony *n* telefonía *f*

teleprinter *n Br* teletipo *m*, teleimpresor *m*

teleprocessing *n* teleprocesamiento *m*, teleproceso *m*

telesales *n* televenta *f*, venta *f* telefónica ❑ **telesales person** televendedor(ora) *m,f*

teleshopping *n* telecompra *f*

teletex *n* COMPTR teletexto *m*

teletypewriter *n US* teletipo *m*, teleimpresor *m*

television *n* televisión *f* ❑ **television advertisement** anuncio *m* de televisión, spot *m* (publicitario); **television advertising** publicidad *f* televisiva; **television audience** *(reached by advertising)* audiencia *f* televisiva *or* de televisión; **television broadcasting** teledifusión *f*; **television campaign** campaña *f* televisiva *or* en televisión; **television channel** cadena *f* de televisión, canal *m* de televisión; **television commercial** anuncio *m* de televisión, spot *m* (publicitario); **television interview** entrevista *f* por televisión; *Br* **television licence** = certificado de haber pagado el impuesto que todo propietario de un televisor ha de pagar, con el que se financian las cadenas públicas; **television network** cadena *f* de televisión; **television report** reportaje *m* televisivo, crónica *f* televisiva; **television sponsoring** patrocinio *m* televisivo; **television station** canal *m* de televisión; **television tie-in** = producto asociado a un programa de televisión; **television viewer** telespectador(ora) *m,f*, televidente *mf*; **television viewing panel** panel *m* de audiencia

teleworker *n* teletrabajador(ora) *m,f*

teleworking *n* teletrabajo *m*

> ❝
>
> The mass adoption of **teleworking** and the death of the City worker is still some way off. Moreover, though **teleworking** projects typically result in 20% better productivity from employees, too many fail because of inflexible management.
>
> ❞

telex 1 *n* télex *m inv*; **to send sth by telex** enviar algo por télex ❑ **telex message** télex *m inv*; **telex transfer** transferencia *f* por télex
  2 *vt (message)* enviar por télex; *(person)* enviar *or* poner un télex a

teller *n* cajero(a) *m,f*

Telnet *n* COMPTR Telnet *m*

temp 1 *n* trabajador(ora) *m,f* temporal administrativo(a) ❑ **temp agency** empresa *f* de trabajo temporal
  2 *vi* hacer trabajo temporal de administrativo(a)

temping *n* trabajo *m* temporal administrativo ❑ **temping agency** empresa *f* de trabajo temporal

template *n* COMPTR plantilla *f*

temporary *adj (employment)* temporal, eventual, *Am* temporario(a); *(employee)* temporal, eventual; *(measures)* provisional, transitorio(a), *Am* temporario(a) ❑ **temporary contract** contrato *m* temporal; CUSTOMS **temporary entry** admisión *f* temporal; COMPTR **temporary file** archivo *m or* fichero *m* temporal; CUSTOMS **temporary importation** importación *f* temporal; **temporary labour** mano *f* de obra temporal, trabajadores *mpl* eventuales; **temporary staff** personal *m* eventual

> ❝
>
> There are a substantial number of boats berthed in EC waters, often under **temporary importation** arrangements and on which VAT has not been paid anywhere in the EC. In many cases, these boats have remained in EC waters for many years and have changed ownership several times. The view is almost certain to be that these tax-free boats should not remain in EC waters unless VAT is paid.
>
> ❞

tenable *adj (post)* ocupable; **the appointment is tenable for a five-year period** la duración del cargo es de cinco años

tenancy *n (right)* arrendamiento *m*, alquiler *m*, *Méx* renta *f*; *(period)* periodo *m* de alquiler *or Méx* renta; **to take up the tenancy on a house** comenzar a alquilar *or Méx* rentar una casa; **during my tenancy of the house** mientras estuve de alquiler *or* de inquilino en la casa ❑ *tenancy agreement* contrato *m* de alquiler *or* arrendamiento *or* *Méx* renta

tenant *n (of house)* inquilino(a) *m,f*; *(of land)* arrendatario(a) *m,f*

ten-cent store *n US* (tienda *f* de) baratillo *m*, *Esp* tienda de "todo a cien"

tendency *n* tendencia *f* (**to** a); **an upward/downward tendency** *(in share prices)* una tendencia alcista/bajista

tender 1 *n (bid)* oferta *f*, licitación *f*; **to make** *or* **put in a tender (for sth)** presentarse a concurso con una oferta (para algo), licitar (por algo); **to invite tenders for a contract, to put a contract out to tender** sacar a concurso el contrato *or* la contratación de algo; **by tender** mediante licitación ❑ *tender document* documento *m* de la oferta, documento de licitación; *tender form* formulario *m or Méx* forma *f* de inscripción para una licitación; *tender pool* conjunto *m* de ofertas presentadas; *tender proposal* propuesta *f* de licitación
  2 *vt* (**a**) *(services)* ofrecer; *(bid, offer)* presentar; *(resignation)* presentar (**b**) *(money)* abonar, entregar
  3 *vi* licitar, presentar una oferta; **to tender for a contract** presentarse a una licitación de contratación, licitar por un contrato

tenor *n FIN (of bill)* vencimiento *m*

tentative *adj (provisional)* provisional, *Am* provisorio(a)

tenure *n (of post)* ocupación *f*; *(of property, land)* tenencia *f*; **during his tenure as chairman** durante su mandato como presidente

term *n* (**a**) **terms** *(conditions)* términos *mpl*, condiciones *fpl*; *(rates, tariffs)* condiciones; **terms and conditions** términos y condiciones; **under the terms of the agreement** de conformidad con lo establecido en el acuerdo; **on easy terms** con facilidades de pago ❑ *terms of credit* condiciones *fpl* de crédito; *terms of delivery* condiciones *fpl* de entrega; *terms of employment* condiciones *fpl* de contrato; *terms of exchange* condiciones *fpl* de cambio; *terms of payment* condiciones *fpl* de pago; *terms of reference (of commission)* competencias *fpl*; ECON *terms of trade* relación *f* de intercambio
  (**b**) FIN *(of bill of exchange)* plazo *m* de vencimiento; **to set** *or* **put a term to sth** fijar un plazo para algo ❑ *term bill* letra *f* a plazo fijo; *term day* día *f* de vencimiento; *term deposit* depósito *m* a plazo; *term draft* letra *f* a plazo fijo; *term loan* préstamo *m* a plazo fijo
  (**c**) *(duration)* periodo *m* de duración **the loan shall be for a term of ten years** el periodo de duración del préstamo será de diez años ❑ INS *term insurance* seguro *m* de vida limitado al plazo contratado, seguro a término; *term of notice* plazo *m* de preaviso; *term of office* mandato *m*

terminable annuity *n* seguro *m* de vida mixto a término fijo

terminal 1 *n* (**a**) *(at airport)* terminal *f*; *(for goods)* terminal *f* (**b**) COMPTR terminal *m*
  2 *adj* INS *terminal bonus* bonificación *f* a vencimiento de póliza; ACCT *terminal loss* pérdida *f* final; ST EXCH *terminal market* mercado *m* terminal; *terminal price* precio *m* a vencimiento

terminate *vt (employee)* despedir; *(project)* suspender; *(contract)* rescindir

termination *n (of employee)* despido *m*; *(of project)* suspensión *f*; *(of contract)* rescisión *f* ❑ *termination of business* cese *m* de la actividad comercial; *termination clause* cláusula *f* resolutoria; *termination of employment* despido *m*

terminator *n* COMPTR terminador *m*

territorial waters *npl* aguas *fpl* territoriales *or* jurisdiccionales

territory *n (of salesperson)* zona *f*

tertiary *adj (industry)* terciario(a), de servicios; *(market)* terciario(a) ❑ *tertiary sector* sector *m* terciario

TESSA *n* (*abbr* **tax-exempt special savings account**) = plan de ahorro británico que permite unos máximos anuales de inversión y de capitalización de intereses exentos de tributación fiscal, que en la actualidad ha sido reemplazado por la ISA

test 1 *n* (**a**) *(of machine, equipment, product)* prueba *f*; *(quality)* control *m*; **to carry out tests on sth** realizar pruebas con algo ❑ *test certificate* certificado *m* de ensayo *or* prueba (**b**) MKTG *(of reaction, popularity)* prueba *f*, test *m* ❑ *test area* área *f* de prueba *or* del test; *test city* ciudad *f* de prueba *or* del test; *test market* mercado *m* de prueba *or* del test; *test shop* tienda *f* de la prueba *or* del test; *test site* lugar *m* de la prueba *or* del test
  2 *vt* (**a**) *(machine, equipment, product)* probar; *(quality)* controlar (**b**) MKTG *(reaction, popularity)* testear

tester *n (person)* verificador(ora) *m,f*, comprobador(ora) *m,f*

testimonial *n* (**a**) MKTG *(in advert)* testimonial *m* ❑ *testimonial advertising* publicidad *f* testimonial (**b**) *(reference)* referencias *fpl*

testing *n (of machine, product)* prueba *f*; *(of quality)* control *m*

test-market *vt* MKTG testear, hacer tests de mercado de

text *n* COMPTR texto *m* ❑ *text block* bloque *m* de texto; *text buffer* buffer *m* de texto; *text editor* editor *m* de texto; *text field* campo *m* de texto; *text file* archivo *m or* fichero *m* de texto; *text layout* formato *m* del texto; TEL *text message (sent by mobile phone)* mensaje *m* de texto; *text mode* modo *m* (de) texto; *text processing* procesamiento *m or* tratamiento *m* de textos; **text processor** procesador *m* de textos; **text wrap** contorneo *m* de texto

text-message *vt* TEL enviar un mensaje de texto a

theoretical inventory *n* inventario *m* teórico

thermal *adj* COMPTR **thermal paper** papel *m* térmico; **thermal printer** impresora *f* térmica

think tank *n* grupo *m* de expertos, equipo *m* de cerebros

> ❝
>
> A leading Taiwan economic **think tank** revised downward Friday its annual economic growth forecast for the island to 2.38% from its earlier 5.21% estimate, citing the more severe than expected economic slowdown.
>
> ❞

third *adj* tercero(a); *(before masculine singular noun)* tercer ❑ US **third class** *(for mail)* = clase económica de correo que se emplea sobre todo para enviar publicidad; **third party, third person** tercero *m*; **third quarter** *(of financial year)* tercer trimestre *m*; **the Third World** el Tercer Mundo

third-class *adj* US *(mail)* = de clase económica, referido principalmente al envío de publicidad

third-generation, 3G *adj* COMPTR, TEL de tercera generación

third-party *adj* INS **third-party insurance** seguro *m* a terceros; **third-party holder** tercero *m* tenedor; INS **third-party liability** responsabilidad *f* frente a terceros; INS **third-party liability insurance** seguro *m* de responsabilidad civil; INS **third-party owner** tomador(ora) *m,f* de un seguro por cuenta ajena; INS **third-party risk** riesgo *m* de daños a terceros

three-button mouse *n* COMPTR *Esp* ratón *m or Am* mouse *m* de tres botones

three-level channel *n* canal *m* (de ventas) de tres niveles

threshold *n (limit)* umbral *m*, límite *m*; **the government has raised tax thresholds** el gobierno ha elevado los umbrales impositivos ❑ IND **threshold agreement** acuerdo *m* de actualización *or* revalorización salarial automática; EU **threshold price** precio *m* umbral

thrift *n* US ≃ entidad *f* de ahorros ❑ **thrift institution** ≃ entidad *f* de ahorros; **thrift shop** = tienda perteneciente a una entidad benéfica en la que se venden artículos de segunda mano

thrive *vi (company, industry)* prosperar

thriving *adj (company, industry)* próspero(a), floreciente

through **1** *prep* US **Monday through Friday** desde el lunes hasta el viernes inclusive

2 *adj* FIN **through bill** conocimiento *m* de embarque directo; **through freight** mercancías *fpl* en tránsito

3 *adv (on telephone)* **to get through to sb** conseguir contactar *or* comunicar con alguien; **to put sb through to sb** comunicar *or* pasar *or Esp* poner a alguien con alguien; **I'll just put you through to her** te paso *or Esp* pongo con ella

throughput *n* (volumen *m* de) producción *f*; COMPTR rendimiento *m*, capacidad *f* de procesamiento

through-the-line *adj* MKTG through the line, = que se vale de todos los medios de publicidad, tanto masivos como selectivos

thumbnail *n* COMPTR miniatura *f*

thumbtack *n* US chincheta *f*, *Am* chinche *m*

tick **1** *n* (**a**) *Br Fam (credit)* **to buy sth on tick** comprar algo fiado (**b**) *(mark)* marca *f*, señal *f*; **to put a tick against sth** marcar algo (con una señal) (**c**) ST EXCH **tick size** variación *f* mínima de precios

2 *vt (on form)* marcar (con una señal); **tick the appropriate box** marque la casilla apropiada

ticket *n* (**a**) *(for plane, train, bus, underground)* billete *m*, *Am* boleto *m*, *esp Am* pasaje *m* (**b**) *(label)* etiqueta *f* (**c**) ❑ ST EXCH **ticket day** día *m* de intercambio de boletas

▶ **tie up** *vt sep (money)* inmovilizar; **my capital is tied up in property** tengo mi capital inmovilizado en bienes inmuebles

tied *adj* **tied agent** agente *m* afecto; **tied loan** préstamo *m* condicionado; **tied outlet** punto *m* de venta exclusivo (de una sola marca)

tied-up capital *n* capital *m* inmovilizado

tie-in *n* MKTG **a movie/TV tie-in** = un producto asociado a una película/un programa televisivo ❑ **tie-in promotion** lanzamiento *m* de promoción conjunta; **tie-in sale** venta *f* condicionada

> ❝
>
> Burger King Corp. won exclusive sponsorship rights to the Backstreet Boys' fall tour and will launch a CD and video **tie-in** in August. ... This is the first national music **tie-in** for Burger King, which is targeting teens and tweens with the promotion. Although the chain did not disclose how it would distribute the CD and video, a **tie-in** with its Big Kids Meal is expected.
>
> ❞

tie-up *n (joint venture)* empresa *f* conjunta

TIFF *n* COMPTR *(abbr* **Tagged Image File Format**) TIFF *m*

tiger economy *n* tigre *m* asiático; **the (Asian) tiger economies** los tigres asiáticos

> **"**
>
> Before the crisis broke, almost everybody was far too starry-eyed about East Asia's economic prospects. Now the mood has swung to the other extreme and many people are being too gloomy. Some myths about the **tiger economies'** success needed to be debunked …
>
> **"**

tight *adj* (**a**) *(schedule)* apretado(a); *(deadline)* ajustado(a) (**b**) *(budget)* ajustado(a), limitado(a); *(credit, discount)* restringido(a); **to work on a tight budget** trabajar con un presupuesto ajustado *or* limitado *or* reducido

tighten *vt (budget)* limitar; *(credit)* restringir

tile *vt* COMPTR *(windows)* poner en mosaico

till *n* caja *f* (registradora); **to do the till** hacer (la) caja ❑ **till receipt** recibo *m* de caja, tíquet *m* de compra

time *n* (**a**) *(in general)* tiempo *m* ❑ **time frame** plazo *m* de tiempo; **time limit** límite *m* de tiempo, tiempo *m* límite, plazo *m* (máximo); **there's a time limit of three weeks** hay un plazo (máximo) de tres semanas; **there's no time limit** no hay límite de tiempo; **the work must be completed within the time limit** el trabajo deberá concluirse en el tiempo límite establecido; **time management** gestión *f or* administración *f* del tiempo; **time to market** plazo *m* de comercialización; **time and methods study** estudio *m* de tiempos y métodos; **time and motion consultant** analista *mf* de tiempos y movimientos; **time and motion studies** análisis *m inv* de tiempos y movimientos; **time and motion study** estudio *m* de tiempos y movimientos; MKTG **time pricing** fijación *f* de precios según la estacionalidad; **time sharing** COMPTR tiempo *m* compartido; *(of property)* tiempo *m* compartido; **time slot** *(in TV schedule)* franja *f* horaria; ST EXCH **time value** valor *m* de tiempo

(**b**) *(by clock)* hora *f*; **time of arrival/departure** hora de llegada/salida ❑ **time card** tarjeta *f* (para fichar); **time clock** máquina *f* de fichar, reloj *m* (para fichar); **time difference** diferencia *f* horaria; **time in lieu** crédito *m* horario, descanso *m* compensatorio; **time off** tiempo *m* libre; **time rate** salario *m* por unidad de tiempo; **time sheet** ficha *f* de horas trabajadas; **time work** trabajo *m* por horas, trabajo *m* a jornal; **time worker** *(paid hourly)* trabajador(ora) *m,f* por horas; *(paid daily)* jornalero(a) *m,f*, trabajador(ora) *m,f* por días

(**c**) *(credit) US* **to buy sth on time** comprar algo a crédito ❑ ST EXCH **time bargain** venta *f* al descubierto; FIN **time bill** letra *f* a plazo fijo; *US* **time deposit** depósito *m* a plazo; **time draft** letra *f* a plazo fijo; **time loan** préstamo *m or* crédito *m* a plazo; INS **time policy** póliza *f* de seguro a término

(**d**) *(hourly wages)* **we pay time and a half on weekends** pagamos un 50% más los fines de semana; **overtime is paid at double time** las horas extras se pagan al doble (de las normales) *or* un 100% más caras

> **"**
>
> Avnet Applied Computing (AAC) … officially opened a new engineering laboratory built to provide a resource-rich environment where original equipment manufacturer customers and AAC engineers can work side-by-side to cut the **time to market** of their designs.
>
> **"**

time-critical *adj* **this project is absolutely time-critical** el tiempo es un factor crucial en este proyecto

timekeeper *n* (**a**) *(supervisor)* controlador(ora) *m,f* de horarios (**b**) *(employee)* **he's a good timekeeper** (siempre) es muy puntual; **he's a bad timekeeper** no es muy puntual

timekeeping *n (in factory)* control *m* de horarios *or* puntualidad; *Br (of employee)* puntualidad *f*; **he was sacked for bad timekeeping** lo echaron del trabajo por impuntualidad

timetable 1 *n* (**a**) *(for transport)* horario *m* (**b**) *(schedule) (for event, project)* programa *m*; *(for talks, reform)* calendario *m*
2 *vt (talks, meeting)* programar

tin parachute *n* indemnización *f* por pérdida de empleo

> **"**
>
> Even less common than gold or silver parachutes are **tin parachutes** – severance plans that cover all of the employees of a company in the event it undergoes a change in control. The value of a **tin parachute** will vary significantly from company to company, says Siske, but will typically provide a severance payment linked to the recipients' years of service and/or their age, often with a cap, such as 1.5 times annual compensation.
>
> **"**

tip 1 *n (cash)* propina *f*
2 *vt* dar (una) propina a

Tipp-Ex® 1 *n* Tipp-Ex® *m*, corrector *m*
2 *vt* **to Tipp-Ex sth out** borrar algo con Tipp-Ex®

TIR *n (abbr* **Transport International Routier)** TIR *m*, transporte *m* internacional por carretera

title *n* (**a**) LAW título *m* de propiedad ❑ **title deed** escritura *f*, título *m* de propiedad (**b**) COMPTR **title bar** barra *f* de título

TL *n* (**a**) *(abbr* **time loan)** préstamo *m or* crédito *m* a plazo (**b**) *(abbr* **total loss)** pérdida *f* total

TM n (abbr **trademark**) marca f registrada

TMT n (abbr **technology, media and telecommunications**) TMT, tecnología, media y telecomunicaciones; **a TMT company** una empresa TMT or del sector TMT

> ❝
>
> The company's story is typical of many of the transformations that took place in the so-called **TMT sector** during the internet frenzy in that it decided to move away from its old defence electronics business to focus on supplying telecoms equipment.
>
> ❞

Tobin tax n FIN tasa f Tobin

toggle COMPTR **1** n **toggle key** tecla f de conmutación; **toggle switch** tecla f or botón m de conmutación

2 vi alternar, conmutar; **to toggle between two applications** pasar de una aplicación a otra pulsando una tecla

token adj (payment, rent) simbólico(a) □ COMPTR **token ring network** red f en anillo, token ring m; IND **token strike** huelga f simbólica

tolerance n (margen m de) tolerancia f □ **tolerance margin** margen m de tolerancia

toll n (**a**) (on bridge, road) peaje m, Méx cuota f □ **toll bridge** puente m de peaje or Méx cuota f; **toll road** carretera f de peaje or Méx cuota f (**b**) US TEL **toll call** llamada f or Am llamado m de larga distancia, Esp conferencia f

toll-free US **1** adj **toll-free number** (número m de) teléfono m gratuito

2 adv (call) gratuitamente

tone n TEL señal f, tono m; **leave a message after the tone** (on answering machine) deje un mensaje después de la señal

toner n (for printer, fax) tóner m □ **toner cartridge, toner cassette** cartucho m de tóner

tonnage n (of ship, port) tonelaje m □ **tonnage certificate** certificado m de arqueo

tonne n tonelada f (métrica)

tool n (implement) herramienta f; **(set of) tools** (juego m de) herramientas fpl; **it has become an essential tool for most businesses** se ha convertido en una herramienta básica para la mayoría de las empresas; **to down tools** (stop working) dejar de trabajar; (go on strike) hacer un paro laboral □ COMPTR **tool bar** barra f de herramientas; **tool palette** paleta f de herramientas

toolbox n COMPTR caja f de herramientas

top 1 n ST EXCH **to buy at the top and sell at the bottom** comprar en máximos y vender en mínimos; **the top of the range** lo mejor de la gama

2 adj **this task should be given top priority** esta tarea debería tener prioridad absoluta □

top copy original m; **top management** los altos directivos; **top price** precio m alto or elevado; **top quality** alta calidad f; **top rate** (of tax) Esp tipo m impositivo más alto, Am tasa f impositiva más alta

3 vt (exceed) superar, sobrepasar; **production topped five tons last month** la producción superó las cinco toneladas el mes pasado; **to top sb's offer** mejorar la oferta de alguien

top-down adj (management style) jerárquico(a) □ MKTG **top-down forecasting** previsión f (de ventas) basada en datos macroeconómicos

> ❝
>
> Forget capital; it's relatively easy to obtain nowadays. Today's scarce, sought-after strategic resource is expertise, which comes in the form of employees. Although organizations have changed mightily from the days of hierarchical, **top-down management**, they still have a long way to go.
>
> ❞

top-heavy adj (structure) sobrecargado(a) en la parte superior; **the company is top-heavy** (with too many senior staff) la empresa cuenta con demasiados altos cargos; (overcapitalized) la empresa está sobrecapitalizada

> ❝
>
> Many corporations have **top-heavy**, vertical organization structures and new ideas just take too long to move through the business process.
>
> ❞

top-of-the-range, US **top-of-the-line** adj de gama alta □ **top-of-the-range item** artículo m de gama alta

top-up card n TEL tarjeta f de recarga, tarjeta recargable

▶ **tot up** vt sep Br sumar

total 1 n total m; **the total comes to $389** el total es de or asciende a 389 dólares

2 adj (amount, cost, output etc) total; **marketing the product accounts for 20% of the total costs** la comercialización del producto supone un 20% de los costos totales □ **total annual expenses** gastos mpl anuales totales; **total assets** activos mpl totales; **total asset value** valor m total del activo; **total care services** servicio m integral de atención al cliente; INS **total constructive loss** pérdida f total constructiva; **total contract value** valor m contractual total, valor m total del contrato; **total distribution cost** costo m or Esp coste m total de distribución; **total exemption** exención f total; **total export sales** volumen m (total) de ventas de exportación, total m de ventas de exportación; **total fixed cost** costo m or Esp coste m fijo total; **total gross income** ingresos mpl brutos totales; **total insured value** valor m total asegurado;

total liabilities pasivo *m* total; **total loss** pérdida *f* total; **total loss settlement** liquidación *f* por pérdida total; **total net income** ingresos *mpl* netos totales; **total payable** total *m* a pagar; **total quality control** control *m* de calidad total; **total quality management** gestión *f* de calidad total; **total sales** volumen *m* (total) de ventas, total *m* de ventas; **total unit cost** costo *m* or *Esp* coste *m* unitario total

3 *vt* (**a**) *(add up)* sumar (**b**) *(amount to)* ascender a

totalize *vt* sumar

touch *n* (**a**) *(communication)* **to be in touch with sb** estar en contacto con alguien; **to get in touch with sb** ponerse en contacto con alguien (**b**) COMPTR **touch screen** pantalla *f* táctil; **touch screen computer** *Esp* ordenador *m* or *Am* computadora *f* con pantalla táctil

touchpad mouse *n* COMPTR *Esp* ratón *m* Touchpad *or* de panel táctil, *Am* mouse *m* Touchpad *or* de panel táctil

touch-sensitive *adj* COMPTR *(screen)* táctil; *(key, switch)* táctil

touch-tone telephone *n* teléfono *m* de tonos

touch-type *vi* mecanografiar al tacto

tour *n* *(by tourist)* recorrido *m*, viaje *m* ◻ **tour guide** *(person)* guía *mf* turístico(a); *(book)* guía *f* turística; **tour operator** operador *m* turístico, tour operador *m*

tourism *n* turismo *m*

tourist *n* turista *mf* ◻ **tourist attraction** atracción *f* turística; **tourist board** patronato *m* de turismo; **tourist centre** centro *m* turístico; **tourist class** clase *f* turista; **tourist facilities** equipamiento *m* turístico, instalaciones *fpl* y servicios *mpl* turísticos; **tourist (information) office** oficina *f* de turismo; **tourist season** temporada *f* turística; **the tourist trade** el sector turístico

tower *n* COMPTR torre *f* ◻ **tower system** equipo *m* de or con torre

town *n* **town and country planning** ordenación *f* urbanística y rural; **town hall** municipio *m*, ayuntamiento *m*; **town planner** urbanista *mf*; **town planning** urbanismo *m*

TQC *n* (*abbr* **total quality control**) control *m* de calidad total

TQM *n* (*abbr* **total quality management**) gestión *f* de calidad total

trackball *n* COMPTR *Esp* ratón *m* or *Am* mouse *m* de bola, trackball *m*

tracker fund *n* *esp Br* ST EXCH fondo *m* indexado, fondo referenciado a un índice

trackpad *n* COMPTR *Esp* ratón *m* or *Am* mouse *m* táctil, trackpad *m*

trade 1 *n* (**a**) *(commerce)* comercio *m* (**in** de); **it's good for trade** es bueno para las ventas; **to do a roaring trade** hacer buen negocio ◻ **trade agreement** acuerdo *m* comercial; **trade balance** balanza *f* comercial; **trade ban** embargo *m* comercial; **trade barriers** barreras *fpl* comerciales; **trade bill** efecto *m* comercial; **trade bloc** bloque *m* comercial; ACCT **trade credit** crédito *m* comercial; ACCT **trade creditor** acreedor *m* comercial; **trade cycle** ciclo *m* económico, coyuntura *f*; ACCT **trade debt** deuda *f* comercial; ACCT **trade debtor** deudor *m* comercial; **trade deficit** déficit *m* (de la balanza) comercial; **trade delegation** delegación *f* comercial; *Br* **Trade Descriptions Act** = ley que prohíbe a las empresas hacer uso de la publicidad engañosa; **trade embargo** embargo *m* comercial; **trade exhibition** exposición *f* comercial, feria *f* (de muestras); **trade fair** feria *f* (comercial *or* de muestras); **trade figures** cifras *fpl* comerciales; **trade gap** déficit *m* (de la balanza) comercial; **trade marketing** marketing *m* al canal de distribución; **trade name** *(of product)* nombre *m* comercial; *(of company)* razón *f* social; **trade negotiations** negociaciones *fpl* comerciales; **trade policy** política *f* comercial; **trade practices** prácticas *fpl* comerciales; **trade restraint** restricción *f* comercial; **trade surplus** excedente *m* or superávit *m* comercial; ST EXCH **trade ticket** boleta *f* (**b**) *(profession)* oficio *m*; **to be in the trade** estar en el oficio; **we only sell to the trade** solo vendemos al por mayor or *Am* al mayoreo; **he's an electrician by trade** su oficio es el de electricista ◻ **trade association** asociación *f* gremial; **trade body** asociación *f* gremial; **trade directory** guía *f* por profesiones; **trade discount** descuento *m* comercial; **trade journal** publicación *f* del sector, *Am* publicación gremial; **trade press** prensa *f* del sector **trade price** precio *m* al por mayor or *Am* al mayoreo; **trade register** registro *m* mercantil; **trade representative** representante *mf* comercial; **trade secret** secreto *m* profesional; *esp Br* **trade union** sindicato *m*; **Trades Union Congress** = confederación nacional de sindicatos británicos; **trade union council** consejo *m* sindical; **trade unionism** sindicalismo *m*; **trade unionist** sindicalista *mf*; **trade union official** funcionario(a) *m,f* sindical (**c**) FIN *(transaction)* operación *f*, transacción *f*

2 *vt* ST EXCH negociar ❏ **traded option** opción *f* negociada

3 *vi* (**a**) *(do business)* comerciar; **he trades in clothing** se dedica a la compraventa de ropa; **the company trades under the name of Prism Ltd** la empresa comercia bajo el nombre de Prism Ltd; **to trade at a loss** vender con pérdidas; **to trade with sb** tener relaciones comerciales *or* comerciar con alguien (**b**) ST EXCH *(shares, commodity)* cotizar (**at** a); *(currency)* cotizar (**at** a); **corn is trading at $2.20** el maíz cotiza a 2,20 dólares

▸ **trade down** *vi* vender para recomprar a la baja

▸ **trade in** *vt sep* entregar como parte del pago

▸ **trade up** *vi* vender para recomprar al alza

trade-in *n* = artículo usado que se entrega como parte del pago ❏ **trade-in allowance** = descuento que se practica por la entrega de un artículo usado al comprar uno nuevo; **trade-in facility** = posibilidad de entregar un artículo usado al comprar uno nuevo; **trade-in price** = cantidad que se recibe por un artículo usado al comprar uno nuevo; **trade-in value** = valor que se le da a un artículo usado al comprar uno nuevo

trademark *n* marca *f* comercial *or* registrada

trade-off analysis *n* MKTG análisis *m inv* de conjunto

trader *n* comerciante *mf*; (**in** de); ST EXCH operador(ora) *m,f* de bolsa *or* bursátil

tradesman *n* (**a**) *(shopkeeper)* pequeño comerciante *m*, tendero *m* (**b**) *(electrician, plumber)* trabajador *m* manual, obrero *m* especializado

trading *n* (**a**) *(commerce)* comercio *m* ❏ ACCT **trading account** cuenta *f* de explotación; **trading bank** banco *m* comercial; **trading capital** capital *m* circulante operativo; **trading company** empresa *f* mercantil; *Br* **trading estate** polígono *m* industrial; **trading hours** *(of shop)* horario *m* comercial; *(on stock exchange)* horario *m* de contratación *or* apertura; **trading licence** licencia *f* comercial; **trading loss** pérdidas *fpl* comerciales; **trading nation** país *m* comercial; **trading partner** socio(a) *m,f* comercial; **trading profit** beneficios *mpl* comerciales; ACCT **trading and profit and loss account** cuenta *f* de explotación y resultados; **trading results** resultados *mpl* comerciales; **trading stamp** cupón *m*, vale *m*; **trading standards** normativa *f* comercial; *Br* **Trading Standards Office** = organismo que vela por el cumplimiento de la normativa comercial; **trading year** ejercicio *m* económico

(**b**) *(on stock exchange)* compraventa *f* de acciones; **trading was heavy today** el volumen de negocio ha sido muy alto hoy ❏ **trading day** día *m* de negociación; **trading floor** parqué *m*;

trading instrument instrumento *m* de negociación; **trading member** miembro *m* del mercado; **trading month** mes *m* de contratación; **trading order** orden *f* de contratación; *US* **trading post** mesa *f* de contratación; **trading range** banda *f* de fluctuación; **prices are stuck in a trading range** los precios están estancados en una banda de fluctuación; **trading room** sala *f* de contratación; **trading session** sesión *f* (de contratación); ST EXCH **trading volume** volumen *m* de contratación *or* de operaciones

> **"**
>
> The platinum price moved higher Thursday with one analyst from Merrill Lynch & Co. New York, observing that the price is meandering in the **trading range** with a slight phasing out of physical metal on the market.
>
> **"**

traffic 1 *n* *(trade)* comercio *m*; *(illegal)* tráfico *m* (**in** de) ❏ MKTG **traffic builder: to be a traffic builder** crear *or* generar tráfico (en el punto de venta)

2 *vi* **to traffic in sth** *(illegally)* traficar con algo; *(legally)* comerciar con algo

train 1 *vt (employee)* dar formación a, formar; **he's training somebody to take over from him** está formando a alguien para que lo releve en el puesto; **she was trained in economics** recibió formación en economía

2 *vi* formarse, estudiar; **to train as an accountant** formarse como contable *or* *Am* contador(ora); **where did you train?** ¿dónde adquiriste tu formación?

trained *adj (person)* cualificado(a); *(engineer, translator)* titulado(a)

trainee *n (in trade)* aprendiz(iza) *m,f*, aprendiz *mf*; *(in profession)* persona *f* en prácticas *or* en formación; *(at lawyer's)* pasante *mf*; *(at accountant's) Esp* contable *mf* or *Am* contador(ora) *m,f* en prácticas; **trainee computer programmer** programador(ora) *m,f* informático(a) en prácticas

traineeship *n (in trade)* aprendizaje *m*; *(in profession)* formación *f*; *(at lawyer's)* pasantía *f*; *(at accountant's)* prácticas *fpl*

training *n* formación *f*; **I've had business training** he recibido formación empresarial ❏ **training centre** centro *m* de formación; **training course** cursillo *m* de formación; **training division** división *f* de formación; **training officer** jefe(a) *m,f* de formación; **training programme, training scheme** programa *m* de formación; **training time** tiempo *m* or periodo *m* de formación

tranche *n (of loan, shares)* tramo *m*; *(of payment)* plazo *m*

> It is noticeable that the French **tranche**, covering 50 per cent of the issue, is being sold by a general offer for sale while the British **tranche**, half as large, is split between an offer and a placing with institutions.

transact vt (deal) realizar, llevar a cabo; (purchase, sale) realizar, efectuar; **to transact business (with sb)** llevar a cabo transacciones comerciales (con alguien)

transaction n (**a**) (deal) transacción f; ST EXCH, FIN operación f; **cash transactions have decreased** las operaciones en efectivo han disminuido ❑ **transaction costs** costos mpl or Esp costes mpl de transacción (**b**) (act of transacting) **transaction of business will continue as normal** la empresa seguirá operando con normalidad

transfer 1 n (**a**) (of employee, goods) traslado m; (of air passenger) transporte m, traslado; FIN, ST EXCH (of shares, capital) traspaso m; (of money) transferencia f ❑ **transfer advice** notificación f or aviso m de transferencia; CUSTOMS **transfer of bonded goods** traslado m de mercancías en depósito or bajo control aduanero; ST EXCH **transfer certificate** certificado m de traspaso (de acciones o valores); **transfer cheque** cheque m de transferencia; ST EXCH **transfer duty** impuesto m sobre transmisiones; ST EXCH **transfer by endorsement** traspaso m mediante endoso; ST EXCH **transfer fee** comisión f de traspaso; ST EXCH **transfer form** orden f de traspaso; FIN **transfer order** orden f de transferencia; **transfer passenger** (between flights) pasajero(a) m,f en tránsito or de paso; **transfer payment** (pago m de) transferencia f; ST EXCH **transfer register** registro m de traspasos; **transfer restrictions** (on investment) restricciones fpl sobre el traspaso
(**b**) ACCT (of debt, entry) traspaso m ❑ **transfer entry** asiento m de traspaso
(**c**) LAW (of property, ownership) transmisión f; (of rights) transmisión, transferencia f ❑ **transfer deed** escritura f de cesión, escritura f de transmisión; Br **transfer tax** (on death) impuesto m de sucesión; (between living persons) impuesto de or sobre transmisiones patrimoniales
(**d**) COMPTR (of data) transferencia f ❑ **transfer rate, transfer speed** velocidad f de transferencia
2 vt (**a**) (employee, goods) trasladar; FIN (shares, capital) traspasar; (money) transferir (**b**) ACCT (debt, entry) traspasar (**c**) LAW (property, ownership) transmitir; (rights) transferir; **she will transfer the rights over to him** le transferirá los derechos (**d**) TEL (call) pasar, transferir; **I'm transferring you now** le paso ahora mismo ❑ Br **transfer charge call** llamada f or Am llamado m a cobro revertido (**e**) COMPTR (data) transferir
3 vi (**a**) (employee) trasladarse; **to transfer to a different department** trasladarse a otro

departamento (**b**) (air passenger) hacer una conexión

transferable adj (document, property, ownership, rights) transferible ❑ **transferable bond** bono m or obligación f transferible; **transferable credit** crédito m transferible; **transferable letter of credit** carta f de crédito transferible; **transferable securities** títulos mpl or valores mpl transferibles; **transferable share** acción f transferible; **transferable skills** capacidades fpl transferibles

transferee n FIN, ST EXCH (of shares, funds, capital) adquiriente mf, beneficiario(a) m,f; LAW (of property, ownership, rights) adquiriente, cesionario(a) m,f

transferor n FIN, ST EXCH (of shares, funds, capital) (parte f) transferente mf; LAW (of property, ownership, rights) transmisor(ora) m,f, cedente mf

tranship = **transship**

transhipment = **transshipment**

transit n tránsito m; **in transit** en tránsito; **goods lost in transit** mercancías fpl perdidas durante el traslado ❑ CUSTOMS **transit entry** importación f temporal; **transit permit** permiso m de tránsito; **transit port** puerto m de tránsito; **transit system** régimen m de tránsito; **transit visa** visado m or Am visa f de tránsito

translate 1 vt traducir (**from/into** de/a)
2 vi (**a**) (person) traducir; **she translates for the EU** traduce para la UE (**b**) (word, expression) traducirse (**as** por)

translation n traducción f ❑ **translation agency** agencia f de traducción

translator n traductor(ora) m,f

transmission n COMPTR (of data) transmisión f ❑ **transmission protocol** protocolo m de transmisión

transparency n (for overhead projector) transparencia f

transport 1 n transporte m; **means of transport** medio m de transporte ❑ **transport advertising** publicidad f en medios de transporte; **transport charges** costos mpl or Esp costes mpl de transporte; **transport company** empresa f de transportes, transportista m; **transport costs** costos mpl or Esp costes mpl de transporte; **transport facilities** servicios mpl de transporte
2 vt transportar

transportation n transporte m

transship, tranship vt transbordar

transshipment, transhipment n transbordo m ❑ **transshipment bill of lading** conocimiento m de transbordo

trash n US COMPTR **trash (can)** papelera f (de reciclaje)

travel 1 n viajes mpl □ **travel agency,** Br **travel agent's** agencia f de viajes; **travel agent** empleado(a) m,f de una agencia de viajes; **travel allowance** Esp dietas fpl de viaje or desplazamiento, Am viáticos mpl (de viaje); **travel documents** documentación f para el viaje; **travel expenses** gastos mpl de viaje; **travel goods** artículos mpl or objetos mpl de viaje
   2 vi viajar; **to travel on business** viajar por negocios

traveling US = **travelling**

traveller, US **traveler** n viajero(a) m,f; (salesman) viajante mf (de comercio) □ **traveller's cheque** cheque m de viaje or Am viajero

travelling, US **traveling 1** n viajes mpl □ **travelling allowance** Esp dietas fpl de viaje or desplazamiento, Am viáticos mpl (de viaje); **travelling expenses** gastos mpl de viaje
   2 adj **travelling salesman** viajante m (de comercio)

treasurer n tesorero(a) m,f □ **treasurer's report** informe m del tesorero

treasury n (funds, place) tesorería f; **the Treasury** (in UK) el Tesoro (Público), ≃ (el Ministerio de) Economía; **the Department of the Treasury** (in US) el Departamento del Tesoro, ≃ (el Ministerio de) Hacienda □ **Treasury bill** letra f del Tesoro; **Treasury bond** bono m del Tesoro; **Treasury note** pagaré m del Tesoro **Treasury savings** bonos mpl de ahorro del Tesoro; **Treasury scrip** resguardo m provisional del Tesoro; US **Treasury Secretary** secretario(a) m,f del Tesoro; **treasury swap** swap m sobre Deuda Pública, swap sobre tipos de interés de las letras del Tesoro; **Treasury warrant** warrant m sobre Deuda Pública

----

"

Goldman Sachs has been notified that the Securities and Exchange Commission plans to pursue a case against it for allegedly trading US **Treasury bonds** based on inside information. ... The $3,000bn **Treasury market** rallied, with 30-year bonds seeing the biggest one-day gain in 14 years.

"
----

treaty n (international) tratado m; (between individuals) contrato m; **they sold the property by private treaty** vendieron el inmueble mediante contrato privado

treble 1 vt triplicar
   2 vi triplicarse

tree n (of data) árbol m □ **tree diagram, tree structure** (diagrama m en) árbol m

trend n tendencia f; **the general trend of the market** la tendencia general del mercado; **house prices are on an upward/downward trend** el precio de la vivienda mantiene una tendencia al alza/a la baja or alcista/bajista □ MKTG

trend analysis análisis m inv de (la) tendencia; **trend reversal** inversión f de la tendencia

triad market n MKTG mercado m de la tríada

trial 1 n (**a**) (test) ensayo m, prueba f; **to give sth a trial** probar algo; **on trial** a prueba; **they gave me a month's trial before taking me on** me tuvieron a prueba durante un mes antes de contratarme □ **trial lot** lote m de prueba; **trial offer** (of product) oferta f especial de lanzamiento; **trial order** pedido m de prueba; **trial period** periodo m de prueba; **trial subscription** suscripción f de prueba
   (**b**) ACCT **trial balance** balance m de comprobación
   (**c**) LAW juicio m; **to stand trial (for sth)** ser procesado(a) (por algo); **to bring sb to trial (for sth)** llevar a alguien a juicio (por algo)
   2 vt probar

tri-band adj TEL de triple banda

tribunal n tribunal m

trickle-down theory n ECON teoría f de la filtración, = teoría según la cual la riqueza de unos pocos termina por revertir en toda la sociedad

----

"

In retirement Galbraith has continued in articles, speeches, and books to argue for strong government, progressive taxes and public spending. He is not a "Third Way" man. He ridiculed the Reaganite **trickle-down theory** of wealth distribution, preferring the earthier phrase "the horse-and-sparrow theory" – "If you feed the horse enough oats, some will pass through to the road for the sparrows.

"
----

trigger 1 n (of change, decision) factor m desencadenante, detonante m; **the strike was the trigger for nationwide protests** la huelga provocó una cadena de protestas por toda el país
   2 vt (reaction) desencadenar; (revolution, protest) hacer estallar; **the crisis has triggered huge numbers of closures** la crisis ha ocasionado el cierre de numerosas empresas

▶ **trigger off** vt sep desencadenar

triple-A rating n ST EXCH calificación f AAA or triple A

triple witching hour n US ST EXCH Fam = sesión bursátil en la que coincide el vencimiento de los contratos de futuros sobre índices bursátiles y las opciones relativas a los mismos

----

"

Note that a trade can be put in by a trader to be executed at the market closing price for a given stock. Regardless of what the price is, the trade will be executed. The deluge of orders on the **triple witching hour** at the market closing price often caused the ticker to be delayed up to a half hour at the closing. _"_

triplicate 1 *n* **in triplicate** por triplicado **2** *vt (document)* hacer tres copias de

troubleshoot *vi (resolve organizational problems)* identificar y resolver problemas; *(repair machines)* reparar averías

troubleshooter *n (for organizational problems)* localizador(ora) *m,f* de problemas; *(for machines)* técnico(a) *m,f* (en averías)

_"_
Mr James has a reputation as a corporate **troubleshooter** capable of reviving the fortunes of struggling companies like Railtrack, a record that has earned him the nickname of the Red Adair of the business world. As well as the Dome, his talents have been turned to Dan-Air, the airline, and the British Shoe Corporation. _"_

troubleshooting *n (for organizational problems)* localización *f* y resolución *f* de problemas; *(for machines)* reparación *f* de averías; COMPTR resolución *f* de problemas

trough *n* ECON *(of graph, cycle)* depresión *f*

truck 1 *n* camión *m* □ **truck driver** camionero(a) *m,f*, CAm, Méx trailero(a) *m,f* **2** *vt* transportar en camión

truckage *n* US *(charge)* gastos *mpl* del transporte en camión

trucker *n* US camionero(a) *m,f*, CAm, Méx trailero(a) *m,f*

true *adj* **true copy** *(of document)* copia *f* fiel; **true discount** verdadero descuento *m*; ACCT **true and fair view** *(of accounts)* imagen *f* fiel; **true sample** muestra *f* fiel

true-false *adj (question)* de verdadero o falso

trust *n* **(a)** LAW *(agreement)* fideicomiso *m*; *(organization)* fundación *f*; **to set up a trust for sb** crear un fideicomiso a nombre de alguien □ **trust account** cuenta *f* de fideicomiso *or* de custodia; **trust deed** contrato *m or* escritura *f* de fideicomiso; **trust fund** fondo *m* fiduciario *or* de fideicomiso **(b)** FIN *(cartel)* trust *m* □ **trust bank** banco *m* fiduciario; **trust company** compañía *f* fiduciaria

trustbuster *n* US *Fam* = encargado de disolver un monolopio

trusted third party *n* COMPTR *(for Internet transactions)* tercero *m* de confianza

_"_
At the moment a mere $200m worth of goods are sold across the Internet each year. All the estimates of this figure reaching

$30 billion by the end of the decade will count for little unless somebody comes up with some kind of 'digital signature' that gives users the same assurance that face-to-face contact, a physical address or even a driving licence does in the real world. Ideally, a digital signature should be guaranteed by some **trusted third party** – eg, a credit-card firm or a government body. _"_

trustee *n* LAW *(of fund, property)* fideicomisario(a) *m,f*, administrador(ora) *m,f* fiduciario(a); *(of charity, institution)* miembro *m* del consejo de administración □ **trustee in bankruptcy** síndico(a) *m,f* de la quiebra

trusteeship *n (of fund, property)* fideicomiso *m*, administración *f* fiduciaria; *(of charity, institution)* administración fiduciaria

try *vt (product)* probar

TTP *n* COMPTR *(abbr* **trusted third party**) *(for Internet transactions)* tercero *m* de confianza

TUC *n (abbr* **Trades Union Congress**) = confederación nacional de sindicatos británicos

turbomarketing *n* MKTG turbomarketing *m*

▸ **turn down** *vt sep (applicant, job, offer)* rechazar

▸ **turn out** *vt sep (goods)* producir

▸ **turn over** *vt sep* FIN facturar; **he turns over £1,000 a week** factura más de 1.000 libras a la semana

▸ **turn round** *vt sep* **(a)** *(order, request, application)* procesar, tramitar; **the stocks are turned round every four months** las existencias se renuevan completamente cada cuatro meses, las existencias tienen una rotación de cuatro meses **(b)** *(economy)* enderezar; *(company)* hacer rentable

turnaround *n* **(a)** *(of order)* ciclo *m* de pedido; **they offer a faster turnaround** ofrecen un servicio más rápido □ **turnaround time** tiempo *m* de respuesta **(b)** *(improvement)* mejora *f* radical

turnkey *adj (project, factory, system)* integral, llave en mano

turnover *n* **(a)** FIN *(of company)* facturación *f*, volumen *m or* cifra *f* de negocio; **his turnover is £100,000 per annum** su facturación es de 100.000 libras al año □ **turnover tax** impuesto *m* sobre el volumen de negocio, impuesto *m* sobre la cifra de negocios **(b)** *(of stock, capital)* rotación *f*; **the staff turnover there is very high** allí la rotación de personal es muy elevada □ **turnover rate** *(for staff)* índice *m* de rotación

turnround *n* **(a)** *(of order)* ciclo *m* de pedido **(b)** *(of passenger ship, plane)* tiempo *m* entre desembarco y embarco; *(for freight)* tiempo *m* de carga y descarga **(c)** *(time taken to complete round trip)* tiempo *m* de ida y vuelta

tutorial n COMPTR tutorial m ❑ *tutorial program* tutorial m

twin-pack selling n MKTG venta f en un pack de dos unidades

2G adj COMPTR,TEL de segunda generación

2.5G adj COMPTR,TEL de segunda generación y media, de generación 2,5

two-level channel n canal m (de ventas) de dos niveles

tycoon n magnate mf; **an oil tycoon** un magnate del petróleo

type 1 n (text) tipo m, letra f
  2 vt (with typewriter) escribir a máquina, mecanografiar; (with word processor) escribir en Esp el ordenador or Am la computadora; **to type sth into the computer** introducir algo en Esp el ordenador or Am la computadora, pasar algo Esp al ordenador or Am a la computadora
  3 vi escribir a máquina, mecanografiar

▶ **type out** vt sep escribir a máquina, mecanografiar

▶ **type up** vt sep (with typewriter) escribir a máquina, mecanografiar; (with word processor) escribir en Esp el ordenador or Am la computadora

typeface n tipo m, letra f

typewriter n máquina f de escribir

typically adv (usually) por lo general, normalmente; **typically, prices range from $1000 to $1500** por lo general, los precios oscilan entre los 1.000 y los 1.500 dólares

typing n (by typewriter) (technique) mecanografía f; (action) mecanografiado m; (by word processor) escritura f en Esp el ordenador or Am la computadora ❑ *typing error* error m mecanográfico; *typing paper* papel m para escribir a máquina; *typing pool* sección f de mecanografía; *typing skills* conocimientos mpl de mecanografía; *typing speed* velocidad f de mecanografiado

typist n mecanógrafo(a) m,f

Uu

UAW n (abbr **United Automobile Workers**) = sindicato estadounidense de trabajadores del sector automovilístico

UBR n (abbr **uniform business rate**) = impuesto municipal británico sobre la tierra o inmueble que ocupa una actividad profesional

UCATT n (abbr **Union of Construction, Allied Trades and Technicians**) = sindicato británico de técnicos y trabajadores del sector de la construcción y similares

UCITS n (abbr **undertakings for collective investment in transferables**) OICVM mpl

UDC n (abbr **underdeveloped country**) PSD m

ullage n CUSTOMS vacío m de seguridad

ultimate adj **ultimate consumer** consumidor(ora) m,f final, usuario(a) m,f (final); **ultimate holding company** sociedad f holding matriz

umbrella n **umbrella committee** comité m coordinador, comisión f coordinadora; **umbrella fund** fondo m paraguas; **umbrella organization** organización f aglutinante; **umbrella trademark** marca f paraguas

> **"**
> Other so-called advantages they were supposed to offer, such as **umbrella funds** that allowed cheap or free switching between sub-funds, lower charges because of the need for only one set of administration for the **umbrella fund**, have failed to transpire.
> **"**

UMTS n TEL (abbr **Universal Mobile Telecommunications System**) UMTS m, SUTM m

UMW n (abbr **United Mineworkers of America**) = sindicato de mineros de EE.UU.

UN n (abbr **United Nations**) **the UN** la ONU

unabsorbed cost n costo m or Esp coste m no absorbido

unaccounted for adj **these sixty pounds are unaccounted for in the balance sheet** estas sesenta libras no aparecen contabilizadas or no están reflejadas en el balance; **there is still a lot of money unaccounted for** queda aún mucho dinero sin contabilizar

unadvertised adj (job) no publicado(a); (meeting, visit) no anunciado(a)

unallocated adj no asignado(a) □ ACCT **unallocated cash** dinero m en efectivo sin justificar; ACCT **unallocated cash report** informe m sobre cantidades de efectivo sin justificar

unallotted adj FIN, ST EXCH (share) no distribuido(a)

unanimous adj (consent, decision) unánime □ **unanimous vote** voto m unánime; **passed by a unanimous vote** aprobado(a) por unanimidad

unappropriated adj (money) sin asignar, disponible □ **unappropriated profits** beneficios mpl no distribuidos ni asignados

unassigned revenue n ingresos mpl no asignados

unaudited adj (figures) sin auditar

unauthorized adj no autorizado(a) □ COMPTR **unauthorized access** acceso m no autorizado

unavailable adj (person, information, services) no disponible; (product) agotado(a), no disponible; **the manager is unavailable** el director no se encuentra disponible

unavoidable costs npl ACCT costos mpl or Esp costes mpl inevitables

unbalanced adj (**a**) ACCT (account) que no cuadra (**b**) FIN (economy) desequilibrado(a)

unbankable adj FIN sin aceptación bancaria, no bancario(a) □ **unbankable bill** efecto m no bancario

unbonded warehouse n CUSTOMS depósito m no aduanero

unbranded adj MKTG sin marca □ **unbranded product** producto m sin marca

unbundle vt (company) desmembrar

unbundling n (of company) desmembramiento m

uncallable adj (bond) no exigible

uncalled adj FIN (capital) suscrito(a) y no desembolsado(a)

uncashed adj (cheque) sin cobrar

unclaimed adj (dividend) no reclamado(a) □ **unclaimed goods** bienes mpl no reclamados, bienes mpl mostrencos

uncommercial adj poco comercial

unconditional adj (acceptance, offer) incondicional □ FIN **unconditional order** orden f incondicional (de pago)

unconfirmed letter of credit *n* carta *f* de crédito no confirmada

unconscionable bargain *n* LAW contrato *m* fraudulento, contrato leonino

unconsolidated *adj* FIN *(debt)* no consolidado(a)

uncovered *adj* FIN *(purchase, sale)* sin garantía de pago; *(cheque)* sin (provisión de) fondos ❑ ST EXCH **uncovered position** posición *f* descubierta

uncrossed *adj Br (cheque)* sin cruzar, no cruzado(a)

UNCTAD *n (abbr* **United Nations Conference onTrade and Development)** UNCTAD *f*

undated *adj* no fechado(a)

underbid *vt* **we underbid them** *(for tender)* presentamos una oferta más baja que la de ellos

underborrow *vi (company)* adquirir *or* tener un nivel insuficiente de endeudamiento

underborrowed *adj (company)* con un nivel insuficiente de endeudamiento

underborrowing *n (of company)* nivel *m* insuficiente de endeudamiento

underbuy *vt (goods)* comprar a menor precio

undercapitalization *n* descapitalización *f*, infracapitalización *f*

undercapitalize *vt* descapitalizar, infracapitalizar

undercapitalized *adj* descapitalizado(a), infracapitalizado(a)

undercharge *vt (customer)* cobrar de menos; **I was undercharged** me cobraron de menos; **she undercharged him by £60** le cobró 60 libras de menos

undercut *vt* **to undercut the competition** vender a precios más baratos que los de la competencia; **they undercut us by £500** hicieron un presupuesto 500 libras más barato que el nuestro

> **"**
>
> Mr O'Leary claimed Ryanair was "Europe's only low-cost airline", with fares **undercutting** its rivals by up to a third. He insisted EasyJet's takeover of Go represented little threat, dismissing that company's chairman, Stelios Haji-Ioannou, as "the son of a billionaire", adding: "He's Greek, I'm Irish. The Greeks have never beaten the Irish at anything. Not even drinking."
>
> **"**

underdeveloped *adj* ECON *(country)* subdesarrollado(a)

underemployed *adj* ECON *(skills, resources)* infrautilizado(a); *(worker)* subempleado(a)

underemployment *n* ECON *(of skills, resources)* infrautilización *f*; *(of workers)* subempleo *m*

underequipped *adj* infradotado(a) (de medios)

underfund *vt* dotar de insuficiente financiación, infrafinanciar

underfunded *adj* infradotado(a) de recursos económicos, infrafinanciado(a), sin suficientes fondos

underground economy *n* economía *f* sumergida

> **"**
>
> But the domestic parts of some countries … are riddled with regulations or government-protected monopolies that stifle competition, stunt growth and drive businesses into the **underground economy**.
>
> **"**

underinsured *adj* infrasegurado(a); **to be underinsured** estar infrasegurado(a)

underlying *adj* subyacente ❑ **underlying asset** activo *m* subyacente; ST EXCH **underlying futures contract** contrato *m* de futuro implícito *or* subyacente; **underlying mortgage** hipoteca *f* subyacente; ST EXCH **underlying security** instrumento *m* subyacente, título *m or* valor *m* subyacente

> **"**
>
> While a convincing proposition on the surface, some believed that such claims encouraged individuals who might not have otherwise invested to make an investment in potentially risky mortgage-backed securities. In one example, marketing materials for a fund promoted a proprietary five-step process that could purportedly assess prepayment expectations of the **underlying mortgages** in a variety of interest-rate scenarios.
>
> **"**

undermanned *adj* sin personal suficiente, escaso(a) de personal

underpaid *adj* mal pagado(a)

underperform **1** *vt (of shares)* tener un rendimiento inferior al de
2 *vi (shares)* tener un bajo rendimiento

underpin *vt (market)* sustentar

underpriced *adj* demasiado barato(a), de precio demasiado bajo

underproduce **1** *vt* no producir suficiente(s)
2 *vi* producir de menos

underproduction *n* ECON producción *f* insuficiente

undersell *vt (person, company)* vender más barato que; *(product, goods)* malvender

undersigned **1** *n* **the undersigned** *(one person)* el abajo firmante; *(more than one person)* los abajo firmantes; **I, the undersigned declare**

that... yo, el abajo firmante, declaro que... **2** *adj* abajo firmante(s)

understaffed *adj* infradotado(a) de personal; **to be understaffed** no tener suficiente personal

understanding *n (agreement)* acuerdo *m*; **to come to** *or* **to reach an understanding (about sth/with sb)** llegar a un acuerdo (sobre algo/con alguien)

understate *vt* ACCT infravalorar

undersubscribed *adj* ST EXCH *(shares)* suscrito(a) en un porcentaje insuficiente; **the share issue was undersubscribed** la emisión de acciones no fue suscrita en su totalidad

undertake *vt (job)* realizar, llevar a cabo; *(project)* emprender; **to undertake responsibility for sth** asumir la responsabilidad de algo; **to undertake to do sth** encargarse de hacer algo

undertaking *n* **(a)** *(enterprise)* empresa *f*, proyecto *m* **(b)** *(promise)* compromiso *m*; **to give an undertaking to do sth** comprometerse a hacer algo □ **undertaking to purchase** compromiso *m* de compra; **undertaking to sell** compromiso *m* de venta

undertax *vt (goods, product)* gravar con un impuesto muy bajo; *(person)* cobrar impuestos muy bajos a

undervaluation *n (of goods)* infravaloración *f*

undervalue *vt (goods)* infravalorar

underwater *adj* US *(share prices)* fuera de dinero □ **underwater option** opción *f* fuera de dinero

― ❝ ―――――――――――――

This provides employees with a guaranteed return within a specified time period, but assures the company that the bonus is paid only if the stock options remain **underwater**.

――――――――――――――― ❞

underweight *vt* FIN infraponderar

underwrite *vt* **(a)** INS *(policy, risk)* suscribir **(b)** ST EXCH *(new issue)* suscribir, garantizar la colocación de **(c)** *(pay for) (project, scheme)* financiar

underwriter *n* **(a)** INS *(of policy, risk)* suscriptor(ora) *m,f* **(b)** ST EXCH *(of new issue)* suscriptor(ora) *m,f*, asegurador(ora) *m,f or* garante *mf* (de la colocación) □ **underwriter agent** agente *mf* subscriptor(ora)

underwriting *n* **(a)** INS *(of policy, risk)* suscripción *f* **(b)** ST EXCH *(of new issue)* garantía *f or* suscripción *f* de emisión □ **underwriting agent** agente *mf* de suscripción; **underwriting commission** comisión *f* de suscripción; **underwriting contract** contrato *m* de suscripción; **underwriting fee** comisión *f* de suscripción; **underwriting share** cuota *f* de riesgo de los

suscriptores; **underwriting syndicate** sindicato *m* de garantía

undifferentiated marketing *n* marketing *m* masivo *or* indiferenciado

undischarged *adj* **(a)** LAW *(bankrupt)* no rehabilitado(a) **(b)** FIN *(debt)* no saldado(a), no liquidado(a)

undisclosed *adj (sum)* no revelado(a) □ **undisclosed principal** mandante *mf or* ordenante *mf* oculto(a)

undiscountable *adj* FIN no descontable

undistributed *adj (earnings, money)* no distribuido(a) □ **undistributed profit** beneficio *m* no distribuido

undo *vt* COMPTR *(command)* deshacer; **undo changes** deshacer cambios □ **undo command** comando *m* deshacer

unearned *adj* **unearned income** rendimientos *mpl* del capital, renta *f* no salarial; **unearned increment** plusvalía *f*

― ❝ ―――――――――――――

Private productive property provides massive **unearned income**, and also frequently forms the basis of economic power. **Unearned income** derives from: (i) rent on buildings or land; (ii) dividends paid from profit of firms to shareholders; and (iii) interest on monetary investments such as deposit accounts or government securities.

――――――――――――――― ❞

uneconomic *adj* **(a)** *(unprofitable)* carente de rentabilidad, antieconómico(a) **(b)** *(wasteful, inefficient)* poco rentable, ineficaz desde el punto de vista económico

uneconomical *adj (wasteful, inefficient)* poco rentable, ineficaz desde el punto de vista económico

unedited *adj* COMPTR *(text)* sin editar

unemployed 1 *npl* **the unemployed** los desempleados, los desocupados, *Esp* los parados **2** *adj* **(a)** *(person)* desempleado(a), desocupado(a), *Esp* parado(a) **(b)** *(capital, funds)* sin utilizar, sin emplear

unemployment *n* desempleo *m*, desocupación *f*, *Esp* paro *m* □ *Br Formerly* **unemployment benefit,** *US* **unemployment compensation** subsidio *m* de desempleo; **unemployment crisis** crisis *f* de desempleo; **unemployment fund** fondo *m* de subsidio de desempleo; **unemployment insurance** seguro *m* de desempleo; **unemployment level, unemployment rate** tasa *f or* índice *m* de desempleo

unendorsed *adj (cheque)* sin endosar, sin endoso

unenforceable *adj* LAW *(contract)* de cumplimiento no exigible

unexchangeable *adj* FIN *(securities)* no canjeable

unfair *adj* **unfair competition** competencia *f* desleal; **unfair dismissal** despido *m* improcedente; **unfair trading** prácticas *fpl* comerciales desleales, comercio *m* desleal

unfavourable, *US* **unfavorable** *adj (conditions, balance of trade, exchange rate)* desfavorable

unforeseen expenses *npl* (gastos *mpl*) imprevistos *mpl*

unformatted *adj* COMPTR *(disk)* sin formatear

unfunded *adj (borrowing)* no consolidado(a) □ FIN **unfunded debt** deuda *f* no consolidada

ungeared *adj (company)* sin financiación crediticia □ **ungeared balance sheet** = balance en el que figura un nivel cero o muy bajo de financiación crediticia

UNICE *n (abbr* **Union of Industrial and Employers' Confederations of Europe)** UNICE *f*

UNIDO *n (abbr* **United Nations Industrial Development Organization)** ONUDI *f*

uniform *adj* **uniform accounting** contabilidad *f* uniforme, contabilidad *f* normalizada; *Br* **uniform business rate** = impuesto municipal sobre la tierra o inmueble que ocupa una actividad profesional; **uniform rate** tarifa *f* única

unilateral *adj (action, decision, contract)* unilateral

unincorporated sector *n* sector *m* de entidades no constituidas en sociedad de capital

uninitialized *adj* COMPTR sin inicializar

uninstall, *US* **uninstal** *vt* COMPTR desinstalar

uninsured *adj* no asegurado(a) (**against** contra)

union *n (trade union)* sindicato *m* □ **union agreement** acuerdo *m* sindical; **union card** carnet *m* sindical; **union claims, union demands** reivindicaciones *fpl* sindicales; **union dues** cuota *f* sindical; *US* **union label** etiqueta *f* de fabricación sindical; **union leader** dirigente *mf* sindical; **union meeting** reunión *f* sindical; **union member** afiliado(a) *m,f* sindical; **union membership** afiliación *f* sindical; **union official** sindicalista *mf*, dirigente *mf* sindical; **union representative** delegado(a) *m,f* sindical; *US* **union shop** = empresa o fábrica en que la afiliación sindical es obligatoria

unionism *n* sindicalismo *m*

unionist *n* sindicalista *mf*

unionization *n* sindicación *f*, *Am* sindicalización *f*

unionize *vt* sindicar, *Am* sindicalizar

unionized *adj* sindicado(a), *Am* sindicalizado(a)

unique *adj* MKTG **unique proposition** característica *f* distintiva *or* única; **unique selling point** *or* **proposition** argumento *m* de venta diferenciador

UNISON *n* = sindicato británico de empleados públicos

unissued *adj (shares, share capital)* no emitido(a)

unit *n* unidad *f*; *(in unit trust)* participación *f*; **each lot contains a hundred units** cada lote contiene cien unidades □ EU **unit of account** unidad *f* de cuenta; **unit of consumption** unidad *f* de consumo; **unit cost** costo *m* or *Esp* coste *m* unitario; **unit of currency** unidad *f* monetaria; **unit holder** *(in unit trust, mutual fund)* partícipe *mf*; **unit of labour** unidad *f* de mano de obra; **unit labour cost** costo *m* or *Esp* coste *m* unitario de la mano de obra; **unit price** precio *m* por unidad; **unit of production** unidad *f* de producción; *Br* **unit trust** fondo *m* de inversión mobiliaria; **unit of weight** unidad *f* de peso

unitary *adj* unitario(a)

United Nations *npl* **the United Nations** las Naciones Unidas □ **United Nations Organization** Organización *f* de las Naciones Unidas

universal *n US* **universal product code** código *m* de barras; COMPTR **Universal Serial Bus** Bus *m* Serial Universal

universe *n* MKTG *(number of people in group or segment)* universo *m*, conjunto *m*

Unix *n* COMPTR Unix *m*

unlawful *adj* ilegal, ilícito(a)

unlimited *adj* ilimitado(a); **the policy offers unlimited cover** la póliza ofrece cobertura ilimitada □ **unlimited company** sociedad *f* de responsabilidad ilimitada; **unlimited liability** responsabilidad *f* ilimitada; **unlimited warranty** garantía *f* ilimitada

unlisted *adj* **(a)** ST EXCH *(share)* no cotizado(a) □ **unlisted company** empresa *f* que no cotiza en Bolsa, empresa no cotizada; **unlisted market** mercado *m* extrabursátil; **unlisted securities** títulos *mpl* no cotizados; **unlisted securities market** segundo mercado *m* **(b)** *US (telephone number)* que no figura en la guía (telefónica) *or Méx* en el directorio (telefónico)

> **“**
> … Sherwood Group (steady at 760p and now capitalised at £140m) is looking too big for the **unlisted securities market** and a move up to the main market may well accompany Tuesday's year-end profits.
> **”**

unload 1 *vt* **(a)** *(ship, truck, goods)* descargar □ **unloading point** *or* **place** punto *m* or lugar *m* de descarga; **unloading port** puerto *m* de descarga **(b)** *(sell off)* deshacerse rápidamente de

2 *vi (ship, truck)* descargar

unlock *vt (assets)* desinmovilizar, liberar

unmarketable *adj (goods)* no comercializable; *(assets)* invendible

unmortgaged *adj* sin hipoteca

unnegotiable *adj (cheque, bill)* no negociable

UNO *n (abbr* **United Nations Organization)** ONU *f*

unofficial *adj (appointment, meeting)* extraoficial ❏ *unofficial strike* huelga *f* no apoyada por los sindicatos; FIN *unofficial price* cotización *f* no oficial

unorganized *adj* IND sin sindicar, *Am* sin sindicalizar

unpack *vt (goods)* desembalar

unpaid *adj* (**a**) *(person, post)* no retribuido(a) ❏ *unpaid leave* baja *f* no retribuida *or* sin sueldo (**b**) *(account, salary, debt)* impagado(a)

unpledged revenue *n* ingresos *mpl* no asignados

unprocessed material *n* materia *f* prima, materia bruta

unproductive *adj (capital)* improductivo(a), ocioso(a); *(work)* improductivo(a) ❏ *unproductive land* tierra *f* improductiva

unproductiveness *n (of work)* improductividad *f*

unprofessional *adj* poco profesional

unprofitable *adj (business)* no rentable; *(discussions, meeting)* infructuoso(a), poco productivo(a)

unquoted *adj Br* ST EXCH *unquoted company* empresa *f* que no cotiza en Bolsa, empresa no cotizada; *unquoted securities* valores *mpl* no cotizados (en Bolsa); *unquoted shares* acciones *fpl* no cotizadas

unreadable *adj* COMPTR ilegible

unrealizable *adj* FIN *(assets)* no liquidable, no realizable

unrealized *adj* FIN *(capital, assets)* no realizado(a); *(gain, loss)* latente

unrecoverable *adj (debt)* irrecuperable

unredeemed *adj* FIN *(loan, mortgage)* no amortizado(a); *(bond)* sin cobrar

unrefined material *n* material *m* en bruto

unregulated market *n* FIN mercado *m* informal

unrest *n (in labour relations)* conflictividad *f*

unsaleable *adj (goods)* invendible

unsecured *adj* sin garantía, no garantizado(a) ❏ *unsecured advance* anticipo *m* sin garantía; *unsecured credit card* = tarjeta de crédito no respaldada por un bien líquido o valor;

unsecured creditor acreedor *m* común *or* sin garantía; *unsecured debenture* obligación *f* sin garantía; *unsecured debt* deuda *f* sin garantía; *unsecured loan* préstamo *m* sin garantía; *unsecured overdraft* sobregiro *m* sin garantía

> **“**
>
> The position of a secured creditor is to be contrasted with that of an **unsecured creditor** who merely has a personal claim to sue for the payment of his debt and to invoke the available legal processes for the enforcement of any judgment that he may obtain.
>
> **”**

unsettled *adj* (**a**) *(market)* inestable, volátil (**b**) *(account, bill)* sin pagar; *(debt)* impagado(a), pendiente (de pago), *Am* impago(a)

unskilled *adj (worker)* no cualificado(a), *Am* no calificado(a); *(job, work)* no especializado(a) ❏ *unskilled labour* mano *f* de obra no cualificada *or Am* calificada; *unskilled labourer* trabajador(ora) *m,f* no cualificado(a) *or Am* calificado(a)

unsocial *adj Br* **to work unsocial hours** trabajar a deshoras

unsold *adj* sin vender

unsolicited application *n (for job)* candidatura *for* solicitud *f* espontánea

unsound *adj (enterprise, investment)* arriesgado(a); *(business)* precario(a); **the project is economically unsound** el proyecto es poco sólido desde el punto de vista económico

unspent *adj (sum, balance)* no utilizado(a)

unstable *adj (market, prices)* inestable

unstamped *adj (letter)* sin franquear, sin sello; *(document)* sin timbrar

unsteady *adj (currency, prices, market)* inestable

unstructured interview *n* MKTG entrevista *f* no estructurada

unsubscribe *vi (from newsletter, mailing list)* darse de baja (**from** de), cancelar la suscripción (**a** de),

unsubscribed *adj (capital)* no suscrito(a)

untaxed *adj (income)* no gravado(a), exento(a) de impuestos; *(goods)* libre *or* exento(a) de impuestos

untradable *adj* ST EXCH no negociable

unweighted *adj* ECON *(index)* no ponderado(a) ❏ *unweighted figures* cifras *fpl* no ponderadas

unzip *vt* COMPTR descomprimir

UP *n (abbr* **unit price)** precio *m* por unidad

up 1 *adj* COMPTR *up arrow* flecha *f* arriba; *up arrow key* tecla *f* de flecha arriba

2 *adv* (**a**) *(higher)* **the price of gold is up** ha subido el precio del oro; **the pound is up ten cents against the dollar** la libra ha ganado diez centavos frente al dólar; **profits are up 25% on**

last year los beneficios superan en un 25% los del pasado año (**b**) **up front** *(pay)* por adelantado

UPC *n US (abbr* **universal product code**) código *m* de barras

update COMPTR **1** *n (of software package)* actualización *f*
   2 *vt* actualizar

upgradable *adj* COMPTR *(hardware, system)* actualizable; *(memory)* ampliable

upgrade COMPTR **1** *n (of hardware, system)* actualización *f*; *(of memory)* ampliación *f* ◻ ***upgrade kit*** kit *m* de actualización
   2 *vt (hardware, system)* actualizar; *(memory)* ampliar

upgradeability *n* COMPTR *(of hardware, system)* capacidad *f* de actualización; *(of memory)* capacidad *f* de ampliación

upgradeable *adj* COMPTR *(hardware, system)* actualizable; *(memory)* ampliable

upkeep *n (maintenance)* mantenimiento *m*; *(cost)* costo *m or Esp* coste *m* del mantenimiento ◻ ***upkeep cost(s)*** gasto(s) *m(pl)* de mantenimiento

upload *vt* COMPTR cargar, subir

upmarket 1 *adj (neighbourhood, restaurant)* elegante; *(newspaper, programme)* dirigido(a) a un público selecto
   2 *adv* **the newspaper wants to move upmarket** el periódico quiere atraer a un público más selecto

upper *adj* **upper case** mayúsculas *fpl*; **upper class** clase *f* alta; **upper limit** límite *m* superior, tope *m* (máximo); **upper price limit** precio *m* máximo

upper-case *adj* en mayúsculas ◻ ***upper-case character*** (letra *f*) mayúscula *f*

UPS *n* COMPTR *(abbr* **uninterruptible power supply**) SAI *m*

upscale *adj US (neighbourhood, restaurant)* elegante; *(newspaper)* dirigido(a) a un público selecto

> **"**
> The **upscale** client is demanding more, and tour operators seeking to capitalize are ripe for the challenge ... "There is an increasing emphasis on experience," says Tauck, echoing what many industry leaders in the **upscale** market are saying about leisure travel. "While they do want service and the finest amenities, **upscale** clients are increasingly sophisticated and want to learn about and engage in a destination," says Tauck.
> **"**

upset price *n US (at auction)* precio *m* de salida

upside *n (trend)* **prices have been on the**

upside los precios han experimentado una tendencia al alza ◻ ST EXCH **upside potential** potencial *m* alcista; ST EXCH **upside risk** riesgo *m* al alza

upstream 1 *adj (company)* abastecedor(ora) ◻ ***upstream product*** insumo *m*, producto *m* previo
   2 *adv* en una fase previa

upswing *n (improvement)* mejora *f*, alza *f* (**in** en); **the Stock Market is on the upswing** la Bolsa está en alza; **there has been an upswing in sales** se ha producido un movimiento ascendente *or* un repunte en las ventas

> **"**
> We now have an outline of the reasons for an **upswing** in economic activity and for an increase in the rate of surplus-value. But the faster the **upswing**, the more bunched replacements will be and the sooner a new crisis will loom on the horizon.
> **"**

uptick *n* (**a**) *(small increase)* ligero repunte *m or* aumento *m*; **last week's uptick in interest rates** el ligero repunte *or* aumento de *Esp* los tipos *or Am* las tasas de interés registrado la pasada semana (**b**) ST EXCH = venta ejecutada a un precio mayor que el anterior

> **"**
> Although the trading statement did not look so far out, analysts also have hopes for an **uptick** in business for the private sector in the Far East and the US later this year. Profits, around £114m in 2001 according to the consensus of forecasts, look set to increase to £130m this year.
> **"**

up-to-date *adj* (**a**) *(most recent)* reciente, actualizado(a); **to bring sb up-to-date on sth** poner a alguien al día (sobre algo) (**b**) *(modern) (machinery, methods)* moderno(a)

uptrend *n* tendencia *f* alcista *or* al alza

upturn *n (in economy)* reactivación *f* (**in** de); *(in production, sales)* repunte *m*, aumento *m*; **there has been an upturn in the market** el mercado ha iniciado una fase de recuperación

upward *adj* FIN **upward market trend** tendencia *f* alcista del mercado; **upward mobility** movilidad *f* social ascendente; FIN **upward movement** movimiento *m* alcista; **upward trend** *or* **tendency** tendencia *f* alcista *or* al alza

upward-compatible *adj* COMPTR compatible con versiones posteriores

urban *adj* urbano(a) ◻ ***urban renewal*** renovación *f* urbana; ***urban transport*** transporte *m* urbano; ***urban unemployment*** desempleo *m* urbano

> **"**
> The panel is tasked with crafting an **urban renewal** plan as part of the government's economic stimulus measures by considering issues including the construction of waste disposal and recycling plants, international airports and disaster refuge areas, as well as making use of vacant lots.
> **"**

urgent adj urgente; **it's not urgent** no corre prisa, SAm no hay apuro

URL n COMPTR (abbr **uniform resource locator**) URL m

Uruguay Round n Ronda f de Uruguay

US 1 n (abbr **United States**) **the US** los EE.UU. **2** adj estadounidense ❑ **US dollar** dólar m estadounidense

usance n BANKING, FIN (time limit) vencimiento m; **at thirty days' usance** con vencimiento a treinta días ❑ **usance bill** letra f con vencimiento fijo

USB n COMPTR (abbr **Universal Serial Bus**) USB m ❑ **USB cable** cable m USB; **USB port** puerto m USB

use vt (product) usar, utilizar

use-by date n fecha f de caducidad

used n (car) usado(a), de segunda mano, de ocasión; (equipment) usado(a), de segunda mano

Usenet n COMPTR Usenet f

user n (of machine, product, telephone) usuario(a) m,f ❑ COMPTR **user ID, user identification** nombre m de usuario; COMPTR **user interface** interfaz m or f de usuario; COMPTR **user language** lenguaje m de usuario; COMPTR **user manual** manual m del usuario; COMPTR **user name** nombre m de usuario; COMPTR **user network** red f de usuarios; MKTG **user panel** panel m de usuarios; COMPTR **user software** software m de usuario; COMPTR **user support** asistencia f técnica al usuario

user-definable adj COMPTR (characters, keys) definible por el usuario

user-friendliness n facilidad f de manejo

user-friendly adj de fácil manejo ❑ **user-friendly software** programa m informático de fácil manejo

> **"**
> El Al's frequent-flyer clubs, Matmid and Loyal Club, are more **user-friendly** now that the carrier has introduced several advantages for its members. Members can now access their account statement via the carrier's Web site by entering their seven-digit membership number along with a PIN code.
> **"**

USM n ST EXCH (abbr **unlisted securities market**) segundo mercado m

USP n MKTG (abbr **unique selling point** or **proposition**) argumento m diferenciador

> **"**
> In other words, it should be offering the potential buyer at least one, possibly only one, clear reason for purchase. In its extreme form, this is an expression of the Unique Selling Proposition, or **USP** ... Very simply, the theory behind this is that any product has some characteristic which can be developed so as to make it unique in its class.
> **"**

USPHS n (abbr **United States Public Health Service**) = servicio de salud pública de EE.UU.

usufruct n LAW usufructo m

usufructary LAW **1** n usufructuario(a) m,f **2** adj usufructuario(a) ❑ **usufructuary rights** derechos mpl de usufructo

usurer n usurero(a) m,f

usurious adj (rate of interest) abusivo(a)

usury n usura f

utility n (a) (service) **(public) utility** (entidad f de) servicio m público ❑ US **utility stocks** acciones fpl en empresas públicas (b) COMPTR utilidad f **utility (program)** utilidad

utilization n utilización f, empleo m

utilize vt utilizar

Vv

vacancy *n* (**a**) *(position, job)* (puesto *m*) vacante *f*; **to fill a vacancy** cubrir una vacante; **the vacancy has been filled** se ha cubierto la vacante; **we have a vacancy for a sales assistant** tenemos una vacante de dependiente; **do you have any vacancies?** ¿tienen algún puesto vacante? (**b**) *(at hotel)* habitación *f* libre **vacant** *adj* (**a**) *(job, position)* vacante; **there are several vacant places to be filled** hay varias vacantes por cubrir; **a secretarial job has become vacant** ha quedado vacante un puesto de administrativo □ **vacant post** (puesto *m*) vacante *f* (**b**) *(room, apartment)* libre □ **vacant possession** propiedad *f* desocupada *or* libre de inquilinos; **apartments sold with vacant possession** venta de apartamentos desocupados

vacate *vt* *(hotel room)* dejar libre; *(house, property)* desalojar; *(job)* dejar vacante

vacation *n* (**a**) *US (holiday)* vacaciones *fpl*; **a month's vacation** un mes de vacaciones; **to be on/go on vacation** estar de/irse de vacaciones; **to get vacation with pay** tener *or* disfrutar de vacaciones remuneradas □ **vacation leave** vacaciones *fpl*, periodo *m* (anual) de vacaciones (**b**) *Br* LAW *(of courts)* periodo *m* vacacional

vacuum pack *n* envase *m* al vacío

vacuum-packed *adj* envasado(a) al vacío

valid *adj* *(contract)* legal; *(passport)* vigente, válido(a); **valid for six months** válido(a) *or* valedero(a) por *or* durante seis meses

validate *vt* *(document)* dar validez a; *(ticket)* validar, picar *(contract)* validar, dar validez a

validation *n* validación *f*

validity *n* validez *f*

valorization *n* FIN valorización *f*

valorize *vt* FIN valorizar

valuable **1** *n* **valuables** objetos *mpl* de valor **2** *adj* valioso(a)

valuate *vt* *US* valorar, tasar, *Am* valuar; **the house was valuated at $100,000** la casa fue valorada *or Am* valuada en 100.000 dólares

valuation *n* FIN (**a**) *(act)* tasación *f*, valoración *f*, *Am* valuación *f*; **to get a valuation of sth** hacer tasar *or* valorar algo; **to make a valuation of sth** tasar *or* valorar algo □ *US* INS **valuation charge** cargo *m* por valorización (**b**) *(price)* **the**

valuation put on the business is £100,000 la empresa está valorada *or Am* valuada en 100.000 libras

valuator *n* tasador(ora) *m,f*

value **1** *n* valor *m*; **to be of value** tener valor; **to be of no value** no tener (ningún) valor, carecer de valor; **to be good/poor value (for money)** tener buena/mala relación calidad-precio; **to go up/down in value** revalorizarse/desvalorizarse; **to set** *or* **put a value on sth** poner precio a algo, valorar algo; **they put a value of £150,000 on the house** valoraron *or* tasaron la casa en 150.000 libras; **of no commercial value** carente de valor comercial; **to the value of...** hasta un valor de...; **what will this do to the value of property?** ¿cómo repercutirá en el valor de la propiedad? □ BANKING **value in account** valor *m* en cuenta; **value added** valor *m* añadido; **value analysis** análisis *m inv* de(l) valor; MKTG **value brand** marca *f* económica; MKTG **value chain** cadena *f* de valor; FIN **value for collection** valor *m* al cobro; **value creation** creación *f* de valor; FIN **value date** fecha *f* de valor; FIN **value day** día *m* de valor; **value engineering** ingeniería *f* del valor; **value in exchange** valor *m* al cambio; **value as a going concern** valor *m* como empresa en funcionamiento; BANKING **value in gold currency** valor *m* oro; **value at liquidation** valor *m* liquidativo; **value at maturity** valor *m* al vencimiento; **value for money audit** auditoría *f* de gestión; **value in use** valor *m* en uso

2 *vt* *(goods, damage)* valorar, tasar, *Am* valuar; **to have sth valued** pedir una valoración *or Am* valuación de algo; **they valued the company at $10 billion** la empresa fue valorada *or Am* valuada en 10.000 millones de dólares

> **❝**
> **Value engineering** (VE) consists of considering the costs of producing a product together with the functions it provides. The objective is to engineer an all-round improvement in value with benefits to both user and supplier. The cost of a product is not, therefore, its value. This can only be arrived at by considering the functions it performs.
> **❞**

value-add *n* valor *m* añadido

value-added *adj* *(product, service)* con valor

añadido ❏ *Br* **value-added tax** impuesto *m* sobre el valor añadido, *Am* impuesto *m* al valor agregado

valued policy *n* INS póliza *m* con valor acordado

valueless *adj* sin valor

valuer *n* tasador(ora) *m,f*

variability *n* variabilidad *f*

variable 1 *n* variable *f*
  2 *adj* variable ❏ **variable costs** costos *mpl or Esp* costes *mpl* variables; **variable expenses** gastos *mpl* variables; EU **variable import levy** gravamen *m* variable a la importación; BANKING **variable rate** *Esp* tipo *m or Am* tasa *f* de interés variable; FIN **variable yield securities** títulos *mpl or* valores *mpl* de renta variable

variable-income *adj (bond, investment)* de renta variable

variable-interest *adj (bond, investment)* de renta variable

variable-rate *adj* **variable-rate interest** *Esp* tipo *m or Am* tasa *f* de interés variable; **variable-rate mortgage** hipoteca *f* (con *Esp* tipo *or Am* tasa) de interés variable; FIN **variable-rate security** título *m or* valor *m* de renta variable;

variable-yield *adj (investments, securities)* de renta variable

variance *n* ACCT desviación *f* ❏ **variance analysis** análisis *m inv* de la varianza

variation *n* variación *f*; **the level of demand is subject to considerable variation** el nivel de la demanda está sujeto a variaciones considerables ❏ INS **variation of risk** variación *f* del riesgo

variety store *n US* almacén *m* popular

VAT *n Br (abbr* **value-added tax**) IVA *m*; **exclusive of** *or* **excluding VAT** sin IVA, sin incluir *or* excluyendo el IVA; **subject to VAT** sujeto(a) a(l) IVA; **to be VAT registered** estar inscrito(a) en el censo del IVA ❏ **VAT credit** crédito *m* IVA; **VAT exempt amount** cantidad *f* exenta de IVA; *Fam* **VAT man** *(department)* departamento *m* de recaudación del IVA; **VAT rate** tipo *m or Am* tasa *f* del IVA; **VAT registration number** número *m* de identificación a efectos de IVA; **VAT return** (hoja *f* de) declaración *f* del IVA; **VAT statement** declaración *f* del IVA

❝
A High Court judge ruled yesterday that the **VAT man** is perfectly entitled to pursue prostitutes. Mr Justice Jacob decided that members of the world's oldest profession should not be allowed to exploit a loophole because of their illegal activities and avoid paying value-added tax. The ruling, while difficult to enforce, raises the prospect of pimps and procurers having to keep accounts for inspection by Customs and Excise, just like any other business. ❞

vault *n* BANKING cámara *f* acorazada, *Am* bóveda *f* de seguridad

VCR *n (abbr* **video cassette recorder**) (aparato *m* de) *Esp* vídeo *m or Am* video *m*

VCT *n (abbr* **venture capital trust**) fondo *m* de capital riesgo

VDU *n* COMPTR *(abbr* **visual display unit**) pantalla *f* de visualización, monitor *m* ❏ **VDU operator** persona *f* que trabaja en pantalla

veep *n US Fam* vice *m,f*, vicepresidente(a) *m,f*

velocity *n* ECON **velocity of circulation of money** velocidad *f* de circulación del dinero

vend *vt* LAW vender

vendee *n* LAW comprador(ora) *m,f*

vendible *adj* LAW vendible

vending machine *n* máquina *f* expendedora

vendor *n* LAW parte *f* vendedora; COMPTR vendedor(ora) *m,f* ❏ **vendor's lien** derecho *m* de retención del vendedor; FIN **vendor placing** = colocación con inversores predeterminados de acciones emitidas como contraprestación para la adquisición de una rama de negocios; FIN **vendor's shares** = acciones emitidas por la empresa adquirente en un "vendor placing"

vendue *n US* pública subasta *f*

venture *n* empresa *f*, operación *f* ❏ **venture capital** capital *m* (de) riesgo; **venture capital company** compañía *f* de capital riesgo; **venture capitalist** capitalista *m f* de riesgo; **venture capital trust** fondo *m* de capital riesgo; **venture team** = equipo de profesionales que intervienen en la compra de una empresa distinta de la suya propia

❝
3i, the UK's largest **venture capital** provider, is pulling back from funding smaller companies that are not involved in technology or other growth areas. … The **venture capitalist** is setting up a special team to manage investments of less than £2m in non-technology companies to "maximise value". This could involve sales and mergers but not a flood of disposals. ❞

verbal *adj (agreement, offer, promise)* verbal

verdict *n* veredicto *m*

verification *n (confirmation)* corroboración *f*, confirmación *f*; *(checking)* verificación *f*, comprobación *f*

verify *vt (confirm)* corroborar, confirmar; *(check)* verificar, comprobar

vertical *adj* vertical ❏ *vertical concentration* concentración *f* vertical; *vertical equity* equidad *f* vertical; *vertical integration* integración *f* vertical; *vertical merger* fusión *f* vertical; ST EXCH *vertical spread* diferencial *m* vertical; *vertical trust* (organization) empresa *f* de integración vertical; US *vertical union* sindicato *m* industrial

> " By a horizontal merger we mean the union of two firms at the same production stage in the same industry, for example the merger of two steel producers or two motor car manufacturers. By a **vertical merger** we mean the union of two firms at different production stages in the same industry, as when a car manufacturer merges with a steel producer. "

vessel *n* (ship) buque *m*, navío *m*

vested interest *n* **to have a vested interest in a business** (personal involvement) tener un interés personal en un negocio; (money invested) tener dinero invertido en un negocio; **vested interests** (advantages, privileges) intereses *mpl* creados; (investments) capital *m* invertido; LAW (rights) derecho *m* adquirido; **there are vested interests in industry opposed to reform** hay (grupos con) intereses creados en el sector industrial que se oponen a la reforma

vet *vt* (person) someter a investigación; (application) investigar; (claims, figures) revisar, contrastar; **she was thoroughly vetted for the job** la investigaron exhaustivamente antes de concederle el empleo; **the committee has to vet any expenditure exceeding £100** cualquier gasto que exceda las 100 libras ha de ser aprobado por la comisión, previa investigación

veto 1 *n* veto *m*; **right** *or* **power of veto** derecho de veto; **to use one's veto** hacer uso del derecho de veto; **to impose a veto on sth** vetar algo **2** *vt* vetar

VGA *n* COMPTR (abbr **Video Graphics Array**) VGA *m*

viability *n* viabilidad *f*

viable *adj* viable; **it's not a viable proposition** no es una propuesta viable

vice-chairman *n* vicepresidente *m*

vice-chairmanship *n* vicepresidencia *f*

vice-chairperson *n* vicepresidente *m*

vice-chairwoman *n* vicepresidenta *f*

vice-presdency *n* vicepresidencia *f*

vice-president *n* (of country, company) vicepresidente(a) *m,f*

video *n* Esp vídeo *m*, Am video *m* ❏ COMPTR *video accelerator card* acelerador *m* de Esp vídeo *or* Am video; COMPTR *video board* placa *f* de Esp vídeo *or* Am video; *video card* tarjeta *f* de Esp vídeo *or* Am video; *video clip* videoclip *m*, clip *m* de Esp vídeo *m or* Am video *m*; *video compact disc* CD *m* de Esp vídeo *or* Am video, *video link* enlace *m* de Esp vídeo *or* Am video; *video recorder* (aparato *m* de) Esp vídeo *m or* Am video *m*

videoconference *n* videoconferencia *f*

videoconferencing *n* videoconferencias *fpl*

videophone *n* videoteléfono *m* ❏ *videophone conference* videoconferencia *f*

videotex *n* COMPTR videotexto *m*

view *vt* COMPTR (codes, document) visualizar

Viewdata® *n* videotexto *m*

viewer *n* COMPTR (program) visualizador *m*

viewphone *n* TEL videoteléfono *m*

violate *vt* (law) violar, vulnerar; (agreement) incumplir

VIP *n* (abbr **very important person**) VIP *mf* ❏ *VIP lounge* sala *f* VIP

viral marketing *n* marketing *m* viral

> " Persuasion works best when it's invisible. The most effective marketing worms its way into our consciousness, leaving intact the perception that we have reached our opinions and made our choices independently. As old as humankind itself, over the past few years this approach has been refined, with the help of the internet, into a technique called **viral marketing**. "

virtual *adj* COMPTR virtual ❏ *virtual reality* realidad *f* virtual

virus *n* COMPTR virus *m inv*; **to disable a virus** desactivar un virus ❏ *virus alert* alerta *f* de virus; *virus check* detección *f* de virus; **to run a virus check on a disk** analizar un disco en busca de virus, efectuar una exploración antivirus de un disco; *virus detection* detección *f* de virus; *virus detector* detector *m* de virus; *virus program* (program containing a virus) programa *m* virus; (antivirus program) programa *m* antivirus

virus-checked *adj* COMPTR explorado(a) para detectar virus; **all downloads are virus-checked** todas las descargas se exploran *or* examinan para detectar virus

virus-free *adj* COMPTR libre de virus

Visa® *n* Visa® *f*; **to pay by Visa**® pagar con Visa® ❏ *Visa*® *card* tarjeta *f* Visa®

visa 1 *n* visado *m*, Am visa *f* **2** *vt* visar

visible ECON **1** *n* **visibles** bienes *mpl* (visibles), productos *mpl*, mercancías *fpl* **2** *adj* *visible balance* balanza *f* comercial;

visible defect defecto *m* visible; **visible exports** exportaciones *fpl* visibles; **visible imports** importaciones *fpl* visibles; **visible reserve** reserva *f* visible; **visible trade** comercio *m* de bienes

> ❝
> The Treasury has stuck to its earlier forecast of a £15 billion current-account deficit this year. It expects a smaller invisibles surplus than before, but the forecasters are a lot more optimistic about **visible trade**: exports are booming.
> ❞

visit 1 *vt (person, place)* visitar
  2 *vi* **to be visiting** estar de visita; *US* **to visit with sb** charlar *or CAm, Méx* platicar con alguien

visiting fireman *n* visitante *mf or* visita *f* importante *(a quien hay que agradar)*

> ❝
> Although Kenyan head of state Daniel Arap Moi kept his cool while on camera, he was reported to be furious on February 7 when he said goodbye to International Monetary Fund **visiting fireman** Jose Fajgenbaum, leaving after a two-week mission in Nairobi.
> ❞

visitor *n* visitante *mf*, visita *f*; **all visitors must report to reception** todos los visitantes deben presentarse en recepción ❑ **visitor attraction** centro *m* de atracción de visitantes, punto *m* de interés turístico; **visitor centre** *(in park, at tourist attraction)* centro *m* de atención al visitante

visual display unit *n* COMPTR pantalla *f* de visualización, monitor *m*

vocational *adj (course, qualification)* de formación profesional ❑ **vocational guidance** orientación *f* profesional; **vocational training** formación *f* profesional

voice *n* COMPTR **voice mail** correo *m* de voz; **voice recognition software** software *m or* programa *m* de reconocimiento de voz; **voice synthesizer** sintetizador *m* de voz

voice-activated *adj* COMPTR activado(a) por la voz

void 1 *adj (deed, contract)* **(null and) void** nulo(a) y sin valor; **to make sth void** dejar algo sin efecto
  2 *vt (deed, contract)* invalidar, anular

voidable *adj* anulable

voidance *n* anulación *f*

volatile *adj (situation, economy, market)* inestable, volátil

volatility *n* inestabilidad *f*, volatilidad *f*

volume *n* volumen *m* ❑ **volume of activity** volumen *m* de actividad; **volume of business** volumen *m* de negocio; ECON **volume of current output** volumen *m* de producción actual;

volume discount descuento *m* por volumen, rappel *m*; **volume of exports** volumen *m* de exportaciones; **volume of imports** volumen *m* de importaciones; COMPTR **volume label** etiqueta *f* de volumen; **volume mailing** envíos *mpl* publicitarios masivos; **volume of output** volumen *m* de producción; **volume of purchases** volumen *m* de compras; **volume of sales** volumen *m* de ventas; **volume of trade** volumen *m* de intercambios (comerciales), volumen *m* comercial

voluntary *adj (a) (unpaid) (work, worker)* voluntario(a); **the shop is run on a voluntary basis** la tienda está a cargo de personas que trabajan en régimen de voluntariado; **many people like to include voluntary work on their CV** a mucha gente le gusta incluir trabajos de voluntariado en su CV ❑ **voluntary group** grupo *m* voluntario
  (b) *(optional)* voluntario(a) ❑ **voluntary arrangement** *(in insolvency proceedings)* acuerdo *m* voluntario; **voluntary bankruptcy** quiebra *f* voluntaria; **voluntary chain** cadena *f* libre *(de establecimientos)*; **voluntary export restraint** limitación *f* voluntaria de las exportaciones; **voluntary insurance** seguro *m* voluntario; **voluntary liquidation** liquidación *f* voluntaria; **the company has gone into voluntary liquidation** la compañía ha iniciado un proceso de liquidación voluntaria; **voluntary redundancy** despido *m* voluntario, baja *f* voluntaria *or* incentivada; **voluntary retail chain** cooperativa *f* de minoristas

vote 1 *n (a) (ballot)* votación *f*; **to put sth to the vote, to take a vote on sth** someter algo a votación ❑ **vote of confidence** voto *m* de confianza; **vote of no confidence** voto *m* de censura; **vote of thanks** voto *m* de gracias; **to propose a vote of thanks to sb** pedir un voto de gracias para alguien **(b)** *(individual vote)* voto *m*; **to give one's vote to sb** dar el voto a alguien, votar a alguien; **to cast one's vote** emitir el voto, votar
  2 *vt* **to vote to do sth** votar hacer algo; **to vote sb in** elegir a alguien (en votación); **to vote sb out** rechazar a alguien (en votación)
  3 *vi* votar (**for/against** a favor de/en contra de); **most of the delegates voted against the chairman** la mayoría de los delegados votaron en contra del presidente; **to vote by a show of hands** votar a mano alzada; **to vote by proxy** votar por poderes

voter *n* votante *mf*

voting 1 *n* votación *f* ❑ **voting paper** papeleta *f* (de voto), voto *m*, *Col* tarjetón *m*, *Méx, RP* boleta *f*; ST EXCH **voting rights** *(of shareholders)* derecho *m* a voto; *Br* **voting shares,** *US* **voting stock** acciones *fpl* con derecho a voto
  2 *adj (member)* con voto ❑ **voting assembly** junta *f* general

voucher *n* (**a**) *(for purchase)* vale *m*, cupón *m* (**b**) *(receipt)* comprobante *m*, resguardo *m* (**c**) ACCT documento *m* contable

VP *n* (*abbr* **vice-president**) vicepresidente(a) *m,f*

VRAM *n* COMPTR (*abbr* **video random access memory**) VRAM *f*

VRM *n* (*abbr* **variable-rate mortgage**) hipoteca *f* (con *Esp* tipo *or Am* tasa) de interés variable

VSAT *n* (*abbr* **very small aperture terminal**) *(terminal)* VSAT *m*; *(station)* VSAT *f*

Ww

W3 n (abbr **World Wide Web**) W3 f, WWW f

wage n **wage(s)** salario m, sueldo m □ **wage(s) agreement** convenio m or acuerdo m salarial; **wage(s) bill** costos mpl or Esp costes mpl salariales, masa f salarial; **wage bracket** categoría f de salarios or salarial; **wage ceiling** techo m salarial; **wage claim** reivindicación f or demanda f salarial; **wage cut** recorte m salarial; **wage differential** diferencia f salarial; **wage drift** desviación f salarial; **wage earner** asalariado(a) m,f; **wage economy** economía f salarial; **wage floor** salario m mínimo; **wage freeze** Esp congelación f or Am congelamiento m salarial; **wage increase** incremento m salarial; **wage inflation** inflación f salarial; ACCT **wages ledger** libro m de gastos de personal; **wage packet** (envelope) sobre m de la paga; (money) salario m; **wage policy** política f salarial; **wage and price index** índice m de precios y salarios; **wage pyramid** pirámide f salarial; **wage rate** salario m, índice m salarial; **wage restraint** moderación f salarial; **wage scale** escala f salarial; **wage settlement** acuerdo m salarial; **wages sheet** nómina f (de la empresa); **wage slip** nómina f, recibo m de sueldo; **wage structure** estructura f salarial; **wage zone** zona f salarial

wage-price spiral n espiral f de precios y salarios

> **❝**
>
> With its inflation still rising, the country on the verge of a perilous **wage-price spiral** and public finances deeply in the red, the Bundesbank has made it clear that it will keep the German economy locked in a vice of high interest rates for as long as it takes to squeeze out inflation.
>
> **❞**

wageworker n US asalariado(a) m,f

WAIS n COMPTR (abbr **wide area information service system**) servidores mpl de información de área amplia

waiter n ST EXCH auxiliar m for subalterno(a) m,f de la Bolsa de Londres

waiting n **waiting list** lista f de espera; **waiting period** (for order) periodo m de espera; (for insurance) plazo m de carencia; **waiting room** sala f de espera; **waiting time** tiempo m de espera

waive vt (condition, law) no tomar en consideración, no aplicar; (rule, requirement) obviar, pasar por alto; (claim, right) renunciar a

waiver n (of condition, law) dispensa f; (of rule, requirement) exención f; (of claim, right) renuncia f

wake-up call n (**a**) (on phone) **I asked the operator for a wake-up call** le pedí a la operadora que me despertara (**b**) (warning) llamada f or Am llamado m de atención

► **walk out** vi (**a**) (strike) ponerse or declararse en huelga (**b**) (leave) salir; **they walked out of the talks** abandonaron la mesa de negociaciones

walkout n (strike) huelga f, plante m; (from meeting) abandono m (en señal de protesta); **to stage a walkout** (workers) abandonar el puesto de trabajo or realizar un plante en señal de protesta; (negotiators) abandonar la sala en señal de protesta

wallpaper n COMPTR papel m tapiz

Wall Street n Wall Street m □ **the Wall Street Crash** el crack or crash del 29

WAN n COMPTR (abbr **wide area network**) red f de área extensa

want ad n US anuncio m por palabras

WAP n TEL (abbr **wireless applications protocol**) WAP m □ **WAP phone** teléfono m WAP

war chest n (of company) reserva f de capital, capital m ocioso; (of trade union) Esp caja f de resistencia, Am fondo m de huelga

warehouse **1** n almacén m, depósito m □ **warehouse book** libro m de almacén; **warehouse charges** gastos mpl de almacenaje; **warehouse keeper** encargado(a) m,f de almacén; **warehouse manager** jefe(a) m,f de almacén; **warehouse receipt** resguardo m de depósito; **warehouse warrant** resguardo m de depósito or de almacén
2 vt almacenar **warehoused goods** bienes mpl almacenados

warehouseman n (owner) almacenista m; (employee) empleado m de almacén, almacenero m; (manager) jefe m de almacén

warehousing n (**a**) (of goods) almacenaje m; (of goods in bond) depósito m □ **warehousing charges** gastos mpl de almacenaje; **warehousing company** empresa f de almacenaje; **warehousing costs** costos mpl or Esp costes mpl de almacenaje; **warehousing entry** certificado m de entrada en almacén; **warehousing system**

sistema *m* de almacenaje (**b**) ST EXCH *(of shares)* acaparamiento *m*

warm *adj* COMPTR ***warm boot, warm start*** arranque *m* en caliente

warning *n* (**a**) *(caution)* advertencia *f*, aviso *m* ❑ COMPTR ***warning message*** mensaje *m* de alerta; IND ***warning strike*** huelga *f* de advertencia (**b**) *(advance notice)* aviso *m*; **we only received a few days' warning** nos avisaron con sólo unos días de antelación (**c**) *(alarm, signal)* alerta *f*

warrant 1 *n* (**a**) LAW *(written order)* mandamiento *m or* orden *f* judicial (**b**) *(for goods)* resguardo *m* de almacén *or* de depósito, warrant *m* (**c**) ST EXCH bono *m* de suscripción, warrant *m* (**d**) *(guarantee)* garantía *f*
  2 *vt* (**a**) *(justify)* justificar; **the costs are too high to warrant further investment** los costos son demasiado elevados como para justificar más inversión (**b**) *(guarantee)* garantizar

warranted *adj (guaranteed)* garantizado(a)

warrantee *n* LAW titular *mf* de una garantía

warrantor *n* LAW garante *mf*

warranty *n (given by manufacturer)* garantía *f*; LAW *(in contract)* garantía *f*; **this printer has a five-year warranty** esta impresora tiene cinco años de garantía; **under warranty** en garantía; **extended warranty** garantía ampliada; **on-site warranty** garantía in situ; **return-to-base warranty** garantía de reparación en el taller del proveedor ❑ ***warranty certificate*** certificado *m* de garantía; ***warranty clause*** cláusula *f* de garantía

wastage *n* (**a**) *(of material)* desperdicio *m*; *(of money)* pérdida *f*, despilfarro *m*; *(wasted material)* material *m* de desecho; **to allow for wastage** tener en cuenta el desperdicio de material (**b**) *(reduction of workforce)* reducción *f* de plantilla *or* personal

waste 1 *n* (**a**) *(of materials, resources, effort)* derroche *m*; *(of money, time)* pérdida *f*, derroche *m* (**b**) *(unwanted material)* desechos *mpl*; *(radioactive, toxic)* residuos *mpl* ❑ ***waste disposal*** eliminación *f* de residuos; ***waste material*** material *m* de desecho; ***waste products*** productos *mpl or* materiales *mpl* de desecho
  2 *vt (materials, resources, money)* derrochar, malgastar; *(time)* perder

wastebasket *n* COMPTR papelera *f*

wasting asset *n* ACCT activo *m* amortizable, posesión *f* que genera pérdidas

❝
There is a series of complex rules for determining the true length of a lease … A lease will usually be a **wasting asset** for the purposes of capital gains tax when its duration does not exceed fifty years.
❞

watchdog *n (organization)* (organismo *m*) regulador *m* ❑ COMPTR ***watchdog program*** programa *m* de vigilancia *or* control

❝
THE US accountancy **watchdog**, the Financial Accounting Standards Board, has proposed toughening the so-called 3% rule that allowed Enron to keep special purpose entities, such as partnerships, off its books by ensuring third-party investors held at least 3% of the entities.
❞

watered stock *n* ST EXCH acciones *fpl* diluidas

waybill *n (in road transport)* hoja *f* de ruta; *(in air or sea transport)* conocimiento *m* de embarque

WB *n (abbr* **waybill**) *(in road transport)* hoja *f* de ruta; *(in air or sea transport)* conocimiento *m* de embarque

weak *adj (currency, economy, market)* débil ❑ ***weak point*** punto *m* débil *or* flaco

weaken 1 *vt (currency, market, prices)* debilitar
  2 *vi (currency, market, prices)* debilitarse

wealth *n* riqueza *f* ❑ ***wealth tax*** impuesto *m* sobre el patrimonio

wealthy 1 *npl* **the wealthy** los ricos
  2 *adj (person, family)* rico(a), pudiente; *(country, city)* rico(a)

wear *n* **wear (and tear)** deterioro *m*, desgaste *m*; **fair wear and tear** desgaste natural por el uso

Web *n* COMPTR **the Web** la Web ❑ ***Web address*** dirección *f* web; ***Web authoring*** creación *f* de páginas web; ***Web authoring program*** programa *m* de creación de páginas web; ***Web authoring tool*** herramienta *f* de creación de páginas web; ***Web browser*** navegador *m*; ***Web cam*** cámara *f* web, webcam *f*; ***Web consultancy*** consultoría *f* sobre páginas web; ***Web design agency*** agencia *f* de diseño de páginas web; ***Web designer*** diseñador(ora) *m,f* de páginas web; ***Web hosting*** hospedaje *m* de páginas web; ***Web page*** página *f* web; ***Web server*** servidor *m* web; ***Web site*** sitio *m* web; ***Web space*** espacio *m* web

webcast COMPTR **1** *n* difusión *f* en Internet, difusión web
  2 *vt* difundir en Internet

webcasting *n* COMPTR difusión *f* en Internet, difusión web

Webmaster *n* COMPTR administrador(ora) *m,f* de (sitio) web, webmaster *mf*

webzine *n* revista *f* electrónica, revista cibernética

week *n* semana *f*

weekday *n* día *m* entre semana

weekly 1 *adj* semanal ❑ ***weekly paper*** semanario *m*; ***weekly pay*** paga *f* semanal; ST EXCH *weekly trading report* informe *m* semanal de operaciones; *weekly wage* salario *m* semanal

2 *adv* semanalmente

weight 1 *n* peso *m*; **weight when empty** peso en vacío, tara *f*; **to sell sth by weight** vender algo al peso □ *weight limit* límite *m* de peso; *weights and measures* pesos *mpl* y medidas; *weight note* nota *f* de peso

2 *vt* ECON *(index, average)* ponderar

weighted *adj* ECON *(index, average)* ponderado(a) □ ACCT *weighted average cost* costo *m* or *Esp* coste *m* medio ponderado; *weighted distribution* distribución *f* ponderada

weighting *n* ECON *(of index, average)* ponderación *f*; ADMIN **London weighting** *(in salary)* = compensación salarial que sirve para equilibrar el coste de la vida en Londres

❝
The weekend starts two days early for many of the capital's pupils today, as NUT members take a day of strike action to campaign for a one- third increase in **London weighting**. Far from "being held hostage", as some have put it, pupils will probably feel the opposite.
❞

welcome *n* COMPTR *welcome message* mensaje *m* de bienvenida; *welcome pack (at conference, in hotel)* paquete *m* de bienvenida

welfare *n esp US (state aid)* ayudas *fpl or* subsidios *mpl* estatales; **to be on welfare** percibir un subsidio del Estado; **people on welfare** las personas que reciben un subsidio del Estado; **the welfare lines are lengthening** el número de personas que reciben una prestación económica del Estado va en aumento; **to stand in the welfare line** recibir una prestación económica *or* un subsidio del Estado □ *welfare benefits* beneficios *mpl or* prestaciones *fpl* sociales; *welfare centre* centro *m* de asistencia social; *welfare check* cheque *m* del subsidio del Estado; *welfare economics* economía *f* del bienestar; *the welfare economy* la economía del bienestar; *welfare office* oficina *f* de la seguridad social; *welfare payment* subsidio *m* del Estado; *welfare service* servicio *m* de asistencia social; *the Welfare State (concept)* el Estado del bienestar; **the government wants to cut back on the Welfare State** el gobierno quiere hacer recortes en el Estado de bienestar; *welfare work* trabajo *m* social; *welfare worker* trabajador(ora) *m,f* social

welfare-to-work *n Br* = programa de inserción laboral en el que los desempleados que perciben un subsidio han de realizar trabajos para la comunidad o cursos de formación de carácter obligatorio

WFTU *n (abbr* **World Federation of Trade Unions)** FSM *f*

wharf 1 *n* muelle *m*, embarcadero *m* □ *wharf dues* muellaje *m*, derechos *mpl* de muelle

2 *vt* (**a**) *(goods) (store)* almacenar en el muelle; *(unload)* desembarcar (en el muelle) (**b**) *(ship)* atracar

3 *vi* atracar

wharfage *n* muellaje *m*, derechos *mpl* de muelle

wharfinger *n* jefe(a) *m,f* del muelle

wheeler-dealer *n Fam* chanchullero(a) *m,f*

wheeling and dealing, wheeler-dealing *n Fam* chanchullos *mpl*, tejemanejes *mpl*

❝
The languishing gold price has not dampened the amount of **wheeling and dealing** going on among local producers. Junior mining company Harmony Ltd., for example, is still solidly in the market to raise 1 billion rand ($128 million) to buy two mines from industry giant AngloGold.
❞

white *adj white goods (kitchen appliances)* (aparatos *mpl* de) línea *f* blanca; ST EXCH *white knight* caballero *m* blanco; PARL *white paper* Libro *m* Blanco; *white squire* escudero *m* blanco

whiteboard *n* pizarra *f* blanca

white-collar *adj* de oficina, administrativo(a) □ *white-collar crime* delito *m* de guante *or* cuello blanco; *white-collar union* sindicato *m* de empleados (de oficina); *white-collar worker* empleado(a) *m,f* de oficina

whizz-kid *n Fam* joven *mf* prodigio; **she's a computer whizz-kid** es un cerebro informático

❝
This seemingly lottery-like sector is famous for being over-crowded by poorly equipped entrepreneurs attracted by well publicised "get-megarich-quick" tales of Internet businesses started by **whizz-kid** teenagers in their parents' garages who then float their companies a couple of years later.
❞

whole-life, whole-of-life *adj* INS **whole-life** *or* **whole-of-life policy** póliza *f* (de seguro) de vida entera; **whole-life** *or* **whole-of-life insurance** seguro *m* de vida entera

wholesale 1 *n* venta *f* al por mayor, *Am* mayoreo *m*; **wholesale and retail** (ventas) al por mayor y al por menor, *Am* mayoreo y menudeo

2 *adj* al por mayor, *Am* al mayoreo □ *wholesale bank* banco *m* mayorista; *wholesale banking* banca *f* mayorista; *wholesale co-operative* cooperativa *f* mayorista; *wholesale customer* cliente(a) *m,f* mayorista; *wholesale dealer*

mayorista *mf*; **wholesale distribution** distribución *f* al por mayor *or Am* al mayoreo; **wholesale firm** empresa *f* mayorista; **wholesale goods** mercancías *fpl* al por mayor *or Am* al mayoreo; BANKING **wholesale market** mercado *m* mayorista; **wholesale price** precio *m* al por mayor *or Am* al mayoreo; **wholesale price index** índice *m* de precios al por mayor *or Am* al mayoreo; **wholesale purchase** compra *f* al por mayor *or Am* al mayoreo; **the wholesale trade** los mayoristas, el sector mayorista

3 *adv (buy, sell)* al por mayor, *Am* al mayoreo; **I can get it for you wholesale** te lo puedo conseguir a precio de mayorista

wholesaler *n* mayorista *mf* ❑ **wholesaler margin** margen *m* del mayorista

wholesaling *n* venta *f* al por mayor, *Am* mayoreo *m*

wholly-owned subsidiary *n* subsidiaria *f* en propiedad absoluta, filial *f* participada al 100%

> ❝
> Multinationals face increasing scrutiny of workplace standards in their foreign suppliers. ... While it may be straightforward to impose a policy in a **wholly-owned subsidiary**, how can contractors be brought into line?
> ❞

wide area network *n* COMPTR red *f* de área extensa

widow's pension *n Esp* pensión *f* de viudedad, *Am* pensión de viudez

wildcard *n* COMPTR comodín *m* ❑ **wildcard character** carácter *m* comodín

wildcat *n* (**a**) **wildcat strike** huelga *f* salvaje (**b**) *US* MKTG *(company)* negocio *m* arriesgado

will *n* testamento *m*; **to make a will** hacer testamento, testar

▸ **wind up** *vt sep (company)* liquidar, disolver; *(account)* cancelar; *(meeting, speech)* concluir; **the business will be wound up by the end of the year** la empresa quedará disuelta a finales de año

windbill *n* FIN letra *f* de favor

windfall *n (unexpected gain)* dinero *m* caído del cielo ❑ **windfall dividends** dividendos *mpl* extraordinarios; **windfall payment** pago *m* extraordinario; **windfall profits** *(of company)* beneficio *m* inesperado; **windfall revenues** ingresos *mpl* extraordinarios; **windfall tax** impuesto *m* sobre ingresos extraordinarios

> ❝
> Sir David Rowland, NatWest's chairman, said yesterday that this was just a "stepping stone" to other deals. The banking and insurance groups yesterday promised their

investors £130m a year in savings, and analysts expect about £100m a year in **windfall revenues**, but this was not enough to quell the doubts of some big shareholders.
> ❞

winding-up *n (of company)* liquidación *f*, disolución *f*; *(of account)* cancelación *f* ❑ **winding-up order** orden *f* de liquidación

window *n* (**a**) *(of shop)* escaparate *m*, *Am* vidriera *f*, *Chile, Col, Méx* vitrina *f*; *(at bank)* ventanilla *f* ❑ **window display** presentación *f* del escaparate; **window dressing** *(in shop)* escaparatismo *m*; ACCT manipulación *f* contable, maquillaje *m* de cuentas
(**b**) COMPTR ventana *f*
(**c**) *Fam (in schedule)* hueco *m*; **I've got a window at 10.30** tengo un hueco a las diez y media; **a window of opportunity** una ocasión *or* oportunidad única
(**d**) *(on envelope)* ventanilla *f* ❑ **window envelope** sobre *m* de ventanilla

> ❝
> Airlines are tricky businesses, as British Airways has unhappily proven. A few delays or technical problems and the wheels could come off. EasyJet clearly sees a **window of opportunity** – it wants to buy big quickly, while traditional carriers struggle to cope with the fallout from September 11.
> ❞

win-win *adj* **a win-win situation** una situación ventajosa para todos

> ❝
> Ariba's Glynn agrees that constant pressure on suppliers is limiting the potential of online trade exchanges. "We've got to change from that single-sided view where we just beat the supplier to death," Glynn says. "We've got to get to that **win-win situation** where both sides feel they are getting better deals."
> ❞

WIP *n (abbr* **work in progress**) productos *mpl* semiterminados

▸ **wipe off** *vt sep (debt)* cancelar; **several millions of pounds were wiped off the value of shares** las acciones vieron reducido su valor en varios millones de libras

wire *vt US* girar

wireless *adj* COMPTR inalámbrico(a) ❑ **wireless mouse** *Esp* ratón *m or Am* mouse *m* inalámbrico

wire service *n* agencia *f* de noticias

withdraw *vt* (**a**) *(money)* sacar, retirar (**from** de); **I would like to withdraw £500 from my account** quisiera retirar 500 libras de mi cuenta (**b**) *(order)* anular

withdrawal n *(of money)* reintegro m, *Esp* retirada f, *Am* retiro m; **to make a withdrawal** efectuar un reintegro ❑ **withdrawal limit** límite m de reintegro (de efectivo), límite de *Esp* retirada or *Am* retiro de fondos; **withdrawal notice** aviso m de reintegro, aviso *Esp* retirada or *Am* retiro de fondos; **withdrawal slip** justificante m de reintegro

withhold vt *(rent, tax)* retener; **to withhold payment** retener el pago

withholding n **the withholding of payments** la retención de los pagos; **the withholding of taxes** la retención de impuestos en origen ❑ *US* **withholding tax** impuesto m retenido origen

without prep LAW **without prejudice** *(on document)* sin perjuicio de los derechos que asisten al abajo firmante; **without recourse** *(on bill of exchange)* sin recurso

with-pack premium n MKTG promoción f en pack or en envase

wizard n (**a**) *Fam (genius)* **a financial wizard** un genio de las finanzas (**b**) COMPTR asistente m

word n COMPTR **word count** recuento m or *Am* conteo m de palabras; **to do a word count** contar las palabras; **word count facility** contador m de palabras; **word processor** procesador m de textos

word-of-mouth advertising n publicidad f boca a boca

word-process vt COMPTR procesar

word-processing n COMPTR tratamiento m or procesamiento m de textos ❑ **word-processing package** software m de tratamiento de textos; **word-processing software** software m de tratamiento or procesamiento de textos

wordwrap n COMPTR salto m de línea automático

work 1 n (**a**) *(labour)* trabajo m; **this report needs more work** hay que elaborar or trabajar más este informe; **to start work, to set to work** ponerse a trabajar ❑ COMPTR **work area** área f de trabajo; **the work ethic** la ética del trabajo; **work flow** flujo m de trabajo; **work flow schedule** programa m de flujo de trabajo; **work in progress** *(unfinished goods)* productos mpl semiterminados; *(sign)* trabajos mpl en curso; **work progress** avance m en el trabajo; **work rate** ritmo m de trabajo; **work standard** norma f laboral; **work study engineer** analista mf de tiempos y movimientos
(**b**) *(employment)* trabajo m, empleo m; **to look for work** buscar empleo or trabajo; **to be out of work** no tener trabajo, estar desempleado(a), *Esp* estar parado(a); **to take time off work** tomarse unos días libres; **she's off work today** hoy tiene el día libre, hoy no trabaja ❑ **work colleague** compañero(a) m,f de trabajo;

work experience *(previous employment)* experiencia f laboral; *Br (placement)* prácticas fpl (laborales); **work permit** permiso m de trabajo
(**c**) *(task)* trabajo m; **to take work home** llevar(se) trabajo a casa; **I'm trying to get some work done** estoy intentando trabajar
(**d**) **works** *(construction)* obras fpl; *(factory)* fábrica f, planta f ❑ **works council** or **committee** comité m de empresa; **works manager** jefe(a) m,f de planta or fábrica; **works owner** propietario(a) m,f de fábrica
2 vt (**a**) *(employee)* **to work sb hard** hacer trabajar mucho a alguien (**b**) *(operate) (machine)* manejar, hacer funcionar
3 vi (**a**) *(person)* trabajar; **he works in advertising** trabaja en publicidad; **we have to work to a budget** tenemos que trabajar ajustándonos a un presupuesto; **to work from home** trabajar desde casa; **to work to rule** hacer huelga de celo (**b**) *(machine)* funcionar (**c**) *(plan, idea, method)* funcionar

> 66
> Flights to France were worst affected as an all day walkout interrupted more than 7,000 flights. Shorter stoppages in Greece, Portugal, Hungary and Italy brought airports to a standstill, and in Switzerland, Belgium, Luxembourg and Austria staff **worked to rule**.
> 99

▶ **work out** 1 vt sep (**a**) *(plan)* elaborar (**b**) *(price)* calcular
2 vi *(total)* **to work out at** salir a/por; **the total works out at £9,000** el total asciende a 9.000 libras

▶ **work up** vt sep **she worked her way up through the company** fue ascendiendo en el escalafón de la empresa; **she worked her way up from secretary to managing director** empezó de secretaria y llegó a directora general

workable adj *(project, plan)* viable, factible

workaholic n *Fam* **to be a workaholic** ser un(a) adicto(a) al trabajo

workday n *(day's work)* jornada f laboral; *(not holiday)* día m laborable, día hábil

worker n trabajador(ora) m,f; **workers and management** los trabajadores y la dirección ❑ **workers' co-operative** cooperativa f obrera; **worker director** = empleado que forma parte del consejo de administración; **worker participation** = participación de los trabajadores en la gestion de la empresa; **worker representation** representación f de los trabajadores

> 66
> Giving employees a greater say in how their companies operate could be an important step towards such a goal, but Laing is opposed to the appointment of **worker**

> **directors**, as is the practice in Scandinavia.
> "I think everybody who joins a company in
> any capacity should, if he's got the capabil-
> ity, be able to reach board level. But I don't
> think you should just appoint somebody
> and say he's a **worker director**. I just don't
> believe in that."
>   **"**

workfare n US = trabajos para la comunidad de carácter obligatorio para desempleados que perciben un subsidio

workforce n (**a**) *(working population)* población f activa (**b**) *(employees)* plantilla f, SAm plantel m

work-in n IND encierro m

working adj *(person)* trabajador(ora) ❑ **working account** cuenta f de explotación; **working agreement** acuerdo m tácito; **working assets** activos mpl circulantes; **working capital** capital m circulante; **working capital cycle** periodo m medio de maduración, duración f del ciclo de explotación; US **working capital fund** fondo m de explotación *(para un fin concreto)*; **working capital requirements** necesidades fpl de capital circulante; **the working class** la clase trabajadora or obrera; **working conditions** condiciones fpl de trabajo; **working copy** copia f de trabajo; **working day** *(hours of work in a day)* jornada f laboral; *(not holiday)* día m laborable, día m hábil; **during a normal working day** en una jornada laboral normal; **Sunday is not a working day** el domingo no es día laborable; **working document** documento m de trabajo; **working environment** entorno m laboral or de trabajo; **working expenses** gastos mpl de explotación; **working group** grupo m de trabajo; **working hours** horario m laboral or de trabajo; **working interest** interés m económico directo; **working lunch** almuerzo m de trabajo; **working man** hombre m que trabaja, hombre trabajador; **working party** comisión f de trabajo; **working population** población f activa; **working week** semana f laboral; **working woman** mujer f que trabaja, mujer trabajadora

work-life balance n conciliación f de la vida laboral y familiar

workload n cantidad f de trabajo; **to have a heavy workload** tener mucho trabajo; **my workload has eased off** ya no tengo tanto trabajo

workman n *(manual worker)* obrero m; *(craftsman)* artesano m

workmanlike adj competente, profesional

workmanship n confección f, factura f; **a fine/shoddy piece of workmanship** un trabajo de excelente/pésima factura

workplace n lugar m de trabajo

work-related stress n estrés m laboral, estrés relacionado con el trabajo

workshare n trabajo m or empleo m compartido; **workshares are becoming more common** los trabajos compartidos se están convirtiendo en una práctica cada vez más habitual

worksharing n reparto m del trabajo, trabajo m compartido; **we have a worksharing arrangement** tenemos un acuerdo de trabajo compartido; **worksharing is becoming popular** el trabajo compartido or el reparto del trabajo se está convirtiendo en una práctica cada vez más generalizada

worksheet n hoja f de trabajo

workshop n taller m

workstation n COMPTR estación f de trabajo

work-to-rule n huelga f de celo, RP trabajo m a reglamento

workweek n US semana f laboral

world n (**a**) *(earth)* mundo m ❑ **the World Bank** el Banco Mundial; **world economy** economía f mundial; **world** or **world's fair** exposición f universal; **world markets** mercados mpl mundiales; **world reserves** reservas fpl mundiales; **world trade** el comercio mundial; **World Trade Organization** Organización f Mundial del Comercio; COMPTR **the World Wide Web** la (World Wide) Web

(**b**) *(domain)* mundo m; **the business world** el mundo de los negocios; **the financial world** el mundo de las finanzas

worldwide 1 adj mundial ❑ **worldwide policy** política f mundial; **worldwide rights** derechos mpl mundiales

2 adv en todo el mundo; **this product is now sold worldwide** este producto se vende ya en todo el mundo

WORM COMPTR *(abbr* **write once read many times***)* WORM

worth 1 n valor m; **the storm did £500 worth of damage to our house** el valor de los daños causados por la tormenta en nuestra vivienda fue de 500 libras; **a week's worth of fuel** combustible para una semana

2 prep **to be worth sth** valer algo; **how much is it worth?** ¿qué valor tiene?; **what is the dollar worth in pounds?** ¿cuál es la equivalencia del dólar en libras?

worthless adj **to be worthless** *(object)* no valer nada, no tener ningún valor; *(advice, suggestion)* no servir para nada

WP n COMPTR (**a**) *(abbr* **word processing***)* tratamiento m or procesamiento m de textos (**b**) *(abbr* **word processor***)* procesador m de textos

wrap 1 vt *(goods)* envolver

2 vi COMPTR *(document)* ajustar las líneas automáticamente

wrist rest n COMPTR apoyamuñecas m inv, reposamuñecas m inv

writ *n* LAW mandato *m* judicial; **to serve a writ on sb** entregar un mandato judicial a alguien ▫ *writ of execution* auto *m* de ejecución

write 1 *vt (letter, name, address)* escribir; *(CD-ROM)* grabar; **to write (sb) a cheque** extender un cheque (a nombre de alguien); *US* **to write sb** escribir a alguien; COMPTR **to write sth to disk** escribir algo en el disco; **to write new business** conseguir nuevos clientes
  2 *vi* escribir; **to write to sb** escribir a alguien
  3 *n* COMPTR *write area* área *f* de escritura; *write access* acceso *m* a escritura; *write density* densidad *f* de escritura; *write protection* protección *f* contra escritura; *write speed* velocidad *f* de escritura

▶ **write away for** *vt insep (order by post)* **to write away for sth** solicitar algo por correo; **I wrote away for a catalogue** solicité un catálogo por correo; **I had to write away for spare parts** tuve que pedir por correo las piezas de recambio

▶ **write down** *vt sep* (**a**) *(make note of)* escribir, anotar (**b**) ACCT *(asset)* rebajar, sanear

▶ **write off** *vt sep* ACCT *(debt)* condonar; *(asset)* anular *or* cancelar en libros

▶ **write up** *vt sep* ACCT *(asset)* aumentar el valor en libros

write-down *n* ACCT *(of asset)* saneamiento *m* ▫ *write-down of accounts receivable* saneamiento *m or* regularización *f* de cuentas a cobrar

write-off *n* ACCT *(of debt)* condonación *f*; *(of asset)* eliminación *f*, cancelación *f*

write-protect *vt* COMPTR proteger contra escritura

write-protected *adj* COMPTR protegido(a) contra escritura

write-up *n* ACCT *(of asset)* aumento *m* del valor en libros

written *adj* **written agreement** acuerdo *m* escrito; **written offer of employment** oferta *f* de empleo por escrito; **written proof** prueba *f* escrita; **written undertaking** compromiso *m* escrito

written-down value *n* ACCT valor *m* contable reducido

wrongful *adj* **wrongful dismissal** despido *m* improcedente; **wrongful trading** comercio *m* ilícito

> **❝**
> Under UK insolvency legislation, if a company goes into insolvent liquidation, a director will be liable for **wrongful trading** (and liable to contribute personally to the company's losses) if, at some time before the commencement of the winding up, the director knew or, perhaps more significantly, ought to have concluded that there was no reasonable prospect that the company would avoid going into insolvent liquidation but continued to trade in any event.
> **❞**

WTO *n* (*abbr* **World Trade Organization**) OMC *f*

WWW *n* COMPTR (*abbr* **World Wide Web**) WWW *f*

WYSIWYG *n* COMPTR (*abbr* **what you see is what you get**) WYSIWYG, = se imprime lo que ves ▫ *WYSIWYG display* visualización *f* WYSIWYG

Xx

X-Dax *n* ST EXCH **the X-Dax (index)** el (índice) Xetra Dax

xerography *n* xerografía *f*

Xerox® **1** *n (machine)* fotocopiadora *f*, xerocopiadora *f*; *(copy)* fotocopia *f*, xerocopia *f* ❑ ***Xerox copy*** fotocopia *f*, xerocopia *f*; ***Xerox machine*** fotocopiadora *f*, xerocopiadora *f*
  2 *vt* fotocopiar, xerocopiar

Xetra-Dax *n* ST EXCH **the Xetra-Dax index** el índice Xetra Dax, = índice bursátil de las 30 empresas más importantes de Alemania

XMCL *n* COMPTR (*abbr* **Extensible Media Commerce Language**) XMCL *m*

XML *n* COMPTR (*abbr* **Extensible Markup Language**) XML *m*

Yy

Yankee bond *n US* FIN bono *m* yankee, = bono denominado en dólares estadounidenses y emitido en Estados Unidos por bancos o sociedades extranjeras

year *n* año *m*; **she earns £40,000 a year** gana 40.000 libras al año; **the year under review** el ejercicio que nos ocupa; ACCT **year ended 31 December 2003** ejercicio cerrado al 31 de diciembre de 2003 ❑ *year of assessment* ejercicio *m* fiscal; ACCT *year to date* (*calendar year*) año *m* hasta la fecha, periodo *m* desde el 1 de enero hasta la fecha; (*financial year*) ejercicio *m* hasta la fecha; **sales are up by 5% for the year to date** (*calendar year*) las ventas han subido un 5% en lo que va de año; (*financial year*) las ventas han subido un 5% en lo que va de ejercicio; *year's profits* beneficios *mpl* del ejercicio; *year's purchase* valor *m* de capitalización de los beneficios

yearbook *n* anuario *m*

year-end *adj* ACCT (*accounts*) de cierre de ejercicio; (*profits, losses*) al cierre del ejercicio ❑ *year-end audit* auditoría *f* de cierre de ejercicio; *year-end closing of accounts* cierre *m* de cuentas del ejercicio, cierre *m* de ejercicio

yearly 1 *adj* anual ❑ *yearly accounts* cuentas *fpl* anuales; *yearly payment* pago *m* anual; *yearly premium* prima *f* anual
2 *adv* anualmente, cada año

year-to-date *adj* ACCT (*for calendar year*) desde el 1 de enero hasta la fecha, en lo que va de año; (*for financial year*) desde el inicio del ejercicio, en lo que va de ejercicio

yellow *adj* **the Yellow Pages®** las Páginas Amarillas®; *yellow sticker* (*Post-it®*) nota *f* adhesiva

yen *n* yen *m*

yes/no question *n* MKTG (*in survey*) pregunta *f* cerrada sí/no

yield 1 *n* (*from investments*) rendimiento *m*, rentabilidad *f*; (*from tax*) producto *m*, recaudación *f* ❑ *yield capacity* capacidad *f* de producción; *yield curve* curva *f* de rendimientos; *yield gap* brecha *f* de(l) rendimiento; *yield to maturity* rendimiento *m* al vencimiento
2 *vt* (*dividend*) arrojar, producir; (*interest*) rendir, producir; (*income*) producir; **the investment bond will yield 5%** el bono de inversión producirá una rentabilidad del 5%

youth *n youth market* mercado *m* juvenil; *youth marketing* marketing *m* dirigido a los jóvenes; *youth unemployment* desempleo *m* or desocupación *f* or *Esp* paro *m* juvenil

YTD ACCT (*abbr* **year to date**) **1** *n* (*calendar year*) año *m* hasta la fecha, periodo *m* desde el 1 de enero hasta la fecha; (*financial year*) ejercicio *m* hasta la fecha
2 *adj* (*for calendar year*) desde el 1 de enero hasta la fecha, en lo que va de año; (*for financial year*) desde el inicio del ejercicio, en lo que va de ejercicio

yuppie *n* yupi *mf*

Zz

zap *vt* COMPTR *(file)* borrar

ZBB *n* ACCT (*abbr* **zero base budgeting**) PBC *m*, presupuesto *m* (de *or* en) base cero

Z chart *n* gráfico *m* Z

zero *n* cero *m* ❑ **zero base budgeting** presupuesto *m* (de *or* en) base cero; **zero coupon bond** bono *m* de cupón cero; **zero defects** cero defectos *mpl*; **zero defects purchasing** compra *f* de productos con cero defectos; ECON **zero growth** crecimiento *m* cero

> **"**
> … the French economy is set to go into recession in the first half of this year with even the most optimistic forecasters predicting **zero growth**.
> **"**

zero-rated *adj (for VAT)* con *Esp* tipo *or Am* tasa cero **books are zero-rated** los libros están sujetos al tipo cero del IVA

zero-rating *n Esp* tipo *m* cero, *Am* tasa *f* cero

Zip® COMPTR *n* **Zip**® **disk** disco *m* Zip®; **Zip**® **drive** unidad *f* Zip®

zip 1 *n US* **zip code** código *m* postal
2 *vt* COMPTR comprimir

zone 1 *n (area)* zona *f*
2 *vt* (**a**) *(subdivide)* dividir en zonas (**b**) *US (classify)* calificar; **they zoned the area for industrial development** la zona fue calificada como área industrial

zoning *n US* calificación *f* urbanística

zoom box *n* COMPTR cuadro *m* de zoom

SUPLEMENTO

Índice

GUÍA DE COMUNICACIÓN EN INGLÉS

Índice

La correspondencia

Esta guía tiene la finalidad de facilitarle la redacción de una carta en inglés. En ella podrá encontrar consejos útiles sobre la disposición de cada parte, las fórmulas de introducción y de cortesía o el formato de la dirección, al igual que muchos modelos de cartas y sugerencias de expresiones que se pueden emplear en la correspondencia personal o comercial, el correo electrónico y los documentos enviados por fax.

Presentación de la carta

La correspondencia administrativa o comercial, influida por el fax y el correo electrónico, obliga a utilizar un estilo directo y conciso. Se empleará preferiblemente un tono cordial y respetuoso, y se evitarán las abreviaturas o las contracciones como **don't**, **I've** o **she'd** en lugar de **do not**, **I have** o **she had/would**, que habrán de utilizarse únicamente en la correspondencia personal o la comunicación oral. El correo electrónico y el fax se caracterizan por un estilo más espontáneo y un registro de lengua menos formal.

Cada párrafo estará formado por tres o cuatro frases como máximo y tratará un solo tema. Hay que evitar mezclar el pasado y el presente dentro de una misma oración y respetar las reglas de concordancia entre los tiempos verbales.

En los países anglosajones la carta de negocios va siempre mecanografiada. Los párrafos van alineados a la izquierda, sin sangría y separados por una línea en blanco. En inglés británico, la fecha, las direcciones y las fórmulas de saludo y de despedida no llevan ningún signo de puntuación. En inglés norteamericano, se coloca una coma antes del año en la fecha, un punto después de las abreviaturas Mr., Ms., etc., dos puntos después de la fórmula de saludo y una coma después de la fórmula de despedida.

Fórmulas de saludo y despedida

La fórmula de despedida varía en función de la fórmula de saludo utilizada. Consulte el cuadro que figura en el reverso.

- Fórmula de saludo

- Fórmula de despedida

Cuando no conocemos el nombre de la persona a la que nos dirigimos:

Dear Sir
Dear Madam

Cuando no sabemos si se trata de un hombre o de una mujer:
Dear Sir or Madam
o
Dear Sir/Madam

Cuando nos dirigimos a una empresa o a una entidad sin indicar el nombre del destinatario:
Dear Sirs (*Br*)
Gentlemen (*US*)

Yours faithfully (*Br*)

En inglés norteamericano, la fórmula de cortesía es siempre en sentido contrario:
Faithfully yours (*US*)

Cuando conocemos el nombre de la persona a la que nos dirigimos:

Dear Mr Jameson
Dear Mrs Lucas
Dear Miss Crookshaw
Dear Ms Greening

(La abreviatura Ms se utiliza cada vez más cuando nos dirigimos a una mujer porque así se evita indicar si se trata de una mujer casada (Mrs) o no (Miss).)

Dear Dr Illingworth

En los Estados Unidos, la abreviatura termina generalmente con un punto:
Mr., Mrs., Ms., Dr.

Cuando nos dirigimos al director de un periódico:
Sir

a un concejal británico:
Dear Councillor Henderson
Dear Councillor Mr/Mrs/Ms
Adams

a un diputado británico:
Dear Mr/Mrs Brown

a un gobernador:
Dear Governor Almanza

a un miembro del Congreso estadounidense:
Sir/Madam Dear Congressman/
Congresswoman Fox
Dear Senator Mitcham

al Primer Ministro:
Dear Sir/Madam
Dear Prime Minister

al Presidente de Estados Unidos:
Sir/Madam
Dear Mr/Madam President

Yours sincerely (*Br*)
Sincerely yours (*US*)
Sincerely (*US*)

Tono más amistoso:
Yours very sincerely (*Br*)

Estilo menos formal:
With best wishes
With kind regards
Kindest regards

Menos frecuente:
Yours respectfully (*Br*)
Respectfully yours (*US*)
Respectfully (*US*)

• Presentación de una carta mecanografiada

Los párrafos van alineados a la izquierda, sin sangría y separados por una línea en blanco.

Cuando se utiliza esta presentación en inglés británico, la dirección, el saludo y la despedida no llevan ninguna puntuación. En inglés norteamericano, el uso es ligeramente distinto y admite que se coloque una coma al final de cada línea de la dirección, al igual que entre el número y la calle.

Este espacio se puede usar para añadir algunas notas como: **Recorded delivery** (*Br*), **Certified mail** (*US*), **Personal**, **Confidential**.

La dirección del remitente figura en la parte superior derecha.

La fecha se coloca a la derecha, debajo de la dirección y dejando una línea en blanco. En Estados Unidos, se invierte el orden del día y del mes (**June 4, 2005**) y el año va separado con una coma.
Asimismo, se puede indicar la fecha en cifras: (*Br*) **4/6/2005**, **4.6.05**, (*US*) **6/4/2005**, **6.4.05**. Y también se suele utilizar la abreviatura del número ordinal correspondiente al día: **1st**, **2nd**, **3rd**, **4th**, **5th**, etc., aunque este uso tiende a desaparecer.

Nombre y/o cargo del destinatario, cuando los conocemos.

Dirección completa del destinatario.

En Estados Unidos, la fórmula de saludo va seguida siempre de dos puntos: **Dear Mr. Wikeley:**

Asunto de la carta. Suele mencionarse como introducción, al inicio de la carta.

En Estados Unidos, la fórmula de despedida va seguida siempre de coma: **Faithfully yours,**

Frase habitual que precede a la fórmula de despedida.

Nombre y apellido completos

La firma aparece a la izquierda debajo de la fórmula de cortesía. Se pueden utilizar distintas firmas: **Robert Clark**, **R Clark**, **RJ Clark**, **Robert J. Clark** (*US*)

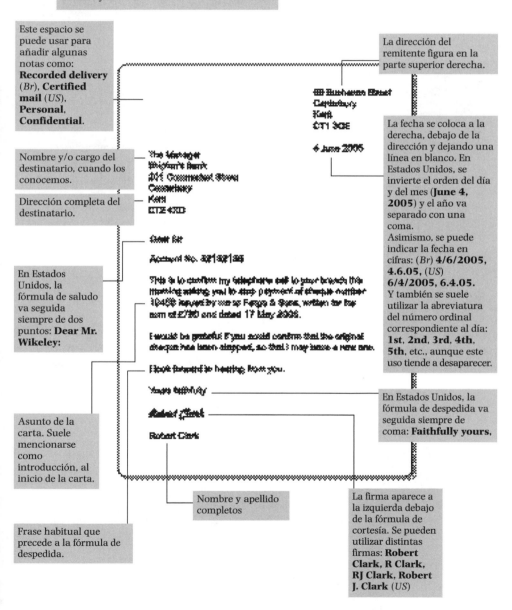

- **Presentación de una carta en papel con membrete**

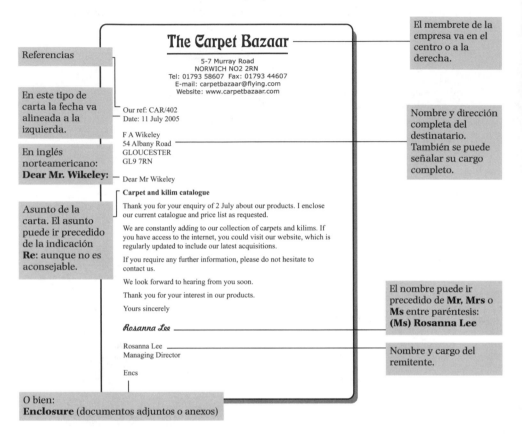

Referencias

En este tipo de carta la fecha va alineada a la izquierda.

En inglés norteamericano:
Dear Mr. Wikeley:

Asunto de la carta. El asunto puede ir precedido de la indicación **Re:** aunque no es aconsejable.

El membrete de la empresa va en el centro o a la derecha.

Nombre y dirección completa del destinatario. También se puede señalar su cargo completo.

El nombre puede ir precedido de **Mr, Mrs** o **Ms** entre paréntesis: **(Ms) Rosanna Lee**

Nombre y cargo del remitente.

O bien:
Enclosure (documentos adjuntos o anexos)

Sobres y direcciones

La dirección tiene que ser lo más precisa posible. Los sitios web de los servicios postales de cada país pueden ser útiles para encontrar la dirección completa de algún particular, de un organismo o empresa, incluso el código postal exacto.

Reino Unido: www.royalmail.com
Estados Unidos: www.usps.gov
Canadá: www.canadapost.ca
Irlanda: www.anpost.ie
Australia: www.auspost.com.au
Nueva Zelanda: www.nzpost.co.nz

Es aconsejable no incluir ningún signo de puntuación y escribir la dirección con mayúsculas especialmente si se trata de Estados Unidos o de Canadá (véanse los modelos siguientes).

- **Dirección en el Reino Unido:**

Mr (Mrs, Ms, Dr, etc.), nombre (o inicial), apellido
(Nombre del lugar y/o) número, calle
Población
CONDADO o CIUDAD PRINCIPAL
CÓDIGO POSTAL

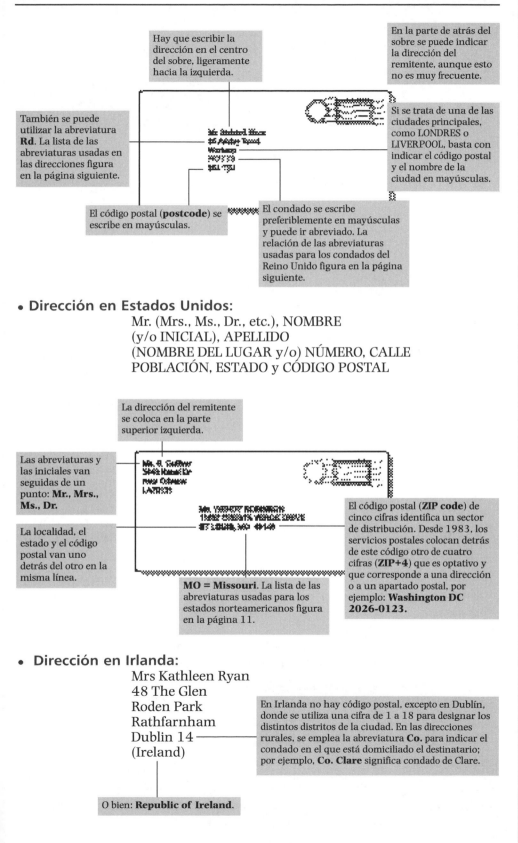

Hay que escribir la dirección en el centro del sobre, ligeramente hacia la izquierda.

En la parte de atrás del sobre se puede indicar la dirección del remitente, aunque esto no es muy frecuente.

También se puede utilizar la abreviatura **Rd**. La lista de las abreviaturas usadas en las direcciones figura en la página siguiente.

Si se trata de una de las ciudades principales, como LONDRES o LIVERPOOL, basta con indicar el código postal y el nombre de la ciudad en mayúsculas.

El código postal (**postcode**) se escribe en mayúsculas.

El condado se escribe preferiblemente en mayúsculas y puede ir abreviado. La relación de las abreviaturas usadas para los condados del Reino Unido figura en la página siguiente.

- **Dirección en Estados Unidos:**
  Mr. (Mrs., Ms., Dr., etc.), NOMBRE
  (y/o INICIAL), APELLIDO
  (NOMBRE DEL LUGAR y/o) NÚMERO, CALLE
  POBLACIÓN, ESTADO y CÓDIGO POSTAL

La dirección del remitente se coloca en la parte superior izquierda.

Las abreviaturas y las iniciales van seguidas de un punto: **Mr., Mrs., Ms., Dr.**

La localidad, el estado y el código postal van uno detrás del otro en la misma línea.

El código postal (**ZIP code**) de cinco cifras identifica un sector de distribución. Desde 1983, los servicios postales colocan detrás de este código otro de cuatro cifras (**ZIP+4**) que es optativo y que corresponde a una dirección o a un apartado postal, por ejemplo: **Washington DC 2026-0123.**

MO = Missouri. La lista de las abreviaturas usadas para los estados norteamericanos figura en la página 11.

- **Dirección en Irlanda:**
  Mrs Kathleen Ryan
  48 The Glen
  Roden Park
  Rathfarnham
  Dublin 14
  (Ireland)

En Irlanda no hay código postal, excepto en Dublín, donde se utiliza una cifra de 1 a 18 para designar los distintos distritos de la ciudad. En las direcciones rurales, se emplea la abreviatura **Co.** para indicar el condado en el que está domiciliado el destinatario; por ejemplo, **Co. Clare** significa condado de Clare.

O bien: **Republic of Ireland**.

- **Dirección en Canadá:**

  Mr & Mrs Fitzgerald
  28 Alpine Boulevard
  St Albert AB T8N 2M7
  (Canada)

  > Las dos primeras letras del código postal canadiense representan la provincia o el territorio.
  > **AB = Alberta.** La lista de las abreviaturas usadas para las provincias y los territorios de Canadá figura en la página siguiente.

- **Dirección en Australia:**

  Gareth Connolly
  55 Elizabeth Street
  Potts Point
  NSW 2020
  (Australia)

  > Abreviatura del estado o del territorio (consultar la lista en la página siguiente).

- **Dirección en Nueva Zelanda:**

  Mr J Hall
  3 Bridge Avenue
  Te Atatu
  Auckland 8
  (New Zealand)

- **Abreviaturas usadas en las direcciones**

Las abreviaturas siguientes se emplean habitualmente en las direcciones. Pueden figurar tanto en el encabezamiento de la carta como en el sobre.

Apt	Apartment	**Mtn**	Mountain
Av o **Ave**	Avenue	**Pde**	Parade
Blvd	Boulevard	**Pk**	Park
Cl	Close	**Pl**	Place
Cres	Crescent	**Plz**	Plaza
Ct	Court	**Rd**	Road
Dr	Drive	**Rdg**	Ridge
Est	Estate	**Rm**	Room
Gdns	Gardens	**Sq**	Square
Gr	Grove	**St**	Street
Hts	Heights	**Ter**	Terrace
La	Lane		

Las abreviaturas **N** (North), **S** (South), **W** (West), **E** (East), **NE** (Northeast), NW (Northwest), **SE** (Southeast) y **SW** (Southwest) también son muy usuales, especialmente en las direcciones de Estados Unidos y Canadá.

Por ejemplo, en Nueva York:

351 W 32ND ST
NEW YORK, NY 10001

> Esta dirección se lee: **three hundred and fifty-one West Thirty-second Street**

en Montreal:

123 MAIN ST NW
MONTREAL QC H3Z 2Y7

> Esta dirección se lee: **one hundred and twenty-three Main Street Northwest**

- **Abreviaturas de los condados del Reino Unido**

Generalmente en los nombres de los condados que terminan en –shire se mantiene la primera sílaba a la que se le agrega una "**s**": **Beds** = Bedfordshire, **Berks** = Berkshire, **Bucks** = Buckinghamshire, **Cambs** = Cambridgeshire, **Gloucs** = Gloucester, **Herts** = Hertfordshire, **Lancs** = Lancashire, **Lincs** = Lincolnshire, **Notts** = Nottinghamshire, **Staffs** = Staffordshire, **Wilts** = Wiltshire.

Excepciones:
Northants = Northamptonshire, **Oxon** = Oxfordshire

Los condados siguientes no se abrevian: Avon, Cleveland, Greater Manchester, Humberside, Kent, Merseyside, Tyne and Wear.

- **Abreviaturas de los estados norteamericanos**

AK	Alaska	**MT**	Montana
AL	Alabama	**NC**	North Carolina
AR	Arkansas	**ND**	North Dakota
AZ	Arizona	**NE**	Nebraska
CA	California	**NH**	New Hampshire
CO	Colorado	**NJ**	New Jersey
CT	Connecticut	**NM**	New Mexico
DC	District of Columbia	**NV**	Nevada
DE	Delaware	**NY**	New York
FL	Florida	**OH**	Ohio
GA	Georgia	**OK**	Oklahoma
HI	Hawaii	**OR**	Oregon
IA	Iowa	**PA**	Pennsylvania
ID	Idaho	**RI**	Rhode Island
IL	Illinois	**SC**	South Carolina
IN	Indiana	**SD**	South Dakota
KS	Kansas	**TN**	Tennessee
KY	Kentucky	**TX**	Texas
LA	Louisiana	**UT**	Utah
MA	Massachusetts	**VA**	Virginia
MD	Maryland	**VT**	Vermont
ME	Maine	**WA**	Washington
MI	Michigan	**WI**	Wisconsin
MN	Minnesota	**WV**	West Virginia
MO	Missouri	**WY**	Wyoming
MS	Mississippi		

- **Abreviaturas de las provincias y los territorios canadienses**

AB	Alberta	**NU**	Nunavut
BC	British Columbia	**ON**	Ontario
MB	Manitoba	**PE**	Prince Edward Island
NB	New Brunswick	**QC**	Quebec
NF	Newfoundland	**SK**	Saskatchewan
NS	Nova Scotia	**YT**	Yukon
NT	Northwest Territories		

- **Abreviaturas de los estados y territorios australianos**

ACT	Australian Capital Territory
NSW	New South Wales
NT	Northern Territory
QLD	Queensland
SA	South Australia
TAS	Tasmania
VIC	Victoria
WA	Western Australia

Modelos de cartas

- Para concertar una reunión

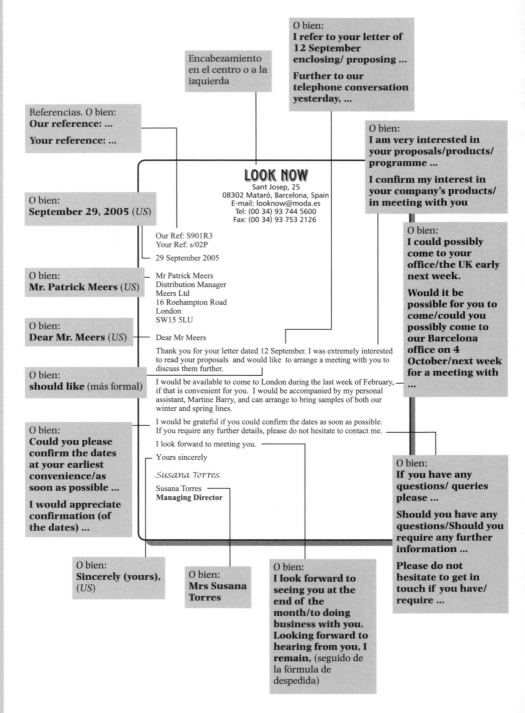

Encabezamiento en el centro o a la izquierda

O bien:
I refer to your letter of 12 September enclosing/ proposing ...

Further to our telephone conversation yesterday, ...

Referencias. O bien:
Our reference: ...
Your reference: ...

O bien:
I am very interested in your proposals/products/ programme ...

I confirm my interest in your company's products/ in meeting with you

O bien:
September 29, 2005 (US)

LOOK NOW
Sant Josep, 25
08302 Mataró, Barcelona, Spain
E-mail: looknow@moda.es
Tel: (00 34) 93 744 5600
Fax: (00 34) 93 753 2126

O bien:
I could possibly come to your office/the UK early next week.

Would it be possible for you to come/could you possibly come to our Barcelona office on 4 October/next week for a meeting with ...

Our Ref: S901R3
Your Ref: s/02P
29 September 2005

O bien:
Mr. Patrick Meers (US)

Mr Patrick Meers
Distribution Manager
Meers Ltd
16 Roehampton Road
London
SW15 5LU

O bien:
Dear Mr. Meers (US)

Dear Mr Meers

Thank you for your letter dated 12 September. I was extremely interested to read your proposals and would like to arrange a meeting with you to discuss them further.

O bien:
should like (más formal)

I would be available to come to London during the last week of February, if that is convenient for you. I would be accompanied by my personal assistant, Martine Barry, and can arrange to bring samples of both our winter and spring lines.

O bien:
Could you please confirm the dates at your earliest convenience/as soon as possible ...

I would appreciate confirmation (of the dates) ...

I would be grateful if you could confirm the dates as soon as possible. If you require any further details, please do not hesitate to contact me.

I look forward to meeting you.

Yours sincerely

Susana Torres

Susana Torres
Managing Director

O bien:
If you have any questions/ queries please ...

Should you have any questions/Should you require any further information ...

Please do not hesitate to get in touch if you have/ require ...

O bien:
Sincerely (yours), (US)

O bien:
Mrs Susana Torres

O bien:
I look forward to seeing you at the end of the month/to doing business with you. Looking forward to hearing from you, I remain, (seguido de la fórmula de despedida)

- ## Después de una reunión

En los países anglosajones, después de un primer contacto, se suele llamar a las personas por su nombre. En tal caso, habría que empezar la carta diciendo **Dear Susana**.

O bien:
There are several points that I would like to discuss further. Firstly, ... Secondly, ...

I agree fully with your proposal to ..., and would like to confirm ...
O bien:
As we agreed/discussed on Wednesday ...

O bien:
I would like to thank you for affording me the opportunity to meet with you and your staff.

O bien:
I would like to arrange another meeting with you to discuss matters/the proposal/ details further, and suggest next Friday/you could come to our London office on ...

I should like to discuss matters further and will phone you early next week/ write to you again.

O bien:
Thank you again for your hospitality/arranging the meeting/your interest in our company. Please contact me/ do not hesitate to contact me, if you have any further questions/need any further information.

- ## Solicitud de información

O bien:
27 February 2005 (*Br*)

Sin puntuación en inglés británico.

O bien:
Thanking you in anticipation ...

Thank you in advance for your help, ...

O bien:
I am writing to ask whether ...

I wish to know whether ...

Could you please send me/advise me/let me know ...

Would you kindly send me/ inform me ...

- ## Respuesta a una solicitud de información

O bien:
Thank you for your enquiry of 13 March about our equipment/services/products ...

In response to your enquiry of 7 April, we have pleasure in enclosing full details of ..., together with our price list.

O bien:
inquiry (*US*)

O bien:
I am enclosing our catalogue for your review.

O bien:
Once again, thank you for your interest in our products.

O bien:
I enclose/I have enclosed our 2005 catalogue and current price list with details of discounts and delivery dates.

O bien:
If you require/Should you require any further information, please contact me. I look forward to hearing from you soon. After you have reviewed our material, we would appreciate your comments, and we will look forward to answering any questions you have about our products.

Meers Ltd

16 Roehampton Road
London
SW15 5LU

Tel: 020 1876 2332
E-mail: Meers@garments.uk
Fax: 020 1876 2334

Our Ref: s/02P
Your Ref: S901R3

Mr Richard Delacroix
8 Fallowfield Road
Walsall
WS5 3DL

17 March 2005

Dear Mr Ramos

Thank you for your recent enquiry about our products.

I enclose our current catalogue and price list and am confident that this literature will provide many of the answers you have requested.

If there is additional information you would like to have regarding our products, please do not hesitate to contact us. We will be most happy to be of assistance.

Thanking you once again for your interest, we look forward to hearing from you.

Yours sincerely

Margaret Meers

Margaret Meers
Assistant Manager

- ## Reclamaciones

Motivo de la queja: indicar el número de pedido, el código del modelo o la información necesaria para identificar la mercancía.

3 Pennybrook Lane
Dollis Hill
London
NW2 6HG

The Customer Services Manager
Blotto & Co.
34 Vine Street
Ashford
Kent
KE8 5HB

1st September 2005

Dear Sir or Madam

Order 324B

I received the above order from you on 30 August 2005. I regret to inform you that there were several items missing from the shipment and other items do not correspond to the original order.

I enclose a list of the wines I have received, as well as a photocopy of the original order form and invoice. I trust you will remedy the situation as quickly as possible.

I look forward to hearing from you within the next 7 days.

Yours faithfully

Jackson Brattel

Mr Jackson Brattel

O bien:
The goods I received were badly damaged.

The goods you sent me were damaged in transit/were damaged on receipt.

The goods you sent me had the following defects: ...

- **Respuesta a una reclamación**

Acuse de recibo de la carta de reclamación del cliente.

O bien:
I refer to your letter dated 3 September 2005 which arrived this morning with the consignment of damaged boxes you advised you would be returning to us.

O bien:
I apologise most sincerely for the inconvenience this has caused you/your company and have dispatched this morning a replacement consignment of … which will reach you by …

Explicación breve y detalle de las medidas tomadas para resolver el problema. O bien:
To compensate for the inconvenience caused to you/your company, we would like …

O bien:
Once more please accept my sincerest apologies.

Please accept my/our sincere apologies once again.

- **Mailing**

O bien:
To whom it may concern: (Br)
Gentlemen: (US)

Introducción de los argumentos destinados a despertar el interés del lector. Otras frases útiles:
Since our service lends itself so well you your type of business, we would appreciate having an opportunity to speak with you or one of your representatives about …

Presentación de la empresa y asunto de la carta. Otras frases útiles:
Our firm recently received an extremely favourable review from/in … which we hope may be of some interest to you.

It is our great pleasure to inform you that our new product line is ready for your inspection.

O bien: **We will look forward to seeing you soon.**

Invitación para que el lector contacte con la empresa. Otras frases útiles:
Please contact me at [nº de teléfono], so that we can arrange a convenient time to meet. I will be looking forward to your call.

Please feel free to either drop in or make an appointment with one of our staff at any time.
Thank you for being a customer of our firm.
We invite you to call for an appointment to visit our display room/factory/shop.

- **Pedido**

O bien:
We would like to place an order for the following items, in the sizes and quantities specified below.

I refer to your letter of 5 June enclosing your catalogue for 2005. I would like to place an order for/to order ...

Please find enclosed our order no. 471 for ...

I wish to order ... as advertised in the July issue of ...

O bien:
Gentlemen: (US)
To whom it may concern: Esta última expresión se utiliza en inglés británico en la correspondencia administrativa cuando no se conoce el nombre del destinatario.

Campoamor, 25
46022 Valencia, Spain
Tel: 00 34 963 572736

Brooke's Books   23 June 2005
188 Belvidere Road
Glasgow
G64 2JP

Dear Sir or Madam

Please send me the following items from your summer catalogue:

10 copies of "Learn English the Easy Way", Intermediate, Scot Press. Ref: 4356K
10 copies of "Improve your Ps and Qs", Scot Press. Ref 5367Q

I enclose a cheque made payable to you for £267.50, which includes the cost of postage and packaging.

I look forward to receiving confirmation of my order, and would be obliged if you would advise me in advance of the planned delivery date.

Yours faithfully

Rodolfo Marín

Rodolfo Marin

O bien:
I enclose a cheque to the amount of £ ... (Br)
I am enclosing a check in the amount of $ ... (US)

O bien:
The enclosed order is based on your current price list, assuming our usual discount of ... on bulk orders.

- **Respuestas**

· Thank you for your order no ... It is receiving our immediate attention and will be dispatched to you by ... Please allow 28 days for delivery.
· This is to acknowledge receipt of your order no. ... dated ..., and to advise you that the goods will be dispatched within 7 working days.
· We acknowledge receipt of your order of 12 July, which will be dispatched within 14 days.
· We cannot accept responsibility for goods damaged in transit.
· I hope we may continue to receive your valued custom.

O bien:
· We regret that we will be unable to fulfil your order for ...
· We regret that the goods you ordered are temporarily out of stock/we no longer stock the goods you ordered.

- Factura

O bien:
Payment is to be made 14 days after receipt of the invoice.

- Carta de reclamación por falta de pago

- Segunda reclamación

Our records indicate that payment on your account is overdue to the amount of £ ... If the amount has already been paid, please disregard this notice. If you have not yet posted your payment, please use the enclosed envelope to send payment in full.

Thank you in advance for your anticipated co-operation in this matter.

On 12 July 2004 we notified you of your overdue account for order no. ...

To date we still have not received payment for the above order.

Please give this matter your most urgent attention. Payment must be made within the next ten days.

O bien:
mailed (*US*)

O bien:
in the amount of ... (*US*)

- **Envío del pago**

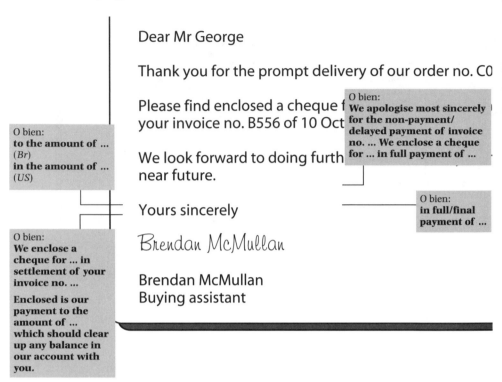

Dear Mr George

Thank you for the prompt delivery of our order no. C0

Please find enclosed a cheque f
your invoice no. B556 of 10 Oct

We look forward to doing furth
near future.

Yours sincerely

Brendan McMullan

Brendan McMullan
Buying assistant

O bien:
to the amount of ...
(*Br*)
in the amount of ...
(*US*)

O bien:
**We enclose a
cheque for ... in
settlement of your
invoice no. ...**

**Enclosed is our
payment to the
amount of ...
which should clear
up any balance in
our account with
you.**

O bien:
**We apologise most sincerely
for the non-payment/
delayed payment of invoice
no. ... We enclose a cheque
for ... in full payment of ...**

O bien:
**in full/final
payment of ...**

- **Solicitud de presupuesto**

24 Oldhay Close
Fulflood
Winchester
SO23 5BY

Mr J. Fargo
Fargo & Sons
93 Hickory Street
Truro
CO1 3GH

14th January 2005

Dear Mr Fargo

I have recently purchased a property in your area and am looking for a reliable builder to undertake
extensive renovations. You have come highly recommended and I hope you will be available to work for
me during the coming months.

I attach a detailed list of the work I have envisaged. Could you please send me an estimate for the
renovations listed? I would also like to know how long the work might take.

I look forward to hearing from you.

Yours sincerely

Kenneth McLough

Kenneth McLough

O bien:
**I would be
grateful if
you could
send ...**

O bien:
**I look
forward to
doing
business
with you.**

Búsqueda de empleo

Carta de presentación

En los países anglosajones la carta de presentación se manda siempre mecanografiada, salvo si el anuncio especifica que la carta sea manuscrita. El papel de la carta tiene que ser el mismo que el del currículum.

Hay que dirigir la carta a la persona responsable, indicando su nombre y cargo si se conocen. No hay que dejar de mencionar las referencias del anuncio y el cargo en el que se está interesado. Si no se adjunta el currículum con la carta, esta deberá contener toda la información útil sobre el candidato: historial académico, experiencia profesional, aptitudes y títulos. Si la carta va acompañada de un currículum, no merece la pena repetir la información que figura en él; en este caso habrá que atraer la atención del lector, poniendo énfasis en la capacitación profesional y demostrando que uno tiene las cualidades requeridas. Se pueden volver a usar algunas palabras clave del anuncio para captar su atención. La experiencia y los títulos que se mencionan deberán corresponder al cargo ofrecido.

El candidato tendrá que mostrar en la carta que conoce la empresa y que esta le interesa. Además, es preciso explicar por qué su experiencia y sus aptitudes se ajustan al perfil buscado. Es importante señalar que está disponible para una entrevista.

El currículum y la carta de solicitud pueden enviarse por correo electrónico. Es preferible mandar asimismo una copia impresa por correo normal.

- **Solicitud de prácticas**

Nombre y cargo del destinatario.

Datos del remitente a la derecha.

Fecha a la izquierda o a la derecha, debajo del número de teléfono y de la dirección electrónica.

Si la carta va dirigida a una empresa norteamericana hay que utilizar la palabra **internship** en lugar de **work placement**.

Situación actual, experiencia, títulos.

Capacitación profesional, cualidades y motivación.

- **Candidatura espontánea**

29 Bletchley Road
Worthing
West Sussex
BN14 7QY

Tel: 01903 990092

Alexander Maxwell
Personnel Manager
Kingsway Ltd
24-28 Finchley Rd
London
N2 0TT

13 December 2005

Dear Mr Maxwell

I wish to enquire about any vacancy you may have in your Sales Department.
Your customer services manager, Don Griffiths, suggested I wrote to you.

As you can see from the enclosed CV, I have a good educational background and
twelve years' experience in sales, both as sales representative and sales
executive.

I am currently working for a software company in Kent, where I have acquired
essential IT skills. I believe this combined experience in sales and computing
would be ideal for the job profile.

Should you consider my application favourably, I should be pleased to attend an
interview at any time.

Yours sincerely

William Brownston

Enclosure

> Es conveniente mencionar, si se conoce, a alguien que trabaja en la empresa.

> O bien:
> **I would like to/I wish to inquire about the possibility of becoming a ... at your factory/ facility/in your company.**

> O bien:
> **I have been/I was given your address by a colleague of mine/ of yours, [nombre de la persona] who has reason to believe you may be recruiting staff (for your sales team).**
>
> **I am seeking a position in sales/publishing at a (high technology) company such as yours.**

> O bien:
> **As you will note from the enclosed CV (Br)/resumé (US), I have specialized in/majored in (US) physics and have participated in significant research.**

> O bien:
> **at your convenience.**
> **I would like to learn more about ..., and I will contact your office early next week to arrange an appointment at your convenience.**

Expresiones útiles

I know how to/I can operate a cash register/a computer/power equipment
I am computer literate/a good communicator/a good organizer
I am a capable linguist/can speak fluent English and German
I have good computer/IT/language/editing/communication/organizational skills
I can learn new tasks and enjoy/can accept a challenge
I enjoy working/can work with a variety of people
I work well in a team, and can also work under pressure
I perform well under stress/am good with difficult customers
I can handle multiple tasks simultaneously

Respuesta a un anuncio

O bien:
I should like to apply for the above post as recently advertised in the July issue of …/which was advertised in today's Daily Post.

I am writing to apply for the above post/for the post of … as advertised in …
I am writing in response to your advertisement in … for …

I would like to be considered for the above post which your company advertised in …

O bien:
The position seems to fit very well with my education, experience, and career interests. According to the advertisement, your position requires excellent communication skills and an MA degree in …

O bien:
and (I) enclose my (current) CV (*Br*)/resumé (*US*) for your consideration.

Asunto de la carta: función o cargo.

O bien:
Thank you for considering my application/for your consideration. If you would like to schedule an interview, please call me at … I will be available at your convenience. I would appreciate the chance to meet with you. You may reach me at the above telephone number or e-mail address.

O bien:
I am confident that I can perform the job effectively and am excited about the idea of working for a dynamic firm. I know your firm seeks only the brightest staff for its team. I also know that I have the training and ability it takes to … My degree in … and my internship experiences have taught me how to …

O bien:
I look forward to talking with you/to discussing matters with you (at a future interview).

Curriculum vitae

Hoy en día un buen currículum destaca si es conciso (dos páginas como máximo). Es aconsejable mencionar la experiencia profesional y los títulos según el cargo y la empresa de que se trate.

El currículum puede seguir un orden cronológico directo o inverso. En este caso, se empieza por el empleo más reciente y se termina por el más antiguo. Esta presentación es la más corriente. Cuando se aspira a un cargo o un sector profesional preciso, también se puede redactar un currículum adaptado al mismo, en el que se insiste más sobre los conocimientos, la capacitación y los resultados alcanzados que sobre la trayectoria profesional.

Se suelen omitir los artículos (**a**, **an** y **the**) y, por otra parte, se pueden usar verbos para describir experiencias, por ejemplo, **managed**, **organized**, **supervised**, **designed**, **co-ordinated**, **developed**, etc. Si se envía el currículum por correo electrónico o si es probable que la empresa lo vaya a digitalizar, es conveniente utilizar sustantivos o palabras clave que el software pueda reconocer, por ejemplo, **management**, **organization**, **supervision**, **design**, **co-ordination**, **development of**, etc.

Es preferible no indicar las referencias en el currículum. Si la empresa las pide, es mejor imprimirlas en una hoja aparte.

Si se manda el currículum por correo electrónico, es preferible escoger un tipo de caracteres sencillo y un cuerpo intermedio, entre 10 y 14 puntos. No hay que incluir tablas o gráficos, ni utilizar caracteres en cursiva o subrayados.

- **Titulado británico con poca experiencia**

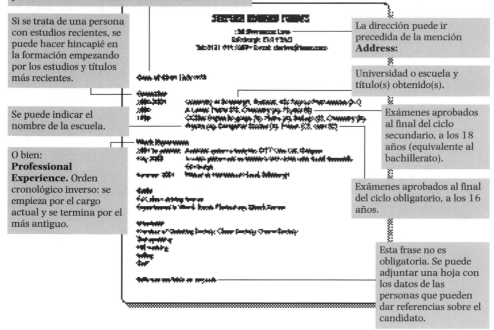

No es indispensable indicar la fecha de nacimiento. Si se quiere, se puede mencionar la nacionalidad, **Nationality:**, y el estado civil, **Single** o **Married**, precedido o no de **Status:** o **Marital Status:**

Si se trata de una persona con estudios recientes, se puede hacer hincapié en la formación empezando por los estudios y títulos más recientes.

Se puede indicar el nombre de la escuela.

O bien: **Professional Experience.** Orden cronológico inverso: se empieza por el cargo actual y se termina por el más antiguo.

La dirección puede ir precedida de la mención **Address:**

Universidad o escuela y título(s) obtenido(s).

Exámenes aprobados al final del ciclo secundario, a los 18 años (equivalente al bachillerato).

Exámenes aprobados al final del ciclo obligatorio, a los 16 años.

Esta frase no es obligatoria. Se puede adjuntar una hoja con los datos de las personas que pueden dar referencias sobre el candidato.

- **Británico con experiencia en un cargo intermedio**

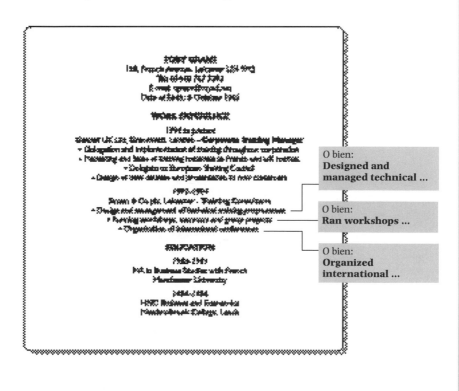

O bien: **Designed and managed technical ...**

O bien: **Ran workshops ...**

O bien: **Organized international ...**

- ## Titulado estadounidense con poca experiencia

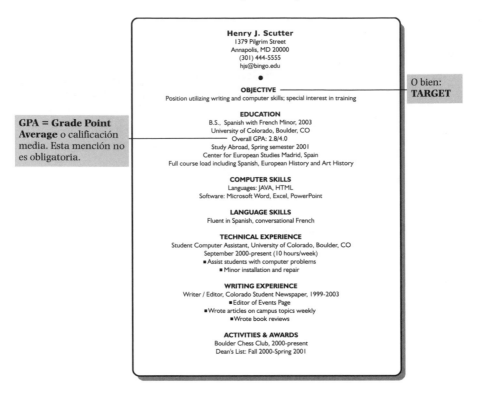

GPA = Grade Point Average o calificación media. Esta mención no es obligatoria.

O bien:
TARGET

Henry J. Scutter
1379 Pilgrim Street
Annapolis, MD 20000
(301) 444-5555
hjs@bingo.edu

OBJECTIVE
Position utilizing writing and computer skills; special interest in training

EDUCATION
B.S., Spanish with French Minor, 2003
University of Colorado, Boulder, CO
Overall GPA: 2.8/4.0
Study Abroad, Spring semester 2001
Center for European Studies Madrid, Spain
Full course load including Spanish, European History and Art History

COMPUTER SKILLS
Languages: JAVA, HTML
Software: Microsoft Word, Excel, PowerPoint

LANGUAGE SKILLS
Fluent in Spanish, conversational French

TECHNICAL EXPERIENCE
Student Computer Assistant, University of Colorado, Boulder, CO
September 2000-present (10 hours/week)
- Assist students with computer problems
  - Minor installation and repair

WRITING EXPERIENCE
Writer / Editor, Colorado Student Newspaper, 1999-2003
- Editor of Events Page
- Wrote articles on campus topics weekly
- Wrote book reviews

ACTIVITIES & AWARDS
Boulder Chess Club, 2000-present
Dean's List: Fall 2000-Spring 2001

- ## Estadounidense con experiencia en un cargo intermedio

O bien:
WORK EXPERIENCE EMPLOYMENT HISTORY

No es necesario incluir esta sección cuando se quiere poner énfasis en la experiencia profesional.

JESSICA O'GARA
725 Boulder Henry Dr.,
Blacksburg, VA 24060
(540) 961-6666
jogara@vt.edu

OBJECTIVE
Product Designer/Manager

EXPERIENCE
Computer Consultant and Systems Designer, Systems Go Inc, Blacksburg, VA, 1997-present
Troubleshoot hardware and software problems
Design and test new operating systems
Head up large team of consultants

Assistant Systems Consultant, Benson Inc, Redmond, WA, 1993-1997
Created Web pages and customized computer systems for clients in the Redmond area

Intern, JCN Corp., Redmond, WA, June-August 1993
Worked as software design engineer intern.

EDUCATION
Bachelor of Science Degree in Computer Science, May 1993
Virginia Polytechnic Institute & State University (Virginia Tech), Blacksburg, VA

COMPUTER SKILLS
Languages and Software : B, CC, Java, HTML, Excel, Word
Operating Systems : Unix, Windows, Mac OS

ACTIVITIES
Society of Manufacturing Engineers
Aircraft Owners and Pilots Association

- **Titulado mexicano sin experiencia**

No es obligatorio mencionar la nacionalidad ni la edad. Estos datos, al igual que el estado civil, se suelen obviar.

- **Español con experiencia en un cargo intermedio**

El fax

Estos son algunos consejos para redactar documentos que se envían por fax:

– deben mencionarse únicamente las informaciones esenciales,

– se puede adoptar un estilo telegráfico y emplear abreviaturas y acrónimos en lugar de ciertas palabras o incluso expresiones enteras, aunque es preciso utilizar las abreviaturas reconocidas como tales (véase p. 29),

– hay que cuidar el tono general del mensaje ya que los mensajes breves y fácticos pueden resultar fríos. Es aconsejable terminar con una fórmula de cortesía amistosa como, por ejemplo, **"Best Wishes"**.

- **En una empresa**

O bien:
Attn: (a la atención de)

Asunto del fax.

Abreviaturas de **Tuesday** y **September**

= **Wednesday morning**

To: Nicholas Rock
Re: Itinerary for visit to Chile

From: Hilary Bronwen
Date: Monday 18 Sept

Pages: 1
CC:

= **Arrive, arrival**

Arrival date now Tues 19 Sept. Arr. Santiago airport, 18.40. Please arrange visit to Benefin Wed a.m. and meeting at your office Wed p.m. Flight Santiago-Buenos Aires Fri 09.00.

= **Wednesday afternoon or evening**

Call Sally a.s.a.p to confirm.

Thanks and regards.

Hilary Bronwen

= **as soon as possible**

- **Para confirmar una reserva**

To: Pinetops Hotel
From: Sebastián Salcedo
Date: 30 Oct 2005
Pages: 1

Las fórmulas de saludo y de despedida no varían.

O bien:
Further to our conversation this morning, I would like to confirm ...

Dear Sir or Madam

Following our telephone conversation this morning, this is to confirm reservation of a double room with en-suite bath for the nights of 17 and 18 November 2005.

Yours faithfully

Sebastián Salcedo

El correo electrónico

El correo electrónico es un medio de comunicación rápido, por lo que el estilo de los mensajes suele ser familiar y telegráfico, y el uso de abreviaturas y acrónimos muy frecuente. Según la netiqueta, es decir, el código de conducta de la red, no es aconsejable escribir un mensaje todo en mayúsculas porque eso podría interpretarse como un signo de mal humor.

Se suelen omitir las fórmulas de introducción clásicas (**Dear ...**). Si uno conoce bien a su interlocutor, puede empezar con una expresión familiar como **Hello** o **Hi**, seguida del nombre de la persona.

- **Mensaje interno**

Fórmula de saludo familiar, sin puntuación, que incluso se puede omitir.

To: Robert <rjones@vpr.co.uk>
From: Alan <ahenderson@vpr.co.uk>
Subject: Budget meeting
Cc: Sharon <smacdonald@vpr.co.uk
Bcc:
Attached:

Hi

I suggest we all get together this week to discuss the budget for the Hillbrook project.

How about Thurs morning, 10a.m?

We should go over the following points: revised budget proposals, clause 2b in contract with Hillbrook and estimate schedules.

Let me know asap if that's OK.

Any comments welcome.

Alan

Si se conoce al interlocutor, puede terminar con una expresión como **Best wishes**, **Regards**, **Thanks**, **Yours** o **Cheers** (*Br*).

- **Mensaje de una empresa a otra**

To: Jack Manley <jmanley@melchior.uk>
From: ahenderson@vpr.co.uk
Subject: Hillbrook Project
Cc:
Bcc:
Attached:

Dear Mr Manley

Please find attached a full proposal, with schedules and cost estimate, for the renovation of Hillbrook House.

If you have any further questions, please do not hesitate to contact us.

We look forward to hearing from you,

Yours sincerely

Alan Henderson

Si no conocemos muy bien a nuestro interlocutor, podemos usar las fórmulas de saludo tradicionales.

- Reserva

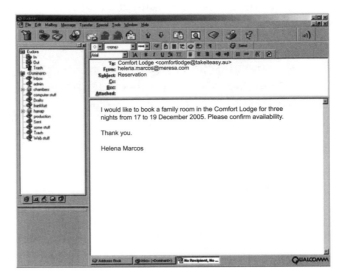

- Mensaje al proveedor de acceso

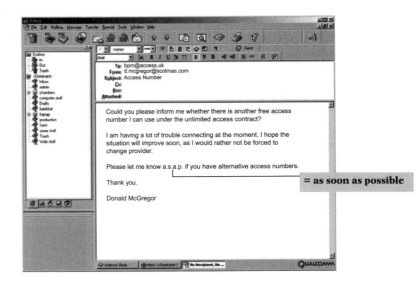

Abreviaturas y acrónimos

• Correspondencia general

a/c	account (cuenta)	**Dir**	director
ack.	acknowledge (acuse de recibo)	**Dr**	Doctor
add.	addendum (adición o apéndice)	**E&OE**	errors and omissions accepted
AGM	annual general meeting (junta		(salvo error u omisión)
	general anual)	**eg**	for example (por ejemplo)
am, a.m.	ante meridiem, morning (antes el	**EGM**	extraordinary general meeting
	mediodía, de la mañana)		(junta general extraordinaria)
AOB	any other business (ruegos y	**enc(s)**	enclosure(s) (documentos
	preguntas)		adjuntos o anexos)
approx.	approximately (aproximadamente)	**ETA**	estimated time of arrival (hora de
APR	annual percentage rate (TAE o		llegada estimada)
	tipo anual efectivo)	**FAO**	for the attention of (a la atención
asap, a.s.a.p.	as soon as possible (lo antes		de)
	posible)	**ff**	following (a continuación de)
av.	average (media)	**HM**	His/Her Majesty (Su Majestad)
bal.	balance (saldo)	**ie, i.e.**	in other words (es decir)
b/d	bankers draft (cheque de banco)	**Inc., Incorp.**	incorporated (S.A.)
bc., bcc.	blind (carbon) copy (CCC o copia	**incl.**	included, including (adjunto(a)(s)
	invisible (o ciega) de cortesía)		o incluido(a)(s))
b/e	bill of exchange (letra de cambio)	**infm., info**	information (información)
bk	bank; book (banco; libro)	**inst**	of this month (del corriente, del
bkcy, bkpt	bankruptcy, bankrupt (quiebra;		mes corriente)
	en quiebra)	**L/C**	letter of credit (carta de crédito)
B/L, bl	bill of lading (conocimiento de	**Ltd**	limited company (sociedad
	embarque)		limitada)
b/s	bill of sale (escritura de	**MD**	managing director (director
	compraventa)		gerente)
BST	British Summer Time (hora oficial	**mgr.**	manager (jefe o responsable)
	de verano en el Reino Unido)	**mtg.**	meeting (reunión o junta)
c.	circa (alrededor de)	**NB**	nota bene (nota)
CB	cash book (libro de caja)	**OD**	overdraft (saldo negativo o
cc	carbon copy (copia a)		deudor)
CEO	chief executive officer (director	**OHP**	overhead projector
	gerente, consejero delegado)		(retroproyector)
CET	Central European Time (hora de	**ono**	or nearest offer (negociable)
	Europa Central)	**p.a.**	per annum (al año o anual)
CFO	chief financial officer (director	**p&p**	postage and packing (gastos de
	financiero)		envío)
chq	cheque	**PAYE**	pay as you earn (retención en
c.i.f., CIF	cost, insurance, freight (coste,		nómina del impuesto sobre la
	seguro y flete)		renta)
C/O	care of; carried over; cash order	**P&L**	profit and loss (pérdidas y
	(en el domicilio de; sigue; orden		ganancias)
	de caja)	**PLC**	public limited company (S.A.)
Co	company; county (empresa;	**pm, p.m.**	post meridiem (después del
	condado)		mediodía, de la tarde o de la
COD	cash on delivery (entrega contra		noche)
	reembolso)	**p.o.**	postal order (giro postal)
Conf	confirm; conference (confirmar;	**pp**	post procurationem, on behalf of
	conferencia)		(en nombre de)
Contd, cont'd	continued (continuación)	**pps**	additonal postscript (postdata
CV	curriculum vitae		adicional)
DD	direct debit (domiciliación	**Pres.**	president (presidente)
	bancaria, (AM) débito bancario)	**Prof.**	professor (catedrático o profesor)
del.	delivery; delivered (entrega;	**ps**	postcript (postdata)
	entregado)	**PTO**	please turn over (sigue)

rc'd	received (recibido)	SO	standing order (domiciliación
re	with reference to (asunto o		bancaria, (*AM*) débito bancario)
	referido a)	tbc	to be confirmed (por confirmar)
Ref	reference (referencia)	ult.	ultimo, last (último(a))
req, reqd	required (requerido)	viz	namely (o sea, es decir)
retd	retired (jubilado)	VP	vice-president (vicepresidente)
sae	stamped addressed envelope	yf	Yours faithfully (atentamente)
	(sobre franqueado)	ys	Yours sincerely (atentamente)
sase	self-addressed stamped envelope		
	(sobre franqueado con la		
	dirección del remitente		

- ## Mensajes SMS y correo electrónico

Adv	advice (consejo)	IMO	in my opinion (en mi opinión)
AFAICT	as far as I can tell (por lo que yo	IOW	in other words (en otras palabras)
	sé)	ISTM	it seems to me (me parece)
AFAIK	as far as I know (que yo sepa)	ITRO	in the region of (alrededor de)
AFK	away from keyboard (indica que	LOL	laughing out loud (me
	alguien abandona momentánea-		desternillo)
	mente el ordenador)	MYOB	mind your own business (no te
AIUI	as far as I understand (si lo he		metas en lo que no te importa)
	entendido bien)	NRN	no reply necessary (no hace falta
B4	before (antes)		respuesta)
BAK	back at keyboard (vuelvo a estar	NW!	no way! (¡de ningún modo!)
	frente al teclado)	OMG	oh my God! (¡Dios mío!)
BBFN	bye bye for now (hasta luego)	OTOH	on the other hand (por otra parte)
BBL	be back later (luego vuelvo)	OTT	over the top (exagerado)
BTW	by the way (por cierto)	PD	public domain (dominio público)
cld	could	PLS	please (por favor)
Doc	document (documento)	POV	point of view (punto de vista)
EOF	end of file (fin del archivo)	prhps	perhaps (tal vez)
F2F	face to face (cara a cara)	ROTFL	rolling on the floor laughing (me
FAQ	frequently asked questions		parto de risa)
	(preguntas más frecuentes)	RTFM	read the fucking manual (léete el
FOC	free of charge (gratuito, gratis)		puto manual)
Foll	following, to follow (siguiente,	RUOK	are you OK? (¿estás bien?)
	sigue)	TIA	thanks in advance (gracias por
FWIW	for what it's worth (por si sirve de		adelantado)
	algo)	TNX	thanks (gracias)
FYI	for your information (para tu	TVM	thanks very much (muchas
	información)		gracias)
HTH	hope this helps (espero que te	urgt	urgent (urgente)
	sirva)	VR	virtual reality (realidad virtual)
IIRC	if I recall correctly (si mal no	WRT	with regard to (en lo que se refiere
	recuerdo)		a)
IMHO	in my humble opinion (en mi		
	modesta opinión)		

El teléfono

- ## Pronunciación de los números de teléfono

20995
Two oh double nine five (*Br*)
Two zero double nine five (*US*)

- ## Para pedir información

– Can I have directory enquiries (*Br*) or directory assistance (*US*) please?
– I'm trying to get through to a London number

– What is the (country) code for Canada?
– How do I get an outside line?

- **Para pedir hablar con alguien**

Hello,
– could I speak to ...?
– can I speak to ...?
– I'd like to speak to ...
– (could I have) extension 593 please?

- **Para contestar a una llamada**

– Robert McQueen speaking, can I help you?
– Hello, this is ...
– Yes, speaking (para confirmar que se es la persona solicitada)
– Hold on/hold please, I'll (just) get him/her.
– I'm sorry, he's/she's not here. Can I take a message?
– I'm afraid he's away on business/out of the office/off sick/on holiday/on vacation (*US*)

- **Para dejar un mensaje**

En un contestador:
– I'm returning your call.
– I'll be in London next week, perhaps we can ...
– I'd like to talk to you about ...
– Could you call me back, so we can discuss ...?

A otra persona:
– Could you ask him/her to call me on ...?
– Could you tell him/her I won't be able to ...?
– I'll call back later.
– I need to speak to him/her urgently.
– Please ask him/her to confirm. Thank you.

- **Para pedir confirmación**

– Could you spell that please?
– Could you speak a bit more slowly please?
– I'm sorry I didn't catch that. Could you repeat that please?
– Let me check, 11 a.m. Wednesday 10th. Yes, that's fine.

- **Para terminar una llamada**

– Thank you, I look forward to seeing you on Wednesday. Goodbye.
– Thank you for your help.

- **Mensaje de un contestador automático**

– We are unable to take your call at the moment. Please leave a message after the tone.
– I am not here at the moment. Please leave a message after the tone.

LAS REUNIONES DE NEGOCIOS EN INGLÉS

Índice

En esta sección se ha incluido una serie de términos y expresiones que pueden servir de utilidad en reuniones o negociaciones.

Los diferentes tipos de reuniones

Annual General Meeting (AGM) *(UK)*	Asamblea General Anual
Annual Stockholders Meeting (ASM) *(EE UU)*	Asamblea General Anual
board meeting	consejo de administración
breakfast meeting *(principalmente en EE UU)*	desayuno de trabajo
business meeting	reunión de negocios
Extraordinary General Meeting (EGM)	Junta General Extraordinaria
staff meeting	reunión de personal
team meeting	reunión de equipo
weekly meeting	reunión semanal
briefing	reunión o sesión informativa
conference	congreso o conferencia
discussion	discusión
negotiation	negociación
seminar	coloquio

La organización de una reunión

to call	convocar
to convene	convocar
to set up	preparar
to arrange	organizar
to postpone	aplazar
to bring forward	adelantar
to adjourn	levantar
to cancel	cancelar
to hold	celebrar

Para la preparación de una reunión de negocios en un país anglosajón, se establece primero la orden del día (**draw up the agenda**) y se distribuye (**circulate**) con antelación a los partcipantes (**participants**). Se designa a una persona, normalmente una secretaria para tomar notas y redactar el acta (**take the minutes**) de la reunión. Durnate la reunión se van discutiendo uno a uno los os asuntos (**items**) o puntos (**points**) de la orden del día. Esta comienza a menudo con las excusas de los ausentes (**Apologies**), seguidas de la aprobación del acta (**Confirmation of Minutes**) durante la que se discute y aprueba (**confirmed**) el acta de la reunión anterior, antes de pasar al tema central de la reunión, cuyo último punto suele ser los asuntos varios (**AOB – any other business; o AOCB – any other competent business**) para permitir a los asistentes plantear otros puntos pertinentes, y finalmente se decide el lugar y la fecha de la siguiente reunión, antes de levantar la sesión.

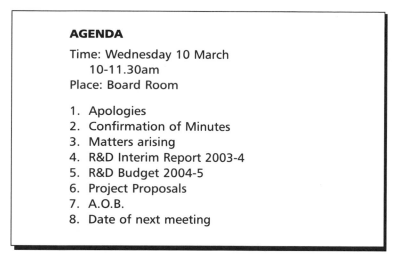

AGENDA

Time: Wednesday 10 March
    10-11.30am
Place: Board Room

1. Apologies
2. Confirmation of Minutes
3. Matters arising
4. R&D Interim Report 2003-4
5. R&D Budget 2004-5
6. Project Proposals
7. A.O.B.
8. Date of next meeting

En el Reino Unido o Estados Unidos se considera una falta de profesionalismo y de cortesía no respetar la orden del día

El desarrollo de una reunión

to agree (with someone/ something)	estar de acuerdo (con alguien/algo)
to brief someone	dar instrucciones a alguien
to decide (on something/ what to do)	decidir (algo/qué hacer)
to disagree (with someone/ something)	no estar de acuerdo (con alguien/algo)
to discuss (a matter/a resolution)	debatir (un asunto/una resolución)
to exchange (ideas/ information	intercambiar (ideas/ información)
motion	moción
to negotiate	negociar
to present (a motion/a proposal)	presentar (una moción/ una propuesta)
to pass (a motion)	aprobar (una moción)
to recap (the main points/what has been agreed so far)	resumir (los puntos principales/lo acordado hasta el momento)
to recommend (action)	recomendar (una acción)
resolution	resolución
to suggest (ideas/ solutions)	sugerir (ideas/soluciones)
to vote (on something/ to do something)	votar (algo/hacer algo)

Resultados positivos		Resultados negativos	
action	acción	**conflict**	conflicto
agreement	acuerdo	**deadlock**	punto muerto
consensus	consenso	**disagreement**	desacuerdo
decision	decisión	**inaction**	inacción
resolution	resolución	**indecision**	indecisión
agreement	acuerdo	**disapproval**	desaprobación
		opposition	oposición

El acta

El acta (**the minutes**) se distribuye a todos los participantes, así como a aquellos que habían sido convocados a la reunión y no pudieron asistir. Tiene habitualmente un estilo impersonal que el que se recapitula lo que se dijo, quién lo dijo, las decisiones tomadas, las acciones a llevar a cabo, etc

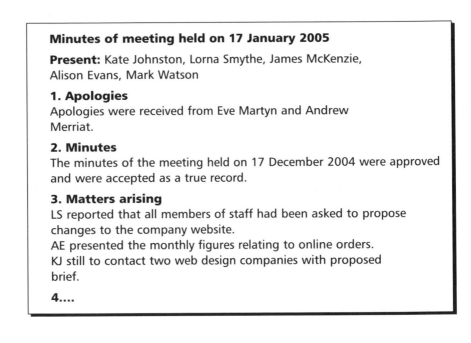

> **Minutes of meeting held on 17 January 2005**
>
> **Present:** Kate Johnston, Lorna Smythe, James McKenzie, Alison Evans, Mark Watson
>
> **1. Apologies**
> Apologies were received from Eve Martyn and Andrew Merriat.
>
> **2. Minutes**
> The minutes of the meeting held on 17 December 2004 were approved and were accepted as a true record.
>
> **3. Matters arising**
> LS reported that all members of staff had been asked to propose changes to the company website.
> AE presented the monthly figures relating to online orders.
> KJ still to contact two web design companies with proposed brief.
>
> **4....**

Expresiones útiles para participar en una reunión

• **Cómo comenzar una reunión**

Para empezar, quisiera hacer algunas consideraciones sobre...
First of all, I'd like to make a few points about...

Quisiera comenzar mi intervención señalando que.../informando sobre.../recordando que.../agradeciendo...
I'd like to start by pointing out that.../telling you about.../reminding you that.../thanking...

- **Cómo pedir opinión**

¿Usted qué opina?
What do you think?

¿Cuál es su postura/punto de vista sobre el asunto?
What's your position/view on the matter?

¿Qué le parece la propuesta?
What do you think of the proposal?

¿Qué opinión le merece el informe?
What's your opinion on the report?

- **Cómo dar una opinión**

En mi opinión,...
In my opinion,...

Desde mi punto de vista, es necesario...
In my view, we need to...

Desde el punto de vista financiero...
From a financial point of view,...

Opino que...
I feel that...

A mi entender/A mi parecer/A mi modo de ver...
In my view/It seems to me that/The way I see it is that...

- **Cómo hacer comentarios y expresar apoyo**

Es una buena idea.
That's a good idea.

Esa es una cuestión importante
That's an important point.

Estoy a favor de esa línea de actuación.
I'm in favour of that line of action.

La propuesta cuenta con mi apoyo.
This proposal has my full support.

- **Cómo recalcar**

Quisiera poner de relieve/subrayar/señalar que...
I'd like to emphasize/stress/point out that...

Quisiera subrayar la importancia/el alcance de...
I'd like to stress the importance/significance of...

- **Cómo insistir**

Quisiera hacer hincapié en el hecho de que...
I'd like to stress that...

Insisto en la necesidad de.../en señalar que...
I must stress the importance of.../I must point out that...

• Cómo expresar cierta reserva

Entiendo lo que quiere decir, pero…
I see what you mean, but…

Bien, ¿pero no cree que…?/De acuerdo, ¿pero no le parece que…?
Point taken, but don't you think…?/Yes, OK, but don't you think… ?

Es cierto, pero…
That's true, but…

• Cómo expresar oposición y desacuerdo

Soy contrario a esa idea.
I am opposed to that idea.

Lo siento, pero no estoy de acuerdo.
I'm sorry but I don't agree.

No estoy convencido de que sea una buena idea.
I'm not convinced it's a good idea.

Puede que sí, pero…
That may well be the case, but …

Estoy de acuerdo hasta cierto punto, pero no estoy seguro de que…
I agree with you up to a point, but I'm not so sure about/not so sure that …

No soy de la misma opinión.
I don't agree.

No comparto ese criterio.
I don't share that point of view.

No me parece la actuación más acertada.
I don't think that's the ideal solution.

• Cómo expresar un desacuerdo profundo

¡De ninguna manera!
Absolutely not!/That's out of the question!

Me opongo radicalmente.
I'm completely against it.

Eso es de todo punto inaceptable.
That's totally unacceptable.

Eso es absolutamente imposible.
That's absolutely impossible.

• Cómo expresar acuerdo

Estoy totalmente de acuerdo (con usted).
I agree (with you) entirely.

Creo que en eso estamos de acuerdo.
I think we are in agreement on that.

Creo que ahí tiene usted toda la razón.
I think you're absolutely right there.

Coincido plenamente con usted.
I agree with you entirely.

Comparto plenamente su opinión.
I share your opinion entirely.

● **Cómo expresar un acuerdo parcial**

Puede que tenga razón.
You could be right.

En líneas generales, estoy de acuerdo con usted, pero me gustaría discutirlo un poco más.
I agree with you on the whole, but I'd like to discuss it a little further.

En principio no estoy en contra, pero creo que...
I'm not against it in principle, but I think ...

● **Cómo pedir más información**

Perdone, no le sigo, ¿podría ser más específico?
I'm sorry, I don't quite follow you. Could you be a little more specific?

Perdone, pero ¿podría explicarlo con más detalle?
I'm sorry, but could you explain in a little more detail?

● **Cómo disipar malentendidos**

Me temo que ha habido un pequeño malentendido.
I'm afraid there seems to have been a slight misunderstanding.

Puede que no me haya explicado muy bien. Lo que quiero decir es que...
Perhaps I didn't explain myself very well. What I mean is that...

Eso no es lo que he dicho exactamente.
That's not quite what I said.

● **Cómo hacer recomendaciones, propuestas y sugerencias**

Recomiendo/propongo/sugiero que...
I recommend/propose/suggest that...

¿Por qué no...?
Why don't we...?

¿Qué les parece si...?
How about if...? o How would you feel about...?

¿No creen que sería mejor...?
Don't you think it might be better to...?

● **Cómo interrumpir o tomar la palabra**

¿Puedo intervenir sobre este punto?
Could I just say something at this point?

¿Me permite hacer un comentario sobre el punto anterior?
I wonder if I might comment on that last point?

Si me permite que le interrumpa, quisiera comentar su última apreciación.
If I could just interrupt you for a moment, I'd like to comment on your last point.

● En caso de interrupción

¿Puedo continuar?
May I go on/continue?

Déjeme terminar.
Let me finish.

Como iba diciendo,...
As I was saying,...

... and then, of course, this could lead to problems in ...
...y además, claro, esto podría causar problemas en...

Sorry to interrupt, but don't you think that ... ?
Perdone que le interrumpa, pero ¿no cree que... ?

Could I just finish making my point and then I'd be interested to hear your view?
Permítame que termine de explicarme y después escucharé encantado su opinión.

OK. Sorry.
Sí, disculpe.

As I was saying, this could lead to problems in the distribution side ...
Como estaba diciendo, esto podría causar problemas en la distribución ...

● Cómo concluir

En conclusión, yo diría que...
In conclusion, I'd like to say that...

Para terminar, quisiera hacer una última observación/un comentario general/unas consideraciones generales sobre...
To finish off, I'd just like to point out one more thing/make a general comment/some general remarks on...

Quisiera cerrar mi intervención expresando mi agradecimiento a.../mi confianza en que...
And finally, I'd like to thank.../to say I'm sure that...

La presidencia de una reunión

chair, chairperson, chairman	presidente
chair, chairperson, chairwoman	presidenta
to chair a meeting	presidir una reunión

Durante años ha suscitado cierto debate la cuestión de cómo designar a la persona que preside una reunión. **Chairman** es el término tradicional y continúa siendo el más frecuente. Debido al número creciente de mujeres que acceden a puestos de responsabilidad, se ha hecho habitual oír **chairperson**, un término más "políticamente correcto" o bien chair, pues ambas palabras son exualmente neutras. **Chairwoman**, el equivalente de **chairman** para una mujer, no ha tenido mucho éxito, y la expresión **Madam Chairman** resulta anticuada y ha veces provoca el ridículo. En generel es conveniente informarse antes de una reunión de cuál es el tratamiento que prefiere usar la persona que ocupa la presidencia.

Expresiones útiles para presidir una reunión

• **Para comenzar la reunión**

Ante todo, gracias por su asistencia.
First of all, thank you all for attending.

Si les parece, podemos comenzar.
Let's get started, shall we?

El Sr. Fernández, Secretario de la reunión, será el encargado de levantar el acta.
Our secretary, Mr Fernández, will be charge of writing up the minutes.

Podemos pasar a abordar los puntos del orden del día.
Let's make a start on the agenda.

• **Para excusar las ausencias**

Han excusado su asistencia don Jaime López y doña Nieves Sánchez.
We've received apologies from Jaime López and Nieves Sánchez.

No estarán presentes los señores Ramírez, González y Garrido, que han disculpado su ausencia.
Mr Ramírez, Mr González and Mr Garrido can't be here today, and have sent their apologies.

• **Questiones diversas**

¿Podemos dar por leída el acta?
Can we take the minutes as read?

¿Alguien quiere hacer alguna observación sobre el acta?
Any matters arising from the minutes?

• **Para fijar los objetivos**

La reunión de hoy tiene como finalidad...
The purpose of today's meeting is to...

El objetivo de esta reunión es decidir...
The aim of this meeting is to decide on...

Les he convocado a esta reunión para intentar llegar a un acuerdo sobre...
I've called this meeting to try to reach an agreement on...

• **El orden del día**

¿Todos han recibido una copia del orden del día?
Has everyone received a copy of the agenda?

El primer punto del orden del día es...
The first item on the agenda is...

• **Para organizar y comenzar una discusión**

Vamos mal de tiempo. Le ruego que sea breve.
We're a bit short of time, so can I ask you to be brief?

Sugiero que empecemos por conocer la opinión de todos los presentes.
I suggest we go round the table and get everybody's views first.

Paula, ¿quiere comenzar usted?
Would you like to start, Paula?

Le paso la palabra a la Sra. Irene García
I'd like to give the floor to Ms Irene García.

• **Para pedir la opinión de los participantes**

¿Cuál es su punto de vista?
What are your views?

¿Qué les parece?
What do you think?

¿Qué opina usted al respecto?
How do you feel about this?

• **Para centrarse en el orden del día**

No nos desviemos del tema que nos ocupa.
Could we stick to the subject?

Creo que este tema debe ser tratado en el epígrafe de asuntos varios.
I think that issue would be best discussed under AOB.

Abordaremos ese tema más tarde, dentro del punto cuarto.
We'll come to that later, under item four.

Creo que nos estamos olvidando de lo fundamental.
I think we're missing the point here.

• **Para asegurarse de que hay acuerdo general**

Entonces, ¿estamos todos de acuerdo?
Do we all agree, then?

¿A todos les parece bien la propuesta?
Is everybody happy with the proposal?

¿Alguien tiene algo que objetar?
Are there any objections to this?

Parece que hay consenso.
We seem to have a consensus.

• **Para concluir en un asunto**

¿Alguien quiere hacer alguna pregunta antes de continuar?
Are there any questions before we go on?

¿Algún otro comentario?
Any other comments?

Si nadie tiene nada más que añadir, podemos pasar al punto cuarto.
If nobody has anything else to add, we can move on to item four.

● **Para continuar**

Pasemos al siguiente punto del orden del día.
Let's move on to the next item on the agenda.

¿Podemos pasar al Informe Anual?
Can we go on to the Annual Report now?

Bien, punto tercero.
Right, item number three.

● **Para aplazar una discusión o una decisión**

Creo que vamos a necesitar más tiempo para discutir esto.
I think we're going to need more time to discuss this.

Quizá deberíamos aplazar la decisión por el momento.
Perhaps we should postpone this decision for now.

● **La votación**

Levanten la mano los que estén de acuerdo.
Can I have a show of hands (on this)?

Sometámoslo a votación.
Let's put it to a vote o Let's vote on it.

¿Quiénes están a favor/en contra?
Those in favour/against?

¿Quiénes apoyan la moción?
Those for the motion?

¿Alguna abstención?
Any abstentions?

Se rechaza/aprueba la propuesta por 6 votos a favor y 3 en contra.
The motion is rejected/The motion is carried by 6 votes to 3.

Se abandona la moción.
The motion is dropped.

● **La finalización de la reunión**

Tendremos que volver sobre este tema en otra ocasión.
We'll have to come back to this another time.

Se nos acaba el tiempo. Debemos ir concluyendo.
We're running out of time. Can we try and come to a conclusion?

Bien, ya casi no nos queda tiempo. Si les parece, voy a hacer un resumen de lo acordado.
OK, our time's nearly up – can I summarize what we've agreed?

● **Resumen**

En resumen, las principales cuestiones que se han discutido son...
To sum up, the main points that have been made are...

Resumiendo lo expuesto hasta el momento, parece que hay acuerdo general sobre...
To sum up then, there seems to be general agreement on...

En conclusión, hemos decidido que...
So, what we've decided is that...

• **Questiones diversas**

¿Algún otro asunto que tratar?
Is there any other business?

¿Hay alguna otra cuestión que quieran discutir?
Is there anything else you want to discuss?

• **La preparación de la próxima reunión**

¿Fijamos una fecha para nuestra próxima reunión? ¿Qué tal el próximo lunes?
Shall we fix a date for our next meeting? How about next Monday?

Nos reunimos otra vez el veintitrés de mayo a la misma hora.
Let's meet again on the twenty-third of May at the same time.

• **Para concluir**

Bueno, creo que eso es todo.
Well, I think that's everything.

Damos por terminada la reunión. Gracias por su asistencia.
That's the end of the meeting. Thank you all for attending.

Las negociaciones

to negotiate	negociar
negotiation	negociación
negotiator	negociador
negotiable	negociable

• **Sugerencias**

I think we should start by stating our overall objectives. We could then move on to present an overview of our respective organizations.
Creo que deberíamos comenzar exponiendo nuestros objetivos generales y después pasar a hacer una descripción general de nuestras respectivas compañías.

Would you go along with that?/ Does that sound OK (to you)?/ Would that fit in with your ideas?
¿Les parece bien?/¿Están de acuerdo?/¿Conformes?

Certainly./ Yes, indeed./ That's fine by me./Well, actually I think we should explore the objectives a little further before we move on to other matters.
Por supuesto./Sí, naturalmente./Sí, la verdad es que creo que deberíamos analizar un poco más los objetivos antes de pasar a tratar otros asuntos.

● Cómo exponer los objetivos

Nuestro principal objetivo es lograr un acuerdo sobre...
Our main objective is to reach an agreement on...

También quisiéramos tratar el tema de...
We'd also like to talk about...

Otro de los objetivos que perseguimos es intercambiar puntos de vista sobre...
Another of our objectives is to exchange views on...

Para expresar lo que se quiere, conviene usar **would like**, que es menos directo y refleja una actitud de mayor colaboración que **want**.

> **We'd like to discuss delivery terms.** ✓
> Queríamos tratar de los términos de la entrega.

> **We want to discuss delivery terms.** ✗
> Queremos tratar de los términos de la entrega.

Asimismo, los auxiliares modales en en condicional como **should**, **could**, **might** y **would** se perciben como menos agresivos. Normalmente se usan con expresiones más tentativas como **I think**, **perhaps**, **maybe**, etc.

> **I think it would be a good idea if we took a ten-minute break.** ✓
> Creo que sería una buena idea hacer un descanso de diez minutos.

> **It's time to take a break for ten minutes.** ✗
> Es hora de hacer un descanso de diez minutos.

> **Perhaps we could begin by giving a brief presentation of our markets.** ✓
> Quizá podríamos comenzar haciendo una pequeña presentación de nuestro mercados.

> **We'll begin by giving a brief presentation of our markets.** ✗
> Comenzaremos con una breve presentación de nuestros mercados.

Lógicamente, se pueden usar las otras frases dadas si se considera necesario ser más firme.

- **Cómo recapitular**

Si le parece, podemos resumir los puntos principales de su exposición.
Perhaps we could just summarize your main points.

Si no he entendido mal, tienen ustedes intención de lanzar...
As I understand it, you're planning to launch...

Si resumimos los puntos principales de su intervención, podemos decir que sus objetivos se centran principalmente en...
So to summarize your main points, you're particularly interested in...

- **Cómo interrumpir para hacer una pregunta**

¿Puedo preguntarle sobre su política de precios?
Could I just ask you a few questions about your pricing policy?

Hay tan sólo unos puntos que me gustaría aclarar antes de seguir adelante.
There are just a few points I'd like to clear up before we move on.

Yes, that sounds interesting – could I just check a couple of things?
Sí, eso parece interesante. ¿Podría aclararme un par de cosas?

> **Yes, of course.**
> Sí, por supuesto.

How many product lines are you proposing to introduce into the market?
¿Cuántas líneas de productos tienen intención de introducir en el mercado?

> **Well, we thought just four or five initially.**
> Pues inicialmente hemos pensado en unas cuatro o cinco.

I see. So when do you think you would introduce your full range?
Ya. Entonces ¿cuándo piensan lanzar la gama completa?

> **Well, that would depend on several factors.**
> Bueno, eso depende de varios factores.

- **Cómo hacer propuestas y encontrar alternativas**

Nuestra propuesta es... *o* **consiste en...**
Our proposal is to...

Lo que nosotros proponemos es...
What we're proposing is that ...

O bien podríamos...
Or we could...

¿Y no sería mejor...?
And wouldn't it be better to ...?

• Cómo articular propuestas y condiciones

No podemos fabricar todos los componentes que necesitan a menos que acepten...
We couldn't manufacture all of the components you need unless you were prepared to accept...

Si nos ofrecieran un mayor descuento, no tendríamos ningún inconveniente en...
If you offered us an improved discount we would be willing to...

• Cómo reaccionar ante una oferta

Uno de los problemas que podrían surgir, en mi opinión, es que...
One of the problems I can foresee with this is that...

El principal problema, a nuestro entender, es...
The main problem as we see it is...

Creo que nos va a resultar muy difícil aceptar esas condiciones.
I think it would be very difficult for us to accept those conditions.

• Cómo rechazar una oferta

No creo que nos compense su propuesta.
I don't think your proposal be worthwhile for us.

No estamos en situación de aceptar esas condiciones.
We're not in a position to accept those conditions.

Comprendo su postura, pero no podemos mejorar nuestra oferta.
I appreciate your position, but I'm afraid we can't improve our offer.

Por regla general, es preferible intentar no imponer el punto de vista personal en las negociaciones) a no ser, claro está que sea ese el objetivo buscado:

That's impossible. ✗
Es imposible.

That might be difficult. ✓
Eso podría ser difícil.

That might not be possible. ✓
Eso quizá no sea posible.

This negotiation is pointless. ✗
Esta negociación es inútil.

I'm not so sure we're going about this in the best way. ✓
No estoy seguro de que este sea el mejor método.

• Cómo articular acuerdos y condiciones

Estaríamos dispuestos a llegar a un acuerdo siempre y cuando ustedes cubran los costes extraordinarios adicionales.
We'd be prepared to agree to that provided that you covered the extra costs involved.

Well, we'd be willing to go ahead and purchase a fleet of 25 cars if you could offer us a good price.
Bien, creo que podríamos comprar una flota de 25 coches si nos ofrecen un buen precio.

I don't see a problem with that – as you know our prices are really very competitive.
No creo que eso sea un problema. Como sabe, nuestros precios son muy competitivos.

Yes, but given the number of cars we're taking, we'd still be looking for some kind of discount.
Sí, pero dado el número de coches que pensamos adquirir, nos gustaría obtener algún tipo de descuento adicional.

Well, we can consider a discount if you are prepared to pay for the transportation costs.
Bueno, podríamos aplicar un descuento si ustedes están dispuestos a pagar los gastos del transporte.

OK, we'll cover them but in that case we'd like a decent discount.
De acuerdo, correremos con los gastos del transporte, pero en ese caso deberán hacernos un buen descuento.

All right. How about 3%?
Muy bien. ¿Qué les parece el 3%?

3%? We had something more like 5% in mind.
¿El 3%? La verdad es que esperábamos un descuento superior al 5%.

I'm not so sure we can go that high – after all our prices are pretty low as they are and margins are very tight.
No creo que podamos ofrecerles tanto. Piensen que nuestros precios son ya muy bajos y los márgenes están muy ajustados.

Well how about this, then? Give us 5% and we'd be willing to sign a one-year maintenance agreement.
Entonces, ¿qué les parece si nos aplican el 5% y firmamos un acuerdo de mantenimiento por un año?

Make that two years and you've got a deal.
Si fuera por dos años, estaríamos conformes.

OK. Done!
De acuerdo, ¡hecho!

TRABAJAR CON UN INTÉRPRETE

Ante la mundialización de los intercambios económicos y comerciales, la interpretación es un medio cada vez más utilizado para facilitar la comunicación entre personas que hablan lenguas diferentes. Para lograr que la mayoría de la gente le entienda, resulta indispensable saber trabajar con un intérprete de manera eficaz.

Existen tres tipos de interpretación:

- Interpretación simultánea
- Interpretación consecutiva
- Interpretación susurrada o *chuchotage*

La **interpretación simultánea** es la modalidad de interpretación más utilizada en conferencias y reuniones de negocios. El orador habla ante un micrófono y su voz se transmite a los intérpretes, que, instalados en cabinas insonorizadas, disponen de auriculares y de un micrófono. Interpretan directamente a la lengua pertinente y los oyentes escuchan la traducción por medio de un casco.

Se recurre a la **interpretación consecutiva** cuando la simultánea resulta imposible por razones prácticas, como por ejemplo durante la visita a una fábrica o en el transcurso de una cena. El intérprete permanece de pie o sentado al lado del orador e interpreta lo que dice cuando éste marca una pausa. Para ello, puede ayudarse tomando notas.

El **chuchotage** es la técnica de interpretación que se utiliza en menos ocasiones. El intérprete se sienta junto a los delegados y, susurrando, traduce simultáneamente lo que se dice.

Cómo presentar una conferencia a un público multilingüe

Si sabe que su conferencia debe ser interpretada a otras lenguas, es importante recordar los siguientes puntos:

- Es necesario tener en cuenta que van a escuchar su discurso personas con culturas diferentes. Recuerde que es muy difícil traducir los chistes y los juegos de palabras y que no todos los pueblos tienen el mismo sentido del humor. Las referencias culturales muy específicas resultan a menudo incomprensibles para los oyentes provenientes de otros países y, por tanto, deberían evitarse. Siempre que sea posible, intente expresarse de manera sencilla, ya que los términos familiares o muy técnicos pueden suponer problemas de traducción.

- Si ya ha redactado su texto, proporcione a los intérpretes un ejemplar. Es preferible hacérselo llegar dos semanas antes de la fecha de su ponencia y, si esto no es posible, es imperativo distribuírselo antes de tomar la palabra, acompañado de copias de todos los documentos que piensa utilizar durante su presentación. También resulta útil entregarles con antelación informaciones de tipo general sobre el tema que se tratará.

- Si interviene en una conferencia donde se utiliza la interpretación simultánea, deberá hablar ante un micrófono. No olvide que el intérprete se encuentra en una cabina insonorizada y que sólo le oye gracias a este aparato. Asegúrese de que su micrófono esta encendido y de que los intérpretes le oyen. Hable en dirección al micrófono sin acercarse demasiado. Mantenga una distancia constante entre su boca y el aparato para evitar las variaciones de volumen. Recuerde que si da la espalda al micrófono para consultar un cuadro o una pantalla situada detrás de usted, el intérprete no oirá nada de lo que usted esté diciendo. Para evitar este tipo de problemas, la mayoría de los conferenciantes que utilizan un retroproyector llevan un micrófono de corbata. Si es su caso, considere que cada vez que roce el micrófono con la mano o con su chaqueta, a oídos del intérprete llegarán únicamente ruidos estridentes.

- Cuando utilice un retroproyector, asegúrese de que los intérpretes puedan ver la pantalla. Es importante comentar los documentos proyectados, ya que, en caso contrario, sólo podrán comprenderlos aquellos que conozcan la lengua en la que están escritos.

- El error más común de los conferenciantes que se dirigen a un público multilingüe consiste en hablar demasiado rápido. Los intérpretes no sólo se contentan con repetir lo que dice, sino que tienen que traducir sus palabras, por lo que necesitan más tiempo que usted. Por otro lado, puede darse el caso de que ciertos delegados cuya lengua materna no se corresponde con la que usted emplea, le escuchen sin recurrir a los intérpretes. Así, es indispensable no adoptar un ritmo demasiado acelerado. Cuanto más rápido hable, menos le entenderán.

- Para mantener un ritmo adecuado, se recomienda marcar una pausa después de cada frase, lo que permite a los oyentes asimilar lo que acaba de exponer y a los intérpretes terminar de traducir. Todo buen conferenciante espera a que los intérpretes hayan acabado de hablar para continuar con su discurso.

- Es esencial expresarse con claridad. Si murmura, los intérpretes se verán ante la imposibilidad de traducir lo que esté diciendo.

Qué hacer y qué no hacer cuando se trabaja con un intérprete

✓ Debe:

- Proporcionar con antelación un ejemplar de su ponencia, junto con copias de todos los documentos que el intérprete vaya a necesitar, principalmente los que se van a proyectar en una pantalla.

- Encender su micrófono y utilizarlo correctamente.

- Hablar lenta y claramente.

✗ No debe:

- Incluir en su ponencia una gran cantidad de chistes o referencias culturales específicas.

- Dar la espalda al micrófono cuando esté comentando documentos proyectados en una pantalla.

- Pasar de un idioma a otro en medio de una frase.

PAÍSES DEL MUNDO

El nombre inglés de los países se encuentra en la segunda columna de la siguiente tabla. Para consultar los términos ingleses de las monedas y las lenguas oficiales, remítase a la tabla correspondiente en el suplemento inglés.

Las abreviaciones de las monedas que figuran en la quinta columna son las abreviaciones estándar internacionales definidas por la ISO. Se utilizan en las operaciones financieras internacionales, en lugar de las abreviaciones de uso local.

Nombre español	Nombre inglés	Nombre local	Lengua(s) oficial(es)	Moneda
Afganistán	Afghanistan	Afghānestān	dari, pashto	1 afgani (AFA) = 100 puls
Albania	Albania	Shqīpëri	albanés	1 lek (ALL) = 100 qindarka
Alemania	Germany	Bundesrepublik Deutschland	alemán	1 euro (EUR) = 100 céntimos
Andorra	Andorra	Andorra	catalán, francés, español	1 euro (EUR) = 100 céntimos
Angola	Angola	Angola	portugués	1 kwanza (AOA) = 100 lwei
Arabia Saudí	Saudi Arabia	Al-'Arabīyah as Sa'ūdīyah	árabe	1 rial (o riyal) saudí (SAR) = 100 halalas
Argelia	Algeria	Al-Jazā'ir (árabe) Algérie (francés)	árabe	1 dinar argelino (DZD) = 100 céntimos
Argentina	Argentina	Argentina	español	1 peso argentino (ARS) = 100 centavos
Armenia	Armenia	Hayastani Hanrapetut'yun	armenio	1 dram (AMD) =100 lumas
Australia	Australia	Australia	inglés	1 dólar australiano (AUD) = 100 centavos
Austria	Austria	Österreich	alemán	1 euro (EUR) = 100 céntimos
Azerbaiyán	Azerbaijan	Azarbaijan	azerí	1 manat azerí (AZM) =100 kepik
Bahamas	The Bahamas	Bahamas	inglés	1 dólar de las Bahamas (BSD) = 100 centavos
Bahráin	Bahrain	Dawlat al-Bahrayn	árabe	1 dinar bahriní (BHD) = 1.000 fils
Bangladesh	Bangladesh	Gana Prajatantri Bangladesh	bengalí	1 taka (BDT) = 100 poisha
Barbados	Barbados	Barbados	inglés	1 dólar de Barbados (BBD) = 100 centavos
Bélgica	Belgium	Belgique (francés) België (flamenco)	flamenco, francés, alemán	1 euro (EUR) = 100 céntimos

Nombre español	Nombre inglés	Nombre local	Lengua(s) oficial(es)	Moneda
Belice	Belize	Belize	inglés	1 dólar de Belice (BZD) = 100 centavos
Benín	Benin	Bénin	francés	1 franco CFA (XOF) = 100 céntimos
Bielorrusia	Belarus	Belarus	bielorruso	1 rublo bielorruso (BYB) =100 kopeks
Birmania ▸ Myanmar	Burma			
Bolivia	Bolivia	Bolivia	español	1 peso boliviano (BOB) = 100 centavos
Bosnia y Hercegovina	Bosnia-Herzegovina	Bosnia-Herzegovina	serbocroata	marco bosnio convertible (BAM) = 100 fenings
Botsuana	Botswana	Botswana	inglés	1 pula (BWP) = 100 thebe
Brasil	Brazil	Brasil	portugués	1 real (BRL) = 100 centavos
Brunéi	Brunei	Brunei	malayo	1 dólar de Brunéi (BND) = 100 sen
Bulgaria	Bulgaria	Bălgarija	búlgaro	1 lev (BGN) = 100 stotinki
Burkina Faso	Burkina Faso	Burkina Faso	francés	1 franco CFA (XOF) = 100 céntimos
Burundi	Burundi	Burundi	francés, kirundi	1 franco de Burundi (BIF) = 100 céntimos
Bután	Bhutan	Druk-Yul	tibetano	1 ngultrum (BTN) = 100 chetrum
Cabo Verde	Cape Verde	Cabo Verde	portugués	1 escudo de Cabo Verde (CVE) = 100 centavos
Camboya	Cambodia	Preah Reach Ana Pak Kampuchea	jemer	1 riel (KHR) = 100 sen
Camerún	Cameroon	Cameroon	francés, inglés	1 franco CFA (XAF) = 100 céntimos
Canadá	Canada	Canada	francés, inglés	1 dólar canadiense (CAD) = 100 centavos
Chad	Chad	Tchad	francés, árabe	1 franco CFA (XAF) = 100 céntimos
Chequia ▸ República Checa				
Chile	Chile	Chile	español	1 peso chileno (CLP) = 100 centavos
China	China	Zhongguo	chino	1 yuan renminbi (CNY) = 10 jiao = 100 fen
Chipre	Cyprus	Kipros (griego) Kibris (turco)	griego, turco	1 libra chipriota (CYP) = 100 (céntimos)

Nombre español	Nombre inglés	Nombre local	Lengua(s) oficial(es)	Moneda
Colombia	Colombia	Colombia	español	1 peso colombiano (COP) = 100 centavos
Comoras	Comoros	Comores	francés, árabe, comorano,	1 franco comorano (KMF) = 100 céntimos
Congo	Congo	Congo	francés	1 franco CFA = 100 céntimos
Congo, República Democrática del	Democratic Republic of Congo	Congo	francés, lingala	1 franco congoleño (CDF) = 100 céntimos
Corea del Norte	North Korea	Chosŏn Minjujuüi In'min Konghwaguk	coreano	1 won norcoreano (KPW) = 100 chun
Corea del Sur	South Korea	Taehan-Min'guk	coreano	1 won surcoreano (KRW) = 100 chun
Costa de Marfil	Côte d'Ivoire (Ivory Coast)	Côte d'Ivoire	francés	1 franco CFA (XOF) = 100 céntimos
Costa Rica	Costa Rica	Costa Rica	español	1 colón costarricense (CRC) = 100 céntimos
Croacia	Croatia	Hrvatska	serbocroata	1 kuna (HRK) = 100 lipa
Cuba	Cuba	Cuba	español	1 peso cubano (CUP) = 100 centavos
Dinamarca	Denmark	Danmark	danés	1 corona danesa (DKK) = 100 øre
Dominica	Dominica	Dominica	inglés, francés, criollo	1 dólar del Caribe Oriental (XCD) = 100 centavos
Ecuador	Ecuador	Ecuador	español	1 dólar estadounidense (USD) = 100 centavos
Egipto	Egypt	Jumhuriyat Misr al-Arabiya	árabe	1 libra egipcia (EGP) = 100 piastras
El Salvador	El Salvador	El Salvador	español	1 colón salvadoreño (SVC) = 100 centavos
Emiratos Árabes Unidos	United Arab Emirates	Ittihād al-Imārāt al-'Arabīyah	árabe, inglés	1 dirham (AED) = 100 fils
Eritrea	Eritrea	Eritrea	tigrinya, árabe	1 nakfa (ERN) = 100 centavos
Eslovaquia	Slovakia	Slovenska Republika	eslovaco	1 corona eslovaca (SKK) = 100 haliere
Eslovenia	Slovenia	Republika Slovenija	esloveno	1 tólar (SIT) =100 stotins
España	Spain	España	español	1 euro (EUR) = 100 céntimos
Estonia	Estonia	Eesti Vabariik	estonio	1 corona estonia (EEK) = 100 senti

Nombre español	Nombre inglés	Nombre local	Lengua(s) oficial(es)	Moneda
Estados Unidos (EE. UU.)	United States of America	United States of America	inglés	1 dólar estadounidense (USD) = 100 centavos
Etiopía	Ethiopia	Ityopiya	amárico	1 birr (ETB) = 100 centavos
Feroe ▸ Islas Feroe				
Filipinas	Philippines	Pilipinas	tagalo, inglés	1 peso filipino (PHP) = 100 centavos
Finlandia	Finland	Suomen Tasavalta	finlandés, sueco	1 euro (EUR) = 100 céntimos
Fiyi	Fiji	Matanitu Ko Viti	inglés	1 dólar de Fiyi (FJD) = 100 centavos
Francia	France	République française	francés	1 euro (EUR) = 100 céntimos
Gabón	Gabon	République gabonaise	francés	1 franco CFA (XAF) = 100 céntimos
Gambia	The Gambia	Gambia	inglés	1 dalasi (GMD) = 100 bututs
Georgia	Georgia	Sakartvelos Respublica	georgiano, ruso	1 lari (GEL) = 100 tetri
Ghana	Ghana	Ghana	inglés	1 cedi (GHC) = 100 pesewas
Grecia	Greece	Elliniki Dimokratia	griego	1 euro (EUR) = 100 céntimos
Groenlandia	Greenland	Grønland (danés), Kalaallit Nunaat	danés, groenlandés	1 corona danesa (DKK) = 100 øre
Guatemala	Guatemala	Guatemala	español	1 quetzal (GTQ) = 100 centavos
Guinea	Guinea	République de Guinée	francés	1 franco guineo (GNF) = 100 centimes
Guinea-Bissau	Guinea-Bissau	Republica da Guiné-Bissau	portugués	1 franco CFA (XOF) = 100 céntimos
Guinea Ecuatorial	Equatorial Guinea	Guinea Ecuatorial	español	1 franco CFA (XAF) = 100 céntimos
Guayana Francesa	French Guiana	Guyane	francés	1 euro (EUR) = 100 céntimos
Guyana	Guyana	Guyana	inglés	1 dólar de Guyana (GYD) = 100 centavos
Haití	Haiti	République d'Haïti	francés	1 gourde o gurda (HTG) = 100 céntimos
Holanda ▸ Países Bajos	Holland			
Honduras	Honduras	Honduras	español	1 lempira (HNL) = 100 centavos
Hungría	Hungary	Magyar Koztarsasag	húngaro	1 forint (HUF) = 100 filler

Nombre español	Nombre inglés	Nombre local	Lengua(s) oficial(es)	Moneda
India (la)	India	Bhārat (hindi)	hindi, inglés	1 rupia india (INR) = 100 paisa
Indonesia	Indonesia	Republik Indonesia	indonesio	1 rupia indonesia (IDR) = 100 sen
Irak, Iraq	Iraq	Jumhouriya al Iraquia	árabe	1 dinar iraquí (IQD) = 1.000 fils
Irán	Iran	Jomhoori-e-Islami-e-Iran	persa	1 rial iraní (IRR)
Irlanda	Ireland	Poblacht na hEireann	gaélico irlandés, inglés	1 euro (EUR) = 100 céntimos
Islandia	Iceland	Ísland	islandés	1 corona islandesa (ISK) = 100 aurar
Islas Feroe	Faroe Islands	Faroyar/ Faeroerne	feroés, danés	1 corona danesa (DKK) = 100 øre
Islas Salomón	Solomon Islands	Solomon Islands	inglés	1 dólar de las Islas Salomón (SBD) = 100 centavos
Israel	Israel	Medinat Israel	hebreo, árabe	1 sheqel (ILS) = 100 agorot
Italia	Italy	Repubblica Italiana	italiano	1 euro (EUR) = 100 céntimos)
Jamaica	Jamaica	Jamaica	inglés	1 dólar de Jamaica (JMD) = 100 centavos
Japón	Japan	Nihon	japonés	1 yen (JPY) = 100 sen
Jordania	Jordan	Al'Urdun	árabe	1 dinar jordano (JOD) = 1.000 fils
Kazajistán, Kazajstán	Kazakhstan	Kazak Respublikasy	kazajo, ruso	1 tenge (KZT) = 100 tiyn
Kenia	Kenya	Jamhuri ya Kenya	suajili, inglés	1 chelín keniano (KES) = 100 centavos
Kirghizistán	Kyrgyzstan	Kyrgyz Respublikasy	kirghiz	1 som (KGS) = 100 tyiyn
Kuwait	Kuwait	Dowlat al-Kuwayt	árabe	1 dinar kuwaití (KWD) = 1.000 fils
Laos	Laos	Lao	laosiano	1 kip (LAK) = 100 at
Lesoto	Lesotho	Lesotho	inglés, sesotho	1 loti (LSL) = 100 lisente
Letonia	Latvia	Latvijas Republika	letón	1 lats (LVL) = 100 santimi
Líbano	Lebanon	Al-Lubnan	árabe	1 libra libanesa (LBP) = 100 piastras
Liberia	Liberia	Liberia	inglés	1 dólar liberiano (LRD) = 100 centavos
Libia	Libya	Lībyā	árabe	1 dinar libio (LYD) = 1.000 dirhams

Nombre español	Nombre inglés	Nombre local	Lengua(s) oficial(es)	Moneda
Liechtenstein	Liechtenstein	Furstentum Liechtenstein	alemán	1 franco suizo (CHF) = 100 céntimos
Lituania	Lithuania	Lietuva	lituano	1 litas (LTL) = 100 centai
Luxemburgo	Luxembourg	Lëtzebuerg (Letz), Luxembourg (francés), Luxemburg (alemán)	francés, alemán	1 euro (EUR) = 100 céntimos
Macedonia	Macedonia	Republika Makedonija	macedonio	1 denar (MKD) = 100 deni
Madagascar	Madagascar	Republikan'i Madagasikara	malgache, francés	1 franco malgache (MGF) = 100 céntimos
Malasia	Malaysia	Federation of Malaysia	malayo	1 ringgit (MYR) = 100 sen
Malaui	Malaŵi	Dziko la Malaŵi	chichewa, inglés	1 kwacha de Malaui (MWK) = 100 tambalas
Maldivas	Maldives	Maldives Divehi Jumhuriya	divehi maldivano	1 rufiyaa (o rupia de Maldivas) (MVR) = 100 laari
Malí	Mali	Mali	francés	1 franco CFA (XOF) = 100 céntimos
Malta	Malta	Malta	inglés, maltés	1 lira maltesa (MTL) = 100 centavos
Marruecos	Morocco	Mamlaka al-Maghrebia	árabe	1 dirham marroquí (MAD) = 100 céntimos
Martinica	Martinique	Martinique	francés, criollo	1 euro (EUR) = 100 céntimos
Mauricio	Mauritius	Mauritius	inglés	1 rupia mauriciana (MUR) = 100 centavos
Mauritania	Mauritania	Mauritanie (francés) Mūrītāniyā (árabe)	árabe	1 ouguiya (MRO) = 5 khoums
México	Mexico	México	español	1 peso mexicano (MXN) = 100 centavos
Micronesia	Micronesia	Micronesia	inglés	1 dólar estadounidense (USD) = 100 centavos
Moldavia	Moldova	Republica Moldove-nească	rumano	1 leu moldavo (MDL) = 100 bani
Mónaco	Monaco	Monaco	francés	1 euro (EUR) = 100 céntimos
Mongolia	Mongolia	Mongol Ard Uls	khalkha	1 tugrik (MNT) = 100 möngö

Nombre español	Nombre inglés	Nombre local	Lengua(s) oficial(es)	Moneda
Mozambique	Mozambique	Republica de Moçambique	portugués	1 metical (MZM)= 100 centavos
Myanmar	Myanmar	Myanmar	birmano	1 kyat (MMK) = 100 pyas
Namibia	Namibia	Namibia	inglés	1 dólar namibio (NAD) = 100 centavos 1 rand sudafricano (ZAR) = 100 centavos
Nauru	Nauru	Naeoro (naurés) Nauru (inglés)	naurés, inglés	1 dólar australiano (AUD) = 100 centavos
Nepal	Nepal	Nepal Adhirajya	nepalés	1 rupia nepalesa (NPR) = 100 paisa
Nicaragua	Nicaragua	Nicaragua	español	1 córdoba oro (NIO) = 100 centavos
Níger	Niger	Niger	francés	1 franco CFA (XOF) = 100 céntimos
Nigeria	Nigeria	Nigeria	inglés, francés	1 naira (NGN) = 100 kobo
Noruega	Norway	Kongeriket Norge	noruego	1 corona noruega (NOK) = 100 øre
Nueva Zelanda	New Zealand	New Zealand	inglés	1 dólar neozelandés (NZD) = 100 centavos
Omán	Oman	Saltanat 'Uman	árabe	1 rial omaní (OMR) = 1.000 baisas
Países Bajos	The Netherlands	Koninkrijk der Nederlanden	neerlandés	1 euro (EUR) = 100 céntimos
Pakistán	Pakistan	Pākistān	urdu, inglés	1 rupia paquistaní (PKR) = 100 paisa
Panamá	Panama	Panamá	español	1 balboa (PAB) = 100 centésimos
Papúa-Nueva Guinea	Papua New Guinea	Papua New Guinea	inglés, neomelanesio	1 kina (PGK) = 100 toea
Paraguay	Paraguay	Paraguay	español	1 guaraní (PYG) = 100 céntimos
Perú	Peru	Perú	español	1 nuevo sol (PEN) = 100 céntimos
Polinesia Francesa	French Polynesia	Territoire de la Polynesie Française	polinesio, francés	1 Franco CFP (XPF) = 100 céntimos
Polonia	Poland	Rzeczpospolita Polska	polaco	1 zloty (PLN) = 100 groszy
Portugal	Portugal	Portugal	portugués	1 euro (EUR) = 100 céntimos
Puerto Rico	Puerto Rico	Puerto Rico	español, inglés	1 dólar estadounidense (USD) = 100 centavos
Qatar	Qatar	Dowlat Qatar	árabe	1 rial (o riyal) (QAR) = 100 dirhams

Nombre español	Nombre inglés	Nombre local	Lengua(s) oficial(es)	Moneda
República Centroafricana	Central African Republic	République Centrafricaine	francés (lengua nacional: sango)	1 franco CFA (XAF) = 100 céntimos
República Checa	Czech Republic	Căeská Republika	checo	1 corona checa (CZK) = 100 haler
República Dominicana	Dominican Republic	República Dominicana	español	1 peso dominicano (DOP) = 100 centavos
Reino Unido	United Kingdom	United Kingdom	inglés	1 libra esterlina (GBP) = 100 peniques
Ruanda	Rwanda	Rwanda	kinyaruanda francés, inglés	1 franco ruandés (RWF) = 100 céntimos
Rumania, Rumanía	Romania	Romănia	rumano	1 leu (ROL) = 100 bani
Rusia	Russia	Rossiya	ruso	1 rublo ruso (RUB) = 100 kopeks

Salomón ▸ Islas Salomón

Nombre español	Nombre inglés	Nombre local	Lengua(s) oficial(es)	Moneda
San Marino	San Marino	San Marino	italiano	1 euro (EUR) = 100 céntimos
Samoa	Samoa	Samoa	samoano, inglés	1 tala (WST) = 100 sene
Senegal	Senegal	Sénégal	francés, wolof	1 franco CFA (XOF) = 100 céntimos
Seychelles	Seychelles	Seychelles	francés, inglés, criollo	1 rupia de Seychelles (SCR) = 100 centavos
Sierra Leona	Sierra Leone	Sierra Leone	inglés	1 leone (SLL) = 100 centavos
Siria	Syria	As-Sūrīyah	árabe	1 libra siria (SYP) = 100 piastras
Singapur	Singapore	Singapore	chino, inglés, malayo, tamil	1 dólar singapurense (SGD) = 100 centavos
Somalia	Somalia	Somaliya	árabe, somalí	1 chelín somalí (SOS) = 100 centavos
Sri Lanka	Sri Lanka	Sri Lanka	cingalés, tamil	1 rupia de Sri Lanka (LKR) = 100 centavos
Suazilandia	Swaziland	Umbouso we Swatini	swazi, inglés	1 lilangeni (SZL) = 100 centavos
Sudáfrica	South Africa	South Africa	inglés, afrikaans	1 rand (ZAR) = 100 centavos
Sudán	The Sudan	As-Sūdān	árabe	1 dinar soudanés (SDD) = 100 piastras
Suecia	Sweden	Konungariket Sverige	sueco	1 corona sueca (SEK) = 100 öre
Suiza	Switzerland	Schweiz (alemán), Suisse (francés), Svizzera (italiano)	francés, alemán, italiano, romanche	1 franco suizo (CHF) = 100 céntimos

Nombre español	Nombre inglés	Nombre local	Lengua(s) oficial(es)	Moneda
Surinam	Suriname	Suriname	neerlandés	1 florín surinamés (SRG) = 100 centavos
Tailandia	Thailand	Prathet Thai	thai	1 baht (THB) = 100 satang
Taiwán	Taiwan	T'aiwan	chino	1 (nuevo) dólar de Taiwán (TWD) = 100 fen
Tanzania	Tanzania	Tanzania	suajili, inglés	1 chelín tanzano (TZS) = 100 centavos
Tayikistán	Tajikistan	Jumkhurii Tojikistan	tayik	1 somoni (TJS) = 100 diram)
Togo	Togo	Togo	francés	1 franco CFA (XOF) = 100 céntimos
Tonga	Tonga	Tonga	inglés, tongano	1 pa'anga (TOP) = 100 seniti
Trinidad y Tobago	Trinidad and Tobago	Trinidad and Tobago	inglés	1 dólar de Trinidad y Tobago (TTD) = 100 centavos
Túnez	Tunisia	Tunisiya	árabe, francés	1 dinar tunecino (TND) = 1. 000 milésimos
Turkmenistán	Turkmenistan	Turkmenostan	turcomano	1 manat turcomano (TMM) = tenge
Turquía	Turkey	Turkiye	turco	1 libra turca (TRL) = 100 kurus
Ucrania	Ukraine	Ukraina	ucraniano, ruso	1 jrivnia UAH = 100 kopiykas
Uganda	Uganda	Uganda	inglés, suajili	1 chelín ugandés (UGX) = 100 centavos
Uruguay	Uruguay	Uruguay	español	1 peso uruguayo (UYU) = 100 centésimos
Uzbekistán	Uzbekistan	Uzbekistan	uzbeko	1 sum (UZS)= 100 tiyin
Vanuatu	Vanuatu	Vanuatu	bislamar, inglés, francés	1 vatu (VUV) = 100 céntimos
El Vaticano	Vatican City	Citta' del Vaticano	italiano	1 euro (EUR) = 100 céntimos
Venezuela	Venezuela	Venezuela	español	1 bolívar (VEB) = 100 céntimos
Vietnam	Vietnam	Viêt-nam	vietnamita	1 dong (VND) = 100 sou
Yemen	Yemen	Al-Yamaniya	árabe	1 rial yemení (YER) = 100 fils
Yibuti	Djibouti	Djibouti	árabe, francés	1 franco de Yibuti (DJF) = 100 céntimos
Yugoslavia	Yugoslavia	Jugoslavija	serbocroata (serbo)	1 dinar yugoslavo (YUN) = 100 paras

Nombre español	Nombre inglés	Nombre local	Lengua(s) oficial(es)	Moneda
Zaire	Zaire			
▸ Congo, República Democrática del				
Zambia	Zambia	Zambia	inglés	1 kwacha zambiano (ZMK) = 100 ngwee
Zimbabue	Zimbabwe	Zimbabwe	inglés	1 dólar de Zimbabue (ZWD) = 100 centavos

Condados ingleses

Condado	Centro administrativo	Abreviatura
Avon	Bristol	
Bedfordshire	Bedford	Beds
Berkshire	Reading	Berks
Buckinghamshire	Aylesbury	Bucks
Cambridgeshire	Cambridge	Cambs
Cheshire	Chester	Ches
Cleveland	Middlesbrough	
Cornwall	Truro	Corn
Cumbria	Carlisle	
Derbyshire	Matlock	Derby
Devon	Exeter	
Dorset	Dorchester	
Durham	Durham	Dur
Essex	Chelmsford	
Gloucestershire	Gloucester	Glos
Greater London	-	
Greater Manchester	-	
Hampshire	Winchester	Hants
Hereford and	Worcester	Worcester
Hertfordshire	Hertford	Herts
Humberside	Hull	
Isle of Wight	Newport	IOW
Kent	Maidstone	
Lancashire	Preston	Lancs
Leicestershire	Leicester	Leics
Lincolnshire	Lincoln	Lincs
Merseyside	Liverpool	
Norfolk	Norwich	
Northamptonshire	Northampton	Northants
Northumberland	Newcastle upon Tyne	Northumb
Nottinghamshire	Nottingham	Notts
Oxfordshire	Oxford	Oxon
Shropshire	Shrewsbury	
Somerset	Taunton	Som
Staffordshire	Stafford	Staffs
Suffolk	Ipswich	
Surrey	Kingston upon Thames	
Sussex, East	Lewes	
Sussex, West	Chichester	
Tyne and Wear	Newcastle	
Warwickshire	Warwick	War
West Midlands	Birmingham	W Midlands
Wiltshire	Trowbridge	Wilts
Yorkshire, North	Northallerton	N Yorks
Yorkshire, South	Barnsley	S Yorks
Yorkshire, West	Wakefield	W Yorks

Escocia

División administrativa	Centro administrativo
Aberdeen City	Aberdeen
Aberdeenshire	Aberdeen
Angus	Forfar
Argyll and Bute	Lochgilphead
Clackmannanshire	Alloa
Dumfries and Galloway	Dumfries
Dundee City	Dundee
East Ayrshire	Kilmarnock
East Dunbartonshire	Kirkintilloch
East Lothian	Haddington
East Renfrewshire	Giffnock
Edinburgh, City of	Edinburgh
Falkirk	Falkirk
Fife	Glenrothes
Glasgow City	Glasgow
Highland	Inverness
Inverclyde	Greenock
Midlothian	Dalkeith
Moray	Elgin
North Ayrshire	Irvine
North Lanarkshire	Motherwell
Orkney Islands	Kirkwall
Perth and Kinross	Perth
Renfrewshire	Paisley
Scottish Borders	Newton St Boswells
Shetland Islands	Lerwick
South Ayrshire	Ayr
South Lanarkshire	Hamilton
Stirling	Stirling
West Dunbartonshire	Dumbarton
Western Isles (Eilean Siar, Comhairle nan)	Stornoway
West Lothian	Livingston

Condados irlandeses

Condado	Centro administrativo
Carlow	Carlow
Cavan	Cavan
Clare	Ennis
Cork	Cork
Donegal	Lifford
Dublin	Dublin
Galway	Galway
Kerry	Tralee
Kildare	Naas
Kilkenny	Kilkenny
Laoighis (Leix)	Portlaoise
Leitrim	Carrick
Limerick	Limerick
Longford	Longford
Louth	Dundalk
Mayo	Castlebar
Meath	Trim
Monaghan	Monaghan
Offaly	Tullamore
Roscommon	Roscommon
Sligo	Sligo
Tipperary	Clonmel
Waterford	Waterford
Westmeath	Mullingar
Wexford	Wexford
Wicklow	Wicklow

País de Gales

División administrativa	Centro administrativo
Anglesey, Isle of	Llangefni
Blaenau Gwent	Ebbw Vale
Bridgend	Bridgend
Caerphilly	Hengoed
Cardiff	Cardiff
Carmarthenshire	Carmarthen
Ceredigion	Aberaeron
Conwy	Conwy
Denbighshire	Ruthin
Flintshire	Mold
Gwynedd	Caernarfon
Merthyr Tydfil	Merthyr Tydfil
Monmouthshire	Cwmbran
Neath Port Talbot	Port Talbot
Newport	Newport
Pembrokeshire	Haverfordwest
Powys	Llandrindod Wells
Rhondda, Cynon, Taff	Clydach Vale
Swansea	Swansea
Torfaen	Pontypool
Vale of Glamorgan	Barry
Wrexham	Wrexham

Irlanda del Norte

División administrativa	Centro administrativo
Antrim	Antrim
Ards	Newtownards
Armagh	Armagh
Ballymena	Ballymena
Ballymoney	Balleymoney
Banbridge	Banbridge
Belfast	
Carrickfergus	Carrickfergus
Castlereagh	Belfast
Coleraine	Coleraine
Cookstown	Cookstown
Craigavon	Craigavon
Derry	
Down	Downpatrick
Dungannon	Dungannon
Fermanagh	Enniskillen
Larne	Larne
Limavady	Limavady
Lisburn	Lisburn
Magherafelt	Magherafelt
Moyle	Ballycastle
Newry and Mourne	Newry
Newtownabbey	Newtownabbey
North Down	Bangor
Omagh	Omagh
Strabane	Strabane

Estados-Unidos: lista de Estados

Abreviaturas: la primera abreviatura indica la forme més frecuente, la segunda corresponde al código postal del estado (ZIP code).

Estado	Abreviaturas	Sobrenombre	Habitantes	Capital
Alabama	Ala; AL	Camellia State, Heart of Dixie	Alabamians	Montgomery
Alaska	AK	Mainland State, The Last Frontier	Alaskans	Juneau
Arizona	Ariz; AZ	Apache State, Grand Canyon State	Arizonans	Phoenix
Arkansas	Ark; AR	Bear State, Land of Opportunity	Arkansans	Little Rock
California	Calif; CA	Golden State	Californians	Sacramento
Colorado	Colo; CO	Centennial State	Coloradans	Denver
Connecticut	Conn; CT	Nutmeg State, Constitution State	Nutmeggers	Hartford
Delaware	Del; DE	Diamond State, First State	Delawareans	Dover
District of Columbia	DC	DC, the District	Washingtonians	Washington

Estado	Abreviaturas	Sobrenombre	Habitantes	Capital
Florida	Fla; FL	Everglade State, Sunshine State	Floridians	Tallahassee
Georgia	Ga; GA	Empire State of the South, Peach State	Georgians	Atlanta
Hawaii	HI	Aloha State	Hawaiians	Honolulu
Idaho	ID	Gem State	Idahoans	Boise
Illinois	Ill; IL	Prairie State, Land of Lincoln	Illinoisans	Springfield
Indiana	Ind; IN	Hoosier State	Hoosiers	Indianapolis
Iowa	IA	Hawkeye State, Corn State	Iowans	Des Moines
Kansas	Kans; KS	Sunflower State, Jayhawker State	Kansans	Topeka
Kentucky	Ky; KY	Bluegrass State	Kentuckians	Frankfort
Louisiana	La; LA	Pelican State, Sugar State, Creole State	Louisianians	Baton Rouge
Maine	ME	Pine Tree State	Downeasters	Augusta
Maryland	Md; MD	Old Line State,	Marylanders	Annapolis
Massachusetts	Mass; MA	Bay State, Old ColonyBay	Staters	Boston
Michigan	Mich; MI	Wolverine State, Great Lake State	Michiganders	Lansing
Minnesota	Minn; MN	Gopher State, North Star State	Minnesotans	St Paul
Mississippi	Miss; MS	Magnolia State	Mississippians	Jackson
Missouri	Mo; MO	Bullion State, Show Me State	Missourians	Jefferson City
Montana	Mont; MT	Treasure State, Big Sky Country	Montanans	Helena
Nebraska	Nebr; NE	Cornhusker State, Beef State	Nebraskans	Lincoln
Nevada	Nev; NV	Silver State, Sagebrush State, Battle Born State	Nevadans	Carson City
New Hampshire	NH	Granite State	New Hampshirites	Concord
New Jersey	NJ	Garden State	New Jerseyites	Trenton
New Mexico	N Mex; NM	Sunshine State, Land of Enchantment	New Mexicans	Santa Fe
New York	NY	Empire State	New Yorkers	Albany
North Carolina	NC	Old North State, Tar Heel State	North Carolinians	Raleigh
North Dakota	N Dak; ND	Flickertail State, Sioux State, Peace Garden State	North Dakotans	Bismarck
Ohio	OH	Buckeye State	Ohioans	Columbus
Oklahoma	Okla; OK	Sooner State	Oklahomans	Oklahoma City
Oregon	Oreg; OR	Sunset State, Beaver State	Oregonians	Salem

Estado	Abreviaturas	Sobrenombre	Habitantes	Capital
Pennsylvania	Pa; PA	Keystone State	Pennsylvanians	Harrisburg
Rhode Island	RI	Little Rhody, Plantation State	Rhode Islanders	Providence
South Carolina	SC	Palmetto State	South Carolinians	Columbia
South Dakota	S Dak; SD	Sunshine State, Coyote State	South Dakotans	Pierre
Tennessee	Tenn; TN	Volunteer State	Tennesseans	Nashville
Texas	Tex; TX	Lone Star State	Texans	Austin
Utah	Utah; UT	Mormon State, Beehive State	Utahans	Salt Lake City
Vermont	Vt; VT	Green Mountain State	Vermonters	Montpelier
Virginia	Va; VA	Old Dominion State, Mother of Presidents	Virginians	Richmond
Washington	Wash; WA	Evergreen State, Chinook State	Washingtonians	Olympia
West Virginia	W Va; WV	Panhandle State, Mountain State	West Virginians	Charleston
Wisconsin	Wis; WI	Badger State, America's Dairyland	Wisconsinites	Madison
Wyoming	Wyo; WY	Equality State	Wyomingites	Cheyenne

Estados y territorios australianos

Nombre	Capital
Australian Capital Territory	Canberra
New South Wales	Sydney
Northern Territory	Darwin
Queensland	Brisbane
South Australia	Adelaide
Tasmania	Hobart
Victoria	Melbourne
Western Australia	Perth

Provincias canadienses

Nombre	Capital
Alberta	Edmonton
British Columbia	Victoria
Manitoba	Winnipeg
New Brunswick	Fredericton
Newfoundland	St John's
Northwest Territories and Nunavut	Yellowknife
Nova Scotia	Halifax
Ontario	Toronto
Prince Edward Island	Charlottetown
Quebec	Quebec City
Saskatchewan	Regina
Yukon Territory	Whitehorse

Español–Inglés
Spanish–English

Aa

A3 *nm (formato de papel)* A3

A4 *nm (formato de papel)* A4

A/A (*abrev de* **a la atención de**) attn

AB *nf Méx* FIN (*abrev de* **aceptación bancaria**) bank acceptance, banker's acceptance

ABA *nf* FIN (*abrev de* **Asociación de Bancos de la Argentina**) Association of Argentine Banks

abajo *adv* **el abajo firmante** the undersigned

abandonar *vt* (**a**) *(proyecto)* to abandon, to axe; *(idea, planes)* to scrap; **han amenazado con abandonar las negociaciones** they have threatened to walk out of the negotiations (**b**) INS *(barco, cargamento)* to abandon

abandono *nm* (**a**) *(de proyecto)* abandonment ❑ UE **abandono de tierras** land set-aside (**b**) INS *(de barco, cargamento)* abandonment

abanico *nm* (**a**) *(gama)* range; **tenemos un amplio abanico de modelos** we have a wide range of models; **un abanico de precios** a range of prices (**b**) BOLSA *(de inversiones)* spread

abaratamiento *nm (de producto)* reduction *o* fall in price; **el abaratamiento de los precios** the reduction *o* fall in prices

> Las técnicas modernas de tratamiento de los tejidos o la rapidez en la entrega han sido algunas de las claves que han empujado a estas cadenas. Por otro lado, factores como la incorporación de la mujer al trabajo, el **abaratamiento** de los costes y el incremento del nivel de vida auguran un aumento en la demanda de estos servicios.

abaratar 1 *vt (precio, coste)* to bring down, to reduce; *(producto)* to reduce the price of
2 abaratarse *vpr (precio, coste)* to fall; *(producto)* to go down in price, to become cheaper

abarrotar *vt CAm, Méx* to monopolize, to buy up

abastecer 1 *vt* to supply (**de** with); **nos abastecen de materias primas** they supply *o* provide us with raw materials
2 abastecerse *vpr* to stock up (**de** on)

abastecimiento *nm* supply; **se ha interrumpido el abastecimiento** they've cut off the supply

abierto, -a *adj* (**a**) *(tienda, archivo)* open; **abierto**

de 9 a 5 *(en letrero)* opening hours: 9 to 5 (**b**) BANCA *(cuenta)* active

abogacía *nf* legal profession; **ejercer la abogacía** to practise law

abogado, -a *nm,f* DER *Br* lawyer, *US* attorney ❑ **abogado defensor** counsel for the defence; **abogado de empresa** company lawyer; **abogado del Estado** public prosecutor

abogar *vi* **abogar por algo** to advocate sth

abonado, -a *nm,f (a teléfono, revista)* subscriber

abonar 1 *vt* (**a**) *(pagar)* to pay; **¿cómo desea abonarlo?** how would you like to pay?; **abonar algo en la cuenta de alguien** to credit sb's account with sth (**b**) *(suscribir)* **abonar a alguien a una revista** to get sb a subscription to a magazine
2 abonarse *vpr (a revista)* to subscribe (**a** to)

abono *nm* (**a**) BANCA, CONT credit entry (**b**) *(para transporte público)* season ticket (**c**) *Méx (plazo)* instalment; **pagar en abonos** to pay by instalments

abortar *vt* INFORM *(programa)* to abort

abrecartas *nm inv* letter opener, paper knife

abrir 1 *vt* (**a**) *(en general)* to open; INFORM *(archivo)* to open; **abrir un nuevo centro comercial** to open a new shopping centre
(**b**) *(iniciar) (cuenta bancaria)* to open; **abrir una línea de crédito** to open a line of credit; DER **abrir diligencias** to instigate proceedings; **abrir la licitación/sesión** to open the bidding/session
(**c**) *(posibilidades)* to open up; **la empresa intenta abrir nuevos mercados en el exterior** the company is trying to open up new markets abroad
2 *vi* to open; **la tienda abre a las nueve** the shop opens at nine (o'clock); **abrimos también los domingos** *(en letrero)* also open on Sundays

abrochadora *nf RP* stapler ❑ **abrochadora industrial** staple gun

abrochar *vt RP* to staple

abrogar *vt* DER to repeal, to abrogate

absentismo *nm Esp* **absentismo (laboral)** *(justificado)* absence from work; *(injustificado)* absenteeism

absorber *vt* (**a**) *(empresa)* to absorb by merger;

Roma Inc. fue absorbida por su mayor competidor Roma Inc. was absorbed by its biggest rival (**b**) FIN *(deudas)* to absorb (**c**) *(consumir)* **esta tarea absorbe mucho tiempo** this task takes up a lot of time; **absorbe mucha mano de obra** it's very labour-intensive

absorción *nf (de empresa)* absorption (by merger)

> ❝
>
> El presidente del órgano sindical, Hilario Álvarez, ha asegurado que con esta decisión la multinacional "ha completado" la operación de **absorción** de Fontaneda por parte de Marbú, también perteneciente a United Biscuits.
>
> ❞

abusar *vi* **abusar de** *(autoridad)* to misuse

abusivo, -a *adj (precio)* extortionate; *(interés)* usurious

abuso *nm (uso excesivo)* abuse (**de** of) ▫ *abuso de autoridad* abuse of authority; *abuso de confianza* breach of trust; *abuso de poder* abuse of power; *abuso de posición dominante* abuse of a dominant position

acabar 1 *vt* to finish, to end; **hemos acabado el trabajo** we've finished the work
2 *vi* to finish, to end
3 **acabarse** *vpr* (**a**) *(agotarse)* to be used up, to be gone; **se nos ha acabado el papel** we're out of paper (**b**) *(terminar)* to finish, to be over

acaparar *vt* (**a**) *(monopolizar)* to corner, to monopolize; **en un año han acaparado el mercado** they've cornered the market in a year (**b**) *(comprar la totalidad de)* to buy up

acceder *vi* **acceder a** *(edificio)* to enter, to gain entry to; INFORM **acceder a una base de datos** to access a database; **desde aquí se puede acceder a Internet** you can log on to the Internet from here

accesibilidad *nf (al mercado)* accessibility

accesible *adj* (**a**) *(producto)* accessible (**b**) *(precio, oferta)* affordable

acceso *nm* (**a**) *(paso)* access (**a** to); **tener acceso a algo** to have access to sth; **tener acceso a información confidencial** to have access to confidential information (**b**) INFORM access; *(a página Web)* hit; **acceso a Internet/escritura** Internet/write access ▫ *acceso aleatorio* random access; *acceso directo* direct access; *acceso remoto* remote access; *acceso secuencial* sequential access

accesorio, -a 1 *adj (gastos)* incidental
2 **accesorios** *nmpl (de producto)* accessories

accidente *nm* accident ▫ *accidente laboral* industrial accident; *accidente de trabajo* workplace accident, occupational accident

acción *nf* (**a**) FIN share; **acciones** *esp Br* shares, *esp US* stock ▫ *acción acumulativa* cumulative share; *acción aurífera* gold share; *acciones bancarias* bank shares; *acciones en cartera* Br own shares held, *US* Treasury stock; *acciones en circulación* outstanding shares; *acción cotizada* listed share; *acciones no cotizadas* unlisted shares; *acciones con derecho a voto* Br voting shares, *US* voting stock; *Esp acciones desembolsadas* paid-up shares; *acción diferida* deferred share; *acciones diversas* miscellaneous shares; *acción de dividendo* dividend share; *acciones especulativas* speculative shares; *acciones excedentes* excess shares; *acción del fundador* founder's share; *acciones de goce* jouissance shares; *acciones de gran liquidez* blue-chip stocks *o* shares; *acción gratuita* bonus share; *acciones industriales* industrial shares; *acciones inmobiliarias* property shares; *acciones liberadas* Esp bonus shares; *Am* paid-up shares; *acción nominativa* registered share; *acciones nuevas* new shares; *acciones ordinarias* equity shares, *Br* ordinary shares, *US* common stock; *acción de oro* golden share; *acciones petroleras* oil shares; *acciones de poco valor* Br penny shares, *US* penny stock; *acción al portador* bearer share; *acciones preferentes* Br preference shares, *US* preferred stock; *acciones preferentes acumulativas* Br cumulative preference shares, *US* cumulative preferred stock; *acciones de primera línea* blue chips; *acciones de propiedad conjunta* joint shares; *acciones de renta fija* Br fixed-interest shares, *US* fixed-income stock; *acción roja* red chip; *acciones sindicadas* syndicated shares; *acción transferible* transferable share
(**b**) DER **acción civil** civil action; *acción judicial* legal action; *acción legal* lawsuit; **iniciar acciones legales contra alguien** to take legal action against sb; *acción popular* action brought by the People

accionar *vt* to activate

accionariado *nm* (**a**) *(conjunto de accionistas)* Br shareholders, US stockholders (**b**) *(posesión de acciones)* share ownership, US stock ownership; **plan de accionariado** employee share ownership plan, US stock ownership plan

> ❝
>
> Y la imaginación puede sustituir al efectivo salarial en algunos casos. Un ejemplo es el sistema de **accionariado** voluntario para empleados de Alcampo o de American Express, que concede acciones gratis a su plantilla. Ésta sólo puede vender un tercio de las mismas pasado el año de su concesión; otro tercio, al segundo año y el último tercio, el tercero. Y cada ejercicio se van recibiendo nuevas acciones bajo el mismo sistema.
>
> ❞

accionarial, *Am* **accionario, -a** *adj* FIN *esp Br* share, *esp US* stock; **paquete** *o* **participación accionarial** *Br* shareholding, *US* stockholding

accionista *nmf* FIN *Br* shareholder, *US* stockholder ❑ **accionista mayoritario** majority *Br* shareholder *o US* stockholder; **accionista minoritario** minority *Br* shareholder *o US* stockholder; **accionista principal** major *Br* shareholder *o US* stockholder; **accionista registrado** registered *Br* shareholder *o US* stockholder

ACE *nm* (*abrev de* **Acuerdo de Complementación Económica**) ECA

acelerador *nm* INFORM accelerator ❑ **acelerador gráfico** graphics accelerator; **acelerador de vídeo** video accelerator

acento *nm* accent ❑ **acento agudo** acute accent; INFORM **acento flotante** floating accent; **acento grave** grave accent

acentuado, -a *adj* (*sílaba*) stressed; (*caracter*) accented

aceptable *adj* acceptable

aceptación *nf* (**a**) BANCA acceptance ❑ **aceptación bancaria** bank acceptance, banker's acceptance; **aceptación definitiva** final acceptance; **aceptación limitada** qualified acceptance (**b**) MKTG **aceptación condicionada** conditional acceptance; **aceptación del consumidor** consumer acceptance; **aceptación de marca** brand acceptability, brand acceptance

aceptante *nmf* BANCA acceptor

aceptar *vt* (*cantidad, entrega, letra*) to accept; (*oferta*) to accept, to take up; **no aceptaron nuestras condiciones** they didn't accept our conditions; **no se aceptan cheques** (*en letrero*) we do not take cheques; **se aceptan donativos** (*en letrero*) donations welcome

aclaratorio, -a *adj* explanatory

acomodado, -a *adj* well-off, affluent

aconsejar *vt* to advise; **aconsejar a alguien (que haga algo)** to advise sb (to do sth); **le pedí que me aconsejara (acerca de)** I asked him for advice (about)

acontecimiento *nm* event ❑ **acontecimiento mediático** media event

acopio *nm* **hacer acopio de** (*existencias, comestibles*) to stockpile

acorazado, -a *adj* **cámara acorazada** strong-room, vault

acordado, -a *adj* agreed (upon); **lo acordado fue que lo pagarían ellos** it was agreed that they would pay

acordar *vt* to agree (on); **acordar hacer algo** to agree to do sth; **acordaron que lo harían** they agreed to do it

acoso *nm* harassment ❑ **acoso moral** mobbing; **acoso sexual** sexual harassment

acrecentar 1 *vt* to increase
2 acrecentarse *vpr* to increase

acreditación *nf* (*de representante*) accreditation; (*de periodista*) press card

acreditado, -a *adj* (*representante*) accredited; **los congresistas acreditados** the official conference delegates

acreditar *vt* (**a**) (*representante*) to accredit (**b**) (*certificar*) to certify; **este diploma lo acredita como traductor jurado** this diploma certifies that he is an official translator; **los interesados deben acreditar que cumplen los requisitos** applicants must provide documentary evidence that they meet the requirements; **el carnet lo acredita como miembro de la delegación** the ID card identifies him as a member of the delegation

acreedor, -ora *nm,f* FIN creditor ❑ **acreedor asegurado** secured creditor; **acreedor comercial** trade creditor; **acreedor común** ordinary creditor; **acreedor con garantía parcial** partly secured creditor; **acreedor hipotecario** mortgagee; **acreedor preferente, acreedor preferencial** preferential creditor, preferred creditor; **acreedor solidario** joint and several creditor

acta *nf* (**a**) (*certificado*) certificate; **acta (de nombramiento)** certificate of appointment ❑ BOLSA **acta de adjudicación** letter of allotment; **acta de constitución** (*de empresa*) formation deed; **acta de inspección** tax inspection report; **acta notarial** affidavit (**b**) **acta(s)** (*de junta, reunión*) minutes; **actas** (*de congreso*) proceedings; **constar en acta** to be minuted; **levantar acta** to take the minutes (**c**) (*acuerdo*) act ❑ UE **Acta de Adhesión** Act of Accession; **acta fundacional** founding treaty; UE **Acta Única (Europea)** Single European Act

actitud *nf* attitude

activación *nf* (**a**) CONT (*de gastos*) capitalization (**b**) (*de alarma, mecanismo*) activation (**c**) (*estímulo*) stimulation; **medidas que pretenden la activación del consumo** measures designed to boost *o* stimulate consumption

activado, -a *adj* (**a**) CONT capitalized (**b**) INFORM enabled; **activado por la voz** voice-activated

activar 1 *vt* (**a**) (*cliente, cuenta*) to activate (**b**) CONT (*gastos*) to capitalize (**c**) INFORM (*opción, función*) to enable (**d**) (*estimular*) (*consumo*) to boost, to stimulate
2 activarse *vpr* (*alarma*) to go off; (*mecanismo*) to be activated; **el mecanismo se activa con la voz** the mechanism is voice-activated

actividad *nf* (**a**) (*trabajo, tarea*) activity; **una ley que regula la actividad de las agencias de viajes** a law that regulates the activities *o* operation of travel agencies; **la empresa desarrolla su actividad en el sector de la construcción** the company operates in the building industry

❏ *actividades auxiliares* support activities; *actividad comercial* business activity; *actividad económica* economic activity; CONT*actividades ordinarias* ordinary activities; *actividad principal* (de una empresa) principal o main activity; *actividad remunerada* paid employment; *actividad secundaria* (de una empresa) secondary activity

(**b**) (en la Bolsa) trading; **el mercado registraba una actividad frenética** there was furious trading on the markets

activo, -a 1 adj (**a**) (dinámico) active (**b**) (que trabaja) **la población activa** the working population; **en activo** in employment

2 nm FIN assets ❏ *activo bruto* gross assets; *activo de caja* bank reserves; *activos en cartera* portfolio assets; *activo circulante* current assets; *activos circulantes* working assets; *activo circulante neto* net current assets; *activo corriente* current assets; *activo diferido* deferred assets; *activo disponible* liquid assets; *activos en divisas* (foreign) currency assets; *activo de explotación* operating assets; *activo ficticio* fictitious assets; *activo fijo* fixed assets; *activos fijos materiales netos* net tangible assets; *activo financiero* financial assets; *activo físico* physical assets; *activo flotante* floating assets; *activo ilíquido* illiquid assets; *activo imponible* chargeable assets; *activo inmaterial* intangible assets; *activo inmovilizado* capital assets; *activos intangibles* intangible assets; *activos invisibles* invisible assets; *activo líquido* liquid assets; *activos monetarios* monetary assets; *activos muebles* movable assets; *activo neto* net assets; *activos principales* core assets; *activos reales* physical assets; *activo realizable* short-term investments in securities; *activos de renta fija* fixed-yield assets; *activos de renta variable* variable-yield assets; *activos sociales* corporate assets; *activo subyacente* underlying asset; *activos tangibles* tangible assets; *activos totales* total assets; Am *activo de trabajo* working assets

> ❝
> El consejero delegado del BBVA insiste en que México es la pieza clave de la estrategia del grupo en la región, por su fuerte crecimiento del PIB y porque concentra el 69% de los **activos** de la región.
> ❞

acto nm (**a**) (acción) act ❏ *acto de conciliación* = formal attempt to reach an out-of-court settlement (**b**) (ceremonia) ceremony ❏ *actos sociales de la empresa* corporate hospitality

actor nm player; **los principales actores del sector** the key players in this industry ❏ *actor económico* economic actor

actual adj (**a**) (del momento presente) present, current; **las tendencias actuales de la economía** current trends in the economy; **el seis del actual** the sixth of this month (**b**) (de moda) modern, up-to-date; **tiene un diseño muy actual** it has a very modern o up-to-date design (**c**) (de interés) topical; **un tema muy actual** a very topical issue

actualizable adj INFORM upgradable, upgradeable

actualización nf (**a**) (de información, datos) updating (**b**) (de tecnología, industria) modernization (**c**) INFORM (de software, hardware) upgrade

actualizado, -a adj (noticias, información) up to date

actualizar vt (**a**) (información, datos) to update (**b**) (tecnología, industria) to modernize (**c**) INFORM (software, hardware) to upgrade

actuar vi (**a**) (obrar) (persona) to act; **actuar dentro de la ley** to act legally (**b**) (operar) (negocio, empresa) to operate

actuarial adj actuarial

actuario, -a nm,f FIN **actuario de seguros** actuary

acuerdo 1 nm (**a**) (determinación, pacto) agreement; **un acuerdo verbal** a verbal agreement; **llegar a un acuerdo** to reach (an) agreement; **no hubo acuerdo** they did not reach (an) agreement; **de común acuerdo** by common consent ❏ *acuerdo arancelario* tariff agreement; *acuerdo de arbitraje* settlement by arbitration; *acuerdo bilateral* bilateral agreement; *acuerdo de colaboración* partnership agreement; *acuerdo comercial* trade agreement; *acuerdo de comercialización* marketing agreement; *acuerdo de comercio justo* fair-trade agreement; *acuerdo de compensación* (de cheque) clearing agreement; *acuerdo compensatorio* offset agreement; *acuerdo contractual* contractual agreement; *acuerdo de doble imposición o tributación* double taxation agreement; *acuerdo escrito* written agreement; *acuerdo financiero* financial deal; *acuerdo formal* formal agreement; *Acuerdo General sobre Aranceles y Comercio* General Agreement on Tariffs and Trade; *acuerdo global* package deal; *acuerdo de indemnización* compensation deal; *acuerdos internacionales de o sobre productos básicos* international commodity agreements; *acuerdo de libre comercio o cambio* free trade agreement; *acuerdo de licencia* licence agreement; *acuerdo marco* general o framework agreement; *acuerdo monetario* monetary agreement; *Acuerdo Monetario Europeo* European Monetary Agreement; *acuerdo de moratoria* standstill agreement; *acuerdo multilateral* multilateral agreement; *acuerdo multilateral de comercio* multilateral trade agreement; *acuerdo mutuo* joint agreement, mutual agreement; *acuerdo de patrocinio* sponsorship agreement, sponsorship deal; BOLSA *acuerdo de permuta* swap agreement; *acuerdo de precios* price agreement; *acuerdo privado* private agreement; *acuerdo de productividad* productivity agreement; *acuerdo recíproco* reciprocal agreement; BOLSA *acuerdo de recompra* repurchase agreement; *acuerdo salarial* pay agreement, pay deal; *acuerdo sindical* union agreement; *acuerdo de subcontratación* subcontracting agreement; BOLSA *acuerdo de swap* swap agreement; *acuerdo tácito* *(de colaboración)* working agreement; *acuerdo sobre tipos de interés futuros* Forward Rate Agreement; *acuerdo de venta* sale agreement

(**b**) *Méx (reunión)* staff meeting

2 de acuerdo *adv* (**a**) *(conforme)* **estar de acuerdo** to agree (**con/en** with/on); **ponerse de acuerdo (con alguien)** to agree (with sb), to come to an agreement (with sb) (**b**) **de acuerdo con** *(conforme a)* in accordance with; **de acuerdo con cifras oficiales...** according to official figures...

acumulación *nf (de capital, existencias)* accumulation, build-up; *(de intereses)* accrual ❑ *acumulación de capital* capital accumulation

acumular **1** *vt (capital, existencias)* to accumulate, to build up; *(intereses)* to accrue, to accumulate; *(deudas)* to run up, to accumulate

2 acumularse *vpr (capital, intereses, deudas)* to accumulate, to build up; *(intereses)* to accumulate, to accrue

acumulativo, -a *adj* cumulative

acuñar *vt (moneda)* to mint

acusar *vt (recibo)* to acknowledge; **acusamos la recepción del paquete** we acknowledge the receipt of your parcel

acuse *nm* **acuse de recibo** *(de pedido, petición)* acknowledgement of receipt, confirmation of receipt; *(escrito)* acknowledgement slip; *(como respuesta a un e-mail)* acknowledgement

adaptador *nm* INFORM adaptor ❑ *adaptador de gráficos mejorado* enhanced graphics adaptor

adaptar **1** *vt* to adapt; **un modelo adaptado a condiciones desérticas** a model adapted to suit desert conditions; **adaptar un servicio a las necesidades del cliente** to customize a service, to tailor a service to the customer's needs

2 adaptarse *vpr* to adapt (**a** to); **adaptarse al mercado/a la demanda** to adapt to the market/to demand; **el nuevo local se adapta a las necesidades de la tienda** the new premises meet *o* are well suited to the shop's requirements

adelantado: por adelantado *adv* in advance; **hay que pagar por adelantado** you have to pay in advance; CONT **facturar a alguien por adelantado** to prebill sb

adelantar **1** *vt* (**a**) *(reunión, viaje)* to bring forward, to put forward; **adelantaron la fecha de la reunión** they brought forward the date of the meeting (**b**) *(dinero) (de sueldo)* to advance; *(por servicios, honorarios)* to pay in advance; **pedí que me adelantaran la mitad del sueldo de julio** I asked for an advance of half of my wages for July

2 adelantarse *vpr (anticiparse)* **se adelantaron a la competencia** they stole a march on their competitors

adelante *adv* (**de ahora**) **en adelante** from now on; **más adelante** later on; *(en texto)* below, later

adelanto *nm* (**a**) *(de dinero)* advance; **pidió un adelanto del sueldo** she asked for an advance on her wages (**b**) *(de reunión, viaje)* bringing forward; **se anunció el adelanto del congreso** it was announced that the date of the conference was being brought forward (**c**) *(anticipación)* **el proyecto lleva dos días de adelanto** the project is two days ahead of schedule

adeudar **1** *vt* (**a**) *(deber)* to owe (**b**) FIN to debit; **adeudar 5.000 euros a una cuenta** to debit 5,000 euros to an account

2 adeudarse *vpr* to get into debt

adeudo *nm* (**a**) FIN debit; **con adeudo a mi cuenta corriente** debited to my current account (**b**) *Méx (deuda)* debt ❑ *adeudos bancarios* bank debts

ADI *nf Arg* FIN *(abrev de* **Agencia de Desarrollo de Inversiones***)* = Argentinian investment development agency

adición *nf* (**a**) *(suma)* addition; **hay que efectuar la adición de todos los gastos** we have to calculate the total cost (**b**) *RP (cuenta) Br* bill, *US* check

adicional *adj* extra, additional

adiestramiento *nm* training

adiestrar *vt* to train

adjudicación *nf* (**a**) BOLSA *(de acciones)* allocation, allotment ❑ *adjudicación de bonos del tesoro* treasury bond auction (**b**) *(de obras)* awarding ❑ *adjudicación por concurso público* competitive tendering

adjudicar *vt* (**a**) BOLSA *(acciones)* to allocate, to allot (**b**) *(contrato)* to award; **les fue adjudicada la construcción del puente** they were awarded the contract to build the bridge

adjudicatario, -a *nm,f* successful bidder; **ser el adjudicatario de algo** to have won the contract for sth

❝

Esta compañía, madrileña y familiar, dedicada a la consultoría financiera, es la **adjudicataria** del mayor complejo hotelero y comercial de la Federación Rusa. La sociedad es la ganadora de un concurso al que se presentaron más de 50 aspirantes. **"**

adjuntar *vt* (**a**) *(a carta)* to enclose; *(a documento)* to append, to attach; **le adjunto a esta carta una lista de precios** I am enclosing a price list with this letter, please find enclosed a price list (**b**) INFORM *(a correo electrónico)* to attach; **adjuntar un archivo a un mensaje** to attach a file to a message

adjunto, -a 1 *adj* (**a**) *(a carta)* enclosed; *(a documento)* appended, attached; **ver mapa adjunto** see the enclosed map (**b**) INFORM *(archivo)* attached (**c**) *(auxiliar)* assistant; **director adjunto** associate director/manager, deputy director/ manager
2 *adv* enclosed; **adjunto le remito el recibo** please find a receipt enclosed

administración *nf* (**a**) *(de empresa, finca)* administration, management; **la administración de la justicia corresponde a los jueces** judges are responsible for administering justice ▫ **administración de empresas** business administration; **administración fiduciaria** trusteeship; **administración de fondos** fund management; **administración judicial** official receivership; **administración del personal** staff management; **administración de recursos** resource management
(**b**) *(oficina)* manager's office
(**c**) **la Administración** *(los órganos del Estado)* the government; *(en EE.UU.)* the Administration ▫ **administración central** central government; **administración fiscal, administración de hacienda** tax authorities, *esp US* tax administration; **administración local** local government, local authority; **administración pública, administraciones públicas** civil service, public authorities

administrador, -ora 1 *nm,f* (**a**) *(de empresa)* manager ▫ INFORM **administrador de red** network administrator; INFORM **administrador de servidores** server administrator; INFORM **administrador de (sitio) web** webmaster (**b**) *(de bienes ajenos)* administrator ▫ **administrador de fincas** property manager
2 *nm* INFORM **administrador de archivos** file manager

administrar *vt* *(empresa, finca)* to manage, to run; *(recursos)* to manage

administrativo, -a 1 *adj* administrative; **personal administrativo** administrative staff
2 *nm,f* office worker, clerical worker

admiración *nf* *(signo ortográfico) Br* exclamation mark, *US* exclamation point

admisión *nf* *(de persona)* admission; *(de solicitudes)* acceptance; **reservado el derecho de**

admisión *(en letrero)* the management reserves the right to refuse admission; **mañana se abre el plazo de admisión de solicitudes** applications may be made from tomorrow ▫ ADUANA **admisión temporal** temporary entry

admitir *vt* (**a**) *(dejar entrar)* to allow in, to admit (**b**) *(aceptar)* to accept; **admitimos tarjetas de crédito** we accept all major credit cards; **admitieron a trámite la solicitud** they allowed the application to proceed; **se admiten propinas** *(en letrero)* gratuities at your discretion (**c**) *(permitir)* to allow, to permit

adopción *nf* *(de moda, decisión)* adoption; **estoy en contra de la adopción de medidas sin consultar al interesado** I'm against taking any steps without consulting the person involved

adoptador, -ora *nm,f* MKTG **adoptadores iniciales** early adopters

adoptar *vt* *(medida, decisión)* to take; **adoptaron medidas para luchar contra el desempleo** they took measures to combat unemployment

adquirido, -a *adj* acquired

adquirir *vt* *(empresa)* to acquire, to take over; **adquirieron el 51% de las acciones de la empresa** they acquired a 51% shareholding in the company

adquisición *nf* (**a**) *(de propiedades, productos, acciones)* purchase; **ayudas para la adquisición de viviendas** financial assistance for house buyers (**b**) *(de empresa)* takeover, acquisition ▫ **adquisición corporativa** corporate buy-out; **adquisición inversa** reverse takeover (**c**) *(cosa comprada)* purchase; **fue una excelente adquisición** it was an excellent buy

adscribir *vt* (**a**) *(asignar)* to assign (**b**) *(destinar)* to appoint; **lo adscribieron a Guadalajara** they sent him to Guadalajara

ADSL *nm* *(abrev de* **asymmetric digital subscriber line)** ADSL

aduana *nf* customs; *(edificio)* customs house; **pasar por la aduana** to go through customs; **derechos de aduana** customs duty ▫ **aduana móvil** mobile customs unit

aduanero, -a 1 *adj* customs; **controles aduaneros** customs controls
2 *nm,f* customs officer

ad valorem *adj inv* *(aranceles, impuestos)* ad valorem

advertencia *nf* warning; **hacer una advertencia a alguien** to warn sb ▫ **advertencia sobre los beneficios** profit warning; **advertencia previa** advance warning

advertir *vt* (**a**) *(notar)* to notice; **no he advertido ningún error** I didn't notice o spot any mistakes (**b**) *(prevenir, avisar)* to warn

AEA *nf (abrev de* **Asociación Española de Agencias de Publicidad**) = Spanish professional organization for advertising agencies, *Br* ≃ AA

AEC *nm* UE FIN (*abrev de* **Arancel Externo Común**) CET

AELC *nf (abrev de* **Asociación Europea de Libre Comercio**) EFTA

AENA *nf (abrev de* **Aeropuertos Españoles y Navegación Aérea**) = Spanish airport authority, *Br* ≃ BAA

AENOR *nf (abrev de* **Asociación Española de Normalización y Certificación**) = Spanish national standards institute, *Br* ≃ BSI, *US* ≃ ANSI

aéreo, -a *adj* air; **línea aérea** airline

aerograma *nm* air(mail) letter

aeropuerto *nm* airport

afianzar *vt (posición, cliente)* to secure; *(relación)* to consolidate; **la empresa ha afianzado su liderazgo en el sector** the company has consolidated its market leadership

afiche *nm Am* poster

afiliación *nf (a organización)* membership; **ha bajado el nivel de afiliación a los sindicatos** union membership has fallen; **se ha incrementado el número de afiliaciones a la Seguridad Social** the number of people registered with the social security system has risen ◻ *afiliación sindical* union membership

afiliado, -a *1 nm,f* member (**a** of); **los afiliados de base** the rank and file members ◻ *afiliado sindical* union member
2 *nf (empresa)* affiliated company

afiliar 1 *vt (federación, sociedad)* to affiliate; *(empleado)* to join
2 afiliarse *vpr (organización)* to affiliate; *(como sindicalista)* to join; **afiliarse a la Seguridad Social** to register with the social security system

afín *adj (industria, producto)* allied

afluencia *nf* influx; **hubo una gran afluencia de público** the attendance was high

AFORE, Afore *nf Méx* FIN (*abrev de* **Administradora de Fondos para el Retiro**) = private pension fund administrator

> 66
> El elevado nivel del desempleo pone en riesgo la viabilidad del sistema de administradoras de fondos para el retiro (**Afore**), que si bien manejan el ahorro de 30.3 millones de trabajadores, en realidad son sostenidas por las aportaciones de solamente 12.3 millones de personas.
> 99

agencia *nf* (**a**) *(empresa)* agency ◻ *agencia de aduanas* customs broker; *agencia de bolsa afiliada* member firm; *agencia de calificación*

crediticia *o* **de riesgos** credit (rating) agency, *US* credit bureau; *agencia de cambio y bolsa* stockbroking firm; *agencia de cobro de deudas* debt collection agency; *agencia de colocación* employment agency, employment bureau; *agencia comercial* commercial agency; *agencia de comunicación* PR agency, PR consultancy; *agencia de contratación* recruitment agency; *agencia de diseño* design agency; *agencia inmobiliaria* estate agency, *Br* estate agent's, *US* real estate office; *agencia marítima* shipping agency; *agencia de marketing directo* direct marketing agency; *agencia de noticias* news agency, press agency; *agencia de prensa* press agency; *agencia de promociones* promotions agency; *agencia de la propiedad (inmobiliaria)* estate agency, *Br* estate agent's, *US* real estate office; *agencia de protección del o al consumidor* consumer protection agency; *agencia de publicidad* advertising agency, ad agency; *agencia de relaciones públicas* PR agency, PR consultancy; *agencia de reservas (de viajes, alojamiento, congresos)* reservations agent; *(de entradas)* booking agency; *agencia de seguros* insurance company; *agencia de traducción* translation agency; *agencia de valores* brokerage house, stockbrokers; *agencia de viajes* travel agency, *Br* travel agent's
(**b**) *(organismo)* agency ◻ *agencia de ayuda humanitaria* aid *o* relief agency; *agencia de cooperación* development agency; *Agencia Espacial Europea* European Space Agency; *Agencia de Protección de Datos* Data Protection Agency; *Esp* **la Agencia Tributaria** *Br* ≃ the Inland Revenue, *US* ≃ the IRS
(**c**) *(sucursal)* branch ◻ *agencia urbana* high street branch

agenda *nf* (**a**) *(de notas, fechas)* diary; *(de anillas)* Filofax®; *(de teléfonos, direcciones)* address book; **agenda (de citas)** appointments diary; **tener una agenda muy apretada** to have a very busy schedule ◻ *agenda de bolsillo* pocket diary; *agenda electrónica* (electronic) personal organizer (**b**) *(de trabajo, reunión)* agenda

agente *nmf* (**a**) *(representante)* agent ◻ *agente de aduanas, agente aduanero, Méx agente aduanal* customs agent, customs broker; *agente afecto* tied agent; *agente auxiliar de bolsa* stockbroker's clerk; *agente de bolsa* stockbroker; *agente de cambio* foreign exchange broker, foreign exchange dealer; *agente de cambio y bolsa* stockbroker; *agente de carga internacional* international freight forwarder; *agente comercial, agente de comercio* commercial agent, mercantile agent; *agente de compras* purchasing agent; *agente de distribución* distribution agent; *agente en exclusiva* sole agent; *agente exportador* export agent; *agente financiero, agente* *fiscal* fiscal agent; *agente de garantía* del credere agent; *agente general de Bolsa* general broker; *agente hipotecario* mortgage broker; *agente inmobiliario* *Br* estate agent, *US* realtor, real estate agent; *agente marítimo* shipping agency; *agente oficial* registered agent; *agente de patentes* patent agent; *agente de prensa* press agent; *agente de la propiedad (inmobiliaria)* *Br* estate agent, *US* real estate agent; *agente publicitario* advertising agent, publicity agent; *agente de seguros* insurance agent; BOLSA *agente de suscripción, agente suscriptor* underwriter agent; *agente único* sole dealer

(**b**) *(funcionario)* officer ❑ *agente de aduanas* customs officer; *agente de inmigración* immigration officer; *agente de seguridad* security officer

(**c**) ECON *agente económico* economic agent; *agentes sociales* social partners

---

❝

Recién llegado al Gobierno, el nuevo ministro de Trabajo, Eduardo Zaplana, se ha mostrado partidario de impulsar cuanto antes el diálogo con los **agentes sociales**, y ha señalado que la reunión con los sindicatos será una de las primeras cosas que haga.

❞

---

agio *nm* ECON agio, speculation

agiotaje *nm* ECON agiotage, speculation

agiotista *nmf* ECON stockjobber

AGN *nf* FIN (*abrev de* **Auditoria General de la Nación**) = Argentinian national audit office, *Br* ≃ National Audit Office, *US* ≃ General Accounting Office

agotado, -a *adj (libro, disco)* out of stock; *(entradas)* sold out

agotar 1 *vt (producto)* to sell out of; *(recursos)* to exhaust, to use up; **hemos agotado todos los ejemplares** we've sold all the copies

2 agotarse *vpr (acabarse)* to run out; *(libro, disco, entradas)* to sell out; **se nos ha agotado ese modelo** that model has sold out

agrandar *vt* INFORM *(ventana)* to maximize

agregado, -a *nm,f (diplomático)* attaché ❑ *agregado comercial* commercial attaché

agresivo, -a *adj (campaña, publicidad)* aggressive

agrícola *adj (sector, política, producto)* agricultural; **región agrícola** farming region

agricultura *nf* agriculture ❑ *agricultura biológica, agricultura ecológica* organic farming; *agricultura extensiva* extensive farming; *agricultura intensiva* intensive farming; *agricultura orgánica* organic farming; *agricultura de subsistencia* subsistence farming

agrimensor, -ora *nm,f* surveyor

agroindustrial *adj (sector, complejo)* agroindustrial

agropecuario, -a *adj* **el sector agropecuario** the agricultural and livestock sector

agroturismo *nm* agrotourism, agritourism, rural tourism

agrupación *nf* group, association ❑ *agrupación temporal de empresas* joint enterprise

agrupamiento *nm* INFORM *(de terminales)* cluster

agrupar *vt* to group (together); **la red agrupa a veinte emisoras locales** the network brings together o is made up of twenty local radio stations

agua *nf* **aguas arriba/abajo** *(en proceso de producción)* upstream/downstream ❑ *aguas costeras* coastal waters; *aguas jurisdiccionales* territorial waters; *aguas territoriales* territorial waters

ahorrador, -ora, 1 *adj* thrifty, careful with money

2 *nm,f* saver

ahorrar 1 *vt* (**a**) *(dinero)* to save; **ahorró tres millones** she saved three million (**b**) *(economizar) (energía)* to save; **lo haremos aquí para ahorrar tiempo** we'll do it here to save time

2 *vi* to save

3 ahorrarse *vpr (dinero)* to save; **nos ahorramos 1.000 pesos** we saved (ourselves) 1,000 pesos

ahorrativo, -a *adj (medida)* money-saving

ahorrista *nmf Andes, RP* saver

ahorro *nm* (**a**) *(menos gasto)* saving; **esta medida supone un ahorro de varios millones** this measure means a saving of several millions; **una campaña para fomentar el ahorro** a campaign encouraging people to save ❑ *ahorro forzoso* forced saving; *ahorro negativo* negative saving; *ahorro público* government budget surplus (**b**) **ahorros** *(cantidad)* savings ❑ *ahorros a plazo fijo* fixed savings

ajetreado, -a *adj* busy; **un día muy ajetreado** a very busy day

ajustado, -a *adj (márgenes)* tight

ajustar 1 *vt (precios, salarios)* to adjust; **ajustar las pensiones al índice de inflación** to index-link pensions

2 ajustarse *vpr* **ajustarse al presupuesto** to keep within the limits of the budget

ajuste *nm* (**a**) *(de precios, salarios)* adjustment; **las medidas de ajuste económico propuestas por el gobierno** the economic measures proposed by the government ❑ FIN *ajuste por apalancamiento* gearing adjustment; *ajuste estacional* seasonal adjustment; *ajuste estructural* structural adjustment; *ajuste fiscal* tax adjustment; **ajuste por inflación** inflation adjustment, adjustment for inflation; **ajuste monetario** monetary adjustment; FIN **ajuste de la paridad** sliding peg; CONT **ajustes por periodificación** accruals and deferred income; **ajuste de plantilla** downsizing; **ajustes presupuestarios** budget adjustments; **ajuste salarial** pay adjustment; **ajuste del tipo de cambio** exchange adjustments

(**b**) RDom, Ven (pago único) = agreed payment for a piece of work

alarma nf (dispositivo) alarm ▫ **alarma antirrobo** (en vehículo) anti-theft o car alarm; (en edificio) burglar alarm; (en ropa) anti-theft tag

albacea nmf DER **albacea (testamentario)** executor

albarán nm Esp delivery note, consignment note, Br docket

ALCA nf ECON (abrev de **Área de Libre Comercio de las Américas**) FTAA, Free Trade Area of the Americas

alcance nm (**a**) (de campaña, anuncio) reach (**b**) (económico) **no está a mi alcance** o **al alcance de mi bolsillo** it's outside my price range

alcanzar 1 vt to reach; (objetivo, resultado) to achieve, to attain, to realise; **el desempleo ha alcanzado un máximo histórico** unemployment is at o has reached an all-time high
2 vi **alcanzar para algo** to be enough for sth; **el sueldo no me alcanza para llegar a fin de mes** my salary isn't enough to make ends meet

alcista 1 adj (**a**) (tendencia) upward (**b**) BOLSA (inversor) bullish; **mercado alcista** bull market; **valores alcistas** stocks whose price is rising
2 nmf BOLSA (inversor) bull, bullish investor

> **"**
> Muchas de estas empresas pusieron los programas en marcha entre 1998 y 2000, cuando el mercado bursátil mantenía una tendencia **alcista** que parecía imparable.
> **"**

aldea nf **la aldea global** the global village

aleatorio, -a adj random

alerta nf alert ▫ INFORM **alerta de virus** virus alert

alfabéticamente adv alphabetically

alfabético, -a adj alphabetical

alfanumérico, -a adj INFORM alphanumeric

alfanúmero nm INFORM alphanumeric string

alfombrilla nf INFORM (para ratón) mouse mat, mouse pad

algol nm INFORM Algol, ALGOL

alimentación nf INFORM **alimentación automática de datos** automatic input; **alimentación**

hoja a hoja cut sheet feed; **alimentación de papel** paper feed

alimentador nm INFORM **alimentador de corriente** power unit; **alimentador de hojas sueltas** sheet feeder; **alimentador hoja a hoja** cut sheet feeder; **alimentador de papel** paper feed

alimentario, -a adj (sector) food-processing; **la industria alimentaria** the food industry

alimenticio, -a adj **la industria alimenticia** the food industry; **productos alimenticios** foodstuffs; **pensión alimenticia** maintenance

alimento nm food ▫ **alimentos básicos** basic foodstuffs, staples; **alimentos infantiles** baby foods; **alimentos transgénicos** GM food

alineación nf (**a**) FIN alignment ▫ **alineación monetaria** monetary alignment (**b**) INFORM alignment

alinear vt (**a**) FIN to align (**b**) INFORM to align

aliviar vt (deuda) to relieve

alivio nm (de deuda) relief

almacén nm (**a**) (para guardar) (de gran tamaño) warehouse, storehouse; (habitación) stockroom ▫ **almacén de envíos** shipping depot; **almacén frigorífico** refrigerated storehouse; **almacén de mercancías** goods depot; **almacén portuario** dock warehouse
(**b**) **(grandes) almacenes** department store
(**c**) Andes, RP (de alimentos) grocer's (shop), grocery store
(**d**) CAm (de ropa) clothes shop

almacenaje nm storage, warehousing

almacenamiento nm (**a**) (de mercancías) storage, warehousing (**b**) INFORM storage ▫ **almacenamiento de datos** data storage; **almacenamiento de información** information storage; **almacenamiento masivo** mass storage

almacenar vt (**a**) (mercancías) to store, to warehouse (**b**) INFORM to store

almacenero, -a nm,f, **almacenista** nmf (**a**) (que almacena) warehouse worker, storekeeper, m warehouseman (**b**) Andes, RP (que vende) grocer

almuerzo nm (**a**) (a mediodía) lunch ▫ **almuerzo de trabajo** working lunch (**b**) (a media mañana) mid-morning snack

alojamiento nm accommodation; **el precio incluye el alojamiento** the price includes accommodation ▫ **alojamiento hotelero** hotel accommodation

alojar vt INFORM **alojar páginas web** to host web pages

alquilado, -a adj (casa, oficina, televisor) rented; (vehículo, traje) hired

alquilar vt (**a**) (dejar en alquiler) (vivienda, oficina, aparato) to rent (out); (vehículo, traje) to rent out, Br to hire out; **le alquilamos nuestra casa**

we rented our house (out) to him; **se alquila** *(en letrero)* to let (**b**) *(tomar en alquiler) (casa, oficina, aparato)* to rent; *(vehículo, traje)* to rent, *Br* to hire

alquiler *nm* (**a**) *(acción) (de vivienda, oficina, aparato)* renting; *(de vehículo)* rental, *Br* hiring; **¿está en venta o en alquiler?** is it for sale or to let?; **coche de alquiler** hire car; **tenemos viviendas de alquiler** we have homes to let □ *alquiler de coches* car rental, *Br* car hire; *alquiler comercial* commercial charter; *alquiler de equipo Br* plant hire, *US* plant leasing; TEL *alquiler de la línea* line rental; *alquiler de oficinas* office rental; *alquiler con opción a compra* rental with option to buy

(**b**) *(precio) (de vivienda, oficina)* rent; *(de aparato)* rental; *(de vehículo)* rental charge, *Br* hire charge

alta *nf* **darse de alta (en)** *(club)* to become a member (of); *(Seguridad Social)* to register (with); **con fecha de hoy causa alta en el club** he is a member of the club as of today; **dar de alta a alguien** *(en teléfono, gas, electricidad)* to connect sb

alternativo, -a *adj* alternative

ALTEX *nfpl Méx (abrev de* **Empresas Altamente Exportadoras***)* high-export firms

altibajos *nmpl* ups and downs; **la economía está sufriendo continuos altibajos** the economy is undergoing a lot of ups and downs

alto, -a *adj* (**a**) *(elevado) (costo, precio, interés)* high; INFORM **un disco duro de alta capacidad** a high-capacity hard disk; **un televisor de alta definición** a high-resolution TV screen; **una inversión de alta rentabilidad** a highly profitable investment □ *alta calidad* high quality, top quality; **de alta calidad** high-quality, top-quality; *alta fidelidad* high fidelity

(**b**) *(en una escala)* **un alto dirigente** a high-ranking leader; **de alto nivel** *(delegación)* high-level □ *alto cargo (puesto)* top position *o* job; *(persona) (en empresa)* top manager; *(en la Administración)* top-ranking official; **los altos cargos** top management; *alta dirección* senior management; *alto directivo (en empresa)* top manager; *(en la administración)* top-ranking official; **los altos directivos** top management; *alto ejecutivo* senior executive

(**c**) *(avanzado)* INFORM **de alto nivel** *(lenguaje)* high-level □ *altas finanzas* high finance; *alta tecnología* high technology

alza *nf (subida)* rise; **un alza en las cotizaciones** a rise in share prices; **al alza: los precios están al alza** prices are rising; **la evolución al alza de las acciones** the rising value of the shares; **la evolución al alza de los precios** the upward trend in prices; **la previsión de la inflación ha sido revisada al alza** the forecast level of inflation has been revised upwards; BOLSA **jugar al**

alza to bull the market; **una empresa en alza** a company that is on its way up

> ❝
>
> Dragados y ACS han acogido con **alzas** bursátiles —la primera se ha revalorizado un 5,48% y la segunda un 5,94% en la última semana— el anuncio de su fusión. "Es una operación buena para ambas compañías, aunque la ecuación de canje de acciones favorece al inversor de ACS", señalan los analistas.
>
> ❞

amañar *vt Fam (cuentas)* to fiddle

amasar *vt (riquezas)* to amass

ámbito *nm* (**a**) *(espacio, límites)* scope; **un problema de ámbito nacional** a nationwide problem; **una ley de ámbito provincial** a law which is applicable at provincial level □ *ámbito competitivo (de empresa)* competitive scope

(**b**) *(ambiente)* world; **una teoría poco conocida fuera del ámbito científico** a theory which is little known outside scientific circles *o* the scientific world

AME *nm (abrev de* **Acuerdo Monetario Europeo***)* EMA

AMI *nm (abrev de* **Acuerdo Multilateral de Inversiones***)* MAI

amistoso, -a *adj (acuerdo)* amicable

amortizable *adj (bonos, acciones)* redeemable; **amortizable en el plazo de un año** redeemable in one year

amortización *nf* (**a**) *(de deuda, préstamo, hipoteca)* repayment, paying-off; *(de inversión, capital)* recouping; *(de bonos, acciones)* redemption; *(de bienes de equipo)* depreciation □ *amortización acumulada* accumulated depreciation; *amortización anticipada* early redemption; CONT *amortización anual* annual writedown, annual depreciation charge; CONT *amortización por anualidades* annual depreciation; CONT *amortización de cuentas por cobrar* writedown of accounts receivable; *amortización lineal* straight-line depreciation; *amortización negativa* negative amortization

(**b**) *(de empleos)* **este cambio implicará la amortización de puestos de trabajo** this change will entail some downsizing

amortizar *vt* (**a**) *(deuda, préstamo, hipoteca)* to repay, to pay off; *(inversión, capital)* to recoup; *(bonos, acciones)* to redeem; *(bienes de equipo)* to depreciate (**b**) *(sacar provecho de)* to get one's money's worth out of; **amortizamos la compra de la fotocopiadora muy rápidamente** the photocopier very soon paid for itself (**c**) *(puesto de trabajo)* to downsize

ampliable *adj* (**a**) *(plazo)* extendible (**b**) INFORM *(memoria)* expandable, upgradable

ampliación nf *(de negocio, producción)* expansion; *(de plazo)* extension; **una ampliación de plantilla** an increase in staff numbers; **la ampliación de la Unión Europea** the enlargement of the European Union ❑ FIN **ampliación de capital** share issue, equity issue; MKTG **ampliación de la gama** range stretching; MKTG **ampliación de marca** brand extension; INFORM **ampliación de memoria** memory expansion; **una ampliación de memoria** a memory upgrade; MKTG **ampliación del mercado** market expansion

> El jueves anunció su segundo drástico plan de reestructuración en ocho meses: 12.300 despidos, cierre de 12 plantas y una **ampliación de capital** de 1.842 millones, con el objetivo de volver a ser rentables en 2006.

ampliar vt **(a)** *(negocio)* to expand, to develop; *(mercado, producción, plantilla)* to expand; **han ampliado el servicio a todo el país** they have extended the service to cover the whole country; **vamos a ampliar el catálogo de productos** we are going to expand o extend our product range; **ampliarán la plantilla del banco** they are going to take on additional staff at the bank, they are going to increase staff numbers at the bank; **no quieren ampliar más la Unión Europea** they don't want to enlarge the European Union any further
(b) FIN *(capital)* to increase
(c) INFORM *(memoria)* to upgrade, to expand

análisis nm inv **(a)** *(de situación, problema)* analysis; **hacer un análisis de algo** to analyse sth ❑ **análisis del camino crítico** critical path analysis; **análisis de carteras** *(de inversiones)* portfolio analysis; MKTG **análisis cluster** *(en estadística)* cluster analysis; **análisis de la competencia** competitor analysis; **análisis competitivo** competitive analysis; **análisis de costo-beneficio** o Esp **coste-beneficio** cost-benefit analysis; **análisis de costos** o Esp **costes** cost analysis; **análisis de costos** o Esp **costes de explotación** operating costs analysis; **análisis cualitativo** qualitative analysis; **análisis cuantitativo** quantitative analysis; MKTG **análisis DAFO** SWOT analysis; **análisis de datos** data analysis; **análisis de la demanda** demand analysis; **análisis demográfico** demographic analysis; **análisis económico** economic analysis; **análisis estadístico** statistical analysis; MKTG **análisis de estilos de vida** lifestyle analysis; **análisis gráfico, análisis de gráficas** chart analysis; FIN **análisis horizontal** horizontal analysis; **análisis de inversiones** investment appraisal; **análisis de medios de comunicación** media research; **análisis de mercados** market analysis; **análisis de métodos de trabajo** methods engineering; **análisis de movimientos** *(en el ámbito laboral)* motion analysis; **análisis de necesidades** needs analysis; MKTG **análisis de las necesidades del mercado** gap analysis; **análisis operativos** operational research; MKTG **análisis de oportunidades y amenazas** opportunity and threat analysis; **análisis de problemas** problem analysis; **análisis del producto** product analysis; **análisis de proyectos** project analysis; **análisis de puestos de trabajo** job analysis; FIN **análisis del punto de equilibrio** break-even analysis; **análisis de rentabilidad** cost-effectiveness analysis; **análisis de riesgos** risk analysis; **análisis de la tasa de rentabilidad** rate of return analysis; BOLSA **análisis técnico** technical analysis; MKTG **análisis de (la) tendencia** trend analysis; **análisis de tiempos y movimientos** time and motion study; **análisis de(l) valor** *(de un producto)* value analysis; **análisis de la varianza** *(en estadística)* variance analysis; **análisis de ventas** sales analysis; **análisis vertical** vertical analysis
(b) INFORM analysis ❑ **análisis numérico** numerical analysis; **análisis de sistemas** systems analysis

analista nmf analyst ❑ **analista financiero** financial analyst; **analista de gráficos** chart analyst; **analista informático** computer analyst; **analista de inversiones** investment analyst; **analista de marketing** marketing analyst; **analista de medios** media analyst; **analista de mercados** market analyst; **analista de métodos de trabajo** methods engineer; INFORM **analista de sistemas** systems analyst; **analista de tiempos y movimientos** time and motion consultant, work study engineer

analizar vt to analyse

analógico, -a adj INFORM analogue

anaquel nm shelf

ancho nm width ❑ INFORM **ancho de banda** bandwidth; **ancho de línea** line width

anexo nm **(a)** *(apéndice)* appendix, annex; DER *(cláusula)* schedule **(b)** INFORM attachment

anilla nf *(en carpeta)* ring

animación nf Am **animación por computadora,** Esp **animación por ordenador** computer animation

animado, -a adj *(mercado)* brisk; **poco animado** quiet

anotación nf *(en registro)* entry ❑ **anotación contable** book entry, accounting entry; **anotación en el registro de compra** purchase entry

anotar vt **(a)** *(escribir)* to write down **(b)** CONT *(entrada)* to enter

antedatar vt *(cheque)* to antedate

antena nf aerial, antenna ❑ **antena parabólica** satellite dish

anteriormente adv previously; **el artículo**

mencionado anteriormente the aforementioned *o* aforesaid item

antes *adv* **antes de impuestos** before-tax, pretax; **cuanto antes** as soon as possible; **lo antes posible** as soon as possible

antiabsorción *adj inv* FIN *(mecanismo, investigación)* anti-merger

anticipado, -a *adj* **pago anticipado** advance payment, prepayment; **por anticipado** in advance; **le agradezco por anticipado su ayuda** *(en despedida de carta)* thanking you in advance for your help

anticipar *vt (dinero)* to advance

anticipo *nm (de dinero)* advance; *(a especialista)* retainer; **recibió cien mil dólares como anticipo por su libro** she received a hundred thousand dollar advance for her book □ *anticipo sin garantía* unsecured advance; *anticipo en metálico* cash advance

antidumping *adj inv* ECON *(medidas, leyes)* antidumping

antieconómico, -a *adj* uneconomic

antiglobalizador, -ora 1 *adj* anti-globalization
2 *nm,f* anti-globalization protester

antigüedad *nf (laboral)* seniority; **un plus de antigüedad** a seniority bonus

antiinflacionista, antiinflacionario, -a *adj* ECON anti-inflationary

antimonopolio *adj inv* ECON anti-trust

antitrust *adj inv* ECON *(medidas, leyes)* anti-trust

antivirus INFORM 1 *adj inv* antivirus
2 *nm inv* antivirus program

anual *adj* annual; **paga una cuota anual de 5.000 pesos** he pays an annual fee of 5,000 pesos; **la economía ha estado creciendo un 5% anual** the economy has been growing at 5% a year

anualidad *nf* annuity, yearly payment □ *anualidad diferida* deferred annuity; *anualidad fija* fixed annuity; SEGUR *anualidad por reversión de renta* reversionary annuity; *anualidad vitalicia* life annuity

anualizar *vt* ECON to annualize

anualmente *adv* annually, yearly

anuario *nm* yearbook

anulación *nf (de pedido, cheque)* cancellation; *(de contrato)* annulment

anular *vt (pedido, cheque)* to cancel; *(contrato)* to annul

anunciante *nmf* advertiser

anunciar 1 *vt* (a) *(notificar)* to announce; **hoy anuncian los resultados** the results are announced today (b) FIN *(pérdidas, ganancias)* to

report, to post (c) *(hacer publicidad de)* to advertise
2 **anunciarse** *vpr (con publicidad)* to advertise; **se anuncian en "El Sol"** they advertise in "El Sol"

anuncio *nm* (a) *(de noticia)* announcement
(b) *(cartel, aviso)* notice □ *anuncio luminoso* illuminated sign
(c) *(publicitario) (en prensa)* advertisement, advert; *(en televisión)* advertisement, commercial, advert □ MKTG *anuncio aislado* solus advertisement; *anuncios breves* classified advertisements; *anuncios clasificados* classified advertisements; MKTG *anuncio exclusivo* solus advertisement; *anuncio impreso* print advertisement; *anuncios por palabras* classified advertisements; *anuncio de periódico* newspaper advertisement; *anuncio publicitario* display advertisement; *anuncio de televisión* television advertisement *o* commercial; *anuncio de trabajo* job advertisement

añadido, -a 1 *adj* added (**a** to)
2 *nm* addition

añadir *vt* to add; **a ese precio hay que añadir el IVA** you have to add *Br* VAT *o* *US* sales tax to that price

año *nm* year; **ganar dos millones al año** to earn two million a year; CONT **año hasta la fecha** year to date □ *año base* base year; *Am año calendario* calendar year; *año en curso* current year; *año fiscal* tax year, *Br* financial year, *US* fiscal year; *Col, Perú año gravable* fiscal year; *año natural* calendar year; *año sabático* sabbatical year

año-hombre *nm* ECON man-year

apagado *nm* INFORM shutdown

apagar INFORM 1 *vt* to shut down; **apagar equipo** *(en menú)* shut down
2 **apagarse** *vpr* to shut down

apaisado, -a *adj (orientación)* landscape

apalancamiento *nm* FIN leverage, *Br* gearing □ *apalancamiento financiero* financial leverage, *Br* financial gearing; *apalancamiento operativo* operating leverage

apartado *nm (párrafo)* paragraph; *(sección)* section □ *apartado de correos, apartado postal, Col apartado aéreo* Post Office box, PO Box

apelación *nf* DER appeal; **interponer una apelación** to lodge *o* make an appeal

apelante DER 1 *adj* **la parte apelante** the appellant party
2 *nmf* appellant

apelar *vi* DER to (lodge an) appeal; **apelar contra algo** to appeal against sth

apellido *nm* surname □ *apellido de casada* married name; *apellido de soltera* maiden name

apéndice *nm (de libro, documento)* appendix

apertura *nf* (**a**) *(de cuenta corriente, negocio)* opening; **han pedido la apertura de un expediente disciplinario** they have requested that disciplinary action be taken (**b**) *(en economía)* **buscan la apertura de mercados en Asia** they are seeking to open up markets in Asia ❑ *apertura económica* economic liberalization

aplazamiento *nm* (**a**) *(de reunión, juicio) (antes de empezar)* postponement; *(ya empezado)* adjournment; **el presidente ordenó el aplazamiento de la reunión** the chairman adjourned the meeting (**b**) *(de pago)* deferment, deferral

aplazar *vt* (**a**) *(reunión, juicio) (antes de empezar)* to postpone; *(ya empezado)* to adjourn (**b**) *(pago)* to defer

aplicación *nf* (**a**) *(de técnica, teoría)* application; *(de plan)* implementation; **una ley de aplicación inmediata** a law that will take immediate effect (**b**) *(uso)* application, use; **las aplicaciones de la energía hidroeléctrica** the different applications o uses of hydroelectric power (**c**) INFORM application ❑ *aplicación activa* current application; *aplicación comercial* business application; *aplicación gráfica* graphics application; *aplicación de negocios* business application (**d**) *Andes (solicitud)* application

aplicar 1 *vt (técnica, teoría)* to apply; *(plan)* to implement
2 *vi Andes (postular)* to apply (**a** for)

apoderado, -a *nm,f* DER proxy (holder), *(official)* representative

apoquinar *Esp Fam* **1** *vt* to fork out, to cough up
2 *vi* to cough up; **aquí hay alguien que no ha apoquinado** someone here hasn't paid their share

aportación *nf* contribution; **hacer una aportación** to contribute; **hizo una aportación de 10.000 pesos** she made a contribution of 10,000 pesos ❑ *aportación anual (a plan de pensiones)* annual contribution; *aportación de capital* capital contribution; *aportación en efectivo* cash contribution; *aportación del trabajador (a plan de pensiones)* employee's contribution

aportar 1 *vt* to contribute; **cada empresa aportará cien millones** each company will contribute a hundred million; **todos los miembros del equipo aportaron ideas** all the members of the team contributed their ideas
2 *vi RP (a seguridad social)* to pay social security contributions

aporte *nm* (**a**) *(aportación)* contribution (**b**) *RP (a seguridad social)* social security contribution

apóstrofo *nm (signo)* apostrophe

apoyamuñecas *nm inv* wrist rest

apoyar *vt (decisión)* to support, to back; **los directivos los apoyaron en su protesta** management supported their protest

apoyo *nm* support, backing; **anunciaron su apoyo a la iniciativa** they declared their support for the initiative; **buscan apoyos económicos para el proyecto** they are seeking funding o financial support for the project

applet *nm* INFORM applet

apreciación *nf (de moneda, acciones)* appreciation

apreciarse *vpr (moneda, acciones)* to appreciate

aprendiz, -iza *nm,f* apprentice; **es aprendiz de carpintero** he's an apprentice carpenter, he's a carpenter's apprentice

aprendizaje *nm* (**a**) *(adquisición de conocimientos)* learning; **el aprendizaje de un oficio** learning a trade (**b**) *(para trabajo)* apprenticeship

apretado, -a *adj* (**a**) *(de tiempo)* busy; **tengo unas tardes muy apretadas** my afternoons are very busy (**b**) *(de dinero)* **vamos muy apretados** things are very tight at the moment, we're very short of money at the moment

aprobación *nf (de proyecto, medida)* approval; *(de ley, moción)* passing; **dio su aprobación al proyecto** he gave the project his approval, he approved the project ❑ *aprobación oficial* formal consent; *aprobación con reservas* qualified approval

aprobar *vt (proyecto, medida)* to approve; *(ley, moción)* to pass

apropiación *nf (incautación, ocupación)* appropriation ❑ DER *apropiación indebida* misappropriation

apropiarse *vpr* **apropiarse (indebidamente) de algo** to misappropriate sth

aprovechamiento *nm (utilización)* use; **el aprovechamiento de la energía eólica** the exploitation of wind power ❑ *aprovechamiento óptimo de recursos* optimum employment of resources

aprovechar *vt (tiempo, dinero)* to make the most of; *(oferta, ocasión)* to take advantage of; *(conocimientos, experiencia)* to use, to make use of

aprovisionar 1 *vt* to supply
2 **aprovisionarse** *vpr* **aprovisionarse de algo** to stock up on sth

aprox. *(abrev de* **aproximadamente***)* approx

aproximación *nf* (**a**) *(acercamiento)* approach; *(de países)* rapprochement (**b**) *(en cálculo)* approximation

aproximadamente *adv* approximately

aproximado, -a adj (cifra, cantidad) approximate; **tengo una idea aproximada del problema** I have a rough idea of the problem

apuntador nm INFORM scrapbook

apunte nm CONT entry

apuro nm (a) (dificultad) tight spot, difficult position; **pasar apuros económicos** to experience financial hardship (b) Am (prisa) **tener apuro** to be in a hurry

APYME nf (abrev de **Asamblea de Pequeños y Medianos Empresarios**) = Argentinian association of small and medium-sized enterprises

arancel nm tariff ◻ **arancel aduanero** customs duty, customs tariff; **arancel aduanero común** common customs tariff; **arancel cuota** tariff-rate quota; **arancel diferencial** differential tariff o duty; **arancel de entrada** import list; UE **arancel externo común** common external tariff; **arancel financiero** revenue tariff; **arancel preferente, arancel preferencial** preferential tariff o duty; **arancel de salida** export list

> ❝
>
> El Gobierno mexicano está investigando a Zara y Bershka, empresas del grupo Inditex, por importar prendas eludiendo los **aranceles** legales. Como medida cautelar, la Administración General de Aduanas mexicana ha anunciado que estas compañías no podrán aplicar el **arancel preferencial** que establece el Tratado de Libre Comercio México–Unión Europea.
>
> ❞

arancelario, -a adj tariff; **barreras arancelarias** tariff barriers; **derechos arancelarios** customs duties

arbitraje nm (a) DER arbitration; **se sometieron al arbitraje de la ONU** they agreed to UN arbitration (b) BOLSA arbitrage, switch trading ◻ **arbitraje de cambio** exchange rate arbitrage; **arbitraje especulativo** risk arbitrage; **arbitraje de índices** index arbitrage

arbitrajista nmf BOLSA arbitrageur, arbitrager

arbitrar vt & vi DER to arbitrate

árbitro, -a nm,f DER arbitrator

árbol nm (a) INFORM tree (b) (estructura) tree diagram, tree structure ◻ **árbol de decisión** decision tree

arcas nfpl (fondos) coffers; **las arcas comunitarias** the EU's coffers; **las arcas públicas** the Treasury

archivado nm (a) (documentos) filing; **sistemas de archivado** filing systems (b) INFORM archiving

archivador nm (a) (mueble) filing cabinet, US file cabinet (b) (cuaderno) ring binder

archivar vt (a) (documentos) to file (b) INFORM to archive (c) (proyecto) (definitivamente) to drop; (temporalmente) to shelve

archivero, -a nm,f, **archivista** nmf archivist, Br filing clerk, US file clerk

archivo nm (a) (lugar) archive ◻ **archivo colgante** suspension file
(b) (documentos) archives
(c) INFORM file ◻ **archivo adjunto** attachment; **archivo ASCII** ASCII file; **archivo de ayuda** help file; **archivo de comandos** command file; **archivo contador** tally file; **archivo de correo (electrónico)** mail file; **archivo de direcciones** address file; **archivo en el disco** disk file; **archivo ejecutable** executable file; **archivo sin formato** flat file; **archivo fuente** source file; **archivo de imagen** image file; **archivo invisible** invisible file; **archivo léeme** read-me file; **archivo maestro** master file; **archivo MP3** MP3 file; **archivo oculto** hidden file; **archivo de salida** output file; **archivo del sistema** system file; **archivo de sólo lectura** read-only file; **archivo temporal** temporary file; **archivo de texto** text file

área nf area ◻ **área de crecimiento** growth area; **área del dólar** dollar area; INFORM **área de escritura** write area; **área de libre comercio** o **cambio** free trade area, free trade zone; **área monetaria** monetary area; **área postal** postal area; **área de producción** shop floor; MKTG **área de prueba** test area; **área telefónica** telephone code area; MKTG **área del test** test area; INFORM **área de trabajo** work area; INFORM **área de visualización** display area

áridos nmpl dry foodstuffs, Br dry goods

arquear vt Am to count, to audit

arqueo nm (a) **arqueo (de caja)** cash count, cash audit (b) (de barco) measurement tonnage

arrancar vt (máquina) to start; INFORM to start up, to boot (up)

arranque nm INFORM boot-up, start-up ◻ **arranque en caliente** warm boot, warm start; **arranque en frío** cold boot, cold start

arrastrar vt INFORM to drag; **arrastrar y soltar** to drag and drop

arreglar vt (a) (reparar) to repair, to fix (b) (solucionar) to sort out

arreglo nm (a) (reparación) repair (b) (acuerdo) agreement; **llegar a un arreglo** to reach an agreement; **con arreglo al derecho internacional** in accordance with international law

arrendador, -ora 1 nm,f lessor
2 nf Méx, Ven **arrendadora financiera** financial leasing company

arrendamiento, arriendo nm (acción de dar o tomar en arriendo) leasing, renting; **estos terrenos están en arrendamiento** this land is being rented o leased; **contrato de arrendamiento** lease; **tomar algo en arrendamiento** to rent o lease sth □ **arrendamiento de bienes de equipo** equipment leasing; **arrendamiento comercial** commercial leasing; **arrendamiento financiero** financial leasing; **arrendamiento de inmuebles** property leasing, US real estate leasing; **arrendamiento a largo plazo** long leasing; **arrendamiento vitalicio** life tenancy

arrendar vt (**a**) (dar en arriendo) to let, to lease; **nos arriendan la oficina** they let o rent the office to us (**b**) (tomar en arriendo) to rent, to lease; **arrendamos sus tierras desde hace años** we have leased his land for years; Am **se arrienda** (en letrero) for o to rent

arrendatario, -a 1 adj leasing
2 nm,f (de alojamiento) tenant, leaseholder; (de local comercial) leaseholder □ **arrendatario vitalicio** life tenant

arriba adv (en un texto) above; **más arriba** above; **el arriba mencionado** the above-mentioned

arriendo = **arrendamiento**

arroba nf INFORM (símbolo) at sign, @ sign; **"juan, arroba mundonet, punto, es"** "juan, at mundonet, dot, es"

artesanal adj (producto) handcrafted; (alimento) produced using traditional methods, handmade; (pesca, agricultura) traditional; **de fabricación artesanal** (producto) handcrafted; (alimento) produced using traditional methods, handmade; **métodos artesanales** traditional methods; **un importante centro artesanal** an important centre for traditional industries

artesano, -a 1 adj **métodos artesanos** traditional methods
2 nm,f craftsman, f craftswoman

artículo nm (**a**) (objeto, mercancía) article, item; **hemos rebajado todos los artículos** all items have been reduced □ **artículos de consumo básicos** basic consumer goods; **artículos especializados** speciality o US specialty goods; **artículos de gama alta** top-of-the-range goods; **artículos de marca** branded goods; **artículos de marca registrada** proprietary goods; **artículos de prestigio** prestige goods; **artículos de primera necesidad** basic commodities; **artículos de uso diario** o **cotidiano** convenience goods; **artículos de venta por correo** mail-order goods; **artículos de viaje** travel accessories
(**b**) (periodístico) article □ **artículo de fondo** editorial; **artículo de periódico** newspaper article
(**c**) (en ley, reglamento) article

asalariado, -a 1 adj salaried
2 nm,f wage earner, salary earner

asamblea nf (reunión) meeting; **convocar una asamblea** to call a meeting; **los trabajadores, reunidos en asamblea, votaron a favor de la** huelga the workers voted for strike action at a mass meeting □ **asamblea de accionistas** shareholders' o US stockholders' meeting; **asamblea de acreedores** creditors' meeting; **asamblea general** general meeting; **asamblea general anual** annual general meeting; **asamblea general extraordinaria** extraordinary general meeting; **asamblea general ordinaria** ordinary general meeting; **asamblea plenaria** plenary assembly

ascender 1 vi (**a**) (aumentar) (precios) to rise, to go up (**b**) (en empleo) to be promoted (**a** to); **ascendió a jefe de producción** he was promoted to production manager (**c**) **ascender a** (totalizar) to come to, to total; **la facturación ascendió a 5.000 millones** turnover came to o totalled five billion; **¿a cuánto asciende el total?** what does the total come to?
2 vt (empleado) to promote; **fue ascendida al puesto de subdirectora** she was promoted to the position of deputy director

ascenso nm (**a**) (de precios) rise; **continúa en ascenso** it continues to rise, it is still on the rise (**b**) (en empleo) promotion

ASCII nm INFORM (abrev de **American Standard Code for Information Interchange**) ASCII

ASEAN nf (abrev de **Asociación de Naciones del Asia Sudoriental**) ASEAN

asegurable adj insurable

asegurado, -a 1 adj insured; (con seguro de vida) insured, Br assured; **está asegurado en cinco millones** it's insured for five million; **está asegurado a todo riesgo** it's fully insured
2 nm,f policy holder

asegurador, -ora 1 adj **compañía aseguradora** insurance company; (de seguros de vida) insurance o Br assurance company
2 nm,f (persona) insurer, underwriter; (de seguros de vida) insurer, Br assurer

asegurar 1 vt to insure (**contra** against, **en** for); **asegurar algo a todo riesgo** (compañía de seguros) to provide comprehensive Br cover o US coverage for sth; (propietario) to take out comprehensive insurance on sth
2 asegurarse vpr to insure oneself, to take out an insurance policy

asequibilidad nf affordability

asequible adj (precio, producto) affordable

asesor, -ora 1 adj advisory
2 nm,f adviser □ **asesor del consumidor** consumer adviser; **asesor de contratación** recruitment consultant; **asesor económico** economic adviser; **asesor financiero** financial adviser; **asesor financiero independiente** Br independent financial adviser, IFA, US certified financial planner, CFP; **asesor fiscal** tax consultant, tax adviser; **asesor de imagen** image consultant; **asesor de inversiones**

investment adviser; ***asesor jurídico*** legal adviser; ***asesor de medios de comunicación*** media consultant; ***asesor de relaciones públicas*** PR consultant; ***asesor de seguros*** insurance adviser; ***asesor técnico*** technical adviser; ***asesor de ventas*** sales consultant

asesoría *nf* (**a**) *(actividad)* consultancy ❑ ***asesoría jurídica*** legal advice (**b**) *(empresa)* ***asesoría contable*** accounting firm; ***asesoría empresarial*** business consultancy; ***asesoría financiera*** financial consultancy; ***asesoría fiscal*** tax consultancy; ***asesoría de imagen y comunicación*** PR company; ***asesoría de inversión*** investment consultancy; ***asesoría jurídica*** legal consultancy

asiento *nm* CONT entry ❑ ***asiento de adeudo*** debit entry; ***asiento de apertura*** opening entry; ***asiento de cargo*** debit entry; ***asiento de cierre*** closing entry; ***asiento compuesto*** compound entry; ***asiento contable*** book entry; ***asiento de contrapartida*** contra entry; ***asiento falso*** false entry; ***asiento en el libro diario*** journal entry; ***asiento de regularización*** adjustment account; ***asiento suplementario*** supplementary entry; ***asiento de traspaso*** transfer entry

asignación *nf* (**a**) *(atribución)* *(de dinero, recursos)* allocation ❑ ***asignación de activos*** asset allocation; ***asignación de costos** o Esp* **costes** cost allocation; ***asignación de fondos*** commitment of funds; ***asignación óptima de recursos*** optimal resource allocation; ***asignación de recursos*** resource allocation; ***asignación de tareas*** job assignment
(**b**) *(cantidad asignada)* allocation; **tenemos una asignación anual de cinco millones de dólares** we have an annual allocation of five million dollars ❑ *CSur* **asignación familiar** = state benefit paid to families for every child, *Br* ≃ child benefit
(**c**) *(de empleado)* **anunciaron su asignación a un nuevo destino** they announced that she was being assigned to a new post

asignar *vt* (**a**) *(atribuir)* **asignar algo a alguien** to assign *o* allocate sth to sb; **le han asignado una oficina en el último piso** he has been assigned *o* allocated an office on the top floor
(**b**) *(destinar)* **asignar a alguien a** to assign sb to; **la asignaron al departamento de relaciones públicas** she was assigned to the public relations department

asíncrono, -a *adj* INFORM asynchronous

asistencia *nf* (**a**) *(ayuda)* assistance ❑ ***asistencia al cliente*** customer support; ***asistencia jurídica*** legal advice; ***asistencia jurídica de oficio*** legal aid; ***asistencia letrada*** legal advice; ***asistencia por línea directa*** hot line support; ***asistencia técnica*** technical assistance, technical backup; INFORM ***asistencia técnica al usuario***

user support; ***asistencia de ventas*** sales support
(**b**) *(presencia)* *(acción)* attendance; *(hecho)* presence; **se ruega confirme su asistencia al acto** *(en invitación)* please let us know whether you will be able to attend
(**c**) *(afluencia)* attendance; **no se tienen datos precisos de asistencia** we do not have an exact attendance figure

asistente 1 *adj* **el público asistente** the audience, everyone present; **los científicos asistentes a un congreso** the scientists attending a congress
2 *nmf* (**a**) *(ayudante)* assistant, helper (**b**) *(presente)* attendee; **los asistentes** those present; **se espera una gran afluencia de asistentes** a high attendance is expected
3 *nm* INFORM (**a**) *(software)* wizard (**b**) ***asistente personal*** *(de bolsillo)* personal assistant

asistido, -a *adj* **asistido por** *Esp* **ordenador** *o Am* **computadora** computer-aided, computer-assisted

asistir *vi* *(acudir)* to attend; **asistir a un acto** to attend an event

asociación *nf* *(grupo, colectivo)* association; **crear una asociación** to form an association ❑ ***asociación de consumidores*** consumer association; ***Asociación Europea de Depositarios Centrales de Valores*** European Central Securities Depositories Association; ***Asociación Europea de Libre Comercio*** European Free Trade Association; ***asociación gremial*** trade association, trade body; ***asociación de libre cambio** o* **comercio** free trade association; ***asociación del personal*** staff association; ***asociación de productores*** producers' association; ***asociación profesional*** professional association; ***asociación de trabajadores*** employee association

asociado, -a 1 *adj* (**a**) *(relacionado)* associated (**b**) *(miembro)* associate; **director asociado** associate director
2 *nm,f* *(miembro)* associate, partner

asociarse *vpr* to form a partnership; **se asoció con varios amigos** he formed *o* entered a partnership with some friends

asterisco *nm* asterisk

astillero *nm* shipyard

asumir *vt* *(hacerse cargo de)* *(puesto)* to take up; **asumir la responsabilidad de algo** to take on *o* assume responsibility for sth; **asumir el mando/control (de)** to take charge/control (of); **el Estado asumirá las pérdidas de la empresa** the State will cover the company's losses

asunto *nm* *(tema)* matter, issue; *(problema)* issue, affair; **necesitamos hablar de un asunto importante** we need to talk about an important matter ❑ ***asuntos de Estado*** affairs of state;

asuntos exteriores foreign affairs; ***asuntos pendientes*** *(en orden del día)* matters pending; ***asuntos públicos*** public affairs; ***asuntos a tratar*** agenda

atacar *vt* MKTG *(mercado)* to attack

atajo *nm* INFORM shortcut □ ***atajo de teclado*** keyboard shortcut

ataque *nm* (**a**) MKTG *(a mercado)* attack □ ***ataque de guerrillas*** guerrilla attack (**b**) BOLSA ***ataque especulativo*** dawn raid

ATE *nf* (*abrev de* **Asociación de Trabajadores del Estado**) = Argentinian union of public-sector workers

atención *nf* (**a**) *(interés)* attention; **a la atención de** for the attention of □ ***atención mediática*** media exposure (**b**) *(servicio)* **horario de atención al público** opening hours □ ***atención al cliente*** customer service, customer care; ***atención simultánea de llamadas*** call holding

> "
> Las empresas no se pueden permitir el lujo de perder clientes. Y esa es la misión del director de **atención al cliente**, el máximo responsable del departamento que hace de puente entre la compañía y el consumidor o usuario.
> "

atender *vt* (**a**) *(cliente)* to serve, to attend to; **¿lo atienden?, ¿lo están atendiendo?** are you being served?; **atiende el negocio personalmente** she looks after the business herself; **el director no puede atenderlo en este momento** the manager isn't available at the moment (**b**) *(centralita, teléfono)* to man

aterrizaje *nm (de avión)* landing

ATM *nm* INFORM (*abrev de* **asynchronous transfer mode**) ATM

atracar *vi (barco)* to dock (**en** at)

atracción *nf* ***atracción turística*** tourist attraction

atractivo, -a **1** *adj (precio, oferta, proposición)* attractive

2 *nm (de producto)* appeal; **su principal atractivo** its main selling point □ ***atractivo para el cliente*** customer appeal; ***atractivo comercial*** market appeal

atraer *vt (atención)* to attract; *(gente)* to attract, to appeal to; **la campaña debería atraer muchos inversores nuevos** the campaign should attract many new investors; **la idea atraerá a los treintañeros** the idea will appeal to thirty-somethings

atrasos *nmpl (de pagos)* arrears; *(de sueldo)* back pay

atribuciones *nfpl (competencias)* powers; **no tengo atribuciones para tomar esa decisión** I

do not have the authority to take that decision

audiencia *nf* (**a**) *(de programa de TV, radio)* **la audiencia del programa ha caído mucho** the programme has lost a lot of viewers/listeners; **un horario de máxima audiencia** a peak viewing/listening time

(**b**) MKTG *(público)* audience □ ***audiencia acumulada*** cumulative audience; MKTG ***audiencia bruta*** gross audience; ***audiencia cautiva*** captive audience; ***audiencia mundial*** global audience; ***audiencia potencial*** share of voice; ***audiencia televisiva, audiencia de televisión*** television audience *(reached by advertising)*; ***audiencia útil*** useful audience

(**c**) DER *(tribunal, edificio)* court □ ***Audiencia Nacional*** = court in Madrid dealing with cases that cannot be dealt with at regional level; ***audiencia provincial*** provincial court; ***audiencia territorial*** regional court

(**d**) DER *(juicio)* hearing □ ***audiencia disciplinaria*** disciplinary hearing; ***audiencia pública*** public hearing

audímetro, audiómetro *nm* TV audiometer, audience-monitoring device

audio *nm* audio

audioconferencia *nf* audioconference

audiómetro = **audímetro**

auditar *vt* FIN to audit

auditor, -ora FIN **1** *adj* **empresa auditora** auditing firm, auditor(s)

2 *nm,f* auditor □ ***auditor de cuentas*** auditor; ***auditor del Estado*** government auditor; ***auditor externo*** external auditor; ***auditor informático*** IT auditor; ***auditor interno*** internal auditor; ***auditor jefe*** audit manager; ***auditor de marketing*** marketing auditor; ***auditor de ventas*** retail auditor

auditoría *nf* FIN (**a**) *(actividad)* auditing; **normas de auditoría** auditing standards

(**b**) *(balance)* audit □ ***auditoría ambiental*** environmental audit; ***auditoría del balance de situación*** balance sheet audit; ***auditoría de cierre de ejercicio*** year-end audit; ***auditoría de cuentas*** audit of accounts; ***auditoría energética*** energy audit; ***auditoría externa*** external audit; ***auditoría fiscal*** tax audit; ***auditoría general*** general audit; ***auditoría de gestión*** value for money audit; ***auditoría informática*** IT audit; ***auditoría interna*** internal audit; ***auditoría de marketing*** marketing audit; ***auditoría medioambiental*** environmental audit; ***auditoría operativa*** operational audit; ***auditoría social*** social audit; ***auditoría tributaria*** tax audit; ***auditoría de ventas*** retail audit, sales audit

(**c**) *(empresa)* auditor(s), auditing firm

auge *nm* **estar en (pleno) auge** to be booming; **el turismo está en un momento de auge**

tourism is booming □ *auge bursátil* stock market boom; *auge económico* economic boom; *auge de inversiones* investment boom

aumentar 1 *vt (ventas, precio, gastos)* to increase; **aumentar la producción** to increase production; **me han aumentado el sueldo** my salary has been increased *o* raised; **eso aumenta nuestros gastos** this adds to our expenses
2 *vi (ventas, precio, gastos)* to increase, to rise; **el desempleo aumentó en un 4%** unemployment rose *o* increased by 4%; **aumentar de precio** to go up *o* increase in price; **aumentar de tamaño** to increase in size

aumento *nm* (**a**) *(de ventas, precio, gastos)* increase, rise; **un aumento del 10%** a 10% increase; **un aumento de los precios** a price rise; **ir** *o* **estar en aumento** to be on the increase □ *aumento encubierto de precio* hidden price increase; *aumento lineal (de sueldo)* across-the-board pay rise; *aumento de personal* staff increase; *aumento de la productividad* increase in productivity; MKTG *aumento del producto* product augmentation; *aumento salarial, aumento de sueldo* salary increase, pay increase *o Br* rise *o US* raise (**b**) *Méx (posdata)* postscript

aunar *vt (esfuerzos)* to join, to pool

auricular *nm* (**a**) *(de teléfono)* receiver, handset (**b**) **auriculares** *(de arco)* headphones; *(de botón)* earphones

ausente *adj* absent; **estará ausente todo el día** he'll be away all day; **está ausente por enfermedad** he's off sick; **trabajador ausente** *(por motivos injustificados)* absentee

ausentismo *nm* **ausentismo laboral** *(justificado)* absence from work; *(injustificado)* absenteeism

austeridad *nf* ECON, FIN austerity

autarquía *nf* autarky, self-sufficiency

autenticación *nf* (**a**) *(de firma, documento)* authentication (**b**) INFORM authentication

autenticar *vt* (**a**) *(firma, documento)* to authenticate (**b**) INFORM to authenticate (**c**) *RP (compulsar)* to check against the original; **una fotocopia autenticada** a certified copy

auténtico, -a *adj (cuadro, diamante)* genuine; *(documento)* authentic

autentificación *nf* (**a**) *(de firma, documento)* authentication (**b**) INFORM authentication

autentificar *vt* (**a**) *(firma, documento)* to authenticate (**b**) INFORM to authenticate

auto *nm* (**a**) DER *(resolución)* judicial decree □ *auto de ejecución* writ of execution; *auto judicial* judicial decree; *auto de prisión* arrest warrant; *auto de procesamiento* committal for trial order; **dictar auto de procesamiento**

contra alguien to commit sb for trial; *auto de quiebra* receiving order (**b**) *esp CSur (vehículo)* car □ *auto de alquiler* rental *o Br* hire car

autoalimentación *nf* INFORM automatic paper feed

autobús *nm* bus

autocartera *nf* FIN *Br* bought-back shares, *US* treasury stock

autodiagnóstico *nm* INFORM self-test

autoedición *nf* INFORM desktop publishing, DTP

autoeditar *vt* INFORM to produce using DTP

autoeditor, -ora *nm,f* INFORM desktop publishing operator, DTP operator

autoempleo *nm* self-employment

autofacturación *nf* self-invoicing

autofinanciación *nf* self-financing

autofinanciar 1 *vt* to self-finance
2 autofinanciarse *vpr* to be self-financed

autoguardado *nm* INFORM automatic backup

autoliquidación *nf* **autoliquidación tributaria** self-assessment

automático, -a *adj (mecanismo, dispositivo)* automatic

automatización *nf* automation

automatizado, -a *adj* automated

automatizar *vt* to automate

autonomía *nf* (**a**) *(de persona, empresa)* autonomy (**b**) *(de vehículo)* range; *(de computadora portátil, teléfono móvil)* battery life; *(de videocámara)* recording time (**c**) *Esp* POL *(territorio)* autonomous region, = largest administrative division, with its own Parliament and a number of devolved powers

autónomo, -a 1 *adj* (**a**) *(independiente)* autonomous (**b**) *(trabajador)* self-employed; *(traductor, periodista)* freelance (**c**) POL *(región, parlamento)* autonomous
2 *nm,f (trabajador)* self-employed person; *(traductor, periodista)* freelance, freelancer

autopista *nf* INFORM **autopista(s) de la información** information (super)highway; *autopista interactiva* interactive highway

autopublicidad *nf* self-advertising

autoridad *nf* (**a**) *(poder)* authority; **ejercer más**

autoridad sobre alguien to exercise more authority over sb
(**b**) *(persona al mando)* **las autoridades** the authorities ❑ **autoridades de defensa de la competencia** competition authorities; **autoridades económicas** economic authorities; **autoridades financieras** financial authorities; **autoridades fiscales** tax authorities; **autoridad portuaria** port authority; **autoridades públicas** public authorities

autorización *nf* (**a**) *(permiso)* authorization; **pedir autorización para hacer algo** to request authorization to do sth; **pidieron autorización para aterrizar** they requested clearance to land ❑ **autorización de acceso** access authorization; **autorización aduanera** customs clearance authorization (**b**) BANCA *(impreso)* mandate form

autorizado, -a *adj (permitido)* authorized; **un distribuidor autorizado** an authorized *o* official distributor

> **"**
> Bruselas defiende que un supermercado podría convertirse en un distribuidor autorizado (de una o varias marcas) si satisface los mismos criterios fijados por el fabricante y este lo acepta.
> **"**

autorizar *vt* (**a**) *(pago, crédito, manifestación)* to authorize; **les autorizó para controlar el presupuesto** she authorized them to monitor the budget (**b**) *(documento)* to authorize

autorregulación *nf* self-regulation

autoseguro *nm* self insurance

autoservicio *nm* (**a**) *(restaurante)* self-service restaurant (**b**) *(supermercado)* supermarket

autosuficiencia *nf (económica)* self-sufficiency

autosuficiente *adj (económicamente)* self-sufficient

autotest *nm* INFORM self-test

auxiliar 1 *adj (personal)* ancillary, auxiliary
2 *nmf* assistant ❑ **auxiliar administrativo** administrative assistant; **auxiliar de oficina** office junior

aval *nm (documento)* guarantee, *US* guaranty; *(para préstamo)* security ❑ **aval bancario** bank guarantee

avalar *vt* (**a**) *(préstamo, crédito)* to guarantee (**b**) *(respaldar)* to endorse; **el consejo avala su candidatura** the board endorses her candidature

avalista *nmf* guarantor ❑ **avalista solidario** joint and several guarantor

avance *nm* INFORM *(de impresora)* **avance automático** automatic feed; **avance de línea** line feed; **avance de página** *(en impresora)* form feed; *(en*

pantalla) page down; **avance del papel** paper advance

aventura *nf* FIN *(empresa)* adventure

avería *nf* SEGUR *(de mercancía)* average ❑ **avería gruesa** general average, gross average; **avería particular, avería simple** particular average

averiarse *vpr (máquina, vehículo)* to break down

avión *nm* plane, *Br* aeroplane, *US* airplane; **en avión** by plane; **por avión** *(en sobre)* airmail ❑ **avión de carga** cargo plane, freight plane; **avión chárter** charter plane; **avión comercial** commercial aircraft; **avión de pasajeros** passenger plane; **avión de pasajeros y carga** passenger and cargo plane

avisador, -ora *nm,f RP* advertiser

avisar *vt (informar)* **avisar a alguien de algo** to let sb know sth, to tell sb (about) sth; **los empleados deben avisar con tres meses de antelación** *(para dejar un trabajo)* employees must give three months' notice; **avisar por megafonía** to page

aviso *nm* (**a**) *(notificación)* notice; **hasta nuevo aviso** until further notice; **sin previo aviso** without notice; **último aviso para los pasajeros del vuelo IB 257** last call for passengers for flight IB 257 ❑ **aviso de abono** credit advice; CONT **aviso de comisión** commission note; **aviso de crédito** credit advice; **aviso de despido** notice of dismissal; FIN **aviso de domiciliación** *(de efectos)* domiciliation advice; **aviso de envío, aviso de expedición** advice note; **aviso de huelga** strike notice; **aviso de pago** remittance advice; **aviso previo** advance notice; SEGUR **aviso de renovación** renewal notice; *Am* **aviso de retiro (de fondos)** notice of withdrawal; **aviso de suspensión de pagos** stop payment advice; **aviso de vencimiento** due-date reminder
(**b**) *Am (anuncio)* advertisement, advert ❑ **aviso clasificado** classified advertisement; **aviso publicitario** advertisement, advert

ayuda *nf* (**a**) *(asistencia)* help, assistance; **prestar ayuda** to help, to assist ❑ INFORM **ayuda contextual** context-sensitive help; INFORM **ayuda en línea, ayuda on-line** on-line help; INFORM **ayuda en pantalla** on-screen help
(**b**) *(económica, alimenticia)* aid, assistance; **un paquete de ayudas a la pequeña empresa** a package of measures to help small businesses ❑ **ayuda al desarrollo** development aid, development assistance; **ayuda económica** economic aid; **ayuda del Estado, ayuda estatal** government aid; **ayuda a la exportación** export aid; *Esp* ADMIN **ayuda familiar** = state financial assistance to those caring for dependents; **ayuda financiera** financial aid, financial assistance; UE **ayuda financiera a medio plazo** medium-term financial assistance; **ayuda**

humanitaria humanitarian aid; *ayuda a la inversión* investment incentive

ayudante *nmf* assistant

ayuntamiento *nm* (**a**) *(corporación) Br* town council, *US* city council (**b**) *(edificio) Br* town hall, *US* city hall

Bb

B2A *(abrev de* **business-to-administration)**
B2A

B2B *(abrev de* **business-to-business)** B2B

B2C *(abrev de* **business-to-consumer)** B2C

backup *nm* INFORM backup

bahía *nf* INFORM bay

baja *nf* **(a)** *(descenso)* drop, fall; **no se descarta una baja en los tipos de interés** a cut in interest rates isn't being ruled out; **a la baja: redondear el precio a la baja** to round the price down; **el precio del cacao sigue a la baja** the price of cocoa is continuing to fall, the slump in the price of cocoa is continuing; **la Bolsa de Madrid sigue a la baja** share prices on the Madrid stock exchange are continuing to fall; **las eléctricas cotizaron ayer a la baja** share prices for the electricity companies fell yesterday; BOLSA **jugar a la baja** to bear the market; **tendencia a la baja** downward trend
 (b) *(cese) (forzado)* redundancy; **la empresa ha sufrido bajas entre sus directivos** *(voluntarias)* a number of managers have left the firm; **dar de baja a alguien** *(en un club, sindicato)* to expel sb; *(en colegio profesional)* to strike sb off; **darse de baja (de)** *(dimitir)* to resign (from); *(salirse)* to drop out (of); INFORM *(de una suscripción)* to unsubscribe (from) □ *baja incentivada* voluntary redundancy; *baja por jubilación* retirement; *bajas naturales* natural wastage *(in job numbers)*
 (c) *(permiso)* leave □ *baja por enfermedad* sick leave; *baja por maternidad* maternity leave; *baja por paternidad* paternity leave; *baja remunerada, baja retribuida* paid leave; *baja no retribuida* unpaid leave; *baja con sueldo* paid leave; *baja sin sueldo* unpaid leave
 (d) *Esp (por enfermedad) (permiso)* sick leave; *(documento)* sick note, doctor's certificate; **estar/darse de baja** to be on/take sick leave

bajar 1 *vt* **(a)** *(reducir) (inflación)* to reduce; *(precios)* to lower, to cut **(b)** *Fam* INFORM *(de Internet)* to download
 2 *vi (precios, acciones, ventas)* to fall, to drop; **bajó la gasolina** the price of *Br* petrol *o US* gasoline fell; **el euro bajó frente a la libra** the euro fell against the pound; **los precios bajaron** prices dropped; **bajó la Bolsa** share prices fell; **han bajado las ventas** sales are down; **este modelo ha bajado de precio** this model has gone down in price, the price of this model has

gone down; **no bajará del millón** it will not be less than *o* under a million
 3 bajarse *vpr Fam* INFORM **bajarse un programa** to download a program

bajista BOLSA **1** *adj (inversor)* bearish; **mercado bajista** bear market
 2 *nmf* bear

bajo, -a 1 *adj (costo, interés, cifra)* low; **los precios más bajos de la ciudad** the lowest prices in the city; **tirando** *o* **calculando por lo bajo** at least, at the minimum; **de baja calidad** poor(-quality) □ INFORM *baja resolución* low resolution
 2 *nm (planta baja) Br* ground floor, *US* first floor; *(local) Br* premises on the ground floor, *US* premises on the first floor

bajón *nm* slump, downturn; **las ventas han dado un bajón** sales have slumped

balance *nm* **(a)** CONT *(documento)* balance sheet □ *balance abreviado* abridged balance sheet; *balance de apertura* opening balance sheet; *balance de cifras de ventas* statement of sales figures; *balance de comprobación* trial balance; *balance condensado* summary balance sheet; *balance consolidado* consolidated balance sheet; *balance contable* balance sheet; *balance de facturas* statement of invoices; *balance final* final statement; *balance fraudulento* fraudulent balance sheet; *balance general de fin de ejercicio* end-of-year balance sheet; *balance de inventario* inventory *o Br* stock check; *balance previsional* forecast balance sheet; *balance de resultados* statement of results; *balance de situación* balance sheet, statement of assets and liabilities, *US* statement of financial position; *balance social* social report
 (b) *Am* ECON *balance de pagos* balance of payments

balanza *nf* ECON *balanza cambiaria* foreign exchange balance; *balanza comercial* (visible) balance of trade, trade balance; *balanza por cuenta corriente* current accounts balance; *balanza de operaciones invisibles* invisible balance; *balanza de pagos* balance of payments; *balanza de pagos por cuenta corriente* balance of payments on current account; *balanza de servicios* balance of services

banca *nf* banking; **la situación de la banca en China** the banking system in China □ *banca en casa* home banking; *Am banca computarizada* computerized banking; **banca corporativa** corporate banking; **banca directa** direct banking; **banca a distancia** remote banking; **banca a domicilio** home banking; **banca electrónica** electronic banking; **banca global** global banking; **banca informatizada** computerized banking; **banca por Internet** Internet banking; **banca de inversión** investment banking; **banca en línea** on-line banking; **banca mayorista** wholesale banking; **banca de negocios** business banking; **banca on-line** on-line banking; **banca para particulares** retail banking; **banca privada** private (sector) banks; **banca telefónica** telephone banking

bancario, -a 1 *adj* bank; **crédito bancario** bank loan; **cuenta bancaria** bank account; **entidad bancaria** bank; **sector bancario** banking sector **2** *nm,f CSur (empleado)* bank clerk

bancarización *nf* banking services coverage, bank usage; **la bancarización de la economía/las operaciones comerciales** the increasing role of banks in the economy/in trade; **nivel de bancarización** bank density

bancarrota *nf* bankruptcy; **declararse en bancarrota** to declare oneself bankrupt; **estar en bancarrota** to be bankrupt; **ir a la bancarrota** to go bankrupt

bancasegurador *nm* bancassurer

bancaseguros *nf inv,* **bancassurance** *nf* bancassurance

banco *nm* (**a**) *(institución financiera)* bank □ **banco aceptante** accepting bank; **banco acreedor** lending bank, creditor bank; **banco central** central bank; UE **Banco Central Europeo** European Central Bank; **banco cobrador** collecting bank; **banco de cobro** collection bank; **banco comercial** commercial bank, trading bank; **banco de comercio** mercantile bank; **banco de compensación** clearing bank; **banco confirmador** confirming bank; **banco cooperativo** co-operative bank; **banco corresponsal** correspondent bank; **banco de crédito** credit bank, lending bank; **banco de crédito inmobiliario** mortgage bank; **banco de depósitos** deposit bank; **banco de descuento** discount bank, discounting bank; **banco emisor** issuing bank; **Banco Europeo de Inversiones** European Investment Bank; **Banco Europeo de Reconstrucción y Desarrollo** European Bank for Reconstruction and Development; **banco fiduciario** trust bank; **banco hipotecario** mortgage bank, Br ≃ building society, US ≃ savings and loan association; **banco industrial** industrial bank; **Banco Interamericano de Desarrollo** Inter-American Development Bank; **Banco Internacional para la Reconstrucción y el Desarrollo** International Bank for Reconstruction and Development; **banco de inversiones** investment bank; **banco en línea** on-line bank;

banco mayorista wholesale bank; **banco mercantil** business bank, Br merchant bank; **el Banco Mundial** the World Bank; **banco nacional** national bank; **banco de negocios** business bank, Br merchant bank; **banco on-line** on-line bank; **banco pagador** paying bank; **banco privado** private bank; **banco registrado** chartered bank; **banco de segundo piso** second-tier bank

(**b**) *(depósito)* bank □ INFORM **banco de datos** data bank; **banco de imágenes** image bank; **banco de memoria** memory bank

Bancomext *nm* (*abrev de* **Banco Nacional de Comercio Exterior**) = Mexican government's development bank in charge of promoting and financing foreign trade

banda *nf* (**a**) *(escala)* band □ Am **banda cambiaria** exchange rate band; **banda de fluctuación** FIN fluctuation band, currency band; BOLSA trading range; **banda impositiva** tax band, tax bracket; **banda de oscilación** fluctuation band, currency band; **banda de precios** price range, price racket; *(tarifas)* rate band; **banda salarial** wage bracket, salary band (**b**) *(cinta)* **banda magnética** magnetic strip

bandeja *nf* tray □ **bandeja de asuntos pendientes** pending tray; **bandeja para cartas** letter tray; **bandeja de la correspondencia** correspondence tray; **bandeja de escritorio** desk tray; **bandeja de papel** paper tray

bandera *nf* flag □ **bandera de conveniencia** flag of convenience

banner *nm* INFORM banner □ **banner publicitario** advertising banner, banner advertisement

banquero, -a *nm,f* banker

Banxico *nm* (*abrev de* **Banco de México**) = Mexican national bank

barato, -a 1 *adj (objeto)* cheap, inexpensive; **ser muy barato** to be very cheap **2** *adv* cheap, cheaply; **me costó barato** it was cheap, I got it cheap; **vender algo barato** to sell sth cheaply

barco *nm* ship □ **barco de carga** cargo boat *o* ship; **barco mercante** merchant ship; **barco de pasajeros** passenger ship

baremo *nm (tabla)* ready reckoner

barra *nf* (**a**) *(signo gráfico)* slash, oblique □ **barra inclinada** forward slash; **barra invertida** backslash; **barra oblicua** slash, oblique (**b**) INFORM **barra de desplazamiento** scroll bar; **barra espaciadora** space bar; **barra de estado** status bar; **barra de estilos** style bar; **barra de herramientas** tool bar; **barra de iconos** icon bar; **barra de menús** menu bar; **barra de navegación** navigation bar; **barra de título** title bar; **barra de tareas** taskbar

barrera *nf* (**a**) *(de control)* barrier □ **barreras**

arancelarias tariff barriers; **barreras no arancelarias** non-tariff barriers; **barreras comerciales** trade barriers; **barrera de entrada** entry barrier; **barrera de salida** exit barrier (**b**) *(nivel)* mark; **superaron la barrera del millón de discos vendidos** sales of their album went over the million mark

> Según los expertos, el diferencial de precios entre los distintos países de la UE "ni es factible, ni deseable". "No es factible porque existen **barreras comerciales** locales y no es deseable porque hay grados de discriminación de precios que son óptimos", explicó Seppo Honkapja, catedrático de la Universidad de Helsinki.

barril *nm* barrel ❑ **barril de petróleo** oil barrel

barrio *nm* area, district, neighbourhood ❑ **barrio comercial** shopping district

base *nf* (**a**) *(fundamento)* basis; **el petróleo es la base de su economía** their economy is based on oil ❑ FIN **base de amortización** depreciable base; **base del costo** *o Esp* **coste** cost base; **base imponible** taxable income, *US* taxable base; **base liquidable** net tax base; **base monetaria** monetary base

(**b**) *(banco, conjunto)* **base de clientes** customer base, client base; **base de clientes potenciales** suspect pool; **base de datos** database; **base de datos de clientes** customer database; **base de datos documental** documentary database; **base de datos relacional** relational database; **base de muestreo** sample base; **base productiva** manufacturing base; **base de proveedores** supplier base

(**c**) *(en partido, sindicato)* **las bases** the grass roots, the rank and file; **afiliado de base** grassroots member

BASIC, Basic *nm* INFORM BASIC, Basic

básico, -a *adj (fundamental)* basic; **el arroz es su alimentación básica** rice is their staple food

basura *adj inv (bono)* junk; *(contrato)* short-term *(with poor conditions)*

baudio *nm* INFORM baud

baza *nf (ventaja)* advantage; **la gran baza del producto es su reducido precio** the product's great advantage is its low price ❑ **baza de negociación** bargaining chip

BBE *nm (abrev de* **Boletín Bursátil Electrónico**) = electronic bulletin of the Mexican stock exchange

BBS *nf* INFORM *(abrev de* **Bulletin Board Service**) BBS

BCE *nm (abrev de* **Banco Central Europeo**) ECB

BCRA *nm (abrev de* **Banco Central de la República Argentina**) Central Bank of Argentina

BCRP *nm (abrev de* **Banco Central de Reserva del Perú**) Central Reserve Bank of Peru

BCV *nm (abrev de* **Banco Central de Venezuela**) Central Bank of Venezuela

beca *nf* scholarship ❑ UE **beca Erasmus** Erasmus scholarship; **beca de investigación** research scholarship

becario, -a *nm,f (en prácticas)* person on a work placement, *US* intern

BEI *nm* UE *(abrev de* **Banco Europeo de Inversiones**) EIB

below-the-line *adj & nm* MKTG below-the-line

beneficiar 1 *vt* to benefit; **con esa medida todos los empleados se verán beneficiados** that measure will benefit all employees

2 beneficiarse *vpr* to benefit; **beneficiarse de** *o* **con algo** to benefit from sth; **el dólar se benefició de la debilidad del euro** the dollar benefited *o* profited from the weakness of the euro

beneficiario, -a *nm,f* (**a**) *(de seguro, subvención, plan de pensiones)* beneficiary ❑ **beneficiario proindiviso** joint beneficiary (**b**) *(de cheque)* payee

beneficio *nm* (**a**) *(ganancia)* profit; **la tienda ya está dando beneficios** the shop is already making a profit ❑ **beneficio por acción** earnings per share; **beneficio por acción después de disolución** fully diluted earnings per share; **beneficio acumulado** cumulative profit; **beneficio aleatorio** contingent profit; **beneficios antes de impuestos** pre-tax profits; **beneficio anual** annual profit; **beneficios básicos por acción** primary earnings per share; **beneficio bruto** gross profit, gross return; **beneficio bruto de explotación** gross operating profit; **beneficios del capital** capital profits; **beneficios comerciales** trading profit; **beneficio contable** book profit; **beneficio después de impuestos** after-tax profit; **beneficios distribuibles** profit balance; **beneficio no distribuido** undistributed profit, retained earnings; **beneficios no distribuidos ni asignados** unappropriated profits; **beneficio económico** economic profit; **beneficios del ejercicio** year's profits; **beneficios excesivos** excess profits *(considered to be too high)*; **beneficio de explotación** operating profit; **beneficios extraordinarios** extraordinary profits, *(unexpected)*; **beneficio imponible** taxable profit; **beneficios imputables** CONT allocable profits; *(en fiscalidad)* chargeable gain; **beneficios líquidos** net profits; **beneficio marginal** marginal profit; **beneficio neto** net profit, net earnings; **beneficio neto de explotación** net operating profit; **beneficio sobre el papel** paper profit; **beneficios previstos** anticipated profit; **beneficio rápido** quick returns; **beneficio real** real profit; **beneficios retenidos** retained earnings, *US* earned surplus; **beneficio teórico** paper profit (**b**) *(bien)* benefit; **a beneficio de** *(gala, concierto)* in aid of; **en beneficio de todos** in everyone's interest; **ello redundó en beneficio nuestro** it was to our advantage ❑ *beneficio para el consumidor o los consumidores* consumer benefit; *beneficios sociales (del estado)* welfare benefits, social benefits; *(de la empresa)* employee benefits, social benefits

benéfico, -a *adj (concierto, partido)* charity, benefit; **una entidad benéfica** a charity, a charitable organization

BERD *nm (abrev de* **Banco Europeo de Reconstrucción y Desarrollo**) EBRD

bianual *adj* (**a**) *(dos veces al año)* biannual, twice-yearly (**b**) *(cada dos años)* biennial

bibliorato *nm RP* lever arch file

biblioteca *nf* INFORM *biblioteca de programas* program library

bienal 1 *adj* biennial
  2 *nf* biennial exhibition

bienes *nmpl (productos)* goods; *(patrimonio)* property ❑ *bienes de capital* capital assets, capital goods; *bienes comunales* common property; *bienes consumibles* consumable goods; *bienes de consumo* consumer goods; *bienes de consumo duraderos* consumer durables, *US* hard goods; *bienes de consumo de rápida rotación* fast-moving consumer goods; *bienes duraderos* durable goods; *bienes de equipo* capital equipment, capital goods; *bienes fungibles (consumibles)* consumables; BOLSA *(intercambiables)* fungibles; *bienes gananciales* shared possessions; *bienes industriales* industrial goods; *bienes inmateriales* intangible assets; *bienes inmuebles* real estate, real property, *US* realty; *bienes de interés cultural* heritage assets; *bienes intermedios* intermediate goods; *bienes mostrencos* unclaimed goods; *bienes muebles* personal property *o* estate, movable property; *bienes muebles tangibles* tangible movables; *bienes personales* personal assets; *bienes de producción* capital goods, producer goods; *bienes públicos* public property; *bienes raíces* real estate, landed property; *bienes no reclamados* unclaimed goods; *bienes suntuarios* luxury goods; *bienes sustitutivos* substitute goods; *Am* *bienes transables* exportable goods; *Am bienes no transables* non-exportable goods

bifurcación *nf* INFORM *(de red)* branch

bilateral *adj* bilateral

billete *nm* (**a**) *(de banco) Br* note, *US* bill; **un billete pequeño** *o Am* **chico** a small (denomination) *Br* note *o US* bill; **un billete grande** *o Chile* **largo** a large (denomination) *Br* note *o US* bill ❑ *billete de banco* banknote
  (**b**) *Esp (de transporte)* ticket ❑ *billete abierto* open ticket; *billete de avión* plane ticket;

billete de ida Br single (ticket), *US* one-way ticket; *billete de ida y vuelta Br* return (ticket), *US* round trip (ticket); *billete de lista de espera* stand-by ticket; *billete sencillo Br* single (ticket), *US* one-way (ticket)
  (**c**) *Andes, Méx Fam (dinero)* dough; **sólo le interesa el billete** she's only interested in money; **esa familia tiene mucho billete** that family's loaded (with money) *o Br* not short of a bob or two

bimensual *adj* twice-monthly

bimestral *adj* (**a**) *(cada dos meses)* two-monthly, bimonthly (**b**) *(que dura dos meses)* two-month

binario, -a *adj* binary

BIRD *nm (abrev* **Banco Internacional para la Reconstrucción y el Desarrollo**) IBRD

birome *nf RP* Biro®, ballpoint (pen)

bisemanal *adj* twice-weekly

bit *nm* INFORM bit ❑ *bit de paridad* parity bit

blando, -a *adj* ECON *(crédito)* soft

blanquear *vt (dinero)* to launder

blanqueo *nm* *blanqueo de capitales, blanqueo de dinero* money laundering

blindaje *nm (de contrato)* penalties for termination; **cláusula de blindaje** golden parachute clause

blíster *nm* blister pack, bubble pack

bloc *nm* pad ❑ *bloc de notas* note pad

bloque *nm* (**a**) ECON, POL bloc ❑ *bloque comercial* trade bloc; *bloque de monedas* currency bloc; *bloque monetario* monetary bloc (**b**) *(edificio)* block; **un bloque de oficinas** an office block (**c**) *(grupo)* block ❑ MKTG *bloque publicitario* advertising break (**d**) INFORM block ❑ *bloque de texto* text block

bloqueado, -a *adj* (**a**) FIN *(cuenta)* frozen; *(divisa, importaciones)* blocked (**b**) INFORM *(pantalla)* frozen; *(archivo, disquete)* locked

bloquear 1 *vt* (**a**) FIN *(cuenta)* to freeze; *(divisa, importaciones)* to block (**b**) INFORM *(archivo, disquete)* to lock
  2 bloquearse *vpr* INFORM *(sistema)* to crash; *(pantalla)* to freeze

bloqueo *nm* (**a**) FIN *(de cuenta)* freezing; *(de divisa, importaciones)* blocking ❑ *bloqueo económico* economic stranglehold (**b**) INFORM *(en sistema)* crash; *(en archivo)* lock ❑ *bloqueo de archivo, bloqueo de fichero* file lock; *bloqueo numérico* numbers lock; *bloqueo del sistema* system crash; *bloqueo de sólo lectura* read-only lock

BMV *nf* FIN *(abrev de* **Bolsa Mexicana de Valores**) = Mexican stock exchange

BN *nm (abrev de* **Banco de la Nación**) = Peruvian national bank

boca a boca 1 *nm* word of mouth
  2 *adj inv* **campaña boca a boca** word of mouth campaign

BOCAS *nmpl Am* FIN (*abrev de* **bonos convertibles en acciones**) convertible debentures

boceto *nm* rough (drawing)

Boden *nmpl Arg* (*abrev de* **Bonos Optativos del Estado Nacional**) = national government bonds (issued in exchange for frozen bank deposits)

boicot *nm* boycott

boicotear *vt* to boycott

boleta *nf* (**a**) BOLSA trade ticket (**b**) *Méx, RP (para votar)* ballot paper

boletín *nm* journal, periodical ◻ *boletín de la Bolsa* stock market report; *boletín interno (de una empresa)* house magazine, in-house journal; *boletín de noticias* news bulletin; *Boletín Oficial del Estado* Official Spanish Gazette, = daily state publication, giving details of legislation *etc*; *boletín de prensa* press release

boleto *nm* (**a**) *Am (para transporte)* ticket ◻ *boleto abierto* open ticket; *boleto de avión* plane ticket; *boleto de ida* *Br* single (ticket), *US* one-way ticket; *boleto de ida y vuelta* *Br* return (ticket), *US* round-trip (ticket); *boleto de lista de espera* stand-by ticket; *Méx* *boleto redondo* *Br* return (ticket), *US* round-trip (ticket) (**b**) *RP* DER *boleto de compra-venta* contract of sale; *boleto de venta* contract of sale

bolígrafo *nm* ballpoint pen, Biro®

bolsa *nf* (**a**) *(mercado financiero)* **bolsa (de valores)** stock exchange, stock market; **la Bolsa de Madrid** the Madrid Stock Exchange; **la bolsa ha subido/bajado** share prices have gone up/down; **jugar a la bolsa** to speculate on the stock market ◻ *bolsa alcista* bull market; *bolsa bajista* bear market; *bolsa de comercio* stock exchange; *bolsa de materias primas* commodities exchange; *Chile, Cuba* *bolsa negra* black market; *bolsa oficial* official market; *bolsa de productos básicos* commodity exchange (**b**) *(beca)* *bolsa de estudios* (study) grant; *bolsa de viaje* travel grant (**c**) *bolsa de trabajo (en universidad, organización)* = list of job vacancies and situations wanted; *(en periódico)* appointments section

bolsillo *nm* **de bolsillo** *(agenda, calculadora, edición)* pocket

bolsín *nm* BOLSA local stock exchange, *US* curb market

bolsista *nmf* BOLSA stockbroker

bolsístico, -a *adj* BOLSA stock market; **actividad bolsística** activity on the stock market

bombo *nm Fam (publicidad)* hype; **le están dando mucho bombo a la nueva película** the new film is getting a lot of hype, they're really hyping the new film

bonanza *nf (prosperidad)* prosperity; **un año de bonanza** a bonanza year

BonDes *nmpl* FIN (*abrev de* **Bonos de desarrollo del Gobierno Federal**) = Mexican government development bonds

bonificación *nf* (**a**) *(aumento)* bonus ◻ *bonificación en efectivo* cash bonus; *bonificación por reversión de renta* reversionary bonus; SEGUR *bonificación a vencimiento de póliza* terminal bonus (**b**) *(descuento)* discount; **me hacen una bonificación del 15%** they give me a 15% discount ◻ *bonificación de intereses (en préstamos)* interest rate subsidy; *bonificación por promoción (de las empresas a los comerciantes)* merchandising allowance

> **"**
> Así consta en el documento sobre las líneas del nuevo modelo de gestión de la formación continua, elaborado por el Ministerio de Trabajo, que establece que todas las empresas que hagan formación tendrán derecho a deducciones en las cotizaciones sociales, podrán elegir qué cualificación quieren dar, con qué contenido, cómo y cuándo. Estas deducciones o "créditos de formación continua" se calcularán multiplicando el número de trabajadores de la empresa por una **bonificación** que se determinará anualmente, con objeto de bonificar a las pymes. Para las empresas de uno a cinco trabajadores, el crédito se dará por centro de trabajo.
> **"**

bonificar *vt* (**a**) **bonificar a alguien** *(con aumento)* to give sb a bonus; *(descuento)* to give sb a discount (**b**) *(apoyar)* to subsidize; **el gobierno bonificará la contratación de trabajadores mayores de 50 años** the government will offer subsidies to companies who take on workers over the age of 50

bonista *nmf* FIN bondholder

bono *nm* (**a**) FIN bond ◻ *bono de ahorro* savings bond; *bonos de ahorro del Tesoro* Treasury savings; *bono basura* junk bond; *bono brady* Brady bond; *bono de caja* short-term bond; *bono convertible* convertible bond; *bono a corto plazo* short-term bond; *bono de cupón cero* zero coupon bond, split coupon bond; *bono con descuento* discount bond; *bono emitido con descuento* original issue discount bond; *bono empresarial* corporate bond; *bono del Estado* government bond; *bono con garantía* secured bond; *bono con garantía hipotecaria* mortgage bond; *bono garantizado* guaranteed bond; *bono global* global bond; *bono hipotecario* secured bond; *bono indexado, bono indizado* indexed bond; *bono a largo*

plazo long-term bond; **bono con opción de amortización anticipada** put bond; **bono al portador** bearer bond, coupon bond; *Am* **bono de prenda** pledge bond; *Méx* **bono de protección al ahorro** savings protection bond; **bono reembolsable de una sola vez** bullet bond; **bono respaldado con oro** gold bond; **bono de responsabilidad general** general obligation bond; **bono sin riesgo** prime bond; *Am* **bono soberano** government bond; **bono del tesoro** treasury bond; **bono con tipo de interés fijo** fixed-rate bond; **bono con tipo de interés flotante** floating-rate bond; **bono transferible** transferable bond; **bono de vencimiento escalonado** serial bond

(b) *(vale)* voucher ▫ **bono restaurante** *Br* luncheon voucher, *US* meal ticket

Bontes *nmpl* FIN *(abrev de* **Bonos del Tesoro***)* = Argentinian treasury bonds

bonus-malus *nm* SEGUR no-claims bonus clause

booleano, -a *adj* INFORM Boolean

boom *nm* boom ▫ **boom inmobiliario** property boom

borrador *nm (escrito)* draft; INFORM draft version; **el borrador de la carta** the draft letter; **hacer un borrador de** to draft ▫ **borrador de acuerdo** draft agreement, heads of agreement; **borrador de contrato** draft contract; **borrador de la declaración de la renta** income tax assessment

borrar *vt* INFORM *(archivo)* to delete, to erase

bosquejo *nm* (rough) sketch

botón *nm* INFORM button ▫ **botón de ayuda** help button; **botón de cancelar** cancel button; **botón de desplazamiento** scroll button; **botón de inicio** start button; *Am* **botón del mouse** mouse button; **botón de opción** option button; *Esp* **botón del ratón** mouse button; **botón de reinicio** reset button, reset switch

boutique *nf* boutique

bóveda *nf Am* **bóveda de seguridad** *(en banco)* vault

boyante *adj (empresa, negocio)* prosperous; *(economía, mercado, moneda)* buoyant

BPA *nm Méx* FIN *(abrev de* **Bono de Protección al Ahorro***)* savings protection bond

bpp INFORM *(abrev de* **bits por pulgada***)* bpi

bps INFORM *(abrev de* **bits por segundo***)* bps

brainstorming *nm* brainstorming session

brecha *nf* gap; **la brecha entre ricos y pobres** the gulfo gap between rich and poor; **abrir brecha en un mercado** to break into a market ▫ **brecha deflacionaria** deflationary gap; **brecha de(l) rendimiento** yield gap

BREM *nm* FIN *(abrev de* **Bono de Regulación Monetaria del Banco de México***)* = monetary

regulation bonds issued by Mexico's national bank

brent *nm* Brent crude

briefing *nm* MKTG briefing

broker *nmf* BOLSA broker ▫ **broker en línea, broker on-line** on-line broker

bruto, -a *adj (sueldo, ingresos)* gross; **gana 1.000 pesos brutos al mes** she earns 1,000 pesos a month gross

búfer = **buffer**

bufete *nm* (a) *(empresa)* **bufete (de abogados)** law firm, law practice (b) *(mueble)* writing desk

buffer, búfer *nm* INFORM buffer ▫ **buffer de memoria** memory buffer; **buffer de salida** output buffer; **buffer de texto** text buffer

bug *nm* INFORM bug

bumerán *adj inv (efecto)* boomerang

buque *nm* ship ▫ **buque de carga** cargo ship; **buque factoría** factory ship; **buque mercante** merchant ship; **buque de pasajeros** passenger ship, liner; **buque de pasajeros y carga** passenger and cargo ship; **buque refrigerado** refrigerated ship; **buque de transporte de contenedores** container ship

burbuja *nf* **burbuja bursátil** stock market bubble; **burbuja inmobiliaria** property bubble

> **"**
>
> Latinoamérica tendrá en 2003 un crecimiento positivo, pero mediocre, según el subdirector gerente del Fondo Monetario Internacional (FMI), Eduardo Aninat, quien avanzó tasas de entre el 1,7% y 1,9%, frente a una proyección anterior del 3%, debido a la incertidumbre generada por la guerra en Irak, el exceso de inversión en sectores como telecomunicaciones e informática y las **burbujas** en los mercados bursátiles.
>
> **"**

burocracia *nf (sistema)* bureaucracy; *(papeleo)* red tape

burocrático, -a *adj* bureaucratic

bursátil *adj* FIN *(índice, operación)* stock market

bursatilización *nf Méx* FIN securitization

bursatilizar *vt Méx* FIN to securitize

bus *nm* INFORM bus ▫ **bus de control** control bus; **bus de direccionamiento, bus de direcciones** address bus; **bus local** local bus; **bus multimedia** multimedia bus; **Bus Serial Universal** Universal Serial Bus

busca *nm Esp* pager

buscador *nm* INFORM *(en Internet)* search engine

buscapersonas *nm inv* pager

buscar 1 *vt* (a) *(en general)* **estoy buscando trabajo** I'm looking for work, I'm job hunting; MKTG

buscar nuevos clientes to prospect for new customers (**b**) *(en diccionario, índice, horario)* to look up; **buscaré la dirección en mi agenda** I'll look up the address in my address book (**c**) INFORM to search for; **buscar y reemplazar algo** to search and replace sth

2 *vi* INFORM **buscar y reemplazar** to search and replace, to find and replace

buseta *nf Col, CRica, Ecuad,Ven* bus

búsqueda *nf* (**a**) *búsqueda de empleo* job hunting (**b**) INFORM search ▫ *búsqueda booleana* Boolean search; *búsqueda hacia adelante* forward search; *búsqueda hacia atrás* backward search

buzón *nm* (**a**) *(para cartas)* post box, *Br* letter box, *US* mailbox; **echar algo al buzón** to post sth, *US* to mail sth ▫ *buzón de voz* voice mail (**b**) INFORM *(de correo electrónico)* (electronic) mailbox, e-mail address ▫ *buzón electrónico* electronic mailbox; *buzones múltiples* multiple mailboxes; *buzón de salida* out box

buzonear *vi (by hand)* to deliver leaflets

buzoneo *nm (by hand)* leafleting, leaflet drop

BVB *nf (abrev de* **Bolsa de Valores de Bolivia**) = Bolivian stock exchange

BVC *nf* (**a**) *(abrev de* **Bolsa de Valores de Caracas**) = Caracas stock exchange (**b**) *(abrev de* **Bolsa de Valores de Colombia**) = Colombian stock exchange

BVL *nf (abrev de* **Bolsa de Valores de Lima**) = Lima stock exchange

BVM *nf (abrev de* **Bolsa de Valores de Montevideo**) = Montevideo stock exchange

byte *nm* INFORM byte

Cc

caballero *nm* (**a**) *(señor, varón)* gentleman (**b**) BOLSA **caballero blanco** white knight; **caballero negro** black knight

cabecera *nf* (**a**) *Esp (de periódico)* masthead (**b**) *(en comercio)* **cabecera de góndola** gondola end

cabeza 1 *nf* **tener cabeza para los negocios** to be a good businessman/businesswoman; **es la cabeza visible de la organización** he's the public face of the organization □ INFORM **cabeza lectora-grabadora** read-write head
2 *nmf* **cabeza de familia** head of the household

cabezal *nm* INFORM **cabezal de impresión** print head

cable *nm* (**a**) *(eléctrico) (para conectar)* cable, lead; *(dentro de aparato)* wire □ INFORM **cable de impresora** printer cable; **cable módem** cable modem; **cable paralelo** parallel cable; **cable USB** USB cable (**b**) *(de fibra óptica)* cable; **un operador de cable** a cable company; **televisión por cable** cable television □ **cable de fibra óptica** fibre-optic cable; **cable óptico** optical cable

cabotaje *nm (marítimo)* coastal shipping; *(aéreo)* cabotage

CAC *nf* *(abrev de* **Cámara Argentina de Comercio***)* Argentine Chamber of Commerce

CAC 40 *nm* CAC 40 index, = Paris Stock Market Index

caché[1] *nf* INFORM **(memoria) caché** cache memory □ **caché externa** external cache

caché[2]**, cachet** *nm* (**a**) *(tarifa de artista)* fee (**b**) *Fam (distinción)* cachet; **estos invitados dan mucho caché al programa** these guests add a real touch of class to the programme

CAD *nm* *(abrev de* **computer-aided design***)* CAD

CAD/CAM *nm* *(abrev de* **computer-assisted design/computer-assisted manufacture***)* CAD/CAM

cadena *nf* (**a**) *(red de establecimientos)* chain □ **cadena de grandes almacenes** retail chain *(of department stores)*; **cadena hotelera, cadena de hoteles** hotel chain; **cadena de supermercados** supermarket chain; **cadena de tiendas** chain of stores
(**b**) *(red)* chain □ **cadena de distribución** chain of distribution, distribution chain; MKTG **cadena de valor** value chain

(**c**) *(de proceso industrial)* line □ **cadena de montaje**, *Méx* **cadena de ensamblaje** assembly line; **cadena de producción** production line
(**d**) *(red de emisoras)* network □ **cadena de televisión** television network
(**e**) INFORM string □ **cadena de bits** bit chain; **cadena de caracteres** character string

caducado, -a *adj* (**a**) *(carné, pasaporte)* out-of-date; *(subscripción)* lapsed (**b**) *(alimento, medicamento)* past its use-by date

caducar *vi* (**a**) *(carné, contrato)* to expire; *(subscripción)* to lapse (**b**) *(alimento, medicamento)* to pass its use-by date

caducidad *nf* **fecha de caducidad** *(de carné, pasaporte)* expiry date; *(de alimento, medicamento)* use-by date

caer 1 *vi (precio, acciones, tipos)* to fall, to drop; **caer en** *Esp* **picado** *o Am* **picada** to plummet
2 caerse *vpr* INFORM *(red, servidor)* to go down; **la red se ha caído** the network is down

caída *nf* (**a**) *(de paro, precios)* fall, drop (**de** in); **se ha registrado una caída del desempleo** there has been a fall *o* drop in unemployment □ **caída en picado**, *Am* **caída en picada** *(de la economía)* free fall; *(de precios)* nose-dive (**b**) *Fam* INFORM *(de red)* crash

caja *nf* (**a**) *(recipiente)* box; *(para transporte, embalaje)* box, crate □ INFORM **caja de herramientas** toolbox
(**b**) *(para dinero)* cash box; **la empresa tiene ocho millones de pesos en caja** the company has eight million pesos in cash □ **caja B** = parallel illegal system of book-keeping; **caja de caudales** safe, strongbox; *RP* **caja chica** petty cash; **caja fuerte** safe, strongbox; **caja para gastos menores** petty cash box; **caja operativa generada** operating cash flow; *Esp* **caja de resistencia** strike fund; **caja de seguridad** safe-deposit box
(**c**) *(entidad financiera)* *Esp* savings bank □ *Col* **Caja Agraria** agricultural credit bank; *Esp* **caja de ahorros** savings bank; **Caja Postal** post office savings bank; **caja rural** agricultural credit bank
(**d**) *(en tienda, supermercado)* till; *(mostrador)* checkout; *(en banco)* cashier's desk; **horario de caja** *(en banco)* banking hours; **para pagar, pasen por la caja número dos** please pay at till number two □ **caja rápida** express checkout; **caja registradora** cash register

(**e**) *(dinero recaudado)* takings; **hacer (la) caja** to cash up; **hacer una caja de 1.000 euros** to have takings of *o* to take in 1,000 euros

> ❝
>
> Recoletos es, sin duda, otro de los interesados por la participación de Telefónica en Antena 3. Quizá sea ahora el único que pueda ir en solitario por ese paquete al contar en **caja** con casi 300 millones de euros tras sus desinversiones y a ello se une la posibilidad de endeudarse.
>
> ❞

cajero, -a 1 *nm,f (en tienda)* cashier; *(en supermercado)* checkout assistant; *(en banco)* teller, cashier
2 *nm* cash machine, cash dispenser □ **cajero automático** cash machine, cash dispenser, ATM; **cajero nocturno** *Br* night safe, *US* night depository

cajón *nm (para transporte, almacenaje)* packing case

calculadora *nf* calculator □ **calculadora de bolsillo** pocket calculator; **calculadora de escritorio** desktop *o* desk calculator

calcular *vt* (**a**) *(cantidades)* to calculate; **calcular la raíz cuadrada de un número** to calculate *o* extract the square root of a number; **calcular mal** to miscalculate; **su fortuna se calcula en 20 millones de dólares** he is estimated to be worth $20 million; **¿cuánto calculas tú que nos costará?** how much do you reckon it will cost us? (**b**) *(para tributación)* to assess; **calcular la renta de alguien** to assess sb's income

calculista *nmf* planner

cálculo *nm* calculation; **equivocarse en los cálculos** to be out in one's calculations; **hacer cálculos** to do some calculations; **según mis cálculos, llegaremos a las cinco** by my reckoning, we'll arrive at five o'clock □ **cálculo aproximado** estimate; **cálculo de costos** *o Esp* **costes** costing; **cálculo de costos** *o Esp* **costes basado en actividades** activity-based costing; **cálculo de costos** *o Esp* **costes directos** direct costing; **cálculo de costos** *o Esp* **costes estándar** standard costing

calderón *nm* TIP paragraph mark

calendario *nm* (**a**) *(de actividades)* schedule, programme; *(de negociaciones, reformas)* timetable; **un calendario muy apretado** a very busy schedule □ **calendario del contribuyente** = timetable for making annual tax returns; **calendario de entrega** delivery schedule; **calendario de pago** payment schedule (**b**) *(sistema anual, objeto)* calendar □ **calendario laboral** = officially stipulated working days and holidays for the year

> ❝
>
> Lo que no puede ser es que cada ciudad española organice una feria. Nosotros necesitamos que exista una oferta internacional. Es muy difícil atraer visitantes extranjeros con tantos certámenes. A nivel internacional existe una serie de **calendarios** fijados y, si queremos tener ferias internacionales, tenemos que ser capaces de colocarnos dentro de estos **calendarios**.
>
> ❞

calidad *nf* (**a**) *(de producto, servicio)* quality; **un género de (buena) calidad** a quality product; **de mala calidad** of poor quality; **de primerísima calidad** highest quality; **una buena relación calidad-precio** good value (for money) □ INFORM **calidad borrador** draft quality; MKTG **calidad de carta** letter quality; **calidad corriente** fair average quality; **calidad estipulada** stipulated quality; INFORM **calidad de impresión** print quality; MKTG **calidad percibida** perceived quality; **calidad de vida** quality of life
(**b**) *(condición)* **actúa en calidad de asesor** he's acting in an advisory capacity; **fue contratado en calidad de experto jurídico** he was employed as a legal expert

calificación *nf* FIN rating □ **calificación bursátil** market rating; **calificación crediticia** credit rating; **calificación de la deuda** debt rating; **calificación financiera** financial rating; **calificación de riesgo** (credit) risk rating, credit scoring; **calificación de solvencia** credit rating; **calificación de valores** bond rating

calificado, -a *adj Am (trabajador)* skilled

calificar *vt (propiedad)* to classify; **se ha calificado el terreno como urbanizable** *Br* the land has been designated as a brownfield site, *US* the land has been zoned for construction

call center *nm* call centre

calle *nf* (**a**) *(en población)* street, road; **echar a alguien a la calle** *(de un trabajo)* to fire *o Br* sack sb (**b**) *(ciudadanía)* **la calle** the public; **¿qué se opina en la calle?** what does the man in the street think?

callejero *nm Esp* street directory, A-Z

CAM *nf (abrev de* **computer-assitted manufacturing***)* CAM

cámara *nf* (**a**) *(entidad, organismo)* chamber □ **cámara de agentes de cambio** stock exchange committee; **cámara agrícola** farmers' association; **Cámara de Comercio (e Industria)** Chamber of Commerce (and Industry); **Cámara de Comercio Internacional** International Chamber of Commerce; **cámara de compensación** clearing house; **cámara de compensación automática** automated clearing house; **cámara de la propiedad** property owners' association

(**b**) *(sala, receptáculo)* chamber ◻ *cámara aco-*
razada strongroom, vault; *cámara frigorífica*
cold-storage room; **un camión con cámara fri-**
gorífica a refrigerated truck *o Br* lorry

cambiar 1 *vt* (**a**) *(alterar, modificar)* to change;
han cambiado la fecha de salida they've changed *o* altered the departure date; **cambiar de**
nombre un archivo to rename a file
  (**b**) *(reemplazar) (batería, pieza)* to change, to replace
  (**c**) *(dinero)* to change; **cambiar dólares en**
euros to change dollars into euros; **¿me podría**
cambiar este billete en monedas, por favor?
could you give me change for this note in coins,
please?
  (**d**) *(intercambiar)* **cambiar algo por algo** to exchange sth for sth; **cambiar un artículo defec-**
tuoso to exchange a faulty item
  2 *vi* **cambiar de manos** *(dinero, vehículo)* to
change hands; **cambiar de táctica** to change
one's tactics; **cambiar de trabajo** to move *o*
change jobs

cambiario, -a *adj* FIN *(mercado)* currency, foreign exchange

cambio *nm* (**a**) *(alteración, modificación)* change;
cambio de actitud change in attitude; **ha ga-**
nado con el cambio de trabajo he has benefited from changing jobs; **el cambio al sistema**
métrico the changeover to the metric system
◻ *cambio de domicilio* change of address;
ECON *cambio estructural* structural change;
MKTG *cambio de marca* brand switch
  (**b**) *(reemplazo, trueque)* exchange; **durante las**
rebajas no se admiten cambios while the sales
are on, goods may not be exchanged; **se admite**
su vieja lavadora a cambio we will take your
old washing machine in part exchange
  (**c**) *(monedas, billetes)* change; **¿tiene cambio?**
have you got some change?; **¿tiene cambio de**
50? have you got change for *o* of 50?; **nos hemos**
quedado sin cambio(s) we're out of change
  (**d**) FIN *(de divisas)* exchange; **(tipo de) cambio**
exchange rate; **ha bajado el cambio del peso**
the (exchange rate of the) peso has fallen; **¿a**
cuánto está el cambio de la libra? what's the
exchange rate for the pound?; **(oficina de)**
cambio *(en letrero)* bureau de change ◻ *cambio*
extranjero foreign exchange; *cambio de inter-*
vención intervention rate; *cambio oficial* official rate
  (**e**) FIN *(de acciones)* price; **los valores eléctricos**
han mantenido el cambio share prices in the
electricity companies have remained steady

cambista *nmf Am* foreign exchange dealer *o*
broker, money broker

CAME *nm Antes (abrev de* **Consejo de Ayuda**
Mutua Económica*)* Comecon

camino *nm* (**a**) *(en planificación de tareas) cami-*
no crítico critical path (**b**) INFORM path

camión *nm* (**a**) *(de mercancías)* truck, *Br* lorry ◻
camión frigorífico refrigerated truck *o Br* lorry
(**b**) *CAm, Méx (autobús)* bus

camionero, -a 1 *adj CAm, Méx* bus; **central ca-**
mionera bus station
  2 *nm,f* (**a**) *(de camión)* truck driver, *Br* lorry driver, *US* trucker (**b**) *CAm, Méx (de autobús)* bus
driver

campaña *nf* (**a**) *(acción organizada)* campaign;
hacer campaña (de/contra) to campaign (for /
against) ◻ *campaña de descrédito* dirty tricks
campaign; *campaña de difamación* smear
campaign; *campaña de imagen de marca*
branding campaign; *campaña informativa* information campaign; *campaña de marketing*
marketing campaign; *campaña de marketing*
promocional promotion marketing campaign;
SEGUR *campana de producción* new business
campaign; *campaña de promoción* promotional campaign; *campaña publicitaria, campaña*
de publicidad advertising campaign; *campaña*
de saturación saturation campaign; *campaña*
televisiva TV campaign, television campaign;
campaña de ventas sales campaign
  (**b**) *(periodo)* **los bancos han incrementado**
sus beneficios con respecto a la campaña
anterior the banks have increased their profits
compared to last (financial) year

campo *nm* (**a**) *(área, ámbito)* field; **es una exper-**
ta en su campo she's an expert in her field (**b**)
INFORM field ◻ *campo memo* memo field; *campo*
numérico numeric field; *campo de texto* text
field

> ❝
>
> Hay que garantizar la coordinación eficaz
> de las **campañas de marketing** desde la
> fase de desarrollo a la de producción con
> proveedores externos y utilizando cual-
> quiera de los canales.
>
> ❞

canal *nm* (**a**) *(medio, vía)* channel ◻ *canal de co-*
municación communications channel
  (**b**) INFORM channel ◻ *canal IRC* IRC channel
  (**c**) MKTG channel ◻ *canal comercial* commercial channel; *canal de comercialización* distribution channel, marketing channel; *canal de*
comunicación de marketing marketing communications channel; *canal de distribución*
distribution channel, channel of distribution;
canal de venta(s) sales channel
  (**d**) TEL channel ◻ *canal de televisión* television
channel; *canal vía satélite* satellite channel

canasta *nf* ECON *RP canasta familiar:* **el precio**
de la canasta familiar the cost of the average
week's shopping; *Am canasta de monedas* basket of currencies

cancelación *nf* (**a**) *(de contrato, vuelo, reunión)*
cancellation ◻ *cancelación de última hora*

late cancellation (**b**) *(de deuda)* settlement (**c**) INFORM cancellation

cancelar 1 *vt* (**a**) *(contrato, vuelo, reunión)* to cancel (**b**) *(deuda)* to settle (**c**) INFORM to cancel, to abort (**d**) *Chile, Ven (compra)* to pay for 2 *vi Chile, Ven (pagar)* to pay

candidato, -a *nm,f* candidate

candidatura *nf (para un cargo)* candidacy; **presentar su candidatura a** to put oneself forward as a candidate for; **su candidatura para el puesto fue rechazada** she was not chosen for the position □ *candidatura espontánea* unsolicited application, on-spec application

canibalización *nf*, **canibalismo** *nm* MKTG cannibalization

canibalizar *vt* MKTG to cannibalize

canje *nm* exchange

canjeable *adj* exchangeable; **un vale canjeable por un regalo** a gift voucher

canjear *vt* to exchange; *(vale, cupón)* to redeem

canon *nm (pago)* royalty, fee, charge □ CONT *canon de alquiler, canon de arrendamiento* lease charges; *canon de bolsa* stock exchange fee

cantidad *nf* (**a**) *(medida)* quantity, amount; **comprar algo en grandes cantidades** to buy sth in large quantities (**b**) *(número)* number; **sumar dos cantidades** to add two numbers o figures together (**c**) *(suma de dinero)* sum (of money) □ *cantidad excedente* sum in excess; CONT *cantidades por pagar* amounts payable

cantina *nf (en fábrica, empresa)* canteen

capacidad *nf* (**a**) *(cabida)* capacity; **unidades de capacidad** units of capacity; **con capacidad para 500 personas** with a capacity of 500 □ INFORM *capacidad de almacenamiento* storage capacity; *capacidad de alojamiento* accommodation capacity; *capacidad de carga* cargo capacity, load-carrying capacity; INFORM *capacidad del disco* disk capacity; INFORM *capacidad de memoria* memory capacity; *capacidad de tráfico (de puerto, aeropuerto)* handling capacity (**b**) *(aptitud, talento, potencial)* ability, capacity; **no tener capacidad para algo/para hacer algo** to be no good at sth/at doing sth □ *capacidad adquisitiva* purchasing power; *capacidad de la deuda* debt capacity; *capacidad directiva* managerial skills; *capacidad de endeudamiento* borrowing capacity o power; *capacidad de fabricación* manufacturing capacity; *capacidad de financiación* financing capacity; *capacidad de generar ingresos* earning capacity o potential; *capacidad de gestión* managerial skills; *capacidad de producción* production capacity; *capacidad real* effective capacity; *capacidades transferibles* transferable skills

capacitación *nf (formación)* training; **cursos de**

capacitación profesional professional training courses

capacitado, -a *adj* qualified; **estar capacitado para algo** to be qualified for sth

capataz, -aza *nm,f* foreman, *f* forewoman □ *capataz general* head foreman; *capataz de obra* site foreman

capitación *nf* FIN capitation

capital *nm* ECON capital; **he invertido un pequeño capital en el negocio de mi hermano** I've invested a small sum in my brother's business; **el capital y los trabajadores** Capital and Labour □ *capital en acciones* share capital, capital stock; *capital en acciones ordinarias* equity o ordinary share capital; *capital activo* active capital; *capital actual* present capital; *capital adicional* new capital; *capital asegurado* sum at risk, sum insured; *capital autorizado* authorized capital; *capital circulante* working capital; *capital circulante neto* net working capital; *capital circulante operativo* trading capital, *US* operating capital; *capital a corto plazo* short-term capital; *capital de desarrollo* development capital; *capital desembolsado* called-up capital; *capital disponible* available capital; *capital emitido* issued capital; *capital escriturado* share capital, *US* capital stock; *capital especulativo* hot money; *capital evadido* flight capital; *capital fijo* fixed capital; *capital físico* physical capital; *capital flotante* floating capital; *capital en fondos* funded capital; *Am capitales golondrina* = speculative capital invested internationally wherever the highest returns are available; *capital humano* human capital; *capital inicial* initial capital, start-up capital, *US* front money; *capital inmovilizado* tied-up capital; *capital insuficiente* insufficient capital; *capital de inversiones* investment capital; *capital invertido* capital invested; *capital a largo plazo* long-term capital; *capital liberado en acciones* paid-up capital; *capital líquido* liquid assets; *capital nominal* nominal capital; *capital ocioso* war chest; *capital privado* private capital; *capital productivo* active capital; *capital propio* stockholders' equity; *capital público* public capital; *capital de reserva* reserve capital; *capital y reservas* capital and reserves; *capital (de) riesgo* venture capital, risk capital; *capital social* share capital, *US* capital stock; *capital social autorizado* authorized (share) capital; *capital suscrito* subscribed capital; *capital totalmente desembolsado* fully paid(-up) capital; *capital utilizado* capital employed

"

El apoyo al desarrollo del sector privado supone uno de los ejes del programa MEDA II, que cuenta con varias líneas de ayuda a las pymes, incluso con el objetivo de incluir operaciones de **capital riesgo** en sus actuaciones con este tipo de empresas, una de las mayores demandas del empresariado árabe para poder iniciar proyectos en el exterior. **"**

capitalismo *nm* capitalism

capitalista 1 *adj* capitalist
2 *nmf* capitalist □ **capitalista de riesgo** venture capitalist

capitalizable *adj* FIN capitalizable

capitalización *nf* FIN capitalization □ **capitalización bursátil** market capitalization; **capitalización de la deuda** debt equity swap

capitalizar *vt* FIN to capitalize

captación *nf* (*de ejecutivos*) headhunting □ **captación de clientes** customer acquisition; **han lanzado una campaña agresiva de captación de nuevos clientes** they have launched an aggressive campaign to attract o win new customers; **captación de fondos** fundraising

captar *vt* (*clientes*) to win, to attract; (*fondos*) to raise; **tratar de captar clientes** to canvass for customers

captura *nf* INFORM □ **captura de datos** data capture; **captura de pantalla** screen capture o dump o shot

carácter *nm* TIP character; **escriba en caracteres de imprenta** (*en impreso*) please print □ **caracteres alfanuméricos** alphanumeric characters; **carácter comodín** wildcard character

característica *nf* (**a**) (*de producto*) feature □ MKTG **característica distintiva, característica única** unique proposition (**b**) RP TEL **característica (telefónica)** area code

carencia *nf* FIN (*de préstamo*) grace period; **período de carencia** grace period

"

El **período de carencia** se fija en los dos primeros años, abonándose por semestres vencidos el interés pactado. Concluido el **período de carencia**, los sucesivos semestres de la prórroga constituirán el período de amortización, venciendo de manera parcial el capital del préstamo, debiendo devolverse una parte del capital, además de los intereses, mediante cuotas semestrales. **"**

carga *nf* (**a**) (*acción*) loading; **zona de carga y descarga** loading and unloading area (**b**) (*cargamento*) (*de avión, barco*) cargo; (*de tren*) freight; **la carga va en la bodega** the cargo goes in the hold □ **carga aérea** air cargo, airfreight; **carga consolidada** consolidated cargo; **carga contenerizada** containerized cargo o freight; **carga embarcada** shipped weight;

carga de retorno homeward cargo o freight, return cargo; **carga seca** dry cargo; **carga segura** safe load; **carga unitaria** breakbulk cargo (**c**) (*peso, capacidad*) load; **no sé si esta viga aguantará tanta carga** I don't know if this beam will be able to take such a heavy load □ **carga completa** full load; **carga especificada** specified load; **carga incompleta** part load; **carga máxima** maximum load; **carga máxima autorizada** maximum authorized load; **carga útil** (*de vehículo*) payload (**d**) (*impuesto*) tax □ **cargas administrativas** administrative costs; **carga financiera** financial cost; **carga fiscal** tax burden; **carga hipotecaria** mortgage charge; **carga impositiva** tax burden; **cargas sociales** social security contributions; **carga territorial** property charge; **carga tributaria** levy

cargado, -a *adj* (*vehículo, mercancías*) loaded, laden; (*mercancías*) loaded

cargamento *nm* (*de buque*) cargo; (*de camión*) load □ **cargamento mixto** mixed cargo; **cargamento perecedero** perishable cargo; **cargamento pesado** deadweight cargo

cargar *vt* (**a**) (*vehículo, mercancías*) to load; **cargar algo de** to load sth with; **cargar algo en un barco/camión** to load sth onto a ship/lorry (**b**) (*adeudar*) (*importe, factura, deuda*) to charge (**a** to); **cargar algo a alguien en su cuenta** to charge sth to sb's account; **cargar de más** to overcharge; **cargar de menos** to undercharge (**c**) INFORM to load

cargo *nm* (**a**) FIN charge; **con cargo a** charged to; **han asignado una nueva partida con cargo a los presupuestos del estado** they have created a new budget heading; **sin cargo adicional** for o at no extra charge; **correr a cargo de** to be borne by, to be chargeable to; **todos los gastos corren a cargo de la empresa** all expenses will be borne by the company; **el seguro se hará cargo de los daños** the insurance will pay for the damage □ **cargo automático** automated withdrawal; **cargo por intereses** interest charge (**b**) (*cuidado*) charge; **está a cargo de la seguridad de la empresa, tiene a su cargo la seguridad de la empresa** he is in charge of o responsible for company security; **tiene a diez trabajadores a su cargo** she has ten people working under her; **las personas a su cargo** (*familiares*) your dependants; **hacerse cargo de** (*asumir el control de*) to take charge of; (*ocuparse de*) to take care of; **se hizo cargo de la gestión de la empresa** she took over the running of the company (**c**) (*empleo*) post, position; **ocupa un cargo importante** she holds an important position o post; **tomar posesión del cargo** to take up the position; (*cargo público*) to take up office □ **cargo directivo** manager; **cargo público:**

ostentar o **ser un cargo público** to hold public office; **varios cargos públicos se han visto involucrados** several people holding public office have been involved

(**d**) *(acusación)* charge; **formular graves cargos contra alguien** to bring serious charges against sb

(**e**) *(buque de carga)* cargo ship, freighter

carguero *nm* cargo ship, freighter

carné, carnet *nm* card ❑ **carné de afiliado** membership card; **carné comunitario** Community carnet; **carné de identidad** identity card; **carné sindical** union card; **carné de socio** membership card

caro, -a 1 *adj* expensive; **ser muy caro** to be very expensive o dear

2 *adv* **costar caro** to be expensive; **nos salió muy caro** it cost us a lot

carpeta *nf* (**a**) *(archivador)* file, folder ❑ **carpeta de anillas** ring binder (**b**) INFORM folder ❑ **carpeta del sistema** system folder

carrera *nf* (**a**) *(estudios)* university course; **hacer la carrera de derecho/económicas** to study law/economics (at university) (**b**) *(profesión)* career

carretera *nf* road; **por carretera** by road; **mapa de carreteras** road map ❑ **carretera de circunvalación** Br ring road, US beltway; Méx **carretera de cuota** toll road; **carretera general** main road; **carretera nacional** Br ≃ A road, US ≃ state highway; **carretera de peaje** toll road

carro *nm* (**a**) Andes, CAm, Carib, Méx *(automóvil)* car (**b**) Méx *(vagón)* car (**c**) *(carrito)* trolley, US cart ❑ INFORM **carro de la compra** shopping trolley, US shopping cart

carrusel *nm* Col FIN **(operación) carrusel** = agreement between various parties successively to buy and sell a bond at predetermined prices

carta *nf* (**a**) *(escrito)* letter; **echar una carta** to Br post o US mail a letter ❑ **carta de adjudicación** allotment letter; **carta de apoyo financiero** (financial) comfort letter; **carta certificada** Br recorded o US certified letter; **cartas credenciales** letters of credence; **carta de crédito** letter of credit; **carta de crédito confirmada** confirmed letter of credit; **carta de crédito contingente** standby letter of credit; **carta de crédito documentaria** documentary letter of credit; **carta de crédito revocable** revocable letter of credit; **carta de crédito standby** standby letter of credit; **carta de crédito transferible** transferable letter of credit; **carta de despido** letter of dismissal; **carta de dimisión** resignation letter; **carta fundacional** founding charter; **carta de garantía** letter of guarantee; **carta general** form letter; **carta de indemnidad** letter of indemnity; **carta de intenciones**

letter of intent; **carta de manifestaciones** *(en auditoría)* letter of representation; **carta de notificación** letter of notification; **carta de pago** receipt; **carta de pedido** order; **carta de porte** consignment note; **carta de porte CIM** CIM waybill; **carta de porte CMR** CMR waybill; **carta de presentación** *(para un tercero)* letter of introduction; *(con currículum)* Br covering letter, US cover letter; **carta de recomendación** reference (letter); **carta de solicitud** *(en Bolsa)* letter of application; **carta urgente** express letter; **carta de venta** bill of sale; **carta verde** green card *(for international car insurance)*

(**b**) *(estatutos)* charter ❑ **carta de fletamiento** charter party

> **"**
> Cuando no se pacte expresamente otra cosa en el acuerdo contractual, se entenderá que los servicios realizados se pagarán al contado, previa presentación del albarán, **carta de porte** u otro documento acreditativo de la recepción de la mercancía en destino debidamente conformado, acompañado de la correspondiente factura.
> **"**

cartel¹ *nm* *(anuncio)* poster; **prohibido fijar carteles** *(en letrero)* post o stick no bills ❑ **cartel publicitario** poster, bill

cartel², cártel *nm* *(de empresas)* cartel ❑ **cartel de precios** price cartel, price ring

cartera *nf* (**a**) FIN portfolio ❑ **cartera de acciones** share portfolio; Am **cartera bruta** credit portfolio; **cartera de clientes** client portfolio; **cartera de control** controlling shareholding; **cartera de crédito** credit portfolio; **cartera discrecional** discretionary portfolio; **cartera de empresas** business portfolio; **cartera indexada** indexed portfolio; **cartera de inversiones** investment portfolio; **cartera de marcas** brand portfolio; **cartera de pedidos** order book; **cartera de productos** product portfolio; **cartera de valores** investment portfolio

(**b**) *(para documentos)* briefcase; *(sin asa)* portfolio

(**c**) *(para dinero)* wallet, US billfold

(**d**) POL *(de ministro)* portfolio; **ocupa la cartera de Defensa** he is the Minister of Defence, he has the Defence portfolio

cartilla *nf* **cartilla de ahorros** savings book, passbook; **cartilla del paro** = registration card issued to the unemployed, Br ≃ UB40

cartucho *nm* *(de tinta, videojuego)* cartridge ❑ **cartucho de tóner** toner cartridge

casa *nf* (**a**) *(hogar)* home; **trabajar en** o **desde casa** to work at o from home

(**b**) *(establecimiento)* company; **este producto lo fabrican varias casas** this product is made by several different companies; **por la compra**

de un televisor, la casa le regala una radio buy one television and we'll give you a radio for free; **¡invita la casa!** it's on the house!; **especialidad/vino de la casa** house speciality/wine □ **casa de apuestas** betting shop; **casa de banca** banking house; *RP* **casa bancaria** savings bank; **casa de cambio** bureau de change; **casa central** head office; **casa de comisiones** commission agency; **casa discográfica** record company; **casa editorial** publishing house; **casa de empeño(s)** pawnshop; **casa exportadora** exporter; **casa importadora** importer; **casa matriz (de** *empresa)* head office; *(de grupo de empresas)* parent company; **casa de préstamo** pawnshop; **casa de subastas** auction house, auctioneer's

cash-flow *nm* cash flow

casilla *nf* (**a**) *(para cartas)* pigeonhole □ *Andes, RP* **casilla de correo** PO Box; *Am* INFORM **casilla de correo electrónico** electronic mailbox; *CAm, Carib, Méx* **casilla postal** PO Box (**b**) *(en un impreso)* box □ INFORM **casilla de verificación** checkbox

casillero *nm (casilla)* pigeonhole; *(mueble)* set of pigeonholes

caso *nm (situación, circunstancias, ejemplo)* case □ DER **caso fortuito, caso de fuerza mayor** act of God; **caso judicial** court case

catalogar *vt* to catalogue

catálogo *nm* catalogue; **comprar algo por catálogo** to buy sth by catalogue □ INFORM **catálogo electrónico** electronic catalogue; **catálogo en línea, catálogo on-line** on-line catalogue; **catálogo de venta por correo** mail-order catalogue

catastro *nm* property register

catástrofe *nf* SEGUR **catástrofe natural** natural disaster

categoría *nf* category; **un hotel de primera categoría** a top-class hotel

catering, cátering *nm* catering

> "
> Iberia confirmó que estudia la venta de su 70% de la empresa de **catering** Iberswiss, de la que Gate Gourmet pose el 30% restante. La intención sería la de integrar todos sus servicios de **catering** en una sola compañía, lo que podría provocar la venta de su filial.
> "

cauce *nm (camino, forma)* **abrir nuevos cauces de diálogo** to open new channels for talks; **los cauces reglamentarios** the correct procedure

caución *nm* (**a**) DER bail □ FIN **caución de indemnidad** indemnity bond (**b**) SEGUR surety

causa *nf* DER case □ **causa civil** lawsuit; **causa criminal** criminal case

cautivo, -a *adj* captive

cazar *vt (ejecutivos)* to headhunt

cazatalentos *nmf inv* (**a**) *(de ejecutivos)* headhunter (**b**) *(de artistas, deportistas)* talent scout

c/c *(abrev de* **cuenta corriente**) c/a

CCI *nf (abrev de* **Cámara de Comercio Internacional**) ICC

Cco INFORM *(abrev de* **con copia**) Bcc

CCSCS *nf (abrev de* **Coordinadora de Centrales Sindicales del Cono Sur**) Southern Cone Trade Union Coordinating Body, = umbrella organization of trade unions of Argentina, Bolivia, Brazil, Chile, Paraguay and Uruguay

CD *nm (abrev de* **compact disc**) CD

CD-I *nm (abrev de* **compact disc interactivo**) CD-I

CD-R *nm* (**a**) *(abrev de* **compact disc recorder**) CD-R (**b**) *(abrev de* **compact disc recordable**) CD-R

CD-ROM *nm (abrev de* **compact disc-read only memory**) CD-ROM

CD-RW *nm (abrev de* **compact disc rewritable**) CD-RW

CDT *nm Andes* FIN *(abrev de* **Certificado de Depósito a Término**) fixed-term certificate of deposit

ceder *vt (traspasar, transferir)* to hand over; *(derechos)* to assign; *(acciones)* to transfer

cédula *nf* document □ **cédula de citación** summons; **cédula hipotecaria** mortgage bond, mortgage debenture; *Am* **cédula de identidad** identity card

CEE *nf Antes (abrev de* **Comunidad Económica Europea**) EEC

celda *nf* INFORM cell

celebrar *vt* (**a**) *(votación, reunión)* to hold; **las entrevistas se celebrarán a principios de mayo** interviews will take place o will be held in early May (**b**) *(contrato, acuerdo)* to enter into, to conclude

celular *Am* **1** *adj* **telefonía celular** *Br* mobile phones, *US* cellphones; **el mercado de la telefonía celular** the *Br* mobile phone o *US* cellphone market
2 *nm Br* mobile (phone), *US* cellphone

censo *nm (de población)* census; *Esp* **censo (electoral)** electoral roll, electoral register □ **censo de contribuyentes** tax roll; **censo de empresas** company census; **censo fiscal** tax roll; **censo de población** population census

censor, -ora *nm,f Esp* FIN **censor de cuentas** auditor; **censor jurado de cuentas** *Br* chartered accountant, *US* certified public accountant

censura *nf Esp* FIN **censura de cuentas** inspection of accounts, audit

centavo *nm (en países anglosajones)* cent; *(en países latinoamericanos)* centavo

céntimo *nm (de euro, bolívar)* cent

central 1 *adj (banco, gobierno)* central
2 *nf (oficina)* headquarters, head office; *(de correos, comunicaciones)* main office; **central (eléctrica)** power station; **central (sindical)** *Br* trade union, *US* labor union ▫ **central de compras** media buying agency; **central de medios** sales agency; **central de reservas** central reservations unit; **central telefónica** telephone exchange

centralita *nf* switchboard ▫ **centralita digital** digital exchange

centralización *nf* centralization

centralizado, -a *adj* centralized

centralizar *vt* to centralize

centrar *vt* (a) INFORM to centre (b) *(dirigir)* **una medida económica centrada en reducir el desempleo** an economic measure aimed at reducing unemployment; **un negocio centrado en el cliente** a customer-focused business

centro *nm* (a) *(establecimiento, organismo)* centre, *US* center; **un importante centro financiero/cultural** an important financial/cultural centre ▫ **centro de asistencia social** welfare centre; **centro de atención telefónica** call centre; **centro de atención al visitante** visitor centre; **centro de beneficios** profit centre; **centro de cálculo** computer centre; **centro comercial** shopping centre *o* mall; **centro comercial electrónico** electronic mall; **centro de comercio** commercial centre; **centro de congresos** conference centre; CONT **centro de costo** *o Esp* **coste** cost centre; CONT **centro de costos** *o Esp* **costes secundarios** secondary cost centre; **centro de distribución** distribution centre; **centro financiero** financial centre; **centro fiscal** tax centre; **centro de formación** training centre; **centro de información** information centre; **centro de llamadas** call centre; **centro de negocios** business centre; CONT **centro principal de costos** *o Esp* **costes** main cost centre; **centro de procesamiento de datos** data processing centre; **centro de trabajo** workplace; **centro turístico** tourist centre
(b) *(de ciudad)* town centre; **ir al centro** to go to town

CEOE *nf (abrev de* **Confederación Española de Organizaciones Empresariales***)* = Spanish employers' association, *Br* ≃ CBI

cereal *nm* grain, cereal

cero *adj inv & nm* zero; **la inflación experimentó un crecimiento cero** there was no increase in the rate of inflation ▫ **cero defectos** zero defects

cerrado, -a *adj (tienda, fábrica) (a diario)* closed, shut; *(permanentemente)* closed (down), shut (down); **cerrado por obras/vacaciones** *(en letrero)* closed for alterations/holidays; **cerrado los fines de semana** *(en letrero)* closed at weekends

cerrar 1 *vt* (a) *(negocio) (a diario)* to close, to shut; *(permanentemente)* to close down, to shut down
(b) BOLSA *(sesión)* to close; **cerrar una posición** to close a position
(c) BANCA *(cuenta)* to close
(d) *(carta, sobre)* to seal; INFORM *(archivo)* to close
(e) *(gestiones, acuerdo)* **han cerrado un trato para...** they've reached an agreement *o* made a deal to...; **cerraron el trato ayer** they wrapped up the deal yesterday
(f) *(signo ortográfico)* to close; **cerrar comillas/paréntesis** to close inverted commas/brackets
2 *vi* (a) *(negocio) (a diario)* to close; *(definitivamente)* to close down; **¿a qué hora cierra?** what time do you close?; **cerramos los domingos** *(en letrero)* closed on Sundays (b) BOLSA to close; **las acciones cerraron a 420 céntimos** the shares closed at 420 cents; **la Bolsa cerró con una caída/subida de dos enteros** the Share Index closed two points down/up

> **❝**
> La Bolsa Mexicana de Valores (BMV) **cerró** ayer en su nivel más elevado desde el 28 de mayo de 2002, cuando el principal indicador accionario nacional se colocó en siete mil 303.57 unidades.
> **❞**

certificación *nf* (a) *(acción)* certification (b) *(documento)* certificate

certificado, -a 1 *adj (documento)* certified; *(carta, paquete)* registered; **enviar un paquete por correo certificado** to send a parcel by registered *Br* post *o US* mail
2 *nm* certificate ▫ **certificado de aduana** customs certificate; **certificado de aeronavegabilidad** certificate of airworthiness; **certificado de ahorro** savings certificate; **certificado de aprobación** certificate of approval; **certificado de aptitud** certificate of proficiency; **certificado de arqueo** tonnage certificate; SEGUR **certificado de averías** damage certificate; **certificado de calidad** quality certificate; **certificado de conformidad** certificate of compliance, certificate of conformity; **certificado de constitución** certificate of incorporation; SEGUR **certificado de daños** damage certificate, certificate of damage; FIN **certificado de depósito** certificate of deposit, bond note; **certificado de depósito jumbo** jumbo certificate of deposit; **certificado de descarga** landing certificate; **certificado de despacho aduanero** clearence certificate, clearence papers; **certificado del destinatario final** end-

user certificate; *certificado de empleo* attestation of employment; *certificado de ensayo* test certificate; *certificado de garantía* guarantee certificate, warranty certificate; *certificado de inscripción* registration certificate; *certificado de inversión* investment certificate; *certificado médico* medical certificate; *certificado notarial* notarial certificate; *certificado de origen* certificate of origin; BOLSA *certificado de participación* participation certificate; *certificado de patente* letters patent; *certificado privilegiado de inversión* preferential investment certificate; *certificado provisional* scrip certificate; *certificado de prueba* test certificate; *certificado de recibo* certificate of receipt; *certificado de registro del barco* ship's certificate of registry; *certificado de residencia* certificate of residence; *certificado de seguridad* security certificate; *certificado de seguro* certificate of insurance, insurance certificate; *certificado de transferencia* certificate of transfer; *certificado de valor* certificate of value

certificar *vt* (a) *(constatar)* to certify (b) *(en correos)* to register

CES *nf* (*abrev de* **Confederación Europea de Sindicatos**) ETUC

cesar 1 *vt* *(destituir)* to dismiss; *(alto cargo)* to remove from office
2 *vi* *(dimitir)* to resign, to step down; **cesó como presidente de la empresa** he resigned *o* stepped down as company chairman

cese *nm* (a) *(detención, paro)* **el cese de la actividad comercial** the termination of business operations; **liquidación por cese de negocio** *(en letrero)* closing-down sale (b) *(destitución)* dismissal; *(de alto cargo)* removal from office

> **"**
> Gateway, el fabricante de ordenadores estadounidense, ha anunciado que recortará cerca de 4.600 empleos, un 25% de su fuerza laboral, como consecuencia del **cese** de sus operaciones en Asia y, posiblemente, en Europa.
> **"**

cesión *nf* *(de derechos)* transfer, assignment □ DER **cesión de bienes** assignment of property; UE **cesión de cuotas** *(pesqueras)* quota hopping

cesionario, -a *nm,f* transferee, assignee

cesta *nf* ECON **la cesta de la compra** the shopping basket, *US* the market basket; INFORM **cesta (de la compra** *o* **de pedidos)** *(en página web)* shopping basket *o US* cart □ ECON **cesta de monedas** basket of currencies

CFR (*abrev de* **Cost and Freight**) CFR

CGR *nf Am* (*abrev de* **Contraloría General de la República**) National Audit Office

chanchullero, -a *nm,f Fam* crook

chanchullo *nm Fam* fiddle; **hicieron un chanchullo para evitar pagar** they worked some fiddle to avoid paying

charla *nf* (a) *(conferencia)* talk (**sobre** about *o* on); **dar una charla** to give a talk (b) INFORM chat

chat *nm* INFORM *(charla)* chat; *(sala)* chat room

chatarra *nf* (a) *(metal)* scrap (metal) (b) *Fam (monedas)* small change

chatarrería *nf* scrapyard

chatarrero, -a *nm,f* scrap (metal) dealer, scrap merchant

chatear *vi Fam* INFORM to chat

chelín *nm Antes* (a) *(en Austria)* schilling (b) *(en el Reino Unido)* shilling

cheque *nm Br* cheque, *US* check; **pagar con cheque** to pay by cheque; **cobrar un cheque** to cash a cheque; **cruzar un cheque** to cross a cheque; **extender un cheque (a alguien)** to make out a cheque (to sb) □ **cheque abierto** open cheque; **cheque bancario** banker's draft, bank cheque; **cheque barrado** crossed cheque; **cheque en blanco** blank cheque; *Am* **cheque de caja** cashier's cheque, banker's draft; **cheque certificado** certified cheque; **cheque cruzado** crossed cheque; **cheque sin fondos** bad cheque; **cheque (de) gasolina** *Br* petrol *o US* gas voucher; *Am* **cheque de gerencia** cashier's cheque, banker's draft; **cheque nominativo** = cheque made out to a specific person; **un cheque nominativo a favor de Carla Gimeno** a cheque made out to Carla Gimeno; **cheque al portador** bearer cheque; **cheque postal** post office cheque, *Br* Girocheque; **cheque de ventanilla** counter cheque; **cheque de viaje,** *Am* **cheque de viajero** traveller's cheque

chequera *nf Br* chequebook, *US* checkbook

chicharro *nm Fam* speculative stocks, cheap stock

chinche *nf Am Br* drawing pin, *US* thumbtack

chincheta *nf Br* drawing pin, *US* thumbtack

chip *nm* INFORM chip □ **chip de memoria** memory chip

chiringuito *nm Fam* chiringuito (financiero) cowboy outfit *(unscrupulous or fraudulent financial intermediary)*

> **"**
> El **chiringuito financiero** de Bilbao gestionado por José Antonio Fernández Echezárraga recogía los ahorros de sus clientes con la promesa de una inversión en renta fija y una rentabilidad media del 5%. Pero luego, Fernández Echezárraga jugaba con esos fondos en Bolsa. Mientras los mercados de valores estuvieron al alza, la doble

cara del **chiringuito** JA Fernández Echezárraga, SL, no quedó al descubierto, pero las fuertes caídas de las acciones en el parqué en estos dos últimos años revelaron el fraude. Medio centenar de afectados han visto esfumarse ahorros de 3,01 millones. **"**

chollo *nm Esp Fam (producto, compra)* bargain

chupatintas *nmf inv Pey* pen pusher

cía., Cía. *(abrev de* **compañía***)* Co

ciber- *pref* INFORM cyber-

cibercafé *nm* INFORM Internet cafe, cybercafe

ciberespacio *nm* INFORM cyberspace

cibernauta *nmf* INFORM Net user

ciberocupa, ciberokupa *nmf Esp* INFORM cybersquatter

ciberocupación, ciberokupación *nf Esp* INFORM cybersquatting

ciclo *nm (periodo)* cycle ❑ **ciclo de distribución** distribution cycle; **ciclo económico** business cycle, economic cycle; **ciclo operativo** operating cycle; MKTG **ciclo de vida familiar** family lifecycle; MKTG **ciclo de vida de la marca** brand lifecycle; MKTG **ciclo de vida del producto** product lifecycle; **ciclo vital** life cycle

ciencias *nfpl* **ciencias económicas** economics; **ciencias empresariales** business studies; **ciencias de la información** media studies; **ciencias políticas** political science

ciento *núm* a o one hundred; **ciento cincuenta** a o one hundred and fifty; **seis/diez por ciento** six/ten percent

cierre *nm* (**a**) *(de fábrica, tienda, colegio) (permanente)* closure; **el horario de cierre de las tiendas** the shops' closing times ❑ IND **cierre patronal** lockout
(**b**) CONT closing-off ❑ **cierre de ejercicio** year-end closing of accounts
(**c**) BOLSA *(de sesión, posición)* close, closing; **precio de cierre** closing price ❑ **cierre al alza** closing high; **cierre a la baja,** *Am* **cierre en baja** bear closing
(**d**) *(administrativo)* closure; **el juez ordenó el cierre del bar** the judge ordered the closure of the bar, the judge ordered the bar to be closed
(**e**) *(mecanismo)* **cierre de combinación** combination lock

CIF 1 *(abrev de* **Cost, Insurance and Freight***)* CIF
2 *nm Esp (abrev de* **Código de Identificación Fiscal***)* = number identifying company for tax purposes

cifra *nf* (**a**) *(signo)* figure; **un código de cuatro cifras** a four-digit code (**b**) *(cantidad)* number, figure; *(de dinero)* sum; **la cifra de desempleados sigue subiendo** the number of unemployed continues to rise; **ingresó la cifra de 100.000 euros** he deposited the sum of 100,000 euros ❑

cifras comerciales trade figures; FIN **cifra de negocio** turnover; **cifras reales** actual figures; FIN **cifra de ventas** sales figures; FIN **cifra de ventas anuales** annual sales figures

"

La confianza crece en todos, excepto en hostelería y turismo. El comercio es el sector con mejores perspectivas; la **cifra de negocio** aumentará en el 50,7 por ciento de las empresas del sector. Le sigue el sector de otros servicios (ocio, consultoría, telecomunicaciones), donde la **cifra de negocio** se incrementará en el 44,9 por ciento de las empresas. En el sector industrial, el 38,6 por ciento de las empresas incrementarán su facturación, mientras que en la construcción este porcentaje es del 31,8 por ciento. Finalmente, la hostelería y el turismo espera un incremento de la **cifra de negocio** en el 24,2 por ciento de las empresas.

"

cinta *nf (de imagen, sonido, ordenadores)* tape ❑ **cinta de audio** audio cassette; **cinta digital** digital tape; **cinta digital de audio** digital audio tape; **cinta magnética** magnetic tape

CIOSL *nf (abrev de* **Confederación Internacional de Organizaciones Sindicales Libres***)* ICFTU

CIP *(abrev de* **Carriage and Insurance Paid To***)* CIP

circuito *nm (eléctrico)* circuit ❑ **circuito integrado** integrated circuit; **circuito lógico** logic circuit

circulación *nf (de moneda, valores, revista)* circulation; **fuera de circulación** out of circulation; **poner en circulación** to put into circulation; **retirar de la circulación** to withdraw from circulation ❑ FIN **circulación de capitales** circulation of capital; FIN **circulación fiduciaria** paper currency; **circulación forzada** forced currency; **circulación masiva** mass circulation; FIN **circulación monetaria** paper currency

circulante *adj* FIN **capital circulante** working capital

circular 1 *nf (notificación)* circular
2 *vi* (**a**) *(moneda)* to be in circulation (**b**) *(capital, dinero)* to circulate

círculo *nm (grupo de personas, instituciones)* circle; **círculos económicos/políticos** economic/ political circles ❑ **círculo de calidad** quality circle

cita *nf (entrevista)* appointment; **una cita de negocios** a business appointment; **pedir cita** to ask for an appointment; **tener una cita** to have an appointment

citación *nf* DER summons

citar 1 *vt* (**a**) *(para reunión)* to make an appointment with; **el jefe convocó una reunión y citó**

a todos los empleados the boss called a meeting to which he invited all his workers; **citar a un candidato para una entrevista** to call o invite a candidate for interview (**b**) DER to summons

2 citarse vpr **citarse (con alguien)** to arrange to meet (sb)

ciudad nf (grande) city; (pequeña) town ▫ **ciudad dormitorio** commuting town, dormitory town

ciudadano, -a nm,f citizen

clase nf (**a**) (grupo, categoría) class; **de primera clase** first-class; **una mercancía de primera clase** a first-class o top-class product; **de segunda clase** second-class

(**b**) (en medio de transporte) class; **primera/segunda clase** first/second class; **viajar en primera/segunda clase** to travel first/second class ▫ **clase económica** economy class; **clase ejecutiva** business class; **clase preferente** first class; Andes **clase salón** (en tren) first class; **clase turista** tourist class

(**c**) (grupo social, profesional, institucional) class ▫ **clase alta** upper class; **clase baja** lower class; **la clase dirigente** the ruling class; **clase media** middle class; **clase media alta** upper middle class; **clase media baja** lower middle class; **clase obrera** working class; **clases pasivas** = pensioners and people on benefit; **clase social** social class; **clase trabajadora** working class

clasificación nf classification ▫ **clasificación arancelaria** customs classification; **clasificación socioeconómica** socio-economic classification; FIN **clasificación de solvencia** credit rating

clasificados nmpl **(anuncios) clasificados** classified advertisements

clasificar vt (datos, documentos) to classify; **clasificar algo por orden alfabético** to put o sort sth in o into alphabetical order

cláusula nf clause ▫ **cláusula adicional** additional clause; **cláusula de arbitraje** arbitration clause; SEGUR **cláusula de no caducidad** non-forfeiture clause; **cláusula de no concurrencia** non-competition clause; **cláusula derogatoria** overriding clause; **cláusula escala móvil** (de salarios) escalator o escalation clause; **cláusula de escape** escape clause, get-out clause; **cláusula de excedentes** excess clause; **cláusula de exclusividad** exclusivity clause; **cláusula de exención de garantía** non-warranty clause; **cláusula de fuerza mayor** force majeure clause; **cláusula de garantía** warranty clause; SEGUR **cláusula de huelga** strike clause; **cláusula de indexación** indexation clause; SEGUR **cláusula de invalidez** disability clause; SEGUR **cláusula de negligencia** negligence clause; **cláusula de penalización** penalty clause; FIN **cláusula de pignoración negativa** negative pledge clause;

cláusula de refinanciación refunding clause; **cláusula de no responsabilidad** non-liability clause; **cláusula de restricción** restrictive clause; **cláusula de revisión (salarial)** wage revision clause, pay review clause; **cláusula de salvaguardia** escape clause, safeguard clause; **cláusula de vencimiento anticipado** (de préstamo hipotecario) acceleration clause

> **❝**
>
> Los salarios crecerán un 0,8% adicional aproximadamente por la activación de las **cláusulas de revisión** recogidas en los convenios colectivos, según la estimación realizada por el secretario de Estado de Economía, Luis de Guindos.
>
> **❞**

clave 1 adj inv (fundamental, esencial) key; **un factor clave** a key factor; **es una fecha clave para la empresa** it's a crucial date for the company

2 nf (**a**) (código) code ▫ **clave de acceso** access code; BANCA **clave de sucursal (bancaria)** (bank) sort code (**b**) (de sistema informático) password; (de caja fuerte) combination

clic, click nm INFORM click; **hacer clic** o **click** to click; **hacer doble clic** o **click** to double-click

clicar INFORM **1** vt to click on
2 vi to click

click = **clic**

cliente, -a 1 nm,f (de negocio) customer; (de contable, abogado) client; (de hotel) guest; **perder/ganar un cliente** to lose/gain a customer/client ▫ MKTG **cliente activo** active customer; MKTG **cliente actual** existing customer; **clientes fijos** customer base; **cliente habitual** regular customer; MKTG **cliente más fiel** hard-core loyal; **cliente mayorista** wholesale customer; **cliente misterioso** mysterious shopper; **cliente particular** retail customer; **cliente de paso** passing customer; **cliente potencial** potential customer; MKTG **cliente de referencia** reference customer; **cliente virtual** virtual customer

2 nm INFORM client ▫ **cliente de correo electrónico** e-mail client

clientela nf (de negocio) customers; (de banco, abogado) clients; (de hotel) guests; (de bar, restaurante) clientele ▫ **clientela fija** customer base; **clientela de paso** passing trade

clip nm (para papel) paperclip ▫ INFORM **clip de vídeo**, Am **clip de video** video clip

clónico, -a 1 adj cloned
2 nm INFORM clone

cluster nm INFORM cluster

CNBV nf FIN (abrev de **Comisión Nacional Bancaria y de Valores**) = Mexican stock market regulatory body

CNMV nf FIN (abrev de **Comisión Nacional del**

Mercado de Valores) = Spanish stock market regulatory body

CNV *nf* FIN (*abrev de* **Comisión Nacional de Valores**) = stock market regulatory body in Argentina, Panama, Paraguay and Venezuela

coacreedor, -ora *nm,f* joint creditor

coarrendatario, -a *nm,f* joint tenant

coarriendo *nm* joint tenancy

coasegurador, -ora *nm,f* co-insurer

coaseguro *nm* co-insurance

coavalista *nmf* joint surety

cobertura *nf* (**a**) *(de servicio)* coverage; **mi teléfono móvil no tiene cobertura aquí** my mobile network doesn't cover this area □ **cobertura mediática** media coverage; **cobertura publicitaria** advertising density; **cobertura social: miles de parados sin cobertura social** thousands of unemployed people who are not receiving benefit; **cobertura de ventas** sales coverage
(**b**) *(de beneficios)* **cobertura del dividendo** dividend cover
(**c**) *(de seguro)* cover □ **cobertura contractual** contractual cover; **cobertura sanitaria** health cover; **cobertura total** full cover
(**d**) FIN security; **cobertura para un crédito/una hipoteca** security for a loan/a mortgage
(**e**) BOLSA **cobertura corta** short hedge; **cobertura a corto plazo** short covering; **cobertura cruzada** cross-hedge; **cobertura de riesgo** hedging

COBOL, Cobol *nm* INFORM COBOL, Cobol

cobrable *adj* cashable

cobrador, -ora *nm,f* *(de deudas, recibos)* collector □ **cobrador de morosos** debt collector

cobrar 1 *vt* (**a**) *(dinero)* to charge; *(cheque)* to cash; *(deuda)* to collect; **cobran 10 euros por página** they charge 10 euros per page; **cantidades por cobrar** amounts due
(**b**) *(sueldo)* to earn, to be paid; *(subsidio)* to claim; **cobra un millón al año** she earns a million a year; **sobrevive cobrando diferentes subsidios** she lives by claiming a number of different benefits; **tengo que ir a cobrar la jubilación** I have to go and draw my pension; **cobro mi pensión por el banco** my pension is paid straight into the bank
(**c**) *(en tienda)* **¿me cobra, por favor?** how much do I owe you?; **cóbrelo todo junto** put it all together, we'll pay for it all together
2 *vi* *(en el trabajo)* to get paid; **cobrarás el día 5 de cada mes** you'll be paid on the 5th of every month; **llevan un año sin cobrar** they haven't had any wages for a year; **cobrar en efectivo** to be *o* get paid (in) cash

cobro *nm* *(de cheque)* cashing; *(de pago)* collection; **llamar a alguien a cobro revertido** *Br* to make a reverse-charge call to sb, *US* to call sb collect □ CONT **cobros por caja** cash receipts; **cobro de comisiones** *(delito)* acceptance of bribes *o* (illegal) commissions; **cobro de deudas** debt collection

coche *nm* (**a**) *(automóvil)* car, *US* automobile □ **coche de alquiler** hire car; **coche de empresa** company car (**b**) *(autobús)* bus (**c**) *(de tren)* coach, *Br* carriage, *US* car

codecisión *nf* IND codetermination

codeudor, -ora *nm,f* joint debtor

codificación *nf* INFORM *(de texto)* encrypting, coding; *(de imagen)* coding

codificado, -a *adj* (**a**) INFORM *(texto)* encrypted, coded; *(imagen)* encoded (**b**) *(emisión de TV)* scrambled

codificador *nm* (**a**) INFORM *(de texto)* encrypter, encoder; *(de imagen)* encoder (**b**) *(para TV de pago)* scrambler

codificar *vt* INFORM *(texto)* to encrypt, to encode; *(imagen)* to encode

código *nm* (**a**) *(de leyes, normas)* code □ **código de circulación** highway code; **código civil** civil code; **código de comercio** commercial law; **código de conducta publicitaria** advertising standards; **código deontológico** code of ethics; **código mercantil** commercial law
(**b**) *(de señales, signos)* code □ **código de barras** bar code; **código de cliente** customer code; **código de identificación** *(de producto)* identification code; *Esp* **código de identificación fiscal** = number identifying company for tax purposes; **código postal** *Br* postcode, postal code, *US* zip code; **código del proveedor** supplier code; **código de seguridad** security code; **código SWIFT** SWIFT code
(**c**) INFORM code □ **código de acceso** access code; **código alfanumérico** alphanumeric code; **código ASCII** ASCII (code); **código binario** binary code; **código de carácter** character code; **código de error** error code; **código fuente** source code; **código máquina** machine code

coeficiente *nm* ratio □ **coeficiente de apalancamiento** leverage *o* *Br* gearing ratio; **coeficiente de caja** cash ratio; **coeficiente de capitalización** capitalization ratio; BOLSA **coeficiente de cobertura** hedge ratio; **coeficiente de endeudamiento** debt-equity ratio; **coeficiente de explotación** operating ratio; **coeficiente de flujo de caja** cash flow rate; **coeficiente de garantía** capital adequacy ratio; **coeficiente de liquidez** liquidity ratio, reserve ratio; **coeficiente de liquidez inmediata** acid test ratio; **coeficiente de paridad** parity ratio; **coeficiente de producción** output ratio; **coeficiente de rendimiento** performance ratio; **coeficiente de riesgo** risk ratio; **coeficiente de**

rotación de existencias inventory *o Br* stock turnover ratio; *coeficiente de solvencia Br* capital adequacy ratio, *US* solvency ratio

cofundador, -ora *nm,f* co-founder

cogarante *nmf* joint surety

coheredero, -a *nm,f* joint heir

coima *nf Andes, RP Fam* bribe, *Br* backhander

cola *nf* INFORM **cola (de impresión)** print queue

colaboración *nf (cooperación)* collaboration; **necesito tu colaboración para escribir el artículo** I need your help to write this article; **trabajaron en estrecha colaboración durante unos meses** they worked in close partnership for several months

colaborador, -ora *nm,f (compañero)* associate, colleague; *(de prensa)* contributor, writer □ *colaborador externo* freelancer

colaborar *vi (empresas)* to collaborate; **colaborar en** *(proyecto)* to take part in; *(revista)* to contribute to

colapsar 1 *vt (actividad)* to bring to a halt, to stop
2 colapsarse *vpr (mercado)* to collapse

colectividad *nf* ECON collectivity

colectivo, -a 1 *adj (responsabilidad, interés)* collective; *(iniciativa)* joint; *(despido)* mass; *(transporte)* public
2 *nm* **(a)** *(grupo)* group; *(en estadística)* collective, population; **un colectivo pacifista** a pacifist group; **el colectivo médico** the medical community **(b)** *Arg, Bol (autobús)* bus

colega *nmf (profesional)* colleague, *US* coworker

colegio *nm* **colegio de abogados** lawyers' association, Bar association

colgar 1 *vt* **colgar el teléfono** to hang up; **me colgó en mitad de la frase** she hung up on me when I was in mid-sentence
2 *vi (hablando por teléfono)* to hang up, to put the phone down; **no cuelgue, por favor** hold the line, please
3 colgarse *vpr* INFORM *(computadora)* to crash; **se me ha colgado** it has crashed

colocación *nf* **(a)** *(empleo)* position, job; **oficina de colocación** employment agency **(b)** BOLSA placing, placement □ *colocación de acciones* placing *o* placement of shares **(c)** MKTG *colocación de producto* product placement

colocar 1 *vt* **(a)** BOLSA *(acciones)* to place; *(dinero)* to invest; **colocaron un millón de títulos** they placed a million in bonds; **coloqué mis ahorros en acciones** I invested my savings in shares **(b)** INFORM *(cursor, imagen)* to position **(c)** *(en un empleo)* to find a job for; **colocar a alguien** to find sb a job
2 colocarse *vpr (en un empleo)* to get a job

columna *nf (de texto, cuenta)* column □ CONT **columna del debe** debit column; **columna del haber** credit column

coma *nf* **(a)** *(signo ortográfico)* comma **(b)** MAT **coma (decimal)** ≃ decimal point; **tres coma cuatro** *(3,4)* three point four *(3.4)* **(c)** INFORM *coma flotante* floating point

comandita: en comandita *adj* **sociedad en comandita** general and limited partnership

comanditar *vt* to finance as a silent partner

comanditario, -a 1 *adj* silent
2 *nm,f* silent partner

comando *nm* INFORM command □ *comando de búsqueda* find command; *comando (de) copiar* copy command; *comando deshacer* undo command; *comando DOS* DOS command; *comando erróneo* bad command; *comando externo* external command; *comando (de) guardar* save command; *comando de inserción* insert command; *comando interno* internal command; *comando de línea* line command; *comando suprimir* delete command

comarca *nf* = administrative unit smaller than a region and larger than a municipality, ≃ district

combinación *nf* **(a)** *(de caja fuerte)* combination **(b)** *(de medios de transporte)* connections; **hay muy buena combinación para llegar al aeropuerto** there's a very good connection to the airport **(c)** BOLSA *combinación de cartera* portfolio mix **(d)** INFORM *combinación de teclas* key combination

comedor *nm (de fábrica)* canteen

comerciabilidad *nf* marketability

comercial 1 *adj* **(a)** *(de empresas)* commercial; *(embargo, disputa, política, déficit)* trade; **relaciones comerciales** trade relations; **aviación comercial** civil aviation; **gestión comercial** business management **(b)** *(que se vende bien)* commercial; **una película muy comercial** a very commercial film
2 *nmf (vendedor, representante)* sales rep □ *comercial de publicidad* advertising agent
3 *nm Am (publicidad)* commercial, *Br* advert

comercialismo *nm* commercialism

comercializable *adj* marketable

comercialización *nf* **(a)** *(de producto)* selling,

marketing ❑ *comercialización a gran escala* mass marketing (**b**) *(de cultura, deporte)* commercialization

comercializador, -ora 1 *adj* **una empresa comercializadora de productos biotecnológicos** a company which markets biotechnology products
  2 *nf (empresa)* marketer

> **"**
>
> El marisqueo y la pesca extractiva serán los sectores más afectados en cuanto al impacto sobre su conjunto, pues el informe estima que el volumen de negocio disminuirá un 90% y un 80%, respectivamente. Sin embargo, será el sector **comercializador**, más amplio, quien sufrirá en mayor medida los efectos del accidente marítimo, al estimarse las pérdidas en 700 millones de euros, aproximadamente.
>
> **"**

comercializar 1 *vt* (**a**) *(producto)* to market (**b**) *(cultura, deporte)* to commercialize
  2 comercializarse *vpr (cultura, deporte)* to become commercialized

comerciante *nmf* (**a**) *(negociante)* tradesman, *f* tradeswoman (**b**) *(tendero)* shopkeeper; **pequeños comerciantes** small businessmen ❑ *comerciante individual* sole trader

comerciar *vi* to trade; **comerciar con armas/pieles** to deal *o* trade in arms/furs; **comerciar en especias** to deal *o* trade in kind

comercio *nm* (**a**) *(de productos)* trade, commerce; **libre comercio** free trade ❑ *comercio asistido por Esp ordenador o Am computadora* computer-aided trading; *comercio de bienes* visible trade; *comercio de cabotaje* coastal trade; *comercio controlado* managed trade; *comercio desleal* unfair trading; *comercio electrónico* e-commerce; *comercio exterior* foreign trade; *comercio fraudulento* fraudulent trading; *comercio ilícito* wrongful trading; *comercio de importación* import trade; *comercio industrial* industrial trade; *comercio interior* domestic trade; *comercio internacional* international trade; *comercio de invisibles* invisible trade; *comercio justo* fair trade; *comercio legítimo* lawful trade; *comercio marítimo* maritime trade; *comercio mayorista* wholesale trade; *comercio minorista* retail trade; *comercio recíproco* reciprocal trade; *comercio transfronterizo* cross-border trade
  (**b**) *(tienda)* shop, store
  (**c**) *(conjunto de tiendas) Br* shops, *US* stores; **el comercio cierra mañana por ser festivo** the *Br* shops *o US* stores are closed tomorrow because it's a holiday

comestible 1 *adj* edible, eatable
  2 comestibles *nmpl* food; **tienda de comestibles** grocer's (shop), grocery store

cometido *nm* (**a**) *(objetivo)* mission, task (**b**) *(deber)* duty

comida *nf* (**a**) *(alimento)* food; **la comida francesa/mexicana** French/Mexican food ❑ *comida basura* junk food; *comidas para empresas* business catering; *comida rápida* fast food (**b**) *Esp, Méx (al mediodía)* lunch ❑ *comida de negocios* business lunch (**c**) *esp Andes (a la noche)* dinner

comienzo *nm* start, beginning; **dar comienzo (a algo)** to start (sth), to begin (sth)

comillas *nfpl* inverted commas, quotation marks ❑ *comillas tipográficas* curly quotes

comisario, -a *nm,f (de muestra)* organizer; *(de exposición)* organizer, curator ❑ SEGUR *comisario de averías* average surveyor; UE *comisario europeo* European Commissioner; *comisario de quiebra* official liquidator

comisión *nf* (**a**) *(delegación)* committee, commission ❑ *comisión de control* monitoring committee; *comisión disciplinaria* disciplinary committee; *comisión ejecutiva* executive committee; *Comisión Europea* European Commission; *Comisión Europea de Normalización* European Standards Commission; *Comisión Internacional de Normas Contables* International Accounting Standards Committee; *comisión de investigación* commission of inquiry, committee of inquiry; *comisión mixta* joint committee, joint commission; *Comisión Nacional Bancaria y de Valores* = Mexican stock market regulatory body; *Comisión Nacional del Mercado de Valores* = Spanish stock market regulatory body; *Comisión Nacional Supervisora de Empresas y Valores* = Peruvian stock market regulatory body; *Comisión Nacional de Valores* = stock market regulatory body in Argentina, Panama, Paraguay and Venezuela; *comisión de normalización* standards commission; *Comisiones Obreras* = Spanish left-wing trade union; *comisión parlamentaria* parliamentary committee; *comisión permanente* standing committee; *comisión de retribuciones* pay commission; *comisión de trabajo* working party
  (**b**) *(por servicios)* commission; **(trabajar) a comisión** (to work) on a commission basis; **recibe** *o* **se lleva una comisión del 5%** she gets 5% commission ❑ *comisión de administración* account charges; *comisión de agencia* agency fee; *comisión por amortización anticipada* exit charge(s); *comisión de apertura (de cuenta)* set-up fee; *(de préstamo)* arrangement fee, front-end fee, *US* loan origination fee; *comisión bancaria* bank fee; *comisión de o por compromiso* commitment fee; *comisión extra (de corredor)* overriding commission; *comisión de garantía* del credere commission; *comisión de gestión* administration fee, management fee;

comisión de mantenimiento account fee; *comisión de negociación* acceptance fee; *comisión de reembolso* back-end fee, redemption fee; BOLSA *comisión de suscripción* underwriting commission, underwriting fee; BOLSA *comisión de traspaso* transfer fee; *comisión de venta* sales commission

❝
31 de las 35 compañías del Ibex tienen **comisión de retribuciones**, que es la encargada de establecer cómo se paga a los consejeros.
❞

comisionista *nmf* commission agent

comité *nm* committee □ BANCA *comité asesor* advisory committee; *comité de auditoría* audit committee; *comité de buen gobierno empresarial* corporate governance committee; *comité consultivo* consultative committee; *comité de disciplina, comité disciplinario* disciplinary committee, disciplinary board; UE *Comité Económico y Social* Economic and Social Committee; *comité ejecutivo* executive committee; IND *comité de empresa* works council; *comité de gestión* management committee; IND *comité intercentros* coordinating *o* joint committee; *comité organizador* organizing committee; *comité permanente* standing committee; *comité de política monetaria* monetary policy committee; UE *Comité de las Regiones* Committee of the Regions

comodín *nm* INFORM wild card

compact *nm* INFORM compact disc □ *compact disc* compact disc

compactación *nf* INFORM compression □ *compactación de ficheros* file compression

compactar *vt* INFORM to compact, to compress

compacto, -a 1 *adj* compact
2 *nm* (**a**) *(aparato)* compact disc player (**b**) *(disco)* compact disc, CD

compañero, -a *nm,f* compañero (de trabajo) colleague, workmate, *US* co-worker □ *compañero de equipo* team-mate

compañía *nf* company; **Fernández y Compañía** Fernández and Company □ *compañía aérea* airline; *compañía aérea nacional* national airline; *compañía de capital riesgo* venture capital company; *compañía discográfica* record company; *compañía eléctrica* electricity company; *compañía fiduciaria* trust company; *compañía financiera* finance company, *Br* finance house; *compañía mercantil* mercantile company; *compañía naviera* shipping company; *compañía petrolera* oil company; *compañía de seguros* insurance company; *compañía de seguros de vida* life insurance company; *compañía de tarifas reducidas (aérea)* low-cost airline; *compañía telefónica*

telephone company; *compañía de vuelos chárter* charter company

❝
...las **compañías** tradicionales –o de red– tienen que hacer frente a un fenómeno de espectacular crecimiento, el de los operadores de bajo coste o **compañías de tarifa reducida**.
❞

comparación *nf* comparison □ *comparación de precios* price comparison

comparar *vt* to compare; **comparar precios** to compare prices, to shop around

comparativa *nf* *(de productos)* product comparison

comparativo, -a *adj* comparative

comparecer *vi* *(ante tribunal)* to appear; **comparecer ante alguien** to appear before sb; **no comparecer** to default

compartición *nf* INFORM *compartición de datos* data sharing; *compartición de impresora* printer sharing

compartir *vt* *(ganancias, gastos)* to share (out); **lo compartieron entre los familiares** they shared it (out) among their relations; **compartir el empleo** to job-share; **compartir oficina con alguien** to share an office with sb

compatibilidad *nf* INFORM compatibility

compatible INFORM **1** *adj* compatible; **compatible con versiones anteriores** backward compatible
2 *nm* compatible computer

compendiar *vt* *(libro, artículo)* to abridge, to abstract

compensación *nf* (**a**) *(indemnización)* compensation; **solicitan una compensación económica por los daños sufridos** they are seeking financial compensation for the damage; **recibió 10 millones en compensación por el fallecimiento de su marido** she received 10 million in compensation for the death of her husband □ *compensación económica* financial compensation; *compensación en efectivo* cash compensation
(**b**) FIN *(sistema)* clearing □ *compensación bancaria* bank clearing

compensar 1 *vt* (**a**) *(contrarrestar)* to make up for, to offset; **compensaron las pérdidas con las ganancias** the profit they made offset their losses
(**b**) *(indemnizar)* **compensar a alguien (de** *o* **por)** to compensate sb (for); **la compensaron con dos millones** she got two million in compensation
(**c**) *(cheque)* to clear; **los cheques tardan tres días en ser compensados** it takes three working days for cheques to clear

(**d**) BOLSA *(en mercado de futuros)* **compensar el riesgo de las fluctuaciones cambiarias** to hedge against currency fluctuations

2 *vi* to be worthwhile; **compensa más comprarlo al por mayor** it pays *o* it's more economical to buy it in bulk

3 compensarse *vpr* **las pérdidas en el Reino Unido se compensan con nuestras ganancias en Europa** European earnings make up for our losses in the UK

compensatorio, -a *adj* compensatory, compensating

competencia *nf* (**a**) *(entre personas, empresas)* competition; **hay mucha competencia por conseguir ese contrato** there's a lot of competition for that contract; **hacer la competencia a alguien** to compete with sb ❑ *competencia desleal* unfair competition; *competencia directa* direct competition; *competencia entre marcas* brand competition; *competencia imperfecta* imperfect competition; *competencia de mercado* market competition; *competencia perfecta* pure competition

(**b**) *(competidores)* **la competencia** the competition; **trabaja para la competencia** he works for the competition

(**c**) *(atribuciones, incumbencia)* **competencias** powers; **no es de mi competencia** it's not my responsibility

(**d**) *(aptitud)* competence, ability; **un profesional de una gran competencia** a very able *o* competent professional

> **"**
> Habrá que esperar el desenlace de esta batalla, en la que el Gobierno debe actuar con el criterio prioritario de defender los intereses de los consumidores y velar por la libre **competencia**.
> **"**

competente *adj (capaz)* competent

competidor, -ora 1 *adj* competitor

2 *nm,f* competitor ❑ *competidor comercial* commercial competitor; *competidor de marca* brand competitor

competitividad *nf* competitiveness ❑ *competitividad de precios* price competitiveness

competitivo, -a *adj* competitive; **productos a precios muy competitivos** products at very competitive prices

complejo *nm (zona construida)* complex ❑ *complejo comercial* shopping complex; *complejo hotelero* hotel complex; *complejo industrial* industrial complex; *complejo turístico* tourist development

complementariedad *nf complementariedad estratégica* strategic fit

complemento *nm* (**a**) *(añadido)* supplement ❑ *complemento salarial* bonus, wage supplement

(**b**) **complementos** *(accesorios)* accessories

completar *vt* (**a**) *(acabar)* to complete (**b**) *(impreso)* to fill out, to fill in

completo, -a *adj* (**a**) *(entero)* complete; **nombre completo** full name (**b**) *(lleno)* full; **todos los hoteles de la ciudad están al completo** all the hotels in town are full; **completo** *(hotel)* no vacancies; *(aparcamiento)* full

componente *nm (pieza)* component

comportamiento *nm* (**a**) *(de acciones)* performance; **el comportamiento de la inflación ha sido muy irregular este año** inflation has fluctuated considerably this year ❑ *comportamiento de la inversión* investment performance

(**b**) MKTG behaviour ❑ *comportamiento de compra* buying behaviour; *comportamiento del comprador* buyer behaviour; *comportamiento del consumidor* consumer behaviour; *comportamiento postcompra* post-purchase behaviour

comportarse *vpr* BOLSA *(acciones)* to perform

> **"**
> Algunos fondos especializados **se han comportado** bien sólo en términos relativos, por ejemplo los especializados en alimentación (-7.66%), o los fondos solidarios (-8.87%), mientras que otros lo han hecho decididamente peor que la media: los fondos tecnológicos acumulan en el año pérdidas del -43%.
> **"**

composición *nf (de texto)* layout

compra *nf* (**a**) *(adquisición)* purchase; **por la compra de una enciclopedia te regalan un televisor** if you buy an encyclopedia, they'll give you a television free; *Esp* **hacer la compra,** *Am* **hacer las compras** to do the shopping; **ir de compras** to go shopping ❑ *compra apalancada* leveraged buyout; *compras centralizadas* central *o* centralized purchasing; BOLSA *compras de cobertura* covering purchases; *compras comparativas* comparison shopping; *compra conjunta* joint purchase; *compra al contado* cash purchase; FIN spot buying; *compra por correo* mail-order purchase; *Am* **compra en cuotas** *Br* hire-purchase, *US* installment plan; CONT *compra de deudas* purchase of debts; *compra directa* direct purchase; *compras especulativas* speculative buying; *compra fantasma* mystery shopping; *compras desde el hogar* in-home shopping; *compra impulsiva, compra por impulso* impulse buy; *compra integral* one-stop shopping; *compras justo a tiempo* just-in-time purchasing; INFORM *compras en línea* electronic shopping; *compra al por mayor* wholesale purchase, bulk buying; *compra oculta* mystery shopping; BOLSA *compra con pacto de reventa* reverse repo operation; BOLSA, FIN **compra a plazo** forward purchase; **compra a plazos** Br hire-purchase, US installment plan; MKTG **compra prevista** destination purchase

(**b**) *(objeto adquirido)* purchase, buy; **esta impresora fue una excelente compra** this printer was a really good buy; **algunos supermercados te llevan la compra a casa** some supermarkets deliver your shopping to your home

comprador, -ora 1 *adj* **fiebre compradora** buying frenzy; **la parte compradora** the buyer **2** *nm,f (adquiriente)* buyer, purchaser; *(en una tienda)* shopper, customer □ **comprador de empresa** organizational buyer; **comprador ficticio** mystery buyer; **comprador impulsivo, comprador por impulso** impulsive buyer o purchaser; MKTG **comprador objetivo** target buyer; **comprador potencial** potential buyer; **comprador de primera vivienda** first-time buyer *(of house)*

comprar *vt* (**a**) *(adquirir)* to buy, to purchase; **se lo compré a un vendedor ambulante** I bought it from a street vendor o seller; **se lo compraron a Ignacio como regalo de despedida** they bought it for Ignacio as a leaving present; **comprar algo al contado** *(en metálico)* to pay cash for sth; *(en un plazo)* to pay for sth all at once o Br on the nail; **comprar a plazos** o Am **en cuotas** to buy on Br hire-purchase o US an installment plan; **comprar al por mayor** to buy wholesale, to buy in bulk

(**b**) *(sobornar)* to buy (off), to bribe

compraventa, compra-venta *nf (intercambio comercial)* trading (**de** in) □ **compraventa de acciones** share dealing, share trading; **compraventa de armas** arms dealing

compresión *nf* INFORM compression □ **compresión de archivos** file compression; **compresión de datos** data compression; **compresión de ficheros** file compression

comprimir *vt* INFORM to compress, to zip

comprobación *nf* checking □ **comprobación aleatoria** random check

comprobador, ora *nm,f* tester

comprobante *nm* (**a**) *(documento)* supporting document, proof (**b**) *(recibo)* receipt □ CONT **comprobante de caja** (petty) cash voucher; **comprobante de compra** proof of purchase, receipt; **comprobante de crédito** credit voucher; **comprobante de envío** proof of postage; **comprobante de gastos** proof of expenditure, receipt; **comprobante de pago** proof of payment; **comprobante de venta** sales receipt, US sales check

comprobar *vt* to check

comprometer 1 *vt* (**a**) *(poner en peligro) (éxito, posibilidades)* to jeopardize; *(inversión)* to compromise (**b**) *(obligar)* **el acuerdo no nos**

compromete a nada the agreement doesn't commit us to anything

2 comprometerse *vpr (asumir un compromiso)* to commit oneself; **se han comprometido a cumplir el acuerdo** they have committed themselves to fulfilling the agreement; **me comprometí a acabarlo cuanto antes** I promised to finish it as soon as possible

compromiso *nm* (**a**) *(obligación)* commitment, undertaking; **sin compromiso** without obligation; **reciba información en su domicilio, sin ningún compromiso** let us send you our brochure without obligation □ **compromiso de compra** undertaking to purchase; **compromiso escrito** written undertaking; **compromiso de venta** undertaking to sell

(**b**) *(acuerdo)* agreement; **patronal y sindicatos alcanzaron un compromiso** management and unions reached an agreement; **presentaron una propuesta de compromiso** they proposed a compromise (**c**) *(cita)* engagement; **tenía un compromiso previo** he had a previous engagement

compulsar *vt (documento)* to check against the original; **una fotocopia compulsada** a certified copy

computación *nf esp Am* computing

computadora *nf*, **computador** *nm esp Am* computer □ **computadora de bolsillo** hand-held computer; **computadora compatible** compatible computer; **computadora doméstica** home computer; **computadora frontal** front-end computer; **computador personal** personal computer; **computadora portátil** laptop computer; **computadora de red** network computer; **computadora de sobremesa** desktop computer

computadorización *nf Am* computerization

computadorizar *vt Am* to computerize

computarización *nf* computerization

computarizar *vt* to computerize

computerización *nf* computerization

computerizar *vt* to computerize

comunicación *nf* (**a**) *(contacto, intercambio de información)* communication; **estar en comunicación con alguien** to be in contact with sb; **ponerse en comunicación con alguien** to get in touch with sb; **los medios de comunicación (de masas)** the (mass) media □ **comunicación horizontal** horizontal communication; **comunicación en línea** on-line communication

(**b**) *(por teléfono)* **se cortó la comunicación mientras hablábamos** we were cut off

(**c**) *(escrito oficial)* communiqué

(**d**) *(ponencia)* paper

(**e**) **comunicaciones** *(transporte)* communications

comunicado *nm* announcement, statement ❏ *comunicado oficial* official communiqué; *comunicado a la prensa, comunicado de prensa* press release

comunicador, -ora *nm,f* communicator; **es un buen comunicador** he's a good communicator

comunicar 1 *vt* (**a**) *(información)* **comunicar algo a alguien** to inform sb of sth; **le comunicaron su despido por escrito** he was informed in writing of his dismissal; **lamentamos tener que comunicarle que…** we regret to inform you that… (**b**) *(sentimientos, ideas)* to convey (**c**) *Am (al teléfono)* to call, to telephone
2 *vi* (**a**) *Esp (teléfono) (estar ocupado)* *Br* to be engaged, *US* to be busy; **está comunicando, comunica** the line's *Br* engaged *o US* busy (**b**) *RP (teléfono) (estar sonando)* to ring (**c**) *(hablar)* to get through; **no consigo comunicar con él** I can't get through to him
3 comunicarse *vpr (hablarse)* to communicate; **se comunican por correo electrónico** they communicate by e-mail; **le cuesta comunicarse con sus compañeros** he finds it difficult to communicate with his colleagues

comunidad *nf* (**a**) *(grupo)* community; **la comunidad científica/educativa** the scientific/education community ❏ *Comunidad Andina* Andean Community, = organization for regional cooperation formed by Bolivia, Colombia, Ecuador, Peru and Venezuela; *comunidad autónoma* autonomous region, = largest administrative division in Spain, with its own Parliament and a number of devolved powers; *Antes Comunidad Económica Europea* European Economic Community; *comunidad empresarial, RP comunidad empresaria* business community; *la Comunidad Europea, las Comunidades Europeas* the European Community; *Antes Comunidad Europea del Carbón y del Acero* European Coal and Steel Community; *comunidad financiera* financial community; *comunidad internacional* international community; *comunidad de propietarios* owners' association; *comunidad de vecinos* residents' association
(**b**) FIN *comunidad de bienes* co-ownership *(between spouses)*

comunitario, -a *adj* UE Community, of the European Union; **política comunitaria** EU *o* Community policy; **los países comunitarios** the EU countries, the Community members

CONASEV *nf* FIN *(abrev de* **Comisión Nacional Supervisora de Empresas y Valores**) = Peruvian stock market regulatory body

conceder *vt (premio, contrato, indemnización)* to award; *(préstamo, subvención, licencia)* to give, to grant

concejo *nm* (**a**) *(ayuntamiento)* (town) council

(**b**) *(municipio)* municipality

concentración *nf (de capital)* concentration ❏ *concentración parcelaria* land consolidation; *concentración urbana* conurbation; *concentración vertical* vertical concentration

concepto *nm* (**a**) *(idea)* concept ❏ *concepto de la marca* brand concept; *concepto de marketing* marketing concept; *concepto publicitario* advertising concept (**b**) *(de una cuenta)* heading, item; **los ingresos por este concepto crecieron un 5%** income under this heading increased by 5%; **en concepto de dietas** by way of *o* as expenses; **recibió 2 millones en concepto de derechos de autor** he received 2 million in royalties

concernir *vi* to concern; **en lo que concierne a…** as regards…

concertación *nf* settlement ❏ IND *concertación social* = process of employer-trade-union negotiations, *Br* ≃ social contract

concesión *nf* (**a**) *(de premio, contrato, indemnización)* award, awarding; *(de préstamo, subvención, licencia)* granting (**b**) *(licencia, franquicia)* licence; **tienen la concesión exclusiva del producto en ese país** they have the exclusive licence for the product in that country; **el servicio de limpieza fue dado en concesión a una empresa privada** the contract for cleaning services was awarded to a private company

concesionario, -a *nm,f (persona con derecho exclusivo de venta)* licensed dealer; *(titular de una concesión)* concessionaire, licensee ❏ *concesionario de automóviles* car dealer *(of particular make)*; *concesionario autorizado* approved dealer

conciliación *nf (en un litigio)* reconciliation; *(en un conflicto laboral)* conciliation ❏ CONT *conciliación de estados bancarios* bank reconciliation

conciliador, -ora IND **1** *adj* conciliatory
2 *nm,f* conciliator

concluir 1 *vt (reunión)* to end, to conclude; *(trabajo, obras)* to finish, to complete
2 *vi* to (come to an) end

conclusión *nf* (**a**) *(de reunión)* end, conclusion; *(de trabajo, obras)* completion (**b**) **conclusiones** *(de informe)* findings

concordato *nm Col, Urug* ECON *(expediente de crisis)* = statement of the economic difficulties of a company, presented to the authorities to justify redundancies

concretar *vt* (**a**) *(precisar)* to specify, to state exactly; **todavía no han concretado su oferta** they haven't made a firm offer yet (**b**) *(concertar)* to fix; **por fin concretaron una fecha para el inicio de las negociaciones** they finally agreed on *o* fixed a starting date for the negotiations

concurrencia *nf* competition; DER **no concurrencia** non-competition clause

concurso *nm (para obra, contrato)* tender; **sacar a concurso** to put to tender ❑ *concurso de adjudicación* tendering process; *concurso público* invitation to tender

> **"**
>
> La Comisión Nacional de la Energía (CNE) **ha sacado a concurso** la campaña de comunicación que, con un presupuesto conjunto de 2,74 millones de euros, pretende ofrecer al consumidor información sobre la plena liberalización de los mercados del gas y la electricidad.
>
> **"**

condición *nf* (**a**) *(término, estipulación)* condition, proviso; **con la** *o* **a condición de que** on condition that; **sin condiciones** unconditional; **las condiciones de un contrato** the terms of a contract ❑ *condiciones de cambio* terms of exchange; *condiciones de contrato* contract terms; *(de empleado)* terms of employment; *condiciones de crédito* credit terms, terms of credit; *condiciones de entrega* terms of delivery; *condiciones de licencia* licencing requirements; *condiciones de pago* payment terms, terms of payment; *condiciones de pago al contado* cash terms; *condición sine qua non* prerequisite; *condiciones de venta* conditions of sale (**b**) *(estado, circunstancia)* condition; **en buenas/malas condiciones** in good/bad condition ❑ *condiciones del mercado* market conditions; *condiciones óptimas* optimum conditions; *condiciones de trabajo* working conditions; *condiciones de vida* living conditions (**c**) *(calidad)* capacity; **en su condición de abogado** in his capacity as a lawyer

condonación *nf (de deuda)* cancellation, remission

> **"**
>
> El Gobierno tiene pensado aliviar una parte de la deuda que Irak tiene contraída con España. El montante de esa **condonación** dependerá en el futuro de lo que hagan los grandes acreedores del país.
>
> **"**

condonar *vt (deuda)* to cancel, to remit, to release

conducir *vt (dirigir) (empresa)* to manage, to run

conducta *nf* behaviour, conduct

conectado, -a *adj* connected (**a** to); **la impresora está conectada a la red** the printer is connected to the network; **estar conectado a Internet** to be on-line, to be on the Internet

conectar 1 *vt (aparato, mecanismo) (con cables)* to connect (**a** *o* **con** (up) to); INFORM **conectar en red** to network; **conectar la impresora** to put the printer on-line

2 *vi* INFORM **conectar y funcionar** plug and play

3 conectarse *vpr* **conectarse a Internet** *(por primera vez)* to get connected to the Internet, to go on-line; *(regularmente)* to go on the Internet, to go on-line

conexión *nf (eléctrica, informática)* connection; **la conexión a la red eléctrica/telefónica no funciona** the mains/telephone connection doesn't work ❑ *conexión aérea* air link; *conexión por carretera* road link; *conexión ferroviaria, conexión por ferrocarril* rail link; INFORM *conexión a Internet* Internet connection; INFORM *conexión por línea conmutada* dial-up connection; INFORM *conexión por línea telefónica* dial-up connection; *conexión postal* postal link; INFORM *conexión en red* networking; INFORM *conexión con tarifa plana* flat-rate connection; *conexión vía satélite* satellite link

confección *nf* (**a**) *(de ropa)* tailoring, dressmaking; **el ramo de la confección** the clothing *o* US garment industry; **un traje/vestido de confección** a ready-to-wear *o* ready-made *o* esp Br an off-the-peg suit/dress (**b**) *(creación)* **productos de confección artesanal** handicrafts

confederación *nf (de personas, bancos)* confederation ❑ *Confederación Europea de Sindicatos* European Trade Union Confederation; *Confederación Internacional de Sindicatos Libres* International Confederation of Free Trade Unions

conferencia *nf* (**a**) *(charla)* talk, lecture (**sobre** on) (**b**) *(reunión)* conference; **celebrar una conferencia** to hold a conference ❑ *conferencia de prensa* press conference (**c**) *(por teléfono)* (long-distance) call ❑ *conferencia a cobro revertido* Br reverse-charge call, US collect call

confiabilidad *nf Am* reliability

confiable *adj Am* reliable

confianza *nf* (**a**) *(seguridad)* confidence (**en** in); **tengo plena confianza en su trabajo** I have the utmost confidence in her work (**b**) *(fe)* trust; **de confianza** trustworthy; **uno de sus colaboradores de confianza** one of his most trusted associates; **una marca de toda confianza** a very reliable brand

confiar *vi* **confiar en alguien** to trust sb; **confiamos en el triunfo** we are confident of winning; **confío en poder conseguirlo** I am confident of being able to achieve it

confidencial *adj* confidential

confidencialidad *nf* confidentiality ❑ *confidencialidad de los datos* data privacy; *confidencialidad profesional* professional confidentiality

configuración *nf* INFORM configuration, settings

configurar *vt* INFORM to configure

confirmación *nf (de billete, reserva)* confirmation

confirmar *vt (billete, reserva)* to confirm; **ha sido confirmado en el cargo** he has been confirmed in his post

conflictividad *nf* unrest ❏ *conflictividad laboral* industrial unrest; *conflictividad social* social unrest

conflicto *nm* conflict; **entrar en conflicto con** to come into conflict with ❏ *conflicto de intereses* conflict of interests; *conflicto laboral* industrial dispute; *conflicto salarial* pay dispute

conformar *vt (cheque)* to authorize

conformidad *nf* (**a**) *(aprobación)* approval; **dio su conformidad** she gave her consent (**b**) *(acuerdo)* **de** *o* **en conformidad con** in accordance with

congelación *nf Esp* freeze, freezing ❏ *congelación de créditos* credit freeze; *congelación de precios* price freeze; *congelación salarial* pay *o* wage freeze

congelado, -a *adj (precios, salarios, cuenta bancaria)* frozen

congelamiento *nm Am* freeze, freezing ❏ *congelamiento de créditos* credit freeze; *congelamiento de precios* price freeze; *congelamiento salarial* pay *o* wage freeze

congelar *vt (precios, salarios, cuenta bancaria)* to freeze

> ❝ ————————————————
> Tras despedir a 17.000 empleados, Siemens estudia **congelar** el sueldo a unos 40.000 empleados en Alemania con salarios superiores a 5.450 euros mensuales, para reducir costes.
> ———————————————— ❞

conglomerado *nm (de hoteles, empresas)* conglomerate

congreso *nm* (**a**) *(de una especialidad)* conference, congress (**b**) *(asamblea nacional)* **el Congreso (de los Diputados)** *(en España)* = the lower house of the Spanish Parliament; **el Congreso** *(en Estados Unidos)* Congress

conjuntamente *adv* jointly, together

conjunto, -a *adj* joint

conmutador *nm* (**a**) *(interruptor)* switch (**b**) *Am (centralita)* switchboard

conocer 1 *vt* (**a**) *(saber acerca de)* to know; **conocer algo a fondo** to know sth well; **dieron a conocer la noticia a través de la prensa** they announced the news through the press (**b**) *(a una persona) (por primera vez)* to meet; *(desde hace tiempo)* to know; **¿conoces a mi jefe?** do you know *o* have you met my boss?; **ha sido**

un placer conocerlo it was a pleasure to meet you
  2 conocerse *vpr (dos o más personas) (por primera vez)* to meet; *(desde hace tiempo)* to know each other; **nos conocimos en la recepción de la embajada** we met at the ambassador's reception

conocimiento *nm* (**a**) *(documento)* **conocimiento aéreo** air waybill; *conocimiento de embarque* bill of lading; *conocimiento de embarque directo* through bill; *conocimiento de embarque de la empresa* house bill; *conocimiento de embarque limpio* clean bill of lading; *conocimiento de embarque marítimo* marine bill of lading; *conocimiento de embarque (de transporte) combinado* combined transport bill of lading; *conocimiento de entrada* inward bill of lading; *conocimiento exterior* outward bill of lading; *conocimiento de trasbordo* transshipment bill of lading
  (**b**) *(saber, nociones)* MKTG *conocimiento de la competencia* competitive awareness; *conocimientos de informática* computer literacy; MKTG *conocimiento de marca* brand familiarity; *conocimientos de mecanografía* typing skills; MKTG *conocimiento del producto* product awareness

conquista *nf (de mercado, nuevos clientes)* conquest

conquistar *vt (mercado, nuevos clientes)* to conquer

consecución *nf (de objetivo)* attainment

conseguir *vt (obtener)* to obtain, to get; *(objetivo)* to achieve; *(acuerdo, préstamo)* to secure

consejero, -a *nm,f* (**a**) *(en asuntos técnicos)* adviser, consultant (**b**) *(de consejo de administración)* member of the board, director ❏ *consejero delegado* chief executive, *esp Br* managing director, *esp US* chief executive officer (**c**) *Esp (de comunidad autónoma)* minister

> ❝ ————————————————
> Los **consejeros delegados** españoles ven incrementar su salario variable. El pago en especie y la mayor implantación de incentivos a largo plazo, son fórmulas para orientar a los ejecutivos hacia la estrategia global de la compañía.
> ———————————————— ❞

consejo *nm* (**a**) *(advertencia)* advice; **dar un consejo** to give some advice *o* a piece of advice
  (**b**) *(organismo)* council; *(reunión)* meeting ❏ *consejo de administración* board (of directors); *(reunión)* board meeting; *Consejo de Asistencia Mutua Económica* Council for Mutual Economic Aid; *consejo de dirección* board (of directors); *(reunión)* board meeting; *consejo económico* economic council; *Consejo de Europa* Council of Europe; *consejo de gobierno*

governing body; **Consejo de Ministros** *(de gobierno)* cabinet; *(reunión)* cabinet meeting; UE Council of Ministers; **consejo regional** regional council; **consejo sindical** trade union council

consenso *nm* consensus

consensuar *vt* to reach a consensus on; **el comité consensuó finalmente la propuesta del presidente** the committee eventually agreed to approve the president's proposal

consentimiento *nm* consent

consigna *nf (para el equipaje)* Br left-luggage office, US checkroom

consignación *nf* (a) *(de mercancías)* consignment, shipment (b) *Col (en banco)* deposit

consignador *nm* consignor

consignar *vt* (a) *(mercancías)* to consign, to dispatch (b) *(equipaje)* to deposit in the Br left-luggage office *o* US baggage room (c) *Col (dinero)* to deposit

consignatario, -a *nm,f* (a) *(de mercancía)* consignee (b) DER *(de depósito)* trustee (c) *(representante)* **consignatario (de buques)** shipping agent

consola *nf* INFORM console ❑ **consola de videojuegos** video games console

consolidación *nf* (a) FIN consolidation ❑ CONT **consolidación por integración global** full consolidation (b) *(de mercancías)* consolidation

consolidado, -a FIN **1** *adj* consolidated
2 *nm* consolidated annuity

consolidador *nm* consolidator ❑ **consolidador de carga aérea** airfreight consolidator; **consolidador de carga marítima** maritime freight consolidator; **consolidador de transporte por carretera** road haulage consolidator

consolidar 1 *vt* FIN to consolidate
2 consolidarse *vpr (precios)* to strengthen, to harden; *(negocio)* to consolidate its position

> En su opinión, la franquicia española **se está consolidando** y se está produciendo lo que sucede en cualquier mercado maduro: "Sólo las más dinámicas están avanzando posiciones".

consorcio *nm* consortium ❑ **consorcio asegurador** insurance pool; **consorcio bancario** bankers' consortium; **consorcio financiero** financial syndicate

constante *adj (crecimiento, proporción)* steady

constar *vi (información)* to appear, to figure (**en** in); **su nombre no consta en esta lista** his name is not on *o* does not appear on this list; **hacer constar algo** to put sth on record; **hacer**

constar en acta to minute

constitución *nf (de grupo empresarial)* creation, setting up; **constitución en sociedad** incorporation

constituir 1 *vt (negocio)* to establish; *(comité)* to constitute; **constituir una empresa en sociedad** to form *o* incorporate a company
2 constituirse *vpr* **constituirse en sociedad anónima** to become a limited company

construcción *nf* (a) *(de edificio)* construction, building; *(de buque)* building; **en construcción** *(edificio, página web)* under construction (b) *(sector)* construction *o* building industry; **trabajadores de la construcción** construction *o* building workers; **una empresa de la construcción** a construction company ❑ **construcción naval** shipbuilding (c) *(creación)* MKTG **construcción de marca** brand building

consular *adj* consular

consulta *nf (pregunta)* query, question; *(búsqueda de información)* consultation; **hicieron una consulta al abogado de la empresa** they consulted the company lawyer; **la propuesta se encuentra en fase de consulta** the proposal is under consultation; **libros de consulta** reference books

consultar *vt* (a) *(persona)* to consult; **tengo que consultarlo con mi abogado** I have to talk to *o* consult my lawyer about it; **consultar a un abogado** to take legal advice (b) *(buscando información) (dato, fecha)* to look up; *(catálogo, manual)* to refer to; *(libro)* to consult

consultor, -ora 1 *adj* consulting
2 *nm,f* consultant ❑ **consultor (en administración) de empresas** management consultant; **consultor financiero** financial consultant; **consultor fiscal** tax consultant; **consultor jurídico** legal adviser; **consultor de marketing** marketing consultant; **consultor medioambiental, consultor de medio ambiente** environmental consultant; **consultor de publicidad** advertising consultant; **consultor de recursos humanos** human resources consultant

consultoría *nf* (a) *(empresa)* consultancy firm ❑ **consultoría en administración de empresas** management consultancy; **consultoría empresarial, consultoría de empresas** business consultancy; **consultoría fiscal** tax consultancy; **consultoría jurídica** legal consultancy; **consultoría de marketing** marketing consultancy; **consultoría medioambiental, consultoría de medio ambiente** environmental consultancy; **consultoría de recursos humanos** human resources consultancy
(b) *(actividad)* consultancy, consulting

consumidor, -ora *nm,f* consumer ❑ **consumidor final** end consumer; **consumidor objetivo** target consumer

consumismo *nm* consumerism

consumista *adj* consumerist, materialistic

consumo *nm* consumption; **se ha disparado el consumo de agua mineral** sales of mineral water have shot up; **bienes/sociedad de consumo** consumer goods/society ▫ **consumo familiar** household consumption; **consumo global** global consumption, overall consumption; **consumo interior** home consumption; **consumo masivo** mass consumption; **consumo privado** private consumption, consumer spending; **consumo público** public *o* government consumption

contabilidad *nf* (**a**) *(oficio)* accountancy, accounting (**b**) *(actividad)* accounting, bookkeeping; **llevar la contabilidad** to keep the accounts; **doble contabilidad** double-entry bookkeeping ▫ **contabilidad analítica** cost accounting; **contabilidad por actividades** activity accounting; **contabilidad automatizada** automatic accounting; **contabilidad de caja** cash basis accounting; **contabilidad por centros de beneficio** profit-centre accounting; **contabilidad de compras** purchase accounting; **contabilidad de costos** *o Esp* **costes** cost accounting; **contabilidad de costos** *o Esp* **costes corrientes** current cost accounting; **contabilidad de costos** *o Esp* **costes directos** direct cost accounting; **contabilidad de costos** *o Esp* **costes históricos** historical cost accounting; **contabilidad de costos** *o Esp* **costes totales** full cost accounting; **contabilidad creativa** creative accounting; **contabilidad financiera** financial accounting; **contabilidad de fusiones** merger accounting; **contabilidad de fusiones y adquisiciones** acquisition accounting; **contabilidad general** financial accounting; **contabilidad de gestión** management accounting; **contabilidad informatizada** computerized accounting; **contabilidad nacional** national accounting; **contabilidad por partida doble** double-entry bookkeeping; **contabilidad por partida simple** single-entry bookkeeping; **contabilidad uniforme** uniform accounting

contabilización *nf* **contabilización de la amortización** depreciation accounting; **contabilización del fondo de negocio** goodwill accounting

contabilizar *vt* (**a**) *(en contabilidad)* to enter, to record (**b**) *(contar)* to count

contable 1 *adj* countable
2 *nmf Esp* accountant ▫ **contable de costes** cost accountant; **contable financiero** financial accountant; **contable de gestión** management accountant

contactar 1 *vt* to contact
2 *vi* **contactar con alguien** to contact sb

contacto *nm* (**a**) *(entre dos cosas, personas)* contact; **ponerse en contacto con** to get in touch with, to contact ▫ MKTG **contacto en frío** cold calling (**b**) *(persona)* contact; **tiene contactos en el ministerio** he has contacts at the ministry

contado: **al contado** *adj & adv* **precio al contado** cash price; **pagar algo al contado** *(en un plazo)* to pay for sth all at once; *(en metálico)* to pay for sth in cash, to pay cash for sth

contador, -ora 1 *nm,f Am* accountant ▫ **contador de costos** cost accountant; **contador financiero** financial accountant; **contador de gestión** management accountant; **contador público** *Br* chartered accountant, *US* certified public accountant
2 *nm* INFORM **contador de palabras** word count facility

contaduría *nf Am* (**a**) *(profesión)* accountancy ▫ **contaduría general** audit office (**b**) *(oficina)* accountant's office; *(departamento)* accounts office

contar 1 *vt (enumerar)* to count
2 *vi* (**a**) *(hacer cálculos)* to count (**b**) **contar con** *(tener, poseer)* **todos nuestros productos cuentan con una garantía de devolución** all our products feature a money-back guarantee (**c**) **contar con** *(tener en cuenta)* to take into account; **tenemos que contar con un 10% extra para transporte** we have to allow an extra 10% for carriage

contenedor *nm (recipiente grande)* container; **contenedor (de escombros)** *Br* skip, *US* Dumpster® ▫ **contenedor de basura** large wheelie bin; **contenedor de vidrio** bottle bank

contener *vt* (**a**) *(encerrar)* to contain; **no contiene CFC** does not contain CFCs (**b**) *(detener, reprimir) (inflación, salarios)* to keep down

contenerización *nf* containerization

contenerizar *vt* to containerize

contenido *nm* (**a**) *(de recipiente)* contents; **una bebida con un alto contenido alcohólico** a drink with a high alcohol content (**b**) *(de discurso, redacción)* content ▫ **contenido editorial** editorial content

contestación *nf* (**a**) *(respuesta)* answer, reply; **en contestación a su pregunta...** to answer your question...; **se ruega contestación** *(en* *invitación)* RSVP (**b**) *(protesta)* protest, opposition; **contestación social/sindical** social/trade union protest *o* opposition

contestador *nm* **contestador (automático)** answering machine, answerphone

contestar 1 *vt* to reply to, to answer; **contestar a una pregunta** to answer a question; **contestar a una carta** to reply to *o* answer a letter 2 *vi (responder)* to reply, to answer; **no contestan** *(al teléfono)* there's no reply *o* answer

contexto *nm* MKTG **contexto de compra** buying situation

contextual *adj* INFORM context-sensitive

contingencia *nf (eventualidad)* contingency, eventuality

contingente *nm (de importación, exportación, producción)* quota

> **"**
>
> El Consejo de Ministros aprobó en su última reunión de 2002 la revalorización de las pensiones en el próximo año, el **contingente** de trabajadores inmigrantes no comunitarios correspondiente a 2003 y las nuevas tarifas eléctricas. El nuevo **contingente** incluye 10.575 ofertas de empleo estable para el cupo de trabajadores extranjeros que establece la Ley de Extranjería.
>
> **"**

continuo, -a *adj (ininterrumpido)* continuous

contorneo *nm* INFORM **contorneo de texto** text wrap

contrabandear *vi* to smuggle

contrabandista *nmf* smuggler

contrabando *nm* (**a**) *(acto)* smuggling; **tabaco de contrabando** contraband cigarettes; **pasar algo de contrabando** to smuggle sth in □ *contrabando de alcohol* alcohol smuggling; *contrabando de armas* gunrunning; *contrabando de tabaco* cigarette smuggling (**b**) *(mercancías)* contraband

contracción *nf (de economía)* downswing, downturn

> **"**
>
> Hoy, las operaciones en el extranjero representan un 70% de nuestra facturación y la presencia en otros países nos permitió contrarrestar la **contracción** del mercado local, que por otro lado ya está maduro y contiene gran cantidad de canales. Queremos aumentar nuestra presencia en países emergentes y continuar creciendo.
>
> **"**

contractual *adj* contractual

contrademanda *nf* DER counterclaim; **presentar** *o* **interponer una contrademanda (contra**

alguien) to file *o* lodge a counterclaim *o* to counterclaim (against sb)

contraer 1 *vt (deuda)* to incur, to contract 2 **contraerse** *vpr (economía)* to shrink

contralor, -ora *nm,f* Am comptroller □ *Contralor General* Comptroller General

contraloría *nf* Am *(oficina)* comptroller's office □ *Contraloría General* National Audit Office

contraoferta *nf* counter-offer, counterbid

contrapartida *nf* CONT balancing entry, cross entry

contraprestación *nf* consideration; **la cuota mensual da derecho a varias contraprestaciones** the monthly subscription entitles you to a number of benefits

> **"**
>
> El consorcio encabezado por Acciona se ha adjudicado el 99,06% de Transmediterránea una vez cerrado el plazo para acudir a la OPA, que ofrecía una **contraprestación** de 45 euros por título. El consorcio tiene la intención de excluir a la naviera de Bolsa, lo que podría producir una OPA de exclusión.
>
> **"**

contraproducente *adj* counterproductive

contraseña *nf* INFORM password

contrata *nf* (fixed-price) contract

contratación *nf* (**a**) *(de personal)* recruitment, hiring; **la ley contempla diferentes modalidades de contratación** the law provides *o* allows for different forms of recruitment; **es urgente la contratación de un abogado** we urgently need to hire a lawyer; **ha bajado la contratación indefinida** the number of (people in) permanent jobs has gone down; **una empresa de contratación artística** a theatrical agency (**b**) *(de servicio, mercancías) (de hotel)* hiring; *(de vuelo)* chartering □ *contratación de obras* (building) contracting (**c**) BOLSA *(de valores)* trading, Br dealing □ *contratación continua* continuous trading; *contratación electrónica* electronic trading, screen trading; *contratación fuera de hora* after-hours trading; *contratación en el parqué* floor trading

> **"**
>
> La **contratación** de las cuatro Bolsas españolas (Madrid, Barcelona, Valencia y Bilbao) subió hasta los 364.779 millones de euros entre enero y agosto, un 1,15% más que en el mismo periodo del año anterior, según informó la Comisión Nacional del Mercado de Valores (CNMV).
>
> **"**

contratante 1 *adj* contracting; **la parte contratante** the contracting party
  2 *nmf* contracting party

contratar *vt* (**a**) *(personal)* to recruit, to hire (**b**) *(póliza de seguros)* to take out; *(servicio, obra, mercancía)* to contract for (**a** with)

contratista *nmf* contractor □ **contratista de obras** building contractor; **contratistas de obras públicas** public works contractor

contrato *nm* contract; **firmar un contrato** to sign a contract; **romper un contrato** to break (the terms of) a contract; **incumplimiento de contrato** breach of contract; **bajo contrato** under contract; **por contrato** contractually □ BOLSA **contrato abierto** open contract; **contrato de adhesión** contract of adhesion; **contrato administrativo** administrative contract; **contrato de admisión a cotización** listing agreement; **contrato de alquiler** *(de vivienda, local comercial)* lease, tenancy agreement; *(de maquinaria)* lease (agreement); **contrato de aprendizaje** contract of apprenticeship, apprentice contract; **contrato de arrendamiento** *(de vivienda, local comercial)* lease, tenancy agreement; *(de maquinaria)* lease (agreement); **contrato basura** short-term contract *(with poor conditions)*; **contrato blindado** golden parachute, cast-iron contract; **contrato de cesión de cuentas a cobrar** factoring agreement; **contrato colectivo** group contract; **contrato de compra a plazos** *Br* hire-purchase agreement, *US* installment plan agreement; **contrato de compraventa** contract of sale; **contrato de correduría** broker's contract; **contrato de distribución** distribution contract; **contrato de distribución exclusiva** exclusive distribution contract; **contrato de exclusividad** exclusive agreement; **contrato exclusivo** sole contract; **contrato de fideicomiso** trust deed; **contrato fijo** permanent contract; **contrato de franquicia** franchise agreement; BOLSA **contrato de futuros** futures contract; BOLSA **contrato de futuro subyacente** underlying futures contract; **contrato indefinido** permanent contract; **contrato laboral** work contract; **contrato de licencia** licensing agreement; **contrato de mantenimiento** maintenance contract; **contrato matrimonial** marriage contract; **contrato mercantil** commercial contract; **contrato por obra y servicio** = work contract for the duration of a specified project; **contrato de obras** building contract; BOLSA **contrato a plazo** forward contract; **contrato en prácticas** work-experience contract; **contrato privado** private contract; **contrato psicológico** psychological contract; BOLSA **contrato de recompra** buyback agreement; **contrato de representación exclusiva** sole agency contract; **contrato de servicios** service agreement *o* contract; **contrato simple** simple contract;

contrato social social contract; **contrato temporal,** *Am* **contrato temporario** temporary *o* short-term *o* fixed-term contract; BOLSA **contrato a término** forward contract; **contrato a tiempo completo** full-time contract; **contrato a tiempo parcial** part-time contract; **contrato de trabajo** employment contract, contract of employment, *US* labor contract; **contrato de transporte** contract of carriage; **contrato de venta** sales contract; **contrato verbal** verbal contract

contribución *nf* (**a**) *(impuesto)* tax; **contribuciones** taxes, taxation; **exento de contribuciones** tax-exempt; **contribuciones a la Seguridad Social** social security contributions □ **contribución directa** direct tax; **contribución indirecta** indirect tax; **contribución rústica** land tax; **contribución urbana** = tax for local services, ≃ council tax (**b**) *(colaboración)* contribution

contribuidor, -ora *nm,f* **contribuidor neto** net contributor

contribuir *vi* (**a**) *(aportar dinero)* to contribute; **contribuyó con 100 millones** he contributed 100 million (**b**) *(colaborar)* to contribute; **todos contribuyeron al triunfo** everyone contributed to the victory

contribuyente *nmf* taxpayer

control *nm (dominio)* control; *(comprobación, verificación)* examination, inspection; **bajo control** under control; **todos los productos pasan un riguroso control** all the products are rigorously inspected *o* examined; **se encarga del control del gasto** he is in charge of controlling expenditure □ INFORM **control de acceso** access control; **control accionarial** controlling interest, controlling share; **control aduanero** customs control; **control de alquileres** rent control; **control de calidad** quality control; **control de calidad total** total quality control; **control de cambios** exchange control; **control de contabilidad** accounting control; **control de costos** *o Esp* **costes** cost control; **control crediticio** credit control; **control de crédito** credit control; INFORM **control del cursor** cursor control; **control estatal** state control; **control de existencias** *Br* stock *o US* inventory control; **control financiero** financial control; **control de gestión** management control; **control de importaciones** import control; **control interno** internal check, internal control; **control monetario** monetary control; **control monopolístico** monopoly control; **control de precios** price control; **control presupuestario** budgetary control; **control de la producción** production control; *Méx* **control de rentas** rent control; **control de stock** *Br* stock *o US* inventory control

> "
> La firma no descarta que se puedan producir movimientos corporativos en el sector en los próximos meses. En su opinión, "el **control accionarial** sigue siendo un problema, ya que los bancos son los accionistas de referencia de las cuatro compañías que cubrimos, pero esta situación podría cambiar este año por la actividad de consolidación".
> "

controlado, -a adj controlled; **controlado por el Estado** state-controlled

controlador, -ora 1 nm,f (persona) controller **2** nm INFORM driver □ **controlador de disco** disk driver; **controlador de impresora** printer driver

controlar vt (organización, gastos, calidad) to control; **la empresa controla el 30% del mercado** the company controls 30% of the market; **medidas para controlar los precios** measures to control prices

convención nf (a) (acuerdo) convention □ **la Convención de Ginebra** the Geneva Convention (b) (asamblea) convention

convenido, -a adj (día, fecha, lugar) agreed; **hicieron lo convenido** they did what they'd agreed

convenio nm agreement □ **convenio aduanero** tariff agreement; IND **convenio colectivo** collective agreement; **convenio de crédito** credit agreement; **convenio de doble imposición** double taxation treaty; **convenio salarial** wage agreement o settlement

convergencia nf ECON convergence

> "
> A menos que se centre toda la atención en lo que los expertos llaman "**convergencia nominal**" —y el enfoque de Brown no lo hace—, el debate se centra en si deshacerse de la libra y sustituirla por el euro proporciona un entorno económico superior.
> "

conversación nf (a) (acción de hablar) conversation (b) **conversaciones** (negociaciones) talks

conversacional adj INFORM (modo) conversational

conversión nf (a) FIN (de valores) conversion □ **conversión de la deuda en capital** debt equity swap; **conversión de moneda** currency conversion (b) INFORM **conversión de archivos** file conversion; **conversión de datos** data conversion

convertibilidad nf FIN convertibility

convertible adj FIN (bono, moneda) convertible

convertir vt (a) FIN (bonos, valores, divisas) to convert (b) INFORM (archivos) to convert

convocante 1 adj **las organizaciones convocantes de la manifestación** the organizations that organized the demonstration **2** nmf (de reunión) convener; (de protesta) organizer; **los convocantes de la huelga** the people who called the strike

convocar vt (a) (reunión) to convene; **convocaron a los accionistas a junta** the shareholders were called to a meeting, a shareholders' meeting was convened (b) (huelga, elecciones) to call; (manifestación) to organize; **convocar a alguien a una manifestación** to call on sb to demonstrate o to attend a demonstration; **convocar a alguien a la huelga** to call sb out on strike

cookie nm o nf INFORM cookie

cooperativa nf (sociedad) co-operative □ **cooperativa agrícola** agricultural co-operative, farming co-operative; **cooperativa de crédito** credit union; **cooperativa mayorista** wholesale co-operative; **cooperativa de minoristas** retailer co-operative; **cooperativa obrera** workers' co-operative; **cooperativa de productores** producers' co-operative; **cooperativa de viviendas** housing co-operative

cooptación nf co-opting; **elegir a alguien por cooptación** to co-opt somebody

> "
> De paso, la CNMV ha suspendido en el ejercicio de su cargo a los cuatro consejeros de Bami en Metrovacesa: Joaquín Rivero Valcarce, Manuel González García, Ignacio López del Hierro y José Gracia Barba, designados por **cooptación** el pasado 19 de julio de 2002, cuando Joaquín Rivero, presidente de Bami, compró el 23,9% de Metrovacesa que estaba en poder del BBVA.
> "

coordinación nf (de esfuerzos, medios, trabajo) coordination

coordinador, -ora nm,f coordinator □ **coordinador de congresos** conference coordinator

coordinar vt (esfuerzos, medios, trabajo) to coordinate

copia nf (a) (reproducción) copy; **hacer una copia de algo** to duplicate sth □ **copia certificada** certified copy; **copia compulsada** attested copy; **copia fiel** true copy; **copia en limpio** fair copy; **copia notarial** notarized copy; **copia en papel** paper copy; **copia de trabajo** working copy (b) INFORM **copia de archivo** archive copy; **copia impresa** printout; **copia maestra** master copy; **copia de seguridad** backup (copy); **copia de seguridad en cinta** tape backup

copiar vt (a) (transcribir) to copy; **copie este texto a máquina** type up (a copy of) this text (b) INFORM to copy; **copiar y pegar algo** to copy and paste sth

coprocesador *nm* INFORM coprocessor ❑ **coprocesador matemático** maths coprocessor

copropiedad *nf (de empresa)* joint ownership, co-ownership; *(multipropiedad)* timesharing

copropietario, -a *nm,f* co-owner, joint owner

copyright *nm* copyright

corchete *nm* (**a**) *(signo ortográfico)* square bracket (**b**) *Chile (para papeles)* staple

corchetear *vt Chile* to staple

corchetera *nf Chile* stapler ❑ **corchetera industrial** staple gun

corona *nf (moneda)* **corona (danesa)** (Danish) krone; **corona (noruega)** (Norwegian) krone

corporación *nf* (**a**) *(organismo público)* corporation, authority ❑ **Corporación Financiera Internacional** International Finance Corporation; **corporaciones locales** local authorities (**b**) *(empresa)* corporation

corporatismo *nm* corporatism

corporatista *adj* corporatist

corporativo, -a *adj* corporate

corrección *nf (de error)* correction ❑ INFORM **corrección de color** colour correction; **corrección de mercado** market correction; *Andes* FIN **corrección monetaria** monetary correction, monetary adjustment

correcto, -a *adj (resultado, texto, información)* correct

corrector, -ora 1 *nm,f (persona)* **corrector de estilo** copy editor
2 *nm (líquido)* correction fluid, Tipp-Ex® ❑ INFORM **corrector de estilo** stylechecker; **corrector de gramática** grammar checker; **corrector ortográfico** spell-checker

corredor, -ora *nm,f* **corredor de apuestas** bookmaker; **corredor de bolsa** stockbroker, broker; **corredor de comercio** registered broker, exchange broker; **corredor de fincas** land agent; **corredor de letras de cambio** bill broker; **corredor de parqué** floor trader; **corredor de productos básicos** commodity broker, commodity dealer; **corredor de seguros** insurance broker

correduría *nf (de bolsa)* brokerage ❑ **correduría de seguros** *(oficina)* insurance broker's

corregir *vt (error)* to correct; INFORM **corregir automáticamente** to autocorrect

correo *nm* (**a**) *(sistema, cartas)* Br post, US mail; **a vuelta de correo** by return (of post); **echar algo al correo** to Br post o US mail sth; **mandar algo por correo** to send sth by Br post o US mail ❑ **correo aéreo** airmail; INFORM **correo basura** junk mail, spam; INFORM **correo caracol** snail mail; **correo certificado** Br recorded delivery, US registered mail; **correo comercial** direct mail; INFORM **correo electrónico** electronic mail, e-mail; **me envió un correo (electrónico)** she e-mailed me, she sent me an e-mail; **me mandó la información por correo electrónico** she e-mailed me the information, she sent me the information by e-mail; **correo entrante** incoming mail; **correo interno** internal mail; **correo postal** ordinary mail; **enviar algo por correo postal** to send sth by Br post o US mail; **correo recibido** incoming mail; Am **correo recomendado** Br registered post, US registered mail; **correo saliente** outgoing mail; **correo terrestre** surface mail; INFORM **correo tortuga, correo tradicional** snail mail; **correo urgente** = special postal service for domestic or international mail which ensures quicker delivery for a higher fee; INFORM **correo de voz** voice mail
(**b**) Am *(organismo)* the Post Office, US the Postal Service; **tengo que ir al correo** I have to go to the post office

Correos *nm Esp (organismo)* the Post Office, US the Postal Service; **tengo que ir a Correos** I have to go to the post office

correr 1 *vi* (**a**) **correr con** *(gastos)* to bear, to meet; *(cuenta)* to pay; **la comida corre a cargo de la empresa** the meal is on the company; **la organización del congreso corrió a cargo de nuestra empresa** our company organized the conference, our company took care of the organization of the conference
(**b**) *(sueldo, renta)* to be payable; **el alquiler corre desde principios de cada mes** the rent is payable at the beginning of each month
(**c**) INFORM *(programa, aplicación)* to run
2 *vt* (**a**) *(riesgo)* to run, to incur; **correr el riesgo de (hacer) algo** to run the risk of (doing) sth (**b**) INFORM *(programa, aplicación)* to run; **no consigo correr este programa** I can't get this program to run properly

correspondencia *nf (relación por correo)* correspondence; *(cartas)* Br mail, US post

corresponder 1 *vi (competer)* **corresponderle a alguien hacer algo** to be sb's responsibility to do sth; **no me corresponde a mí enjuiciar su trabajo** it's not my place to judge his work
2 **corresponderse** *vpr* (**a**) *(escribirse)* to correspond (**b**) *(ser equivalente)* to correspond (**con/a** with/to); **ambas cantidades no se corresponden** the two figures don't correspond

corresponsal *nmf* PRENSA correspondent ❑ **corresponsal de negocios** business correspondent

corretaje *nm* (**a**) *(trabajo)* brokerage, broking ❑ **corretaje electrónico** e-broking (**b**) *(comisión)* broker's commission

> ❝
> En los países desarrollados, se espera que la mitad de todas las actividades bancarias y el 80% de todas las actividades de

corretaje se efectúen en línea. Para las economías emergentes, las cifras van del 30% para las operaciones bancarias electrónicas al 40% para el **corretaje electrónico.**

"

corriente 1 adj (**a**) (cuenta) current (**b**) (mes, año) current

2 nf (tendencia) trend, current; BOLSA **una corriente alcista/bajista** an upward/downward trend

3 nm (mes en curso) **el 10 del corriente** the 10th of this month

4 al corriente adv **estoy al corriente del pago de la hipoteca** I'm up to date with my mortgage repayments; **estoy al corriente de la marcha de la empresa** I'm aware of how the company is doing; **mantener/poner a alguien al corriente (de algo)** to bring/keep sb up to date (on sth); **tenemos que poner al corriente nuestras bases de datos** we have to bring our databases up to date; **ponerse al corriente** to bring oneself up to date

corro nm BOLSA ring, US pit; **el ambiente en los corros bursátiles madrileños era de pesimismo** traders in the Madrid stock exchange were in a pessimistic mood ❑ **corro a viva voz** open outcry

corromper INFORM **1** vt to corrupt

2 corromperse vpr to become corrupted

cortafuegos nm inv INFORM firewall

cortar 1 vt (**a**) (recortar) (gastos) to cut back (**b**) INFORM to cut; **cortar y pegar** cut and paste

2 vi (interrumpirse) **se cortó la comunicación** I was/we were etc cut off; **la comunicación telefónica se cortó por culpa de la tormenta** the phone lines went down because of the storm

corte nm (**a**) (pausa) break ❑ **corte publicitario** commercial break (**b**) Am (reducción) cut, cutback ❑ **corte presupuestario** budget cut; **corte salarial** wage o pay cut

cortesía nf (obsequio) **el vino es cortesía del restaurante** the wine comes with the compliments of the house

corto, -a adj **a corto plazo** short-term

coseguro nm co-insurance

costar vi (dinero) to cost; **¿cuánto cuesta?** how much is it?; **me costó 300 pesos** it cost me 300 pesos; **costó muy barato** it was very cheap

costas nfpl DER **costas (judiciales)** legal expenses

coste = costo

costeo nm **costeo por absorción** absorption costing; **costeo total** full costing

costo, Esp **coste** nm (de producción) cost; (de un objeto) price; **cuatro semanas de prueba sin costo alguno** four weeks on approval free of charge; **la relación costo-beneficio** the cost-

benefit ratio; **al costo** at cost ❑ **costos above-the-line** above-the-line costs; **costos por actividades** activity-based costing; **costos acumulados** cumulative costs; **costos de administración** administration costs; **costos administrativos** administrative costs; **costo de adquisición** acquisition cost; **costos de almacenaje** warehousing costs; **costo del capital** capital cost; **costos de cierre** (de negocio) closing-down costs; **costos de compra** purchasing costs; **costos de conservación** (de bienes) holding costs; **costos controlados** managed costs; BOLSA **costo de conversión** conversion cost; **costo corriente** current cost; **costos de desarrollo** development costs; **costo diferencial** marginal cost; **costo directo** direct cost; **costos discrecionales** discretionary costs; **costo de distribución** distribution cost; **costo económico** economic cost; **costo efectivo** actual cost; **costos de entrada** (de embarcación) inward charges; **costos escalonados** step costs; **costo estándar** standard cost; **costos de explotación** operating costs; **costo de fabricación** manufacturing cost; **costos fijos** fixed costs; **costo fijo total** total fixed cost; **costos de financiación** finance costs; **costo financiero** financial cost; **costo histórico** historical cost; **costo incremental** incremental cost; **costo indirecto** indirect cost; **costos iniciales** initial o starting costs; **costo de la mano de obra** labour cost; **costo de mano de obra directa** direct labour cost; **costo de mantenimiento** maintenance cost; **costo marginal** marginal cost; **costo medio ponderado** weighted average cost; **costo neto** net cost; **costo objetivo** target cost; **costo oculto** hidden cost; **costo de oportunidad** opportunity cost; **costos de producción** production costs; **costos de promoción** promotional costs; **costos publicitarios** advertising costs; **costo real** real cost; **costo de reposición** replacement cost; **costo, seguro y flete** cost, insurance and freight; **costos semivariables** mixed costs; **costo social** social cost; **coste total de distribución** total distribution cost; **costos de transacción** transaction costs; **costos de transporte** transport costs; **costo unitario** unit cost; **costo unitario medio,** Am **costo unitario promedio** average unit cost; **costo unitario total** total unit cost; **costos variables** variable costs; **costo de ventas** cost of sales; **costo de (la) vida** cost of living

cotejar vt to collate

cotidiano, -a adj daily; **el trabajo cotidiano** day-to-day tasks

cotización nf (**a**) BOLSA price, quotation; **la cotización de apertura/al cierre** the opening/closing price; **ha mejorado la cotización del euro** the euro has strengthened; **el barril de petróleo alcanzó una cotización de 19 dólares** the

price of oil reached 19 dollars a barrel ❑ *cotiza-ciones al cierre* closing quotations; *cotización al contado* spot quotation; *cotización inme-diata* actual quotation; *cotización en el merca-do* market quotation; *cotización nominal* nominal quote; *cotización oficial* official quo-tation; *cotización a plazo, cotización a térmi-no (de cambio de divisa)* forward rate
　(**b**) *(de trabajador, empresa)* contribution ❑ *coti-zación a la Seguridad Social* social security contribution

cotizado, -a *adj* BOLSA *(acción, empresa)* listed, *Br* quoted

cotizar 1 *vt* (**a**) BOLSA *(valorar)* to list, *Br* to quote; **las acciones de la empresa cotizan cinco en-teros menos que ayer** the company's shares are five points down on yesterday (**b**) *(pagar)* to pay; **cotiza un 5% de su salario a la seguri-dad social** she pays 5 % of her salary in national insurance contributions
　2 *vi* (**a**) *(pagar)* to contribute; **los trabajadores tienen que cotizar a la seguridad social** em-ployees have to pay Social Security contribu-tions (**b**) BOLSA *(empresa, valores)* **cotizar en Bolsa** to be listed *o Br* quoted on the Stock Ex-change; **sus acciones cotizan a 10 euros** their shares are listed *o Br* quoted at 10 euros; **cotizar al alza** to bull
　3 cotizarse *vpr (valores, bonos)* **cotizarse a 20 euros** to be listed *o Br* quoted at 20 euros; **el dó-lar se cotiza a un euro** one dollar is worth one euro

❝────────────────

Tras conocerse la decisión, los precios del petróleo se desplomaron hasta su nivel más bajo de los últimos cinco meses. El ba-rril del brent llegó a **cotizar** a 23,35 dólares. Una vez asimilada la decisión, el petróleo se recuperó hasta volver a superar los 24 dó-lares, en los niveles similares a los de la vís-pera.

────────────────❞

couché *adj* **papel couché** coated (magazine) paper

coyuntura *nf* **coyuntura económica** economic situation *o* climate

cpp INFORM (*abrev de* **caracteres por pulgada**) cpi

cps INFORM (*abrev de* **caracteres por segundo**) cps

CPT (*abrev de* **Carriage Paid To**) CPT

CPU *nf* INFORM (*abrev de* **Central Processing Unit**) CPU

crack, crash *nm* FIN crash; **el crack del '29** the Wall Street Crash ❑ *crack bursátil* stock mar-ket crash

creación *nf (de empleo, mercado, riqueza)* crea-tion; *(de sistema, empresa)* setting up, establish-ment; **la creación de páginas Web** the creation

of Web pages, Web page authoring ❑ MKTG *crea-ción de imagen* image building; *creación de va-lor* value creation

creador, -ora *nm,f* BOLSA *creador de mercado* market maker; *creador de opinión* opinion for-mer *o* leader

crear *vt (empleo, mercado, riqueza)* to create; *(sis-tema, empresa)* to set up, to establish

creatividad *nf* creativity

creativo, -a 1 *adj* creative
　2 *nm,f* **creativo (de publicidad)** copywriter, creative

crecer *vi* to grow; **nuestra cuota de mercado ha crecido en un 5% en el último año** our mar-ket share has grown by 5% in the last year

crecimiento *nm* growth ❑ *crecimiento de beneficios* earnings growth; *crecimiento del capital* capital growth; *crecimiento cero* zero growth; *crecimiento económico* economic growth; *crecimiento interno* internal growth; *crecimiento mediante adquisiciones* external growth; *crecimiento del mercado* market growth; *crecimiento nulo* zero growth; *creci-miento orgánico* organic growth; *crecimiento de la población* population growth; *crecimien-to sostenible* sustainable growth; *crecimiento de ventas* sales growth

❝────────────────

El Producto Interior Bruto (PIB) de la zona euro registró un **crecimiento nulo** en el pri-mer trimestre del año en relación al periodo anterior, según las estimaciones difundidas hoy por la Oficina Europea de Estadísticas (Eurostat), que confirma las cifras provisio-nales publicadas el 15 de mayo.

────────────────❞

crediticio, -a *adj* credit; **entidad crediticia** credit institution, lender

❝────────────────

En la evolución de Banesto en el primer tri-mestre, destacó el crecimiento del 13,7 por ciento en su inversión **crediticia** total, que ascendía a 29.591 millones de euros al tér-mino de marzo, y sobre todo resaltó el incre-mento del 16,8% en la concesión de préstamos al sector privado y del 36% en hipotecas.

────────────────❞

crédito *nm (posibilidad de obtener dinero)* credit; *(préstamo)* loan; **(comprar algo) a crédito** (to buy sth) on credit; **pedir un crédito** to ask for a loan ❑ *crédito abierto* open-ended credit; *crédito ampliado* extended credit; *Méx crédito de avío* agricultural loan; *crédito bancario* bank loan; **continúa el crecimiento en el crédito bancario** bank lending continues to grow; *crédito blando* soft loan; SEGUR *crédito y*

caución credit and suretyship insurance; **crédito comercial** trade credit; **crédito de comprador** buyer credit; **crédito al consumo** consumer credit; **crédito contingente** standby credit; **crédito a corto plazo** short-term credit; **crédito en cuenta** account credit; **crédito al desarrollo** development loan; **crédito en descubierto** overdrawn credit facility; **crédito de descuento** discount loan; **crédito diferido** deferred credit; **crédito documentario** documentary credit; **crédito dudoso** doubtful loan; **crédito de empalme** bridging loan; **crédito a la exportación** export credit; **crédito fiscal** tax credit; **crédito gratuito** free credit; **crédito hipotecario** mortgage (loan); **crédito horario** time in lieu, US compensatory time; **crédito a la importación** import credit/loan; **crédito incobrable** non-performing loan; **crédito inmobiliario** mortgage, property loan; **crédito interbancario** interbank loan; **crédito sin intereses** interest-free credit/loan; **crédito a largo plazo** long-term credit/loan; **crédito a medio plazo** medium-term credit/loan, intermediate credit/loan; **crédito oficial** official credit/loan; **crédito permanente** permanent credit; **crédito personal** personal loan; **crédito a plazo fijo** fixed-term credit/loan; **crédito a plazos** instalment loan; **crédito preferencial** preferential credit; **créditos presupuestarios** budget appropriations; **crédito prorrogado** extended credit; **crédito de proveedor** supplier credit; **crédito provisional** provisional loan, conditional loan; **crédito puente** bridge loan, bridging loan; **crédito renovable de interés variable** rollover credit; **crédito rotativo** revolving credit; **crédito sindicado** syndicated loan; **crédito transferible** transferable credit/loan; **crédito vivienda** home loan

crisis nf inv crisis; **la crisis en el mercado de valores** the stock market crisis ❑ **crisis bursátil** market crisis; **crisis de desempleo** unemployment crisis; **crisis del dólar** dollar crisis; **crisis económica** economic crisis, recession; **crisis energética** energy crisis; **crisis financiera** financial crisis; **crisis de mercado** market crisis; **crisis del petróleo** oil crisis

criterio nm (norma) criterion; **celebraron una reunión para unificar criterios** they held a meeting to agree on their criteria ❑ UE **criterios de convergencia** convergence criteria; **criterios de seguridad** safety standards; **criterios de selección** selection criteria

crónico, -a adj (escasez, desempleo) chronic

crudo, -a 1 adj (petróleo) crude
  2 nm crude (oil) ❑ **crudo brent** Brent crude

cruzado, -a adj (cheque) crossed

cruzar vt (cheque) to cross

cuadrar 1 vi (números, cuentas) to tally, to add up, to agree; **tus cálculos no cuadran con los míos**

your calculations don't tally with mine; **estas cuentas no cuadran** these accounts don't balance
  2 vt (cuentas) to balance

cuadro nm (**a**) (en una empresa) **cuadros dirigentes** top management, senior executives; **cuadros intermedios** middle management; **cuadros de mando** top management, senior executives; **cuadros medios** middle management
  (**b**) (gráfico) chart, diagram ❑ **cuadro de análisis por funciones** funtional analysis chart; **cuadro sinóptico** tree diagram
  (**c**) INFORM box ❑ **cuadro de cierre** close box; **cuadro de diálogo** dialog box; **cuadro de selección** selection box
  (**d**) **en cuadro: la empresa está en cuadro tras la marcha del equipo directivo** the company has been caught seriously short after its entire management team left

> ❝
>
> La eficacia de una economía moderna se basa, en gran medida, en sus técnicos y **cuadros medios**. Este tipo de formación tiene la ventaja de que se adapta a las pequeñas y medianas empresas, que constituyen la trama de casi todos los países de América Latina; sin embargo, estos **cuadros** no se han desarrollado suficientemente en la región. Una causa por la cual la formación técnica profesional, por lo menos en México, no ha producido los resultados que de ella se esperaban, pese al gran interés de los actores de la vida económica, es la atracción que ejerce la licenciatura como el único nivel profesional socialmente prestigiado.
>
> ❞

cualidad nf quality; **las cualidades que buscamos en nuestros candidatos** the qualities we are looking for in our candidates

cualificado, -a adj skilled

cualitativo, -a adj qualitative

cuantía nf (**a**) (suma) amount, quantity; **una cuantía sin precisar** an unspecified amount (**b**) (alcance) extent; **un problema de menor cuantía** a relatively insignificant o minor problem (**c**) DER claim, amount claimed

cuantificar vt to quantify

cuantitativo, -a adj quantitative

cuartil nm quartile

cuarto, -a 1 núm fourth; **la cuarta parte** a quarter ❑ **el cuarto mundo** the Fourth World; **cuarto trimestre** fourth quarter
  2 nm (parte) quarter

cuasidinero nm, Arg **cuasimoneda** nf BOLSA near money

cubierto, -a *adj* (**a**) BOLSA *(posición)* covered (**b**) **estar a cubierto** *(con saldo acreedor)* to be in the black (**c**) *(vacante)* filled

cubrir *vt* (**a**) *(proteger)* to cover; **esta póliza nos cubre contra cualquier accidente** this policy covers us against all accidents (**b**) *(gastos)* to cover; **el presupuesto no cubre todos los gastos** the budget doesn't cover all the expenses; **cubrir gastos** *(exactamente)* to break even (**c**) *(puesto, vacante)* to fill; **hay veinte solicitudes para cubrir tres plazas** there are twenty applications for three jobs

cuelgue *nm Fam* INFORM crash

cuello *nm* **cuello de botella** bottleneck

cuenta *nf* (**a**) *(depósito de dinero)* account; **abrir/cerrar una cuenta** to open/close an account; **abónelo/cárguelo en mi cuenta, por favor** please credit/debit *o* charge it to my account; **me han abonado el sueldo en cuenta** they've paid my salary into my account; **he cargado el recibo en tu cuenta** I've charged the bill to your account; **ingresó el cheque en su cuenta** she paid the cheque into her account ❑ **cuenta abierta** active account; **cuenta de afectación** appropriation account; **cuenta de agio** agio account; *Esp* **cuenta de ahorros** savings account; *Esp* **cuenta de ahorro vivienda** = tax-exempt savings account used for paying deposit on a house; **cuenta de anticipos** imprest account; **cuenta bancaria** bank account; **cuenta de caja** cash account; **cuenta de capital** capital account; **cuenta de cliente** BANCA customer account; *(con gestor de inversiones)* client account; **cuenta comercial** business account; **cuenta de compensación** clearing account; **cuenta conjunta** joint account; **cuenta corriente** *Br* current account, *US* checking account; **cuenta de crédito** credit account; **cuenta de custodia** trust account; **cuenta de depósito** deposit account; **cuenta de depósito en garantía** escrow account; **cuenta en descubierto** overdrawn account; BOLSA short account; **cuenta discrecional** discretionary account; **cuenta en divisas** foreign currency account; **cuenta de explotación** operating statement; **cuenta extranjera** foreign account; **cuenta de fideicomiso** trust account; **cuenta fiduciaria** fiduciary account; **cuenta de giros** giro account; **cuenta inactiva** dead *o* dormant account; **cuenta indistinta** joint account; **cuenta de inversiones** investment account; **cuenta mancomunada** joint account; **cuenta numerada** numbered account; **cuenta personal** personal account; **cuenta a plazo fijo** deposit account; **cuenta de plica** escrow account; **cuenta de no residente** external account, non-resident account; **cuenta de reserva** reserve account; **cuenta transitoria** suspense account; **cuenta a la vista** instant access account; *Esp* **cuenta vivienda** =

tax-exempt savings account used for paying deposit on a house

(**b**) CONT **cuentas** *(ingresos y gastos)* accounts; **las cuentas de esta empresa no son nada transparentes** this company's books *o* accounts are not very transparent; **llevar las cuentas** to keep the books; **cuentas por cobrar/pagar** accounts receivable/payable ❑ **cuenta acreedora** *(con acreedor)* creditor account; *(con crédito)* account with a credit balance; **cuentas anuales** annual accounts; **cuentas anuales definitivas** final accounts; **cuentas certificadas** certified accounts; **cuenta de cliente** trade debtor account; **cuenta por** *o* **a cobrar** account receivable; **cuenta de compras** purchase account; **cuenta de conciliación** reconciliation account; **cuentas consolidadas** consolidated accounts; **cuenta de contrapartida** contra account; **cuenta de control** control account; **cuenta corriente de la balanza de pagos** external account; **cuentas por debajo de la línea** below-the-line accounts; **cuenta detallada** itemized account; **cuenta deudora** *(con deudor)* debtor account; *(con deudas)* account with a debit balance; **cuenta de existencias** inventory *o Br* stock account; **cuenta de explotación** trading account, *US* operating account; **cuenta de explotación y resultados** trading and profit and loss account; **cuenta de gastos** expense account; **cuentas de gastos de explotación** operational cost accounts; **cuenta general de gastos** nominal account; **cuentas generales** general accounts; **cuentas de gestión** management accounts; **cuenta de ingresos y gastos** income and expenditure account; **cuentas nacionales** national accounts; **cuenta de orden** memo account; **cuenta a** *o* **por pagar** account payable; **cuentas de patrimonio** equity accounts; **cuenta pendiente** outstanding account; **cuenta de pérdidas y ganancias** *Br* profit and loss account *o* statement, *US* income account *o* statement; **cuentas de periodificación** accrual accounts; **cuenta de producción** manufacturing account; **cuenta provisional de resultados** *Br* interim profit and loss statement, *US* interim income statement; **cuenta rendida** account rendered; **cuenta de resultados** *Br* profit and loss account *o* statement, *US* income account *o* statement; **cuenta de resultados consolidada** consolidated profit and loss account, *US* consolidated income statement; **cuenta subsidiaria** subsidiary account; **cuenta de tesorería** cash statement; **cuenta transitoria** clearing account, suspense accounts; **cuenta de ventas** sales account

(**c**) *(cliente, negocio)* account; **se encarga de las grandes cuentas de la empresa** she looks after the company's most important accounts ❑ **cuenta clave** key account; **cuenta institucional** agency account; **cuenta de publicidad** advertising account (**d**) *(de electricidad, teléfono)* bill; *(en restaurante)* *Br* bill, *US* check; **¡la cuenta, por favor!** could I have the *Br* bill *o US* check, please?; **pagar 10 euros a cuenta** to pay 10 euros down; **pasar la cuenta** to send the bill

(**e**) *(acción de contar)* count; **tenemos que hacer cuentas de los gastos** we have to tot up *o* work out what we've spent; **vamos a echar cuentas de cuánto te debo** let's work out how much I owe you; **llevar la cuenta** to keep count; **salir a cuenta** to work out cheaper

(**f**) INFORM account ❏ *cuenta con acceso telefónico* dial-up account; *cuenta de correo (electrónico)* e-mail account; *cuenta por línea conmutada* dial-up account

(**g**) *(responsabilidad)* **el vino corre de mi cuenta** the wine's on me; **trabajar por cuenta propia/ajena** to be self-employed/an employee; **el número de trabajadores por cuenta propia** the number of self-employed

cuentapropista *nmf RP* self-employed person

> " ────────
>
> Los **cuentapropistas** tuvieron su momento de auge con la privatización de las empresas públicas a comienzos de los 90. Por entonces muchos cobraron la indemnización o se anotaron en los retiros voluntarios para intentar otro tipo de salida. En aquellos años se multiplicaron en Buenos Aires las canchas de padel, las cadenas de lavado de ropa y los maxiquioscos. Pero hacia finales de la década, el avance de los shoppings y los hipermercados que expresan la concentración del comercio en pocas manos terminó con la ilusión de mucha gente de trabajar de manera independiente.
>
> ──────── "

cuerpo *nm* (**a**) *(de documento)* body (**b**) TIP point; **letra de cuerpo diez** ten point font

cuestionar *vt* to query, to question

cuestionario *nm* questionnaire ❏ MKTG *cuestionario piloto* pilot questionnaire; *cuestionario de satisfacción del cliente* customer satisfaction questionnaire

CUFIN *nf Méx* (*abrev de* **Cuenta de Utilidad Fiscal Neta**) net tax income account

CUIL *nm* (*abrev de* **Código Único de Identificación Laboral**) Unique Work Identification Number, = identification number given to all employees in Argentina for tax and social security purposes

CUIT *nm* (*abrev de* **Código Único de IdentificaciónTributaria**) UniqueTax Identification Code = tax identification number in Argentina

cultura *nf* *(en empresa)* culture ❏ *cultura empresarial* *(de empresa)* corporate culture; *(en la sociedad)* enterprise culture

cumbre *nf (reunión)* summit; **la cumbre del G7** the G7 summit

cumplimentar *vt (impreso)* to fill in *o* out

cumplimiento *nm* (**a**) *(de contrato, obligaciones)* fulfilment; *(de la ley)* observance; *(de órdenes)* carrying out; **en cumplimiento del artículo 34** in compliance with article 34; **una disposición de obligado cumplimiento** a compulsory regulation (**b**) *(de objetivo)* achievement, fulfilment (**c**) *(de plazo)* expiry

cumplir 1 *vt (contrato, obligaciones)* to fulfil; *(ley)* to observe; *(orden)* to carry out; *(objetivo)* to achieve; **cumplí las instrucciones al pie de la letra** I followed the instructions to the letter; **los que no cumplan las normas serán sancionados** anyone failing to comply with *o* abide by the rules will be punished; **esta máquina cumple todos los requisitos técnicos** this machine complies with *o* meets all the technical requirements; **los candidatos deben cumplir los siguientes requisitos** the candidates must meet *o* satisfy the following requirements; **hacer cumplir algo** to enforce sth

2 *vi* (**a**) *(plazo, garantía)* to expire; **el plazo de matriculación ya ha cumplido** the deadline for registration is already up *o* has already expired (**b**) **cumplir con** *(norma, condición)* to comply with, to meet; *(obligación)* to fulfil; **este producto no cumple con la normativa europea** this product doesn't comply with *o* meet European standards; **varios países cumplen con los requisitos para acceder al mercado único** several countries fulfil the criteria *o* meet the terms for joining the single market

3 cumplirse *vpr* **mañana se cumple el plazo de presentación de solicitudes** the deadline for applications expires tomorrow

cuña *nf (de radio)* short advertisement

cuota *nf* (**a**) *(contribución)* *(a entidad, club)* membership fee, subscription; *(a Hacienda)* tax (payment); *(a sindicato)* dues ❏ *cuota de abono (de teléfono)* line rental; *cuota de admisión* admission fee; *cuotas de amortización* amortization charges, depreciation charges; *cuota compensatoria (en comercio internacional)* countervailing duty, compensatory duty; INFORM *cuota de conexión (inicial)* setup charge *o* fee; *(periódica)* subscription rate; *cuota impositiva* tax payable; *cuota de ingreso* entrance fee; *cuota de inscripción (en congreso)* registration fee; *cuota mínima* minimum payment; *cuotas de la seguridad social* social security contributions, *Br* ≃ National Insurance contributions; *cuota del seguro* insurance rate; *cuota sindical* union dues

(**b**) *Am (plazo)* instalment; **comprar en cuotas** to buy on *Br* hire-purchase *o US* an installment plan; **pagar en cuotas** to pay in instalments ❏ *cuota inicial* down payment (**c**) *(cupo)* quota; UE **las cuotas lácteas/pesqueras** milk/fishing quotas ❑ *cuota de audiencia (en televisión)* audience share; *cuota de exportación* export quota; *cuota de mercado* market share; *cuota de muestreo* sampling quota; *cuota de pantalla (en televisión)* audience share; *cuota de producción* production quota; *cuota de ventas* sales quota

(**d**) *Méx (importe)* toll; **autopista de cuota** *Br* toll motorway, *US* turnpike

> **"**
>
> Con ello, se consolida como el líder del mercado de telefonía móvil brasileño, con una **cuota de mercado** media estimada del 56% en sus áreas de operaciones, gracias a la oferta más avanzada de servicios de última generación y una exitosa oferta comercial unificada bajo la marca Vivo.
>
> **"**

cupo *nm* (**a**) *(cantidad máxima)* quota (**b**) *(cantidad proporcional)* share ❑ *cupo de ventas* sales quota

cupón *nm* coupon ❑ FIN *cupón cero* zero coupon; *cupón de compra (de producto)* (purchase) voucher; BOLSA warrant, detachable warrant facility; *cupón corrido* accrued interest; *cupón de descuento* discount voucher, money-off coupon; *cupón de pedido* order form; *cupón de respuesta* reply slip, reply coupon

CURP *nf Méx* (*abrev de* **Clave Única de Registro de Población**) = tax identification number, tax ID number

currículo, currículum (vitae) *nm* curriculum vitae, *Br* CV, *US* résumé

cursillo *nm* short course; **un cursillo de formación** a training course

curso *nm* (**a**) *(año académico)* year ❑ *curso académico* academic year; *curso escolar* school year (**b**) *(lecciones)* course; **un curso de inglés/informática** an English/computing course ❑ *curso por correspondencia* correspondence course; *curso intensivo* crash course; *curso de reciclaje* training course; *curso de secretariado* secretarial course (**c**) *(circulación)* **billete/moneda de curso legal** legal tender ❑ *curso forzoso* forced currency

cursor *nm* INFORM cursor

curva *nf (línea, forma, gráfico)* curve; **una curva de temperatura/producción** a temperature/production curve ❑ *curva de aprendizaje* learning curve; *curva del ciclo de vida* lifecycle curve; *curva de costos o Esp costes* cost curve; *curva de crecimiento* growth curve; *curva de demanda* demand curve; MKTG *curva de distribución normal* normal distribution curve; *curva de eficacia* efficiency curve; MKTG *curva de experiencia* experience curve; *curva de inversión* investment curve; *curva de la oferta* supply curve; *curva de precios* price curve; *curva de productividad* productivity curve; *curva de rendimientos* yield curve; *curva salarial* salary curve; *curva de ventas* sales curve

custodia *nf* FIN custody ❑ *custodia global* global custody; *custodia segura* safe custody

CV *nm* (*abrev de* **currículum vitae**) *Br* CV, *US* résumé

Dd

DAF (*abrev de* **Delivered At Frontier**) DAF

DAFO *nm* MKTG (*abrev de* **debilidades, amenazas, fortalezas y oportunidades**) SWOT

dañado, -a *adj (mercancía, producto)* damaged, spoilt

dañar 1 *vt (mercancía, producto)* to damage, to spoil
  2 dañarse *vpr (mercancía, producto)* to be *o* get damaged, to be *o* get spoilt

daños *nmpl* damage; **los daños se calculan en miles de euros** the damage may run to thousands of euros; **daños y perjuicios** damages ❑ *daños corporales* bodily injury; *daños ecológicos* environmental damage; *daños estructurales* structural damage; *daños indemnizables* compensable loss; *daños medioambientales* environmental damage

DAT *nf* INFORM (*abrev de* **digital audio tape**) DAT

dato *nm (hecho, cifra)* piece of information, fact; **lo que necesitamos son datos concretos** what we need is hard facts; **el alto desempleo es un dato que hay que tener en cuenta** the high level of unemployment is a factor which has to be borne in mind; **aún no cuentan con todos los datos** they do not yet have all the information at their disposal; **datos (personales)** (personal) details; **déjenos sus datos y nos pondremos en contacto con usted** leave us your details and we will get in touch with you ❑ *datos administrativos* administrative details; *datos bancarios* bank details; *Am* *datos computarizados* computerized data; *datos demográficos* demographic data; *datos digitales* digital data; *datos estadísticos* statistical data; *datos geodemográficos* geodemographic data; *datos informatizados* computerized data; *datos numéricos* numerical data; *datos secundarios* secondary data; *datos sociodemográficos* sociodemographic data

DAX *nm* Dax index, Frankfurt Stock Market Index

DCV *nm* FIN (*abrev de* **Depósito** *o* **Depositario Central de Valores**) CSD

DDP (*abrev de* **Delivered Duty Paid**) DDP

DDU (*abrev de* **Delivered Duty Unaid**) DDU

debajo *adv* MKTG **por debajo de la línea** below-the-line

debate *nm* debate

debatir 1 *vt* to discuss, to debate
  2 *vi* **debatir sobre algo** to discuss *o* debate sth

debe *nm* debit; **debe y haber** debit and credit; **anotar algo en el debe de una cuenta** to enter sth on the debit side of an account; **los reintegros se reflejan en el debe de su cuenta** withdrawals are shown in the debit colum

deber *vt (adeudar)* to owe; **deber algo a alguien** to owe sb sth, to owe sth to sb; **me deben medio millón de pesos** they owe me half a million pesos; **¿qué** *o* **cuánto le debo?** how much is it?, how much does it come to?

debidamente *adv* properly; **devuelva la solicitud debidamente cumplimentada a esta dirección** return the application form, properly completed, to this address; **ya fueron debidamente informados de los trámites que debían seguir** they were duly informed of the procedures to follow

débil *adj (de economía, moneda)* weak

debilidad *nf (de economía, moneda)* weakness ❑ MKTG *debilidades, amenazas, fortalezas y oportunidades* strengths, weaknesses, opportunities and threats

debilitar 1 *vt (economía, moneda)* to weaken, to debilitate
  2 debilitarse *vpr (moneda, economía)* to weaken

debitar *vt* to debit; **debitar algo de la cuenta de alguien** to debit sth to sb's account

débito *nm (debe)* debit; *(deuda)* debt ❑ *débito acumulado* cumulative debit; *Am* *débito bancario* direct debit; *débito diferido* deferred debit; *Bol, RP* *débito directo* direct debit; *débito inmediato* immediate debit

decadencia *nf* decline; **en decadencia** *(industria)* declining

decidir *vt* to decide; **decidir hacer algo** to decide to do sth; **el juez decidirá si es inocente o no** the judge will decide *o* determine whether or not he is innocent

decisión *nf* decision; *(de juez)* ruling; **tomar una decisión** to make *o* take a decision ❑ *decisión conjunta* joint decision; *decisión de alto nivel* high-level decision; MKTG *decisión de compra* buying decision, purchase decision; *decisión por mayoría* majority decision

declaración *nf (ante la autoridad, en público)*

statement; **no hizo declaraciones a los medios de comunicación** he didn't make any statement to the media; **prestar declaración** to give evidence; **tomar declaración (a)** to take a statement (from) ❏ *declaración de aduanas* customs declaration; *declaración conjunta (de la renta)* joint filing; *(para informar públicamente)* joint statement; *declaración de dividendos* declaration of dividend; ADUANA *declaración de entrada* declaration inwards; *declaración de exportación* export declaration; *declaración de gastos* statement of expenditure, statement of expenses; *declaración de Hacienda* (income) tax return; *declaración de impacto ambiental* environmental impact statement; *declaración de importación* import declaration; *declaración del impuesto sobre la renta* income tax return; *declaración de intenciones* declaration of intent; *declaración del IVA* VAT return; *declaración jurada* sworn statement; *declaración de (la) misión* mission statement; BOLSA *declaración de opciones* declaration of options; *declaración del patrimonio* = inventory of property, drawn up for tax purposes; SEGUR *declaración de pérdidas* statement of loss; *declaración de pérdidas y ganancias* P & L form; *declaración de principios* statement of principle; *declaración de quiebra* declaration of bankruptcy, adjudication of *o* in bankruptcy; *declaración de la renta* (income) tax return; **hacer la declaración de la renta** *Br* to send in *o US* to file one's tax return; ADUANA *declaración de salida* declaration outwards; SEGUR *declaración de siniestro* notification of claim; *declaración de solvencia* declaration of solvency; *declaración tributaria* tax return; ADUANA *declaración del valor* declaration of value

declarado, -a *adj (ingresos, renta)* declared

declarar 1 *vt* **(a)** *(ante la autoridad)* to declare; **declarar el patrimonio** to declare one's property; **¿tú declaras (a Hacienda) todo lo que ganas?** do you declare all your earnings (to the Tax Inspector)? **(b)** *(en tribunal)* **declarar culpable/ inocente a alguien** to find sb guilty/not guilty; **declarar a alguien en quiebra** to declare sb bankrupt **(c)** ADUANA to declare; **¿algo que declarar?** *(en aduana)* anything to declare?
2 *vi* DER to testify, to give evidence; **declarar ante un tribunal** to testify before a tribunal; **lo llamaron a declarar** he was called to give evidence
3 declararse *vpr* **declararse en huelga** to go on strike; **declararse en quiebra** to declare oneself bankrupt

declinar *vi (economía, industria)* to decline

declive *nm* decline; **una industria en declive** a declining industry

decodificación = **descodificación**

decodificador = **descodificador**

decodificar = **descodificar**

decomisar *vt* to confiscate, to seize

decrecer *vi (disminuir) (en intensidad, importancia)* to decrease, to decline; *(en tamaño, cantidad)* to fall, to drop; **el desempleo decreció en un 2%** unemployment has fallen by 2%

decreciente *adj (tasa, porcentaje, tipo)* declining, decreasing, falling; **una tendencia decreciente** a downward trend; **por *o* en orden decreciente** in descending order

dedicado, -a *adj* dedicated

dedicar 1 *vt (tiempo)* to spend
2 dedicarse *vpr* **(a)** **dedicarse a** *(profesión)* **¿a qué se dedica usted?** what do you do for a living?; **se dedica a la enseñanza** she works as a teacher **(b)** **dedicarse a** *(actividad, persona)* to spend time on; **dejé la empresa para dedicarme a mi familia** I left the company so that I could spend more time with my family

deducción *nf* deduction; **hacer una deducción de algo** to make a deduction from sth; **hacemos una deducción de 150 euros del precio original** we'll deduct 150 euros from the original price ❏ *deducción de la cuota (fiscal)* tax credit; *deducción fiscal* tax deduction; *deducción de la base imponible* income tax allowance; *deducción de los rendimientos del trabajo* earned income allowance

deducible *adj (dinero, gastos)* deductible

deducir *vt* to deduct (**de** from); **me deducen del sueldo la seguridad social** national insurance is deducted from my salary

defaultear *vt Arg (deuda)* to default on

defecto 1 *nm* defect (**en** in) ❏ *defecto de diseño* design fault; *defecto de fábrica, defecto de fabricación* manufacturing defect; *defecto sustancial* material defect; *defecto visible* visible defect
2 por defecto *adv* INFORM by default

defectuoso, -a *adj (mercancía, producto)* defective, faulty

defender 1 *vt* to defend; **defender los derechos/intereses de alguien** to defend sb's rights/interests
2 defenderse *vpr* **(a)** *(protegerse)* to defend oneself (**de** against) **(b)** *(apañarse)* to get by; **se defiende en inglés** he can get by in English

defensor, -ora 1 *adj* **(a)** *(en tribunal)* **abogado defensor** counsel for the defence **(b)** *(partidario)* **siempre fue defensor de una legislación más dura** he always advocated tougher legislation; **asociaciones defensoras de los consumidores** consumer *o* consumers' associations
2 *nm,f* **(a)** *(de ideas)* advocate, champion; **un firme defensor de la libre empresa** a strong advocate of free enterprise ❏ *defensor del cliente (en actividades financieras)* financial

ombudsman (**b**) *(abogado)* counsel for the defence ❑ **defensor de oficio** court-appointed defence lawyer

deficiente *adj* (**a**) *(producto)* poor-quality, substandard (**b**) *(cantidad)* insufficient, inadequate

déficit *nm (económico)* deficit ❑ **déficit de la balanza comercial** trade gap, trade deficit; **déficit de la balanza de pagos** balance of payments deficit, external deficit; **déficit de caja** cash deficit; **déficit cero** zero deficit; **déficit comercial** trade gap, trade deficit; **déficit de explotación** operating deficit; **déficit exterior** external deficit; **déficit financiero** financial imbalance; **déficit inflacionista, déficit inflacionario** inflationary gap; **déficit presupuestario** budget deficit; **déficit público** public deficit; **déficit del sector público** public sector deficit

❝

En España, no sólo los socialistas sino algunos expertos piensan que la obsesión por el **déficit cero** es desaconsejable cuando la economía está deprimida. No es este el caso concreto de nuestro país, cuyo PIB crece a un ritmo del 2,3%, pero las dudas sobre la sostenibilidad de este auge relativo y aislado les mantienen en una continua agitación.

❞

definible *adj* INFORM **definible por el usuario** *(caracteres, teclas)* user-definable

definitivo, -a *adj (concluyente, final)* final, definitive; **los resultados definitivos** the final results

deflación *nf* FIN, ECON deflation

deflacionario, -a, deflacionista *adj* FIN, ECON deflationary

deflactor *nm* FIN, ECON deflator

defraudar *vt (estafar)* to defraud; **defraudar al fisco** *o* **a Hacienda** to practise tax evasion

degradación *nf (de mando, cargo)* demotion

degradar *vt (mando, cargo)* to demote, to downgrade

delegación *nf* (**a**) *(autorización)* delegation; **asumió la gestión de la empresa por delegación de su padre** his father entrusted him with the running of the company (**b**) *(comisión)* delegation ❑ **delegación comercial** *(de un país)* trade delegation (**c**) *Esp (sucursal)* office ❑ **delegación de Hacienda** = head tax office *(in each province)*; **delegación regional** regional office, area office

delegado, -a *nm,f (representante, en congreso)* delegate; *Esp (director de zona)* representative ❑ *Esp* **delegado del Gobierno** = person representing central government in each province; **delegado de personal** staff representative; **delegado de seguridad** safety officer; **delegado**

de seguridad e higiene health and safety representative; **delegado sindical** union representative

delegar 1 *vt* (**a**) *(funciones)* to delegate; **delegar algo en alguien** to delegate sth to sb (**b**) *(representante)* to delegate; **delegar a alguien para hacer algo** *o* **para que haga algo** to delegate sb to do sth
2 *vi* to delegate; **delegar en alguien para hacer algo** to delegate sth to sb

delimitación *nf (de funciones, tareas, responsabilidades)* delimitation, demarcation

delineante *nmf Br* draughtsman, *f* draughtswoman, *US* draftsman, *f* draftswoman

delito *nm* crime, criminal offence ❑ **delito de guante** *o* **cuello blanco** white-collar crime; **delito financiero** financial crime; **delito fiscal** tax offence

demanda *nf* (**a**) *(petición)* request; *(reivindicación)* demand; **atender las demandas de los trabajadores** to respond to the workers' demands ❑ **demanda de empleo** *(solicitud)* job application; **demanda salarial** wage claim
(**b**) *(en economía)* demand; **hay mucha demanda de informáticos** there is a great demand for computer specialists; **la demanda de trabajo en el sector turístico es muy alta** jobs in the tourist industry are in high demand; **la oferta y la demanda** supply and demand ❑ **demanda agregada** aggregate demand; **demanda de consumo** consumer demand; **demanda externa** external demand; **demanda global** overall demand; **demanda interna** domestic *o* internal demand; **demanda del mercado** market demand; **demanda prevista** *(de producto)* projected demand; MKTG **demanda primaria** primary demand
(**c**) *(en derecho)* lawsuit; *(por daños y perjuicios)* claim; **interponer** *o* **presentar una demanda contra** to take legal action against; **presenté una demanda contra la constructora por daños y perjuicios** I sued the builders for damages; **una demanda por difamación** a libel suit

❝

Papademos añadió que la recuperación económica está en marcha en varias partes del mundo, lo que debería contribuir a incrementar la **demanda externa**, lo que, a su vez, contrarrestará los efectos de la pérdida de competitividad por los precios, en alusión a la fuerte apreciación del euro.

❞

demandante 1 *nmf* (**a**) DER plaintiff (**b**) *(solicitante)* **demandante de empleo** job seeker, job hunter
2 *adj* DER **la parte demandante** the plaintiff

demandar *vt* (**a**) *(legalmente)* **demandar a alguien (por)** to sue sb (for); **demandar a**

alguien por daños y perjuicios to sue sb for damages (**b**) *(pedir, requerir)* to ask for, to seek; **los sindicatos demandan una mejora salarial** the unions are demanding a wage rise

demo INFORM *adj & nf* demo

demografía *nf* demography

demográfico, -a *adj (estudio, instituto)* demographic; **crecimiento demográfico** population growth

demora *nf* delay; **el vuelo sufre una demora de una hora** the flight has been delayed by one hour; **la demora en el pago conlleva una sanción** delay in payment will entail a penalty

demostración *nf (de sistema, equipo, producto)* demonstration; **hacer una demostración** to give a demonstration ▫ **demostración en el punto de venta** in-store demonstration

denegar *vt (permiso, visado, préstamo)* to refuse; **me han denegado el crédito** they turned down my loan application; **le ha sido denegado el visado** her visa application has been turned down

denominación *nf (nombre)* name ▫ **denominación de origen** = certification that a product (e.g. wine) comes from a particular region and conforms to certain quality standards; **denominación social** company name

densidad *nf* INFORM density; **alta/doble densidad** high/double density ▫ **densidad de escritura** write density

denuncia *nf* (**a**) *(acusación)* accusation; *(condena)* denunciation; **un artículo/programa de denuncia** an exposé (**b**) *(a la policía)* report; **hacer** *o* **poner** *o* **presentar una denuncia contra alguien** to report sb to the police; **presentar una denuncia por** *o* **de robo** to report a robbery *o* theft

departamento *nm* (**a**) *(en empresa, organización)* department ▫ **departamento de administración** administration department; **departamento administrativo** administrative department; **departamento de análisis de métodos de trabajo** methods office; **departamento de atención al cliente** customer service department; **departamento central de compras** central purchasing department; **departamento de cobros, departamento de cobranzas** collecting department; **departamento de comercio exterior** international division; **departamento de compras** purchasing department, buying department; **departamento de contabilidad** accounts department; **departamento de control de calidad** quality control department; **departamento creativo** creative department; **departamento de créditos** loan department; **departamento de crédito documentario** documentary credit department; **departamento de diseño** design department; **departamento de envíos, depar-**tamento de expedición dispatch department, forwarding department; **departamento de exportación** export department; **departamento de facturación** billing *o* invoice department; **departamento financiero** finance department; **departamento informático** computer department; **departamento de investigación** research department; **departamento jurídico** legal department; **departamento de mantenimiento** maintenance department; **departamento de marketing** marketing department; MKTG **departamento de medios** media department; **departamento de negociación de bonos** bond-trading department; **departamento de opciones** options desk; **departamento de pedidos** order department; **departamento de personal** personnel department; **departamento de producción** production department; **departamento de publicidad** advertising *o* publicity department; **departamento de reclamaciones,** SAm **departamento de reclamos** complaints department; **departamento (de servicio) postventa** after-sales department; **departamento de recursos humanos** human resources department; **departamento técnico** technical department; **departamento de valores** securities department; **departamento de ventas** sales department

(**b**) *(en tienda)* department; **departamento de caballeros** menswear department

(**c**) *(ministerio)* ministry, department ▫ **Departamento de Estado** Department of State, State Department

dependiente, -a *nm,f Br* sales assistant, shop assistant, *US* sales clerk

depositante *nmf* depositor

depositar *vt (en banco)* to deposit; **depositar algo como garantía** to deposit sth as security; CONT **depositar las cuentas anuales** to file the annual accounts

depositaría *nf* depositary fee

depositario, -a 1 *nm,f* (**a**) *(de dinero)* custodian; **depositario (de una garantía)** pledge holder, pledgee (**b**) *(de mercancías)* warehousekeeper **2** *nm* FIN *(de valores)* depository, depositary ▫ **Depositario Central de Valores** Central Securities Depository

depósito *nm* (**a**) FIN *(en cuenta bancaria)* deposit ▫ **depósito bancario** bank deposit; *Am* **depósito directo** = payment directly into a bank account, *US* direct deposit; **depósito disponible** sight deposit, *US* demand deposit; **depósito en efectivo** cash deposit; BOLSA **depósito de garantía** initial margin; **depósito de garantía mínimo** margin requirement; **depósito indistinto** joint deposit; **depósito interbancario** interbank deposit; **depósito mínimo** minimum deposit; **depósito a plazo** term deposit, *US* time deposit; **depósito a plazo fijo** *Br* fixed(-term) deposit, *US* time deposit; ***depósitos públicos*** public deposits; *Col **depósito a término fijo*** *Br* fixed(-term) deposit, *US* time deposit; ***depósito a un día*** overnight loan; ***depósito a la vista*** sight deposit, *US* demand deposit

(**b**) *(de documentos)* FIN ***Depósito Central de Valores*** Central Securities Depository; ***depósito legal*** copyright deposit, legal deposit

(**c**) *(almacén) (de mercancías)* depot, warehouse ▫ ***depósito aduanero*** bonded warehouse; ***depósito aduanero interior*** inland clearance depot; ***depósito de contenedores*** container depot; ***depósito de distribución*** distribution depot; ***depósito franco*** free warehouse; ***depósito de recepción*** receiving depot; ***depósito de transporte por carretera*** road haulage depot

(**d**) *(fianza)* deposit; **dejar una cantidad en depósito** to leave a deposit

depreciación *nf* FIN depreciation ▫ ***depreciación de la moneda, depreciación monetaria*** currency depreciation; CONT ***depreciación por saldos decrecientes*** declining balance depreciation

depreciar FIN **1** *vt* to (cause to) depreciate **2 depreciarse** *vpr* to depreciate

depresión *nf* (**a**) *(económica, del mercado)* depression (**b**) *(en gráfico, ciclo)* trough

deprimido, -a *adj (zona, industria, economía)* depressed

> **❝**
> El mercado bursátil lleva semanas **deprimido** por desalentadores pronósticos de ganancias corporativas, escándalos de contabilidad fraudulenta y las posibilidades de nuevos ataques.
> **❞**

depuración *nf* (**a**) CONT ***depuración de saldos contables*** verification and adjustment of account balances (**b**) INFORM debugging

depurador *nm* INFORM debugger

depurar *vt* INFORM to debug

DEQ *(abrev de* **Delivered Ex Quay***)* DEQ

derecho *nm* (**a**) *(leyes, estudio)* law; **conforme** *o* **según derecho** according to the law ▫ ***derecho administrativo*** administrative law; ***derecho civil*** civil law; ***derecho comunitario*** Community law, EU law; ***derecho concursal*** insolvency law; ***derecho contractual*** contract law; ***derecho escrito*** statute law; ***derecho financiero*** financial law; ***derecho fiscal*** tax law; ***derecho internacional*** international law; ***derecho laboral*** labour law; ***derecho marítimo*** maritime law; ***derecho mercantil*** commercial law; ***derecho de patentes*** patent law; ***derecho de sociedades*** company law, corporate law; ***derecho del trabajo*** labour law

(**b**) *(prerrogativa)* right; **los derechos y obligaciones del consumidor** the rights and responsibilities of the consumer; **esta tarjeta me da derecho a un 5% de descuento** this card entitles me to a 5% discount; **miembro de pleno derecho** full member; **reservados todos los derechos** all rights reserved; **tener derecho a algo** to have a right to sth, to be entitled to sth ▫ ***derecho de acceso*** right of entry; ***derechos de antena*** broadcasting rights; ***derecho de apelación*** right of appeal; ***derechos de autor (potestad)*** copyright; ***derechos de compra*** purchasing rights; ***derechos conyugales*** marital rights; ***derechos de distribución*** distribution rights; ***derechos exclusivos*** exclusive rights, sole rights; ***derechos exclusivos de venta*** exclusive *o* sole selling rights; ***derechos de explotación*** concession; ***derechos de fabricación*** manufacturing rights; ***derechos de giro*** drawing rights; ***derecho de huelga*** right to strike; ***derechos de imagen*** image rights; ***derechos internacionales*** international rights; ***derechos mundiales*** worldwide rights; ***derecho de posesión*** possessory right; ***derecho de preferencia*** BOLSA *(de accionistas)* pre-emption right; DER *(de acreedor)* preferential claim, preferential right; BOLSA ***derecho preferente*** pre-emptive right; ***derecho de prioridad*** BOLSA *(de accionistas)* pre-emption right; DER *(de acreedor)* preferential claim, preferential right; BOLSA ***derecho prioritario*** pre-emptive right; ***derechos de propiedad*** proprietary rights; BOLSA ***derecho de recompra*** repurchase right; ***derecho de retención*** DER *(del acreedor)* general lien; DER ***derecho de retención del vendedor*** vendor's lien; ***derechos secundarios*** *(de propiedad intelectual)* ancillary rights; ***derechos sociales*** *(de ciudadano)* social entitlements; BOLSA ***derecho de suscripción*** subscription right; DER ***derecho de tanteo*** first refusal; ***derechos de usufructo*** usufructuary rights; BOLSA ***derecho al valor de rescate*** contingent value right; ***derechos de venta en el extranjero*** foreign rights; ***derecho a voto*** *(de accionistas)* voting rights

(**c**) **derechos** *(tasas)* duties, taxes; *(profesionales)* fees ▫ ***derechos de aduana*** customs duty; ***derechos arancelarios*** customs duty; ***derechos de autor*** *(dinero)* royalties; ***derechos compensatorios*** *(en importaciones)* countervailing duties, compensatory duties; ***derechos consulares*** consular fees; ***derechos de entrada*** import duty; ***derechos de exportación*** export duty; ***derechos de importación*** import duty; ***derechos de inscripción*** registration fees; ***derechos de muelle*** wharf dues; ***derechos de navegación*** shipping dues; ***derechos de patente*** patent royalty; ***derechos petroleros*** oil royalties; ***derechos portuarios, derechos de puerto*** harbour dues; ***derechos de registro*** registration fees; *pagados al registro)* registry fees

> "
> De todas formas, Toyota se opuso hace un
> año a que el Grupo Bergé se quedara con
> los **derechos de importación** en exclusiva
> para España de Daihatsu, marca en la que
> posee el 55%.
> "

derivado *nm* (**a**) *(producto)* spin-off (**b**) BOLSA
derivative

derogar *vt (ley)* to repeal

derrochar *vt (dinero, fuerzas)* to squander, to
waste

derroche *nm (despilfarro)* squandering, waste

DES *(abrev de* **Delivered Ex Ship**) DES

desaceleración *nf* slow down, slowing
(down); **una desaceleración del crecimiento
económico** a slowdown in economic growth
❑ *desaceleración económica* economic slowdown

desacelerar 1 *vt (proceso, cambio)* to slow
down
   2 desacelerarse *vpr* to slow down

desactivar *vt* INFORM to disable, to deactivate

desahorro *nm* dissaving, negative saving

desajuste *nm (económico)* imbalance

desaparecido, -a *adj (extinto)* **la desaparecida
Sociedad de Naciones** the now defunct League
of Nations

desarrollado, -a *adj (país, proyecto)* developed

desarrollador, -ora *nm,f* INFORM developer
   ❑ *desarrollador de software* software developer

desarrollar 1 *vt* (**a**) *(economía, sector, comercio)*
to develop (**b**) *(realizar) (actividad, trabajo, proyecto)* to carry out (**c**) *(crear) (prototipos, técnicas, estrategias)* to develop
   2 desarrollarse *vpr (evolucionar)* to develop

desarrollo *nm* (**a**) *(evolución, mejora)* development; **el desarrollo económico** economic development; **países en vías de desarrollo**
developing countries ❑ *desarrollo económico*
economic development; *desarrollo exterior*
overseas development; *desarrollo industrial*
industrial development; *desarrollo del mercado* market development; *desarrollo profesional* career development; *desarrollo
regional* regional development; *desarrollo
sostenible,* Am *desarrollo sustentable* sustainable development
   (**b**) *(realización) (de actividad, trabajo, proyecto)*
carrying out
   (**c**) *(creación) (de prototipos, técnicas, estrategias)*
development ❑ MKTG *desarrollo de concepto*
concept development; *desarrollo de nuevos
productos* new product development; *desarrollo del producto* product development;

desarrollo simultáneo de productos simultaneous product development

desayuno *nm* **desayuno de trabajo** working
breakfast

desbordamiento *nm* INFORM overflow

descanso *nm* (**a**) *(reposo)* rest; **día de descanso**
day off; **los lunes cerramos por descanso semanal** we don't open on Mondays ❑ *descanso
compensatorio* time in lieu (**b**) *(pausa)* break;
cinco minutes de descanso a five-minute break

descapitalización *nf* FIN undercapitalization

descapitalizado, -a *adj* FIN undercapitalized

descapitalizar FIN **1** *vt* to undercapitalize
   2 descapitalizarse *vpr* to be undercapitalized

> "
> Lo que sucede al recorrerse el impuesto a
> toda la cadena, es que se retrasan los flujos
> de efectivo porque los productores y distri-
> buidores primero pagarán los impuestos, y
> luego los recuperarán y esta situación
> eventualmente puede **descapitalizar** a al-
> gunas empresas y hacer que produzcan
> menos tequila, o que produzcan una bebi-
> da de menor calidad.
> "

descarga *nf* (**a**) *(de mercancías)* unloading; **zonas de carga y descarga** loading and unloading
areas (**b**) INFORM *(acción)* downloading; **una descarga** a download

descargable *adj* INFORM downloadable

descargar 1 *vt* (**a**) *(vaciar) (cargamento, vehículo,
barco)* to unload, to discharge (**b**) INFORM to
download; **descargar un programa de la Red**
to download a program from the Net
   2 descargarse *vpr* INFORM to download; **el programa tarda mucho en descargarse** this program takes a long time to download

descargo *nm* FIN *(de deuda)* discharge, settlement

descartar *vt (posibilidad, idea)* to rule out; *(plan)*
to reject

descatalogar *vt* MKTG **lo han descatalogado**
they've dropped it from their catalogue

descender 1 *vi* (**a**) *(nivel, precios)* to fall, to drop
(**b**) *(en el trabajo)* to be demoted
   2 *vt (en el trabajo)* to demote; **lo han descendi-
do de categoría** he's been demoted

descenso *nm (de precio, nivel)* fall, drop, decline;
**la tasa de desempleo experimentó un espec-
tacular descenso** there was a spectacular drop
in the unemployment rate; **ir en descenso** to be
falling *o* decreasing *o* on the decline

descentralización *nf* decentralization

descentralizar 1 *vt* to decentralize
   2 descentralizarse *vpr* to become decentral-
ized

descifrar *vt* INFORM to decrypt

descodificación, decodificación *nf* INFORM decoding

descodificador, decodificador *nm (aparato)* decoder; *(para televisión)* unscrambler

descodificar, decodificar *vt (mensaje)* to decode; *(emisión televisiva, acústica)* to unscramble

descompresión *nf* INFORM decompression, unzipping

descomprimir *vt* INFORM to decompress, to unzip

desconectado, -a *adj* INFORM off-line

desconectar *vt (máquina)* to disconnect

descontar *vt* (**a**) *(cantidad)* to deduct; **me lo descontarán de mi sueldo** it will be deducted from my salary; **facturaré 5.000 euros brutos, pero a eso habrá que descontarle gastos** I'll make 5,000 euros gross, but I'll have to take off the costs from that (**b**) *(hacer un descuento de)* to discount; **me descontaron el 5% del precio de la lavadora** they gave me a 5% discount on the (price of the) washing machine (**c**) FIN *(letra de cambio)* to discount

desconvocar *vt (huelga, manifestación, reunión)* to call off, to cancel

descremación *nf* MKTG *(de mercado)* skimming

descremar *vt* MKTG *(mercado)* to skim

describir *vt (trazar) (trayectoria, subida)* to chart

descripción *nf (de mercancías)* description

descubierto *nm* FIN *(de empresa)* deficit; *(de cuenta bancaria)* overdraft; **tengo un descubierto de 2.000 euros** I have an overdraft of 2,000 euros; **al** *o* **en descubierto** overdrawn; **tener la cuenta al** *o* **en descubierto** to be overdrawn □ *descubierto bancario* bank overdraft

descuento *nm* (**a**) *(rebaja)* discount; **un descuento del 5%** 5% off; **con descuento** at a discount; **artículos con descuento** discounted items; **hacer descuento** to give a discount □ *descuento no acumulativo por volumen* non-cumulative quantity discount; *descuento adicional* additional discount; *descuento bancario* bank discount; *descuento comercial* trade discount; *descuento por compra al por mayor* bulk discount; *descuento contractual* contractual allowance; *descuento al distribuidor* distributor discount; *descuento duro* hard discount; *descuento de facturas* invoice discounting; *descuento por fidelidad, descuento por fidelización* (customer) loyalty discount; *descuento de grupo* group discount; *descuento impositivo* tax credit; *descuento por liquidación* settlement discount; *descuento de prima* premium discount, premium rebate; *descuento de promoción* promotional discount;

descuento por pronto pago cash discount; *descuento de temporada* seasonal discount; *descuento por volumen* volume discount (**b**) FIN *(de letra de cambio)* discount

desdolarización *nf* ECON dedollarization

desechable *adj (envase)* disposable, non-returnable

desecho *nm* **material de desecho** waste products; **desechos** *(residuos)* waste products □ *desechos industriales* industrial waste; *desechos nucleares* nuclear waste; *desechos radiactivos* radioactive waste

deseleccionar *vt* INFORM to deselect

desembalar *vt* to unpack

desembarcar **1** *vt (pasajeros)* to disembark; *(mercancías)* to unload
2 *vi (de barco, avión)* to disembark; **desembarcarán por la puerta C** you will disembark through gate C

desembarco *nm* **su desembarco en el mercado español** their arrival on the Spanish market; **antes de su desembarco en el consejo de administración** prior to their gaining a presence on the board

> En la actualidad el Grupo Correo precisaría volver al endeudamiento para poder afrontar en solitario esa operación. El grupo vasco, tras la fusión con Prensa Española, vio incrementar su deuda hasta los 260 millones de euros, una cantidad que le impediría, quizá, afrontar el **desembarco** en Antena 3.

desembolsar *vt* to pay out

desembolso *nm* payment; *(gasto inicial)* outlay; **la operación supuso un desembolso de 100 millones** the operation cost 100 million; **obtuvo una ganancia de 50.000 euros con un desembolso inicial de 25.000 euros** he made a return of 50,000 euros on an initial outlay of 25,000 euros □ *desembolso inicial* initial expenditure

desempleado, -a **1** *adj* unemployed, jobless
2 *nm,f* unemployed person; **lo peor para un desempleado es el aislamiento** the worst thing for someone who is out of work is the isolation; **los desempleados** the unemployed □ *los desempleados de larga duración* the long-term unemployed

desempleo *nm* (**a**) *(falta de trabajo)* unemployment; **una de las tasas de desempleo más altas de Europa** one of the highest unemployment rates in Europe □ *desempleo cíclico* cyclical unemployment; *desempleo estructural* structural unemployment; *desempleo estacional* seasonal unemployment;

desempleo generalizado mass unemployment; **desempleo juvenil** youth unemployment; **desempleo de larga duración** long-term unemployment; **desempleo masivo** mass unemployment; **desempleo urbano** urban unemployment
 (**b**) *(subsidio)* unemployment benefit; **cobrar el desempleo** to receive unemployment benefit

desencadenante 1 *adj* **los factores desencadenantes de...** the factors which brought about...
 2 *nm* **el desencadenante de la tragedia** what brought about the tragedy

desencadenar *vt (conflicto, reacción)* to trigger

desencriptación *nf,* **desencriptado** *nm* COMPUT **desencriptación de datos** data decryption

deseo *nm* (**a**) MKTG *(de compra)* desire; **necesidades y deseos** needs and wants (**b**) *(en carta, obsequio)* wish; **con mis/nuestros mejores deseos** (with my/our) best wishes

desestimación *nf* DER *(de apelación)* dismissal, rejection

desestimar *vt* DER to reject, to turn down; **el Supremo desestimó el recurso** the Supreme Court rejected *o* dismissed the appeal

desfalcador, -ora *nm,f* embezzler

desfalcar *vt* to embezzle

desfase *nm (diferencia)* gap; **hay un desfase entre la oferta y la demanda** supply is out of step with demand ❑ **desfase horario** *(tras vuelo)* jet lag

desfavorable *adj (balanza comercial, tipos)* unfavourable

desfragmentación *nf* INFORM defragmentation

desglosar *vt (cifras, gastos, estadísticas)* to break down; **una factura desglosada** an itemized bill

desglose *nm (de cifras, gastos, estadísticas)* breakdown ❑ **desglose de actividades** operations breakdown

desgravable *adj* tax-deductible

> **"**
> El respaldo fiscal a los salarios más bajos se traduce en un aumento de la reducción fiscal por rentas del trabajo de un 17%, que deja la cantidad **desgravable** para los trabajadores con ingresos hasta 8.200 euros al año en 3.500 euros. Para los salarios superiores a 13.000 euros el aumento de esta reducción es menor, de un 7% y se sitúa en 2.400 euros.
> **"**

desgravación *nf* deduction, allowance; **una inversión con derecho a desgravación** a tax-deductible investment; **una desgravación del**
15% a reduction in your tax of 15%; **las desgravaciones por hijo o familiar a cargo** the allowances for a dependent child or relative ❑ **desgravaciones sobre bienes de capital** capital allowances; **desgravación fiscal** tax relief; **desgravación por I+D** R&D tax credit

desgravar 1 *vt* **los alquileres desgravan un 5%** 5% of rent can be claimed against tax
 2 *vi* to be tax-deductible; **¿las minusvalías físicas desgravan?** are there any tax allowances for physical disabilities?
 3 desgravarse *vpr (gastos)* to be tax-deductible

deshacer *vt* INFORM to undo

designado, -a *adj* **la persona designada** the appointee

designar *vt* (**a**) *(nombrar)* to appoint; **han designado a Gómez para el cargo** Gómez has been appointed to the post (**b**) *(fijar, determinar)* to name, to fix; **falta por designar una fecha y un lugar** a date and place have yet to be set *o* decided

desigual *adj* (**a**) *(trato)* different (**b**) *(contrato)* one-sided

desinflación *nf* ECON disinflation

desinflacionario, -a, desinflacionista *adj* ECON disinflationary

desinstalación *nf* INFORM deinstallation

desinstalador *nm* INFORM deinstaller

desinstalar *vt* INFORM to deinstall, to uninstall

desintegración *nf (de empresa, organización)* break-up

desintermediación *nf* disintermediation

desinversión *nf* FIN disinvestment, divestment ❑ **desinversión marginal** marginal disinvestment

desinvertir *vi* FIN to disinvest

> **"**
> Muchas empresas **están desinvirtiendo** en sus activos inmobiliarios situados en el centro de las ciudades con el fin de trasladarse a la periferia.
> **"**

desmaterialización *nf (de valores)* dematerialization

desmembración *nf,* **desmembramiento** *nm (de empresa, conglomerado)* break-up

desmembrar 1 *vt (empresa, conglomerado)* to break up
 2 desmembrarse *vpr* to break up, to fall apart

desmonetización *nf* FIN demonetization, demonetarization

desmonetizar *vt* FIN to demonetize, to demonetarize

desmotivar 1 *vt* to demotivate

2 desmotivarse *vpr* to get o become discouraged

desmutualización *nf* FIN demutualization

desmutualizarse *vpr* FIN to demutualize

desnacionalización *nf* denationalization, privatization

desnacionalizar *vt* to denationalize, to privatize

desocupación *nf (desempleo)* unemployment
❑ **desocupación generalizada, desocupación masiva** mass unemployment

desocupado, -a *adj* (**a**) *(sin empleo)* unemployed (**b**) *(vivienda)* empty

desorbitado, -a *adj (precio, beneficios)* exorbitant, inflated

despachar 1 *vt* (**a**) *(enviar) (mercancía)* to dispatch, to ship; *(paquete, envío postal)* to send; **le despacharemos el pedido por mensajero** we'll send your order by courier
(**b**) *(en tienda) (atender)* to serve; *(vender)* to sell; **¿lo despachan?** are you being served?; **no se despachan bebidas alcohólicas a menores de 18 años** *(en letrero)* alcohol is not for sale to persons under the age of 18
(**c**) *(tratar) (asunto, negocio)* to deal with; **despachó los asuntos del día con su secretario** she dealt with the day's business with her secretary
(**d**) *Am (en aeropuerto)* to check in
2 *vi* (**a**) *(sobre un asunto)* **despachar con alguien (sobre algo)** to have a meeting with sb (about sth) (**b**) *(en una tienda)* to serve; **¿hasta qué hora despachan?** what time are you open till?

despacho *nm* (**a**) *(oficina) (fuera de casa)* office; *(en casa)* study; **muebles y material de despacho** office furniture and stationery; **un despacho de abogados** a law firm, *US* a law office
(**b**) *(en aduanas)* **despacho aduanero, despacho de aduana(s)** customs clearance; **despacho de entrada** clearance inward(s); **despacho de salida** clearance outward(s)
(**c**) *(de mercancías)* dispatch
(**d**) *(comunicado) (oficial)* dispatch; *(de prensa)* communiqué; **un despacho de agencia** a news agency report
(**e**) *Am Formal (en carta)* **su despacho** = formulaic phrase which appears immediately below name of addressee at head of formal letter

despedir 1 *vt (de empleo) (por cierre, reducción de plantilla)* to make redundant, to lay off; *(por razones disciplinarias)* to fire, to dismiss
2 despedirse *vpr* to leave one's job

desperdicio *nm (de material)* wastage

despido *nm* (**a**) *(expulsión)* dismissal; **su falta de disciplina precipitó su despido** his lack of discipline led to his dismissal; **la reestructuración de la empresa significó docenas de despidos** the restructuring of the company meant dozens of redundancies o lay-offs ❑ **despido colectivo** mass redundancy; **despido forzoso** compulsory redundancy; **despido improcedente** *(por incumplimiento de contrato)* wrongful dismissal; *(por ir contra el derecho laboral)* unfair dismissal; **despido inmediato** summary dismissal; **despido libre** dismissal without compensation; **despido masivo** mass dismissal, mass redundancy; **despido voluntario** voluntary redundancy
(**b**) *(indemnización)* redundancy money o payment

> **"**
> Cada año se producen en España más de 275.000 rescisiones de contratos indefinidos. Una parte, mínima, corresponde a prejubilaciones, otra a **despidos** disciplinarios procedentes (que no conllevan indemnización para el trabajador), una proporción similar se refiere a **despidos** tramitados mediante expedientes de regulación de empleo, y la gran mayoría (más de 200.000), a **despidos** individuales "puros y duros".
> **"**

despilfarro *nm (de dinero)* squandering, waste; *(de energía, agua, recursos)* waste

desplazar 1 *vt* (**a**) *(trasladar)* to move (**a** to); **desplazaron la sede de la empresa a otro edificio** they moved the firm's headquarters to another building (**b**) *(tomar el lugar de)* to take the place of; **fue desplazado de su puesto por alguien más joven** he was pushed out of his job by a younger person; **el correo electrónico está desplazando al correo convencional** electronic mail is taking over from conventional mail
2 desplazarse *vpr* (**a**) *(viajar)* to travel; **desplazarse diariamente al lugar de trabajo** to commute (to work) (**b**) INFORM *(por la pantalla)* to scroll; **desplazarse hacia arriba/abajo** to scroll up/down

desplegable *adj* INFORM *(menú)* drop-down, pull-down

desplegar *vt* INFORM *(menú)* to pull down

despliegue *nm* **despliegue mediático** media hype

desplomarse *vpr (divisa, Bolsa, precios)* to collapse

desplome *nm (de cotización, precios, mercado)* slump, collapse; **el desplome del euro** the slump in the value of the euro, the collapse of the euro; **el desplome de las bolsas asiáticas** the crash of o slump in the Asian stock markets

> **"**
> Esta operación explica el **desplome** bursátil que está sufriendo hoy la petrolera en el parqué. Al inicio de la sesión, la cotización de Repsol YPF cedía un 4,65%, el mayor

descenso de todas las cotizadas, hasta los 13,55 euros. El precio más alto al que se cruzaban operaciones sobre este valor era de 13,60 euros, en tanto que el cambio mínimo se fijaba en 13,35. **"**

desregulación *nf* deregulation

desregular *vt* to deregulate

destajo *nm* **(trabajo a) destajo** piecework; **trabajar a destajo** *(por trabajo hecho)* to do piecework; *(mucho)* to work flat out

destinar *vt* **(a)** *(cantidad, fondos)* to allocate; **un 10% de los beneficios fue destinado a I+D** 10% of profits were allocated to R&D **(b)** *(empleado)* to post, to assign; *(temporalmente)* to attach; **han destinado a Elena al departamento de marketing** Elena has been assigned to the marketing department

destinatario, -a *nm,f* **(a)** *(de carta, paquete, mercancía)* addressee; **destinatario desconocido** *(en carta)* not known at this address **(b)** *(de giro o transferencia bancarios)* payee

destino *nm* **(a) (lugar de) destino** destination; **(ir) con destino a** (to be) bound for *o* going to; **pasajeros con destino a Chicago, embarquen por puerta 6** passengers flying to Chicago, please board at gate 6 **(b)** *(empleo, plaza)* posting; **estar en expectativa de destino** to be awaiting a posting; **le han dado un destino en las Canarias** he's been posted to the Canaries

destitución *nf* dismissal

destituir *vt* to dismiss

destreza *nf* skill

> **"**
> Un trabajador atractivo es el poseedor de un portafolio de habilidades y **destrezas**, así como de experiencias aplicables a situaciones complejas. Es un productor de conocimientos que los aplica a procesos de negocios, y que con su labor, agrega valor a la organización. **"**

desviación *nf* **(a)** *(en estadística)* deviation ❑ **desviación absoluta media** mean absolute deviation; **desviación estándar** standard deviation; **desviación media** mean deviation; **desviación salarial** wage drift; **desviación típica** standard deviation **(b)** CONT, FIN **desviación en los gastos generales** overhead variance; **desviación neta** net variance; **desviación presupuestaria** budgetary variance **(c)** DER **desviación de fondos públicos** diversion of public funds

desvío *nm* TEL **desvío (automático) de llamadas** *o* Am **llamados** (automatic) call forwarding

detallar *vt* **(a)** *(factura, cuenta, gastos)* to itemize, to break down **(b)** *(historia, hechos)* to detail

detalle 1 *nm* *(pormenor, dato)* detail; **para más detalles, llame al teléfono…** for further details please call…
2 al detalle *adv* retail; **en este almacén no se vende al detalle** we don't sell retail in this warehouse

detallista 1 *adj* *(meticuloso)* meticulous, thorough
2 *nmf* *(minorista)* retailer

detección *nf* INFORM **detección de errores** error detection; **detección de virus** virus detection

detector *nm* INFORM **detector de virus** virus detector

detener *vt* *(parar)* to arrest, to halt; **medidas para detener la inflación** measures to arrest *o* halt inflation

deterioro *nm* *(daño)* damage; **la mercancía no sufrió deterioro alguno** the goods were undamaged

determinado, -a *adj* *(preciso, concreto)* given; **a un precio determinado** at a given price

determinar *vt* *(fecha, precio, lugar)* to decide, to fix; **en fecha aún sin** *o* **por determinar** on a date that has yet to be decided *o* fixed; **reuniones para determinar los términos del acuerdo** meetings to settle the terms of the agreement

detonante *nm* trigger; **la subida de los precios del pan fue el detonante de la revuelta** the rise in bread prices was what sparked off *o* triggered the rebellion

deuda *nf* *(financiera)* debt; **tiene deudas pendientes con un proveedor** he owes money to a supplier; **contraer una deuda** to take on debt; **contrajo deudas (por valor) de varios millones** he ran up debts (to the tune) of several million; **pagar** *o* **saldar una deuda** to pay off *o* settle a debt ❑ **deuda amortizable** repayable debt; **deudas bancarias** bank debts; **deuda de cobro dudoso** doubtful debt; **deuda comercial** trade debt; **deuda consolidada** consolidated debt, funded debt; **deuda no consolidada** unfunded debt; **deuda de** *o* **por consumo** consumer debt; **deudas contables** book debts; **deuda a corto plazo** short-term debt; **deuda de entresuelo** mezzanine debt; **deuda del Estado** *(títulos)* government stock; *(concepto)* public debt; **deuda exterior, deuda externa** foreign debt, overseas debt; **deuda fiscal** tax liability; **deuda flotante** floating debt; **deuda sin garantía** unsecured debt; **deuda garantizada** secured debt; **deuda de honor** debt of honour; **deudas incobrables** bad debt; **deuda interior, deuda interna** internal debt; **deuda a largo plazo** long-term debt; **deuda líquida** liquid debt; **deudas pendientes** outstanding debts; **deuda perpetua** irredeemable bond; **deuda preferente** preferential debt, preferred debt; **deuda prioritaria** senior debt; **deuda privilegiada** privileged debt; **deuda pública** *(títulos)* government stock; *(concepto)* public debt; **deuda tributaria** tax payable, tax due; **deuda vencida** debt due

deudor, -ora 1 *adj* debtor; **la compañía deudora** the debtor company; **la parte deudora se declaró insolvente** the debtor declared himself insolvent

2 *nm,f* debtor ▫ **deudor comercial** trade debtor; **deudor hipotecario** mortgagor; **deudor en posesión** debtor in possession; **deudor solidario** joint and several debtor

devaluación *nf* devaluation

devaluar 1 *vt* to devalue; **devaluaron el euro un 3%** the euro was devalued by 3%
2 devaluarse *vpr (moneda)* to fall (in value); *(precios)* to fall; *(bienes, terrenos)* to go down in value, to depreciate

devengar *vt (intereses, dividendos)* to yield, to accrue; *(sueldo)* to earn; **un depósito a plazo que devenga altos intereses** a fixed-term deposit that yields *o* pays a high rate of interest; **ingresos devengados durante el ejercicio** income earned *o* accrued during the *Br* financial *o US* fiscal year

devolución *nf (de compra)* return; *(de dinero)* refund; *(de préstamo)* repayment; **declaraciones de la renta con derecho a devolución** = income tax returns with entitlement to a refund; **el plazo de devolución del préstamo es de doce años** the loan is repayable over (a period of) twelve years; **no se admiten devoluciones** *(en letrero)* no refunds (given); **devolución de monedas** *(en letrero de máquinas expendedoras)* refund, coin return ▫ **devolución de compra** purchase return; FIN **devolución fiscal** tax rebate, tax refund; **devolución lineal** fixed-rate rebate

devolver *vt (producto defectuoso, cheque)* to return; *(préstamo, crédito)* to repay, to pay back; *(lo alquilado)* to take back, to return; **si no queda satisfecho, le devolvemos el dinero** if you're not satisfied, we'll refund you *o* give you back the money; **me devolvieron la carta por un error en las señas** the letter was returned to me because it was not properly addressed

devorar *vt* INFORM *(números, datos)* to crunch

DG *nf* EU *(abrev de* **Dirección General***)* DG

día *nm* **(a)** *(periodo de tiempo)* day ▫ BOLSA **día de apertura** opening day; **día de baja (por enfermedad)** sick day; **día contable** accounting day; **día de deuda** pay-by date; **día festivo,** *Am* **día feriado** (public) holiday, *Br* bank holiday, *US* legal holiday; **día de fiesta** holiday; **día de gracia** day of grace; **día hábil** working day, business

day; **día de huelga** day of action; **día laborable** working day; **día libre** day off; **tener/tomarse un día libre** to have/take a day off; BOLSA **día de liquidación** settlement day; BOLSA **día de negociación** trading day; **día de pago** payment day; **día de pago de intereses** interest day, interest payment date; *Am* **día patrio** national holiday *(commemorating important historical event)*; BOLSA **día del reporte** contango day; **Día del trabajador, Día del trabajo** Labour Day; **día de trabajo** working day; **me pagan por día de trabajo** I get paid for each day's work; **día útil** working day; FIN **día de valor** value day; **día de vencimiento** *(de letra)* term day
(b) *(corriente)* **estar al día** to be up to date; **estamos al día de todos nuestros pagos** we're up to date with all our payments; **poner algo/a alguien al día** to update sth/sb; **ya me han puesto al día sobre la situación de la empresa** they've already updated me *o* filled me in on the company's situation

> **"**
> La moneda de Estados Unidos ignoró un reporte de la firma de colocación laboral Challenger, Gray & Christmas, Inc, que dijo que la cantidad de recortes de empleos anunciada por los empleadores de Estados Unidos cayó 42 por ciento en noviembre, un mes que tuvo menos **días hábiles** por los feriados del Día de Acción de Gracias.
> **"**

diáfano, -a *adj (oficina)* open-plan

diagrama *nm* diagram, chart ▫ **diagrama en árbol, diagrama arbóreo** tree diagram, tree structure; **diagrama de barras** bar chart; **diagrama del ciclo de pedido** order flowchart; **diagrama circular** pie chart; **diagrama de flujo** flow chart; **diagrama de producción** production flowchart; **diagrama de sectores** pie chart

día-hombre *nm* man-day

diálogo *nm* **(a)** *(negociación)* dialogue **(b)** INFORM dialogue

diapositiva *nf* slide, transparency

diario, -a 1 *adj (rutina, vida)* daily; **el funcionamiento diario del negocio** the day-to-day running of the business; **ganaba 100 diarios dólares** she earned $100 a day
2 *nm* **(a)** *(periódico)* newspaper, daily **(b)** *(relación día a día)* diary ▫ MKTG **diario de compras** purchase diary **(c)** *(gasto)* daily expenses

dictado *nm* dictation; **escribir al dictado** to take dictation

dictáfono *nm* Dictaphone®

dictamen *nm (informe)* report ▫ **dictamen pericial** expert's report; CONT **dictamen con reservas** qualified report

dictar *vt* **(a)** *(texto, carta)* to dictate **(b)** DER *(sentencia, fallo)* to pronounce, to pass

dieta(s) *nf(pl) Esp* expense *o* subsistence allowance, *US* per diem ❑ **dieta(s) de alojamiento** accommodation allowance; **dieta(s) de desplazamiento** travel allowance; **dieta(s) de kilometraje** ≃ milleage allowance; **dieta(s) de viaje** travel allowance, travelling allowance

difamación *nf (verbal)* slander; *(escrita)* libel

diferencia *nf* **diferencia horaria** time difference; FIN **diferencia horizontal** horizontal spread; **diferencias negativas de cambio** exchange loss; **diferencias positivas de cambio** exchange gain; **diferencia salarial** wage differential

diferenciación *nf* differentiation ❑ MKTG **diferenciación por líneas** line differentiation; **diferenciación del producto** product differentiation

diferencial 1 *adj (tarifa, arancel)* differential
2 *nm* (**a**) ECON differential ❑ **diferencial de inflación** inflation differential; **diferencial de precios** price differential; **diferencial de salarios, diferencial salarial** wage *o* pay differential; MKTG **diferencial semántico** semantic differential; **diferencial de** *Esp* **tipos** *o Am* **tasas de interés** interest rate differential (**b**) BOLSA spread ❑ **diferencial de precios** price spread; **diferencial vertical** vertical spread

> ❝
> El **diferencial de inflación** de España con la media de los países de la Unión Monetaria se redujo a siete décimas en octubre, dos menos que un mes antes, según datos facilitados hoy por el Instituto Nacional de Estadística (INE).
> ❞

diferir *vt (posponer)* to defer

digital *adj* INFORM digital

digitalización *nf* INFORM digitization

digitalizador *nm* INFORM digitizer ❑ **digitalizador de imágenes** image digitizer

digitalizar *vt* INFORM to digitize

dígito *nm* digit

diligencia *nf* **diligencia debida** due diligence

dilución *nf* FIN *(del valor de las acciones)* dilution ❑ **dilución de capital** equity dilution

dimisión *nf* resignation; **presentar la dimisión** to hand in one's resignation

dimitir *vi* to resign; **dimitió de su cargo como secretario** he resigned from his post as secretary

dinámica *nf* (**a**) *(situación, proceso)* dynamics; **la dinámica de nuestra empresa** the dynamics of our company; **entramos en una dinámica de desarrollo económico** we are beginning a process of economic development ❑ **dinámica de equipo** team dynamics; **dinámica de grupo** group dynamics; **dinámica del mercado** market dynamics; **dinámica de productos** product dynamics (**b**) MKTG **dinámica de grupo de discusión** focus group interview

dinámico, -a *adj* (**a**) *(empresa, ejecutivo, economía)* dynamic (**b**) INFORM dynamic

dinero *nm* money; **¿pagará con dinero o con tarjeta?** will you be paying in cash or by credit card?; **hacer dinero** to make money ❑ **dinero B** undeclared money; **dinero bancario** bank money; **dinero barato** cheap money; **dinero bien invertido** smart money; **dinero en circulación, dinero circulante** money in circulation, active money; **dinero al contado** spot cash; **dinero contante (y sonante)** hard cash; **dinero a corto plazo** money at short notice; **dinero de curso legal** legal tender; **dinero en efectivo** (ready) cash; CONT **dinero en efectivo sin justificar** unallocated cash; **dinero electrónico** e-cash, e-money, electronic cash, electronic money; **dinero especulativo** hot money; **dinero fácil** easy money; **dinero falso** counterfeit money; **dinero fraccionario** divisional money; **dinero fresco** new money; **dinero para gastos** spending money; **dinero interbancario** interbank money; **dinero mercancía** commodity money; **dinero en metálico** cash; **dinero negro** black money; **dinero (de) plástico** plastic (money); **dinero sucio** dirty money; **dinero suelto** loose change; **dinero a la vista** call money, money at call

diodo *nm* diode ❑ **diodo emisor de luz** LED, light-emitting diode

diplomacia *nf (disciplina, carrera, tacto)* diplomacy ❑ **diplomacia del dólar** dollar diplomacy

diplomado, -a *adj* qualified

diputación *nf Esp* **diputación provincial** = governing body of a province in Spain, *Br* ≃ county council

dir. *(abrev de* **director***)* dir

dirección *nf* (**a**) *(mando, gestión)* management ❑ **dirección centralizada** centralized management; **dirección de división** divisional management; **dirección por excepción** management by exception; **dirección general** general management; **dirección de hoteles** hotel administration, hotel management; **dirección de línea** line management; **dirección de marketing** marketing management; **dirección de materiales** materials management; **dirección por objetivos** management by objectives
(**b**) *(directivos) (de empresa)* management; **la dirección del hotel** the hotel management
(**c**) *(organismos)* UE **Dirección General** Directorate General; **Dirección General de Aviación Civil** ≃ Federal Aviation Administration; *RP* **Dirección General Impositiva** *Br* ≃ Inland Revenue, *US* ≃ IRS
(**d**) *(oficina) (de empresa)* manager's office ❑

dirección comercial commercial department; *dirección general* head office

(**e**) *(domicilio)* address; **deme su nombre y dirección, por favor** could you tell me your name and address, please? ❑ *dirección de entrega* delivery address, *esp US* shipping address; *dirección de la oficina* office address; *dirección del remitente* return address; *dirección telegráfica* telegraphic address; *dirección de trabajo* business address

(**f**) INFORM address ❑ *dirección de correo (electrónico)* e-mail address, mail address; *dirección electrónica (de correo)* e-mail address; *(de página)* web page address; *dirección de Internet* Internet address; *dirección IP* IP address; *dirección de memoria* memory address; *dirección web* web address

direccionador *nm* INFORM router

direccionamiento *nm* INFORM addressing ❑ *direccionamiento directo* direct addressing

direccionar *vt* INFORM to address

directiva *nf* (**a**) *(en empresa)* board (of directors) (**b**) *(ley de la UE)* directive ❑ *directiva comunitaria* community directive

directivo, -a 1 *adj (funciones, personal)* managerial; **un cargo directivo** a management post *o* position

2 *nm,f (jefe)* manager ❑ *directivo de banco de inversión* investment banker; *directivo de empresa* executive officer; *directivo de rango inferior* junior executive

> ❝
>
> En los últimos meses, las prejubilaciones y reestructuraciones en la empresa han generado una bolsa de **directivos** en paro que buscan nuevas salidas profesionales. Las empresas de selección y los cazatalentos señalan varias opciones en las que estos profesionales pueden seguir desarrollando sus carreras.
>
> ❞

directo, -a *adj* direct

director, -ora *nm,f (de empresa)* director; *(de hotel, banco)* manager; *(de periódico)* editor ❑ *director adjunto* associate director/manager, deputy director/manager; *director de atención al cliente* customer relations manager; *director de banco* bank manager; *director comercial* marketing manager; *director de comunicación* communications director/manager; *director creativo* creative director; *director de cuentas* account director/manager, *US* account executive; *director de cuentas clave* key-account manager; *director de departamento* department manager, departmental manager; *director de división* divisional director; *director ejecutivo* executive director; *director de exportaciones* export director/

manager; *director financiero* financial director, finance director, chief financial officer; *director financiero corporativo* corporate finance manager; *director en funciones* acting manager; *director general* general manager; *director general adjunto* assistant general manager, deputy managing director; *director gerente* managing director, chief executive, *esp US* chief executive officer; *director de grupo* group manager; *director de hotel* hotel manager; *director de inversiones* investment officer, *US* money manager; *director de marca* brand manager; *director de marketing* marketing manager; *director de mercado* market manager; *director de obra* site manager; *director operativo* operations manager; *director de personal* personnel manager, staff manager; *director de publicidad* advertising director/manager; *director de recursos humanos* human resources manager; *director regional* regional director/manager; *director de relaciones públicas* communications director/manager; *director de RR.HH.* HR manager; *director de sucursal* branch manager; *director técnico* technical director/manager; *director de ventas* sales director/manager

directorio *nm* (**a**) *(lista de direcciones)* directory ❑ *directorio comercial, directorio de empresas* business directory (**b**) *Andes, CAm, Carib, Méx* *directorio (de teléfonos)* telephone directory, phone book (**c**) INFORM directory ❑ *directorio electrónico* electronic directory (**d**) *directorio ejecutivo* executive board

directriz *nfpl* guideline; **seguir las directrices marcadas** to follow the established guidelines ❑ EU *directrices para el empleo* employment guidelines

dirigente 1 *adj (en empresa)* management; **la clase dirigente** the ruling class

2 *nmf (de partido, asociación)* leader; *(de empresa)* manager ❑ *dirigente sindical (cargo superior)* union leader; *(representante)* union official

dirigido, -a *adj* (**a**) *(carta, paquete)* **dirigido a** addressed to (**b**) MKTG **una campaña publicitaria dirigida a un público joven** an advertising campaign targeting young people (**c**) *(economía)* state-controlled

dirigir 1 *vt* (**a**) *(estar al cargo de)* to manage, to run (**b**) *(dedicar, encaminar)* **dirigir unas palabras a alguien** to speak to sb, to address sb; **dirige sus esfuerzos a incrementar los beneficios** she is directing her efforts towards increasing profits, her efforts are aimed at increasing profits (**c**) *(carta, paquete)* to address (**d**) INFORM *(mensaje)* to address

2 dirigirse *vpr* **dirigirse a** *(hablar con)* to address, to speak to; *(escribir a)* to write to; **me dirijo a usted para solicitarle...** I'm writing to you to request... **diríjase al apartado de**

correos 42 write to PO Box 42

discado *nm Andes, RP* TEL dialling ▢ *discado directo* direct dialling

discapacidad *nf* disability; ▢ *discapacidad física* physical disability; *discapacidad psíquica* mental disability

discar *vt Andes, RP* TEL to dial

disciplina *nf disciplina fiscal* fiscal discipline

disciplinario, -a *adj* disciplinary

disco *nm* INFORM disk ▢ *disco de arranque* start-up disk, boot disk; *disco compacto* compact disc; *disco compacto interactivo* compact disc interactive, interactive compact disc; *disco compacto regrabable* CD-R, compact disc rewritable; *disco de copia* copy disk; *disco de demostración* demo disk; *disco de destino* destination disk, target disk; *disco duro* hard disk; *disco externo* external drive; *disco fijo* fixed disk; *disco de instalación* installation disk; *disco maestro* master disk; *disco magnético* magnetic disk; *disco óptico digital* digital optical disk; *disco original* source disk; *disco de programa* program disk; *disco del sistema* system disk; *disco de sólo lectura* read-only disk; *disco versátil digital* digital versatile disk; *disco de* ESP *vídeo o Am* **video digital** digital video disk; *disco Zip®* Zip® disk

discográfica *nf Esp* record company

discográfico, -a *adj (casa, industria)* record

discrepancia *nf* (**a**) *(desacuerdo)* disagreement; **expresó su discrepancia con el comité** she made clear her disagreement with the committee (**b**) *(diferencia)* discrepancy; **una discrepancia en las cuentas** a discrepancy in the accounts

discriminación *nf* discrimination ▢ *discriminación de género* gender discrimination; *discriminación positiva* positive discrimination; ECON *discriminación en el precio* price discrimination; *discriminación racial* racial discrimination; *discriminación sexual* sex discrimination

disculpa *nf (excusa, perdón)* apology; **pedir disculpas a alguien (por)** to apologize to sb (for); **les pido disculpas por el retraso** I apologize for the delay

disculpar 1 *vt* **rogamos disculpen las molestias** we apologize for any inconvenience; **disculpen la tardanza** I'm sorry for being late
 2 disculparse *vpr* to apologize

discurso *nm* speech ▢ *discurso de clausura* closing speech

discusión *nf (conversación, debate)* discussion; **en discusión** under discussion

discutir *vt (hablar sobre)* to discuss; **podemos discutir ese asunto en la próxima reunión** we can discuss the matter at the next meeting

diseñador, -ora *nm,f* designer ▢ *diseñador de anuncios* commercial designer; *diseñador gráfico* graphic designer; *diseñador industrial* industrial designer; *diseñador multimedia* multimedia designer; *diseñador de páginas web* Web designer

diseñar *vt (producto)* to design; **diseñaron una estrategia para hacerse con el mercado** they designed a strategy to capture the market

diseño *nm (de producto)* design; **ropa de diseño** designer clothes ▢ INFORM *diseño asistido por Esp* **ordenador** *o Am* **computadora** computer-aided design; *diseño gráfico* graphic design; *diseño industrial* industrial design; *diseño de página* page design; *diseño del producto* product design; *diseño registrado* registered design

diskette *nm* INFORM diskette, floppy disk

disminución *nf (de demanda, producción, inversiones, exportaciones)* decrease, decline, fall; **la disminución del desempleo** the decrease in unemployment; **una disminución salarial** a decrease *o* drop in wages; **ir en disminución** to be on the decline *o* decrease

disminuir *vi (demanda, producción, inversiones, exportaciones)* to decline, to decrease, to fall; **medidas para que disminuyan los costes** cost-cutting measures; **no disminuye la euforia inversora** investor enthusiasm continues unabated

disolución *nf (de empresa)* dissolution, winding up; *(de grupo empresarial)* splitting up, break-up

> ❝
> La operadora holandesa KPN ha reducido su endeudamiento en 630 millones de euros tras la venta de sus actividades de cable en República Checa y la **disolución** de su filial Vision Networks, informó la empresa.
> ❞

disolver 1 *vt (empresa)* to dissolve, to wind up; *(grupo empresarial)* to split up, to break up
 2 disolverse *vpr (sociedad)* to be dissolved; *(grupo empresarial)* to split up, to break up

dispararse *vpr (precios, inflación, ventas)* to soar, to shoot up

disponer *vt* (**a**) *(colocar)* to arrange; **disponer algo por orden alfabético** arrange sth in alphabetical order (**b**) *(arreglar, preparar)* to arrange; **dispuso todo para el viaje** he made all the arrangements for the journey (**c**) *(establecer)* to provide, to state; **según lo dispuesto en el artículo 5** as provided in section 5

disponibilidad *nf (de plazas, producto, servicio)* availability; **¿qué disponibilidad tiene?** *(en entrevista de empleo)* how many hours would you be able to work?; **disponibilidad inmediata**

(en oferta de empleo) must be able to start immediately

disponible *adj (producto, persona)* available; **disponible en versiones para Mac o PC** available for Mac or PC; **no tenemos habitaciones/plazas disponibles** we don't have any rooms/places available; **el director no está disponible en estos momentos** the manager is not available at the moment

disposición *nf* **(a)** *(en contrato, tratado)* provision; *(orden)* order; *(norma)* regulation; **disposiciones administrativas** administrative orders/regulations; **el medicamento cumple con las disposiciones legales** the drug complies with the legal requirements □ *disposición adicional* additional provision; *disposición especial* special provision; *disposiciones testamentarias* provisions of a will; *disposición transitoria* temporary provision

(b) *(uso)* disposal; **a disposición de** at the disposal of; **estoy a tu disposición** I am at your disposal; *Formal* **quedo a su entera disposición para cualquier información adicional** I will be pleased to provide any further information you may require; **poner algo a disposición de alguien** to put sth at sb's disposal

(c) FIN *(de fondos)* utilization; BANCA *(de crédito)* drawdown

(d) *(del teclado)* layout

dispositivo *nm* INFORM *(mecanismo)* device □ *dispositivo de almacenamiento* storage device; *dispositivo de entrada* input device; *dispositivo de entrada y salida* input/output device; *dispositivo de manos libres* hands-free device; *dispositivo periférico* peripheral device, peripheral unit; *dispositivo de salida* output device

disputa *nf* dispute □ *disputa comercial* commercial dispute; *disputa legal* legal dispute

disquete *nm* INFORM diskette, floppy disk □ *disquete original* source disk; *disquete de sólo lectura* read-only disk; *disquete virgen sin formatear* blank unformatted disk

disquetera *nf* INFORM disk drive, floppy (disk) drive

distancia *nf* **a larga distancia** *(llamada)* long-distance

distintivo *nm* **(a)** *(señal)* badge **(b)** *(marca)* distinguishing mark o characteristic

distorsión *nf* MKTG *distorsión selectiva* selective distortion

distribución *nf* **(a)** *(de mercancías)* distribution □ *distribución comercial* commercial distribution; *distribución domiciliaria (de propaganda)* door-to-door delivery; *distribución exclusiva* exclusive distribution; *distribución física* physical distribution; *distribución intensiva* intensive distribution; *distribución*

justo a tiempo just-in-time distribution, JIT distribution; *distribución en mano (de propaganda)* distribution by hand; *distribución en masa* mass distribution; *distribución al por mayor* wholesale distribution; *distribución mayorista y minorista* wholesale and retail distribution; *distribución numérica* numerical distribution; *distribución ponderada* weighted distribution; *distribución selectiva* selective distribution

(b) *(de trabajo, beneficios, dividendos)* distribution; **una distribución bastante desigual de los beneficios** a rather uneven distribution of the profits □ *distribución de la plusvalía* capital gains distribution; *distribución de la riqueza* distribution of wealth

(c) *(de edificio)* layout □ *distribución aproximada* rough layout; *distribución de la planta* plant layout

distribuidor, -ora 1 *adj* **una red distribuidora** a distribution network

2 *nm,f* *(empresa)* distributor, *Br* stockist □ *distribuidor autorizado* authorized distributor, authorized dealer; *distribuidor local* local agent

distribuir *vt* **(a)** *(mercancías, productos)* to distribute; **una empresa que distribuye material de papelería** a firm distributing stationery materials **(b)** *(trabajo, beneficios, dividendos)* to distribute; **distribuir la riqueza más justamente** to share out o distribute wealth more justly

distrito *nm* district □ *Distrito Federal (en México)* Federal District *(= Mexico City)*; *(en Venezuela)* Federal District *(= Caracas)*; *distrito postal* postal district

diversificación *nf* diversification □ FIN *diversificación de cartera* portfolio diversification; *diversificación de productos* product diversification; FIN *diversificación de riesgos* risk spreading

diversificar 1 *vt* to diversify; **debemos diversificar la producción/nuestros servicios** we should diversify production/our services

2 diversificarse *vpr* to diversify

diversos, -as *adj (gastos)* miscellaneous, sundry

dividendo *nm* FIN dividend; **cobrar/repartir dividendos** to be paid/to distribute dividends; **dar/obtener dividendos** to pay/to receive dividends □ *dividendo por acción* earnings per share; *dividendo en acciones* share dividend, stock dividend, *US* scrip dividend; *dividendo acumulado* accrued dividend; *dividendo acumulativo* cumulative dividend; *dividendo bruto* gross dividend; *dividendo complementario* final dividend; *dividendo a cuenta* interim dividend; *dividendo en efectivo* cash dividend; *dividendo expresado en bruto* grossed-up dividend; *dividendo extraordinario* bonus dividend, windfall dividend; **dividendo neto** net dividend; **dividendo preferente, dividendo preferencial** preferential dividend, *Br* preference dividend

❝
El Banco Popular pagará el primer **dividendo** activo a cuenta del ejercicio de 2003 desde el próximo 1 de octubre, por un importe de 0,395 euros brutos, según informó el banco a la Comisión Nacional del Mercado de Valores (CNMV).
❞

dividir *vt (repartir)* to share out, to divide; **el resto de los beneficios fue dividido entre los empleados** the rest of the profits were shared out *o* divided among the employees

divisa *nf (moneda)* currency; **divisas** foreign exchange; **una divisa fuerte/débil** a strong/weak currency; **la principal fuente de divisas** the main source of foreign currency; **fuga de divisas** flight of capital □ *divisa bloqueada* blocked currency; *divisa convertible* convertible currency; *divisa débil* soft currency; *divisa fuerte (estable, convertible)* hard currency; *divisa de reserva* reserve currency

división *nf* (**a**) *(departamento)* division □ *división de exportación* export division; *división de formación* training division (**b**) *(repartición)* division □ *división del trabajo* division of labour

divulgación *nf (de información financiera)* disclosure □ *divulgación de cuentas* disclosure of accounts

DNI *nm (abrev de* **documento nacional de identidad***)* ID card

DNS *nm* INFORM *(abrev de* **Domain Name System***)* DNS

doble 1 *adj* double □ UE *doble circulación (de divisas)* dual circulation; INFORM *doble clic* double-click; **hacer doble clic** to double-click; BOLSA *doble cotización* dual listing; *doble divisa* dual currency; *doble imposición* double taxation; BOLSA *doble opción* double option; *doble seguro* double insurance; *doble tributación* double taxation

2 *nm* **el doble** twice as much/many; **gana el doble** she earns twice as much; **los domingos cobro el doble** I get double time on Sundays

documentación *nf* (**a**) *(identificación) (de persona)* papers, identification; *(de vehículo, cargamento, mercancías)* documents (**b**) *(información)* information; *(manuales de uso)* documentation (**c**) *(investigación)* documentation, research; **equipo de documentación** research team

documentalista *nmf* documentalist

documento *nm* (**a**) *(escrito)* document □ *documentos aduaneros* customs papers; *documentos de a bordo* ship's papers; BANCA *documento de cancelación* memorandum of satisfaction; *documentos comerciales* commercial documents; *documentos de domiciliación* domiciliation papers; *documentos de embarque* shipping documents; *documentos de identificación* identification papers; *documentos de los impuestos especiales* excise documents; *documento interno de la empresa* internal company document; *documento legal* legal document; *documento de licitación* tender document; *documento modelo* standard document; *documento nacional de identidad* identity card; *documento normativo* policy paper; *documento de la oferta* tender document; *documento oficial* official document; *documento original* master document; CONT original document; *documento de pago* document of payment; *documento de política general* policy document; *documento de trabajo* working document; *documento de transporte* transport document; DER *documento de venta* bill of sale (**b**) INFORM document □ *documento original* source document

dólar *nm* dollar □ *dólar estadounidense* US dollar

dolarización *nf* ECON dollarization

domiciliación *nf Esp* domiciliación (bancaria) *(de cantidad variable)* direct debit; *(de cantidad fija)* banker's order, *Br* standing order; **pagar mediante domiciliación (bancaria)** to pay by direct debit/by standing *o* banker's order □ *domiciliación de nóminas* = payment of salary directly into employee's bank account; *domiciliación de pagos* direct debit; *domiciliación de recibos* direct debit

❝
El pago de las cuotas podrá hacerse mediante **domiciliación de pagos** a favor del Ayuntamiento, o bien en efectivo en las dependencias municipales. A tal efecto se entregará a cada contribuyente un impreso de **domiciliación de pagos**.
❞

domiciliar *vt* (**a**) *Esp (pago) (de una cantidad variable)* to pay by direct debit; *(de una cantidad fija)* to pay by banker's order *o* standing order; **domiciliar la nómina** *o* **el sueldo** to have one's salary paid into a bank account (**b**) *Méx (carta)* to address

domicilio *nm (dirección)* address; **cambio de domicilio** change of address; **reparto a domicilio** home delivery; **vender a domicilio** to sell door-to-door □ *domicilio comercial* business address; *domicilio conyugal* matrimonial home; *domicilio de facturación* invoicing address; *domicilio fijo* permanent address; *domicilio fiscal* tax domicile; *domicilio habitual* usual residence; *domicilio particular* private residence; **domicilio social** registered office

dominio *nm* (**a**) INFORM domain ❏ *dominio público* public domain (**b**) *(de idiomas)* command; **para el puesto requerimos dominio de al menos dos lenguas** the post requires mastery of at least two languages; **un buen dominio de inglés** a good command of English

donación *nf* donation, gift; **hacer donación de algo a alguien** to donate sth to sb ❏ *donación inter vivos* gift inter vivos

donador, -ora *nm,f (de bienes, capital)* donor

donante *nmf* donor

donativo *nm* donation; **dar** *o* **hacer un donativo a alguien** to give *o* make a donation to sb

dormir *vi* INFORM to sleep

dorso *nm (de cheque, impreso)* back; **al dorso, en el dorso** on the back; **véase al dorso** see overleaf

DOS *nm* INFORM *(abrev de* **disk operating system***)* DOS

dossier *nm (informe)* dossier, file

dotación *nf* (**a**) *(de dinero, medios)* **una beca con una dotación de 5.000 euros** a scholarship worth 5,000 euros; **la fábrica necesita mayor dotación de maquinaria** the factory needs to be better equipped with machinery ❏ *dotación presupuestaria* budget allocation; *dotación presupuestaria global* overall budget (**b**) *(de personal)* staff, personnel; **un hotel con poca dotación** an understaffed hotel

dotar *vt* (**a**) *(con medios)* to equip; **dotaron todas las sucursales con sistemas de alarma** they equipped all the branches with alarm systems
(**b**) *(con personal)* to staff; **dotar algo de** *(hotel, tienda)* to staff sth with
(**c**) *(con dinero)* **actos benéficos para dotar de fondos (a) una organización humanitaria** charity events to raise funds for a humanitarian organization; **la beca está dotada con 15.000 dólares** the scholarship is worth $15,000; **el premio fue dotado con 100.000 pesos** the prize was set at 100,000 pesos

dotes *nfpl (naturales)* qualities; *(aprendidas)* skills ❏ *dotes para la comunicación* communication skills; *dotes de gestión* management skills; *dotes de mando* leadership qualities *o* skills

dpi INFORM *(abrev de* **dots per inch***)* dpi

dpto. *(abrev de* **departamento***)* dept; **dpto. de personal** personnel dept

dracma *nm o nf* Antes drachma

DRAM *nf* INFORM *(abrev de* **Dynamic Random Access Memory***)* DRAM

drive *nm* INFORM drive

driver *nm* INFORM driver

DTP *nm* INFORM *(abrev de* **desktop publishing***)* DTP

DUA *nm (abrev de* **Documento Único Aduanero***)* single customs document

dueño, -a *nm,f (propietario)* owner; *(de casa alquilada)* landlord, *f* landlady; **cambiar de dueño** to change hands

dumping *nm* ECON dumping; **hacer dumping** to dump, to practise dumping ❏ *dumping social* social dumping

duopolio *nm* ECON duopoly

dúplex *adj & nm inv* TEL duplex

duplicado *nm* duplicate (copy); **por duplicado** in duplicate

duplicar 1 *vt* (**a**) *(cantidad, número)* to double (**b**) *(documento)* to duplicate
2 duplicarse *vpr* to double

duración *nf (de hipoteca, seguro)* term; *(de alquiler)* duration; *(de campaña, spot publicitario)* length; **la duración del cargo es de cinco años** the appointment is for a five-year period; **de larga duración** *(desempleado)* long-term ❏ *duración del ciclo de explotación* working capital cycle; *duración del ciclo de pedido* order cycle time; *duración de(l) vuelo* flight time

duradero, -a *adj (bienes)* durable

DVD *nm (abrev de* **Disco Versátil Digital***)* DVD

E

EBIT *nm* FIN (*abrev de* **earnings before interest and tax**) EBIT

EBITDA, ebitda *nm* FIN (*abrev de* **earnings before interest, taxes, depreciation and amortization**) EBITDA

> La nota discordante en el panorama de Internet europeo ha llegado de la mano de Terra, que obtuvo un **ebitda** negativo de 120 millones de euros y unas pérdidas netas de 2.009 millones de euros, los mayores números rojos de un grupo europeo de Internet.

e-business *nm* e-business

echar *vt* (**a**) *(empleado)* **echar a alguien (de)** to sack sb (from) (**b**) *(carta)* to post, *US* to mail; **echar algo al correo** to put sth in the post, to post sth, *US* to mail sth

Ecofin *nm* UE (*abrev de* **Consejo de Ministros de Economía y Finanzas**) ECOFIN

ecológico, -a *adj* (**a**) *(deterioro, equilibrio)* environmental; *(desastre)* ecological (**b**) *(alimentos)* organic; *(detergente, producto)* environmentally-friendly, green

e-commerce *nm* e-commerce

econométra *nmf* econometrician

econometría *nf* econometrics

econométrico, -a *adj* econometric

economía *nf* (**a**) *(actividad productiva)* economy □ **economía abierta** open economy; **economía del bienestar** welfare economy; **economía capitalista** capitalist economy; **economía dirigida** command economy, controlled economy; **economía doméstica** housekeeping; **economía dormida** sleeping economy; **economía de la especulación** bubble economy; **economía globalizada** globalized economy; *Am* **economía informal** black economy; **economía de (libre) empresa** enterprise economy; **economía de libre mercado** free-market economy; **economía madura** mature economy; **economía de mercado** market economy; **economía mixta** mixed economy; **economía mundial** global economy, world economy; **economía natural** natural economy; **economía participada** share economy; **economía planificada** planned economy; **economía**

de pleno empleo full-employment economy; **economía salarial** wage economy; **economía social de mercado** social market economy; **economía socialista** socialist economy; **economía de subsistencia** subsistence economy; **economía sumergida** black economy; **economía de trueque** barter economy

(**b**) *(ciencia, estudio)* economics □ **economía aplicada** applied economics; **economía del bienestar** welfare economics; **economía de empresas** business economics; **economía familiar** home economics; **economía medioambiental** environmental economics; **economía política** political economics

(**c**) *(situación económica) (de persona, familia)* finances

(**d**) *(ahorro)* saving; **por economía de espacio** to save space; **hacer algo con gran economía de medios** to do sth with the optimum use of resources; **hacer economías** to economize, to make economies □ **economía de escala** economy of scale

económicamente *adv* (**a**) *(relacionado con la economía)* economically; **un país económicamente pobre** an economically backward country (**b**) *(relacionado con el dinero)* financially; **económicamente, no tenemos problemas** we have no problems financially (**c**) *(con ahorro)* cheaply, inexpensively

economicismo *nm* economism

economicista *adj* economicist

económico, -a *adj* (**a**) *(de la economía)* economic; *(del dinero)* financial; **la política económica del gobierno** the government's economic policy; **una empresa con problemas económicos** a company with financial problems (**b**) *(barato)* cheap, inexpensive; **pagándolo al contado sale más económico** it works out cheaper if you pay in cash (**c**) *(rentable) (método, máquina)* economical

economista *nmf* economist

economizar 1 *vt* to save, to economize on **2** *vi (ahorrar dinero)* to economize

ecotasa *nf (impuesto)* ecotax, green tax

ecoturismo *nm* ecotourism

ECSDA *nf* FIN (*abrev de* **European Central Securities Depositories Association**) ECSDA

ecu *nm Antes* UE (*abrev de* **unidad de cuenta europea**) ECU, ecu

ecuación *nf* equation ❑ *ecuación de benefi-cios* profit equation; *ecuación de costos* *oEsp* *costes* cost equation; *ecuación de (la) deman-da* demand equation; *ecuación de ventas* sales equation

ed. (**a**) (*abrev de* **editor**) ed (**b**) (*abrev de* **edición**) ed, edn (**c**) (*abrev de* **edificio**) bldg

edad *nf* age; **dividir un grupo por edades** to divide a group by age ❑ *edad de jubilación* re-tirement age; *edad límite* age limit; *edad nor-mal de jubilación* normal retirement age

edición *nf* (**a**) (*acción de publicar*) publication; **Ediciones Herrero** Herrero Publications; **edi-ción (a cargo) de Jorge Urrutia** (*en libro*) edited by Jorge Urrutia
(**b**) (*ejemplares publicados*) edition; **nueva edi-ción revisada y ampliada** new edition revised and enlarged ❑ *edición abreviada* abridged edition; *edición anotada* annotated edition; *edición de bolsillo* pocket edition; *edición crí-tica* critical edition; *edición electrónica* elec-tronic publishing; *edición facsímil* facsimile edition; *edición limitada* limited edition; *edi-ción de lujo* deluxe edition; *edición pirata* pi-rate edition; *edición príncipe* first edition
(**c**) INFORM editing
(**d**) (*celebración periódica*) **la décima edición del festival** the tenth festival; **los cursos de verano cumplen su vigésima edición** the sum-mer courses are now in their twentieth year

edificable *adj* suitable for building on; **lo de-clararon edificable** it was classified as suitable for development, *US* it was zoned for building

edificio *nm* building ❑ *edificio de administra-ción* administration building, administrative building; *edificio inteligente* intelligent *o* smart building; *edificio de oficinas* office building

editar *vt* (**a**) (*publicar*) (*libro, periódico, revista*) to publish; (*disco, vídeo*) to release (**b**) (*modificar*) (*texto, programa, grabación*) to edit (**c**) INFORM to edit

editor, -ora **1** *adj* publishing; **empresa editora** publishing company
2 *nm,f* (**a**) (*que publica*) (*libro, periódico, revista*) publisher (**b**) (*que modifica*) (*texto, programa, gra-bación*) editor
3 *nm* INFORM editor ❑ *editor de enlaces* link edi-tor; *editor de HTML* HTML editor; *editor de iconos* icon editor; *editor de texto(s)* text edi-tor; *editor de vínculos* link editor

editorial **1** *adj* (*casa, sector, proyecto*) publishing
2 *nf* (*empresa*) publisher, publishing house *o* company
3 *nm* (*en periódico*) editorial, *esp Br* leader

editorializar *vi* to editorialize

EEE *nm* (*abrev de* **espacio económico europeo**) EEA

efectividad *nf* (**a**) (*eficacia*) effectiveness ❑ *efectividad publicitaria* advertising effective-ness; *efectividad de las ventas* sales effective-ness (**b**) (*validez*) **tendrá efectividad desde el próximo lunes** it will take effect as from next Monday

efectivo, -a **1** *adj* (**a**) (*producción, beneficio*) ef-fective (**b**) **hacer efectivo** (*cheque*) to cash; (*di-nero, crédito*) to pay; (*pago*) to make; **hacer efectivo un ingreso en una cuenta bancaria** to make a deposit in a bank account
2 *nm* (*dinero*) cash; **en efectivo** in cash; **pagos/premios en efectivo** cash payments/prizes; **pagar/cobrar en efectivo** to pay/be paid in cash ❑ *efectivo en caja* *Br* cash in hand, *US* cash on hand; *efectivo disponible* available funds

> **"**
> Las aportaciones **en efectivo** es la manera más habitual de las donaciones empresa-riales, seguidas a bastante distancia por las aportaciones en especie y la dedicación del tiempo laboral de los propios trabaja-dores.
> **"**

efecto *nm* (**a**) FIN (*documento*) bill ❑ *efecto ban-cario* bank bill *o* draft; *efecto no bancario* un-bankable bill *o* draft; *efectos en cartera* bills in hand; *efectos a cobrar* bills receivable; *efecto al cobro* bill for collection; *efecto comercial* trade bill; *efectos comerciales en eurodivisas* euro-commercial paper; *efectos comerciales de primera clase* first-class paper; *efectos del estado* government securities; *efecto de favor* accommodation bill; *efecto impagado* over-due bill; *efecto interbancario* bank draft; *efec-to en moneda extranjera* bill in foreign currency; *efecto negociable* negotiable paper; *efectos a pagar* bills payable; *efecto al porta-dor* bearer bill; *efectos públicos* government securities; *efecto a la vista* sight paper *o* draft
(**b**) (*consecuencia, resultado*) effect; **las me-didas contra el desempleo no han surtido efecto** the measures against unemployment haven't had any effect *o* haven't been effective ❑ *efecto bola de nieve* snowball effect; *efecto bumerán, efecto bumerang* boomerang ef-fect; *efecto de dientes de sierra* see-saw ef-fect; FIN *efecto dilutivo* dilutive effect; MKTG *efecto experiencia* experience effect; MKTG *efecto halo* halo effect; MKTG *efecto indirecto* indirect effect; *efecto de sustitución* substitu-tion effect
(**c**) (*vigencia*) effect; **con efecto desde** with ef-fect from; **con efecto retroactivo** retroactive-ly; **la subida salarial tendrá efecto retroactivo a partir del 1 de mayo** the pay increase is back-dated to 1 May; **dejar un contrato sin efecto** to render a contract (null and) void; **¿desde cuán-do tiene efecto esa norma?** how long has that law been in force?

(**d**) *(finalidad)* **al efecto, a dicho efecto, a tal efecto** to that end; **rogamos contacte con nosotros; a tal efecto le adjuntamos...** you are requested to contact us, and to that end please find attached...; **a efectos legales, esta empresa ya no existe** as far as the law is concerned *o* in the eyes of the law, this company no longer exists; **a efectos fiscales, estos ingresos no cuentan** this income is not counted for tax purposes, this income is not taxable; **a todos los efectos el propietario es usted** for all practical purposes you are the owner
(**e**) *efectos personales* personal effects

efectuar *vt (compra, pago, venta)* to make; *(operación, estudio)* to carry out

eficacia *nf (de medida, gestión)* effectiveness; *(de persona, organización)* efficiency □ *eficacia del marketing* marketing efficiency

eficaz *adj (medida, gestión)* effective; *(persona, organización)* efficient

eficiencia *nf* efficiency □ *eficiencia absoluta* absolute efficiency; *eficiencia económica* economic efficiency; *eficiencia máxima* maximum efficiency; *eficiencia operativa* operational efficiency

eficiente *adj* efficient

EFTA *nf (abrev de* **European Free Trade Association**) EFTA

EGA *nm* INFORM *(abrev de* **enhanced graphics adaptor**) EGA

egreso *nm Am* outgoing; **ingresos y egresos** income and expenditure

ejecución *nf* (**a**) *(realización) (de trabajo, orden)* carrying out; *(de plan, proyecto)* implementation; *(de pedido)* fulfilment (**b**) DER *(de hipoteca)* foreclosure (**c**) INFORM *(de programa)* execution, running

ejecutable INFORM **1** *adj* executable
2 *nm* executable file, exe file

ejecutar *vt* (**a**) *(realizar) (trabajo, orden)* to carry out; *(plan, proyecto)* to implement, to carry out *(pedido)* to fulfil (**b**) BOLSA *(opción)* to exercise (**c**) DER *(hipoteca)* to foreclose (on) (**d**) INFORM *(programa)* to execute, to run

ejecutivo, -a 1 *adj* executive
2 *nm,f (persona)* executive; **un alto ejecutivo** a top executive □ *ejecutivo de cuentas* account executive; *ejecutivo de marketing* marketing executive; *ejecutivo de publicidad* advertising executive; *ejecutivo de ventas* sales executive

ejemplar *nm (de libro, diario)* copy; *(de revista)* issue, number □ *ejemplar informativo* information copy; *ejemplar de muestra* specimen copy; *ejemplar de regalo (libro)* complimentary copy

ejercer 1 *vt* (**a**) *(profesión)* to practise; *(cargo)* to hold; **ejerció la presidencia de la empresa** durante años he was *Br* chairman *o US* president of the company for years; **ejercer funciones de secretario** to act as secretary (**b**) *(poder, derecho)* to exercise (**c**) BOLSA *(opción)* to exercise
2 *vi* to practise (one's profession); **ejercer de** *o* **como** to practise *o* work as

ejercicio *nm* (**a**) FIN *Br* financial year, *US* fiscal year □ *ejercicio contable* accounting year; *año en curso* current year; *ejercicio económico Br* financial year, *US* fiscal year; *ejercicio fiscal* tax year, *US* tax period; *ejercicio financiero Br* financial year, *US* fiscal year; *ejercicio presupuestario* budgetary year
(**b**) BOLSA *(de opción)* exercise
(**c**) *(de profesión)* practising; *(de cargo, funciones)* carrying out; **se le acusa de negligencia en el ejercicio de sus funciones** he has been accused of negligence in carrying out *o* in the performance of his duties; **un abogado en ejercicio** a practising lawyer
(**d**) *(de poder, derecho)* exercising; **el ejercicio del voto** the use of one's vote

> **"**
> El sector de la franquicia alcanzará una facturación de 16.150 millones de euros en el presente **ejercicio**, el 15,5 por ciento más que los 13.991 millones facturados en 2002, según las previsiones realizadas por la consultora especializada en franquicias Tormo y Asociados.
> **"**

elaboración *nf* (**a**) *(de producto)* manufacture, production; **proceso de elaboración** *(industrial)* manufacturing process (**b**) *(de plan, programa)* drawing up; *(de estudio, informe)* preparation *(de idea, teoría)* working out, development □ *elaboración del presupuesto* budgeting

elaborar *vt* (**a**) *(producto)* to make, to manufacture (**b**) *(plan, presupuesto, programa)* to draw up; *(estudio, informe)* to prepare; *(idea, teoría)* to work out, to develop; *(censo)* to conduct, to take

elasticidad *nf* ECON *(de mercado, precios, demanda)* elasticity

elástico, -a *adj* ECON *(mercado, oferta, demanda)* elastic

electrónico, -a *adj* electronic

elegibilidad *nf* eligibility

elevado, -a *adj (precio, inflación)* high; *(impuesto)* high, heavy; *(descuento)* deep; **consiguieron elevados beneficios** they made a large profit

elevar 1 *vt* (**a**) *(aumentar) (precio, nivel)* to raise; *(ventas, ganancias)* to increase (**b**) *(presentar) (queja, recurso)* to lodge, to present; *(propuesta)* to submit, to present; **elevar a público** *(documento)* to execute in a public deed, to notarise
2 elevarse *vpr* **elevarse a** *(gastos, cifra)* to amount *o* come to

eliminación *nf (de residuos)* disposal; *(de fronteras, obstáculos)* removal, elimination

eliminar *vt (residuos)* to dispose of; *(fronteras, obstáculos)* to remove, to eliminate

e-mail *nm* e-mail

embalaje *nm* (**a**) *(acción)* packing, packaging (**b**) *(material)* packaging ❑ *embalaje de burbujas* bubble pack, bubble wrap; *embalaje hermético* vacuum packaging, airtight packaging; *embalaje original* original packaging

embalar *vt* to pack, to package

embarcar 1 *vt (mercancías)* to take on, to load; *(personas)* to board
2 *vi (persona)* to board
3 embarcarse *vpr (persona)* to board, to embark

embargar *vt* DER *(bienes)* to seize, to impound *(because of unpaid debt)*; *(vivienda)* to foreclose on

embargo *nm* (**a**) DER *(de bienes)* seizure; *(de vivienda)* foreclosure (**b**) POL *(económico)* embargo; **levantar un embargo** to lift or raise an embargo ❑ *embargo comercial* trade embargo

embarque *nm (de personas)* boarding; *(de mercancías)* loading ❑ *embarque parcial* part shipment

emergente *adj* ECON emerging

emilio *nm Fam* INFORM e-mail (message)

emisión *nf* (**a**) BOLSA, FIN *(de acciones, papel moneda)* issue ❑ *emisión de acciones* share issue; *emisión de acciones liberadas* scrip issue; *emisión de acciones nuevas* new issue; *emisión de bonos* bond issue; *emisión convertible* conversion issue; *emisión con derecho preferente de suscripción* rights issue; *emisión fiduciaria* fiduciary issue; *emisión gratuita de acciones* bonus issue, capitalization issue; *emisión de obligaciones* debenture issue; *emisión de papel moneda* note issue; *emisión en serie* block issue (**b**) *(transmisión)* broadcasting ❑ *emisión vía satélite* satellite broadcasting

> 66
> Para encontrar la fuente de la primera divergencia hay que remontarse al nacimiento de Jazztel, una compañía que basó su financiación en la **emisión de bonos** de alta rentabilidad. La legislación española no permitía este esquema, así que la operadora tuvo que buscar acogida en un país cuya normativa lo contemplase. Reino Unido fue la elección y Londres es, desde entonces, su sede.
> 99

emisor, -ora *adj* BOLSA, FIN issuing; **la entidad emisora** the issuing body

emisora *nf* (**a**) BOLSA, FIN issuing body (**b**) *(de radio)* radio station ❑ *emisora vía satélite* satellite station

> 66
> El mercado accionario nacional fue impulsado por los favorables reportes financieros de las **emisoras**, y también por la caída de los réditos nacionales, que obligan a los fondos de inversión a posicionarse en instrumentos de mayor rentabilidad.
> 99

emitir *vt* (**a**) FIN *(acciones, papel moneda, póliza)* to issue *(préstamo, bonos)* to float (**b**) *(programa de radio o TV)* to broadcast

emoticón, emoticono *nm* INFORM smiley, emoticon

empaque *nm Am (envase)* packaging

empaquetado *nm* packaging ❑ *empaquetado automático* automatic packaging; *empaquetado manual* manual packaging

empaquetar *vt* to package

empeñar 1 *vt (bienes)* to pawn
2 empeñarse *vpr (endeudarse)* to get into debt

empeño *nm (de bienes)* pawning; **casa de empeño(s)** pawnshop

empezar 1 *vt (proyecto, campaña)* to start
2 *vi* to start; **empezó con 500 euros a la semana** she started on 500 euros a week; **empezar a fabricarse** to go into production

emplazamiento *nm* location ❑ MKTG *emplazamiento exclusivo* solus site; *emplazamiento preferente* special position

empleabilidad *nf* employability

empleable *adj* employable

empleado, -a 1 *adj* employed
2 *nm,f* employee; **sólo empleados y personal autorizado** *(en letrero)* staff and authorized personnel only ❑ *empleado de banca, empleado de banco,* SAm *empleado bancario* bank clerk; *empleado del estado* civil servant; *empleado de oficina* white-collar worker; *Méx empleado de planta* permanent employee; *empleado público* public employee

empleador, -ora *nm,f* employer

emplear 1 *vt* (**b**) *(contratar)* to employ (**a**) *(usar) (herramienta, recursos, método)* to use, to employ; *(tiempo, dinero)* to spend
2 emplearse *vpr (colocarse)* to find a job

empleo *nm* (**a**) *(trabajo)* employment; *(puesto)* job; **economía de pleno empleo** full-employment economy; **la precariedad del empleo** job insecurity; **estar suspendido de empleo y sueldo** to be suspended without pay ❑ *empleo compartido* job sharing; *empleo fijo* permanent job; *empleo juvenil* youth employment; *empleo real* actual employment; *empleo* *temporal* temporary employment (**b**) *(uso)* use; **modo de empleo** instructions for use

emprendedor, -ora 1 *adj* enterprising; **se necesita ejecutivo dinámico y emprendedor** dynamic and enterprising executive required
2 *nm,f* entrepreneur

emprender *vt (trabajo, proyecto)* to undertake; *(ataque, ofensiva)* to launch; **emprender acciones judiciales contra alguien** to initiate legal proceedings against sb

empresa *nf* (**a**) *(sociedad)* company; **montó su propia empresa** he started his own business; **la pequeña y mediana empresa** small and medium-sized businesses; **la libre empresa** free enterprise □ **empresa de almacenaje** warehousing company; **empresa de alquiler** hire company, rental company; **empresa asociada** associate company, associated company; *(perteneciente al mismo grupo)* sister company; **empresa auditora** audit company; **empresa común** joint venture (company); **empresa de comunicación** PR company; **empresa conjunta** joint venture (company); **empresa cotizada (en Bolsa)** listed company, *Br* quoted company; **empresa no cotizada (en Bolsa)** unlisted company, *Br* unquoted company; **empresa elaboradora de alimentos** food manufacturer; **empresa estatal** state-owned company; **empresa de estudios de mercado** market research company; **empresa exportadora** export company; **empresa de factoring** *o* **factoraje** factoring company, factoring agent; **empresa fantasma** dummy company; **empresa filial** affiliated company, subsidiary; **empresa de importación-exportación** import-export company; **empresa importadora** import company; **empresa de información comercial** mercantile agency; **empresa de investigación** research company; **empresa de investigación de mercado** market research company; **empresa júnior** junior enterprise, = firm set up and run by business studies students; **empresa manufacturera** manufacturing company; **empresa de marketing** marketing company; **empresa matriz** parent company; **empresa mayorista** wholesale firm; **empresa mercantil** trading company; **empresa minorista** retail company; **empresa mixta** mixed company; **empresa multinacional** multinational company; **empresa de paquetería** parcel delivery company; **empresa privada** *(que no cotiza en Bolsa)* private company; **la empresa privada** private enterprise, the private sector; **empresa pública** state-owned company, public sector firm; **la empresa pública** the public sector; **empresa puntera** blue-chip company; **empresa punto com** dot.com (company); **empresa de relaciones públicas** PR company; **empresa de reciente creación** start-up company; **empresa de salvamento** salvage company; **empresa de**

seguridad security firm; **empresa de servicio público** public utility (company), *US* public service corporation; **empresa de servicios** service company; **empresa de servicios de tierra** ground handling agent; **empresa de software** software company; **empresa de sondeos de opinión** polling company; **empresa subsidiaria** subsidiary company, ancillary; **empresa de telecomunicaciones** telecommunications company; **empresa de trabajo temporal** temp agency, temping agency; **empresa transitaria** freight forwarder; **empresa transnacional** global player; **empresa de transporte aéreo** airfreight company; **empresa de transporte por carretera** road haulage company; **empresa de transporte combinado** combined transport company; **empresa de transportes, empresa transportista** transport company; **empresa unipersonal** sole trader, one person business; **empresa de venta al detalle** retail company; **empresa de venta por correo** mail-order company
(**b**) *(dirección)* employer, company; **las negociaciones con la empresa** the negotiations with the employer
(**c**) *(acción)* enterprise, undertaking; **se embarcó en una peligrosa empresa** he embarked on a risky enterprise *o* undertaking

empresariado *nm* employers

> **"**
>
> Al dar a conocer su plan de gestión o plan estratégico para el período 2003-2005, la presidenta de Fedecámaras señaló que el **empresariado** "no permitirá que el país siga por un despeñadero". Y lamentó que Venezuela se ubique entre las primeras naciones con mayor inflación y recesión económica; y en los últimos lugares de competitividad.
>
> **"**

empresarial 1 *adj (estructura, crisis, líder)* business; **estudios empresariales** management *o* business studies; **organización empresarial** employers' organization
2 **empresariales** *nfpl Esp* business studies

empresario, -a 1 *adj RP (estructura, crisis, líder)* business; **el mundo empresario** the business world
2 *nm,f* (**a**) *(patrono)* employer; *(hombre, mujer de negocios)* businessman, *f* businesswoman; **las organizaciones de empresarios** employers' organizations; **los pequeños empresarios** owners of small businesses, small businesspeople □ **empresario individual** sole trader, *US* sole proprietor (**b**) *(de teatro)* impresario

empréstito *nm* FIN debenture loan □ **empréstito de consolidación** funding loan; **empréstito de conversión** conversion loan; **empréstito en divisas** foreign currency loan; **empréstito**

forzoso forced loan; *empréstito con garantía de oro* gold loan; *empréstito indexado, empréstito indizado* indexed loan; *empréstito de obligaciones* debenture loan; *empréstito público* public loan

emulación *nf* INFORM emulation ◻ *emulación de terminal* terminal emulation

emular *vt* INFORM to emulate

encabezamiento *nm (de escrito, lista, apartado)* heading; *(de carta) (fórmula de saludo)* opening, salutation; *(en documento electrónico)* header

encajar *vi (concordar) (datos)* to tally

encaje *nm* BANCA reserve ◻ *encaje legal* legal reserve

encargado, -a 1 *adj* responsible (**de** for), in charge (**de** of); **está encargado de cerrar la oficina** he's responsible for locking up the office, it's his job to lock up the office
2 *nm,f (de tienda, negocio)* manager, *f* manageress; *(en fábrica)* (shop) foreman; **póngame con el encargado** can I speak to the person in charge, please? ◻ *encargado de almacén (responsable de existencias)* inventory *o Br* stock controller; *(responsable de almacén)* warehouse keeper; *encargado de compras* business buyer; *encargado de facturación* invoice clerk; *encargado de marketing* marketer; *encargado de sección* department *o* departmental manager

encargar 1 *vt* (**a**) *(producto)* to order; *(proyecto)* to commission (**b**) *(poner al cargo de)* **encargar a alguien de algo, encargar algo a alguien** to put sb in charge of sth
2 encargarse *vpr* **encargarse de algo** *(ocuparse)* to deal with sth; *(estar a cargo de)* to be in charge of sth; **se encarga de las facturas** she deals with *o* handles the invoicing; **él se encargaba de la tienda** he looked after the shop, he was in charge of the shop; **yo me encargaré de eso** I'll take care of *o* see to that; **encargarse de hacer algo** to undertake to do sth

encargo, *RP* **encargue** *nm (de producto)* order; *(de proyecto)* commission; **hacer un encargo a alguien** to order sth from sb; *Esp* **mobiliario (hecho) de encargo** furniture made to order; **trabajar por encargo** to work to order *o* on commission

encarte *nm (folleto)* insert

encender *vt (aparato)* to switch on; *(motor)* to start up

encierro *nm (protesta)* sit-in; *(contra posible cierre)* work-in

encomienda *nf CAm, SAm (paquete)* parcel; **empresa de encomiendas** parcel delivery company

encriptación *nf* INFORM encryption

encriptar *vt* INFORM to encrypt

encuesta *nf* survey, opinion poll; **hacer** *o* **realizar una encuesta** to carry out *o* conduct a survey ◻ *encuesta a consumidores* consumer survey; *encuesta por correo* postal survey, mail survey; *encuesta por muestreo* sample survey; *encuesta de opinión* opinion poll; *encuesta piloto* pilot survey; *encuesta de población activa* = survey of the economically active population; *encuesta postal* postal survey, mail survey; *encuesta de precios* price survey; *encuesta sociológica* sociological survey; *encuesta telefónica* telephone survey

encuestado, -a *nm,f* respondent

encuestador, -ora *nm,f* pollster

encuestar *vt* to poll, to survey

enderezar *vt (economía)* to turn round

endeudado, -a *adj* indebted, in debt

endeudamiento *nm* indebtedness ◻ *endeudamiento excesivo* overborrowing; *endeudamiento remunerado* interest-bearing loans

endosante *nmf* FIN *(de documento, cheque)* endorser

endosar *vt* FIN *(documento, cheque)* to endorse

endosatario, -a *nm,f* FIN endorsee

endoso *nm* FIN *(de documento, cheque)* endorsement ◻ *endoso en blanco* blank endorsement

energía *nf* energy; **fuentes de energía** sources of energy ◻ *energías alternativas* alternative energy sources; *energía atómica* nuclear power *o* energy; *energía eléctrica* electric energy; *energías renovables* renewable forms of energy

enfermedad *nf* illness, disease ◻ *enfermedad laboral* occupational disease *o* illness; *enfermedad profesional* occupational disease *o* illness *(officially recognized as such)*; *enfermedad relacionada con el estrés* stress-related illness

> **"**
> Con esta medida, los autónomos podrán acceder a la prestación por accidente de trabajo desde el cuarto día, y no desde el decimosexto como pasa ahora. Si se trata de **enfermedad profesional**, gozarán de cobertura social desde el día siguiente al de la baja.
> **"**

enfoque *nm* approach ◻ *enfoque de marketing* marketing approach; *enfoque publicitario* advertising approach

engrapadora, engrampadora *nf Méx, CAm, Bol, Perú* stapler ◻ *engrapadora industrial* staple gun

engrapar *vt Am* to staple

enlace *nm* (**a**) INFORM, TEL link ◻ *enlace de comunicación, enlace de comunicaciones* communications link; *enlace directo* hot link;

enlace hipertextual hypertext link; **enlace por mar** sea link; **enlace telefónico** telephone link; *Esp* **enlace de vídeo,** *Am* **enlace de video** video link **(b)** *(persona)* **sirvió de enlace en las negociaciones** he acted as mediator in the negotiations ❑ *Esp* **enlace sindical** shop steward

enmendar *vt (texto, moción, ley)* to amend

enmienda *nf (de texto, moción, ley)* amendment

ensamblado, -a 1 *adj (producto)* assembled **2** *nm* assembly

ensamblador, -ora *adj* INFORM *(lenguaje)* assembly

ensamblaje *nm* assembly

ensamblar *vt* **(a)** *(piezas)* to assemble **(b)** INFORM to assemble

ensayo *nm (prueba)* test; **el nuevo prototipo será sometido a ensayo** the new prototype will undergo testing ❑ FARM **ensayo clínico** clinical trial

enseña *nf* flagship

enseñanza *nf (educación)* education; *(actividad docente)* teaching ❑ **enseñanza asistida por** *Esp* **ordenador** *o Am* **computadora** computer-aided learning, computer-assisted learning

enseres *nmpl (muebles, accesorios)* fixtures; *(herramientas, utensilios)* implements ❑ **enseres domésticos** household goods

entablar *vt (negociaciones)* to enter into, to open; *(conversación)* to strike up; *(relaciones)* to establish; **entablar juicio contra alguien** to start court proceedings against sb

entero *nm* BOLSA point; **Prunosa subió dos enteros** Prunosa gained two points

entidad *nf (organización)* body; *(empresa)* firm, company; **las entidades públicas** public bodies ❑ **entidad con ánimo de lucro** profit-making organization, *US* for-profit organization; **entidad sin ánimo de lucro** not-for-profit organization, *Br* non-profit(-making) organization; **entidad aseguradora** insurance company; **entidad bancaria** bank, banking house; **entidad benéfica** charitable organization, charity; **entidad comercial** business concern, business enterprise; **entidad de crédito** credit *o* lending institution; **entidad financiera** financial institution

entorno *nm* **(a)** *(ambiente)* environment; **el entorno familiar/social** the home/social environment; **fuentes bien informadas del entorno del presidente** well-informed sources close to the president; **España y los países de su entorno** Spain and her European neighbours ❑ MKTG **entorno de la compra** purchase environment; **entorno empresarial** corporate environment; **entorno laboral** working environment; **entorno de marketing** marketing environment; **entorno de trabajo** working environment **(b)** INFORM environment

entrada *nf* **(a)** *(acción)* entry; **están en contra de su entrada en la organización** they're opposed to him joining the organization ❑ **entrada de capital** capital inflow; **entrada de divisas** foreign exchange inflow; **entrada en el mercado** market entry; **entrada en vigor: hoy se cumple un año de la entrada en vigor de la ley** it is a year today since the act came into force **(b)** ADUANA *(en un país)* entry **(c)** CONT **anotar una entrada** to enter up an item ❑ **entradas de caja** cash receipts; **entradas y salidas de caja** cash receipts and payments **(d)** INFORM input ❑ **entrada continua** continuous input; **entrada de datos** data entry, data input; **entrada manual** manual input; **entrada y salida** input-output, I/O **(e)** *Esp (pago inicial)* down payment, deposit; **hay que pagar un millón de entrada** you have to put down a million as a deposit

entrante *nm (en un mercado)* entrant

> ❝
> El informe del mercado liberalizado Omel constata la dificultad que tienen los nuevos **entrantes** en el sector eléctrico para incrementar su cuota de mercado. Buen ejemplo de ello es Gas Natural, el nuevo **entrante** más activo.
> ❞

entrar *vi* **(a)** *(incorporarse)* **entrar en** *(empresa)* to start at; *(club, partido político)* to join; **entrar en la Unión Europea** to join the European Union; **entró a trabajar hace un mes** she started work a month ago **(b)** INFORM to log on; **entrar en un sistema** to log onto a system

entrega *nf* **(a)** *(de pedido, paquete)* delivery; **pagadero a la entrega** payable on delivery ❑ **entrega atrasada** late delivery; **entrega contrarreembolso** cash on delivery; **entrega por correo** postal delivery; **entrega a domicilio** home delivery; **entrega a domicilio gratuita** free home delivery; **entrega escalonada** staggered delivery; **entrega gratuita** free delivery; **entrega incompleta** short delivery; **entrega inmediata** immediate delivery; BOLSA spot delivery; **entrega en el mismo día** same-day delivery; **entrega a plazo, entrega a término** BOLSA forward delivery; FIN future delivery; **entrega urgente** express delivery **(b)** *(pago)* **entrega inicial** down payment, deposit

entregar *vt (pedido, paquete, correspondencia)* to deliver; *(informe, solicitud)* to hand in; **una carta certificada hay que entregarla en mano** a registered letter must be delivered to the addressee in person

entrevista *nf* (**a**) *(de trabajo, para encuesta)* interview; **hacer una entrevista a alguien** to interview sb ▫ *entrevista asistida por Esp ordenador o Am computadora* computer-aided interview; *entrevista por competencias* competency-based interview; *entrevista de despedida* exit interview; MKTG *entrevista estructurada* structured interview; *entrevista a fondo* depth interview; *entrevista en grupo* group interview; *entrevista en profundidad* depth interview; *entrevista de salida* exit interview; *entrevista por televisión* television interview; *entrevista de trabajo* job interview (**b**) *(cita)* meeting; **celebrar** *o* **mantener una entrevista con alguien** to hold a meeting with sb

❝
A pesar de que la **entrevista por competencias** es el procedimiento de selección más utilizado hoy en día, según los puestos y los perfiles, es conveniente no ceñirse exclusivamente a este método a la hora de evaluar al sujeto y decantarse por un conjunto de técnicas diversas. De esta forma, se puede, y es conveniente completar, con un test de personalidad, casos prácticos, Assessment, entrevistas estructuradas, solución de casos en dinámicas de grupos, etc.
❞

entrevistado, -a *nm,f* interviewee; **uno de cada tres entrevistados…** *(en encuesta)* one in three people interviewed…

entrevistador, -ora *nm,f* interviewer

entrevistar 1 *vt (para un empleo, encuesta)* to interview
2 entrevistarse *vpr (reunirse)* to have a meeting (**con** with)

envasado *nm (en cajas)* packing; *(en paquetes)* packaging, packing; *(en bolsas)* bagging; *(en latas)* canning; *(en botellas)* bottling ▫ *envasado de alimentos* food packaging; *envasado al vacío* vacuum packaging

envasar *vt (en cajas)* to pack; *(en paquetes)* to package, to pack; *(en bolsas)* to bag, to put in bags; *(en latas)* to can; *(en botellas)* to bottle; **envasar al vacío** to vacuum-pack

envase *nm* (**a**) *(envasado) (en cajas)* packing; *(en paquetes)* packaging, packing; *(en bolsas)* bagging; *(en latas)* canning; *(en botellas)* bottling (**b**) *(recipiente)* container; *(botella)* bottle; **envases de plástico/cartón** plastic/cardboard containers ▫ *envases alimentarios* food packaging; *envase desechable* disposable container; *envase familiar* economy pack; *envase de muestra* dummy pack; *envase de presentación* presentation pack; *envase retornable* returnable bottle; *envase no retornable, envase sin retorno* non-returnable bottle

enviar *vt (paquete, mercancías)* to send; **enviar algo por avión** to airfreight sth, to send sth by air; **enviar algo por barco** to ship sth; **enviar algo por correo aéreo** to airmail sth, to send sth by airmail; **enviar algo por correo electrónico** to e-mail sth, to send sth by e-mail; **enviar algo por fax** to fax sth, to send sth by fax; **enviar una factura a alguien** to bill sb, to invoice sb

envío *nm* (**a**) *(de paquete, mercancías)* dispatch, shipment; *(de dinero)* remittance; **en el albarán figura la fecha y la hora de envío** the date and time of delivery is stated on the delivery note; **el precio no incluye gastos de envío** the price does not include postage and *Br* packing *o US* handling ▫ *envío directo* drop shipment; *envío de fondos* remittance of funds; *envío de mercancías por mar* maritime shipment; *envíos publicitarios masivos* volume mailing; *envío de puerto a puerto* port-to-port shipment (**b**) *(mercancías)* shipment, consignment

envoltorio *nm (de producto)* packaging; *(de regalo)* wrapping

envolver *vt (paquete)* to wrap

EONIA *nm* FIN (*abrev de* **Euro Overnight Index Average**) EONIA

EPA *nf* (*abrev de* **encuesta de población activa**) = Spanish survey of economically active population

EPS *nm* INFORM (*abrev de* **encapsulated PostScript**) EPS

equidad *nf* ECON *equidad horizontal* horizontal equity; *equidad vertical* vertical equity

equilibrar 1 *vt (cuentas, presupuesto)* to balance
2 equilibrarse *vpr (cuentas, presupuesto)* to be balanced

equilibrio *nm (estabilidad)* balance; **el gobierno busca el equilibrio presupuestario** the government is seeking a balanced budget

equipaje *nm Br* luggage, *US* baggage; **hacer el equipaje** to pack ▫ *equipaje de mano* hand luggage

equipamiento *nm equipamiento industrial* industrial equipment; *equipamiento de serie (de automóvil)* standard features; *equipamiento turístico* tourist facilities

equipar *vt (edificio, institución)* to equip; (**con** with)

equipo *nm* (**a**) *(de trabajadores, profesionales)* team; **trabajar en equipo** to work as a team; **trabajo en equipo** teamwork ▫ *equipo creativo* creative team; *equipo de dirección* management team; *equipo de diseño* design team; *equipo de expertos* expert panel; *equipo de marketing* marketing team; *equipo de promociones* promotion team; *equipo de ventas* sales team

(b) *(equipamiento)* equipment ❑ *equipo informático* computer equipment; *equipo de mantenimiento* maintenance equipment; *equipo de oficina* office equipment; *equipo pesado* heavy equipment; *equipo de o con torre* tower system

equivalente 1 *adj* equivalent (**a** to)
  2 *nmpl* FIN *equivalentes en efectivo* cash equivalents

equivocación *nf* mistake; **cometer una equivocación** to make a mistake; **por equivocación** by mistake

equivocado, -a *adj* wrong

ERE *nm* (*abrev de* **expediente de regulación de empleo**) redundancy plan, workforce adjustment plan

ergonomía *nf* ergonomics

ergonómico, -a *adj* ergonomic

ERP *nm* (*abrev de* **Enterprise Resource Planning**) ERP

> **"**
>
> Muchos empresarios y directivos conocen ya lo que es un Entreprise Resource Planning (el sistema de gestión de dato único que utilizan la mayoría de las empresas líderes a nivel mundial). Sin embargo, no está claro que las empresas entiendan siempre cuál es realmente su problema. Los modernos sistemas de gestión —el **ERP** es probablemente el más utilizado— requieren un cambio de mentalidad en la empresa que, si no se consigue, pone en gran riesgo una inversión muy importante.
>
> **"**

error *nm* (**a**) *(falta, equivocación)* mistake, error; **por error** by mistake; **salvo error u omisión** errors and omissions excepted ❑ *error administrativo* clerical error; *error aleatorio* random error; *error de cálculo* miscalculation; *error de gestión* management error; *error de imprenta* misprint; *error judicial* miscarriage of justice; *error mecanográfico* typing error; *error de muestreo* sampling error; *error de selección* selection error; *error tipográfico,* Am *error de tipeo* keying error
  (**b**) INFORM error; *(en un programa)* bug ❑ *error de disco* disk error; *error de sintaxis* syntax error; *error del sistema* system error; *error de software* software bug, software error

E/S INFORM (*abrev de* **entrada/salida**) I/O

esbozo *nm* rough (drawing)

escala *nf* (**a**) *(para medir, ordenar)* scale; **a escala nacional/mundial** on a national/worldwide scale ❑ *escala de gravamen, escala del impuesto, escala impositiva* tax schedule, tax scale; MKTG *escala de medición de actitudes* attitude scale; *escala móvil* sliding scale; *escala*

de precios price scale; *escala salarial* salary scale, pay scale (**b**) *(de buque)* port of call

escalonado, -a *adj* staggered, phased

escalonar *vt* to stagger, to phase

escándalo *nm (financiero)* scandal

escanear *vt* INFORM to scan

escaneo *nm* INFORM scan

escáner *nm* INFORM scanner ❑ *escáner de mano* hand-held scanner; *escáner de páginas* page scanner; *escáner plano, escáner de sobremesa* flatbed scanner

escaparate *nm (de tienda)* (shop) window, display window; **la Exposición Universal será un escaparate para el país** the Universal Exhibition will be a showcase for the country

escaparatismo *nm* window dressing

escaparatista *nmf* window dresser

escape *nm* INFORM **tecla de escape** escape key

escasez *nf (de materiales, recursos, personal)* shortage ❑ *escasez de existencias* inventory *o Br* stock shortage; *escasez de mano de obra* labour shortage; *escasez personal* shortage of staff; *escasez de viviendas* housing shortage

escaso, -a *adj (recursos, medios)* limited, scant; *(trabajo)* scarce; **escasos de personal** undermanned

escisión *nf* spin-off, split

escribano, -a *nm,f Andes, CRica, RP* notary (public)

escribir 1 *vt (carta, nombre, dirección)* to write, **escribir algo en** *Esp* **el ordenador** *o Am* **la computadora** to type sth (up)
  2 *vi* to write; **escribir a máquina** to type

escrito 1 *adj* written; **por escrito** in writing
  2 *nm* (**a**) *(documento)* document; **envió un escrito de protesta al ayuntamiento** he sent a letter of protest to the council (**b**) DER brief ❑ *escrito de acusación formal* indictment

escritorio *nm* (**a**) *(mesa)* desk (**b**) *esp Am (oficina)* office (**c**) INFORM desktop ❑ *escritorio activo* active desktop

escritura *nf* DER deed; **firmar una escritura** to sign a deed ❑ *escritura de cesión* deed of assignment, transfer deed; *escritura de compraventa* deed of sale; *escritura de constitución (de empresa)* formation deed, deed of incorporation, charter; *escritura ejecutable* enforceable deed; *escritura de hipoteca, escritura hipotecaria* mortgage deed; *escritura notarial* notarized deed; *escritura de propiedad* title deed, deed of title; *escritura pública* public instrument; *escritura de transmisión* transfer deed; *escritura de traspaso* deed of transfer

escudo *nm Antes (moneda)* escudo

escuela *nf escuela de comercio* business

school; **escuela de hostelería** catering school; **Escuela Oficial de Idiomas** = Spanish State language-teaching institute; **escuela de secretariado** secretarial college; **escuela de turismo** school of tourism; **escuela universitaria** = section of a university which awards diplomas in a vocational discipline (e.g. engineering, business) after three years of study

esferográfico *nm Col, Ecuad* ballpoint pen

eslogan *nm* slogan ❑ **eslogan publicitario** advertising slogan

espaciado, -a 1 *adj* **hacer los renglones menos espaciados** to reduce the space between the lines, to make the lines closer together
  2 *nm* INFORM spacing ❑ **espaciado de caracteres** character spacing

espaciar *vt* INFORM to space

espacio *nm* **(a)** *(lugar)* space ❑ MKTG **espacio aislado** *(para anuncio)* solus position; INFORM **espacio en disco** disk space; **Espacio Económico Europeo** European Economic Area; MKTG **espacio exclusivo** *(para anuncio)* solus position; **espacio de exposición** display space; **espacio en el lineal** shelf space; **espacio para oficinas** office space; **espacio publicitario** advertising space; INFORM **espacio Web** Web space
  (b) *(en texto)* space; **a dos espacios, a doble espacio** double-spaced; **cuatro folios a un espacio** four single-spaced sheets ❑ **espacio en blanco** blank; TIP **espacio indivisible** hard space

especialidad *nf* **(a)** *(en actividad)* speciality, *US* specialty ❑ **especialidad farmacéutica** patent medicine **(b)** *(culinaria) (en restaurante, de región)* speciality, *US* specialty **(b)** *(en estudios) US* major, = main subject of degree; *(en conocimientos)* specialist field

especialista *nmf* specialist **(en** in) ❑ **especialista en marketing** marketer; **especialista en marketing industrial** industrial marketer; **especialista de producto** product specialist; **especialista en usuarios finales** end-user specialist

especialización *nf* specialization

especializado, -a *adj* specialized **(en** in); **un abogado especializado en casos de divorcio** a lawyer specializing in divorce cases; **un restaurante especializado en carnes a la brasa** a restaurant whose speciality is barbecued meats; **mano de obra especializada** skilled labour; **obrero especializado** skilled worker; **no especializado** *(mano de obra)* unskilled

especializar 1 *vt* to specialize
  2 especializarse *vpr* to specialize **(en** in)

especie *nf* **en especie** in kind; **pagar en especie** to pay in kind; **rendimientos** *o* **retribuciones en especie** benefits in kind

especificación *nf* specification ❑ **especificaciones de patente** patent specifications

especificar *vt* to specify; **por favor, especifique claramente el modo de pago** please state clearly the method of payment

específico *nm (medicamento)* patent medicine

espectro *nm* spectrum ❑ **espectro de marketing** marketing spectrum

especulación *nf (económica, financiera)* speculation ❑ **especulación al alza** bull speculation; **especulación a la baja** bear speculation; **especulación bursátil** stock market speculation, speculation on the stock exchange; **especulación en divisas** currency speculation; **especulación inmobiliaria** property speculation

especulador, -ora *nm,f* speculator ❑ **especulador bajista, especulador a la baja** bear; **especulador ciervo** stag; **especulador a corto plazo** day trader; **especulador en divisas** currency speculator

especular *vi* **especular con/en algo** to speculate in sth; **especular con terrenos/la propiedad** to speculate in land/property; **especular en Bolsa** to speculate on the Stock Market *o* Exchange

especulativo, -a *adj (comercio, economía, actividad)* speculative

> **“**
>
> SCH ha adquirido acciones de Unión Fenosa representativas del 3,8% de su capital, con lo que eleva su participación en la eléctrica al 20,3%. El grupo gallego, en tanto, desmintió que haya 'inflado' sus cuentas y atribuyó la volatilidad de sus títulos en Bolsa a movimientos **especulativos**.
>
> **”**

espera *nf* **en espera de, a la espera de** awaiting, waiting for; **seguimos a la espera de su respuesta** we await your reply

esperado, -a *adj (previsto)* expected; **fue el resultado esperado** it was the result they expected

esperar 1 *vt* **(a)** *(aguardar)* to wait for; **esperaré a que vuelva** I'll wait till she gets back **(b)** *(tener esperanza de)* **espero poder ayudar** I hope I can be of some help **(c)** *(tener confianza en)* to expect; **no esperábamos esta reacción** we didn't expect this reaction; **espero discreción de usted** I expect discretion from you, I expect you to be discreet
  2 *vi* to wait; **espere un momento, no cuelgue** hold the line, please

espionaje *nm* espionage, spying ❑ **espionaje industrial** industrial espionage

espiral *nf (escalada)* spiral ❑ **espiral inflacionaria,** *Esp* **espiral inflacionista** inflationary spiral

espíritu *nm* **espíritu de empresa** entrepreneurship; **espíritu de equipo** team spirit

espuma *nf* (**a**) **subir como la espuma** *(precios, Bolsa)* to shoot up, to rocket; **el negocio crecía como la espuma** the business went from strength to strength (**b**) *(gomaespuma)* foam rubber ❑ *Urug* **espuma de plast** polyurethane foam; **espuma de poliuretano** polyurethane foam

esquemático, -a *adj (dibujo, plano)* schematic; **un resumen esquemático** an outline; **un resumen muy/demasiado esquemático** a very simplified/an oversimplified summary

esquirol, -ola *nm,f Esp* scab, *Br* blackleg

estabilidad *nf (de mercado, economía)* stability ❑ **estabilidad económica** economic stability; **estabilidad en el empleo** job security; **estabilidad de precios** price stability; **estabilidad en el tipo de cambio** exchange rate stability

estabilización *nf (de precios, mercado, economía)* stabilization

estabilizar 1 *vt (precios, mercado, economía)* to stabilize
2 estabilizarse *vpr (precios, mercado, economía)* to stabilize, to become (more) stable; **el índice de la Bolsa se ha estabilizado en 1.100 puntos** the Share Index has stabilized at 1,100 points

estable *adj (situación, empleo)* stable

establecer 1 *vt* (**a**) *(iniciar) (sistema)* to establish, to set up; *(negocio, sucursal)* to set up; *(relaciones, comunicación)* to establish; **establecer contactos profesionales** to network (**b**) *(estipular)* to state, to stipulate; **las normas del club establecen que...** the club rules state that...; **según establece la ley...** as stipulated by law...
2 establecerse *vpr* (**a**) *(empresario)* to set up a business; **voy a establecerme por mi cuenta** I'm going to set up on my own *o* set up my own business (**b**) *(empresa, fábrica)* to locate; **las nuevas empresas que se han establecido en la región** the new businesses which have located in the region

establecimiento *nm* (**a**) *(negocio)* establishment; *(local)* premises ❑ **establecimiento comercial** commercial *o* business establishment (**b**) *(creación) (de sistema, negocio)* establishment ❑ **establecimiento de contactos profesionales** networking; **establecimiento de la llamada** *o Am* **del llamado** call connection

estación *nf* (**a**) *(para trasportes)* station ❑ **estación de carga** freight depot; **estación de llegada** arrival station; **estación marítima** harbour station; **estación de mercancías** goods station, freight station; **estación receptora** receiving station; **estación de salida** forwarding station (**b**) INFORM **estación base** *(para portátil)* docking station; **estación de trabajo** workstation

estacional *adj (empleo, demanda, fluctuaciones)* seasonal

> **"**
>
> Los pedidos en la industria alemana cayeron un 0,6% en febrero respecto a enero, mes en el que registraron un fuerte alza del 4,1%, según cifras provisionales corregidas de variaciones **estacionales** difundidas hoy por el Ministerio de Economía y Trabajo.
>
> **"**

estadística *nf* (**a**) *(ciencia)* statistics (**b**) *(dato)* statistic; **se basa en estadísticas** it is based on statistical data ❑ **estadísticas demográficas** demographics; **estadística de población** population statistics

estadístico, -a 1 *adj* statistical
2 *nm,f* statistician

estado *nm* (**a**) *(situación, condición)* condition; **el estado de su cuenta arroja un saldo positivo** your account is in credit ❑ **estado civil** marital status, civil status
(**b**) FIN *(documento)* **estado de caja** cash statement; **estado de conciliación** reconciliation statement; **estado de cuenta** statement of account; **estado financiero** statement of affairs; **estado financiero consolidado** consolidated balance sheet; CONT **estado de flujo de caja** cash flow statement; CONT **estado de origen y aplicación de fondos** statement of sources and applications of funds, statement of changes in financial position; CONT **estado provisional** interim statement
(**c**) *(gobierno, división territorial)* state; **temas de estado** affairs of state; **el Estado** the State ❑ **el Estado del bienestar** the Welfare State; UE **estado miembro** member state; **estado tapón** buffer state; **Estados Unidos (de América)** United States (of America); **Estados Unidos Mexicanos** United Mexican States

estadounidense, *Méx* **estadunidense**
1 *adj* American, US
2 *nmf* American

estafar *vt (a empresa, organización)* to defraud; **estafó millones a la empresa** he defrauded the company of millions

estampadora *nmf* INFORM **estampadora de CD-ROM** CD-ROM writer, CD-ROM burner

estampar *vt* **estampar la firma** to sign one's name

estampilla *nf* (**a**) *(para marcar)* rubber stamp (**b**) *Am (de correo)* (postal) stamp

estancado, -a *adj (economía, comercio, precios)* stagnant; *(negociación)* in (a) deadlock, at a standstill; *(proyecto)* at a standstill

estancamiento *nm (de economía)* stagnation; *(de negociaciones)* deadlock; **temen el estancamiento del proyecto** they're afraid the project will come to a standstill

estancar 1 *vt (progreso, negocio)* to bring to a standstill; *(negociación)* to deadlock

2 estancarse *vpr (economía)* to stagnate; *(progreso, negocio, proyecto)* to come to a standstill; *(negociaciones)* to reach deadlock, to come to a standstill

estándar 1 *adj (diseño, tamaño)* standard; *(producto)* off-the-shelf

2 *nm* standard □ **estándar de costos** cost standard; **estándar técnico** technical standard; **estándar de vida** standard of living

estandarización *nf* standardization

estandarizar *vt* to standardize

estanflación *nf* ECON stagflation

estante *nm* shelf

estantería *nf (conjunto)* shelves, shelving; *(para libros)* bookcase; *(tabla)* shelf

estatal *adj (empresa)* state-owned, state-controlled; *(colegio, universidad)* state

estatuto *nm (de asociación, organismo)* constitution, statutes; *(de club)* constitution, rules □ **estatutos sociales** *Br* articles of association, *US* articles of incorporation, *US* corporate by-laws; **estatuto de los trabajadores** labour code, = Spanish law governing labour relations and workers' rights

esterlina *adj* **libra esterlina** pound sterling

estibador *nm* stevedore, *Br* docker, dock worker, *Am* longshoreman

estilo *nm* style □ **estilo de gestión** management style; **estilo de vida** lifestyle

estimación *nf (cálculo aproximado)* estimate □ **estimación de la base imponible** assessment of taxable income; **estimaciones presupuestarias** budget estimates

estimar *vt* (**a**) *(evaluar)* to estimate; **estimar el valor de algo** to estimate the value of sth (**b**) DER *(recurso)* to allow, to uphold

estimular *vt (economía, ventas)* to stimulate, to boost; *(inversión)* to encourage, to stimulate

> **"**
> Fracasa el objetivo del Gobierno de **estimular** la contratación con un tiempo inferior a la ordinaria. El número de hombres ocupados parcialmente cae respecto al año 1997. Las mujeres representan más del 80 por ciento de estos contratos.
> **"**

estímulo *nm* (**a**) *(aliciente)* incentive; *(ánimo)* encouragement; **servir de estímulo** to act *o* serve as an incentive; **medidas de estímulo a la creación de empleo** measures to encourage job creation (**b**) MKTG stimulus

estipulación *nf (en contrato, tratado)* stipulation, provision

estipular *vt* to stipulate; **según lo estipulado en** *o* **por el artículo doce...** as stipulated in article twelve...

estraperlista *nmf* black marketeer

estrategia *nf* strategy □ **estrategia competitiva** competitive strategy; **estrategia de comunicaciones** communication strategy; **estrategia de consolidación** consolidation strategy; **estrategia creativa publicitaria** creative copy strategy; **estrategia de crecimiento** growth strategy; **estrategia departamental** functional strategy; **estrategia de diferenciación** differentiation strategy; **estrategia de distribución intensiva** intensive distribution strategy; **estrategia de diversificación** diversification strategy; **estrategia económica** economic strategy; **estrategia empresarial** business strategy; **estrategia financiera** financial strategy; **estrategia global** global strategy; **estrategia globalizadora** globalization strategy; **estrategia de imitación** me-too strategy; MKTG **estrategia de juego** gameplan; **estrategia de lanzamiento** launch strategy; **estrategia de marca** brand strategy; **estrategia de marketing** marketing strategy; **estrategia operativa** operations strategy; **estrategia de penetración (en el mercado)** (market) penetration strategy; **estrategia de posicionamiento** positioning strategy; **estrategia de precios** pricing strategy; **estrategia publicitaria, estrategia de publicidad** advertising strategy; **estrategia de relaciones públicas** communication strategy; **estrategia de ventas** sales strategy

estratégicamente *adv* strategically

estratégico, -a *adj* strategic

estrella *adj inv (producto, marca)* flagship

estrellarse *vpr* **con su último lanzamiento se estrellaron** their last product launch was a disaster

estropear 1 *vt (mercancías)* to damage; *(alimentos)* to spoil

2 estropearse *vpr (máquina)* to break down; *(alimentos)* to spoil

estructura *nf (organización)* structure □ INFORM **estructura del archivo** file structure; **estructura de bloque** block structure; **estructura del capital** capital structure; **estructura de costos** cost structure; **estructura directiva** managerial structure; INFORM **estructura de directorio** directory structure; **estructura empresarial** corporate structure; INFORM **estructura en estrella** star structure; INFORM **estructura del fichero** file structure; **estructura de gestión** managerial structure; **estructura del mercado** market structure; **estructura de**

poder power structure; **estructura de precios** price structure; **estructura salarial** salary structure, wage structure

estructurado, -a adj MKTG (entrevista) structured

estuche nm (de instrumento, gafas, reloj) case; **en estuche** (como presentación) boxed

estudiar vt (asunto) to study; (oferta, propuesta) to study, to consider; (mercado) to explore; **el gobierno estudia la posibilidad de subir las pensiones** the government is studying the possibility of raising pensions; **después de estudiar tu propuesta he decidido no aceptarla** having considered your proposal, I've decided not to accept it; **el informe estudia el estado actual de la producción industrial** the report surveys the current state of the manufacturing industry

estudio nm (a) (investigación) study; **hacer un estudio de algo** to survey sth □ MKTG **estudio AIO** AIO study; MKTG **estudio de actitudes** attitude survey; MKTG **estudio de audiencia** audience study; **estudio de campo** field study; **estudio de casos** case study; MKTG **estudio de comportamiento** behavioural study; MKTG **estudio del comportamiento del consumidor** consumer behaviour study; **estudio de comunicaciones** communications study; MKTG **estudio cualitativo** qualitative study; MKTG **estudio cuantitativo** quantitative study; MKTG **estudio de eficacia del marketing** marketing efficiency study; **estudio de impacto** impact study; **estudio de impacto ambiental** environmental impact study; **estudio de marketing** marketing study; **estudio de medios** media analysis; MKTG **estudio de mercado** market survey; **estudio de métodos** method study, methods analysis; **estudio monográfico** case study; MKTG **estudio de la motivación** motivation study; MKTG **estudio motivacional** motivational study; **estudio de movimientos** motion study; **estudio de necesidades** needs study; MKTG **estudio de las necesidades del mercado** gap study; MKTG **estudio de la notoriedad** awareness study; MKTG **estudio de posicionamiento** positioning study; **estudio piloto** pilot study; **estudio preliminar** preliminary study; MKTG **estudio de recuerdo** recall study; **estudio de tiempos y métodos** time and methods study; **estudio de tiempos y movimientos** time and motion study; **estudio de ventas** retail panel; **estudio de viabilidad** feasibility study

(b) **estudios** (educación) studies □ **estudios de administración de empresas, estudios de gestión empresarial** management studies; **estudios de posgrado** postgraduate studies o education; **estudios secundarios** secondary education; **estudios superiores** higher education

(c) (oficina) (de arquitecto) office, studio; RP (de abogado) office, practice

etapa nf (trayecto, fase) stage, phase; **por etapas** in stages

Ethernet® nf INFORM Ethernet®

ética nf ethics □ **ética empresarial** business ethics; **ética profesional** (professional) ethics; **ética del trabajo** work ethic

ético, -a adj ethical

etiqueta nf (a) (en envase, producto, prenda) (pegada o cosida) label; (colgada o atada) tag, label □ **etiqueta de calidad** quality label; **etiqueta de dirección** address label; **etiqueta de garantía** guarantee label; **etiqueta de identificación** identification label; **etiqueta identificativa del equipaje** luggage label; **etiqueta de marca blanca** own-brand label; **etiqueta de origen** label of origin; **etiqueta del precio** price tag; **etiqueta de promoción** promotional label; **etiqueta de seguridad** security tag
(b) INFORM (en HTML) tag

etiquetado, etiquetaje nm labelling □ **etiquetado de precios** price labelling

etiquetar vt (a) (objeto) to label (b) INFORM (en HTML) to tag

ETT nf (abrev de **Empresa de Trabajo Temporal**) temp agency, temping agency

> ❝
> "Las **ETT** han pasado de gestionar el 16% del empleo temporal en 2000 a gestionar el 14%". No obstante, el presidente de la patronal de las **ETT** explicó que el menor número de contratos gestionado por este tipo de empresas no ha implicado una reducción del número global de contratos temporales suscritos en España, que hasta noviembre de 2002 registró un crecimiento del 2% respecto a mismo periodo precedente
> ❞

ETVE nf FIN (abrev de **entidad de tenencia de valores extranjeros**) Spanish holding company

euforia nf (en la Bolsa) euphoria; **los mercados viven un momento de euforia** we are currently going through a period of stock-market euphoria

Euribor nm FIN (abrev de **Euro InterBank Offered Rate**) EURIBOR

> ❝
> El índice **Euribor**, que es utilizado como principal referencia para fijar el tipo de interés de los préstamos hipotecarios concedidos por las entidades de crédito españolas, subió en agosto al 2,279%, por segundo mes consecutivo, tras haber alcanzado en junio un mínimo histórico con el 2,014%.
> ❞

euro *nm (moneda)* euro; **la zona** *o* **el territorio (del) euro** the euro zone

eurobanco *nm* Eurobank

eurobarómetro *nm* UE Eurobarometer

eurobono *nm* Eurobond

Eurocard® *nf* Eurocard®

eurocertificado *nm* eurocertificate

eurocheque *nm* Eurocheque

eurócrata *nmf* Eurocrat

eurocrédito *nm* Eurocredit

eurodiputado, -a *nm,f* Euro-MP, MEP

eurodivisa *nf* Eurocurrency

eurodólar *nm* Eurodollar

Eurolandia *n* Euroland

eurolibra *nf* Eurosterling

euromercado *nm* Euromarket

europeo, -a *adj & nm,f* European

europréstamo *nm* Euroloan

EuroStoxx *nm* BOLSA Euro Stoxx

euroyen *nm* Euroyen

evaluación *nf (de daños, pérdidas, costo)* assessment, evaluation; *(de empleados)* appraisal □ *evaluación comparativa* benchmarking; *evaluación del consumidor* consumer audit; *evaluación de costo* cost assessment; *evaluación de la demanda* demand assessment; *evaluación económica* economic appraisal; *evaluación financiera* financial appraisal; *evaluación de impacto ambiental* environmental impact assessment; *evaluación de mercado* market appraisal; *evaluación de necesidades* needs assessment; *evaluación del personal (ejercicio)* staff appraisal; *(resultado)* personnel rating; MKTG *evaluación postcompra* post-purchase evaluation; *evaluación de proyectos de capital* capital project evaluation; *evaluación del rendimiento* performance appraisal; *evaluación de riesgos* risk assessment; *evaluación del siniestro* loss assessment; *evaluación del trabajo* job evaluation

evaluar *vt (daños, pérdidas, costo)* to assess

evasión *nf evasión de capitales* capital flight; *evasión de divisas* capital flight; *evasión de impuestos, evasión fiscal* tax evasion; *(legal)* tax avoidance

evento *nm* event □ *eventos para empresas* corporate events

eventual **1** *adj (trabajador, empleo)* casual, temporary; *(cargo)* temporary; *(gastos, ingresos)* incidental; **un contrato de trabajo eventual** a temporary (employment) contract
2 *nmf (trabajador)* casual *o* temporary worker

eventualidad *nf (hecho incierto)* eventuality; **estamos preparados para cualquier eventua-**

lidad we are prepared for every eventuality *o* contingency

evitable *adj* avoidable

exacción *nf (de impuestos)* exaction, collection, levy □ *exacción a la exportación* export levy; UE *exacciones reguladoras agrícolas* agricultural levies

exacto, -a *adj (justo, preciso)* exact; *(preciso)* accurate, precise; *(correcto)* correct, right; **3 metros exactos** exactly 3 metres; **no sé la fecha exacta** I don't know the exact date; **para ser exactos** to be precise

examen *nm* **(a)** *(de documentos, mercancías)* inspection, examination **(b)** *(en escuela, universidad)* exam, examination

examinar *vt* **(a)** *(documentos, mercancías)* to inspect, to examine **(b)** *(en escuela, universidad)* to examine

excedente **1** *adj* **(a)** *(producción)* surplus **(b)** *(funcionario)* on leave; *(profesor)* on sabbatical
2 *nm (de producción, existencias)* surplus □ *excedentes agrícolas* agricultural surpluses, surplus produce; *excedente comercial* trade surplus; CONT *excedente de efectivo* cash surplus; CONT *excedentes líquidos* cash overs; *excedente monetario* monetary surplus; *excedente productivo* productivity surplus; CONT *excedente de tesorería* cash surplus

> ❝
>
> Por mercados, los datos definitivos de Eurostat para el periodo enero−julio de este año muestran una caída del 10% en las exportaciones de la UE hacia EE UU y del 7% hacia Japón; mientras que en el capítulo de las importaciones destaca la caída del 16% en las compras a Estados Unidos, que permite aumentar el **excedente comercial** de los Quince con este país hasta 37.800 millones de euros, un 8,6% más que en los mismos meses de 2002.
>
> ❞

exceder *vt* to exceed, to surpass; **excede en dos kilos el peso permitido** it is two kilos over the weight limit; **una cifra que excede con mucho la deuda externa del país** a figure well in excess of the country's foreign debt

excepcional *adj (extraordinario)* exceptional

excesivo, -a *adj* excessive; **se pagan precios excesivos** people pay inflated prices, *Br* people pay over the odds; ECON **consumo excesivo** overconsumption

exceso *nm (de gastos, peso)* excess, surplus □ ECON *exceso de capacidad* overcapacity, excess capacity; *exceso de demanda* excess demand; *exceso de empleados* overstaffing, overmanning; *exceso de importaciones* import surplus; *exceso de liquidez* excess liquidities; *exceso*

de oferta excess supply; **exceso de personal** overstaffing, overmanning; **exceso de peso** excess weight; BANCA **exceso de reservas** excess reserves

> "
> Horst Köhler, director gerente del organismo financiero, dijo que ese tema es preocupante porque no hay certidumbre sobre el rumbo ni la solidez del repunte económico mundial: aunque hay signos de recuperación, también existe **exceso de capacidad** en el mundo y podrían retroceder las bolsas.
> "

exclamación nf (signo ortográfico) exclamation mark, US exclamation point

exclusividad nf (de uso, derechos) exclusivity

exclusivo, -a adj (producto) exclusive; (derecho, distribuidor) exclusive, sole; (distribución) sole

exención nf (de impuestos, obligación) exemption; (a norma) waiver ❑ **exención fiscal** tax exemption; **exención parcial** partial exemption; **exención total** total exemption

exento, -a adj exempt; **exento de impuestos** tax-exempt, exempt from taxes

exhibir vt (productos, objetos) to exhibit

exigencia nf demand

exigible adj (a) (por ley) enforceable (b) FIN (bono) callable; **no exigible** uncallable

exigir vt to demand, to call for; **exigen una subida salarial** they are calling for a wage increase

exiliado, -a, Am **exilado, -a** nm,f **exiliado fiscal** tax exile

eximir vt (de obligaciones, impuestos) to exempt (**de** from)

existencias nfpl inventory, Br stock; **quedan muy pocas existencias en el almacén** there isn't much inventory o Br stock in the warehouse; **en existencias** in stock; **quedarse sin existencias (de algo)** to run out (of sth); **reponer (las) existencias** to restock ❑ **existencias al cierre** closing inventory o Br stock; **existencias disponibles** inventory o Br stock in hand; **existencias en divisas** foreign currency holding; **existencias excedentarias** surplus inventory o Br stock; **existencias finales** closing inventory o Br stock; **existencias iniciales** opening inventory o Br stock; **existencias salientes** outgoing inventory o Br stock; **existencias de seguridad** safety stock

éxito nm success; **tener éxito** to be successful; **ser un éxito de ventas** to be a best seller

exitoso, -a adj successful

expandible adj INFORM expandable

expandir 1 vt (a) (empresa, mercado, negocio) to expand (b) INFORM to expand

2 **expandirse** vpr (empresa, mercado, negocio) to expand, to grow

expansión nf (a) (de empresa, mercado, negocio) expansion, growth; **un periodo de expansión económica** a period of economic expansion o growth; **en expansión** expanding; **un sector económico en franca expansión** a fast-growing o rapidly-growing sector of the economy ❑ **expansión monetaria** currency expansion; **expansión de ventas** sales expansion (**b**) INFORM expansion

expansionista adj expansionist

expectativa nf expectation; **los resultados de la empresa no cumplieron las expectativas de la comunidad financiera** the company's performance did not confirm the financial community's expectation; **contra toda expectativa** against all expectations

expedición nf (a) (envío) dispatch, shipment (b) (de documento) issue, issuing; **fecha de expedición** date of issue

expedidor, -ora nm,f (empresa) sender, dispatcher; (empleado) shipping clerk

expediente nm (a) (documentación) dossier; (ficha) file ❑ **expediente del cliente** client file

(**b**) (investigación) inquiry; **abrir expediente a alguien** (castigar) to take disciplinary action against sb; (llevar a juicio) to start proceedings against sb; **formar** o **instruir expediente a un funcionario** to impeach a public official ❑ **expediente disciplinario** disciplinary action

(**c**) Esp ECON **expediente de crisis** = statement of the economic difficulties of a company, presented to the authorities to justify redundancies; **expediente de regulación de empleo** redundancy plan, workforce adjustment plan

> "
> El efecto negativo que está teniendo esta "regulación asimétrica" es uno de los argumentos principales en los que la compañía basa el **expediente de regulación de empleo** (ERE) que tiene previsto presentar esta misma semana ante la Dirección General de Trabajo.
> "

expedir vt (a) (carta, pedido, mercancías) to send, to dispatch (**b**) (pasaporte, certificado) to issue

experiencia nf experience; **no es necesaria experiencia** (en anuncio) no experience necessary ❑ **experiencia laboral** work experience

experimentar vt (a) (pérdidas) to incur (**b**) (dificultades) to undergo, to experience; **el Ibex 35 ha experimentado una fuerte subida** there has been a sharp rise in the Ibex 35 index

experto, -a 1 adj expert; **es experta en temas**

medioambientales she's an expert on environmental matters

2 *nm,f* expert ❑ *experto en comunicaciones* communications expert; *experto en gestión* management expert; *experto en informática* computer expert; *experto en marketing* marketing expert; *experto sectorial* industry expert

expirar *vi (tener vencimiento)* to expire

explorar *vt (mercado, posibilidades)* to explore

explotación *nf* (**a**) *(acción) (de recursos)* exploitation; *(de fábrica, negocio)* running, operation; *(de yacimiento)* mining; *(agrícola)* farming; *(de petróleo)* drilling; **tiene el negocio en régimen de explotación** he has the business on lease; **explotación forestal** forestry
(**b**) *(instalaciones)* **explotación agrícola** farm; *explotación agropecuaria* arable and livestock farm; *explotación ganadera* livestock farm; *explotación industrial* industrial concern; *explotación minera* mine; *explotación petrolífera* oilfield
(**c**) *(de trabajadores)* exploitation

exponer *vt* (**a**) *(ideas, razones)* to set out, to state; *(propuesta)* to present (**b**) *(a la vista) (cuadro, obra)* to exhibit; *(objetos en vitrinas)* to display

exportable *adj* exportable

exportación *nf* (**a**) *(acción)* export, exportation; **una empresa de exportación de cerámica** a ceramics export company; **productos de exportación** export goods ❑ INFORM *exportación de datos* data export (**b**) *(mercancía)* export ❑ *exportaciones invisibles* invisible exports; *exportaciones visibles* visible exports

exportador, -ora 1 *adj* exporting; **país exportador** exporting country, exporter; **una compañía exportadora de objetos de artesanía** a company exporting handicrafts
2 *nm,f* exporter

exportar *vt* (**a**) *(productos)* to export (**a** to) (**b**) INFORM to export (**a** to)

exposición *nf* (**a**) *(feria)* **exposición (comercial)** trade show, trade fair ❑ *exposición universal* international exhibition, world fair (**b**) *(de objetos en vitrina)* display ❑ *exposición del producto* product display (**c**) *(de ideas, razones)* setting out, statement; *(de propuesta)* presentation

expositor, -ora 1 *nm,f (en feria)* exhibitor
2 *nm (para productos)* display stand, display unit; **un expositor giratorio de libros** a revolving book display o stand ❑ *expositor de folletos* leaflet holder, leaflet stand; *expositor giratorio* spinner; *expositor en el punto de compra* point-of-purchase display; *expositor en el punto de venta* point-of-sale display

expropiación *nf* expropriation ❑ *expropiación forzosa* expropriation, *Br* compulsory purchase

expuesto, -a *adj (producto, objeto)* on display

ext. *(abrev de* **extensión***) (de línea telefónica)* ext

extender *vt* (**a**) *(cheque)* to make out, to write (out); *(documento)* to draw up; **le extenderé un cheque** I'll write you (out) a cheque, I'll make out a cheque to you (**b**) *(prolongar)* to prolong, to extend

extensión *nf* (**a**) *(de línea telefónica)* extension (**b**) INFORM *(de archivo)* extension (**c**) *(ampliación)* extension; **se concedió una extensión del plazo** an extension was granted ❑ *extensión de marca* brand extension

exterior *adj (asuntos, comercio)* foreign, external; **una empresa de comercio exterior** an import-export company

externalización *nm* outsourcing

externalizar *vt* to outsource

externo, -a *adj (deuda)* external

extinción *nf* (**a**) *(de derechos, patente)* lapse (**b**) *(de plazo, obligaciones)* termination, end

extinguirse *vpr (derecho, patente)* to lapse

extornar *vt* SEGUR *(prima)* to return

extorno *nm* SEGUR *(de prima)* return

extra 1 *adj* (**a**) *(adicional)* extra; **horas extras** overtime (**b**) *(de gran calidad)* top quality, superior; **chocolate extra** superior quality chocolate
2 *nm* (**a**) *(gasto)* extra (**b**) INFORM add-on
3 *nf Esp Fam (paga)* = additional payment of a month's salary or wages

extracontable *adj* CONT *(partida)* off-balance sheet, non-accounting

extracto *nm* **extracto bancario** bank statement; *extracto de cuenta* bank statement; CONT statement of account; *extracto mensual* monthly statement

extraer *vt* (**a**) INFORM *(archivo comprimido)* to extract (**b**) *(carbón, mineral)* to mine (**de** from); *(petróleo)* to extract (**de** from)

extraíble *adj* INFORM *(disco)* removable

extranjero, -a 1 *adj* foreign, overseas
2 *nm,f (persona)* foreigner
3 *nm (territorio)* **en** o **por el extranjero** abroad; **está de viaje en** o **por el extranjero** she's

away on a trip abroad; **ir al extranjero** to go abroad

extraoficial *adj* unofficial

extraordinaria *nf Esp (paga)* = additional payment of a month's salary or wages

extraordinario, -a *adj (congreso, asamblea, junta)* extraordinary; **hacer gastos extraordinarios** to have extra expenses

extrapolación *nf* extrapolation

extrapolar *vt* to extrapolate; **a partir de los datos hemos extrapolado algunas conclusiones** based on the data, we have extrapolated some conclusions

EXW (*abrev de* **Ex Works**) EXW

Ff

FAB (*abrev de* **Franco a Bordo**) FOB

fábrica *nf* factory; **viene instalado de fábrica** it's pre-installed; **tiene un defecto de fábrica** it has a manufacturing defect ❑ *fábrica de automóviles* car factory; *fábrica de cerveza* brewery; *fábrica de conservas* canning plant, cannery; *fábrica modelo* model factory; *Fábrica Nacional de Moneda y Timbre* = Spanish national mint; *fábrica de papel* paper mill; *fábrica piloto* pilot factory; *fábrica siderúrgica* iron and steelworks

fabricación *nf* manufacture; **un automóvil de fabricación nacional** a domestically produced car; **licencia/proceso de fabricación** manufacturing licence/process ❑ *fabricación asistida por Esp ordenador o Am computadora* computer-aided *o* computer-assisted manufacture; *fabricación integrada por Esp ordenador o Am computadora* computer-integrated manufacture; *fabricación en serie* mass production

fabricante **1** *adj* manufacturing; **la empresa fabricante** the manufacturer
2 *nmf* manufacturer, maker ❑ *fabricante de alimentos* food manufacturer; *fabricante de automóviles* car manufacturer; *fabricante de equipo original* original equipment manufacturer

fabricar *vt* to manufacture, to make; **fabricar en serie** to mass-produce; **fabricado en China** (*en etiqueta*) made in China

fachada *nf* (*de tienda*) shop front, *US* storefront

fácil *adj* easy; **dinero fácil** easy money; **de fácil manejo** user-friendly

facilidad *nf facilidades de crédito* credit facilities; *facilidades de crédito a corto plazo* short-term credit facilities; *facilidad de manejo* user-friendliness; *facilidades de pago* easy (payment) terms; BOLSA *facilidades de permuta, facilidades de swap* swap facilities; *facilidad de uso* user-friendliness; **destaca por su facilidad de uso** it is particularly user-friendly

facilitador, -ora *nm,f* (*de reunión, dinámica de grupo*) facilitator

facilitar *vt* (**a**) (*simplificar*) to facilitate, to make easy; **esta máquina nos facilita mucho la tarea** this machine makes the job a lot easier (for us); **su radicalismo no facilitó las negociaciones** her inflexibility did not make the negotiations any easier

(**b**) (*reunión*) to facilitate
(**c**) (*proporcionar*) to provide; **nos facilitaron toda la información que necesitábamos** they provided us with all the information we needed; **la nota de prensa facilitada por el portavoz del gobierno** the press release made available by the government spokesman

facsímil, facsímile *adj & nm* facsimile

factible *adj* feasible

factor *nm* (**a**) (*elemento*) factor; **el precio del petróleo es el factor clave** the price of oil is the key factor ❑ *factor de control* controlling factor; *factor del costo* cost factor; *factor de crecimiento* growth factor; *factor de demanda* demand factor; *factor económico* economic factor; *factor humano* human factor; *factor de ocupación* load factor; ECON *factores de producción* factors of production, production factors; *factor riesgo* risk factor; *factor de seguridad* safety factor
(**b**) MAT factor
(**c**) FIN (*empresa*) factor, factoring company

factora *nf* FIN (*empresa*) factor, factoring company

factoraje, factoring *nm* FIN factoring

factura *nf* (**a**) (*por mercancías, trabajo realizado, servicios*) invoice; (*de luz, teléfono*) bill; **extender una factura** to issue an invoice; **pasar** *o* **presentar una factura** to send an invoice ❑ *factura comercial* commercial invoice; ACCT *factura de comisión* commission note; ACCT *factura de compra* purchase invoice; *factura conforme* approved invoice; *factura de consignación* consignment invoice; *factura consular* consular invoice; *factura contabilizada* booked invoice; *factura detallada* itemized bill; *factura energética* energy consumption bill; *factura de flete* freight note; *factura de hotel* hotel bill; *factura original* original invoice; *factura pro forma, factura proforma* pro-forma invoice; *factura de venta* sales invoice
(**b**) (*hechura*) workmanship

facturación *nf* (**a**) FIN (*ventas*) turnover; **una facturación anual de 1.000 millones** an annual turnover of 1,000 million ❑ *facturación del grupo* group turnover (**b**) (*cobro*) invoicing, billing (**c**) (*de equipaje*) checking-in; **mostrador de facturación** check-in desk

facturar vt (**a**) FIN (capital) to turn over; **facturaron 4.000 millones** they had a turnover of 4,000 million (**b**) (cobrar) **facturarle a alguien algo** to invoice o bill sb for sth (**c**) (equipaje) to check in

facultad nf (**a**) (poder, capacidad) **su cargo no le da facultad para autorizar compras** his position doesn't allow him to authorize purchases ❑ **facultad de decisión** decision-making power (**b**) (centro universitario) faculty ❑ **facultad de ciencias empresariales** business college

falencia nf Am (bancarrota) bankruptcy

falla nf (**a**) (en producto) fault, defect; Am (en método, proyecto) flaw ❑ **falla de fabricación** manufacturing fault; **falla mecánica** mechanical fault (**b**) Am INFORM **falla de software** software failure; **falla del sistema** system failure

fallar vi (**a**) (fracasar, flaquear) to fail; (no funcionar) to stop working; (plan) to go wrong; **nos fallaron las previsiones** our forecasts were out (**b**) (sentenciar) **fallar a favor/en contra de alguien** to find in favour of/against sb

fallo nm (**a**) Esp (en producto) fault; (en método, proyecto) flaw ❑ **fallo de fabricación** manufacturing fault; **fallo mecánico** mechanical fault (**b**) Esp INFORM **fallo del sistema** system failure; **fallo de software** software failure (**c**) (veredicto) (de juez) ruling; (de jurado) verdict; (en concurso) decision ❑ **fallo absolutorio** acquittal; **fallo judicial** court ruling

falsificación nf (**a**) (acción) (de firma, pasaporte) forgery; (de contabilidad, documentos) falsification (**b**) (pasaporte, firma, billete) forgery

falsificado, -a adj (firma, pasaporte) forged; (contabilidad, documentos) falsified

falsificar vt (firma, pasaporte) to forge; (contabilidad, documentos) to falsify; (billete) to forge, to counterfeit

falso, -a adj (**a**) (firma) forged; (billete) forged, counterfeit; (pasaporte) forged, false; (cheque) dud (**b**) (afirmación, información, rumor) false, untrue

falta nf (**a**) (de recursos, material, trabajo) (total) lack; (escasez) shortage; **sin falta** without fail; **hemos de entregar este proyecto el lunes sin falta** this project has to be handed in on Monday without fail ❑ **falta de existencias** inventory o Br stock shortage; **falta de pago** nonpayment; **falta de personal** staff shortage (**b**) (defecto de fábrica) defect, flaw (**c**) (infracción laboral) offence ❑ **falta grave** serious offence; **falta leve** minor offence

faltante nm Am **faltante de caja** cash shortage

falto, -a adj **falto de** lacking in, short of; **estamos faltos de recursos** we are short of resources; **faltos de personal** short-staffed

familiar adj (**a**) (ayuda, negocio, ingresos) family

(**b**) (tamaño) family-sized; **un envase familiar** a family pack

fantasma adj (empresa) bogus

FAO nf (abrev de **Food and Agriculture Organization**) FAO

FAS 1 (abrev de **Free Alongside Ship**) FAS **2** nm inv (abrev de **Fondo de Asistencia Social**) = Spanish social welfare fund

fase nf stage, phase; **el proyecto está en fase de estudio** the project is still being researched ❑ **fase de crecimiento** growth phase; MKTG **fase de decadencia** (de producto) decline stage; MKTG **fase de desarrollo** (de producto) development stage; **fase de fabricación** manufacturing stage; MKTG **fase de introducción** (de producto) introduction stage; **fases del proyecto** project milestones; MKTG **fase de viabilidad** feasibility stage

favorable adj favourable

favorecer vt (ser beneficioso para) (comercio, país) to benefit; **esta política favorece a los más pobres** this policy works in favour of the poorest

favorito, -a 1 nm,f (candidato) favourite, frontrunner **2** nm INFORM bookmark, favorite

fax nm (**a**) (aparato) fax (machine); **mandar algo por fax** to fax sth ❑ **fax de papel normal** plain paper fax (machine); **fax de papel térmico** thermal paper fax (**b**) (documento) fax; **mandar un fax** to send a fax

FCA (abrev de **free carrier**) FCA

fe nf **de buena fe** in good faith

fecha nf date ❑ FIN **fecha de amortización** (de bonos) redemption date; BOLSA **fecha base** base date; **fecha de caducidad** (de alimentos) use-by date, Br expiry date, US expiration date; (de medicamento) use before date; CONT **fecha de cierre** closing date; **fecha de consumo preferente** best-before date; FIN **fecha de ejercicio** (de opción) exercise date; **fecha de emisión** date of issue; **fecha de entrada en vigor** effective date; **fecha de entrega** date of delivery, delivery date; **fecha de expedición** date of issue; **fecha de la factura** date of invoice; **fecha de facturación** billing date, invoice date; **fecha de finalización** (de obra, venta) completion date; **fecha de finalización de la contrata** contract date, contractual date; **fecha de la firma** date of signature; **fecha de ingreso** (en cuenta) remittance date; **fecha de inicio** starting date; **fecha límite** deadline, closing date; **fecha límite de edición** copy deadline; **fecha límite de venta** sell-by date; **fecha de nacimiento** date of birth; Am **fecha patria** national holiday (commemorating important historical event); BANCA **fecha de presentación** (de cheque) presentation date; **fecha de recepción** date of receipt;

fecha tope deadline, closing date; FIN **fecha (de) valor** value date; FIN **fecha de vencimiento** *(de inversión, póliza)* due date, maturity date; *(de pago)* due date; *(de opción)* option day

fechar *vt (carta, cheque)* to date; **no fechado** undated

FED *nm* UE *(abrev* **Fondo Europeo de Desarrollo**) EDF

FEDER *nm* UE *(abrev de* **Fondo Europeo de Desarrollo Regional**) ERDF

federación *nf* federation ▢ **federación deportiva** sports federation; **federación empresarial, federación patronal** employers' federation; **federación de sindicatos** federation of unions, union federation

federal *adj* federal

FEM *nf (abrev de* **Federación Europea del Metal**) EMF

FEOGA *nm* UE *(abrev de* **Fondo Europeo de Orientación y de Garantía Agrícola**) EAGGF, European Agriculture Guidance and Guarantee Fund

feria *nf* (**a**) *(exhibición)* fair ▢ **feria del automóvil** car show, motor show; **feria comercial** trade fair, trade show; **feria de ganado** cattle fair; **feria del libro** book fair; **feria de muestras** *(actividad)* trade fair, trade show; *(instalaciones)* exhibition centre (**b**) RP **feria judicial** holiday *(when the courts are closed)*

> Reflexionar sobre el futuro del sector aeroespacial español y mostrar los proyectos de investigación más relevantes en curso son los principales objetivos de la **Feria** de la Industria Aeronáutica y del Espacio, AEROTEC 2003, que celebrará su decimotercera edición del 15 al 19 de diciembre.

feriado, -a *Am* **1** *adj* **día feriado** (public) holiday **2** *nm* (public) holiday; **abierto domingos y feriados** open on Sundays and public holidays

feroz *adj (competencia)* fierce, keen

ferrocarril *nm* (**a**) *(sistema, red)* railway, US railroad; **por ferrocarril** by rail (**b**) *(tren)* train

festivo, -a **1** *adj* **día festivo** (public) holiday **2** *nm* (public) holiday; **abierto domingos y festivos** open on Sundays and public holidays

FGD *nm* FIN *(abrev de* **fondo de garantía de depósitos**) Deposit Guarantee Fund

FIAB *nf (abrev de* **Federación Iberoamericana de Bolsas**) Ibero-American Federation of Exchanges

fiabilidad *nf* reliability; *(de persona)* reliability, trustworthiness

fiable *adj* reliable; *(persona)* reliable, trustworthy

fiador, -ora *nm,f* guarantor, surety

FIAMM *nm* FIN *(abrev de* **Fondo de Inversión en Activos del Mercado Monetario**) = Br unit trust *o* US mutual fund restricted to the currency market

fianza *nf* (**a**) *(depósito)* deposit; *(garantía)* surety ▢ **fianza de contratista** contract bond; *Am* **fianza de cumplimiento** performance bond; **fianza de ejecución de un contrato** performance bond; **fianza específica** excise bond; **fianza de licitación** bid bond (**b**) DER *(por delito)* bail; **bajo fianza** on bail

fiar *vt & vi (en tienda)* to sell on credit; **en esta tienda no se fía** *(en letrero)* no credit (given here)

fibra *nf* fibre ▢ **fibra óptica** optical fibre

ficha *nf (tarjeta)* (index) card; *(con detalles personales)* file, record card ▢ **ficha del cliente** customer record; **ficha de horas trabajadas** time sheet; **ficha del proveedor** supplier file; **ficha técnica** *(de producto)* technical specifications sheet, product information sheet

fichar *vi (en el trabajo) (al entrar)* to clock in, US to punch in; *(al salir)* to clock out *o* off, US to punch out

fichero *nm* (**a**) *(conjunto de fichas)* file ▢ **fichero de tarjetas** card index, card-index file (**b**) *(mueble)* filing cabinet; *(cajón)* filing cabinet drawer; *(caja)* card index box (**c**) INFORM file ▢ **fichero abierto** open file; **fichero activo** active file; **fichero adjunto** attachment; **fichero de archivo** archive file; **fichero ASCII** ASCII file; **fichero de ayuda** help file; **fichero de comandos** command file; **fichero contador** tally file; **fichero de correo (electrónico)** mail file; **fichero de direcciones** address file; **fichero de domiciliación** domiciliation file; **fichero ejecutable** executable file; **fichero sin formato** flat file; **fichero fuente** source file; **fichero de imagen** image file; **fichero invisible** invisible file; **fichero léeme** read-me file; **fichero por lotes** batch file; **fichero maestro** master file; **fichero MP3** MP3 file; **fichero oculto** hidden file; **fichero de salida** output file; **fichero del sistema** system file; **fichero de sólo lectura** read-only file; **fichero temporal** temporary file; **fichero de texto** text file

fidedigno, -a *adj* reliable

fideicomisario, -a *nm,f* DER trustee

fideicomiso *nm* DER *(acuerdo)* trust; *(administración)* trusteeship

fideicomitente *nmf* DER trustor

fidelidad *nf* loyalty ▢ **fidelidad del cliente** customer loyalty; **fidelidad del consumidor** consumer loyalty; **fidelidad a la marca** brand loyalty; **fidelidad total** hard-core loyalty

fidelización *nf* building of customer loyalty; **programa de fidelización** loyalty programme

fidelizar *vt* **fidelizar a los clientes** to build customer loyalty

fiduciario, -a *adj & nm,f* FIN, DER fiduciary

fiel *adj (cliente)* loyal

fiesta *nf (día)* public holiday; **ser fiesta** to be a public holiday; **hacer fiesta** to be on holiday ▫ *Am* **fiesta patria** national holiday *(commemorating important historical event)*

figura *nf* DER **figura (jurídica)** legal concept

fijación *nf* **fijación estratégica de objetivos** strategic targeting; **fijación de precios** pricing, price setting; **fijación de precios a la baja** price undercutting; **fijación de precios competitivos** competitive pricing; **fijación de precios con descuento** discount pricing; **fijación de precios desleales** predatory pricing; **fijación de precios según la estacionalidad** time pricing; **fijación del precio en función del costo** cost pricing; **fijación de precios según la localización geográfica** location pricing; **fijación del precio óptimo** target pricing; **fijación del precio del oro** gold fixing; **fijación de precios por paquetes de productos** product bundling pricing; **fijación de precios psicológicos** odd-even pricing; **fijación de precios según la tasa de rentabilidad** rate of return pricing; **fijación de precios por zona geográfica** geographic pricing

fijado, -a *adj (convenido) (precio, fecha)* appointed; **se terminará dentro del plazo fijado** it will be finished within the stated time

fijar *vt (convenir) (fecha, precio)* to set, to fix; **vamos a fijar una fecha para la reunión** let's set *o* fix a time for the meeting; **les corresponde a ellos fijar sus propios objetivos de producción** it's up to them to set their own production targets

fijo, -a *adj* (**a**) *(precio)* fixed, set (**b**) *(empleado, trabajo)* permanent; *(cliente)* regular; **estoy fijo en la empresa** I've got a permanent job in the company ▫ **fijo discontinuo** (employee) on a permanent seasonal contract

fila *nf* INFORM *(en hoja de cálculo)* row

filiación *nf* (**a**) *(datos personales)* personal details (**b**) *(parentesco)* relationship

filial 1 *adj (empresa)* subsidiary, affiliated
  2 *nf* subsidiary, affiliated company ▫ **filial comercial** sales company, sales subsidiary; **filial de comercialización** marketing subsidiary; **filial de ventas** sales subsidiary

> ❝
> Una empresa de tamaño pequeño o mediano puede tener un mercado global, pero en cada país tiene sólo unos 10 clientes, con lo que no se justifica instalar una fábrica, en cualquier caso, sí es posible una **filial comercial** con asistencia técnica.
> ❞

filosofía *nf (ideas)* philosophy ▫ **filosofía de ventas** sales philosophy

filtro *nm* (**a**) INFORM *(para monitor)* filter ▫ **filtro de pantalla** glare filter, glare screen (**b**) INFORM *(software)* filter (**c**) *(de llamadas)* screening

FIM *nm* FIN *(abrev de* **Fondo de Inversión Mobiliaria**) *Br* unit trust, *US* mutual fund

fin *nm (de mes, año, reunión)* end; **a fin** *o* **fines de mes** at the end of the month; **nuestros resultados de fin de año** our year end results ▫ INFORM **fin de línea** line end

final *nm (terminación)* end; **a finales de** at the end of

finalización *nf (de contrato, trabajo)* completion; *(de reunión)* closing

financiación *nf,* *Am* **financiamiento** *nm* financing, funding; **problemas en la financiación del proyecto a corto plazo** problems in the short-term financing *o* funding of the project ▫ **financiación ajena** external financing; **financiación cero** zero percent financing; **financiación a corto plazo** short-term financing; **financiación de la deuda** debt financing; **financiación de entresuelo** mezzanine finance; **financiación de equipo** equipment financing; **financiación a largo plazo** long-term financing; **financiación mediante arriendo** lease financing; **financiación mediante déficit** deficit financing; **financiación mediante la emisión de acciones** equity financing; **financiación con tipo de interés fijo** fixed-rate financing

> ❝
> Alguna marca ya está aplicando en España la fórmula de **financiación cero**, muy extendida en EE UU, por la que se aplazan los pagos sin cobrar intereses.
> ❞

financiar *vt* (**a**) *(proyecto, organismo)* to fund, to finance (**b**) *(compra)* to offer credit facilities for; **le financiamos su vehículo** we'll provide the credit for you to buy your car

financiero, -a 1 *adj* financial
  2 *nm,f (persona)* financier

finanzas *nfpl (actividades)* finance; *(fondos)* finances; **el ministro de finanzas** the finance minister; **las altas finanzas** high finance; **las finanzas de la empresa** the company's finances ▫ **finanzas mundiales** global finance

finca *nf* (**a**) *(bien inmueble)* property ▫ **finca rústica** rural property; **finca urbana** urban property (**b**) *Col* **finca raíz** real estate

finiquitar *vt (deuda)* to settle; *(trabajador)* to pay off

finiquito *nm (de deuda)* settlement; *(por despido)* redundancy settlement; **dar finiquito** *(saldar cuenta)* to close o settle; *(concluir)* to finish, to wind up

firma *nf* (**a**) *(rúbrica)* signature; **estampó su firma** he signed (his name), he wrote his signature □ **firma colectiva** joint signature; **firma digital, firma electrónica** digital signature (**b**) *(acción)* signing; **la firma de un acuerdo** the signing of an agreement (**c**) *(empresa)* firm

firmante 1 *adj* **las partes firmantes de un acuerdo** the signatories to an agreement
2 *nmf* signatory; **el abajo firmante** the undersigned □ **firmante conjunto** co-signatory

firmar 1 *vt (documento, cheque)* to sign
2 *vi* to sign

firme *adj (mercado)* firm; **en firme** *(acuerdo, oferta, venta)* firm; **tenemos un acuerdo en firme para intercambiar información** we have a firm agreement to exchange information; **una respuesta en firme** a definite answer

firmware *nm* INFORM firmware

fiscal 1 *adj* (**a**) *(del fisco)* fiscal, tax; **asesor/ fraude fiscal** tax adviser/evasion (**b**) DER **el ministerio fiscal** *Br* ≃ Office of the Director of Public Prosecutions, *US* ≃ Attorney General's Office
2 *nmf* (**a**) DER *Br* ≃ public prosecutor, *US* ≃ district attorney □ **Fiscal General del Estado** *Br* ≃ Director of Public Prosecutions, *US* ≃ Attorney General

fiscalidad *nf (impuestos)* taxation; **países con distintos regímenes de fiscalidad** countries with different tax regimes

> **❝**
> La ventaja española es, en este caso, la neutralidad sea cual sea la **fiscalidad** aplicada en la nación fuente de las ganancias de capital o dividendo, frente a la actitud de otros países que obligan a las empresas a pagar a sus Haciendas respectivas la diferencia.
> **❞**

fisco *nm Fam* **el fisco** the taxman

flecha *nf* INFORM **flecha abajo** down arrow; **flecha arriba** up arrow; **flecha derecha** right arrow; **flecha de desplazamiento** scroll arrow; **flecha izquierda** left arrow

fletamiento, fletamento *nm (de barco, avión)* charter, chartering

fletar *vt (barco, avión)* to charter; *(mercancías)* to freight

flete *nm (transporte, carga)* freight; *(precio)* freight, shipping costs; **flete en destino** freight forward; **enviar algo por flete** to send sth by freight □ **flete aéreo** airfreight; **flete falso** dead freight; **flete de ida** outward freight; **flete**

interior inland freight; **flete marítimo** maritime freight; **flete de retorno, flete de vuelta** return freight, home freight

flexibilidad *nf (de presupuesto, precio, enfoque)* flexibility □ **flexibilidad de horarios** *(requisito)* ability to work flexible hours; *(derecho)* flexible hours, flexitime

flexible *adj (presupuesto, enfoque, horario)* flexible

flojo, -a *adj (mercado, negocio)* slack; **las ventas están muy flojas** sales are very slack

floppy *nm* INFORM **floppy (disk)** floppy disk

floreciente *adj (negocio, economía)* flourishing, thriving

florín *nm* (**a**) *Antes (moneda holandesa)* guilder (**b**) *(moneda húngara)* forint

flota *nf* (**a**) *(de barcos)* fleet □ **flota mercante** merchant fleet; **flota pesquera** fishing fleet (**b**) *(de vehículos)* fleet, pool

flotación *nf* ECON *(de divisa)* flotation, float □ **flotación limpia** clean float; **flotación sucia** dirty float

flotante *adj* ECON *(divisa, tipo de cambio)* floating

flotar *vi* ECON **hacer flotar una divisa** to float a currency

flote: **a flote** *adv* **mantener a flote** to keep afloat; **mantenerse a flote** to stay afloat

fluctuación *nf (de mercado, moneda, precio)* fluctuation □ **fluctuación de las acciones** share fluctuation; **fluctuaciones anuales** annual variations; **fluctuación de la Bolsa** Stock Market fluctuation; **fluctuación de divisas** currency fluctuation; **fluctuación estacional** *(ajuste)* seasonal adjustment; **fluctuación máxima** maximum fluctuation; **fluctuación del mercado** market fluctuation; BOLSA **fluctuación de precios** price fluctuation

fluctuante *adj (mercado, moneda, precio)* fluctuating

fluctuar *vi (mercado, moneda, precio)* to fluctuate

flujo *nm (de información, dinero)* flow □ **flujo de caja** cash flow; **flujo de caja descontado** discounted cash flow; **flujo de caja incremental** incremental cash flow; **flujo de caja neto** net cash flow; **flujo de entrada de caja** cash inflow; **flujo de fondos** cash flow; **flujo de salida de caja** cash outflow; **flujo de tesorería** cash flow; **flujo de trabajo** work flow

fluorescente *adj* **rotulador fluorescente** highlighter (pen)

FMI *nm (abrev de* **Fondo Monetario Internacional***)* IMF

FOB *(abrev de* **Free on Board***)* FOB □ **FOB puerto de embarque** FOB port of embarkation

folio nm (**a**) (hoja de papel) leaf, sheet (A4 size); **tamaño folio** A4-sized (**b**) CONT (hoja) folio

folleto nm (librito) brochure, booklet; (hoja suelta) leaflet ❑ **folletos corporativos** corporate literature; BOLSA **folleto de emisión** (de acciones) prospectus; **folleto informativo** (sobre una empresa, producto) information booklet; **folletos de promoción** promotional literature; **folleto publicitario** publicity brochure; **folletos publicitarios** sales literature

fomentar vt to encourage, to promote; **medidas para fomentar el ahorro** measures to encourage saving

fondo nm (**a**) (de dinero) fund; **a fondo perdido** (préstamo) non-returnable; (subvención) outright; **no estamos dispuestos a invertir a fondo perdido** we're not prepared to pour money down the drain ❑ **fondo administrado** managed fund; **fondo de amortización** sinking fund; **fondo de capital riesgo** venture capital trust; **fondo cautivo** captive fund; **fondo de cohesión** cohesion fund; **fondo (colocado) en paraíso fiscal** offshore fund; **fondo de comercio** goodwill; BOLSA **fondo de compensación** compensation fund; **fondo de compensación interterritorial** interterritorial compensation fund; **fondo para contingencias** contingency fund; CONT **fondo contra contingencias y pérdidas** contingency and loss provision; **fondo de crecimiento** growth fund; **fondo de crédito permanente** evergreen fund; **fondo discrecional** discretionary fund; **fondo de emergencia** contingency fund; **fondo de estabilización** equalization fund; **fondo ético** ethical fund; UE **Fondo Europeo de Desarrollo** European Development Fund; UE **Fondo Europeo de Desarrollo Regional** European Regional Development Fund; **fondo fiduciario, fondo de fideicomiso** trust fund; **fondo fijo de caja** imprest fund; **fondo de futuros y opciones** futures and options fund; **fondo de garantía** guarantee fund; **fondo de garantía de crédito** credit guarantee fund; **fondo de garantía de depósitos** deposit guarantee fund; **fondo gestionado** managed fund; Am **fondo de huelga** strike fund; **fondo indexado** indexed fund, index-linked fund, esp Br tracker fund; **fondo de índice** index fund; **fondo de inversión** investment fund; **fondo de inversión en activos del mercado monetario** money market fund; **fondo de inversión de alto riesgo** hedge fund; **fondo de inversión autorizado** authorized investment fund; **fondo de inversión en bolsa** market fund; **fondo de inversión cerrado** closed-end investment fund; **fondo de inversión colectiva** investment fund; **fondo de inversión ético** ethical investment fund; **fondo de inversión gestionado** managed investment fund; **fondo de inversión inmobiliaria** real estate investment fund; **fondo de inversión mobiliaria** Br unit trust, US mutual fund; **fondo de inversión de renta fija** fixed income (investment) fund; **fondo de inversión de renta variable** equity (investment) fund, Br unit trust; **fondo de maniobra** working capital; **Fondo Monetario Internacional** International Monetary Fund; **fondo de oro** gold pool; **fondo paraguas** umbrella fund; **fondo de pensiones** pension fund; **fondo de previsión** provident fund; **fondo referenciado** indexed fund, index-linked fund, esp Br tracker fund; **fondo de renta** income fund; **fondo de renta fija** non-equity fund, bond fund; **fondo de renta variable** equity (investment) fund; **fondo de reserva** reserve fund, guarantee fund; **fondo rotativo** revolving fund; **fondo de seguro mixto** endowment (fund); UE **Fondo Social Europeo** European Social Fund; **fondo de subsidio de desempleo** unemployment fund; **fondo vitalicio** life annuity (**b**) **fondos** (capital) funds; **nos hemos quedado sin fondos** our funds have run out; **un cheque sin fondos** a bad cheque; **estar mal de fondos** (persona) to be badly off; (empresa) to be short of funds; **recaudar fondos** to raise funds ❑ **fondos ajenos** borrowed funds, borrowings; **fondos bloqueados** frozen funds; **fondos disponibles** disposable funds; **fondos de la empresa** company funds; UE **fondos estructurales** structural funds; **fondos propios** (de accionistas) (shareholders') equity; **fondos públicos** public funds; **fondos reservados** secret funds

> "
>
> Los datos de suscripciones de **fondos de inversión** en España siguen la misma tónica desde principios de año. Las campañas masivas de captación de dinero a través de garantizados organizadas por la gran banca han provocado que estos productos acaparen el incipiente apetito por la Bolsa. Han canibalizado a los fondos de Bolsa puros que, aunque empiezan a recibir dinero, lo hacen en una proporción muy limitada, y en el año aún registran salidas de capital.
>
> "

forjar vt (reputación) to build up

forma nf (**a**) (manera) way, manner; **de forma fraudulenta/ilegal** fraudulently/illegally ❑ **forma de compra** purchase method; **forma de pago** method of payment (**b**) Méx (formulario) form ❑ **forma en blanco** blank form; **forma de reserva** reservation form; **forma de respuesta** reply form; **forma de solicitud** application form

formación nf (**a**) (educación) training; **sin formación académica** with little formal education ❑ **formación en alternancia** sandwich courses; **formación asistida por** Esp **ordenador** o

Am **computadora** computer-based training; **formación de cargos de gestión** management training; **formación continua** in-service training; **formación en la empresa** in-house training, *Br* in-company training; **formación industrial** *(en la empresa)* industrial training; **formación en el lugar de trabajo** in-house training, *Br* in-company training; **formación ocupacional** occupational training; **formación del personal** staff training; **formación práctica** hands-on training; **formación profesional** professional *o* vocational training
(**b**) *(creación)* formation

formal *adj (oficial)* formal; **un requisito formal** an official requirement

formalidad *nf (requisito)* formality; **es una mera formalidad** it's just a formality ▫ **formalidades administrativas** administrative formalities; **formalidades aduaneras** customs procedure

formalmente *adv* formally

formar 1 *vt* (**a**) *(empresa, comité)* to form; **formar un equipo** to make up a team; **formar una asociación cultural** to set up a cultural organization (**b**) *(empleado)* to train
2 **formarse** *vpr (empleado)* to train; *(estudiante)* to be educated

formateado, -a INFORM 1 *adj* formatted
2 *nm (proceso)* formatting

formatear *vt* INFORM to format

formateo *nm* INFORM formatting ▫ **formateo de salida** output formatting

formato *nm (de libro, documento)* format ▫ **formato apaisado** landscape; **formato de archivo** file format; **formato ASCII** ASCII format; **formato de fichero** file format; **formato de imagen** image format; **formato de impresión** print format; **formato de página** page format; **formato de papel** paper format; **formato de retrato** portrait; **formato del texto** text layout; **formato vertical** portrait

fórmula *nf (en carta)* **fórmula de despedida** standard ending; **fórmula de saludo** standard opening

formulario *nm* form; **rellenar un formulario** to fill in *o* out a form ▫ **formulario de anulación** *(de pedido)* cancellation form; **formulario en blanco** blank form; **formulario de cancelación** *(de pedido)* cancellation form; **formulario de cheque** cheque form; INFORM **formulario de datos** input form, data entry form; **formulario de entrada en almacén** inventory *o* Br stock received form; **formulario de gastos** expenses claim form; **formulario de inscripción** *(para una licitación)* tender form; **formulario de pedido** order form; **formulario de reclamación**, *SAm* **formulario de reclamo** *(de póliza de seguros)* claim form; **formulario de reserva** reservation form;

formulario de respuesta reply form; **formulario de salida de almacén** inventory *o* Br stock issue form; **formulario de solicitud** application form; **formulario de solicitud de crédito** credit application form; **formulario de suscripción de acciones** share application form, share subscription form

foro *nm (lugar de discusión)* forum ▫ **foro de debate** forum for debate; INFORM **foro de discusión** discussion group

fortalecer 1 *vt (economía, moneda)* to strengthen; **el acuerdo fortalecerá las relaciones entre los dos países** the agreement will strengthen relations between the two countries
2 **fortalecerse** *vpr (economía, moneda)* to strengthen

fortaleza *nf (de economía, moneda)* strength; *(temporal) (de mercado, precios)* buoyancy ▫ MKTG **fortalezas de la marca** brand strengths; **fortalezas del producto** product strengths

> **❝**
> El euro se ha disparado hoy hasta los 1,16 dólares con un avance del 1%, frente a los 1,1521 de ayer por su **fortaleza** frente al yen ante el interés de inversores japoneses en bonos públicos europeos.
> **❞**

fotocopia *nf* (**a**) *(objeto)* photocopy; **hacer una fotocopia de** to make *o* take a photocopy of (**b**) *(procedimiento)* photocopying

fotocopiadora *nf* (**a**) *(máquina)* photocopier (**b**) *(tienda)* copy shop

fotocopiar *vt* to photocopy

fracasar *vi (plan, proyecto, negociaciones)* to fail; *(producto)* to be a failure; **el modelo fracasó en Europa** the model was a failure in Europe

fracaso *nm (de plan, proyecto, negociaciones)* failure; **fue un fracaso comercial** it was a commercial failure

fracción *nf* FIN *(de acción)* fraction

fraccionamiento *nm* FIN **fraccionamiento de acciones** share splitting

fracción *nf Am* **fracción arancelaria** customs code

fraccionar *vt* (**a**) FIN *(acciones)* to split (**b**) *(pago)* to split up into instalments

frágil *adj (objeto)* fragile

fragmentación *nf* INFORM fragmentation ▫ **fragmentación del disco** disk fragmentation

fragmentado, -a *adj* INFORM *(disco duro)* fragmented

fragmentar INFORM *vt (disco duro)* to fragment

franchising *nm* franchising

franco, -a 1 *adj* (**a**) *(sin impuestos)* free; **puerto franco** free port; **franco de porte** *(carta)*

postpaid; *(pedido)* carriage-paid; **franco a bordo** free on board; **franco al costado del buque** free alongside ship; **franco muelle** free alongside *o* at quay; **franco sobre camión** free on truck; **franco sobre vagón** free on rail (**b**) **estar franco de servicio** *(de permiso)* to be off duty; *CSur, Méx* **me dieron el día franco** they gave me the day off
 2 *nm* (**a**) *(moneda)* franc ▫ *Antes* ***franco belga*** Belgian franc; *Antes* ***franco francés*** French franc; ***franco suizo*** Swiss franc (**b**) *CSur, Méx (permiso)* **esta semana tengo franco** I'm off work this week; **ayer tuvimos franco** we had the day off yesterday

franja *nf (de salarios, impuestos)* band ▫ ***franja de edad*** age bracket; ***franja horaria*** *(en programación de televisión)* time slot; *(huso horario)* time zone; ***franja (horaria) de máxima audiencia*** prime time, *Br* peak time

franqueadora *nf Br* franking machine, *US* postage meter

franquear *vt (correo)* to attach postage to; *(con máquina)* to frank; **enviar un sobre franqueado** send a stamped (addressed) envelope; **a franquear en destino** *(en sobre)* postage paid, post-paid, *Br* ≃ Freepost®

franqueo *nm* postage; **franqueo pagado** postage paid, post-paid, *Br* ≃ Freepost®

franquicia *nf* (**a**) *(tienda)* franchise (**b**) *(exención)* exemption ▫ ***franquicia aduanera*** duty-free entry; ***franquicia postal*** exemption from postage, free postage (**c**) *(en seguro) Br* excess, *US* deductible

franquiciado, -a *nm,f* franchisee, franchiseholder

franquiciador, -ora *nm,f* franchiser

franquiciar *vt* to franchise

fraude *nm* fraud ▫ ***fraude fiscal*** tax fraud; ***fraude informático*** computer fraud; ***fraude con tarjetas de crédito*** credit card fraud

fraudulentamente *adv* fraudulently, by fraudulent means

fraudulento, -a *adj* fraudulent

frecuencia *nf* MKTG frequency ▫ ***frecuencia absoluta*** absolute frequency; ***frecuencia de compra*** purchase frequency

frecuentar *vt (lugar)* to frequent; *(negocio, tienda)* to patronize

frecuente *adj* frequent

free-lance *nmf* freelance; **trabajar como free-lance** to work freelance, to freelance

freeware *nm* INFORM freeware

frenar *vt (inflación, gastos, desempleo)* to curb; **los altos tipos de interés frenan a los inversores** the high interest rates are deterring investors

freno *nm (contención)* check, curb; **la inflación es un freno al crecimiento** inflation holds back growth; **poner freno a algo** to curb sth

friccional *adj (desempleo)* frictional

frigorífico, -a *adj* **cámara frigorífica** cold store; **camión frigorífico** refrigerated *Br* lorry *o US* truck; *RP* **planta frigorífica** meat processing plant

frontal *nm* **frontal del lineal** *(de distribución)* shelf facing

frontera *nf (entre países)* border, frontier; *(entre estados federados, regiones)* border

fruto *nm* **dar fruto** *(trabajo, esfuerzo)* to pay off

FSE *nm* UE *(abrev de* **Fondo Social Europeo**) ESF

FSM *nf (abrev de* **Federación Sindical Mundial**) WFTU

FTP INFORM *(abrev de* **file transfer protocol**) FTP; **hacer FTP** to do FTP ▫ ***FTP anónimo*** anonymous FTP

fuente *nf* (**a**) *(origen)* source ▫ ***fuente de alimentación*** *(para máquina)* power supply; INFORM ***fuente de datos*** data source; ***fuente de financiación*** backer; ***fuente de ingresos*** source of income; ***fuente de riqueza*** source of wealth (**b**) INFORM *(de letra)* font ▫ ***fuente por defecto*** default font; ***fuente de impresora*** printer font; ***fuente de mapa de bits*** bitmap font; ***fuente OCR*** OCR font; ***fuente PostScript®*** PostScript® font; ***fuente predeterminada*** default font

fuerte *adj (economía, divisa)* strong; *(temporalmente) (mercado, precios)* **es una empresa fuerte en el sector** the company is strong in this sector

fuerza *nf* (**a**) *(de mercado, divisa, economía)* strength (**b**) **fuerza mayor** *(en seguros)* force majeure; **un caso de fuerza mayor** an act of God (**c**) **fuerzas** *(grupo)* forces; **las principales fuerzas sociales** the main interest groups in society ▫ ***fuerzas económicas*** economic forces; ***fuerzas del mercado*** market forces; ***fuerzas productivas*** productive forces

fuga *nf* **fuga de capitales** capital flight, flight of capital; **fuga de cerebros** brain drain; **fuga de divisas** capital flight

función *nf* (**a**) *(de máquina, persona)* function; **la función del coordinador es hacer que todo discurra sin contratiempos** the coordinator's job *o* function is to make sure everything goes smoothly; **desempeña las funciones de portavoz** he acts as spokesperson; **director en funciones** acting director; **entrar en funciones** *(en empresa, organización)* to take up one's post; **en función de los ingresos** *(prestaciones)* earnings-related ▫ ECON ***función de la demanda*** demand function; ***funciones directivas*** *(ejecutivas)* executive functions; *(de gestión)* managerial functions; ***funciones de gestión***

managerial functions; *funciones ministeriales* ministerial functions
  (**b**) INFORM function ❑ *función (de) guardar* save function; *función (de) repetir* repeat function

funcional *adj (práctico)* functional

funcionamiento *nm* operation, functioning; **explicó el funcionamiento de la empresa** she explained how the company works; **entrar/estar en funcionamiento** *(sistema)* to come into/be in operation; *(máquina)* to start/be (working *o* running); **poner algo en funcionamiento** *(sistema)* to put sth into operation; *(máquina)* to start sth (working)

funcionar *vi (machine)* to work, to run; *(plan, idea, método)* to work; **no funciona** *(en letrero)* out of order

funcionario, -a *nm,f* (**a**) **funcionario (público)** *(de la Administración central)* civil servant; *(profesor, bombero, enfermero)* public sector worker; **un alto funcionario** a senior civil servant ❑ *funcionario de aduanas* customs official, customs officer; *funcionario de Correos* *Br* Post Office worker, *US* mail service worker; *funcionario de Hacienda* tax official; *funcionario de prisiones* prison officer; *funcionario sindical* trade union official
  (**b**) *(de organismo internacional)* employee, staff member
  (**c**) *RP (de empresa)* employee, worker

fundación *nf* (**a**) *(creación, establecimiento)* foundation, establishment (**b**) *(organización)* foundation, trust; **una fundación benéfica** a charitable foundation *o* trust

fundacional *adj* **carta fundacional** charter

fundado, -a *adj (empresa)* founded, established; **H. Rodríguez, fundada en 1957**

H. Rodríguez (est 1957)

fundador, -ora 1 *adj* founding
  2 *nm,f* founder

fundar 1 *vt (empresa)* to found, to set up
  2 **fundarse** *vpr (crearse, establecerse)* to be founded

fundir 1 *vt (empresas)* to merge
  2 **fundirse** *vpr (empresas)* to merge

fungible *adj (consumible)* disposable; BOLSA *(título)* fungible

furgoneta *nf* van ❑ *furgoneta de reparto* delivery van

fusión *nf* (**a**) *(de empresas, bancos)* merger, amalgamation ❑ *fusiones y adquisiciones* mergers and acquisitions; *fusión impropia* vertical merger; *fusión propia* horizontal merger; *fusión vertical* vertical merger (**b**) INFORM merge ❑ *fusión de archivos* file merge

fusionar 1 *vt* (**a**) *(empresas, bancos)* to merge, to amalgamate (**b**) INFORM to merge
  2 **fusionarse** *vpr* to merge, to amalgamate

"
La compañía aérea suiza ha anunciado que despedirá a 3.000 empleados de su área de catering y **se fusionará** con la aerolínea de vuelos regionales Crossair para hacer frente al descenso de la demanda en el sector. La alemana Lufthansa ha paralizado el 10% de su flota.
"

futuro *nm* (**a**) *(de persona, empresa)* future; **ese negocio no tiene futuro** there's no future in that business (**b**) BOLSA **futuros** futures ❑ *futuros financieros* financial futures; *futuros y opciones* futures and options

Gg

G-3 *nm (abrev de* **Grupo de los tres***)* G-3, = economic bloc formed by Colombia, Mexico and Venezuela

G7 *nm (abrev de* **Grupo de los Siete***)* G7

G8 *nm (abrev de* **Grupo de los Ocho***)* G8

gajes *nmpl Fam* **gajes del oficio** occupational hazards

galopante *adj (inflación, ritmo)* galloping

gama *nf (de productos, precios)* range; **de gama alta** high-end, *Br* top-of-the-range, *US* top-of-the-line; **un modelo de gama baja** a low-end *o* an economy *o* a budget model; **una computadora de gama baja** an entry-level computer; **de gama media** middle of the range, mid-range □ *gama de modelos* range of models

ganancia *nf (rendimiento)* profit; *(ingreso)* earnings; **ganancias y pérdidas** profit and loss □ *ganancia bruta* gross profit, gross earnings; *ganancia cambiaria* exchange premium; *ganancias de capital* capital gains; *ganancia inesperada* windfall profit; *ganancias invisibles* invisible earnings; *ganancia líquida, ganancia neta* net profit, net earnings; *ganancias sobre el papel* paper profits; *ganancia total* gross profit, gross earnings

ganar 1 *vt (sueldo, dinero)* to earn; **gana dos millones al año** she earns *o* she's on *o* she makes two million a year
2 *vi (lograr dinero)* to earn money; *Am* **ganar bien** to be well paid
3 ganarse *vpr* **ganarse la vida** to earn a *o* one's living

ganchito, gancho *nm Col (para papeles)* staple

ganga *nf* snip, bargain; **se lo dejo a precio de ganga** I'll let you have it for a knockdown price

garante *nmf (de productos)* warrantor; *(de créditos)* guarantor, surety; **salir garante** to act as guarantor □ DER *garante solidario* joint and several guarantor

garantía *nf* **(a)** *(de producto, servicio)* guarantee, warranty; **una garantía de tres años, tres años de garantía** a three-year guarantee *o* warranty; **estar en garantía** to be under guarantee □ *garantía ampliada* extended guarantee, extended warranty; *garantía de calidad* quality assurance; *garantía contractual* contractual guarantee; *garantía de devolu-*

ción money-back guarantee; *garantía de finalización* completion guarantee; *garantía ilimitada* unlimited warranty; *garantía limitada* limited warranty; *garantía sobre piezas y mano de obra* parts and labour warranty; *garantía de reembolso (del dinero)* money-back guarantee; *garantía total* full warranty; *garantía de por vida* lifetime guarantee
(b) *(de préstamo)* security □ *garantía bancaria* bank guarantee; *garantía de crédito* proof of credit; *garantía del crédito de comprador* buyer credit guarantee; *garantía de créditos para la exportación* export credit guarantee; *garantía hipotecaria* mortgage security; *garantía legal* legal guarantee; *garantía de opción de compra* call warrant; *garantía pignoraticia, garantía prendaria* collateral (security)

garantizado, -a *adj (cheque, deuda)* guaranteed

garantizar *vt* **(a)** *(producto, aparato)* to guarantee; **les garantizaron el televisor por un año** they guaranteed the television for a year, they gave them a year's guarantee for the television **(b)** *(deuda, préstamo)* to guarantee, to secure; BOLSA *(emisión)* to underwrite

garete *nm Fam* **ir** *o* **irse al garete** to go down the drain, to go to pot

gastar 1 *vt (dinero)* to spend (**en** on)
2 *vi* to spend (money); **gastar de más** *o* **en exceso** to overspend

gasto *nm (dinero gastado)* spending, expenditure; **el gasto educativo/militar** *(de país)* spending on education/defence; **correr con los gastos (de algo)** to meet *o* bear the cost (of sth), to pay (for sth); **cubrir gastos** to cover costs, to break even; **no reparar en gastos** to spare no expense □ *gasto adicional* additional expenditure; *gastos administrativos* administrative expenses; *gastos de almacenamiento, gastos de almacenaje* storage charges, warehouse charges; *gastos amortizables* deferred charges, capitalised expenses; *gastos anuales totales* total annual expenses; *gastos bancarios* bank charges; CONT *gastos de caja* cash expenditure; *gastos de capital* capital outlay, capital expenditure; *gastos de cobro* collection charges, collection fees; *gastos de comercialización* marketing costs; *gasto de* o *en consumo* consumer expenditure; *gasto* *corriente* current expenditure; *gastos deducibles* tax-deductible expenses, allowable expenses; *gastos no deducibles* disallowable expenses; *gastos de descarga* landing charges; *gastos de desplazamiento* relocation expenses, settling-in allowance; *gastos devengados* accrued charges, accrued expenses; *gastos diferidos* deferred charges; *gastos directos* direct expenses; *gastos de distribución* distribution costs; *gastos diversos* miscellaneous expenses, sundry expenses; *gastos documentarios* documentary charges; CONT *gastos en efectivo* cash expenditure; *gastos de embalaje* packaging costs, packing costs; *gastos de entrega* forwarding charges; *gastos de envío* shipping charges, delivery charges; *gastos de explotación* operating costs o expenses; CONT *gastos extraordinarios* extraordinary expenses; *gastos fijos* fixed costs; *gastos fijos directos* direct fixed costs; *gasto financiado mediante déficit* deficit spending; *gastos financieros* financial expenses; *gasto fiscal* public spending, fiscal spending; *gastos de franqueo* postage costs; *gastos generales* general expenses, overhead costs; *gastos generales y de administración* general and administrative expenses; *gastos generales de fabricación* factory *Br* overheads o *US* overhead; *gastos de gestión* handling charges; *gastos del hogar* household expenses; *gastos imprevistos* incidental costs, incidental expenses; *gastos imputables* chargeable expenses; *gastos de mantenimiento* maintenance costs; *gastos de marketing* marketing spend; *gastos menores* out-of-pocket expenses; *gastos netos de capital* net capital expenditure; *gastos de oficina* office expenses; *gastos de personal* personnel expenses, staff costs; *gastos postales* postal charges; *gastos preliminares* preliminary expenses; *gastos de primer establecimiento* start-up expenses; CONT *gastos de producción* production *Br* overheads o *US* overhead; *gastos de publicidad, gastos publicitarios* advertising costs, advertising expenses; *gastos de publicidad above-the-line o general* above-the-line expenditure; *gastos de publicidad below-the-line* below-the-line costs; *gasto público* public spending, public expenditure; *gastos de puesta en marcha* start-up costs; *gastos repercutibles* chargeable expenses; *gastos de representación* entertainment allowance, entertainment expenses; *gasto social* social expenditure; *gastos de seguro* insurance charges; *gastos soportados* incurred expenditure, incurred expenses; *gastos de tramitación* handling charges; *gastos de transporte* transport costs; *gastos de traslado* (de empleado) relocation expenses; *gastos variables* variable expenses; *gastos varios* miscellaneous expenses; *gastos de venta* selling costs; *gastos de viaje* travel expenses, travelling expenses

GATT *nm* (*abrev de* **General Agreement on Tariffs and Trade**) GATT

GB *nm* INFORM (*abrev de* **gigabyte**) GB

generado, -a *adj* **generado por** *Esp* **ordenador** o *Am* **computadora** computer-generated

general *adj* (*director, asamblea, tendencia*) general; (*huelga*) all-out; **una regla de aplicación general** a blanket rule; **mi valoración general es negativa** my overall opinion of it is negative

generalizado, -a *adj* (*sentimiento, problema*) widespread; (*incremento, reducción*) across-the-board

generar *vt* (*ingresos, intereses*) to generate; (*empleo*) to create; **generado por** *Esp* **ordenador** o *Am* **computadora** computer-generated; **el turismo genera millones de dólares cada año** tourism generates millions of dollars each year

genérico, -a 1 *adj* generic
  2 *nm* (*medicamento*) generic drug; MKTG (*producto*) generic

género *nm* (*productos*) merchandise, goods

genuino, -a *adj* (*artículo*) genuine

geodemografía *nf* MKTG geodemographics

geodemográfico, -a *adj* MKTG geodemographic

geográfico, -a *adj* MKTG geographic

geomarketing *nm* geomarketing

gerencia *nf* management

gerente *nmf* manager ❑ *gerente de crédito* credit manager; *gerente de división* divisional manager; *gerente de empresa* company manager; *gerente de informática* computer manager; *gerente de línea* line manager; *gerente de oficina* office manager; *gerente de planta* (*en grandes almacenes*) floor manager; *gerente de procesamiento de datos* data processing manager; *gerente de publicidad* advertising manager; *gerente técnico* technical manager

gestión *nf* (**a**) (*administración*) management; **es responsable de la gestión diaria del negocio** he is responsible for the day-to-day running of the business ❑ *gestión de activos (financieros)* (financial) asset management; *gestión de caja* cash management; *gestión de calidad* quality management; *gestión de calidad total* total quality management; *gestión del cambio* change management; MKTG *gestión de los canales de distribución* channel management; *gestión de cartera* portfolio management; MKTG *gestión de clientes principales* key-account management; *gestión de cobro* = collection of outstanding payments; *gestión de comunicación* communications management; *gestión conjunta* joint management; *gestión del conocimiento* knowledge management; *gestión por consenso* consensus management;

gestión de costos cost management; *gestión de(l) crédito* credit management; *gestión de crisis* crisis management; MKTG *gestión de cuentas clave* key-account management; *gestión de la demanda* demand management; *gestión de la distribución física* physical distribution management; *gestión eficiente* effective management; *gestión de empresas* business management; *gestión estratégica* strategic management; *gestión de existencias* inventory o Br stock management; *gestión de exportaciones* export management; *gestión financiera* financial management; *gestión financiera de las sociedades* corporate finance; *gestión del flujo de caja* cash flow management; *gestión de fondos* fund management; *gestión de gastos menores* petty cash management; *gestión de inversiones* investment management; *gestión logística* logistics management; *gestión de la mano de obra* manpower management; *gestión de la marca* brand management; *gestión matricial* matrix management; *gestión múltiple de carteras* multiple management; *gestión de oficinas* office management; *gestión operativa* operations management; *gestión de personal* personnel management; *gestión de la producción* production management; *gestión de producto* product management; *gestión de proyectos* project management; *gestión de recursos* resource management; *gestión de recursos humanos* human resource management; *gestión de red* network management; *gestión de relaciones públicas* communications management; *gestión de riesgos* risk management; *gestión de servicios de restauración* hospitality management; *gestión de stocks* inventory o Br stock control; *gestión de tesorería* cash management; *gestión del tiempo* time management; *gestión de ventas* sales management

(**b**) INFORM *gestión de archivos* file management; *gestión de bases de datos* database management; *gestión de datos* data management; *gestión de documentos* document handling; *gestión de ficheros* file management; *gestión de memoria* memory management; *gestión de sistemas* systems management

(**c**) *(diligencia)* **tengo que hacer unas gestiones en Hacienda** I have a few things to do at the tax office; **las gestiones del negociador fracasaron** the negotiator's efforts came to nothing

gestionar *vt* (**a**) *(tramitar)* to arrange; **gestionar un préstamo** to arrange a loan; **gestionar un visado** to arrange o to get a visa; **están gestionando el traspaso del jugador** they're arranging the transfer of the player (**b**) *(administrar)* to manage; **gestiona la empresa con eficacia** she manages o runs the business well

gestor, -ora 1 *adj* **el equipo gestor del proyecto** the project management team

2 *nm,f* **gestor (administravivo)** = person who carries out dealings with public bodies on behalf of private customers or companies, combining the roles of solicitor and accountant
◻ *gestor de carteras* portfolio manager; *gestor de fondos* fund manager; BANCA *gestor de particulares* general account manager; *gestor de riesgos* risk manager

3 *nm* INFORM *gestor de archivos* file manager; *gestor de correo* mail manager; *gestor de memoria* memory manager; *gestor de red* network manager

GIF *nm* INFORM *(abrev de* **graphics interchange format)** GIF

gigabyte *nm* INFORM gigabyte

gigante 1 *adj* **de tamaño gigante** giant-sized
2 *nm (empresa)* giant

girador, -ora *nm,f* FIN drawer

girar 1 *vi* FIN **girar a la vista** to draw at sight; **girar en descubierto** to write a cheque without sufficient funds
2 *vt* (**a**) FIN to draw (**b**) *(enviar) (dinero)* to send, to remit

giratorio, -a *adj* revolving

giro *nm* (**a**) *(de dinero en efectivo)* money order, remittance; **poner un giro** to send a money order; **le envió 100 euros por giro** she sent him a money order for 100 euros ◻ *giro postal* money order, Br postal order; *giro postal internacional* international money order; *giro telegráfico:* **poner un giro telegráfico a alguien** to wire money to sb
(**b**) FIN *(de letras, órdenes de pago)* draft ◻ *giro bancario* banker's cheque, banker's draft; *giro a la vista* sight draft, demand draft

global *adj* (**a**) *(solución, enfoque, estrategia)* global; *(aumento)* overall; INFORM **una búsqueda global** a global search; **por un importe global de 10 millones** for a total sum of 10 milllion (**b**) *(mundial)* global, worldwide; **una economía global** a global economy

globalifóbico, -a *Fam* 1 *adj* anti-globalization
2 *nm,f* anti-globalization protester

❝
Zedillo fue quien acuñó, durante su mandato (1994-2000), el término de "**globalifóbicos**" para definir a las miles de personas que desde la última década se manifiestan en cada cita de líderes mundiales para protestar por las condiciones de pobreza en el mundo.
❞

globalización *nf* globalization
globalizar *vt* *(internacionalizar)* to globalize
gobernante *adj* governing

gobernanza *nf* governance ❑ *gobernanza corporativa* corporate governance

gobernar *vt* to govern

gobierno *nm* government; **buen gobierno** *(de empresa)* (corporate) governance ❑ *gobierno electrónico* e-government; *gobierno nacional* national government

góndola *nf (en supermercado)* gondola

gopher *nm* INFORM gopher

GPRS *nm*TEL (*abrev de* **General Packet Radio Service**) GPRS

GPS *nm* (*abrev de* **Global Positioning System**) GPS

grabadora *nf (magnetófono)* tape recorder ❑ INFORM *grabadora de CD-ROM* CD-ROM writer; *grabadora de discos compactos* compact disc recorder

grabar *vt* INFORM *(documento)* to save; *(CD-ROM)* to write, to burn

grado *nm* (**a**) *(en escala)* degree ❑ MKTG *grado de notoriedad* awareness rating (**b**) *(rango)* grade

graduado, -a *nm,f (de universidad)* graduate; **graduado en economía/derecho** economics/law graduate

gráfica *nf (figura)* graph, chart; *(dibujo)* diagram ❑ *Méx* **gráfica de pastel,** *SAm* **gráfica de tarta** pie chart

gráfico, -a **1** *adj (artes, diseño, representación)* graphic; **reportaje gráfico** photo story, illustrated feature; **reportero gráfico** press photographer
2 *nm* (**a**) *(figura)* graph, chart; *(dibujo)* diagram ❑ *gráfico de actividades* activity chart; *gráfico de barras* bar chart; *gráfico financiero* financial chart; *SAm* *gráfico de tarta* pie chart; *gráfico de ventas* sales chart (**b**) *gráficos informáticos* computer graphics; *gráficos para presentaciones* presentation graphics, business graphics
3 *nm,f RP* printer

grafista *nmf* graphic designer, graphic artist

grampa *nf Am (para papeles)* staple

gran *ver* **grande**

grande **1** *adj (de tamaño)* big, large; *(en importancia)* great; **un periódico de gran difusión** a newspaper with a large circulation; **un puesto de una gran responsabilidad** a position of great responsibility; **los grandes bancos** the major banks; **las grandes empresas** the major companies; **el gran Buenos Aires/Santiago** greater Buenos Aires/Santiago, the metropolitan area of Buenos Aires/Santiago ❑ *grandes almacenes* department store; *Gran Bretaña* Great Britain; *Esp* *gran superficie* hypermarket, large retail outlet

2 *nm (persona, entidad importante)* **uno de los grandes del sector** one of the major players in the industry

granel: a granel *adj & adv (sin envase)* loose; *(en gran cantidad)* in bulk; **vender/comprar vino a granel** to sell/buy wine from the barrel

granelero *nm* **(barco) granelero** bulk carrier

grano *nm (cereal)* grain

grapa *nf (para papeles)* staple; **sujetar con grapas** to staple

grapadora *nf Esp, Méx, Carib* stapler ❑ *grapadora industrial* staple gun

grapar *vt* to staple

gratificación *nf (monetaria) (por un trabajo)* bonus; *(propina)* gratuity

gratis **1** *adj inv* free; **ser gratis** to be free
2 *adv* (for) free, free of charge; **el viaje me salió gratis** the journey didn't cost me anything

gratuitamente *adv* free (of charge)

gratuito, -a *adj* free; **harán la entrega de forma gratuita** they will deliver free of charge

gravable *adj* taxable

gravamen *nm (impuesto)* tax; **libre de gravamen** unencumbered, free from encumbrances ❑ *gravamen hipotecario* mortgage charge; UE *gravamen variable a la importación* variable import levy

gravar *vt (con impuestos)* to tax; **el local está gravado con una fuerte hipoteca** the premises are heavily mortgaged

gris *adj (mercado, zona)* grey

grupaje *nm* groupage

grupo *nm (de personas, empresas)* group ❑ *Grupo Andino* Andean Group, = group promoting economic integration of Bolivia, Ecuador, Colombia, Peru and Venezuela; *grupo asegurador* insurance group; *grupo de compra* purchasing group; MKTG *grupo de control* control group; *grupo cooperativo* co-operative group; *grupo de discusión* MKTG panel; INFORM discussion group; *grupo de edad* age group; *grupo empresarial* business group, combine; *grupo estratégico* strategic group; *grupo de estudio* study group; *grupo de expertos* think tank; *grupo financiero* financial group; *grupo de hoteles* hotel group; *grupo industrial* industrial group; *grupo de interés económico* economic interest group; *grupo de medios de comunicación* media group; *grupo de minoristas* retailers' group; *grupo multimedia* multimedia group; INFORM *grupo de noticias* newsgroup; *Grupo de los Ocho* Group of Eight; *grupo de presión* pressure group, lobby; MKTG *grupo de referencia* reference group; *Grupo de los Siete* Group of Seven; *grupo socioeconómico* socio-economic group; **grupo socioprofesional** socio-professional group; **grupo de trabajo** task force, working group; **Grupo de los Tres** Group of Three, = economic bloc formed by Colombia, Mexico and Venezuela

guagua *nf Cuba, PRico, RDom (autobús)* bus

guardar *vt* INFORM to save; **guardar cambios** to save changes; **guardar automáticamente** to autosave

gubernamental *adj* government; **organización no gubernamental** non-governmental organization

guerra *nf* **guerra económica** economic warfare; INFORM **guerra de llamaradas, guerra de mensajes ofensivos** flame war; **guerra de precios** price war

guía 1 *nf* **guía de calles** street directory; **guía de carga** consignment note; *Am* **guía (de carga) aérea** air waybill, air bill; **guía comercial, guía de empresas** commercial directory; **guía de profesiones** trade directory; *Esp, RP* **guía telefónica, guía de teléfonos** telephone book, telephone directory; **guía turística** tour guide **2** *nmf* **guía turístico** tour guide

guillotina *nf (para papel)* guillotine

guión, guion *nm (símbolo) (corto)* hyphen; *(más largo)* dash ❑ **guión de fin de línea** line end hyphen

guita *nf Esp, RP Fam* dough, *Br* dosh

Hh

haber *nm* (**a**) CONT credit (side) (**b**) **haberes** assets; **confiscaron sus haberes** they confiscated his assets

habilidad *nf* skill; **una de sus muchas habilidades** one of his many skills; **su habilidad para vender** his salesmanship □ *habilidades principales* core competences, core skills; *habilidad técnica* technical skill

habitación *nf* **no hay habitaciones (libres)** *(en hotel)* there are no vacancies

hábito *nm (costumbre)* habit □ *hábito de compra* buying habit, purchasing habit; *hábito de consumo* consumption habit

habitual *adj (comportamiento, respuesta)* habitual; *(cliente)* regular; **seguir el procedimiento habitual** to follow the usual procedure

hacienda *nf* **(el Ministerio de) Hacienda** *Br* ≃ the Treasury, *US* ≃ the Department of the Treasury; **declarar algo a Hacienda** to declare sth (to the taxman *o Br* Inland Revenue *o US* IRS) □ *hacienda pública:* **un delito contra la hacienda pública** a case of tax evasion

hacker *nmf* INFORM hacker

hardware *nm* INFORM hardware

HD INFORM (**a**) *(abrev de **hard disk**)* HD (**b**) *(abrev de **high density**)* HD

hecho, -a **1** *adj* **hecho a mano** handmade; **hecho a máquina** machine-made
2 *nm* FIN **hecho imponible** taxable event, taxable transaction

heredable *adj* inheritable

heredar *vt* (**a**) *(recibir)* to inherit (**de** from); (**b**) *Méx (legar)* to bequeath

heredero, -a *nm,f* heir, *f* heiress □ DER *heredero universal* residuary legatee

herencia *nf (de bienes)* inheritance; **dejar algo en herencia a alguien** to leave *o* bequeath sth to sb □ *herencia yacente* unclaimed estate, estate in abeyance

herramienta *nf* tool □ *herramienta para la creación de páginas web* Web authoring tool; *herramienta de marketing* marketing tool; *herramienta de producción* production tool; *herramienta de ventas* sales tool

heterogéneo, -a *adj* heterogeneous

hexadecimal *adj* INFORM hexadecimal

higiene *nf (en el trabajo)* health; **seguridad e higiene** health and safety

hiperenlace *nm* INFORM hyperlink

hiperinflación *nf* hyperinflation

hipermedia *nf* INFORM hypermedia

hipermercado *nm* hypermarket

hipertexto *nm* INFORM hypertext

hipertextual *adj* INFORM **enlace hipertextual** hypertext link

hipoteca *nf* mortgage, home loan; **levantar una hipoteca** to pay off a mortgage □ *hipoteca abierta* blanket mortgage; *hipoteca cerrada* closed-end mortgage; *hipoteca flexible* flexible mortgage; *hipoteca a interés fijo* fixed-rate mortgage; *hipoteca a interés variable* variable-rate mortgage; *hipoteca con pagos progresivos* graduated payment mortgage; *hipoteca de segundo grado* second mortgage; *hipoteca subyacente* underlying mortgage

hipotecable *adj* mortgageable

hipotecar *vt* to mortgage

> **"**
>
> Con las cifras en la mano, Barcelona se sitúa en la cabeza del ranking con 10.273 inmuebles **hipotecados**, seguida de Madrid (8.080 fincas), Valencia (3.424), Alicante (3.097) y Málaga (2.211). Es también en estas cinco provincias donde se concentra casi la mitad del total **hipotecado** en España (nada menos que el 47,2%), siendo Madrid la que encabeza la lista, a pesar de tener menos hipotecas que Barcelona.
>
> **"**

hipotecario, -a *adj* mortgage; **crédito hipotecario** mortgage (loan)

historial *nm (de empleado)* service record; *(de organización)* track record □ *historial crediticio, historial de crédito* credit history

hogar *nm (domicilio)* home; *(unidad familiar)* household; **en más de la mitad de los hogares del país** in more than half of the households in the country; **el consumo medio por hogar subió un 3%** average consumption per household *o* family rose by 3% □ *hogar conyugal* marital home

hoja *nf* (**a**) *(de papel)* sheet (of paper); *(de libro)* page □ *hoja de almacén* inventory *o Br* stock

sheet; *hoja de asistencia* attendance sheet; *hoja de contabilidad* accounting entry sheet o form; *hoja de embarque* *(para transporte de mercancías)* cart note; *hoja informativa* *(de producto, asociación, gobierno)* fact sheet, information sheet; *(boletín)* newsletter; *hoja de pedido* order form; *hoja de propaganda* flyer, flier; *hoja de reclamación* complaint form; *hoja de reserva* reservation sheet; *hoja de ruta* consignment note; *hoja de servicios* service record; MKTG *hoja de sugerencias* comments(s) card; *hoja de tareas* task sheet; *hoja de trabajo* worksheet; *Col hoja de vida* curriculum vitae, *US* résumé
  (b) INFORM *hoja de cálculo* spreadsheet; *hoja de cálculo con gráficos* graphics spreadsheet; *hoja de estilos* style sheet

holding *nm* holding company

hombre *nm hombre de negocios* businessman

homogéneo, -a *adj* homogeneous

homologar *vt* to certify, to obtain official certification

homólogo, -a *nm,f* counterpart, opposite number

honorario, -a **1** *adj (miembro)* honorary
  2 honorarios *nmpl* fees, *Formal* honorarium
  ❑ *honorarios de asesoría, honorarios de consultoría* consultancy fees

honorífico, -a *adj (miembro)* honorary

hora *nf* hour; **(pagar) por horas** (to pay) by the hour; **cobra 80 euros por hora** she charges 80 euros an hour ❑ *hora de embarque* boarding time; *hora estimada de llegada* estimated time of arrival, E.T.A.; *hora estimada de partida* estimated time of departure, E.T.D.; *horas extra(s), horas extraordinarias (tiempo)* overtime; *(pago)* overtime pay; **hacer horas extra(s)** to do o work overtime; *hora de llegada* arrival time; *hora local* local time; *hora máquina* machine hour; *horas de mayor audiencia (de TV)* peak hours; *horas de mayor consumo (de gas, electricidad)* peak hours; *horas de oficina* office hours; *Am hora pico (de tráfico)* rush hour; *(de agua, electricidad)* peak times; *hora prevista de llegada* ETA; *hora prevista de salida* ETD; *Esp hora punta (de tráfico)* rush hour; *(de agua, electricidad)* peak times; *Esp horas punta (de tráfico)* peak hours; *hora de salida* departure time; *horas de trabajo* working hours; *horas valle* off-peak hours

hora-hombre *nf* man-hour

horario, -a *nm (de actividad) Br* timetable, *US* schedule; TEL **una llamada hecha en horario diurno/nocturno** a daytime/evening call ❑ BOLSA *horario de apertura* trading hours; *horario de atención (al público) (en oficina)* opening hours; **horario de atención: de 9 a 6** *(al teléfono)* lines open between 9 and 6; *horario bancario* banking hours; *horario comercial* opening hours, business hours; *horario no comercial* non-trading hours; *Esp horario continuo, Am horario corrido* = working day with no lunch break, and an earlier finishing time; *horario flexible* flexitime, flextime; *horario intensivo* = working day with no lunch break, and an earlier finishing time; *horario laboral* working hours; BOLSA *horario oficial de negociación* mandatory quote period; *horario de oficina* office hours; *horario partido* = working day with long (2-3 hour) lunch break, ending at 7-8 p.m.; *horario de tarifa reducida* off-peak hours; *horario de trabajo (de empleado)* working hours; *(de empresa)* business hours; *horario de trabajo flexible* flexible working hours; *horario de verano* summer working hours; *horario de visita (de atracción turística)* opening hours

horizontal *adj* INFORM *(orientación)* landscape

hospedaje *nm* INFORM hosting ❑ *hospedaje de páginas web* Web hosting

hospedar *vt* INFORM *(páginas web)* to host

host *nm* INFORM host

hostal *nm* guesthouse, cheap hotel

hostelería, *Am* hotelería *nf (sector)* hotel and catering industry

hostelero, -a *adj* **sector hostelero** hotel and catering industry

hostil *adj (OPA)* hostile

hotel *nm* hotel ❑ *hotel de aeropuerto* airport hotel; *hotel de empresas, hotel de negocios* business hotel

hotelería = hostelería

HTML *nm* INFORM *(abrev de* **hypertext markup language**) HTML ❑ *HTML dinámico* dynamic HTML

HTTP *nm* INFORM *(abrev de* **hypertext transfer protocol**) HTTP ❑ *HTTP seguro* secure HTTP

hueco *nm (en mercado)* gap, opening

> **"**
> No ha sido fácil, pero Lourdes Fuentes se ha hecho un **hueco** en el sector inmobiliario. Empezó alquilando pisos de amigos y hoy dirige su firma, Roan.
> **"**

huelga *nf* strike; **estar en huelga** to be on strike; **declararse en huelga** to go on strike; **hacer huelga** to strike; **ir a la huelga** to go on strike; **los trabajadores en huelga** the strikers ❑ *huelga de advertencia* warning strike; *huelga de apoyo* sympathy strike; *huelga de brazos caídos* sit-down (strike); *huelga de celo Br* work-to-rule, *US* slowdown; *huelga de correos* postal strike; *huelga escalonada* staggered strike; *huelga de estibadores* dock strike; *huelga general* general strike; *huelga indefinida* indefinite strike; *huelga oficial* official strike; *huelga patronal* lockout; *huelga postal* postal strike; *huelga salvaje* wildcat strike; *huelga simbólica* token strike; *huelga de solidaridad* sympathy strike

huelguista *nmf* striker

hundimiento *nm (de mercado, precios, divisa)* collapse

hundirse *vpr (mercado, precios, divisa)* to collapse

I i

IAE *nm* (*abrev de* **Impuesto sobre Actividades Económicas**) = Spanish tax paid by professionals and shop owners

IAPC *nm* UE (*abrev de* **Índice Armonizado de Precios de consumo**) HICP

IBEX, Ibex *nm* IBEX index, = Madrid Stock Market Index

IBB *nm* FIN (*abrev de* **Índice de la Bolsa de Bogotá**) IBB index, = Bogotá Stock Market Index

IBC *nm* FIN (*abrev de* **Índice Bursátil Caracas**) IBC index, = Caracas Stock Market Index

IBI *nm* FIN *Esp* (*abrev de* **Impuesto sobre Bienes Inmuebles**) property tax, = annual tax on property paid to local authorities

ICO *nm* (*abrev de* **Instituto de Crédito Oficial**) = Spanish government body which provides credit to projects at home and abroad

icono, *Am* **ícono** *nm* INFORM icon

I+D *nf* (*abrev de* **investigación y desarrollo**) R & D

identidad *nf* identity; **la identidad corporativa de la empresa** the company's corporate identity

identificación *nf* identification; **la identificación, por favor** may I see your papers, please?

identificador *nm* INFORM identifier

IDIPC *nm* FIN (*abrev de* **Índice de dividendos-Índice de Precios y Cotizaciones**) IDIPC index, = Mexican dividend index

IGBC *nm* FIN (*abrev de* **Índice General de la Bolsa de Colombia**) IGBC index, = Colombian Stock Market Index

IGBVL *nm* FIN (*abrev de* **Índice General de la Bolsa de Valores de Lima**) IGVBL index, = Lima Stock Market Index

IGPA *nm* FIN (*abrev de* **Índice General de Precios de Acciones**) IGPA index, = Chilean Stock Market Index

iguala *nf* FIN retainer, retaining fee

igualación *nf* (*de cantidades*) equalization, equalizing; **piden la igualación de salarios** they are asking for salaries to be made the same

igualar *vt* to make equal, to equalize; **les han igualado los sueldos** they've brought their salaries into line with each other, they've started paying them the same salary; **intentan igualar**

sus productos a los de la competencia they are trying to match their products to those of their competitors

igualdad *nf* equality; **la igualdad ante la ley** equality before the law; **piden un trato de igualdad** they are asking for equal treatment □ *igualdad de derechos* equal rights; *igualdad de oportunidades* equality of opportunity, *Br* equal opportunities, *US* equal opportunity; *igualdad de retribuciones, igualdad salarial* equal pay, pay equity

ilegal 1 *adj* illegal
  2 *nmf* (*trabajador*) illegal worker, *US* illegal

ilegalmente *adv* illegally

ilícito, -a *adj* illicit

ilimitado, -a *adj* unlimited

ilustración *nf* (*dibujo*) illustration; **illustraciones** (*para anuncio*) artwork

ilustrador, -ora *nm,f* illustrator

imagen *nf* (**a**) (*de producto, empresa*) image; **quieren proyectar una imagen positiva** they want to project a positive image □ *imagen corporativa, imagen de empresa* corporate image; CONT *imagen fiel* true and fair view; *imagen de marca* brand image; *imagen del producto* product image; *imagen pública* public image
  (**b**) INFORM image □ *imagen digitalizada* digitized image; *imágenes generadas por Esp ordenador o Am computadora* computer-generated images; *imágenes prediseñadas* clip art

IME *nm* UE (*abrev de* **Instituto Monetario Europeo**) EMI

imitación *nf* imitation □ *imitación de marca* brand imitation

imitar *vt* (*producto, marca*) to imitate

impacto *nm* impact; **el impacto político del cierre de una fábrica** the political impact *o* fallout of the closure of a factory □ *impacto ambiental* environmental impact; MKTG *impacto en el lineal* shelf impact

impagado, -a 1 *adj* unpaid
  2 *nm* unpaid bill

impago, -a 1 *adj Am* (*no pagado*) unpaid; **los salarios impagos** the unpaid wages; **los obreros impagos** the workers who haven't been paid; **factura impaga** unpaid *o* outstanding invoice

2 *nm* non-payment, default; **el impago de una multa** non-payment of a fine

imperar *vi (práctica, tendencia)* to prevail; **las prácticas que imperan en la banca europea** current practices in European banking

imperfecto, -a *adj (defectuoso)* imperfect

implementación *nf* implementation

implementar *vt* to implement

implícito, -a *adj (costos)* implicit; *(intereses)* discounted

imponer *vt* **(a)** *(embargo, controles, prohibición)* to impose; **la situación económica impone las condiciones del mercado** market conditions are dictated by the economic situation; **el juez le impuso una pena de dos años de cárcel** the judge sentenced him to two years' imprisonment; **le impusieron la difícil tarea de sanear las finanzas de la empresa** he was charged with the difficult task of straightening out the company's finances
(b) *(tributos, cargas fiscales)* to impose

imponible *adj* FIN taxable; **base imponible** taxable income

importación *nf* **(a)** *(acción)* importing, importation; **la importación de alimentos** the importing *o* importation of foodstuffs; **de importación** imported □ *importación temporal* temporary importation, temporary admission
(b) *(artículo)* import; **un aumento de las importaciones** an increase in imports □ *importaciones invisibles* invisible imports; *importación libre de derechos, importación libre de impuestos* duty-free import; *importaciones paralelas* parallel imports; *importaciones visibles* visible imports
(c) INFORM *importación de datos* data import

importador, -ora **1** *adj* importing; **empresa importadora** importing company
2 *nm,f* importer

importar *vt* **(a)** *(productos, materias primas)* to import **(de** from**) (b)** INFORM to import **(de** from**) (c)** *(sujeto: factura, coste)* to amount to, to come to; **la factura importa 5.000 pesos** the bill comes to 5,000 pesos

importe *nm* amount; **un cheque por un importe de dos millones** a cheque to the amount of two million; **ayudas por un importe cercano a los 5.000 millones** aid to the tune of almost 5,000 million; **devolvió el importe íntegro del préstamo** he repaid the loan in full; **una inversión por un importe máximo de 100 millones** a maximum investment of 100 million □ *importe bruto* gross amount; *importe neto* net amount; *importe a pagar* sum payable

imposición *nf* **(a)** *(acción) (de impuesto)* imposition; **tras la imposición de una pena de diez años** after he had been sentenced to ten years'

prison □ *imposición de precios* price fixing
(b) *(impuesto)* taxation; **doble imposición** double taxation □ *imposición directa* direct taxation; *imposición indirecta* indirect taxation; *imposición en régimen de evaluación global* presumptive taxation
(c) *(en banco)* deposit; **hacer** *o* **efectuar una imposición** to make a deposit □ *imposición a plazo* fixed-term deposit

impositivo, -a *adj (carga)* tax; **política impositiva** tax *o* taxation policy

> **❝**
> La Comisión Europea ha hecho inventario de los paraísos fiscales que tientan a las empresas en los 10 países llamados a ingresar en la UE el 1 de mayo de 2004. Tres decenas de regímenes ofrecen considerables ventajas **impositivas** a unos inversores extranjeros que, como en el sector automovilístico, ya han comenzado a trasladar su producción al Este.
> **❞**

impresión *nf* printing; **impresión a una/dos caras** one-/two-sided printing □ INFORM *impresión en calidad borrador* draft quality printing; *impresión en color* colour printing; *impresión por líneas* line printout; *impresión subordinada* background (mode) printing

impreso, -a **1** *adj* printed; **impreso en México** printed in Mexico
2 *nm* **(a)** *(formulario)* form; **rellenar un impreso** to fill in *o* out a form □ *impreso en blanco* blank form; *impreso de declaración de la renta* tax form; *impreso de reserva* reservation form; *impreso de respuesta* reply form; *impreso de solicitud (de acciones, empleo, crédito)* application form **(b)** **impresos** *(en sobre)* printed matter

impresora *nf* INFORM printer □ *impresora de agujas* dot matrix printer; *impresora de chorro de tinta* inkjet printer; *impresora en color* colour printer; *impresora de inyección* bubble-jet (printer); *impresora láser* laser printer; *impresora de líneas* line printer; *impresora de margarita* daisy-wheel printer; *impresora matricial* dot matrix printer; *impresora en paralelo* parallel printer; *impresora PostScript®* PostScript® printer; *impresora en serie* serial printer; *impresora térmica* thermal printer

imprevistos *nmpl (gastos)* unforeseen expenses

imprimir **1** *vt (libro, documento)* to print (out); **imprimir algo a todo color** to print sth in full colour
2 *vi* to print

improductivo, -a *adj (tierra, trabajo)* unproductive

imprudencia *nf* DER *imprudencia temeraria* criminal negligence

impuesto, -a *nm* tax; **pagar impuestos** to pay tax *o* taxes; **cinco millones antes de impuestos** five million before tax; **beneficios antes de impuestos** pre-tax profits; **libre de impuestos** *(alcohol, cigarrillos)* tax-free, duty-free □ *impuesto sobre actividades económicas* = Spanish tax paid on businesses with a turnover of more than €1 million; *impuesto adicional* surtax, additional tax; *impuesto a o sobre artículos de lujo* tax on luxury goods; *impuestos atrasados* back tax; *impuesto sobre los beneficios* profit tax; *impuesto de capitación* capitation tax; *impuesto sobre el capital* capital tax; *impuesto sobre la cifra de negocios* turnover tax; *impuesto de circulación* road tax; *impuesto complementario* surtax; *impuesto a o sobre la compra* purchase tax; *impuesto al consumo, impuesto sobre el consumo* consumption tax; *impuesto degresivo* degressive tax; *impuesto diferido* deferred tax; *impuesto directo* direct tax; *impuesto sobre dividendos* dividend tax; *impuesto de donaciones y sucesiones* gift and inheritance tax; *impuesto ecológico* green tax, ecotax; *impuesto encubierto* hidden tax; *impuesto de espectáculos* entertainment tax; *impuestos especiales* excise duty, excise tax *impuesto sobre la exportación* export tax; *impuesto extraordinario* exceptional tax; *impuesto sobre las ganancias de capital* capital gains tax; *impuesto indirecto* indirect tax; *impuesto a la inflación* inflation tax; *impuesto de lujo* luxury tax; *impuesto de matriculación* = tax paid on a new car; *impuesto municipal* local tax; *impuesto sobre la nómina* payroll tax; *impuesto sobre el patrimonio* wealth tax; *impuesto de o sobre plusvalías, impuesto sobre la plusvalía* capital gains tax; *impuesto progresivo* progressive tax; *impuesto sobre la propiedad inmobiliaria* property tax; *impuesto sobre la renta (de las personas físicas)* personal income tax; *impuesto retenido en la fuente o en origen* tax deducted at source, *US* withholding tax; *impuesto de sociedades* corporate (income) tax, *Br* corporation tax; *impuesto de sucesión, impuesto sobre sucesiones* *(tras fallecimiento)* inheritance tax, *US* estate tax; *impuesto de o sobre transmisiones* transfer tax; *impuesto sobre transmisiones patrimoniales* capital transfer tax; *impuesto único* single tax; *impuesto sobre el valor* tax on value; *Am impuesto al valor agregado, Esp impuesto sobre el valor añadido Br* value-added tax, *US* ≃ sales tax; *impuesto sobre ventas* output tax; *impuesto sobre el volumen de negocio* turnover tax

impulsar *vt (productividad, ventas, economía)* to stimulate, to boost; **las claves que impulsan el sector** the key drivers for the industry

impulsivo, -a *adj* MKTG *(reacción)* impulsive

imputable *adj* CONT *(beneficio)* attributable

inactivo, -a *adj* **(a)** *(mercado)* sluggish, quiet **(b)** *(fábrica, máquina)* idle

inalámbrico, -a 1 *adj* cordless
2 *nm (teléfono)* cordless phone

inauguración *nf (de tienda, negocio)* opening

incapacidad *nf* DER incapacity □ *incapacidad laboral* industrial disability *o Br* disablement; *incapacidad laboral transitoria* temporary disability; *incapacidad legal* legal incapacity; *incapacidad permanente* invalidity; *incapacidad temporal* temporary disability

incentivar *vt* to encourage; **ayudas estatales para incentivar la producción agrícola** state aid to encourage agricultural production; **estar incentivado fiscalmente** to have tax advantages

incentivo *nm* incentive; **incentivos** *(en sueldo)* incentive pay; **un incentivo para la compra de viviendas** an incentive for people to buy their own home □ MKTG *incentivo de compra* buying incentive; *incentivo en efectivo* cash incentive; *incentivo a la exportación* export incentive; *incentivo fiscal* tax incentive; *incentivo a la producción* production incentive; *incentivo de ventas* sales incentive

incluido, -a *adj (franqueo, servicio)* included; **IVA incluido** inclusive of VAT; **hasta el 31 de diciembre incluido** up to and including 31 December

incluir *vt* **(a)** *(comprender)* to include; **el precio incluye el IVA** the price includes VAT **(b)** *(adjuntar)* to enclose

inclusive *adv* **hasta el 31 de diciembre inclusive** up to and including 31 December

incobrable *adj* irrecoverable; **deuda inco-brable** bad debt

incomparecencia *nf* DER failure to appear; **el juicio se suspendió por incomparecencia de una de las partes** the trial was suspended because one of the parties failed to appear in court

incompatible *adj* (**a**) INFORM incompatible (**b**) *(cargo)* **estos dos puestos son incompatibles** the two posts cannot be held by the same person at the same time

incondicional *adj (aceptación, oferta)* unconditional

inconvertible *adj* FIN inconvertible

incorporación *nf (unión, adición)* addition; **incorporaciones a la plantilla** additions to the staff; **la escasa incorporación de la mujer al mercado laboral** the low number of women in the labour market; **su incorporación tendrá lugar el día 31** *(a un puesto)* he starts work on the 31st ▫ FIN **incorporación de reservas** capitalization of reserves

incorporado, -a *adj* built-in; **con DVD incorporado** with built-in DVD

incoterm *nm (abrev de* **international commercial term***)* incoterm

incremento *nm (de precios, salario, actividad)* increase, increment ▫ ECON **incremento neto acumulado** aggregate net increment; **incremento porcentual** percentage increase; MKTG **incremento de precio** *(dentro de una gama)* price step; **incremento salarial** salary increase

incumplimiento *nm (de pago)* default ▫ **incumplimiento de contrato** breach of contract; **incumplimiento de las normas** breach of discipline

incumplir *vt (contrato)* to breach, to break

incurrir *vi* **incurrir en** *(gastos)* to incur; **incurrimos en muchos gastos en nuestro viaje por Asia** we incurred a lot of expenses during our Asian trip

indebidamente *adv* **apropiarse indebidamente de algo** to misappropriate sth; **usar algo indebidamente** to misuse sth

indebido, -a *adj* **apropiación indebida** misappropriation; **uso indebido** misuse

indefinido, -a *adj (tiempo)* indefinite; *(contrato)* permanent; *(acuerdo)* open-ended

indemnización *nf (compensación)* (financial) compensation, indemnity ▫ DER **indemnización por daños y perjuicios** damages; **indemnización por despido** severance pay, *Br* redundancy pay; SEGUR **indemnización por fallecimiento** death benefit

indemnizar *vt* to compensate (**por** for); **le indemnizaron con varios millones** he was given several million in compensation

independiente *adj* (**a**) *(asesor, ingresos, minorista)* independent (**b**) INFORM stand-alone

indexación *nf* FIN indexation, index-linking

indexado, -a *adj* FIN index-linked

indexar *vt* FIN to index, to index-link

indicado, -a *adj (marcado)* specified; **se entregará en la fecha indicada por el cliente** it will be delivered on the date specified by the client; **la fecha indicada en el párrafo anterior** the date indicated in the previous paragraph

indicador, -ora *nm (signo)* indicator; **ese fallo es un indicador de la poca calidad del producto** that fault shows the poor quality of the product ▫ **indicadores avanzados** leading indicators; **indicador de beneficios** profit indicator; **indicador bursátil** (stock) market indicator; **indicador de calidad** quality indicator; **indicador económico** economic indicator; **indicador estadístico** statistical indicator; **indicador de mercado** market indicator; **indicador de rentabilidad** profitability indicator; **indicadores de tendencia** leading indicators

indicativo, -a *nm* TEL *Br* dialling code, *US* area code ▫ **indicativo internacional** international dialling code

índice *nm* (**a**) BOLSA *(lista de precios)* index ▫ **índice bursátil** stock (market) index, share (price) index; **índice de cotización** share (price) index; **índice Ibex** Ibex index; **índice Nikkei** Nikkei index
(**b**) *(indicador)* index; *(proporción)* rate ▫ **índice de ahorro** savings ratio; **índices arancelarios** tariff level indices; UE **Índice Armonizado de Precios al Consumo** Harmonized Index of Consumer Prices; **índice de audiencia** audience ratings; MKTG **índice de conocimiento** *(de producto)* rate of awareness; **índice del costo** *o Esp* **coste de la vida** cost-of-living index; **índice de crecimiento** growth index; **índice de desempleo** unemployment rate; **índice económico** economic indicator; **índice estacional** seasonal index; **índice de popularidad** popularity rating; **índice de precios** price index; *Am* **Índice de Precios al Consumidor,** *Esp* **Índice de Precios al Consumo** *Br* Retail Price Index, *US* Consumer Price Index; **índice de precios al por mayor** wholesale price index; **índice de precios del mercado** market price list; *Am* **Índice de Precios al Productor** Producer Price Index; **índice de precios y salarios** wage and price index; **índice de producción** rate of production; MKTG **índice de recuerdo** recall rate; MKTG **índice de renovación** rate of renewal; **índice de rentabilidad** profitability index; **índice de rotación** turnover rate; **índice salarial** wage rate; SEGUR **índice de siniestralidad** loss ratio; **índice de ventas** sales ratio
(**c**) *(señal, indicio)* sign, indicator; **el número de llamadas es índice del interés despertado** the

number of calls is a sign of how much interest has been generated
  (**d**) *(de libro)* index; **índice (de materias)** (table of) contents ▫ *índice alfabético* alphabetical index; *índice onomástico* index of proper names; *índice temático* subject index

indirecto, -a *adj (impuesto, costo)* indirect; **la fábrica creará 500 empleos indirectos** the factory will create 500 indirect jobs

individual *adj* individual

individualmente *adv* individually; **se venden individualmente** they're sold individually *o* singly

indización *nf* FIN indexation, index-linking

«
Los métodos de fijación del salario mínimo varían de un país a otro. En una gran parte de los Quince, esta cantidad se fija a partir de una **indización** automática sobre el salario mínimo de años anteriores y revisiones periódicas del mismo. En España, Grecia y Portugal, el gobierno fija cada año esta cantidad de acuerdo con sus previsiones sobre la tasa de inflación.
                                                                    »

indizar *vt* (**a**) FIN to index, to index-link (**b**) INFORM to index

inducción *nf* MKTG *inducción a la compra* buying inducement

industria *nf* industry; **una industria en expansión** a growth industry ▫ *la industria agroalimentaria* the food and agriculture industry; *industria agropecuaria* agribusiness; *la industria alimentaria* the food industry; *industria artesanal* cottage industry; *industria del automóvil, industria automovilística* car industry; *industria de bienes de consumo* consumer industry; *industria clave* key industry; *industria de la construcción* building industry; *industria editorial* publishing (industry); *industria en expansión* growth industry; *industria ligera* light industry; *industria manufacturera* manufacturing industry; *industria maquiladora* in-bond industry; *industria del ocio* leisure industry; *industria pesada* heavy industry; *industria del petróleo, industria petrolífera* oil industry, petroleum industry; *industria petroquímica* petrochemical industry; *industria de precisión* precision industry; *industria primaria* primary industry; *industria secundaria* secondary industry; *industria de servicios* service industry; *industria subvencionada* subsidized industry; *industria textil* textile industry; *industria de transformación* manufacturing industry; *industria del turismo* tourist industry

industrial 1 *adj (explotación, maquinaria, reconversión)* industrial

2 *nmf (empresario)* industrialist

industrialismo *nm* industrialism

industrialización *nf* industrialization

industrializado, -a *adj* industrialized

industrializar 1 *vt* to industrialize
  2 industrializarse *vpr* to industrialize, to become industrialized

ineficaz *adj* (**a**) *(de bajo rendimiento)* inefficient (**b**) *(de baja efectividad)* ineffective

ineficiencia *nf* (**a**) *(bajo rendimiento)* inefficiency (**b**) *(baja efectividad)* ineffectiveness

ineficiente *adj* (**a**) *(de bajo rendimiento)* inefficient (**b**) *(de baja efectividad)* ineffective

inercia *nf* inertia

inestabilidad *nf* (**a**) *(de construcción)* instability (**b**) *(de régimen, economía)* instability (**c**) *(de carácter)* instability (**d**) *(de tiempo)* changeability

inestable *adj (economía, mercado, precios)* volatile, unstable

infectar INFORM **1** *vt* to infect
  2 infectarse *vpr* to become infected

inferior 1 *adj* (**a**) *(menor)* **es inferior a la media** it's below average; **se vende a un precio inferior al del mercado** it's being sold for a below-the-market price (**b**) *(producto, calidad)* inferior (**c**) *(en rango)* inferior
  2 *nm (en escala laboral)* subordinate

inflación *nf* ECON inflation ▫ *inflación estructural* structural inflation; *inflación galopante* galloping inflation; *inflación inercial* inertial inflation; *inflación interanual* year-on-year inflation; *inflación monetaria* monetary inflation; *inflación de precios* price inflation; *inflación salarial* wage inflation; *inflación subyacente* underlying inflation

«
El Índice de Precios de Consumo (IPC) subió un 0,3% en agosto, con lo que el acumulado del año se situó en el 1,4% y la **inflación interanual** baja una décima, hasta el 2,9%, según datos hechos públicos hoy por el Instituto Nacional de Estadística (INE).
                                                                    »

inflacionario, -a *adj* ECON inflationary

inflacionismo *nm* ECON inflationism

inflacionista *adj Esp* ECON inflationary

inflar *vt (cifras)* to inflate

infoadicto, -a *nm,f Fam* INFORM infoaddict

infografía *nf* INFORM computer graphics

infografista *nmf* INFORM computer graphics artist

infolio *nm* CONT folio

información *nf* (**a**) *(conocimiento)* information;

(noticias) news; **para mayor información, visite nuestra página web** for more information visit our website; **una información** *(un dato)* an item *o* a piece of information; *(una noticia)* an item *o* a piece of news; **información (telefónica)** *Br* directory enquiries, *US* directory assistance, *US* information ❑ **información bursátil** market report; **información comercial** business information; *(sobre marketing)* marketing information; **información confidencial** classified information; **información económica** economic information; *(noticias)* business news, financial news; **información financiera** financial information; *(noticias)* financial news; *(informes contables)* financial reporting; **información horaria** speaking clock; **información de mercado** market information; MKTG **información primaria** primary data; **información privilegiada** insider information; **información en el punto de compra** point-of-purchase information; **información en el punto de venta** point-of-sale information; MKTG **información secundaria** secondary data

(**b**) INFORM *(datos)* data

(**c**) *(oficina)* information office; **(el mostrador de) información** the information desk

informar 1 *vt* **informar a alguien (de)** to inform *o* tell sb (about); **tenemos el placer de informarle que...** we are pleased to inform *o* advise you that...; **informar de sus conclusiones (a alguien)** to report one's findings (to sb)

2 informarse *vpr* **me informaré y luego te llamo** I'll call you once I've found out the details; **informarse de** *o* **sobre** to find out about

informática *nf* computing, information technology, IT; **el departamento de informática** the IT department; **se requieren conocimientos de informática** candidates should be computer-literate ❑ **informática de gestión** business computing; **informática personal** personal computing

informático, -a 1 *adj* computer; **red informática** computer network

2 *nm,f* computer specialist, IT specialist; **según nuestros informáticos...** according to our IT people...

informativo, -a 1 *adj* (**a**) **folleto informativo** information booklet (**b**) *(útil)* informative; **es muy informativo** it's very informative

2 *nm (en radio, televisión)* news (bulletin)

informatización *nf* computerization

informatizado, -a *adj* computerized

informatizar 1 *vt* to computerize

2 informatizarse *vpr* to become computerized; **empresas que aún no se han informatizado** companies which have yet to computerize their operations

informe 1 *nm (documento, estudio)* report (**sobre**

on *o* about); **han solicitado el informe de un técnico** they have asked for a report from an expert ❑ **informe anual** annual report; **informe de auditoría** auditor's report; **informe de auditoría con salvedades** qualified report; **informe de auditoría sin salvedades** unqualified report; CONT **informe de caja** cash report (form); **informe conjunto** joint report; **informe del consejo de administración** directors' report, report of the board of directors; **informe de coyuntura** interim report; **informe de daños** damage report; BOLSA **informe diario del mercado** daily trading report; **informe financiero** financial report; **informe de gestión** management report; **informe de la junta directiva** directors' report, report of the board of directors; **informe oficial** official report; **informe del presidente (del consejo de administración)** chairman's report; **informe resumido** summary report; BOLSA **informe semanal de operaciones** weekly trading report; **informes por segmentos** segment reporting; **informe de (la) situación** status report; **informe del tesorero** treasurer's report; **informe de ventas** sales report; **informe de viabilidad** feasibility report

2 informes *nmpl (sobre comportamiento)* report; *(para un empleo)* reference(s)

infracapitalizado, -a *adj* FIN undercapitalized

infracapitalizar *vt* FIN to undercapitalize

infracción *nf* offence ❑ **infracción penal** criminal offence; **infracción tributaria** breach of tax regulations

infradotado, -a *adj (sin financiación)* underfunded; *(sin recursos materiales)* under-resourced; *(sin personal)* understaffed

infraestructura *nf (de organización, país)* infrastructure

infraponderar *vt* FIN to underweight

infrarrojo, -a *adj* INFORM infrared

infrautilización *nf (de recursos, conocimientos)* underuse, underutilization

infrautilizado, -a *adj (recursos, conocimientos)* underused, underutilized

infravalorar 1 *vt* to undervalue, to underestimate; CONT to understate

2 infravalorarse *vpr* to undervalue oneself

infructuoso, -a *adj (reunión, discusiones)* unsuccessful, fruitless

ingeniería *nf* engineering ❑ **ingeniería asistida por** *Esp* **ordenador** *o* *Am* **computadora** computer-assisted engineering, CAE; **ingeniería de caminos, ingeniería civil** civil engineering; **ingeniería de diseño** design engineering; **ingeniería financiera** financial engineering; **ingeniería humana** human engineering; **ingeniería industrial** mechanical engineering; **ingeniería de producción** production engineering; **ingeniería de sistemas** systems engineering; **ingeniería de software asistida por** *Esp* **ordenador** *o* *Am* **computadora** computer-assisted software engineering, CASE; **ingeniería del valor** value engineering

ingeniero, -a 1 *nm,f* engineer ❑ **ingeniero civil,** *Esp* **ingeniero de caminos, canales y puertos** civil engineer; **ingeniero de campo** field engineer; **ingeniero de diseño** design engineer; **ingeniero industrial** industrial engineer; **ingeniero informático** computer engineer; **ingeniero de programas** software engineer; **ingeniero de sistemas** systems engineer; **ingeniero superior** = engineer who has done a full five-year university course; **ingeniero técnico** = engineer who has done a three-year university course rather than a full five-year course; **ingeniero de ventas** sales engineer
2 *nm Andes, CAm, Carib, Méx* = title used to address businessmen and professionals (even if they are not actually qualified as an engineer)

ingresar 1 *vt* (a) *Esp (en banco)* to deposit, to pay in, to bank; **los pagos me los ingresan en mi cuenta** the money is paid into my account, the payments are credited to my account (b) *(ganar)* to make, to earn; **la empresa ingresa varios millones cada día** the company makes several million a day
2 *vi* **ingresar en** *(asociación)* to join; *(universidad)* to enter

ingreso *nm* (a) *Esp (de dinero)* deposit; **realizó un ingreso** she made a deposit ❑ **ingreso en efectivo** cash deposit
(b) **ingresos** *(de empresa)* income, earnings, revenue; *(de persona)* income, earnings ❑ **ingresos acumulados** accrued income; **ingresos por alquileres** rental income; **ingresos anticipados** prepaid income; **ingresos anuales** annual income, annual earnings; **ingresos por arrendamientos** rental income; **ingresos brutos** gross income; **ingresos brutos totales** total gross income; **ingresos corrientes** current earnings; **ingresos devengados** accrued income; **ingresos diarios** *(en tienda)* daily takings; **ingresos diferidos** deferred income; **ingresos diversos** sundry income; **ingresos en divisas** foreign currency earnings; **ingresos del Estado** government revenue; **ingresos de explotación** operating income; **ingresos por exportaciones** export earnings, export revenue; **ingresos extraordinarios** extraordinary income; **ingresos familiares** family income; **ingresos fijos** fixed income; **ingresos financieros netos** net interest income; **ingreso fiscal** tax revenue, tax receipts; **ingresos independientes** independent income; **ingresos íntegros** gross earnings; **ingresos por intereses y dividendos** interest and dividend income; **ingresos internos** internal revenue; **ingresos marginales** marginal

revenue; **ingresos medios** average revenue; **ingresos netos** net income; **ingresos netos totales** total net income; **ingresos del petróleo** oil revenue; **ingresos previstos** projected income; **ingresos procedentes de inversiones mobiliarias** income from security investments, investment income; *Am* **ingresos promedio** average revenue; **ingresos por publicidad** advertising revenue; **ingresos regulares** regular income; **ingresos del sector público** public sector earnings; **ingresos sujetos a gravamen** taxable income; **ingresos teóricos** notional income; **ingresos totales** aggregate income

inicial 1 *adj* initial
2 *nf* (a) *(letra)* initial (b) *Ven (pago)* down payment

inicialización *nf* INFORM initialization

inicializar *vt* INFORM to initialize

iniciar *vt (debate, discusión)* to start off, FORMAL to initiate; *(negociaciones)* to open, to enter into; **iniciar un pleito contra alguien** to bring legal proceedings against sb

iniciativa *nf* (a) *(propuesta)* proposal, initiative ❑ **iniciativas gubernamentales** government action; **la iniciativa privada** private enterprise (b) *(cualidad, capacidad)* initiative

inicio *nm* INFORM home

inmediato, -a *adj (entrega)* immediate; *(acceso)* instant

INMEX *nm* FIN *(abrev de* **Índice México***)* INMEX index, = Mexican Stock Market Index

inmobiliaria *nf* (a) *(agencia)* Br estate agency o agent's, US real estate agency (b) *(constructora)* property developer

inmobiliario, -a *adj* **agente inmobiliario** Br estate agent, US realtor; **propiedad inmobiliaria** real estate

inmovilización *nf* FIN *(de capital)* tying-up ❑ **inmovilizaciones financieras** fixed investments; **inmovilizacions inmateriales** intangible fixed assets; **inmovilizaciones materiales** tangible fixed assets

inmovilizado, -a FIN 1 *adj (capital)* tied up
2 *nm (activo)* fixed assets ❑ **inmovilizado fijo** tangible fixed assets; **inmovilizado inmaterial** intangible fixed assets; **inmovilizado material** tangible fixed assets

inmovilizar *vt (capitales)* to tie up

inmueble 1 *adj* **bienes inmuebles** real property, real estate, US realty
2 *nm (propiedad)* property; *(edificio)* building ❑ **inmueble rural, inmueble rústico** rural property; **inmueble urbano** urban property

inmunidad *nf* immunity ❑ **inmunidad tributaria** immunity from taxation

inmunización *nf* **inmunización financiera** financial immunization

innovación *nf* innovation ▢ *innovación continua* continuous innovation; *innovación de productos* product innovation

innovador, -ora 1 *adj* innovative
2 *nm,f* innovator

INPC *nm* FIN *Méx* (*abrev de* **Índice Nacional de Precios al Consumidor**) *Br* RPI, *US* CPI

input *nm* INFORM input

inquilino, -a *nm,f* tenant

Insalud *nm* *Esp* (*abrev de* **Instituto Nacional de la Salud**) *Br* ≃ NHS, *US* ≃ Medicaid

inscripción *nf* (*en censo, registro*) registration ▢ *inscripción on-line, inscripción en línea* online registration; *inscripción de la propiedad inmobiliaria* land registration

inserción *nf* (**a**) (*acción*) (*de texto, párrafo*) insertion; (*de anuncio*) insertion, placing; (*elemento insertado*) insert ▢ INFORM *inserción de carácter* character insert; *inserción publicitaria* advertising insert (**b**) *inserción laboral* employment; **un programa de inserción laboral** an employment scheme; **ayudas para favorecer la inserción laboral de inmigrantes** subsidies to help immigrants into employment, subsidies to help immigrants find work

> ❝
> La **inserción laboral** de las personas discapacitadas de Gipuzkoa es la razón de ser del Grupo Gureak, organización promovida por la asociación Atzegi, activa desde 1975 y con una fuerza laboral cifrada actualmente en más de 2.600 empleados repartidos en 30 centros de trabajo, con amplias instalaciones y avanzados medios técnicos que, combinados con una adecuada adaptación de los puestos de trabajo y secuenciación de los procesos productivos, posibilitan una amplia y competitiva oferta.
> ❞

insertar *vt* (*texto, párrafo, anuncio*) to insert

insolvencia *nf* insolvency

insolvente *adj* insolvent

> ❝
> A falta de un inversor y con una deuda de 75 millones de euros, Grundig ha tenido que declararse **insolvente**. Un nuevo fracaso empresarial que se añade a la ya larga lista de empresas germanas, cerca de 32.000, que suspendieron pagos en el último año y que están poniendo seriamente en peligro a la economía alemana.
> ❞

inspección *nf* (*de mercancías, local, documentos*) inspection ▢ *inspección aduanera* customs inspection, customs examination; *inspección de calidad* quality control inspection; *inspección*

de fábrica factory inspection; *inspección fiscal, inspección de Hacienda* tax inspection; *inspección sanitaria* environmental health inspection; *Inspección de Trabajo* *Br* ≃ Health and Safety Executive, *US* ≃ Occupational Safety & Health Administration

inspeccionar *vt* (*mercancías, local, documentos*) to inspect

inspector, -ora *nm,f* inspector ▢ *inspector de aduanas* customs officer, customs inspector; *inspector fiscal, inspector de Hacienda* tax inspector, *Br* inspector of taxes; *inspector de sanidad* health inspector; *inspector de seguros* insurance inspector; *inspector de trabajo* factory inspector; *inspector de tributos* tax inspector, *Br* inspector of taxes

instalación *nf* (**a**) (*de maquinaria, equipamiento*) installation
(**b**) INFORM (*de programa*) installation
(**c**) **instalaciones** (*lugar*) **el acto se celebró en las instalaciones de la empresa** the ceremony took place on company premises ▢ *instalaciones y accesorios* fixtures and fittings; *instalaciones de almacenamiento* storage facilities; *instalaciones deportivas* sports facilities; *instalaciones y enseres* fixtures and fittings; *instalaciones multimedia* multimedia facilities; *instalaciones portuarias* port facilities, harbour facilities; *instalaciones de producción* production facilities; *instalaciones y servicios turísticos* tourist facilities

instalador *nm* INFORM installer

instalar 1 *vt* (**a**) (*maquinaria, equipamiento*) to install (**b**) INFORM (*programa*) to install
2 instalarse *vpr* (*empresa, fábrica*) to locate (**en**) to

institución *nf* (**a**) (*organización*) institution ▢ *institución benéfica* charitable organization; *institución crediticia* loan company, *US* loan office; *institución inversora, institución inversionista* investment institution (**b**) *instituciones* (*del Estado*) institutions

instituto *nm* (*corporación*) institute ▢ *Instituto Monetario Europeo* European Monetary Institute

instrucción *nf* (**a**) INFORM instruction (**b**) DER (*investigación*) preliminary investigation; (*curso del proceso*) proceedings (**c**) **instrucciones** (*órdenes, explicación*) instructions ▢ *instrucciones de envío* forwarding instructions; *instrucciones de facturación* invoicing instructions; *instrucciones de uso* instructions for use, directions for use

instrumental *nm* instruments ▢ *instrumental médico* surgical instruments; *instrumental técnico* technical equipment

instrumento *nm* FIN instrument ▢ *instrumento de cobertura de riesgos* hedging instrument;

instrumento de comercio instrument of commerce; *instrumento de deuda* debt instrument; *instrumento financiero* financial instrument; *instrumento de gestión* management tool; *instrumento de inversión* investment instrument; *instrumento negociable* negotiable instrument; *instrumento de negociación* trading instrument; *instrumento de renta fija* fixed-interest instrument; *instrumento subyacente* (*título*) underlying security

insuficiencia *nf (escasez) insuficiencia de capital* capital shortfall; *insuficiencia de liquidez* cash shortage

insuficiente *adj* insufficient

insumos *nmpl* (**a**) *(bienes)* raw materials; **un producto fabricado a partir de insumos chilenos** a product manufactured using Chilean materials (**b**) *(suministros)* supplies; **la dotación de insumos para los hospitales** the provision of supplies to hospitals

> 66
>
> Entre la gran mayoría de empresas que anticiparon inversiones, un 32 por ciento lo hará para ampliar su capacidad de producción, en tanto que 27% buscará modernizarse y otro 22% apuntará al desarrollo de nuevos productos. Sólo 13% de las inversiones se canalizarán al reemplazo de viejos equipos y un 4% a la producción de **insumos**.
>
> 99

intangible 1 *adj (activo, bien)* intangible 2 **intangibles** *nmpl* intangibles

> 66
>
> Cada vez se percibe con más claridad el peso creciente de las industrias y servicios basados en el Conocimiento dentro de las economías actuales. Este recurso está jugando un importante papel y esto se percibe en el hecho de que la inversión en **intangibles** está creciendo mucho más rápidamente que la inversión física, en que las organizaciones con más conocimiento presentan mayores ventajas competitivas y las personas con más información obtienen, en general, mejores empleos y remuneraciones mejores.
>
> 99

integración *nf* ECON integration ❑ *integración económica* economic integration; *integración horizontal* horizontal integration; *integración progresiva* forward integration; *integración regresiva* backward integration; *integración vertical* vertical integration

integrado, -a *adj* integrated

integrante *nmf (de organización)* member

intelectual *adj* intellectual

inteligente *adj (sistema, edificio)* intelligent; *(tarjeta)* smart

intención *nf* MKTG *intención de compra* intention to buy

intento *nm* attempt; **en un intento de reanudar las negociaciones** in a bid o an attempt to reopen negotiations

interactivo, -a *adj* INFORM interactive

interanual *adj* year-on-year

> 66
>
> Pese a esta dinámica respuesta del sector de la construcción "que ha permitido que los incrementos de precios no hayan sido mayores", el precio de la vivienda en España ha crecido un 60% desde 1997 (una media de un 10% anual) y los datos más recientes apuntan un incremento **interanual** del 17,5% en 2003.
>
> 99

interbancario, -a *adj* interbank; **mercado interbancario** interbank market

intercambiar *vt (objetos, ideas)* to exchange; *(lugares, posiciones)* to change, to swap

intercambio *nm* (**a**) *(de mercancías, ideas)* exchange ❑ *intercambio comercial* trade; INFORM *intercambio de datos* data exchange; INFORM *intercambio dinámico de datos* dynamic data exchange; INFORM *intercambio electrónico de datos* electronic data interchange (**b**) FIN *intercambio de acciones* share swap; *intercambio de la deuda* debt swap

intercentros *adj inv* IND **comité intercentros** central works committee

interdepartamental *adj* interdepartmental

interés *nm* (**a**) FIN *(de crédito, inversión)* interest; **a bajo interés** *(crédito)* low-interest; **pagar intereses** to pay interest; **producir un interés del 5%** to bear o yield 5% interest ❑ *interés acumulable* cumulative interest; *interés acumulado* accrued interest; *interés anual bruto* gross annual interest return; *interés asegurable* insurable interest; *intereses atrasados* back interest; *interés bancario* bank interest; *interés compuesto* compound interest; *interés a corto plazo* short-term interest; *interés de demora* penalty interest, late-payment interest; *interés deudor* debit interest; *interés devengado* accrued interest; *interés económico directo* working interest; *interés a largo plazo* long-term interest; *interés minoritario* minority interest; *interés de mora, interés moratorio* penalty interest, late-payment interest; *intereses pagaderos* interest payable; *intereses pagados* interest paid; *intereses percibidos* interest received; *interés simple* simple interest; *intereses vencidos* interest due (**b**) **intereses** *(económicos)* interests; **los**

intereses españoles en Latinoamérica Spanish interests in Latin America; **tiene intereses en una empresa del sector** he has interests o a stake in a company in that sector; **su hermana administra sus intereses** her sister looks after her financial interests

interesante adj (oferta, precio, proposición) interesting, attractive

interfaz, interface nm o nf INFORM interface ❏ **interfaz, gráfico** graphical interface; **interfaz paralelo** parallel interface; **interfaz de serie** serial interface; **interfaz de usuario** user interface

interior 1 adj (**a**) (nacional) (comercio, política) domestic (**b**) (no costero) inland
2 nm (**a**) (de país) interior, inland area (**b**) (parte de dentro) **en el interior** inside

interlineado nm TIP line spacing

intermediación nf (**a**) (en conflicto) intervention, mediation; **por intermediación de** through the intervention o mediation of (**b**) FIN intermediation

intermediario, -a nm,f intermediary ❏ **intermediario comercial** middleman; **intermediario de crédito** credit broker; **intermediario financiero** financial intermediary

internacional adj (mercado, vuelo) international

internauta nmf INFORM Internet user

Internet nf INFORM the Internet; **acceso a/dirección de Internet** Internet access/address

interno, -a 1 adj (**a**) (dentro de organización) internal; (de la empresa) in-house (**b**) (dentro de un país) (asuntos, comercio, mercado) domestic, internal
2 nm RP (extensión) (telephone) extension; **interno 28, por favor** extension 28, please

interponer vt DER to lodge, to make; **interponer un recurso (de apelación) contra algo** to lodge o make an appeal against sth, to appeal against sth

interpretar 1 vt (**a**) (entender, explicar) to interpret; **interpretar mal** to misinterpret (**b**) (traducir) to interpret
2 vi (traducir) to interpret

intérprete nmf interpreter ❏ **intérprete de conferencias** conference interpreter; **intérprete jurado** = interpreter qualified to work in court; **intérprete simultáneo** simultaneous interpreter

interrogación nf (signo) question mark

interrogatorio nm (preguntas) questioning

interrumpir vt (service) to suspend; (producción) to halt

intervención nf (**a**) (acción, participación) intervention (**b**) (discurso) speech; (pregunta)

question; (comentario) remark, comment (**c**) FIN (de cuentas) auditing; Am **el ministro decidió la intervención de la empresa** the minister decided the company should go into administration

intervencionismo nm ECON interventionism

intervencionista adj & nmf ECON interventionist

intervenir 1 vt (**a**) FIN (inspeccionar) (cuentas) to audit (**b**) Am (institución privada) to put into administration
2 vi (actuar) to intervene

interventor, -ora nm,f (**a**) FIN (financiero) controller, US comptroller ❏ **interventor de cuentas** auditor; **Interventor General** Br ≃ Comptroller and Auditor General, US ≃ Comptroller General (**b**) Am (administrador) administrator (appointed by the government)

intracomunitario, -a adj intra-Community, within the EU; **ventas intracomunitarias** internal EU sales, intra-Comunity sales

intranet nf INFORM Intranet

intro nm INFORM enter (key), return (key)

introducción nf (**a**) (de novedad, medida, política, producto) introduction; **la introducción de la moneda única** the introduction of the single currency **precio especial de introducción** special introductory price (**b**) INFORM (de datos) entry

introducir 1 vt (**a**) (medida, reformas) to introduce, to bring in (**b**) (nuevos productos) to introduce, to bring out (**c**) INFORM (datos) to enter
2 introducirse vpr **introducirse en** (mercado) to penetrate, to break into

intruso, -a nm,f INFORM intruder

inundar 1 vt (mercado) to flood; **inundaron el mercado con imitaciones baratas** they flooded the market with cheap imitations
2 inundarse vpr **el mercado se ha inundado de imitaciones** the market has been flooded with imitations

invalidación nf (de documento, contrato) invalidation; (de cheque) cancellation

invalidar vt (documento) to invalidate; (contrato) to void; (cheque) to cancel

invalidez nf (**a**) (de persona) disability, invalidity ❏ **invalidez permanente** permanent disability; **invalidez temporal** temporary disability (**b**) (de contrato, documento) invalidity

inválido, -a adj (**a**) (persona) disabled (**b**) (contrato, documento) invalid (**c**) INFORM (nombre) invalid

inventariar vt to make an inventory of

inventario nm inventory; **hacer un inventario (de algo)** to draw up o take an inventory (of sth); **hacer inventario** (en almacén, tienda) Br to stocktake, US to conduct an inventory audit; **cerrado por inventario** (en letrero) closed for inventory o Br stocktaking ❑ **inventario conta-ble** book inventory; **inventario constante** perpetual inventory; **inventario de enseres** inventory of fixtures; **inventario final** ending inventory, closing inventory; **inventario físico** physical inventory; **inventario de mercancías** inventory of goods; **inventario periódico** periodic inventory; **inventario permanente** perpetual inventory

inversión nf (a) FIN investment ❑ **inversión bursátil** stock market investment; **inversión de capital** capital investment, capital expenditure; **inversión en capital fijo** fixed investment; **inversión en capital social** equity investment; **inversión a corto plazo** short-term investment; **inversión directa** direct investment; **inversión directa extranjera** foreign direct investment; **inversión ética** ethical investment; **inversión del exterior** inward investment; **inversión en el exterior** outward investment; **inversión extranjera** foreign investment, overseas investment; **inversión indirecta** indirect investment; **inversión inicial** initial investment; **inversiones institucionales** institutional investment; **inversiones a largo plazo** long-term investments; **inversiones on-line** o **en línea** on-line investing; **inversión en paraíso fiscal** offshore investment; **inversión principal** core holding; **inversión privada** private investment; **inversión en productividad** productivity investment; **inversión en renta fija** fixed-income investment; **inversión con tipo de interés fijo** fixed-rate investment; **inversión con tipo de interés flotante** floating-rate investment; **inversión en títulos cotizados** quoted investment; **inversión en valores del Estado** gilt-edged investment; **inversión en valores de renta fija** bond investment
(b) (del orden) reversal, inversion ❑ **inversión de la tendencia** trend reversal

inversor, -ora, Col, Méx **inversionista** 1 adj **los países inversores en la región** the countries that have invested in the region; **ha habido un gran esfuerzo inversor en el sector** there has been heavy investment in the sector
2 nm,f investor ❑ **inversor extranjero** foreign investor; **inversor institucional** institutional investor; **inversor on-line, inversor en línea** on-line investor; **inversor minoritario** minority investor; **inversor privado** private investor

invertir 1 vt (dinero) to invest; **invirtieron cinco millones en maquinaria nueva** they invested five million in new machinery
2 vi to invest (**en** in); **invertir en bolsa** to invest on the stock market

investigación nf (a) (estudio) **investigación científica** scientific research; **investigación y desarrollo** research and development
(b) MKTG research ❑ **investigación sobre actitudes** attitude research; **investigación AIO**

AIO research; **investigación de la audiencia** audience research; **investigación continua** continuous research; **investigación cualitativa** qualitative research; **investigación cuantitativa** quantitative research; **investigación económica** economic research; **investigación de marketing** marketing research; **investigación de mercado** market research; **investigación motivacional** motivational research; **investigación de precios** pricing research; **investigación de producto** product research; **investigación de ventas** sales research
(c) (de incidente, problema, delito) inquiry, investigation; **se ha abierto una investigación sobre el incidente** an inquiry o an investigation into the incident has been opened; **comisión de investigación** committee of inquiry ❑ **investigación judicial** judicial inquiry

investigador, -ora 1 adj **comisión investigadora** committee o board of inquiry; **un equipo investigador** a research team
2 nm,f researcher ❑ **investigador de mercado** market researcher

investigar 1 vt (a) (estudiar) to research, to do research into (b) (indagar) to investigate; **un equipo investiga las causas del accidente** a team is investigating the causes of the accident (c) (candidato) to vet
2 vi to do research (**sobre** into o on)

inyección nf (de dinero) injection ❑ **inyección de capital** capital injection; **una inyección de capital extranjero** an injection of foreign capital

inyectar vt (dinero) to inject (**en**) into

IP nm INFORM (abrev de **Internet protocol**) IP

IPC nm FIN (a) (abrev de Esp **Índice de Precios al Consumo,** Am **Índice de Precios al Consumidor**) Br RPI, US CPI (b) Méx (abrev de **Índice de Precios y Cotizaciones**) IPC index, = Mexican Stock Market Index

IPCA nm FIN, UE (abrev de **Índice de Precios al Consumo Armonizado**) HICP

IPP nm Am FIN (abrev de **Índice de Precios al Productor**) Producer Price Index

IPyC nm Méx FIN (abrev de **Índice de Precios y Cotizaciones**) IPC index, = Mexican Stock Market Index

IRPF nm (abrev de **Impresto sobre la Renta de las Personas Físicas**) personal income tax

IRF nm FIN (abrev de **Instrumentos de Renta Fija**) fixed-interest instruments

irrecuperable adj (deuda) unrecoverable, irrecoverable

irregularidad nf (en contabilidad) irregularity ❑ **irregularidad administrativa** administrative o procedural irregularity; **irregularidad contable** accounting irregularity

irrevocable *adj* irrevocable

ISAI *nm Méx* (*abrev de* **Impuesto sobre adquisición de inmuebles**) property tax

ISBN *nm* (*abrev de* **International Standard Book Number**) ISBN

isla *nf* MKTG (*para productos*) island

ISO *nf* (*abrev de* **International Standards Organization**) ISO

ítem *nm* (*elemento*) item; (*en test*) question

❑ INFORM *ítem de menú* menu item

itinerancia *nf* TEL (*de móvil*) roaming

itinerario *nm* route, itinerary

IVA *nm* (*abrev de* **impuesto sobre el valor añadido,** *Am* **impuesto al valor agregado**) *Br* VAT, *US* ≃ sales tax

izquierdo, -a *adj* left; **el margen izquierdo** the left-hand margin

Jj

Java *nm* INFORM Java

jefe, -a *nm,f (persona al mando)* boss; *(de una sección)* manager □ **jefe de almacén** warehouse manager; **jefe de compras** purchasing manager, head buyer; **jefe de equipo** team leader; **jefe de fábrica** works manager; **jefe de formación** head of training; **jefe de grupo** group leader; **jefe de personal** human resources manager, HR manager, head of personnel; **jefe de planta** plant manager; **jefe de prensa** press officer; **jefe de producción** production manager; **jefe de producto** product manager; **jefe de proyecto** project manager; **jefe de recursos humanos** human resources manager, HR manager, head of personnel; **jefe de redacción** editor-in-chief; **jefe de relaciones públicas** public relations manager; **jefe de selección de personal** recruitment manager, head of recruitment; **jefe de ventas** sales manager; **jefe de zona** area manager

jerga *nf* jargon; **la jerga administrativa/publicitaria** administrative/advertising jargon; **la jerga de Internet** netspeak

jet-lag *nm* jet lag; **tener jet-lag** to be jet-lagged

jornada *nf* (**a**) *(día)* day; **una jornada de huelga** a day of strike action; **una jornada de lucha** a day of protest □ **jornada laboral** working day; **una jornada laboral de ocho horas** an eight-hour day; **una jornada laboral de 35 horas/de 1.700 horas** a 35-hour week/a working year of 1,700 hours
(**b**) *(horario de trabajo)* **media jornada** half day □ **jornada completa** full working day; **un empleo a jornada completa** a full-time job; **jornada continua, jornada intensiva** = working day from early morning to mid-afternoon with only a short lunch break; **jornada partida** = working day with lunch break of several hours, finishing in the evening; **jornada reducida** part-time work; **contratos de trabajo con jornada reducida** part-time contracts

jornalero, -a *nm,f* day labourer

JPEG *nm* INFORM *(abrev de* **Joint Photographic Experts Group**) JPEG

jubilación *nf* (**a**) *(fin del trabajo)* retirement □ **jubilación anticipada** early retirement; **jubilación forzosa** compulsory retirement; **jubilación voluntaria** voluntary retirement (**b**) *(pensión)* pension

jubilado, -a 1 *adj* retired
2 *nm,f Br* pensioner, *US* retiree

jubilar 1 *vt* **jubilar a alguien (de)** to pension sb off (from), to retire sb (from)
2 jubilarse *vpr* to retire

judicatura *nf* (**a**) *(cargo)* office of judge (**b**) *(institución)* judiciary

judicial *adj* judicial; **el poder judicial** the judiciary; **recurrir a la vía judicial** to go to o have recourse to law

juego *nm (conjunto de objetos)* set □ INFORM **juego de caracteres** character set

juez *nmf*, **juez, -a** *nm,f* DER judge □ **juez de alzado** appeal court judge; **juez de apelaciones** appeal court judge; **juez de conciliación** conciliation magistrate; **juez de instrucción** examining magistrate; **juez de paz** Justice of the Peace; **juez de primera instancia** examining magistrate

jugar *vi* **jugar a** o **en la Bolsa** to speculate (on the Stock Exchange); **jugar al alza** to try to bull the market, to speculate on share prices rising; **jugar a la baja** to try to bull the market, to speculate on share prices falling

juicio *nm* DER trial; **llevar a alguien a juicio** to take sb to court □ **juicio civil** civil action; **juicio oral** hearing; **juicio sumarísimo** summary trial

junta *nf* (**a**) *(grupo, comité)* committee; *(de empresa, examinadores)* board □ **junta arbitral** arbitration panel o board; **junta de conciliación** conciliation board; **junta consultiva** advisory board; *Urug* **junta departamental** provincial government; **junta directiva** board of directors; **junta de directores generales** general management committee; **junta de síndicos** board of trustees
(**b**) *(reunión)* meeting □ **junta de accionistas** shareholders' meeting; **junta general** general meeting; **junta general de accionistas** shareholders' meeting; **junta general anual** annual general meeting; **junta general extraordinaria** extraordinary general meeting; **junta de portavoces** = meeting of the party spokespersons in a parliament or council to discuss a particular issue
(**c**) *Esp (gobierno autónomo)* = government and administrative body in certain autonomous regions

jurado, -a 1 *adj (declaración)* sworn **2** *nm (grupo)* jury **3** *nm,f (miembro)* juror, jury member

jurídico, -a *adj* legal; **asesor jurídico** legal adviser

jurisdicción *nf* (**a**) *(autoridad)* jurisdiction; **tener jurisdicción sobre algo** to have jurisdiction over sth ▫ **jurisdicción mercantil** commercial jurisdiction (**b**) *(territorio)* jurisdiction

jurisdiccional *adj* **aguas jurisdiccionales** territorial waters

justicia *nf* (**a**) *(derecho)* justice; **administrar justicia** to administer justice (**b**) *(organización)* **la justicia española** the Spanish legal system; **la persigue la justicia británica** she is being sought by the British courts

justificación *nf* (**a**) *justificación documental* documentary evidence *o* support (**b**) INFORM justification ▫ **justificación a la derecha** right justification; **justificación a la izquierda** left justification

justificado, -a *adj* INFORM justified

justificante *nm (de gastos)* voucher ▫ *justificante de compra* receipt; *justificante médico* doctor's note *o* certificate; *justificante de reintegro* withdrawal slip

justificar *vt* (**a**) *(gastos, transacciones)* to support; **todos los gastos deberán ser justificados debidamente** all expenses must be duly supported (**b**) *(probar, razonar)* to justify (**c**) INFORM to justify

justiprecio *nm* fair price

justo, -a *adj* (**a**) *(presupuesto)* tight (**b**) *(comercio, juicio)* fair (**c**) **justo a tiempo** *(distribución, producción)* just in time

> ❝
> En Japón el sistema **Justo a Tiempo** ha sido un logro de esa nación sobre el mercado mundial, ya que el cumplimiento en los plazos de entrega de sus productos es una de las características que lo hacen líderes de la economía contemporánea. El **Justo a Tiempo** no es una función solamente en las empresas, ni una campaña indicando que se acabó el tiempo, es una verdadera filosofía gerencial.
> ❞

juzgar *vt* DER to judge, to try

Kk

K *nm* INFORM (*abrev de* **kilobyte**) K

Kb *nm* INFORM (*abrev de* **kilobyte**) Kb

kbps INFORM (*abrev de* **kilobytes por segundo**) kbps

keynesiano, -a *adj & nm,f* ECON Keynesian

kilobit *nm* INFORM kilobit

kilobyte *nm* INFORM kilobyte

kilometraje *nm (de vehículo)* ≃ mileage; **sin límite de kilometraje** *(vehículo alquilado)* unlimited mileage

kit *nm (conjunto)* kit, set ❑ INFORM *kit de actualización* upgrade kit; INFORM *kit de conexión* connection kit

krugerrand *nm* Krugerrand

Ll

laborable 1 *adj* **día laborable** *(hábil)* working day, workday; *(de semana)* weekday
  2 *nm (día hábil)* working day; *(día de la semana)* weekday

laboral *adj (semana, jornada, horario, condiciones)* working; *(derecho, costos, mercado)* labour; *(conflicto, accidente)* industrial

laguna *nf (en leyes, reglamento)* loophole ◻ **laguna fiscal** tax loophole; **laguna legal** legal flaw *o* loophole

laissez-faire *nm* ECON laissez-faire

LAN *nf* INFORM *(abrev de* **local area network)** LAN

lana *nf Andes, Méx Fam* dough, cash

lanzamiento *nm (de producto)* launch

lanzar *vt (producto)* to launch

lapicera *nf CSur* ballpoint (pen), Biro®

lápiz *nm* pencil ◻ INFORM **lápiz óptico** light pen; *Chile* **lápiz de pasta** ballpoint pen

lapso *nm* space, interval; **en el lapso de unas semanas** in the space of a few weeks ◻ **lapso de tiempo** time lag

laptop *nm* INFORM laptop (computer)

láser 1 *adj inv (impresora, rayo)* laser
  2 *nm inv* laser ◻ **láser disc** laser disc

Latibex *nm* BOLSA Latibex index, = index of Latin American stocks traded in Spain

laudo *nm* DER **laudo (arbitral)** arbitration ruling

LCD *(abrev de* **liquid crystal display)** LCD

lealtad *nf* MKTG **lealtad a la marca** brand loyalty

leasing *nm* FIN *(sistema)* leasing; *(documento)* lease; **tener algo en leasing** to lease sth

> Respecto a los métodos de financiación, el más habitual en nuestro país es el contrato con mantenimiento (58,4%). El **leasing** y el efectivo son las otras fórmulas más habituales. La fórmula del **leasing** está mucho más extendida en Suecia (50,4%), Noruega (41,9%) y Suiza (40,9%). Sin embargo, el contrato con mantenimiento se utiliza más en Reino Unido (63,4%), Holanda (62,3%) y Luxemburgo (56%).

lector, -ora 1 *nm,f (de libros)* reader; **nuestros**

lectores our readers *o* readership
  2 *nm* INFORM *(aparato)* reader ◻ **lector de CD-ROM** CD-ROM drive; **lector de código de barras** bar-code scanner *o* reader; **lector de correo (electrónico)** (e-)mail reader; **lector de disco compacto** compact disc player; **lector de documentos** document reader; **lector de DVD** DVD player; **lector de microfilms** microfilm reader; **lector de noticias** news reader; **lector de OCR** OCR reader; **lector off-line** off-line reader; **lector óptico** optical scanner *o* reader; **lector óptico de caracteres** optical character reader; **lector de tarjetas inteligentes** smart card reader; **lector de tarjetas magnéticas** magnetic card reader
  3 *nf Andes, RP* INFORM **lectora de CD-ROM** CD-ROM drive

lectura *nf* INFORM **de sólo lectura** read-only ◻ **lectura óptica** optical reading

LED *nm* INFORM *(abrev de* **light-emitting diode)** LED

legado *nm* legacy, bequest

legal *adj* (**a**) *(relativo a la ley)* legal (**b**) *(que cumple con la ley)* lawful

legalidad legality, lawfulness

legalización *nf* legalization

legalizar *vt* to legalize; *(firma)* to authenticate

legalmente *adv* legally, lawfully

legar *vt* to bequeath

legible *adj* legible; INFORM **legible por** *Esp* **ordenador** *o Am* **computadora** machine-readable

legislación *nf* legislation; **la legislación española en la materia** Spanish law *o* legislation on the matter ◻ **legislación aduanera** customs legislation; **legislación bancaria** banking legislation *o* law; **legislación sobre carteles** cartel law; **legislación laboral** labour *o* employment legislation; **legislación mercantil** mercantile legislation; **legislación monetaria** exchange control legislation; **legislación tributaria** tax legislation

legislar *vi* to legislate

legislativo, -a *adj* legislative

legítimo, -a *adj (conforme a derecho)* lawful; *(sucesor, propietario)* rightful

lenguaje *nm* INFORM language ◻ **lenguaje de alto nivel** high-level language; *Am* **lenguaje**

assembler assembly language; ***lenguaje de autor*** authoring language; ***lenguaje de bajo nivel*** low-level language; ***lenguaje comando, lenguaje de comandos*** command language; ***lenguaje comercial*** business language; ***lenguaje ensamblador*** assembly language; ***lenguaje Java®*** Java script®; ***lenguaje macro*** macro language; ***lenguaje máquina*** machine language; ***lenguaje natural*** natural language; ***lenguaje de programación*** programming language; ***lenguaje de usuario*** user language

lesión *nf* injury ❑ ***lesiones por esfuerzo repetitivo, lesiones por movimiento repetitivo*** repetitive strain *o* stress injury

Letes *nfpl Arg* (*abrev de* **Letras del Tesoro**) Treasury bills

> **"**
> A fines de 2001, y ante la negativa del FMI a desembolsar una cuota del blindaje (1.260 millones de dólares) y la caída de la recaudación, el gobierno de Fernando de la Rúa decidió emitir 2.300 millones en Letras del Tesoro (**Letes**) para pagar diversos gastos del Estado. Y fijó, por decreto y con resoluciones del ministro Domingo Cavallo, que obligatoriamente las AFJP debían adquirir esos títulos con el dinero que tuvieran en sus cajas y a medida que iban venciendo sus plazos fijos en bancos.
> **"**

letra *nf* (**a**) FIN **letra (de cambio)** bill *o* letter of exchange; **girar una letra** to draw a bill of exchange; **protestar una letra** to protest a bill ❑ ***letra aceptada*** accepted bill, acceptance; ***letra no atendida*** overdue bill; ***letra avalada*** guaranteed bill; ***letra (de cambio) comercial*** commercial bill; ***letra (de cambio) interior*** inland bill; ***letra (de cambio) de la máxima garantía*** fine (trade) bill; ***letra al cobro*** bill for collection; ***letra a corto plazo*** short bill; ***letra descontada*** discounted bill; ***letra documentaria*** documentary bill; ***letra domiciliada*** domiciled bill; ***letra a largo plazo*** long-dated bill; ***letra limpia*** clean bill; ***letra muerta*** dead letter; ***letra a plazo fijo*** fixed-term bill *o* draft, time draft; ***letra del Tesoro*** Treasury bill; ***letra con vencimiento*** usance bill; ***letra a la vista*** sight bill, demand bill
(**b**) *(signo)* letter ❑ ***letra pequeña,*** *Am* ***letra chica*** small print
(**c**) *(en imprenta)* type, typeface ❑ ***letra bastardilla*** italic type, italics; ***letra capitular*** drop cap; ***letra cursiva*** italic type, italics; ***letra de imprenta*** *(impresa)* print; *(en formulario)* block capitals; **escriba en letra de imprenta** please write in block capitals; ***letra itálica*** italic type, italics; ***letra mayúscula*** capital letter, uppercase letter; **en letra(s) mayúscula(s)** in capitals *o* capital letters, in upper case; ***letra minúscula***

small letter, lower-case letter; **en letra(s) minúscula(s)** in small letters, in lower case; ***letra de molde*** *(impresa)* print; *(en formulario)* block capitals; ***letra negrita*** bold (face); ***letra redonda*** roman type; ***letra redondilla*** roman type; ***letra versalita*** small capital

levantar *vt* (**a**) **el presidente levantó la sesión** *(terminarla)* the chairman brought the meeting to an end; *(aplazarla)* the chairman adjourned the meeting; **si no hay más preguntas, se levanta la sesión** *(en reunión)* if there are no more questions, that ends the meeting (**b**) *(dar un empuje a)* **no ha conseguido levantar la economía** he hasn't managed to get the economy back on its feet

levante *nm* ADUANA *(de mercancías)* release

> **"**
> El **levante** de la mercancía en el puerto o aeropuerto de destino se autorizará, previas las comprobaciones que se estimen oportunas, con la presentación en las dependencias de la Sección de Vigilancia Fiscal del Ejemplar de **Levante** de la declaración de tráfico interinsular.
> **"**

ley *nf* (**a**) *(norma)* law; *(parlamentaria)* act; **leyes** *(derecho)* law ❑ ***ley antimonopolio*** antitrust law; ***leyes arancelarias*** tariff laws; ***leyes fiscales*** tax laws; ***leyes laborales*** labour *o* employment laws; ECON ***la ley de la oferta y de la demanda*** the law of supply and demand; ***ley de rendimientos decrecientes*** law of diminishing returns; ***ley de silencio*** gag law; ***Ley de Sociedades Anónimas*** = Spanish Companies Act
(**b**) **la ley** *(la justicia)* the law; **la igualdad ante la ley** equality before the law
(**c**) *(de metal precioso)* **de ley** *(oro)* = containing the legal amount of gold; *(plata)* sterling

libelo *nm* libel

liberación *nf* *(de fondos)* release; *(de recursos)* freeing (up); *(de hipoteca)* redemption

liberalismo *nm* ***liberalismo económico*** economic liberalism, free-market economics

liberalización *nf* (**a**) *(de régimen, leyes)* liberalization (**b**) *(de economía, sector)* deregulation; **la liberalización de precios** the abolition of price controls

liberalizar *vt* *(economía, sector)* to deregulate; **liberalizar los precios** to abolish price controls

liberar *vt* *(fondos)* to release; *(recursos)* to free (up); *(hipoteca)* to redeem

libertad *nf* freedom ❑ ECON ***libertad de circulación de capitales*** free movement of capital; ***libertad de circulación de trabajadores*** free movement of workers; ***libertad de comercio*** freedom of trade; ***libertad de comunicación*** freedom of communication; ***libertad de horarios***

(comerciales): **las tiendas tienen libertad de horarios** shops can open when they like; *libertad de información* freedom of information; *libertad de movimientos* freedom of movement; *libertad de prensa* freedom of the press; DER *libertad provisional* bail

LIBOR, Líbor *nf o nm* FIN (*abrev de* **London Inter-Bank Offer Rate**) LIBOR

libra *nf (moneda)* pound ❏ *libra esterlina* pound sterling

librado, -a *nm,f* FIN drawee

librador, -ora *nm,f* FIN drawer

libramiento *nm* FIN order of payment

librancista *nmf* FIN bearer

libranza *nf* (**a**) FIN order of payment (**b**) *(tiempo libre)* **día de libranza** time off

librar 1 *vt* FIN to draw
2 *vi Esp (no trabajar)* to be off work; **libro los lunes** I get Mondays off

libre *adj* (**a**) ECON *libre cambio* free trade; *(de divisas)* floating exchange rates; *libre circulación de capitales* free circulation of capital; *libre circulación de mercancías* free movement of goods; *libre circulación de personas* free movement of people; *libre circulación de trabajadores* free movement of labour; *libre comercio* free trade; *libre competencia* free competition; *libre empresa* free enterprise; *libre mercado* free market
(**b**) **libre de** *(exento)* exempt from; **libre de franqueo** post-free; **libre de impuestos** *(alcohol, cigarrillos)* tax-free, duty-free
(**c**) *(tiempo)* free, spare; **mañana tengo el día libre** I've got the day off tomorrow; **tengo dos horas libres** I have two hours spare
(**d**) *(independiente)* **trabajar por libre** to work freelance

> 66
>
> Dijo que la UE debe avanzar en las reformas de su Política Agraria Común para favorecer el **libre comercio** mundial sin medidas proteccionistas para sus productos ni subsidios a países miembros, que impiden el desarrollo agrícola y comercial de naciones más pobres.
>
> 99

librecambista 1 *adj* free-market
2 *nmf* free-marketeer

librería *nf* INFORM library ❏ *librería de programas* program library

libreta *nf* **libreta (de ahorros)** savings book, passbook ❏ *libreta del banco* bank book; *RP libreta de cheques* chequebook

libro *nm* BOLSA *libro de acciones, libro de accionistas* share register, shareholder register, *US* stock ledger; *libro de actas* minute book; *libro*

de almacén warehouse book; PARL *Libro Blanco* white paper; CONT *libro de caja* (general) cash-book; CONT *libro de compras* purchase ledger; *libro de contabilidad* account book, book of account; CONT *libro de devoluciones* returns book, returns ledger; CONT *libro diario (para transacciones)* journal, day book; *libro electrónico* e-book; *libro de gastos* cash paid book; *libro de gastos menores* petty cash book; *libro de inventario* inventory *o Br* stock book; *libro de inventarios y balances* balance book; CONT *libro mayor* general ledger, nominal ledger; CONT *libro mayor de compras* bought *o* purchase ledger; CONT *libro mayor de ventas* sales ledger; *libro de muestras* sample book; *libros oficiales de comercio* mandatory books of account; *libro de pedidos* order book; *libro de reclamaciones* complaints book; *libro registro de acciones* share ledger; *libro registro de facturas emitidas* bill book; *libro registro de ventas e ingresos* income and expenditure account, revenue account; *libro de reservas* reservations book

licencia *nf* (**a**) *(para fabricación)* licence; *(de software, vídeo)* licence agreement; *(para cadena de radio, TV)* franchise ❏ *licencia bancaria* banking charter; *licencia comercial* trading licence; INFORM *licencia de empresa* corporate licence; *licencia exclusiva* exclusive licence; *licencia de exportación* export licence; *licencia de fabricación* manufacturing licence; *licencia fiscal* = official authorization to practise a profession; *licencia de importación* import licence; *licencia de obras* planning permission; *licencia de venta* selling licence
(**b**) *Am (en el trabajo)* leave; **estar de licencia** to be off work ❏ *RP licencia por enfermedad* sick leave; *RP licencia por maternidad* maternity leave

licenciado, -a *nm,f* (**a**) *(de universidad)* graduate; **licenciado en económicas/derecho** economics/law graduate; **es licenciado en Derecho por la Universidad de Córdoba** he has a law degree from the University of Córdoba (**b**) *Andes, CAm, Carib, Méx (forma de tratamiento)* = form of address used to indicate respect; **el licenciado Pérez** Mr Pérez

licenciar 1 *vt Am (en universidad)* to confer a degree on
2 licenciarse *vpr (en universidad)* to graduate; **me licencié en derecho por la Universidad de Salamanca** I obtained a law degree from the University of Salamanca

licenciatura *nf* degree; **licenciatura en económicas/derecho** economics/law degree

licitación *nf* tender; **estar en licitación** to be out to tender; **salir a licitación** to be put out to tender; **un proceso de licitación** a call for tenders ❏ *licitación pública* competitive bidding

licitador, -ora *nm,f* bidder

licitar 1 *vt (sacar a concurso)* to put out to tender **2** *vi (en subasta)* to bid

> **"**
>
> Renfe **licitó** este viernes el mayor pedido de trenes de su historia, que incluye la compra de hasta 70 nuevos trenes de Alta Velocidad (Ave) y que, en conjunto, supondrá una inversión mínima de 1.183 millones de euros. En concreto, la compañía ferroviaria sacó a concurso la compra de entre 32 y 40 trenes de Alta Velocidad y Altas Prestaciones, con capacidad para circular a una velocidad máxima de 300 kilómetros a la hora por un importe de 825 millones.
>
> **"**

líder 1 *adj* leading; **la empresa es líder en el sector** it is the leading company in the industry **2** *nmf (de clasificación, mercado)* leader □ MKTG **líder de la categoría** category leader; **líder del mercado** market leader; **líder de opinión** opinion leader; **líder en precios** price leader; **líder sindical** union leader

LIFFE *nm* FIN *(abrev de* **London International Financial Futures Exchange***)* LIFFE

limitación *nf* limitation, limit □ **limitación de daños** damage limitation; **limitaciones presupuestarias** budget constraints *o* restrictions; **limitación voluntaria de las exportaciones** voluntary export restraint

limitado, -a *adj* limited; **sociedad limitada** private limited company

limitar *vt* to limit, to restrict

límite *nm* **(a)** *(tope)* limit □ FIN **límite al alza** limit up; BOLSA **límites de apertura** opening range; FIN **límite a la baja** limit down; **límite de carga** load limit; FIN **límite de crédito** credit limit, credit ceiling; **límite de descubierto** overdraft limit; **límite de edad** age limit; **límite de endeudamiento** borrowing limit; **límite de gastos** spending limit; **límite de peso** weight limit; **límite de posición** position limit; **límite presupuestario** budgetary limit; **límite de reintegro** withdrawal limit; **límite superior** upper limit **(b)** *(como adjetivo) (precio, edad)* maximum; **fecha límite de entrega: 15 de junio** deadline for submissions: 15 June

línea *nf* **(a)** FIN **línea de crédito** credit line, line of credit; **línea de descubierto autorizada** authorized overdraft facility **(b)** **línea (aérea)** airline; **una línea de vuelos charter** a charter airline □ **línea aérea de bandera** flag airline **(c)** *(en comercio)* line; □ **línea blanca** white goods; **línea marrón** brown goods; **línea de productos** product line **(d)** *(estilo, tendencia)* style; **de línea clásica** classical □ **línea de conducta** course of action;

línea de investigación line of inquiry **(e)** *(categoría)* **de primera línea** *(producto)* first-rate; *(marca, empresa)* top **(f)** *(de telecomunicaciones)* line; **cortar la línea (telefónica)** to cut off the phone; **no hay** *o* **no tenemos línea** the line's dead □ **línea abierta** open line; **línea arrendada** leased line; **línea de asistencia técnica** support line, helpline; **línea caliente** *(de atención al cliente)* hot line; **línea conmutada** dial-up line; **línea dedicada** dedicated line; **línea directa** direct line; **línea exterior** outside line; **línea privada** private line; **línea RDSI** ISDN line; *RP* **líneas rotativas** *(centralita)* switchboard; **línea terrestre** land line **(g)** INFORM line; **en línea** on-line; **fuera de línea** off-line □ **línea de base** baseline; **línea de comando** command line; **línea de estado** status line

lineal 1 *adj* **(a)** *(de la línea)* linear; **no lineal** non-linear **(b)** *(aumento, descenso)* steady **2** *nm (en supermercado)* shelf

> **"**
>
> "A veces el fabricante sigue pagando por tener una determinada posición en el **lineal** o estantería; pero ahora se va más a que el supermercado comparta toda la información que obtiene de sus clientes con el fabricante y éste se encargue de hacer estudios sobre categorías y de aprovisionarlo automáticamente." De hecho, las marcas sólo pagan por la introducción de novedades. "Nosotros, apoyándonos en los estudios que encargamos, aconsejamos a los supermercados dónde situar nuestros productos, la cantidad de ellos que debe tener el **lineal** y qué otras marcas deberían estar situadas al lado", cuenta Unzalu, de Unilever Bestfoods.
>
> **"**

lingote *nm* ingot □ **lingote de oro** gold ingot

liquidable *adj* FIN *(bonos)* redeemable; *(activos)* realizable

liquidación *nf* **(a)** *(pago)* settlement; *(de hipoteca)* redemption; **hacer la liquidación de una cuenta** to settle an account □ **liquidación de activos** asset-stripping; **liquidación de averías** average adjustment; **liquidación de bienes** liquidation of assets; **liquidación complementaria** additional tax assessment; **liquidación definitiva** final assessment; **liquidación de la deuda** liquidation of the debt; **liquidación en efectivo** cash settlement; **liquidación final** final settlement; **liquidación del préstamo** settlement of the loan **(b)** *(de empresa)* liquidation, winding-up □ **liquidación forzosa** compulsory liquidation **(c)** *(rebaja)* **liquidación (de existencias)** clearance sale; **estar de liquidación** to be having a clearance sale ❑ *liquidación por cese de negocio* closing-down sale, *US* closeout; *liquidación por fin de temporada* end-of-season sale; *liquidación por reforma* = sale before a shop is closed for renovation; *liquidación por traspaso* = sale before a business is sold to new management

(**d**) *(finiquito)* redundancy settlement

liquidador, -ora *nm,f* liquidator ❑ *liquidador de averías* average adjuster

liquidar *vt* (**a**) *(pagar) (deuda, préstamo)* to settle; *(hipoteca)* to redeem (**b**) *(negocio, sociedad)* to liquidate, to wind up (**c**) *(rebajar)* to sell off, *US* to close out; **liquidar existencias** to have a stock clearance sale

liquidez *nf* FIN liquidity ❑ *liquidez de cartera* portfolio liquidity; *liquidez primaria* primary liquidity; *liquidez secundaria* secondary liquidity

líquido, -a 1 *adj* FIN *(neto)* net
2 *nm* (**a**) FIN liquid assets (**b**) *líquido corrector* correction fluid, Tippex®

lira *nf* Antes *(moneda)* lira

liso, -a *adj (papel)* plain

lista *nf (de activos, pasivos, nombres)* list ❑ *lista de características* attribute list; INFORM *lista de correo* mailing list; *lista de correos* *Br* poste restante, *US* general delivery; MKTG *lista de destinatarios* mailing list; INFORM *lista de distribución* mailing list; ADUANA *lista de embarque, Am lista de empaque (de paquetes)* packing list; *lista de llegadas* arrivals list; MKTG *lista de mailing* mailing list; *lista negra* blacklist; BOLSA *lista oficial* official list; *lista de precios* price list; *lista de salidas* departure list; *lista de suscriptores* subscription list

listado, -a 1 *adj Am* BOLSA listed, *Br* quoted
2 *nm (lista)* list ❑ *listado de precios* price list

❝
En Latinoamérica, el nivel de compañías **listadas** en la bolsa es muy pequeño en comparación con el tamaño de los países.
❞

listar *vt* to list

listero, -a *nm,f* Fam INFORM list member

listín *nm Esp* **listín (de teléfonos)** (telephone) directory

litigante *adj & nmf* litigant

litigar *vi* to go to law

litigio *nm* (**a**) DER court case, lawsuit (**b**) *(disputa)* dispute; **en litigio** in dispute; **entrar en litigio con alguien** to enter into a dispute with sb

llamada *nf* TEL call; **hacer una llamada** to make a phone call; **tienes dos llamadas en el contestador** you have two messages on your answering machine ❑ *llamada a cobro revertido*

Br reverse-charge call, *US* collect call; **hacer una llamada a cobro revertido** *Br* to make a reverse-charge call, *US* to call collect; *llamada en espera* call waiting; *llamada en frío* cold call; *llamada internacional* international call; *llamada de larga distancia* toll call; *llamada local* local call; *llamada telefónica* telephone call, phone call; *llamada urbana* local call

llamado *nm Am* TEL call; **hacer un llamado** to make a phone call; **tienes dos llamados en el contestador** you have two messages on your answering machine ❑ *llamado por cobrar o Ecuad, Urug a cobrar Br* reverse-charge call, *US* collect call; *llamado a cobro revertido* *Br* reverse-charge call, *US* collect call; **hacer un llamado a cobro revertido** *Br* to make a reverse-charge call, *US* to call collect; *llamado en espera* call waiting; *llamado en frío* cold call; *llamado de larga distancia* toll call; *llamado local* local call; *llamado telefónico* telephone call, phone call

llamar 1 *vt* (**a**) *(por teléfono)* to phone, to call; **llamar más tarde** to call back, *Br* to ring back (**b**) *(convocar)* to summon, to call; **el jefe me llamó a su despacho** the boss summoned o called me to his office
2 *vi (por teléfono)* to phone, to call

llamarada *nf* INFORM flame

llave *nf* (**a**) *(signo ortográfico)* curly bracket (**b**) *RP* **llaves** *(en compra inmobiliaria)* occupancy fee *(paid when keys are handed over)* (**c**) **llave en mano** *(sistema, proyecto)* turnkey

❝
La experiencia adquirida por la empresa de software en proyectos nacionales e internacionales le ha permitido desarrollar soluciones verticales, en muchos casos **llave en mano**, para varios sectores: confección y distribución de prendas, cadenas de tiendas, franquicias, constructoras, aceiteras y alquiler de coches, entre otros.
❞

llegada *nf (de mercancías, persona, avión)* arrival

llegar *vi* (**a**) *(persona, vehículo, encargo)* to arrive; **no me ha llegado aún el paquete** the parcel still hasn't arrived, I still haven't received the parcel (**b**) **llegar a** *(acuerdo, conclusión)* to come to, to reach; **el importe total de la reparación no llega a 5.000 pesos** the total cost of the repairs is less than o below 5,000 pesos

llevar *vt* (**a**) *(dirigir)* to be in charge of; *(negocio)* to look after, to run
(**b**) *(ocuparse de)* to handle, to deal with; **este asunto lo lleva el departamento de ventas** this matter is being handled by the sales department; **llevar la contabilidad** to keep the books
(**c**) *Esp (cobrar)* to charge; **¿qué te llevaron por la revisión del coche?** how much o what did

they charge you for servicing the car?

(**d**) *(transportar)* to carry; **el taxi los llevó al aeropuerto** the taxi took them to the airport; **¿cómo van a llevar la carga al puerto?** how are they going to transport *o* get the cargo to the port?

(**e**) **llevar a cabo** *(plan, estrategia, política)* to implement; *(estudio)* to carry out

lluvia *nf* MKTG *lluvia de ideas* brainstorming

lobby *nm* lobby

local 1 *adj (administración, hora, llamada)* local **2** *nm (establecimiento)* premises ❏ **local comercial** business premises

localización *nf* INFORM localization

localizador *nm* (**a**) INFORM *(de página Web)* URL (**b**) *Méx (buscapersonas)* pager

localizar *vt* (**a**) *(encontrar)* to locate, to find; **localizar una llamada** to trace a call; **llevo horas intentando localizarlo** I've been trying to get hold of him for hours (**b**) INFORM to localize

lock-out *nm* IND lockout

lógico, -a *adj* INFORM logical

logística *nf* logistics; **la logística desempeña un papel fundamental en nuestra empresa** logistics plays a vital role in our company; **la logística de la operación es bastante complicada** the logistics of the operation are quite complicated

❝
Las firmas de **logística** prevén aumentar su plantilla un cinco por ciento en 2004. Comerciales con experiencia, mozos de almacén y carretilleros son los perfiles más demandados en este sector, que ya cuenta con sistemas de evaluación para todos sus empleados, retribución variable y planes de sucesión. ❞

logotipo, logo *nm* logo

lograr *vt (objetivo)* to achieve; *(puesto)* to get, to obtain; *(resultado)* to obtain, to achieve; **lograr hacer algo** to manage to do sth

logro *nm* achievement

longitudinal *adj* MKTG *(estudio)* longitudinal

lote *nm* (**a**) BOLSA, FIN lot; **en lotes** in lots (**b**) *(en subastas)* lot (**c**) *(conjunto)* batch ❏ *lote económico* economic batch; *lote de prueba* trial lot (**d**) *Am (solar)* plot (of land)

lucrativo, -a *adj (rentable)* profitable; *(para generar beneficios)* profit-making; **una organización con fines no lucrativos** a not-for-profit organization, *Br* a non-profit(-making) organization

lucro *nm* profit, gain; **una asociación sin ánimo de lucro** a not-for-profit organization, *Br* a non-profit(-making) organization ❏ *lucro cesante* loss of earnings

lugar *nm* place ❏ *lugar de encuentro* meeting place; *lugar de entrega* place of delivery; *lugar de envío* place of shipment; *lugar de nacimiento (en formulario)* place of birth; *lugar de origen* place of origin; *lugar de pago* place of payment; *lugar de recogida (de cargamento, pasajeros)* pick-up point; *lugar de residencia (en formulario)* place of residence; *lugar de trabajo* workplace, place of work

lugarteniente *nmf* deputy

lujo *nm* luxury; **de lujo** luxury; **un hotel de lujo** a luxury hotel

lunes *nm lunes negro* Black Monday

Mm

macro *nf* INFORM macro

macroeconomía *nf* macroeconomics

madurez *nf (de mercado)* maturity

maestro, -a *nm,f (en oficio)* master; **maestro carpintero/albañil** master carpenter/builder

magistratura *nf* **(a)** *(tribunal)* tribunal; **llevar a alguien a magistratura** to take sb to court □ *Esp* **magistratura de trabajo** industrial tribunal **(b)** DER **la magistratura** *(jueces)* judges, the magistracy, ≃ the Bench

magnate *nm* magnate, tycoon □ **magnate del petróleo** oil baron, oil tycoon; **magnate de la prensa** press baron, press magnate

mail *nm* INFORM e-mail; **enviar un mail a alguien** to e-mail sb

mailing *nm* mailing, *Br* mailshot; **hacer un mailing** to do a mailing o *Br* mailshot □ **mailing masivo** mass mailing

maletín *nm (de mano)* briefcase

malgastar *vt (dinero, tiempo)* to waste

malo, -a *adj* **mala fama** bad name; **mala fe** bad faith; **mala gestión** bad management; **mala reputación** bad name

malvender *vt* to sell (too) cheaply, to undersell

malversación *nf* **malversación (de fondos)** embezzlement, misappropriation (of funds)

malversador, -ora *nm,f* **malversador (de fondos)** embezzler

malversar *vt* to embezzle, to misappropriate

mancomunado, -a *adj* joint

mancomunadamente *adj* jointly

mancomunar *vt* to pool (together)

> ❝
> La junta de accionistas también nombró una representación **mancomunada** integrada por la secretaria del consejo, María del Carmen García Robledo, y el presidente en funciones, Rubén Manso Olivar. Esta representación contó con el voto favorable del 77,67% de los accionistas.
> ❞

mancomunidad *nf* association

mandamiento *nm* DER writ □ **mandamiento de arresto** arrest warrant; **mandamiento de**

detención arrest warrant; **mandamiento judicial** writ

mandar 1 *vt (enviar)* to send; **mandar algo a alguien** to send sb sth, to send sth to sb; **mandar algo (por correo)** to post sth, *esp US* to mail sth; **mandar algo por fax** to fax sth; **mandar un correo electrónico a alguien** to e-mail sb **2** *vi (dirigir)* to be in charge

mandato *nm (orden, precepto)* order, command □ DER **mandato judicial** writ

mando *nm* **mando intermedio** middle manager; **mandos intermedios** middle management

manejar *vt (máquina, mandos)* to operate; *(herramienta)* to use

manejo *nm (de máquina, mandos)* operation; *(de herramientas)* use; **de fácil manejo** *(máquina, aparato)* easy-to-use; *(programa)* user-friendly; **instrucciones de manejo** instructions for use

manifiesto *nm (de barco, avión)* manifest □ **manifiesto de aduanas** customs manifest; **manifiesto de entrada** inward manifest; **manifiesto de flete** freight manifest; **manifiesto de salida** outward manifest

manipulación *nf (de datos)* manipulation □ **manipulación contable** massaging the accounts; **manipulación de divisas** currency manipulation

manipulador, - ora *nm,f (operario)* handler □ **manipulador de alimentos** food handler; **manipulador de material** material handler

> ❝
> El perfil tipo del empleado del sector industrial corresponde a un hombre soltero, de cerca de 28 años. Las categorías profesionales más demandadas son las de peón en el que trabajan más de la mitad (52 por ciento) de los contratados. Les siguen como puestos más habituales los de **manipulador de alimentos** (8 por ciento de los empleados), ayudante de almacén (7 por ciento) y **manipulador de material** (6 por ciento).
> ❞

mano *nf* **a mano** manually; **de primera mano** brand new; **de segunda mano** second-hand □ TEL **manos libres** hands-free; **mano de obra** *(trabajadores)* labour, workers; *(trabajo manual)* labour; **la mano de obra barata** cheap labour costs; *mano de obra contratada* contract labour; *mano de obra cualificada* skilled labour *o* workers; *mano de obra no cualificada* unskilled labour *o* workers; *mano de obra directa* direct labour; *mano de obra especializada* skilled labour *o* workers; *mano de obra extranjera* foreign labour; *mano de obra semicualificada* semi-skilled labour *o* workers; *mano de obra temporal* temporary labour *o* workers

mantener *vt* (**a**) *(económicamente)* to support (**b**) *(conversación, negociaciones, diálogo)* to hold; **mantener correspondencia con alguien** to correspond with sb; **mantener contactos con alguien** to be in contact with sb (**c**) *(producción, tipos de cambio)* to maintain; *(precios)* to keep up; **mantener los precios bajos** to keep prices down

mantenimiento *nm (de máquina, equipos, edificio)* maintenance; **gastos de mantenimiento** maintenance costs; **manual de mantenimiento** service manual; **servicio de mantenimiento** maintenance service □ *mantenimiento periódico* routine maintenance; *mantenimiento planificado* planned maintenance

manual 1 *adj (trabajo, obrero)* manual
2 *nm* manual □ *manual de instrucciones* instruction manual; *manual de mantenimiento* service manual; *manual técnico* technical handbook; *manual de uso* instruction manual; *manual del usuario* user's manual

manualmente *adv* manually

manufactura *nf* (**a**) *(actividad)* manufacture (**b**) *(fábrica)* factory (**c**) **manufacturas** *(producto)* manufactured goods

manufacturado, -a *adj* manufactured; **productos manufacturados** manufactured goods

manufacturar *vt* to manufacture

manufacturero, -a *adj* manufacturing; **la industria manufacturera** manufacturing industry

mapa *nm* INFORM **mapa de bits** bit map; **mapa de caracteres** character map

maqueta *nf* (**a**) *(reproducción)* model (**b**) *(de libro)* dummy

maquetación *nf* INFORM page layout

maquetar *vt* INFORM to do the layout of

maquilador, -ora 1 *adj* **planta maquiladora** bonded assembly plant *(set up by a foreign firm near the US border)*, US maquiladora (plant), in-bond plant
2 *nf* CAm, Méx bonded assembly plant, US maquiladora (plant), in-bond plant

“
Entrevistado en el puerto de Ensenada, donde participó en el acto Exportuaria Ensenada 2003, el funcionario federal aseguró que 50 por ciento de los empleos desaparecidos en Baja California se relacionan con la industria **maquiladora** de exportación, por la falta de crecimiento en este sector.
„

maquillaje *nm (manipulación)* massaging □ *maquillaje de cuentas* creative accounting, window dressing

maquillar *vt (cifras)* to massage; **intentaron maquillar las pérdidas** they tried to massage the figures to hide the losses

máquina *nf (aparato)* machine; **escribir a máquina** to type; **escrito a máquina** typewritten; **hecho a máquina** machine-made □ *máquina de cambio* change machine; *máquina de escribir* typewriter; *máquina expendedora* vending machine; *máquina herramienta* machine tool; *máquina registradora* cash register

maquinaria *nf* (**a**) *(aparatos)* machinery □ *maquinaria agrícola* agricultural *o* farming machinery; *maquinaria industrial* industrial machinery; *maquinaria pesada* heavy machinery (**b**) *(de gobierno, organización)* machinery □ *maquinaria administrativa* administrative machinery; *maquinaria económica* economic machinery

marca *nf* (**a**) *(de producto)* brand; *(de vehículo)* make □ *marca blanca* own brand; *marca de la casa* own brand, US house brand; *marca clave* key brand; *marca comercial* trademark; *marca conocida* name brand; *marca de consumo* consumer brand; *marca del distribuidor* distributor's brand; *marca económica* economy brand, value brand; *marca de fábrica* trademark; *marca del fabricante* manufacturer brand; *marca de familia* family brand; *marca genérica* generic brand; *marca líder* brand leader; *marca de lujo* luxury *o* premium brand; *marca paraguas* umbrella trademark; *marca principal* core brand; *marca propia* own brand; *marca registrada* registered trademark; *marca registrada del fabricante* maker's trademark; *marca secundaria* secondary brand
(**b**) *(señal)* mark □ *marca de certificación* certification mark

“
Los productos bajo marcas de distribuidores o **marca blanca** doblarán su cuota de mercado en España en los próximos años, pasando de un 22% actual a más de un 40%. Así lo estima PWC Consulting en un informe en el que destaca que, si no se toman medidas ahora, la distribución convertirá en dueña del mercado.
„

marcación *nf*, **marcado** *nm* TEL dial, dialling □ *marcación automática* autodial, automatic dialling; **marcación directa** direct dialling; **marcación rápida** speed dial

marcador nm (**a**) INFORM (de página web) bookmark (**b**) Am (rotulador) felt-tip pen; Méx (fluorescente) highlighter (pen)

marcar vt (**a**) (poner marca en) to mark; **¿qué precio marca la etiqueta?** what is the price on the label?; **el euro ha marcado un nuevo mínimo frente al dólar** the euro has fallen to another all-time low against the dollar (**b**) (número de teléfono) to dial (**c**) RP (en el trabajo) **marcar tarjeta** (a la entrada) to clock in; (a la salida) to clock out

marcha nf (**a**) (partida) departure; **ha anunciado su marcha de la empresa** she has announced that she will be leaving the company (**b**) (funcionamiento) **poner en marcha** (máquina) to start; (proyecto) to start, to launch; **puesta en marcha** (de proyecto) launch, start; (de empresa) start-up

marco 1 nm (**a**) (ámbito) framework; **dentro del marco de la UE** within the framework of the EU (**b**) (moneda) Antes **marco alemán** Deutschmark, German mark; **marco finlandés** markka
   2 adj inv **acuerdo marco** general o framework agreement

margen nm margin ❑ **margen antes de impuestos** pre-tax margin; **margen de beneficio(s)** profit margin; **un producto con un alto margen de beneficio** a high-margin product; **margen de beneficio neto** net profit margin; **margen bruto** gross profit margin, pre-tax margin; **margen comercial** mark-up; **margen de contribución** contribution margin; **margen de crédito** credit margin; **margen del distribuidor** distributor's margin; **margen de error** margin of error; **margen de explotación** operating margin; **margen de fluctuación** fluctuation margin; **margen de ganancia** profit margin; **margen de ganancia neta** net profit margin; **margen del importador** importer's margin; **margen de intermediación** financial margin; **margen del mayorista** wholesaler margin; **margen neto** net margin; **margen neto de intereses** net interest margin; **margen operacional** operating margin; **margen de rendimiento** yield spread; **margen de segmento** segment margin; BOLSA **margen de seguridad** safety margin; **margen de tolerancia** tolerance (margin)

stocks. Concretamente, afirma que los resultados responden a la bajada de precios, gracias a las productividades y existencias en gestión.
   ❞

marginal adj (negocio, beneficio, costo) marginal

marital adj DER marital

marítimo, -a adj (comercio, derecho, seguro) maritime; **transporte marítimo** shipping, transport by ship

marketing, márketing nm marketing ❑ **marketing de afinidad** affinity marketing; **marketing bancario** bank marketing; **marketing creativo** creative marketing; **marketing directo** direct marketing; **marketing ecológico** green marketing; **marketing electrónico** e-marketing; **marketing estratégico** strategic marketing; **marketing financiero** financial marketing; **marketing global** global marketing; **marketing de guerrilla** guerrilla marketing; **marketing de incentivos** incentive marketing; **marketing industrial** industrial marketing; **marketing interactivo** interactive marketing; **marketing interno** internal marketing; **marketing mix** marketing mix; **marketing multinacional** multinational marketing; **marketing de nichos** niche marketing; **marketing de nuevos productos** new product marketing; **marketing on-line** on-line marketing; **marketing operativo** operational marketing; **marketing de permiso** permission marketing; **marketing personalizado** customized marketing; **marketing de posventa** after-sales marketing; **marketing de segmentación** niche marketing; **marketing selectivo** selective marketing; **marketing social** social marketing; **marketing telefónico** telemarketing; **marketing viral** viral marketing

masa nf (**a**) ECON **masa monetaria** money supply; **masa salarial** (total) wage bill (**b**) **en masa** (distribución) mass (**c**) MKTG **masa crítica** critical mass

masivo, -a adj (despidos, circulación) mass

máster nm (título) Master's (degree); **un máster en economía** a Master's (degree) in economics

matasellos nm inv (marca) postmark

materia nf **materia prima** raw material

material nm (**a**) (sustancia) material ❑ **material de desecho** waste material
   (**b**) (equipo) materials; **materiales y mano de obra** materials and labour ❑ **materiales de construcción** building materials; **material fungible** consumables; **material de laboratorio** laboratory materials; **material móvil** (de ferrocarril) rolling stock; **material de oficina** office supplies; **material técnico** technical equipment
   (**c**) MKTG (información) material ❑ **material de exposición** promotional material; **material de**

promoción promotional material; **material publicitario** advertising material; **material de regalo** giveaway material

matricial *adj* INFORM *(impresora)* dot matrix

matrícula *nf* (**a**) *(importe)* enrolment fee, registration fee (**b**) *(documento)* registration document (**c**) *(de vehículo)* Br number plate, US license plate (**d**) *(de barco)* registration (document); **un barco con matrícula de Liberia** a ship registered in Liberia

matriz 1 *nf* (**a**) *(empresa)* parent company (**b**) *Esp (de talonario)* (cheque) stub, Br counterfoil (**c**) INFORM matrix □ **matriz activa** active matrix (**d**) MKTG **matriz de Boston** Boston matrix; **matriz crecimiento-cuota** growth-share matrix
2 *adj (empresa)* parent; **casa matriz** *(empresa)* parent company; *(sede)* head office

maximización *nf (de beneficios)* maximization

maximizar *vt (beneficios)* to maximize

máximo, -a 1 *adj (capacidad, cantidad)* maximum; **en un plazo máximo de diez días** within ten days
2 *nm* maximum; **trabajan un máximo de 35 horas** they work a maximum of 35 hours; **las ventas han alcanzado un máximo histórico** sales have reached an all-time high; **la Bolsa ha alcanzado un nuevo máximo** the Stock Market reached a new high; **los beneficios alcanzaron su máximo en julio** profits peaked in July

> ❝
>
> La bolsa ha subido con fuerza, pese a las dudas que provocaron los resultados empresariales conocidos este mediodía en Estados Unidos, y el Ibex se ha quedado a 50 puntos de **máximos** anuales. El volumen de negocio reducido ha vuelto a ser muy reducido.
>
> ❞

mayor 1 *adj* **al por mayor** wholesale; **un almacén de venta al por mayor** a wholesaler's; **comprar al por mayor** to buy wholesale
2 *nm* ledger

mayoreo *nm Am* wholesale; **vender al mayoreo** to sell wholesale; **venta al mayoreo** wholesale

mayoría *nf* majority □ **mayoría absoluta** absolute majority; **mayoría de bloqueo** blocking majority; MKTG **mayoría inicial** early majority; **mayoría simple** simple majority; MKTG **mayoría tardía** late majority

mayorista 1 *adj* wholesale
2 *nmf* wholesaler □ **mayorista importador** import wholesaler

mayúscula *nf* capital letter, upper-case letter; **en mayúsculas** in capitals *o* capital letters, in upper case □ **mayúsculas fijas** caps lock

MB INFORM *(abrev de* **megabyte***)* MB

Mb INFORM *(abrev de* **megabit***)* Mb

MBA *nm (abrev de* **Master of Business Administration***)* MBA

MBps INFORM *(abrev de* **megabytes por segundo***)* MBps

Mbps INFORM *(abrev de* **megabits por segundo***)* Mbps

mecánicamente *adv* mechanically

mecánico, -a 1 *adj* mechanical
2 *nm,f (persona)* mechanic

mecanismo *nm* (**a**) *(de máquina)* mechanism (**b**) *(sistema)* mechanism; **un mecanismo automático de revisión salarial** a procedure *o* system for automatic salary reviews □ **mecanismo bancario** banking mechanism; **mecanismo de descuento** discount mechanism; **mecanismo de la oferta y la demanda** supply and demand mechanism; **mecanismo presupuestario** budgetary mechanism; *Antes* **mecanismo de los tipos de cambio** exchange rate mechanism

mecanización *nf* mechanization

mecanizar *vt* to mechanize

mecanografía *nf* typing □ **mecanografía al tacto** touch-typing

mecanografiar *vt* to type; **mecanografiar al tacto** to touch-type

mecanógrafo, -a *nm,f* typist

mecenazgo *nm* patronage

media 1 *nf (promedio)* average, mean □ **media ponderada** weighted mean; **media proporcional** proportional mean
2 *nmpl (medios de comunicación)* media

mediación *nf* mediation; **por mediación de** through

mediador, -ora *nm,f* mediator

mediano, -a *adj* (**a**) *(en tamaño)* medium-sized (**b**) *Am (de promedio) (ingresos, rendimiento)* average (**c**) *Am (intermedio)* medium; **a mediano plazo** in the medium term

mediar *vi (intervenir)* to mediate (**entre/en** between/in)

medición *nf (cálculo)* measurement □ **medición de la audiencia** audience measurement

medida *nf* (**a**) *(disposición)* measure, step; **adoptar** *o* **tomar medidas** to take measures *o* steps □ **medida de ahorro** economy measure; **medidas arancelarias** tariff measures; **medidas no arancelarias** non-tariff measures; **medidas de austeridad** austerity measures; **medidas disciplinarias** disciplinary measures; **medida económica** economic measure; **medidas de emergencia** emergency measures; **medida fiscal** fiscal measure; **medida monetaria**

money measurement; *medidas proteccionis-tas* protectionist measures; *medidas de seguridad* safety measures o precautions (**b**) *(dimensión)* measurement

> Detalló que entre los instrumentos que el gobierno federal aplica para reactivar el mercado interno y el crecimiento económico está el aprovechamiento de los tratados comerciales que México tiene en el mundo, así como la aplicación de **medidas arancelarias** en los casos en que algún sector productivo esté en riesgo.

medio, -a 1 *adj* (**a**) *(de promedio) (ingresos, rendimiento)* average; **el consumo medio por habitante** the average consumption per head of population (**b**) *(intermedio)* medium; **a medio plazo** in the medium term
2 *nm* (**a**) *(sistema, manera)* means ❑ *medio de almacenamiento* storage medium; BOLSA *medio de cambio* medium of exchange; *medio de comunicación* means of communication; *los medios de comunicación* the media; *medios de comunicación electrónicos* electronic media; *los medios de comunicación de masas* the mass media; *los medios de difusión* the media; *medios digitales interactivos* interactive digital media; *medio de pago* means of payment; *medios de producción* means of production; *medio publicitario* advertising medium; *medio de transporte* means of transport (**b**) **medios** *(recursos)* means, resources; **no cuentan con los medios económicos para realizarlo** they lack the means o the (financial) resources to do it ❑ *medios financieros* financial means

mega *nm Fam* INFORM meg, megabyte

megabit *nm* INFORM megabit

megabyte *nm* INFORM megabyte

mejora *nf* (**a**) *(progreso)* improvement; **una mejora radical** a radical improvement, a complete turnaround ❑ *mejora continua* continous improvement; *mejora del producto* product improvement o augmentation (**b**) INFORM *(de imagen, calidad)* enhancement

mejorado, -a *adj* INFORM *(imagen, calidad)* enhanced

mejorar *vt* (**a**) *(producción, condiciones)* to improve; **mejorar la oferta de alguien** to improve on o top sb's offer; **debemos intentar mejorar las cifras del año pasado** we must try to better last year's figures (**b**) INFORM *(imagen, calidad)* to enhance

melodía *nf* MKTG *(de anuncio)* jingle

membrete *nm* letterhead, heading

memorándum, memorando *nm (nota)* memorandum, memo

memoria *nf* (**a**) *(informe)* **memoria (anual)** *(de empresa)* (annual) report; *(notas de auditoría)* notes to the annual accounts (**b**) INFORM memory ❑ *memoria de acceso aleatorio* random access memory; *memoria buffer* buffer memory; *memoria de datos* data memory; *memoria de disco* disk memory; *memoria disponible* available memory; *memoria expandida* expanded memory; *memoria extendida* extended memory; *memoria intermedia* buffer; *memoria RAM* RAM; *memoria ROM* ROM; *memoria de sólo lectura* read-only memory

mencionar *vt* to mention; **en el mencionado estudio se afirma que...** in the above-mentioned study it is stated that...

menor *adj* (**a**) *(cambio, problema)* minor (**b**) **al por menor** retail; **vender al por menor** to retail; **puntos de venta al por menor** retail outlets

menoreo *nm Am* retail; **comercio al menoreo** retail trade

menorista = **minorista**

mensaje *nm* (**a**) *(comunicación)* message ❑ MKTG *mensaje central* core message; *mensaje por correo electrónico* e-mail message; *mensaje emocional* emotional message; *mensaje publicitario* advertisement; *mensaje SMS* SMS (message); *mensaje telefónico* telephone message; *mensaje de texto* text message (**b**) INFORM message ❑ *mensaje de alerta* alert message; *mensaje de ayuda* help message; *mensaje de bienvenida* welcome message; *mensaje de error* error message; *mensaje ofensivo* flame; *mensaje rebotado* bounce(d) message; *mensaje del sistema* system prompt

mensajería *nf* (**a**) *(de paquetes, cartas)* courier service (**b**) INFORM messaging

> El grupo de **mensajería**, logística y transporte rápido TNT Post Group (TPG) alcanzó un beneficio neto de 145 millones de euros en el segundo trimestre de 2002, lo que supone un incremento del 17,9% respecto al mismo período del año anterior, informó la empresa.

mensajero, -a *nm,f (portador)* messenger; *(de mensajería)* courier

mensual *adj* monthly

mensualidad *nf* (**a**) *(sueldo)* monthly salary (**b**) *(pago)* monthly payment o instalment; **lo puede pagar en seis mensualidades** you can pay for it in six monthly instalments

mensualmente *adv* monthly

mentor, -ora *nm,f* mentor

menú *nm* INFORM menu ❏ **menú de archivo** file menu; **menú de ayuda** help menu; **menú desplegable** drop-down o pull-down menu; **menú de fichero** file menu; **menú de impresión** print menu; **menú (de) inicio** start menu; **menú de opciones** options menu

menudear *vi & vt Andes, Méx* to sell retail

menudeo *nm Andes, Méx* retailing; **vender al menudeo** to sell retail; **venta al menudeo** retailing

❝

Las ventas al **menudeo** aumentaron en julio pasado 3.8 por ciento en términos reales en relación con igual mes del año pasado, donde destacan las de farmacias, supermercados, papelerías y librerías, gaseras y refacciones para vehículos.

❞

mercado *nm* (**a**) ECON, MKTG *(lugar)* market ❏ **mercado actual** existing market; **mercado de alquiler** rental market; **mercado de bienes de capital** capital goods market; **mercado cautivo** captive market; **mercado de cereales** grain market; **mercado competitivo** competitive market; **mercado común** common market; **Mercado Común Centroamericano** Central American Common Market, = Central American free trade agreement between Costa Rica, El Salvador, Guatemala, Honduras and Nicaragua; **Mercado Común del Sur** Mercosur, = South American free trade agreement between Argentina, Brazil, Paraguay and Uruguay; **mercado de consumo** consumer market; **mercado de control** control market; **mercado de distribución** distribution market; **mercado emergente** emerging market; **mercado de empresa** business market; **mercado en expansión** growth market; **mercado de exportación** export market; **mercado exterior** foreign market; **mercado extrabancario** nonbank market; **mercado financiero** financial market; **mercado genérico** generic market; **mercado global** global market; **mercado hipotecario** mortgage market; **mercado industrial** industrial market; **mercado de la información** information market; **mercado inmobiliario** housing market, property market; **mercado interbancario** interbank market; **mercado interior, mercado interno** domestic o home market; **mercado juvenil** youth market; **mercado laboral** labour market; **mercado libre** free market, open market; **mercado de masas** mass market; **mercado mayorista, mercado al por mayor** wholesale market; **mercado monetario libre** open money market; **mercado monopolizado** monopoly market; **mercado muerto** dead market; **mercado mundial** world market; **mercado nacional** domestic o national market;

mercado negro black market; **mercado objetivo** target market; **mercado del petróleo** oil market; **mercado potencial** available o potential market; **mercado principal** core market; **mercado de prueba** test market; **mercado de referecia** benchmark market; **mercado de segunda mano** second-hand market; **mercado target** target market; **mercado de trabajo** labour o job market; UE **mercado único** single market

(**b**) BOLSA **mercado de acciones** stock o share market; **mercado alcista, mercado al alza** bull market; **mercado a la baja, mercado bajista** bear market; **mercado bursátil** stock market; **mercado de cambios** exchange market; **mercado de cambio doble** dual exchange market; **mercado de cambio de moneda** currency exchange market; **mercado de capitales** capital market; **mercado al contado** spot market; *Esp* **mercado a crédito** = market for transactions involving deferred payment; **mercado deprimido** heavy market; **mercado de derivados** derivative market; **mercado de descuento** discount market; **mercado de divisas** currency market, foreign exchange market; **mercado de divisas a plazo** forward exchange market; **mercado de divisas a término** forward exchange market; **mercado de eurodivisas** euro-currency market; **mercado extrabursátil** over-the-counter market, unlisted securities market; **mercados financieros** financial markets; **mercado fuera de hora** after-hours market; **mercado de futuros** futures market; **mercado de futuros financieros** financial futures market; **mercado gris** grey market; **mercado informal** unregulated market; **mercado de intermediarios** middleman's market; **mercado de inversiones** investment market; **mercado de materias primas** commodity market; **mercado de metales** metal(s) market; **mercado monetario** money market; *Col* **mercado mostrador** over-the-counter market, unlisted securities market; **mercado de nuevas emisiones** new issue market; **mercado de opciones** options market; **mercado del oro** gold market; **mercado paralelo** parallel market; **mercado primario** primary market; **mercado de productos básicos** commodity market; **mercado de renta fija** fixed-interest market; **mercado de renta variable** equity o equities market; **mercado secundario** secondary market; **mercado terminal** terminal market; **mercado a término** spot market; **mercado de valores** securities market; **mercado de valores del Estado** government securites market, *Br* gilts market, gilt-edged market; **mercado de vendedores** seller's market

❝

La detención del ex presidente iraquí Sadam Husein ha traído nuevos máximos anuales a los **mercados** europeos e incluso permitió, durante unas horas, apuntalar al dólar. En el Bolsa de Madrid, el Ibex 35 ha logrado un nuevo máximo anual pero no ha podido mantener al cierre la cota de los 7.500 puntos que ha rebasado esta mañana. **"**

mercadotecnia *nf* marketing ❑ *mercadotecnia directa* direct marketing; *mercadotecnia ecológica* green marketing; *mercadotecnia electrónica* e-marketing; *mercadotecnia estratégica* strategic marketing; *mercadotecnia global* global marketing; *mercadotecnia industrial* industrial marketing; *mercadotecnia personalizada* customized marketing; *mercadotecnia telefónica* telemarketing; *mercadotecnia viral* viral marketing

mercancía *nf* merchandise, goods; **transporte de mercancías** freight transport ❑ *mercancías al contado* spot goods; *mercancías de contrabando* contraband (goods); *mercancías de exportación* export goods; *mercancías extranjeras* foreign goods; *mercancías a granel* bulk goods; *mercancías de importación* import goods; *mercancías al por mayor* wholesale goods; *mercancías paletizadas* palletized goods; *mercancías peligrosas* hazardous products; *mercancías perecederas* perishable goods, perishables; *mercancías en tránsito* goods in transit

mercantil *adj* mercantile, commercial

mercantilismo *nm* ECON mercantilism

merchandising *nm* merchandising

Mercosur *nm* (*abrev de* **Mercado Común del Sur**) Mercosur, = South American free trade agreement between Argentina, Brazil, Paraguay and Uruguay

mérito *nm* merit

merma *nf* (*de ingresos, productividad*) fall; (*de calidad*) deterioration; **se ha producido una merma en los ingresos** there has been a reduction o fall in income, income has fallen

MerVal *nm* (**a**) (*abrev de* **Mercado de Valores de Buenos Aires**) Buenos Aires Securities Market (**b**) (*abrev de* **Índice del Mercado de Valores de Buenos Aires**) MerVal index, = Buenos Aires Securities Market Index

mes *nm* month ❑ BOLSA *mes de entrega* delivery month; *mes natural* calendar month

mesa *nf* (**a**) (*mueble*) table; (*de oficina, despacho*) desk ❑ *mesa de negociaciones* negotiating table; *mesa redonda* round table; *mesa de reuniones* conference table (**b**) (*comité*) board, committee; (*en un debate*) panel (**c**) Am *mesa de dinero* money market desk

meta *nf* (*objetivo*) target, goal

metal *nm* (*material*) metal ❑ *metales y*

minerales hard commodities; *metales preciosos* precious metals

metódico, -a *adj* methodical

método *nm* method ❑ CONT *método de amortización lineal* straight-line depreciation method; *método del camino crítico* critical path method; *método contable* accounting method; *método de distribución* distribution method; *método de fabricación* manufacturing method; *método de funcionamiento* method of operation; *método de inventario* inventory method; CONT *método lineal* straight-line method; MKTG *método de muestreo* sampling method; CONT *método de partida doble* double-entry method; CONT *método de partida simple* single-entry method; *método no probabilístico* non-probability method; CONT *método del saldo decreciente* diminishing balance method; *método de selección* selection method; *método de sondeo* polling method

metodología *nf* methodology

métrico, -a *adj* metric

metro *nm* (*unidad*) metre ❑ *metro cuadrado* square metre; *metro cúbico* cubic metre; *metro lineal* linear metre

MexDer *nm* (*abrev de* **Mercado Mexicano de Derivados, S.A. de C.V**) Mexican derivatives exchange o market

MHz (*abrev de* **megahercio**) MHz

Mibor, mibor *nm* FIN (*abrev de* **Madrid Inter-Bank Offered Rate**) Mibor

"
El euribor y **mibor**, principales índices de referencia utilizados por el mercado para calcular el tipo de las hipotecas experimentaron en octubre su quinta rebaja consecutiva, hasta situarse en el 3,126% y 3,127%, respectivamente. Con el nuevo recorte, los dos índices se colocan en las cotas más bajas registradas desde el mes de julio de 1999, cuando el euribor se situó en el 3,030% y el **mibor** en el 3,018%, respectivamente. **"**

microchip *nm* microchip

microcomputadora *nf* Am microcomputer

microcrédito *nm* microcredit

microeconomía *nf* microeconomics

microeconómico, -a *adj* microeconomic

microempresa *nf* microenterprise, microbusiness

"
Los microcréditos —préstamos de pequeña cuantía— tratan de facilitar la puesta en marcha de pequeños negocios

denominados **microempresas**, que en la actualidad ocupan entre el 40% y el 60% de la población activa de los países iberoamericanos. **"**

microficha nf microfiche

microfilm, microfilme nm microfilm

microinformática nf microcomputing

microordenador nm Esp microcomputer

micropréstamo nm microloan

microprocesador nm microprocessor

microprocesamiento nm microprocessing

miembro nm (integrante) member; **los países miembros de la OCDE** OECD member states o countries ❑ **miembro asociado** associate member; **miembro del comité ejecutivo** executive member; **miembro del consejo (de administración)** board member; **miembro corporativo** corporate member; **miembro fundador** founder member; **miembro de la junta** board member; **miembro liquidador** clearing member; **miembro permanente** permanent member; **miembro de pleno derecho** full member

mil núm thousand; **mil millones** a billion

millón nm million

mina nf (a) (de mineral) mine (b) (cosa rentable) gold mine ❑ **mina de oro** gold mine, money spinner

mineral 1 adj mineral
    2 nm (a) (sustancia) mineral (b) (mena) ore; **mineral de hierro** iron ore

minería nf (a) (técnica) mining (b) (sector) mining industry (c) INFORM **minería de datos** data mining

minicomputadora nm Am minicomputer

MiniDisc® nm inv MiniDisc®

minimizar vt (gastos, pérdidas, riesgos) to minimize

mínimo, -a 1 adj (a) (lo más bajo posible o necesario) (salario, tarifa, tipo) minimum; **el número mínimo de acciones** the minimum number of shares (b) (muy pequeño) (valor) minimal
    2 nm minimum; **un mínimo de dos años de experiencia** a minimum of two years' experience; **reducir algo al mínimo** to reduce sth to a minimum; **la inflación ha alcanzado un mínimo histórico** inflation is at an all-time low; **la oficina funciona con un mínimo de personal** the office is run by a skeleton staff ❑ **mínimo familiar** (en impuestos) dependent family tax exemption; **mínimo de mercado** market minimum; **mínimo personal** (en impuestos) personal tax exemption

miniordenador nm Esp minicomputer

ministerial adj (cartera, orden) ministerial;

equipo ministerial cabinet

ministerio nm Br ministry, US department ❑ **Ministerio de Agricultura** Ministry of Agriculture, Br ≃ Department for Environment, Food and Rural Affairs, US ≃ Department of Agriculture; **Ministerio de Asuntos Exteriores** Ministry of Foreign Affairs, Br ≃ Foreign Office, US ≃ State Department; **Ministerio de Economía** Ministry of Economic Affairs, Br ≃ Treasury, US ≃ Treasury Department; **Ministerio de Hacienda** Ministry of Economic Affairs, Br ≃ Treasury, US ≃ Treasury Department; **Ministerio de Industria** Ministry of Industry, Br ≃ Department of Trade and Industry; **Ministerio de Trabajo** Ministry of Employment, Br ≃ Department of Employment, US ≃ Department of Labor

ministro, -a nm,f Br minister, US secretary ❑ **Ministro de Agricultura** Minister of Agriculture, Br ≃ Minister for the Environment, Food and Rural Affairs, US ≃ Secretary of Agriculture; **Ministro de Comercio** Minister of Trade, Br ≃ Secretary of State for Trade and Industry, US ≃ Secretary of Commerce; **Ministro de Economía** Minister for Economic Affairs, Br ≃ Chancellor of the Exchequer, US ≃ Secretary of the Treasury; **Ministro de Hacienda** Minister for Economic Affairs, Br ≃ Chancellor of the Exchequer, US ≃ Secretary of the Treasury; **Ministro de Industria** Minister for Industry, Br ≃ Secretary of State for Trade and Industry; **Ministro de Trabajo** Minister of Employment, Br ≃ Secretary of State for Employment, US ≃ Secretary of Labor

minitorre nf INFORM mini tower

minoría nf minority; **estar en minoría** to be in a minority ❑ **minoría de bloqueo** blocking minority

minorista, Chile, Méx **menorista 1** adj retail; **comercio minorista** retail trade
    2 nmf retailer ❑ **minorista independiente** independent retailer

"

Con respecto a abril de 2002 y entre los Estados para los que hay datos disponibles, las ventas del comercio **minorista** crecieron en todos los países, excepto en Portugal, donde bajaron un 0,6%, y en Bélgica, con un 0,3%. Las tasas de crecimiento más fuertes se registraron en Austria (7,3%), Suecia (4,7%) e Irlanda (4,6%).

"

minoritario, -a adj minority; **un grupo minoritario** a minority group

minúsculas nfpl lower case; **en minúsculas** in lower case

minusvalía nf capital loss

minuta nf (factura) fee

miopía *nf miopía en (el) marketing* marketing myopia

misceláneo, -a *adj* miscellaneous

misión *nf* (**a**) *(delegación)* mission □ *misión diplomática* diplomatic delegation *o Br* mission (**b**) *(declaración)* mission

mixto, -a *adj (capital)* mixed; **financiación mixta** public-private financing

mobbing *nm* bullying, mobbing

mobiliario *nm* furniture □ *mobilario de oficina* office furniture

moción *nf (en asamblea, debate)* motion; **presentar una moción** to present *o* bring a motion, *Br* to table a motion

modalidad *nf modalidad de pago* method of payment

modelo 1 *adj (fábrica)* model
   2 *nm* (**a**) *(producto)* model; **nuestro último modelo** our latest model □ MKTG *modelo AIDA* AIDA model; *modelo familiar* family model; *modelo de muestra* demonstration model; MKTG *modelo de prestigio* prestige model
   (**b**) *(ejemplo)* specimen □ *modelo de factura* specimen invoice; *modelo de firma* specimen signature
   (**c**) *(teórico)* model □ *modelo del camino crítico* critical path model; MKTG *modelo de comportamiento de compra* buying *o* purchasing behaviour model; *modelo corporativo* corporate model; *modelo de decisiones* decision model; *modelo econométrico* econometric model; *modelo económico* economic model; *modelo matemático* mathematical model

módem *nm* INFORM modem □ *módem externo* external modem; *módem fax* fax modem; *módem interno* internal modem; *módem RDSI* ISDN modem

moderación *nf* moderation □ *moderación salarial* wage restraint

moderado, -a *adj (precio ingresos, aumento)* moderate

moderador, -ora *nm,f (de debate)* moderator, facilitator

moderar *vt (debate)* to moderate, to facilitate

modernización *nf* modernization

modernizar 1 *vt* to modernize
   2 modernizarse *vpr* to modernize

moderno, -a *adj (maquinaria, método, diseño)* modern, up-to-date

modificación *nf* modification, alteration; **han introducido una serie de modificaciones en la ley** they introduced a number of amendments to the law

modificar *vt* to modify, to alter

modo (**a**) *modo de empleo* instructions for use

(**b**) INFORM mode □ *modo de arranque* start-up mode; *modo continuo* continous mode; *modo (de) diálogo* dialogue mode; *modo gráfico* graphic mode; *modo de inserción* insert mode; *modo de reposo* sleep *o* standby mode; *modo de sobreescribir* overwrite mode; *modo de texto* text mode

molestia *nf* **(les rogamos) disculpen las molestias (causadas)** we apologize for any inconvenience (caused); **ocasionar** *o* **causar molestias a alguien** to cause sb trouble

moneda *nf* (**a**) *(pieza)* coin; **moneda de un euro** one-euro coin □ *moneda falsa* counterfeit coin
   (**b**) *(divisa)* currency □ *moneda común* common currency; *moneda controlada* managed currency; *moneda convertible* convertible currency; *moneda corriente* legal tender; *moneda de cuenta* currency of account; *moneda de curso legal* legal tender; *moneda débil* weak currency; *moneda escasa* scarce currency; *moneda extranjera* foreign currency; *moneda fiduciaria* fiat currency; *moneda fraccionaria* fractional money; *moneda fuerte* strong currency; *moneda inflacionista* inflationary currency; *moneda internacional* international currency; *moneda nacional* national *o* local currency; UE *moneda única* single currency; UE *Antes* **moneda verde** green currency

monedero *nm* purse □ *monedero electrónico* electronic purse

monetario, -a *adj* monetary

monetarismo *nm* ECON monetarism

monetarista *adj & nmf* ECON monetarist

monitor *nm* INFORM monitor □ *monitor digital* digital display; *monitor de pantalla plana* flat monitor, flat-screen monitor

monitorear *vt* to monitor

monitoreo *nm* monitoring

monopólico = **monopolista**

monopolio *nm* monopoly; **tener el monopolio de algo** to have a monopoly of *o* on sth; **formar un monopolio** to form a monopoly □ *monopolio comercial* commercial monopoly; *monopolio del Estado* state monopoly; *monopolio de explotación* operating monopoly; *monopolio de fabricación* manufacturing monopoly; *monopolio industrial* industrial monopoly; *monopolio de ventas* sales monopoly

monopolista, monopolístico, -a, monopólico, -a *adj* monopolist; **control monopolista** monopoly control

monopolizar *vt (mercado)* to monopolize, to corner

monopsonio *nm* ECON monopsony

montaje *nm (de máquina, estructura)* assembly

montante *nm* total (amount) ❑ UE ***montantes compensatorios*** compensatory amounts

montar *vt* (**a**) *(ensamblar) (máquina, mueble)* to assemble (**b**) *(organizar) (negocio, empresa)* to set up, to start up; *(tienda)* to open; *(exposición)* to organize

monto *nm* total

moratoria *nf* moratorium

mordida *nf CAm, Méx Fam (soborno)* bribe, *Br* backhander; **cobrar mordida** to receive a bribe *o Br* backhander

morosidad *nf* defaulting; **se ha disparado el índice de morosidad** the percentage of bad debt has shot up

> **❝**
> Los bancos contaban con 146.017 millones en hipotecarios, un 19,4% más, lo que significa que las cajas siguen ganando cuota de mercado a sus competidores y no parecen dispuestas a seguir los insistentes consejos del gobernador del Banco de España, que pide un freno en esta materia para evitar una **morosidad** futura.
> **❞**

moroso, -a 1 *adj* defaulting
  2 *nm,f* defaulter, bad debtor

mosaico *nm* INFORM **poner en mosaico** to tile

mostrador *nm (en tienda)* counter; *(en aeropuerto)* desk ❑ ***mostrador de caja*** cash desk; ***mostrador de facturación*** check-in desk; ***mostrador de información*** information desk; ***mostrador de recepción*** reception desk; ***mostrador de reservas*** reservation desk; ***mostrador de saldos*** bargain counter; ***mostrador de ventas*** sales counter

motivación *nf* motivation; **la motivación del consumidor/del personal** consumer/staff motivation

motivador *nm* MKTG ***motivador de compra*** purchasing motivator

motivar *vt (estimular)* to motivate

motivo *nm (causa)* reason (**de** for); **la situación económica se ha vuelto a convertir en motivo de preocupación** the economy has once again become a cause for concern ❑ MKTG ***motivo de compra*** buying motive

motor *nm* (**a**) *(máquina)* engine, motor (**b**) *(fuerza)* driving force; **el motor de la economía** the driving force in the economy ❑ ***motor de crecimiento*** growth driver (**c**) INFORM ***motor de búsqueda*** search engine

mouse *nm inv Am* INFORM mouse ❑ ***mouse inalámbrico*** wireless mouse; ***mouse de infrarrojos*** infrared mouse; ***mouse óptico*** optical mouse

móvil 1 *adj (teléfono)* mobile
  2 *nm* mobile

movilización *nf* (**a**) *(de capital)* mobilization (**b**) *(de obreros)* protest, industrial action; **han anunciado movilizaciones** they have announced that they will take industrial action

movilizar 1 *vt* (**a**) *(capital)* to mobilize (**b**) *(recursos, equipo, personal)* to deploy (**c**) *(como protesta)* to mobilize
  2 movilizarse *vpr (obreros)* to mobilize

movimiento *nm* (**a**) *(en negocio, mercado, empresa)* activity; *(de personal, mercancías)* turnover; *(en cuenta bancaria)* transaction; *(en contabilidad)* operation; **había poco movimiento en el parqué** there was little activity on the trading floor; **últimos movimientos** *(opción en cajero automático)* print mini-statement ❑ FIN ***movimiento alcista*** upward movement; FIN ***movimiento a la baja*** downward movement; ***movimiento de capitales*** capital movements; ***movimiento de personal*** staff turnover
  (**b**) IND *(hecho por empleado)* motion

MP3 *nm (abrev de* **MPEG1 Audio Layer 3***)* MP3; **reproductor de MP3** MP3 player

MPEG *nm* INFORM *(abrev de* **Moving Pictures Expert Group***)* MPEG

MS-DOS *nm* INFORM *(abrev de* **Microsoft Disk Operating System***)* MS-DOS

mudanza *nf* move; **una empresa de mudanzas** a furniture remover

mudarse *vpr* to move

mueble *adj* **bienes muebles** movable property

muellaje *nm* wharf dues

muelle *nm* (**a**) *(en puerto)* dock, quay, wharf; **en muelle** ex dock, ex quay, ex wharf (**b**) *(de carga y descarga)* loading bay

muerto, -a *adj (mercado, periodo)* dead

muestra *nf* (**a**) *(exposición)* display, exhibition
  (**b**) *(de producto)* sample; **una muestra gratuita** *o* **de regalo** a free sample ❑ ***muestra de promoción*** promotional sample
  (**c**) *(en estadística, marketing)* sample ❑ ***muestra aleatoria*** random sample; ***muestra no aleatoria*** non-random sample; ***muestra de área*** area sample; ***muestra de control*** check sample; ***muestra de cuota*** quota sample; ***muestra dirigida*** purposive sample; ***muestra estándar*** standard sample; ***muestra estratificada*** stratified sample; ***muestra fiel*** true sample; ***muestra por grupos*** cluster sample; ***muestra piloto*** pilot sample; ***muestra probabilística*** probability sample; ***muestra no probabilística*** non-probability sample; ***muestra representativa*** representative sample, cross-section; ***muestra testigo*** check sample

muestrario *nm* pattern book

muestreo *nm* MKTG sampling ❑ ***muestreo de aceptación*** acceptance sampling; ***muestreo aleatorio*** random sampling; ***muestreo no***

aleatorio non-random sampling; *muestreo por áreas* area sampling; *muestreo de conveniencia* convenience sampling; *muestreo por cuotas* quota sampling; *muestreo dirigido* purposive sampling; *muestreo estratificado* stratified sampling; *muestreo por grupos* cluster sampling; *muestreo intencional* judg(e)ment sampling; *muestreo probabilístico* probability sampling; *muestreo no probabilístico* non-probability sampling

mujer *nf mujer de negocios* businesswoman; *mujer trabajadora* working woman

multiconferencia *nf* TEL conference call

multidifusión *nf* INFORM, TV multicast

multidivisa *nf* UE multicurrency

multifuncional *adj* multifunctional

multilateral *adj* multilateral

multimedia INFORM **1** *adj inv* multimedia **2** *nm o nf* multimedia

multinacional *adj & nf* multinational

múltiple *adj* multiple

múltiplex *adj inv & nm inv* TEL multiplex

multipropiedad *nf* multiple ownership

multipuesto *adj inv* INFORM multi-terminal, multi-station

multitarea *adj inv & nf* INFORM multitasking

multiusuario *adj* INFORM multi-user

mundial *adj (política, economía, líder)* world; *(tratado, organización)* worldwide

mundialización *nf* globalization

mundo *nm* (**a**) *(la Tierra, el universo)* world; **ha vendido miles de discos en todo el mundo** she has sold thousands of records worldwide *o* all over the world (**b**) *(ámbito, actividad)* world; **el mundo empresarial** *o* **de los negocios,** *RP* **el mundo empresario** the business world

municipal *adj (elecciones)* municipal, local; *(impuesto)* local, *Br* council, *US* municipal

municipio *nm* (**a**) *(corporación)* local council (**b**) *(edificio)* town hall, *US* city hall (**c**) *(territorio)* town, municipality

mutua *nf Br* friendly society, *US* mutual benefit society ❑ *mutua de accidentes* mutual accident insurance company; *mutua de seguros* mutual insurance company

mutualidad *nf (asociación) Br* friendly society, *US* mutual benefit society

mutuo, -a *adj* mutual; **de mutuo acuerdo** by mutual *o* joint agreement

Nn

naciente *adj (industria, empresa)* fledgling

nación *nf (pueblo, país)* nation ❏ ECON *nación acreedora* creditor nation; ECON *nación deudora, nación endeudada* debtor nation; ECON *nación más favorecida* most favoured nation; *Naciones Unidas* United Nations

nacional *adj (gobierno, renta, línea aérea)* national; *(mercado, noticias)* domestic, home; *(vuelo)* domestic; **consuma productos nacionales** buy British/Spanish/*etc* products

nacionalización *nf (de banca, bienes)* nationalization

nacionalizar 1 *vt (banca, bienes)* to nationalize **2 nacionalizarse** *vpr* **nacionalizarse español** to become a Spanish citizen, to acquire Spanish nationality

NAFTA *nm (abrev de* **North American FreeTrade Agreement)** NAFTA

narcodólares *nmpl* narcodollars

Nasdaq *nm* BOLSA *(abrev de* **National Association of Securities Dealers Automated Quotation)** Nasdaq

natural *adj* **(a)** *(recursos, bajas, economía)* natural **(b)** *(año, mes)* calendar; **30 días naturales de vacaciones** 30 working days' holiday *o US* vacation

navegación *nf* **(a)** *(en río, mar, aire)* navigation **(b)** INFORM *(en página web)* navigation; **navegación por Internet** surfing the Net

navegador *nm* INFORM (Web) browser

navegar *vi* INFORM **navegar por Internet** to surf *o* browse the Net

naviera *nf (compañía)* shipping company

naviero, -a *adj* shipping

navío *nm* vessel

necesidad *nf (en general)* need; **en caso de necesidad** in case of need; **atendemos las necesidades de la pequeña empresa** we cater for the needs of small companies; **un artículo de primera necesidad** a basic *o* staple commodity ❏ *necesidades de capital circulante* working capital requirements; *necesidades de crédito* borrowing requirements

necesitar *vt* to need, to require; **se necesita camarero/dependiente** *(en letrero)* waiter/shop assistant wanted

negativa *nf (a sugerencia, oferta, propuesta)* refusal; **su negativa a negociar** their refusal to negotiate

negativo, -a *adj (amortización, tipos de interés)* negative; **el saldo de su cuenta es negativo** your account is in debit

negligencia *nf* negligence ❏ *negligencia grave* gross negligence; *negligencia profesional* professional negligence

negociable *adj (sueldo, tarifa, letra de cambio)* negotiable

negociación *nf* **(a)** *(para obtener acuerdo)* negotiation; **estar en negociaciones con alguien** to be in negotiation with sb ❏ *negociación colectiva* collective bargaining; *negociación colectiva libre* free collective bargaining; *negociaciones comerciales* trade negotiations; *negociación salarial* pay bargaining **(b)** BOLSA trading ❏ *negociación al alza* bull trading; *negociación a la baja* bear trading; *negociación electrónica* electronic trading; *negociación de futuros* futures trading; *negociación en línea* on-line trading; *negociación de opciones* options trading; *negociación a plazo* forward trading *o* dealing; *negociación telefónica* telephone dealing; *negociación a término* forward trading *o* dealing; *negociación a última hora* late trading **(c)** *Méx (empresa)* business

> “
> El euro se mantuvo sin grandes cambios en una jornada de escasa **negociación**, si bien perdió la marca de los 1,14 dólares al mismo tiempo que algunos inversores no ven un cambio de tendencia a su favor.
> ”

negociado, -a *adj* BOLSA *(acciones)* traded

negociador, -ora 1 *adj* negotiating; **una comisión negociadora** a negotiating committee **2** *nm,f* negotiator

negociar 1 *vt (acuerdo, préstamo, precio)* to negotiate **2** *vi* **(a)** *(en discusión)* to negotiate, to bargain **(con** with) **(b)** *(comerciar)* to do business **(con** with)

negocio *nm* **(a)** *(empresa)* business; **un negocio rentable** a profitable business ❏ *negocio familiar* family business

(**b**) *(transacción)* deal, (business) transaction; **hacer negocio** to do well; **un negocio redondo** a great bargain, an excellent deal
(**c**) **negocios** *(actividad)* business; **el negocio principal de la empresa** the company's core business; **el mundo de los negocios** the business world; **un viaje de negocios** a business trip; **hacer negocios con** to do business with; **estoy aquí por cuestiones de negocios** I'm here on business ◻ *negocios transfronterizos* cross-border business
(**d**) *RP (tienda)* store

negrita IMPRENTA **1** *adj* **letra negrita** bold (type), bold face
2 *nf* bold (type), boldface; **en negrita** in bold, in boldface

nervioso, -a *adj* BOLSA *(mercado)* nervous, jumpy

netear *vt Fam* FIN to net out, to net against

netiqueta *nf* INFORM netiquette

neto, -a 1 *adj (beneficio, ingresos, peso)* net
2 *nm* **neto patrimonial** net worth

neuronal *adj* INFORM neural

nicho *nm* MKTG niche ◻ *nicho de mercado* niche market

NIF *nm Esp* (*abrev de* **Número de Identificación Fiscal**) = tax identification number, tax ID number

nivel *nm* level, standard; **un alto nivel de desempleo/ingresos** high unemployment/income; **estar al nivel/por debajo del nivel exigido** to be up to/below standard; **a nivel europeo** at a European level; **una campaña realizada a nivel mundial** a worldwide campaign; **una reunión al más alto nivel** a meeting at the highest level, a top-level meeting ◻ INFORM *nivel de acceso* access level; *nivel de existencias* inventory *o Br* stock level; *nivel general de precios* general price level; *nivel general de salarios* general wage level; *nivel de incorporación (a empleo)* entry level; *nivel mínimo de existencias* minimum stock level; *nivel de necesidades* need level; *nivel óptimo* optimum; *niveles de personal* staffing levels; *nivel de precios* price point *o* level; *nivel salarial* salary level *o* grade; *nivel de ventas previsto* forecast sales level; *nivel de vida* standard of living, living standards

nivelación *nf (de impuestos)* equalization; **están pidiendo la nivelación de salarios con el resto del sector** they are calling for their salaries to be brought into line with the rest of the industry

nivelar *vt (impuestos)* to bring to the same level, to equalize; **quieren nivelar los sueldos con los de la empresa privada** they want to bring salaries into line with those in the private sector

nodo *nm* INFORM node

nombramiento *nm* appointment

nombrar *vt (para cargo, comisión)* to appoint, to nominate

nombre *nm* (**a**) *(de persona, empresa, cuenta)* name; **a nombre de** *(carta, sobre, paquete)* addressed to; *(cheque)* made out to; *(cuenta bancaria)* in the name of; **las acciones están a mi nombre** the shares are in my name; **quiero abrir una cuenta a nombre de mi hijo** I'd like to open an account for my son; **en nombre de** *(representando a)* on behalf of ◻ *nombre y apellidos* full name; INFORM *nombre de archivo* file name; INFORM *nombre de campo* field name; *nombre comercial* trade name; *nombre completo* full name; *nombre del depositario* nominee name; INFORM *nombre de dominio* domain name; INFORM *nombre de fichero* file name; *nombre genérico* generic name; *nombre de pila* first *o* Christian name; *nombre del puesto* job title; *nombre registrado* registered name; *nombre de soltera* maiden name; INFORM *nombre de usuario* user name
(**b**) *(fama)* name; **tener buen/mal nombre** to have a good/bad name

nómina *nf* (**a**) *(lista de empleados)* payroll; **estar en nómina** to be on the payroll *o* staff (**b**) *(pago)* wage packet, wages (**c**) *(hoja de salario)* pay slip

> **"**
> Los directivos españoles han sido los europeos que más han ajustado sus subidas salariales anuales a la inflación del país. 252.000 euros es la **nómina** media que perciben los máximos responsables de las empresas, que siguen recibiendo la mayor parte de su retribución en fijo.
> **"**

nominación *nf* nomination

nominal 1 *adj* nominal
2 *nm* ECON face value, nominal value

nominar *vt* to nominate

norma *nf (patrón, modelo)* standard; *(regla)* rule, regulation; **este producto no cumple la norma europea** this product does not meet European standards; **tenemos por norma contratar únicamente profesionales** our policy is to hire professionals only; **esa es la norma que se sigue en el sector** that is standard practice in the industry ◻ *normas contables* accounting rules; *normas de la empresa* company rules; *normas fiscales* tax rules; *normas internas* internal regulations; *normas laborales* work standard; *normas de obligado cumplimiento* compulsory standards; *normas presupuestarias* budgetary standards; *normas de seguridad* safety regulations

normalización *nf* standardization

normalizar *vt* to standardize

normativa *nf* regulations; **según la normativa vigente** under current rules *o* regulations ❑ *normativa comercial* trading standards; *normativa fiscal* tax regulations *o* rules; *normativa laboral* employment regulations

nota *nf* (**a**) *(apunte)* note; **tomar nota de algo** to note sth down ❑ *nota de abono* credit note *o* memo; *nota aclaratoria* explanatory note; *nota de adeudo* debit advice; *nota bene* nota bene, N.B.; *nota de cargo* debit note; *nota de cobertura* cover note; *nota de consignación* consignment note; *nota de cortesía* compliments slip; *nota de entrega* delivery note, *Br* docket; *nota de envío* dispatch note; *nota de liquidación* settlement note; *nota al margen* marginal note; *nota de peso* weight note; *nota a pie de página* footnote; *nota de prensa* press release; *Méx nota de remisión* delivery note; FIN *nota simple* = uncertified copy of registry entry; *nota de venta* sales note (**b**) *(memorándum)* memo, memorandum ❑ *nota interna* internal memo (**c**) *(cuenta) (en restaurante) Br* bill, *US* check ❑ *Méx nota de consumo* expenses claim; *nota de gastos* expenses claim

notaría *nf Esp, CAm, Carib, Méx* (**a**) *(profesión)* profession of notary (**b**) *(oficina)* notary's office

notarial *adj Esp, CAm, Carib, Méx* notarial

notario, -a *nm,f Esp, CAm, Carib, Méx* notary (public)

noticia *nf* (**a**) *(información, hecho)* news; **una noticia** a piece of news (**b**) **las noticias** *(programa)* the news

noticiario, *Am* **noticiero**, *Andes, RP* **noticioso** *nm (programa)* news

notificación *nf* notification ❑ *notificación de abono en cuenta* payment advice; *notificación bancaria* bank notification; BOLSA *notificación de ejercicio* exercise notice; *notificación oficial* formal notice; *notificación de transferencia* transfer advice

notificar *vt* to notify; **nos notificó la congelación de salarios** he gave us notice that salaries were to be frozen

notoriedad *nf* MKTG *notoriedad de la marca* brand awareness

‟
"Con una audiencia acumulada de 37.000 millones de telespectadores, este acontecimiento es una ocasión única para consolidar la **notoriedad de la marca** Danone en el mundo y especialmente en todos los países en los que ya está implantado el grupo".
„

novación *nf* remortgaging *(with original lender*

on different terms), novation

novato, -a *nm,f* novice, beginner; INFORM newbie

núcleo *nm* centre; **un núcleo de pobreza** an area with an extremely high level of poverty, an area where poverty is concentrated ❑ *núcleo duro* hard core; *núcleo industrial* industrial centre; *núcleo de producción* production centre

nuevo, -a 1 *adj* new; **es el nuevo director** he's the new manager; **los nuevos medios (de comunicación)** the new media ❑ *nueva economía* new economy; *nueva empresa* start-up company; **la nueva empresa está dando impulso a la economía** start-up companies are boosting the economy
2 *nm,f* newcomer

‟
Cuando se dio la mega-fusión entre America Online y Time Warner se creyó que el mundo presenciaba el triunfo o la prueba contundente de la supremacía de la **nueva economía** sobre la economía tradicional. La compra de AOL finalmente se cerró en 106 mil 200 millones de dólares. Bajo otro cristal de observación, hoy podría interpretarse como la primera señal de la reconcentración del poder empresarial. ¿Se trata de un retorno al pasado?
„

nulidad *nf (no validez)* nullity

nulo, -a *adj* null and void, invalid; **nulo y sin valor** null and void

numerar *vt* to number

numérico, -a *adj* numerical, numeric

número *nm* number ❑ INFORM *número de acceso* access number; *número de afiliación a la Seguridad Social Br* National Insurance number, *US* social security number; INFORM *número ASCII* ASCII number; *número de cheque* cheque number; *número de cuenta* account number; TEL *número directo* direct-dial number; *número de empleados* staffing level; *número de extensión* extension number; *número de fax* fax number; *Esp número de identificación fiscal* = tax identification number, tax ID number; *número de identificación personal* PIN (number); INFORM *número de Internet* Internet number; *RP número de interno* extension number; INFORM *número IP* IP number; *número de lote* BOLSA lot number; INFORM batch number; *número de matrícula* registration number; *números negros* the black; **en números negros** in the black; **siguen a la espera de los números negros** they are still waiting to make a profit; *número de pedido* order number; *número redondo* round figure; *número de referencia* reference number; *número de referencia del cliente* customer reference number; INFORM *número de registro* registration number; *número de reserva* booking o registration number; *números rojos* the red; **en números rojos** in the red; *número secreto* personal identification number; *número de serie* serial number; *número de solicitud* application number; *número de sucursal (de banco)* sort code; *número de tarjeta de crédito* credit card number; *número de teléfono* telephone number; *número de teléfono gratuito* Br Freephone number, US toll-free number; *número de vuelo* flight number

> 66
>
> Empresas que estaban implantadas en Argentina, que ya han pasado la crisis, están ahora en **números negros**. Seguramente, no alcanzaremos el 11% de crecimiento de las exportaciones que apuntamos en marzo pasado, pero la actividad será claramente positiva.
>
> 99

Oo

objetividad *nf* objectivity

objetivo, -a 1 *adj (público, precio)* target
  2 *nm (finalidad)* objective, aim; *(en cifras concretas)* target; **la medida tiene como objetivo facilitar la comunicación** the aim of the measure is to make communication easier, the measure is aimed at making communication easier □ *objetivo de beneficios* profit target; *objetivo global* overall objective; *objetivos de inversión* investment objectives; *objetivo a largo plazo* long-term objective; *objetivo de producción* production target; *objetivo publicitario* advertising target; *objetivo de ventas* sales target, sales objective

objeto *nm* (**a**) *(cosa) objetos personales* personal effects; *objetos de valor* valuables; *objetos de viaje* travel goods (**b**) *objeto social (de empresa)* corporate objects

obligación *nf* (**a**) FIN *(título)* bond, debenture □ *obligación del Estado* government bond; *obligación con garantía hipotecaria* collateralized mortgage obligation; *obligación sin garantía* unsecured debenture; *obligación sin garantía prendaria* naked debenture; *obligación garantizada* secured debenture; *obligación hipotecaria* debenture bond; *obligación nominativa* registered debenture o bond; *obligación participativa* participating bond; *obligaciones perpetuas* irredeemable bonds; *obligación de segundo rango* second debenture; *obligación simple* simple debenture; *obligación del Tesoro* Treasury bond, *Br* gilt; *obligación transferible* transferable bond
  (**b**) FIN *(pasivo) obligaciones a corto plazo* short-term liabilities
  (**c**) *(compromiso)* obligation, engagement; **cumplir con sus obligaciones** to fulfil one's obligations

> De los 5.852 millones de euros invertidos, 3.555 están en bonos a cinco años; 1.500, en bonos a tres años; 646, en **obligaciones** a diez o más años y 351, en letras del tesoro. En cualquier caso, y para el futuro inmediato, el gobierno tiene intención de plasmar en un reglamento tanto los valores que han de formar parte de 'la cartera', como su gestión.

obligacionista *nmf* FIN bondholder, debenture holder

obligado, -a 1 *adj* **obligado por contrato** bound by contract
  2 *nm* **obligado tributario** = party liable to pay tax

obligatorio, -a *adj* compulsory, obligatory

obra *nf (solar en construcción)* building site □ *obras públicas* public works

obrero, -a 1 *adj* **clase obrera** working class; **movimiento obrero** labour movement
  2 *nm,f* manual worker; *(en fábrica)* worker; *(en obra)* labourer □ *Am* **obrero calificado,** *Esp* **obrero cualificado** skilled worker; **obrero industrial** factory worker

obsequio *nm* gift, present □ *obsequio de empresa* corporate gift; *obsequio promocional* free gift

observación *nm* MKTG *observación personal* personal observation

obsolescencia *nf* obsolescence □ *obsolescencia incorporada* built-in obsolescence; *obsolescencia planificada* planned obsolescence; *obsolescencia programada* built-in obsolescence

obsoleto, -a *adj* obsolete

obtener *vt (cargo, información)* to get, to obtain; *(resultado)* to achieve, to obtain; *(ganancias)* to make; *(ventaja)* to gain, to obtain; **obtuvieron un precio muy alto por la venta del inmueble** they secured a high price when they sold the property

ocasión *nf* (**a**) *(oportunidad)* opportunity, chance; **una ocasión única** *o* **de oro** a golden opportunity (**b**) *(ganga)* bargain; **artículos de ocasión** bargains; **automóviles de ocasión** secondhand *o* used cars

OCDE *nf (abrev de* **Organización para la Cooperación y el Desarrollo Económico***)* OECD

ocio *nm (tiempo libre)* leisure; **la industria del ocio** the leisure industry

ocioso, -a *adj (empleado)* idle; *(capital)* unproductive

OCR *nm* INFORM *(abrev de* **optical character recognition***)* OCR

octavilla *nf* pamphlet, leaflet

OCU *nf (abrev de* **Organización de Consumidores y Usuarios***)* = Spanish consumers' association

ocultación *nf* FIN *ocultación de activos* concealment of assets; DER *ocultación de pruebas* concealment, non-disclosure

ocultar *vt* FIN *(bienes)* to conceal

ocupación *nf* (**a**) *(de edificio)* occupation; *(de cargo)* tenure; **los hoteles registraron una ocupación del 80 por ciento** the hotels reported occupancy rates of 80 percent □ INFORM *ocupación ilegal de dominios* cybersquatting (**b**) *(empleo)* occupation, job

ocupado, -a *adj* (**a**) *(atareado)* busy; **tengo toda la tarde ocupada** I'm busy all afternoon (**b**) *(teléfono)* Br engaged, US busy; *Méx, RP* **dar ocupado** to be Br engaged o US busy

ocupante *nmf* occupant, Br occupier; **ocupante ilegal de viviendas** squatter

ocupar **1** *vt* (**a**) *(tomar posesión de)* to occupy (**b**) *(cargo, puesto)* to hold (**c**) *(dar trabajo a)* to find o provide work for; **el sector turístico ocupa a la mayoría de la población del litoral** most of the people who live on the coast are employed in the tourist industry
2 ocuparse *vpr* **ocuparse de algo/alguien** to deal with sth/sb, to attend to sth/sb; **un contable se ocupa de las cuentas de la empresa** an accountant deals with o looks after the company's accounts

OEMA *nf* UE *(abrev de* **Oficina Europea del Medio Ambiente**) EEB

ofensiva *nf* offensive, attack

oferente *nmf* offeror

oferta *nf* (**a**) *(propuesta, ofrecimiento)* offer □ SEGUR *oferta de cobertura* offer of cover; *oferta en efectivo* cash offer; *oferta de empleo* job offer; *ofertas de empleo (en anuncio)* situations vacant, job opportunities; *oferta en firme* firm offer; *oferta de precio* price proposal; *Esp* *oferta pública de empleo* = announcement of job vacancies in civil service; *oferta de trabajo* job offer; *ofertas de trabajo (en anuncio)* situations vacant, job opportunities
(**b**) MKTG *(de producto)* **oferta (especial)** special offer; **estar de** o **en oferta** to be on offer □ *oferta en cupones* coupon offer; *oferta de descuento* money-off deal; *oferta de devolución (del dinero)* money-back offer; *oferta especial* special offer; *oferta especial de lanzamiento* trial offer; *oferta de introducción, oferta de lanzamiento* introductory offer; *oferta de muestras* sampling offer; *oferta de ocasión* bargain offer; *oferta de promoción* promotional offer; *oferta de reembolso (del dinero)* money-back offer
(**c**) BOLSA *oferta de acciones para empleados* Br share offer to employees, US stock offer to employees; *oferta inicial* initial stock; *oferta pública de acciones* public (share) offering; *oferta pública de adquisición (de acciones)* takeover bid; *oferta pública de adquisición amistosa* friendly takeover bid; *oferta pública de adquisición hostil* hostile takeover bid; *oferta pública inicial* initial public offering, IPO; *oferta pública de intercambio de acciones* public exchange offer; *oferta pública de venta de acciones* public offering; *oferta de venta directa de acciones* offer by prospectus
(**d**) *(en subastas)* bid; *(licitación)* tender □ *oferta final* closing bid; *oferta de precio* price bid
(**e**) ECON *(suministro)* supply; **la oferta y la demanda** supply and demand □ *oferta monetaria* money supply
(**f**) *(selección)* choice; **no hay much oferta en el mercado** there isn't much market choice

> **"**
> Terra, filial de Internet de Telefónica, será excluida del índice selectivo Ibex 35 a partir del próximo 24 de julio como consecuencia de la **oferta pública de adquisición** (opa) que lanzó la matriz el pasado 28 de mayo, según ha anunciado la Sociedad de Bolsas.
> **"**

ofertante *nm,f* offeror

off line *adv* INFORM off line

oficial¹ **1** *adj* official; **seguir los trámites oficiales** to go through (the) official channels; **su nombramiento se hará oficial mañana** his appointment will be made official tomorrow
2 *nmf* **oficial pagador** paymaster

oficial², **-ala** *nm,f* skilled worker, *m* journeyman; **oficial montador** journeyman fitter; **oficial electricista** skilled electrician

oficialmente *adv* officially

oficina *nf* office; **puedes llamarlo a la oficina** you can phone him at the office □ *oficina de atención al cliente* front office; *oficina de cambio (de moneda)* bureau de change; *oficina central* headquarters, main office, *US* home office; *oficina central de compras* central purchasing office; *oficina de clasificación del correo* mail room; *oficina de correos* post office; *oficina de distribución* distribution agency; *oficina de empleo* employment bureau, *Br* Jobcentre; **Oficina Europea del Medio Ambiente** European Environmental Bureau; *oficina de expedición* forwarding office; *oficina de Hacienda* tax office; *oficina de información* information bureau; **Oficina Internacional del Trabajo** International Labour Office; *Esp* **Oficina de Justificación de la Difusión** ≃ *Br* Audit Bureau of Circulation, *US* Audit Bureau of Circulations; *oficina de orientación profesional* careers office; *Esp* **Oficina de Patentes y Marcas** ≃ patent office; *oficina de prensa* press office; *oficina principal (de banco)* main

branch; **oficina de recepción** *(de mercancías)*
receiving office; **oficina de reclamaciones,** *Am*
oficina de reclamos complaints office; **oficina
de la seguridad social** social security office;
oficina de turismo tourist (information) office

oficinista *nmf* office worker, clerk

oficio *nm* (**a**) *(profesión manual)* trade; **de oficio**
by trade □ **oficio manual** manual trade (**b**) *(trabajo)* job (**c**) DER **de oficio** *(abogado)* court-
appointed, legal aid

ofimática *nf* (**a**) *(técnicas informáticas)* office IT,
office automation (**b**) *(material de oficina)* office
computer equipment

ofrecer *vt* (**a**) *(proporcionar, dar)* to offer; **me
han ofrecido el puesto de gerente** they've offered me the job of manager; **¿cuánto te ofrecen por la casa?** how much are they offering
you for the house? (**b**) *(en subastas)* to bid;
¿qué ofrecen por esta mesa? what am I bid
for this table? (**c**) *(prestar)* to offer; **la empresa
comenzó a ofrecer sus servicios al público en
noviembre** the company began offering its services to the public in November

OIC *nf (abrev de* **Organización Internacional del
Comercio)** ITO

OICV *nf (abrev de* **Organización Internacional
de Comisiones de Valores)** IOSCO, International Organization of Securities Commissions

OICVM *mpl (abrev de* **Organismos de Inversión
Colectiva en Valores Mobiliarios)** UCITS

OIT *nf (abrev de* **Organización Internacional del
Trabajo)** ILO

OJD *nf (abrev de* **Oficina de Justificación de la
Difusión)** = Spanish audience measurement
organization, ≃ ABC

ola *nf* **una ola de ventas** a sales wave; **una ola
de visitantes** a flood of visitors

oligopolio *nm* ECON oligopoly

> **"**
>
> En los próximos días debería quedar defini-
> da la venta de 58.6% de la petrolera Perez
> Companc a la estatal brasileña Petrobras,
> en momentos que el gobierno argentino
> analiza la operación por cuestiones de **oli-
> gopolio**. Perez Companc se negociaba
> con una caída de 5.5% a 1.72 pesos por
> acción.
>
> **"**

oligopsonio *nm* ECON oligopsony

OMA *nf Am* FIN *(abrev de* **Operación de Mercado
Abierto)** OMO, open market operation

OMC *nf (abrev de* **Organización Mundial del Comercio)** WTO

ómnibus *nm Cuba, Urug (urbano)* bus; *Andes,
Cuba, Urug (interurbano, internacional) Br* coach,
US bus

ONG *nf inv (abrev de* **Organización No Gubernamental)** NGO

ONGD *nf (abrev de* **Organización No Gubernamental de Desarrollo)** NGDO

on line *adv* INFORM on line

ONU *nf (abrev de* **Organización de las Naciones
Unidas)** UN, UNO

ONUDI *nf (abrev de* **Organización de las Naciones Unidas para el Desarrollo Industrial)**
UNIDO

OPA *nf (abrev de* **oferta pública de adquisición)**
takeover bid; **lanzar una OPA sobre** to launch a
takeover bid for □ **OPA amistosa** friendly takeover bid; **OPA hostil** hostile takeover bid

> **"**
>
> Los italianos Quarta y Astrim, que lanzaron
> una **OPA** por el 75% de la inmobiliaria en
> febrero, han extendido la operación hasta
> el 100% de las acciones.
>
> **"**

opar *vt (intentar adquirir)* to launch a takeover bid
for; *(adquirir)* to take over

> **"**
>
> Otra compañía tecnológica que protagoni-
> zó el fuera de hora fue PeopleSoft, la com-
> pañía **opada** por Oracle, que se situó en
> 20,13 dólares, un 3,8% por encima del
> cierre de la jornada, debido a sus anuncios
> del día: recortes de plantilla, plan de recom-
> pra de acciones y previsiones de ventas
> para 2003 y 2004.
>
> **"**

opción *nf* (**a**) BOLSA option □ **opción sobre acciones** *Br* share option, *US* stock option; **opción
de adquisición** option to buy, purchase option;
opción americana American-style option; **opción con beneficio implícito** in-the-money option; **opción de compra** call option, buyer's
option; **opción de compra de acciones** *Br* share
option, *US* stock option; **opción de compra y
venta** put and call option; **opción al descubierto** naked option; **opción con dinero** in-the-
money option; **opción en dinero** at-the-money
option; **opción sobre divisas** FX option, foreign exchange option, foreign currency option; **opción europea** European-style option;
opción fuera de dinero underwater option;
opción de futuros futures option; **opción sobre índice (bursátil)** index option; **opción negociada** traded option; **opción a la par** at-the-
money option; **opción vencida** lapsed option;
opción de venta put option, seller's option
(**b**) *(elección)* option □ **opciones de amortización** repayment options; **opciones de crédito**
credit options
(**c**) INFORM option □ **opción de guardar** save
option; **opción de impresión** print option;

opción del menú menu option

opcional *adj* optional

OPEP *nf* (*abrev de* **Organización de Países Exportadores de Petróleo**) OPEC

operación *nf* (**a**) *(actividad)* operation; **van a cerrar sus operaciones comerciales en Argentina** they are to close down their operations in Argentina ◻ *operaciones bancarias* banking; *operaciones bancarias en paraísos fiscales* offshore banking; *operación comercial* business operation; *operación contable* accounting operation; *operaciones en el extranjero* overseas business; *operaciones internacionales* international operations

(**b**) FIN *(transacción)* transaction; **una operación de ingreso** a deposit; **una operación de reintegro** a withdrawal ◻ *operación comercial* business transaction; *operación de descuento* discount operation

(**c**) BOLSA transaction, deal ◻ *operación de apertura* opening transaction; *operación bursátil* stock exchange transaction, stock market transaction; *operaciones al cierre* closing trade; *operación de cobertura* hedge transaction; *operación de compensación* clearing transaction; *operación al contado* cash deal, spot deal, spot transaction; *operaciones al contado* spot trading; *operación en divisas* exchange transaction; *operaciones en divisas* foreign exchange trading, forex trading; *operación de divisas a plazo o a término* forward exchange transaction; *operación de mercado abierto* open market operation; *operación a prima* option deal; *operación sujeta a impuestos* taxable transaction

operador, -ora 1 *nm,f* (**a**) BOLSA trader ◻ *operador de posición* position trader (**b**) *(de una máquina)* operator ◻ *Esp* **operador de ordenadores,** *Am* **operador de computadoras** computer operator; *operador del sistema* SYSOP, systems operator; *operador de teclado* keyboard operator (**c**) TEL operator

2 *nm* (**a**) *(empresa)* operator ◻ *operador telefónico* telephone operator, telephone company; *operador turístico* tour operator (**b**) INFORM *operador booleano* Boolean operator

3 *nf* TEL operator

operar 1 *vi (realizar una actividad)* to operate; **los países donde operamos** the countries in which we operate

2 *vt Am (máquina)* to operate

operario, -a *nm,f (trabajador)* worker, operative; *(de máquina)* operator

operativo, -a *adj* (**a**) *(que funciona)* operative, functional, operational; **medidas operativas** operational measures; **el servicio será operativo desde el viernes** the service will be operational from Friday; **una gran capacidad operativa** a large operating capacity (**b**) INFORM

operating; **el sistema operativo** the operating system

OPI *nf* (**a**) *(abrev de* **Oferta Pública Inicial***)* IPO (**b**) *(abrev de* **Oferta Pública de Intercambio de acciones***)* PEO, Public Exchange Offer

opinión *nf* opinion ◻ *opinión de auditoría* auditor's opinion; *opinión editorial* editorial opinion; *la opinión pública* public opinion

oportunidad *nf* (**a**) *(posibilidad)* opportunity; **las oportunidades de promoción son excelentes** the opportunities for advancement are excellent

(**b**) MKTG opportunity; **oportunidades y amenazas** opportunities and threats; **oportunidades de ver/oír** opportunities to see/hear (**c**) **oportunidades** *(en gran almacén)* bargains

optativo, -a *adj* optional, *US* elective

óptica *nf* (**a**) *(ciencia)* optics (**b**) *(tienda)* optician's (shop) (**c**) *(punto de vista)* point of view

óptico, -a *adj* INFORM optical

optimización *nf* optimization ◻ *optimización de beneficios* profit optimization

optimizador *nm* INFORM optimizer

optimizar *vt* to optimize

óptimo, -a *adj* optimum, optimal

opulento, -a *adj (rico)* affluent; *(abundante)* abundant

OPV *nf* (*abrev de* **oferta pública de venta (de acciones)**) public offering

> **❝**
>
> Cuando la junta de accionistas apruebe la propuesta del comité de dirección el próximo lunes, los ejecutivos valorarán el potencial de sus empleados para asignar a cada uno las opciones que le correspondan. Mientras en el caso de los directivos el precio se fijó teniendo en cuenta el de la **OPV,** 8,9 euros, ahora se considerará el precio medio de las acciones durante los treinta días posteriores a la aprobación del plan, con un cinco por ciento de descuento.
>
> **❞**

órdago *nm* BOLSA greenmail

orden¹ *nm* (**a**) *(secuencia, colocación correcta)* order ◻ *orden alfabético* alphabetical order; INFORM *orden ascendente* ascending order; INFORM *orden descendente* descending order; *orden del día* agenda; **el primer punto del orden del día** the first item on the agenda (**b**) *(normalidad, disciplina)* order; **llamar a alguien al orden** to call sb to order

orden² *nf* (**a**) *(de pedido, transacciones)* order; **cheque a la orden** cheque to order ◻ *orden de compra* purchase order; *orden de domiciliación bancaria, Am orden de débito bancario* direct debit mandate; **orden de entrega** delivery order; FIN **orden incondicional (de pago)** unconditional order; **orden de pago** payment order; BANCA *(documento)* mandate form; **orden de pago de dividendos** dividend mandate; FIN **orden de transferencia** transfer order

(**b**) BOLSA order ▫ **orden abierta** good-till-cancelled order; **orden bursátil** stock exchange order; **orden de compra** buy order, buying order; **orden condicional** contingent order; **orden de contratación** trading order; **orden discrecional** discretionary order; **orden de futuros** futures order; **orden limitada** limit order; **orden al mercado** market order; **orden (de) stop** stop loss, stop order, stop-loss order; **orden todo o nada** all-or-none order; **orden de traspaso** *(documento)* transfer form; **orden de venta** sell order

(**c**) DER *(mandato, disposición)* **orden de embargo** sequestration order; **orden de expropiación forzosa** expropriation order, *Br* compulsory purchase order; ADUANA **orden de inspección** inspection order; **orden judicial** court order, warrant; **orden de liquidación** winding-up order; **orden ministerial** ministerial order

ordenación *nf* (**a**) *(de recursos, edificios)* planning ▫ **ordenación del suelo** town planning regulations, *US* zoning regulations (**b**) INFORM sort ▫ **ordenación ascendente** ascending sort; **ordenación descendente** descending sort; **ordenación inversa** reverse sort

ordenador *nm Esp* computer; **pasar algo a ordenador** to key sth up (on a computer) ▫ **ordenador de bolsillo** hand-held computer; **ordenador compatible** compatible computer; **ordenador doméstico** home computer; **ordenador frontal** front-end computer; **ordenador personal** personal computer; **ordenador portátil** laptop computer; **ordenador de red** network computer; **ordenador de sobremesa** desktop computer

ordenamiento *nm* **ordenamiento jurídico** legal system

ordenante *nmf* FIN instructing party, initiator

ordenar 1 *vt* (**a**) *(poner en orden secuencial)* to arrange, to put in order; **ordenar alfabéticamente** to put in alphabetical order; **ordenar por temas** to arrange by subject (**b**) INFORM to sort; **ordenar algo alfabéticamente** to alphasort sth (**c**) *(mandar)* to order; **ordenar a alguien que haga algo, ordenar a alguien hacer algo** to order sb to do sth
2 *vi* to give orders

organigrama *nm* (**a**) *(de organización, empresa)* organization chart, organizational chart, organigram ▫ **organigrama de árbol** organization tree; **organigrama directivo** management chart (**b**) *(esquema)* flow chart, flow diagram

> La reestructuración anunciada ayer da como resultado el **organigrama** más simple de la historia de Telefónica. La operadora tendrá tres divisiones operativas, dos direcciones de apoyo y 20 directivos en el primer nivel. Además, se crea una nueva unidad de filiales.

organismo *nm (entidad)* body, organization ▫ **organismo consultivo** advisory body; **organismo profesional** professional body; **organismo regulador** regulatory body, watchdog

organización *nf* (**a**) *(gestión)* organization, organizing; **¿quién se encargó de la organización del congreso?** who is in charge of organizing the conference? ▫ **organización de eventos** event(s) management

(**b**) *(estructura de una empresa)* **organización por departamentos** functional layout, functional organization; **organización lineal** line organization; **organización matricial** matrix organization; **organización y métodos** organization and methods; **organización del personal** staff organization; **organización de los turnos** shift pattern

(**c**) *(organizadores)* **la organización** the organizers; **damos las gracias a la organización del congreso** we would like to thank the conference organizers

(**d**) *(organismo)* organization ▫ **organización con ánimo de lucro** profit-making organization, *US* for-profit organization; **organización sin ánimo de lucro** not-for-profit organization, *Br* non-profit(-making) organization; **organización benéfica** charity (organization), charitable organization; **organización de consumidores** consumer organization, consumer group; **organización empresarial** employers' association, employers' organization; **organización no gubernamental** non-governmental organization; **organización no gubernamental de desarrollo** non-governmental development organization; **organización patronal** employers' association, employers' organization; **organización política** political organization; **organización sindical** trade union

(**e**) *(organismos internacionales)* **Organización para la Cooperación y el Desarrollo Económico** Organization for Economic Cooperation and Development; **Organización de Estados Americanos** Organization of American States; **Organización Internacional de Normalización** International Standards Organization; **Organización Internacional del Trabajo** International Labour Organization; **Organización Mundial del Comercio** World Trade Organization; **Organización de las Naciones Unidas** United Nations Organization; **Organización de Países Exportadores de Petróleo** Organization of

Petroleum Exporting Countries; *Organización para la Seguridad y Cooperación en Europa* Organization for Security and Cooperation in Europe

organizador, -ora 1 *adj* organizing
  2 *nm,f* organizer ❏ *organizador de eventos* event(s) manager

organizar *vt (evento, reunión, viaje)* to organize; **no contamos con los medios adecuados para organizar un congreso** we don't have the facilities to hold a conference here

organizativo, -a *adj* organizational

órgano *nm (institución)* *órgano de conciliación* conciliation service

orientación *nf* (**a**) *(de negocio)* orientation ❏ *orientación al o hacia el mercado* market orientation, marketing orientation; *orientación al o hacia el producto* product orientation; *orientación a o hacia las ventas* sales orientation
  (**b**) *(información)* guidance, advice ❏ *orientación profesional,* CSur *orientación vocacional* careers guidance, careers advice
  (**c**) INFORM orientation ❏ *orientación horizontal* horizontal o landscape orientation; *orientación vertical* vertical o portrait orientation

orientado, -a *adj* oriented; **orientado al mercado juvenil** orientated o directed towards the youth market; INFORM **orientado a objeto** object-oriented; INFORM **orientado a usuario** user-oriented

origen *nm* origin; **país de origen** country of origin; **los aceites de origen español** oils from Spain

originador *nmf* FIN originator

original 1 *adj (documento)* original
  2 *nm (documento)* original, master copy

oro *nm* **1** gold; **oro de 18 quilates** 18-carat gold ❏ *oro acuñado* gold coin; *oro en lingotes* gold bullion; *oro en moneda de curso legal* gold currency
  2 *adj inv* gold

oscilación *nf (variación)* fluctuation; **la oscilación de los precios** the fluctuation in prices ❏ *oscilación máxima* maximum fluctuation; *oscilación mínima* minimum fluctuation

oscilar *vi (variar)* to fluctuate

> **"**
> En un sondeo realizado por Dow Jones Newswires a 18 economistas, los encuestados proyectaron un crecimiento para la economía durante el tercer trimestre respecto del segundo. Las estimaciones de crecimiento **oscilaron** entre un 0.8% y 2.5% sobre una base ajustada por estación. Los datos oficiales se publicarán el miércoles.
> **"**

otorgar *vt* (**a**) *(licencia, concesión)* to grant (**b**) DER to sign, *Espec* to execute (**c**) *(ley)* to pass, *Espec* to promulgate

overbooking *nm* overbooking

pabellón *nm (bandera)* **pabellón de conveniencia** flag of convenience

PAC *nf* UE *(abrev de* **Política Agrícola Común)** CAP

pack *nm* pack; **un pack de seis** a six-pack ❏ **pack familiar** economy pack; **pack de presentación** presentation pack

pacto *nm* agreement, pact; **hacer/romper un pacto** to make/break an agreement; **cumplir un pacto** to fulfil an agreement ❏ *Pacto Andino* Andean Pact; **pacto de** *o* **entre caballeros** gentleman's agreement; UE *Pacto de Estabilidad y Crecimiento* Stability and Growth Pact; **pacto de productividad** productivity deal; BOLSA **pacto de recompra** repurchase agreement; **pacto social** social contract

paga *nf (sueldo)* salary, pay; *(dinero)* pay packet, *US* pay envelope; **tenemos 14 pagas al año** we have 14 salary payments a year; **hoy nos dan la paga** we get paid today ❏ *paga doble* = two months' salary or wages, including a "paga extra"; *paga extra, paga extraordinaria* = additional payment of a month's salary or wages; *paga de Navidad* = additional payment of a month's salary or wages at Christmas; *paga neta* take-home pay; *paga semanal* weekly pay; *paga y señal (fianza)* deposit

pagadero, -a *adj* payable; **pagadero a 90 días/a la entrega** payable within 90 days/on delivery; **pagadero en efectivo** payable in cash; **pagadero a la vista** payable at sight; **pagadero contra entrega/por adelantado** payable on delivery/in advance; **pagadero al portador** payable to bearer; **pagadero a la orden** payable to order

pagado, -a *adj* paid; **estar muy bien/mal pagado** to be highly paid/underpaid; **pagado por adelantado** prepaid; **con el franqueo pagado** postage paid, post-paid, *Br* post-free

pagador, -ora 1 *adj* paying; **agente pagador** payer

2 *nm,f* payer; *(de obreros)* paymaster; **ser buen/mal pagador** to be a good/bad payer

pagar 1 *vt (precio, alquiler, factura, multa)* to pay; *(deuda, hipoteca)* to pay off; *(dividendo, indemnización)* to pay out; **pagar algo en efectivo** to pay cash for sth, to pay for sth in cash; **pagar 400 pesos a alguien** to pay sb 400 pesos; **los jubilados no pagan las medicinas** pensioners don't pay for prescriptions

2 *vi* to pay; **pagar por adelantado** to pay in advance; **pagar a plazos** to pay by *o* in instalments; **pagar con cheque/tarjeta (de crédito)** to pay by cheque/credit card; **pagar mediante transferencia bancaria** to pay by bank transfer; **pagar en especie** to pay in kind; **pagar en euros/dólares** to pay in euros/dollars; **pagar en efectivo** *o* **en metálico** to pay (in) cash; **pagar contra reembolso** to pay on delivery; **páguese al portador** pay to bearer

pagaré *nm* FIN promissory note, IOU ❏ *pagaré bancario* banker's note; *pagaré garantizado* secured note; *pagaré a medio plazo* medium-term note; *pagaré del préstamo* loan note; *pagaré del Tesoro* Treasury note, currency note; *pagaré a la vista* demand note

> "
>
> Las subastas de **Pagarés del Tesoro** fueron reduciéndose y la última se realizó en 1990. Las subastas de letras han aumentado, y hoy la Letra del Tesoro es la base del mercado monetario español, que cuenta además con una creciente oferta de **pagarés** de empresa y de otros instrumentos de renta fija a corto plazo. Con la emisión de Letras del Tesoro y su colocación entre el público, la dependencia directa del Estado en la banca para su financiación disminuyó considerablemente.
>
> "

página *nf* (**a**) *(de libro, publicación)* page ❏ *las Páginas Amarillas*® the Yellow Pages®; *página central* centrefold; *página de portada (de fax)* cover page, cover sheet (**b**) INFORM page; **avanzar/retroceder una página** to page down/up ❏ *página de búsqueda* search engine; *página inicial, página de inicio* home page; *página personal* (personal) home page; *página web* Web page

paginación *nf* pagination

paginar *vt* to paginate

pago, -a 1 *adj* RP *(trabajador)* paid

2 *nm* payment; **realizar** *o* **efectuar un pago** to make a payment; **incumplir** *o* **no satisfacer un pago** to default on a payment; **previo pago de 100 euros** on payment of 100 euros; **tener pagos atrasados** to be in arrears; **un cliente de pago** a paying customer; **por pronto pago** for prompt payment ❑ *pago por adelantado* advance payment, prepayment; *pago adicional* additional payment; *pago anticipado* advance payment; *pago anual* yearly payment; *pago aplazado* deferred payment; *pago atrasado* late payment; *pago compensatorio* compensating payment; *pago al contado* cash payment; *pago a cuenta* payment on account, interim payment, progress payment; *pago diferido* deferred payment; *pago contra documentos* cash against documents; *pago en efectivo* cash payment; *pago electrónico* electronic payment; *pago contra embarque* cash on shipment; *pago a la entrega* cash on delivery; *pagos escalonados* staggered payments; *pago en especie* payment in kind; *pago extraordinario* windfall payment; *pagos de final de mes* end-of-month payments; *pago fraccionado* payment by instalments; *pago inicial* down payment; *pago insuficiente* short payment; *pago en metálico* cash payment; *pago parcial* partial payment; *pagos periódicos* periodic payments; *pago recibido* inward payment; *pago contra reembolso* payment on delivery; *pago con tarjeta* card payment; *pago total* full discharge; *pago de transferencia* transfer payment

país *nm* country ❑ *país acreedor* creditor country; *países desarrollados* developed countries; *país deudor, país endeudado* debtor country; *país exportador* exporting country; *países firmantes* signatory countries; *país importador* importing country; *países industrializados* industrialized countries; *país miembro* member country; *país de origen* country of origin; *países subdesarrollados* underdeveloped countries; *países en vías de desarrollo* developing countries

palabra *nf* word ❑ INFORM *palabra clave* keyword

palacio *nm palacio de congresos* conference centre; *palacio de exposiciones* exhibition centre

palé, palet *nm* pallet

paleta *nf* INFORM palette ❑ *paleta gráfica* graphics palette

paletización *nf* palletization

paletizar *vt* to palletize

palmtop *nm o nf* palmtop

pancarta *nf pancarta (publicitaria)* banner

panel *nm* (**a**) MKTG *(de personas)* panel ❑ *panel de audiencia* television viewing panel; *panel de consumidores* consumer panel; *panel de distribuidores* distributor panel; *panel de usuarios* user panel (**b**) INFORM *panel de control* control panel

pantalla *nf* INFORM screen; **en pantalla** on screen; **trabajar en pantalla** to work on

screen ❑ *pantalla de arranque* start-up screen; *pantalla de ayuda* help screen; *pantalla de cristal líquido* (en monitor) LCD screen, liquid crystal screen; (en cámara) liquid crystal display; *pantalla LCD* LCD screen; *pantalla de matriz activa* active matrix display; *pantalla plana* flat screen; *pantalla táctil* touch screen

pantallazo *nm* INFORM *Fam* screen shot, screen dump

papel *nm* (**a**) *(material)* paper; *(hoja)* sheet of paper ❑ *papel carbón*, RP *papel carbónico* carbon paper; *papel continuo* continuous paper; *papel couché, papel cuché* coated paper; *papel de impresora* printer paper; *papel con membrete* headed (note)paper; *papel sin membrete* plain paper; *papel de pagos al Estado* = special stamps for making certain payments to the State; *papel perforado* perforated paper; *papel sellado* stamped paper, = paper bearing an official stamp to show that the corresponding tax has been paid; INFORM *papel tapiz* wallpaper; *papel térmico* thermal paper; *papel timbrado* stamped paper, = paper bearing an official stamp to show that the corresponding tax has been paid

(**b**) FIN *(efecto)* paper ❑ *papel comercial* commercial paper, trade bill; *papel del Estado* government bonds; *papel moneda* paper money, paper currency, US bank paper; Am *papel de renta fija* fixed-interest bond; Am *papel de renta variable* equity

> **❝**
> Las acciones de Jazztel procedían de fuertes pérdidas durante los últimos meses del año pasado y primeros de este debido en una gran parte a la afluencia de nuevo **papel** procedente del canje de sus bonos de alta rentabilidad por nuevas acciones. La operadora emitió el año pasado un total de 457,3 millones de acciones ordinarias para hacer frente al canje de sus bonos.
> **❞**

papeleo *nm* paperwork; **papeleo (burocrático)** red tape

papelera *nf* INFORM *(en Windows)* recycle bin; *(en Macintosh)* Br wastebasket, US trash can

papelería *nf* **material** *o* **artículos de papelería** stationery

papeleta *nf (de votación)* ballot paper

paquete *nm* (**a**) *(postal)* parcel, package (**b**) *(conjunto)* package; **el paquete incluye un seguro médico privado** *(en condiciones laborales)* the package includes private health insurance ❑ *paquete de beneficios (para empleado)* remuneration package, benefits package, compensation package; *paquete de bienvenida (en congreso, de empresa)* welcome pack; *paquete de medidas* package of measures;

paquete de prestaciones extrasalariales benefits package; **paquete turístico** package tour

(**c**) MKTG *(de productos en venta)* pack □ **paquete de muestra** sample pack; **paquete con promoción** bonus pack

(**d**) BOLSA bundle, lot □ **paquete de acciones, paquete accionarial** bundle *o* lot of shares

(**e**) INFORM package □ **paquete de comunicaciones** communications package; **paquete de contabilidad** accounting package, accounts package; **paquete de gestión de proyectos** project management package; **paquete integrado** integrated package; **paquete de software** software package

> ❝
> En caso de producirse la compra del **paquete accionarial**, el primer socio, con un 25% de las participaciones de la sociedad, y por tanto, principal grupo en TUI AG sería la Institutionelle Investoren, una compañía alemana de inversiones centrada principalmente en el negocio de los planes de pensiones.
> ❞

par *nf* FIN **a la par** at par; **emitir acciones a la par** to issue shares at par; **el dólar cotiza a la par con el euro** the dollar is trading at par with the euro; **sobre la par** above par; **bajo par** below par

parabólica *nf* satellite dish

parado, -a 1 *adj* (**a**) *(inactivo)* dull, slack; **el negocio está parado** business is dull (**b**) *Esp (sin empleo)* unemployed, out of work; **estar parado** to be unemployed, to be out of work

2 *nm,f Esp (desempleado)* unemployed person; **los parados** the unemployed, the jobless; **los parados de larga duración** the long-term unemployed

paraíso fiscal *nm* tax haven; **inversiones en paraísos fiscales** offshore investments; **tener algo en un paraíso fiscal** to keep sth offshore *o* in a tax haven

parámetro *nm (dato, valor)* parameter

parcela *nf* plot (of land)

parche *nm* INFORM patch

parcial *adj* partial; **trabajar a tiempo parcial** to work part-time

paréntesis *nm inv* (round) bracket □ **paréntesis angular** angle bracket

paridad *nf* (**a**) FIN parity; **la paridad del dólar con el euro** the dollar/euro exchange rate □ **paridad de cambio, paridad cambiaria** parity of exchange; **paridad fija** fixed parity; **paridad monetaria** monetary parity; **paridad móvil** sliding peg; **paridad del poder adquisitivo** purchasing power parity; **paridad en el tipo de cambio** exchange rate parity (**b**) *(igualdad)*

equality; **reclaman la paridad de salarios** they are demanding equal pay (**c**) INFORM parity

paro *nm* (**a**) *(cesación) (acción)* shutdown; *(estado)* stoppage; **los trabajadores realizaron un paro de diez minutos para condenar el último atentado** the workers staged a ten-minute stoppage in protest at the latest attack □ **paro técnico** *(de máquina)* downtime

(**b**) *Am (huelga)* strike, stoppage; **estar en** *o* **de paro** to be on strike; **hacer paro** to strike; **los trabajadores en paro** the strikers □ **paro de brazos caídos** sit-down (strike); **paro cívico** community protest; **paro general** general strike; **paro indefinido** indefinite strike; **paro laboral** industrial action

(**c**) *Esp (desempleo)* unemployment; **estar en (el) paro** to be unemployed □ **paro cíclico** cyclical unemployment; **paro encubierto** hidden unemployment, concealed unemployment; **paro estructural** structural unemployment; **paro friccional** frictional unemployment; **paro juvenil** youth unemployment; **paro registrado** registered unemployment, official unemployment

(**d**) *Esp (subsidio)* Br unemployment benefit, US unemployment compensation; **apuntarse al paro** to register as unemployed, Br to sign on; **cobrar el paro** to claim *o* receive Br unemployment benefit *o* US unemployment compensation

parque *nm* (**a**) *(instalaciones)* park □ **parque comercial** Br retail park, US shopping mall; **parque empresarial** business park; **parque tecnológico** technology park (**b**) *(de medios, utensilios)* **parque automovilístico,** RP **parque automotor** car fleet; *Esp* **parque de ordenadores,** *Am* **parque de computadoras** computer population

parqué *nm* BOLSA (trading) floor

> ❝
> Algunos de los principales valores del **parqué** madrileño, que ayer fueron de los más castigados, han conseguido levantar el precio de sus títulos y empujar al Ibex hacia arriba.
> ❞

párrafo *nm* paragraph

parte¹ *nm (informe)* report; **dar parte (a alguien de algo)** to report (sth to sb) □ **parte de accidente** *(para aseguradora)* (accident) claim form; **parte facultativo** medical report; **parte médico** medical report

parte² *nf* (**a**) *(participación)* share; **vendió su parte del negocio** she sold her share *o* part of the business

(**b**) DER *(en juicio, transacción)* party; **no hubo acuerdo entre las partes** the two sides were unable to reach an agreement □ **la parte acusadora** the plaintif; **parte agraviada** aggrieved party; **parte compradora** buyer; **parte contratante** party to the contract; **parte incumplidora** defaulting party; **partes interesadas** interested parties; **parte morosa** defaulting party; **parte perjudicada** aggrieved party; **parte vendedora** seller, vendor

participación *nf* FIN *(acción, cuota)* share; *(de fondo)* unit; *(inversión)* interest, investment, shareholding; **quieren una participación en los beneficios** they want a share in the profits; **tiene una participación del 10% en la sociedad** he has a 10% interest in the company □ **participación accionarial,** *Am* **participación accionaria** shareholding; **participación en el capital** participating interest; **participación de control** golden share; **participación de los empleados en los beneficios** *(de la empresa)* employee profit-sharing; **participación mayoritaria** majority holding, majority interest; **participación minoritaria** minority holding, minority interest; **participación recíproca** cross-holding; **participación societaria** equity participation, equity holding

> **❝**
> La riqueza financiera de los hogares se halla concentrada, por un lado, en lo que atesoran en efectivo y depósitos (42% del total) y, por otro, en la tenencia de acciones y **participaciones societarias** (37% del total).
> **❞**

participante *nmf (en mercado, negociación)* participant

participar FIN **1** *vi* to have a share; **participar de los beneficios** to have a share in the profits; **varias personas participan en la empresa** several people have shares in the company
2 *vt* **una empresa participada por varias sociedades** a business in which several companies have shareholdings

> **❝**
> El Servicio de Defensa de la Competencia (SDC), dependiente del Ministerio de Economía, ha abierto un expediente sancionador a Gas Natural por el contrato suscrito en julio de 2001 con su **participada** Enagas.
> **❞**

partícipe *nmf (en fondo de inversión)* unit holder

> **❝**
> Los **partícipes** han optado por Fondos de Inversión en Activos del Mercado Monetario (FIAMM) cuya volatilidad y riesgo es inferior, y también sus comisiones, lo que repercute directamente en la cuenta de resultados de las gestoras.
> **❞**

partida *nf* **(a)** CONT *(entrada)* item, entry □ **partida del balance de situación** balance sheet item; **partida de caja** cash item; **partidas de capital** capital items; **partida consolidada** consolidated entry; **partida extraordinaria** extraordinary item; **partida del haber** credit item; **partida informativa** reminder entry; **partida inversa** reverse entry; **partida presupuestaria** budget item; **se ha recortado la partida presupuestaria para la vivienda** the budget allocation for housing has been cut
(b) *(de mercancías)* batch
(c) *(documento)* certificate □ **partida de defunción** death certificate; **partida de matrimonio** marriage certificate; **partida de nacimiento** birth certificate
(d) *(marcha, salida)* departure

> **❝**
> El comisario europeo Erkki Likkanen recordó que existe una **partida** para el fomento de la sociedad de la información de 10.000 millones de euros para el periodo 2000-2006, procedentes de los fondos estructurales, lo que supone el 7,3% del total de lo presupuestado por este concepto.
> **❞**

pasabordo *nm Col* boarding pass

pasaje *nm esp Am* ticket; **el pasaje cuesta 1.000 dólares** the ticket costs 1,000 dollars, the fare is 1,000 dollars □ **pasaje abierto** open ticket; **pasaje de avión** plane ticket; **pasaje de ida** *Br* single (ticket), *US* one-way ticket; **pasaje de ida y vuelta** *Br* return (ticket), *US* round-trip (ticket); **pasaje de lista de espera** stand-by ticket

pasajero, -a *nm,f* passenger □ **pasajero en lista de espera** standby passenger; **pasajero en tránsito** transfer passenger

pasante *nmf (de abogado)* articled clerk

pasantía *nf (en abogacía)* traineeship, *Br* articles

pasaporte *nm* passport

pasar *vt* **(a)** *(al teléfono)* **pasar a alguien con alguien** to put sb through to sb; **pasar una llamada** *o Am* **un llamado a alguien** to transfer a call to sb **(b)** *(transcribir)* **pasar un documento** *Esp* **al ordenador** *o Am* **a la computadora** to type *o* key a document (up) on the computer

pasarela *nf* INFORM gateway □ **pasarela de correo (electrónico)** mail gateway

PASCAL, Pascal *nm* INFORM PASCAL, Pascal

pase *nm (permiso)* pass □ **pase de prensa** press pass

paseo *nm* BOLSA **paseo aleatorio** random walk (theory)

pasillo *nm (en comercio)* aisle

pasivo, -a *nm* **1** FIN liabilities □ **pasivo circulante** current liabilities; **pasivo contingente**

contingent liabilities; **pasivo corriente** current liabilities; **pasivo a corto plazo** short-term liabilities; **pasivo diferido** deferred liabilities; **pasivo exigible** current liabilities; **pasivo exigible a largo plazo** deferred liabilities; **pasivo a largo plazo** long-term liabilities; **pasivo a medio plazo** medium-term liabilities; **pasivo total** total liabilities

2 *nm,f Urug (pensionista)* senior citizen, *Br* (old age) pensioner

> **❝**
> El grupo asegurador Zurich Financial Services anunció unos 3.400 millones de dólares de pérdidas en el ejercicio de 2002 frente a un **pasivo** de 387 millones del año anterior por la debilidad de los mercados bursátiles y el bajo nivel récord de los tipos de interés.
> **❞**

pasta *nf Esp Fam (dinero)* dough, *Br* dosh; **ganar mucha pasta** to earn big money

patentado, -a *adj* patent, patented

patentar *vt* to patent

patente *nf* (**a**) **patente (de invención)** patent; **presentar una solicitud de patente** to file a patent application (**b**) *(certificado)* **patente de navegación** certificate of registration (**c**) *RP (de auto) Br* registration number, *US* license number (**d**) *Chile (cuota)* membership fee, *Br* subscription

patrimonial *adj* **las ganancias patrimoniales del anterior ejercicio** the previous year's capital gains; **la situacion patrimonial de la empresa** the company's situation as regards its assets

patrimonio *nm (bienes) (personal)* estate, assets; *(de empresa)* assets; **el patrimonio de la empresa asciende a mil millones de dólares** the company has net assets of one billion dollars ◻ **patrimonio contable** book equity, book assets; **patrimonio neto** shareholders' equity; **patrimonio neto negativo** negative net worth; **patrimonio personal** personal assets; **patrimonio social** social *o* corporate assets

patrocinador, -ora 1 *adj* sponsoring; **la empresa patrocinadora del encuentro** the company sponsoring the event

2 *nm,f* sponsor

patrocinar *vt* to sponsor

patrocinio *nm* sponsorship ◻ **patrocinio corporativo** corporate sponsorship; **patrocinio televisivo** television sponsorship

patrón, -ona 1 *nm,f (de obreros)* boss; *(empresario)* employer

2 *nm* ECON *(medida)* standard ◻ **patrón internacional** international standard; **patrón monetario** currency standard; **patrón oro** gold standard

patronal 1 *adj (empresarial)* management; **organización patronal** employers' organization

2 *nf (organización)* employers' organization; **la patronal del turismo** the tourist operators' association *o* organization; **negociaciones entre la patronal y los sindicatos** negotiations between employers and the unions

patronato *nm (dirección)* board of trustees; *(con fines benéficos)* trust ◻ **patronato de turismo** tourist board

pausa *nf* **pausa publicitaria** commercial break

PC *nm (abrev de* **personal computer**) PC

PCGA *nmpl (abrev de* **principios de contabilidad generalmente aceptados**) GAAP

PCMCIA *nf* INFORM *(abrev de* **PC memory card international association**) PCMCIA

PDA *nm* INFORM *(abrev de* **personal digital assistant**) PDA

PDF *nm* INFORM *(abrev de* **portable document format**) PDF

peaje *nm* (**a**) *(importe)* toll; **autopista de peaje** *Br* toll motorway, *US* turnpike (**b**) *(lugar)* toll barrier

PEC *nm* UE *(abrev de* **Pacto de Estabilidad y Crecimiento**) SGP

pedido *nm* (**a**) *(de producto)* order; **hacer un pedido (a alguien)** to place an order (with sb); **sólo se fabrica sobre pedido** they are manufactured exclusively to order ◻ **pedido abierto** open indent; **pedido atrasado** back order; **pedido cerrado** closed order; **pedidos conjuntos** joint ordering; **pedido por correo** mail order; **pedido de exportación** export order; **pedido en firme** firm order; **pedido general** blanket order; **pedido al por mayor** bulk order; **pedido de prueba** trial order; **pedido por teléfono** telephone order; **pedido urgente** rush order

(**b**) *Am (petición)* request; **a pedido de** at the request of

pedimento *nm Méx* customs document *(for imports and exports)*

pedir *vt* (**a**) *(solicitar)* to ask for, to request; **pedir algo a alguien** to ask sb for sth; **pedir a alguien que haga algo** to ask sb to do sth; **pedir prestado algo a alguien** to borrow sth from sb; **piden demasiado dinero por la empresa** they're asking too much for the company (**b**) *(mercancías)* to order; **pedir algo a alguien** to order sth from sb

pegar *vt* INFORM to paste (**en** into/onto)

peligrosidad *nf* **plus de peligrosidad** danger money

penalización *nf (sanción)* penalty ◻ **penalización por pago anticipado** prepayment penalty; **penalización por retraso en la entrega** late delivery penalty; **penalización por retraso en el pago** late payment penalty

penalizar vt to penalize

pendiente 1 adj (negociaciones, causa judicial) pending; (deuda, pago, factura) outstanding; **estar pendiente de algo** (a la espera de) to be waiting for sth, to be awaiting sth
  2 pendientes nmpl Am (asuntos) unresolved matter; **la lista de pendientes es enorme** there is an enormous backlog of matters to be dealt with

penetración nf (en mercado) penetration; **un país con escasa penetración de Internet** a country with low Internet penetration □ **penetración de mercado** market penetration

> En la cesta de los alimentos congelados, los envasados como el pescado preparado, los precocinados, etc., ganan peso progresivamente respecto a los vendidos a granel, llegando a una participación de mercado del 64% en volumen, con un crecimiento del 2% respecto al año anterior. En el 2002, los congelados envasados tuvieron una **penetración** del 96,3%, frente al 83,1% de los congelados a granel.

penetrar 1 vi **penetrar en** (mercado) to penetrate, to break into; **no consiguen penetrar en el mercado europeo** they have been unable to penetrate the European market
  2 vt (mercado) to penetrate, to break into; **han penetrado el mercado latinoamericano** they have broken into o penetrated the Latin American market

pensión nf pension; **cobrar una pensión** to be on a pension □ **pensión alimentaria, pensión alimenticia** maintenance allowance; **pensión asistencial** = benefit paid to people with low incomes, Br ≃ income support; **pensión contributiva** contributory pension; **pensión no contributiva** non-contributory pension; **pensión del Estado** state pension; **pensión de invalidez** disability pension; **pensión de jubilación** retirement pension; **pensión privada** private pension; **pensión retributiva** earnings-related pension; **pensión suplementaria** supplementary pension; **pensión vitalicia** life pension; **pensión de viudedad** widow's pension

pensionarse vpr Am to start drawing one's pension

> El procesamiento de la información no permite distinguir a los trabajadores que **se pensionaron** bajo la nueva Ley del Instituto Mexicano del Seguro Social (IMSS), que establece el mecanismo de capitalización individual y los que **se pensionaron** bajo la Ley de 1973, bajo el régimen de reparto. **"**

pensionista nmf (jubilado) pensioner

pequeño, -a adj small □ **pequeño accionista** small shareholder; **pequeño ahorrador** small saver; **pequeño comerciante** small trader; **pequeña empresa** small business; **la pequeña empresa** small businesses; **pequeño empresario** small businessman; **pequeño inversor** small investor; **pequeñas y medianas empresas** small and medium-sized enterprises

percentil nm percentile

percepción nf MKTG perception □ **percepción de marca** brand perception; **percepción selectiva** selective perception

perder 1 vt (a) (clientes, valor, empleo, dinero) to lose; **han perdido mucha cuota de mercado** they have lost a lot of market share (b) (tren, vuelo, oportunidad) to miss (c) (tiempo) to waste
  2 perderse vpr (cosecha) to fail

pérdida nf (a) FIN loss; **la empresa anunció pérdidas por valor de 2 millones de euros** the company announced losses o a loss of 2 million euros; **arrojar pérdidas** to run at a loss; **salir de pérdidas** to get out of the red; **tener pérdidas** to make a loss □ **pérdida atribuible** loss attributable; **pérdida bruta** gross loss; **pérdidas comerciales** trading loss; SEGUR **pérdida efectiva total** actual total loss; **pérdidas de explotación** operating loss; **pérdida final** terminal loss; **pérdida fiscal** tax loss; **pérdidas y ganancias** profit and loss; **pérdida neta** net loss; **pérdidas por operaciones en divisas** foreign exchange loss; **pérdida sobre el papel** paper loss; SEGUR **pérdida parcial** partial loss; **pérdida presunta** presumptive loss; **pérdida teórica** paper loss; SEGUR **pérdida total** total loss; SEGUR **pérdida total constructiva** total constructive loss
  (b) (de material, productos) **pérdida de datos** data loss; **pérdida de existencias** stock wastage; **pérdida en ruta** loss in transit
  (c) (de clientes, empleo) loss; **el cierre provocará la pérdida de cientos de puestos de trabajo** the closure will cause the loss of hundreds of jobs
  (d) (de tiempo, dinero) waste; **invertir en esos fondos es una pérdida de dinero** investing in those funds is a waste of money

perecedero, -a adj (productos) perishable; **productos perecederos** perishables

perfeccionar vt (habilidad, oficio) to improve

perfil nm (a) (de candidato, cliente) profile; **buscan licenciados con un perfil comercial** they are looking for graduates with a background in sales □ **perfil de la empresa** company profile; BANCA **perfil de patrimonio personal** personal assets profile (**b**) MKTG **perfil del consumidor** consumer profile; **perfil demográfico** demographic profile; **perfil geodemográfico** geodemographic profile; **perfil del mercado** market profile; **perfil de producto** product profile; **perfil psicológico** psychological profile; **perfil sociodemográfico** sociodemographic profile

>
> Explicó que la nueva política de precios se basa en una estructura segmentada de tarifas por reserva que varían en función del **perfil** de negocio y de alcance geográfico de la aerolínea. De esta forma las reservas, apuntó, se dividen en estándar o Premium dependiendo de la importancia que posean para la aerolínea y valor añadido que aporte el Sistema Global de Distribución (GDS, por sus siglas en inglés) al proceso de venta.
>

periférico, -a INFORM **1** adj peripheral
  2 nm peripheral (device) □ **periférico de entrada** input device; **periférico externo** external device; **periférico de impresora** printer peripheral; **periférico de salida** output device; **periférico en serie** serial device

periódico, -a 1 adj (regular) regular, periodic
  2 nm newspaper, paper □ **periódico en CD-ROM** CD-ROM newspaper; **periódico digital** online newspaper, digital newspaper; **periódico electrónico** electronic newspaper; **periódico gratuito** giveaway paper

periodificación nf **periodificación contable** time period adjustment

periodismo nm journalism

periodista nmf journalist

periodístico, -a adj journalistic

periodo, período nm period; **durante un periodo de tres meses** for a period of three months □ **periodo de amortización** depreciation period; **periodo de carencia** (de préstamo) grace period; **periodo de cobro** collection period; **periodo contable** accounting period; **periodo del crédito** credit period; UE **periodo de doble circulación** dual circulation period; **periodo de espera** (de pedido) waiting period; **periodo de exención fiscal** tax holiday; **periodo fiscal** tax period, US fiscal period; **periodo de gracia** grace period, period of grace, days of grace; **periodo de liquidación** settlement period; **periodo medio de cobro** debtors' turnover; **periodo medio de maduración** working capital cycle; **periodo medio de pago** creditors' turnover; **periodo muerto** dead period; **periodo de preaviso** notice period; **periodo de prueba** (de producto) trial period; (de candidato) probation, trial period; **periodo de prueba gratuito** free trial period; **periodo de**

recuperación (de inversión) payback period; **periodo de reflexión** (en ventas) cooling-off period

peritaje nm, **peritación** nf (**a**) (trabajo) expert work; **antes de comprar el inmueble encargaron un peritaje** before buying the property they got it surveyed (**b**) (informe) expert's report

peritar vt (inmueble) to value, to survey; (daños) to assess the value of

perito 1 adj expert; **ser perito en algo** to be an expert in sth
  2 nm (experto) expert; **un perito en contabilidad** an accountancy expert □ **perito agrícola** agronomist; **perito agrónomo** agronomist; **perito judicial** legal expert; **perito tasador de seguros** insurance adjuster; **perito tasador de siniestros** loss adjuster

perjudicado, -a 1 adj affected; DER **la parte perjudicada** the injured o aggrieved party
  2 nm,f DER **el perjudicado** the injured o aggrieved party

perjudicar vt to damage, to harm; **esa decisión perjudica nuestros intereses** this decision damages our interests

permisible adj permissible, acceptable, allowable

permiso nm (**a**) (autorización) permission; **dar permiso a alguien para hacer algo** to give sb permission to do sth; **pedir permiso para hacer algo** to ask permission to do sth
  (**b**) (documento) licence, permit □ **permiso aduanero, permiso de aduanas** customs visa; **permiso de aterrizaje** landing permit; **permiso de carga** loading permit; **permiso de descarga** landing order; **permiso de entrada** entry permit; **permiso de exportación** export permit, export licence; **permiso de importación** import permit, import licence; ADUANA **permiso de inspección** bill of sight; **permiso de residencia** residence permit; **permiso de salida** exit permit; **permiso de trabajo** work permit; **permiso de tránsito** transit permit
  (**c**) (en empleo) leave (of absence); **estar de permiso** to be on leave □ **permiso por asuntos familiares** family leave; **permiso por maternidad** maternity leave; **permiso por paternidad** paternity leave

permitir 1 vt (autorizar) to allow, to permit; **permitir a alguien hacer algo** to allow sb to do sth; **no se permite fumar** (en letrero) no smoking
  2 permitirse vpr **no pueden permitírselo** they can't afford it

permuta nf (**a**) (de bienes) exchange; (de trabajos) (job) swap (**b**) BANCA, BOLSA swap □ **permuta de acciones** equity swap; **permuta de activos** asset swap; **permuta de divisas** currency swap; **permuta financiera** swap; **permuta financiera de divisas** cross-currency swap

persona *nf* DER party ◻ *persona clave* key person; *persona de contacto* contact person; *persona física* individual entity; *persona jurídica, persona legal, Méx persona moral* legal person, artificial person

personal 1 *adj (privado)* personal, private; **para uso personal** for personal use; **personal e intransferible** non-transferable
   2 *nm (trabajadores)* staff, personnel ◻ *personal administrativo* administrative staff, back office staff, clerical staff; *personal asalariado* salaried staff; *personal de asistencia de ventas* sales support staff; *personal auxiliar* support staff; *personal clave* key staff; *personal contratado* contract staff; *personal directivo* managerial staff; *personal eventual* temporary staff; *personal de gestión* managerial staff; *personal de mantenimiento* maintenance staff; *personal mínimo* skeleton staff; *personal de oficina* office staff; *personal sustituto* replacement staff; *personal de ventanilla* counter staff; *personal de ventas* sales force, sales staff; *personal de vuelo* flight personnel

personalidad *nf* DER *personalidad jurídica* legal status

personalizable *adj* INFORM customizable

personalizar *vt* INFORM to customize

perspectiva *nf (posibilidad)* prospect; **las perspectivas de crecimiento** the prospects for growth; **un empleo con buenas perspectivas** a job with prospects ◻ *perspectivas económicas* economic prospects; *perspectivas de mercado* market prospects; *perspectivas de trabajo* job prospects

pesacartas *nm inv* letter scales

pesado, -a *adj (industria, maquinaria)* heavy

PESC *nf* UE *(abrev de* **Política Exterior y de Seguridad Común***)* CSFP

peseta *nf Antes* peseta

pesificación *nf RP* pesification

peso *nm* **(a)** *(carga)* weight; **peso en vacío** weight when empty; **vender algo al peso** to sell sth by weight; **el peso de la deuda** *(externa)* the debt burden ◻ *peso bruto* gross weight; *peso cargado* laden weight; *peso escurrido*

net weight; *peso estándar* standard weight; *peso imponible* chargeable weight; *pesos y medidas* weights and measures; *peso medio* average weight; *peso mínimo* minimum weight; *peso muerto* dead weight; *peso neto* net weight; *Am peso promedio* average weight; *peso total* full weight
   (b) *(fuerza, influencia)* weight; **el vicepresidente tiene mucho peso en la organización** the vice president carries a lot of weight in the organization
   (c) *(moneda)* peso
   (d) *Am Fam (dinero)* **en ese trabajo no gana un peso** she earns next to nothing in that job; **no tengo un peso** I'm broke

petición *nf* **(a)** *(acción)* request; **hacer una petición (de algo)** to make a request (for sth); **a petición de** at the request of **(b)** DER *(escrito)* petition

petrodivisa *nm* petrocurrency

petrodólar *nm* petrodollar

petróleo *nm* oil, petroleum ◻ *petróleo crudo* crude oil

petrolero, -a 1 *adj* oil; **compañía petrolera** oil company; **yacimiento petrolero** oilfield
   2 *nm* oil tanker

petrolífero, -a *adj* oil; **yacimiento petrolífero** oilfield

petroquímico, -a *adj* petrochemical; **productos petroquímicos** petrochemicals

PGC *nm Esp (abrev de* **Plan General de Contabilidad***)* General Accounting Plan

PIB *nm (abrev de* **producto** *Esp* **interior** *o Am* **interno bruto***)* GDP

picada *nf Am,* **picado** *nm Esp* **caer en picada** to drop sharply, to plummet; **la caída en picado del PIB** the sharp drop in GDP

pie *nm* **pie de foto** caption; INFORM *pie de página* footer

pieza *nf (de mecanismo)* part ◻ *pieza de recambio, pieza de repuesto* spare part, *US* extra

pignoración *nf* FIN pledging

pignorar *vt* FIN to pledge

pignoraticio, -a *adj* FIN **préstamo pignoraticio** collateral loan

PIN *nm (abrev de* **personal identification number***)* **(número de) PIN** PIN (number)

pin *nm* INFORM pin

pinchar 1 *vt* **(a)** *(burbuja financiera, inmobiliaria)* to burst **(b)** INFORM to click on; **pinche el icono** click on the icon
   2 *vi* **(a)** *(burbuja financiera, inmobiliaria)* to burst **(b)** INFORM to click; **pinche en el icono** click on the icon
   3 pincharse *vpr (burbuja financiera, inmobiliaria)* to burst

pionero, -a 1 *adj* pioneer, pioneering
  2 *nm,f* pioneer

piquete *nm (de huelguistas)* picket; **un piquete de veinte personas** twenty pickets; **había un piquete en el exterior de la fábrica** there was a picket (line) outside the factory ◻ *piquete informativo* = picket concerned with raising awareness and informing workers about the need for industrial action; *piquete móvil* flying picket

pirámide *nf pirámide salarial* wage pyramid

pirata 1 *adj (software, CD, edición)* pirate
  2 *nmf* INFORM **pirata (informático)** *(que accede sin autorización)* hacker; *(que copia sin autorización)* software pirate

piratear 1 *vi* INFORM to crack
  2 *vt* (**a**) *(propiedad intelectual)* to pirate (**b**) INFORM *(programa) (desproteger)* to hack into, to crack into; *(hacer copia ilegal)* to pirate

piratería *nf (de programas, vídeos, ropa)* piracy ◻ *piratería informática (copias ilegales)* software piracy; *(acceso no autorizado)* hacking

piso *nm Am (nivel más bajo)* low

> **"**
>
> Mediante su política monetaria, el Banco de México (Banxico) ha logrado contener el crecimiento de los precios y el rendimiento de los títulos gubernamentales, que hace poco llegaron a mínimos históricos. En la última subasta de agosto, la tasa líder de los Cetes quedó en 4.65 por ciento, y de esta forma se separó sólo 51 centésimas de su **piso** histórico: 4.14 por ciento.
>
> **"**

pista *nf pista de auditoría* audit trail

PITEX *nm Méx (abrev de Programa de Importación Temporal)* temporary importation programme

píxel *nm* INFORM pixel

pixelado, -a *adj* INFORM *(imagen)* pixellated

pizarra *nf pizarra blanca* whiteboard; *pizarra de conferencia* flip chart

placa *nf* INFORM board ◻ *placa del bus* bus board; *placa de circuito integrado* integrated circuit board; *placa de la CPU* CPU board; *placa de expansión* expansion board; *placa madre* motherboard; *Esp placa de vídeo, Am placa de video* video board

plan *nm* plan ◻ *plan de actuación* action plan; *plan de ahorro* savings plan, savings scheme; *plan de amortización (de deuda, préstamo)* repayment plan; *(de bienes de equipo)* depreciation schedule; *plan de austeridad* austerity programme; *plan contable* accounting plan; *plan de contratación (de empleados)* recruitment plan; *plan de creación de empleo* job creation

scheme; *plan de desarrollo* development plan; *plan económico* economic plan; *plan de empresa* business plan; *plan de estabilización* stabilization plan; *plan estratégico de negocio* strategic business plan; *plan de fidelización* loyalty scheme; *plan de financiación* funding plan; *plan financiero* financial plan; *plan de formación en la empresa o en el lugar de trabajo Br* in-company training scheme, *US* internship program; *Esp Plan General de Contabilidad* General Accounting Plan; *plan global* overall plan; *plan de incentivos* incentive scheme; *plan de inversiones* investment plan; *plan de jubilación* pension plan, pension scheme, retirement savings plan; *plan maestro* master plan; *plan maestro de producción* master production schedule; *plan de marketing* marketing plan; *plan de medidas* action plan; *plan de medios (con objetivos)* media plan; *(con calendario detallado)* media schedule; *plan de muestreo* sampling project; *plan de negocio* business plan; *plan de participación en los beneficios* profit-sharing scheme; *plan de pensiones* pension scheme, pension plan; *plan de pensiones de empleo o empresa* employee pension plan, *Br* occupational pension scheme; *plan previsional* forecast plan; *plan quinquenal* five-year plan; *plan de recuperación empresarial* company recovery plan; *plan de reestructuración* restructuring plan; *Bol, Col, Ven Plan Único de Cuentas* standardized accounting procedure

planear *vt & vi* to plan

planificación *nf* planning ◻ *planificación a corto plazo* short-term planning; *planificación de la distribución* distribution planning; *planificación de la empresa* company planning; *planificación empresarial* corporate planning; *planificación estratégica* strategic planning; *planificación financiera* financial planning; *planificación fiscal* tax planning; *planificación a largo plazo* long-term planning; *planificación de la mano de obra* manpower planning; *planificación de marketing* marketing planning; *planificación de medios* media planning; *planificación operativa* operational planning; *planificación de precios* price plan; *planificación presupuestaria* budget planning; *planificación de la producción* production planning; *planificación de productos* product planning; *planificación de los requerimientos de materiales* material requirements planning; *planificación de las ventas* sales planning

planificador, -ora *nm,f* planner ◻ *planificador de marketing* marketing planner; *planificador de medios* media planner

planificar *vt* to plan

planning *nm* (**a**) *(en pared)* planner (**b**) *(planificación)* schedule, agenda

plano *nm (diseño, mapa)* plan ❑ *plano de calles* street map; *plano de planta* floor plan

planta *nf (fábrica)* plant ❑ *planta de automóviles* car factory, car plant; *planta envasadora, planta de envase* packaging plant; *planta de fabricación* manufacturing plant; *planta industrial* industrial unit; *planta de montaje* assembly plant; *planta de producción* production plant; *planta refrigeradora* refrigeration plant

plante *nm (protesta)* walkout; **ayer hubo un plante en la fábrica** workers in the factory downed tools yesterday

plantel *nm SAm (de empresa)* staff; **estar en plantel** to be on the payroll, to be a permanent member of staff ❑ *plantel fijo* permanent staff; *plantel reducido* reduced staff

plantilla *nf* (**a**) *(de empresa)* staff; **estar en plantilla** to be on the payroll, to be a permanent member of staff; **reducir la plantilla** to downsize ❑ *plantilla fija* permanent staff; *plantilla reducida* reduced staff (**b**) INFORM template

plástico *nm Fam (tarjeta de crédito)* plastic (money)

plata *nf* (**a**) *(metal)* silver ❑ *plata de ley* sterling silver; *plata en lingotes* silver bars, silver bullion (**b**) *Am Fam (dinero)* cash, *Br* dosh; **ganar mucha plata** to earn big money

plataforma *nf* (**a**) INFORM platform (**b**) *(de vehículo)* flat bed ❑ *plataforma de carga (de camión)* load bed

plaza *nf* (**a**) *(puesto de trabajo)* position, job; **han sido cubiertas todas las plazas** all the positions have been filled ❑ *plaza en propiedad* permanent post *(in public service)*; *plaza vacante* vacancy
(**b**) *(mercado)* market, marketplace; BOLSA stock exchange; **la plaza neoyorquina abrió a la baja hoy** the New York stock exchange opened down today; **en plaza** on the market; *Arg* **los negocios volvieron a realizarse dentro de una plaza firme** trading resumed in a steady market
(**c**) MKTG *(en marketing mix)* place

plazo *nm* (**a**) *(de tiempo)* **en el plazo de un mes** within a month; **mañana termina el plazo de subscripción** the deadline for subscription is tomorrow; **cumplir un plazo** to meet a deadline; **a corto/medio/largo plazo** in the short/medium/long term; **una solución a corto/largo plazo** a short-/long-term solution; **invertir dinero a plazo fijo** to invest money for a fixed term ❑ SEGUR *plazo de carencia* waiting period; *plazo de comercialización* time to market; *plazo de entrega* delivery time; *plazo de entrega garantizado* guaranteed delivery period; *plazo máximo* time limit; *plazo de preaviso* term of notice; *plazo de prescripción* lapsing period;

plazo previsto target date; *plazo de tiempo* time frame
(**b**) *(de dinero)* instalment; **comprar a plazos** to buy on *Br* hire purchase *o US* an installment plan; **pagar a plazos** to pay in instalments ❑ *plazos de la hipoteca* mortgage (re)payments; *plazo mensual* monthly instalment

pleiteante *nmf* DER litigant

pleitear *vi* DER to litigate, to conduct a lawsuit

pleito *nm* DER *(litigio)* lawsuit; **entablar un pleito contra alguien** to start *o* institute proceedings against sb, to bring a lawsuit against sb; **ganar/perder un pleito** to win/lose a case *o* lawsuit

plenario, -a *adj* **sesión plenaria** plenary

pleno, -a 1 *adj* full, complete; **miembro de pleno derecho** full member ❑ *pleno empleo* full employment; *plenos poderes* plenary powers
2 *nm (reunión)* plenary meeting

plica *nf (sobre)* sealed envelope

plóter, plotter *nm* INFORM plotter

plug-in *nm* INFORM plug-in

pluma *nf (estilográfica)* (fountain) pen; *Carib, Méx (bolígrafo)* (ballpoint) pen ❑ *Méx pluma atómica* ballpoint (pen); *pluma estilográfica* fountain pen; *Méx, Ven pluma fuente* fountain pen

plurianual *adj* over several years

pluriempleo *nm* moonlighting; **el pluriempleo es común en la región** having more than one job is common in the region

plurisectorial *adj* cross-industry

plus *nm* bonus ❑ *plus de antigüedad* seniority bonus; *plus familiar* family allowance; *plus de peligrosidad* danger money, *US* danger pay; *plus de productividad* productivity bonus

plusvalía *nf (tras venta)* capital gain; ECON *(aumento de valor)* surplus value ❑ *plusvalía imputable* chargeable gain

> **"**
>
> Paradójicamente este último grupo mediático formaba parte del accionariado de RTL hasta diciembre de 2001, fecha en la que vendió su pequeña participación a Bertelsmann, lo que le reportó importantes **plusvalías**.
>
> **"**

PNB *nm* ECON *(abrev de* **producto nacional bruto***)* GNP

población *nf* (**a**) *(ciudad)* town, city; *(pueblo)* village (**b**) *(personas, animales)* population ❑ *población activa* working population, workforce; *población básica, población estable* basic population; *población prevista* projected population

> La tasa de paro de la zona euro aumentó una décima en marzo respecto al mes anterior y se situó en el 8,7% de la **población activa**, hasta 12,2 millones de personas, según los datos publicados hoy por la Oficina Europea de Estadística (Eurostat).

poder *nm* (**a**) *(autoridad, capacidad)* power; **actuar con plenos poderes** to act with full powers; **estar en el poder** to be in power; **hacerse con** *o* **tomar el poder** to seize power; **perder el poder** to lose power ❑ *poder adquisitivo* purchasing power; *poder adquisitivo del consumidor* consumer purchasing power; *poder de compra* purchasing power; *poderes discrecionales* discretionary powers; *poder ejecutivo* executive power; *(el gobierno)* executive; *poderes extraordinarios* emergency powers; *los poderes fácticos* the centres of power in society; *poder judicial* legislative power; *(los jueces)* judiciary; *poder legislativo* judicial power; *(las cortes)* legislature; *poder de negociación* bargaining power; *poder para tomar decisiones* decision-making power; *poder de ventas* selling power

(**b**) *(posesión, control)* **estar en poder de alguien** to be in sb's hands; **el inmueble pasó a poder del banco** ownership of the property was transferred to the bank

(**c**) *(autorización)* power, authorization, proxy; **poder (notarial)** *(documento)* power of attorney; **dar poderes a alguien para que haga algo** to authorize *o* empower sb to do sth; **tener plenos poderes para hacer algo** to be fully authorized *o* empowerd to do sth; *Esp* **por poderes**, *Am* **por poder** by proxy

polígono industrial *nm Br* industrial estate, trading estate, *US* industrial area

política *nf* (**a**) *(arte de gobernar)* politics

(**b**) *(modo de gobernar, táctica)* policy; **adoptar una política** to adopt a policy ❑ UE *Política Agrícola Común* Common Agricultural Policy; *política de austeridad* austerity policy; *política cambiaria, política de cambio* exchange policy; *política comercial* trade policy; *política contable* accounting policy; *política de contratación de personal* staffing policy; *política crediticia* lending policy; *política de distribución* distribution policy; *política de dividendos* dividend policy; *política económica* economic policy; *política editorial* editorial policy; *política de empleo* employment policy; *política de empresa* company policy; *política de estabilización* stabilizing policy; *política exterior* foreign policy; UE *Política Exterior y de Seguridad Común* Common Foreign and Security Policy; *política fiscal* fiscal policy; *política inflacionista, política inflacionaria* inflationary policy; *política de inversiones* investment policy; *política de libre comercio, política de libre cambio* free trade policy; *política de marca* brand policy; *política de marketing* marketing policy; *política medioambiental* environmental policy; *política de mercado abierto* open-market policy; *política de mínima intervención estatal* laissez-faire policy; *política monetaria* monetary policy; *política mundial* worldwide policy; UE *Política Pesquera Común* Common Fisheries Policy; *política de precios* price policy, pricing policy; *política presupuestaria* budgetary policy; *política de productos* product policy; *política de promociones* promotional policy; *política de puertas abiertas* open-door policy; *política de rentas* incomes policy; *política salarial* pay policy, wage policy; *política de ventas* sales policy

político, -a 1 *adj (de gobierno)* political
   2 *nm,f* politician

politología *nf* political science

politólogo, -a *nm,f* political scientist

polivalencia *nf (de empleado)* multiskilling

póliza *nf* (**a**) *(de seguro)* (insurance) policy; **póliza de incendios/de vida** fire /life insurance policy; **suscribir una póliza** to take out a policy ❑ *póliza abierta* open policy; *póliza de accidentes* accident policy; *póliza combinada* mixed policy; *póliza conjunta* joint policy; *póliza de crédito* loan agreement; *póliza estándar* standard policy; *póliza de fidelidad (de empleados)* fidelity scheme; *póliza flotante* floating policy; *póliza con franquicia* excess policy; *póliza integral* blanket policy; *póliza liberada, póliza con prima* paid-up policy; *póliza de prima única* single premium policy; *póliza provisional* cover note; *póliza de seguros* insurance policy; *póliza de seguro marítimo* marine insurance policy; *póliza de seguro de vida* life insurance policy, (life) assurance policy; *póliza de tipo mixto* endowment policy; *póliza a todo riesgo* all-in policy, comprehensive policy

(**b**) *(sello de Estado)* = stamp on a document showing that a certain tax has been paid; *(impuesto) Br* stamp duty, *US* tax duty

ponderación *nf* ECON weighting

ponderado, -a *adj* ECON *(índice, media)* weighted

> La rentabilidad media **ponderada** obtenida por los fondos de inversión en los últimos doce meses fue negativa y los ahorradores perdieron una media del 4,61 por ciento de su patrimonio.

ponderar *vt* ECON to weight

POP *nm* INFORM (*abrev de* **post office protocol**) POP

porcentaje *nm* percentage; **nos dan un porcentaje sobre las ventas** we get a percentage of the sales

porción *nf* portion

portada *nf* INFORM *(de página Web)* home page

portador, -ora *nm,f* bearer; **al portador** to the bearer

portadora *nf* INFORM,TEL carrier ❑ *portadora de datos* data carrier

portafolio *nm*, **portafolios** *nm inv (carpeta)* file; *(maletín)* briefcase, attaché case ❑ *Am portafolio de inversión* investment portfolio

portal *nm* INFORM portal

portapapeles *nm inv* INFORM clipboard

portátil 1 *adj* portable
2 *nm* laptop, portable (computer)

portavoz *nmf (persona)* spokesperson, spokesman, *f* spokeswoman

porte *nm* (**a**) *(gasto de transporte)* transport costs, carriage; **los portes corren a cargo del destinatario** carriage is payable by the addressee; **pagar los portes** to pay the carriage ❑ *portes debidos* Br carriage forward, US freight collect; **enviar algo a portes debidos** to send sth Br carriage forward o US freight collect; *porte neto* net register tonnage; *portes pagados* freight paid, Br carriage paid; **enviar algo a portes pagados** to send sth freight paid o Br carriage paid; *porte y seguro pagados* freight and insurance paid, Br carriage and insurance paid
(**b**) *(transporte)* carriage, transport; **una empresa de portes y mudanzas** Br a removal firm, US a moving firm
(**c**) *RP (permiso)* permit, licence; **¿usted tiene porte de armas?** do you have a gun licence?

porvenir *nm* future; **se está labrando su porvenir** she is carving out a future for herself; **el porvenir de la empresa** the future of the company, the company's future

poseedor, -ora *nm,f (de acciones)* owner, holder; *(de inmueble)* owner

poseer *vt* (**a**) *(ser dueño de)* to own; **posser el 51% de las acciones** to own 51% of the shares
(**b**) DER to possess

posesión *nf* (**a**) *(acción, efecto)* possession; **el inmueble ha pasado a posesión de sus antiguos dueños** ownership of the property has passed back to its previous owners; **tomar posesión de** *(cargo)* to take up; *(propiedad)* to take possession of ❑ DER *posesión efectiva* actual possession (**b**) *(cosa poseída)* possession; **tuvo que vender todas sus posesiones** she had to sell all her possessions

posibilidad *nf* (**a**) *(circunstancia)* possibility, chance (**b**) *(recursos económicos)* **posibilidades**

(económicas) financial means o resources; **comprar un inmueble no entra dentro de nuestras posibilidades** we don't have the means o we can't afford to buy a property

posible 1 *adj* possible; **un posible cliente** a prospective client, a prospect; **en cuanto le sea posible** at your earliest convenience; **hacer posible algo** to make sth possible; **su intervención hizo posible el acuerdo** his intervention made the agreement possible; **lo antes posible** as soon as possible
2 posibles *nmpl* (financial) means

posición *nf* (**a**) *(lugar)* position; **la empresa ha consolidado su posición como líder del mercado** the company has consolidated its position as the market leader ❑ *posición competitiva* competitive position; *posición estratégica* strategic position
(**b**) BOLSA position; **tomar una posición larga/corta** to take a long/short position, to go long/short; **cerrar una posición** to close a position; **perder posiciones** to fall back ❑ *posición abierta* open position; *posición alcista* bull position; *posición bajista* bear position; *posición corta* short position; *posición cubierta* covered (short) position; *posición descubierta* uncovered position; *posición larga* long position
(**c**) *(categoría) (social)* status; *(económica)* situation; **está en una posición económica difícil** he's in a difficult financial situation

posicionamiento *nm* MKTG positioning ❑ *posicionamiento de calidad* quality positioning; *posicionamiento competitivo* competitive positioning; *posicionamiento estratégico* strategic positioning; *posicionamiento de marca* brand positioning; *posicionamiento en el mercado* market positioning; *posicionamiento del precio* price positioning; *posicionamiento de producto* product positioning

posicionar 1 *vt* MKTG *(producto)* to position
2 posicionarse *vpr (empresa)* to position oneself; **nuestro producto se ha posicionado entre los mejores del mundo** our product now ranks among the best in the world

> ❝
> Los jóvenes que nacieron en EE UU en la década de los setenta hicieron de los Levi's el uniforme de su generación. A partir de entonces, estos vaqueros **se posicionaron** en todo el mundo.
> ❞

positivo, -a 1 *adj (número, respuesta, resultado)* positive; **saldo positivo** credit balance
2 *nm* BOLSA **cerrar en positivo** to close up

> ❝
> El Popular fue el único banco que **cerró en positivo**, al sumar un 0,14%, mientras que BBVA acabó al mismo cambio que ayer, 9,8

euros. SCH se dejó un 0,12% y Bankinter restó un 0,58%. ⸻ **„**

posponer *vt (aplazar)* to postpone; **pospondremos la reunión para mañana** we will postpone the meeting until tomorrow

postal 1 *adj* postal; **los servicios postales** the postal services
2 *nm Esp* **postal exprés** express delivery, *Br* ≃ special delivery

póster *nm* MKTG poster

poste restante *nm RP Br* poste restante, *US* general delivery

post-it® *nm inv* Post-it®

postor, -ora *nm,f* bidder; **vender al mejor postor** to sell to the highest bidder

PostScript® *nm* INFORM PostScript®

posventa, postventa *adj inv* after-sales; **servicio posventa** after-sales service

potencial 1 *adj* potential; **un cliente potencial** a prospective client, a potential customer, a prospect
2 *nm* potential ◻ BOLSA **potencial alcista** upside potential; BOLSA **potencial bajista** downside potential; **potencial de clientes** potential customer base; **potencial de crecimiento** growth potential; **potencial de desarrollo** development potential; **potencial de exportación** export potential; **potencial importador** import potential; **potencial industrial** industrial potential; **potencial de mercado** market potential; **potencial publicitario** advertising potential; **potencial de ventas** sales potential

p.p. **(a)** *(abrev de* **por poder***)* pp **(b)** *(abrev de* **porte pagado***)* c/p

PPA *nf* ECON *(abrev de* **Paridad del Poder Adquisitivo***)* PPP, Purchasing Power Parity

PPP INFORM *(abrev de* **point-to-point protocol***)* PPP

ppp INFORM *(abrev de* **puntos por pulgada***)* dpi

práctica *nf* **(a)** *(experiencia)* practice; **se aprende con la práctica** it comes with practice **(b)** *(aplicación)* practice; **llevar algo a la práctica, poner algo en práctica** to put sth into practice **(c)** **prácticas (laborales)** training, *Br* work experience, *US* internship; **contrato en prácticas** *Br* work-experience contract, *US* internship **(d)** *(uso)* **prácticas comerciales** trade practices; **prácticas comerciales desleales** unfair trading; **prácticas restrictivas** restrictive practices

practicar *vt (profesión)* to practise; **practica la abogacía desde hace diez años** she has been practising law for ten years

práctico, -a *adj (estilo, enfoque)* practical

Practicum *nm* practicum training

precariedad *nf* **la precariedad en el empleo** job insecurity; **una situación de precariedad económica** a precarious financial situation

precario, -a *adj* **un empleo precario** an insecure job with poor pay and conditions

precarización *nf* **la precarización del empleo** the casualization of labour

precarizar *vt* to casualize

precinto *nm* seal ◻ **precinto aduanero** customs seal

precio *nm* price; **subir los precios** to put prices up; **bajar los precios** to bring prices down; **subir de precio** to go up *o* rise *o* increase in price; **bajar de precio** to go down *o* fall *o* decrease in price; **el precio ha subido en un 10%** the price has gone up *o* risen *o* increased by 10%; **el precio ha bajado en un 10%** the price has gone down *o* fallen *o* decreased by 10%; **el precio del dinero** the cost of borrowing; **vender algo a precio reducido** to sell sth at a reduced price; **¿a qué precio está el oro?** what is the price of gold? ◻ BOLSA **precio de apertura** opening price; **precio aproximado** approximate price; **precio autorizado** authorized price; **precio bruto** gross price; **precio de catálogo** catalogue price, list price; BOLSA **precio de cierre** closing price; **precio completo** full price; **precio de compra** purchase price; BOLSA **precio comprador** bid price, *US* bidding price; **precio al contado** cash price; BOLSA spot price; **precio controlado** controlled price; FIN **precio de conversión** *(de bonos)* conversion price; **precio de costo,** *Esp* **precio de coste** cost price; **comprar algo a precio de costo** to buy sth at cost price; BOLSA **precio de cotización** listed price, *Br* quoted price; **precios cruzados** cross-pricing; **precio con descuento** discount price; MKTG **precio desleal** predatory price; BOLSA **precio de ejercicio** *(de opciones)* exercise price, strike price, striking price; BOLSA **precio de emisión** issue price; **precio especial** special price; **precio de exportación** export price; **precio de fábrica** factory price, manufacturer's price; **precio facturado** invoice price; **precio del flete** freight price; **precio franco en almacén** price ex warehouse; **precio franco en fábrica** price ex works; **precio de importación** import price; **precio indicativo** guide price; UE *(en PAC)* target price; **precio de lanzamiento** introductory price; **precio de liquidación** closing-down price; BOLSA settlement price; **precio de lista** list price; **precio de lujo** premium price; **precio marcado** marked price; **precio máximo** maximum price; **precio máximo autorizado** ceiling price; **precio al por mayor** trade price, wholesale price; **precio mediano** mean price, middle price; **precio medio** average price; **precio de mercado** market price; **precio mínimo**

minimum price; BOLSA floor price; *(en subasta)* reserve price; UE **precio mínimo garantizado** intervention price; **precio en muelle** landed cost; **precios múltiples** *(según el mercado)* multiple pricing; BOLSA **precio nominal** nominal price; **precio normal** regular price, standard price; UE **precio objetivo** *(en PAC)* target price; **precio de oferta** offer price; BOLSA *(comprador)* bid price, *US* bidding price; ECON supply price; **precio oficial** official price; BOLSA **precio de opción** option money, option price; MKTG **precio óptimo** optimal price; **precio del petróleo** oil price; BOLSA **precio a plazo** forward price; **precio preferente, precio preferencial** preferential price; MKTG **precio de prestigio** prestige price; *Am* **precio promedio** average price; **precio de promoción** promotional price; MKTG **precio psicológico** psychological price; MKTG **precio psicológico óptimo** optimal psychological price; BOLSA **precio real** actual price; **precio rebajado** reduced price, sale price; MKTG **precio de reclamo** loss leader price; **precio recomendado por el fabricante** manufacturer's recommended price; **precio de reembolso** *(de bonos, acciones)* redemption price; **precio de referencia** reference price; **precio de rescate** call price, redemption price; **precio de saldo** bargain price; **precio de salida** *(en subasta)* starting price, *US* upset price; BOLSA asking price, *US* asked price; **precio de salida a Bolsa** issue price; **precio simbólico** nominal o token amount; **precio de subasta** auction price; UE **precio subvencionado** support price; **precio de suscripción** *(a publicación)* subscription rate; BOLSA **precio a término** forward price; **precio en las tiendas** street price; **precio tope** top o ceiling price; UE **precio umbral** threshold price; **precio por unidad, precio unitario** unit price; **precio a vencimiento** terminal price; **precio de venta** selling price, sale price; **precio de venta al público** retail price; **precio de venta al público recomendado** recommended retail price

precisión *nf* precision

predecesor, -ora *nm,f* predecessor

predicción *nf* forecast, prediction ❑ **predicción bursátil** stock market forecast

predisposición *nf* MKTG **predisposición del consumidor** buyer readiness

preferencia *nf* (**a**) MKTG *(predilección)* preference ❑ **preferencia del consumidor** consumer preference; **preferencia de marca** brand preference (**b**) **preferencias aduaneras** customs preferential duty

preferente *adj* (**a**) *(prioritario)* preferential; *(acción, dividendo)* preference (**b**) *(en transporte)* **clase preferente** club class

prefijo *nm* **prefijo (telefónico)** *Br* dialling code, *US* area code, dial code

preformateado, -a *adj* INFORM preformatted

pregunta *nf* MKTG question ❑ **pregunta abierta** open question, open-ended question; **pregunta cerrada** closed question; **pregunta de control** control question, check question; **pregunta escalonada** scaled question; **preguntas más frecuentes** frequently asked questions

preinstalado, -a *adj* INFORM *(software)* preinstalled

prejubilación *nf* = voluntary redundancy before entitlement to early retirement, with agreed benefits and/or additional payments, partly funded by the government

> ❝
>
> En el expediente de regulación llevado a cabo en 1999, Telefónica rebajó la edad de **prejubilación** hasta los 52 años. Entre esa edad y los sesenta años, los empleados que salieran de la empresa tenían derecho a cobrar el setenta por ciento de su salario. Y entre los sesenta años y los sesenta y cinco años, —edad legal de jubilación—, los trabajadores tenían derecho a cobrar el cuarenta por ciento del salario. Después pasaban a lo legalmente establecido en la jubilación.
>
> ❞

prejubilado, -a 1 *adj* **trabajadores prejubilados** workers who have accepted early retirement *(through a "prejubilación" agreement)* **2** *nm,f* early-retired person *(through a "prejubilación" agreement)*

prejubilar 1 *vt* **prejubilar a alguien** to give someone early retirement *(through a "prejubilación" agreement)* **2 prejubilarse** *vpr* to take early retirement *(through a "prejubilación" agreement)*

premercadeo *nm Col* BOLSA pre-marketing

premio *nm* award, prize ❑ **premio de antigüedad** length-of-service award; **premio de jubilación** retirement award

prenda *nf* *(señal, garantía)* pledge, lien; **dejar algo en prenda** to leave sth as a pledge; **ofrecer en prenda** to pledge; **prenda sobre acciones** lien on shares

prendario, -a *adj* **garantía prendaria** collateral (security)

prender *Am* INFORM **1** *vt* to switch on, to power up **2 prenderse** *vpr* to switch itself on, to power up

prensa *nf* *(periódicos, periodistas)* press ❑ **prensa especializada** specialist press; **prensa financiera** financial press; **prensa nacional** national press; **prensa del sector** trade press

preparar 1 *vt* to prepare; *(informe, documento, plan)* to draw up; *(pedido, paquete)* to make up; **la empresa está preparada para la expansión**

the company is geared up for expansion

  2 prepararse *vpr* to prepare oneself, to get ready; **la empresa se prepara para la expansión** the company is gearing up for expansion

preponderante *adj (factor)* overriding

preprogramado, -a *adj* INFORM preprogrammed

prescripción *nf* DER expiry, lapsing, prescription

preseleccionar *vt (candidatos)* to shortlist; **estar preseleccionado para algo** to be shorlisted for sth

presencia *nf* (**a**) *(aspecto)* **buena presencia** smart appearance (**b**) MKTG **presencia en el mercado** market exposure, market presence

> La recesión en Latinoamérica, con epicentro en Argentina, está lastrando fundamentalmente las cotizaciones de los gigantes bancarios españoles, BBVA y BSCH, con fuerte **presencia** en el área. Las inversiones de las dos entidades en la zona –cerca de 15.000 millones de dólares (más de 1,2 billones de pesetas)–, que hasta no hace demasiado habían favorecido un fuerte crecimiento de los márgenes por la buena marcha del negocio en la región, están castigando el precio de las acciones de ambas entidades.

presencial *adj (curso, clase)* on-site

presentación *nf* (**a**) *(entrega) (de letra de cambio, cheque, factura)* presentation, presentment; **pagadero a su presentación** payable on demand, payable upon presentation (**b**) *(exposición) (de planes, presupuestos)* presentation; *(de producto)* launch (**c**) MKTG display ◻ **presentación del escaparate** window display; **presentación masiva** mass display (**d**) INFORM **presentación preliminar** (print) preview

presentar 1 *vt* (**a**) *(entregar) (letra de cambio, factura, cheque, informe)* to present; *(solicitud)* to make, to submit; *(moción)* to propose; *(dimisión)* to tender, to hand in; *(queja, reclamación)* to lodge, to register; **presentar una letra para su aceptación** to present a bill for acceptance; **presentar cargos/una demanda contra alguien** to bring charges/an action against sb (**b**) *(exhibir por primera vez) (planes, presupuestos)* to present; *(producto)* to launch

  2 presentarse *vpr (personarse)* to turn up, to appear; **mañana preséntate en el departamento de contabilidad** go to the accounts department tomorrow; **preséntese en mi oficina** report to my office

presente 1 *adj* (**a**) *(asistente, que está delante)* present; **yo estuve presente en la reunión** I was present at the meeting (**b**) *(en curso)* current; **del presente mes** of this month

  2 *nmf (en un lugar)* **los/las (aquí) presentes** everyone present; **invitó a los presentes a acudir a la próxima reunión** he invited everyone present to attend the next meeting

  3 *nm (corriente)* **el presente** *(mes)* the current month; *(año)* the current year

  4 *nf (escrito)* **por la presente le informo...** I hereby inform you...; **por la presente le informamos de que ha rebasado el límite de su crédito** we should advise you that you have exceeded your credit limit

presidencia *nf* (**a**) *(de nación)* presidency (**b**) *(de empresa, organización, reunión)* chairmanship; **ocupa la presidencia del banco** he is chairman of the bank; **durante la presidencia de la Señora Molina** under the chairmanship of Ms Molina (**c**) *Méx* **presidencia municipal** *(corporación)* town council; *(edificio)* town hall

presidente, -a *nm,f* (**a**) *(de nación)* president; **presidente (del Gobierno)** prime minister (**b**) *(de organización, reunión)* chairman, *f* chairwoman; *(de empresa)* chairman, *f* chairwoman, *US* president ◻ **presidente de honor** honorary president *o* chairman (**c**) *(del parlamento)* speaker (**d**) *(de tribunal)* presiding judge ◻ **presidente del tribunal supremo** chief justice (**e**) *Méx* **presidente municipal** *(alcalde)* mayor

presidir *vt (organización, empresa)* to be chairman of; *(reunión)* to chair

presión *nf* (**a**) *(fuerza)* pressure; **los precios del cobre han experimentado nuevas presiones** copper prices came under renewed pressure ◻ ECON **presión fiscal** fiscal pressure; **presión fiscal en frío** fiscal drag; **presión inflacionista, presión inflacionaria** inflationary pressure (**b**) *(coacción, influencia)* pressure; **meter presión a alguien** to put pressure on sb

presionar 1 *vt* to pressurize, to put pressure on; **un grupo de financieros fue a presionar al ministro** a group of financiers went to lobby the minister

  2 *vi* to lobby; **los ecologistas están presionando para que se cierre la fábrica** ecologists are lobbying for the closure of the plant

prestación *nf* (**a**) *(de servicio) (acción)* provision; *(resultado)* service

  (**b**) *(subsidio)* benefit ◻ **prestaciones por desempleo** unemployment benefit; **prestaciones en efectivo** cash benefits; **prestaciones para los empleados** employee benefits; **prestación por enfermedad** sickness benefit; **prestaciones familiares** family benefits; **prestación por incapacidad, prestación por invalidez** *Br* incapacity benefit, *US* disability benefit; **prestación por maternidad** maternity benefit; **prestaciones de la seguridad social** social security benefits

  (**c**) **prestaciones** *(de producto, vehículo)* performance features

prestado, -a *adj* borrowed, on loan; **pedir dinero prestado a alguien** to borrow money from sb

prestamiento *nm Méx* loan

prestamista *nmf* (money) lender ▫ *prestamista hipotecario* mortgage lender

préstamo *nm* (**a**) *(acción)* lending ▫ *préstamo y arriendo* lend-lease
(**b**) *(cantidad)* loan; **pedir un préstamo** to ask for a loan; **suscribir un préstamo** to take out a loan; **negar un préstamo a alguien** to refuse sb a loan ▫ *préstamo avalado* guaranteed loan; *préstamo bancario* bank loan; *préstamo comercial* commercial loan; *préstamo condicionado* tied loan; *préstamo consolidado* consolidated loan; *préstamo a corto plazo* short-term loan; *préstamo del Estado* government loan; *préstamo fiduciario* unsecured loan; *préstamo a fondo perdido* outright loan; *préstamo con garantía* loan on collateral, secured loan; *préstamo sin garantía* loan without security, unsecured loan; *préstamo con garantía prendaria* collateral loan; *préstamo garantizado* secured loan, guaranteed loan; *préstamo hipotecario* mortgage loan; *préstamo inmobiliario Br* property loan, *US* real estate loan; *préstamo con interés* interest-bearing loan; *préstamo sin intereses* interest-free loan; *préstamo a largo plazo* long-term loan; *préstamo mercantil* commercial loan; *préstamo en moneda extranjera* currency loan; *préstamo participativo* participating loan; *préstamo perpetuo* perpetual loan; *préstamo personal* personal loan; *préstamo pignoraticio* collateral loan; *préstamo a plazo fijo* fixed-term loan; *préstamo de refinanciación* refunding loan; *préstamo remunerado* interest-bearing loan; *préstamo sindicado* syndicated loan; *préstamo a la vista* call loan

> "
> Una de las primeras medidas de reconversión adoptadas fue la suscripción, en mayo de 2002, de un **préstamo sindicado** por 300 millones con vencimiento en 2007. Este préstamo vino a sustituir a otro de la misma cuantía, que el grupo había firmado tres años antes para pagar las compras de OMSA y Navidul y que tenía peores condiciones.
> "

prestar *vt* (**a**) *(dinero)* to lend, to loan; **prestar algo a alguien** to lend sth to sb, to lend sb sth; **prestar dinero con interés** to lend money at interest (**b**) *(servicio)* to provide

prestatario, -a *nm,f* FIN borrower

presupuestal = **presupuestario**

presupuestar *vt* to budget; **hemos presupuestado 100.000 euros para publicidad** we have budgeted 100,000 euros for advertising; **han presupuestado la construcción del museo en cien millones de euros** they have calculated that the museum will cost a hundred million euros to build

presupuestario, -a *Am* **presupuestal** *adj* budgetary; **déficit presupuestario** budget deficit

presupuesto *nm* (**a**) *(dinero disponible)* budget; **equilibrar** *o* **ajustar el presupuesto** to balance the budget; **estamos dentro del presupuesto** we are within budget; **salirse del presupuesto** to overspend one's budget; **ya hemos sobrepasado el presupuesto** we are already over budget, we have already exceeded the budget ▫ *presupuesto de adquisiciones* purchase budget; *presupuesto anual* annual budget; *presupuesto (de o en) base cero* zero base budgeting; *presupuesto de beneficios* revenue budget; *presupuesto de caja* cash budget; *presupuesto de capital* capital budget; *presupuesto de compras* purchase budget; *presupuesto comunitario* common budget; *presupuesto continuo* continuous budget; *presupuesto corporativo* corporate budget; *presupuesto de explotación* operating budget; *presupuesto de explotación previsto* forecast operating budget; *presupuesto familiar* household budget; *presupuesto flexible* flexible budget; *presupuesto para gastos generales* overhead budget; *presupuesto para gastos de representación* expense budget; *presupuesto general* master budget; *Presupuestos (Generales) del Estado* national budget; *presupuesto de marketing* marketing budget; *presupuesto para patrocinios* sponsorship budget; *presupuesto de producción* production budget; *presupuesto para promociones* promotion budget; *presupuesto provisional* interim budget; *presupuesto de publicidad* advertising budget; *presupuesto de ventas* sales budget
(**b**) *(cálculo de costes)* estimate, quotation, quote; **pedir (un) presupuesto (para algo/para hacer algo)** to ask for an estimate (for sth/for doing sth); **me han dado un presupuesto de dos millones** they've given me an estimate of two million

prevención *nf* **prevención laboral** occupational risk prevention; **prevención de riesgos** risk prevention, risk reduction

> "
> Mientras tanto, se estimulará la inversión en **prevención de riesgos** y se aumentará el control del cumplimiento de la normativa en esta materia. Lo incomprensible es lo poco que se ha hecho hasta ahora para que se cumpla la legislación vigente.
> "

prever *vt* (**a**) *(predecir)* to forecast, to predict; **prevé unas ventas de dos millones de euros** he forecasts sales of two million euros (**b**) *(anticipar)* to provide for, to make provision for; **el proyecto de ley prevé la reducción de las subvenciones** the bill provides for subsidies to be reduced; **este riesgo no está previsto en la póliza** this risk is not provided for in the policy

previo, -a *adj* (**a**) *(anterior)* prior; **tener un compromiso previo** to have a prior engagement; **sin previo aviso** without prior warning *o* notice (**b**) *(condicionado a)* subject to; **previo acuerdo de las partes interesadas** subject to the agreement of the interested parties; **previo pago de 100 pesos** on payment of 100 pesos

previsión *nf* (**a**) *(predicción)* forecast; **esto no entraba en nuestras previsiones** we hadn't foreseen *o* predicted this ◻ **previsión de beneficios** profit forecast, earning forecast; **previsión de cash-flow** cash flow forecast; **previsión cualitativa** qualitative forecast; **previsión cuantitativa** quantitative forecast; **previsión de la demanda** demand forecast; **previsión económica** economic forecast; **previsión de flujo de caja** cash flow forecast; **previsión de mano de obra** manpower forecast; **previsión de mercado** market forecast; **previsión presupuestaria** budget forecast; **previsión sectorial** industry forecast; **previsión de ventas** sales forecast *o* projection; **previsión de ventas y beneficios** sales and profit forecast

(**b**) **en previsión de** *(anticipándose a)* in anticipation of; **subieron los precios en previsión de una inflación más alta** they raised their prices in anticipation of increased inflation

(**c**) *Andes, RP* **previsión social** social security

previsto, -a *adj* *(planeado)* planned; **tienen previsto construir un polígono industrial en este solar** an industrial estate is planned for this site; **el crecimiento previsto de la economía** the projected growth of the economy; **está previsto que lleguemos a las nueve de la noche** we're scheduled to arrive at 9pm

prima *nf* (**a**) FIN, BOLSA *(pago adicional)* premium ◻ **prima autoliquidable** self-liquidating premium; **prima de cancelación** redemption fee, redemption premium; **prima de control** control premium; **prima de conversión** conversion premium; **prima del dólar** dollar premium; **prima de emisión** share premium, issue premium; **prima por iliquidez** illiquidity premium; **prima de reembolso** redemption fee, redemption premium; **prima de** *o* **por riesgo** risk premium

(**b**) *(bonificación en sueldo)* bonus; **recibir una prima** to get a bonus ◻ **prima en efectivo** cash bonus; **prima de fin de año** end-of-year bonus; *Col* **prima legal** = additional payment of a month's salary or wages at Christmas; **prima de producción** output bonus; **prima de**

productividad productivity bonus, incentive bonus; **prima de rendimiento** performance-related bonus

(**c**) SEGUR premium ◻ **prima anual** annual premium, yearly premium; **prima neta, prima pura** pure premium; **prima de renovación** renewal premium; **prima del seguro** insurance premium

> ❝
>
> Más importante aún, según el grupo de accionistas, es que el sobreprecio incluye lo que se denomina la "**prima de control**", que no es más que una cantidad extra que el comprador está dispuesto a pagar para poder adquirir el control de una empresa cuando no quiere o no puede comprar todas sus acciones.
>
> ❞

primer, primero, -a *adj* *(en orden)* first; *(en importancia, calidad)* main; **la primera empresa del sector** the leading company in the sector; **productos de primera calidad** top-quality products; **productos de primera necesidad** basic necessities ◻ MKTG **primeros adoptadores** early adopters; **primera clase** first class; MKTG **primera mayoría** early majority; **primer ministro** prime minister; **el primer mundo** the First World; **primera opción de compra** right of first refusal; **primer trimestre** first quarter; **primer vicepresidente** senior vice-president

primicia *nf* *(noticia)* scoop, exclusive; **una gran primicia informativa** a real scoop *o* exclusive

primordial *adj* fundamental; *(objetivo)* overriding; **reducir el paro es un asunto primordial** cutting unemployment is a top priority

principal 1 *adj* main, principal; **nuestro principal competidor** our main competitor

2 *nm* FIN principal; **principal e interés** principal and interest

principio *nm* *(fundamento, ley)* principle ◻ CONT **principio de correlación de ingresos y gastos** matching principle; CONT **principio del devengo** accruals concept; **principios económicos** economic principles; **principio de empresa en marcha** going-concern concept; **principio de Peter** Peter principle; CONT **principio de prudencia** conservatism concept; CONT **principio de uniformidad** consistency concept

prioridad *nf* priority; **tener prioridad (sobre)** to have *o* take priority (over); **este asunto tiene la máxima prioridad** this matter has top priority

privado, -a 1 *adj* private; **privado** *(en letrero)* staff only; **en privado** in private

2 *nm Am (despacho)* private office

privatización *nf* privatization, sell-off

privatizar *vt* to privatize, to sell off

privilegio *nm* INFORM *privilegios de acceso* access privileges

probar *vt* (**a**) *(máquina, producto)* to test; **probar algo sobre el terreno** to field-test sth (**b**) *(degustar)* to taste, to try

problema *nm* problem ❑ *problemas financieros* financial difficulties; *problemas de liquidez* cash flow problems; *problemas de partida* teething troubles; *problema de software* software problem

procedimiento *nm* (**a**) *(método)* procedure; **¿cuál es el procedimiento correcto?** what's the correct procedure? ❑ *procedimiento contable* accounting procedure; *procedimiento normalizado de trabajo* standard operating procedure
(**b**) DER *(tramitación)* *procedimiento arbitral, procedimiento de arbitraje* procedure by arbitration; *procedimiento de despido* dismissal procedure; *procedimiento disciplinario* disciplinary procedure; *procedimiento judicial* legal proceedings; *procedimiento de quiebra* bankruptcy proceedings; *procedimiento de resolución de conflictos* grievance procedure

procesado, -a **1** *nm,f* accused, defendant
2 *nm* (**a**) *(de materias primas, desechos)* processing ❑ *procesado de alimentos* food processing (**b**) INFORM processing ❑ *procesado continuo* continuous processing; *procesado de datos* data processing; *procesado secuencial* sequential processing

procesador *nm* INFORM processor ❑ *procesador frontal* front-end processor; *procesador de imágenes* image processor; *procesador RISC* RISC processor; *procesador de datos* data processor; *procesador de textos* word processor

procesamiento *nm* (**a**) *(de materias primas, desechos)* processing (**b**) INFORM processing ❑ *procesamiento automático de datos* automatic data processing, ADP; *procesamiento de datos* data processing; *procesamiento de textos* word processing (**c**) DER prosecution

procesar *vt* (**a**) *(pedido, solicitud)* to process (**b**) *(productos, desechos)* to process (**c**) INFORM to process (**d**) DER to prosecute; **procesar a alguien por algo** to prosecute sb for sth

proceso *nm* (**a**) *(operación, método)* process ❑ *proceso comercial* commercial process; *proceso de compra* purchasing process; *proceso de distribución* distribution process; *proceso de fabricación* manufacturing process; *proceso operativo* operating process; *proceso de toma de decisiones* decision-making process
(**b**) INFORM processing ❑ *proceso automático de datos* automatic data processing; *proceso de datos* data processing; *proceso de textos* word processing
(**c**) DER *(juicio)* trial; *(causa)* lawsuit; **abrir un**

proceso contra alguien to bring an action *o* proceedings against sb ❑ *proceso civil* civil action; *proceso de quiebra* bankruptcy proceedings

procurador, -ora *nm,f* (**a**) DER attorney (**b**) *Am procurador general del Estado o de la nación o de la república* Br ≃ Director of Public Prosecutions, *US* ≃ Attorney General; *Méx procurador general de justicia* Minister of Justice (**c**) *Méx (representante) procurador del consumidor* consumer ombudsman

producción *nf (acción)* production; *(cantidad producida)* output, production; **se ha incrementado la producción de acero** steel production has increased; **representa un 25% de la producción** this represents 25% of the total output; **producción por persona/hora** output per person/hour; **esta máquina tiene una producción de 6.000 unidades por hora** this machine has an output of 6,000 items per hour ❑ *producción ajustada* lean production; *producción en cadena* assembly line production; *producción conjunta* joint production; *producción continua* continuous (flow) production; *producción excedentaria* surplus production; *producción global (total)* aggregate production; *producción insuficiente* underproduction; *producción JIT, producción justo a tiempo* JIT production, just-in-time production; *producción por lotes* batch production; *producción de máquina* machine production; *producción máxima* maximum output, peak output; *producción mínima* minimum output; *producción prevista* planned production; *producción primaria* primary production; *producción secundaria* secondary production; *producción en serie* mass production; *producción total* total production

producir *vt* (**a**) *(productos agrícolas, recursos naturales)* to produce (**b**) *(manufacturar)* to produce; **no producimos suficientes piezas de recambio** we aren't producing enough spare parts; **la fábrica produce 100 unidades diarias** the factory produces 100 units a day; **producir en exceso** to overproduce (**c**) *(intereses, dividendos, resultados)* to yield; **este negocio produce grandes pérdidas** this business is making huge losses

productividad *nf* productivity ❑ *productividad marginal* marginal productivity; *productividad marginal decreciente* diminishing marginal productivity

productivo, -a *adj* (**a**) *(trabajador, método)* productive; *(encuentro)* productive, fruitful (**b**) *(inversión, negocio)* profitable

producto *nm* product; **son productos de alta calidad** they are high-quality products *o* goods ❑ *producto acabado* finished product; *productos agrícolas* agricultural produce; BOLSA *productos agrícolas básicos* soft commodities; *productos agrícolas nacionales* home produce; *productos alimenticios* food products, foodstuffs; MKTG *producto aumentado* augmented product; *producto bancario* banking product; *producto bandera* flagship product; *producto básico* staple (commodity); *productos de calidad* quality goods; *producto cautivo* captive product; *producto de consumo* consumer product; *producto derivado* spin-off (product); *productos derivados del petróleo* oil products; *productos desechables* disposable goods; *productos de desecho* waste products; *producto ecológico* green product; *producto estrella* flagship product; *producto final* end product, final product; *producto financiero* financial product; MKTG *producto gancho* follow-me product; *producto genérico* generic product; MKTG *producto de imitación* me-too product, copycat product; *producto industrial* industrial product; *producto innovador* innovative product; *producto insignia* flagship product; *Esp* *producto interior bruto* gross domestic product; *Esp* *producto interior neto* net domestic product; *Am* *producto interno bruto* gross domestic product; *Am* *producto interno neto* net domestic product; *producto de inversión* investment product; *producto con licencia* licensed product; *producto de lujo* luxury *o* premium product; *producto manufacturado* manufactured product; *producto de marca* branded product, brand name product; *producto sin marca* unbranded product; *producto de marca blanca* own-brand product; *producto nacional* (*renta nacional*) national product; (*producto no importado*) domestic product; *producto nacional bruto* gross national product; *producto nacional neto* net national product; MKTG *producto perro* dog; *productos petrolíferos* petroleum products; *producto de prestigio* prestige product; *producto de primera necesidad* staple (product); *producto principal* main product; MKTG *producto de rápida rotación* fast mover; *producto reexportado* re-export; *producto secundario* secondary product; *producto semiacabado, producto semielaborado* semi-finished product; *producto semimanufacturado* semi-manufactured product; *productos semiterminados* semi-finished goods; *productos vendibles* saleable goods; *productos de venta al detalle* o *al por menor* retail goods

productor, -ora 1 *adj* producing; **país productor de petróleo** oil-producing country

2 *nm,f* (*fabricante*) producer ▫ *productor de software* software producer

profesión *nf* (*empleo, ocupación*) profession; (*en formularios*) occupation; **de profesión** by profession; **por favor, indique su nombre y profesión** please state your name and occupation ▫ *profesión liberal* liberal profession

profesional 1 *adj* (**a**) (*de la profesión*) professional (**b**) (*eficaz*) professional; **es muy profesional en su trabajo** she works in a very professional manner

2 *nmf* (*trabajador liberal*) professional ▫ *profesional autónomo* self-employed worker; *profesional independiente* independent contractor

profesionista *nmf* *Méx* professional

proforma, pro forma *adj* pro forma

programa *nm* (**a**) (*planificación*) programme, schedule ▫ *programa de acción, Esp programa de actuación* action programme; *programa de ajuste estructural* structural adjustment programme; *programa de creación de empleo* job creation scheme; *programa para el desarrollo* development programme; *programa de fidelización* loyalty programme; *programa de formación* training programme, training scheme; *programa de formación para licenciados* graduate training scheme; *programa intensivo* crash programme; *programa de inversiones* investment programme; *programa de investigación* research programme; *programa de mantenimiento* maintenance programme; *programa de medidas* action programme; *programa de producción* production schedule; *programa de reducción de la deuda* debt reduction programme; *programa de ventas* sales programme; *programa de viajeros frecuentes* frequent flyer programme

(**b**) INFORM program ▫ *programa activo* active program; *programa antivirus* antivirus program; *programa de autoedición* desktop publishing program; *programa de configuración* set-up program; *programa de control* watchdog program; *programa de conversión* conversion program; *programa de creación de páginas web* Web authoring program; *programa de dibujo* draw program; (*no vectorial*) paint program; *programa de dominio público* public domain program; *programa de facturación* invoicing program; *programa informático* computer program; *programa de vigilancia* watchdog program; *programa virus* virus program

programación *nf* (**a**) *(de proyecto, aconteci-miento)* scheduling ❑ **programación de la producción** production scheduling; **programación publicitaria** advertising schedule (**b**) INFORM programming ❑ *Am* **programación de computadoras** computer programming; **programación informática** computer programming; **programación lineal** linear programming; *Esp* **programación de ordenadores** computer programming

programador, -ora *nm,f* INFORM *(persona)* programmer ❑ **programador informático** computer programmer

programar 1 *vt* (**a**) *(actividades, proyecto)* to schedule, to plan; **han programado una reunión para el lunes** they have scheduled a meeting for Monday (**b**) INFORM to program
2 *vi* INFORM to program

progresar *vi* to progress, to make progress; **progresar en** to make progress in

progresividad *nf* FIN *(fiscal)* progressiveness, progressive nature ❑ **progresividad en frío** fiscal drag

progresivo, -a *adj* (**a**) *(desarrollo, crecimiento)* progressive, gradual; *(aumento salarial)* incremental (**b**) *(impuesto)* progressive, graduated

progreso *nm (adelanto, avance)* progress; **hacer progresos** to make progress

prohibición *nf (efecto)* ban; *(acción)* banning; **han levantado la prohibición de pescar en el mar del Norte** they have lifted the ban on fishing in the North Sea; **lo hizo a pesar de la prohibición expresa de sus jefes** he did it in spite of the fact that his bosses had expressly forbidden him to ❑ **prohibición de exportación** export ban, export prohibition; **prohibición sobre la importación** import ban, import prohibition

prohibitivo, -a *adj* (**a**) *(norma, ley)* prohibitive (**b**) *(precio)* prohibitive

prolongar 1 *vt (contrato, plazo)* to extend
2 prolongarse *vpr* to go on, to continue; **la reunión se prolongó más de lo previsto** the meeting went on for longer than expected

promedio 1 *nm (media)* average; **escribe un promedio de cinco libros al año** on average, he writes five books a year; **hacer** *o* **sacar el promedio de algo** to find the average of sth ❑ **promedio de ventas** sales average
2 *adj inv Am* average

promoción *nf* (**a**) MKTG *(de producto)* promotion; *(hecha por un individuo)* endorsement ❑ **promoción de actividades** event promotion; **promoción especial** special promotion; **promoción de eventos** event promotion; **promoción de precios** price promotion; **promoción del producto** product promotion; **promoción en el punto de compra** point-of-purchase promotion; **promoción en el punto de venta**

point-of-sale promotion; **promoción de ventas** sales promotion
(**b**) *(ascenso)* promotion ❑ **promoción interna** internal promotion

promocional *adj* promotional

promocionar *vt* (**a**) *(producto) (a nivel empresarial)* to promote; *(a nivel individual)* to endorse (**b**) *(empleado)* to promote

promotor, -ora 1 *adj* promoting
2 *nm,f* promoter ❑ **promotor inmobiliario** *Br* property developer, *US* real estate developer; **promotor de ventas** sales promoter

> **❝**
>
> La banca acelera los créditos a **promotores inmobiliarios**. Así lo muestran los datos del Banco de España, que dan un crecimiento interanual en septiembre del 41,4%, cuando el ritmo de las hipotecas está en el 23%. Banca y expertos descartan un frenazo, aunque ven cierta moderación para el próximo año.
>
> **❞**

promover *vt* (**a**) *(impulsar, fomentar)* to promote; **promover el crecimiento económico** to promote economic growth (**b**) *(ascender)* **promover a alguien a** to promote sb to

pronosticar *vt* to predict, to forecast; **han pronosticado unas ventas de dos millones de euros** sales of two million euros have been forecast; **los sindicatos pronostican un año conflictivo** the unions are predicting trouble in the year ahead

pronóstico *nm (predicción)* forecast

pronunciado, -a *adj (descenso, aumento)* marked

propaganda *nf* (**a**) *(publicidad)* advertising; **hacer propaganda de algo** to advertise sth; **un folleto de propaganda** an advertising leaflet (**b**) *(prospectos)* publicity leaflets; *(por correo)* junk mail

propensión *nf* ECON **propensión al ahorro** propensity to save; **propensión al consumo** propensity to consume

propiedad *nf* (**a**) *(derecho)* ownership; **tener algo en propiedad** to own sth ❑ **propiedad colectiva** common ownership, collective ownership; **propiedad individual** individual ownership; **propiedad industrial** patent rights; **propiedad intelectual** copyright; **propiedad privada** private ownership; **propiedad pública** public ownership; **propiedad de la tierra** land ownership
(**b**) *(bienes)* property ❑ **propiedad en alquiler** rental property; **propiedad colectiva** joint property; **propiedad comunal** communal property; **propiedad del Estado** government property; **propiedad inmobiliaria** real estate,

immovable property; **propiedad privada** private property; **propiedades tangibles** physical property

propietario, -a 1 *adj* proprietary
2 *nm,f* (**a**) *(de bienes)* owner ◻ **propietario de bienes inmuebles** property owner; **propietario de fábrica** works owner; **propietario individual** individual owner; **propietario legal** legal owner; **propietario legítimo** rightful owner, lawful owner; **propietario de vivienda** home owner (**b**) *(de cargo)* holder

propina *nf* tip; **dar propina (a alguien)** to tip (sb)

propio, -a *adj (en propiedad)* own; **tener negocio propio** to have one's own business; **se requiere vehículo propio** *(en anuncio laboral)* own car required

proponer *vt* (**a**) *(servicio, precio, moción)* to propose, to suggest (**b**) *(candidato)* to nominate; **han propuesto su nombre para el cargo de consejero delegado** his name has been put forward for the post of chief executive

proporción *nf* proportion; **en una proporción de cuatro a uno** in a ratio of four to one

proporcionar *vt* (**a**) *(servicio, ayuda)* to provide; **proporcionar algo a alguien** to provide sb with sth; **proporcionar apoyo financiero a algo** to give financial backing to sth (**b**) *(beneficios)* to return; **proporcionar un buen rendimiento** to bring a good return (**c**) *(ajustar)* **proporcionar algo a algo** to adapt sth to sth; **deben proporcionar los gastos a los ingresos** they ought to keep their spending proportionate to their income

propuesta *nf (proposición)* proposal; *(de empleo)* offer; **presentar una propuesta al consejo de administración** to put a proposal to the board; **me hicieron una propuesta de trabajo** they made me a job offer ◻ **propuesta de ley** bill; **propuesta no de ley** = motion for debate presented to parliament by someone other than the government; **propuesta de licitación** tender proposal; **propuesta de negocio** business proposition; **propuesta de pago** payment proposal

prorrateado, -a *adj* pro rata; **el sueldo es de 20.000 euros prorrateados** the salary is 20,000 euros pro rata

prórroga *nf (de plazo, crédito, contrato)* extension; **les concedieron dos semanas de prórroga para la entrega del proyecto** they were given a two-week extension for handing in the project

prorrogar *vt* to extend; **han prorrogado el plazo dos semanas más** the deadline has been extended by a further two weeks

prospecto *nm* BOLSA **prospecto de emisión** *(de acciones)* prospectus

prosperar *vi (negocio, empresa, economía)* to prosper, to thrive

prosperidad *nf* prosperity

próspero, -a *adj (negocio, empresa, economía)* prosperous, thriving

protagonista *nmf (de mercado)* key player; **¿cuáles son los protagonistas en este mercado?** who are the key players in this market?

protección *nf* (**a**) *(defensa)* protection ◻ **protección del consumidor** consumer protection; **protección del empleo** employment protection, job protection; **protección del medio ambiente** environmental protection
(**b**) INFORM protection ◻ **protección de archivos** file protection; **protección por contraseña** password protection; **protección contra copia** copy protection; **protección contra escritura** write protection; **protección de datos** data protection; **protección de ficheros** file protection

proteccionismo *nm* ECON protectionism

proteccionista ECON **1** *adj* protectionist
2 *nmf* protectionist

protector, -ora 1 *adj* protective
2 *nm* INFORM **protector de pantalla** screensaver

proteger *vt* (**a**) ECON *(productos)* to protect (**b**) INFORM to protect; **proteger contra escritura** to write-protect

protegido, -a (**a**) *(amparado, a salvo)* protected; **protegido contra la inflación** inflation-proof; **protegido por las leyes** protected by law; **protegido por los derechos de autor** subject to copyright (**b**) INFORM protected; **protegido contra copia** copy-protected; **protegido contra escritura** write-protected; **protegido por contraseña** password-protected

protesta *nf (queja, manifestación)* protest; **en señal de protesta** in protest ◻ **protesta del capitán** ship's protest; **protestas laborales** industrial action; **protesta del mar** ship's protest

protestar *vt (letra de cambio)* to protest

protesto *nm* DER protest ◻ **protesto por falta de aceptación** protest for non-acceptance; **protesto por falta de pago** protest for non-payment; **protesto de letra** noting bill of exchange

protocolo *nm* INFORM protocol ◻ **protocolo de comunicación** communications protocol; **protocolo de descarga** download protocol; **protocolo de Internet** Internet protocol; **protocolo POP** POP protocol; **protocolo SSL** SSL protocol; **protocolo de transferencia de archivos** *o* **ficheros** file transfer protocol; **protocolo de transmisión** transmission protocol

prototipo *nm* prototype

proveedor, -ora 1 *nm,f* supplier ◻ **proveedor**

secundario secondary supplier
2 *nm* INFORM *proveedor de acceso (a Internet)* (Internet) access provider; *proveedor de presencia en Internet* Internet presence provider; *proveedor de servicios (de Internet)* (Internet) service provider

> 66
>
> El fabricante de detergentes Bilore ha enviado a los sindicatos un plan de futuro que pretende una reestructuración de plantilla y la obtención de financiación a largo plazo por siete millones de euros para sanear su balance y cumplir los pagos a los **proveedores**.
>
> 99

proveer 1 *vt* (**a**) *(abastecer)* to supply, to provide; **proveer a alguien de algo** to provide o supply sb with sth; **la empresa provee de acceso a Internet al ministerio** the company acts as Internet service provider for the Ministry (**b**) *(puesto, cargo)* to fill
2 proveerse *vpr* **proveerse de** *(abastecerse)* to stock up on

provisión *nf* CONT provision ◻ *provisión por depreciación* provision for depreciation; *provisión para deudas incobrables* bad debt provision; *provisión de fondos* provision of capital; *provisión para impuestos* tax provision; *provisión para insolvencias* provision for bad debts; *provisión para riesgos* provision for liabilities

provisional, *Am* **provisorio, -a** *adj* provisional, interim

provisionar *vt* CONT to provide for

provisorio = **provisional**

proxy *nm* INFORM proxy

proyección *nf* (**a**) *(de película)* screening, showing ◻ *proyección de diapositivas* slide show (**b**) *(trascendencia)* importance; **la proyección internacional de una empresa** the international presence o profile of a company

proyectar *vt* (**a**) *(operación)* to plan (**b**) *(edificio)* to plan; *(puente, obra)* to design

proyecto *nm* (**a**) *(plan, empresa)* project; **el proyecto está a punto de concluir** the project is nearing completion; **tener en proyecto hacer algo** to be planning to do sth ◻ *proyecto piloto* pilot project (**b**) *(borrador)* draft ◻ *proyecto de acuerdo* draft agreement; *proyecto de ley* bill; *proyecto de presupuesto* draft budget

proyector *nm* projector ◻ *proyector de diapositivas* slide projector; *proyector multimedia* multimedia projector; *proyector de opacos* *Br* episcope, *US* opaque projector; *proyector de transparencias* overhead projector, OHP

prueba 1 *nf* (**a**) *(de maquinaria, producto)* test; **sometemos todos nuestros productos a exigentes pruebas** all our products undergo thorough testing ◻ *prueba de aceptación* acceptance test; *prueba en el banco* benchtest; *prueba de campo* field test; *prueba de conformidad* compliance test; *prueba de rendimiento* performance test; *prueba de rendimiento del producto* product performance test; *prueba sobre el terreno* field trial, field test
(**b**) MKTG *(de respuesta, aceptación)* test ◻ *prueba comparativa* comparative test; *prueba del concepto* concept test; *prueba del consumidor* consumer test; *prueba de copy* copy test; *prueba gratuita* free trial; *prueba previa* pretest; *prueba de texto* copy test; *prueba de viabilidad* feasibility test
(**c**) *(documento)* DER piece of evidence; **pruebas** evidence, proof ◻ *prueba escrita* written proof
(**d**) *(examen académico)* test; **el examen consta de una prueba escrita y otra oral** the exam has an oral part and a written part ◻ *prueba de aptitud* aptitude test
2 a prueba *adj (trabajador)* on probation; *(producto comprado)* on approval; **comprar algo a prueba** to buy sth on approval; **venta a prueba** sale on approval; **contratar a alguien a prueba** to take sb on probation

PSI *nm* INFORM *(abrev de* **Proveedor de Servicios Internet***)* ISP

psicográfico, -a *adj* MKTG *(datos, perfil)* psychographic

psicología *nf* psychology ◻ *psicología industrial* industrial psychology; *psicología publicitaria* advertising psychology

psicométrico, -a *adj (test, examen)* psychometric

publicación *nf (actividad, escrito)* publication ◻ *publicación financiera* financial journal; *Am publicación gremial* trade journal; *publicación periódica* periodical; *publicación del sector* trade journal; *publicación trimestral* quarterly

publicar *vt (libro, revista)* to publish; *(prospecto)* to issue; **la revista se publica trimestralmente** the magazine is published quarterly

publicidad *nf* (**a**) *(difusión)* publicity; **nos proporcionará publicidad gratuita del producto** it will give us free publicity for the product
(**b**) MKTG *(promoción)* advertising; *(en televisión)* adverts, commercials; **una campaña de publicidad** an advertising campaign; **hacer publicidad** to advertise; **trabaja en publicidad** she works in advertising ◻ *publicidad above-the-line* above-the-line advertising; *publicidad en aeropuertos* airport advertising; *publicidad below-the-line* below-the-line advertising; *publicidad boca a boca* word-of-mouth advertising; *publicidad con o en carteles* poster

advertising; **publicidad comparativa** comparative advertising; **publicidad competitiva** competitive advertising; **publicidad cooperativa** co-operative advertising; **publicidad corporativa** corporate advertising; **publicidad directa** direct advertising; **publicidad engañosa** misleading advertising; **publicidad estática** static advertising; **publicidad general** above-the-line advertising; **publicidad genérica** generic advertising; **publicidad impresa** print advertising; **publicidad informativa** informative advertising; **publicidad institucional** institutional advertising; **publicidad de marca** brand advertising; **publicidad en medios de comunicación** media advertising; **publicidad en medios de transporte** transport advertising; **publicidad en prensa** newspaper advertising; **publicidad de producto** product advertising; **publicidad en el punto de compra** point-of-purchase advertising; **publicidad en el punto de venta** point-of-sale advertising; **publicidad en radio** radio advertising; **publicidad de respuesta directa** direct response advertising; **publicidad en revistas selectas** prestige advertising; **publicidad por saturación** saturation advertising; **publicidad subliminal** subliminal advertising; **publicidad televisiva** television advertising; **publicidad testimonial** testimonial advertising; **publicidad en vallas** billboard advertising; **publicidad visual** display advertising
    (**c**) *(folletos)* advertising material

publicista *nmf* advertising agent

publicitar *vt (producto, marca)* to advertise

“

Estas ofertas y promociones **se han publicitado** a través de unos folletos que la cadena de hipermercados ha distribuido en diferentes ambientes, especialmente en bares, cafeterías y restaurantes, aunque no en sus propios establecimientos.

”
---

publicitario, -a 1 *adj* advertising; **pausa publicitaria** commercial break
    2 *nm,f* advertising agent

público, -a 1 *adj* (**a**) *(transporte, servicio)* public; **en público** in public (**b**) *(del Estado)* public; **el sector público** the public sector
    2 *nm* (**a**) *(en espectáculo)* audience □ **público cautivo** captive audience (**b**) *(comunidad, gente)* public; **el gran público** the (general) public; **abierto al público** open to the public; **trabajar de cara al público** to work directly with the public

publirreportaje *nm (en televisión)* infomercial, advertorial; *(en revista)* advertorial, advertising feature

PUC *nm Bol, Col, Ven (abrev de* **Plan Único de**

Cuentas) standardized accounting procedure

pudiente 1 *adj* wealthy, well-off
    2 *nmf* wealthy person

puente *nm* (**a**) *(días festivos)* ≃ long weekend *(consisting of a public holiday, the weekend and the day in between)*; **hacer puente** = to take an extra day off to join a public holiday with the weekend (**b**) *(en aeropuerto)* **puente aéreo** (air) shuttle (**c**) INFORM bridge

puerta *nf* INFORM gate

puerto *nm* (**a**) *(de mar)* port, harbour □ **puerto abierto** open port; **puerto comercial** commercial port; **puerto de contenedores** container port; **puerto de descarga** unloading port; **puerto de destino** port of destination; **puerto de embarque** port of shipment, port of loading; **puerto de entrada** port of entry; **puerto franco** free port; **puerto libre** free port; **puerto de llegada** port of arrival; **puerto de mar** sea port; **puerto petrolero** oil port; **puerto privado** independent port; **puerto de salida** port of departure; **puerto seco** inland clearance depot; **puerto de tránsito** transit port, port of transit
    (**b**) INFORM port □ **puerto de comunicaciones** comms port; **puerto de expansión** expansion port; **puerto de la impresora** printer port; **puerto del módem** modem port; **puerto paralelo** parallel port; **puerto del ratón** mouse port; **puerto de salida** output port; **puerto (en) serie** serial port; **puerto USB** USB port

puesta *nf* **puesta en circulación** *(de moneda)* introduction; **puesta al día** updating; **puesta en marcha** *(de máquina)* starting, start-up; *(de acuerdo, proyecto)* implementation; **la puesta en marcha del euro** the introduction of the euro

puesto *nm* (**a**) *(empleo)* **puesto (de trabajo)** post, position, job; **había cuatro candidatos para el puesto de gerente** there were four candidates for the position of manager; **el puesto sigue vacante** the post is still vacant; **escalar puestos** to work one's way up □ **puesto clave** key post, key position; **puesto directivo, puesto de gestión** managerial position; **puesto de trabajo fijo** permanent post; **puesto vacante** opening, vacancy
    (**b**) *(en exhibición, feria)* stand, booth

“

Hidafa, una sociedad inmobiliaria propiedad de la familia Gómez Sainz, ha adquirido un 5,2% del capital de Cortefiel. Se trata de una inversión financiera a medio o largo plazo. Hidafa se plantea elevar su participación hasta el 10%. De momento, el grupo inmobiliario ha informado a Cortefiel de que no pedirá un **puesto** en el consejo de administración.

”
---

puja *nf (acción)* bidding; *(cantidad)* bid

pujar 1 *vi* to bid (**por** for)
 2 *vt* to bid

pulsación *nf* INFORM keystroke, tap; **pulsaciones por minuto** keystrokes *o* characters per minute

pulsar *vt* INFORM to press

pulso *nm* TEL pulse

punta *adj inv* **hora punta** rush hour; **tecnología punta** state-of-the-art technology

puntero, -a 1 *adj* leading; **una de las empresas punteras en el sector** one of the leading companies in the industry; **un país puntero en agricultura biológica** a world leader in organic farming
 2 *nm* INFORM pointer

punto 1 *nm* (**a**) *(unidad) (en índice, bolsa)* point; **el índice Dow Jones ha subido seis puntos** the Dow Jones index is up six points; **los tipos de interés bajarán un punto** interest rates will go down by one (percentage) point ▫ *punto básico* basis point; MKTG *punto de cuota de mercado* share point; *punto oro* gold point; *punto porcentual* percentage point
 (**b**) *(lugar)* point ▫ *punto de carga* loading point; *punto de compra* point of purchase; *punto de descarga* unloading point; *punto de distribución* distribution outlet; *punto de entrega* delivery point; INFORM *punto de inserción* insertion point; *punto de interés turístico* visitor attraction; *punto de referencia* benchmark; *punto de reunión* meeting point; *punto único de compra* *(concepto)* one-stop shopping; *punto de venta* point of sale; **en el punto de venta** at the point of sale; **tenemos puntos de venta en todo el país** we have (sales)

outlets across the country; *punto de venta autorizado* authorized dealer; *punto de venta electrónico* electronic point of sale; *punto de venta exclusivo* *(de una sola marca)* tied outlet
 (**c**) *(asunto, parte)* point; **pasemos al siguiente punto** let's move on to the next point; **tenemos los siguientes puntos a tratar** we have the following items on the agenda ▫ *puntos en común* common ground; *punto débil, punto flaco* weak point; *punto fuerte* strong point
 (**d**) *(estado, fase)* point ▫ CONT *punto de equilibrio* break-even point; *punto muerto* *(en negociaciones)* deadlock; **estar en un punto muerto** to be deadlocked; *punto de saturación* saturation point
 (**e**) *(signo ortográfico) (al final de frase)* Br full stop, US period; *(sobre i, j, en dirección de correo electrónico)* dot; **dos puntos** colon ▫ *punto y coma* semicolon
 2 **punto com** *nf inv (empresa)* dotcom

puntuación *nf* MKTG *(en estudio de mercado)* score

puntualidad *nf* punctuality; **al jefe le indigna su falta de puntualidad** the boss is annoyed by his poor timekeeping

PVP *nm* (*abrev de* **precio de venta al público**) retail price ▫ *PVP recomendado* RRP

PYME, pyme *nf* (*abrev de* **Pequeña y Mediana Empresa**) SME

> **"**
> La mayoría de las **pymes** españolas descuidan su imagen corporativa, que suele consistir en el desarrollo de un logotipo y poco más.
> **"**

quebrado, -a *nm,f* bankrupt

quebranto *nm* **quebranto de la disciplina** breach of discipline; **quebrantos económicos** monetary losses

quebrar *vi (empresa)* to go bankrupt, to fail

> **"**
> En este caso es inevitable acordarse de Andersen, la que fuera una de las mayores firmas de auditoría del mundo, y que **quebró** por sus conexiones con el caso de la eléctrica Enron, que suspendió pagos en 2002.
> **"**

queja *nf* complaint; **presentar una queja** to make *o* lodge a complaint

quejarse *vpr* to complain; **se quejó por la lentitud de la conexión** he complained about how slow the connection was

quiebra *nf (de empresa)* bankruptcy; *(en Bolsa)* crash; **ir a la quiebra** to go bankrupt; **la operación llevó a la empresa a la quiebra** the deal bankrupted the business; **declarar a alguien en quiebra** to adjudicate *o* declare sb bankrupt; **declararse en quiebra** to file for bankruptcy ❑ **quiebra culpable** bankruptcy due to mismanagement; **quiebra fraudulenta** fraudulent bankruptcy; **quiebra técnica** technical bankruptcy; **quiebra voluntaria** voluntary bankruptcy

quincenal *adj* fortnightly

quincenalmente *adv* fortnightly, every two weeks

quórum *nm* quorum; **hay quórum** we have a quorum, we are quorate; **no hay quórum** we are inquorate

Rr

racionalización *nf (de gastos, industria)* rationalization

racionalizar *vt (gastos, industria)* to rationalize

radicarse *vpr (establecerse)* to settle (**en** in)

radio *nf (medio)* radio

radiomensaje *nm RP* pager

ralentización *nf* slowing down, slowdown □ *ralentización económica* economic slowdown

> La **ralentización** de la inflación en los meses pasados dio al BCE espacio para recortar los tipos de interés hasta el 2%, el nivel más bajo en más de 50 años como fórmula para relanzar el crecimiento y eludir la recesión.

ralentizar 1 *vt* to slow down
 2 ralentizarse *vpr* to slow down

RAM *nf* INFORM (*abrev de* **random access memory**) RAM □ *RAM dinámica* dynamic RAM

ramificación *nf* INFORM branch

rango *nm (profesional)* rank; **de alto rango** high-ranking; **tener un rango inferior a alguien** to be junior to sb □ *rango de precios* price range

ranking *nm* **el ranking de las 30 empresas con más facturación** the list of the 30 companies with the highest turnover; **el ranking de accidentes laborales** the industrial accidents league table; **ocupa el sexto puesto en el ranking mundial** it is ranked sixth in the world

ranura *nf* INFORM slot □ *ranura de expansión* expansion slot; *ranura para tarjeta* card slot

rápido, -a *adj* quick; **gracias por su rápida respuesta** thank you for your prompt reply

rappel *nm* volume discount

rasgo *nm* MKTG *rasgo distintivo (de producto)* unique selling point *o* proposition

rastreador *nm* INFORM crawler

ratificación *nf* ratification

ratificar *vt (tratado, convenio)* to ratify

rating *nm* (**a**) FIN credit rating (**b**) *Am (de audiencia)* ratings

ratio *nf* ratio □ *ratio contable* accounting ratio; *ratio de distribución* distribution ratio;

ratio de explotación de activos asset utilization ratio; *ratio financiero* financial ratio; *ratio de frecuencia* frequency rate

ratón *nm Esp* INFORM mouse □ *ratón inalámbrico* wireless mouse; *ratón de infrarrojos* infrared mouse; *ratón óptico* optical mouse

raya *nf* (**a**) TIP dash (**b**) *Méx (sueldo)* pay, wages

razón *nf* (**a**) *razón social* company name, trade name (**b**) *(en letrero)* **razón aquí** apply within (**c**) *Am (ratio)* *razón de deuda, razón de endeudamiento* debt ratio (**d**) *Col, Méx, Ven (recado)* message; **no está, ¿quiere dejarle razón?** he's not in, do you want to leave a message?

razonable *adj (oferta, precio)* reasonable

RDSI *nf* TEL (*abrev de* **Red Digital de Servicios Integrados**) ISDN

reabastecer *vt (tienda)* to restock

reabrir 1 *vt* to reopen
 2 reabrirse *vpr* to reopen

reacción *nf (de clientes)* feedback; *(de precios)* reaction

reaccionar *vi* to react

reactivación *nf (de economía, negocio)* recovery, revival

> Las cifras de la Asociación Hipotecaria Española (AHE) reflejan una ligera **reactivación** del crédito si se comparan con el aumento del 22% de marzo, el 21,5% de febrero y el 21,2% en enero. El volumen de créditos hipotecarios concedidos en los cuatro primeros meses del año fue de 26.390 millones de euros, cifra que supera en un 7% al importe registrado en igual período del año anterior.

reactivar 1 *vt (economía, negocio)* to revive
 2 reactivarse *vpr* to recover

readmitir *vt* to accept, to take back

reajuste *nm (de precios, impuestos, salarios)* change, adjustment □ *reajuste de plantilla* downsizing

realidad *nf* INFORM *realidad virtual* virtual reality

realizable *adj* FIN realizable

realización *nf* (**a**) *(ejecución)* *(de esfuerzo, viaje,* *inversión)* making; *(de investigación, encuesta)* carrying out; *(de plan, reformas)* implementation; *(de transferencia)* execution (**b**) FIN realization ▫ **realización de beneficios** profit-taking

realizar *vt* (**a**) *(ejecutar) (esfuerzo, viaje, inversión)* to make; *(investigación, encuesta)* to carry out, to conduct; *(plan, reformas)* to implement; *(transferencia)* to execute (**b**) FIN *(bienes, beneficios)* to realize

realquilar *vt* to sub-let

reanudar **1** *vt (debate, negociaciones)* to reopen, to resume; *(conversación, actividad)* to resume
  2 reanudarse *vpr (debate, negociaciones)* to reopen, to resume; *(conversación, actividad)* to resume

reaprovisionamiento *nm (de tienda)* restocking

reaprovisionar *vt (tienda)* to restock

reaseguradora *nf* reinsurer

> **❝**
>
> Allianz afirmó que durante el primer trimestre de 2003 ha rebajado su porcentaje en la primera **reaseguradora** del mundo del 22,4% al 20% y añadió que, por el momento, no hay planes para seguir desprendiéndose de acciones de esta compañía. La **reaseguradora**, por su parte, ha reducido su participación en Allianz del 21% al 20%.
>
> **❞**

reasegurar *vt* to reinsure

reaseguro *nm* reinsurance

rebaja *nf* (**a**) *(descuento)* discount, reduction; **me hicieron una rebaja del 5%** they gave me a 5% discount o reduction, they gave me 5% off (**b**) *(recorte, reducción)* reduction, cut; **una rebaja de los tipos de interés** a cut in interest rates (**c**) *(en tienda)* **las rebajas** the sales; **estar de rebajas** to have a sale on; **grandes rebajas** *(en letrero)* massive reductions

rebajado, -a *adj (precio)* reduced, discounted; *(producto)* reduced, discounted, cut-price, *US* cut-rate

rebajar *vt* (**a**) *(precio)* to reduce, to cut; *(producto)* to discount, to mark down; **han rebajado los precios a la mitad** prices have been reduced o cut by half; **me rebajaron el 10%** they gave me 10% off (**b**) *(tipo de interés)* to reduce, to cut

rebotar **1** *vt Méx, RP (cheque)* to bounce
  2 *vi* (**a**) *Méx, RP (cheque)* to bounce (**b**) INFORM to bounce

recadero, -a *nm,f* errand boy, *f* errand girl

recado *nm* message; **le dejé un recado en el contestador** I left a message (for her) on her answering machine

recalentamiento *nm (de economía)* overheating

recalentar **1** *vt (economía)* to overheat
  2 recalentarse *vpr (economía)* to overheat

recambiar *vt* to replace

recambio *nm* (**a**) *(acción)* replacement (**b**) *(repuesto)* spare part

recarga *nf (de móvil)* top-up

recargo *nm* surcharge, additional o extra charge; **pagaron un recargo del 15%** they paid a 15% surcharge ▫ **recargo a la importación** import surcharge

recaudación *nf* (**a**) *(colecta)* collection ▫ **recaudación de fondos** fundraising; **recaudación de impuestos** tax collection (**b**) *(cantidad)* takings; *(de venta)* proceeds ▫ **recaudación anual** annual revenue; **recaudación de impuestos, recaudación tributaria** tax revenues, tax receipts

recaudador, -ora *nm,f* **recaudador de fondos** fundraiser; **recaudador de impuestos** tax collector

recaudar *vt (deudas)* to collect; *(impuestos)* to collect, to raise; *(fondos)* to raise

recepción *nf* (**a**) *(de carta, paquete)* receipt; **el pago se efectuará a la recepción del envío** payment will be made on receipt of the goods (**b**) *(de hotel)* reception (**c**) *(fiesta)* reception

recepcionista *nmf* receptionist

recesión *nf* ECON recession

recesivo, -a *adj* ECON recessionary

rechazar *vt (propuesta, candidato)* to reject; *(oferta, solicitud)* to reject, to turn down; *(trabajo)* to turn down

recibir **1** *vt (carta, llamada, respuesta)* to receive, to get; *(subsidio, propuesta, sugerencia)* to receive; *Formal* **reciba mi más cordial o sincera felicitación** please accept my sincere congratulations
  2 recibirse *vpr Am (graduarse)* to graduate, to qualify (**de** as)

recibo *nm* (**a**) *(recepción)* receipt; **al recibo de tu carta...** on receipt of your letter...; **acusar recibo de** to acknowledge receipt of (**b**) *(documento) (de compra)* receipt, *US* sales slip; *(de servicio)* receipt; *(del gas, de la luz)* bill ▫ **recibo de aduanas** customs receipt; **recibo de caja** till receipt; **recibo de depósito europeo** European Depository Receipt

reciclaje *nm* (**a**) *(de residuos)* recycling (**b**) *(profesional)* retraining

reciclar **1** *vt* (**a**) *(material)* to recycle (**b**) *(empleado)* to retrain
  2 reciclarse *(profesionalmente)* to retrain

reciente *adj* recent

recíproco, -a *adj* reciprocal

reclamación *nf* **(a)** *(queja)* complaint; **hacer una reclamación** to make a complaint **(b)** *(a un seguro, contrato)* claim ❑ *reclamaciones contractuales* contractual claims; *reclamación por daños* damage claim; *reclamación fraudulenta* false claim; *reclamación impugnada* contested claim; *reclamación por siniestro* accident claim

reclamante *nmf* claimant

reclamar 1 *vt (indemnización, deuda, retención)* to claim
2 *vi (quejarse)* to complain

reclamo *nm* **(a)** *(para atraer)* inducement ❑ *reclamo publicitario* advertising gimmick; *reclamo de ventas* loss leader **(b)** *Am (queja)* complaint **(c)** *Am (a un seguro, contrato)* claim ❑ *reclamos contractuales* contractual claims; *reclamo por daños* damage claim; *reclamo fraudulento* false claim; *reclamo impugnado* contested claim; *reclamo por siniestro* accident claim

recobrar 1 *vt* to recover
2 recobrarse *vpr* to recover **(de** from); **la empresa aún no se ha recobrado de la crisis** the company still hasn't recovered from the crisis

recogida *nf recogida de datos* data capture, data collection; *recogida de equipajes* baggage reclaim

recolocación *nf (de empleado)* outplacement

❝

Vía Digital ha destinado 420.708 euros a la **recolocación** de 168 profesionales despedidos que decidieron acogerse a este programa que gestionará Creade. Directivos, responsables de equipo y técnicos y comerciales integran este grupo para el que se ha establecido un período de **recolocación** de seis meses.

❞

recomendación *nf (referencia)* **(carta de) recomendación** letter of recommendation

recomendado, -a *adj Am (carta, paquete)* registered; **enviar un paquete recomendado** to send a parcel by registered *Br* post *o US* mail

recomendar *vt* to advise, to recommend

recompra *nf (de acciones)* buyback, repurchase; *(de productos)* buyback

recomprar *vt (acciones)* to repurchase

reconfigurar *vt* INFORM to reconfigure

reconocido, -a *adj (negocio)* established; **un empresario de reconocida trayectoria** a businessman with a proven track record

reconocimiento *nm* **(a)** FIN *reconocimiento de deuda* acknowledgement of debt **(b)** INFORM recognition ❑ *reconocimiento de caracteres*

character recognition; *reconocimiento del habla* speech recognition; *reconocimiento óptico de caracteres* optical character recognition; *reconocimiento de voz* voice recognition **(c)** MKTG recognition ❑ *reconocimiento de marca* brand recognition; *reconocimiento de la necesidad* need recognition

reconsiderar *vt (política)* to reconsider

reconstrucción *nf (de economía)* reconstruction

recontratación *nf Am* re-employment

recontratar *vt Am* to re-employ

reconversión *nf (de empresa, economía)* restructuring ❑ *reconversión industrial* rationalization of industry

reconvertir *vt (empresa, economía)* to restructure; *(industria)* to rationalize

recopilar *vt* to collect, to gather

recordatorio *nm (aviso)* reminder ❑ *recordatorio de pago* payment reminder, prompt note

recorrer *vt* INFORM *(texto)* to scroll through

recorrido *nm (turístico)* tour

recortar *vt (precios, producción)* to cut (back); **hay que recortar gastos** we'll have to cut (down) our expenditure

❝

Los mercados financieros y muchos analistas esperan que la entidad europea **recorte** de nuevo los tipos de interés antes de terminar este semestre, después de que los rebajara en un 0,25% porcentual en marzo hasta el 2,50%.

❞

recorte *nm* **(a)** *(reducción)* cut, cutback ❑ *recorte de gastos* spending cuts; *recorte de personal* job cuts, staff cutbacks; *recorte presupuestario* budget cut; *recorte salarial* wage cut, pay cut **(b)** *(de periódico, revista)* clipping, *Br* cutting ❑ *recorte de prensa* press clipping, *Br* press cutting

rectificación *nf (de error)* rectification

rectificar *vt (error)* to rectify

recuento *nm* count; **hacer el recuento de** to count (up) ❑ INFORM *recuento de palabras* word count; *recuento de población* population count

recuerdo *nm* MKTG recall ❑ *recuerdo asistido, recuerdo ayudado* aided recall; *recuerdo de marca* brand name recall

recuperable *adj (deuda)* recoverable

recuperación *nf* **(a)** *(de economía, mercado, moneda)* recovery; *(de precios, acciones)* recovery, rally ❑ *recuperación empresarial* corporate recovery **(b)** INFORM *(de información perdida)* recovery; *(de información almacenada)* retrieval ❑ *recuperación de datos* data retrieval

recuperar 1 *vt* (**a**) *(recobrar) (fianza)* to recover, to get back; *(horas de trabajo, pérdida)* to make up; **no recuperaron el dinero invertido** they didn't get back *o* recoup the money they invested (**b**) INFORM *(información perdida)* to recover

2 recuperarse *vpr (economía, mercado, moneda)* to recover, to pick up; *(precios, acciones)* to recover, to rally

recurrente *nmf* DER appellant

recurrir DER **1** *vt* to appeal against
  2 *vi* to appeal

recurso *nm* (**a**) DER appeal; **presentar recurso (ante)** to appeal (against) ❑ *recurso de apelación* appeal; *recurso de casación* High Court appeal; *recurso contencioso administrativo* = court case brought against the State
  (**b**) *(bien, riqueza)* resource ❑ CONT *recursos ajenos (a largo plazo)* loan capital; *recursos del Estado* government resources; *recursos financieros* financial resources; *recursos hídricos* water resources; *recursos insuficientes* insufficient resources; *recursos líquidos* liquid resources; *recursos presupuestarios* budgetary resources; *recursos propios* (shareholders') equity

> **“**
>
> El gobernador del Banco de España, Jaime Caruana, admitió que Eurobank, entidad financiera intervenida por el supervisor desde el pasado 25 de julio, ha permanecido durante seis meses con **recursos propios** inferiores a los 18 millones de euros que establece el mínimo legal y aseguró que la actuación realizada por el organismo que dirige ha sido llevada a cabo con prontitud y diligencia.
>
> **”**

red *nf* (**a**) *(sistema)* network, system ❑ *red de comercialización* marketing network; *red de comunicaciones* communication network; *red de distribución* distribution network; *red ferroviaria* rail network; *red integrada de transporte* integrated transport network; *red telefónica* telephone network; *red de ventas* sales network; *red vía satélite* satellite network
  (**b**) INFORM network; **la Red** *(Internet)* the Net ❑ *red en anillo* ring network; *red de área extensa* wide area network; *red de área local* local area network; *red ciudadana* freenet; *red de datos* (data) network; *red digital de servicios integrados* integrated services digital network; *red en estrella* star network; *red informática* computer network; *red local* local (area) network; *red multimedia* multemedia network; *red neuronal* neural network; *red de transmisión de datos* datacomms network; *red de usuarios* user network

redacción *nf* (**a**) *(acción)* writing ❑ *redacción publicitaria* copy editing (**b**) *(departamento)* editorial team *o* staff

redactar *vt (contrato, orden del día)* to draw up, to draft

redactor, -ora *nm,f* PRENSA *(escritor)* writer; *(editor)* editor ❑ *redactor creativo* copywriter; *redactor de informativos* news editor; *redactor de publicidad* copywriter

redención *nf (de hipoteca)* repayment, redemption

redescuento *nm Am* FIN rediscount; **tasa de redescuento** rediscount rate

redimensionamiento *nm (en empresa)* downsizing

redimensionar *vt* to downsize

> **“**
>
> La decisión cautelar de suspender pagos, con el objetivo de negociar con proveedores y entidades financieras el aplazamiento de la deuda y de mantener la actividad **redimensionando** la empresa y reorientándola hacia Europa y hacia el turismo de salud y el ecoturismo, se hizo irremediable.
>
> **”**

redimir *vt (hipoteca)* to repay, to redeem

redireccionar *vt* INFORM to readdress

rediscado *nm Andes, RP* TEL *rediscado automático* autoredial

rediseñar *vt (producto, proceso)* to reengineer

rediseño *nm* reengineering ❑ *rediseño de los procesos de negocio* business process reengineering

redistribución *nf (de riqueza)* redistribution; *(de recursos, personal)* redeployment

redistribuir *vt (riqueza)* to redistribute; *(recursos, personal)* to redeploy

rédito *nm* yield

redondear *vt (cifra, precio) (al alza)* to round up; *(a la baja)* to round down

reducción *nf (disminución)* cut, reduction; **piden la reducción de la jornada laboral** they are asking for working hours to be shortened ❑ *reducción fiscal* tax cut, tax reduction; *reducción de gastos* cost cutting, cost reduction; **han anunciado una reducción de gastos** they have announced that they are going to cut costs; *reducción de impuestos* tax cut, tax reduction; *reducción de los márgenes de beneficio* profit reduction; *reducción de precios* *(acción)* price-cutting; *(resultado)* price cut; *reducción de la presión fiscal* easing of tax pressure; *reducción tributaria* tax cut, tax reduction

reducido, -a adj (tarifa, plantilla, precio) reduced

reducir 1 vt (gastos, costes, impuestos, plantilla) to cut, to reduce; (producción) to cut (back on); **reducir drásticamente** (precios, costos, impuestos) to slash; **reducir al mímino** (gastos) to minimize; **reducir la plantilla** to downsize
  2 reducirse vpr (beneficios, rentas, presupuesto) to go down, to fall

reembalar vt to repackage

reembolsable, rembolsable adj (gastos) reimbursable; (fianza, dinero) refundable

reembolsar, rembolsar vt (gastos) to reimburse; (fianza, dinero) to refund

reembolso, rembolso nm (de gastos) reimbursement; (de fianza, dinero) refund; **contra reembolso** cash on delivery, US collect (on delivery) ▢ **reembolso diferido** deferred rebate

reempaquetar vt to repackage

reemplazar, remplazar vt to replace

reenvío nm (reexpedición) forwarding ▢ INFORM **reenvío de correo (electrónico)** mail forwarding

reequipar vt to retool

reescribir vt to rewrite

reestructuración nf (a) (de empresa) restructuring (b) (de deuda) restructuring

reestructurar vt (a) (empresa) to restructure (b) (deuda) to restructure

reexpedición nf (de cartas) forwarding

reexpedir vt to forward, to send on

reexportación nf (actividad) re-exportation; (producto) re-export

reexportar vt to re-export

ref. (abrev de **referencia**) ref

referencia nf (a) (mención, base de comparación) reference; **con referencia a su consulta del 5 de mayo,...** (en carta) with reference to your inquiry of 5 May,... (b) **referencias** (para puesto de trabajo) reference, testimonial; (para banco) reference; **nos complacerá dar referencias de usted** we would be delighted to give you a reference

refinanciación nf, **refinanciamiento** nm refinancing

> En países como Brasil y Colombia se discute −ante negociaciones inminentes− si la **refinanciación** de la deuda multilateral argentina y cierta moderación en las metas de superávit primario (3% en 2004) fueron favores excepcionales concedidos a un país en bancarrota, o si pueden servir de precedente.

refinanciar vt to refinance

reflación nf ECON reflation

reflacionar vt ECON to reflate

reflotamiento nm, **reflotación** nf FIN (de empresa, banco) saving; **un acuerdo para el reflotamiento del sector** an agreement aimed at saving the industry

reflotar vt FIN (empresa, banco) to save, to bail out

reforma nf (a) (modificación) reform ▢ **reformas estructurales** structural reforms; **reforma fiscal** tax reform; **reforma monetaria** monetary reform (b) (en local, vivienda) alterations; **cerrado por reformas** (en letrero) closed for alterations

reforzar vt (moneda, economía) to strengthen

refrendar vt to countersign

refrescar vt INFORM to refresh

refresco nm INFORM refresh ▢ **refresco de pantalla** (screen) refresh

refrigeración nf (de alimentos) refrigeration (de máquinas, motores) cooling

refrigerar vt (alimentos) to refrigerate; (máquina, motor) to cool

refugio nm FIN **refugio fiscal** tax shelter; **refugio tributario** tax shelter

regalía nf royalty ▢ **regalía petrolera** oil royalty

regalo nm (obsequio) gift; **compras tres y te dan uno de regalo** if you buy three, you get one free

regatear 1 vt (precio) to haggle over
  2 vi (negociar el precio) to haggle

regateo nm haggling

regentar vt (negocio) to run, to manage

régimen (pl regímenes) nm (sistema) regime, system ▢ **régimen de financiación** financing scheme; **régimen fiscal** tax system, tax regime; **régimen de tránsito** transit system

región nf (a) (área) region (b) (administrativa) region

regional adj regional

registrador, -ora nm,f registrar ▢ **registrador de la propiedad** land registrar, recorder of deeds

registrar 1 vt (a) (nombre, empresa, marca, acciones) to register; (information) to log; (patente) to take out; **registrar como propiedad intelectual** to copyright (b) INFORM (programas) to register (c) (experimentar) **la empresa ha registrado un aumento de las ventas** the company has recorded an increase in sales; **los precios han registrado un incremento del 10% durante el último año** prices show a 10% increase on last

year (**d**) *Am (certificar)* to register
2 registrarse *vpr (en hotel)* to check in

registro *nm* (**a**) *(inscripción) (de nombre, empresa, marca, acciones)* registration
(**b**) *(relación)* record, log; **llevar el registro de algo** to keep a record of sth ❑ *registros contables* accounting records
(**c**) FIN *(libro)* register ❑ *registro de caja* cash book; *registro de cuentas por cobrar* accounts receivable ledger; *registro de cuentas por pagar* accounts payable ledger; *registro de efectos a cobrar* bills receivable ledger; *registro de efectos a pagar* accounts payable ledger; *registro de facturas de compra* purchase invoice ledger; *registro de nóminas* pay ledger
(**d**) *(oficina)* registry (office) ❑ *registro catastral* land register; *registro civil* registry (office); *registro de comercio* trade register office; *registro mercantil* trade register office; *registro de la propiedad* land registry office; *registro de la propiedad industrial* trade mark registry office, patent office; *registro de la propiedad intelectual* copyright registry office
(**e**) BOLSA *registro de acciones, registro de accionistas* share register, shareholder register, *US* stock ledger
(**f**) INFORM *(de memoria)* register; *(dato)* record

regla *nf (norma)* rule, regulation; **en regla** in order ❑ *reglas de funcionamiento* operating rules

reglamentación *nf* (**a**) *(acción)* regulation (**b**) *(reglas)* rules, regulations ❑ *reglamentación laboral* labour regulations, *US* labor code

reglamento *nm (normas)* regulations, rules

regrabable *adj* INFORM rewritable

regresivo, -a *adj* FIN regressive

regulación *nf (de actividad, economía)* regulation ❑ *regulación de empleo* workforce adjustment; *regulación de precios* price regulation

regulador, -ora 1 *adj (organismo)* regulatory
2 *nm* regulator, watchdog

regular *vt (actividad, economía, precios)* to regulate; **el precio está regulado por la oferta y la demanda** the price is regulated by supply and demand

regularización *nf* CONT adjusting entry

regularizar *vt* CONT to adjust

rehabilitación *nf* FIN *(de negocio en quiebra)* discharge ❑ *rehabilitación del quebrado* discharge in bankruptcy

rehabilitar *vt* FIN *(negocio en quiebra)* to discharge

rehusar *vt (oferta, petición)* to refuse

reincorporación *nf* return (**a** to)

“
El ministro de Trabajo, Eduardo Zaplana, también se ha comprometido a extender la bonificación total de la cuota de la Seguridad Social a las mujeres que hayan sido madres durante el año posterior a su **reincorporación** al mercado laboral y a reformar la ley de familias numerosas. Estas medidas se unen a la reforma del IRPF, que entrará en vigor en 2003, que ya recoge ventajas fiscales para las mujeres trabajadoras, como el aumento de las deducciones por el cuidado de menores.
”

reincorporar 1 *vt (a puesto)* to reinstate (**a** in)
2 reincorporarse *vpr* **¿cuándo te reincorporas?** when will you be coming back o returning to work?

reiniciar, reinicializar *vt* INFORM *(ordenador)* to reboot, to restart; *(impresora)* to reset

reinstaurar *vt (ley)* to reinstate

reintegrar 1 *vt* (**a**) *(a un puesto)* to reinstate (**a** in) (**b**) *(gastos)* to reimburse, to refund; *(préstamo)* to repay (**c**) *(documento)* to put an official stamp on
2 reintegrarse *vpr* to return (**a** to); **se reintegró a la vida laboral** she returned to work

reintegro *nm (de gastos)* reimbursement, refund; *(de préstamo)* repayment; *(en banco)* withdrawal ❑ *reintegro en efectivo* cash withdrawal

reintentar *vt* INFORM to retry

reinvertir *vt* to reinvest

reivindicación *nf* claim, demand; **el salario mínimo es una reivindicación histórica de los sindicatos** a minimum wage is one of the trade unions' traditional demands ❑ *reivindicación principal* main claim; *reivindicación salarial* pay claim; *reivindicación sindical* union demand

reivindicar *vt (derechos, salario)* to claim, to demand; **reivindican el derecho a sindicarse** they are demanding the right to join a union

rejilla *nf* (**a**) *(en gráfico)* grid ❑ *rejilla gerencial* managerial grid (**b**) INFORM *rejilla de datos* input grid

relación 1 *nf* (**a**) *(ratio)* ratio ❑ *relación calidad-precio* quality-price ratio; **tener buena / mala relación calidad-precio** to be good/poor value for money; *relación capital-producto* capital-output ratio; *relación capital-trabajo* capital-labour ratio; *relación contable* accounting ratio; *relación costo-beneficio, Esp relación coste-beneficio* cost-benefit ratio; *relación deudas-capital propio* leverage; BOLSA *relación precio-beneficio* price-earnings ratio; BOLSA

relación riesgo-rendimiento risk-reward ratio (**b**) *(lista)* list ❑ *relación de clientes* client list (**c**) *(comunicación, trato)* relationship ❑ *relaciones con los clientes* customer relations; *relaciones comerciales (vínculos)* business links; *(comercio)* trade; **tener relaciones comerciales con alguien** to trade with sb; ECON *relación de intercambio* terms of trade; *relaciones internacionales* international relations; *relaciones interpersonales* interpersonal skills; *relaciones laborales* industrial relations, labour relations; *relaciones públicas (actividad)* public relations, PR
(**d**) **relaciones** *(contactos)* contacts, connections; **tener buenas relaciones** to be well connected
2 *nmf inv* **relaciones públicas** *(persona)* public relations officer, PR officer, communications officer

relacional *adj* relational

relanzamiento *nm* relaunch

relanzar *vt* to relaunch

relativo, -a *adj (proporción, valor)* relative

relegar *vt (a un puesto más bajo)* to demote

relevo *nm (sustituto)* relief; **tomar el relevo** to take over

rellenar *vt (documento, impreso)* to fill in o out

reloj *nm* (**a**) *(para fichar)* time clock (**b**) INFORM clock ❑ *reloj del sistema* system clock

remarcado *nm* TEL *remarcado automático* autoredial

rematar *vt (en subasta)* to auction

remate *nm (subasta)* auction

rembolsable = **reembolsable**

rembolsar = **reembolsar**

rembolso = **reembolso**

remesa *nf (de productos)* shipment, consignment; *(de dinero)* remittance ❑ *remesa documentaria* documentary remittance

----

❝
Las **remesas** de Estados Unidos a México se duplicaron en los últimos cinco años y siguen creciendo de tal forma que para finales del 2003 serán la segunda fuente de ingresos en dólares del país, después de las exportaciones de petróleo y por delante del turismo extranjero y de la inversión privada directa.
❞

----

remitente *nmf* sender

remitir *vt* (**a**) *(enviar)* to send; **adjunto le remito mi currículum vitae** I enclose *Br* my CV o *US* my resumé (**b**) *(reexpedir) (carta, e-mail)* to forward (**c**) *(trasladar)* to refer; **remitiré tu solicitud al director** I'll refer your application to the

director; **remitir a un cliente a otro departamento** to refer a customer to another department (**d**) *(pago)* to remit; **sírvase remitir la diferencia mediante un cheque** *(en carta)* kindly remit the balance by cheque

rémora *nf* FIN *rémora fiscal* fiscal drag

removible *adj* INFORM *(disco)* removable

remplazar = **reemplazar**

remuneración *nf* remuneration; **cobra una alta remuneración por sus servicios** she charges a high fee for her services; **remuneración: a convenir** o **negociar** *(en anuncio)* salary o remuneration to be agreed, salary negotiable

remunerado, -a *adj* (**a**) *(trabajo)* paid; **bien remunerado** well paid; **mal remunerado** badly paid; **no remunerado** unpaid (**b**) FIN *(deuda)* interest-bearing

remunerar *vt* to remunerate

remunerativo, -a *adj* remunerative

rendimiento *nm* (**a**) FIN *(rentabilidad) (de inversión)* yield, return; **preferiría una inversión con un mayor rendimiento** I would prefer a better return on investment; **rendimientos pasados no garantizan rendimientos futuros** past performance is not a guarantee of future results ❑ *rendimiento actuarial bruto* gross actuarial return; *rendimiento anual* annual return; *rendimiento bruto* gross yield; *rendimiento bruto al vencimiento* gross redemption yield; *rendimiento del capital* return on capital; *rendimiento del capital empleado* return on capital employed, ROCE; *rendimiento del capital invertido* return on capital invested, ROCI; *rendimiento cero* nil return, zero return; *rendimiento corriente* current yield, current return; *rendimiento del cupón* coupon yield; *rendimiento del dividendo* dividend yield; *rendimientos en efectivo* cash returns; *rendimiento explícito equivalente* bond equivalent yield; *rendimiento fijo* fixed yield; *rendimiento de la inversión* return on investment, ROI; *rendimiento marginal sobre el capital* marginal return on capital; *rendimiento medio* average yield, average return; *rendimiento neto* net return, net yield; *rendimiento (neto) anual* compound (net) annual return; *rendimiento nominal* nominal yield, nominal return; *Am rendimiento promedio* average yield, average return; *rendimiento sostenido (de recursos)* sustained yield; *rendimientos del trabajo* earned income; *rendimiento al vencimiento* yield to maturity; *rendimiento de ventas* return on sales, ROS
(**b**) *(productividad) (de máquina, empresa)* performance; *(de trabajador)* productivity; **tener un bajo rendimiento** *(acciones)* to underperform; **trabajar a pleno rendimiento** to work at full capacity ❑ *rendimiento global* aggregate output; *rendimiento máximo* capacity output

> El Tribunal Superior de Justicia de Cataluña (TSJC) ha avalado el despido de un trabajador por emplear el ordenador de su trabajo para jugar al "solitario", circunstancia que descubrió la empresa al colocarle un programa informático para controlar su actividad y **rendimiento** laboral.

rendir 1 *vi* (**a**) *(inversión, negocio)* to be profitable (**b**) *(máquina, empresa)* to perform well; *(trabajador)* to be productive
2 *vt (interés)* to yield

renegociación *nf* renegotiation

renegociar *vt* to renegotiate

renovación *nf (de pasaporte, contrato, suscripción)* renewal ◻ **renovación urbana** urban renewal

renovar *vt (pasaporte, contrato, suscripción)* to renew; **la empresa ha renovado su imagen** the company has brought its image up to date

renta *nf* (**a**) *(ingresos)* income; **vivir de (las) rentas** to have an independent income ◻ **renta per cápita** per capita income; **renta del capital** capital income; **renta disponible** disposable income; **renta disponible per cápita** disposable personal income; **renta familiar** family income; **renta fija** fixed income; **renta gravable** taxable income; **renta por habitante** per capita income; **renta imponible** taxable income; **renta íntegra** gross income; **renta nacional** national income; **renta neta** net income; **renta no salarial** unearned income; **renta del trabajo** earned income; **renta vitalicia** life annuity (**b**) *(intereses)* interest ◻ **renta fija** fixed (interest) rate; **acciones de renta fija** fixed-interest shares; **renta variable** variable (interest) rate; **acciones de renta variable** variable-interest shares; **los mercados de renta variable** the equity markets (**c**) *(alquiler) (dinero)* rent; *(acción)* rental, renting ◻ *Méx* **renta de carros** car rental, *Br* car hire; **renta teórica** notional rent

rentabilidad *nf* (**a**) *(de actividad, sector, empresa)* profitability; **debemos estudiar la rentabilidad del proyecto antes de tomar ninguna decisión** we must consider the cost-effectiveness of the project before making any decisions; **el negocio tiene muy poca rentabilidad** the business is not very profitable (**b**) *(interés)* yield, return; **rentabilidades pasadas no garantizan rentabilidades futuras** past performance is not a guarantee of future results; **un bono de alta rentabilidad** a high-yield bond ◻ **rentabilidad bruta** gross yield; **rentabilidad del capital** return on capital; **rentabilidad cero** nil return, zero return; **rentabilidad corriente** current yield, current return; **rentabilidad del dividendo** dividend yield;

rentabilidad fija fixed yield; **rentabilidad de la inversión** return on investment, ROI; **rentabilidad media** average yield, average return; **rentabilidad neta** net return, net yield; **rentabilidad (neta) anual** compound (net) annual return; **rentabilidad nominal** nominal yield, nominal return; **rentabilidad de los recursos propios** return on equity; **rentabilidad sostenida** *(de recursos)* sustained yield; **rentabilidad al vencimiento** yield to maturity

rentabilizar *vt* to make profitable; **rentabilizaron la inversión inicial en dos años** it took them two years to make a profit on their initial investment

rentable *adj (actividad, empresa, inversión)* profitable; **la manera más rentable de hacerlo** the most cost-efficient way of doing it

rentar 1 *vt* (**a**) *(rendir)* to produce, to yield; **esa inversión no me renta mucho** my earnings on that investment aren't very high (**b**) *(dejar en alquiler) (vivienda, oficina, aparato)* to rent (out); *(vehículo, traje)* to rent (out), *Br* to hire out (**c**) *(tomar en alquiler) (vivienda, oficina, aparato)* to rent; *(vehículo, traje)* to rent, *Br* to hire
2 *vi* to be profitable

renuncia *nf* (**a**) *(dimisión)* resignation (**b**) *(de derecho, reivindicación)* waiver

renunciar *vi* (**a**) *(dimitir)* to resign (**b**) **renunciar a** *(derecho)* to give up, to waive; *(reivindicación)* to give up, to renounce

reorganización *nf* reorganization

reorganizar *vt* to reorganize

reparación *nf* (**a**) *(arreglo)* repair; **en reparación** under repair (**b**) *(compensación)* redress ◻ **reparación legal** legal redress

reparar *vt (vehículo, aparato)* to repair

repartidor, -ora *nm,f (de publicidad)* deliverer

repartir 1 *vt* (**a**) *(propaganda)* to deliver (**b**) *(dividendo, trabajo, beneficios)* to distribute
2 *vi (como proveedor)* to deliver; **repartimos a domicilio** we do home deliveries

reparto *nm* (**a**) *(de dividendos)* distribution; *(de herencia)* division; ◻ *Esp* ECON **reparto de beneficios** profit-sharing; ECON **reparto de dividendos** dividend payout; **reparto del mercado** market division; **reparto de la riqueza** distribution of wealth; **reparto del trabajo** work-sharing; *Am* ECON **reparto de utilidades** profit-sharing (**b**) *(a domicilio)* delivery; **el camión del reparto** the delivery van ◻ **reparto a domicilio** home delivery

repatriación *nf* FIN *(de capitales)* repatriation

repatriar *vt* FIN *(capitales)* to repatriate

repercutir *vt* FIN *(IVA)* to charge, to pass on; **IVA repercutido** output VAT

repetición *nf* MKTG *repetición de compra*

repeat pruchase; *repetición de venta* repeat sale

repetitivo, -a *adj* repetitive

replanteamiento *nm (de política, situación)* reappraisal, reassessment

replantear *vt (política, situación)* to reappraise, to reassess

repo *nm o nf Am (abrev de* **repurchase agreement)** repo

reponer *vt (existencias)* to replace; *(pérdidas)* to cover

reportar *CAm, Méx, Ven* **1** *vt (informar)* to report **2** *vi* **reportar a alguien** to report to sb

> 66
>
> Según datos estadísticos de Pemex Refinación, estos grupos **reportaron** un crecimiento de 16 por ciento, promedio anual, en su volumen de ventas en el Distrito Federal. Esa alza, explican expertos, es como consecuencia del Bando Informativo Número Ocho (del Programa Nacional de Desarrollo Urbano del Distrito Federal), que entró en vigor hace casi tres años.
>
> 99

reporte *nm Am (informe)* report ❑ *reporte financiero* financial report; *reporte de ventas* sales report

reporto *nm Méx* FIN repo, repurchase

reposamuñecas *nm inv* INFORM wrist rest

reposar *vi* INFORM to sleep

reposición *nf (de existencias)* replacement

reposicionamiento *nm* MKTG repositioning

reposicionar *vt* MKTG *(producto)* to reposition

representación *nf* **(a)** *(delegación)* representation; **acudió a la reunión en representación de sus compañeros** he attended the meeting on behalf of his colleagues, he represented his colleagues at the meeting; **el banco tiene representación en la junta directiva** the bank is represented on the board ❑ *representación paritaria* joint representation; *representación de los trabajadores* workers' representation **(b)** *(comercial)* representation; **tener la representación de** to act as a representative for ❑ *representación exclusiva* sole agency; **tener la representación exclusiva de Rover** to be sole agent for Rover

representante *nmf* representative; *(comercial)* (sales) rep ❑ *representante autorizado* authorized agent o representative; *representante comercial* sales representative; *representante exclusivo* sole representative; *representante en el extranjero* foreign representative, overseas representative; *representante del fabricante* manufacturer's representative; *representante fiscal* tax

representative; *representante oficial* appointed representative; *representante sindical* union rep o representative; *representante de los trabajadores* employee representative

representar *vt* **(a)** *(actuar en nombre de)* to represent, to act for, to act on behalf of; **representó al sindicato en la reunión** he represented the union at the meeting **(b)** *(empresa, producto)* to represent **(c)** *(mediante gráfica)* to chart

representativo, -a *adj (muestra)* representative

reprocesado *nm* reprocessing

reprocesar *vt* to reprocess

reproducción *nf (copia)* reproduction ❑ INFORM *reproducción en tiempo real* streaming

reproductor, -ora **1** *adj* **un aparato reproductor de DVD** a DVD player **2** *nm* **reproductor de discos compactos** compact disc player, CD player; *reproductor de DVD* DVD player; *reproductor de MP3* MP3 player

reprogramable *adj* INFORM reprogrammable

reprogramación *nf* ECON *(de deuda)* rescheduling

reprogramar *vt* **(a)** ECON *(deuda)* to reschedule **(b)** INFORM to reprogram

repuesto *nm* **(pieza de) repuesto** spare (part)

repuntar *vi* FIN *(valor, precio)* to rally, to recover

repunte *nm* FIN *(de valores, precios)* rally, recovery; **la economía ha tenido un repunte al alza** the economy has rallied; **un repunte inflacionista** o **de la inflación** a slight rise in inflation; **un repunte navideño de las ventas** a slight upturn in sales over the Christmas period

> 66
>
> La pérdida de competitividad de la economía mexicana en un contexto internacional incierto, el **repunte** de los bonos del Tesoro estadounidense, junto con la baja de rendimientos financieros nacionales, mermaron la entrada de divisas a nuestro país e hicieron que el superpeso perdiera el paso.
>
> 99

reputación *nf* reputation, name

requerimiento *nm* request; **el informe fue elaborado a requerimiento de la comisión** the report was written at the request of the committee ❑ *requerimientos de caja* cash requirements; FIN *requerimiento de capital* call (up), call for capital; DER *requerimiento judicial* injunction

requisito *nm* requirement; **cumplir los requisitos** to fulfil the requirements; **reúne todos los requisitos** it meets o satisfies all the requirements; **un requisito previo** a prerequisite; **el dominio del alemán es requisito indispensable**

a knowledge of German is essential

resaltador *nm Col, RP (fluorescente)* highlighter

resaltar *vt (con fluorescente)* to highlight

resarcir 1 *vt* **resarcir a alguien (de)** to compensate sb (for); **la aseguradora lo resarció por los daños sufridos** the insurance company paid him compensation *o* compensated him for the damage caused
  2 resarcirse *vpr* **resarcirse de** *(pérdidas)* to recoup

rescatable *adj* FIN *(acciones)* redeemable

rescatar *vt* **(a)** FIN *(acciones)* to redeem **(b)** *(póliza de seguros)* to surrender **(c)** *(barco, cargamento)* to salvage

rescate *nm* **(a)** FIN *(de acciones)* redemption **(b)** *(de póliza de seguros)* surrender **(c)** *(de barco, cargamento)* salvage

rescindir *vt (contrato)* to rescind, to cancel

rescisión *nf (de contrato)* cancellation, termination

> **"**
>
> En su oferta a los empleados, pendiente de la ratificación de la asamblea de trabajadores, Xfera ha propuesto un 43 por ciento del sueldo actual durante el próximo año, con compromiso de recolocación al final del periodo, a los trabajadores que acepten la **rescisión** de sus contratos.
>
> **"**

reserva *nf* **(a)** *(de hotel, avión)* reservation, booking; **hacer una reserva** to make a reservation *o* booking ▫ **reserva anticipada** advance booking; **reserva automática** automated reservation; **reserva de grupo** group booking
  (b) ECON, FIN, CONT reserve; **la Reserva Federal** *(en Estados Unidos)* the Federal Reserve ▫ **reservas bancarias** bank reserves; **reservas de caja** cash reserves; **reservas de divisas** foreign currency reserves; **reservas estatutarias** reserves required by *Br* articles of association *o US* company's bylaws; **reservas para imprevistos** contingency reserve; **reserva legal** statutory reserve, legal reserve; **reserva metálica** bullion reserve; **reservas monetarias** monetary reserves; **reservas monetarias internacionales** international monetary reserves; **reservas mundiales** world reserves; **reserva obligatoria** mandatory reserve, statutory reserve; **reserva oculta** secret reserve; **reservas de oro** gold reserves; **reservas de petróleo** oil reserves; **reservas sociales** *(en empresa)* company reserves

reservación *nf Am* reservation; **hacer una reservación** to make a reservation

reservado, -a *adj* **(a)** *(mesa, plaza)* reserved; **reservados todos los derechos** copyright reserved **(b)** *(información)* confidential

reservar *vt* **(a)** *(billete, habitación)* to book, to

reserve **(b)** *(apartar)* to set aside; **la habitación está reservada para reuniones** this room is set aside for meetings

resguardo *nm (de compra)* receipt, *US* sales slip; *(de cheque)* stub, *Br* counterfoil ▫ **resguardo de almacén** *(de mercancías)* (warehouse) warrant; **resguardo de depósito,** *Esp* **resguardo de ingreso** deposit slip; BOLSA, FIN **resguardo provisional** *(de acciones)* script

residencia *nf (domicilio)* residence; **permiso de residencia** residence permit ▫ **residencia habitual** normal place of residence

residente 1 *adj* resident
  2 *nmf (ciudadano)* resident ▫ **residente fiscal** resident for tax purposes

residuos *nmpl* waste ▫ **residuos industriales** industrial waste; **residuos tóxicos** toxic waste

resistencia *nf* MKTG **resistencia del consumidor** consumer resistance

resolución *nf* **(a)** *(de crisis)* resolution; *(de disputa, conflicto)* settlement, resolution ▫ DER **resolución judicial** court ruling; **resolución de problemas** problem solving; INFORM troubleshooting **(b)** *(moción)* resolution **(c)** INFORM *(de imagen)* resolution; **alta resolución** high resolution

resolver *vt (crisis)* to resolve; *(problema)* to solve; *(disputa, conflicto)* to settle, to resolve

respaldar *vt (proyecto, empresa, candidatura)* to back, to support

respaldo *nm (de proyecto, empresa, candidatura)* backing, support ▫ **respaldo financiero** financial backing *o* support

responder 1 *vt* to answer
  2 *vi* **responder (a algo)** *(pregunta, llamada)* to answer (sth); *(carta, saludo)* to answer (sth), to reply (to sth); **responder de las deudas de alguien** to be liable for sb's debts

responsabilidad *nf* **(a)** *(obligación)* responsibility; **tienen una responsabilidad para con los accionistas** they have a responsibility to the shareholders; **tener la responsabilidad de algo** to be responsible for sth; **puesto de responsabilidad** senior position; **exigir responsabilidades a alguien por algo** to call sb to account for sth ▫ FIN **responsabilidades contingentes** contingent liabilites; **responsabilidad corporativa** corporate responsibility; **responsabilidad ministerial** ministerial responsibility; **responsabilidades del puesto** *(en empleo)* job description; **responsabilidad social corporativa** corporate social responsibility
  (b) DER liability ▫ **responsabilidad civil** civil liability, public liability, third-party liability; **responsabilidad civil de productos** product liability; **responsabilidad colectiva** collective liability; **responsabilidad conjunta** joint liability; **responsabilidad contractual** contractual

liability; **responsabilidad de la empresa** employer's liability; **responsabilidad del fabricante** manufacturer's liability; SEGUR **responsabilidad frente a terceros** third-party liability; **responsabilidad ilimitada** unlimited liability; **responsabilidad limitada** limited liability; **responsabilidad solidaria** joint and several liability

> **"**
> La Audiencia de Pontevedra ha ratificado la sentencia del juzgado de Cambados y ha decidido que el joven Armando Cacabelos, que está incapacitado desde 1999 cuando le cayó encima una plancha de hierro mientras trabajaba en una obra, es el responsable del accidente por una acción imprudente, por lo que la empresa y la compañía aseguradora quedan eximidas de **responsabilidad civil**.
> **"**

responsable 1 adj (**a**) (con control, autoridad) responsible (**de** for); (**ante**) to (**b**) (con seriedad) responsible; **tener una actitud responsable hacia el medio ambiente** to be environmentally responsible (**c**) DER liable
2 nmf (**a**) DER liable person; **los responsables** those liable (**b**) (encargado) person in charge; **soy el responsable de la sección de ventas** I'm in charge of the sales department □ **responsable político** policymaker

respuesta nf (**a**) (contestación) answer, reply; **en respuesta a** in reply to (**b**) (reacción) response □ MKTG **respuesta al estímulo** stimulus response; **respuesta de ventas** sales response

resquicio nm **un resquicio legal** a loophole in the law

restaurar vt INFORM (recuperar) to restore

restitución nf (**a**) (en cargo) reinstatement (**b**) (devolución) return, restitution □ **restitución a la exportación** export refund

restituir vt (**a**) (en cargo) to reinstate (**b**) (devolver) to return

resto nm rest, remainder; **pague 100 euros ahora y el resto más tarde** you pay 100 euros now, the rest later; **le enviaremos el resto de su pedido en un plazo máximo de diez días** the balance of your order will be supplied within ten days □ **resto de serie** remainder

restricción nf (de gastos, producción) restriction; **se han impuesto restricciones a la importación de vehículos extranjeros** restrictions have been placed on the importing of foreign vehicles □ INFORM **restricciones de acceso** access restrictions; **restricciones de cambio** exchange restrictions; **restricción comercial** trade restraint; **restricciones al crédito** credit restrictions; **restricciones a la exportación** export restrictions; **restricciones a la importación** import restrictions

restrictivo, -a adj restrictive

restringir vt (gastos, producción) to restrict

resultado nm (**a**) (efecto) result; **los resultados económicos han sido muy positivos** the economic results have been very positive □ **resultados comerciales** trading results; **resultados diferidos** deferred results; **resultado neto** net result (**b**) INFORM (de búsqueda) hit

resumen nm summary □ **resumen de compras** purchase report

resumir vt (abreviar) to summarize

RETA nm Esp (abrev de **Régimen Especial de Trabajadores Autónomos**) = special social security scheme for the self-employed

retención nf (**a**) (por impuestos) deduction, Br stoppage; **las retenciones fiscales han disminuido** the amount of tax deducted from wages at source has gone down □ **retención (de impuestos) en origen** tax deduction at source (**b**) (de un pago) withholding (**c**) MKTG **retención selectiva** selective retention

> **"**
> El reglamento fija que no se practicará **retención** sobre rendimientos del trabajo a los contribuyentes solteros o divorciados, con hijos a cargo, y que cobren menos de 10.750 euros al año.
> **"**

retener vt (**a**) (por impuestos) to deduct; **el fisco me retiene el 20% del sueldo** 20% of my salary goes in tax (**b**) (pago) to withhold

retirada nf (**a**) (de dinero, fondos) withdrawal (**b**) (del mercado) (de moneda) withdrawal (from circulation); (de producto) withdrawal; (de producto defectuoso) recall; **se ha ordenado la retirada del mercado del producto** they have ordered the product to be withdrawn from o taken off the market □ **retirada estratégica** strategic withdrawal

retirar 1 vt (**a**) (de una cuenta) to withdraw; **retirar dinero del banco** to withdraw money from the bank (**b**) (del mercado) (moneda) to withdraw (from circulation); (producto) to withdraw; (producto defectuoso) to recall
2 retirarse vpr (**a**) (jubilarse) to retire (**b**) (de negociaciones, acuerdo) to withdraw (**de** from), to pull out (**de** of)

retiro nm (**a**) (jubilación) retirement (**b**) (pensión) pension (**c**) Am (de dinero) withdrawal

reto nm challenge

> **"**
> "Los resultados del estudio muestran que la externalización de las funciones de compra está aquí para quedarse" según Juan Carlos Marco, director asociado de Accenture. "Sin embargo, de cara al futuro, el principal

reto será obtener algo más que un simple ahorro de costes. La externalización de las funciones de compra debe acompañar claras ventajas estratégicas y competitivas".   **"**

retornable *adj (envase)* returnable; **no retornable** non-returnable

retorno *nm* (**a**) *(devolución)* return (**b**) INFORM return ▫ **retorno automático** soft return; **retorno manual** hard return (**c**) *Am* FIN *(de inversión)* return ▫ **retorno sobre activos** return on assets; **retorno sobre el capital invertido** return on invested capital; **retorno sobre la inversión** return on investment; **retorno sobre el patrimonio** return on equity

retracción *nf* ECON *(de la demanda)* reduction, fall; *(del mercado)* shrinking; **se ha producido una retracción de las inversiones** there has been a drop in investments

retractilado, -a 1 *adj* shrink-wrapped
    2 *nm* shrink-wrapping

retractilar *vt* to shrink-wrap

retraerse *vpr* ECON *(demanda, inversiones)* to fall

retrasar 1 *vt (demorar)* to delay, to hold up; **la huelga ha retrasado nuestro calendario por lo menos un mes** the strike has put our schedule back at least a month; **retrasaron la fecha de la reunión** the meeting was postponed, the date of the meeting was put back
    2 retrasarse *vpr* **retrasarse en los pagos** to get into arrears

retraso *nm* (**a**) *(demora)* delay; **la reunión comenzará con un retraso de 20 minutos** there will be a 20-minute delay before the meeting; **llegar con (15 minutos de) retraso** to be (15 minutes) late; **el proyecto lleva dos semanas de retraso** the project is two weeks behind schedule (**b**) *(subdesarrollo)* backwardness; **llevar (siglos de) retraso** to be (centuries) behind

retribución *nf (pago)* payment, remuneration; **en retribución por sus servicios** as payment for your services ▫ **retribución completa** full pay; **retribución en especie** benefit in kind; **retribución justa** fair pay **retribuciones salariales** salaries

retribuido, -a *adj (trabajo)* paid; **no retribuido** unpaid

retribuir *vt* to pay

retroactivamente *adv* retroactively

retroactivo, -a *adj (ley)* retrospective, retroactive; *(pago)* backdated; **con efecto** *o* **con carácter retroactivo** retroactively

retroarriendo *nm* lease-back

retroceso *nm* INFORM backspace ▫ **retroceso de página** page up

retroiluminación *nf* INFORM *(de pantalla)* backlight

retroiluminado, -a *adj* INFORM *(pantalla)* backlit

retroingeniería *nf* IND reverse engineering

retroproyector *nm* overhead projector, OHP

reunión *nf* meeting; **hacer** *o* **celebrar una reunión** to have *o* hold a meeting ▫ **reunión del comité** committee meeting; **reunión del consejo** board meeting; **reunión de departamento** departmental meeting; **reunión del G7** G7 meeting; **reunión del G8** G8 meeting; **reunión de grupo** group meeting; **reunión de la junta** board meeting; **reunión de negocios** business meeting; **reunión del personal** staff meeting; **reunión sindical** union meeting; **reunión de ventas** sales meeting

reunir 1 *vt* (**a**) *(fondos)* to raise (**b**) *(requisitos, condiciones)* to meet, to fulfil; **no reúne los requisitos necesarios para el puesto** she doesn't meet the requirements for the post
    2 reunirse *vpr* to meet; **reunirse con alguien** to meet sb, *esp US* to meet with sb

revaloración *nf* revaluation

revalorar *vt* to revalue

revalorización *nf* (**a**) *(de productos, inversión, acciones)* appreciation ▫ **revalorización de activos** restatement of assets (**b**) *(de moneda)* revaluation

revalorizar 1 *vt (moneda)* to revalue
    2 revalorizarse *vpr* (**a**) *(productos, inversión, acciones)* to appreciate (**b**) *(moneda)* **la libra se revalorizó frente al dólar** the pound rose against the dollar

revaluación *nf (de moneda)* revaluation

revender *vt (productos, bienes)* to resell

reventa *nf (de productos, bienes)* resale

reventar *vt* **reventar los precios** to make massive price cuts

revisar *vt* (**a**) *(examinar) (cuentas, cifras, documento)* to check (**b**) *(con regularidad) (máquina)* to service (**c**) *(modificar)* to revise; **han revisado sus previsiones de crecimiento** they've revised their growth forecasts; **las pensiones han sido revisadas al alza/a la baja** pensions have been adjusted upwards/downwards (**d**) *(analizar) (situación, política)* to review

revisión *nf* (**a**) *(examen) (de cuentas, cifras, documento)* check (**b**) *(con regularidad) (de máquina)* service (**c**) *(modificación)* review; **han hecho una revisión de las cifras de crecimiento** the growth figures have been revised; ▫ **revisión de los precios** price review **revisión salarial** salary review (**d**) *(análisis) (de situación, política)* review ▫ **revisión estratégica** strategic review; **revisión financiera** financial review

revista *nf* (**a**) *(publicación)* magazine ▫ **revista**

del consumidor consumer magazine; *revista de empresa* in-house magazine (**b**) *(inspección)* **pasar revista a** to review; **el informe pasa revista a la situación del sector agrícola** the report reviews the situation of the farming industry

revocación *nf (de sentencia, contrato)* revocation

revocar *vt (sentencia, contrato)* to revoke

revuelo *nm (publicitario)* hype; **se lanzó el producto con gran revuelo publicitario** the product was launched in a blaze of publicity

RFC *nm Méx (abrev de* **Registro Federal de Contribuyentes**) = tax identification number, tax ID number

rico, -a **1** *adj (persona, país)* rich
2 *nm,f* **los ricos** the rich, the wealthy

riesgo *nm* risk; **correr el riesgo de...** to run the risk of...; **a todo riesgo** *(seguro, póliza)* (fully) comprehensive; **aseguró la casa a todo riesgo** she took out comprehensive home insurance ▫ BOLSA **riesgo alzista, riesgo al alza** upside risk; BOLSA **riesgo bajista, riesgo a la baja** downside risk; **riesgo calculado** calculated risk; FIN **riesgo cambiario** exchange risk, currency exposure, currency risk; **riesgo colectivo** collective risk; SEGUR **riesgos combinados** mixed risks; BANCA **riesgo de contraparte** counterparty risk; **riesgo crediticio** credit risk; SEGUR **riesgo de daños a terceros** third-party risk; IND **riesgo laboral** occupational hazard; SEGUR **riesgo de mar** sea risk; FIN **riesgo de mercado** market risk; SEGUR **riesgo moral** moral hazard; FIN **riesgo país** country risk; **riesgo percibido** perceived risk; SEGUR **riesgo de siniestro** loss risk; SEGUR **riesgo suscrito** risk subscribed; **riesgo de tipo de cambio** foreign exchange risk

> 66
> Las diferentes medidas económicas y sociales que se habían puesto en marcha (para muchos simples parches) no han logrado frenar una caída del PIB –que superó el 13% entre enero y marzo de 2002–, ni evitar que el paro alcanzara una tasa récord del 22% o que el **riesgo país** esté situado en los 6.275 puntos.
> 99

riguroso, -a *adj (control)* strict, tight; *(análisis)* rigorous; **las entradas se darán en riguroso orden de llegada** the tickets will be issued strictly on a first come first served basis

riqueza *nf* wealth

RISC INFORM *(abrev de* **reduced instruction set computer**) RISC

ritmo *nm (velocidad)* pace; **la economía está creciendo a un buen ritmo** the economy is growing at a healthy pace *o* rate; **llevan un**

ritmo de trabajo agotador they have a punishing work rate

rival *adj & nmf* rival

rivalidad *nf* rivalry

roaming *nm* TEL roaming

robo *nm (hurto)* theft; *(atraco)* robbery; *Fam* **¡qué robo!** what a rip-off!

robótica *nf* robotics

rol *nm Chile* FIN **rol único tributario** tax identification number

ROM *nf* INFORM *(abrev de* **read only memory**) ROM

rompehuelgas *nmf inv Fam* scab, *Br* blackleg

romper **1** *vt (acuerdo, negociaciones)* to break
2 romperse *vpr (negociaciones, relaciones)* to break down

ronda *nf (de conversaciones, visitas)* round ▫ *Ronda de Uruguay* Uruguay Round

rotación *nf (política, sistema)* rotation; *(cambio, alternancia)* turnover ▫ *rotación de activos* asset turnover; *rotación del capital* capital turnover; *rotación de empleos* job rotation; *rotación de existencias* inventory turnover, *Br* stock turnover; *rotación de personal* staff turnover

rotulador *nm* felt-tip pen ▫ *rotulador fluorescente* highlighter (pen)

router *nm* INFORM router

royalty *nm* royalty

RSC *nf (abrev de* **Responsabilidad Social Corporativa**) CSR, corporate social responsibility

> 66
> Un repaso a las prácticas de los cien mayores gestores de activos del mundo (según Global Investor) permite constatar que buena parte aplica criterios **RSC** al diseño de carteras; algunos, como Barclays Global Investors, declaran que el análisis de las prácticas **RSC** constituye una parte esencial de su política de inversión.
> 99

rubro *nm Am (a) (apartado)* heading; CONT item; **rubro presupuestal 2005: educación, salud, seguridad pública** 2005 budget headings: education, health, law and order (**b**) *(campo)* area, field; **preparamos empresas líderes en su rubro** we provide training for companies which are leaders in their field

> 66
> En ese sector operan firmas importantes como Kasdorf, Ford, Alba y otras dedicadas a variados **rubros**, que van desde metalúrgicas, cueros y derivados hasta químicas y productos para el agro. Aunque también quedan lotes vacíos a disposición.
> 99

RUC *nm RP* (*abrev de* **Registro Único de Contri-buyentes**) = tax identification number, tax ID number

rueda *nf* (**a**) *rueda de prensa* press conference (**b**) *Am* BOLSA (trading) session; **la rueda se movió con alta volatilidad** trading was very volatile ❑ *rueda electrónica* electronic trading

ruego *nm* **ruegos y preguntas** *(en orden del día)* any other business, AOB; **al final tendremos tiempo para los ruegos y preguntas** we'll have time for questions (and answers) at the end

ruido *nm* INFORM noise

ruina *nf* *(quiebra)* ruin; **estar en la ruina** to be ruined; **la epidemia ha supuesto la ruina de muchos ganaderos** the epidemic has ruined many cattle farmers

ruptura *nf* *(de relaciones, conversaciones)* breaking-off

RUT *nm Chile* FIN (*abrev de* **Rol Único Tributario**) tax identification number

ruta *nf* *(itinerario)* route ❑ INFORM *ruta de acceso a los datos* data path; *ruta aérea* air route, airway; *ruta comercial* trade route; INFORM *ruta de correo (electrónico)* mail path; INFORM *ruta de flujo* flow path; *ruta turística* scenic route

rutina *nf* (**a**) *(costumbre)* routine; **de rutina** routine (**b**) INFORM routine

rutinario, -a *adj (actividad, vida)* routine

Ss

S.A. (*abrev de* **sociedad anónima**) *Br* ≃ PLC, *US* ≃ Inc

sacar *vt* (**a**) *(obtener)* **sacar dinero del banco** to take money out of the bank, to withdraw money from the bank; **sacar beneficios** to make a profit (**b**) *(nuevo producto, modelo, libro)* to bring out; **sacar algo al mercado** to put sth on the market; **sacar a Bolsa** to float; **sacar algo a concurso** to invite tenders for sth, to put sth out to tender

SAI *nm* INFORM (*abrev de* **sistema de alimentación ininterrumpida**) UPS

sala *nf* (**a**) *(habitación)* BOLSA *sala de cambios* dealing room; INFORM *sala de chat* chat room; *sala de contratación* trading room; *sala de embarque* *(en aeropuerto)* departure lounge; *sala de espera* waiting room; *(en aeropuerto)* lounge; *sala de exposiciones* exhibition hall; *sala de juntas* conference room; *sala de recepción* reception room; *sala de reuniones* conference room, meeting room; *sala de subastas* auction room; *sala VIP* VIP lounge
  (**b**) DER *(lugar)* court(room); *(magistrados)* bench ❑ *sala de lo civil* civil court; *sala de lo penal* criminal court

salarial *adj* pay; **congelación salarial** pay freeze; **incremento salarial** pay rise, pay increase; **política salarial** wage(s) policy, pay policy

salario *nm* salary, wage(s) ❑ *salario atrasado* back pay; *salario base, salario básico* basic salary; *salario bruto* gross salary; *salario diferido* deferred pay; *salario fijo* fixed salary; *salario inicial* starting salary; *salario mínimo (interprofesional)* minimum wage; *salario neto* net salary; *salario nominal* nominal wages; *salario real* real salary; *salario semanal* weekly wage; *Esp salario social* = benefit paid by local authorities to low-income families; *salario por unidad de tiempo* time rate

saldar *vt (cuenta, deuda)* to settle, to pay off

saldo *nm* (**a**) *(de cuenta)* balance; **saldo a favor/en contra** credit/debit balance; **dispone de un saldo a su favor de 100 dólares** you're in credit to the amount of $100; **la balanza comercial entre los dos países arroja un saldo favorable a Japón** the trade balance between the two countries is tipped in Japan's favour ❑ *saldo acreedor* credit balance; *saldo acumulado* cumulative balance; *saldo anterior* balance brought forward; *saldo de apertura* opening balance; *saldo bancario* bank balance; *saldo de caja* cash balance; *saldo cero* nil balance; *saldo de cuenta* account balance; *saldo decreciente* diminishing balance; *saldo en descubierto* overdrawn account; *saldo deudor* debit balance; *saldo disponible* balance available, available balance; *saldo final de la cuenta* closing account balance; *saldo de final de mes* end-of-month balance; *saldo insuficiente* insufficient funds; *saldo medio* average (bank) balance; *saldo negativo* debit balance; *saldo pendiente* outstanding balance; *saldo positivo* credit balance, positive balance; **presentan un saldo positivo de 10.000 millones de euros en la balanza comercial** they have a balance of trade surplus of 10,000 million euros; *saldo vivo* outstanding balance
  (**b**) **saldos** *(restos de mercancías)* remnants; *(rebajas)* sale; **de saldo** bargain

> ❝
> Entre febrero de 2002 y febrero de 2003, el **saldo vivo** del crédito hipotecario aumentó un 21,5%, pasando de los 320.422 millones de euros del primer año a los 389.251 en 2003, según la Asociación Hipotecaria Española.
> ❞

salida *nf* (**a**) *(partida)* departure; **salidas nacionales/internacionales** *(en aeropuerto)* domestic/international departures ❑ *salida a Bolsa (de empresa)* flotation
  (**b**) FIN *(de divisas, capital)* outflow
  (**c**) *(producción)* output; *(posibilidades)* market; **dar salida a** *(producto)* to find an outlet for; **este producto tiene mucha salida** *(posibilidades de venta)* there's a big market for this product; *(se vende)* this product sells well; **este producto no tiene salida** *(posibilidades de venta)* there's no market for this product; *(no se vende)* this product doesn't sell
  (**d**) INFORM *(de datos, información)* output
  (**e**) INFORM *(en hardware)* *salida paralela* parallel output; *salida de serie* serial output
  (**f**) CONT **salidas** outgoings ❑ *salidas de caja* cash outgoings
  (**g**) **salidas** *(posibilidades laborales)* openings, opportunities; **carreras con salidas** university courses with good job prospects

saliente *adj* (**a**) *(correo, llamada telefónica)* outgoing (**b**) *(presidente, ministro)* outgoing

salir 1 *vi* (**a**) *(marcharse)* to leave; **salir del trabajo a las siete** to leave work at seven; **salir de viaje** to go away (on a trip)
(**b**) *(aparecer) (publicación, producto, modelo)* to come out; **salir al mercado** to come onto the market
(**c**) *(resultar)* **¿te salen las cuentas?** do all the figures tally?; **salir perdiendo** to lose out; **salir a** to work out at; **salimos a 20 dólares por cabeza** it came to *o* worked out at $20 each; **salir más barato** to work out cheaper; **salir caro** to be expensive
(**d**) INFORM *(de programa)* to quit, to exit; *(de servidor remoto)* to log off, to log out; **salir de un programa** to quit *o* exit a program
2 salirse *vpr (marcharse)* **salirse (de)** to leave

salón *nm* (**a**) *(para reuniones, ceremonias)* hall ◻ *salón de actos* assembly hall, assembly room; *salón de congresos* conference hall; *RP salón de fiestas* function room; *salón de sesiones* committee room (**b**) *(feria)* show, exhibition ◻ *salón del automóvil* motor show; *salón de la informática* computer fair

saltarse *vpr* **saltarse algo** *(omitir intencionadamente)* to skip sth

salto *nm* INFORM *salto de línea* line break; *salto de línea automático* wordwrap; *salto de página* page break; *salto de párrafo* paragraph break

salvaguarda = **salvaguardia**

salvaguardar *vt* to safeguard

salvaguardia, salvaguarda *nf (garantía)* safeguard

salvaje *adj (competencia)* cut-throat; *(huelga)* wildcat

salvapantallas *nm inv* INFORM screen saver

sanción *nf* (**a**) *(penalización)* sanction, penalty; DER *(por incumplir contrato)* forfeit; **imponer sanciones (económicas) a** *(país)* to impose (economic) sanctions on (**b**) *(aprobación)* sanction; **todavía no ha recibido la sanción oficial** it hasn't yet been given official sanction

sancionar *vt* (**a**) *(penalizar) (a un país)* to impose sanctions on (**b**) *(aprobar)* to sanction

saneamiento *nm* (**a**) CONT write-down (**b**) ECON *(de moneda)* stabilization; *(de economía)* refloating; *(de empresa)* turnaround; *(de cuenta)* regularization; **el saneamiento de las cuentas públicas** the reform *o* restructuring of public finances

sanear *vt* (**a**) CONT to write down (**b**) ECON *(moneda)* to stabilize; *(economía)* to refloat; *(empresa)* to turn around; *(cuenta)* to regularize; **sanear las cuentas públicas** to reform *o* restructure public finances

sangrado *nm* TIP indent

sangrar *vt* TIP to indent

sangría *nf* (**a**) TIP indentation (**b**) *(ruina)* drain; **los continuos accidentes laborales son una sangría para la empresa** the constant accidents among its employees are a drain on the company's resources

satélite *nm* satellite ◻ *satélite de telecomunicaciones* telecommunications satellite

satisfacción *nf* (**a**) *(agrado, gusto)* satisfaction; **espero que todo sea de su satisfacción** *o* **esté a su satisfacción** I hope everything is to your satisfaction ◻ *satisfacción del cliente* customer satisfaction; *satisfacción del consumidor* consumer satisfaction; *satisfacción laboral* job satisfaction (**b**) *(de deuda)* payment, settlement

satisfacer *vt* (**a**) *(cumplir) (requisitos, exigencias)* to meet, to satisfy; **un producto que satisface nuestras necesidades** a product which meets *o* satisfies our needs (**b**) *(deuda)* to satisfy, to settle

saturación *nf (de mercado)* saturation

saturado, -a *adj (mercado)* saturated, glutted; **el mercado está saturado de importaciones** the market is saturated *o* glutted with imports; **las líneas telefónicas están saturadas** the telephone lines are busy *o* jammed

saturar 1 *vt (mercado)* to saturate, to glut
2 saturarse *vpr* to become saturated (**de** with); **el mercado se ha saturado de importaciones** the market has been saturated *o* glutted with imports

SCSI INFORM *(abrev de* **small computer system interface***)* SCSI

SDRAM *nf* INFORM *(abrev de* **synchronous dynamic random access memory***)* SDRAM

sección *nf (parte)* section; *(en contrato)* article; *(en tienda)* department; **la sección de discos** the record department

secretario, -a *nm,f* (**a**) *(administrativo)* secretary ◻ *secretario de dirección* secretary to the director; *secretario ejecutivo* executive secretary; *secretario particular* private secretary; *secretario personal* personal assistant, PA; *secretario de prensa* press secretary
(**b**) *(político) (en Latinoamérica)* Br minister, US secretary ◻ *secretario de Estado (en España)*

Br junior minister, *US* under-secretary; *(en Latinoamérica) Br* cabinet minister, *US* secretary; *(en Estados Unidos)* Secretary of State; **secretario general** General Secretary

secreto, -a 1 *adj* secret

2 *nm (noticia, información)* secret; **mantener algo en secreto** to keep sth secret ▫ **secreto bancario** banking confidentiality; **secreto de Estado** State secret; **secreto profesional** trade secret; **secreto sumarial, secreto del sumario: decretar el secreto sumarial** *o* **del sumario** = to deny access to information relating to a judicial inquiry

sector *nm* (**a**) *(división)* section; **todos los sectores de la sociedad** all sections of society

(**b**) ECON industry, sector; **el líder del sector** the industry leader ▫ **sector de artículos de lujo** luxury goods industry; **sector bancario** banking sector, banking; **sector básico** basic industry; **sector clave** key sector; **sector de las comunicaciones** communications sector; **sector de la construcción** building sector; **sector de distribución en masa** mass distribution sector; **sector económico** economic sector; **sector empresarial**, *RP* **sector empresario** business sector, corporate sector; **sector en expansión** growth sector; **sector de la hostelería (y restauración)** hospitality business; **sector hotelero** hotel industry; **el sector mayorista** the wholesale trade; **sector primario** primary sector; **sector privado** private sector; **sector público** public sector; **sector de la sanidad** health sector; **sector secundario** secondary sector; **sector servicios** service sector; **sector terciario** tertiary sector; **sector turístico** tourist trade

(**c**) INFORM *(de disco, pantalla)* sector ▫ **sector dañado** bad sector

secuelas *nfpl* consequences

secuencia *nf* INFORM sequence

secuencial *adj* INFORM sequential

secundar *vt (moción, propuesta)* to second

secundario, -a *adj* secondary

sede *nf (de organización, empresa)* headquarters, head office; *(de congreso)* venue ▫ **sede administrativa** administrative headquarters; **sede central** general headquarters, main office; **sede regional** regional headquarters; **sede social** headquarters, head office

segmentación *nf* MKTG segmentation ▫ **segmentación por beneficios** benefit segmentation; **segmentación por comportamiento** behaviour segmentation; **segmentación demográfica** demographic segmentation; **segmentación por estilos de vida** lifestyle segmentation; **segmentación estratégica** strategic segmentation; **segmentación geodemográfica** geodemographic segmentation;

segmentación geográfica geographic segmentation; **segmentación del mercado** market segmentation; **segmentación por necesidades** needs-based segmentation; **segmentación sociodemográfica** sociodemographic segmentation

segmento *nm* MKTG *(franja)* segment ▫ **segmento demográfico** demographic segment; **segmento de edad** age bracket; **segmento geodemográfico** geodemographic segment; **segmento geográfico** geographic segment; **segmento de mercado** market segment; **segmento sociodemográfico** sociodemographic segment

seguimiento *nm (de clientes, pedidos)* follow-up; *(control)* monitoring; **hacer el seguimiento de un proceso** to monitor a process ▫ **seguimiento telefónico** telephone follow-up

> Para lograr una óptima colocación del material de comunicación y el buen desarrollo de la promoción, el departamento de Nuevas Tecnologías ha desarrollado un nuevo programa de control de campaña que permite realizar el control y **seguimiento** del proceso promocional on-line. Un servicio que aporta a MC y Osborne numerosas ventajas en la gestión y comunicación del proceso promocional.

segundo, -a 1 *adj* second; **de segunda (categoría)** second-rate; **de segunda mano** second-hand; INFORM **en segundo plano** *(tarea, datos)* background ▫ FIN **segundo endosante** second endorser; **segunda hipoteca** second mortgage; **segundo mercado** secondary market; **segundo trimestre** second quarter

2 *nf* FIN **segunda de cambio** second of exchange

seguridad *nf* (**a**) *(ausencia de peligro)* safety; **la seguridad de los pasajeros es nuestra prioridad** passenger safety is our priority ▫ **seguridad e higiene laboral** health and safety at work *o* in the workplace; **seguridad laboral** occupational safety; **seguridad vial** road safety

(**b**) *(protección)* security; **el personal de seguridad** the security staff ▫ **Seguridad Social** Social Security; **seguridad de los datos** data security

(**c**) *(estabilidad)* security; **una inversión que ofrece seguridad** a safe *o* secure investment

seguro, -a 1 *adj* (**a**) *(sin peligro) (inversión)* safe, secure (**b**) *(protegido, estable) (trabajo, transacción electrónica, servidor)* secure

2 *nm* (**a**) *(contrato)* insurance; **contratar** *o* **hacerse un seguro** to take out insurance ▫ **seguro de accidentes** accident insurance, *US* casualty insurance; **seguro de accidentes laborales** industrial accident insurance; **seguro de amortización** loan repayment insurance;

seguro de asistencia en carretera roadside assistance insurance; ***seguro de asistencia en viaje*** travel insurance; ***seguro del automóvil*** car insurance; ***seguro básico*** basic cover; ***seguro de cambio*** exchange rate hedge; ***seguro de cancelación*** cancellation insurance; ***seguro de capitalización*** universal life insurance; ***seguro de cartera*** portfolio insurance; ***seguro de la casa*** buildings insurance; ***seguro colectivo*** group insurance; ***seguro contributivo*** contributory insurance; ***seguro de crédito*** credit insurance; ***seguro de crédito y caución*** bad debt insurance; ***seguro de desempleo*** unemployment insurance; ***seguro de discapacidad*** disability insurance; ***seguro de enfermedad*** health insurance, *US* health plan; ***seguro de flete*** freight insurance; ***seguro de hogar*** buildings insurance; ***seguro de *o* contra incendios*** fire insurance; ***seguro individual de accidentes*** personal accident insurance; ***seguro marítimo*** marine insurance, maritime insurance; ***seguro médico*** medical insurance, health insurance; ***seguro multirriesgo*** comprehensive insurance; ***seguro mutuo*** joint insurance; ***seguro de préstamo*** loan insurance; ***seguro de responsabilidad civil*** third-party liability insurance; ***seguro de responsabilidad civil de productos*** product liability insurance; ***seguro de responsabilidad civil profesional*** professional indemnity insurance; ***seguro de responsabilidad empresarial*** employer's liability insurance; ***seguro a terceros*** third-party insurance; ***seguro a término (fijo)*** term life insurance; ***seguro a todo riesgo*** comprehensive insurance; ***seguro de viaje*** travel insurance; ***seguro de vida*** life insurance, *Br* life assurance; ***seguro de vida mixto*** endowment insurance; ***seguro voluntario*** voluntary insurance **(b)** *(prestación social)* ***seguro de desempleo*** unemployment benefit; ***seguro de incapacidad*** disability benefit; ***seguro de invalidez*** disability benefit; ***seguro de paro*** unemployment benefit

Seis Sigma *nm* Six Sigma

selección *nf (acción)* selection; **una prueba de selección de candidatos** a candidate selection test; **test de selección múltiple** multiple-choice test □ MKTG ***selección aleatoria*** random selection; ***selección de personal*** recruitment

seleccionar *vt* **(a)** *(candidato)* to select **(b)** INFORM *(opción)* to select; *(text)* to highlight; **seleccionar un bloque de texto** to block text

selectivo *nm* BOLSA **(índice) selectivo** blue-chip index

selecto, -a *adj (producto)* select

selector *nm* INFORM chooser

sellar *vt (contrato, acuerdo)* to seal

sello *nm* **(a)** *(timbre)* stamp □ ***sello de correos, sello postal*** postage stamp
(b) *(tampón)* rubber stamp; *(marca)* stamp □ ***sello de calidad*** quality seal, seal of quality; ***sello de caucho*** rubber stamp; ***sello de recibo*** receipt stamp
(c) *(lacre)* seal
(d) *(compañía)* ***sello discográfico*** record label; ***sello editorial*** imprint
(e) *Andes, Ven (de moneda)* reverse

semana *nf* week; **entre semana** during the week; **fin de semana** weekend; **dos veces por semana** twice a week, twice weekly □ ***semana laboral*** *Br* working week, *US* workweek

semanal *adj* weekly

semanalmente *adv* weekly

semanario *nm (publicación semanal)* weekly

semestralmente *adv* half-yearly, semiannually

semiacabado, -a *adj* semi-finished

semicualificado, -a, *Am* **semicalificado, -a** *adj* semi-skilled

semielaborado, -a *adj* semi-finished

sencillo, -a **1** *adj* **(a)** *(billete, pasaje)* *Br* single, *US* one-way **(b)** *(habitación)* single; **habitación sencilla** single room
2 *nm Andes, CAm, Méx Fam (cambio)* loose change, small change

sensibilidad *nf* MKTG ***sensibilidad de marca*** brand sensitivity; ***sensibilidad al precio*** price sensitivity

sentencia *nf* DER *(judicial)* judgement; **dictar *o* pronunciar sentencia** to deliver judgement; **visto para sentencia** ready for judgement □ ***sentencia ejecutoria*** enforceable judgement; ***sentencia firme*** final judgement

seña **1** *nf RP (señal)* deposit
2 señas *nfpl (dirección)* address

señal *nf* **(a)** *(tono telefónico)* tone □ ***señal de comunicando*** *Br* engaged tone, *US* busy signal; *Méx* ***señal de libre*** *Br* dialling tone, *US* dial tone; ***señal de llamada*** ringing tone; ***señal de *o* para marcar*** *Br* dialling tone, *US* dial tone; ***señal de ocupado*** *Br* engaged tone, *US* busy signal
(b) *(fianza)* deposit; **dar *o* dejar una señal** to leave a deposit
(c) INFORM ***señal digital*** digital signal
(d) *(marca, huella)* mark

separación *nf (de empresas fusionadas)* demerger ❑ **separación en divisiones** *(en gran empresa)* divisionalization

separado, -a *adj* **por separado** separately

separador *nm* INFORM separator

serie *nf (producción)* run, batch; **este coche es de la primera serie que se fabricó** this car is from the first batch that was produced; **fabricación en serie** mass production; **con ABS de serie** with ABS as standard ❑ **serie de prueba** pilot run

serpiente *nf* FIN **serpiente monetaria** currency snake, monetary snake

servicio *nm* (**a**) *(prestación, asistencia, sistema)* service; **hubo que recurrir a los servicios de una agencia inmobiliaria** we had to use the services of *Br* an estate agent *o US* a real estate office; **el servicio postal/hospitalario** the postal/hospital service; **estamos a su servicio para lo que necesite** we are at your service if you need anything ❑ *Méx* **Servicio de Administración Tributaria** *Br* ≃ Inland Revenue, *US* ≃ IRS; **servicio de aduanas** customs service; **servicios de apoyo** support services; **servicio de asesoramiento, servicio de asesoría** advisory service; **servicio de asistencia** *(telefónica)* help line, help desk; **servicio de asistencia social** welfare service; **servicio de asistencia técnica** technical support; **servicio de atención al cliente** customer service department; **servicio de atención de llamadas** *o Am* **llamados** answering service; **servicios bancarios** banking services; **servicio de consultoría** consultancy service; **servicio de descubierto** overdraft facility; **servicio de la deuda** *Br* debt service, *US* debt servicing; **servicio a domicilio** home delivery service; **servicios de empresa** business services; **servicio de entrega** delivery service; INFORM **servicio de filmación** service bureau; **servicios financieros** financial services; **servicio de información** information service; **servicio de información telefónica** *Br* directory enquiries, *US* directory assistance; **servicio integral** full service; **servicio integral de atención al cliente** total care service; **servicio en línea** on-line service; **servicio de llamada en espera** call waiting service; **servicio de lujo** premium service; **servicio de mensajería** courier service; **servicio de mercancías** goods service; **servicios mínimos** *(en huelga)* skeleton service; **servicio de orientación profesional** careers service; **servicio de paquetería** parcel service; **servicio de pasajeros** passenger service; **servicio de portes** porterage service; **servicios portuarios integrados** integrated port facilities; **servicio postal** postal service; **servicio posventa** after-sales service; **servicio público** public service, public utility; **servicio rápido** prompt service; **servicios sociales**

social services; **servicio técnico** technical assistance; **servicio de telebanco** remote banking; **servicio telegráfico** telegraph service; **servicio de transporte** transport service, *US* transportation service; **servicio de transporte aéreo** air freight service; **servicio de transporte de mercancías** freight service; **servicios de ventanilla** *(en banco)* counter services

(**b**) *(funcionamiento)* service; **entrar en servicio** to come into service; **estar fuera de servicio** *(averiado)* to be out of order

(**c**) *(turno)* duty; **estar de servicio** to be on duty

(**d**) *(en restaurante) (atención al cliente)* service; *(recargo)* service charge; **servicio no incluido** service is not included

(**e**) **servicios** *(sector terciario)* services; **una empresa de servicios** a services company; **el sector servicios** the service sector

servidor *nm* INFORM server ❑ **servidor de archivos** file server; **servidor caché** proxy; **servidor de correo (electrónico)** mail server; **servidor de ficheros** file server; **servidor FTP** FTP server; **servidor de grupos de noticias** news server; **servidor de red** network server; **servidor remoto** remote server; **servidor seguro** secure server; **servidor Web** Web server

servir *vt* (**a**) *(prestar servicio a)* to serve; **¿en qué puedo servirle?** *(en tienda, mostrador)* what can I do for you? (**b**) *(suministrar) (mercancías)* to supply; **nuestra empresa sirve a toda la zona** our company serves *o* supplies the whole area; **le serviremos el pedido en el acto** we'll bring you your order immediately

sesión *nf* (**a**) *(reunión)* meeting, session; **abrir/levantar la sesión** to open/adjourn the meeting ❑ **sesión informativa** *(para presentar algo)* briefing; *(después de una misión)* debriefing; **sesión plenaria** *(de organización)* plenary (session) (**b**) BOLSA session ❑ **sesión de apertura** opening session; **sesión de cierre** closing session

SET® *nm* INFORM *(abrev de* **secure electronic transaction***)* SET®

s.e.u.o. *(abrev de* **salvo error u omisión***)* E & OE

SGC *nf (abrev de* **Sociedad Gestora de Carteras***)* portfolio management company

❝ ─────────────
Gescartera fue creada en 1992 como gestora de patrimonios. Era lo que en la jerga del mundo financiero se denomina una **SGC** —sociedad gestora de carteras— (de las que hay miles en España).
───────────── ❞

SGML *nm* INFORM *(abrev de* **Standard Generated Markup Language***)* SGML

shareware *nm* INFORM shareware

SIBOIF *nf (abrev de* **Superintendencia de Bancos y de Otras Instituciones Financieras***)* =

Nicaraguan stock market regulatory body

SICAV *nf* FIN (*abrev de* **sociedad de inversión de capital variable**) ≃ OEIC, ≃ ICVC

signatario, -a 1 *adj* signatory
2 *nm,f* signatory □ **signatario autorizado** authorized signatory

signo *nm* (*en la escritura*) mark □ **signo de admiración** exclamation mark; **signo del dólar** dollar sign; **signo de exclamación** exclamation mark; **signo (de) igual** *Br* equals sign, *US* equal sign; **signo de interrogación** question mark; **signo de puntuación** punctuation mark

siguiente *adj* (**a**) (*posterior*) next; **eso está explicado en el capítulo siguiente** that is explained in the next chapter (**b**) (*a continuación*) following; **se aceptan los siguientes sistemas de pago** the following methods of payment are acceptable

silencio *nm* silence □ **silencio administrativo** = lack of official response to a request, claim etc within a given period, signifying refusal or tacit assent, depending on circumstances

SIM *nf* FIN (*abrev de* **sociedad de inversión mobiliaria**) investment company

simbólico, -a *adj* (*precio, pago*) nominal, token

símbolo *nm* symbol □ **símbolo del dólar** dollar sign; **símbolo del euro** euro sign; **símbolo de la libra** pound sign; MKTG **símbolo de marca** brand mark

SIMCAV *nf* FIN (*abrev de* **sociedad de inversión mobiliaria de capital variable**) ≃ OEIC, ≃ ICVC

SIMM *nm* INFORM (*abrev de* **single in-line memory module**) SIMM

simulación *nf* INFORM simulation

simulador *nm* INFORM simulator

simular *vt* (*copiar, emular*) to simulate

sindicado, -a *adj* (**a**) (*trabajador*) **estar/no estar sindicado** to be/not to be unionized (**b**) FIN (*préstamo, crédito*) syndicated

sindical *adj Br* (trade) union, *US* (labor) union; **dirigente sindical** union leader; **organización sindical** *Br* trade-union *o US* labor-union organization

sindicalismo *nm* unionism, *Br* trade unionism

sindicalista 1 *adj* union
2 *nmf* union member, *Br* trade unionist

sindicar, *Am* **sindicalizar 1** *vt* to unionize
2 sindicarse *vpr* to join a union

sindicato *nm* (**a**) (*de trabajadores*) union, *Br* trade union, *US* labor union □ *Méx* **sindicato blanco, sindicato charro** = union which serves the interests of the employers rather than of the workers; **sindicato general** general union; **sindicato sectorial** industrial union, industry

union (**b**) FIN **sindicato de bancos** banking syndicate; **sindicato de garantía** underwriting syndicate

síndico, -a *nm,f* (*administrador*) (official) receiver □ **síndico de la Bolsa** Chairman of the Stock Exchange

sinergia *nf* synergy

sinérgico, -a *adj* synergistic

siniestralidad *nf* accident rate; SEGUR claims ratio, loss ratio

> **"**
>
> Los últimos datos del año pasado sobre **siniestralidad** laboral desvelan que los accidentes laborales mortales aumentaron un nueve por ciento respecto al año anterior. La Asociación Nacional de Entidades Preventivas Acreditadas (ANEPA) ha denunciado que todavía existen muchas empresas españolas que no le dan la suficiente importancia a la prevención de riesgos laborales.
>
> **"**

siniestro *nm* (**a**) (*daño, catástrofe*) disaster; (*accidente de coche*) accident; (*incendio*) fire (**b**) SEGUR loss □ **siniestro máximo previsible** maximum foreseeable loss; **siniestro total** total loss; **el taxi fue declarado siniestro total** the cab was declared a write-off

sintaxis *nf inv* INFORM syntax

sintonía *nf* MKTG (*de anuncio*) jingle

sistema *nm* (**a**) (*estructura, método*) system □ **sistema aduanero** customs system; **sistema de almacenaje** warehousing system; **sistema de apertura retardada** time lock; **sistema de asistencia social** social welfare system; **sistema bancario** banking system; **sistema de compensación** clearing system; **sistema contable** accounting system; **sistema de contratación electrónica** screen trading system; **sistema de control de existencias** inventory *o Br* stock control system; CONT **sistema de costo** *o Esp* **coste estándar** standard cost accounting; CONT **sistema de costo** *o Esp* **coste integral** absorption costing; **sistema de distribución** distribution system; **sistema de doble precio** dual pricing; **sistema electrónico de transferencia de fondos** electronic funds tranfer system; **sistema de evaluación integral** full assessment system; **sistema fiscal** tax system; CONT **sistema de fondo fijo** imprest system; **sistema de gestión** management system; **sistema impositivo** tax system; **sistema integrado de gestión** integrated management system; **Sistema Interbancario de Compensación** *Br* Bankers' Automated Clearing System, *US* Automated Clearing House; **sistema de intercambio local** Local Exchange Trading Scheme; **sistema legal** legal system; **sistema de mesa compartida** hot desking; **sistema métrico (decimal)** metric system; **sistema monetario** monetary system; **Sistema Monetario Europeo** European Monetary System; **sistema de pago** method of payment, means of payment; **sistema piramidal de distribución** pyramid scheme; **sistema de primas** bonus scheme; **sistemas y procedimientos** systems and procedures; **sistema de seguridad social** social security system; **sistema telefónico** telephone system; **sistema tributario** tax system; **sistema de trueque** barter system

(**b**) INFORM system ❑ **sistema de archivo** file system; **sistema de archivos jerárquicos** hierarchical file system; **sistema auxiliar** backup system; **sistema central** host computer; **sistema de copias de seguridad** backup system; **sistema experto** expert system; **sistema de gestión de archivos** file management system; **sistema de gestión de bases de datos** database management system; **sistema informático** computer system; BOLSA **sistema informático de contratación** computerized trading system; **sistema de gestión de la información** management information system; **sistema multiusuario** multi-user system; **sistema de nombres de dominio** domain name system; **sistema operativo** operating system; **sistema operativo de gestión** management operating system; **sistema operativo de red** network operating system; **sistema de procesamiento de datos** data processing system; **sistema en red** networked system

sistemático, -a *adj* systematic

sitio *nm* (**a**) *(lugar)* place (**b**) INFORM site ❑ **sitio de archivos** archive site; **sitio espejo** mirror site; **sitio FTP** FTP site; **sitio réplica** mirror site; **sitio web** website

situación *nf (circunstancias)* situation ❑ **situación financiera** financial situation; **situación patrimonial** *(de empresa)* financial situation

S.L. *(abrev de* **sociedad limitada**) *Br* ≃ Ltd, *US* ≃ Inc

> ❝
> El rector de la Universidad Carlos III de Madrid (UC3M), Gregorio Peces-Barba, se comprometió hoy a mediar entre la dirección de la empresa Limpiezas Ortiz, **S.L.**, encargada del servicio de limpieza del centro universitario, y los trabajadores de la misma, que hoy cumplen su segunda día de huelga indefinida, informó la confederación General del Trabajo (CGT).
> ❞

slot *nm Am* INFORM slot

SMAC *nm (abrev de* **Servicio de Mediación, Arbitraje y Conciliación**) = Spanish arbitration service for the resolution of industrial disputes, *Br* ≃ ACAS, *US* ≃ FMCS

SME *nm (abrev de* **Sistema Monetario Europeo**) EMS

SMS *nm* TEL *(abrev de* **short message service**) SMS; **un mensaje SMS** an SMS

SMTP *nm* INFORM *(abrev de* **Simple Mail Transfer Protocol**) SMTP

soberanía *nf* **la soberanía del consumidor** consumer sovereignty

sobornar *vt* to bribe

soborno *nm* (**a**) *(acción)* bribery (**b**) *(dinero, regalo)* bribe

sobre *nm (para cartas)* envelope ❑ **sobre burbuja** bubble envelope; **sobre franqueado** prepaid envelope; **sobre con ventanilla** window envelope

sobrecapitalización *nf* FIN overcapitalization

sobrecapitalizar *vt* FIN to overcapitalize

sobrecarga *nf* (**a**) *(exceso de carga)* excess load ❑ **sobrecarga permitida** permissible overload (**b**) *(saturación)* overload ❑ **sobrecarga de información** information overload; **sobrecarga de trabajo** excessive workload

sobrecargar *vt* (**a**) *(mercado)* to overload (**b**) *(de trabajo)* to overburden

sobrecontratación *nf (de vuelo)* overbooking

sobrecontratar *vt (vuelo)* to overbook

sobrecosto, *Esp* **sobrecoste** *nm* CONT cost overrun

sobredesarrollo *nm* ECON overdevelopment

sobreempleo *nm* ECON overemployment

sobreescribir *vt* INFORM to overwrite

sobreestadía *nf (en transportes)* demurrage

sobreestimar *vt* to overestimate

sobregiro *nm* overdraft

sobreimposición *nf* FIN overtaxation

sobreindustrialización *nf* ECON overindustrialization

sobrepasar *vt (presupuesto)* to exceed

sobreprima *nf* SEGUR additional premium; *(por alto riesgo)* loaded premium

sobreproducción *nf* overproduction

sobreseer *vt* DER to dismiss

sobreseimiento *nm* DER dismissal

sobrevaloración *nf* FIN *(de activos, acciones, moneda)* overvaluation; CONT overstatement

sobrevalorar *vt* FIN *(activos, acciones, moneda)* to overvalue; CONT to overstate

sociedad *nf* (**a**) FIN *(empresa)* company ❑ **sociedad anónima** *Br* public (limited) company, *US* incorporated company; **sociedad de arrendamiento financiero** leasing company; **sociedad**

de cartera holding (company); *sociedad colectiva* general partnership; *sociedad comanditaria, sociedad en comandita* general and limited partnership; *sociedad de comercio internacional* international trading corporation; *sociedad cotizada en Bolsa* listed company, *US* publicly traded company; *sociedad dependiente* subsidiary company; *sociedad depositaria* depository company; *sociedad dominante* controlling company; *sociedad emisora* issuing company; *sociedad gestora* management company; *sociedad gestora de carteras* portfolio management company; *sociedad inmobiliaria* property company; *sociedad instrumental* special purpose company; *sociedad de inversión* investment company; *sociedad de inversión de capital variable* open-ended investment company; *sociedad de inversión mobiliaria* investment trust; *sociedad limitada* private limited company; *sociedad mediadora del mercado de dinero* discount house; *sociedad mercantil* trading corporation; *sociedad mixta* joint venture; *sociedad mutua de seguros* mutual insurance company; *sociedad patrimonial* holding company; *sociedad rectora de la Bolsa* stock exchange governing company; *sociedad de responsabilidad limitada* limited (liability) company; *sociedad unipersonal* single-shareholder company; *sociedad de valores* securities firm *o* house
(**b**) *(asociación)* society
(**c**) *(organización social)* society ❑ *sociedad de consumo* consumer society; *sociedad de la información* information society; *sociedad de libre empresa* enterprise society; *la sociedad de la opulencia* the affluent society; *sociedad de trueque* barter society

> **❝**
> Para la consumación del fraude sus autores controlaban un entramado de **sociedades instrumentales** registradas en España, que carecen de domicilio social conocido y que estaban constituidas por testaferros, que aparecen formalmente como titulares de la actividad comercial fraudulenta.
> **❞**

socio, -a *nm,f* (**a**) *(de empresa)* partner ❑ *socio capitalista Br* sleeping partner, *US* silent partner; *socio comanditario Br* sleeping partner, *US* silent partner; *socio comercial* trading partner; *socio fundador* founding partner; *socio gerente* active partner; *socio industrial* industrial partner; *socio nominal* nominal partner; *socio secreto* secret partner (**b**) *(accionista)* member ❑ *socio mayoritario* majority shareholder (**c**) *(de club, asociación)* member

socioeconómico, -a *adj* socio-economic

sociología *nf* sociology

sociológico, -a *adj* sociological

software *nm* INFORM software; **paquete de software** software package ❑ *software de aplicación* application software; *software de autoedición* DTP software; *software de comunicaciones* communications software; *software de contabilidad* accounting software; *software de correo electrónico* e-mail software; *software empresarial* business software; *software de gráficos* graphics software; *software integrado* integrated software; *software multiusuario* multi-user software; *software de OCR* OCR software; *software para presentaciones* presentation software; *software de red* network software; *software de servidor* server software; *software de sistema* system software; *software de transmisión de datos* datacomms software; *software de tratamiento de texto* word-processing package; *software de usuario* user software

solar *nm (terreno)* vacant lot, undeveloped plot (of land), development site

solicitante *nmf (de préstamo, patente, empleo)* applicant; *(de prestaciones sociales)* claimant

solicitar *vt (información, permiso)* to request (**a** from); *(préstamo, patente, empleo)* to apply for (**a** to)

solicitud *nf* (**a**) *(petición) (de información, permiso)* request; *(de empleo, préstamo, acciones, seguros)* application; **en estos momentos no podemos atender su solicitud** we are unable to respond to your request at this time (**b**) *(documento)* application form

solidario, -a *adj* DER *(obligación, compromiso)* mutually binding; *(responsabilidad)* joint and several

sólido, -a *adj (posición, inversión, negocio)* sound

soltar *vt* INFORM to drop

solvencia *nf (económica)* solvency

solvente *adj (económicamente)* solvent

someter *vt* **someter algo a la aprobación de alguien** to submit sth for sb's approval; **someter algo a votación** to put sth to the vote; **sometieron la estructura a duras pruebas de resistencia** the structure was subjected to stringent strength tests

sondear *vt* to sound out; *(mediante encuesta)* to poll; **sondeó el parecer de los miembros del comité** he sounded out the opinions of the committee members

sondeo *nm* (opinion) poll, survey ❑ *sondeo de opinión* opinion poll

soportar *vt* INFORM to support

soporte *nm* (**a**) *(asistencia)* support ❑ *soporte técnico* technical support (**b**) INFORM medium; **el**

documento se facilita en soporte informático the document is available in electronic form; **una edición en soporte electrónico** an electronic edition ❑ *soporte físico* hardware; *soporte lógico* software; *soporte magnético* magnetic (storage) media; *soporte de salida* output medium (**c**) MKTG **soporte (publicitario** o **mediático)** (media) vehicle

sorteo *nm* BOLSA *(por exceso de demanda de acciones)* ballot

sostenibilidad *nf* ECON *(de desarrollo)* sustainability

sostenible *adj* ECON *(desarrollo, recursos)* sustainable

spot *nm* **spot (publicitario)** (television) commercial o advert

spread *nm* BOLSA option spread

SPVS *nf* (*abrev de* **Superintendencia de Pensiones, Valores y Seguros**) = Bolivian stock market regulatory body

stand *nm (en feria)* stand

stock *nm (de productos)* inventory, Br stock ❑ *stock disponible* inventory o Br stock in hand

subalterno, -a 1 *adj (empleado)* auxiliary **2** *nm,f* subordinate

subarrendador, -ora *nm,f* subletter, sublessor

subarrendamiento *nm (actividad)* subletting, subleasing; *(contrato)* subtenancy, sublease

subarrendar *vt* to sublet, to sublease

subarrendatario, -a *nm,f* subtenant, sublessee

subasta *nf* (**a**) *(venta pública)* auction; **sacar algo a subasta** to put sth up for auction; **vender en subasta** to auction off, to sell at auction ❑ *subasta pública* public auction (**b**) *(contrata pública)* tender; **sacar algo a subasta** to put sth out to tender

subastar *vt* (**a**) *(obra de arte)* to auction (**b**) *(contrato, obras)* to put out to tender

subcapitalización *nf* thin capitalisation

subcomité *nm* subcommittee

subcontratación *nf* subcontracting

subcontratar *vt* to subcontract

❝
El Instituto Nacional de Estadística (INE) **ha subcontratado** este año por primera vez la encuesta de innovación tecnológica en las empresas españolas, decisión que ha provocado malestar entre algunas compañías por los datos altamente sensibles que han tenido que proporcionar. De hecho, una de ellas presentó una denuncia ante la Fiscalía Anticorrupción que fue archivada.
❞

subcontratista *nmf* subcontractor

subcontrato *nm* subcontract

subdesarrollado, -a *adj* ECON underdeveloped

subdesarrollo *nm* ECON underdevelopment

subdirector, -ora *nm,f (de empresa)* deputy director; *(de comercio)* assistant manager

subdirectorio *nm* INFORM subdirectory

súbdito, -a *nm,f (ciudadano)* citizen, national

subempleado, -a *adj* (**a**) *(trabajador)* underemployed (**b**) *(recursos)* underutilized, underemployed

subempleo *nm* (**a**) *(de trabajador)* underemployment (**b**) *(de recursos)* underutilization, underemployment

subida *nf* Esp *(aumento)* increase, rise ❑ *subida de sueldo* pay rise, US pay raise

subir 1 *vt* (**a**) *(aumentar) (precio, impuestos)* to put up, to increase, to raise (**b**) *Fam* INFORM to upload **2** *vi* (**a**) *(aumentar) (precios, acciones)* to rise, to go up; **subió la gasolina** the price of petrol went up o rose; **el euro subió frente a la libra** the euro went up o rose against the pound; **han subido las ventas** sales are up; **este modelo ha subido de precio** this model has gone up in price, the price of this model has gone up; **el coste total no subirá del millón** the total cost will not be more than o over a million (**b**) *(cuenta, importe)* **subir a** to come o amount to

subliminal *adj* subliminal

submenú *nm* INFORM submenu

subordinado, -a 1 *adj* subordinate (**a** to) **2** *nm,f* subordinate

subproducto *nm (de proceso industrial)* by-product

subrogación, *Chile* **subrogancia** *nf* DER subrogation; *(de hipoteca)* = transfer of mortgage to another lender, varying the interest rate but retaining the original term and amount to be repaid

subrogar *vt* DER to subrogate; **subrogar una hipoteca** = to transfer a mortgage to another lender, varying the interest rate but retaining the original term and amount to be repaid

subrutina *nf* INFORM subroutine

subscribir = **suscribir**

subscripción = **suscripción**

subscriptor, -ora = **suscriptor**

subsidiaria *nf (empresa)* subsidiary

subsidiariedad *nf* subsidiarity

subsidiario, -a *adj (empresa, cuenta)* subsidiary

subsidio *nm* benefit, allowance ❑ *subsidio de desempleo* Br unemployment benefit, US unemployment compensation; *subsidio por discapacidad* disability allowance; *subsidios a* *las empresas* business subsidies; **subsidio de enfermedad** sickness benefit; **subsidio del Estado** welfare payment; **subsidio de invalidez** disability allowance, *Br* invalidity benefit; **subsidio de maternidad** maternity benefit

subtítulo *nm (de apartado)* subheading

subvención *nf (para proteger precios, una industria)* subsidy; *(para un proyecto)* grant ❑ **subvención de capital** capital grant; **subvención al desarrollo** development grant; **subvención del Estado** government grant; **subvención de explotación** operating subsidy; **subvención a la exportación** export subsidy

subvencionar *vt (precios, industria)* to subsidize; *(proyecto, actividad cultural)* to provide financial support for; **el proyecto está subvencionado por el gobierno** the project is financed by a government grant

subyacente *adj* underlying

sucesor, -ora *nm,f* successor

sucursal *nf (de banco, empresa)* branch

sueldo *nm (de profesional, oficinista)* pay, salary; *(de obrero)* pay, wage; **a sueldo** *(empleado)* salaried; **me han subido el sueldo** they've given me a pay rise *o US* raise; **pidió una semana sin sueldo** he asked for a week's unpaid leave ❑ **sueldo anual** annual pay, annual salary/wage; **sueldo base** basic pay, basic salary/wage; **sueldo bruto** gross pay, gross salary/wage; **sueldo fijo** fixed pay, fixed salary/wage; **sueldo mínimo** minimum wage; **sueldo neto** take-home *o* net pay, after-tax *o* net salary/wage

suelto, -a 1 *adj* **(a)** *(no envasado)* loose **(b)** *(dinero)* **25 céntimos sueltos** 25 cents in loose change **2** *nm* loose change

sufrir *vt (experimentar)* to undergo, to experience; **la empresa ha sufrido grandes pérdidas** the company has incurred *o* made big losses; **la Bolsa sufrió una caída** the stock market fell

SUGEVAL *nf (abrev de* **Superintendencia General de Valores***)* = Costa Rican stock market regulatory body

sujetapapeles *nm inv* paper clip

sujeto, -a 1 *adj* **estar sujeto a** to be subject to; **estar sujeto a tributación** *(ingresos, empresa)* to be subject to tax; *(persona)* to be liable for tax **2** *nm* **sujeto pasivo** taxpayer

suma *nf (de conocimientos, datos)* total, sum; *(de dinero)* sum; **la suma de los gastos asciende a 4.000 pesos** total expenditure was 4,000 pesos ❑ CONT **suma anterior** amount brought forward

sumar *vt* **(a)** *(añadir)* to add; **súmale diez** add ten; **suma y sigue** *(en contabilidad)* carried forward **(b)** *(dar como resultado)* to add up to, to make; **con esta suman ocho** that makes (it) eight

suministrar *vt (productos, servicios)* to supply; **suministrar algo a alguien** to supply sb with sth, to supply sth to sb

suministro *nm (de productos, servicios)* supply ❑ **suministro eléctrico** electricity supply, power supply

superar *vt (cantidad, número)* to exceed; **la demanda supera la oferta** demand exceeds supply; **la marca que supera en ventas a todas las demás** the brand that outsells all the others; **queremos superar los resultados del año pasado** we want to improve on *o* beat last year's results

superávit *nm* ECON surplus ❑ **superávit adquirido** acquired surplus; **superávit comercial** trade surplus; **superávit presupuestario** budget surplus; CONT **superávit de tesorería** cash surplus

supercomputadora *nf Am* supercomputer

supercuenta *nf* FIN high-interest account

superficie *nf* **(a)** *(extensión)* area ❑ **superficie comercial** commercial floor space; **superficie de ventas** sales area **(b)** **gran superficie** *(hipermercado)* superstore, large retail outlet

> **"**
>
> Los 16 licenciatarios a los que GDM ha otorgado permisos para fabricar y distribuir el merchandising de Operación Triunfo, han puesto en circulación cerca de 100 artículos que se venderán en más de 700 establecimientos de todo el país, entre ellos los centros comerciales de El Corte Inglés, **grandes superficies** y tiendas de regalos.
>
> **"**

superintendencia *nf* **Superintendencia de Bancos y de Otras Instituciones Financieras** = Nicaraguan stock market regulatory body; **Superintendencia de Compañías** = Ecuadoran stock market regulatory body; **Superintendencia General de Valores** = Costa Rican stock market regulatory body; **Superintendencia de Pensiones, Valores y Seguros** = Bolivian stock market regulatory body; **Superintendencia de Valores** = stock market regulatory body in Colombia and El Salvador; **Superintendencia de Valores y Seguros** Securities and Insurance Supervisor, = Chilean stock market regulatory body

superior, -ora 1 *adj* **productos de calidad superior** superior-quality products **2** *nm (jefe)* superior; **ser el superior de alguien** to be sb's senior, to be senior to sb

supermercado *nm* supermarket

superordenador *nm Esp* supercomputer

superproducción *nf* ECON overproduction

SUPERVAL *nf (abrev de* **Superintendencia de Valores***)* = Salvadoran stock market regulatory body

Supervalores nf (abrev de **Superintendencia de Valores**) = Colombian stock market regulatory body

supervisar vt to supervise

supervisión nf supervision

supervisor, -ora 1 adj (cargo) supervisory; (organismo) regulatory
2 nm,f supervisor □ **supervisor de crédito** credit controller
3 nm (de mercado, sector) regulator, watchdog □ **supervisor bancario** bank regulator, banking regulator

> **"**
> El principal objetivo del **supervisor bancario** es salvaguardar la estabilidad del sistema financiero, mediante la estrecha vigilancia de la solvencia y actuación de las entidades, lo que no impide que puedan existir entidades mal gestionadas o ineficientes.
> **"**

suplemento nm (**a**) (recargo) supplement, extra (charge); (de billete, pasaje) excess fare □ **suplemento por reserva** booking fee (**b**) (de periódico, revista) supplement (**c**) INFORM add-on

suponer vt (constituir) to account for; **el vino supone el 5% de todas las exportaciones** wine accounts for 5% of all exports

supremo, -a adj **productos de calidad suprema** top-quality products

suprimir vt (**a**) (puestos de trabajo, servicio) to cut; (ley, impuesto) to abolish; (gastos) to cut out (**b**) INFORM (palabras, texto) to delete

surtido, -a 1 adj (abastecido) **la tienda está bien surtida** the shop is well stocked
2 nm (**a**) (gama) range (**b**) (de galletas, bombones) assortment

surtir 1 vt (proveer) to supply (**de** with)
2 surtirse vpr (proveerse) **surtirse de** to stock up on

suscribir, subscribir 1 vt (**a**) FIN (acciones) to subscribe for; (póliza, préstamo) to take out (**b**) (ratificar, apoyar) to endorse; **suscribo lo dicho por el presidente** I endorse o second the president's remarks (**c**) Formal (firmar) **el que suscribe** the undersigned
2 suscribirse vpr (a publicación) to subscribe (**a** to)

> **"**
> El problema al que deben hacer frente los jóvenes para **suscribir** un préstamo es demostrar su solvencia lo cual no siempre es posible por lo que lo más habitual es que necesiten el aval de alguien que se responsabilice de la deuda en caso de que el joven no puede hacer frente a su devolución.
> **"**

suscripción, subscripción nf (**a**) (a publicación) subscription □ **suscripción colectiva** group subscription; **suscripción de prueba** trial subscription (**b**) FIN (de acciones) subscription; **oferta pública de suscripción de acciones** public offering of shares; **es obligatoria la suscripción de un seguro** it is obligatory to take out insurance; **debe acreditar la suscripción de una póliza de seguros** you must provide proof of insurance

suscriptor, -ora, subscriptor, -ora nm,f subscriber

susodicho, -a adj aforementioned, aforesaid

suspender vt (**a**) (interrumpir) (pago) to suspend; (producción) to halt; (proyecto) to put on hold (**b**) (cancelar) (vuelo, reunión) to cancel (**c**) (aplazar) (reunión, sesión) to adjourn (**d**) (sancionar) (trabajador) to suspend; **suspender a alguien de empleo y sueldo** to suspend sb without pay

suspensión nf (**a**) (interrupción) (de pago) suspension; (de producción) halt; **ordenó la suspensión del proyecto** he ordered the project to be put on hold □ **suspensión de pagos** temporary receivership, Br ≃ administration order, US ≃ Chapter 11; **declarar la suspensión de pagos** Br ≃ to petition for an administration order, US ≃ to file for Chapter 11
(**b**) (cancelación) (de vuelo, reunión) cancellation
(**c**) (aplazamiento) (de reunión, sesión) adjournment
(**d**) (sanción) (de trabajador) suspension □ **suspensión de empleo y sueldo** suspension without pay

sustitución nf replacement, substitution; **la sustitución del presidente por alguien sin experiencia fue un error** replacing the president with a person who had no experience was a mistake; **trabajar haciendo sustituciones** to temp (for sb ill or on leave)

sustituir vt to replace, to substitute; **sustituyó a su secretaria** he replaced his secretary; **han sustituido la moneda nacional por el dólar** the national currency has been replaced by the dollar; **la sustituyó como presidenta de la empresa** he took her place as president of the company; **tuve que sustituirle durante su enfermedad** I had to stand in o substitute for her while she was ill

sustituto, -a nm,f replacement, substitute (**de** for); **ha sido designado sustituto de Pérez en la presidencia** he has been appointed to stand in o substitute for Pérez as president

SUTM nm TEL (abrev de **Sistema Universal de Telecomunicaciones Móviles**) UMTS

SVGA nm INFORM (abrev de **Super Video Graphics Array**) SVGA

SVS *nf* (*abrev de* **Superintendencia de Valores y Seguros**) = Chilean stock market regulatory body

swap *nm* BANCA, BOLSA swap ❏ *swap de deuda* debt swap; *swap de Deuda Pública* treasury swap; *swap de divisas* currency swap; *swap de Esp tipos o Am tasas de interés* interest rate swap

Tt

tabla *nf (lista, gráfico)* table □ **tablas de actividad económica** economic activity tables; **tablas actuariales** actuarial tables; **tabla de decisión** decision table; **tablas de esperanza de vida** life expectancy tables; **tabla estadística** statistical table; **tabla de imputaciones** table of account codes; SEGUR **tablas de mortalidad** mortality tables; **tabla de** *Esp* **tipos** o *Am* **tasas de interés** interest table; SEGUR **tablas de valor actual** present value tables

tableta *nf* INFORM tablet □ **tableta gráfica** graphics tablet

tablón *nm* **tablón de anuncios** *Br* notice board, *US* bulletin board; INFORM bulletin board

tabulador *nm* (a) *(tecla)* tabulator, tab (key) (b) *(carácter)* tab character

tabular 1 *vt* (a) *(texto)* to set the tabs for (b) *(datos, cifras)* to tabulate
2 *vi (en un texto)* to set the tabs

tachar *vt* to cross out, to delete

táctica *nf* tactics □ **táctica defensiva** defensive tactics

táctil *adj* INFORM touch-sensitive

TAE *nm o nf* FIN *(abrev de* **tasa anual equivalente**) APR

tajada *nf Fam* share, cut; **sacar tajada de algo** to get one's cut of sth

taller *nm* (a) *(lugar de trabajo)* workshop □ **talleres gráficos** print shop, printing works (b) *(sección de fábrica)* shop □ **taller de máquinas** machine shop; **taller de montaje** assembly shop, assembly workshop (c) *(cursillo, seminario)* workshop

talón *nm* (a) *Esp (cheque) Br* cheque, *US* check; **extender un talón (a alguien)** to write (sb) a cheque, to make out a cheque (to sb) □ **talón bancario** banker's cheque; **talón en blanco** blank cheque; **talón cruzado** crossed cheque; **talón devuelto** bounced cheque; **talón sin fondos** bad cheque; **talón nominativo** = cheque made out to a specific person; **un talón nominativo a favor de...** a cheque payable to..., a cheque made out to the order of...; **talón al portador** bearer cheque
(b) *(resguardo)* stub, *Br* counterfoil

talonario *nm (de cheques) Br* chequebook, *US* checkbook; **talonario (de recibos)** receipt book □ **talonario de depósitos, talonario de pagos** paying-in book; **talonario de vales** book of vouchers

tamaño *nm* (a) *(de producto)* size; **lo tenemos en varios tamaños** we have it in various sizes; **de gran tamaño** large; **de pequeño tamaño** small, small-sized; **de tamaño mediano** medium, medium-sized; **un paquete (de) tamaño familiar** a family-size o family-sized pack; **de tamaño gigante** giant-sized □ **tamaño económico del lote** economic lot size; **tamaño del lote** lot size; **tamaño del mercado** market size (b) INFORM,TIP *(de letra)* (point) size

tampón *nm (sello)* stamp; *(almohadilla)* ink pad

tancaje *nm (almacenamiento)* tankage

tanto *nm* **tanto por ciento** percentage

tapete *nm* INFORM mouse mat, mouse pad

taquigrafía *nf* shorthand

taquigrafiar *vt* to write (down) in shorthand

taquigráfico, -a *adj* shorthand

taquimecanografía *nf* shorthand and typing

taquimecanógrafo, -a *nm,f* shorthand typist

tara *nf* (a) *(defecto)* defect; **artículos con tara** seconds (b) *(peso)* tare □ **tara real** actual tare

tarea *nf* (a) *(trabajo)* task (b) INFORM task □ **tarea en segundo plano** background task

target *nm* MKTG *(objetivo)* target; *(grupo)* target group □ **target de marketing** marketing target

> **"**
> La Asociación para la Investigación de Medios de Comunicación, AIMC, ha presentado un ambicioso estudio de consumo de marcas en España, AIMC Marcas que pretende conocer a fondo los hábitos del consumidor más allá de su consumo de medios, para que las agencias puedan obtener una mejor definición del **target** y puedan también planificar mejor las campañas.
> **"**

tarifa *nf* (a) *(precio)* charge; *(de profesional)* fee; *(de servicio telefónico, postal)* rate □ **tarifas de alquiler** rental o *Br* hire charges; INFORM **tarifa de alta** joining fee; **tarifa completa** *(por un servicio)* full rate; CONT **tarifa constante** straight-line rate; **tarifa diferencial** differential rate; **tarifa económica** cheap rate; **tarifa eléctrica** electricity charges; **tarifa fija** flat fee; *(en factura)* standing charges; **tarifa de flete** freight rate; **tarifa máxima** peak rate; **tarifa mínima** minimum charge, minimum rate; INFORM **tarifa plana** flat rate; **tarifas postales** postal rates; FIN **tarifa preferente, tarifa preferencial** preferential rate; **tarifas profesionales** professional fees; **tarifas publicitarias** advertising rates; **tarifa punta** peak rate; **tarifa reducida** reduced rate; **tarifa por servicio** service charge; **tarifa de temporada baja** off-season rate; **tarifa única** flat rate

(**b**) *(arancel)* tariff ❑ UE **tarifa exterior común** common external tariff; **tarifa preferente, tarifa preferencial** preferential tariff

(**c**) *(de transportes)* fare ❑ **tarifa apex** Apex fare; **tarifa reducida** reduced fare

tarifación *nf* rating ❑ SEGUR **tarifación de flota** fleet rating

tarifar *vt (fijar precio)* to price

tarifario, -a *adj (sistema)* pricing; *(ajuste, incremento)* price

tarjeta *nf* (**a**) *(para presentación, pagos, transporte)* card ❑ MKTG **tarjeta affinity** affinity (credit) card; **tarjeta American Express®** American Express® card; **tarjeta Amex®** Amex card; **tarjeta bancaria** bank card, banker's card; **tarjeta con banda magnética** swipe card; **tarjeta de compra** *(de crédito)* credit card; *(de tienda)* store card; **tarjeta de control (horario)** clocking-in card; **tarjeta de crédito** credit card; **tarjeta de crédito garantizada** secured credit card; **tarjeta de débito** debit card; **tarjeta de descuento** discount card; **tarjeta de embarque** boarding card, boarding pass; **tarjeta de empresa** corporate card, company card; MKTG **tarjeta de fidelización** loyalty card; **tarjeta inteligente** smart card; **tarjeta MasterCard®** MasterCard® card; **tarjeta monedero** electronic wallet; **tarjeta oro** gold card; TEL **tarjeta (de) prepago** prepaid card; TEL **tarjeta de recarga** top-up card; *Am* **tarjeta de reloj** clocking-in card; **tarjeta de respuesta** reply card; **tarjeta SIM** *(de teléfono)* SIM card; **tarjeta teléfonica, tarjeta de teléfono** phonecard; **tarjeta de visita** business card; **tarjeta Visa®** Visa® card

(**b**) INFORM card ❑ **tarjeta aceleradora** accelerator card; **tarjeta aceleradora gráfica** graphics accelerator card; **tarjeta adaptadora** adapter card; **tarjeta de ampliación (de memoria)** (memory) expansion card *o* board; **tarjeta controladora del disco** disk controller card; **tarjeta de expansión (de memoria)** (memory) expansion card *o* board; **tarjeta de fax** fax card; **tarjeta gráfica** graphics card; **tarjeta magnética** magnetic card; **tarjeta de memoria** memory card; **tarjeta del módem** modem card; **tarjeta de monitor** display card; **tarjeta perforada** perforated card; **tarjeta RDSI** ISDN card; **tarjeta de red** network card; **tarjeta de registro** registration card; **tarjeta SCSI** SCSI card; **tarjeta de sonido** sound card; **tarjeta de**

Esp **vídeo** *o Am* **video** video card

tasa *nf* (**a**) *(índice)* rate ❑ CONT **tasa de absorción de los gastos generales** overhead absorption rate; **tasa de actividad** activity ratio; CONT **tasa de actualización** net present value rate, NPV rate; **tasa de acumulación** accrual rate; MKTG **tasa de adopción** *(de producto)* rate of adoption, rate of uptake; **tasa de amortización** depreciation rate; **tasa básica** base rate; **tasa de cobertura** cover ratio; CONT **tasa de contribución** contribution ratio; **tasa de crecimiento** rate of growth, growth rate; **tasa de crecimiento económico** economic growth rate; **tasa de depreciación** rate of depreciation; **tasa de descuento** discount rate, discounted rate; **tasa de desempleo** unemployment rate, unemployment level; **tasa de endeudamiento** debt ratio; **tasa de inflación** rate of inflation, inflation rate; **tasa interna de rendimiento** *o* **rentabilidad** *o* **retorno** internal rate of return, IRR; **tasa neta de beneficio** net profit ratio; **tasa de participación** participation rate; MKTG **tasa de penetración** penetration rate, rate of penetration; MKTG **tasa de pérdida de clientes** rate of churn; **tasa de quiebras** failure rate; MKTG **tasa de rechazo** refusal rate; BANCA, BOLSA **tasa de recompra** repo rate, repurchase rate; MKTG **tasa de reconocimiento** recognition score; **tasa de rendimiento** *o* **rentabilidad** rate of return; **tasa de rendimiento** *o* **rentabilidad de bonos** bond yield; **tasa de rendimiento** *o* **rentabilidad contable** accounting rate of return; **tasa de rendimiento económico** *o* **rentabilidad económica** economic rate of return

(**b**) *Am* **tasa (de interés)** (interest) rate ❑ **tasa anual equivalente** annual percentage rate, annualized percentage rate; **tasa básica** base rate; **tasa a corto plazo** *(en letras de cambio)* short rate; **tasa de descuento** discount rate, discounted rate; **tasa efectiva anual** effective annual rate; **tasa interbancaria de referencia** interbank reference rate; **tasa de interés bancario** bank rate; **tasa de interés básica** base lending rate; **tasa de interés a corto plazo** short-term interest rate; **tasa de interés de créditos** lending rate; **tasa de interés del dinero** money rate; **tasa de interés fijo** fixed interest rate; **tasa de interés flotante** floating rate; **tasa de interés hipotecario** mortgage rate; **tasa de interés interbancaria** interbank interest rate; **tasa de interés a largo plazo** long-term interest rate; **tasa de interés negativa** negative interest rate; **tasa de interés nominal** nominal interest rate; **tasa de interés de préstamos** lending rate; **tasa de interés promedio** average interest rate on deposits; **tasa de interés variable** variable interest rate; **tasa de oferta interbancaria** interbank offered rate; **tasa preferencial** prime (lending) rate

(**c**) *Am* **tasa de cambio** rate of exchange, exchange rate; **tasa de cambio del dólar** dollar (exchange) rate; **tasa de cambio fija** fixed exchange rate; **tasa de cambio múltiple** multiple exchange rate; **tasa de cambio oficial** official exchange rate; **tasa de conversión** conversion rate

(**d**) *Am (escala, en impuestos)* **tasa impositiva** tax rate, rate of taxation; **tasa del IVA** VAT rate

(**e**) *(impuesto)* tax ❏ **tasas de aeropuerto** airport tax; **tasa municipal** ≃ *Br* council tax, ≃ *US* municipal tax; **tasas portuarias** port charges, port dues

> **"**
> Los analistas dijeron que la decisión de ayer, y la evaluación de que el riesgo está equilibrado entre una caída y una aceleración de la inflación, significan que el banco central prepara el terreno para una eventual subida de las **tasas de interés**.
> **"**

tasación *nf* (**a**) *(de propiedad, objeto de valor)* valuation; **hacer la tasación de un inmueble** to value a property (**b**) *(para seguro, subasta)* valuation, appraisal ❏ SEGUR **tasación de daños** loss adjusting

tasador, -ora *nm,f* valuer ❏ SEGUR **tasador de daños** claims adjuster; **tasador de la propiedad** property valuer; **tasador de seguros** insurance adjuster

tasar *vt* (**a**) *(valorar) (objeto de valor, propiedad)* to value; **tasaron la casa en treinta millones** they valued the house at thirty million (**b**) *(para seguro, subasta)* to value, to appraise; *(daños)* to adjust

TBS *nf* (*abrev de* **Tasa Básica de la Superintendencia Bancaria**) = Colombian interbank rate

TCP/IP *nm* INFORM (*abrev de* **transmission control protocol/Internet protocol**) TCP/IP

TCRM *nf Col* (*abrev de* **Tasa de Cambio Representativa del Mercado**) Market Representative Foreign Exchange Rate, = official exchange rate on the Colombian foreign exchange spot market

techo *nm (tope)* ceiling; **tocar techo** *(inflación, precios)* to reach a ceiling, to peak; **la crisis ha tocado techo** the worst of the recession is behind us ❏ **techo de producción** output ceiling; **techo salarial** wage ceiling

tecla *nf* **tecla de acceso directo** shortcut key; **tecla alt** alt key; **tecla de atajo** shortcut key; **tecla de avance de página** page down key; **tecla de ayuda** help key; **tecla de bloqueo de desplazamiento** scroll lock key; **tecla de bloqueo de mayúsculas** shift lock key, caps lock key; **tecla de bloqueo numérico** num lock key; **tecla de borrado** delete key; **tecla de comando** command key; **tecla de conmutación** toggle key; **tecla de control** control key; **tecla de cursor** cursor key; **tecla de desplazamiento**

scroll key; **tecla de desplazamiento (del cursor)** arrow key; **tecla de encendido** power-on key; **tecla enter** enter key; **tecla de escape** escape key; **tecla fin** end key; **tecla de flecha abajo** down arrow key; **tecla de flecha arriba** up arrow key; **tecla de flecha derecha** right arrow key; **tecla de flecha izquierda** left arrow key; **tecla de función** function key; **tecla de inicio** home key; **tecla de inserción** insert key; **tecla de interrupción** break key; **tecla intro** enter key; **tecla de mayúsculas** shift key; **tecla de mayúsculas fijas** caps lock key; **tecla de movimiento (del cursor)** arrow key; **tecla multifuncional** multifunctional key; **tecla numérica** number key; **tecla de opción** option key; **tecla personalizada** hot key; *Am* **tecla de prendido** power-on key; **tecla de retorno** return key; **tecla de retroceso** backspace key; **tecla de retroceso de página** page up key; **tecla de suprimir** delete key; **tecla de tabulación** tab key

teclado *nm* keyboard ❏ **teclado alfanumérico** alphanumeric keypad; **teclado AZERTY** AZERTY keyboard; **teclado expandido** expanded *o* enhanced keyboard; **teclado extendido** extended keyboard; **teclado inalámbrico** cordless keyboard; **teclado infrarrojo** infrared keyboard; **teclado multifuncional** multifunctional keyboard; **teclado numérico** numerical keypad

teclear 1 *vt* to key (in), to type (in); **teclee su número secreto** key in *o* enter your PIN number **2** *vi* to type

teclista *nmf* INFORM keyboarder

técnica *nf* (**a**) *(procedimiento)* technique ❏ **técnicas de auditoría asistida por** *Esp* **ordenador** *o Am* **computadora** computer-aided audit techniques; **técnicas de comercialización** marketing techniques; **técnicas de dirección de empresas** management techniques; **técnica de estudios de opinión** opinion measurement technique; **técnicas de gestión** management techniques; **técnicas de marketing** marketing techniques; **técnicas de merchandising** merchandising techniques; **técnicas de secretariado** secretarial skills; **técnica de ventas** sales technique

(**b**) *(tecnología)* technology; **los grandes avances de la técnica** great advances in technology

técnico, -a 1 *adj (asesor, problema, servicio)* technical

2 *nm,f* technician ❏ **técnico de informática** computer technician; **técnico de mantenimiento** maintenance engineer; **técnico de ventas** sales technician

tecnología *nf* technology; **de alta tecnología** high-tech; **las nuevas tecnologías** new technologies ❏ **tecnologías de la información** information technology; **tecnología punta** state-of-the-art technology

TEF *nf* INFORM (*abrev de* **transferencia electrónica de fondos**) EFT

tejido *nm (estructura, sistema)* fabric; **el tejido social/industrial del país** the social/industrial fabric of the country

> "
> Las pequeñas y medianas empresas son la base de la economía española. Más del 99% de su **tejido** empresarial lo constituyen sociedades con menos de 250 trabajadores.
> "

telebanca *nf* remote banking □ **telebanca electrónica** on-line banking

telecompra *nf* home shopping, teleshopping

telecomunicaciones *nfpl* telecommunications

teleconferencia *nf* teleconference

telecos *nfpl Fam* telecoms

telediario *nm Esp* (television) news

telefax *nm inv* fax

telefonear *vt & vi* to call, to phone, *Br* to ring

telefonía *nf* telephony □ **telefonía celular** cellular telephony; **el mercado de la telefonía celular** the cellphone market; **telefonía fija** fixed telephony; **telefonía por Internet** Internet telephony; **telefonía móvil** mobile telephony; **el mercado de la telefonía móvil** the mobile phone market

telefonista *nmf* switchboard operator, telephonist

teléfono *nm* (**a**) *(aparato, sistema)* telephone, phone; **coger el teléfono** to answer *o* pick up the phone; **estar al teléfono** to be on the phone; **hablaré con ella por teléfono** I'll speak to her on the phone; **llamar por teléfono a alguien** to phone sb; **te llaman por teléfono** there's someone on the phone for you; **tengo que llamar por teléfono** I've got to make a phone call; **ponerse al teléfono** to come to the phone □ *Am* **teléfono celular** mobile (tele)phone, *US* cellphone; **teléfono directo** direct-dial (tele)phone; **teléfono inalámbrico** cordless (tele)phone; **teléfono por Internet** Internet (tele)phone; **teléfono interno** internal (tele)phone; *Am* **teléfono monedero** payphone; **teléfono móvil** mobile (tele)phone, *US* cellphone; **teléfono rojo** hot line; **teléfono WAP** WAP phone
(**b**) *(número)* telephone number; **dar el teléfono a alguien** to give one's telephone number to sb □ **teléfono gratuito,** *Esp* **teléfono 900** ≃ *Br* Freephone® number, *US* toll-free number

telegénico, -a *adj* telegenic

telegrafiar *vt & vi* to telegraph

telegráfico, -a *adj* telegraphic

telégrafo *nm* telegraph

telegrama *nm* telegram

teleimpresor *nm Br* teleprinter, *US* teletypewriter

telemarketing *nm* telemarketing, telephone marketing

telemática *nf* telematics

telemático, -a *adj* telematic

teleproceso *nm* INFORM teleprocessing

telespectador, -ora *nm,f* (television) viewer

teletexto *nm* Teletext®

teletipo *nm* (**a**) *(aparato)* *Br* teleprinter, *US* teletypewriter (**b**) *(texto)* Teletype® (message)

teletrabajador, -ora *nm,f* teleworker, telecommuter

teletrabajar *vt* to telecommute

teletrabajo *nm* teleworking, telecommuting

> "
> El 6,5% de las empresas españolas tienen contratados a trabajadores que realizan **teletrabajo**, es decir, que desarrollan un porcentaje alto de su actividad profesional desde su domicilio particular. Estos empleados representan el 1,1% del total de los empleados de las sociedades mercantiles en nuestro país. El 37,1% de los empleados españoles tienen acceso a Internet desde su puesto de trabajo y en el 38% de las empresas conectadas a la red lo está en la totalidad de su plantilla.
> "

televendedor, -ora *nm,f* telesales person

televenta *nf* (**a**) *(por teléfono)* telesales, telephone selling (**b**) *(por televisión)* home shopping, teleshopping

televidente *nmf* (television) viewer

televisión *nf* (**a**) *(medio, sistema, aparato)* television □ **televisión por cable** cable television; **televisión a la carta** TV on demand; **televisión digital** digital television; **televisión por** *o* **vía satélite** satellite television (**b**) *(empresa)* television company; **las televisiones privadas** private television companies

télex *nm inv (sistema)* telex; *(mensaje)* telex (message); **enviar** *o* **mandar algo por télex** to telex sth

telnet *nm* INFORM Telnet

tematizar *vt* to theme

> "
> Para 2004, otros tres hoteles, en Costa del Sol, Menorca y Mallorca, **tematizarán** sus instalaciones, hasta hacer un total de 2.500 habitaciones con este nuevo concepto de alojamiento.
> "

temporada *nf* season; **de temporada** *(fruta, trabajo, ropa)* seasonal; **de fuera de temporada** off-season ▫ **temporada alta** high season, peak season; **temporada baja** low season; **temporada turística** tourist season

temporal *adj (situación, actividad, ubicación)* temporary; *(contrato)* temporary, fixed-term

temporalero = **temporero**

temporario *adj Am* temporary

temporero, -a *Chile, Esp,* **temporalero, -a** *Méx* **1** *adj* seasonal
2 *nm,f* seasonal worker

tendencia *nf (corriente, movimiento)* trend; *(inclinación)* tendency; **las últimas tendencias de la moda** the latest fashion trends; **hay una tendencia a contratar trabajadores más jóvenes** there's a tendency to employ younger workers ▫ **tendencia alcista** uptrend, upward trend; **tendencia a la baja** downtrend, downward trend; **tendencias de consumo** consumer trends; **tendencia creciente** growth trend; **tendencias económicas** economic trends; **tendencia empresarial** business trend; **tendencia general** general trend; **tendencias del mercado** market trends; **tendencia de ventas** sales trend, trend in sales

tendero, -a *nm,f* shopkeeper, *US* storekeeper

tenedor, -ora *nm,f (poseedor)* holder ▫ **tenedor de acciones** *Br* shareholder, *US* stockholder; CONT **tenedor de libros** bookkeeper; **tenedor de participaciones accionariales** nominee *Br* shareholder *o US* stockholder; **tenedor de póliza** policy-holder

teneduría *nf* CONT **teneduría (de libros)** bookkeeping

tenencia *nf (a) (posesión)* possession ▫ **tenencia de participaciones accionariales** nominee *Br* shareholding *o US* stockholding **(b)** *Méx (impuesto)* road tax

teoría *nf* theory ▫ CONT **teoría de la contingencia** contingency theory; ECON **teoría cuantitativa del dinero** quantity theory (of money); **teoría de las decisiones** decision theory; **teoría de gestión empresarial** management theory; **teoría de la información** information theory; BOLSA **teoría monetaria** monetary theory; **teoría del paseo aleatorio** random walk (theory)

teórico, -a *adj (caso, conocimientos)* theoretical; *(renta)* notional

tercer ver **tercero**

tercerización *nf Am* outsourcing

tercerizar *vt Am* to outsource

tercero, -a **1** *adj* third ▫ **la tercera edad** senior citizens; **durante la tercera edad** in old age; **el Tercer Mundo** the Third World; FIN **tercero**

tenedor third-party holder; **tercer trimestre** *(de año fiscal)* third quarter
2 *nm (mediador, parte interesada)* third party; **seguro a terceros** third-party insurance, liability insurance

terciario, -a *adj (sector)* tertiary

terciarización *nf Am* outsourcing

terciarizar *vt Am* to outsource

terminación *nf (de trabajo)* completion

terminado, -a *adj (trabajo)* finished, done

terminal **1** *nm* INFORM terminal ▫ **terminal inteligente** intelligent terminal, smart terminal; **terminal de pago electrónico** electronic payment terminal; **terminal de punto de venta** point-of-sale terminal; **terminal remoto** remote terminal
2 *nf (de aeropuerto)* terminal ▫ **terminal aérea** air terminal; **terminal de carga** freight terminal; **terminal de contenedores** container terminal; **terminal de pasajeros** passenger terminal; **terminal de vuelo** air terminal

terminar **1** *vt (acabar) (reunión)* to close, to end; *(proyecto, tarea)* to complete, to finish; **dar por terminado algo** *(discurso, reunión, discusión, visita)* to bring sth to an end *o* a close
2 *vi* to end, to finish; **para terminar, debo agradecer…** finally, I would like to thank…

término **1** *nm (fin)* end; **al término de la reunión se ofrecerá una rueda de prensa** there will be a press conference at the conclusion of the meeting
2 a término *adj (negociación, compra, entrega)* forward
3 términos *mpl (condiciones)* terms; **en términos reales** in real terms; **los términos del acuerdo** the terms of the agreement ▫ **términos del contrato (de trabajo)** conditions of employment

terrateniente *nmf* landowner

terreno *nm* **(a)** *(suelo)* land ▫ **terreno edificable** land suitable for development; **terreno rústico** *(como calificación)* land unsuitable for development; **terrenos rústicos** landed property; **terreno urbanizable** land suitable for development; **terreno no urbanizable** land unsuitable for development **(b)** *(parcela, solar)* plot (of land), *US* lot; **tenemos unos terrenos en el pueblo** we have some land in the village **(c) sobre el terreno** in the field; **estudiar algo sobre el terreno** to study sth in the field

territorial *adj (unidad, ordenamiento)* territorial

territorio *nm* territory; **por todo el territorio nacional** across the country, nationwide ▫ **territorio exclusivo** *(de franquicia)* exclusive territory; **territorio de ventas** sales territory

tesorería *nf* **(a)** *(cargo)* treasurership **(b)** *(oficina)* treasurer's office

tesorero, -a *nm,f* treasurer

Tesoro *nm el Tesoro Público* the Treasury

test *nm* (**a**) MKTG *(prueba)* test ❑ **test ciego** blind test; **test del consumidor** consumer test; **test de copy** copy test; **test de mercado** market test; **test monádico** monadic test; **test de preferencias** preference test; **test de producto** product test; **test de reconocimiento** recognition test; **test de recuerdo** recall test (**b**) *(examen)* test; **tipo test** *(examen, pregunta)* multiple-choice

testaferro *nm* front man

testamentaría *nf* (**a**) *(documentos)* documentation *(of a will)* (**b**) *(bienes)* estate, inheritance

testamentario, -a 1 *adj* **las disposiciones testamentarias** the terms of the will
2 *nm,f* executor

testamento *nm* will; **hacer testamento** to make a will

testar, testear *vt* MKTG to test

texto *nm* *(palabras)* text ❑ **texto impreso** printed text; **texto original** source text; **texto publicitario** *(sobre libro)* blurb

TI *nf(pl)* INFORM *(abrev de* **Tecnología(s) de la Información***)* IT

tiburón *nm* FIN *Fam* (corporate) raider

TIC *nfpl* *(abrev de* **Tecnologías de la Información y la Comunicación***)* ICT, information and communications technologies

> " A partir de la segunda mitad de la década de los noventa, las economías desarrolladas se han caracterizado por la progresiva implantación de las Tecnologías de la Información y la Comunicación (**TIC**) en el conjunto de las actividades económicas, tanto de producción como de distribución y consume. "

ticket *nm* **ticket (de compra)** receipt

tiempo *nm* time; **a tiempo completo/parcial** *(trabajar, trabajo)* full-time/part-time ❑ INFORM **tiempo de acceso** access time; INFORM **tiempo de acceso al disco** disk access time; **tiempo de carga** loading time; **tiempo compartido** *(de propiedad)* time sharing; INFORM time sharing; INFORM **tiempo de conexión** connect time; **tiempo de contacto (personal)** face time; **tiempo de entrega** delivery time; MKTG lead time; **tiempo de espera** waiting time; **tiempo de formación** training time; **tiempo libre** time off; **tiempo mínimo** *(de horario flexible)* core time; **tiempo muerto** idle time; INFORM **tiempo de proceso** processing time; **tiempo de producción** (production) lead time; INFORM **tiempo real** real time; **en tiempo real** real-time; **tiempo de**

respuesta turnaround time; INFORM response time

tienda *nf* shop, store ❑ **tienda de aeropuerto** airport shop; **tienda de artículos usados, tienda de artículos de segunda mano** second-hand shop; **tienda bandera** flagship store; *Méx* **tienda de departamentos** department store; **tienda especializada** specialist retailer; **tienda estrella** flagship store; **tienda de fábrica** factory outlet, *Br* factory shop; **tienda insignia** flagship store; **tienda libre de impuestos** duty-free shop; **tienda on-line, tienda en línea** on-line shop; **tienda de saldos** discount store, *US* discount house; **tienda virtual** virtual store *o* shop

> " La OCU recomienda utilizar la tarjeta únicamente en **tiendas virtuales** con páginas seguras (suelen identificarse con un icono en forma de candado), protegidas por sistemas de encriptación. De otro modo, la información sobre los datos personales y los de la tarjeta podrían ser capturados en la red y utilizados por terceras personas. "

tierra *nf* (**a**) *(superficie)* land; **viajar por tierra** to travel by land (**b**) *(en agricultura)* land ❑ **tierra improductiva** unproductive land (**c**) *(lugar de origen)* **vino/queso de la tierra** local wine/cheese

TIFF *nm* INFORM *(abrev de* **Tagged Image File Format***)* TIFF

TIIE *nf* *(abrev de* **Tasa de Interés Interbancaria de Equilibrio***)* = Mexican interbank rate

tilde *nf* (**a**) *(acento gráfico)* accent (**b**) *(de la ñ)* tilde

timador, -ora *nm,f* confidence trickster, swindler

timar *vt* (**a**) *(estafar)* **timar (algo) a alguien** to swindle sb (out of sth) (**b**) *(engañar)* to cheat, to con; **¿cinco mil por eso?, ¡te han timado!** five thousand for that?, you've been done *o* had *o* ripped off!

timbre *nm* *(de documentos)* (official) stamp; *(de impuestos)* seal; *CAm, Méx (de correos)* stamp ❑ **timbre fiscal** revenue stamp

timo *nm* *(estafa)* swindle; **¡qué timo!** what a rip-off!

tinta *nf* ink

TIP *nf Am* *(abrev de* **Tasa de Interés Promedio***)* average interest rate on deposits

tipear *Am* 1 *vt* *(documento)* to type; *(datos)* to key (in)
2 *vi* *(documento)* to type; *(datos)* to key

tipo *nm* (**a**) *Esp* FIN **tipo (de interés)** (interest) rate ❑ **tipo de actualización** discount rate; **tipo básico** base rate; **tipo a corto plazo** short rate; *tipo del crédito a la exportación* export credit rate; *tipo de descuento* discount rate, discounted rate; *tipo de descuento bancario* bank discount rate; *tipo efectivo anual* effective annual rate; *tipo de interés bancario* bank rate; *tipo de interés básico* base rate; *tipo de interés a corto plazo* short-term interest rate; *tipo de interés de créditos* lending rate; *tipo de interés para depósitos interbancarios* interbank deposit rate; *tipo de interés del dinero* money rate; *tipo de interés fijo* fixed (interest) rate; *tipo de interés flotante* floating interest rate; *tipo de interés hipotecario* mortgage rate; *tipo de interés interbancario* interbank interest rate; *tipo de interés a largo plazo* long-term interest rate; *tipo de interés negativo* negative interest rate; *tipo de interés nominal* nominal interest rate; *tipo de interés oficial* official rate of interest; *tipo de interés de préstamos* lending rate; *tipo de interés variable* variable o floating interest rate; *tipo medio interbancario en euros* Euro Interbank Offered Rate; *tipo preferencial* prime (lending) rate; *tipo de referencia* reference rate

(b) *tipo de cambio* exchange rate, rate of exchange; *tipo de cambio actual* current exchange rate; *tipo de cambio al contado* spot exchange rate; *tipo de cambio cruzado* exchange cross rate; *tipo de cambio de divisas* foreign exchange rate; *tipo de cambio del dólar* dollar (exchange) rate; *tipo de cambio fijo* fixed exchange rate; *tipo de cambio múltiple* multiple exchange rate; *tipo de cambio oficial* official exchange rate; *tipo de cambio paralelo* parallel rate of exchange; BOLSA *tipo comprador, tipo de compra* (de acciones) buying quotation, buying rate

(c) (en impuestos) *tipo de gravamen* tax rate, rate of taxation; *tipo de gravamen máximo* top rate of tax, top tax rate; *tipo de gravamen mínimo* minimum tax rate; *tipo impositivo* tax rate, rate of taxation; *tipo impositivo mínimo* minimum tax rate; *tipo impositivo especial* special rate of taxation; *tipo impositivo máximo* top rate of tax, top tax rate; *tipo impositivo real* effective tax rate; *tipo del IVA* VAT rate; *tipo de retención* withholding rate

(d) TIP type, typeface

> ❝
> La Asociación Hipotecaria Española (AHE), en la que están los bancos y las cajas, calcula que esta rebaja de medio punto en los **tipos** supondrá como término medio pagar 2,63 euros menos en cada mensualidad por cada 10.000 euros de préstamo hipotecario que esté firmado para un periodo de 20 años.
> ❞

tipografía nf typography

tipográfico, -a adj typographical, printing; **industria tipográfica** printing industry

Tipp-Ex® nm inv Tipp-Ex®

tiquet, tique nm **tiquet (de compra)** (till) receipt

TIR 1 nm (abrev de **Transports Internationaux Routiers**) TIR
2 nf (abrev de **Tasa Interna de Retorno**) IRR, internal rate of return

tira nm **tira y afloja: firmaron el acuerdo tras meses de tira y afloja** they signed the agreement after months of hard bargaining

tirada nf (número de ejemplares) print run

titulación nf (académica) qualifications ▫ *titulación profesional* professional qualifications

titulado, -a 1 adj (diplomado) qualified; (licenciado) with a degree; **titulado en ciencias económicas** with a degree in economics
2 nm,f (diplomado) holder of a qualification; (licenciado) graduate ▫ *titulado superior* (university) graduate

titular 1 adj (profesor) tenured; **miembro titular** full member; **el juez titular** = the judge assigned to a particular court
2 nmf (de tarjeta, acciones, cuenta) holder ▫ *titular de garantía* warrantee; *titular de licencia* licence holder; *titular de patente* patentee, patent holder; *titular de tarjeta de crédito* credit card holder

titularización nf FIN securitization

titularizador, -ora 1 adj FIN (sociedad, agente, vehículo) securitizing
2 nf securitizer

titularizar vt FIN to securitize

titulización nf FIN securitization

titulizar vt FIN to securitize

> ❝
> Unión Fenosa, la tercera eléctrica española, ha decidido **titulizar** parte de los recibos de la luz que cobra a sus clientes españoles para anticipar el ingreso de 238 millones de euros, según los datos registrados en la Comisión Nacional del Mercado de Valores (CNMV).
> ❞

título nm (a) (de derecho, obligación) (documento) deed ▫ *título de préstamo* loan certificate; *título de propiedad* title deed
(b) FIN security ▫ *título de acción* Br share certificate, US stock certificate; *títulos no cotizados* unlisted o Br unquoted securities; *título de deuda pública* government bond, Br gilt; *títulos emitidos* issued securities; *títulos del Estado* government securities, government stock; *títulos fungibles* fungible securities; *títulos a largo plazo* long-dated securities; *títulos de*

máxima garantía gilt-edged stock, gilt-edged securities; *títulos negociables* negotiable securities; *título a la orden* instrument to order; *título al portador* bearer paper, bearer bond; *título de renta alta* income stock; *títulos de renta fija* fixed-rate securities, *US* fixed-income securities; *títulos de renta variable* variable-rate securities, *US* variable-income securities; *título subyacente* underlying security; *títulos de transferencia de ingresos* pass-through securities; *títulos transferibles* transferable securities
  (**c**) *(de estudiante) (licenciatura)* degree; *(diploma)* diploma ◻ *título académico* academic degree; *título universitario* university degree

TLC, *Méx* **TLCAN** *nm* (*abrev de***Tratado de Libre Comercio de América del Norte**) NAFTA

TLC CA-EU *nm* (*abrev de***Tratado de Libre Comercio entre Centroamérica y Estados Unidos**) CAFTA

TLC G3 *nm Méx* (*abrev de***Tratado de Libre Comercio entre los Estados Unidos Mexicanos, la República de Colombia y la República de Venezuela**) = free trade agreement between Mexico, Colombia and Venezuela

tocar *vt* **tocar fondo** *(alcanzar el punto más bajo)* to reach rock bottom; *(si se prevee una recuperación)* to bottom out

todo, -a 1 *adj* **con todo incluido** *(precio)* all-in, all-inclusive; **cuesta 4.000 euros, todo incluido** it costs 4,000 euros all-in; **a todo riesgo** *(seguro)* (fully) comprehensive; **se vende en todo el mundo** it's sold worldwide
  2 *pron Esp* **todo a cien** *(tienda) Br* ≃ pound shop, *US* ≃ nickel-and-dime store

tolerancia *nf (en material, producto)* tolerance; **margen de tolerancia** (margin of) tolerance

toma 1 *nf* (**a**) FIN *(de participación)* acquisition (**b**) *toma de decisiones* decision-making; *toma de posición o posiciones* position taking
  2 *nm Fam* **toma y daca** give and take

tomador, -ora *nm,f* payee ◻ *tomador de muestras* sampler; *tomador de seguro* policyholder

tonelada *nf* **tonelada (métrica)** metric ton, tonne ◻ *toneladas de arqueo* registered tonnage; *tonelada de flete* freight ton

tonelaje *nm* tonnage ◻ *tonelaje de registro bruto* gross registered tonnage; *tonelaje de registro neto* net registered tonnage

tóner *nm* toner

tono *nm* TEL tone; ◻ *tono de marcado o de marcar,* *Andes, RP* *tono de discado o de discar Br* dialling *o US* dial tone

tope 1 *nm (límite)* limit, ceiling, cap ◻ *tope máximo* upper limit
  2 *adj inv* **fecha tope** deadline

topo *nm* INFORM,TIP bullet

tormenta *nf* *tormenta de ideas* brainstorming session; *tormenta monetaria* monetary crisis

torre *nf* INFORM tower

tostar *vt Fam (CD)* to burn

total 1 *adj (cifra, gasto, producción)* total; *(garantía, pago)* full; **el importe total de las inversiones** the total amount of the investments
  2 *nm (suma)* total ◻ CONT *total actualizado* running total; *total de contribuyentes* tax base; *total ingresos* gross income; *total neto* net total; *total a pagar* total payable; *total de ventas* total sales; *total de ventas de exportación* total export sales

totalidad *nf* **la totalidad del presupuesto** the entire budget; **los accionistas son italianos en su totalidad** all the shareholders are Italian

tour operador *nm* tour operator

traba *nf* obstacle; **los altos impuestos suponen trabas a la inversión** high taxes act as a disincentive to investment

trabajador, -ora 1 *adj* hard-working; **ser muy trabajador** to be a hard worker, to work hard
  2 *nm,f* worker ◻ *trabajador autónomo* self-employed person; *Am* *trabajador calificado* skilled worker; *Am* *trabajador no calificado* unskilled worker; *trabajador cualificado* skilled worker; *trabajador no cualificado* unskilled worker; *trabajador por cuenta ajena* employee, salaried worker; *trabajador por cuenta propia* self-employed person; *trabajador a domicilio* home worker; *trabajador estacional* seasonal worker; *trabajador eventual* casual worker, *US* contingent worker; *trabajadores eventuales* temporary labour; *trabajador externo* outside worker; *trabajador por horas* time worker; *trabajador manual* manual worker; *trabajador de producción* production worker; *trabajador semicualificado, Am* *trabajador semicalificado* semi-skilled worker; *trabajadores sindicalizados* organized labour; *trabajador social* social worker, *esp US* welfare worker; *trabajador a tiempo completo* full-time worker, full-timer; *trabajador a tiempo parcial* part-time worker, part-timer; *trabajador por turnos* shift worker

trabajar 1 *vi* (**a**) *(persona)* to work; **trabajar a tiempo parcial/completo** to work part time/full time; **trabajar por cuenta propia/ajena** to be self-employed/an employee (**b**) *(máquina)* to work; **la central trabaja ya a pleno rendimiento** the power station is now operating at maximum capacity (**c**) **trabajar con** *(tienda)* to sell; *(fábrica)* to make, to produce; *(editorial)* to publish
  2 *vt (comercializar) (producto, género, marca)* to sell; **sólo trabajan ropa para niños** *(tienda)* they only sell children's clothes; *(fábrica)* they only make children's clothes

trabajo *nm* (**a**) *(tarea, actividad, práctica)* work; **no tener trabajo, estar sin trabajo** to be out of work ❏ **trabajo administrativo** administrative work; **trabajo de campo** field work; **trabajo diurno** day work; MKTG **trabajo de documentación** desk research; **trabajo de o en equipo** teamwork; **trabajo eventual** casual work; **trabajo de fábrica** factory work; **trabajo físico** physical work, manual labour; **trabajo por horas** time work; **trabajo infantil** child labour; **trabajo intelectual** intellectual work; **trabajo de investigación** research work; **trabajo manual** manual labour, manual work; **trabajo de máquina** machine work; **trabajo de noche** night work; **trabajo de oficina** office work, clerical work; **trabajo de producción** productive labour; *CSur* **trabajo a reglamento** *Br* work-to-rule, *US* slowdown; **trabajo remunerado** paid work; **trabajo social** social work, *esp US* welfare work; **trabajo temporal** temporary work; **trabajo a tiempo completo** full-time work; **trabajo a tiempo parcial** part-time work; **trabajo por turnos** shift work; **trabajo voluntario** voluntary work
(**b**) *(empleo)* job; **buscar/encontrar trabajo** to look for/find a job; **un trabajo fijo** a permanent job; **un trabajo de oficina** an office job
(**c**) *(lugar)* work; **en el trabajo** at work
(**d**) ECON, POL labour

trading *nm* BOLSA trading

traducción *nf* translation ❏ **traducción asistida por** *Esp* **ordenador** *o Am* **computadora** computer-aided translation; **traducción automática** machine translation; **traducción simultánea** simultaneous translation

traducir *vt & vi* to translate (**de/a** from/into)

traductor, -ora *nm,f* translator ❏ **traductor jurado,** *RP* **traductor público** sworn translator; **traductor simultáneo** simultaneous translator

tráfico *nm* (**a**) *(de vehículos)* traffic ❏ **tráfico aéreo** air traffic; **tráfico de cabotaje** coastal traffic; **tráfico marítimo** maritime traffic; **tráfico rodado** road traffic (**b**) *(comercio, movimiento)* traffic ❏ **tráfico de armas** arms dealing *o* trafficking; **tráfico de influencias** influence peddling, *US* graft; **tráfico de mercancías** freight traffic, goods traffic; INFORM **tráfico de la red** network traffic

trailero, -a *nm,f CAm, Méx Br* lorry driver, *US* truck driver

tramitación *nf (factura, pedido, solicitud)* processing; **está en tramitación** it is being processed

tramitar *vt (factura, pedido, solicitud)* to process

trámite *nm* formality; **sólo quedan un par de trámites más** there are only a few formalities left; **es sólo cuestión de trámite** it's purely routine, it's just a formality; **los trámites burocráticos** the bureaucratic procedures ❏ **trámites aduaneros** customs formalities

tramo *nm (de impuesto, renta, edad)* bracket, band; *(de tarifa)* band; *(de préstamo, acciones)* tranche ❏ **tramo impositivo** tax bracket; BOLSA **tramo minorista** retail tranche; **tramo de renta** income bracket

transacción *nf* transaction ❏ BOLSA **transacción al alza** bull transaction; BOLSA **transacción a la baja** bear transaction; **transacción bancaria** bank transaction; **transacción cambiaria** exchange transaction; **transacción de capital** capital transaction; BOLSA **transacción de cierre** closing transaction; **transacción comercial** commercial transaction; **transacción de crédito** credit transaction; **transacción electrónica** electronic transaction; **transacción electrónica segura** secure electronic transaction; **transacciones entre empresas** intercompany transactions; **transacción financiera** financial transaction; **transacción fraudulenta** fraudulent transaction; BOLSA **transacción de futuros** futures transaction; BOLSA **transacciones con información privilegiada** insider dealing, insider trading; **transacción con tarjeta de crédito** credit card transaction

transar *vt Am* to trade

transbordar, trasbordar *vi (de mercancías)* to transship, to tranship

transbordo, trasbordo *nm (de mercancías)* transshipment, transhipment

transferencia, trasferencia *nf (de datos, recursos, dinero)* transfer; **quiero hacer una transferencia de 1.000 euros a esta cuenta** I'd like to transfer 1,000 euros to this account ❏ **transferencia de acciones** stock transfer; INFORM **transferencia de archivos** file transfer; **transferencia automática** automatic transfer; **transferencia bancaria** bank transfer, *Br* giro transfer; INFORM **transferencia de datos** data transfer; **transferencia de divisas** foreign exchange transfer, FX transfer; **transferencia electrónica** electronic transfer; **transferencia electrónica de fondos** electronic funds transfer; **transferencia (electrónica de fondos) en el punto de venta** electronic funds transfer at point of sale; INFORM **transferencia de ficheros** file transfer; **transferencia de fondos** remittance of funds; **transferencia interbancaria**

interbank transfer; *transferencia de moneda extranjera* foreign currency transfer; *transferencia telegráfica* telegraphic transfer; *transferencia por télex* telex transfer

transferible, trasferible *adj (datos, derechos, recursos)* transferable

transferir, trasferir *vt (datos, derechos, recursos)* to transfer

tránsito *nm* (**a**) *(de vehículos)* traffic; ❏ *tránsito aduanero* customs transit; *tránsito rodado* road traffic (**b**) *(paso)* transit; **un área de tránsito** a transit area; **pasajeros en tránsito hacia Roma** *(en aeropuerto)* passengers with connecting flights to Rome

transitorio, -a *adj (régimen, medida)* transitional, interim; *(periodo, fase)* transitional; *(solución, residencia)* temporary

transmisión, trasmisión *nf* (**a**) *(de señal, datos)* transmission; **una red de transmisión de datos** a data transmission network ❏ *transmisión electrónica de datos* data communications (**b**) DER *(de derechos, poderes)* transfer

transmitir, trasmitir *vt* (**a**) *(señal, datos)* to transmit, to send (**b**) *(derechos, poderes)* to transfer

transparencia, trasparencia *nf* (**a**) *transparencia fiscal* flow-through tax system (**b**) *(para retroproyector)* transparency, OHP slide

transportar *vt* *(mercancías, pasajeros)* to transport

transporte *nm* transport, transportation; **empresas de transporte por carretera** road transport companies, *Br* hauliers, *US* haulers; **servicios de transporte de viajeros** passenger transport services ❏ *transporte aéreo* air transport; *transporte por carretera* road transport, road haulage; *transporte ferroviario* rail transport; *transporte interior de mercancías* inland haulage; *transporte marítimo* maritime transport; *transporte marítimo en contenedores* container shipping; *transporte de mercancías* freight transport; *transporte público* public transport, *US* mass transit; *transporte terrestre* land transport; *transporte urbano* urban transport; *transporte urgente* urgent transport service

transportista *nmf* transport company, haulage company, carrier

trasbordar = **transbordar**

trasbordo = **transbordo**

trasferencia = **transferencia**

trasferible = **transferible**

trasferir = **transferir**

trasladar 1 *vt* (**a**) *(empleado)* to transfer, to relocate; *(empresa)* to relocate (**b**) *(reunión, fecha)* to postpone, to move back (**c**) *(petición, información)* to refer (**d**) CONT **trasladar al siguiente ejercicio** to carry over (to the following year)
2 **trasladarse** *vpr* to relocate, to move; **se han trasladado a nuevas dependencias** they have relocated to new premises

traslado *nm* (**a**) *(de empleado)* transfer, relocation; *(de empresa)* relocation (**b**) *(de petición, información)* **dar traslado a una solicitud** to refer a petition

trasmisión = **transmisión**

trasmitir = **transmitir**

trasparencia = **transparencia**

traspasar *vt* (**a**) *(negocio)* to sell *(as a going concern)*; **se traspasa** *(en cartel)* for sale (**b**) FIN *(acciones, capital)* to transfer (**c**) CONT *(deuda, asiento)* to transfer

traspaso *nm* (**a**) *(de negocio)* sale *(as a going concern)* (**b**) FIN *(de acciones, capital)* transfer ❏ BOLSA *traspaso mediante endoso* transfer by endorsement (**c**) CONT *(de cuenta, asiento)* transfer (**d**) POL *traspaso de competencias* devolution

trastienda *nf (de tienda)* backroom

tratado *nm* treaty ❏ *Tratado de Libre Comercio* NAFTA

tratamiento *nm* (**a**) *(de material, producto)* treatment ❏ *tratamiento de residuos* waste treatment *o* processing (**b**) INFORM processing ❏ *tratamiento (electrónico) de datos* (electronic) data processing; *tratamiento de imagen* image processing; *tratamiento por lotes* batch processing; *tratamiento de textos* word processing (**c**) *(título)* form of address

tratar 1 *vt (sustancia, tejido, alimento)* to treat
2 *vi* (**a**) *(tener relación)* **tratar con alguien** to deal with sb; **tengo que tratar con todo tipo de gente** I have to deal with all sorts of people; **sabe cómo tratar a los clientes difíciles** she's good at handling difficult customers (**b**) *(comerciar)* to deal (**en** in)

trato *nm* (**a**) *(acuerdo)* deal; **cerrar** *o* **hacer un trato** to do *o* make a deal; **¡trato hecho!** it's a deal!; **un trato justo** a fair deal (**b**) *(negociación)* **estar en tratos con alguien** to be in talks *o* negotiation with sb (**c**) *Am* *trato nacional* national treatment

tren *nm* train ❏ *tren de carga* *Br* goods train, *US* freight train; *tren de mercancías* *Br* goods train, *US* freight train; **tren mixto** passenger and goods train; **tren de pasajeros** passenger train; **tren de pasajeros y mercancías** passenger and goods train

tribunal *nm (de justicia)* court; **llevar a alguien/ acudir a los tribunales** to take sb/to go to court ◻ **Tribunal de Apelación** *Br* Court of Appeal, *US* Court of Appeals; **tribunal de arbitraje** arbitration tribunal; **tribunal de comercio** commercial tribunal; **Tribunal de Cuentas** *(español)* ≃ National Audit Office; *(europeo)* Court of Audit; **Tribunal Europeo de Derechos Humanos** European Court of Human Rights; **tribunal federal** federal court; **Tribunal Internacional de Justicia** International Court of Justice; **tribunal de justicia** law court; *UE* **Tribunal de Justicia de las Comunidades Europeas, Tribunal de Justicia Europeo** European Court of Justice, Court of Justice of the European Communities; **tribunal laboral** industrial tribunal; **tribunal de primera instancia** court of first instance

tributación *nf* (**a**) *(impuestos)* tax ❙ (**b**) *(sistema)* taxation ◻ **tributación conjunta** joint taxation; **tributación ecológica** green taxation; **tributación progresiva** progressive taxation; **tributación regresiva** regressive taxation

tributar *vi FIN (person)* to pay taxes; *(fondo, bien, premio)* to be taxable

> **❝**
>
> De este modo, mucho se ha avanzado desde que en 1987 se acometiera la primera legislación en materia de planes de pensiones. Hoy día, la decisión de ahorro frente a la de consumo goza de una neutralidad fiscal hasta el punto de no **tributar** hasta el momento final de la recuperación del fondo.
>
> **❞**

tributario, -a *adj (sistema, derecho)* tax

tributo *nm (impuesto)* tax ◻ **tributos territoriales** land charges

trimestral *adj* quarterly

trimestralmente *adv* quarterly

trimestre *nm (tres meses)* quarter

triplicar 1 *vt* to triple, to treble; **las exportaciones de frutas triplican las de carne** exports of fruit are three times *o* treble those of meat **2 triplicarse** *vpr* to triple, to treble

trituradora *nf* **trituradora (de documentos)** (document) shredder

triturar *vt (papel)* to shred

TRM *nf Col (abrev de* **Tasa Representativa del Mercado**) Representative Market Rate, = exchange rate between the dollar and the Colombian peso

trueque *nm (de productos, bienes)* barter

trust *nm* trust, cartel

turismo *nm* tourism; **hemos tenido un 10% más de turismo** we have had 10% more visitors; **hacer turismo (por)** to go touring (round) ◻ **turismo de aventura** adventure tourism; **turismo de calidad: atraer al turismo de calidad** to attract 'top-end' tourists; **turismo ecológico** ecotourism; **turismo rural** rural tourism; **casas** *o* **viviendas de turismo rural** rural holiday properties; **turismo verde** ecotourism, green tourism

turista 1 *nmf* tourist **2** *adj inv* **clase turista** tourist *o* economy class

turno *nm* (**a**) *(de trabajo)* shift; **trabajar por turnos** to work shifts; **turno de día/noche** day/night shift; **turno partido** split shift ◻ **turno entrante** oncoming shift, incoming shift; **turno de oficio** = order in which lawyers are assigned legal-aid cases; **turno de piquete** picket duty; **turno saliente** outgoing shift ❙ (**b**) *(orden)* **hay un turno establecido para las vacaciones** there's a rota for *Br* holidays *o US* vacations

tutorial *nm INFORM* tutorial (program)

Uu

UDI *nf Méx (abrev de* **Unidad de Inversión**) index-linked investment unit

Udibono *nm Méx (abrev de* **Bono de Desarrollo del Gobierno Federal en Unidades de Inversión**) = index-linked bond denominated in investment units

UE *nf (abrev de* **Unión Europea**) EU

UEM *nf* UE *(abrev de* **Unión Económica y Monetaria**) EMU

UEN *nf (abrev de* **Unidad Estratégica de Negocio**) SBU

ultimación *nf* completion; **para la ultimación de los detalles** to finalize the details

ultimar *vt* to complete; **ultimar los detalles** to finalize the details

último, -a *adj* (**a**) *(en una serie, en el tiempo)* last; **los últimos diez años** the last ten years □ *último pago* final payment; *último plazo* final instalment; *última voluntad* last wish(es) (**b**) *(más reciente)* latest, most recent; **nuestro último modelo** our latest model (**c**) *(definitivo)* **es mi última oferta** it's my last o final offer □ *último aviso de pago* final demand

umbral *nm (nivel básico)* threshold; **llegar al umbral del pleno empleo** to reach the threshold of full employment □ *umbral impositivo* tax threshold; *umbral de la pobreza* poverty line; *umbral de precios* price threshold; FIN *umbral de rentabilidad* break-even point

>
> Amazon, ahora que parece haber alcanzado el **umbral de rentabilidad** sobre los 3.500 millones de dólares de facturación anual, deberá mostrar que puede seguir creciendo (camino de los 100 millones de clientes online) sin abandonar dicha senda y, junto con las otras puntocom que comienzan a demostrar la viabilidad de su negocio, deberá mostrarse como una alternativa factible a la vieja guardia de la tecnología, cuyo crecimiento, excepción hecha de Microsoft, parece mostrar signos de flojera.
>

UMTS *nm* TEL *(abrev de* **Universal Mobile Telecommunications System**) UMTS

unánime *adj* unanimous

UNCTAD *nf (abrev de* **United Nations Conference on Trade and Development**) UNCTAD

UNICE *nf (abrev de* **Union of Industrial and Employers' Confederations of Europe**) UNICE

unidad *nf* (**a**) *(elemento, sección)* unit; **25 pesos la unidad** 25 pesos each □ *unidad de compras* purchasing unit; *unidad de costeo, unidad de costo* cost unit; *unidad estratégica de negocio* strategic business unit; *unidad de fabricación* factory unit; *unidad de mano de obra* unit of labour; *unidad de producción* production unit, unit of production (**b**) *(medida)* unit □ *unidad de cuenta* unit of account; *Antes* UE *unidad de cuenta europea* European Currency Unit; *unidad de consumo* unit of consumption; *unidad monetaria* unit of currency; *unidad de peso* unit of weight (**c**) INFORM *unidad de CD-ROM* CD-ROM drive; *unidad central de proceso, Am unidad central de procesamiento* central processing unit; *unidad de disco* disk drive; *unidad de disco duro* hard drive; *unidad de disco óptico* optical drive; *unidad de disquetes* floppy (disk) drive; *unidad interna* internal unit; *unidad predeterminada, unidad por defecto* default drive

unilateral *adj* unilateral

unión *nf (asociación)* union □ *unión aduanera* customs union; *unión económica* economic union; UE *Unión Económica y Monetaria* Economic and Monetary Union; UE *Unión Europea* European Union; UE *Unión Monetaria Europea* European Monetary Union; *unión temporal de empresas, RP unión transitoria de empresas* joint venture

unipersonal *adj (sociedad)* single-shareholder

unipersonalidad *nf* single-shareholder status

unir 1 *vt* INFORM *(archivos)* to merge
2 unirse *vpr (dos empresas en una)* to merge, to amalgamate

unitario, -a *adj (costo, precio)* unit

UNIX *nm* INFORM *(abrev de* **Uniplexed Information and Computing System**) UNIX

UPA *nf Am (abrev de* **Utilidad Por Acción**) eps, earnings per share

urbanismo *nm* town planning, city planning

urbanista *nmf* town planner, city planner

urgente *adj (asunto, caso)* urgent

URL *nm* INFORM (*abrev de* **uniform resource locator**) URL

usado, -a *adj (de segunda mano)* used, second-hand, *esp US* pre-owned

usar *vt (aparato, herramienta, producto)* to use; *(ropa, talla)* to wear; **usar indebidamente** to misuse

USB *nm* INFORM (*abrev de* **Universal Serial Bus**) USB

Usenet *nf* INFORM Usenet

uso *nm (utilización)* use; **uso indebido** misuse

usuario, -a *nm,f* user ❑ *usuario experto* power user; *usuario final* end user; INFORM *usuario registrado* registered user

usufructo *nm* DER usufruct

usura *nf* usury

usurero, -a *nm,f* usurer

usurpación *nf* usurping ❑ *usurpación de marca* brand piracy

UTE *nf* (*abrev de* **Unión Temporal de Empresas,** *RP* **Unión Transitoria de Empresas**) joint venture, JV

> **❝**
> El Ministerio de Defensa ha adjudicado a Telefónica la mayor parte del contrato de sus servicios de telecomunicaciones por un importe conjunto de unos 73 millones de euros, mientras que la Unión Temporal de Empresas (**UTE**) formada por BT, Vodafone y Neosky ha conseguido un contrato de servicios de Internet por 1,46 millones de euros.
> **❞**

utilidad 1 *nf* INFORM utility (program) **2 utilidades** *nfpl Am* FIN profits ❑ *utilidades netas* net profit

utilización *nf* use, utilization; **de fácil utilización** easy to use

utilizar *vt* to use, to utilize

Vv

vacacional *adj Br* holiday, *US* vacation; **periodo vacacional** *Br* holiday *o US* vacation period

vacaciones *nfpl Br* holiday, *US* vacation; **estar/ irse de vacaciones** to be/go on *Br* holiday *o US* vacation; **tener derecho a treinta días de vacaciones pagadas** to be entitled to thirty days' paid annual leave *o Br* holiday *o US* vacation ❑ *vacaciones fiscales* tax holiday

vacante 1 *adj (puesto, plaza)* vacant; **queda vacante el cargo de secretario general** the post of secretary general has fallen vacant; **el puesto que dejó vacante en el equipo** the vacancy he left in the team
2 *nf* vacancy, opening; **cubrir** *o* **ocupar una vacante** to fill a vacancy ❑ *vacante laboral* job vacancy

vacío, -a 1 *adj (recipiente, espacio)* empty
2 *nm* **envasar al vacío** to vacuum-pack ❑ *vacío legal* legal vacuum

vagón *nm (de pasajeros) Br* carriage, *US* car; *(de mercancías)* wagon ❑ *vagón cisterna* tanker, tank wagon; *vagón de mercancías Br* goods wagon *o* van, *US* freight car; *vagón de pasajeros* passenger *Br* carriage *o US* car; *vagón de primera* first-class *Br* carriage *o US* car; *vagón restaurante* dining car, *Br* restaurant car; *vagón de segunda* second-class *Br* carriage *o US* car

vale *nm (bono, cupón)* coupon, voucher ❑ *vale de comida Br* luncheon voucher, *US* meal ticket; *vale de compra (por devolución)* credit note; *(como regalo)* gift token, gift voucher, *US* gift certificate; *vale de descuento* discount coupon *o* voucher, money-off voucher; *vale de regalo* gift token, gift voucher, *US* gift certificate

validación *nf (de documento)* validation

validar *vt (documento, tarjeta de crédito, hipótesis, resultado)* to validate; **varios ensayos clínicos validan la eficacia de este medicamento** several clinical trials have validated *o* confirmed the effectiveness of this medicine

validez *nf (de documento)* validity

valioso, -a *adj* valuable

valla *nf* *valla publicitaria* billboard, *Br* hoarding

valor *nm* **(a)** *(precio, utilidad, mérito)* value; **se hicieron con acciones por valor de 70.000 euros** they bought up 70,000 euros worth of shares;

perder valor to go down in value; **sin valor** worthless; **tener mucho valor** to be very valuable, to be worth a lot ❑ CONT *valor de los activos* asset value; CONT *valor actual* current value, present value; *valor actual neto* net present value; *valor en aduana* customs value; *Am* ECON *valor agregado* added value; *valor de alquiler* rental value; *valor de amortización* redemption value; ECON *valor añadido* added value; *valor asegurable* insurable value; *valor asegurado* insured value; *valor bruto* gross value; *valor al cambio* value in exchange; *valor capitalizado* capitalized value; *valor catastral* = value of a property recorded in the land register, *Br* ≃ rateable value, *US* ≃ assessed value; *valor al cobro* value for collection; *valor comercial* commercial value; *valor de compra* purchase value; *valor contable* book price, book value; *valor contractual total* total contract value; BANCA *valor en cuenta* value in account; *valor declarado* declared value; *valor descontado* discounted value; *valor económico añadido* economic value added; *valor en efectivo* cash value; *valor de emisión* issue value; *valor equivalente (teoría)* comparable worth; *valor en factura* invoice value; *valor de fragmentación* break-up value; *valor inicial* initial value; BOLSA *valor intrínseco* intrinsic value; *valor justo de mercado* fair market value; *valor legal* legal value; *valor en libros* balance sheet value; *valor de liquidación* settlement value; *valor liquidativo* value at liquidation; *valor marginal* marginal value; *valor de mercado* market value; BANCA *valor del mismo día* same-day value; *valor monetario previsto* expected monetary value; *valor mínimo* minimal value; *valor neto* net value; CONT *valor neto actual* current net value; CONT *valor neto contable o en libros* net book value, *US* carrying value; CONT *valor neto de realización* net realizable value; *valor nominal (de billetes, cheques, acciones)* face value, nominal value, *US* face amount; BOLSA par value; *valor original* original value; BANCA *valor oro* value in gold currency; *valor de paridad* parity value; *valor patrimonial negativo* negative equity; *valor patrimonial neto* net asset value; *valor percibido* perceived value; *valor previsto* expected value; *valor real* actual value; *valor realizable neto* net realizable value; *valor registrado* registered value; *valor de rentabilidad* profitability value; SEGUR *valor de reposición* replacement value; SEGUR *valor de rescate* surrender value; *valor residual* salvage value; *valor residual neto* net residual value; *valor de reventa* resale value; *valor temporal, valor tiempo* extrinsic value; BOLSA *valor de tiempo* time value; *valor total del activo* total asset value; *valor total asegurado* total insured value; *valor total del contrato* total contract value; BOLSA *valor al vencimiento* maturity value, value at maturity; *valor de venta* sale value

(b) BOLSA **valores** *(de inversión)* securities □ *valores admitidos a cotización en Bolsa* listed securities, listed stock, *Br* quoted securities; *valores bancarios* bank shares, *US* bank stocks; *valores de cartera* portfolio securities; *valores cíclicos* cyclical stocks; *valores no cotizados (en Bolsa)* unlisted o *Br* unquoted securities; *valores de crecimiento* growth stock(s); *valores defensivos* defensive stocks; *valores especulativos* speculative securities; *valores de inversión* investment securities, investment stock; *valores líquidos* liquid securities; *valores de máxima garantía* gilt-edged stock, gilt-edged securities; *valores negociables* negotiable securities; *valores nominativos* registered securities, registered stock; *valores realizables* realizable securities; *valores de renta fija* fixed-rate securities, *Br* fixed-interest securities, *US* fixed-income securities; *valores de renta variable* variable-rate securities, *Br* variable-interest securities, *US* variable-income securities; *valores subyacentes* underlying securities; *valores con tipo de interés flotante* floating-rate securities; *valores transferibles* transferable securities

> En diciembre de 2003, los diez primeros **valores** movieron 39.568 millones, el 82,64% del total. A Telefónica correspondieron 9.222 millones, el 19,26% del total; a SCH, 7.023 millones, el 14,67%, y a BBVA, 5.405 millones, el 11,29%.

valoración *nf (de negocio, propiedad, obra de arte)* valuation; *(de pérdidas, daños)* assessment, estimation; **hicieron una valoración de los daños** they assessed the damage □ *valoración de activos* asset valuation; *valoración de daños* damage survey; *valoración de existencias* stock valuation; *valoración de méritos* merit rating; *valoración del rendimiento* performance rating; *valoración de la situación financiera* financial review, financial healthcheck

valorar *vt (negocio, propiedad, obra de arte)* to value, to make a valuation of; *(daños)* to assess, to estimate; **la casa está valorada en 25 millones** the house is valued at 25 million

valuación *nf Am* valuation

valuar *vt Am* to value

VAN *nm* CONT *(abrev de* **Valor Actual Neto**) NPV

vanguardia *nf* **estar a la vanguardia de los avances tecnológicos** to be at the cutting edge of technological progress; **tecnología de vanguardia** state-of-the-art technology

variabilidad *nf* variability

variable *adj & nf* variable

variación *nf* variation; **el nivel de la demanda está sujeto a variaciones considerables** the level of demand is subject to considerable variation; **apenas ha habido variación en la Bolsa esta semana** there has been hardly any change in the stock market this week □ *variaciones cíclicas* cyclical variations; BOLSA *variación al cierre* closing range; *variación del costo* o *Esp* *coste* cost variance; *variaciones estacionales* seasonal variations; BOLSA *variación mínima de precios* tick size; BOLSA *variación neta* net change; CONT *variación en el precio de venta* selling price variance; SEGUR *variación del riesgo* variation of risk

variedad *nf* variety; **hay gran variedad de modelos** there is a wide variety of models

vehículo *nm* vehicle □ *vehículo de carga* freight vehicle; *vehículo comercial* commercial vehicle; *vehículo de gran tonelaje* *Br* heavy goods vehicle, *US* heavy freight vehicle; *vehículo industrial* industrial vehicle; *vehículo pesado* *Br* heavy goods vehicle, *US* heavy freight vehicle

velocidad *nf* (a) INFORM speed □ *velocidad de ejecución* execution speed; *velocidad de escritura* write speed; *velocidad de impresión* print speed; *velocidad del procesador* processor speed; *velocidad de proceso* processing speed; *velocidad de refresco* refresh rate; *velocidad de refresco de imágenes* image refresh rate; *velocidad de reloj* clock speed; *velocidad de transferencia* transfer rate, transfer speed; *velocidad de transmisión (en módem)* baud rate; *velocidad de transmisión de datos* data throughput speed; *velocidad de visualización* display speed

(b) □ ECON *velocidad de circulación del dinero* velocity of circulation of money; *velocidad-renta de circulación del dinero* income velocity of circulation

vencedero, -a *adj* FIN payable

vencer *vi (garantía, contrato, seguro)* to expire; *(bono, inversión, deuda)* to mature; *(deuda)* to fall due; **el plazo para entregar las solicitudes vence el 15 de mayo** the closing date o the deadline for sending in applications is 15 May

vencido, -a *adj (garantía, contrato, seguro)* expired; *(bono, deuda)* mature; *(pago)* due; **liquidable a mes vencido** payable monthly in arrears

vencimiento *nm (de garantía, contrato, plazo, seguro)* expiry, expiration; *(de bono, inversión, deuda)* maturity; *(de deuda, pago)* due date, falling due; **al vencimiento del préstamo** when the loan falls due *o* matures; **deuda con vencimiento a un año** debt with a maturity of one year; **opciones que pueden ejercitarse en cualquier momento hasta la fecha de vencimiento** options that can be exercised at any time up to maturity ❑ **vencimiento a corto plazo** short-term maturity; **vencimiento a largo plazo** long-term maturity; **vencimiento medio** average due date; **vencimiento a medio plazo** medium-term maturity; **vencimiento a plazo fijo** fixed maturity; **vencimiento del préstamo** loan maturity; *Am* **vencimiento promedio** average due date; **vencimiento a la vista** sight maturity

vendedor, -ora *nm,f (en general)* seller; *(de coches, seguros)* sales person, *m* salesman, *f* saleswoman; *(dependiente)* shop *o* sales assistant, *US* sales clerk; *(en terminología legal)* vendor; **el mayor vendedor de juguetes del país** the biggest seller of toys in the country ❑ BOLSA **vendedor en descubierto** short seller; **vendedor a domicilio** door-to-door salesman

vender 1 *vt (a) (productos)* to sell; **se vende** *(en letrero)* for sale; **este modelo se vende mucho** this model is selling very well; **vendieron la casa para pagar deudas** the house was sold (off) to pay debts; BOLSA **vender a término** *o* **futuro** to sell forward **(b)** *(idea, proyecto)* to sell **2** *vi (producto, autor)* to sell; **eso no vende hoy día** that doesn't sell these days

vendible *adj* saleable, sellable

venta *nf* **(a)** *(actividad)* selling; *(acción concreta)* sale; **de venta en tiendas especializadas** on sale in specialist shops *o* at specialist retailers; **estar en venta** to be for sale; **poner a la venta** *(casa)* to put up for sale; *(producto)* to put on sale; **salir a la venta** *(producto)* to go on sale; **el equipo de ventas** the sales team ❑ **venta ambulante** street vending; BOLSA **venta a la baja** bear sale; **venta por catálogo** mail-order selling; **venta a comisión** commission sale; **venta condicionada** tie-in sale; **venta por correo, venta por correspondencia** mail order, mail-order retailing, mail-order selling; **venta a crédito** credit sale; MKTG **venta cruzada** scrambled merchandising, scrambled retailing; BOLSA **venta al** *o* **en descubierto** short selling; **venta directa** *(actividad)* direct selling; *(un caso concreto)* direct sale; **venta a domicilio** door-to-door selling; **venta especulativa** speculative selling; **venta en firme** firm sale; **venta forzosa** compulsory sale, forced sale; **venta indirecta** indirect selling; MKTG **venta por inercia** inertia selling; **venta on-line, venta en línea** on-line selling, on-line retailing; **venta al por mayor** wholesale; **venta al por mayor en pequeña** escala small wholesale selling; **venta al por menor** retail; **venta a pérdida** below-cost selling, predatory selling; MKTG **venta personal** personal selling; **venta piramidal** pyramid selling; BOLSA **venta a plazo** forward sale; **venta a plazos** sale by instalments; **venta promocional** promotional sale; **venta pública** public sale; **venta en pública subasta** auction sale; *Méx* **venta de refacciones** replacement sale; **venta por referencias** reference sale; **venta de repuestos** replacement sale; **venta selectiva** selective selling; **venta telefónica** telesales, telephone sales; BOLSA **venta a término** forward sale

(b) *(cantidad)* sales; **la venta de hoy ha sido importante** sales have been strong today; **han aumentado/caído las ventas** sales have risen/fallen; **una novela que arrasa en ventas** a novel with phenomenal sales ❑ **ventas de exportación** export sales; **ventas al por menor** retail sales; *Am* **ventas de menudeo** retail sales; **ventas en el mercado interior** home sales; **ventas por metro de lineal** shelf yield; **ventas nacionales** domestic sales; **ventas previstas** anticipated sales; **ventas por teléfono** telephone sales

> ❝
>
> El Parlamento Europeo deja por ahora libertad a los Estados miembros para tolerar o no tolerar la modalidad comercial de venta por debajo de coste (**venta a pérdida**). [...] En la actualidad, sólo seis países de la UE permiten este tipo de venta, mientras que otros países como España, Alemania, Austria, Bélgica, Francia, Italia, Grecia, Irlanda y Portugal, lo prohíben expresamente.
>
> ❞

ventaja *nf* advantage; **tiene la ventaja de que es más manejable** it has the advantage of being easier to handle; **una de las ventajas de su trabajo son los vuelos baratos** cheap air travel is one of the perks of his job ❑ ECON **ventaja absoluta** absolute advantage; MKTG **ventaja comparativa** comparative advantage; **ventaja competitiva** *(of product)* competitive advantage *o* edge; *(of country)* competitive advantage; **ventajas fiscales** tax benefits

ventajoso, -a *adj (acuerdo, condiciones)* advantageous, favourable

ventana *nf* INFORM window ❑ **ventana activa** active window; **ventana de ayuda** help window; **ventana desplegable** pull-down window; **ventana de diálogo** dialogue window; **ventana de edición** editing window; **ventana de gráficos** graphics window; **ventana de texto** input box

ventanilla *nf* **(a)** *(en oficina, banco)* window ❑ **ventanilla única** one-stop service, = Spanish system, designed to simplify citizens' dealings with the administration, whereby official documents can be obtained from a single office (**b**) *(en sobre)* window

verbal *adj (acuerdo, oferta)* verbal

veredicto *nm* verdict

verificación *nf* (**a**) *(de autenticidad)* verification (**b**) *(de funcionamiento)* checking, testing; *(de buen estado)* checking

verificador, -ora *nm,f (de funcionamiento, buen estado)* checker

verificar *vt* (**a**) *(verdad, autenticidad)* to verify, to check (**b**) *(funcionamiento)* to check, to test; *(buen estado)* to check

versalita(s) *nf(pl)* TIP small caps, small capitals

versión *nf* INFORM version ❏ *versión definitiva* final copy; *versión impresa* hard copy

vertical *adj* (**a**) *(estructura, integración, fusión)* vertical (**b**) *(formato, orientación)* portrait

vetar *vt* to veto

veto *nm* veto; **poner veto a algo** to veto sth

VGA *nm* INFORM *(abrev de **video graphics array**)* VGA

vía 1 *nf (medio, proceso)* **por vía terrestre** *(correo)* by surface mail; **por vía oficial/judicial** through official channels/the courts; **por la vía rápida** *(procedimiento, solicitud)* fast-track **2** *prep* via; **conexión vía satélite** satellite link

viabilidad *nf* viability, feasibility

viable *adj (proyecto, sistema)* viable, workable

viajante *nmf* **viajante (de comercio)** (commercial) traveller, travelling salesperson

viajar *vi* to travel

viaje *nm (trayecto)* journey, trip; **son once días de viaje** it's an eleven-day journey; **en sus viajes al extranjero** on his journeys *o* travels abroad; **estar/ir de viaje** to be away/go away (on a trip); **agencia/gastos de viaje** travel agency/expenses ❏ *viaje de ida* outward journey; *(de barco)* outward voyage; *viaje de ida y vuelta* esp Br return journey *o* trip, US round trip; *viajes de incentivos* incentive travel; *viaje de negocios* business trip; *Méx viaje redondo* esp Br return journey *o* trip, US round trip; *viaje de vuelta* return journey; *viaje de vuelta a casa* homeward journey

viajero, -a *nm,f* traveller ❏ *viajero frecuente (de avión)* frequent flyer

viáticos *nmpl Am* expense *o* subsistence allowance, *US* per diem ❏ *viáticos por alojamiento* accommodation allowance; *viáticos de desplazamiento* travel allowance; *viáticos de kilometraje* ≃ mileage allowance; *viáticos (de viaje)* travel allowance, travelling allowance

vicepresidente, -a *nm,f (de comité, empresa)* vice-chairman, *US* vice-president

vida *nf* (**a**) *(de maquinaria, aparato, automóvil)* life; **tiene una vida útil de 20 años** it has a useful life of 20 years, it's designed to last for 20 years ❏ *vida de anaquel, vida en estantería* shelf life; *vida media* average life, mean lifetime; *vida útil (de maquinaria, producto)* useful life (**b**) *(necesidades materiales)* **la vida está muy cara en Japón** the cost of living is very high in Japan; **ganarse la vida** to earn a living

ʻʻ

Los productos tienen una **vida útil** estimada que no se puede forzar. Los móviles son los que tienen una vida más corta; después, los productos informáticos –entre dos y tres años– y luego los reproductores de DVD, de música, cámaras de vídeo, etcétera.

ʼʼ

vídeo *Esp*, **video** *Am nm (sistema, cinta)* video; *(aparato)* video (recorder), VCR ❏ *vídeo corporativo* corporate video; *vídeo publicitario* promotional video

videoclip *nm* video clip

videoconferencia *nf* videoconference; **videoconferencias** videoconferencing

videoteléfono *nm* videophone

videotexto *nm*, **videotex** *nm inv* videotext

vidriera *nf Am (en tienda)* (shop) window, display window

vigente *adj (ley)* in force; *(contrato, tarifa)* current; **según la normativa vigente…** according to the current regulations *o* the regulations currently in force…; **el contrato estará vigente durante tres años** the contract will run *o* be valid for three years

vigor *nm* **en vigor** *(ley, reglamento)* in force; *(contrato, tarifa)* current; **el acuerdo en vigor** the agreement in force, the current agreement; **entrar en vigor** to come into force, to take effect; **con la entrada en vigor de la nueva normativa** when the new regulations come into force *o* take effect

vinculante *adj* binding

vínculo *nm* (**a**) *(comercial)* link (**b**) INFORM link

violación *nf (de ley, derechos, acuerdo)* infringement, violation ❏ *violación de los derechos de autor* copyright infringement; *violación de la ética profesional* professional misconduct

violar *vt (ley, derechos, acuerdo)* to infringe, to violate

VIP *nmf (abrev de **very important person**)* VIP

virgen *adj (disco)* blank

virtual *adj* INFORM virtual

virus *nm inv* INFORM virus ❏ *virus informático* computer virus

visa *nf Am* visa ❏ *visa de entrada* entry visa;

visa de salida exit visa; *visa de tránsito* transit visa

visado *nm* visa ◻ *visado de entrada* entry visa; *visado de salida* exit visa; *visado de tránsito* transit visa

visar *vt (con iniciales)* to initial, to endorse

visita *nf* (**a**) *(en general)* visit *(breve)* call; ◻ MKTG *visita en frío* cold call; *visita de negocios* business call; MKTG *visita sin previo aviso* cold call; *visita de seguimiento* follow-up visit (**b**) *(de turismo)* visit ◻ *visita guiada* guided tour; *visita turística:* hacer una visita turística de la ciudad to do some sightseeing in the city (**c**) *(visitante)* visitor (**d**) INFORM *(a página Web)* hit

visitante *nmf* visitor

visitar *vt (cliente)* to visit, to call on

vista *nf* (**a**) FIN a la vista on sight, on demand; **pagadero a la vista** payable at sight; **a pagar a 30 días vista** payable within 30 days (**b**) *(perspicacia, discreción)* **tiene vista para las antigüedades** she has a good eye for antiques (**c**) DER hearing ◻ *vista oral* oral proceedings

visto bueno *nm* dar el visto bueno (a algo) to approve (sth), to give (sth) the go-ahead

visualización *nf* INFORM display ◻ *visualización WYSIWYG* WYSIWYG display

visualizador *nm* INFORM viewer

visualizar *vt* INFORM to display, to view

vitalicio, -a 1 *adj (renta, pensión)* life; **cargo vitalicio** position held for life
2 *nm* (**a**) *(pensión)* life annuity (**b**) *(seguro)* life insurance policy

vitrina *nf* (**a**) *(expositor)* showcase, glass case (**b**) *Chile, Col, Méx (ventana)* (shop) window, display window

viudedad *nf* pensión de viudedad *(para mujer)* widow's pension; *(para hombre)* widower's pension

vivero *nm* vivero (de empresas) business incubator

> ❝
>
> Redepyme es un **vivero** de pequeñas y medianas empresas nacidas a través de los cursos de creación de empresas que, financiados por el Fondo Social Europeo y el Ministerio de Ciencia y Tecnología, imparte la Escuela de Organización Industrial (EOI) desde hace cinco años. En ese tiempo se han puesto en marcha más de dos mil quinientas pymes que dan empleo a diez mil trabajadores.
>
> ❞

vivienda *nf (casa)* home; *(alojamiento)* housing; **primera/segunda vivienda** first/second home; **el precio de la vivienda** house prices; **la carestía de las viviendas en la capital** the high cost of housing in the capital; **se ha recortado la partida presupuestaria para la vivienda** the budget allocation for housing has been cut ◻ *vivienda habitual* normal place of residence; *vivienda de protección oficial, Col, CRica, Méx, Perú vivienda de interés social* = low-cost home subsidized by the government; *vivienda pública de alquiler* = low-cost home subsidized by the government, *Br* ≃ council house/flat; *vivienda de renta limitada* = government-subsidized home with fixed maximum rent; *viviendas sociales* = low-cost housing subsidized by the government; *vivienda unifamiliar* single-family home

volante *nm* (**a**) volante (publicitario) advertising leaflet (**b**) *Esp (del médico)* (referral) note

volátil *adj (situación, economía, precio)* volatile

volatilidad *nf (de situación, economía, precio)* volatility

volcado *nm* INFORM *volcado de memoria* memory dump; *volcado de pantalla* screen dump

volumen *nm (nivel, cantidad)* volume ◻ *volumen de actividad* volume of activity; *volumen de audiencia* audience size; *volumen comercial* volume of trade; *volumen de compra* purchase volume; BOLSA *volumen de contratación* trading volume; *volumen de exportaciones* volume of exports; *volumen de importaciones* volume of imports; *volumen de intercambios (comerciales)* volume of trade; *volumen de mercado (de un producto)* market size; *volumen de negocio* turnover; *volumen de negocio anual* annual turnover; *volumen de negocio previsto* projected turnover; BOLSA *volumen de operaciones* trading volume; *volumen óptimo de pedido* economic order quantity; *volumen de producción* volume of output; *volumen de producción actual* volume of current output; *volumen total de ventas* total sales; *volumen total de ventas de exportación* total export sales; *volumen de ventas* sales volume

> ❝
>
> Según datos facilitados por FYVAR, la facturación del sector del reclamo publicitario actualmente es de 950 millones de euros. Esto supone que el **volumen de negocio** ha aumentado en los últimos 5 años un 188%. Además, se prevé que la facturación del sector aumente entre un 10 y un 15% en 2003.
>
> ❞

voluntario, -a *adj (trabajo, trabajador)* voluntary

votación *nf* vote; **someter algo a votación** to put sth to the vote; **un nuevo sistema de votación** a new voting system ◻ *votación a mano alzada* show of hands; *votación por mayoría* majority vote

votante *nmf* voter

votar **1** *vt (candidato)* to vote for; *(ley)* to vote on; **votar a un partido** to vote for a party; **¿qué has votado, sí o no?** how did you vote, yes or no?
2 *vi* to vote; **votar a favor de/en contra de alguien** to vote for/against sb

voto *nm* (**a**) *(en elección)* vote; **tres votos a favor/en contra** three votes in favour/against; **personas con derecho a voto** those with the right to vote ▫ **voto de calidad** casting vote; **voto de censura** vote of no confidence; **voto de confianza** vote of confidence; **voto por correo** postal vote; **voto por delegación** block vote; **voto de gracias** vote of thanks; **voto** *unánime* unanimous vote
(**b**) *(derecho a votar)* **tener voto** to have a vote
(**c**) *(papeleta)* ballot paper, voting paper

voz *nf* voice; **tener voz y voto** to have a say

VRAM *nf* INFORM (*abrev de* **video random access memory**) VRAM

vuelo *nm* flight ▫ **vuelo chárter** charter flight; **vuelo directo, vuelo sin escalas** direct flight

vuelta *nf*, *Am* **vuelto** *nm* small change

vulneración *nf (de acuerdo, derechos)* infringement

vulnerar *vt (acuerdo, derechos)* to infringe

WAP *nm* INFORM (*abrev de* **Wireless Application Protocol**) WAP

warrant *nm* BOLSA *(de acciones)* warrant ❏ *warrant sobre Deuda Pública* Treasury warrant

Web, web¹ *nf (World Wide Web)* **la Web** the Web

web² *nm o nf* **(página) web** website

WWW *nf (abrev de* **World Wide Web**) WWW

xerocopia *nf* Xerox (copy), photocopy

xerocopiadora *nf* Xerox machine

xerografía *nf* xerography

XML *nm* INFORM (*abrev de* **Extensible Markup Language**) XML

yacimiento *nm (mineral)* deposit ❏ *yacimiento de petróleo, yacimiento petrolífero* oilfield

yen *nm* yen

yupi *nmf* yuppie

Z z

ZEE *nf* (*abrev de* **Zona Económica Exclusiva**) EEZ, Exclusive Economic Zone

zócalo *nm* INFORM socket

zona *nf* area, zone ❑ *zona aduanera* customs zone; *zona de carga* (*para barcos*) loading dock; *zona de carga y descarga* loading bay; *zona comercial* shopping area; *zona de despacho aduanero* customs clearance area; *zona económica exclusiva* exclusive economic zone; *zona edificada* built-up area; *zona de exposición* (*de productos*) display area; *zona euro* euro zone; *zona franca* duty-free zone, free zone; *zona fronteriza* frontier zone; *zona gris* grey zone; *zona de la libra esterlina* sterling area; *zona de libre comercio o cambio* free trade area; *zona monetaria* monetary area; *zona salarial* wage zone; *zona de urgente reindustrialización* = region given priority status for industrial investment, *Br* ≃ enterprise zone; *zona de ventas* (*sección de representante*) sales area; (*sección de hipermercado*) sales floor

El principal instrumento de la Unión Europea para lograr la **zona de libre cambio** mediterránea en 2010 es el programa MEDA, una especie de Plan Marshall para los países de la otra orilla del Mediterráneo, destinado a compensar los esfuerzos financieros que están haciendo estas naciones en sus programas de liberalización económica.

zonificar *vt* to zone

SUPPLEMENT

Contents

SPANISH COMMUNICATION GUIDE

Contents

Letters

When sending a letter or other written communication, particular attention should be paid to the grammar and spelling as these are sensitive topics. Spelling mistakes and grammatical errors in a letter are considered very bad form, even in private correspondence.

The style should be simple and clear. Use paragraphs to make your ideas easier to follow.

Beginnings

The opening greetings and endings used in letters written in Spanish follow certain well-established rules:

- If you do not know the person you are writing to, whether you know their name or not, or if you know them only slightly:

  Estimado señor ———— When preceded by another word (***Estimado, Muy, Distinguido***), *señor* and *señora* are written in lower case.
  Estimada señora
  Señor, Señora
  Señorita ———— *Señorita* is used for an unmarried young woman, but it is somewhat old-fashioned nowadays. If in doubt, use *Señora*.
  Muy señor mío
  Distinguido señor ———— More formal.

- When you are unsure whether the recipient of the letter is male or female and when the letter is addressed to a company rather than to an individual:

  Estimados señores
  Señores
  Muy señores míos

- When writing to the head of a company or institution:

  Señor Director
  Señora Directora

  Señor Presidente
  Señora Presidenta

- When you know the person you are writing to and want to sound less formal:

  Estimado señor (López)
  Estimada señora (Martín) ———— The abbreviations *Sr., Sra., Srta.* can be used before the surname
  Estimada señorita (Alsina)

- When you are writing to a colleague you do not know or know only slightly:

  Estimado colega
  Estimada colega

  Querido amigo ———— The titles ***Querido amigo*** and ***Querida amiga*** are still slightly formal and are not used between friends but between colleagues or acquaintances.
  Querida amiga

- When you are writing to a colleague with whom you are on first name terms:

  Querido Federico
  Querida Rosa

Endings

The complimentary close should correspond in form and tone to the opening greeting.

- The most neutral endings are:

  Le/Lo saluda atentamente
  Se despide atentamente
  Reciba un cordial saludo de
  Reciba un atento saludo de

- If you want to end on a more respectful note, such as when writing to a superior:

  Quedo a su entera disposición.
  Reciba un respetuoso saludo de
  Respetuosamente le/lo saluda

- If you want to show your gratitude:

  Agradeciendo de antemano su atención
  Le hago partícipe de mi más sincero agradecimiento.(formal)

- Simplified and more informal endings are becoming more common. The following endings can be found more and more in everyday business letters, e-mails and faxes:

  Atentamente
  Cordialmente (more friendly)
  Un (afectuoso) saludo (even more friendly)

Addresses

- In Spanish addresses you will often find no word for "street", only the actual name of the street, unless it is called, for example, "Avenida" or "Paseo". You can also see the abbreviation C/ for "Calle". The house number comes after the street name, and the postcode precedes the name of the town or city.

  Gran Vía, 13
  28005 Madrid

- Some countries use different names to refer to "street". In Perú "Jirón" is often used, and in Colombia a street can be referred to as "Carrera", followed by a number, which is the street number.

  Carrera 3, 17

- You will often see a number followed by superscript ^{a} or ^{o}, given after the house number. This indicates which floor of a building the apartment is situated on. For example, the third floor in the following example:

  Gran Vía, 13 3ª

  If a third number is given, this refers to the door number:

  Gran Vía, 13, 3º 1ª

- In Latin America this information is often given in full:

  Insurgentes 28, 3er. piso, despacho 305

  or sometimes the floor number is omitted:

  Insurgentes 28, despacho 305   or
  Insurgentes 28-305

Envelopes

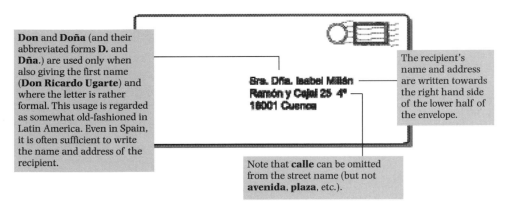

Don and **Doña** (and their abbreviated forms **D.** and **Dña.**) are used only when also giving the first name (**Don Ricardo Ugarte**) and where the letter is rather formal. This usage is regarded as somewhat old-fashioned in Latin America. Even in Spain, it is often sufficient to write the name and address of the recipient.

Sra. Dña. Isabel Millán
Ramón y Cajal 25 4º
16001 Cuenca

The recipient's name and address are written towards the right hand side of the lower half of the envelope.

Note that **calle** can be omitted from the street name (but not **avenida**, **plaza**, etc.).

It is standard practice to write a return address on the back of the envelope at the top, in case the letter gets lost.

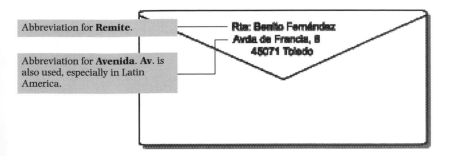

Abbreviation for **Remite**.

Abbreviation for **Avenida**. **Av.** is also used, especially in Latin America.

Rte: Benito Fernández
Avda de Francia, 8
45071 Toledo

Model letters

- **Business to business (general)**

Business correspondence in Spanish has become somewhat less formal in style under the influence of the English language.

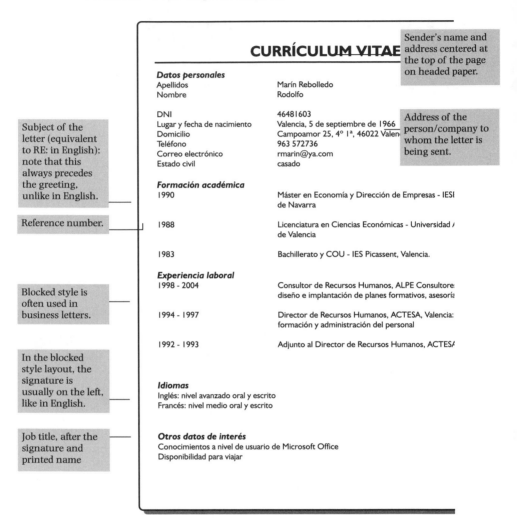

Sender's name and address centered at the top of the page on headed paper.

Subject of the letter (equivalent to RE: in English): note that this always precedes the greeting, unlike in English.

Reference number.

Blocked style is often used in business letters.

In the blocked style layout, the signature is usually on the left, like in English.

Job title, after the signature and printed name

Address of the person/company to whom the letter is being sent.

CURRÍCULUM VITAE

Datos personales
Apellidos   Marín Rebolledo
Nombre   Rodolfo

DNI   46481603
Lugar y fecha de nacimiento   Valencia, 5 de septiembre de 1966
Domicilio   Campoamor 25, 4° 1ª, 46022 Valen
Teléfono   963 572736
Correo electrónico   rmarin@ya.com
Estado civil   casado

Formación académica
1990   Máster en Economía y Dirección de Empresas - IESI
              de Navarra

1988   Licenciatura en Ciencias Económicas - Universidad /
              de Valencia

1983   Bachillerato y COU - IES Picassent, Valencia.

Experiencia laboral
1998 - 2004   Consultor de Recursos Humanos, ALPE Consultore:
              diseño e implantación de planes formativos, asesoría

1994 - 1997   Director de Recursos Humanos, ACTESA, Valencia:
              formación y administración del personal

1992 - 1993   Adjunto al Director de Recursos Humanos, ACTES/

Idiomas
Inglés: nivel avanzado oral y escrito
Francés: nivel medio oral y escrito

Otros datos de interés
Conocimientos a nivel de usuario de Microsoft Office
Disponibilidad para viajar

Useful phrases:

En respuesta a su carta del ...
Acusamos recibo de su carta del ...
Le agradecemos su interés y quedamos a su entera disposición.

- **Placing an order**

The letter placing an order needs to specify the items required, as well as the conditions of delivery and payment.

The abbreviation **núm**. is also frequent, particularly in Latin America.

List of items ordered.

Terms of delivery.

Payment terms.

Useful phrases:

Rogamos (que) nos envíen los artículos siguientes ...
Les remitimos el pedido n°...
Agradeceremos que se sirvan anotar el siguiente pedido ...

- **Informing a customer**

TECNO-MEDIA

Gomis, 28
08023 Barcelona
http:\\www.tecnomedia.com

Barcelona, 10 de junio de 2005

Señor:

Tenemos el placer de informarle que a partir de este mes puede consultar nuestro catálogo y realizar su pedido directamente desde nuestro sitio Web.

La seguridad de nuestro sitio web está garantizada. Si desea beneficiarse de nuestros servicios en línea, bastará con que se registre en la siguiente dirección:

http:\\www.tecnomedia.com

Esperamos que este nuevo servicio sea de su entera satisfacción.

Le saluda atentamente,

Alicia Cabezas

Alicia Cabezas
Responsable del sitio web

Useful phrases:

Le informamos de que ...
Queremos anunciarle que ...
Quedamos a su entera disposición para cualquier consulta que desee hacer.
Le rogamos (que) tome nota de nuestra nueva dirección.
La tienda abrirá sus puertas el ... en nuestra nueva dirección.

- **Letter of complaint**

If you want your letter of complaint to be effective, in Spanish as in English, it is essential to remain polite and not simply to use the letter to give full vent to your anger.

For serious complaints, or if a first letter has been ignored, it is standard practice to send this type of letter by recorded delivery ("correo certificado con acuse de recibo").

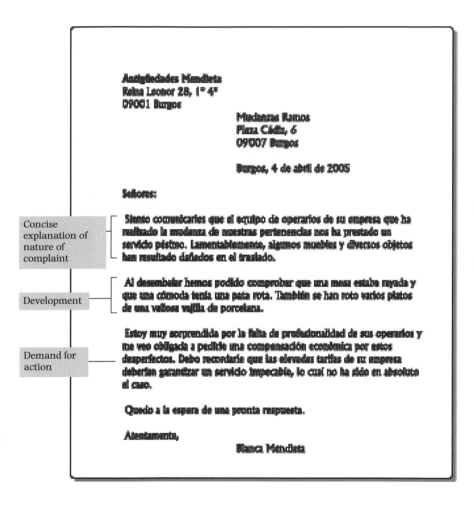

Concise explanation of nature of complaint

Development

Demand for action

Useful phrases:

Me dirijo a ustedes para protestar por ...
Deseo expresarle mi más enérgica queja por ...
Le escribo para expresar mi protesta por el mal funcionamiento de ...
Rogamos se subsane de inmediato esta situación.
Siento comunicarles que he recibido un pésimo servicio por parte de su empresa.
Les ruego (que) anulen mi pedido y me reembolsen la cantidad de ...
Estamos francamente sorprendidos por su falta de profesionalidad.

- **Dealing with a customer complaint**

When replying to a customer complaint, it is necessary to give an explanation of what happened. If the complaint is justified, the company must apologize and offer a solution.

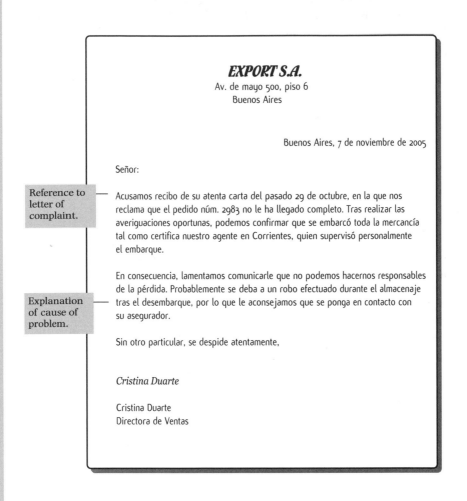

EXPORT S.A.
Av. de mayo 500, piso 6
Buenos Aires

Buenos Aires, 7 de noviembre de 2005

Señor:

Reference to letter of complaint.

Acusamos recibo de su atenta carta del pasado 29 de octubre, en la que nos reclama que el pedido núm. 2983 no le ha llegado completo. Tras realizar las averiguaciones oportunas, podemos confirmar que se embarcó toda la mercancía tal como certifica nuestro agente en Corrientes, quien supervisó personalmente el embarque.

Explanation of cause of problem.

En consecuencia, lamentamos comunicarle que no podemos hacernos responsables de la pérdida. Probablemente se deba a un robo efectuado durante el almacenaje tras el desembarque, por lo que le aconsejamos que se ponga en contacto con su asegurador.

Sin otro particular, se despide atentamente,

Cristina Duarte

Cristina Duarte
Directora de Ventas

Useful phrases:

Lamentamos sinceramente este error.
Le rogamos disculpe las molestias que le hayamos podido ocasionar.
Le reiteramos nuestra más sincera disculpa y quedamos a su entera disposición.
Hemos tomado medidas para que no vuelva a producirse tan lamentable situación.
Esperamos solucionar cuanto antes este contratiempo.

- ### Invoice

A company is free to choose the layout of its invoices, provided all the essential information is included.

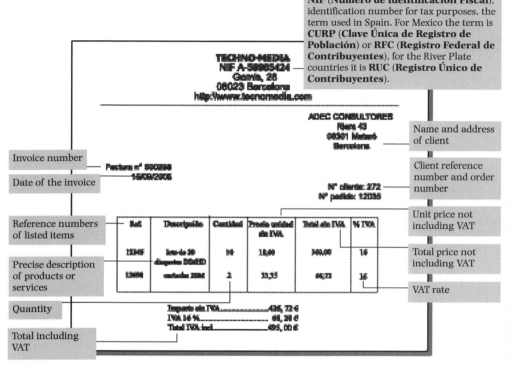

- ### Reply to invoice

You only need to reply to an invoice if you are contesting it.

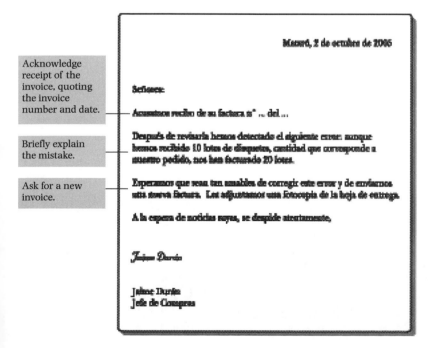

Useful phrases:

Acusamos recibo de su factura n° ...
Revisada la mercancía, hemos descubierto que cinco piezas presentaban desperfectos.
Tras verificar la factura que acaban de enviarnos, hemos constatado que su importe no corresponde a nuestro pedido.

- **Sales promotion letter**

This type of letter is sent to many potential clients as part of a mailshot. The style is very direct and tries to sound as personal as possible. In addition to the standard greetings, various other greetings might be used: "Apreciado cliente", "Estimado consumidor", etc.

Note the typical greeting.

Direct, conversational style.

Querido amigo:

Seguramente en más de una ocasión ha soñado con nadar en su propia piscina, pero ha desistido al imaginar costos elevadísimos e innumerables problemas de instalación. Pero...¿ Y si fuera más fácil de lo que piensa?

¡Olvide sus temores! **Todopiscinas**, empresa líder en el mercado, puede convertir su sueño en realidad.

Le presentamos la única piscina del mercado de bajo costo y fácil mantenimiento. Nuestras piscinas de poliéster, de gran solidez y completamente impermeables, están dotadas de un eficaz sistema de filtrado con limpiafondos automático.

Usted no tiene que preocuparse de nada: nosotros nos encargamos de la instalación en tan sólo una semana, y le ofrecemos una garantía de veinte años. Disponemos de la piscina que mejor se adapta a sus necesidades y a su bolsillo.

¿Qué está esperando? Llame ahora y solicite un presupuesto gratuito.

¡Somos especialistas!

Useful phrases:

Estamos seguros de que ...
Nos complace anunciarles que ...
Esperamos que esta información sea de su interés.
Le ofrecemos la mejor relación calidad-precio del mercado.
Esperamos contar pronto con usted entre nuestros clientes.

Employment

Cover letter

A cover letter ("carta de presentación") is quite formal in its presentation. It should be printed or typed unless the employer specifically asks that it be handwritten. (Some Spanish companies use the services of a graphologist to analyse applicants' handwriting.) The letter should be concise, properly structured in paragraphs and have the standard opening and closing formulas. You should cover the following points:

- Point out what you consider important in your CV
- Add information about your goals and aspirations
- Explain why you are interested in the company
- Convince the reader that you are the right person for the job

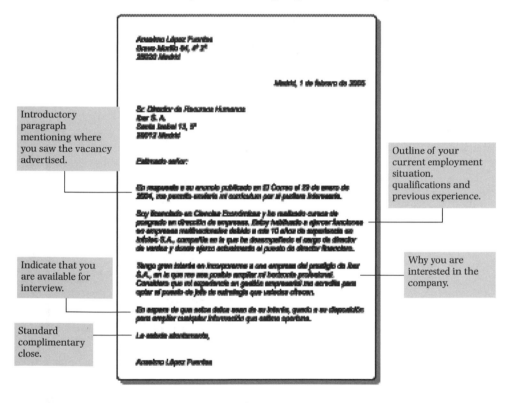

Introductory paragraph mentioning where you saw the vacancy advertised.

Outline of your current employment situation, qualifications and previous experience.

Indicate that you are available for interview.

Why you are interested in the company.

Standard complimentary close.

Useful phrases:

Me dirijo a ustedes para solicitar el puesto de secretaria anunciado en *El Correo de Quito* el ...

Cuento con varios años de experiencia en una empresa con sucursales en todo el territorio nacional.

A lo largo de mis cinco años de experiencia en la empresa X, he adquirido sólidos conocimientos de ...

A la espera de que mi candidatura sea de su interés, reciba un cordial saludo de ...

Quedo a la espera de su atenta respuesta a fin de concertar una entrevista personal.

Curriculum vitae

The presentation of a CV in Spanish is in many ways similar to a British CV or American résumé. The following differences should be respected:

- Only mention hobbies if they add something personal to your profile or if they are particularly relevant to the job. It is assumed that everybody likes reading, going to the cinema, listening to music and travelling.
- Do not include referees on your CV: references are not commonly used in Spain and Latin America except for certain occupations where personal recommendation would be expected, such as catering, cleaning, child care, construction, etc.

- **Experienced (Spanish)**

Documento Nacional de Identidad. In Latin America the equivalent is **Cédula de Identidad Nacional.** In Mexican CVs you'll often see the personal identification number for tax purposes, **RFC** or **CURP**.

CURRÍCULUM VITAE

Datos personales

Apellidos	Marín Rebolledo
Nombre	Rodolfo
DNI	46481603
Lugar y fecha de nacimiento	Valencia, 5 de septiembre de 1966
Domicilio	Campoamor 25, 4° 1ª, 46022 Valencia
Teléfono	963 572736
Correo electrónico	rmarin@ya.com
Estado civil	casado

Formación académica

1990	Máster en Economía y Dirección de Empresas - IESE, Universidad de Navarra
1988	Licenciatura en Ciencias Económicas - Universidad Autónoma de Valencia
1983	Bachillerato y COU - IES Picassent, Valencia.

Experiencia laboral

1998 - 2004	Consultor de Recursos Humanos, ALPE Consultores, Barcelona: diseño e implantación de planes formativos, asesoría a empresas
1994 - 1997	Director de Recursos Humanos, ACTESA, Valencia: selección, formación y administración del personal
1992 - 1993	Adjunto al Director de Recursos Humanos, ACTESA, Valencia

Idiomas
Inglés: nivel avanzado oral y escrito
Francés: nivel medio oral y escrito

Otros datos de interés
Conocimientos a nivel de usuario de Microsoft Office
Disponibilidad para viajar

- **Experienced (American)**

> If you are not Spanish, specify your nationality.

- **Experienced (British)**

- ## Recent graduate (Mexican)

IGNACIO MENÉNDEZ BRAVO

DATOS PERSONALES
Nacido el 7/1/80
Lugar: Puebla
Estado civil: soltero
Nacionalidad: mexicana

DIRECCIÓN ACTUAL
Paseo del Río 14
C.P. 71010 Puebla
Tel.: 01 (2) 434 55 21
imenendez@uni3.com

Formación

2002 – 2003	Maestría en Mercadotecnia Internacional (Programa All-America impartido por la CONCAMIN, Confederación de Cámaras Industriales de México
1998 – 2002	Diplomado en Estudios Empresariales, Universidad Autónoma de Guadalajara
1994 – 1998	Bachillerato Instituto Ignacio Zaragoza

Experiencia profesional

enero – agosto 2004	CIES S.L., Puebla Coordinador comercial: preparación de ofertas y promociones, seguimiento de pedidos.
octubre – diciembre 2003	Arco S.A., Polígono Industrial Malpica, Puebla Prácticas en el departamento de mercadotecnia: seguimiento de clientes y proveedores
julio – septiembre 2003	Vendedor en Electrodomésticos Torres, Puebla

Idiomas
Francés: hablado y escrito
Inglés: nivel medio

Formación complementaria

septiembre 2002	Curso de Gestión Económica Financiera (Cepyme)
julio – agosto 2000	Diploma de instructor de tiempo libre, EPAJ (Escuela Poblana de Actividades pata Jóvenes), Tehuacán
agosto 93 – junio 94	Curso académico en Inglaterra

- ## Recent graduate (American)

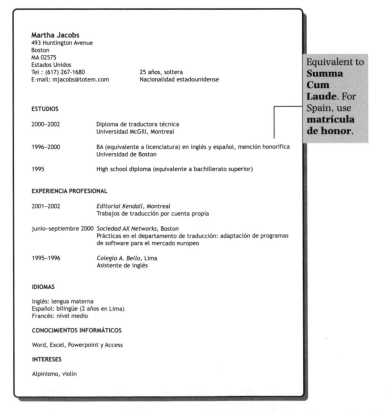

Martha Jacobs
493 Huntington Avenue
Boston
MA 02575
Estados Unidos
Tel : (617) 267-1680
E-mail: mjacobs@totem.com

25 años, soltera
Nacionalidad estadounidense

ESTUDIOS

2000–2002	Diploma de traductora técnica Universidad McGill, Montreal
1996–2000	BA (equivalente a licenciatura) en inglés y español, mención honorífica Universidad de Boston
1995	High school diploma (equivalente a bachillerato superior)

EXPERIENCIA PROFESIONAL

2001–2002	*Editorial Kendall*, Montreal Trabajos de traducción por cuenta propia
junio–septiembre 2000	*Sociedad AX Networks*, Boston Prácticas en el departamento de traducción: adaptación de programas de software para el mercado europeo
1995–1996	*Colegio A. Bello*, Lima Asistente de inglés

IDIOMAS

Inglés: lengua materna
Español: bilingüe (2 años en Lima)
Francés: nivel medio

CONOCIMIENTOS INFORMÁTICOS

Word, Excel, Powerpoint y Access

INTERESES

Alpinismo, violín

Equivalent to **Summa Cum Laude**. For Spain, use **matrícula de honor**.

- Recent graduate (British)

The name of this document varies from country to country. **Licencia de manejo** is used in Mexico, for example, while **permiso de conductor** is used in the River Plate area.

Faxes

Faxes, which are by definition a form of rapid communication, can generally be drafted in a more casual and concise way than letters.

The endings of faxes are usually short and simplified.

- **Business**

Fax

Para: Julián Buera   **De:** Ramón Sala
Fax: 91 456 78 32   **Fecha:** 28 de mayo de 2005
Teléf.: 91 456 78 31   **Pág.:** 1
Ref.: próxima reunión   **CC:** Marta Cueto

It is not necessary to use an opening greeting when you know the person well.

La reunión se celebrará el martes 15 de octubre. Nosotros nos encargaremos de reservar su billete de avión y su habitación de hotel.

Short ending.

Cordialmente,

R. Sala

The word **pasaje** would be more appropriate in Latin America.

- **Booking a hotel room**

The greeting should be used if you don't know the person or if you know them only slightly.

Fax

Para: Hotel   **Condal De:** Ramón Sala
Fax: 93 432 67 45   **Fecha:** 28 de mayo de 2005
Teléf.: 93 432 67 23   **Pág.:** 1
Ref.: reserva 15-17 octubre   **CC:** Marta Cueto

Señor:

Tras nuestra conversación telefónica de esta mañana, le confirmo la reserva de una habitación con baño del 15 al 17 de octubre de 2005.

El Sr. Buera llegará el lunes 15 de octubre después del mediodía.

Abonaremos la factura a su recepción.

Atentamente,

R. Sala

Alternative endings:
Saludos
Saludos cordiales
Cordialmente

E-mail

- E-mail is becoming more and more widely used in the working environment of the Spanish-speaking world, although it is probably not yet as well established a method of business correspondence as it is in the English-speaking world.

- E-mails in Spanish are often written in slightly less telegraphic style than tends to be the case in English, this being mainly due to the fact that Spanish contains fewer of the abbreviated forms that characterize so much of this type of communication in English. Endings are usually rather informal.

- The same rules of "netiquette" apply as in English, so avoid typing entire words in capital letters as this is equivalent to shouting.

- The symbol @ is pronounced "arroba" in Spanish.

- **To a business colleague**

Archivo Edición Ver Insertar Formato Herramientas Mensaje Ayuda

Enviar Cortar Copiar Pegar Deshacer Comprobar Ortografía Adjuntar Prioridad

Para: Julia Fuentes
CC:
Asunto: informe financiero

Times New Roman   12

Hola, Julia.

Un par de preguntas rápidas sobre el informe:

1) ¿Quieres que ponga los precios en libras esterlinas o en euros?
2) ¿Incluyo un apartado sobre mercados extranjeros?

Gracias

Alfonso

The message is brief and to the point.

Informal greeting. It can also be omitted.

- ## Business to business

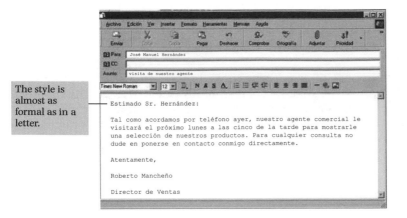

The style is almost as formal as in a letter.

Estimado Sr. Hernández:

Tal como acordamos por teléfono ayer, nuestro agente comercial le visitará el próximo lunes a las cinco de la tarde para mostrarle una selección de nuestros productos. Para cualquier consulta no dude en ponerse en contacto conmigo directamente.

Atentamente,

Roberto Mancheño

Director de Ventas

- ## To an online technical support service

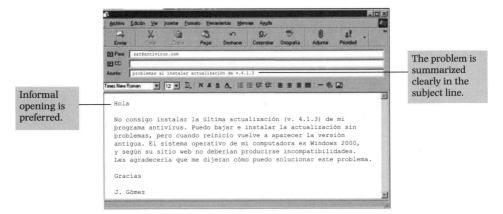

The problem is summarized clearly in the subject line.

Informal opening is preferred.

Hola

No consigo instalar la última actualización (v. 4.1.3) de mi programa antivirus. Puedo bajar e instalar la actualización sin problemas, pero cuando reinicio vuelve a aparecer la versión antigua. El sistema operativo de mi computadora es Windows 2000, y según su sitio web no deberían producirse incompatibilidades. Les agradecería que me dijeran cómo puedo solucionar este problema.

Gracias

J. Gómez

Abbreviations and acronyms

AA	a la atención de (for the attention of)	**CIF**	Código de Identificación Fiscal (tax ID number)
AB	aceptación bancaria (bank acceptance, banker's acceptance)	**Co.**	compañía (company)
admón.	administración (administration)	**cpp**	caracteres por pulgada (characters per inch)
affmo., afmo.	afectísimo (faithfully; sincerely)	**C.P., cp**	código postal (*Br* postcode, *US* zip code)
aprox.	aproximadamente (approximately)		
art.	artículo (article)	**cps**	caracteres por segundo (characters per second)
atte.	atentamente (faithfully; sincerely)		
Av., Avda.	avenida (avenue)	**cta.**	cuenta (account)
c/	cuenta (account) ; calle (street)	**cte.**	corriente (instant)
cap.	capítulo (chapter)	**cto.**	crédito (credit)
c/c	cuenta corriente (current account)	**ctra.**	carretera (road)
Cco	con copia (blind carbon copy)	**c/u**	cada uno (per item)
cf., cfr.	confróntese (confer, compare)	**CV**	curriculum vitae
ch/	cheque	**D.**	don (Mr)
cía., Cía.	compañía (company)	**Dª.**	doña (Mrs)

dcha.	derecha (right)	**p.**	página (page)
dir.	director	**p.a.**	por autorización (on behalf of)
DNI	documento nacional de identidad	**pág.**	página (page)
	(ID card)	**PD**	posdata (PS)
Dña.	doña (Mrs)	**p.ej.**	por ejemplo (e.g)
doc.	documento (document)	**p.o., po**	por orden (on behalf of)
dpto.	departamento (department)	**pp.**	páginas (pages)
Dr.	doctor	**p.p.**	por poder (on behalf of); porte
Dra.	doctora (doctor)		pagado (carriage paid)
dto.	descuento (discount)	**ppp**	puntos por pulgada (dots per inch)
DUA	Documento Único Aduanero	**pral.**	principal
	(single customs document)	**pza.**	plaza (square)
d/v	días vista (within ... days)	**PVP**	precio de venta al público (retail
ed.	edición (edition); edificio (building)		price)
ej.	ejemplo (example)	**PYME, pyme**	Pequeña y Mediana Empresa
e.m.	en mano (by hand)		(small and medium-sized
e.p.d.	en paz descanse (RIP)		enterprise)
e.p.m.	en propia mano (by hand)	**q.e.p.d.**	que en paz descanse (RIP)
ETT	Empresa de Trabajo Temporal	**ref.**	referencia (reference)
	(temping agency)	**Rte.**	remite (sender)
etc.	etcétera (etc)	**RUT**	Rol Único Tributario (tax ID
ext.	extensión (extension)		number)
f. , fra.	factura (invoice)	**S.A.**	sociedad anónima (*Br* PLC, *US* Inc)
gp, g.p.	giro postal (postal order)	**s.e.u.o.**	salvo error u omisión (errors and
gral.	general		omissions excepted)
gtos.	gastos (expenses)	**sig.**	siguiente (following)
hnos.	hermanos (brothers)	**S.L.**	sociedad limitada (*Br* Ltd, *US* Inc)
incl.	inclusive (including)	**s/n**	sin número (no number)
I+D	investigación y desarrollo	**Sr.**	señor (Mr)
	(research and development)	**Sra.**	señora (Mrs)
id.	ídem (ditto)	**Sres.**	señores (Messrs)
IVA	impuesto sobre el valor añadido,	**Srta.**	señorita (Miss)
	Am impuesto al valor agregado	**TAE**	tasa anual equivalente (annual
	(VAT)		percentage rate)
L	letra de cambio (bill of exchange)	**tel. , teléf.**	teléfono (telephone)
Lda.	licenciada (graduate)	**Ud.**	usted (you)
Ldo.	licenciado (graduate)	**Uds.**	ustedes (you)
Lic.	licenciado, -a (graduate)	**UTE**	Unión Temporal de Empresas
MN, mn	moneda nacional (national		(joint venture)
	currency)	**v.**	véase (see)
nº	número (number)	**V.° B.°**	visto bueno (approved)
NB	nota bene	**Vd.**	usted (you)
NIF	Número de Identificación Fiscal	**Vda.**	viuda (widow)
	(tax ID number)	**Vds.**	ustedes (you)
núm.	número (number)	**v.g., v.gr.**	verbigracia (e.g.)
O/	orden (order)	**vid.**	véase (see)
O/P	orden de pago (payment order)	**vol.**	volumen (volume)

Telephone calls

Pronunciation of telephone numbers

When giving their telephone numbers, Spanish people either say the numbers one by one or, preferably, in pairs: 91 417 43 22: "noventa y uno, cuatro uno siete, cuatro tres, dos dos" or "noventa y uno cuatro diecisiete cuarenta y tres veintidós". This can be a little confusing and you may have to ask them to repeat, one number at a time.

Typical Phrases

- **Asking for information from the operator or switchboard:**

– ¿Me podría dar el número de los bomberos, por favor?
– ¿Me puede dar el número de Pablo Castillo Díaz, de Linares? No sé la calle.
– ¿Cuál es el prefijo *or* (MÉX) la clave de Italia, por favor?
– ¿Qué prefijo *or* (MÉX) clave tengo que marcar para llamar al extranjero *or* (AM) exterior?

- **Answering the telephone:**

Informally:

– (ESP) ¿Sí? *or* (MÉX) ¿Bueno? *or* (RP) ¿Hola? *or* (ANDES, CARIB) ¿Alo?
(To which the caller replies:
– ¿Está Miguel? *or* Hola, Miguel. Soy Pedro *etc*)

More formally:

– ¿Diga? *or* ¿Sí, dígame? *or* (RP) ¿Oigo?

In a company or institution:

– Ministerio de Educación y Cultura, ¿buenos días/buenas tardes?
– MC Traducciones, ¿en qué puedo ayudarle?

- **Asking to speak to someone:**

– Quisiera hablar con la señora Carmen Jiménez.
– ¿El señor Bustamante, por favor?
– ¿Me puede (ESP) poner *or* (AM) comunicar con el departamento de contabilidad?
– ¿Me (ESP) pone *or* (AM) comunica con la extensión *or* (RP) el interno 321, por favor?

> pronounced **trescientos vientiuno**

- **Phrases used by a receptionist or secretary taking a call:**

– ¿Quién le llama, por favor?
– ¿De parte de quién?

When putting a caller through:

– Le paso *or* (MÉX) Lo comunico.
– No cuelgue *or* (ESP) No se retire *or* (RP) No corte.

When the caller cannot be connected immediately:

– (ESP) Comunica *or* (AM) Da ocupado.
– No contesta. No cuelgue *or* (ESP) No se retire *or* (RP) No corte, por favor, lo sigo intentando.

Asking the caller if he or she wishes to leave a message:

– ¿Quiere dejarle un mensaje *or* (ESP) recado?

To which the caller may reply:

– ¿Le podría decir que me llame cuando vuelva, por favor?
– No, gracias. Vuelvo (*or* volveré) a llamar más tarde.

- **Recorded messages:**

If you have to deal with the answering machine, the usual recorded message while waiting to get through is:

– Todas nuestras líneas están ocupadas en estos momentos. Por favor, espere (*or* siga a la espera) y en breve atenderemos su llamada.

If you have to leave a message, you will hear the following standard set of sentences:

– Ha llamado al número ... En estos momentos no podemos atender su llamada. Deje su nombre y su número de teléfono después de la señal y nos pondremos en contacto con usted lo antes posible. Gracias

– Este es el contestador de ... *or* (MÉX) Esta es la contestadora de... En estos momentos no estoy en casa. Por favor, deja *or* (RP) dejá tu mensaje después de la señal.

– Sergio Ruiz y María Aguirre. Deja *or* (RP) Dejá tu mensaje.

WORKING WITH AN INTERPRETER

In today's international business environment, interpretation is becoming increasingly common as a means of helping people from different countries to communicate. In order to get your message across to an international audience, it is essential to understand how best to work with interpreters.

There are three types of interpreting:

- Simultaneous
- Consecutive
- Whispering

Simultaneous is the most common form for conferences and business meetings. A microphone relays the speaker's voice to the interpreters who are sitting in soundproof booths. They then interpret instantaneously into the relevant language and the delegates listen to the interpretation via headsets.

Consecutive is used when simultaneous interpretation would not be practical, eg for factory visits or over dinner. The interpreter stands or sits next to you and interprets what you have said after you have said it, sometimes taking notes.

Whispering is the least common form of interpretation. The interpreter sits next to the delegates and whispers the translation of the presentation while it is being made.

Making a Presentation to an International Audience

If you know that your presentation is being interpreted into other languages, bear in mind the following points:

- Adapt the content of your speech to reflect the fact that it will be listened to by people from different cultures. Jokes rarely translate well and may even seem inappropriate to people from certain cultures. Culture-specific references are also usually meaningless to delegates from other countries. Colloquial or very technical language can be hard to translate, so stick to everyday vocabulary wherever possible.

- If you have written your speech out in advance, always provide a copy for the interpreters. Ideally, they should receive it a couple of weeks before the presentation, but if this is impossible, at least distribute it to them just before you speak, along with copies of any overheads or other documents you may be discussing. Background information on the subject of the presentation is also useful if provided in advance of the conference.

- When using simultaneous interpretation, you will be speaking into a microphone. The sound from the microphone is what the interpreters hear, and if they cannot hear what you are saying, they cannot interpret it. First, make sure your microphone is switched on and the interpreters can hear you. Direct your voice towards the microphone, but slightly over the top of it rather than straight at it. Remain at a constant distance from the microphone – if you keep moving towards it and then away, the volume will keep going up and down. When turning to point to a screen behind you, remember that if you speak with your back to the microphone, it will not pick up what you say. To avoid this problem, people using transparencies often wear a small microphone attached to their tie or lapel. If you are using one of these, remember that if you brush against it with your hand or jacket while speaking, the interpreters will only be able to hear a loud crackling noise.

- When using an overhead projector, make sure the screen is positioned so that the interpreters can see it. It is important to take the audience through the content of each transparency, otherwise only those people who speak the language in which they are written will understand them.

- The most common mistake made by people speaking to an international audience is to speak too quickly. Interpreters don't simply repeat what you say, they have to translate it first, so they inevitably need more time than you do. Consider also, that many European languages (including Spanish) are up to one third longer than English. Furthermore, there may be delegates listening to your speech in the language you are making it in, even though it is their second language.

- One way to ensure you keep to a reasonable pace is to pause at the end of every sentence. This allows the listeners to digest what you have said and gives the interpreters time to finish translating. A good speaker will wait until he or she hears that the interpreters have stopped speaking before continuing with his or her presentation.

- It is essential to speak clearly. Interpreters can only translate what they hear; if you mumble they will not be able to communicate your message.

If you bear all these points in mind next time you attend a multilingual conference or business meeting, you will be doing your bit to improve international communication and understanding.

Do's and don'ts when working with an interpreter

✓ **Do:**

- Provide a copy of your speech, transparencies and reference material in advance.
- Switch your microphone on and use it correctly.
- Speak slowly and clearly.

✗ **Don't:**

- Use too many jokes or culture-specific references.
- Turn away from the microphone when speaking about transparencies.
- Change language in the middle of a sentence.

NATIONS OF THE WORLD

Please note that the Spanish name for the countries has been given in the second column. In order to find the Spanish terms for the currencies and languages, please refer to the corresponding table in the Spanish supplement.

Note also that the abbreviations given for currencies are the internationally recognised standard abbreviations established by the ISO and used in international financial transactions, rather than locally used abbreviations.

English name	Spanish name	Local name	Official language(s)	Currency
Afghanistan	Afganistán	Afghānestān	Dari, Pushtøu	1 Afghani (AFA) = 100 puls
Albania	Albania	Shqïpëri	Albanian	1 Lek (ALL) = 100 qindarka
Algeria	Argelia	Al-Jazā'ir (Arabic), Algérie (French)	Arabic	1 Algerian Dinar (DZD) = 100 centimes
Andorra		Andorra	Catalan, French, Spanish	1 Euro (EUR) = 100 cents
Angola	Angola	Angola	Portuguese	1 Kwanza (AOK) = 100 lwei
Argentina	Argentina	Argentina	Spanish	1 Peso (ARS) = 100 centavos
Armenia	Armenia	Hayastani Hanrapetut'yun	Armenian	1 Dram (AMD) =100 luma
Australia	Australia	Australia	English	1 Australian Dollar (AUD) = 100 cents
Austria	Austria	Österreich	German	1 Euro (EUR) = 100 cents
Azerbaijan	Azerbaiyán	Azarbaijan	Azeri (Azerbaijan)	1 Manat (AZM) =100 kepik
The Bahamas	Bahamas	Bahamas	English	1 Bahamian Dollar (BSD) = 100 cents
Bahrain	Bahráin	Dawlat al-Bahrayn	Arabic	1 Bahrain Dinar (BHD) = 1,000 fils
Bangladesh	Bangladesh	Gana Prajatantri Bangladesh	Bengali	1 Taka (BDT) = 100 poisha
Barbados	Barbados	Barbados	English	1 Barbados Dollar (BBD) = 100 cents
Belarus	Bielorrusia	Belarus	Belarussian	1 Rouble (BYB) =100 kopeks
Belgium	Bélgica	Belgique (French), België (Flemish)	Flemish, French, German	1 Euro (EUR) = 100 cents
Belize	Belice	Belize	English	1 Belize Dollar (BZD) = 100 cents
Benin	Benín	Bénin	French	1 CFA Franc (XOF) = 100 centimes
Bhutan	Bután	Druk-Yul	Dzongkha	1 Ngultrum (BTN) = 100 chetrum
Bolivia	Bolivia	Bolivia	Spanish	1 Boliviano (BOB) = 100 centavos

English name	Spanish name	Local name	Official language(s)	Currency
Bosnia-Herzegovina	Bosnia y Hercegovina	Bosnia-Herzegovina	Serbo-Croat paras	1 Bosnian convertible mark (BAM) = 100 fening
Botswana	Botsuana	Botswana	English	1 Pula (BWP) = 100 thebe
Brazil	Brasil	Brasil	Portuguese	1 Real (BRL) = 100 centavos
Brunei	Brunéi	Brunei	Malay	1 Brunei Dollar (BND) = 100 sen
Bulgaria	Bulgaria	Bãlgarija	Bulgarian	1 Lev (BGL) (*pl* Leva) = 100 stotinki
Burkina Faso	Burkina Faso	Burkina Faso	French	1 CFA Franc (XOF) = 100 centimes
Burma ▸ Myanmar	Birmania			
Burundi	Burundi	Burundi	French, Kirundi	1 Burundi Franc (BIF) = 100 centimes
Cambodia	Camboya	Preah Reach Ana Pak Kampuchea	Khmer	1 Riel (KHR) = 100 sen
Cameroon	Camerún	Cameroon	English, French	1 CFA Franc (XAF) = 100 centimes
Canada	Canadá	Canada	English, French	1 Canadian Dollar (CAD) = 100 cents
Cape Verde	Cabo Verde	Cabo Verde	Portuguese	1 Escudo Caboverdiano (CVE) = 100 centavos
Central African Republic	República Centroafricana	République Centrafricaine	French, Sango	1 CFA Franc (XAF) = 100 centimes
Chad	Chad	Tchad	French, Arabic	1 CFA Franc (XAF) = 100 centimes
Chile	Chile	Chile	Spanish	1 Chilean Peso (CLP) = 100 centavos
China	China	Zhongguo	Chinese	1 Renminbi Yuan (CNY) = 10 jiao = 100 fen
Colombia	Colombia	Colombia	Spanish	1 Colombian Peso (COP) = 100 centavos
Comoros	Comoras	Comores	French, arabic, Comorian	1 Comorian Franc (KMF) = 100 centimes
Congo	Congo	Congo	French	1 CFA Franc (XAF) = 100 centimes
Congo, Democratic Republic of	Congo, República Democrática	Congo	French, Lingala	1 New Zaïre (ZRN) = 100 makuta
Costa Rica	Costa Rica	Costa Rica	Spanish	1 Costa Rican Colón (CRC) (*pl* Colones) = 100 céntimos
Côte d'Ivoire	Costa de Marfil	Côte d'Ivoire	French	1 CFA Franc (XOF) = 100 centimes
Croatia	Croacia	Hrvatska	Serbo-Croat	1 Kuna (HRK) = 100 lipas
Cuba	Cuba	Cuba	Spanish	1 Cuban Peso (CUP) = 100 centavos

English name	Spanish name	Local name	Official language(s)	Currency
Cyprus	Chipre	Kipros (Greek), Kibris (Turkish)	Greek, Turkish	1 Cyprus Pound (CYP) = 100 cents
Czech Republic	Chequia, República checa	Česká Republika	Czech	1 Korună (CZK) = 100 halér
Denmark	Dinamarca	Danmark	Danish	1 Danish Krone (DKK) (*pl* Kroner) = 100 øre
Djibouti	Yibuti	Djibouti	Arabic, French	1 Djibouti Franc (DJF) = 100 centimes
Dominica	Dominica	Dominica	English, French, Creole	1 East Caribbean Dollar (XCD) = 100 cents
Dominican Republic	República Dominicana	República Dominicana	Spanish	1 Dominican Republic Peso (DOP) = 100 centavos
Ecuador	Ecuador	Ecuador	Spanish	1 US dollar (USD) = 100 cents
Egypt	Egipto	Jumhuriyat Misr al-Arabiya	Arabic	1 Egyptian Pound (EGP) = 100 piastres
El Salvador	El Salvador	El Salvador	Spanish	1 Colón (SVC) (*pl* Colones) = 100 centavos
Equatorial Guinea	Guinea Ecuatorial	Guinea Ecuatorial	Spanish	1 CFA Franc (XAF) = 100 centimes
Eritrea	Eritrea	Eritrea	Tigrinya, Arabic	1 nakfa (ERN) = 100 centimes
Estonia	Estonia	Eesti Vabariik	Estonian	1 Kroon (EEK) = 100 senti
Ethiopia	Etiopía	Ityopiya	Amharic	1 Ethiopian Birr (ETB) = 100 cents
Faroe Islands	Islas Feroe	Faroyar/ Faeroerne	Faroese, Danish	1 Danish Krone (DKK) (*pl* Kroner) = 100 øre
Fiji	Fiyi	Matanitu Ko Viti	English	1 Fiji Dollar (FJD) = 100 cents
Finland	Finlandia	Suomen Tasavalta	Finnish, Swedish	1 Euro (EUR) = 100 cents
France	Francia	République française	French	1 Euro (EUR) = 100 cents
French Guiana	Gabón	Guyane française	French, Creole	1 Euro (EUR) = 100 cents
French Polynesia	Polinesia Francesa	Territoire de la Polynésie française	Polynesian, French	1 CPA Franc (XPF) = 100 centimes
Gabon	Gabón	République gabonaise	French	1 CFA Franc (XAF) = 100 centimes
The Gambia	Gambia	Gambia	English	1 Dalasi (GMD) = 100 butut
Georgia	Georgia	Sakartvelos Respublica	Georgian, Russian	1 Lari (GEL) = 100 tetri
Germany	Alemania	Bundesrepublik Deutschland	German	1 Euro (EUR) = 100 cents
Ghana	Ghana	Ghana	English	1 Cedi (GHC) = 100 pesewas
Greece	Grecia	Elliniki Dimokratia	Greek	1 Euro (EUR) = 100 cents

English name	Spanish name	Local name	Official language(s)	Currency
Greenland	Groenlandia	Grønland (Danish), Kalaallit Nunaat	Danish, Greenlandic	1 Danish Krone (DKK) (pl Kroner) = 100 øre
Guatemala	Guatemala	Guatemala	Spanish	1 Quetzal (GTQ) (pl Quetzales) = 100 centavos
Guinea	Guinea	République de Guinée	French	1 Guinea Franc (GNF) = 100 centimes
Guinea-Bissau	Guinea-Bissau	Republica da Guiné-Bissau	Portuguese	1 CFA Franc (GWP) = 100 centimes
Guyana	Guyana	Guyana	English	1 Guyana Dollar (GYD) = 100 cents
Haiti	Haití	République d'Haïti	French	1 Gourde (HTG) = 100 centimes
Holland ▶ Netherlands, The	Holanda			
Honduras	Honduras	Honduras	Spanish	1 Lempira (HNL) = 100 centavos
Hungary	Hungría	Magyar Koztarsasag	Hungarian	1 Forint (HUF) = 100 fillér
Iceland	Islandia	Ísland	Icelandic	1 Króna (ISK) = 100 aurar (*sing* eyrir)
India	India	Bhārat (Hindi)	Hindi, English	1 Indian Rupee (INR) = 100 paisa
Indonesia	Indonesia	Republik Indonesia	Bahasa Indonesia	1 Rupiah (IDR) = 100 sen
Iran	Irán	Jomhoori-e-Islami-e-Iran	Farsi	1 Iranian Rial (IRR)
Iraq	Irak, Iraq	Jumhouriya al Iraquia	Arabic	1 Iraqi Dinar (IQD) = 1,000 fils
Ireland	Irlanda	Poblacht na hEireann	Irish, English	1 Euro (EUR) = 100 cents
Israel	Israel	Medinat Israel	Hebrew, Arabic	1 Shekel (ILS) = 100 agorot (*sing* agora)
Italy	Italia	Repubblica Italiana	Italian	1 Euro (EUR) = 100 cents
Ivory Coast ▶ Côte d'Ivoire	Costa de Marfil			
Jamaica	Jamaica	Jamaica	English	1 Jamaican Dollar (JMD) = 100 cents
Japan	Japón	Nihon	Japanese	1 Yen (JPY) = 100 sen
Jordan	Jordania	Al'Urdun	Arabic	1 Jordanian Dinar (JOD) = 1,000 fils
Jugoslavia ▶ Yugoslavia	Yugoslavia			
Kampuchea ▶ Cambodia	Camboya			
Kazakhstan	Kazajistán, Kazajstán	Kazak Respublikasy	Kazakh, Russian	1 Tenge (KZT) = 100 tiyn
Kenya	Kenia	Jamhuri ya Kenya	(Ki) Swahili, English	1 Kenyan shilling (KES) 100 cents

English name	Spanish name	Local name	Official language(s)	Currency
Kuwait	Kuwait	Dowlat al-Kuwayt	Arabic	1 Kuwaiti Dinar (KWD) = 1,000 fils
Kyrgyzstan	Kirghizistán	Kyrgyz Respublikasy	Kyrgyz	1 Som (KGS) = 100 tyiyn
Laos	Laos	Lao	Lao	1 Kip (LAK) = 100 at
Latvia	Letonia	Latvijas Republika	Latvian	1 Lats (LVL) (*pl* Lati) = 100 santimi (*sing* santims)
Lebanon	Líbano	Al-Lubnān	Arabic	1 Lebanese Pound/Livre (LBP) = 100 piastres
Lesotho	Lesoto	Lesotho	English, Sesotho	1 Loti (*pl* Maloti) (LSL) = 100 lisente (*sing* sente)
Liberia	Liberia	Liberia	English	1 Liberian Dollar (LRD) = 100 cents
Libya	Libia	Lībyā	Arabic	1 Libyan Dinar (LYD) = 1,000 dirhams
Liechtenstein	Liechtenstein	Furstentum Liechtenstein	German	1 Swiss Franc (CHF) = 100 centimes
Lithuania	Lituania	Lietuva	Lithuanian	1 Litas (LTL) (*pl* litai) = 100 centai (*sing* centas)
Luxembourg	Luxemburgo	Lëtzebuerg (Letz), Luxembourg (French), Luxemburg (German)	French, German, Letzebuergesch	1 Euro (EUR) = 100 cents
Macedonia	Macedonia	Republika Makedonija	Macedonian	1 Denar (MKD) = 100 deni
Madagascar	Madagascar	Republikan'i Madagasikara	Malagasy, French	1 Malagasy Franc (MGF) = 100 centimes
Malawi	Malaui	Dziko la Malaŵi	Chichewa, English	1 Kwacha (MWK) = 100 tambala
Malaysia	Malasia	Federation of Malaysia	Bahasa Malaysia	1 Malaysian Ringgit (MYR) = 100 cents
Maldives	Maldivas	Maldives Divehi Jumhuriya	Divehi	1 Rufiyaa (MVR) = 100 laari
Mali	Malí	Mali	French	1 CFA Franc (XOF) = 100 centimes
Malta	Malta	Malta	English, Maltese	1 Maltese Lira (MTL) = 100 cents
Martinique	Martinica	Martinique	French, Creole	1 Euro (EUR) = 100 cents
Mauritania	Mauritania	Mauritanie (French), Mūrītāniyā (Arabic)	Arabic	1 Ouguiya (MRO) = 5 khoums
Mauritius	Mauricio	Mauritius	English	1 Mauritian Rupee (MUR) = 100 cents
Mexico	México	México	Spanish	1 Mexican Peso (MXN) = 100 centavos
Micronesia	Micronesia	Micronesia	English	1 US Dollar (USD) = 100 cents
Moldova	Moldavia	Republica Moldove-nească	Moldavian	1 Leu (MDL) (*pl* lei) = 100 bani

English name	Spanish name	Local name	Official language(s)	Currency
Monaco	Mónaco	Monaco	French	1 Euro (EUR) = 100 cents
Mongolia	Mongolia	Mongol Ard Uls	Halh Mongol	1 Tugrik (MNT) = 100 möngö
Morocco	Marruecos	Mamlaka al-Maghrebia	Arabic	1 Dirham (MAD) = 100 centimes
Mozambique	Mozambique	República de Moçambique	Portuguese	1 Metical (MZM) = 100 centavos
Myanmar	Myanmar	Myanmar	Burmese	1 Kyat (MMK) = 100 pyas
Namibia	Namibia	Namibia	English	1 Namibian Dollar (NAD) = 100 cents
Nauru	Nauru	Naeoro (Nauruan), Nauru (English)	Nauruan, English	1 Australian Dollar (AUD) = 100 cents
Nepal	Nepal	Nepal Adhirajya	Napali	1 Nepalese Rupee (NPR) = 100 paisa
The Netherlands	Países Bajos	Koninkrijk der Nederlanden	Dutch	1 Euro (EUR) = 100 cents
New Zealand	Nueva Zelanda	New Zealand	English	1 New Zealand Dollar (NZD) = 100 cents
Nicaragua	Nicaragua	Nicaragua	Spanish	1 Córdoba Oro (NIO) = 100 centavos
Niger	Níger	Niger	French	1 CFA Franc (XOF) = 100 centimes
Nigeria	Nigeria	Nigeria	English, French	1 Naira (NGN) = 100 kobo
North Korea	Corea del Norte	Chosōn Minjujuüi In'min Konghwaguk	Korean	1 Won (KPW) = 100 chon
Norway	Noruega	Kongeriket Norge	Norwegian	1 Norwegian Krone (NOK) = 100 øre
Oman	Omán	Saltanat 'Uman	Arabic	1 Omani Rial (OMR) = 1,000 baiza
Pakistan	Pakistán	Pākistān	Urdu, English	1 Pakistan Rupee (PKR) = 100 paisa
Panama	Panamá	Panamá	Spanish	1 Balboa (PAB) = 100 centésimos
Papua New Guinea	Papúa-Nueva Guinea	Papua New Guinea	English, Tok Pisin, Hiri Motu	1 Kina (PGK) = 100 toea
Paraguay	Paraguay	Paraguay	Spanish	1 Guaraní (PYG) = 100 céntimos
Peru	Perú	Perú	Spanish	1 New Sol (PEN) = 100 centavos
Philippines	Filipinas	Pilipinas	Filipino, English	1 Philippine Peso (PHP) = 100 centavos
Poland	Polonia	Rzeczpospolita Polska	Polish	1 Złoty (PLN) = 100 groszy
Portugal	Portugal	Portugal	Portuguese	1 Euro (EUR) = 100 cents

English name	Spanish name	Local name	Official language(s)	Currency
Puerto Rico	Puerto Rico	Puerto Rico	Spanish, English	1 US Dollar (USD) 100 cents
Qatar	Qatar	Dowlat Qatar	Arabic	1 Qatar Riyal (QAR) = 100 dirhams
Romania	Rumania, Rumanía	Romānia	Romanian	1 Leu (ROL) (*pl* Lei) = 100 bani
Russia	Rusia	Rossiya	Russian	1 Rouble (RUR) = 100 kopeks
Rwanda	Ruanda	Rwanda	(Kinya) Rwanda, French, English	1 Rwanda Franc (RWF) = 100 centimes
Samoa	Samoa	Samoa	Samoan, English	1 Tala (WST) = 100 sene
San Marino	San Marino	San Marino	Italian	1 Euro (EUR) = 100 cents
Saudi Arabia	Arabia Saudí	Al-'Arabīyah as Sa'ūdī yah	Arabic	1 Saudi Arabian Riyal (SAR)= 20 qursh = 100 halala
Senegal	Senegal	Sénégal	French, Wolof	1 CFA Franc (XOF) =100 centimes
Seychelles	Seychelles	Seychelles	Creole French, English, French	1 Seychelles Rupee (SCR) = 100 cents
Sierra Leone	Sierra Leona	Sierra Leone	English	1 Leone (SLL) = 100 cents
Singapore	Singapur	Singapore	Chinese, English, Malay, Tamil	1 Singapore Dollar (SGD) = 100 cents
Slovakia	Eslovaquia	Slovenska Republika	Slovak	1 Koruna (SSK) = 100 haliere
Slovenia	Eslovenia	Republika Slovenija	Slovene	1 Tolar (SIT) =100 stotin
Solomon Islands	Islas Salomón	Solomon Islands	English	1 Solomon Islands Dollar (SBD) = 100 cents
Somalia	Somalia	Somaliya	Arabic, Somali	1 Somali Shilling (SOS) = 100 cents
South Africa	Sudáfrica	South Africa	English, Afrikaans	1 Rand (ZAR) = 100 cents
South Korea	Corea del Sur	Taehan-Min'guk	Korean	1 Won (KRW) = 100 chon
Spain	España	España	Spanish	1 Euro (EUR) = 100 cents
Sri Lanka	Sri Lanka	Sri Lanka	Sinhala, Tamil	1 Sri Lankan Rupee (LKR) = 100 cents
The Sudan	Sudán	As-Sūdān	Arabic	1 Sudanese Dinar (SDD) = 100 piastre
Suriname	Surinam	Suriname	Dutch	1 Surinam Guilder (SRG) = 100 cents
Swaziland	Suazilandia	Umbouso we Swatini	Swazi, English	1 Lilangeni (SZL) (*pl* Emalangeni) = 100 cents
Sweden	Suecia	Konungariket Sverige	Swedish	1 Swedish Krona (SEK) = 100 øre
Switzerland	Suiza	Schweiz (German), Suisse (French), Svizzera (Italian)	French, German, Italian, Romansch	1 Swiss Franc (CHF) = 100 centimes
Syria	Siria	As-Sūrīyah	Arabic	1 Syrian pound (SYP) = 100 piastres

English name	Spanish name	Local name	Official language(s)	Currency
Taiwan	Taiwán	T'aiwan	Chinese	1 New Taiwan Dollar (TWD) = 100 fen
Tajikistan	Tayikistán	Jumkhurii Tojikistan	Tajik	1 Somoni (TJS) = 100 diram
Tanzania	Tanzania	Tanzania	(ki)Swahili, English	1 Tanzanian Shilling (TZS) = 100 cents
Thailand	Tailandia	Prathet Thai	Thai	1 Baht (THB) = 100 satang
Togo	Togo	Togo	French	1 CFA Franc (XOF) = 100 centimes
Tonga	Tonga	Tonga	English, Tongan	1 Pa'anga (TOP) = 100 seniti
Trinidad and Tobago	Trinidad y Tobago	Trinidad and Tobago	English	1 Trinidad and Tobago Dollar (TTD) = 100 cents
Tunisia	Túnez	Tunisiya	Arabic, French	1 Tunisian Dinar (TND) = 1,000 millimes
Turkey	Turquía	Türkiye	Turkish	1 Turkish Lira (TRL) = 100 kurus
Turkmenistan	Turkmenistán	Turkmenostan	Turkmenian	1 Manat (TMM) = 100 tenge
Uganda	Uganda	Uganda	English, Kiswahili	1 Uganda Shilling (UGX) = 100 cents
Ukraine	Ucrania	Ukraina	Ukrainian, Russian	1 Hryvina (UAH) = 100 kopiykas
United Arab Emirates	Emiratos Árabes Unidos	Ittihād al-Imārāt al-'Arabīyah	Arabic, English	1 Dirham (AED) = 100 fils
United Kingdom	Reino Unido	United Kingdom	English	1 Pound Sterling (GBP) = 100 pence
United States of America	Estados Unidos	United States of America	English	1 US Dollar (USD) = 100 cents
Uruguay	Uruguay	Uruguay	Spanish	1 New Uruguayan Peso (UYU) = 100 centésimos
Uzbekistan	Uzbekistán	Uzbekistan	Uzbek	1 Sum (UZS) = 100 tiyin
Vanuatu	Vanuatu	Vanuatu	Bislama, English, French	1 Vatu (VUV) = 100 centimes
Vatican City	El Vaticano	Citta' del Vaticano	Italian	1 Euro (EUR) = 100 cents
Venezuela	Venezuela	Venezuela	Spanish	1 Bolívar (VEB) (*pl* bolívares) = 100 céntimos
Vietnam	Vietnam	Viêt-nam	Vietnamese	1 Dông (VND) = 100 sou
Yemen	Yemen	Al-Yamaniya	Arabic	1 Yemeni Riyal (YER) = 100 fils
Yugoslavia	Yugoslavia	Jugoslavija	Serbo-Croat (Serbian)	1 New Dinar (YUN) = 100 paras
Zaire	Zaire	▸ Congo, Democratic Republic of		
Zambia	Zambia	Zambia	English	1 Kwacha (ZMK) = 100 ngwee
Zimbabwe	Zimbabue	Zimbabwe	English	1 Zimbabwe Dollar (ZWD) = 100 cents

Sources of English Quotes
Fuentes de las citas en inglés

A
ABC1 *Marketing* 1999
ABOVE-THE-LINE *The Guardian* 2001
ACCRUED *Business Wire* 2001
ACTUALS *Healthcare Financial Management* 2001
ADSPEND *Marketing* 1998
ADVERTORIAL *Marketing* 1999
AFFINITY *The Guardian* 2000
AFLOAT *DSN Retailing Today* 2001
AFTER-SALES *The Guardian* 2001
AIM *The Guardian* 1999
ANCHOR STORE *PR Newswire* 2001
ARTICLE *Business Wire* 2000
A-SHARE *The Economist* 1999
ASPIRATIONAL *Marketing* 1999
AVC *Moneywise* 1999

B
B2B *http://news.bbc.co.uk* 2000
BABY *The Economist* 1998
BACS *The Guardian* 2000
BAD *South China Morning Post* 1999
BANCASSURANCE *The Observer* 1999
BANNER *Marketing* 1998
BARGAINING *Aftermarket Business* 2000
BELOW-THE-LINE *Marketing* 1998
BEST-PERCEIVED *Marketing* 1998
BIG *The Guardian* 2002
BI-MEDIA *MediaGuardian* 2001
BLITZ *The Drum* 1998
BORROWING *The Financial Times* 2000
BRAIN-DRAIN *Computer Weekly* 1999
BRAND-LED *Marketing Week* 1999
BREAK-EVEN *The Guardian* 2001
BUILD *Marketing* 1998
BULL *Bloomberg Money* 1999
BULLISH *Chemical Market Reporter* 2001
BUNDLE *Video Store* 2000
BUSINESS *Your Business* 1994
BUYBACK *The Observer* 1999
BUYING *The Observer* 2001

C
CAPITAL *www.campbellharrison.co.uk* 2003

CEILING *Business Times* 2002
CHAEBOL *Korea Times* 1999
CHAPTER 11 *PR Newswire* 2002
CHARITY *PR Newswire* 2000
CHURN *The Guardian* 2002
CLICKS-AND-MORTAR *http://news.bbc.co.uk* 2000
COLLATERAL *The Financial Times* 2002
COLLECTIVE *The Wall Street Journal* 2002
COMMODITY *Bloombery Money* 1999
COMPETITIVE *Brandweek* 2000
CONSUMER *Computer Weekly* 2001
CONTRARIAN *The Guardian* 2001
COOLING-OFF PERIOD *Newsbytes* 2000
CORPORATE *CNN Money* 2002
COST-OF-LIVING *Journal of Accountancy* 2000
COUNTERBID *Investors Chronicle* 1999
CREDIT *The Scotsman* 1999
CROSS-HOLDING *The Guardian* 1999
CUSTOMER-DRIVEN *The Guardian* 2002
CYBERSQUATTING *The Guardian* 2001

D

DAILY *PR Newswire* 2000
DAUGHTER COMPANY *PR Newswire* 2002
DEAD *The Guardian* 2001
DEBTOR *Challenge* 2000
DECISION-MAKING *Win News* 2001
DECONTROL *The Guardian* 2000
DEED *The Guardian* 2001
DEFAULT *Newsbytes* 2000
DEMERGER *The Guardian* 2002
DEMOGRAPHICS *http://news.bbc.co.uk* 2000
DEMUTUALIZE *The Guardian* 1999
DEPRESSED *The Guardian* 2001
DEPTH *www.decisionanalyst.com* 2001
DESKILL *New Statesman* 2000
DIGITAL *The Irish Times* 1999
DIRTY *CFO* 2001
DIVERSIFY *The Financial Times* 1999
DOG *Marketing Week* 1999
DOLLARIZATION *Foreign Policy* 2001
DOTCOM *The Guardian* 2002
DOWNSIZING *http://news.bbc.co.uk* 2001
DRAWDOWN *The Financial Times* 1999
DRESS-DOWN FRIDAY *The Observer* 2002

E

EARNOUT *America's Network* 2000
E-BUSINESS *The Guardian* 2001
E-COMMERCE *Sloan Management Review* 2000

EDGAR *PS Newswire 2000*
EEOC *Business Horizons* 2000
E-GOVERNMENT *Accountancy Age* 2002
ELECTRONIC *Business Wire* 2000
E-MARKETER *Business Wire* 2001
EMOTIONAL *Marketing* 1999
EMPLOYMENT *The Financial Times* 2002
EMPOWERMENT *The Guardian* 2002
ENDOWMENT *The Financial Times* 2002
ENTERPRISE *DSN Retailing Today* 2000
E-TAILER *PR Newswire* 2001
EURO-CURRENCY *Profile Data* 2002
EXCLUSIVITY *Business Wire* 2001
EX-GROWTH *The Financial Times* 2002
EXPANDING *The Guardian* 2002
EXTRAORDINARY *The Financial Times* 2002

F

FACE *Broadcasting & Cable* 1999
FACTORING *The Financial Times* 2002
FANNIE MAE *The Guardian* 2001
FAT CAT *The Guardian* 2002
FEATHERBED *The Guardian* 2001
FED *Emerging Markets Week* 2001
FEDERAL *Business Wire* 2001
FIAT (MONEY) *Federal Reserve Board* 2002
FIRST-TIME *Sunday Business Post* 2003
FLAGSHIP *Accountancy Age* 2002
FLEET STREET *The Guardian* 2002
FLEXIBLE *The Guardian* 2001
FLOOR *Moneywise* 1999
FOCUS *The Guardian* 2002
FOOTFALL *Marketing* 1999
FOOTSIE *The Financial* 2002
FOREIGN *AFX Europe* 2002
FOREX *The Observer* 1999
FORTUNE 500 *PR Newswire* 2002
FREE *The Guardian* 2002
FRONT-END *The Scotsman* 2000
FULL *Accountancy Age* 2002
FUTURES *Business Wire* 2000

G

GAGGING ORDER *The Guardian* 2000
GAP *The Guardian* 2002
GATEKEEPER *Elements of Marketing* 1987
GAZUMPING *New Statesman* 1999
GILT-EDGED *The Guardian* 2001
GLASS CEILING *The Scotsman* 2002
GLOBAL *Marketing* 1998

GLOBALIZED ECONOMY *Financial Post* 2002
GNOME *New Statesman* 2000
GOODWILL *CFO Magazine for Senior Financial Executives* 2000
GREENFIELD SITE *The Guardian* 2002
GROW *Unigram X APT Data Services Ltd,* 1993

H
HAIRCUT *Los Angeles Business Journal* 2000
HANDS-ON *The Guardian* 2002
HATCHET MAN *The Industry Standard* 2001
HEADHUNT *Scotland on Sunday* 2002
HEDGE *The Financial Times* 2002
HIGHLY-GEARED *The Financial Times* 2002
HOLDING *The Financial Times* 2002
HORSE-TRADING *Communications Today* 2001
HOSTILE TAKEOVER BID *The Guardian* 2002
HURDLE RATE *Graphic Arts Monthly* 2000

I
IFA *The Guardian* 2002
INCENTIVIZE *The Observer* 2002
INDEMNIFY *PR Newswire* 2002
INDEX *The Irish Times* 1999
INDICATOR *Applied Economics* Griffiths, Alan & Wall, Stuart, Longman 1990
INELASTIC *Industry Standard* 2000
INFLATIONARY *The Financial Times* 2002
INFLUENCE PEDDLING *Insight* 2001
INFORMAL ECONOMY *Private Banker International* 2001
INFORMATION *The Guardian* 2002
INSIDER *The Financial Times* 2002
INSTANT-ACCESS *The Financial Times* 2002
INTEGRATION *The International Economy* 2001
INTERIM *The Financial Times* 1999
INTERNATIONAL *PR Newswire* 2002
INTRAPRENEUR *PR Newswire* 2000
INVISIBLE *The Guardian* 2002
IPO *The Times* 1999
ISA *Daily Telegraph* 2002
ISDN *Computer Weekly* 2001

J
JOB *Career Development Quarterly* 2001
JUMBO *Investment Dealers' Digest* 2001
JUNK *Financial Post* 2002
JUST-IN-TIME *The Economist* 1991

K
KEIRETSU *The Guardian* 2000
KERB *Dow Jones Newswires* 2002

KEY-ESCROW *The Irish Times* 1999
KITING *Business Wire* 2001

L
LADDERED PORTFOLIO *Medical Economics* 2002
LAME DUCK *The Guardian* 2002
LAUNDER *BBC Monitoring Service* 2002
LAW *New Statement* 1998
LAYOUT *Marketing* 1999
LEARNING CURVE *Business Wire* 2002
LEISURE INDUSTRY *The Guardian* 2002
LEVERAGED *The Guardian* 2002
LIFFE *The Financial Times* 2002
LINEAR *Marketing* 1999
LIQUIDITY *Date and publisher unknown*
LLOYD'S NAME *The Guardian* 2002
LOCAL *The Guardian* 2001
LOYALTY *Debrief* 1998

M
MAILSHOT *The Guardian* 2002
M&A *Venture Capital Journal* 1999
MANIPULATE *American Metal Market* 2000
MARGIN *Purchasing* 2001
MARKET *American Enterprise* 2000
MARKET-DRIVEN *The Guardian* 2002
MARZIPAN LAYER *www.thisismoney.com* 2000
MASTERBRAND *Marketing* 1998
MATTRESS MONEY *The Observer* 2001
M-COMMERCE *TelecomWorldWire* 2002
MEANS-TEST *The Guardian* 2000
MEDIA *Yahoo Media Relations* 2003
MEDIA-FRIENDLY *The New York Observer* 2001
MENTORING *The Guardian* 2002
MERIT *HR Magazine* 2000
MEZZANINE *Investment Dealers' Digest* 2000
MICROMANAGE *Travel Weekly* 2001
MIND SHARE *Multichannel News* 2000
MISBRAND *PR Newsire* 2001
MISERY INDEX *www.worldbank.org* 2000
MISSION *The Guardian* 2001
MISSION-CRITICAL *The Guardian* 2000
MONEY *The Guardian* 1999
MORAL HAZARD *British Medical Journal* 2000
MOST-FAVOURED NATION *European Report* 2000
MOUSETRAP *Business Horizons* 2001
MOVER *Real Estate Weekly* 2000
MPC *The Guardian* 1999
MUST-HAVE *Professional Builder* 2001
MUTUAL *New Statesman* 2000

N

NARROW *The Guardian* 1999
NATURAL *Newsbytes News Network* 2001
NEGATIVE *Asian Economic News* 2001
NEST EGG *Medical Economics* 2002
NET *Investors Chronicle* 1999
NETWORKING *Training and Development* 2001
NICHE *Travel Weekly* 2002
NINE-TO-FIVER *Infoworld* 2000
NOTICE *Internet World* 2000
NUISANCE TAX *Contra Costa Times* 2002

O

OFF-BRAND *National Home Center News* 2000
OFFICIALESE *The Scotsman* 2001
OFT *Business Wire* 2001
ON-LINE *Marketing* 1999
OPEN *Labor History* 2001
OPPORTUNITY *Marketing* 1999
ORGANIC GROWTH *The Guardian* 2002
OUTLOOK *Emerging Markets Week* 2001
OUTPLACEMENT *Business Wire* 2001
OUTREACH *The Independent* 2002
OUTSOURCING *Journal of Management* 2000
OUTTURN *OECD Economic Outlook* 2000
OVERBOUGHT *The Guardian* 1999
OVERTIME *Newsbytes* 2000

P

P *Elements of Marketing* 1987
PAC MAN DEFENSE *www.jonesday.com* 2002
PAID-UP *Principles of Hotel and Catering Law* Pannet, A., Cassell, 1992
PAPER *The Guardian* 1999
PARLAY *Brandweek* 2001
PATERNITY LEAVE *The Industry Standard* 2001
PAYE *The Independent* 2001
PAYROLL *Workforce* 2002
PEOPLE-FOCUSED *PR Newswire* 2000
PERCEPTION *Marketing* 1999
PERK *The Industry Standard* 2002
PERMATEMP *Workforce* 2000
PERSONAL *The Scotsman* Date unknown
PETER PRINCIPLE *Medical Economics* 2002
PINK *The Independent* 2002
PITCH *Marketing* 1998
PLANNED *Morality and the Market-place* Griffiths, Brian., Hodder &
   Stoughton, 1989
PLAYER *Marketing Week* 1999
POACH *Electronic Times* 2000
POISON PILL *CFO* 2001

POLICY WONK *New York Observer* 2001

PONZI SCHEME *Los Angeles Business Journal* 2001

PORTFOLIO *The Guardian* 2002

POSTER *PR Newswire* 2000

POVERTY *The Economist* 1991

POWER *PR Newswire* 2000

POWERBROKER *The Guardian* 2002

PREDATORY *Airline Industry Information* 2000

PRESELL *Brandweek* 2001

PRICE *The Observer* 1999

PRICE-ELASTIC *Rival States, Rival Firms* Henley, J.; Strange, S.; Stopford, J., Cambridge University Press, 1992

PROACTIVE *The Independent* 2002

PROBLEM CHILD *Computergram International* Date and publisher unknown

PROFIT *The Guardian* 1999

PROFIT-TAKING *First Call/Thomson Financial Insiders' Chronicle* 2000

PROJECT *Electronic Designs* 2000

PROSPECT *PR Newswire* 2000

PRUDENCE CONCEPT *Public Sector Accounting* Pendlebury, Maurice & Jones, Rowan, Pitman Publishing, 1992

PUNTER *The Guardian* 2001

PURCHASING *KBS Open Learning MBA Programme,* BPP Publishing Ltd, 1989

PYRAMID *The Guardian* 2001

Q

QUANGO *New Statesman* 2001

QUICK *Human Resource Strategies* Salaman, G.; Mabey, C.; Hamblin, H.; Thompson; Cameron, S.; Iles, P., Open University Press, 1992

R

RAKE OFF *Dollar & Sense* 2001

R AND D *The Birmingham Magazine* 1990

RATE *Communications News* 2000

RAT RACE *The Independent* 2002

REAL *The Independent* 1989

REBRANDING *Marketing* 1999

RECALL *Advertising: What It Is And How To Do It* White, R., McGraw-Hill Book Company, 1993

RECAPITALIZE *Investors Chronicle* 1999

RECEIVER *Eurofood* 2001

RECESSIONARY *Clothes Show,* Redwood Publishing Company, 1991

RED *The Guardian* 2002

REDEMPTION *Investors Chronicle* 1999

REENGINEERING *The Independent* 2002

REFLATION *New Statesman* 2002

REFUSAL *The Independent* 2002

REGULATORY *A Right Approach to Economics?* Hardy, Peter, Hodder & Stoughton Ltd, 1991

RELOCATION *The Industry Standard* 2000

REMUNERATION *The Guardian* 2002

REPOSITION *[Dawson International plc: Annual report]*, 1993

REPOSITIONING *Hotel & Motel Management* 2001

RESERVE *Applied Economics in Banking and Finance* Partington, Oxford University Press, 1989

RESTRUCTURING *PR Newswire* 2002

RETAIL *Nation's Restaurant News* 2001

RETRAIN *Microsoft Word: Training Guide* Andralojc, Hari; Lambden, Anne; Walker, Pauline., Pitman Publishing, 1990

RETROACTIVE *The Art Newspaper*, Umberto Allemandi & Company, 1992

REVOLVING *Consumers and Credit* London National Consumer Council, 1980

RIG *Insight on the News* 2000

RIGHTSIZE *PR Newswire* 2002

RIP-OFF *Internet Magazine* 2001

ROADSHOW *Marketing* 1999

ROBBER BARON *The Chief Executive* 2002

ROGUE TRADER *The Independent* 2002

RSI *American Fitness* 2001

RUST BELT *The Independent* 2002

S

SALESMANSHIP *The Guardian* 2001

SANDBAG *The National Post* 1999

SATCASTER *CIRCOM Regional Newsmonthly* 2003

SAYE *The Independent* 2002

SCORCHED EARTH POLICY *http://news.bbc.co.uk* 2000

SEASONALLY *The Independent* 2002

SELF-ASSESSMENT *The Independent* 2002

SELF-INSURANCE *Entrepreneur* 2000

SERPS *Challenge* 2000

SET-ASIDE *European Report* 2000

SEXY *Brandweek* 2000

SHAKE-UP *Computer Weekly* 2001

SHELF *The Independent* 2002

SHORT *Financial Management* 2002

SHORTFALL *The Independent* 2002

SHOWCASE *Business Wire* 2000

SHRINKAGE *PR Newswire* 2001

SICK *HR Magazine* 2000

SIGHT *Brandweek* 2000

SLUSH FUND *Japan Policy and Politics* 2001

SMEAR CAMPAIGN *The Guardian* 2003

SNAIL MAIL *Newsbytes* 2000

SOFT *Econtent* 2001

SOUNDBITE *The Independent* 2002

SPAM *Newsbytes* 2001

SPEND *Food & Drink Weekly* 2002

SPIN *The Independent* 2002

SPIN-OFF *The Guardian* 1999

SQUARE *The Independent* 2002

STAG *Newsbytes* 1999

STAKEHOLDER *The Independent* 2002

STANDSTILL *American Metal Market* 2001

STATE-OF-THE-ART *Business Wire* 2000

STEERING COMMITTEE *The Guardian* 2001

STOCKBROKER *The Guardian* 2000

STRAPLINE *BBC Worldwide* 2002

STREAMLINE *The Guardian* 2002

STRIP MALL *Kiplinger's Personal Finance Magazine* 2000

SUNRISE INDUSTRY *The Guardian* 2001

SWAPTION *The Guardian* 1999

SWEAT EQUITY *Black Enterprise* 2000

SWOT *Business Horizons* 1999

T

TAKER *Los Angeles Business Journal* 2000

TAPER RELIEF *The Guardian* 2001

TAX *The Guardian* 1999

TAXMAN *The Independent* 2002

TEETHING TROUBLES *Internet Magazine* 2000

TELECOMMUTING *InfoWorld* 2001

TELEWORKING *Computer Weekly* 2000

TEMPORARY *Accountancy* Institute of Chartered Accountants, 1992

THINK TANK *Asian Economic News* 2001

TIE-IN *Nation's Restaurant News* 2000

TIGER ECONOMY *The Economist* 1998

TIME *Business Wire* 2000

TIN PARACHUTE *Journal of Accountancy* 2001

TMT *The Independent* 2002

TOP-DOWN *Business Wire* 2002

TOP-HEAVY *Managing Innovation* Date and publisher unknown

TQM *Education Management in the 1990s* Osborne, Allan; Davies, Brent; West-Burnham, John; Ellison, Linda, Longman Group UK Ltd, 1990

TRADING *American Metal Market* 2000

TRANCHE *The Independent* 1989

TREASURY *American Metal Market* 2000

TRICKLE-DOWN THEORY *The Guardian* 2002

TRIPLE WITCHING HOUR *The Risks Digest* 1987

TROUBLESHOOTER *The Independent* 2002

TRUSTED THIRD PARTY *The Economist* 1998

U

UMBRELLA *The Independent* 2002

UNDERCUT *The Guardian* 2002

UNDERGROUND ECONOMY *The Economist* 1998

UNDERLYING *Investors Chronicle* 1999

UNDERWATER *www.fed.org* 2001

UNEARNED INCOME *Introductory Sociology* Sheard, K.; Stanworth, M.; Bilton, T.; Jones, P.; Bonnet, K., Macmillan Publishers Ltd, 1992

UNLISTED *The Daily Telegraph* 1992

UNSECURED *Principles of Modern Contemporary Law* Gower., Sweet & Maxwell Ltd, 1992

UPSCALE *Travel Agent* 2000

UPSWING *Burharin's Theory of Equilibrium* Tarbuck, Kenneth J., Pluto Press, 1989

UPTICK *The Independent* 2002

URBAN *Japan Policy and Politics* 2001

USER-FRIENDLY *Travel Agent* 2000

USP *Advertising: What It Is And How To Do It* White, R., McGraw-Hill Book Company, 1993

V

VALUE *R&D Management: Managing Projects and New Projects* Date and publisher unknown

VAT *The Independent* 2002

VENTURE *The Financial Times* 1999

VERTICAL *Economics* Begg, David; Fischer, Stanley; Dornbusch, Rudiger., McGraw-Hill Book Company, 1991

VIRAL MARKETING *The Guardian* 2002

VISIBLE *The Economist* 1990

VISITING FIREMAN *The Indian Ocean Newsletter* 2000

W

WAGE-PRICE SPIRAL *The Daily Telegraph* 1992

WASTING ASSET *Drafting Business Leases* Lewison, Kim. Longman Group UK Ltd, 1993

WATCHDOG *The Independent* 2002

WEIGHTING *The Independent* 2002

WHEELING AND DEALING *American Metal Market* 2001

WHIZ-KID *Private Banker International* 2000

WHOLLY-OWNED SUBSIDIARY *Financial Times* Date unknown

WINDFALL *The Guardian* 1999

WINDOW *The Guardian* 2002

WIN-WIN *Purchasing* 2000

WORK *The Guardian* 2002

WORKER *Advice From the Top* Oates, David & Ezra, Derek., David & Charles Publishers plc, 1989

WRONGFUL *Computer Weekly* 2000

Z

ZERO *The Scotsman* Date unknown

Fuentes de las citas en español
Sources of Spanish Quotes

A

ABARATAMIENTO *Expansión y Empleo* 2003
ABSORCIÓN *Expansión y Empleo* 2003
ACCIONARIADO *Expansión y Empleo* 2002
ACTIVO *La Gaceta de los Negocios* 2003
ADJUDICATARIO *Cinco Días* 2002
AFORE *El Financiero (México)* 2003
AGENTE *Expansión y Empleo* 2002
ALCISTA *Expansión y Empleo* 2003
ALZA *El País (España)* 2003
AMPLIACIÓN *El País (España)* 2003
ARANCEL *Cinco Días* 2003
ATENCIÓN *Expansión y Empleo* 2003
AUTOCARTERA *El Mundo (España)* 2003
AUTORIZADO *El Mundo (España)* 2003

B

BARRERA *Expansión y Empleo* 2002
BONIFICACIÓN *Cinco Días* 2003
BURBUJA *La Gaceta de los Negocios* 2003

C

CAJA *La Gaceta de los Negocios* 2003
CALENDARIO *Cinco Días* 2003
CAMPAÑA *Estrategias* 2004
CAPITAL *Cinco Días* 2003
CARENCIA *Infoconsumo.es*
CARTA *aecoc.es (Asociación Española de Codificación Comercial)*
CATERING *El Mundo (España)* 2003
CERRAR *El Financiero (México)* 2003
CESE *Expansión y Empleo* 2001
CHIRINGUITO *Cinco Días* 2002
CIFRA *Expansión y Empleo* 2003
CLÁUSULA *El Mundo (España)* 2003
COMANDITA *El Mundo (España)* 2003
COMERCIALIZADOR *La Vanguardia* 2003
COMISIÓN *El País (España)* 2003
COMPAÑÍA *El País (España)* 2003
COMPETENCIA *El Mundo (España)* 2003
COMPORTARSE *El País (España)* 2001
CONCURSO *www.consumer.es* 2003
CONDONACIÓN *La Gaceta de los Negocios* 2003
CONGELAR *Expansión y Empleo* 2001
CONSEJERO *Expansión y Empleo* 2002
CONSOLIDAR *Expansión y Empleo* 2003

EURIBOR *Banco de España (nota informativa)* 2003
EXCEDENTE *Cinco Días* 2003
EXCESO *El Financiero (México)* 2003
EXPEDIENTE *El País (España)* 2003
EXPOSITOR *Expansión y Empleo* 2002

F
FERIA *El Mundo (España)* 2003
FILIAL *Cinco Días* 2003
FINANCIACIÓN *El País (España)* 2003
FISCALIDAD *Cinco Días* 2003
FONDO *Cinco Días* 2003
FORTALEZA *La Gaceta de los Negocios* 2003
FUSIONAR *Expansión y Empleo* 2001

G
GLOBALIFÓBICO *El Economista* 2003

H
HIPOTECAR *El Mundo (España)* 2003
HUECO *Expansión y Empleo* 2001

I
IMPOSITIVO *Cinco Días* 2003
IMPUESTO *Cinco Días* 2003
INCENTIVAR *El Mundo (España)* 2003
INDIZACIÓN *Expansión y Empleo* 2003
INFLACIÓN *Cinco Días* 2003
INSERCIÓN *Estrategias* 2003
INSOLVENTE *Cinco Días* 2003
INSUMOS *Clarín* 2003
INTANGIBLE *Estrategias* 2003
INTERANUAL *Cinco Días* 2003

J
JUSTO *www.coninpyme.org*

L
LEASING *Expansión y Empleo* 2002
LETES *Clarín* 2003
LEVANTE *Boletín Oficial de Canarias* 1995
LIBRE *El Economista* 2003
LICITAR *El Mundo (España)* 2003
LINEAL *El Mundo (España)* 2002
LISTADO *Poder* 2002
LLAVE *Cinco Días* 2003
LOGÍSTICA *Expansión y Empleo* 2003

M

MANCOMUNAR *El Mundo (España)* 2003
MANIPULADOR *Expansión y Empleo* 2003
MAQUILADOR *La Jornada* 2003
MARCA *El Mundo (España)* 2002
MARGEN *El Mundo (España)* 2003
MÁXIMO *Expansión* 2003
MEDIDA *La Jornada* 2003
MENSAJERÍA *El Mundo (España)* 2002
MENUDEO *El Economista* 2003
MERCADO *Cinco Días* 2003
MIBOR *El Mundo (España)* 2002
MICROEMPRESA *Expansión y Empleo* 2001
MINORISTA *El Mundo (España)* 2003
MOROSIDAD *El País (España)* 2003

N

NEGOCIACIÓN *El Mundo (España)* 2003
NÓMINA *Expansión y Empleo* 2003
NOTORIEDAD *www.france.diplomatie.fr* 1998
NUEVO *Excelsior* 2001
NÚMERO *Cinco Días* 2003

O

OBLIGACIÓN *Expansión y Empleo* 2003
OFERTA *El Mundo (España)* 2003
OLIGOPOLIO *El Economista* 2003
OPA *Cinco Días* 2003
OPAR *Expansión* 2003
OPV *Expansión y Empleo* 2000
ORGANIGRAMA *Cinco Días* 2003
OSCILAR *El Economista* 2003

P

PAGARÉ *ExpansiónDirecto (Curso de Bolsa)*
PAPEL *Cinco Días* 2003
PAQUETE *La Gaceta de los Negocios* 2003
PARQUÉ *Cinco Días* 2003
PARTICIPACIÓN *Cinco Días* 2003
PARTICIPAR *El Mundo (España)* 2003
PARTÍCIPE *Cinco Días* 2003
PARTIDA *Cinco Días* 2003
PASIVO *El Mundo (España)* 2003
PENETRACIÓN *Estrategias* 2003
PENSIONARSE *El Heraldo de México* 2003
PERFIL *El Economista* 2003
PERMUTA *El Colombiano* 2003
PISO *El Financiero (México)* 2003
PLUSVALÍA *La Gaceta de los Negocios* 2003
POBLACIÓN *Cinco Días* 2003
PONDERADO *www.noticiasdenavarra.labolsa.com* 2003

SUPERVISOR *El Mundo (España)* 2003
SUBSCRIBIR *Dinero y Derechos* 2002

T
TARGET *Estrategias* 2003
TASA *El Diario de Hoy* 2003
TEJIDO *El País (España)* 2003
TELETRABAJO *Estrategias* 2003
TEMATIZAR *Expansión* 2003
TIC *Estrategias* 2003
TIENDA *Dinero y Derechos* 2001
TIPO *El País (España)* 2003
TITULIZAR *Cinco Días* 2003
TRAMITACIÓN *Expansión y Empleo* 2002
TRANSPORTISTA *Estrategias* 2001
TRIBUTAR *Actualidad Económica* 2003

U
UMBRAL *www.baquía.com* 2003
UTE *El Mundo (España)* 2003

V
VALOR *El Mundo (España)* 2004
VENTA *www.constituciondesociedades.com* 2002
VIDA *Emprendedores* 2003
VIVERO *Expansión y Empleo* 2001
VOLUMEN *Estrategias* 2003

Z
ZONA *Cinco Días* 2003